HUDSON'S

Contents

Hudson's Historic Houses & Gardens

Publisher	Kate Kaegler
Production Manager	Sarah Phillips
Administrator	Deborah Coulter
Sales	Alex Sargeant
HHG Design	Jamieson Eley
HHG Director	Kelvin D Ladbrook
Production	PDQ Digital Media
Print Management	Bluepoint
Printer	St Ives
UK Trade Sales	Portfolio Books
UK Distribution	NBN International
US Distribution	Globe Pequot

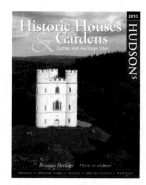

PUBLISHED BY:

Heritage House Group
Ketteringham Hall
Wymondham
Norfolk
NR18 9RS
Tel: 01603 813319
Fax: 01603 814992
Email: hudsons@hhgroup.co.uk
Web: www.hudsonsguide.co.uk

2010

In 2010, visitors see parts of the building never seen before, and other highlights this year include special displays of rarely-seen treasures from the vaults, extensive new displays highlighting the contribution and taste of Duchess Georgiana and of the 3rd Earl of Burlington, and an exhibition celebrating the 90th birthday of Deborah Devonshire, the Dowager Duchess and youngest of the famed Mitford sisters.

At the same time, the 1st Duke of Devonshire's building is being cleaned, and all its services replaced. This work is part of the continuing Masterplan, instigated by the present (12th) Duke of Devonshire soon after he inherited the title in 2004. It is the biggest project of conservation, restoration and renewal for the house since the 6th Duke's alterations in the 1830s, and is designed to make the building fit for its many purposes in the 21st century.

The principal funder of the project, the charitable Chatsworth House Trust, which receives all admission and event income from visitors, was set up and endowed by the Devonshire Family in 1981, to ensure the long-term survival of Chatsworth 'for the benefit of the public'. The Masterplan is the boldest expression yet of the Trust's commitment to current and future visitors. Here the Duke, and other members of the Masterplan team, introduce the current phase of work.

Tsar Nicholas Ist of Russia by Dawe

Diamond tiara, on display in 2010

Deborah Devonshire by Lucian Freud

Wedding of future 11th Duke and Duchess, 1941

From the spring of 2010, 62 years after opening to visitors commercially in 1949, Chatsworth presents a refreshed visitor route around the house, encompassing restored rooms, new spaces and views, better access and more substantial displays from the famous collections.

Duke of Devonshire

Chatsworth REVEALED

Introduction by the Duke of Devonshire

Before Amanda and I even came to live at Chatsworth in 2006, we already knew that the services would have to be completely replaced. They dated from 1959, when my parents moved into Chatsworth, and were coming to the end of their useful life. We were also aware of some unsatisfactory parts of the visitor route, particularly the lack of access to all floors for less able people. So we knew of the need for some work within the building. Further thought and discussion led us to address the fact that the 300 year old exterior facades had never been cleaned, and so vulnerable stone work was in urgent need of cleaning and repair. And finally, we were developing a few ideas of our own about how we would like to show parts of the house to visitors and changes we wanted to make to our private accommodation.

We realised that to satisfy all of these ambitions we would need far sighted and experienced professional help. After months visiting architects' offices and then interviewing four different practices, we chose Peter Inskip, of Inskip and Jenkins, as the architect and leader of the whole project, with David Mlinaric and Jonathan Bourne advising on decoration, room layouts and reorganisation. Rupert Symmons of Fanshawes was appointed as the Project Director, and Sean Doxey, Comptroller at Chatsworth, and Sarah Montgomery, General Manager, took the lead on the Chatsworth side. This phase of work has involved more than 200 contractors on site at different times, each bringing their specific skills to bear on the varied needs of the project, and many other experts, from lighting designers to furniture conservators and silk weavers, have also left their mark.

They have been helped by a huge range of people at Chatsworth, from the entire collections, archive and textile team, led by Matthew Hirst, housekeepers and outstanding craftsmen and women, to the communication and education departments.

Chatsworth South Front

DUKE, DUCHESS AND OTHER MASTERPLAN DESIGN TEAM MEMBERS, FROM LEFT TO RIGHT:
Rupert Symmons – Project Manager, Jonathan Bourne – Art Historian, Denna Garrett – Private Secretary to Duchess, David Mlinaric – Interiors expert, Duchess of Devonshire, Duke of Devonshire, Peter Inskip – Architect, Snug the dog

Oak stairs - original roof lantern revealed

Oak stairs - early 20th century inner skylight, now removed

Pointing cracks in stonework

6

We have all been mindful that this huge project runs alongside our busy day jobs, which for most of us is the management and improvement of Chatsworth, its collections and landscape, principally for the enjoyment of our visitors. So we have involved visitors in the Masterplan wherever we can, by explaining the work being undertaken, and they have been able to see how their admission money has been spent; the resulting interest and goodwill has been very encouraging.

Earlier projects completed in the last three years have included the re-presentation of the State Apartments and the Sculpture Gallery, fascinating to research and realise, and well received by visitors. As this main, current, phase of the Masterplan unfolds indoors and outside, under the monumental scaffolding, I think the most exciting of all the new developments has been the creation of the new North Sketch Gallery on the second floor.

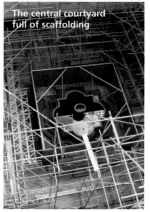

The central courtyard full of scaffolding

A corner of the free-standing scaffold on the North front

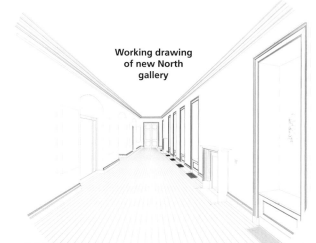

Working drawing of new North gallery

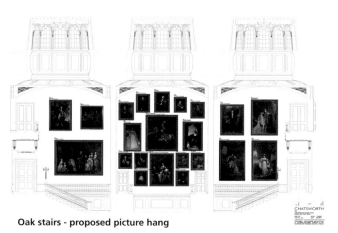

Oak stairs - proposed picture hang

This was Peter Inskip's brilliant solution to improving the visitor route, and reducing the number of stairs visitors encounter, by creating a wide corridor along the north side of the central courtyard to match the 19th century galleries on the south and west sides, where visitors will now see changing displays, before they survey the new hang of family and royal portraits spanning 300 years, on the walls of the completely restored early 19th century Oak Stair with its wonderful lantern opened up once again after 75 years.

Outside, as the North Front and the central courtyard are unveiled, cleaned of the ravages of three centuries of weather and almost two centuries of industrial pollution, the warm stone glows as if new. It is possible to imagine what the 1st Duke's palace will look like in 2012, when the West and South facades have been cleaned, and their richly carved vases, trophies, columns and other carved decoration restored. It will be a thrilling sight.

None of this vital work could even have been considered if my parents had not been so brilliantly successful in turning Chatsworth from the sombre, empty and financially insecure establishment they inherited in 1950, into a thriving and profitable business. Run by the charitable Chatsworth House Trust, which my father set up and endowed in 1981, today it

The North gallery beginning to take shape, July 2009

is directly funded by the hundreds of thousands of people who visit every year.

Without this secure financial grounding the Masterplan, representing a £14million investment by the charity over five years, simply could not have happened. Generations of visitors are now reaping the benefits of my parents' wisdom and good stewardship, and for that all who enjoy Chatsworth must be eternally grateful. Amanda and I are proud now to be carrying their baton.

Duke of Devonshire

Chatsworth, West front

Rediscovering Chatsworth

The Masterplan represents an exciting period of change at Chatsworth, the latest development in a history of innovation and change spanning five centuries. Due to the scale and nature of the project, and the international importance of Chatsworth, a full and comprehensive planning application was submitted to the Peak District National Park Authority and passed by them. Consultation took place in advance with English Heritage, The Peak District National Park Authority and other statutory advisors as required by law.

One of the principal aims of the Masterplan is to enable greater access to areas of the house previously inaccessible to visitors, whilst enabling visitors using wheelchairs, or requiring a lift, to share this experience which has previously been difficult to arrange. More than £½ million has been spent on upgrading the lift and making other access improvements to ensure all visitors can see the same parts of the house. The creation of a new gallery on the second floor of the North Front will for the first time provide the opportunity to circumnavigate the courtyard at this level, which is greatly enhanced by the opening-up of 12 false windows along the West and South Sketch Galleries. These galleries date to the 1830s, forming part of the alterations made by the architect Sir Jeffry Wyatville but their windows were blocked as soon as made, to allow for the display of the collection of old master drawings, hung

18th century wallpaper revealed

19th century mason's drawings found on removed window panels

here until the early 20th century. In 2011, a new old master drawings gallery will open in the house, with the appropriate low light condition, to show a rotating selection from this rarely-seen part of the collection.

Construction of Chatsworth house was begun by Bess of Hardwick in 1552, although the building that survives today was essentially built in two phases between 1680 and 1707 (the main square block of the house, for the 1st Duke) and in the 1820-30s (north wing, sketch galleries and internal remodelling, for the 6th Duke). One of the fascinating aspects of the Masterplan is the unique opportunity to record the structural alterations that have occurred within the house and have been hidden from view behind later wallpaper and plasterwork or under the floorboards. The building works are being monitored by a team of archaeologists, led by Oliver Jessop, who are specialists in the survey and interpretation of historic buildings. From this archaeological recording, it is apparent that recycling has been going on at Chatsworth for over 300 years: for example a whole partition constructed in 1707 on the second floor of the North Front was entirely constructed from reused Oak beams, probably from the earlier Elizabethan house. There have also been numerous unexpected discoveries, including dated signatures from former tradesmen, rolled up newspapers, letters and a strip of floral blue flock wallpaper, which was found behind a 19th century partition, dated to the mid-18th century.

The South and West Sketch Galleries have always been relatively dull spaces with blinds on their skylights and the windows overlooking the courtyard blocked. These windows have been opened up during the current phase of the Masterplan allowing spectacular views onto the courtyard with its great trophies carved by Samuel Watson for the 1st Duke ; the removal of the wooden boards blocking the external windows also revealed what must be regarded as one of the most significant discoveries made so far. Along the South Sketch, wooden doors and shutters had been reused to block the windows, one of which contained a fragment of handmade wallpaper and a large chalk signature, dated April 1836. In contrast, the West windows were blocked with custom made panels, each constructed from smaller reused pine boards found to contain pencil and ink architectural drawings and a date of 1838. Initial observations suggest that many of the drawings correspond with walls in the West Garden. It would appear that following the completion of the new garden layout, the working drawings used by the stone masons were reused by the joiners working inside the house to block the windows; another example of recycling!

The three galleries now form impressive spaces in which to display works of art, both old and new, and to tell the story of different collectors in the Devonshire Family. More than 650 metres of striped silk has been specially woven for us by Claremont Textiles, for the walls and curtains of the galleries.

From the newly revealed windows, visitors have the best view of the cleaned court-yard, and particularly the east wall, with the 1st Duke's magnificent carved stone military trophies, now clean, conserved and any losses carefully replaced. Stone conservators have also dismantled and

North front column, before cleaning

North front column, after cleaning

A carved sphinx, before cleaning

A carved sphinx, after cleaning

restored the sphinxs and trophies on the 1st Duke's entrance court, now the private garden, with magnificent results, and the next two years will see further work on the other facades of the building.

The internal heating and electrical services are being upgraded to meet the needs of the 21st century and during the excavation of the exterior pipe trenches further discoveries have been unearthed including impressive stone lined culverts

and archaeological artefacts such as bottle glass, pottery and animal bone.

Discoveries made during the Masterplan have not only added to our understanding of the development of Chatsworth, but they offering new information which complements the documentary records we already had. The findings will inform our future interpretation of the building to visitors.

Central courtyard before cleaning

Duchess Georgiana by Cosway, before cleaning

Conserving the collection

In addition to the restoration of the building and the renewal of essential services, the Masterplan has provided an opportunity to conserve some of the Devonshire Collection's most important works of art, using the expertise of many of the country's finest specialist conservators.

The newly presented South Sketch Gallery focuses on the life of the 5th Duke and Duchess Georgiana, and includes an important group of furniture by 18th-century cabinet maker David Roentgen (who worked for Catherine the Great of Russia among others). This group contains a huge mahogany cylinder bureau, revolving desk chair, writing table and gentleman's dressing table, which are all being painstakingly conserved, and the gilt bronze mounts cleaned of layers of accumulated dust and verdigris. A pair of Regency chandeliers, originally from Georgiana's London home, Devonshire House, have been cleaned and returned to their original matched appearance, and a full-length portrait of Georgiana as the Goddess Diana flying through the clouds by Maria Cosway, is one of many significant paintings being cleaned for visitors to enjoy.

One of the most striking is the group portrait of the 3rd Earl of Burlington with his family by J.B. Van Loo. The painting has travelled round most of the Burlington and Devonshire family houses since it was first delivered to Burlington House in time for Christmas 1739. The heavily discoloured varnish and layers of dirt have been cleaned, and structural problems attended to, to prepare it for its new home on the Oak Stairs, where it last hung in 1850.

Much gilt wood furniture, designed and made for the Devonshire family in the 18th century by renowned craftsmen like William Kent and François Hervé, is being cleaned and conserved. Replacement gold leaf has been applied to damaged areas and carefully toned to match the original which has been consolidated to ensure its future survival.

In addition to projects brought about by the Masterplan, the usual annual programme of conservation work continues. A pair of late 17th-century Verre Eglomise mirrors, made for the 1st Duke are on display following two years of work. Also, an important pair of desks made by Andre-Charles Boulle have been conserved and placed at the centre of the State Music Room display, surrounded by other examples of this form of marquetry decoration using tortoiseshell and brass.

Many of these objects have not previously been on display to visitors at Chatsworth. Whether well known or newly on view, every project offers new insights into this internationally important collection, and discoveries made during conservation work will be shared with visitors as often as possible.

With thanks to the Duke of Devonshire, Oliver Jessop, Matthew Hirst, Diane Naylor, Jonathan Bourne, Peter Inskip, Matthew Bullen, Simon Seligman.
All images courtesy Chatsworth House Trust.

Roentgen desk

3rd Earl of Burlington, family portrait by Van Loo

Cleaning test on sleeve, before conservation; detail of Van Loo painting

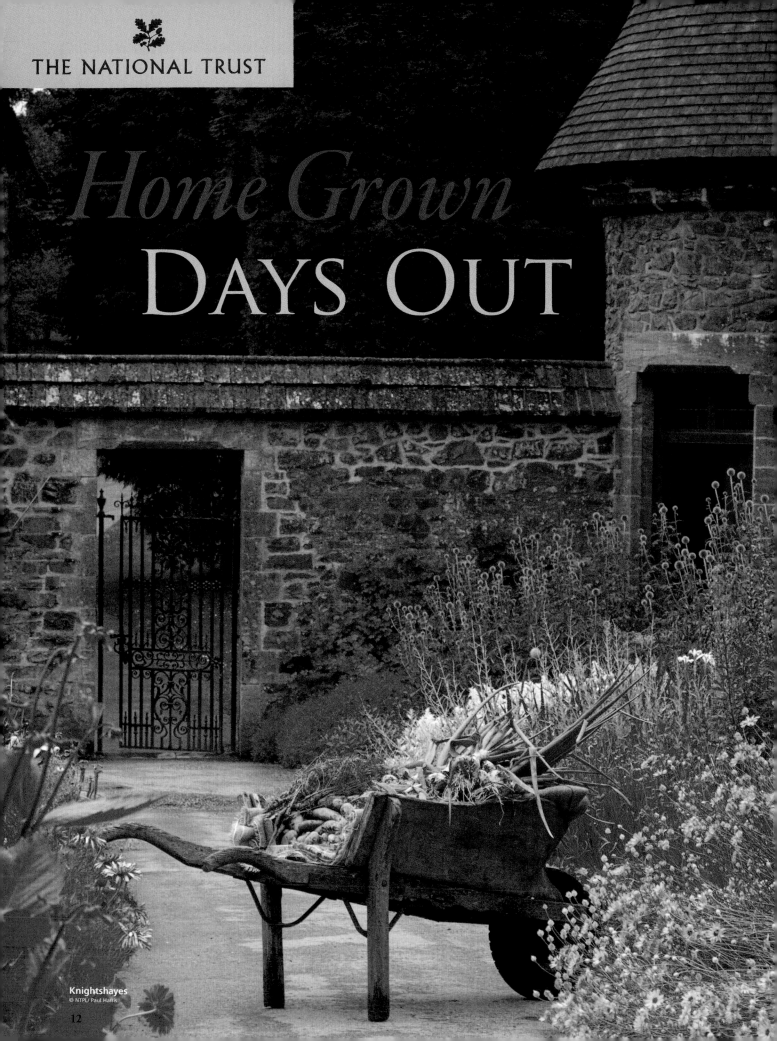

Home Grown DAYS OUT

Knightshayes
© NTPL/ Paul Harris

The National Trust cares for over 200 historic gardens; ranging from wide expanses of parkland landscaped by the likes of "Capability" Brown to small, intimate 'outdoor rooms' brimming with perfume and colour.

With such variety on offer you'll find spaces to relax and unwind in, gardens that inspire and entertain, and travel through nearly 400 years of history. At every turn you'll experience the simple pleasures of seeing, smelling and touching, you'll discover new ideas and plant names and tap into the stories and histories of the great designers, gardeners and owners.

This year why not join the National Trust's campaign to celebrate local and seasonal food and visit one of the Trust's kitchen gardens. Have your senses seduced by the sights and smells of ripening fruit and vegetables, pick up ideas for your own allotment or vegetable plot and enjoy tasting the difference in our restaurants and cafes where food is prepared using ingredients picked at the peak of their freshness and flavour.

Here's a quick glimpse at 20 of the top kitchen gardens in the National Trust's care. We promise a visit will be time well spent, as you're sure to find something to delight and inspire.

Arlington Court, Devon

After exploring the eccentric Victorian interiors of the house, make time to discover the walled kitchen garden. Experience fantastic sights in this fully working garden where a wide range of herbs, fruits and vegetables are grown. Discover the glass house where varieties of tomatoes and chillies are grown, or walk down soft grass paths outside and spot traditional glass cloches. For the chance to taste some of the delicious soft fruits that grow in the orchard order a cream tea with strawberry conserve or raspberry preserve in the tea-room. Even the cheese scones come with Gardeners' Relish sourced from the garden.

Barrington Court, Somerset

The one acre kitchen garden was established in the 1920s and has been in continuous use ever since. The garden produces a diverse crop, including yellow raspberries, neat rows of lettuce and beetroot as well as exotic fig trees – there's plenty to admire. Produce is principally grown for the National Trust restaurant, which has a special seasonal menu reflecting what is flourishing in the garden. There's also the opportunity to try Barrington's apple juice and scrumptious homemade cider; made with fruit from the trees in the orchards. The apples in the cider are milled and pressed on 200-year old cider presses and fermented in old oak barrels.

Arlington Court

Barrington Court

Calke Abbey
© NTPL/ Stephen Robson

Beningbrough Hall, North Yorkshire

This dramatic red brick Georgian mansion boasts one of the Trust's most productive walled gardens. There are over 35 cultivated varieties of Victorian and local apples. Cherries, plums, redcurrants and gooseberries grow in fan-trained and bush arrangements. The vegetables are a mixture of Victorian and more modern varieties of tomatoes and pumpkins, all of which can be found in dishes in the restaurant. Peaches, figs and nectarines are grown in the greenhouse as well as a root crop of liquorice and ten varieties of vines, which separate the beds and walls. For a chance to take the taste of Beningbrough home with you, apple chutney, pear and ginger chutney, Victoria plum and gooseberry jams are all available for sale in the restaurant.

Berrington Hall, Herefordshire

Berrington Hall is beautifully sited above a wide valley with sweeping views to the Brecon Beacons. An elegant house set in parkland designed by the celebrated 'Capability Brown'. The walled kitchen garden houses a renowned collection of apple trees, including the National Collection of Historic Hereford and Marches Apples, many of which are no longer in general cultivation.

Calke Abbey, Derbyshire

At Calke there's plenty to keep a keen gardener entertained; the 18th century physic garden otherwise known as the lower kitchen garden was originally planned as a medicinal herb garden. This plot has now been restored as a working kitchen garden, divided into rotating beds for potatoes, legumes and root crops. There's also an abundance of soft fruits with blackcurrants and redcurrants amongst the favourites grown for the kitchens at Calke.

© NTPL/ Rupert Truman

Berrington Hall

© NTPL/ Stephen Robson

Beningbrough Hall

14

Clumber Park, Nottinghamshire

The spectacular glasshouses, one of the longest in Trust ownership at 450ft, and the immense Lime Tree Avenue hint at the grandeur that was Clumber in it's heyday. And although the house was demolished in 1938, the past is instantly brought to life in the organically managed Kitchen Garden. Visit the Edwardian glasshouses where vines, figs, peaches and nectarines are grown and explore outside plots where perennial vegetables such as asparagus and over 20 varieties of rhubarb grow. Alongside modern hybrids, "heritage" or "heirloom" varieties of fruit and vegetables are grown, including (appropriately for Clumber which is part of Sherwood Forest), varieties "outlawed" under European Union legislation. There are also 70 different apple varieties in the orchard, most of which are native to Nottinghamshire and the surrounding counties.

Chartwell, Kent

Discover the produce that fed Britain's greatest statesman in Chartwell's walled garden. Restored in 2004 the garden is back to its former glory and the result is a charming garden full of many varieties of the fruit, vegetables and flowers that were grown there in Churchill's time. Planting schemes have been redesigned to closely reflect the tastes of Sir Winston and his wife Clementine. What's more, you can see what tickled the Churchill's taste buds with all the dishes in the restaurant created from produce in the garden.

Felbrigg Hall, Norfolk

Felbrigg is a gardener's delight with a decorative and productive walled garden, Victorian pleasure garden and rolling landscape park. The kitchen garden is laid out around a pond and divided into four potagers of mixed vegetables and their traditional companions. Herb borders are planted either side of the 18th century dovecote and provide a sensory delight, and the New Orchard is planted with varieties of fruit that were known to have been grown in the garden during the 19th century.

For information on properties protected by The National Trust log on to www.nationaltrust.org.uk

Clumber Park

Chartwell

Gibside

Hinton Ampner

Gibside, Newcastle upon Tyne

A 400 acre 'forest garden' designed in the 18th century, Gibside combines woodland and open spaces with atmospheric buildings. Take time to explore the ruins of the orangery, bathhouse and hall or take a stroll down the oak lined Long Walk and take in the dramatic Column of Liberty. The kitchen garden is a place of calm but also enthusiastic planting; with a wonderful array of heritage vegetables grown, many of which are supplied to the property restaurant. A visit to the Gibside Larder is also a must-do with the region's finest award-winning food on sale, including produce from local National Trust estates.

Ham House & Garden, Richmond upon Thames

One of a series of grand houses and palaces along the River Thames, Ham House is an unusually complete survival of the 17th century; a place where time has truly stood still. The kitchen garden in front of the orangery is very productive and produce is served daily in the orangery café. The process of restoration is ongoing in the kitchen garden and will eventually include beds of vegetables, herbs and flowers bordered by box and topiary, with a central path of espaliered fruits.

Hinton Ampner, Hampshire

Best known for its fine gardens Hinton is a masterpiece of 20th century garden design. Crisply manicured lawns and fine topiary are cleverly combined with informal planting – giving the gardens a lovely relaxing feel to them. The walled garden is now a hive of activity after being opened to the public only 3 years ago. Vegetables and soft fruits are thriving in their new home and a herb garden has been recently planted, featuring varieties used for medicinal purposes as well as for cooking.

Knightshayes Court, Devon

The vast garden at Knightshayes was the family's passion and they packed it with rare trees and shrubs, creating the celebrated 'Garden in the Wood'. The newly restored kitchen garden, now fully productive, supplies fresh organic heritage varieties of vegetables and fruit to the property's restaurant. It's stepped walls and fairy tale turrets make its structure unique in the country. The vines in the garden also allow the property to make their own label 'Knightshayes' wine.

Llanerchaeron, Ceredigion

A rare example of a self-sufficient 18th century estate, Llanerchaeron has survived virtually unaltered. The double walled fruit and vegetable garden boasts plum trees lining the walls, plots of rhubarb and asparagus, a soft fruit cage, and an extensive range of herbs which complement the rows of legumes and root vegetables. Historic apple varieties, including the 200 year old 'Northern Greening', can be found on the orchard lawn. Visit during October when the trees are ripe for the harvest and you're sure to have your senses seduced. And if you've not got your dinner planned then do not fret as fruit and vegetables, as well as lamb, beef and pork, which are reared on the home farm within yards of the garden, are available to buy.

Oxburgh Hall, Norfolk

Oxburgh Hall is certainly a place of mystery and intrigue and as you step through the Tudor gatehouse you will truly feel as though you have stepped back in time. The garden has a stunning Victorian French parterre, Catholic chapel, walled orchard and kitchen garden. The Victorian Orchard boasts plums and quinces amongst its many delights and the kitchen garden is home to a vast array of wonderful vegetables, including pumpkins, radishes, courgettes and asparagus.

Scotney Castle, Kent

The celebrated gardens, designed around the ruins of a 14th century moated castle, feature spectacular displays of rhododendrons, azaleas and kalmia in May and June. Wisteria and roses ramble over the ruins in summer, and trees and shrubs provide rich colour in autumn. There's also chance to see restoration in action in the kitchen garden where the fruit and vegetable beds have been entirely dug over and a 10 year project is underway to get the life blood of this garden flowing once more.

Sizergh, Cumbria

An imposing medley of a medieval Castle and an Elizabethan country residence. Sizergh's kitchen garden comprises of beds of cut flowers and soft fruits including strawberries and raspberries, as well as herbs and vegetables. On the site of the old kitchen garden stands the present-day orchard. The orchard is a curious mixture of eating, cooking and crab apples, several varieties of plum and damson trees (many of which were planted over 30 years ago), the unusual quince and medlar and an assortment of ornamentals. Seasonal recipes dominate the restaurant and are filled with fresh produce from the garden.

Sizergh
© NTPL/ Val Corbett

Trengwainton Gardens
© NTPL/ Stephen Robson

Trengwainton Gardens, Cornwall

Intimately linked to the picturesque stream which runs the length of the garden there are paths leading up to a terrace and summerhouse where you'll get splendid views across Mount's Bay to The Lizard. The walled gardens contain many rare and unusual species which are difficult to grow anywhere else in the country – visitors can now view previously closed sections of the garden from a newly built viewing platform. The kitchen garden is now in full production for the first time in many years and a wide range of vegetables, fruit and herbs are now being grown.

Tyntesfield, North Somerset

A glorious Victorian extravaganza awaits all who visit. The magic extends to the gardens where you can explore the formal terraced gardens and the wonderful walled kitchen garden. Highly productive since 1837 the protected environment of the garden and the skills of a Victorian workforce would have ensured fruit and vegetables for the house all year round. Today visitors can see peaches and other soft fruits being grown in the 19th century glasshouses as well as a wide variety of vegetables, and there's even the opportunity to take some tasty souvenirs home.

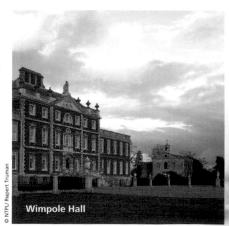

Wimpole Hall
© NTPL/ Rupert Truman

Upton House, Warwickshire

At the heart of Upton's magnificent gardens lies the terraced kitchen garden which dates from 1695. Still supplying the house with fruit and vegetables, it's laid out traditionally with long rows. Unusual crops include old traditional vegetables that have found new popularity such as kohlrabi and luxury crops like asparagus and globe artichokes. The new soft fruit section flourishes with bumper crops of redcurrants, worcesterberrys and boysenberries, and in one record day, over 45 kilos of gooseberries were picked. So make the most of Upton's bounty of produce and purchase goods from the garden in the restaurant.

Wimpole Hall, Cambridgeshire

After discovering the county's grandest house make your way to the two acre kitchen garden. The recreated Sir John Soane glasshouse is used to grow over 12,000 bedding plants for the parterre garden followed by tomato and peppers, including a few of the staggering 60 varieties of tomatoes grown for the property's Tomato Day in August. And if a trip to the glasshouse gets your mouth watering you'll be pleased to know that as well as supplying the restaurant, surplus produce is available to buy.

Sally Williams and Laura Brown

© NTPL/ Ian Shaw

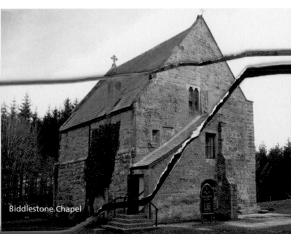

Brodsworth Hall

The opulent interior of the King's Bedroon, Dover Castle, Kent

History just got exciting! Forget the stuffy, uptight museums of your childhood and instead join us to experience England's fascinating history as it is brought to life for a new generation to explore and discover.

English HERITAGE

Discover Days Out with a Difference!

The Drawing Room, Osborne House, Isle of Wight

Walk in the footsteps of a Queen in the recently re-created Elizabethan Garden at **Kenilworth Castle**, originally built for Queen Elizabeth I by Robert Dudley; explore Charles Darwin's home Down House, where he lived and worked for over 40 years; uncover the mystery behind England's most famous pre-historic site **Stonehenge** or simply relax as you meander through the luxurious surroundings of some of the most historically important stately homes in England. With over 400 sites of historical significance to explore, English Heritage brings to life the reality of history in all its luxury or gritty realism to uncover the passion, mystery and intrigue of England's colourful past.

With significant investment and a creative modern approach to the interpretation of England's precious artefacts and sites, English Heritage has brought its properties into the 21st century with imaginative presentations and interactive displays, exhibits and commentary.

There really is something to interest everyone no matter what your age or interests. From storybook castles, breathtaking stately homes, gorgeous gardens, and impressive art collections to interactive children's play areas. England's fascinating heritage is just waiting to be discovered!

Journey Back to the 12th Century at Dover Castle. Behind the doors of the Great Tower of England's largest castle a spectacular transformation has taken place.

Originally created by Henry II as a statement of royal power, the tower has now been brought back to its former glory by a team of English Heritage historians. They have spent the past two years researching what the inside of the 12th-century royal palace at Dover would have looked like. Based on their findings, a group of 141 craftsmen and artisans have painstakingly recreated the opulent interiors alongside more than 1,000 artefacts including furniture, kitchenware, garments, goblets and swords.

It is the largest historically researched medieval re-creation ever attempted in Britain and gives visitors a truly authentic experience. Undeniably it was originally built to impress and today's visitors are sure to be struck by its power, opulent interiors and, sumptuous colours of Dragon's Blood red, green and bright blue. Costumed characters and the latest film technology also bring to life some of the famous inhabitants including King Henry II, Prince John and the court Jester.

Dover Castle, Kent

Children get hands-on with interactive learning displays, Dover Castle

Kit Surrey, lead historical set designer, putting finishing touches to an 180-foot long wall hanging depicting the Norman Conquest, the design of which is inspired by the Bayeux Tapestry, Dover Castle

Two English Heritage members of staff putting final touches to a backcloth for the high table, the centrepiece of the Guest Hall where Henry would have dined and entertained foreign pilgrims and dignitaries, Dover Castle

Become a Member and Discover Even More.
Becoming an English Heritage member is just the beginning of a wonderful adventure. Not only can members enjoy free entry to 400 places of historic interest, plus the numerous benefits listed below but, they also get the chance to experience something a little special with our exclusive Members events.

From guided tours with a chance to see behind some of the doors usually closed to the public, to hands-on craft workshops, to battlefield hikes where historical landscapes will be brought life with commentary by historical experts. At English Heritage membership really does offer something extra special. **Members' benefits include:**
- Free entry to 400 places of historic interest, plus free entry for up to 6 accompanied children within your family group under 19
- Free or reduced price entry to an exciting calendar of historical events
- Free full colour guide detailing each property
- Free quarterly edition of Heritage Today magazine

Alongside all of these wonderful experiences you'll also be supporting the essential work of preserving, restoring and exhibiting England's fascinating legacy for years to come.

Find out more about becoming a member at www.english-heritage.org.uk or call 0870 333 1184
All images © English Heritage

The Gardens and pavillion at Wrest Park, Bedfordshire

The fountain at the Elizabethan garden at Kenilworth Castle, Warwickshire © English Heritage / Alun Bull

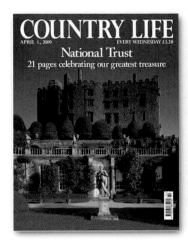

During the 13th century the heiress Lady Dervorgilla of Galloway married the wealthy English knight John Balliol. The couple, among the wealthiest in the realm, appear to have been happy and devoted to one another. After John's death in 1269 Devorgilla decided to found a Cistercian abbey where the memory of their love would be preserved forever. And – in a gesture considered the height of romance – she arranged that when her own time came she would be buried with a casket containing John's embalmed heart clutched to her breast. As a tribute to this tale of marital devotion the monks agreed that their beautiful buildings and lands should be known as **Sweetheart Abbey.**

Further east stand the Borders Abbeys, of Dryburgh, Jedburgh, Kelso and Melrose. The abbey church at **Jedburgh** still stands to roof height and, despite a series of misfortunes including being used as a French artillery base in the late 1540s, is both pretty and impressive. Among its most attractive features is a cloister garden, laid out in 1986 and planted with flowers and herbs of the sort favoured for their scents and curative qualities by the Augustinian canons who once lived at the abbey. One of the strangest stories linked to Jedburgh is that when the congregation gathered there in 1285 for the wedding of Alexander III to Yolande de Dreux a ghost appeared and foretold the king's demise. His death the following year turned out to be a watershed, triggering events that led to the ill-fated reign of Lady Devorgilla's grandson, King John Balliol, then to the Wars of Independence. These

Jedburgh

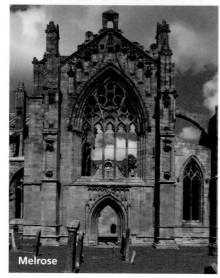

Melrose

wars, and the troubled relations between Scotland and England, meant the Borders Abbeys endured repeated raids and burnings for around 250 years.

In 1322 **Melrose** was sacked by the army of Edward II but was rebuilt with the assistance of Robert I. Indeed, while his body lay at Dunfermline his heart was buried at Melrose. This was thanks to a deathbed plea to his friend 'the Good Sir James of Douglas' to take his heart on a Crusade. The knight gave his life to fulfil the monarch's wish, and fell fighting the Moors in Spain in 1331, after which the heart was

returned. On a rather different note the abbey has delightful carved stonework, including a much-loved depiction of a pig playing the bagpipes. Another fascinating carving is at the island priory of **Inchmahome**, on the Lake of Mentieth – which is particularly lovely when the bluebells are out. Here is an effigy of Earl Walter of Mentieth and his countess Mary; he lies facing her with his legs crossed, which was a sign that he was a Crusader.

Inchmahome, reached by a pleasant boat ride, was later a place of refuge for the young Mary, Queen of Scots, sent there for safety in case the English attempted to capture her after defeating the Scots at the calamitous battle of Pinkie in 1547. A little over 20 years later, the queen again took refuge in a religious house, this time **Dundrennan Abbey**, near the Solway Firth. It followed her defeat at the battle of Langside in 1568, when she was ousted by forces acting in the name of her infant son, James VI. The abbey is now an attractive, but modest ruin, but its place in history is of special poignancy as it was there that Mary spent her last day on Scottish soil before fleeing to England where her plotting eventually resulted in her execution.

Also in the south west of Scotland is **Whithorn Priory** and remains a place of great significance to Scottish Christians. Whithorn is regarded as the 'Cradle of Christianity' as many believe it was there that St Ninian, who died around 432 AD, first brought the faith to the country and set about converting the southern Picts.

Sweetheart Abbey

Earl and Countess of Mentieth

Museum Whithorn Priory

Glasgow Cathedral

The priory's award-winning museum is also highly popular for its world-famous collection of early Christian carved stones. Among them is Scotland's oldest known Christian monument, with its inscription in memory of a 5th century man named Latinus and his unnamed four-year-old daughter.

Shifting offshore, one of the most remarkable and spiritual locations in Scotland is **Iona Abbey**. Founded by St Columba and a dozen companions in 563 AD it grew to become pivotal to the church in Scotland and one of the most important monasteries of early medieval Europe. A renowned centre of learning and a place where exquisite artwork was produced, the abbey has a wonderful collection of carved crosses and grave slabs. Many of the grave slabs carry the effigies of mighty warriors and kings – depicted gripping the swords, and sometimes with the galleys aboard which they sailed the sea lanes from Ireland, through the Hebrides and on to the north. Iona, a small island just off Mull, was once so revered that pilgrims would travel many hundreds of miles to be close to relics of St Columba, which were believed to have miraculous powers. A 19th century restoration project means the abbey church is a complete structure, and an active centre of Christian worship, though the relics are long gone, removed to safer places due to Viking raids.

While so many medieval ecclesiastical sites are now ruins there are exceptions, such as the **Dunblane Cathedral** in central Scotland. However, to see the fullest and most impressive expression of the medieval stonemason's art takes a visit to **Glasgow Cathedral**. It is the only mainland cathedral to have survived the Reformation largely intact and was breathtaking in its ambition. This is probably thanks to a decision by the 13th century Bishop Bondington to rebuild the existing church as a wondrous celebration of God in stone – and a fit place for pilgrims wishing to venerate the relics of St Kentigern, affectionately known by locals as St Mungo.

In addition to their religious resonance, some of abbeys and cathedrals are imbued with a deeply held sense of Scottish nationhood – none more so the **Arbroath**. The abbey's fine ruins, dramatic east-coast location, and unusual origin – having been dedicated by King William the Lion to his childhood friend the English martyr St Thomas Becket, who was murdered in 1170 – are enough reason to pay a visit. But, what rockets it into the heritage super league, is its close association with the Declaration of Arbroath, arguably the most famous document in Scottish history. It was, in fact, a letter sent to the Pope in 1320 by 40 nobles, barons and freemen which outlined the case for Robert I in the Wars of Independence and explained why they were resisting the seemingly overwhelming might of England. Its words have inspired many down the centuries and will doubtless continue to do so long into the future...

'… it is in truth not for glory, nor riches, nor honours that we are fighting, but for freedom – for that alone, which no honest man gives up but with life itself.'

Iona

Historic Scotland offer various products as a means to exploring their properties for great value. Ask staff at their properties about the Historic Scotland Explorer Pass or Historic Scotland Membership.

All images © Crown Copyright reproduced courtesy of Historic Scotland.

Great Things at the GREAT

View of The Great Glasshouse

In the ten years since opening, the gardens have developed to become the most visited in Wales – indeed, readers of Gardeners' World recently voted them the number one garden to visit in Wales.

Laid out on the site of a Regency estate, the gardens blend old and new with panache, and, taking advantage of the natural beauty of the surrounding hills and woodlands, have become an intellectually and sensually stimulating place to spend a few hours. Encircled in a series of lakes, the gardens roll out from the gatehouse, Norman Foster & Partners' first ever wooden building. From here, the visitor can choose to walk up through the broadwalk, a dramatically modern take on the traditional British herbaceous border; to turn towards the Japanese garden and then browse through fascinating displays of flowering plant evolution, both outside and in the tropical glasshouse situated within the double-walled garden; or to follow the course of the lakes and wander through the slate beds to the wild garden, an informally planted area which is alive with bees, butterflies and other insects on a warm summer's day.

Whichever route they take, the visitor will inevitably end up in the Great Glasshouse, the largest single-span glasshouse in

the world. Designed again by Norman Foster & Partners, the structure is dramatic in itself; a simple elliptical dome built into an existing hilltop, but on a scale that is only really apparent from inside. The drama of the building is enhanced by the landscape design by Kathryn Gustafson; with a valley sloping down from the main entrance, surrounded by stone terraces, to a tumbling waterfall and interior lake. But it is the planting which makes the house so spectacular.

The house contains an unrivalled collection of plants from the five mediterranean climate regions of the world – the Western Cape of South Africa, South Western Australia, California, Central Chile and the Mediterranean basin itself. Almost a thousand different plant species – and nearly 3,000 plants – have established happily in the house, and jostle for space in a naturalistic display designed to evoke their original habitat.

The diversity of plants in the mediterranean climate regions is legendary; almost 20% of all the world's plant species occur in these regions (out of an estimated total of 250,000), while the combined extent of all the regions is less than 2% of the world's total landmass. In addition, the vegetation has very high levels of

The National Botanic Garden of Wales, opened to visitors in 2000, was the first national botanic garden to open in the 21st century, and the first to be created in Britain for nearly 200 years.

GLASSHOUSE

endemism (species confined to or occurring only in these particular regions) and is highly threatened by habitat loss, overexploitation and by competition from introduced (non-native) plant species, as well as man's interference in the natural fire cycle. All these factors combine to make the glasshouse a particularly fascinating place to spend an hour or two.

The glasshouse reaches its peak in mid-spring, when increasing day-length, warmer temperatures and plentiful water supplies combine to provide ideal flowering conditions for many of the plants within. On a sunny day, the house is alive with colour, and with fabulous scents arising from both flowers and leaves – aromatic oils contained within them are released on warm days, and combine to make a heady perfume.

Among the most outstanding plants on display are the South African proteas and woody daisies, the Australian grevilleas and banksias, the Chilean alstroemerias, the Californian ceanothus, sages and irises, and the range of lavenders, rosemaries and rock-roses in the Mediterranean. Perhaps the most endangered habitat of the world, the Canary Islands laurel forest, is represented around the margins of the lake. The vegetation here is of a type once found throughout the Mediterranean basin, but now clings on only in the islands off the west coast of Africa and southern Europe, where forests growing on high mountain slopes encourage water droplets to condense from surrounding clouds and trickle to the ground, providing a year-round supply of water for both trees and people. Once cleared, whether for agriculture, building or tourism, the forests no longer act as a natural reservoir; as a result, over 160 plant species from this habitat are threatened with extinction.

The National Botanic Garden of Wales hopes to use such stories to raise awareness among its visitors of the importance of plants to the well-being of themselves and of all humanity. Although something like 80% of the world's population is still entirely dependent on plants for medicines, and all of us are dependent on them for the food we eat and the air we breathe, we none-theless tend to take them for granted. By gathering together several fascinating collections, and displaying them to beautiful effect, NBG Wales aims to educate and enthral.

Religious men left many evocative monuments to their faith in these hills and mountains like the great Cisterian house of Valle Crucis Abbey near Llangollen

Or how about glorious **St Winifrede's Chapel**, a holy well and chapel dating to the early sixteenth century located in Holywell, Flintshire, though the site was a place of pilgrimage from at least 1115!

Probably the best-known abbey in Wales is **Tintern Abbey** in the wooded Wye Valley of south-east Wales. Despite the shell of this grand structure being open to the skies, Tintern Abbey is the best-preserved medieval abbey in Wales and visitors have been flocking to this river bank for hundreds of years to admire Tintern's grace and sublime beauty. There's still a lot going on at Tintern Abbey 500 years on. A major two-year programme of conservation work is nearing completion on the iconic thirteenth century west front – one of the great glories of Gothic architecture in Britain.

Tintern Abbey

Tintern Abbey

For more information on Cadw, visit www.cadw.wales.gov.uk. All images Cadw. Crown Copyright

The Landmark Trust is a building preservation charity that rescues and restores historic buildings at risk and gives them a sustainable future by offering them as inspiring places to spend a holiday.

The Landmark Trust
Living in History

750 YEARS OF LANDMARKS

Landmark's buildings trace our shared history and architecture, through periods of inspiration and conflict, through lives both celebrated and unremarkable. Staying in these buildings give us a better understanding of the lives of our forebears and perhaps even a better appreciation of the world we live in ourselves.

Time spent in an old building is never wasted, especially when you have it all to yourself to enjoy, without opening times or roped off areas to worry about. These pages show just a small selection of Landmark's 186 buildings in Britain and Italy through the centuries.

MEDIEVAL 1200-1485

1300
Morpeth Castle, Northumberland

This gatehouse is all that is left of Lord Greystoke's once mighty castle overlooking the River Wansbeck. (Sleeps 7)

1450
Wortham Manor, Devon

A great hall and exceptionally fine late medieval joinery survive in this manor house. (Sleeps 15)

1478
New Inn, Peasenhall, Suffolk

Dating from the time when purpose-built inns were new-fangled, New Inn today offers three self contained cottages. (Sleeps 4, 4 and 5)

TUDOR 1485-1603

1500
Abbey Gatehouse, Tewkesbury

This sturdy gatehouse guards the precincts of the great abbey of this ancient town between the Cotswold and Malvern Hills. (Sleeps 2)

1534
Laughton Place, East Sussex

A mighty tower is all that remains of the Pelhams' once great mansion, in this area later sought out both by opera buffs and the Bloomsbury set. (Sleeps 4)

c1535
Fish Court, Hampton Court Palace

Just off Henry VIII's Great Kitchen, his Officers of the Pastry once plied their craft in this apartment at the heart of the Palace. (Sleeps 6)

1579
Dolbelydr, Denbighshire

Henry Salesbury, author of the first Welsh grammar book, lived here. (Sleeps 6)

1590
Castle of Park, Dumfries and Galloway

This is a typical Scottish laird's tower house, built at a time when defence was still a consideration. (Sleeps 7)

You can book a holiday in any of Landmark's buildings online at: **www.landmarktrust.org.uk**. The iconic Landmark Trust Handbook, a detailed gazetteer of their buildings, can also be ordered on online or by telephoning **01628 825925**. It costs £10, refundable against a booking.

STUART 1603-1714

1713
Queen Anne's Summerhouse, Bedfordshire

This gracious folly is built of the finest brickwork and has the generous proportions of the English Baroque.
(Sleeps 2)

GEORGIAN 1714-c1800

1720
Princelet Street, London

Part of the development of Spitalfields just outside the city walls, this house once housed Huguenot silk weavers.
(Sleeps 6)

1741
Gothic Temple, Buckinghamshire

James Gibbs designed this homage to ancient liberties for Lord Cobham, at the heart of Capability Brown's landscape at Stowe.
(Sleeps 4)

REGENCY c1800-1837

1815
Swiss Cottage, Devon

A perfect example of the English Picturesque, designed by Jeffrey Wyatville within Humphry Repton's gardens at Endsleigh.
(Sleeps 4)

1825
The House of Correction, Lincolnshire

In this stern era, architecture was sometimes intended to lead the idle and disorderly to mend their ways, as here at Folkingham.
(Sleeps 4)

VICTORIAN 1837-1901

1847
Fort Clonque, Alderney

Reached by a causeway, Fort Clonque was built to allow Britain's new steam-powered warships to take on coal.
(Sleeps 13)

1849
Alton Station, Staffordshire

This is the only Italianate station-master's house on the 'Knotty' or North Staffordshire railway. The fine waiting room is now part of the accommodation. (Sleeps 6)

1850s
Casa Guidi, Florence

This apartment is furnished to reflect the residency of the poets Elizabeth Barratt and Robert Browning, who lived here for many years.
(Sleeps 6)

1877
Appleton Water Tower, Norfolk

Queen Victoria's fear of cholera led her to instruct the construction of this water tower on the Sandringham Estate, incorporating rooms for a custodian.
(Sleeps 4)

TWENTIETH CENTURY 1901+

1920
Steward's House, Oxford

Partaking of the eclectic Jacobethan style which dominated late-Victorian Oxford, this house is in the precincts of that ancient debating society, the Oxford Union.
(Sleeps 2)

1926
Howthwaite, Cumbria

This solid house stands above the Wordsworths' Dove Cottage, Landmark's presence there helping to protect the landscape they loved so much.
(Sleeps 7)

New offerings
from HISTORIC

Norwich Cathedral

The author and poet, Robert Louis Stevenson once declared, "Mankind was never so happily inspired as when it made a cathedral". Today, despite being centuries old, these atmospheric architectural giants continue to provide intrigue and inspiration for visitors. This is largely thanks to the conservation and restoration work carried out by dedicated teams and their desire to keep the buildings 'alive' with services, concerts and guided tours.

Chichester Cathedral celebrated its 900th anniversary in 2008 but in no way could it be accused of being stuck in the past. There are at least three services held here every day, regular concerts, exhibitions and guided tours often accompanied by the transporting sounds of the choir. If you visit as part of a

group, book on one of the specialist tours; from discovering the cathedral's breathtaking Norman and Gothic architecture dating back to 1108, to the extensive art collection. In addition to the 12th-century Chichester Reliefs, two sculptures depicting part of the story of the raising of Lazarus, the cathedral is known for its collection of world-class modern art with work by Marc Chagall, Graham Sutherland, John Piper and Cecil Collins. These paintings, tapestries and stained glass breathe new life into the stone walls.

In fact, this year the Chapter at Chichester announced the plan to commission a major new artwork to mark the centenary of the birth of Walter Hussey (1909-1985), Dean of Chichester from 1955 to 1977 and described by the art historian Kenneth Clark as, "the last great patron of art in the Church of England".

Today, despite being centuries old, these atmospheric architectural giants continue to provide intrigue and inspiration for visitors.

CATHEDRALS

Hussey believed that the cathedral "should be an inspiration to all who come here" and that contemporary art of a high quality only enriched a heritage setting. The brief for the new piece is a contemporary image of Christ after the resurrection designed to express "new life, transformation and hope". The commission has attracted interest from some of the most famous names in the international art world including Antony Gormley, Jaume Plensa, Cornelia Parker, Mark Wallinger, Ana Maria Pacheco and Dorothy Cross and you'll be able to see the winning piece when it is installed at the front of the nave in 2010.

World-class art and culture available to all, and for free, is something perhaps you'd only expect in larger cities such as London or Manchester. However at **Peterborough Cathedral** in Cambridgeshire you'll find all this and more. The Norman cathedral, famous as the set of the 1982 BBC series The Barchester Chronicles starring Alan Rickman, was recently voted the sixth favourite landmark in the UK and there is certainly plenty going on to keep the 100,000 visitors every year happy.

In addition to the regular services and daily evensong, there are special services held at Easter, Christmas (don't miss the Messiah concert), on St Peter's Day and in remembrance of Katharine of Aragon who was buried here in 1536. However, this is much more than a place of worship. On a tour of the cathedral, prepare to stand in awe as you gaze up at the magnificent West Front or the beautiful hand-painted nave ceiling. Make your way past the dramatic hanging crucifix that frames the choir stalls and the imposing marble altar in the sanctuary and learn more about the cathedral in the interactive 'Story of the Abbey' exhibition. For those with a head for heights, brave the cathedral's tower tour

Chichester

Peterborough

Peterborough

from which you're rewarded with views over the scenic Cambridgeshire landscape. Those that prefer to keep their feet firmly on the ground can relax in the new coffee shop or in the Deanery Gardens, open to the public on selected dates from April through to June. The cathedral's grounds also play host to the Peterborough Heritage Festival and the beautiful cloisters are often used for battle re-enactments.

Such re-enactments today are great fun but battles and war are often part of a cathedral's history. **Norwich Cathedral** has survived riot, war, plague and fire since its foundation in 1096 by the Norman Bishop, Herbert de Losinga, to today welcome all within its ancient walls.

With the second tallest spire in the country, the cathedral completely dominates the Norwich skyline and inside the superlatives continue: the largest

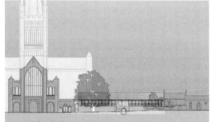
Norwich Cathedral - Hostry

monastic cloister in England and the world's largest collection of medieval roof bosses. In addition to one of the 45-minute tours starting in the nave, organ recitals and concerts are also commonplace as the cathedral upholds a proud tradition of choral worship that stretches back to 1096.

In fact the Song School and Music Library are housed in the Hostry, an exciting new development for Norwich Cathedral, designed by Sir Michael Hopkins. It lies within the footprint of the medieval Hostry, or guest hall, and Hopkins has sensitively maintained the aesthetics of the original building using materials found in the cathedral such as oak, limestone and glass. The original medieval entrance arch has also been preserved and incorporated into the design so that you can follow in the footsteps of past pilgrims visiting the priory. Inside creative writing and poetry workshops take place in the specially designed classroom, exhibitions in the Encounter Space and a film on the cathedral's past and present in the Locutory.

Hopkins is also responsible for the airy Refectory which opened in 2004. This

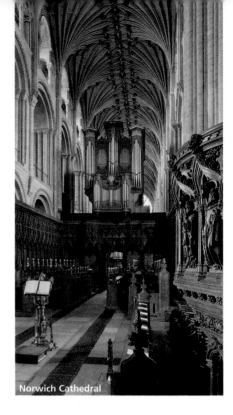
Norwich Cathedral

modern, award-winning restaurant attracts quite a crowd with its quality, fresh, locally-sourced produce. However, Norwich isn't the only cathedral serving fine fare; **St Paul's Cathedral** in London has a new restaurant which is fast becoming the place to taste the best British seasonal ingredients. Architect Wells Mackereth has transformed a corner of the crypt into a light dining room that

Cathedrals Index
Check websites for details of events

Below L to R: Norwich, Peterborough, Liverpool, Chichester, St Davids, St Pauls, St Edmundsbury

St Paul's Cathedral

Café, St Paul's Cathedral

serves traditional afternoon tea, or lunch between 12-3pm. With two courses for £18 and three courses for £22 it certainly won't break the bank, and will leave you nicely replete to fully explore Christopher Wren's masterpiece which celebrates its 300th anniversary. This is the fourth cathedral to stand on the site (there has been a cathedral dedicated to St Paul here since 604AD) and was built after the Great Fire of London destroyed its predecessor. History literally oozes out of every pore of this building and many important services have taken place within the walls including the wedding

of Prince Charles and Lady Diana, the thanksgiving service for HM The Queen's Golden Jubilee and the funerals of Lord Nelson and Sir Winston Churchill.

With its world-class reputation it is little wonder that renowned orchestras, musicians and choirs line up to perform at St Paul's. Christmas here is a particularly magical time; evocatively lit and perfectly atmospheric, the acoustics of this great British landmark ensures that the music embraces you. With acoustics in mind, no visit would be complete without climbing the 259

steps up the dome to the Whispering Gallery, so named because of the ability for a whisper against its walls to be audible on the opposite side. Continue up to the Stone Gallery and the Golden Gallery, which at 280ft affords panoramic views of the capital.

The Supertour also comes highly recommended and can last up to two hours as you take in the cathedral floor and normally out of bounds areas such as the Quire and the geometric staircase. Finally descend to the crypt which holds over 200 memorials including the tomb of Christopher Wren. Above his tomb an inscription reads, Lector, si monumentum requiris, circumspice (Reader, if you seek his monument, look around you).

From Butterflies to Broad Beans...

the wonders of the

KITCHEN

Sandringham 1935 Tapestry aerial view walled gardens behind house

Not since the Blitz have our gardens been so brimming with fruit and vegetables. This time it's not victory that we're digging for - now it's all about choice and lifestyle. We are witnessing one of the largest gardening trends since 'Ground Force' inspired the country to deck over its green and pleasant land; sales of vegetable seeds far outstrip those of flower seeds and ownership of an allotment is a social cachet. The nation's heritage of kitchen gardening is certainly one to be proud of, and nowhere is it better demonstrated than at many of the properties featured in Hudson's – most of which are once again sustaining families and enterprises with their wonderful produce!

The earliest form of recorded kitchen garden in this country is the potager - the name being a derivation from the everyday (literally) soup, or pottage, made from the vegetables and herbs that were grown. The mainstay of this soup was cabbage (also known as colewort or worts) which was boiled up with onions and parsley plus some pungent herbs such as hyssop, mustard seed and garlic to give it some flavour. The cabbage, which was nearer to kale than modern day cabbage, had to be sown up to four times a year to provide sufficient quantities to meet the needs of both master and knave. The juxtaposition of vegetables, herbs and flowers gave the whole plot a decorative as well as utilitarian feel which was further enhanced by the use of dwarf hedging to edge the beds. In some of the larger gardens of the 15th and 16th century the layout of these potagers were extremely elaborate affairs - reflecting the taste for formality and symmetry within the garden.

It wasn't until the end of the 17th century that hedges were gradually replaced with substantial and magnificent walls; built partly for keeping out vermin, but also in order that owners could `pull the curtains` on the goings on in the kitchen garden. As the rest of the gardens were landscaped with less formality and symmetry, the kitchen garden's drill square layout was completely out of kilter and would have jarred the senses of any respectful landowner and his guests. The walling also created the perfect microclimate for bringing on early vegetables and it enabled the construction of magnificent glasshouses for growing the more `exotic' crops.

Some of these `bastions of bountifulness' were truly large scale operations – **Castle Howard's Walled Garden** covered an area of 10 acres in 1750. It took a regiment of gardeners to upkeep, but was productive enough to feed

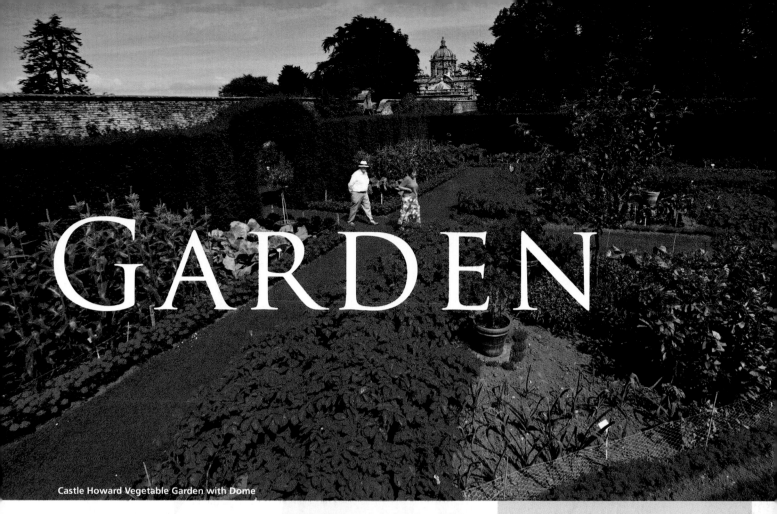

GARDEN

Castle Howard Vegetable Garden with Dome

Walled Garden Gates, Sandringham

the Howard family, guests and servants and still have enough left over for a market stall in York. Although the kitchen garden survived until the early 20th century, it wasn't until 2005 that the Head Gardener, Brian Deighton, inspired by the potager at Chateau Villandry in the Loire Valley, decided to create an ornamental potager within the site of the original walled garden. Wherever possible the original heritage varieties grown in the gardens heyday were used and the triumphant result has become an official `destination' in the tour guide!

Apple picking, Sandringham

Pumpkin loaf cake
Supplied by Sandringham

Ingredients

- 200g (7 oz) plain flour
- 1 1/4 teaspoons bicarbonate of soda
- 1 teaspoon salt
- 1 teaspoon ground cinnamon
- 1/2 teaspoon ground nutmeg
- 255g (9 oz) pureed pumpkin
- 200g (7 oz) dark brown soft sugar
- 110ml (4 fl oz) buttermilk
- 1 egg
- 2 tablespoons butter, softened

Preparation method

1. Preheat oven to 180 C / Gas mark 4.
2. Sift the flour, bicarbonate of soda, salt, cinnamon and nutmeg into a large bowl.
3. Mix in the pumpkin, brown sugar, buttermilk, egg and butter until well blended. Pour into a 23x12cm (9x5 in) loaf tin and smooth the top.
4. Bake for 1 hour in preheated oven, or until a cocktail stick inserted into the centre comes out clean.

Artichokes, Hartland Abbey

Hartland Abbey Apple and Marmalade Tart - Serves 4 - 6

Shortcrust Pastry ingredients

- 6oz (175g) plain flour
- 3 1/2oz (100g) butter, chopped
- 1 teaspoon sugar
- 3 tablespoons (3 x 15ml) cold water
- 7 inch (18cm) flan tin

Put flour, butter and sugar in processor and pulse until like breadcrumbs. With motor running pour in water and blend until it makes a ball. Turn off immediately. Put in plastic bag in fridge for about 30 mins and then roll out on floured surface to fit the tin. Put the tin in the fridge again for another 30 minutes for the pastry to settle and then trim the top. Bake blind (line pastry with greaseproof paper with rice or baking beans on top) at 400F/200C/gas 6 until cooked. If in Aga bake on bottom of Top RH oven.

Filling

- 2lb (900g) cooking apples (or puree from deep freeze)
- 2 tablespoons sugar
- 2 tablespoons (2 x 15ml) water
- 1 tablespoon marmalade
- 2 eating apples
- 2 tablespoons apricot jam, melted with 1 tbsp water and sieved

Peel and chop cooking apples (preferably Bramleys) and cook, covered, with 2 tbsps water until pureed. When nearly cooked remove lid to make puree drier and thicker. Stir in sugar and marmalade and remove from heat to cool a little before filling pastry case. Cover top with cored (not peeled), thinly sliced eating apples arranged in a nice pattern. Glaze with jam and return to oven 375F/190C/gas 5 for 5 - 10 minutes. Serve cold, warm or hot.

Middle vegetable garden, Hartland Abbey

King Edward VII laid out an eight-acre walled Kitchen Garden at **Sandringham** in Norfolk to produce all the fruits, vegetables and cut flowers for the house. Rising costs in the post-war years forced the closure of the garden but, in recent years, a small experimental vegetable plot has been reinstated. The garden provides vegetables and herbs for the restaurant which serves more than two hundred lunches every day in the late summer. As all gardeners will know from experience, there are inevitable gluts which challenge the chefs to produce increasingly ingenious ways to use courgettes, squash and apples.

The Walled Vegetable Garden at **Hartland Abbey** was established by resident monks in the 12th century to provide a sheltered setting to grow their fruit and vegetables. Being only a mile from the ferociously windy Atlantic coast, during the 18th century more sheltered walled gardens were built further up the valley, as they are today. Up until the First World War, fifteen gardeners were gainfully employed. Unfortunately, as was the case in many gardens, a lot of these soldiers never returned and as a result the gardens fell into decline. During the last war the Abbey became a refuge for evacuated school children who tasted the success of the gardens but it wasn't until the 1990's that a programme of restoration meant that these great gardens were not lost forever. Sir Hugh and Lady Stucley together with their wonderful gardener, Joanne Mitchell, have slowly restored these beautiful gardens and glasshouses to their former glory. Once again paths, edged by bright blue catmint and purple alliums, are neatly clipped with herbaceous perennials and roses filling the outer beds. The walls are covered in climbing roses and fruit trees while serried rows of artichokes divide the planting and an explosion of fruit and vegetables awaits the visitor in summer.

sunflowers and nasturtiums in high summer. Clearly the Walled Garden at **Hartland** is in the midst of a renaissance.

The gastronomic potential of a working kitchen garden is immense – with food metres instead of food miles, visitors are assured of the freshest and tastiest food available. Coupled with fine cafes and restaurants in beautiful surroundings, the marriage of garden and eatery is one made in heaven. **Forde Abbey Gardens** in Somerset is one such garden on a green mission and the two-acre walled garden produces enough salad, vegetables and fruit to provide for the owning family and the tearoom. The established and historic working kitchen garden and orchard at **Tiverton Castle**, Devon produces seasonal fruit and vegetables for use in the Castle kitchens and for the lucky holiday visitors staying in the Castle Apartments. The Castle has many unusual recipes including one for Elderflower Cordial and an even better one for using it!

The garden at **Doddington Hall** in Lincoln boasts an award winning Farm Shop and Café which unusually specialise in wonderful varieties of broad bean, a particular favourite of the owner, that they grow in the recently restored walled kitchen garden.

Painswick Rococo Gardens in Gloucestershire feature a large kitchen garden surrounded by 125 espalier fruit trees. The vegetables are mainly heritage but all produce is used in the restaurant which has perfected its own unusual recipe for Chocolate Courgette Cake. At Mannington Gardens in Norfolk, the Kitchen Garden supplies all the salad produce on sale at the wonderfully named Greedy Goose Tearooms.

Fruit growing was a particular passion of the Victorians and complex heating arrangements were built into many walled gardens to grow dates, pineapples and bananas. The kitchen garden at **Clovelly Court** in Devon is a classic example of a lovingly restored Victorian

Beautiful squashes of all shapes and sizes, neat rows of lettuces in red and green, multi coloured spinach, beetroot, onions, carrots and peas, old varieties of climbing runner and French beans winding their way up hazel sticks, are all intermingled with rows of rusty

Doddington Farm Shop and Cafe, Doddington Hall

Elderflower Cordial
Supplied by Tiverton Castle
Ingredients
- 12 elder flower heads (approx.)
- 3 sliced oranges
- 1 sliced lemon
- 3 lbs sugar
- 2 oz tartaric or citric acid
- 3 pints boiling water

Mix all together in large container and leave for three or four days, stirring in passing. Strain and bottle. Dilute to taste.

This freezes well. It is very refreshing, particularly with fizzy water. It is also delicious in SILKS - 1 measure of cordial, 1 measure of gin, and top up with fizzy water and ice.

Chocolate Courgette Cake
Supplied by Painswick Rococo Garden
Ingredients
- 175g/6oz plain chocolate
- 2 large eggs
- 175ml/6fl oz vegetable oil
- 200g/7oz self-raising flour
- 1/2 teaspoon salt
- 115g/4oz caster sugar
- 225g/8oz peeled weight courgettes, grated
- 55g/2oz walnuts, chopped

Preheat the oven to 180°C/350°F/Gas 4. Grease and flour a 20cm/8in round cake tin. Melt the chocolate in a bowl set over a pan of barely simmering water or in a microwave, and set aside. In a large bowl, whisk together the eggs and oil. Measure the flour, salt and sugar into another bowl, and mix together. Gradually add this mixture to the whisked egg and oil, and beat together well. Stir in the melted chocolate, then the grated courgettes and nuts. Mix well and pour into the prepared cake tin. Bake for 1 hour or until the cake is well risen and is firm and springy to the touch in the centre. Allow to cool in the tin for 10 minutes before turning out on a wire rack.

Ripon Garden

Clovelly Court Gardens

walled kitchen garden with magnificent lean-to glasshouses sheltering peaches, apricots, vines including Muscat grapes. The unique maritime microclimate of the garden allows the growth of tender and exotic plants which are grown to organic principles. Visitors are always delighted that the produce is for sale. The Victorian Garden at **St Mary's House & Gardens**, West Sussex was laid out in the 1890s, and has the original 140-foot fruit wall, heated pineapple pits and stove house. Fruit grown in

abundance is used in ingenious ways at **Combermere Abbey** on the Cheshire/Shropshire borders, home to the world's only Fruit Tree Maze. Planted in 1993, in the beautifully restored walled gardens, this unusual feature has redcurrants, gooseberries, crab apples, apples and pears. The fruit is harvested each year and made into jams, jellies and chutneys under the 'The Walled Garden Collection' label which is on sale to visitors.

Another area that is attracting more and more attention from visitors is education and training. The insatiable desire for information and gardening tips for use on allotments or back gardens is swelling the numbers booking onto courses. **Pashley Manor Gardens** in East Sussex will be repeating the successful Kitchen Garden Weekend in 2010. Experts will offer advice and there is a focus on how the produce from the garden is used in the café. The current kitchen garden was designed and planted in 1990 but is a re-creation of how the long-lost Victorian potager might have been; espaliered pear trees, vine arches and sweet peas co-existing happily with vegetables and herbs.

As might be expected, **Cambridge University Botanic Garden** is forefront in horticultural education and has opened a new Schools Garden where schoolchildren can grow their own fruit and vegetables. It is not a model kitchen garden but working plot run by green-fingered youngsters, which offers lots to learn for both children and visitors. The garden is open whenever a school is not working. At The **Alnwick Garden** in Northumberland, children of all ages have helped to create the Roots and Shoots teaching garden within the walls of the old kitchen garden. On certain days, visitors can enjoy gardening workshops and demonstrations which cater for schools, families and gardeners with special interests.

This hands-on approach to garden visiting is also very apparent at the **Ripon Workhouse Garden** where a team of volunteers is gradually bringing the old workhouse

Clovelly Court Gardens

Walled Garden, Combermere Abbey Maze

Julia Butterfly, Berkeley Castle

Swallowtail Butterfly, Berkeley Castle

garden back to something like the 1890's original. Admirably they are also using varieties true to the provenance of the garden and utilising wildlife friendly methods. Wildlife is also very much evident at the walled kitchen garden at **Berkeley Castle** in Gloucestershire where a tropical paradise has been established, which attracts beautiful butterflies from all over the world. Butterflies are hatched on the premises and then bred throughout the summer.

The kitchen garden is once again back where it belongs and proving that it is an essential ingredient for every garden - no matter of size or importance. Those property owners lucky enough to already have a programme of restoration and utilisation of the garden, whether true to the original or not, are now reaping the undoubted benefits through happy and content visitors who have sampled the fruits of their enterprise.

Jonathan Wild

The roots and shoots vegetable garden in the Alnwick Garden

The Great Conservatory, Syon Park
© Reg McKenna

London

England's vibrant capital city contains not just the 'must-see' attractions such as Buckingham Palace and the Tower of London, but also many smaller and no less interesting properties. London's parks are the lungs of the city. From Regent's Park in the north to Battersea Park south of the river, via Hyde Park and St James's it is possible to walk for miles, hardly touching a pavement.

Tulip Stairs © National Maritime Museum

Southside House

LONDON

t Paul's Cathedral © St Paul's Cathedral / Peter Smith

Spencer House © Spencer House / Mark Fiennes

Capel Manor gardens

London – England

■ **Owner**

Chiswick House and Gardens Trust and English Heritage

■ **Contact**

Visits:
House Manager
Chiswick House
Burlington Lane
London W4 2RP

Tel: 020 8995 0508
E-mail: customers@
english-heritage.org.uk

Venue Hire and Hospitality:
Hospitality Co-ordinator
Tel: 07787 435010

■ **Location**

MAP 19:C8
OS Ref: TQ210 775

Burlington Lane
London W4.

Rail: ½ mile NE of Chiswick Station.

Tube:
Turnham Green, ¾ mile

Bus: 190, E3.

■ **Opening Times**

Summer
1–30 April, Daily,
10am–5pm.
1 May–31 October,
Sun–Wed & BHs,
10am–5pm.

Winter
1 November–31 March,
available for group tours
- please call for details.
Closed 21 December–31
March.

■ **Admission**

Adult	£5.00
Child (5–15yrs)	£2.50
Conc	£4.30
Family	£12.50

Groups (11+)
15% discount.

EH Members free.

Opening times and prices are valid until 31st March 2010, after this date details are subject to change please see www.english-heritage.org.uk or www.chgt.org.uk for the most up-to-date information.

CHISWICK HOUSE AND GARDENS ⊞

www.english-heritage.org.uk/chiswickhouse

Chiswick House is internationally renowned as one of the first and finest English Palladian villas. Lord Burlington, who built the villa from 1725–1729, was inspired by the architecture and gardens of ancient Rome and this house is his masterpiece. His aim was to create a fit setting to show his friends his fine collection of art and his library. The opulent interior features gilded decoration, velvet walls and painted ceilings. The important 18th century gardens surrounding Chiswick House have, at every turn, something to surprise and delight the visitor from the magnificent cedar trees to the beautiful Italianate gardens with their cascade, statues, temples, urns and obelisks.

The Chiswick House & Gardens Trust (reg. charity 1109239) has been set up to lead a major restoration project to restore the historic gardens and improve visitor facilities. Visit www.chtg.org.uk for details.

2010 sees the culmination of a major project to restore the gardens to their former glory, including the conservatory and its world-famous camellia collection and over 1600 new trees planted. A new modern airy cafe opens in spring 2010.

- ℹ WCs. Filming, plays, photographic shoots.
- 🎁
- ⊤ Private & corporate hospitality.
- ♿
- ☕
- 🚶 Personal guided tours must be booked in advance.
- 🎧 Free audio tours in English, French & German.
- 🅿 Free if booked in advance. Tel: 020 7973 3485.
- 🐕 Guide dogs in grounds.
- 🔔
- 🎭

© English Heritage / Jonathan Bailey

ELTHAM PALACE AND GARDENS ⊞

www.english-heritage.org.uk/eltham

© English Heritage / Jonathan Bailey

The epitome of 1930s chic, Eltham Palace dramatically demonstrates the glamour and allure of the period.

Bathe in the light flooding from a spectacular glazed dome in the Entrance Hall as it highlights beautiful blackbean veneer and figurative marquetry. It is a tour de force only rivalled by the adjacent Dining Room – where an Art Deco aluminium-leafed ceiling is a perfect complement to the bird's-eye maple walls. Step into Virginia Courtauld's magnificent gold-leaf and onyx bathroom and throughout the house discover lacquered, 'ocean liner' style veneered walls and built-in furniture.

A Chinese sliding screen is all that separates chic Thirties Art Deco from the medieval Great Hall. You will find concealed electric lighting, centralised vacuum cleaning and a loud-speaker system that allowed music to waft around the house. Authentic interiors have been recreated by the finest contemporary craftsmen. Their appearance was painstakingly researched from archive photographs, documents and interviews with friends and relatives of the Courtaulds.

Outside you will find a delightful mixture of formal and informal gardens including a rose garden, pergola and loggia, all nestled around the extensive remains of the medieval palace.

New to the Palace: RAEC exhibition.

Opening times and prices are valid until 31st March 2010, after this date details are subject to change please see www.english-heritage.org.uk for the most up-to-date information.

ℹ️ WCs. Filming, plays and photographic shoots.

🛍️

❄️

🍽️ Exclusive private and corporate hospitality.

♿ WCs.

☕

🚶 Guided tours on request.

🎧 Free. English, German & French.

P Coaches must book.

🐕 Guide dogs only.

🔔

🎭

Owner
English Heritage

Contact
Eltham Palace
Court Yard
Eltham
London SE9 5QE

Visits:
Administrator
Tel: 020 8294 2548
E-mail: customers@
english-heritage.org.uk

Venue Hire and Hospitality:
Hospitality Manager
Tel: 020 8294 2577

Location
MAP 19:F8
OS Ref. TQ425 740

M25/J3, then A20 towards Eltham. The Palace is signposted from A20 and from Eltham High Street.
A2 from Central London.

Rail: 30 mins from Victoria or London Bridge Stations to Eltham or Mottingham, then 15 mins walk.

Opening Times
1 April–31 October,
Sun–Wed,
10am–5pm.

1 November–
31 December,
Sun–Wed,
11am–4pm.

Closed 1–31 January.

1 February–31 March
Sun–Wed
11am–4pm.

Eltham Palace is also open on Saturdays; 8 May, 19 June and 11 Sep.

The property may close at short notice, please ring in advance for details

Venue Hire and Hospitality
English Heritage offers exclusive use of the Palace on Thu, Fri or Sat for daytime conferences, meetings and weddings and in the evenings for dinners, concerts and receptions.

Admission
House and Gardens

Adult	£8.50
Child	£4.30
Conc.	£7.20
Family (2+3)	£20.50

Gardens only

Adult	£5.30
Child	£2.70
Conc.	£4.50

EH Members free.

Group discount available.

Conference/Function

ROOM	MAX CAPACITY
Great Hall	300 standing 200 dining
Entrance Hall	100 seated
Drawing Room	120 standing 80 theatre-style
Dining Room	10 dining

■ Owner
English Heritage

■ Contact
Kenwood House
Hampstead Lane
London NW3 7JR

Visits:
The House Manager
Tel: 020 8348 1286
E-mail: customers@
english-heritage.org.uk

■ Location
MAP 20:K1
OS Ref. TQ271 874

M1/J2. Signed off A1, on leaving A1 turn right at junction with Bishop's Ave, turn left into Hampstead Lane. Visitor car park on left.

Bus: London Transport 210.

Rail: Hampstead Heath.

Underground:
Archway or Golders Green Northern Line then bus 210.

■ Opening Times
1 April–31 March, daily. 11.30am–4pm.

Closed 24–26 December & 1 January.

The Park opens earlier and stays open later, please see site notices. House and grounds free; donations welcome. Pre-booked group tours available.

Venue Hire and Hospitality
Events are available for up to 100 guests in the Service Wing. Please ring Company of Cooks on 020 8341 5384.

■ Admission
House & Grounds
Free. Donations welcome.

Opening times and prices are valid until 31st March 2010, after this date details are subject to change please see www.english-heritage.org.uk for the most up-to-date information.

KENWOOD HOUSE ▦

www.english-heritage.org.uk/kenwoodhouse

Kenwood, one of the treasures of London, is an idyllic country retreat close to the popular villages of Hampstead and Highgate.

The house was remodelled in the 1760s by Robert Adam, the fashionable neo-classical architect. The breathtaking library or 'Great Room' is one of his finest achievements.

Kenwood is famous for the internationally important collection of paintings bequeathed to the nation by Edward Guinness, 1st Earl of Iveagh. Some of the world's finest artists are represented by works such as a Rembrandt *Self Portrait*, Vermeer's *The Guitar Player; Mary, Countess Howe* by Gainsborough and paintings by Turner, Reynolds and many others.

As if the house and it's contents were not riches enough, Kenwood stands in 112 acres of landscaped grounds on the edge of Hampstead Heath, commanding a fine prospect towards central London. The meadow walks and ornamental lake of the park, designed by Humphry Repton, contrast with the wilder Heath below.

WCs. Concerts, exhibitions, filming. No photography in house.

Exclusive private and corporate hospitality.

Available on request (in English). Please call for details.

West Lodge car park (Pay & Display) on Hampstead Lane. Parking for the disabled.

Free when booked in advance on 020 7973 3485.

Guide dogs only.

© National Maritime Museum

ROYAL OBSERVATORY, NATIONAL MARITIME MUSEUM & QUEEN'S HOUSE

www.nmm.ac.uk

The Royal Park at Greenwich provides a beautiful backdrop to the architectural landscape of Greenwich, now a World Heritage Site and a commanding view over London. The Tudor palace, in which Henry VIII, Mary Tudor and Elizabeth I were born, is now covered by the 17th-century Old Royal Naval College with its Painted Hall and Chapel.

Illustrated above is Flamsteed House (Wren 1675), built to accommodate the first Astronomer Royal. It was restored in 2006 with new presentations of significant time-keepers, including those of John Harrison, and the story of Greenwich Mean Time. The Meridian Line, Longitude 0°, is marked in the courtyard as the base point for the calculation of the World's time zones and the 1833 timeball still drops punctually at 1 o'clock. The new Peter Harrison Planetarium features shows and an Astronomy Centre with a café.

The modern National Maritime Museum charts Britain's history of seafaring and empire. Nelson's uniform is on display and portraits and artefacts from various military and civil expeditions tell the human stories behind many great events. Contemporary themes are tackled including the ocean environment, slavery and travel at sea. Stained glass from the destroyed Baltic Exchange is in a separate memorial gallery. There are frequent events and talks for adults and children.

The Queen's House (Inigo Jones 1635) is significant as the first classical house in England. Introducing the Palladian style to England, it was called a 'House of Delights' by Henrietta Maria and was used for court entertainments and balls. The Great Hall, Orangery and 'Tulip' stairs provide an elegant setting for fine and contemporary art displays, occasional exhibitions and private functions.

■ Owner
National Maritime Museum

■ Contact
Bookings Unit
National Maritime Museum
Park Row
Greenwich
London SE10 9NF

Tel: 020 8858 4422
Fax: 020 8312 6632

Visit Bookings:
Tel: 020 8312 6608
Fax: 020 8312 6522
E-mail:
bookings@nmm.ac.uk

Venue Hire:
Rebecca Hawksworth
Tel: 020 8312 8517
Fax: 020 8312 6572
E-mail:
events@nmm.ac.uk

■ Location
MAP 19:E7
OS Ref. TQ388 773

Within Greenwich Park on the S bank of the Thames at Greenwich. Travel by river cruise or Docklands Light Railway (Cutty Sark station).

Rail: London Bridge to Greenwich 8 mins

M25 (S) via A2. From M25 (N) M11, A12 and Blackwall Tunnel.

■ Opening Times
Daily, 10am–5pm (later opening in summer for Meridian Line). Last admission 30 mins prior. Varies at New Year and Marathon Day (25 April).

Closed 24–26 December.

Gallery talks and drama (see notices on arrival).

■ Special Exhibitions
Art for the Nation (all year)

Toy Boats (1 May–31 Oct)

New Visions contemporary art

■ Admission
Free admission except for Planetarium shows.

© National Maritime Museum

© National Maritime Museum

Conference/Function

ROOM	SIZE	MAX CAPACITY
Queen's House	40' x 40'	Dining 120 Standing 200
Observatory, Octagon Rm	25' x 25'	Dining 60 Standing 150
Observatory, Planetarium		Dining 110 Standing 150
NMM Upper Deck	140' x 70'	Dining 500 Standing 750
NMM Lecture Theatre		Conference 130
Queen's House Observatory		Daytime business meetings 12–50

 No photography in galleries   Partial. WC.    Limited for coaches. Assistance dogs only.

Owner
Dean & Chapter of
St Paul's Cathedral

Contact
The Chapter House
St Paul's Churchyard
London EC4M 8AD
Tel: 020 7246 8350
 020 7236 4128
Fax: 020 7248 3104
E-mail: chapter@
stpaulscathedral.org.uk

Location
MAP 20:N7
OS Ref. TQ321 812

Central London.
Underground:
St Paul's, Mansion
House, Blackfriars, Bank.
Rail: Blackfriars,
City Thameslink.
Air: London Airports.

Opening Times
Mon–Sat, 8.30am–
4.30pm, last admission
4pm.
Guided tours: Mon–Sat,
10.45am, 11.15am,
1.30pm & 2pm.
Tours of the Triforium:
Mon & Tues, 11.30am &
2pm. Fri, 2pm.
All tours are subject to
an additional charge.

Cathedral Shop & Café:
Mon–Sat, 9am–5pm,
Shop Sun,10am–4.30pm,
Cafe Sun,12pm–4pm.

Restaurant:
Mon–Sat, Lunch 12pm–
3pm, Afternoon tea
3pm–4.30pm. Sun,
12pm–3pm.

Service Times
Mon–Sat, 7.30am
Mattins 8am Holy
Communion (said),
12.30pm Holy
Communion (said)
5pm Choral Evensong

Sun: 8am Holy
Communion (said)
10.15am Choral Mattins
& sermon, 11.30am
Choral Eucharist &
sermon, 3.15pm Choral
Evensong & sermon
6pm Evening service

The Cathedral may be
closed to tourists on
certain days of the year.
It is advisable to phone
or check our website for
up-to-date information.

Admission
Adult	£11.00
Child	£3.50
OAP	£10.00
Student	£8.50
Family	£25.50

Groups (10+)
Adult	£10.00
Child	£3.00
OAP	£9.00
Student	£7.50

(Subject to change).

Conference/Function

ROOM	MAX CAPACITY
Wren Suite	100 (standing)

Beneath the Dome

ST PAUL'S CATHEDRAL
www.stpauls.co.uk

St Paul's, with its world-famous Dome, is an iconic feature of the London skyline, but there is much more to Sir Christopher Wren's masterpiece than its impressive façade.

A spiritual focus for the nation since its first service in 1697, many important events have taken place within its walls, from State funerals of Lord Nelson, the Duke of Wellington and Sir Winston Churchill to the wedding of the Prince of Wales to Lady Diana Spencer and the Thanksgiving services for Her Majesty the Queen's Golden Jubilee and 80th Birthday.

The results of the Cathedral's programme of cleaning and repair, now in its final stages, are breathtaking.

The West front, once blackened and damaged, now rises majestically at the top of Ludgate Hill and details previously hidden stand out crisp and proud. The interior has been transformed by state-of-the-art restoration techniques and the light that now floods the space, highlights the luminescent Portland stone and brings mosaics, carvings and sculpture to life. In the Dome, exquisite 18th century paintings by Sir James Thornhill, showing scenes from the life of St Paul, have been returned to their original beauty.

The pinnacle of any trip to St Paul's is the winding journey up the spiral staircase to the Whispering Gallery, to experience its unique acoustic effects before climbing up and out to the Stone and Golden Galleries, which afford a panoramic view of London that is second to none.

The High Altar & Quire

Down the Nave

 No photography, video or mobile phones.

 Partial.
 Licensed.

 None for cars, limited for coaches.

Guide dogs only.

© Spencer House / Mark Fiennes

SPENCER HOUSE

www.spencerhouse.co.uk

Spencer House, built 1756–66 for the first Earl Spencer, an ancestor of Diana, Princess of Wales (1961–97), is London's finest surviving 18th century town house. The magnificent private palace has regained the full splendour of its late 18th century appearance, after a painstaking ten-year restoration programme.

Designed by John Vardy and James 'Athenian' Stuart, the nine State rooms are amongst the first neo-classical interiors in Europe. Vardy's Palm Room, with its spectacular screen of gilded palm trees and arched fronds, is a unique Palladian set-piece, while the elegant mural decorations of Stuart's Painted Room reflect the 18th century passion for classical Greece and Rome. Stuart's superb gilded furniture has been returned to its original location in the Painted Room by courtesy of the V&A and English Heritage. Visitors can also see a fine collection of 18th century paintings and furniture, specially assembled for the house, including five major Benjamin West paintings, graciously lent by Her Majesty The Queen.

The State rooms are open to the public for viewing on Sundays. They are also available on a limited number of occasions each year for private and corporate entertaining during the rest of the week.

© Spencer House / Mark Fiennes

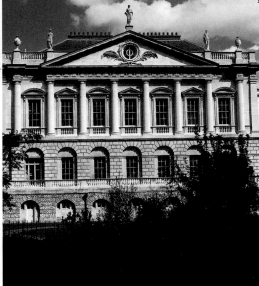

© Spencer House / Mark Fiennes

ℹ No photography inside House or Garden.

🍽 House only, ramps and lifts. WC.

♿ Obligatory. Comprehensive colour guidebook.

P None.

■ Contact

Jane Rick
Director
Spencer House
27 St James's Place
London SW1A 1NR

Tel: 020 7514 1958
Fax: 020 7409 2952
Recorded Info Line:
020 7499 8620
Email:
tours@spencerhouse.co.uk

■ Location

MAP 20:L8
OS Ref. TQ293 803

Central London:
off St James's Street,
overlooking
Green Park.

Underground:
Green Park.

■ Opening Times

All Year (except January & August) Suns, 10.30am–5.45pm.

Last tour 4.45pm.

Regular tours throughout the day. Maximum number on each tour is 20.

Mon mornings for pre-booked groups only. Group size: min 15–60.

Open for private and corporate hospitality except during January & August.

■ Admission

Adult   £9.00
Conc.*   £7.00

*Students, Members of the V&A, Friends of the Royal Academy, Tate Members and senior citizens (only on production of valid identification), children under 16. No children under 10 admitted.

Prices include guided tour.

Garden
For updated information on opening dates for the restored 18th century garden view:
www.spencerhouse.co.uk
or telephone the recorded information line: 020 7499 8620.

Conference/Function

ROOM	MAX CAPACITY
Receptions	400
Lunches & Dinners	126
Board Meetings	24
Theatre-style Meetings	100

Owner
The Duke of Northumberland

Contact
Estate Office
Syon House
Syon Park
Brentford
TW8 8JF

Tel: 020 8560 0882
Fax: 020 8568 0936
E-mail: info@
syonpark.co.uk

Location
MAP 19:B8
OS Ref. TQ173 767

Between Brentford and
Twickenham, off the A4,
A310 in SW London.

SAT NAV Ref TW7 6AZ

Rail: Kew Bridge or
Gunnersbury
Underground then
Bus 237 or 267.

Air: Heathrow 8m.

Opening Times
Syon House
17 March–31 October
Wed, Thur, Sun & BHs
11am–5pm
(open Good Fri &
Easter Sat).

Other times by
appointment for groups.

Gardens only
April–October
Daily, 10.30am–5pm
November–March
Sats & Suns, &
New Year's day,
10.30am–4pm or dusk,
whichever is earlier.

Last admissions House &
Gardens 1 hr before
closing.

Admission
House and Gardens
Adult	£9.00
Child	£4.00
Conc.	£8.00
Family (2+2)	£20.00

Group bookings (15–50)
Adult	£8.50
Conc.	£7.50
School Group	£2.00

**Gardens & Great
Conservatory**
Adult	£4.50
Child	£2.50
Conc.	£3.50
Family (2+2)	£10.00

Group bookings (15–50)
Price on application
(please telephone).

Syon Park Ventures &
The Lovaine Trust reserve
the right to alter opening
times.

Conference/Function
ROOM	SIZE	MAX CAPACITY
Great Hall	50' x 30'	120
Great Conservatory	60' x 40'	150
Northumberland Room	35' x 20'	60
Marquee		1000

SYON PARK 🏛

www.syonpark.co.uk

Described by John Betjeman as the 'Grand Architectural Walk', Syon House and its 200-acre park is the London home of the Duke of Northumberland, whose family, the Percys, have lived here for 400 years.

Originally the site of a late medieval monastery, excavated by Channel 4's *Time Team*, Syon Park has a fascinating history. The present house has Tudor origins but contains some of Robert Adam's finest interiors, which were commissioned by the 1st Duke in the 1760s. The private apartments and State bedrooms are available to view. The house can be hired for filming and photo shoots subject to availability.

Within the 'Capability' Brown landscaped park are 40 acres of gardens which contain the spectacular Great Conservatory designed by Charles Fowler in the 1820s. The House and Great Conservatory are available for corporate and private hire.

The Northumberland Room in Syon House is an excellent venue for conferences, meetings, lunches and dinners (max 60). The State Apartments make a sumptuous setting for dinners, concerts, receptions, launches and wedding ceremonies (max 120). Marquees can be erected on the lawn adjacent to the house for balls and corporate events. The Great Conservatory is available for summer parties, launches, filming, photoshoots and wedding receptions (max 150).

© Tony Marshall

- ℹ️ No photography in house. Indoor adventure playground.
- 🛍️ Garden centre.
- ✻
- ⍾
- ♿ Partial.
- 🍽️
- 🏃 By arrangement.
- 🎧
- 🅿️
- 📷
- 🦮 Guide dogs only.
- 🔔
- ❄️
- 🛡️

2 WILLOW ROAD

HAMPSTEAD, LONDON NW3 1TH
Tel: 020 7435 6166 **E-mail:** 2willowroad@nationaltrust.org.uk
Owner: The National Trust **Contact:** The Custodian
The former home of Ernö Goldfinger, designed and built by him in 1939. A three-storey brick and concrete rectangle, it is one of Britain's most important examples of modernist architecture and is filled with furniture also designed by Goldfinger. The interesting art collection includes works by Henry Moore and Max Ernst.
Location: MAP 20:J2, OS Ref. TQ270 858. Hampstead, London.
Open: 13 Mar–31 Oct, Thur, Fri, Sat, Sun, 12 noon–5pm; 6 Nov–28 Nov, Sat & Sun, 12 noon–5pm. Open Good Friday. Entry by timed tour only at 12 noon, 1 & 2pm. Places on tours limited and available on a first come first served basis on the day. Non-guided viewing 3–5pm with timed entry when busy.
Admission: Adult £5.50, Child £2.75, Family £13.75. Joint ticket with Fenton House £8. Private groups are welcome to book visits between Mar–Nov outside public opening times. Groups must be 5+, booking essential. Free to NT Members.
Small ground floor area accessible. Filmed tour of whole house available.

18 FOLGATE STREET

Spitalfields, East London E1 6BX
Tel: 020 7247 4013 www.dennissevershouse.co.uk
Owner: Spitalfields Historic Buildings Trust **Contact:** Mick Pedroli
A time capsule furnished and decorated to tell the story of the Jervis family, Huguenot silk weavers from 1724–1919.
Location: MAP 20:P6, OS Ref. TQ335 820. ½m NE of Liverpool St. Station. E of Bishopsgate (A10), just N of Spitalfields Market.
Open/Admission: Every Mon evening (except BH), by Candlelight, 'Silent Night'. Times vary with light of seasons, booking necessary. £12. Every Sunday, 12–4pm (last adm 3.15pm). £8. Mons following first & third Sun, 12–2pm. £5. Individual & group/corporate booking possible. Christmas prices, £15/£10/£8 per person.
Partial. Obligatory by private bookings.

ALBERT MEMORIAL

Princes Gate, Kensington Gore SW7 2AN
Tel: Bookings – 020 7495 0916. Enquiries – 020 7495 5504
E-mail: customers@english-heritage.org.uk
An elaborate memorial by George Gilbert Scott to commemorate the Prince Consort.
Location: MAP 20:J8, OS Ref. TQ266 798. Victoria Station 1½m, South Kensington Tube ½m.
Open: All visits by booked guided tours; first Sun of the month Mar–Dec, 2pm & 3pm. Tours last 45 mins.
Admission: Adult £4.50, Conc £4. Booking advisable for groups (10+). (2007 prices). Opening times and prices are valid until 31st March 2010, after this date details are subject to change please see www.english-heritage.org.uk for the most up-to-date information.

APSLEY HOUSE

See page 51 for full page entry.

BANQUETING HOUSE

The Banqueting House, Horse Guards, Whitehall, London SW1A 2ER
Tel: General Enquiries: 0844 482 7777 **Functions:** 020 3166 6150 / 6151
Email: groupsandtraveltrade@hrp.org.uk www.banqueting-house.org.uk
Owner: Historic Royal Palaces
This revolutionary building, is the first in England to be designed in a Palladian style by Inigo Jones. The Banqueting House is most famous for one real life drama, the execution of Charles I.
Location: MAP 20:M8, OS Ref. TQ302 80, Underground: Westminster, Embankment and Charing Cross. Rail: Charing Cross. Boat: Embankment Pier.
Open: All year, Mon–Sat, 10am–5pm. Last admission 4.30pm. Closed 24 Dec–1 Jan, Good Friday and other public holidays. NB. Liable to close at short notice for Government functions.
Admission: Enquiry line for admission prices: 0844 482 7777.
Concerts. No photography inside. WCs. By arrangement. Video and audio guide. Limited.

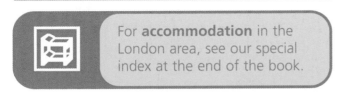
For **accommodation** in the London area, see our special index at the end of the book.

Albert Memorial, Hyde Park

BENJAMIN FRANKLIN HOUSE

36 Craven Street, London WC2N 5NF

Tel: 020 7839 2006 (Box Office) **www.BenjaminFranklinHouse.org**

Owner: The Friends of Benjamin Franklin House **Contact:** Dr Marcia Balisciano

Benjamin Franklin's only surviving residence. A dynamic museum and educational facility. The 'museum as theatre' Historical Experience takes visitors on a journey through this Grade I listed heritage 'gem', blending live interpretation, cutting-edge lighting, sound and visual projection to tell the rich story of Franklin in London in his own words.

Location: MAP 20:N7, OS Ref. TQ302 804. Nr Charing Cross Station.

Open: All year: Wed–Sun, 10.30am–5pm. Historical Experience Show, 12 noon, 1, 2, 3.15 and 4.15pm.

Admission: Adult £7, Child up to 16yrs Free.

🅣 ▦ ❋ ♿

BLEWCOAT SCHOOL 🌿

23 Caxton Street, Westminster, London SW1H 0PY

Tel: 020 7222 2877

Owner: The National Trust **Contact:** Janet Bowden

Built in 1709 at the expense of William Green, a local brewer, to provide an education for poor children. Used as a school until 1926, it is now the NT London Gift Shop and Information Centre.

Location: MAP 20:L9, OS Ref. TQ295 794. Near the junction with Buckingham Gate.

Open: All year: Mon–Fri, 10am–5.30pm. 6 Nov–18 Dec: Sat, 10am–4pm. Closed BHs.

BOSTON MANOR HOUSE

Boston Manor Road, Brentford TW8 9JX

Tel: 0845 456 2824 **E-mail:** info@cip.org.uk

Owner: Hounslow Cultural & Community Services

A fine Jacobean house built in 1623.

Location: MAP 19:B7, OS Ref. TQ168 784. 10 mins walk S of Boston Manor Station (Piccadilly Line) and 250yds N of Boston Manor Road junction with A4 Great West Road, Brentford.

Open: Apr–end Oct: Sat, Sun & BHs, 2.30–5pm. Park open daily.

Admission: Free.

BRUCE CASTLE MUSEUM

Haringey Libraries, Archives & Museum Service, Lordship Lane, London N17 8NU

Tel: 020 8808 8772 **Fax:** 020 8808 4118 **E-mail:** museum.services@haringey.gov.uk

Owner: London Borough of Haringey

A Tudor building. Sir Rowland Hill (inventor of the Penny Post) ran a progressive school at Bruce Castle from 1827.

Location: MAP 19:E6, OS Ref. TQ335 906. Corner of Bruce Grove (A10) and Lordship Lane, 600yds NW of Bruce Grove Station.

Open: All year: Wed–Sun & Summer BHs (except Good Fri), 1–5pm. Organised groups by appointment.

Admission: Free.

BUCKINGHAM PALACE

London SW1A 1AA

Tel: 020 7766 7300 **E-mail:** bookinginfo@royalcollection.org.uk

Owner: Official Residence of Her Majesty The Queen

Contact: Ticket Sales & Information Office

Buckingham Palace is the official London residence of Her Majesty The Queen and serves as both home and office. Its 19 State Rooms, which open for eight weeks a year, form the heart of the working palace. The garden walk offers superb views of the Garden Front of the Palace and the 19th-century lake.

Location: MAP 20:L8, OS Ref. TQ291 796. Underground: Green Park, Victoria, St James's Park.

Open: Contact information office.

Admission: Contact information office.

BURGH HOUSE

New End Square, Hampstead, London NW3 1LT

Tel: 020 7431 0144 **Buttery:** 0207 794 2905 **Fax:** 020 7435 8817

E-mail: info@burghhouse.org.uk **www.burghhouse.org.uk**

Owner: London Borough of Camden **Contact:** General Manager

A Grade I listed building of 1703 in the heart of old Hampstead with original panelled rooms, "barley sugar" staircase banisters and a music room. Child-friendly, refurbished Hampstead Museum, permanent and changing exhibitions. Prize-winning terraced garden. Regular programme of concerts, art exhibitions, and meetings. Receptions, seminars and conferences. Rooms for hire. Special facilities for schools visits. Wedding ceremonies and receptions.

Location: MAP 20:J2, OS Ref. TQ266 859. New End Square, E of Hampstead Underground station.

Open: All year: Wed–Sun, 12 noon–5pm. Sats by appointment only. BH Mons, 2–5pm. Closed Christmas fortnight, Good Fri & Easter Mon. Groups by arrangement. Buttery: Tues–Fri, 11am–6pm. Sat–Sun, 9.30am–6pm. BHs, 11am–6pm.

Admission: Free.

▦ 🅣 ♿ Ground floor & grounds. WC. ▦ Licensed buttery. ⑪ 🅕 By arrangement. 🅟 None. ▦ By arrangement. 🦮 Guide dogs only. ▲ ❋ ♿

CAPEL MANOR GARDENS
BULLSMOOR LANE, ENFIELD EN1 4RQ

www.capelmanorgardens.co.uk

Tel: 08456 122122 **Fax:** 01992 717544

Owner: Capel Manor Charitable Organisation **Contact:** Customer Services

These extensive, richly planted gardens are delightful throughout the year offering inspiration, information and relaxation. The gardens include various themes - historical, modern, walled, rock, water, sensory and disabled and an Italianate Maze, Japanese Garden and 'Gardening Which?' demonstration and trial gardens. Capel Manor is London's only specialist college for land based studies including Horticulture, Garden Design, Arboriculture, Environmental Conservation, Animal Care, Floristry and Saddlery.

Location: MAP 19:E4, OS Ref. TQ344 997. Minutes from M25/J25. Tourist Board signs posted.

Open: Daily in summer: 10am–6pm. Last ticket 4.30pm. Check for winter times.

Admission: Adult £5.50, Child £2.50, Conc. £4.50, Family £13.50. Charges alter for special show weekends and winter months.

▦ ❋ ♿ Grounds. WC. ▦ ⑪ 🅟 ▦ 🦮 In grounds, on leads. ❋ ♿

For unique **Civil wedding** venues see our index at the end of the book.

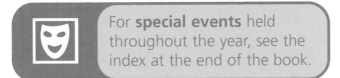

For **special events** held throughout the year, see the index at the end of the book.

CAREW MANOR DOVECOTE

Church Road, Beddington SM6 7NH
Tel: 020 8770 4781 **Fax:** 020 8770 4777 **E-mail:** valary.murphy@sutton.gov.uk
www.sutton.gov.uk
Owner: London Borough of Sutton **Contact:** Ms V Murphy
An early 18th century octagonal brick dovecote with around 1200 nesting boxes and the original potence (circular ladder). Opened for tours with the adjacent late medieval Grade I listed Great Hall of Carew Manor.
Location: MAP 19:D9, OS Ref. TQ295 652. Just off A232 at entrance to Beddington Park.
Open: Tours: Suns only – please ring 020 8770 4781 for dates for 2010.
Admission: Adult £4, Child £2.

CARLYLE'S HOUSE 💐

24 Cheyne Row, Chelsea, London SW3 5HL
Tel: 020 7352 7087 **E-mail:** carlyleshouse@nationaltrust.org.uk
Owner: The National Trust **Contact:** The Custodian
Atmospheric home of the writer Thomas Carlyle and his wife Jane from 1834–1881. There is a small walled garden and the surrounding streets are rich in literary and artistic associations.
Location: MAP 20:K10, OS Ref. TQ272 777. Off the King's Road and Oakley Street, or off Cheyne Walk between Albert Bridge and Battersea Bridge on Chelsea Embankment.
Open: 10 Mar–31 Oct: Wed–Fri (incl. Good Fri), 2–5pm; Sat, Sun & BH Mons, 11am–5pm. Last admission 4.30pm.
Admission: Adult £5.10, Child £2.60, Family £12.80. Free to NT Members. Tel for groups visits and guided tours.
By arrangement for groups.

CHAPTER HOUSE ♯

East Cloisters, Westminster Abbey, London SW1P 3PA
Tel: 020 7654 4900 **E-mail:** customers@english-heritage.org.uk
www.english-heritage.org.uk/chapter
Owner: English Heritage **Managed by:** Dean & Chapter of Westminster
The Chapter House, built by the Royal masons c1250 and faithfully restored in the 19th century, contains some of the finest medieval sculpture to be seen and spectacular wall paintings. The building is octagonal, with a central column, and still has its original floor of glazed tiles, which have been newly conserved. Its uses have varied and in the 14th century it was used as a meeting place for the Benedictine monks of the Abbey as well as for Members of Parliament.
Location: MAP 20:M8, OS Ref. TQ301 795.
Open: Throughout the year: 10am–4pm, Mon–Sat. Closed Good Fri, 24–26 Dec & 1 Jan. May be closed at short notice on state and religious occasions. Major restorations are planned for 2009/2010. Please see website for information before planning a visit.
Admission: Free. Opening times and prices are valid until 31st March 2010, after this date details are subject to change please see www.english-heritage.org.uk for the most up-to-date information.

CHISWICK HOUSE ♯

See page 52 for full page entry.

COLLEGE OF ARMS

Queen Victoria Street, London EC4V 4BT
Tel: 020 7248 2762 **Fax:** 020 7248 6448 **E-mail:** enquiries@college-of-arms.gov.uk
Owner: Corp. of Kings, Heralds & Pursuivants of Arms **Contact:** The Officer in Waiting
Mansion built in 1670s to house the English Officers of Arms and their records.
Location: MAP 20:O7, OS Ref. TQ320 810. On N side of Queen Victoria Street, S of St Paul's Cathedral.
Open: Earl Marshal's Court only; open all year (except BHs, State and special occasions) Mon–Fri, 10am–4pm. Group visits (up to 10) by arrangement only. Record Room: open for tours (groups of up to 20) by special arrangement in advance with the Officer in Waiting.
Admission: Free (groups by negotiation)

EASTBURY MANOR HOUSE 💐

Eastbury Square, Barking, Essex IG11 9SN
Tel: 020 8724 1000 **Fax:** 020 8724 1003 **E-mail:** eastburyhouse@lbbd.gov.uk
www.barking-dagenham.gov.uk
Owner: The National Trust **Contact:** Julie Packham
A fine example of a medium sized Tudor gentry house with attractive grounds. Intriguing Gunpowder Plot connections. Open to visitors all year. Heritage and arts activities and events. Available for education days, business conferences and Civil Wedding and Partnership ceremonies. Managed by the London Borough of Barking and Dagenham.
Location: MAP 19:F7, OS TQ457 838. In Eastbury Square off Ripple Road off A13. Bus: 287, 368 or 62. Underground: Upney (10 mins walk).
Open: All year: Mons & Tues and 1st & 2nd Sat of the month, 10am–4pm.
Admission: Adult £2.50, Child 65p, Conc. £1.25, Family £5. Groups (15+) by arrangement: £2pp. Free to NT Members.
WCs. Licensed. In Eastbury Square. On leads.

ELTHAM PALACE ♯

See page 53 for full page entry.

©NTPL/Nadia MacKenzie

FENTON HOUSE 💐

HAMPSTEAD GROVE, HAMPSTEAD, LONDON NW3 6RT

Tel/Fax: 020 7435 3471 **Infoline:** 01494 755563
E-mail: fentonhouse@nationaltrust.org.uk
Owner: The National Trust **Contact:** The Custodian
A delightful late 17th century merchant's house which contains an outstanding collection of porcelain, needlework, pictures and furniture. The Benton Fletcher Collection of early keyboard instruments is also housed here. The walled garden has a formal lawn and walks, an orchard and vegetable garden.
Location: MAP 20:J2, OS Ref. TQ262 860. Visitors' entrance on W side of Hampstead Grove. Hampstead Underground station 300 yds.
Open: 20 Mar - 31 Oct: Wed–Fri, 2–5pm; Sat, Sun & BHs, 11am–5pm. Groups at other times by appointment.
Admission: Adult £6, Child £3, Family £15, Groups (15+) £5.10. Joint ticket with 2 Willow Road, £8. Garden only: Adult £1. Free to NT Members.
Special Events: Summer concerts on Thurs lunchtimes and evenings, Apple Day fair Sun 3 Oct.
No picnics in grounds. Partial. Licensed. By arrangement. Demonstration tours. None. Guide dogs only. Send SAE for details.

See which properties offer **educational facilities** or **school visits** in our index at the end of the book.

FORTY HALL

FORTY HILL, ENFIELD, MIDDLESEX EN2 9HA

www.enfield.gov.uk/fortyhall

Tel: 020 8363 8196 **Fax:** 020 8367 9098 **E-mail:** forty.hall@enfield.gov.uk
Contact: London Borough of Enfield **Contact:** Gavin Williams
Step back in time and discover Enfield's heritage in this beautiful Grade One listed Jacobean House and Gardens built in 1632 for Sir Nicholas Rainton, Lord Mayor of London. Forty Hall today is a location for festivals, events and guided tours throughout the year and a museum of Enfield's history. The Hall is open Wed - Sun 11am to 4pm. Admission Free. Estate & grounds open daily dawn to dusk.
Location: MAP 19:E5, OS Ref. TQ336 985. 1m from M25/J25, just off A10. Tourist Board sign posted.
Open: All year: Wed–Sun, 11am–4pm.
Admission: Free. Groups welcome.

⬚ ⬚ Partial. WCs. ⬚ ⬚ By arrangement. 🅿 Ample for cars. Limited for coaches.
⬚ ⬚ In grounds, on leads. ⬚ ⬚

THE FOUNDLING MUSEUM

40 Brunswick Square, London WC1N 1AZ
Tel: 020 7841 3600 **Fax:** 020 7841 3601
Owner: The Foundling Museum
Site of London's first home for abandoned children. Established in 1739. The museum charts the history of the Foundling Hospital and its residents.
Location: MAP 20:M6, OS Ref. TQ303 822. Underground: Russell Square.
Open: Tues–Sat, 10am–6pm; Sun, 12 noon–6pm.
Admission: Adult £5, Child up to 16yrs Free, Conc. £4. Special rates for groups & schools.

FULHAM PALACE & MUSEUM

Bishop's Avenue, Fulham, London SW6 6EA
Tel: 020 7736 3233
Owner: London Borough of Hammersmith & Fulham & Fulham Palace Trust
Former home of the Bishops of London (Tudor with Georgian additions and Victorian Chapel). Set in gardens with a collection of rare trees. Museum, contemporary art gallery.
Location: MAP 20:I12, OS Ref. TQ240 761.
Open: Museum: Mons & Tues, 12 noon–4pm; Sats, 11am–2pm; Suns, 11.30am–3.30pm. Café: daily, 9am–5pm.
Admission: Palace & Gardens: Free.

GUNNERSBURY PARK & MUSEUM

Gunnersbury Park, London W3 8LQ
Tel: 020 8992 1612 **Fax:** 020 8752 0686 **E-mail:** gp-museum@cip.org.uk
Owner: Hounslow and Ealing Councils **Contact:** Lynn Acum
Built in 1802 and refurbished by Sydney Smirke for the Rothschild family.
Location: MAP 19:B7, OS Ref. TQ190 792. Acton Town Underground station. ¼m N of the junction of A4, M4 North Circular.
Open: Apr–Oct: daily: 11am–5pm. Nov–Mar: daily: 11am–4pm. Victorian kitchens summer weekends only. Closed Christmas Day & Boxing Day. Park: open dawn–dusk.
Admission: Free. Donations welcome.

HAM HOUSE & GARDEN ❧

HAM ST, RICHMOND-UPON-THAMES, SURREY TW10 7RS

www.nationaltrust.org.uk/hamhouse

Tel: 020 8940 1950 **Fax:** 020 8439 8241 **E-mail:** hamhouse@nationaltrust.org.uk
Owner: The National Trust **Contact:** The Property Manager
One of a series of grand houses and palaces alongside the River Thames, Ham House and Garden is an unusually complete survival of the 17th century. Rich in history and atmosphere, Ham was mainly created by the charismatic Elizabeth, Duchess of Lauderdale, who was deeply embroiled in the politics of the English Civil War and restoration of the monarchy. With lavish interiors unique historical features and outstanding art collections, Ham is a treasure trove waiting to be discovered. The gardens are a rare example of 17th century garden design.
Location: MAP 19:B8, OS Ref. TQ172 732. 1½ m from Richmond and 2m from Kingston. On the S bank of the River Thames, W of A307 at Petersham between Richmond and Kingston. Bus: TfL 371 (outside Richmond station) to Kingston, alight Ham Street by Royal Oak Pub, then 1/2ml walk. Rail/Tube: Richmond 1 1/2ml by footpath, 2ml by road.
Open: House: 13 Feb–28 Feb - only 'Sneak Preview' tours of selected rooms (30 minutes duration) available until the house opens fully on 13 March (maximum 20 tickets per tour).

Sat–Wed, 12noon–3.30pm; 1– 12 Mar - only 'Sneak Preview' tours. Sat & Sun, 12noon–3.30pm; 13 Mar–31 Oct (free flow), Sat–Wed, 12noon–4pm. Garden, Shop & Cafe: 1 Jan–7 Feb, Sat & Sun, 11am–4pm; 13 Feb–31 Oct, Sat–Wed, 11am–5pm; 1 Nov–19 Dec, Sat & Sun, 11am–5pm. Closed 1 Jan. Open Good Friday. Special Christmas openings.
*Admission: House & Garden: Adult £10.40, Child £5.80, Family £26.60. Garden only: Adult £3.50, Child £2.35, Family £9.25. Free to NT members. Family group tickets include 2 adults and children under 16. Pre-booked groups during opening hours (15+) Adult £8. Pre- booked groups outside normal hours, £14. *includes a voluntary donation of at least 10%; visitors can, however, choose to pay the standard prices which are displayed at the property and at www.nationaltrust.org.uk.
Special Events: Themed guided tours, open-air theatre and cinema, Christmas events. New and exciting Discovery Room and free Voyages Map for families. In 2010 Ham House and Garden will be celebrating its 400th anniversary.

⬚ ⬚ ⬚ ⬚ WCs. ⬚ Licensed. ⬚ Licensed. ⬚ By arrangement. 🅿 Limited for coaches.
⬚ ⬚ Guide dogs only. ⬚ ⬚

HANDEL HOUSE MUSEUM
25 BROOK STREET, LONDON W1K 4HB
www.handelhouse.org

Tel: 020 7495 1685   **Fax:** 020 7495 1759   **E-mail:** mail@handelhouse.org
Owner: The Handel House Trust Ltd   **Contact:** Shuk Kwan Liu
Handel House Museum is a beautifully restored Georgian townhouse where the famous composer George Frideric Handel lived for 36 years and composed timeless masterpieces such as *Messiah* and *Zadok the Priest*. The elegantly refurbished interiors create the perfect setting for 18th-century fine art and furniture, evoking the spirit of Georgian London. Portraits and paintings of Handel and his contemporaries illustrate Handel's London life and the House is as vibrant with music as it was in Handel's day. Weekly Thursday evening recitals and regular weekend events are held in Handel's intimate music room (booking recommended).
Location: MAP 20:K7, OS Ref. TQ286 809. Central London, between New Bond St and Grosvener Square. Entrance in Lancashire Court. Bond Street Tube.
Open: All year, Tue–Sat, 10am–6pm (8pm Thur). Sun, 12 noon–6pm. Closed Mon. Groups by arrangement. Last entry 30 mins before closing.
Admission: Adult £5, Child £2 (Free on Sat), Conc. £4.50. The Art Fund cardholders Free.
ⓘ No inside photography. ▣ ▣ ⓘ By arrangement. ▦ Guide dogs only. ✸ ♨

HONEYWOOD MUSEUM
Honeywood Walk, Carshalton SM5 3NX
Tel/Fax: 020 8770 4297   **E-mail:** lbshoneywood@btconnect.com
www.sutton.gov.uk   www.friendsofhoneywood.co.uk
Owner: London Borough of Sutton   **Contact:** The Curator
Local history museum in a 17th century listed building next to the picturesque Carshalton Ponds, containing displays on many aspects of the history of the London Borough of Sutton plus a changing programme of exhibitions and events on a wide range of subjects. Attractive garden at rear.
Location: MAP 19:D9, OS Ref. TQ279 646. On A232 approximately 4m W of Croydon.
Open: Wed–Fri, 11am–5pm. Sat, Suns & BH Mons, 10am–5pm. Free admission to shop and tearooms.
Admission: Adult £1.60, Child 80p, under 5 Free. Groups by arrangement.
▣ ▣ Ground floor. WC. ▣ ⓘ ▣ Limited. ▦ ▦ Guide dogs only. ✸ ♨

JEWEL TOWER ⌗
Abingdon Street, Westminster, London SW1P 3JX
Tel: 020 7222 2219   **E-mail:** customers@english-heritage.org.uk
www.english-heritage.org.uk/jeweltower
Owner: English Heritage   **Contact:** Visitor Operations Team
Built c1365 to house the personal treasure of Edward III. One of two surviving parts of the original Palace of Westminster. Now houses an exhibition on 'Parliament Past and Present'. The second floor now includes new illustrated panels, telling the story of this small but important building.
Location: MAP 20:M8, OS Ref. TQ302 794. Opposite S end of Houses of Parliament (Victoria Tower).
Open: 1 Apr–1 Nov: daily, 10am–5pm. 2 Nov–31 Mar: daily, 10am–4pm. Closed 24–26 Dec & 1 Jan.
Admission: Adult £3, Child £1.50, Conc. £2.60. EH Members free. Group discount available. Opening times and prices are valid until 31st March 2010, after this date details are subject to change please see www.english-heritage.org.uk for the most up-to-date information.
▣ ▦ ✸ ♨

DR JOHNSON'S HOUSE
17 Gough Square, London EC4A 3DE
Tel: 020 7353 3745   **E-mail:** curator@drjohnsonshouse.org
Owner: The Trustees
Fine 18th century house, once home to Dr Samuel Johnson, the celebrated literary figure, famous for his English dictionary.
Location: MAP 20:N7, OS Ref. TQ314 813. N of Fleet Street.
Open: Oct–Apr: Mon–Sat, 11am–5pm. May–Sept: Mon–Sat, 11am–5.30pm. Closed BHs.
Admission: Adult £4.50, Child £1.50 (under 10yrs Free), Conc. £3.50. Family £10. Groups: £3.50.

KEATS HOUSE
KEATS GROVE, HAMPSTEAD, LONDON NW3 2RR
www.cityoflondon.gov.uk/keatshousehampstead

Tel: 020 7332 3868   **E-mail:** keatshouse@cityoflondon.gov.uk
Owner: City of London   **Contact:** The Manager
This Grade I listed Regency house is where the poet John Keats lived from 1818 to 1820 with his friend Charles Brown. Here he wrote 'Ode to a Nightingale' and met and fell in love with Fanny Brawne. Suffering from tuberculosis, Keats left for Italy, where he died at the age of 25. Leaving his beloved Fanny in Hampstead, she wore his engagement ring until she died, now on display at the house. Their love story has been immortalised in the Jane Campion film, *Bright Star*, released in 2009.
The museum runs regular poetry readings, talks and events suitable for families throughout the year.

Location: MAP 20:K3, OS Ref. TQ272 856. Hampstead, NW3. Nearest Underground: Belsize Park & Hampstead.

Open: Keats House has recently reopened after the successful Magic Casements project funded by the Heritage Lottery Fund. Our opening hours are Easter–31 Oct, Tue–Sun, 1pm to 5pm. 1 Nov–Easter, Fri–Sun, 1pm–5pm. School parties and pre booked groups by arrangement. The house is also open on BH Mons.

Admission: Adults £5.00, Concessions £3.00 Children 16 and under are free. Tickets are valid for one year.
▣ ▣ WC Ground floor & garden. ▣ None. ▦ ▦ Guide dogs only. ♨

© Historic Royal Palaces

© Historic Royal Palaces

© Historic Royal Palaces

KENSINGTON PALACE
LONDON W8 4PX

www.kensington-palace.org.uk

Tel Information line: 0844 482 7777   **Email:** groupsandtraveltrade@hrp.org.uk
Venue Hire and Corporate Hospitality: 020 3166 6104

Owner: Historic Royal Palaces

Generations of royal Women have shaped this stylish palace. Opening Easter 2010 Kensington will be transformed into an enchanted palace. Through the State Apartments there are stunning installations from leading and new fashion designer interwoven with the palace's own enchanting history. The birthplace and childhood home of Queen Victoria, the palace first became a royal residence for William and Mary in 1689. The famous Orangery was built in 1704 by Queen Anne, and George II's wife, Queen Caroline, another keen gardener, added further improvements. Today, the palace houses a stunning permanent display of fashionable and formal dresses, the Royal Ceremonial Dress Collection, which includes dresses worn by Diana, Princess of Wales. Also on view, Diana, Fashion and Style a unique collection of dresses, including seven recently loaned and never before displayed at Kensington Palace. This display charts the early days from the 1983.

Location: MAP 20:I8, OS Ref. TQ258 801 In Kensington Gardens. Underground: Queensway on Central Line, High Street Kensington on Circle & District Line.

Open; Mar–Oct: daily, 10am–6pm (last admission 5pm) Nov–Feb: daily, 10am–5pm (last admission 4pm) Closed 24–26 Dec.

Admission: Telephone Information Line for admission prices: 0844 482 7777. Advance Ticket Sales: 0844 482 7799. Group bookings 0844 482 7770. Quote Hudson's.

ⓘ No photography indoors. ▣ ⊤ ⊥ Partial. WCs. ☞ ⏹ 🅵 By arrangement. ⌂ 🅿 Nearby. ▣ Please book, 0844 482 7777. ⌧ ⌘

© Nigel Iskander/HRP/newsteam.co.uk

Venetian Blackamoor figures once owned by Princess Margaret

KENWOOD HOUSE ⌗

See page 54 for full page entry.

LITTLE HOLLAND HOUSE

40 Beeches Avenue, Carshalton SM5 3LW
Tel: 020 8770 4781   **Fax:** 020 8770 4777
E-mail: valary.murphy@sutton.gov.uk
www.sutton.gov.uk
Owner: London Borough of Sutton   **Contact:** Ms V Murphy
The home of Frank Dickinson (1874–1961) artist, designer and craftsman, who dreamt of a house that would follow the philosophy and theories of William Morris and John Ruskin. Dickinson designed, built and furnished the house himself from 1902 onwards. The Grade II* listed interior features handmade furniture, metal work, carvings and paintings produced by Dickinson in the Arts and Crafts style.
Location: MAP 19:D9, OS Ref. TQ275 634. On B278 1m S of junction with A232.
Open: First Sun of each month & BH Suns & Mons (excluding Christmas & New Year), 1.30–5.30pm.
Admission: Free. Groups by arrangement, £4pp (includes talk and guided tour).
ℹ No photography in house. ♿ Ground floor. ✆ By arrangement.
🐕 Guide dogs only. ✱

MARBLE HILL HOUSE ⌗
RICHMOND ROAD, TWICKENHAM TW1 2NL

www.english-heritage.org.uk/marblehillhouse

Tel: 020 8892 5115   **E-mail:** customers@english-heritage.org.uk
Owner: English Heritage   **Contact:** Visitor Operations Team
This beautiful villa beside the Thames was built in 1724–29 for Henrietta Howard, mistress of George II. She entertained many of the poets and wits including Pope. The villa was inspired by the 16th century Italian architect, Palladio. This beautifully presented house contains an important collection of paintings and furniture, including some pieces commissioned for the villa when it was built. A recent installation recreates the Chinese wallpaper hung in the Dining Room in 1751.
Location: MAP 19:B8, OS Ref. TQ174 736. A305, 600yds E of Orleans House.
Open: 1 Apr–31 Oct, Sat 10am–2pm; Sun & Bank Hols.10am–5pm Guided tours at 12pm on Sat; 11am & 2.30pm on Sun. 1 Nov–31 Mar Available for group tours - please call for details.
Admission: Adult £4.40, Child £2.20, Conc. £3.70, Family £10.50. EH Members free. Group discount available. Opening times and prices are valid until 31st March 2010, after this date details are subject to change please see www.english-heritage.org.uk for the most up-to-date information.
📷 🍴 ♿ 🛗 🅿 🐕 On leads. ▲ ⛵

MORDEN HALL PARK ✿

Morden Hall Road, Morden SM4 5JD
Tel: 020 8545 6850   **Fax:** 020 8417 8091
E-mail: mordenhallpark@nationaltrust.org.uk
Owner: The National Trust   **Contact:** The Property Manager
Former deer park centred around historic snuff mills and rose garden featuring an extensive network of waterways, ancient hay meadows and wetlands. Second-hand bookshop.
Location: MAP 19:D8, OS Ref. TQ261 684. Off A24 and A297 S of Wimbledon, N of Sutton.
Open: All year: daily. NT gift shop & Riverside Café: 10am–5pm (closed: 25/26 Dec & 1 Jan). Car park closes 6pm.
Admission: Free.

WILLIAM MORRIS GALLERY

Lloyd Park, Forest Road, Walthamstow, London E17 4PP
Tel: 020 8527 3782   **Fax:** 020 8527 7070
Owner: London Borough of Waltham Forest   **Contact:** The Keeper
Location: MAP 19:F6, OS Ref. SQ372 899. 15 mins walk from Walthamstow tube (Victoria line). 5–10 mins from M11/A406.
Open: Tue–Sat and first Sun each month, 10am–1pm and 2–5pm.
Admission: Free for all visitors but a charge is made for guided tours which must be booked in advance.

© English Heritage

MYDDELTON HOUSE GARDENS
BULLS CROSS, ENFIELD, MIDDLESEX EN2 9HG

www.leevalleypark.org.uk

Tel: 08456 770 600
Owner: Lee Valley Regional Park Authority
Created by the famous plantsman and Fellow of the Royal Horticultural Society, E A Bowles, the gardens contain year round interest. From the January snowdrops, through the springtime flowering daffodils to the summer roses and beyond to the autumn crocus, there's always something in the gardens to interest the visitor. The gardens are an ideal place to draw, paint, photograph or picnic. Woodland walks. Carp lake. National Collection of award-winning Bearded Iris. Guided walks available.
Location: MAP 19:D4, OS Ref. TQ342 992. ¼m W of A10 via Turkey St. ¾m S M25/J25.
Open: Every day (except Christmas). Apr–Sept: 10am–4.30pm, Oct–Mar: 10am–3pm. Last admission 30 mins before closing.
Admission: Adult £3.10, Conc. £2.60. Prices subject to change April 2010. Separate charge for guided walks.
📷 🍴 ♿ Some paths.💺 ✆ Please ring 01992 702 200. 🅿 🐕 Guide dogs only. ✱

THE OCTAGON, ORLEANS HOUSE GALLERY

Riverside, Twickenham, Middlesex TW1 3DJ
Tel: 020 8831 6000   **Fax:** 020 8744 0501   **E-mail:** galleryinfo@richmond.gov.uk
Owner: London Borough of Richmond-upon-Thames   **Contact:** The Curator
Outstanding example of baroque architecture by James Gibbs c1720. Art gallery.
Location: MAP 19:B8, OS Ref. TQ168 734. On N side of Riverside, 700yds E of Twickenham town centre, 400yds S of Richmond Road. Vehicle access via Orleans Rd only.
Open: Tue–Sun, 1–5.30pm, Sun & BHs, 2–5.30pm (Oct–Mar closes 4.30pm). Closed Mons. Garden: open daily, 9am–sunset.
Admission: Free.

OSTERLEY PARK AND HOUSE ✤
JERSEY ROAD, ISLEWORTH, MIDDLESEX TW7 4RB
www.nationaltrust.org.uk/osterley

Tel: 020 8232 5050   **Fax:** 020 8232 5080

E-mail: osterley@nationaltrust.org.uk

Owner: The National Trust   **Contact:** Visitor Services Manager

With a spectacular mansion surrounded by gardens, park and farmland, Osterley is one of the last surviving country estates in London. Once described as the 'palace of palaces', Osterley was created in the late 18th century by architect and designer Robert Adam for the Child family to entertain and impress their friends and clients. Today you can explore the dazzling interior with handheld audio visual guides which bring the House to life in a completely new way. Outside the gardens are being restored to the 18th century glory and offer a delightful retreat from urban life

Location: MAP 19:B7, OS Ref. TQ146 780. On A4 between Hammersmith and Hounslow. Main gates at junction of Thornbury and Jersey Roads. If using SatNav, please enter 'Jersey Road' as well as 'TW7 4RB'. Bus: TfL H28, H91 to within 1 mile. Rail: Isleworth (1.5 miles). Tube: Osterley (Piccadilly Line - 1 mile).

Open: House: 3 Mar–31 Oct: Wed–Sun & BHs, 12–4.30pm. 4–19 Dec: Sat & Sun, 12–3.30pm. Garden: 3 Mar–31 Oct: Wed–Sun & BHs, 11am–5pm. Park: All year, daily, 8am–7.30pm (closes 6pm in winter).

*Admission: House and Garden: Adult £8.80, Child £4.40, Family £22, Group (15+) £7.50. Garden: Adult £3.85, Child £1.95. Park: Free. Car Park: £3.50. Free to NT Members. *includes a voluntary 10% donation but visitors can choose to pay the standard prices displayed at the property and on the website.

Special Events: Please see website for event details.

ℹ️ No photography inside House. 📷🎧♿Partial. WCs. 🍴Licensed. 🎧🅿 Limited for coaches. ■☒ Guide dogs only in House and Garden. Dogs on leads in park. ▲✱▦

PALACE OF WESTMINSTER

London SW1A 0AA

Tel: 020 7219 3000 / 0870 906 3773   **Info:** 020 7219 4272

Fax: 020 7219 5839   **Contact:** Information Office

The first Palace of Westminster was erected on this site by Edward the Confessor in 1042 and the building was a royal residence until a devastating fire in 1512. After this, the palace became the two-chamber Parliament for government – the House of Lords and the elected House of Commons. Following a further fire in 1834, the palace was rebuilt by Sir Charles Barry and decorated by A W Pugin.

Location: MAP 20:M8, OS Ref. TQ303 795. Central London, W bank of River Thames. 1km S of Trafalgar Square. Underground: Westminster.

Open: Aug–Sept (please ring for details). At other times by appointment. Please telephone Info line.

Admission: Aug–Sept: Adult £12, Conc. £8, Child £5 (under 5yrs Free), At other times Free.

PITZHANGER MANOR-HOUSE

Walpole Park, Mattock Lane, Ealing W5 5EQ

Tel: 020 8567 1227   **Fax:** 020 8567 0595

E-mail: pmgallery&house@ealing.gov.uk   www.ealing.gov.uk/pmgalleryandhouse

Owner: London Borough of Ealing   **Contact:** Zoë Archer

Pitzhanger Manor House is a restored Georgian villa, once owned and designed by the architect Sir John Soane (1753–1837). Rooms in the house have been restored using Soane's highly individual ideas in design and decoration. Exhibitions of contemporary art are programmed year-round, sited in the adjacent Gallery and often also in the House.

Location: MAP 19:B7, OS Ref. TQ176 805. Ealing, London.

Open: All year: Tue–Fri, 1–5pm. Sat, 11am–5pm. Summer Sunday Openings, please ring for details. Closed Christmas, Easter, New Year and BHs.

Admission: Free.

🎧♿ By arrangement. 🎧 ■ ☒ In grounds, on leads. ▲✱

RED HOUSE ✤
RED HOUSE LANE, BEXLEYHEATH DA6 8JF

Tel: 020 8304 9878 (Booking line: Tues–Sat, 9.30am–1.30pm)

Owner: The National Trust

Commissioned by William Morris in 1859 and designed by Philip Webb, Red House is of enormous international significance in the history of domestic architecture and garden design. The garden was designed to "clothe" the house with a series of sub-divided areas that still clearly exist today. Inside, the house retains many of the original features and fixed items of furniture designed by Morris and Webb, as well as wall paintings and stained glass by Edward Burne-Jones.

Location: MAP 19:G8, OS Ref. TQ48 1750. Off A221 Bexleyheath. Visitors directions can be given on how to reach the property when booking. Nearest rail station Bexleyheath, 10 mins' walk.

Open: 3 Mar–28 Nov, Wed–Sun, 11am–4.45pm. 3 Dec–19 Dec, Fri–Sun only. Open Easter Sun, Good Fri, BH Mons. Ring 0208 304 9878 to book tours. Self guided viewing from 1.30pm, no need to book.

Admission: Adult £6.90, Child £3.45, Family £17.25. NT Members Free.

ℹ️WC. ♿ Ground floor only. 📷🎧■🅿 No parking on site. Disabled drivers can pre-book (limited parking). Parking at Danson Park (15 min walk). Parking charge at weekends and BHs. See Danson House (Kent section).■☒

ROYAL OBSERVATORY NATIONAL MARITIME MUSEUM & QUEEN'S HOUSE

See page 55 for full page entry.

ST GEORGE'S CATHEDRAL, SOUTHWARK

Westminster Bridge Road, London SE1 7HY
Tel: 020 7928 5256   **Fax:** 020 7202 2189
E-mail: info@southwark-rc-cathedral.org.uk   **Contact:** Canon James Cronin
Neo-Gothic rebuilt Pugin Cathedral bombed during the last war and rebuilt by Romily Craze in 1958.
Location: MAP 20:N9, OS Ref. TQ315 794. Near Imperial War Museum. ½m SE of Waterloo Stn.
Open: 8am–6pm, every day, except BHs.
Admission: Free.

ST JOHN'S GATE
MUSEUM OF THE ORDER OF ST JOHN
ST JOHN'S GATE, LONDON EC1M 4DA

www.sja.org.uk/museum

Tel: 020 7324 4005   **Fax:** 020 7336 0587   **E-mail:** museum@nhq.sja.org.uk
Owner: The Order of St John   **Contact:** Pamela Willis
Early 16th century Gatehouse (built 1504), Priory Church and Norman Crypt. The remarkable history of the Knights Hospitaller, dedicated to caring for the sick and dating back to the 11th century, is revealed in collections including furniture, paintings, armour, stained glass and other items. Notable associations with Shakespeare, Hogarth, Edward Cave, Dr Johnson, Dickens, David Garrick and many others. In Victorian times, St John Ambulance was founded here and a modern interactive gallery tells its story.
Location: MAP 20:N6, OS Ref. TQ317 821. St. John's Lane, Clerkenwell. Nearest Underground: Farringdon.
Open: Closed for refurbishment 2009-10. Reopening summer 2010: Mon–Sat 10am–5pm. See website for further details.
Admission: Museum Free. Tours of the building: £5, OAP £4 (donation).
▢ ⃞ Ground floor. WC. 🗗 ▣ 🗗 Guide dogs only. ✳   Reg. Charity No. 1077265
Supported by the National Lottery through the Heritage Lottery Fund.

ST PAUL'S CATHEDRAL

See page 56 for full page entry.

SIR JOHN SOANE'S MUSEUM

13 Lincoln's Inn Fields, London WC2A 3BP
Tel: 020 7405 2107   **Fax:** 020 7831 3957   **www.soane.org**
Owner: Trustees of Sir John Soane's Museum   **Contact:** Julie Brock
The celebrated architect Sir John Soane built this in 1812 as his own house. It now contains his collection of antiquities, sculpture and paintings.
Location: MAP 20:M6, OS Ref. TQ308 816. E of Kingsway, S of High Holborn.
Open: Tue–Sat, 10am–5pm. 6–9pm, first Tue of the month. Closed BHs & 24 Dec.
Admission: Free. Possible charge for first Tue. Groups must book.

SOUTHSIDE HOUSE 🏛
3 WOODHAYES ROAD, WIMBLEDON, LONDON SW19 4RJ

www.southsidehouse.com

Tel: 020 8946 7643   **E-mail:** info@southsidehouse.com
Owner: The Pennington-Mellor-Munthe Charity Trust   **Contact:** The Administrator
Described by connoisseurs as an unforgettable experience, Southside House provides an enchantingly eccentric backdrop to the lives and loves of generations of the Pennington Mellor Munthe families. Maintained in traditional style, without major refurbishment, and crowded with the family possessions of centuries, Southside offers a wealth of fascinating family stories.
Behind the long façade are the old rooms, still with much of the original furniture and a superb collection of art and historical objects. John Pennington-Mellor's daughter, Hilda, married Axel Munthe, the charismatic Swedish doctor and philanthropist. The preservation of the house was left to their youngest son who led a life of extraordinary adventure during the Second World War. Malcolm Munthe's surviving children continue to care for the property.
The gardens are as fascinating as the house, with a series of sculptural "rooms" linked by water and intriguing pathways.

Location: MAP 20:D8, OS Ref. TQ234 706. On S side of Wimbledon Common (B281), opposite Crooked Billet Inn.
Open: Easter Sat–3 Oct: Weds, Sats, Suns & BH Mons. Closed during Wimbledon fortnight last week in June/first week in July. Guided tours on the hour 2, 3 & 4pm. Other times throughout the year by arrangement with the Administrator for groups of 15 or more.
Admission: Adult £5, Child £2.50 (must be accompanied by an adult), Conc. £4, Family £10.
ⓘ No photography inside house. ⃞ Unsuitable. 🗗 Obligatory. 🅿 Limited. ▣
🗗 In grounds on leads. ⬚

© NTPL/Geoffrey Frosh

Southside House

SUTTON HOUSE ❧

2 & 4 HOMERTON HIGH STREET, HACKNEY, LONDON E9 6JQ

Tel: 020 8986 2264 **E-mail:** suttonhouse@nationaltrust.org.uk

Owner: The National Trust   **Contact:** The Custodian

A rare example of a Tudor red-brick house, built in 1535 by Sir Ralph Sadleir, Principal Secretary of State for Henry VIII, with 18th century alterations and later additions. Restoration revealed many 16th century details, even in rooms of later periods. Notable features include original linenfold panelling and 17th century wall paintings.

Location: MAP 20:P3, OS Ref. TQ352 851. At the corner of Isabella Road and Homerton High St.

Open: Historic rooms: 4 Feb–19 Dec 2010: Thur–Sun, 12.30–4.30pm. Café, Shop & Art Gallery: 4 Feb–19 Dec 2010: Thur–Sun, 12 noon–4.30pm. Last admission 4pm. Open BH Mons, closed Good Fri.

Admission: Adult £2.90, Child 80p, Family £6.60. Group £2.70. Free to NT Members.
⬚ Second-hand book shop. ⬚ Ground floor only. WC. ⬚⬚⬚ ⬚ None. ⬚⬚⬚

SPENCER HOUSE
See page 57 for full page entry.

SYON PARK 🏛
See page 58 for full page entry.

THE TOWER BRIDGE EXHIBITION

Tower Bridge, London SE1 2UP

Tel: 0207 403 3761 **Fax:** 020 7357 7935

Owner: Corporation of London   **Contact:** Emma Parlow

One of London's most unusual and exciting exhibitions is situated inside Tower Bridge. Enjoy spectacular views from the high level walkways.

Location: MAP 20:P8, OS Ref. TQ337 804. Adjacent to Tower of London, nearest Underground: Tower Hill.

Open: 1 Apr–30 Sep: 10am–5.30pm (last ticket). 1 Oct–31 Mar: 9.30am–5pm (last ticket). Closed 24–26 Dec.

Admission: Adult £6, Child £3, Conc. £4.50. (Prices may change April 2008.)

© HRP 2007 / Stephen Pond/HRP/newstream.co.uk

© HRP 2007 / Stephen Pond/HRP/newstream.co.uk

TOWER OF LONDON
LONDON EC3N 4AB

www.tower-of-london.org.uk

Tel Information Line: 0844 482 7777 **Email:** groupsandtraveltrade@hrp.org.uk
Venue Hire and Corporate Hospitality: 020 3166 6207
Owner: Historic Royal Palaces

The ancient stones reverberate with dark secrets, priceless jewels glint in fortified vaults and pampered ravens strut the grounds. The Tower of London, founded by William the Conqueror in 1066–7, is Britain's most visited historic site. Despite a grim reputation for a place of torture and death, there are so many more stories to be told about the Tower. An intriguing cast of characters have played their part From 2009, Henry VIII: Dressed to Kill. Journey back with Henry through his historic reign at this spectacular exhibition of his armour and weapons brought together for the first time in modern history.

Location: MAP 20:P7, OS Ref. TQ336 806, Underground: Tower Hill on Circle/District Line. Docklands Light Railway: Tower Gateway Station. Rail: Fenchurch Street Station and

London Bridge Station. Bus: 15, 25, 42, 78, 100, D1, RV1. Riverboat: From Embankment Pier, Westminster or Greenwich to Tower Pier. London Eye to Tower of London Express.

Open: Summer: 1 Mar–31 Oct, Daily, Tues–Sat: 9am–6pm (last admission 5pm), Mons & Suns: 10am–6pm (last admission 5pm). Winter: 1 Nov–28 Feb, Tues–Sat: 9am–5pm, Mons & Suns: 10am–5pm (last admission 4pm). Closed 24–26 Dec and 1 Jan. Buildings close 30 minutes after last admission.

Admission: Telephone Information Line for admission prices: 0844 482 7777. Advance Ticket Sales: 0844 482 7799. Group bookings: 0844 482 7770. Quote Hudson's.
ℹ No photography in Jewel House. ⬚ ☎ 020 3166 6311. ⬚ Partial. WCs.
⬚ Licensed ⬚ Licensed ⬚ Yeoman Warder tours are free and leave front entrance every ½ hr. ⬚ ⬚ None for cars. Coach parking nearby. ⬚ To book 0844 482 7777.
⬚⬚⬚

WELLINGTON ARCH ⌗
HYDE PARK CORNER, LONDON W1J 7JZ

www.english-heritage.org.uk/wellingtonarch

Tel: 020 7930 2726 **Venue Hire and Hospitality:** 020 7973 3292
E-mail: customers@english-heritage.org.uk
Owner: English Heritage **Contact:** Visitor Operations Team
Set in the heart of Royal London, Wellington Arch is a landmark for Londoners and visitors alike. George IV originally commissioned this massive monument as a grand outer entrance to Buckingham Palace. Visit the balconies just below the spectacular bronze sculpture for glorious views over London.
Location: MAP 20:L8, OS Ref. TQ285 798. Hyde Park Corner Tube Station.
Open: 1 Apr–31 Oct Wed–Sun & Bank Hols 10am–5pm. 1 Nov–31 Mar Wed–Sun 10am–4pm. Closed 24–26 Dec and 1 Jan. Last admission 1/2 hour before closing.
The property may close at short notice, please ring in advance for details.
Admission: Adult £3.50, Child £1.80, Conc. £3.00. Groups (11+) 15% discount. Joint ticket available with Apsley House: Adult £7.30, Child £3.70, Conc. £6.20. EH Members free. Opening times and prices are valid until 31st March 2010, after this date details are subject to change please see www.english-heritage.org.uk for the most up-to-date information.

◻ ⊤ ♿ ⬛ Mondays for groups only. ✲ ♨

THE 'WERNHER COLLECTION' AT RANGER'S HOUSE ⌗
CHESTERFIELD WALK, BLACKHEATH, LONDON SE10 8QX

www.english-heritage.org.uk/rangershouse

Tel: 020 8853 0035 **E-mail:** customers@english-heritage.org.uk
Owner: English Heritage **Contact:** House Manager
A truly hidden gem, in South East London's Greenwich Park, Ranger's House is home to the Wernher Collection - a sumptuous arrangement of glittering silver and jewels, paintings and porcelain. A wonderful day out for any art enthusiast, there are nearly 700 works on display.
Location: MAP 4:I2, OS Ref. TQ388 768. N of Shooters Hill Road.
Open: 1 Apr–30 Sep, Mon–Wed, entry by guided tours only at 11.30am and 2.30pm. Pre-booking advisable on 020 8853 0035. 1 Apr–30 Sep, Sun, 11am–5pm. 1 Oct–31 Mar Available for group tours - please call for details. The property may close at short notice, please ring in advance for details.
Admission: Adult £5.70, Child £2.90, Conc. £4.80. EH Members free. Group discount available. Opening times and prices are valid until 31st March 2010, after this date details are subject to change please see www.english-heritage.org.uk for the most up-to-date information.

ⓘ WC. ⊤ ♿ ⬛ ⬛ ⬛ Guide dogs only.

WESTMINSTER CATHEDRAL

Victoria, London SW1P 1QW
Tel: 020 7798 9055 **Fax:** 020 7798 9090 **www.westminstercathedral.org.uk**
Owner: Diocese of Westminster **Contact:** Revd Canon Christopher Tuckwell
The Roman Catholic Cathedral of the Archbishop of Westminster. Spectacular building in the Byzantine style, designed by J F Bentley, opened in 1903, famous for its mosaics, marble and music. Bell Tower viewing gallery has spectacular views across London.
Location: MAP 20:L9, OS Ref. TQ293 791. Off Victoria Street, between Victoria Station and Westminster Abbey.
Open: All year: 7am–7pm. Please telephone for times at Easter & Christmas.
Admission: Free. Tower lift/viewing gallery charge: Adult £5. Family (2+4) £11. Conc. £2.50

◻ ♿ Ground floor. ⬛ ⬛ Booking required. ⬛ None. ⬛ Worksheets & tours.
⬛ Guide dogs only. ✲

WHITEHALL

1 Malden Road, Cheam SM3 8QD
Tel/Fax: 020 8643 1236 **E-mail:** whitehallcheam@btconnect.com
www.sutton.gov.uk www.friendsofwhitehallcheam.co.uk
Owner: London Borough of Sutton **Contact:** The Curator
A Tudor timber-framed house, c1500 with later additions, in the heart of Cheam Village conservation area. Displays on the history of the house and the people who lived here, plus nearby Nonsuch Palace, Cheam School and William Gilpin (Dr Syntax). Changing exhibition programme and special event days throughout the year. Attractive rear garden features medieval well from c1400. Tearoom features homemade cakes.
Location: MAP 19:C9, OS Ref. TQ242 638. Approx. 2m S of A3 on A2043 just N of junction with A232.
Open: Wed–Fri, 2–5pm; Sat 10am–5pm; Sun & BH Mons, 2–5pm. Tearoom closes 4.30pm.
Admission: Adult £1.60, Child (6-16yrs) 80p, under 5yrs Free. Groups by appt. Free admission to shop and tea room.

◻ ♿ Ground floor. ⬛ ⬛ ⬛ ⬛ Guide dogs only. ✲ ♨

Westminster Cathedral

The Drawing Room, Arundel Castle, Sussex

South East

Eight counties make up this region. In each you can find world-famous properties such as Windsor Castle, Blenheim Palace and Leeds Castle – and lesser known treasures such as Belmont, Broughton Castle and Great Dixter House and Gardens that give a deeper insight into britain's heritage and history both architectural and horticultural.

Rousham House, Oxfordshire

Berkshire
Buckinghamshire
Hampshire
Kent
Oxfordshire
Surrey
Sussex
Isle of Wight

BUCKINGHAMSHIRE

OXFORDSHIRE

BERKSHIRE

SURREY

KENT

HAMPSHIRE

SUSSEX

ISLE OF WIGHT

Danson House, Kent

The Hermitage , Painshill Park

Herstmonceux Castle, Sussex

■ **Owner**
The Crown Estate

■ **Contact**
The Savill Garden
Wick Lane
Englefield Green
Surrey TW20 0UU

Tel: 01784 435544
Fax: 01784 439746
E-mail: enquiries@
theroyallandscape.co.uk

■ **Location**
MAP 3:G2
OS Ref. SU977 706

Sign posted off A30,
M25 Junction 13 or M4
Junction 6.

Rail: Windsor Central or
Egham.

■ **Opening Times**
Daily. March–October:
10am–6pm.
November–February:
10am–4:30pm.
Closed Christmas Day
and Boxing Day.

■ **Admission**
Nov 09–Feb 10
Adult	£5.75
Child under 6	Free
Child (6–16yrs)	£2.00
Seniors	£5.25
Groups (10+)	£4.50

Groups should pre-book.

Family ticket concessions
available. For prices from
March 2010, please
telephone or email.

Guided tours available at
additional cost.

Annual Memberships
available from £40.

■ **Special Events**
A brief guide to some of
the popular annual
highlights:

Feb–Mar:
Camellias and daffodils in
The Glades.

Apr–May:
Azalea and
rhododendrons. Easter
events and Spring Gardens
Week.

June–Jul:
Rose Garden, Hidden
Gardens and Golden
Jubilee Garden. Celebration
of the Rose events. Art
Week.

Aug–Sept:
Herbaceous borders, the
Dry Garden and
hydrangeas.

Oct–Nov:
The New Zealand Garden
and Autumn Wood.

Dec–Jan:
The Winter Garden,
Mahonia National
Collection and a packed
programme of Christmas
festivities in the Savill
Building.

See our website for
updates about our exciting
events programme.

The Summer Gardens

THE SAVILL GARDEN
(WINDSOR GREAT PARK, BERKSHIRE)
www.theroyallandscape.co.uk

World-renowned 35 acres of ornamental gardens and woodland, including National Collections and rare international species, The Savill Garden provides a wealth of beauty and interest in all seasons.

Spring in The Savill Garden is heralded by hosts of daffodils, marvellous magnolias and the wonderful perfume of the varieties of rhododendrons and azaleas. Summer brings a contrast of colour with the vibrancy of the grand Herbaceous Borders and the tranquil, pastel shades of the Golden Jubilee Garden. The glorious displays of autumn in the Garden are a joy to behold, before attention turns to the striking new additions to the Winter Garden.

Do not miss the exciting new Rose Garden, which will be unveiled in June 2010. The contemporary design will create an intense sensory experience with roses especially chosen for their scent, strong colours and repeat flowering.

The Queen Elizabeth Temperate House is another must-see element. The Temperate House provides an ideal environment to grow particularly tender plants, including examples of rhododendrons and mahonias from the National Collections. The Temperate House also showcases original and unusual seasonal plant displays which offer continuous floral interest and vitality throughout the year.

Visit the iconic Savill Building, with its award winning grid-shell roof structure, fabricated from sustainable sources from forests within Windsor Great Park. This impressive visitor centre is the gateway to The Royal Landscape, and also offers excellent shopping, an art gallery, exhibitions and a restaurant, managed by Leith's.

Glenn Dale Azalea Display

The Savill Building

i	Film & photographic shoots.		Licensed.
	Plant centre.		For groups, by appointment.
		P	
	Grounds. WC.		Guide dogs only.

©NT/Nick White

BASILDON PARK ❧

BASILDON PARK, LOWER BASILDON, READING, BERKSHIRE RG8 9NR

www.nationaltrust.org.uk/basildonpark

Tel: 0118 984 3040 **Fax:** 0118 976 7370 **E-mail:** basildonpark@nationaltrust.org.uk

Owner: The National Trust **Contact:** The Administrator

This beautiful Palladian mansion stars as 'Netherfield' in the recent feature film adaptation of Jane Austen's classic novel *Pride and Prejudice*. It is an elegant, classical house designed in the 18th century by John Carr of York and set in rolling parkland in the Thames Valley. The house has rich interiors with fine plasterwork, pictures and furniture, and includes an unusual Octagon Room and decorative Shell Room. Basildon Park has connections with the East through its builder and was the home of a wealthy industrialist in the 19th century. Flower gardens, tearoom, 400 acres of parkland with woodland walks.

Location: MAP 3:E2 OS Ref. SU611 782. 2½m NW of Pangbourne, W of A329, 7m from M4/J12.

Open: House: 10 Mar–31 Oct, 11am–5pm plus 1–12 Dec, 11am–4pm, daily except Mon & Tue (open BH Mons). Park, Gardens, Tearoom & Shop, as House, plus 10 Feb–7 Mar, 11am–3pm & 3 Nov–19 Dec, 11am–3pm, daily except Mon & Tue (open BH Mons).

*Admission: House, Park & Garden: Adult £8.80 Child £4.40 Family £20.35. Park & Garden only: Adult £5 Child £2.50 Family £11, Groups (15+) by appointment: Adult £7, Child £3.50. Free to NT Members. All information correct at time of going to print. *includes a voluntary 10% donation but visitors can choose to pay the standard prices displayed at the property and on the website.

🖼 🔲 🅿 In grounds. 📷 By appointment. 🐕 On leads, in grounds only. ▲ ▼

DORNEY COURT 🏛

Nr WINDSOR, BERKSHIRE SL4 6QP

www.dorneycourt.co.uk

NEW OPENING TIMES FROM 2010

Tel: 01628 604638 **E-mail:** palmer@dorneycourt.co.uk

Owner/Contact: Mrs Peregrine Palmer

Just a few miles from the heart of bustling Windsor lies "one of the finest Tudor Manor Houses in England", *Country Life*. Grade I listed with the added accolade of being of outstanding architectural and historical importance, the visitor can get a rare insight into the lifestyle of the squirearchy through 550 years, with the Palmer family, who still live there today, owning the house for 450 of these years. The house boasts a magnificent Great Hall, family portraits, oak and lacquer furniture, needlework and panelled rooms. A private tour on a 'non-open day' takes around 1½ hours, but when open to the public this is reduced to around 50 mins. The adjacent 13th century Church of St James, with

Norman font and Tudor tower can also be visited, as well as the adjoining Plant Centre in our walled garden where light lunches and full English cream teas are served in a tranquil setting throughout the day. Highly Commended by Country Life – The Nation's Finest Manor House – 2006.

Location: MAP 3:G2, OS Ref. SU926 791. 5 mins off M4/J7, 10mins from Windsor, 2m W of Eton.

Open: April–May, Mon–Fri inclusive. Bank holiday Sundays and Mondays in May.

Admission: Adult: £7.50, Child (10yrs +) £5.00. Groups 10 or more: £6.50 when house is open to public. Private group rates at other times.

ℹ Film & photographic shoots. No stiletto heels. 🌿 Garden centre. ⊤ Wedding receptions. 🔲 Garden centre. 🖼 📷 🅿 🍴 🐕 Guide dogs only. ✳

Savill Garden

DONNINGTON CASTLE ⌗

Newbury, West Berkshire RG14 2
Tel: 01424 775705   **E-mail:** customers@english-heritage.org.uk
www.english-heritage.org.uk/donnington
Owner: English Heritage
Built in the late 14th century, the twin-towered gatehouse of this heroic castle survives amid some impressive earthworks.
Location: MAP 3:D2, OS Ref. SU461 692. 1m N of Newbury off B4494.
Open: All year: Any reasonable time (exterior viewing only).
Admission: Free. Opening times and prices are valid until 31st March 2010, after this date details are subject to change please see www.english-heritage.org.uk for the most up-to-date information.
▣ ■ ▣ On leads. ▣

ETON COLLEGE 🏛

Windsor, Berkshire SL4 6DW
Tel: 01753 671177   **Fax:** 01753 671029   **www.etoncollege.com**
E-mail: r.hunkin@etoncollege.com
Owner: Provost & Fellows   **Contact:** Rebecca Hunkin
Eton College, founded in 1440 by Henry VI, is one of the oldest and best known schools in the country. The original and subsequent historic buildings of the Foundation are a part of the heritage of the British Isles and visitors are invited to experience and share the beauty of the ancient precinct which includes the magnificent College Chapel, a masterpiece of the perpendicular style.
Location: MAP 3:G2, OS Ref. SU967 779. Off M4/J5. Access from Windsor by footbridge only. Vehicle access from Slough 2m N.
Open: Daily during the school's holidays and Wednesdays, Fridays, Saturdays & Sundays during term time between March & early October: Times vary, please check with the Visits Office. Pre-booked groups welcome all year.
Admission: Guided tours only at 14.00hrs & 15.15hrs for interested individuals. Groups by appointment only. Rates vary according to type of tour. ▣
▣ ▣ ▣ Ground floor. WC. ▣ ■ Limited. ▣ Guide dogs only. ▣

SAVILL GARDEN

See page 72 for full page entry.

---

giftaid it Some properties will be operating the Gift Aid on Entry scheme at their admission points. Where the scheme is operating, visitors are offered a choice between paying the standard admission price or paying the 'Gift Aid Admission' which includes a voluntary donation of at least 10%. Gift Aid Admissions enable the charity to reclaim tax on the whole amount paid* - an extra 28% - potentially a very significant boost to property funds. Money raised from paying visitors in this way will go towards restoration projects at the property and will be very welcome.
Where shown, the admission prices are inclusive of the 10% voluntary donation where properties are operating the Gift Aid on Entry scheme, but both the standard admission price and the Gift Aid Admission will be displayed at the property and on their website.

*Gift Aid donations must be supported by a valid Gift Aid declaration and a Gift Aid declaration can only cover donations made by an individual for him/herself or for him/herself and members of his/her family.

SHAW HOUSE
CHURCH ROAD, NEWBURY, BERKSHIRE RG14 2DR
www.shawhouse.org.uk

Tel: 01635 279279
E-mail: shawhouse@westberks.gov.uk
Owner: West Berkshire District Council
Built in 1581 by Newbury clothier Thomas Dolman, this fine Elizabethan building was recently restored through a £6million project. The stories and characters from Shaw House's varied past are bought to life in the exhibition. Wheelie Do activities throughout the house, including a Civil War board game. Exciting events programme.
Location: MAP 3:D2, OS Ref. SU 47573 68363. Near Newbury.
Open: 13 Feb–31 Mar: Sat & Sun, 11am–4pm. 1 Apr–31 Jul: Sat & Sun, 11am-5pm. 1–31 Aug: Wed–Sun, 11am–5pm. 1 Sept–19 Dec: Sat & Sun, 11am–4pm. And some days in school holidays.
Admission: Adult £5.00, Child £2.50, Conc. £4.00. Discounts apply for West Berkshire Residents Card Holders.
▣ ▣ Partial. WCs. ▣ ▣ By arrangement. ■ Limited. ▣ Guide dogs only. ▣

WINDSOR CASTLE

Windsor, Berkshire SL4 1NJ
Tel: 020 7766 7304   **E-mail:** bookinginfo@royalcollection.org.uk
Owner: Official Residence of Her Majesty The Queen
Contact: Ticket Sales & Information Office
Windsor Castle, along with Buckingham Palace and the Palace of Holyroodhouse in Edinburgh, it is one of the official residences of Her Majesty The Queen. The magnificent State Rooms are furnished with some of the finest works of art from the Royal Collection.
Location: MAP 3:G2, OS Ref. SU969 770. M4/J6, M3/J3. 20m from central London.
Open: Contact information office.
Admission: Contact information office.

Windsor Castle

STOWE HOUSE 🏛

www.shpt.org

Stowe owes its pre-eminence to the vision and wealth of two great owners. From 1715 to 1749 Viscount Cobham, one of Marlborough's Generals, continuously improved his estate, calling in the leading designers of the day to lay out the Gardens and commissioning several leading architects – Vanburgh, Gibbs, Kent and Leoni – to decorate them with garden temples. From 1750 to 1779 Earl Temple, his nephew and heir, continued to expand and embellish both the House and Gardens. As the estate was expanded, and political and military intrigues followed, the family eventually fell into debt, resulting in two great sales – 1848 when all the contents were sold and 1922 when the contents and the estate were sold off separately. The House is now part of a major public school, since

1923, and owned by Stowe House Preservation Trust, since 2000. Over the last four years, through the Trust, the House has under gone two phases of a six phase restoration – the North Front and Colonnades, the Central Pavilion and South Portico and the absolutely spectacular Marble Saloon, dating from the 1770s. Around the mansion is one of Britain's most magnificent and complete landscape gardens, taken over from the School by the National Trust in 1989. The Gardens have since undergone a huge, and continuing, restoration programme, and with the House restoration, Stowe is slowly being returned to its 18th century status as one of the most complete neo-classical estates in Europe.

Jerry Hardman-Jones / SHPT

ℹ️ Indoor swimming pool, sports hall, tennis court, squash courts, astroturf, parkland, cricket pitches and golf course.

🍸 International conferences, private functions, weddings, and prestige exhibitions. Catering on request.

♿ Visitors may alight at entrance, tel. 01280 818229 for details. Allocated parking. WC. 'Batricars' available (from NT – tel. 01280 818825).

☕ NT tearooms.

🍴 Morning coffee, lunch and afternoon tea available at the House by pre-arrangement only, for up to 80.

🚶 For parties of 15–60 at group rate. Tour time: house and garden 2½–4½ hrs, house only 1¼ hrs.

🅿️ Ample.

♿

🐕 In grounds on leads.

🔔 Civil Wedding Licence.

📷 Available.

❄️ House open to groups all year, tel for details.

🛡 Please check website for 2010 events: www.stoweevents.co.uk

■ Owner
Stowe House
Preservation Trust

■ Contact
Visitor Services Manager
Stowe School
Buckingham
MK18 5EH

Tel: 01280 818229
Fax: 01280 818186
House only
E-mail:
amcevoy@stowe.co.uk

■ Location
MAP 7:C10
OS Ref. SP666 366

From London, M1 to
Milton Keynes, 1½ hrs
or Banbury 1¼ hrs,
3m NW of Buckingham.

Bus: Buckingham 3m.

Rail: Milton Keynes 15m.

Air: Heathrow 50m.

■ Opening Times
House:
Easter & Summer
School Holidays.
Wed–Sun 12noon–5pm
(last admission 4pm),
Guided tour at 2pm &
also in term times, please
check website or
telephone for further
details 01280 818166.

■ Admission
House (including optional tour)
Check website for
admission prices.
www.shpt.org

Open to private groups
(15–60 persons), all year
round at discounted rates.
Please telephone 01280
818229 to pre-book.

Visit both the Landscape
Gardens and the House.
For Landscape Gardens
opening times telephone
01280 822850 or visit
www.nationaltrust.org.uk/
stowegardens
Joint tickets available.

Conference/Function

ROOM	MAX CAPACITY
Roxburgh Hall	350
Music Room	100
Marble Hall	200
State Dining Rm	200

BUCKINGHAMSHIRE

ASCOTT

Wing, Leighton Buzzard, Buckinghamshire LU7 0PS
Tel: 01296 688242   **Fax:** 01296 681904
E-mail: info@ascottestate.co.uk   **www.ascottestate.co.uk**
Owner: The National Trust   **Contact:** Resident Agent

Originally a half-timbered Jacobean farmhouse, Ascott was bought in 1876 by the de Rothschild family and considerably transformed and enlarged. It now houses a quite exceptional collection of fine paintings, Oriental porcelain and English and French furniture. The extensive gardens are a mixture of the formal and natural, containing specimen trees and shrubs, as well as an herbaceous walk, lily pond, Dutch garden and remarkable topiary sundial.

Location: MAP 7:D11, OS Ref. SP891 230. ½ m E of Wing, 2m SW of Leighton Buzzard, on A418.
Open: House & Garden: 23 Mar–25 Apr: daily except Mons, 2–6pm. 27 Apr–22 Jul: Tues–Thurs, 2–6pm. 27 Jul–10 Sept daily except Mons, 2–6pm. Last admission 5pm.
Admission: Adult £8.40, Child £4.20. Garden only: £4.20, Child £2.10. No reduction for groups which must book. NT members free (except NGS days) 3 May & 30 Aug.
🔲 Ground floor & grounds with assistance. 3 wheelchairs available. WCs.
🅿 220 metres. 🐕 In car park only, on leads.

BOARSTALL DUCK DECOY

Boarstall, Aylesbury, Buckinghamshire HP18 9UX
Tel: 01280 822850 (Assistant Property Manager – Stowe Mon–Fri)
E-mail: boarstalldecoy@nationaltrust.org.uk
Owner: The National Trust   **Contact:** Assistant Property Manager – Stowe

A rare survival of a 17th century decoy in working order, set on a tree-fringed lake, with nature trail and exhibition hall. Demonstrations with the decoy man and his dog on request. New! New nature trail including glorious bluebell woods in season.

Location: MAP 7:B11, OS Ref. SP624 151. Midway between Bicester and Thame, 2m W of Brill.
Open: 3 Apr–29 Aug: Sats & Suns, 10am–4pm; 7 Apr–25 Aug: Weds, 3.30–6pm; BH Mons 10am–4pm. Displays on Sats, Suns, & BH Mons: 11am & 3pm; Weds: 3.30pm. Bird walks and woodland talks occasionally, please telephone for details. Please telephone for winter opening details. Free to NT members.
Admission: Adult £2.60, Child £1.25. Family £6.50. Groups (6+) must book: £2.20.
🔲 Partial. 🎁🅿 Free ■ By arrangement. Suitable for school groups. Pond dipping, interpretation, environment and conservation learning. 🐕 In car park only, on leads.

BOARSTALL TOWER

Boarstall, Aylesbury, Buckinghamshire HP18 9UX
Tel: 01280 822850 (Mon–Fri)   **E-mail:** boarstalltower@nationaltrust.org.uk
Owner: The National Trust   **Contact:** Assistant Property Manager – Stowe

The stone gatehouse of a fortified house long since demolished. It dates from the 14th century, and was altered in the 16th and 17th centuries, but retains its crossloops for bows. The gardens are surrounded by a moat on three sides.

Location: MAP 7:B11, OS Ref. SP624 141. Midway between Bicester and Thame, 2m W of Brill.
Open: Sat 3 Apr; Mon 5 Apr; Mon 3 May; Mon 31 May, Sat 28 Aug, Mon 30 Aug, 11–5pm. Open Wed 2–5pm, 2 Jun–25 Aug.
Admission: Adult £2.60, Child £1.50. Free to NT members.
ℹ Accessible WC. 🔲 Ground floor & garden (steps to entrance). 🅿 🐕 In car park only.

BUCKINGHAM CHANTRY CHAPEL

Market Hill, Buckingham
Tel: 01280 822850 (Mon–Fri)   **Fax:** 01280 822437
E-mail: buckinghamchantry@nationaltrust.org.uk
Owner: The National Trust   **Contact:** Assistant Property Manager – Stowe

15th-Century chapel, restored by Gilbert Scott in 1875. Now a secondhand book shop. The oldest building in Buckingham with a fine Norman doorway.

Location: MAP 7:B10, OS Ref. SP693 340. In narrow lane, NW of Market Hill.
Open: Available for private function hire. Open Sat & Tues, 9.30am–3pm.
Admission: Free. Donations welcome.
ℹ No WCs. 🔲 Secondhand books 🖥 🔲 ✳

CHENIES MANOR HOUSE 🏛
CHENIES, BUCKINGHAMSHIRE WD3 6ER
www.cheniesmanorhouse.co.uk

Tel: 01494 762888   **E-mail:** macleodmatthews@btinternet.com
Owners: Mrs E MacLeod Matthews & Mr C MacLeod Matthews
Contact: Susan Brock

Home of the MacLeod Matthews family, this 15th & 16th century Manor House with fortified tower is the original home of the Earls of Bedford, visited by Henry VIII and Elizabeth I. She was a frequent visitor, first coming as an infant in 1534 and as Queen she visited on several occasions, once being for a six week period. The Bedford Mausoleum is in the adjacent church. The House contains tapestries and furniture mainly of the 16th and 17th centuries, hiding places, and a collection of antique dolls. Art Exhibitions are held throughout the season in the newly restored 16th century Pavilion with its unusual cellars. The Manor is surrounded by enchanting gardens, famed for the spring display of tulips, which have been featured in many publications and on television. From early June there is a succession of colour in the Tudor Sunken Garden, The White Garden, Herbaceous Borders and Fountain Court. The Physic Garden contains a wide selection of medicinal and culinary herbs. The Parterre has a Gazebo which was used in an adaptation of BBC 'Little Dorrit' by Charles Dickens, also an ancient oak and complicated Yew Maze, while the Kitchen Garden is in Victorian style with unusual vegetables and fruit. Attractive dried and fresh flower arrangements decorate the house.

Location: MAP 7:D12, OS Ref TQ016 984. N of A404 between Amersham & Rickmansworth. M25–Ext 18 3m
Open: 1 Apr–29 Oct: Wed & Thurs and BH Mons, 2–5pm. Last entry to House: 4.15pm.
Admission: House & Garden: Adult £5.50, Child £3, Garden only: Adult £4, Child £2, Groups (20+) by arrangement throughout the year (half price during Oct).
🔲 ✳ 🖥 Delicious home made teas in the Garden Room. 🎁 🅿 🐕
🌼 Easter 5 Apr – BH Mon, 2–5pm – Fun for Children, a special Easter Event. The first mention of the distribution of Eggs was at Chenies. 18 Apr 2-5pm, Sun – Tulip Festival. Hundreds of Bloms tulips arranged throughout the House with hundreds of tulips and also in the Gardens. 3 May, BH Mon, 2–5pm, more stunning tulips throughout the House & Gardens. 31 May, BH Mon, 2–5pm, House & Garden open, also the The British Driving Society 10am–4pm, contact Shirley Higgins (01923 267919). This will be a competitive event with many classes, including trade vehicles. 18 Jul, Sun 10am–5pm, Plant & Garden Fair, (Manor opens from 2pm). Rare & Exceptional Plants, 70 Specialist Nurseries. Garden Books, Sculpture, Garden accessories. Lunch and Refreshments. Children's entertainer. 30 Aug, BH Mon, 2–5pm. Special Entertainment. 27 & 28 Oct, 2–5pm, 'Spooks & Surprises', fun for Children.

CHILTERN OPEN AIR MUSEUM

Newland Park, Gorelands Lane, Chalfont St Giles, Buckinghamshire HP8 4AB
Tel: 01494 871117   **Fax:** 01494 872774
Owner: Chiltern Open Air Museum Ltd   **Contact:** Phil Holbrook
A museum of historic buildings showing their original uses including a blacksmith's forge, stables, barns etc.
Location: MAP 3:G1, OS Ref. TQ011 938. At Newland Park 1½ m E of Chalfont St Giles, 4½ m from Amersham. 3m from M25/J17.
Open: Apr–Oct: daily. Please telephone for details.
Admission: Adult £7.50, Child (5–16yrs) £5.00, Child under 5yrs Free, OAP £6.50, Family (2+2) £22.00. Groups discount available on request. 2009 prices.

Chenies Manor House

CLAYDON ❧
MIDDLE CLAYDON, Nr BUCKINGHAM MK18 2EY

Tel: 01296 730349   **Fax:** 01296 738511   **Infoline:** 01494 755561
E-mail: claydon@nationaltrust.org.uk
Owner: The National Trust   **Contact:** The House and Premises Manager
Home of the Verney family for more than 400 years, the extraordinary interiors of Claydon House, built 1759–69, represent a veritable three-dimensional pattern book of 18th-century decorative styles. Outstanding features include lavish wood carving in the Chinese Room and the fine grand staircase. Claydon has strong associations with Florence Nightingale, sister-in-law to Sir Harry Verney. Claydon is set within 21 hectares of unspoilt parkland with far-reaching views. The courtyard contains a second-hand bookshop and craft galleries, as well as a restaurant and tearoom (not NT). The gardens are open to visitors at an additional charge.

Location: MAP 7:C11, OS Ref. SP720 253. In Middle Claydon, 13m NW of Aylesbury, signposted from A413 and A41. 3½ m SW of Winslow.
Open: House: 24 Mar–31 Oct, daily except Thu & Fri (open Good Friday), 1–5pm, last admission 4.30pm. Grounds, Garden, Bookshop, Church & facilities: As house, 12 noon–5pm.
Admission: Adult £6.35, Child £3.05, Family £15.65. Groups: Adult £6 (£1.50 extra for guided tour) Gardens: Adult £3.50, including NT Members, under 5s free.
ℹ No photography. No pushchairs. No backpacks. No large bags. 📷 Second-hand books, pottery & art gallery. 🅃 ♿ Partial. WCs. ☕ Licensed 🍴 Licensed 🍴 For groups only, by arrangement. 🅿 Limited for coaches. ■ ▦ In parkland only, on leads. ▣ ▨ For details visit www.nationaltrust.org.uk.

Claydon House

CLIVEDEN ❦
TAPLOW, MAIDENHEAD SL6 0JA

Tel: 01628 605069 **Infoline:** 01494 755562 **Fax:** 01628 669461
E-mail: cliveden@nationaltrust.org.uk
Owner: The National Trust **Contact:** Property Manager

152 hectares of gardens and woodland. A water garden, 'secret' garden, herbaceous borders, topiary, a great formal parterre, and informal vistas provide endless variety. The garden statuary is one of the most important collections in the care of The National Trust and includes many Roman antiquities collected by 1st Viscount Astor. The Octagon Temple (Chapel) with its rich mosaic interior is open on certain days, as is part of the house (see below).

Location: MAP 3:F1, OS Ref. SU915 851. 3m N of Maidenhead, M4/J7 onto A4 or M40/J4 onto A404 to Marlow and follow signs. From London by train take Thames Train service from Paddington to Burnham (taxi rank and office adjacent to station).

Open: Estate, Garden, Shop, Refreshment kiosk: 13 Feb–31 Mar, daily 11am–5pm; 1 Apr–30 Oct, daily 11am–5.30pm; 31 Oct–23 Dec, daily 11am–4pm. House (part) & Chapel: 1 Apr–28 Oct. Thurs & Sun, 3–5.30pm. Admission to house by timed ticket, from Information Centre only. Woodlands: 2 Jan–31 Mar, daily 11am–4pm; 1 Apr–30 Oct, daily 11am–5.30pm; 31 Oct–23 Dec, daily 11am–4pm. eat at The Orangery: 1 Mar–30 Oct, daily 11am–5pm; 31 Oct–19 Dec, Sat/Sun 11am–3pm. Some areas of formal gardens may be roped off when ground conditions are bad.

Admission: Grounds: Adult £8 Child £4, Family £20, Groups (must book) £6.80 House: £1 extra, Child 50p extra. Mooring charge on Cliveden Reach.

⊡ 🖼 🖳 WCs. 🍽 Licensed. 🍴 Licensed. 🎫 By arrangement. 🅿 Limited for coaches. 🦮 Guide dogs only 🔲 🔶

The King's Head, Aylesbury

COWPER & NEWTON MUSEUM
Home of Olney's Heritage, Orchard Side, Market Place, Olney MK46 4AJ
Tel: 01234 711516 **E-mail:** cowpernewtonmuseum@btconnect.com
www.cowperandnewtonmuseum.org.uk
Owner: Board of Trustees **Contact:** Mrs A Pickard, House Manager

Once the home of 18th century poet and letter writer William Cowper and now containing furniture, paintings and personal belongings of both Cowper and his ex-slave trader friend, Rev John Newton (author of "Amazing Grace"). Attractions include two peaceful gardens and Cowper's restored summerhouse. Costume gallery, important collection of bobbin lace, and local history displays, from dinosaur bones to WW2. Visit website for our events.

Location: MAP 7:D9, OS Ref. SP890 512. On A509, 6m N of Newport Pagnell, M1/J14.
Open: 1 Mar–23 Dec: Tue–Sat & BH Mons, 10.30am–4.30pm. Closed on Good Fri.
Admission: Adult £4, Conc. £3.25, Child (5–16) £1, Under 5's Free, Family (2+2) £9, Groups (inc. introductory talk) £4.50, Guided Tour £5.50, Refreshments £1.50, Annual Family Membership £26.

ℹ No photography. ⊡ 🖼 🖳 Gardens. 🎫 By arrangement. 🔲 🦮 Guide dogs only. 🔶

FORD END WATERMILL
Station Road, Ivinghoe, Buckinghamshire
Tel: 01296 661997 **Contact:** John Wallis

The Watermill, a listed building, was recorded in 1616 but is probably much older.
Location: MAP 7:D11, OS Ref. SP941 166. 600 metres from Ivinghoe Church along B488 (Station Road) to Leighton Buzzard.
Open: Easter Mon–end Sept: 2nd & 4th Suns of each month & BHs, 2.30–5.30pm. Milling between 3–5pm on BHs and the 2nd Sun in May (National Mills Day) and 4th Sun in July and Sept.
Admission: Adult £1.50, Child 50p (5–15yrs). Schools: Child 75p, Adults Free.

HUGHENDEN MANOR ❧
HIGH WYCOMBE HP14 4LA

Tel: 01494 755573 **Infoline:** 01494 755565 **Fax:** 01494 474284
E-mail: hughenden@nationaltrust.org.uk
Owner: The National Trust **Contact:** The General Manager

Hughenden Manor offers a vivid insight into the charismatic personality and colourful private life of the most unlikely Victorian Prime Minister, Benjamin Disraeli, who lived here from 1848–1881. The formal gardens have been recreated based on the original designs of of Mary Anne Disraeli and there are beautiful walks through the surrounding park and woodland. Hughenden's secret wartime past is revealed in our Second World War room in the cellars, with interactive exhibits and eye-witness accounts.

Location: MAP 3:F1, OS 165 Ref. SU866 955. 1½ m N of High Wycombe on the W side of the A4128. Bus: Arriva 300 High Wycombe to Aylesbury. Rail: High Wycombe train station 2 miles.

Open: House: 17 Feb–31 Oct, 12–5pm (11.20am by guided tour only). Wed–Sun & BH Mon. Open Good Fri. On BHs and busy days entry is by timed ticket. Open 7 days a week for summer school holidays. 3 Nov–19 Dec 11–3pm. Wed–Sun. Gardens, shop and restaurant: open same days as house, 11am–5pm until 31 Oct, 11am–4pm from 3 Nov–19 Dec. Park & Woodland: All year.

***Admission:** House & Garden: Adult £8.00, Child £4.10, Family £20. Garden only: Adult £3.20, Child £2.20. Park & Woodland Free. Groups: Adult £6.90. No groups at weekends or BHs. £1 off if arriving by public transport. Free to NT Members. *includes a voluntary 10% donation but visitors can choose to pay the standard prices displayed at the property and on the website.

⬚ ⚥ ♿ Partial. WCs. 🍴 Licensed 🎦 For booked groups. 🅿 Limited for cars. 🔲 🚶 Guide dogs only. ❄ ♿

THE KING'S HEAD ❧

King's Head Passage, Market Square, Aylesbury, Buckinghamshire HP20 2RW
Tel: 01296 381501 **E-mail:** kingshead@nationaltrust.org.uk
Owner: The National Trust **Contact:** The Visitor Development Manager

This enchanting restored coaching inn dates from 1455 and its noteworthy architectural features include medieval stained glass windows, extensive timber framing and a central cobbled courtyard. It has strong associations with the Civil War, Oliver Cromwell stayed there in 1651, and with the Rothschild family. There is a second-hand bookshop, coffee shop and the Farmers' Bar is run by the Chiltern Brewery.

Location: MAP 7:C11, OS Ref. SP818 138. At NW corner of Aylesbury Market Square.
Open: All year: Tues–Sat. No Visitor Reception and no Mon opening from 2010. Bookshop & coffee shop 10.30am–4pm. Farmers' Bar licensing hours all year. Guided tours on Wed, Fri & Sat at 2pm.
Admission: Adult £3.20 (incl tour) booking necessary. £2.60 for groups of over 15 people. NT members Free. Child £1.50.

🎦 ♿ Partial. WC. ⚐ Licensed. 🎦 Obligatory. 🅿 None. 🔲 🚶 Guide dogs only. ❄ ♿

LONG CRENDON COURTHOUSE ❧

High St, Long Crendon, Buckinghamshire HP18 9AN
Tel: 01280 822850 (Mon–Fri) **E-mail:** stowegarden@nationaltrust.org.uk
www.nationaltrust.org.uk
Owner: The National Trust **Contact:** Assistant Property Manager – Stowe

A fantastic opportunity to see very clearly a 15th century building. The exposed timber beams and early oak floorboards are a rare sight. New! Local History Display (inside).

Location: MAP 7:B11, OS Ref. SP698 091. 3miles N of Thame.
Open: 3 Apr–26 Sept, 11am–6pm, Sat & Sun; 7 Apr–29 Sept, 2pm–6pm, Wed.
Admission: Adult £1.60, Child 55p. Free to NT Members.

ℹ

NETHER WINCHENDON HOUSE 🏛

Nether Winchendon, Nr Aylesbury, Buckinghamshire HP18 0DY
Tel: 01844 290101 **Fax:** 01844 290199
www.netherwinchendonhouse.com **www.timelessweddingvenues.com**
Owner/Contact: Mr Robert Spencer Bernard

Medieval and Tudor manor house. Great Hall. Dining Room with fine 16th century frieze, ceiling and linenfold panelling. Fine furniture and family portraits. Home of Sir Francis Bernard Bt (d1779), the last British Governor of Massachussetts Bay. Continuous family occupation since mid-16th century. House altered in late 18th century in the Strawberry Hill Gothick style. Interesting garden (5 acres) and specimen trees.

Location: MAP 7:C11, OS Ref. SP734 121. 2m N of A418 equidistant between Thame & Aylesbury.
Open: 28 April - 31 May (not Saturdays) & 30 Aug 2010 all 2.30–5.30pm. Conducted tours only at 1/4 to each hour. Groups at any time by prior written agreement (£10 per person, no concessions, minimum charge £300).
Admission: Adult £8, OAP £5 (no concessions at weekends or BHs), Child (under 12) Free. HHA free (not on special groups).

🎦 ♿ Please tel in advance. WC. ⚐ By arrangement. 🎦 Obligatory. 🅿 🚶 ❄ ♿

PITSTONE WINDMILL ❧

Ivinghoe, Buckinghamshire
Tel: 01442 851227 **Group organisers:** 01296 668223 **Fax:** 01442 850000
E-mail: pitstonemill@nationaltrust.org.uk
Owner: The National Trust

One of the oldest post mills in Britain restored by volunteers.

Location: MAP 7:D11, OS Ref. SP946 158. 1/2 m S of Ivinghoe, 3m NE of Tring. Just W of B488.
Open: 6 Jun–30 Aug, Sun & BHs, 2.30–6pm. Last admission, 5.30pm.
Admission: Adult £2, Child £1, Family £5. Free to NT members.

ℹ No WC. ♿ Difficult access. 🅿

STOWE HOUSE 🏛

See page 75 for full page entry.

© NT/Paul Watson

STOWE LANDSCAPE GARDENS & PARK

Nr BUCKINGHAM, BUCKINGHAMSHIRE MK18 5DQ

www.nationaltrust.org.uk/stowegardens

Tel: 01280 822850 **Infoline:** 01494 755568 **Fax:** 01280 822437
Group Visits: 01280 822850 **E-mail:** stowegarden@nationaltrust.org.uk
Owner: The National Trust **Contact:** The Property Manager

Nestling amongst spectacular views and vast open spaces there are magical secret corners, hidden meanings, and over 40 monuments and temples waiting to be discovered. Visitors can also take a tour of Stowe House or explore the 750 acres of surrounding historic parkland, including the restored 250 acre Deer Park. Stowe is the perfect setting for a family picnic or those seeking peace and tranquility, with walks and trails for all to enjoy. With the changing seasons, continuing restoration and a calendar of events for all the family, each visit provides something new to discover. A beautiful creation of the 18th century, Stowe is one of Europe's foremost landscape gardens. What's new: Restoration of Sleeping Wood complete.

Location: MAP 7:C10, OS Ref. SP665 366. Off A422 Buckingham – Banbury Rd. 3m NW of Buckingham.

Open: Gardens & Shop: 2 Jan–28 Feb, 10.30am–4pm, Sat & Sun; 3 Mar–31 Oct, 10.30am–5.30pm, Wed–Sun; 6 Nov–19 Dec, 10.30am–4pm, Sat & Sun. Tearooms: 2 Jan–28 Feb, 10.30am–3.30pm, Sat & Sun; 3 Mar–31 Oct, 10.30am–5pm, Wed–Sun; 6 Nov–19 Dec, 10.30am–3.30pm, Sat & Sun. Last admission 1½hrs before closing. Shop additionally open: 3 Nov–17 Dec, 11am–3pm, Wed–Fri. Open BH Mons. May close in extreme weather conditions. CLOSED SAT 29 MAY. House not NT. Parkland open all year dawn to dusk.

*Admission: Gardens: Adult £7.50, Child £3.80, Family £18.80, Groups £6.40. Free to NT Members. 15% discount for booked groups. House (not NT) admission payable at NT reception.. *includes a voluntary 10% donation but visitors can choose to pay the standard prices displayed at the property and on the website.

WCs. Free in gardens, 11am and 2pm most days. By arrangement for groups. Limited for coaches In grounds, on leads.

© NT / Waddesdon Manor/Barry Keen

© NT / Waddesdon Manor/Mike Fear

WADDESDON MANOR

Nr AYLESBURY, BUCKINGHAMSHIRE HP18 0JH

www.waddesdon.org.uk

Tel: 01296 653211 **Booking & Info:** 01296 653226 **Fax:** 01296 653212
E-mail: waddesdonmanor@nationaltrust.org.uk
Owner: The National Trust

Waddesdon Manor was built by Baron Ferdinand de Rothschild in the 19th century to display his superb collection of art treasures and entertain the fashionable world. The Victorian garden is considered one of the finest in Britain with its parterre, seasonal displays, aviary, fountains and statuary. The Wine Cellars contain thousands of bottles of wine dating back to 1868. A full programme of events is organised throughout the year including family and study days. With two licensed restaurants, shops, a woodland playground and conveniently situated for London and Oxford Waddesdon offers a memorable day out for all the family.

Location: MAP 7:C11, OS Ref. SP740 169. Car: Between Aylesbury & Bicester, off A41. Rail: Aylesbury 6m.

Open: Gardens, Aviary, Restaurants, Shops & Woodland Playground: 2 Jan–28 Mar: Sats & Suns; 31 Mar–31 Dec (inc. 20, 21, 27 & 28 Dec. excl. 24,25 & 26 Dec) Wed–Sun & BH Mons, 10am–5pm. House & Gardens, Wine Cellars, Woodland Playground, Shops & Restaurants: 31 Mar–31 Oct, Wed–Sun & BH Mons, 12noon–4pm (11am Sats & Suns). Last rec adm. 2.30pm. Bachelors' Wing: 31 Mar–31 Oct: Wed–Fri 12noon–4pm. Limited space, entry cannot be guaranteed. Christmas Season (East Wing decorated for the festive season) 17 Nov–31 Dec (inc. 20, 21, 27 & 28 Dec. excl. 24,25 & 26 Dec), Wed–Fri 12 noon–4pm. Sats & Suns 11am–4pm. Timed tickets to house available. Booking fee £3 per transaction. Please call Booking Office or book on-line free of charge.

Gift Aid Admission: House & Gardens, Wine Cellars, Aviary, Woodland Playground, Shops & Restaurants: Adult Wed–Fri: £13.20, Sats, Suns & BHs: £15.00. Child† Wed–Fri: £9.35, Sats, Suns & BHs: £11.00. Gardens, Aviary, Woodland Playground, Shops & Restaurants: Adult Wed–Fri:£5.50, Sats, Suns & BHs: £7.00. Child† Wed–Fri: £2.75, Sats, Suns & BHs: £3.50. Bachelors' Wing: £3.30. †Child (5–16 yrs). Children under 5 Free. Group rates available.

No photography in House. NT members free. HHA Members free entry to grounds. RHS members free to grounds in Mar, Sept & Oct. Children welcomed under parental supervision in the House. Babies must be carried in a front-sling. WCs. Parking. Licensed. Licensed. By arrangement. Assistance dogs only. Wine Tasting, Special Interest Days, Family Events. Please telephone 01296 653226 for details.

WEST WYCOMBE PARK ⅍

WEST WYCOMBE, HIGH WYCOMBE, BUCKINGHAMSHIRE HP14 3AJ

Tel: 01494 513569

Owner: The National Trust   **Contact:** The Head Guide

A perfectly preserved rococo landscape garden, created in the mid-18th century by Sir Francis Dashwood, founder of the Dilettanti Society and the Hellfire Club. The house is among the most theatrical and Italianate in England, its façades formed as classical temples. The interior has Palmyrene ceilings and decoration, with pictures, furniture and sculpture dating from the time of Sir Francis.

Location: MAP 3:F1, OS Ref. SU828 947. At W end of West Wycombe S of the A40. Bus: Arriva 40 High Wycombe - Stokenchurch. Rail: High Wycombe train station 2.5 miles.

Open: House & Grounds: 1 Jun–31 Aug: daily except Fri & Sat, 2–6pm. Weekday entry by guided tour only every 20 mins (approx), last admission 5.15pm. Grounds only: 1 Apr–31 May: daily except Fri & Sat, 2–6pm.

Admission: House & Grounds: Adult £7.60, Child £3.90, Family £19.10. Groups £6.30. Grounds only: Adult £3.90, Child £2.20. Free to NT Members. Groups by arrangement. Note: The West Wycombe Caves and adjacent café are privately owned and NT members must pay admission fees.

🖪 ⓕ Obligatory on weekdays. ⓟ Limited for coaches. ▣ Guide dogs only.

WOTTON HOUSE

Wotton Underwood, Aylesbury, Buckinghamshire HP18 0SB
Tel: 01844 238363   **Fax:** 01844 238380   **E-mail:** david.gladstone@which.net
Owner/Contact: David Gladstone

The Capability Brown Pleasure Grounds at Wotton, currently undergoing restoration, are related to the Stowe gardens, both belonging to the Grenville family when Brown laid out the Wotton grounds between 1750 and 1767. A series of man-made features on the 3 mile circuit include bridges, follies and statues.

Location: MAP 7:B11, OS Ref. 468576, 216168. Either A41 turn off Kingswood, or M40/J7 via Thame. Rail: Haddenham & Thame 6m.

Open: 7 Apr – 8 Sept: Weds only, 2–5pm. Also 5 Apr, 3 May, 3 Jul, 7 Aug, 4 Sept: 2–5pm.

Admission: Adult £6, Child Free, Conc. £3. Groups (max 25).

ⓕ Obligatory. ⓟ Limited. ▣

WYCOMBE MUSEUM

Priory Avenue, High Wycombe, Buckinghamshire HP13 6PX
Tel: 01494 421895   **E-mail:** museum@wycombe.gov.uk
Owner: Wycombe District Council   **Contact:** Grace Wison

Set in historic Castle Hill House and surrounded by peaceful and attractive gardens.

Location: MAP 3:F1, OS Ref. SU867 933. Signposted off the A404 High Wycombe/Amersham road. The Museum is about 5mins walk from the town centre and railway station.

Open: Mon–Sat, 10am–5pm. Suns, 2–5pm. Closed BHs.

Admission: Free.

 See which properties offer **educational facilities** or **school visits** in our index at the end of the book.

Cliveden

■ **Owner**
Lord Montagu

■ **Contact**
John Montagu Building
Beaulieu
Brockenhurst
Hampshire SO42 7ZN

Tel: 01590 612345
Fax: 01590 612624
E-mail: info@
beaulieu.co.uk

■ **Location**
MAP 3:C6
OS Ref. SU387 025

M27 to J2, A326, B3054
follow brown signs.

Bus: Local service within
the New Forest.

Rail: Stations at
Brockenhurst 7m away.

■ **Opening Times**
Summer
May–September
Daily, 10am–6pm.

Winter
October–April
Daily, 10am–5pm.

Closed Christmas Day.

■ **Admission**
All year

Individual rates upon
application.

Groups (15+)
Rates upon application.

■ **Special Events**
April 25
Boat Jumble

May 15/16
Spring Motormart &
Autojumble

September 11/12
International Autojumble

October 31
Fireworks Spectacular

All enquiries should be
made to our Special
Events Booking Office
where advance tickets can
be purchased. The
contact telephone is
01590 612888.

BEAULIEU 🏛

www.beaulieu.co.uk

The Beaulieu Estate has been owned by the same family since 1538 and is still the private home of the Montagus. Thomas Wriothesley, who later became the 1st Earl of Southampton, acquired the estate at the time of the Dissolution of the Monasteries when he was Lord Chancellor to Henry VIII.

Palace House, overlooking the Beaulieu River, was once the Great Gatehouse of Beaulieu Abbey with its monastic origins reflected in the fan vaulted ceilings of the 14th Century Dining Hall and Lower Drawing Room. The rooms are decorated with furnishings, portraits and treasures collected by past and present generations of the family. Visitors can enjoy the fine gardens or take a riverside walk around the Monks' Mill Pond.

Beaulieu Abbey was founded in 1204 when King John gave the land

to the Cistercians and although most of the buildings have now been destroyed, much of the beauty and interest remains. The former Monks' Refectory is now the local parish church and the Domus, which houses an exhibition and video presentation of monastic life, is home to beautiful wall hangings.

Beaulieu also houses the world famous National Motor Museum which traces the story of motoring from 1894 to the present day. 250 vehicles are on display including legendary world record breakers plus veteran, vintage and classic cars and motorcycles.

The modern Beaulieu is very much a family destination with many free and unlimited rides on a transportation theme to be enjoyed, including a mile long, high-level monorail and replica 1912 London open-topped bus.

Conference/Function

ROOM	SIZE	MAX CAPACITY
Brabazon (x3)	40' x 40'	85 (x3)
Domus	69' x 27'	150
Theatre		200
Palace House		60
Motor Museum		250

BEAULIEU ...

Catering and Functions

Beaulieu also offers a comprehensive range of facilities for conferences, company days out, product launches, management training, corporate hospitality, promotions, film locations, exhibitions and outdoor events.

The National Motor Museum is a unique venue for drinks receptions, evening product launches and dinners or the perfect complement to a conference as a relaxing visit.

The charming 13th century Domus hall with its beautiful wooden beams, stone walls and magnificent wall hangings, is the perfect setting for weddings, conferences, dinners, buffets or themed evenings.

Palace House, the ancestral home of Lord Montagu is an exclusive setting for smaller dinners, buffets and receptions. With a welcoming log fire in the winter and the coolness of the courtyard fountain in the summer, it offers a relaxing yet truly 'stately' atmosphere to ensure a memorable experience for your guests whatever the time of year.

A purpose-built theatre, with tiered seating, can accommodate 200 people whilst additional meeting rooms can accommodate from 20 to 200 delegates. Bespoke marquees can also be erected in a charming parkland setting, for any event or occasion. With the nearby Beaulieu River offering waterborne activities and the Beaulieu Estate, with its purpose-built off road course, giving you the opportunity of indulging in a variety of country pursuits and outdoor management training, Beaulieu provides a unique venue for your conference and corporate hospitality needs.

For further information please call 01590 614769/87 or visit www.leithsatbeaulieu.co.uk

ℹ️ Allow 3 hrs or more for visits. Last adm. 40 mins before closing. Helicopter landing point. When visiting Beaulieu arrangements can be made to view the Estate's vineyards. Visits, which can be arranged between Apr–Oct, must be pre-booked at least one week in advance with Beaulieu Estate Office.

Palace House Shop and Kitchen Shop plus Main Reception Shop.

Disabled visitors may be dropped off outside Visitor Reception before parking. WC. Wheelchairs can be provided free of charge in Visitor Reception by prior booking.

🍴 The Brabazon restaurant seats 250.

Attendants on duty. Guided tours by prior arrangement for groups.

🅿️ 1,500 cars and 30 coaches. During the season the busy period is from 11.30am to 1.30pm. Coach drivers should sign in at Information Desk. Free admission for coach drivers plus voucher which can be exchanged for food, drink and souvenirs.

Professional staff available to assist in planning of visits. Services include introductory talks, films, guided tours, rôle play and extended projects. In general, educational services incur no additional charges and publications are sold at cost. Information available from Education at Beaulieu, John Montagu Building, Beaulieu, Hants SO42 7ZN.

In grounds, on leads only.

THE ABBEY CHURCH OF SS MARY AND ETHELFLAEDA

Church Lane, Romsey, Hants SO51 8EP
Tel: 01794 513125 **Email:** romsey.abbey@lineone.net
Website: www.romseyabbey.org.uk
Owner: Vicar and Church Wardens **Contact:** Hazel, Parish Secretary
This Parish Church is set in the centre of Romsey in peaceful grounds. Romsey Abbey is a magnificent predominantly Norman building with many unique features. Lord Louis Mountbatten is buried in the Abbey.
Location: MAP 3:C5. OS Ref: SU 353 212. M27/J3. Centre of Romsey.
Open: All year 8am–6pm. Times may vary for services and special events.
Admission: Free entry, suggested donations. Entry by ticket for some events, concerts etc.
🔲 ♿ 🅯 By arrangement 🅿 Limited. Coaches dropping off only 🔳 🖼 Guide dogs only
❄ Open all year. 💷 €

Broadlands

JANE AUSTEN'S HOUSE
CHAWTON, ALTON, HAMPSHIRE GU34 1SD

www.jane-austens-house-museum.org.uk

Tel: 01420 83262 **E-mail:** enquiries@jahmusm.org.uk
Owner: Jane Austen Memorial Trust **Contact:** Ann Channon
17th century house where Jane Austen wrote or revised her six great novels. Contains many items associated with her and her family, documents and letters, first editions of the novels, pictures, portraits and furniture. Recreated Historic kitchen. Pleasant garden, suitable for picnics, bakehouse with brick oven and wash tub, houses Jane's donkey carriage. Learning Centre.
Location: MAP 3:E4, OS Ref. SU708 376. Just S of A31, 1m SW of Alton, signposted Chawton.
Open: Jan/mid Feb: Sats & Suns, 10.30am–4.30pm. Mar–end May: daily, 10.30am–4.30pm. June–Aug: daily, 10am–5pm. Sept–end Dec: daily, 10.30am–4.30pm. Closed 25/26 December.
Admission: Fee charged.
🔲 Bookshop. 🍽 ♿ Ground floor & grounds. WC. 🖼 Opposite house.
🅿 Opposite house. 🔳 🖼 Guide dogs only. ❄ 💷

AVINGTON PARK 🏛
WINCHESTER, HAMPSHIRE SO21 1DB

www.avingtonpark.co.uk

Tel: 01962 779260 **E-mail:** enquiries@avingtonpark.co.uk
Owner/Contact: Mrs S L Bullen
Avington Park, where Charles II and George IV both stayed at various times, dates back to the 11th century. The house was enlarged in 1670 by the addition of two wings and a classical Portico surmounted by three statues. The State rooms are magnificently painted and lead onto the unique pair of conservatories flanking the South Lawn. The Georgian church, St. Mary's, is in the grounds.
Avington Park is a privately owned stately home and is a most prestigious venue in peaceful surroundings. It is perfect for any event from seminars, conferences and exhibitions to wedding ceremonies and receptions, dinner dances and private parties. The Conservatories and the Orangery make a delightful location for summer functions, whilst log fires offer a welcome during the winter. Excellent caterers provide for all types of occasion, ranging from breakfasts and light lunches to sumptuous dinners. All bookings at Avington are individually tailor-made and only exclusive use is offered. Several rooms are licensed for Civil wedding ceremonies and a delightful fully-equipped apartment is available for short stays.
Location: MAP 3:D4, OS Ref. SU534 324. 4m NE of Winchester ½m S of B3047 in Itchen Abbas.
Open: May–Sept: Suns & BH Mons plus Mons in Aug, 2.30–5.30pm. Last tour 5pm. Other times by arrangement, coach parties welcome by appointment all year.
Admission: Adult £4.75, Child £2.
ℹ Conferences. 🍽 ♿ Partial. WC. 🖼 🅯 Obligatory. 🅿
🖼 In grounds, on leads. Guide dogs only in house. 🔼 💷

BASING HOUSE

Redbridge Lane, Basing, Basingstoke RG24 7HB
Tel: 01256 467294
Owner: Hampshire County Council   **Contact:** Alan Turton
Ruins, covering 10 acres, of huge Tudor palace. Recent recreation of Tudor formal garden.
Location: MAP 3:E3, OS Ref. SU665 526. 2m E from Basingstoke town centre. Signposted car parks are about 5 or 10 mins walk from entrance.
Open: Apr–Sept: Wed–Sun & BHs, 2–6pm.
Admission: Adult £2, Conc. £1.

BEAULIEU 🏠   *See pages 82/83 for double page entry.*

BISHOP'S WALTHAM PALACE ♯

Bishop's Waltham, Hampshire SO32 1DH
Tel: 01489 892460   **E-mail:** customers@english-heritage.org.uk
www.english-heritage.org.uk/bishop
Owner: English Heritage   **Contact:** Visitor Operations Team
The ruins of a medieval palace (together with later additions) used by Bishops and senior clergy of Winchester as they travelled through their diocese. Winchester was the richest diocese in England, its properties were grandiose and extravagantly appointed. The ground floor of the Farmhouse is occupied by the Bishop's Waltham Town Museum.
Location: MAP 3:D5, OS Ref. SU552 174. In Bishop's Waltham, 5 miles NE from M27/J8.
Open: Grounds: 1 May–30 Sept: Sun–Fri, 10am–5pm. Farmhouse: open by request.
Admission: Free. Opening times and prices are valid until 31st March 2010, after this date details are subject to change please see www.english-heritage.org.uk for the most up-to-date information.
🔲 🔣 **P** 🔣 Grounds only, on leads. 🔺

BREAMORE HOUSE & MUSEUM 🏠

BREAMORE, FORDINGBRIDGE, HAMPSHIRE SP6 2DF

www.breamorehouse.com

Tel: 01725 512468   **Fax:** 01725 512858   **E-mail:** breamore@btinternet.com
Owner/Contact: Michael Hulse
Elizabethan manor with fine collections of pictures and furniture. Countryside Museum takes visitors back to the time when a village was self-sufficient.
Location: MAP 3:B5, OS Ref. SU152 191. W Off the A338, between Salisbury and Ringwood.
Open: Easter weekend; Apr: Tue & Sun; May–Sept: Mon, Tue, Wed, Thur, Sun & BHs. House 2–5pm. Countryside Museum: 1–5.30pm. Last tour of house 4pm.
Admission: Combined ticket for house and museum: Adult £8, Child £6, OAP £7, Family £19.
🔲 🔣 Ground floor & grounds. WCs. 🔳 🔣

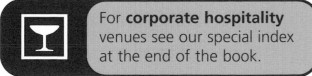

For **corporate hospitality** venues see our special index at the end of the book.

Calshot Castle

©English Heritage

BROADLANDS

Romsey, Hampshire SO51 9ZD
www.broadlands.net
Owner: Lord & Lady Brabourne
Broadlands, the historic home of the late Earl Mountbatten of Burma, is undergoing major remedial work over the next two years and will be closed to visitors throughout 2010. Outdoor events continue to be held, please see website for details.

CALSHOT CASTLE ♯

Calshot, Fawley, Hampshire SO4 1BR
Tel: 02380 892023 or 02380 892077   **E-mail:** customers@english-heritage.org.uk
www.english-heritage.org.uk/calshot
Owner: English Heritage   **Contact:** Hampshire County Council
Henry VIII built this coastal fort in an excellent position, commanding the sea passage to Southampton. The fort houses an exhibition and recreated pre-World War I barrack room.
Location: MAP 3:D6, OS Ref. SU489 025. On spit 2 miles SE of Fawley off B3053.
Open: 1 Apr–30 Sep, daily 10am–4pm.
Admission: Adult £2.50, Child £1.50, Conc. £1.80, Family £6. EH Members Free. Group discount available. Opening times and prices are valid until 31st March 2010, after this date details are subject to change please see www.english-heritage.org.uk for the most up-to-date information.
ℹ️ WCs. 🔲 🔣 Partial. **P** 🔣

ELING TIDE MILL

The Toll Bridge, Eling, Totton, Southampton, Hampshire SO40 9HF
Tel: 023 8086 9575   **E-mail:** info@elingtidemill.org.uk
Owner: Eling Tide Mill Trust Ltd & New Forest District Council
Contact: Mr David Blackwell-Eaton
Location: MAP 3:C5, OS Ref. SU365 126. 4m W of Southampton. ½m S of the A35.
Open: All year: Wed–Sun and BH Mons, 10am–4pm. Closed 25/26 Dec.
Admission: Adult £2.30, Child £1.30, OAP £1.80, Family £6. Group rates on application. Prices may change Apr 2008. Please telephone for details.

© Colin Roberts

© Exbury Gardens

EXBURY GARDENS & STEAM RAILWAY 🏛
EXBURY, SOUTHAMPTON, HAMPSHIRE SO45 1AZ
www.exbury.co.uk

Tel: 023 8089 1203 **Fax:** 023 8089 9940

Owner: The Rothschild Family **Contact:** Estate Office

HHA/Christie's *Garden of the Year* 2001. A spectacular 200-acre woodland garden showcasing the world famous Rothschild Collection of rhododendrons, azaleas magnolias, camellias, rare trees and plants. Enchanting river walk, ponds and cascades. Daffodil Meadow, Rock and Heather Gardens, exotic plantings and herbaceous borders ensure year-round interest. Superb autumn colour, with National Collection of *Nyssa* and *Oxydendrum*. The Steam Railway enchants visitors of all ages, passing through a Summer Garden, and featuring a bridge, tunnel and viaduct. Licensed for Civil weddings in three venues on site. Excellent Restaurant and Tearooms.

Location: MAP 3:D6, OS Ref. SU425 005. 20 mins Junction 2, M27 west. 11m SE of Totton (A35) via A326 & B3054 & minor road. In New Forest.

Open: 13 Mar–7 Nov: daily, 10am–5pm (dusk in Nov). Please call for details of Santa Steam Specials in December.

Admission: Adult £8.50, Child (3–15yrs) £1.50, OAP £8, Group £7.50, Family (2+3) £19; Railway +£3.50, Unlimited rides £4.50. Child under 3yrs Free. Buggy tours +£3.50/£4. RHS Members Free Mar & Sept.

▣ ▣ ▣ ▣ ▣ ▣ Licensed. ▣ By arrangement. ▣ ▣ ▣ In grounds, on leads. ▣
▣ 19 Apr–31 May, The Glory of The Garden; 9 Oct–7 Nov, Festival of Autumn Colour; 25 –31 Oct, Exbury Ghost Train.

FORT BROCKHURST ⌗

Gunner's Way, Gosport, Hampshire PO12 4DS

Tel: 02392 581059 **E-mail:** customers@english-heritage.org.uk

www.english-heritage.org.uk/fortbrockhurst

Owner: English Heritage **Contact:** Visitor Operations Team

This 19th-century fort was built to protect Portsmouth. Today it displays extraordinary objects found at sites across the region, including stonework, jewellery, textiles and furniture from various periods. Tours of the fort explain the exciting history of the site and the legend behind the ghostly activity in cell no.3.

Location: MAP 3:E6, OS196, Ref. SU596 020. Off A32, in Gunner's Way, Elson on N side of Gosport.

Open: The fort opens 11am–3pm on the 2nd Sat of every month, 1 Apr–30 Sept. The new Collections Resource Centre will also be open.

Admission: Free. Opening times and prices are valid until 31st March 2010, after this date details are subject to change please see www.english-heritage.org.uk for the most up-to-date information.

ⓘ WCs. ▣ ▣ Dogs on leads (restricted areas).

FURZEY GARDENS

Minstead, Lyndhurst, Hampshire SO43 7GL

Tel: 023 8081 2464 **Fax:** 023 8081 2297

Owner: Furzey Gardens Charitable Trust **Contact:** Maureen Cole

Location: MAP 3:C5, OS Ref. SU273 114. Minstead village ½m N of M27/A31 junction off A337 to Lyndhurst.

Open: Mar–Oct: daily, 10am–5pm.

Admission: Please contact property for prices.

Exbury Gardens , Festival of Autumn Colour

GILBERT WHITE'S HOUSE & THE OATES MUSEUM

THE WAKES, HIGH STREET, SELBORNE, ALTON GU34 3JH

www.gilbertwhiteshouse.org.uk

Tel: 01420 511275   **E-mail:** info@gilbertwhiteshouse.org.uk
Owner: Oates Memorial Trust   **Contact:** Duty Manager

Gilbert White's House & The Oates Museum is the charming 18th century home of the famous naturalist, the Rev. Gilbert White (1720-1793), which also houses an exhibition about Captain Lawrence Oates, and his part in Scott's ill fated expedition in 1911. Over 20 acres of gardens, an elegant Tea Parlour and Museum shop.

Open: 1 Jan–23 Dec: Tue–Sun, 11am–5pm. Also open Mons Jun, Jul and Aug and BH Mon.

Admission: Adults £6.95, Conc. £5.95, Child £1.50 (2009 prices). Reductions are available for pre-booked groups of over 10 people, including a free introductory talk.

ℹ️ No photography in house. 📷 ♿ Partial. 🐕 By arrangement.
🅿️ Guide dogs only.

Fort Brockhurst

GREAT HALL & QUEEN ELEANOR'S GARDEN

CASTLE AVENUE, WINCHESTER SO23 8PJ

www.hants.gov.uk/greathall

Tel: 01962 846476   **Bookings:** Online
Owner: Hampshire County Council   **Contact:** Custodian

The only surviving part of Henry III's medieval castle at Winchester, this 13th century hall was the centre of court and government life. The Round Table, closely associated with the legend of King Arthur, has hung here for over 700 years. Queen Eleanor's garden is a faithful representation of the medieval garden visited by Kings and Queens of England.

Location: MAP 3:D4, OS Ref. SU477 295. Central Winchester. SE of Westgate archway.
Open: Daily. Closed 25/26 Dec and for Civic events – see website for details.
Admission: Free. Donations appreciated towards the upkeep of the Great Hall.

ℹ️ 📷 ♿ By arrangement.

HIGHCLERE CASTLE, GARDENS & EGYPTIAN EXHIBITION
HIGHCLERE, NEWBURY, BERKSHIRE RG20 9RN

www.highclerecastle.co.uk

Tel: 01635 253210 **Fax:** 01635 255315 **E-mail:** theoffice@highclerecastle.co.uk
Owner: Earl of Carnarvon **Contact:** The Castle Office
Visit this spectacular Victorian Castle set in a 'Capability Brown' Park. The Gardens include a Monk's Garden, Secret Garden and a new Arboretum. Explore the new Egyptian Exhibition in the Castle Cellars; follow the Path to Discovery; marvel at what Lord Carnarvon and Howard Carter found in 1922 in Egypt.
Location: MAP 3:D3, OS Ref. SU445 587. M4/J13 – A34 south. M3/J8 – A303 –A34 north. Air: Heathrow M4 45 mins. Rail: Paddington – Newbury 45 mins.
Open: Easter Opening 2010: every day 28 Mar–11 Apr. Summer Opening: 4 Jul–2 Sept, Sun–Thur.
Admission: Castle & Exhibition: Adult: £15, Child: £9, Conc. £13.50, Family (2+3/1+4) £40. Each element available separately; Group Rates available. Grounds & Gardens only; Adult £4, Child £1. Private Guided tours by arrangement.

HINTON AMPNER ❧
BRAMDEAN, ALRESFORD, HAMPSHIRE SO24 0LA

www.nationaltrust.org.uk

Tel: 01962 771305 **Fax:** 01962 793101
E-mail: hintonampner@nationaltrust.org.uk
Owner: The National Trust **Contact:** The Property Manager
Best known for its fine garden, Hinton Ampner is an elegant country house with an outstanding collection of furniture, paintings and object d'art. House was remodelled after a fire in 1960.
The garden is widely acknowledge as a masterpiece of 20th century design with formal and informal planting.
Location: MAP 3:E4, OS Ref. SU597 275. M3/J9 follow signs to Petersfield. On A272, 1m W of Bramdean village, 8m E of Winchester.
Open: House: 13 Mar–31 Oct: Mon, Tues, Wed, Sat & Sun, 11.30am–5pm. Garden: 15 Mar–2 Nov, daily except Thur & Fri, 11am–5pm.
Admission: House & Garden: Adult £8.25, Child (5–16yrs) £4.10 Garden only: Adult £7.05, Child (5–16yrs) £3.45, Free to NT Members. *includes a voluntary 10% donation but visitors can choose to pay the standard prices displayed at the property and on the website.
Special Events: Range of special events in the house and parkland throughout the year. Contact the property or National Trust website for details.
WCs. Licensed. By arrangement. Limited for coaches. Guide dogs only.

©NT/Nick White

HOUGHTON LODGE GARDENS 🏛
STOCKBRIDGE, HAMPSHIRE, SO20 6LQ

www.houghtonlodge.co.uk

Tel: 01264 810502 **Fax:** 01264 810063 **E-mail:** info@houghtonlodge.co.uk
Owner/Contact: Captain & Mrs Martin Busk
A haven of peace above the tranquil beauty of the River Test. Grade II* Gardens with fine trees surround an enchanting and unique example of an 18th Century "Cottage Ornè". Chalk Cob walls enclose traditional Kitchen Garden with espaliers, herbs and heated greenhouses, hydroponicum and orchid collection. Gardens both formal and informal. Popular TV/Film location. For an additional £2.50 enjoy the 14 acres adjoining the garden which provide an experience of the natural world with meadow walks through the peaceful and unspoiled surroundings of the River Test and meet Tom, Dick and Harry, our new Alpacas. Licensed for Civil Weddings.
Location: MAP 3:C4, OS Ref. SU344 332. 1½m S of Stockbridge (A30) on minor road to Houghton village.
Open: 1st Mar–31st Oct, Thu–Tue,10am to 5pm. Weds & House by appointment only.
Admission: Adult £5, Children under 14 Free. Coach Tours and Groups welcome on any day by appointment only – special rates if booked in advance.
Self-service teas & coffees, home-made cakes. Obligatory, by arrangement. In grounds, on short leads.

HURST CASTLE ⚏

Keyhaven, Lymington, Hampshire SO41 0TP
Tel: 01590 642344 **E-mail:** customers@english-heritage.org.uk
www.english-heritage.org.uk/hurstcastle
Owner: English Heritage **Contact:** (Managed by) Hurst Castle Services
This was one of the most sophisticated fortresses built by Henry VIII, and later strengthened in the 19th and 20th centuries, to command the narrow entrance to the Solent. There is an exhibition in the castle, and two huge 38-ton guns form the fort's armaments.
Location: MAP 3:C7, OS196 Ref. SZ318 897. 1½ m walk on shingle spit from Milford-on-Sea.
Open: 1 Apr–31 Oct: daily, 10.30am–5.30pm. Café: open Apr–May weekends & Jun–Sept: daily.
Admission: Adult £3.50, Child £2.20, Conc. £3.20. EH Members free. Group discount available. Opening times and prices are valid until 31st March 2010, after this date details are subject to change please see www.english-heritage.org.uk for the most up-to-date information.
WCs. Dogs on leads (restricted areas).

Highclere

KING JOHN'S HOUSE & HERITAGE CENTRE

CHURCH STREET, ROMSEY, HAMPSHIRE SO51 8BT

www.kingjohnshouse.org.uk

Tel: 01794 512200 **E-mail:** annerhc@aol.com
Owner: King John's House & Tudor Cottage Trust Ltd **Contact:** Anne James
Three historic buildings on one site: Medieval King John's House, containing 14th-century graffiti and rare bone floor, Tudor Cottage complete with traditional tea room and parlour. Beautiful period gardens, special events/exhibitions and children's activities. Gift shop and Tourist Information Centre. Receptions and private/corporate functions.
Location: MAP 3:C5, OS Ref. SU353 212. M27/J3. Opposite Romsey Abbey, next to Post Office.
Open: Apr–Sept: Mon–Sat, 10am–4pm. Oct–Mar: Heritage Centre only. Limited opening on Sundays. Evenings also for pre-booked groups.
Admission: Adult £2.50, Child 50p, Conc. £2. Heritage Centre only: Adult £1.50, Child 50p, Conc. £1. Discounted group booking by appointment.
🏠 🌣 🖬 Partial. 🖭 🗷 By arrangement.
🅿 Off Latimer St with direct access through King John's Garden.
🖩 🖬 Guide dogs only. ❄ 🖵

MEDIEVAL MERCHANT'S HOUSE ♯

58 French Street, Southampton, Hampshire SO1 0AT
Tel: 02380 221503 **E-mail:** customers@english-heritage.org.uk
www.english-heritage.org.uk/medievalmerchant
Owner: English Heritage **Contact:** Visitor Operations Team
The life of a prosperous merchant in the Middle Ages is vividly evoked in this recreated, faithfully restored 13th-century townhouse.
Location: MAP 3:D5, OS Ref. SU419 112. 58 French Street. ¼m S of Bargate off Castle Way. 150yds SE of Tudor House.
Open: 1 Apr–30 Sept: Sun only, 12 noon–5pm.
Admission: Adult £3.80, Child £1.90, Conc. £3.20. EH Members free. Opening times and prices are valid until 31st March 2010, after this date details are subject to change please see www.english-heritage.org.uk for the most up-to-date information.
🖬 Partial. 🗷 Obligatory. 🏠 🖬

Medieval Merchants House

MOTTISFONT 🥬

MOTTISFONT, Nr ROMSEY, HAMPSHIRE SO51 0LP

www.nationaltrust.org.uk/mottisfont

Tel: 01794 340757 **Fax:** 01794 341492 **Recorded Message:** 01794 341220
E-mail: mottisfont@nationaltrust.org.uk
Owner: The National Trust **Contact:** General Manager
Step into another world when you visit this historic estate with its handsome old house and tranquil ground set alongside the fast flowing River Test. Mottisfont is home to the National Collection of Old Fashioned Roses (at their best in June), and a stunning 20th century art collection.
Location: MAP 3:C5, OS185 Ref. SU327 270. Signposted off A3057 Romsey to Stockbridge road, 4½m N of Romsey. Also signposted off B3084 Romsey to Broughton. Station: Dunbridge (U) ¾m.
Open: Garden, Shop & Cafe: 6–28 Feb, 6 Nov–19 Dec Weekends only. 15–21 Feb, every day 11am–4pm. House, Garden, Shop & Cafe: 1–25 Mar, Sat–Thur, 11am–5pm (House Timed Tours 12 & 2pm). 27 Mar–18 Apr, every day 11am–5pm. 19 Apr–30 May, Sat–Thur, 11am–5pm. 31 May–6 Jun, every day 11am–5pm. 7 Jun–20 June, every day 11am–8pm (House closes at 5pm). 21 Jun–24 Oct, Sat–Thurs, 11am–5pm (Open Fri 25 June). 25–31 Oct, every day 11am–5pm. Car park gates close at 6pm or dusk if earlier. 8.30pm 7–20 Jun. Access to some shows in the house may be limited due to functions.
*Admission: Adult £8.50, Child (5-18yrs) £4.20, Family £21. Group discount, rate on application. Free to NT Members. *includes a voluntary 10% donation but visitors can choose to pay the standard prices displayed at the property and on the website.
🏠 🌣 🖬 WCs. 🖭 Licensed. 🍴 Licensed. 🗷 By arrangement. 🅿 Limited for coaches. 🖬 Guide dogs only. 🔺 🖵

NETLEY ABBEY ♯

Netley, Southampton, Hampshire SO31 5DG
Tel: 02392 378291 www.english-heritage.org.uk/netleyabbey
Owner: English Heritage **Contact:** Portchester Castle
A peaceful and beautiful setting for the extensive ruins of this 13th-century Cistercian monastery converted in Tudor times for use as a house. Even in ruins, the abbey continues to be influential, inspiring Romantic writers and poets.
Location: MAP 3:D6, OS Ref. SU453 089. In Netley, 4 miles SE of Southampton, facing Southampton Water.
Open: 1 Apr–30 Sept: daily, 10am–6pm. 1 Oct–31 Mar '10: Sat & Sun, 10am–3pm. Closed 24–26 Dec & 1 Jan.
Admission: Free. Opening times and prices are valid until 31st March 2010, after this date details are subject to change please see www.english-heritage.org.uk for the most up-to-date information.
🖬 🅿 🖬 ❄

NORTHINGTON GRANGE ♯

New Alresford, Hampshire SO24 9TG
Tel: 01424 775705 **E-mail:** customers@english-heritage.org.uk
www.english-heritage.org.uk/northingtongrange
Owner: English Heritage **Contact:** 1066 Battle Abbey
Northington Grange and its landscaped park as you see it today, formed the core of the house as designed by William Wilkins in 1809. It is one of the earliest Greek Revival houses in Europe.
Location: MAP 3:E4, OS 185, SU562 362. 4 miles N of New Alresford off B3046 along farm track – 450 metres.
Open: Exterior only: 1 Apr–31 May: daily, 10am–6pm. 1 Jun–31 Jul: daily 10am–3pm. 1 Aug–30 Sep: daily, 10am–6pm. 1 Oct–31 Mar '10: daily, 10am–4pm. Closes 3pm Jun & Jul for opera evenings. Closed 24–26 Dec & 1 Jan.
Admission: Free. Opening times and prices are valid until 31st March 2010, after this date details are subject to change please see www.english-heritage.org.uk for the most up-to-date information.
🖬 🅿 🖬 On leads. 🖵

PORTCHESTER CASTLE ⌗

Portsmouth, Hampshire PO16 9QW
Tel/Fax: 02392 378291 **E-mail:** customers@english-heritage.org.uk
www.english-heritage.org.uk/portchester
Owner: English Heritage **Contact:** Visitor Operations Team
The rallying point of Henry V's expedition to Agincourt and the ruined palace of King Richard II. This grand castle has a history going back nearly 2,000 years and the most complete Roman walls in northern Europe. Exhibition telling the story of the castle and interactive audio tour.
Location: MAP 3:E6, OS196, Ref. SU625 046. On S side of Portchester off A27, M27/J11.
Open: 1 Apr–30 Sept: daily, 10am–6pm. 1 Oct–31 Mar '10: daily, 10am–4pm. Closed 24–26 Dec & 1 Jan.
Admission: Adult £4.30, Child £2.20, Conc. £3.70. Family £10.80. 15% discount for groups (11+). EH Members Free. Opening times and prices are valid until 31st March 2010, after this date details are subject to change please see www.english-heritage.org.uk for the most up-to-date information.
ⓘ WCs. Exhibition. 🎫 ♿ 🔄 P 🔲 ♿ On leads. ❄

PORTSMOUTH CATHEDRAL

Portsmouth, Hampshire PO1 2HH
Tel: 023 9282 3300 **Fax:** 023 9229 5480
E-mail: rosemary.fairfax@portsmouthcathedral.org.uk **Contact:** Rosemary Fairfax
Maritime Cathedral founded in 12th century and finally completed in 1991. A member of the ship's crew of Henry VIII's flagship *Mary Rose* is buried in Navy Aisle.
Location: MAP 3:E6, OS Ref. SZ633 994. 1½ m from end of M275. Follow signs to Historic Ship and Old Portsmouth.
Open: 7.45am–6pm all year. Sun service: 8am, 9.30am, 11am, 6pm. Weekday: 6pm (Choral on Tues and Fris in term time).
Admission: Donation appreciated.

ST AGATHA'S CHURCH
MARKET WAY, PORTSMOUTH PO1 4AD

Tel: 02392 837050
Owner: St Agatha's Trust **Contact:** Fr J Maunder (Tel/Fax: 01329 230330)
A grand Italianate basilica of 1894 enriched with marble, granite and carved stone. The apse contains Britain's largest sgraffito mural, by Heywood Sumner c1901. Fine furnishings, untouched by Vatican II, by Randoll Blacking, Sir Ninian Comper, Sir Walter Tapper, Martin Travers, Norman Shaw and others. Described by Pevsner as containing *"one of Portsmouth's few major works of art"*.
Location: MAP 3:D3, OS Ref. SU640 006. On route for Historic Ships. Near Cascades Centre car park.
Open: All year, Sats, 10am–4pm. Suns, 10am–2pm (High Mass 11am). Jun–Aug, Weds, 10.30am–3pm. Other times by appointment – 01329 230330.
Admission: No charge.
ⓘ Available for hire – concerts, exhibitions & filming. Has featured in 'Casualty'.
🎫 ♿ Partial. WCs. 🔲 📷 By arrangement. P Limited. 🔲 ♿ ❄

SANDHAM MEMORIAL CHAPEL ❧
BURGHCLERE, Nr NEWBURY, HAMPSHIRE RG20 9JT

Tel/Fax: 01635 278394 **E-mail:** sandham@nationaltrust.org.uk
www.nationaltrust.org.uk/sandham
Owner: The National Trust **Contact:** The Custodian
This 1920's chapel was built for artist Stanley Spencer to fill with paintings inspired by his Great War experiences. Influenced by Giotto's Arena Chapel in Padua, Spencer took five years to complete this, his finest work. The Chapel garden has an orchard and faces Watership Down. No artificial lighting inside.
Location: MAP 3:D3, OS Ref. SU463 608. 4m S of Newbury, ½m E of A34, W end of Burghclere. Taxi: available from Newbury Bus or Train Stations. Bus: 5 miles from Newbury Bus Station. Rail: 4 miles from Newbury train station.
Open: 6–28 Mar, Sat & Sun, 11am–3pm; 31 Mar– 3 Oct, Wed–Sun, 11am–5pm plus BH Mons. 6–31 Oct, Wed–Sun, 11am–3pm; 6 Nov–19 Dec, Sat & Sun, 11am–3pm.
Admission: Adult £4, Child £2. NT Members free.
ⓘ No photography inside the Chapel. No toilet or refreshment facilities on site, telephone for details of nearest pubs, service stations etc. ♿ Partial, Portable ramps available – suitable for manual wheelchairs. 📷 By arrangement. P Limited. 🔲 ♿ Guide dogs only. ❄

Portchester Castle

© S.S.P.T.

STRATFIELD SAYE HOUSE

STRATFIELD SAYE, HAMPSHIRE RG7 2BZ

www.stratfield-saye.co.uk

Tel: 01256 882882 **Fax:** 01256 881466

Owner: The Duke of Wellington **Contact:** The Administrator

After the Duke of Wellington's victory against Napoleon at the Battle of Waterloo in 1815, the Duke chose Stratfield Saye as his country estate. The house provides a fascinating insight into how the 1st Duke lived and contains many of his possessions. It is still occupied by his descendents and is a family home rather than a museum. Over the last six years there has been an extensive programme of restoration and conservation. Of particular interest are many pieces of fine French furniture, porcelain and some rare examples of Print Rooms.

Location: MAP 3:E2, OS Ref. SU700 615. Equidistant from Reading (M4/J11) & Basingstoke (M3/J6) 1½m W of the A33.

Open: 9–13 Apr, (Easter) & 15 Jul–9 Aug 2010: daily, 11.30am (Sats & Suns, 10.30am) 3.30pm last admission all days.

Admission: Weekends: Adult £9.50, Child £5, OAP/Student £8.50. Weekdays: Adult £7, Child £4, OAP/Student £6. Groups by arrangement only.

WC. Obligatory. Guide dogs only.

© NTPL/James Mortimer

The Vyne

TITCHFIELD ABBEY

Titchfield, Southampton, Hampshire PO15 5RA

Tel: 02392 378291 **E-mail:** customers@english-heritage.org.uk

www.english-heritage.org.uk/titchfield

Owner: English Heritage **Contact:** The Titchfield Abbey Association

Remains of a 13th-century abbey overshadowed by the grand Tudor gatehouse. Reputedly some of Shakespeare's plays were performed here for the first time. Under local management of Titchfield Abbey Society.

Location: MAP 3:D6, OS Ref. SU542 067. ½m N of Titchfield off A27.

Open: 1 Apr–30 Sept: daily, 10am–5pm. 1 Oct–31 Mar '10: daily, 10am–4pm. Closed 24–26 Dec & 1 Jan.

Admission: Free. Opening times and prices are valid until 31st March 2010, after this date details are subject to change please see www.english-heritage.org.uk for the most up-to-date information.

On leads.

© NT / David Watson

THE VYNE

SHERBORNE ST JOHN, BASINGSTOKE RG24 9HL

www.nationaltrust.org.uk

Tel: 01256 883858 **Infoline:** 01256 881337 **Fax:** 01256 881720

E-mail: thevyne@nationaltrust.org.uk

Owner: The National Trust **Contact:** The Property Manager

A 16th century house and estate and a treasure trove of history, set within beautiful gardens, with lake and woodland walks. Originally built as a great Tudor 'power house', The Vyne was visited by King Henry VIII on at least three occasions and was home to the Chute family for over 350 years. Dramatic improvements and changes have made The Vyne a fascinating microcosm of changing fads and fashions over five centuries. The house is filled with a vast indigenous collection of furniture, paintings, ornaments and *objets d'art*. The attractive gardens and grounds feature an ornamental lake, one of the earliest summer-houses in England and woodland walks. A newly developed wetlands area with new bird hide attracts a wide diversity of wildlife.

Location: MAP 3:E3, OS Ref. SU639 576. 4m N of Basingstoke between Bramley & Sherborne St John.

Open: House: 13 Mar–31 Oct, Sat & Sun, 11am–5pm; 15 Mar–27 Oct, Mon–Wed, 1–5pm. House, Christmas opening: 4 Dec–19 Dec; Mon–Wed, Sat & Sun, 11am–3pm. Gardens, Shop & Restaurant: 6 Feb–7 Mar, Sat & Sun, 11am–5pm; 15 Feb–19 Feb, Mon–Fri, 11am–5pm; 13 Mar–31 Oct, Mon–Wed, Sat & Sun, 11am–5pm; 4 Dec–19 Dec, Mon–Wed, Sat & Sun, 11am–3pm. Open Good Fri and BH Mons, 11am–5pm (inc. house). Guided tours of house for groups (25–50) by appointment only, 15 Mar–27 Oct: Mon, Tue & Wed, 11am–12noon. During busy periods timed tickets may be issued for entry to house.

***Admission:** House & Grounds: Adult £9.50, Child £4.75, Family £23.65. Grounds only: Adult £5.80, Child £2.90. Reduced rate when arriving by cycle or public transport (applies to house & grounds ticket only). *includes a voluntary 10% donation but visitors can choose to pay the standard prices displayed at the property and on the website. Groups £8.

No photography in house.

©NT/David Watson

WINCHESTER CITY MILL

BRIDGE STREET, WINCHESTER

www.nationaltrust.org.uk/winchestercitymill

Tel/Fax: 01962 870057 **E-mail:** winchestercitymill@nationaltrust.org.uk

Owner: The National Trust **Contact:** Anne Aldridge

Spanning the River Itchen and rebuilt in 1744 on an earlier medieval site, this corn mill has a chequered history. The machinery is completely restored making this building an unusual survivor of a working town mill. It has a delightful island garden and impressive mill races roaring through the building.

Location: MAP 3D:4, OS Ref. SU486 293. M3/J9 & 10. City Bridge near King Alfred's statue. 15 min walk from station.

Open: 13–21 Feb daily. 6 –12 Mar, Sat & Sun, 13 Mar–24 Oct Wed–Sun, 25 Oct–24 Dec, daily. All half terms and summer holidays, daily 10.30am–4.30pm. Last Admission half an hour before closing.

Admission: *Gift Aid: Adult £4, Child £2, Family (2+2) £10. NT & H & IOW WLT members Free. * includes a voluntary 10% donation – but visitors can choose to pay the standard prices displayed at the property and on the NT website.

By arrangement. Nearby public car park.

WINCHESTER CATHEDRAL

1 The Close, Winchester SO23 9LS

Tel: 01962 857225 **Fax:** 01962 857201 **E-mail:** visits@winchester-cathedral.org.uk

www.winchester-cathedral.org.uk

Owner: The Dean and Chapter **Contact:** Group Visits Co-ordinator

Explore more than 1000 years of England's past. Walk in the footsteps of kings, saints, pilgrims, writers and artists in Europe's longest medieval Cathedral. Uncover the secrets of how a diver saved the Cathedral from collapse and learn why Jane Austen came to be buried in the nave. See the Winchester Bible, the finest of all the great 12th-century manuscripts, illuminated in gold and lapis lazuli, and tour the crypt to find Antony Gormley's sculpture *'Sound II'*. The Cathedral Café with its open-air terrace and Cathedral views has won awards for its architecture and food. The Cathedral Shop has a unique range of gifts and souvenirs, including CDs featuring the Cathedral Choir.

Location: MAP 3:D4, OS Ref. SU483 293. Winchester city centre.

Open: Daily 8.30am–6pm (5.30pm Sun). Times may vary for services and special events.

Admission: Adult £5, Conc. £4. Student/Language Schools £3. Conc. for booked groups (2009).

Licensed. In grounds, on leads. Fairs and markets, concerts and theatre, lectures tours and even an ice rink! See website for details.

WOLVESEY CASTLE

College Street, Wolvesey, Winchester, Hampshire SO23 8NB

Tel: 02392 378291 **E-mail:** customers@english-heritage.org.uk

www.english-heritage.org.uk/wolvesey

Owner: English Heritage **Contact:** Portchester Castle

The fortified palace of Wolvesey was the chief residence of the Bishops of Winchester and one of the greatest medieval buildings in England. Wolvesey Castle was frequently visited by medieval and Tudor monarchs and was the scene of the wedding feast of Philip of Spain and Mary Tudor in 1554

Location: MAP 3:D4, OS Ref. SU484 291. ¾m SE of Winchester Cathedral, next to the Bishop's Palace; access from College Street.

Open: 1 Apr–30 Oct: daily, 10am–5pm.

Admission: Free. Opening times and prices are valid until 31st March 2010, after this date details are subject to change please see www.english-heritage.org.uk for the most up-to-date information.

On leads.

© Britainonview / - Britain on View

Winchester Cathedral

CHARTWELL ❦

www.nationaltrust.org.uk/chartwell

The family home of Sir Winston Churchill from 1924 until the end of his life. He said of Chartwell, simply 'I love the place – a day away from Chartwell is a day wasted'. With magnificent views over the Weald of Kent it is not difficult to see why.

The rooms are left as they were in Sir Winston & Lady Churchill's lifetime with daily papers, fresh flowers grown from the garden and his famous cigars. Photographs and books evoke his career, interests and happy family life. Museum and exhibition rooms contain displays, sound recordings and superb collections of memorabilia, including gifts, uniforms and family photographs, and give a unique insight into Sir Winston's political career and personal life.

The garden studio contains Sir Winston's easel and paintbox, as well as many of his paintings. Terraced and water gardens descend to the lake, the gardens also include a golden rose walk, planted by Sir Winston and Lady Churchill's children on the occasion of their golden wedding anniversary, and the Marlborough Pavilion decorated with frescoes depicting the battle of Blenheim. Visitors can see the garden walls that Churchill built with his own hands, as well as the pond stocked with the golden orfe he loved to feed.

The Mulberry Room at the restaurant can be booked for meetings, conferences, lunches and dinners. Please telephone for details.

- Conference and function facilities.
- Partial. WCs.
- Licensed.
- By arrangement.
- P In grounds, on leads.

■ Owner
The National Trust

■ Contact
The Visitor Services Manager
Chartwell
Mapleton Road
Westerham
Kent TN16 1PS

Tel: 01732 866368 (infoline)
01732 868381
Fax: 01732 868193
E-mail: chartwell@ nationaltrust.org.uk

■ Location
MAP 19:F11
OS Ref. TQ455 515

2m S of Westerham, forking left off B2026.

Bus: 246 from Bromley South, 401 from Sevenoaks (All services Suns & BHs only). Please check times.

■ Opening Times
13 Mar–30 Jun and 1 Sept–31 Oct, Wed–Sun & BHs, 11am–5pm.

1 Jul–31 Aug, Tues–Sun, 11am–5pm.

Last admission at 4.15pm

■ Winter Opening
Garden, Shop & Restaurant:
4 Nov–12 Mar 2010, Wed–Sun, 11am–4pm.
Closed 25 Dec.
Open BH Mons

■ *Admission
House, Garden & Studio
Adult	£11.80
Child	£5.90
Family	£29.50

Pre-booked groups (minimum 15)
Adult	£9.80
Child	£4.90

Garden & Studio only
Adult	£5.90
Child	£2.95
Family	£14.75

Winter Gardens
Adult	£3.00
Child	£1.50

*includes a voluntary donation but visitors can choose to pay the standard prices displayed at the property and on the website.

■ Special Events
Including school holiday activities, themed lunches and Christmas Market. Please see www.nationaltrust.org.uk for further details.

CHIDDINGSTONE CASTLE 🏠

www.chiddingstonecastle.org.uk

Chiddingstone Castle is located in the heart of the beautiful village of Chiddingstone, which dates from 1453. It lies between Sevenoaks and Tunbridge Wells and is conveniently located close to the M25 (Junction 5 – Sevenoaks or Junction 6 – Oxted). We welcome individuals, families and can accommodate pre-booked groups for guided tours (minimum 15 people). There is ample parking available, and a beautifully restored Victorian Tearoom.

Set in 35 acres of unspoilt grounds with a growing Japanese theme, including a lake, waterfall, rose garden and woodland, this attractive country house originates from the 1550s when High Street House, as the Castle was known, was home to the Streatfeild family. Several transformations have since taken place and the present building dates back to 1805 when Henry Streatfeild extended and remodelled his ancestral home in the "castle style" which was then fashionable. Rescued from creeping dereliction in 1955 by the gifted antiquary

Denys Bower, the Castle became home to his amazing and varied collections. With a genius for discovering masterpieces before they had been recognised, he amassed a stunning collection of Japanese armour, swords and lacquer as well as Egyptian antiquities, Buddhist artefacts, Jacobean manuscripts and paintings. Today, you can still enjoy Denys's eclectic collections as well as exhibitions devoted to both the castle and local history.

Our craft and activity rooms enable children to have a hands-on, fun approach in relating to the Castle's collections. In addition we have a busy programme of family activity days throughout the year (see our website) Japanese, Victorian or Egyptian themed interactive performances, arts and crafts, nature trails, Taiko Drumming workshops and face-painting. Pre-booking is not necessary. These are included in our normal entrance price, or free to annual Family Pass holders.

ℹ️ Museum, weddings, business and private functions, scenic gardens and lake, picnics. Fishing available.

🍽️ Available for special events. Licensed for Civil Ceremonies. Wedding receptions.

♿ Partial (grounds unsuitable). WC.

🅿️ Ample for cars. Limited for coaches, please book.

🏫 We welcome visits from schools who wish to use the collections in connection with classroom work.

🐕 In grounds, on leads.

🔔

🎭 Regular musical concerts – please refer to website for further details.

COBHAM HALL

www.cobhamhall.com

Cobham Hall is now a leading Girls Boarding and Day School, and has been visited by several English monarchs from Elizabeth I to Edward VIII. Charles Dickens used regularly to walk through the grounds from his house in Higham to the Leather Bottle Public House in Cobham Village.

Cobham Hall is one of the largest, finest and most important houses in Kent, it is an outstanding beautiful red brick mansion in Elizabethan, Jacobean, Carolean and 18th century styles, it yields much interest to the students of art, architecture and history. The Elizabethan Wings were begun in 1584, whilst the central section, which contains the Gilt Hall, was wonderfully decorated by John Webb. Further rooms were decorated by James Wyatt in the 18th century.

In 1883 the Hon Ivo Bligh, later the 8th Earl of Darnley, led the victorious English cricket team against Australia bringing the Ashes home to Cobham.

Gardens

Originally landscaped for the 4th Earl of Darnley by Humphrey Repton, the park has recently been restored by the Cobham Ashenbank Management Scheme. This includes restoration of the many fascinating features: The Aviary, The Bastion, The Orangerie, The Pump House and Repton's Seat.

The gardens are beautiful at all times of the year, but especially so in Spring, when snowdrops, celandines and a myriad of daffodils bloom throughout the park.

■ Special Events

April 2, 4 & 5
Easter Opening
(+ House Open 2–5pm)

April 11 & July 18
National Garden Scheme
Donation £2.50 per person for Entrance to the Grounds; Children F.O.C.
(+ House Open 2–5pm)

July 11
EllenorLions Hospices
Charity Walk

August 5
Summer Stroll @ 7pm
(Guided Tour and Refreshments – £7 per person)
Please telephone to book
(+ House Open 2–5pm)

Conferences, business or social functions, 150 acres of parkland for sports, corporate events, open air concerts, sports centre, indoor swimming pool, art studios, music wing, tennis courts, helicopter landing area. Filming and photography. No smoking.

In-house catering team for private, corporate hospitality and wedding receptions. (cap. 120).

In areas. House tour involves 2 staircases, ground floor access for w/chairs.

Cream teas 2–5pm on open days. Other meals by arrangement.

Obligatory guided tours; tour time 1½hrs. Tours also arranged outside standard opening times.

By Agreement.

Ample. Pre-booked coach groups are welcome any time.

Guide dogs only.

18 single and 18 double with bathroom. 22 single and 22 double without bathroom. Dormitory's. Groups only.

■ Owner
Cobham Hall

■ Contact
Mrs Sarah Poole ACMI BII
Household & Functions Manager
Cobham Hall
Cobham
Kent DA12 3BL

Tel: 01474 823371
Fax: 01474 825904
E-mail: catering@
cobhamhall.com

■ Location
MAP 4:K2
OS Ref. TQ683 689
Situated adjacent to the A2/M2. ½m S of A2 4m W of Strood. 8m E of M25/J2 between Gravesend & Rochester.

London 25m
Rochester 5m
Canterbury 30m

Rail: Ebblesfleet 2m, Meopham 3m
Gravesend 5m
Taxis at both stations.

Air: Gatwick 45 mins.
Heathrow 60 mins,
Stansted 50 mins.

■ Opening Times
2, 4–5 & 11 April;
30 May;
4, 11, 18 & 25 July;
1, 8, 15, 22 &
29 August;
24 October.

Pre-booked parties of 10 or more/ coach tours only
16–18 February;
30–31 March;
1, 6–8, 13–15 April;
1–3, 29–31 June;
6–8, 13–15, 20–22 &
27–29 July;
3–5, 10–12, 17–19 &
24–26 August;
19–21 & 26–28 October

House & Shop
2–5pm (5.30pm Shop).
Last tour at 4pm.

Garden
Closes at 6pm.

Cream Teas available
2–5pm.

Dates could change, please telephone to confirm.

■ Admission
Adult	£5.50
Child (4–14yrs.)	£4.50
Conc.	£4.50
Self-guided tour of gardens only	£2.50

Historical/Conservation tour of Grounds
(by arrangement)
Adult	£5.50
Child (4–14yrs.)	£4.50
Conc.	£4.50

Conference/Function

ROOM	SIZE	MAX CAPACITY
Gilt Hall	41' x 34'	180
Wyatt Dining Rm	49' x 23'	135
Clifton Dining Rm	24' x 23'	75
Activities Centre	119' x 106'	300

DANSON HOUSE

www.dansonhouse.org.uk

In 1995 this Palladian villa by Robert Taylor was deemed the most significant building at risk in London. Following extensive restoration by English Heritage it has been returned to its former Georgian glory.

Completed in 1766, Danson was built for wealthy merchant Sir John Boyd. The house was designed to reflect its original purpose, that of a country house dedicated to entertainment. The sumptuous interior decoration tells stories that reveal the passion of Boyd for his wife and the love they shared.

The principal floor takes in the austere Entrance Hall that would have held Boyd's collection of souvenir sculpture from the Grand Tour. The exquisitely gilded Dining Room presents a set of wall paintings by Charles Pavillon. The octagonal Salon houses the only known portrait of Boyd in an original painting that has been reframed to the design of William Chambers. Chambers also made considerable changes to the house shortly after it was completed. The impressive Library is home to a George England organ, built for the house, and still in working order. Further displays relating to the history of the house and its inhabitants can be found on the bedroom level.

The principal floor is licensed for civil wedding ceremonies and can accommodate up to 65 guests. There is a programme of events throughout the whole year. Please telephone for details. Round off your visit with a light lunch and homemade cakes in the popular Breakfast Room, and indulge in our imaginatively stocked gift shop.

 Two.

 WCs.

Licensed.

 By prior arrangement. Please telephone 020 8298 6951.

P Limited for coaches. Parking here for The Red House see London section (15 mins walk).

 For events and functions.

THE HOME OF CHARLES DARWIN ⊞

www.english-heritage.org.uk/darwin

A visit to the Home of Charles Darwin, Down House, is a fascinating journey of discovery for all the family. It was here that Charles Darwin worked on his scientific theories and wrote his groundbreaking theory, On the Origin of Species by Means of Natural Selection. Down House was also Darwin's home for 40 years and his family's influence can be felt throughout, remaining much as it did when they lived here.

See the actual armchair in which Darwin wrote his groundbreaking theory of evolution and wander the family rooms on the ground floor. His study is much the same as it was in his lifetime and is filled with belongings that give you an intimate glimpse into both his studies and everyday life.

Now visitors can enjoy new interpretation of the house and grounds in celebration of the 200th anniversary of Darwin's birth in February 2009. Developments include a new hand-held multimedia tour of the house and gardens as well as a new exhibition suite on the first floor. Visitors can also explore Darwin's rare Beagle collection, including his field notebooks, letters and diary, in digital format using exciting new touch-screen interactives. A full-scale replica of Darwin's cramped cabin aboard HMS Beagle truly brings his dramatic journey of discovery around the globe to life.

Outside, enjoy a stroll along the famous Sandwalk, which Darwin paced daily in search of inspiration. Then take time to explore the extensive gardens before finishing your day by sampling the delicious selection of home-made cakes in the tea room.

ℹ️ WCs.

☕ Free.

🅿️ Limited.

In grounds.

Owner
English Heritage

Contact
Visitor Operations Team
Down House
Luxted Road
Downe
Kent BR6 7JT

Tel: 01689 859119
Fax: 01689 862755
E-mail: customers@
english-heritage.org.uk

Location
MAP 19:F9
OS Ref. TQ431 611

In Luxted Road, Downe, off A21 near Biggin Hill.

Rail: From London Victoria or Charing Cross.

Bus: Orpington (& Bus R8) or Bromley South (& Bus 146). Bus R8 does not run on Sundays or BHs.

Opening Times
1 April–30 June:
Wed–Sun & BHs,
11am–5pm.
1 July–31 August: daily,
11am–5pm (grounds open until 6pm).
1–31 September:
Wed–Sun, 11am–5pm.
1 November–20
December: Wed–Sun,
11am–4pm.
21 December–31
January: Closed.
1 Feb–31 Mar:
Wed–Sun,11am–4pm.

Admission
Adult	£8.80
Child	£4.40
Conc.	£7.50
Family (2+3)	£22.00

EH Members Free.

Groups (11+)
15% discount

Opening times and prices are valid until 31st March 2010, after this date details are subject to change please see www.english-heritage.org.uk for the most up-to-date information.

Tour leader and coach driver have free entry. 1 extra place for every 20 additional people.

Tearoom and shop on site.

South East – England

Owner
English Heritage

Contact
Visitor Operations Team
Dover Castle
Dover
Kent CT16 1HU
Tel: 01304 211067
E-mail: customers@
english-heritage.org.uk

**Venue Hire and
Hospitality:**
Hospitality Manager
Tel: 01304 209889

Location
MAP 4:O4
OS Ref. TR325 419
Easy access from A2 and
M20. Well signed from
Dover centre and east
side of Dover.
2 hrs from
central London.
Rail: London Charing
Cross or Victoria
1.5hrs.
Bus: 0870 6082608.

Opening Times
Summer
1 April–31 July: daily,
10am–6pm.
1–31 August: daily,
9.30am–6pm.
1–30 September: daily,
10am–6pm.
1–31 October: daily,
10am–5pm.
1 November–31 January
2011: Thur–Mon,
10am–4pm.
1 February–31 March:
daily, 10am–4pm.
Closed 24–26 Dec & 1 Jan.
Note: Last admission ½ hr
before closing.
Secret Wartime Tunnels
tour – time ticket system
in operation; last tour 1
hour before closing.

*Admission
Adult	£13.40
Child	£6.70
Conc.	£11.40
Family (2+3)	£33.50

EH Members Free.
Includes Secret Wartime
Tunnels tour. Additional
charges for members and
non-members may apply
on event days.

Groups: 15% discount for
groups (11+). Free entry
for tour leader and coach
driver. One free place for
every additional 20 paying.

Opening times and prices
are valid until 31st March
2010, after this date
details are subject to
change please see
www.english-
heritage.org.uk for the
most up-to-date
information.

©English Heritage

DOVER CASTLE ⌗
www.english-heritage.org.uk/dovercastle

Explore over 2,000 years of history at Dover Castle! Immerse yourself in the medieval world and royal court of King Henry II as you step inside the newly re-presented Great Tower. Experience the incredible colour and opulence of medieval court life as you wander through richly furnished rooms and be transported to a world of courtly intrigue and royal ambition. Meet the characters central to Henry II's world, and listen out for gossiping whispers in dark corners as members of the court discuss the king's rebellious family. Unravel the dynastic struggles of Henry II and his sons and discover the real story of the 'Devil's Brood'.

Also journey deep into the White Cliffs and discover the complex maze of Secret Wartime Tunnels. Through sight, sound and smells, relive the wartime drama of a wounded pilot fighting for his life in the underground hospital. Discover what life would have been during the planning days of the Dunkirk evacuation and Operation Dynamo under the command of Admiral Ramsay and Sir Winston Churchill, as you are led around the network of tunnels and casements housing the communications centre.

Above ground, enjoy magnificent views of the White Cliffs from Admiralty Lookout and explore the Fire Command Post, re-created as it would have appeared 90 years ago in the last days of the Great War. Also see a Roman Lighthouse and Anglo-Saxon church, as well as an intriguing network of medieval underground tunnels, fortifications and battlements. The land train will help you around this huge site. Throughout the summer there are many fun events taking place, bringing the castle to life through colourful enactments and living history.

©English Heritage

ℹ	WCs. No flash photography within the Great Tower.
	Two.
♿	WCs.
☕	
🍴	Licensed.
🚶	Tour of tunnels: timed ticket system. Last tour 1 hr before closing.
P	Ample.
	Free visits available for schools. Education centre. Pre-booking essential.
🐕	On leads.
❄	
🎭	

Venue Hire and Hospitality
English Heritage offers
exclusive use of the Castle
Keep or Tunnels in the
evenings for receptions,
dinners, product launches
and themed banquets.

Conference/Function
ROOM	MAX CAPACITY
The Castle Keep	standing 120 dining 90
Keep Yard Café	theatre-style 150
Secret Wartime Tunnels	standing 120 dining 80 theatre-style 80
Marquee on Palace Green	standing 400 dining 265

Opening times and prices are subject to change; please check the
English Heritage website for up-to-date information.

FINCHCOCKS MUSICAL MUSEUM

www.finchcocks.co.uk

The Grade 1 house is an outstanding example of Baroque Georgian architecture, renowned for its brickwork and with an east façade attributed to Thomas Archer. It has remained remarkably unaltered through the centuries. Finchcocks is set in an unspoilt Kentish landscape; the beautiful garden has wide lawns, deep shrub borders and a walled 'pleasure garden' with a circle of whitebeams – the perfect setting for outdoor events and receptions.

Finchcocks was acquired in 1971 by Richard Burnett, leading exponent of the period piano, and houses his celebrated collection of over 100 historical keyboards, of which over forty are in full playing order. These are played whenever the house is open. Many of the instruments can also be seen in films such as Pride and Prejudice and Sense and Sensibility. There is also a fascinating permanent exhibition

of pictures, prints and ephemera on the theme of the eighteenth century pleasure gardens such as Vauxhall and Ranelagh.

Finchcocks plays host to a wide range of events. There are informal demonstrations/recitals on all Open Days, as well as for groups, who can visit in the day or evening.

There are regular concerts and fairs and a wide educational programme with opportunity for playing the instruments.

It provides a lovely and unusual setting for wedding ceremonies and receptions, as well as private functions and corporate entertaining. It runs a lively Christmas programme with the atmospheric cellar restaurant providing excellent catering; and a marquee can be used for larger events.

Music events, conferences, seminars, promotions, archery, ballooning, filming, television. Instruments for hire. No videos in house, photography by permission only.

Private and corporate entertaining, weddings.

Limited. WC. Suitable for visually handicapped.

Licensed. Picnics permitted in grounds.

By arrangement.

Musical tours/recitals. Tour time: 2½–4 hrs.

Pre-booked groups (25–100) welcome from Mar–Dec.

Opportunity to play instruments. Can be linked to special projects & National Curriculum syllabus.

Assistance dogs only.

Music a speciality.

■ Owner
Mr Richard Burnett MBE

■ Contact
Mrs Katrina Burnett
Goudhurst,
Kent TN17 1HH

Tel: 01580 211702
Fax: 01580 211007
E-mail: info@
finchcocks.co.uk

■ Location
MAP 4:K4
OS Ref. TQ701 366

1m S of A262, 2m W of Goudhurst. 5m from Cranbrook, 10m from Tunbridge Wells, 45m from London (1½ hrs).

Rail: Marden 6m (no taxi), Paddock Wood 8m (taxi), Tunbridge Wells 10m (taxi).

■ Opening Times
Easter–end Sept: Suns & BH Mons, in addition Wed & Thurs in Aug, 2–6pm.

Groups & individuals: Mar–Dec, by appointment. Closed Jan–Feb.

■ Admission
Adults day £10, Adults eve £12, Child £5 (under 5's admitted free), Student £7, Family £22 (with school-age children).

Garden only:
Adult £3, Child 50p.

■ Owner
Groombridge Asset
Management

■ Contact
The Estate Office
Groombridge Place
Groombridge
Tunbridge Wells
Kent TN3 9QG

Tel: 01892 861444
Fax: 01892 863996
E-mail: office@
groombridge.co.uk

■ Location
MAP 4:J4
OS Ref. TQ534 375
Groombridge Place
Gardens are located on
the B2110 just off the
A264. 4m SW of
Tunbridge Wells and 9m E
of East Grinstead.

Rail: London Charing
Cross to Tunbridge Wells
55mins. (Taxis).

Air: Gatwick.

■ Opening Times
Summer
Gardens
27 March–6 November
Daily, 10am–5.30pm (or
dusk if earlier).

The house is not open
to the public.

■ Admission
Please visit our website
www.groombridge.co.uk
for up to date admission
prices.

■ Special Events
April 2–5
Easter Eggstravaganza.

May 2-3
The Myth and Magic of
Robin Hood with Famous
Bow of Burning Gold.

June 26-27
40's weekend with Spa
Valley Railway.

July 11
Wings, Wheels and
Steam.

August 1
Balloon, Bikes & Ferraris.

September 25-26
Fairies & Crystals.

For a full list of our events
please visit our website
www.groombridge.co.uk

GROOMBRIDGE PLACE GARDENS

www.groombridge.co.uk

There's magic and mystery, history and intrigue, romance and peace at this beautiful venue – which provides such an unusual combination of a traditional heritage garden with the excitement, challenge and contemporary landscaping of the ancient woodland – appealing to young and old alike.

First laid out in 1674 on a gentle, south-facing slope, the formal walled gardens are set against the romantic backdrop of a medieval moat, surrounding a classical Restoration manor house (not open to the public) and were designed as outside rooms. These award-winning gardens include magnificent herbaceous borders, the enchanting White Rose Garden with over 20 varieties of white roses, a Secret Garden with deep shade and cooling waters in a tiny hidden corner, Paradise Walk and Oriental Garden,

the Knot Garden and Nut Walk and the Drunken Garden with its crazy topiary. The gardens feature wonderful seasonal colour throughout spring, summer and autumn.

In complete contrast on a high hillside above the walled gardens and estate vineyard is the Enchanted Forest, where quirky and mysterious gardens have been developed in the ancient woodland by innovative designer, Ivan Hicks, to challenge the imagination. Children love the Dark Walk, Tree Fern Valley, Village of the Groms, the Serpent's Lair and the Mystic Pool, the Romany Camp, Double Spiral and the Giant Swings Walk. There are also Birds of Prey flying displays three times a day, a canal boat cruise to and from the Forest – plus a full programme of special events.

ℹ️ Film location.

🛍️

✼

🍷

♿ Partial. WCs.

🍴 Licensed.

🚶 By arrangement.

🅿️ Limited for coaches.

🐕 Guide dogs only.

🔔

🦉

HALL PLACE & GARDENS 🏛

www.hallplace.org.uk

A fine Grade I listed country house built in 1537 for Sir John Champneys, a wealthy merchant and former Lord Mayor of London. The house boasts a panelled Tudor Great Hall, overlooked by a minstrel's gallery, and various period rooms. The 17th century additions and improvements by Sir Robert Austen include a vaulted Long Gallery and splendid Great Chamber with a fine plaster ceiling.

Managed by Bexley Heritage Trust, this beautiful estate of 65 hectares stands on the banks of the River Cray at Bexley. Surrounding the house are award winning formal gardens with magnificent topiary, enclosed gardens and inspirational herbaceous borders. In the walled gardens there is a nursery selling plants grown in the Hall Place gardens, and a sub-tropical glasshouse where you can see ripening bananas in mid-winter.

The house has been recently restored and was fully open to the public for the first time in 2009. New displays include an introduction to the house's history, children's gallery of Tudor life, and exhibits from Bexley's extensive museum collection, as well as contemporary art exhibitions. The new visitor centre in the grounds offers a riverside tea room and a gift shop, as well as tourist information.

There is an extensive programme of events, art-based activities, concerts and theatre in the house and gardens. Several rooms are available to hire for meetings and events, including the Great Hall and Great Chamber, which are also licensed for civil wedding ceremonies. Bexley Heritage Trust runs a popular education and outreach service and organized activities during the school holidays.

Parts of the historic estate are occasionally used for filming and private hire. For this reason it is sometimes necessary to close certain areas of the house and gardens. We recommend that you call in advance of your visit before travelling a long distance or to see a particular feature.

■ Owner
Bexley Heritage Trust

■ Contact
Mrs Janet Hearn-Gillham
Hall Place & Gardens
Bourne Road
Bexley
Kent DA5 1PQ

Tel: 01322 526574
Fax: 01322 522921
E-mail:
info@hallplace.org.uk

Website
www.bexleyheritagetrust
.org.uk

■ Location
MAP 19:G8
OS Ref. TQ502 743

On the A2 less than 5m from the M25/J2 (London bound).

■ Opening Times
House:
January-March - open Wednesday-Sunday
April-November - open seven days a week.
December - open Tuesday-Saturday
Open 10am Monday-Saturday
Open 11am Sunday and Bank Holidays
Closed 4pm 1st November-31st March
Closed 4.45pm 1st April-31st October
(Last entry 30 minutes before closing.)

Visitor Centre:
Open seven days a week all year.
Open Monday-Saturday 10am
Open Sunday and Bank Holidays 11am
Closed 4.15pm 1st November-31st March
Closed 5pm 1st April-31st October
Tea Room last orders 30 minutes before Visitor Centre closes.
House and Visitor Centre closed Christmas Day, Boxing Day and New Year's Day. Christmas Eve and New Year's Eve closed 1pm.

Gardens:
Open throughout the year from 9am until dusk. Nursery shop with plants for sale. Gardens closed Christmas Day and New Year's Day.

■ Admission
Free. Charge may apply on special event days. Prearranged guided tours (10+) £6 per person. Please telephone 020.8298.6951, or e-mail groupbookings@bexleyheritagetrust.org.uk.

 House, lift & WC.
 Licensed.
 By arrangement (10+).

 Guide dogs only.

■ **Contact**
Ann Watt
Hever Castle
Hever
Edenbridge
Kent TN8 7NG

Infoline: 01732 865224
Fax: 01732 866796
E-mail:
mail@HeverCastle.co.uk

■ **Location**
MAP 19:G12
OS Ref. TQ476 450

Exit M25/J5 & J6
M23/J10 30 miles from
central London, 1½m S of
B2027 at Bough Beech,
3m SE of Edenbridge.

Rail: Hever Station 1m
(no taxis), Edenbridge
Town 3m (taxis).

■ **Opening Times**
1 March–19 December

Main Season
April–October, daily,
10.30am–5pm.
Last exit 6pm.

Winter
March, November and
December, please see
website for details.

■ **Admission**
Individual
Adult	£13.00
Senior	£11.00
Child	£7.00
Family	£33.00

Gardens only
Adult	£10.50
Senior	£9.00
Child	£6.50
Family	£27.50

GROUP
Adult	£10.50
Senior	£9.50
Student	£8.80
Child	£5.90

Gardens only
Adult	£8.50
Senior	£8.00
Student	£7.40
Child	£5.65

**Christmas Shop
& Restaurant**
Free entry December

Groups (15+)
Available on request.

Pre-booked private guided
tours are available before
opening, during season.

HEVER CASTLE & GARDENS 🏛
www.hevercastle.co.uk

Hever Castle dates back to 1270, when the gatehouse, outer walls and the inner moat were first built. 200 years later the Bullen (or Boleyn) family added the comfortable Tudor manor house constructed within the walls. This was the childhood home of Anne Boleyn, Henry VIII's second wife and mother of Elizabeth I. There are many items relating to the Tudors, including two Books of Hours (prayer books) signed and inscribed by Anne Boleyn. The Castle was later given to Henry VIII's fourth wife, Anne of Cleves.

In 1903, the estate was bought by the American millionaire William Waldorf Astor, who became a British subject and the first Lord Astor of Hever. He invested an immense amount of time, money and imagination in restoring the castle and grounds. Master craftsmen were employed and the castle was filled with a fine collection of paintings, furniture and tapestries. The Miniature Model Houses exhibition, a collection of 1/12 scale model houses, room views and gardens, depicts life in English Country Houses.

Gardens
Between 1904–8 over 30 acres of formal gardens were laid out and planted; these have now matured into one of the most beautiful gardens in England. The unique Italian Garden is a four acre walled garden containing a magnificent collection of statuary and sculpture. The glorious Edwardian Gardens include the Rose Garden and Tudor Garden, a traditional yew maze and a 110 metre herbaceous border. There are several water features including a water maze and a 38 acre lake with rowing boats. There is also an Adventure Play Area, the Hever Shop with an exquisite array of gifts, and a full programme of special events throughout the season including Jousting Tournaments and Falconry.

ℹ️ Suitable for filming, conferences, corporate hospitality, weddings, product launches. Outdoor heated pool, tennis court and billiard room. No photography in house.

🛍 Gift, garden & book.

🍽 Exclusive use of Private Residence for Corporate Hospitality, Weddings and Golfing. Restaurants are also available for private functions and weddings.

♿ Access to gardens, ground floor only (no ramps into Castle), restaurants, gift, garden & book shops, and water maze. Wheelchairs available. WC.

🍴 Two licensed restaurants. Supper provided during open air theatre season. Pre-booked lunches and teas for groups.

🚶 Pre-booked tours in mornings. 1 Mar–19 Dec. Tour time 1 hr. Tours in French, German, Dutch, Italian and Spanish (min 20). Garden tours in English only (min 15). Audio tours.

🅿 Free admission and refreshment voucher for driver and courier. Please book, group rates for 15+.

◼ Welcome (min 15). Private guided tours available (min 20). 1:6 ratio (up to 8 year olds); 1:10 9yrs+. Free preparatory visits for teachers during opening hours. Please book.

🐕 In grounds, on leads.

🔔

❄ Private Residence.

❄ Call infoline: 01732 865224.

Conference/Function

ROOM	SIZE	MAX CAPACITY
Dining Hall	35' x 20'	70
Breakfast Rm	22' x 15'	12
Sitting Rm	24' x 20'	20
Pavilion	96' x 40'	250
Moat Restaurant	25' x 60'	75

©NTPL/Robert Morris

IGHTHAM MOTE ❧

www.nationaltrust.org.uk/ighthammote

Beautiful moated manor house covering nearly 700 years of history from medieval times to the 1960s. Discover the stories and characters associated with the house from the first owners in 1320 to Charles Henry Robinson, the American businessman who bequeathed Ightham Mote to the National Trust in 1985.

Following the completion of the largest conservation project ever undertaken by the National Trust on a house of this age and fragility, it is now possible to enjoy the most extensive visitor route open since Ightham Mote's acquisition by the Trust. This includes the refurbished Great Hall and Jacobean staircase, along with the Old Chapel, Crypt, Tudor Chapel with painted ceiling, Drawing Room with Jacobean

fireplace, frieze and 18th century hand-painted Chinese wallpaper, Victorian Billiards Room and the apartments of Mr Robinson. A special exhibition 'Conservation in Action' explains the project and gives insights into the techniques and skills used.

Extensive gardens with lakes and woodland walk. Surrounding 550 acre estate also provides many country walks including way-marked routes.

Free introductory talks, garden and tower tours. Varied events programme including children's events and lecture lunches through the season. Group and Educational Tours available, plus educational facility. For details please telephone: 01732 810378 Ext. 100.

©NTPL/Nadia Mackenzie

©NTPL/Andrew Butler

Ground floor. WC.

On leads, Estate only.

■ Owner
The National Trust

■ Contact
The Property Manager
Ightham Mote
Mote Road
Ivy Hatch
Sevenoaks
Kent TN15 0NT

Tel: 01732 810378
Info: 01732 811145
Fax: 01732 811029
E-mail: ighthammote@
nationaltrust.org.uk

■ Location
MAP 19:H11
OS Ref. TQ584 535

6m E of Sevenoaks off A25. 2½m S of Ightham off A227.

■ Opening Times
House
13 Mar–31 Oct, daily except Tues & Wed, 11am–5pm
(last entry 4.30pm).

1 Nov–19 Dec, Thurs–Sun, 11am–3pm (partial ground floor access) Great Hall decorated for Christmas. (last entry 2.45pm).

Gardens & Shop
13 Mar–31 Oct, daily except Tues & Wed, 10.30am–5pm.

1 Nov–19 Dec, Thurs–Sun, 11am–3pm (partial gardens/courtyard access).

Restaurant
13 Mar–31 Oct, daily except Tues & Wed, 10.30am–5pm.

1 Nov–19 Dec, Thurs–Sun, 11am–3pm (except when function ongoing).

20 Dec–30 Dec every day except 23/24/25 Dec.

Estate
All year, dawn–dusk.

■ *Admission
Adult	£11.00
Child	£5.50
Family	£27.50
Groups (booked)	
Adult	£9.40
Child	£4.70

*includes a voluntary donation but visitors can choose to pay the standard prices displayed at the property and on the website.

■ Owner

The National Trust

■ Contact

Property Manager
Knole
Sevenoaks
Kent TN15 0RP

Tel: 01732 462100
Info: 01732 450608
Fax: 01732 465528
E-mail: knole@
nationaltrust.org.uk

■ Location

MAP 19:H10
OS Ref. TQ532 543

M25/J5. 25m SE of
London. Just off A225 at
S end of High Street,
Sevenoaks, opposite St
Nicholas' Church.

Rail: ½hr from London
Charing Cross to
Sevenoaks.

Bus: Arriva 402 Tunbridge
Wells–Bromley North.

■ Opening Times

House:

13 March–31 October,
Wed–Sun, inc Bank Hol
Mons, 12pm–4pm.

**Shop, Tearoom &
Courtyards:**

13 March–5 April,
Wed–Sun, inc Bank Hol
Mons, 10.30am–5pm.

6 April–3 October,
Tues–Sun, inc Bank Hol
Mons, 10.30am–5pm

6–31 October, Wed–Sun,
inc Bank Hol Mons,
10.30am–5pm

Garden
6 April to 28 September,
Tuesdays only,
11am–4pm.

Last admission to house
and garden is 30 mins
before closing.

**Christmas Shop,
Tearoom & Courtyards:**
3 Nov to 19 Dec, Wed to
Sun, 11am–4pm.

Park
Deer park has pedestrian
access all year round.

■ *Admission

House
Adult	£10.50
Child	£5.25
Family	£26.25

Groups (pre-booked 15+)
Adult	£9.00
Child	£4.50

Garden
Adult	£5.00
Child	£2.50

NT members Free.

Parking £2.50

Park Free to pedestrians

*includes a voluntary Gift Aid
donation but visitors can
choose to pay the standard
prices displayed at the
property and on the website.

■ Special Events

Please telephone or visit
website for details.

KNOLE 🦌

www.nationaltrust.org.uk/knole

Knole's fascinating historic links with Kings, Queens and the nobility, as well as its literary links with Vita Sackville-West and her friend Virginia Woolfe, make this one of the most intriguing houses in England. Thirteen superb state-rooms are laid out much as they were in the 18th century to impress visitors by the wealth and status of the Sackville family, who continue to live at Knole. The house includes Royal Stuart furniture, paintings by Gainsborough, Van Dyck and Reynolds as well as many 17th century tapestries.

The house inspired Vita Sackville-West, who was born at Knole, to write her best-selling novel "The Edwardians" and was also the setting for Virginia Woolf's famous novel "Orlando".

Knole is set at the heart of the only remaining medieval deer park in Kent, where Sika and Fallow deer still roam freely amongst ancient

oak, beech and chestnut trees, as they have since the days of Henry VIII.

Relax in the original Brew House with a cup of tea or enjoy a delicious lunch before browsing through the well-stocked shop full of local produce, exquisite gifts and its large collection of books, including those by Vita Sackville-West, her son Nigel Nicolson, and Virginia Woolf.

Visit on a Tuesday between April and September and enjoy a leisurely stroll through Lord Sackville's private garden. The garden provides the most beautiful view of the house and allows visitors to observe the outside of the Orangery and the Chapel. Witness the changing seasons in the garden from spring through to the autumn.

i Amateur outdoor photography welcomed.

Full range of NT goods and souvenirs of Knole.

Partial, WCs.

Licensed.

Guided tours for pre-booked groups, by arrangement. Short guides to the house available in French, Dutch & German.

P Limited parking for coaches.

Welcome. Contact Education Officer.

Guide dogs only.

Park open all year to pedestrians.

LEEDS CASTLE

www.leeds-castle.com

Set in 500 acres of beautiful parkland and gardens, Leeds Castle is one of the country's finest historic properties and is also one of the Treasure Houses of England.

A Norman fortress and a royal palace to the medieval and Tudor Kings and Queens of England, the development of Leeds Castle continued well into the 20th century. The last private owner, the Hon Olive, Lady Baillie, bought the castle in 1926, restored the castle and furnished its beautiful interiors.

The castle has a fine collection of paintings, tapestries and antiques and is also home to an unusual dog collar museum. The park and grounds include the colourful and quintessentially English Culpeper Garden, the delightful Wood Garden, and the terraced Lady Baillie Garden with its views over the tranquil Great Water. The Aviary houses approximately 100 rare and endangered species from around the world and next to the Vineyard can be discovered the Maze with its secret underground grotto. The Knights' Realm playground delights younger visitors and the new 'World of Wings' free flying bird displays add more interest.

A highly popular and successful programme of special events is arranged throughout the year, details of which can be found on the website.

 Residential conferences, exhibitions, sporting days, clay shooting off site, laser shooting, falconry, field archery, golf, croquet and heli-pad. Talks can be arranged for horticultural, viticultural, historical and cultural groups.

Corporate hospitality, large scale marquee events, wedding receptions, buffets and dinners.

Land train for elderly/disabled, wheelchairs, wheelchair lift, special rates. WC.

 Restaurant, group lunch menus. Refreshment kiosks.

 Guides in rooms. French, Spanish, Dutch and German speaking guides.

 For hire in English, French, Spanish, German and Japanese.

 Free parking.

 Workshops, outside normal opening hours, private tours. Teacher's resource pack and worksheets.

€

Owner
Leeds Castle Foundation

Contact
Leeds Castle
Maidstone
Kent ME17 1PL

Tel: 01622 765400
Fax: 01622 735616

Location
MAP 4:L3
OS Ref. TQ835 533

From London to A20/M20/J8, 40m, 1 hr. 7m E of Maidstone, ¼m S of A20.

Rail: South Eastern Trains available, London–Bearsted.

Coach: Nat Express coach and admission from Victoria.

Opening Times
Summer
1 April–30 September
Daily, 10am–4.30pm (last adm).

Winter
1 October–31 March
Daily, 10am–3pm (last adm).

Castle & Grounds
Closed 3 July, 6 and 7 November and 25 December 2010. Always check our website for up to date opening times before your visit.

Admission
Castle, Park & Gardens
Individuals (valid 1 year)*
Adult   £16.50
Child (4–15yrs)   £9.50
OAP/Student   £13.50
Visitor with disabilities
(1 carer Free)   £13.50

*2009 prices, subject to change.

Group 15+
Adult   £12.00
Child (4–15yrs)   £8.50
OAP/Student   £11.50
Visitor with disabilities
(1 carer Free)   £11.50

A guidebook is published in English, French, Dutch, Spanish, Italian, Russian, Japanese and Mandarin.

Please check website prior to your visit.

A programme of special events are held throughout the year, please visit www.leeds-castle.com/events

Conference/Function

ROOM	SIZE	MAX CAPACITY
Fairfax Hall	19.8 x 6.7m	180
Gatehouse	9.8 x 5.2m	70
Terrace	8.9 x 15.4m	80
Castle Boardroom	9.7 x 4.8m	30
Castle Dining Rm	13.1 x 6.6m	70

South East – England

■ Owner
Viscount De L'Isle

■ Contact
Penshurst Place
Penshurst
Nr Tonbridge
Kent TN11 8DG
Tel: 01892 870307
Fax: 01892 870866
E-mail: enquiries
@penshurstplace.com

■ Location
MAP 19:H12
OS Ref. TQ527 438

From London M25/J5
then A21 to
Hildenborough, B2027
via Leigh; from Tunbridge
Wells A26, B2176.

Visitors entrance at SE
end of village,
S of the church.

Bus: Arriva 231, 233
from Tunbridge Wells
and Edenbridge.

Rail: Charing Cross/
Waterloo–Hildenborough,
Tonbridge or Tunbridge
Wells; then bus or taxi.

■ Opening Times
6 Mar–28 Mar:
Sats & Suns only.
29 March–31 October
Daily.

House
Daily, 12 noon–4pm.

Grounds
Daily, 10.30am–6pm.
Last entry 5pm.

Shop
Open all year.

Winter
Open to Groups by
appointment only
(see Guided Tours).

■ Admission
House & Gardens
Adult	£9.50
Child*	£6.00
Family (2+2)	£25.00

Groups (pre-booked 15+)
Adult	£7.50
Child	£4.50

Garden only
Adult	£7.50
Child*	£5.50
Family (2+2)	£22.00

Garden Season Ticket
£40.00

**Garden Family Season
Ticket** (2+2), additional
child £6.50 each. £65.00

House Tours
(pre-booked 15+)
Adult	£9.50
Child	£5.00

Garden Tours
(pre-booked 15+)
Adult	£9.50
Child	£6.00

House & Garden Tours
Adult	£15.00
Child (5–16 yrs)	£9.00
*under 5s Free.

Conference/Function

ROOM	SIZE	MAX CAPACITY
Sunderland Room	45' x 18'	100
Baron's Hall	64' x 39'	250
Buttery	20' x 23'	50

©David Sellman/Penshurst Place

PENSHURST PLACE & GARDENS
www.penshurstplace.com

Penshurst Place is one of England's greatest family-owned stately homes with a history going back six and a half centuries.

In some ways time has stood still at Penshurst; the great House is still very much a medieval building with improvements and additions made over the centuries but without any substantial rebuilding. Its highlight is undoubtedly the medieval Baron's Hall, built in 1341, with its impressive 60ft-high chestnut-beamed roof.

A marvellous mix of paintings, tapestries and furniture from the 15th, 16th and 17th centuries can be seen throughout the House, including the helm carried in the state funeral procession to St Paul's Cathedral for the Elizabethan courtier and poet, Sir Philip Sidney, in 1587. This is now the family crest.

Gardens
The Gardens, first laid out in the 14th century, have been developed over successive years by the Sidney family who first came to Penshurst in 1552. A twenty-year restoration and re-planting programme under-taken by the 1st Viscount De L'Isle has ensured that they retain their historic splendour. He is commemorated with an Arboretum, planted in 1991. The gardens are divided by a mile of yew hedges into "rooms", each planted to give a succession of colour as the seasons change, with a major restoration project taking place on the Victorian double Herbaceous border 2009–11. There is also a Venture Playground, Woodland Trail, Toy Museum and a Gift Shop.

A variety of events in the park and grounds take place throughout the season.

i Adventure playground & parkland & riverside walks. Product launches, garden parties, photography, filming, fashion shows, receptions, archery, clay pigeon shooting, falconry, parkland for hire. Conference facilities. No photography in house.

Private banqueting, wedding receptions.

Limited. Virtual tour of first floor of house, garden leaflet guide. Wheelchairs available - book in advance. Disabled and elderly groups may alight at private entrance. WC.

Licensed tearoom serving light lunches, cream teas and other refreshments. 2 & 3 course dining menu available in the banqueting function room.

Guided tours of House available by arrangement before the House opens to the public. Garden tours available 10.30am–4.30pm. Pre-booked freeflow (non-guided) visits available throughout opening hours.

P Ample. Double decker buses to park from village.

All year by appointment, discount rates, education room and teachers' packs.

Assistance dogs only

SQUERRYES COURT

www.squerryes.co.uk

Squerryes Court is a beautiful 17th century manor house which has been the Warde family home since 1731. It is surrounded by 10 acres of attractive and historic gardens which include a lake, restored parterres and an 18th century dovecote. Squerryes is 22 miles from London and easily accessible from the M25. There are lovely views and peaceful surroundings. Visitors from far and wide come to enjoy the atmosphere of a house which is still lived in as a family home.

There is a fine collection of Old Master paintings from the Italian, 17th century Dutch and 18th century English schools, furniture, porcelain and tapestries all acquired or commissioned by the family in the 18th century. General Wolfe of Quebec was a friend of the family and there are items connected with him in the Wolfe Room. The Tapestry Room has been re-decorated with the kind support of Farrow and Ball.

Gardens

These were laid out in the formal style but were re-landscaped in the mid 18th century. Some of the original features in the 1719 Badeslade print survive. The family have restored the formal garden using this print as a guide. The garden is lovely all year round with bulbs, wild flowers and woodland walks, azaleas, summer flowering herbaceous borders and roses.

i	Suitable for conferences, product launches, filming, photography, outside events, garden parties. No photography in house. Picnics permitted by the lake.
	Small.
	Wedding receptions (marquee).
	Limited access in house and garden. WCs.
	Lunches and light refreshments on open days. Licenced.
	For pre-booked groups (max 55), small additional charge. Tour time 1 hr. Wine tasting groups by arrangement 45 mins–1 hr. Additional charge.
P	Limited for coaches.
	On leads, in grounds.

■ Owner
John St A Warde Esq

■ Contact
Mrs P A White
Administrator
Squerryes Court
Westerham
Kent TN16 1SJ

Tel: 01959 562345
Fax: 01959 565949
E-mail: enquiries
@squerryes.co.uk

■ Location
MAP 19:F11
OS Ref. TQ440 535

10 min from M25/J5 or 6
Off A25, ½m W from
centre of Westerham

London 1–1½ hrs.

Rail: Oxted Station 4m.
Sevenoaks 6m.

Air: Gatwick,
30 mins.

■ Opening Times
Summer
1 Apr–30 Sept, Wed,
Sun & BH Mons,
12.30–5.00pm. Last
admission 4.30pm

NB. Pre-booked groups
welcome any day except
Saturday.

Grounds
11.30am–5pm

Last admission 4.30pm.

NB. Pre-booked groups
welcome any day except
Saturday.

Winter
October–31 March
Closed.

■ Admission
House & Garden
Adult   £7.00
Child (under 16yrs) £4.00
Senior   £6.50
Family (2+2)   £14.00

Groups (20+)
Adult   £6.00
Child (under 16yrs) £3.50

Wine Tasting
(inc. House & Garden)
Adult   £9.50

NEW FOR 2009:
Housekeeping and
Conservation Lectures (inc.
tour and gardens) £8.50

Garden only
Adult   £4.50
Child (under 16yrs) £2.50
Senior   £4.00
Family (2+2)   £9.00

Groups (20+, booked)
Adult   £4.00
Child (under 16yrs) £2.50

Conference/Function

ROOM	SIZE	MAX CAPACITY
Hall	32' x 32'	70
Green Dining Room	20' x 25' 6"	50

BELMONT HOUSE & GARDENS 🏛

BELMONT PARK, THROWLEY, FAVERSHAM ME13 0HH

www.belmont-house.org

Tel: 01795 890202 **Fax:** 01795 890042 **E-mail:** administrator@belmont-house.org
Owner: Harris (Belmont) Charity **Contact:** administrator@belmont-house.org

Belmont is an elegant 18th century house with views over the rolling Kentish North Downs. Its hidden gardens range from a Pinetum complete with grotto, a walled ornamental garden, a walled kitchen garden with Victorian greenhouse leading to a yew-lined walk to the family pets' graveyard.

Its very special collections echo its ownership by the Harris family since 1801 and include mementos of their travels and posts in India and Trinidad. The house was designed by Samuel Wyatt and includes many novel architectural details. In addition it has one of the most extensive collections of clocks in private hands in the country.

Location: MAP 4:M3, OS Ref. TQ986 564. 4½m SSW of Faversham, off A251.

Open: 31 Mar–30 Sept. House: Sats, Suns & BH Mons. Tours at 2.15pm, 2.45pm, 3.30pm. Group tours weekdays by appointment. Pre-booked specialist clock tours last Sat of month, Apr–Sept. Gardens are open all year round.

Admission: House & Garden: Please check website for prices.

ℹ No photography in house. 🅾 👶 🚽 ♿ Partial. WC. 📷 👤 Obligatory.
🅿 Limited for coaches. 🐕 In grounds on leads. ✳

CHART GUNPOWDER MILLS

Chart Mills, Faversham, Kent ME13 7SE

Tel: 01795 534542 **E-mail:** ticfaversham@btconnect.com

Owner: Swale Borough Council **Contact:** Peter Garner

Oldest gunpowder mill in the world. Supplied gunpowder to Nelson for the Battle of Trafalgar, and Wellington at Waterloo.

Location: MAP 4:M3, OS Ref. TQ615 015. M2/J6. W of town centre, access from Stonebridge Way or South Road.

Open: Apr–Oct: Sat, Sun & BHs, 2–5pm, or by arrangement.

Admission: Free.

🅾 🅿

© English Heritage

DEAL CASTLE ⌗

VICTORIA ROAD, DEAL, KENT CT14 7BA

www.english-heritage.org.uk/dealcastle

Tel: 01304 372762 **Venue hire and Hospitality:** 01304 209889
E-mail: customers@english-heritage.org.uk
Owner: English Heritage **Contact:** Visitor Operations Team

Crouching low and menacing, the huge, rounded bastions of this austere fort, built by Henry VIII, once carried 119 guns. A fascinating castle to explore, with long, dark passages, battlements and a huge basement. The interactive displays and exhibition give an interesting insight into the castle's history.

Location: MAP 4:O3, OS Ref. TR378 522. SE of Deal town centre.

Open: 1 Apr–30 Sept: daily, 10am–6pm (closes 5pm Sat). 1 Oct–31 Mar: Closed.

Admission: Adult £4.30, Child £2.20, Conc. £3.70. Family £10.80. EH Members free. Group discount available. Opening times and prices are valid until 31st March 2010, after this date details are subject to change please see www.english-heritage.org.uk for the most up-to-date information.

ℹ WCs. 🅾 🚽 Exclusive private & corporate hospitality. ♿🎧
🅿 Coach parking on main road. 📷🐕⬆

DODDINGTON PLACE GARDENS

Doddington, Nr Sittingbourne, Kent ME9 0BB
Tel: 01795 886101 **www.doddingtonplacegardens.co.uk**
Owner: Mr & Mrs Richard Oldfield **Contact:** Mrs Richard Oldfield
10 acres of landscaped gardens in an area of outstanding natural beauty.
Location: MAP 4:L3, OS Ref. TQ944 575. 4m N from A20 at Lenham or 5m SW from A2 at Ospringe, W of Faversham.
Open: Easter Sun–end Sept: Suns 2–5pm, BH Mons, 11am–5pm.
Admission: Adult £4.50, Child £1. Groups (10+) £3.50.

DOVER CASTLE   *See page 98 for full page entry.*

DYMCHURCH MARTELLO TOWER

Dymchurch, Kent TN29 0TJ
Tel: 01304 211067 **E-mail:** customers@english-heritage.org.uk
www.english-heritage.org.uk/dymchurch
Owner: English Heritage **Contact:** Dover Castle
Built as one of 74 such towers to counter the threat of invasion by Napoleon, Dymchurch is perhaps the best example in the country. Fully restored, you can climb to the roof which is dominated by an original 24-pounder gun complete with traversing carriage.
Location: MAP 4:M4, OS189, Ref. TR102 294. In Dymchurch, access from High Street.
Open: Aug BH & Heritage Open Days.
Admission: Free. Opening times and prices are valid until 31st March 2010, after this date details are subject to change please see www.english-heritage.org.uk for the most up-to-date information.

EASTBRIDGE HOSPITAL OF ST THOMAS

25 High Street, Canterbury, Kent CT1 2BD
Tel: 01227 471688 **Fax:** 01227 781641 **E-mail:** info@eastbridgehospital.org.uk
www.eastbridgehospital.org.uk **Contact:** The Bursar
Medieval pilgrims' hospital with 12th century undercroft, refectory and chapel.
Location: MAP 4:N3, OS189, Ref. TR148 579. S side of Canterbury High Street.
Open: All year (except Good Fri, Christmas Day & Boxing Day): Mon–Sat, 10am–4.45pm. Includes Greyfriars Franciscan Chapel, House & Garden. Easter Mon–end Sept: Mon–Sat, 2–4pm.
Admission: Adult £1, Child 50p, Conc. 75p.

FINCHCOCKS MUSICAL MUSEUM   *See page 99 for full page entry.*

GOODNESTONE PARK GARDENS

Goodnestone Park, Nr Wingham, Canterbury, Kent CT3 1PL
Tel/Fax: 01304 840107 **E-mail:** fitzwalter@btinternet.com
www.goodnestoneparkgardens.co.uk
Owner/Contact: Margaret, Lady FitzWalter
The garden is approximately 14 acres, set in 18th century parkland. A new gravel garden was planted in 2003. There are many fine trees, a woodland area and a large walled garden with a collection of old-fashioned roses, clematis and herbaceous plants, a new water feature has been installed in 2009. Jane Austen was a frequent visitor, her brother Edward having married a daughter of the house.
Location: MAP 4:N3, OS Ref. TR254 544. 8m ESE of Canterbury, 1½m E of B2046, at S end of village. The B2046 runs from the A2 to Wingham, the gardens are signposted from this road.
Open: Suns only 12–4pm from 14 Feb, Tues–Fri from 23 March–1st Oct 11am–5pm, Sundays 12–5pm. Closed Sat & Mon except BH Mons. Groups welcome any day with prior notice.
Admission: Adult £5, Child (6–16yrs) £1 (under 6 Free), OAP £4.50, Student £3, Family Ticket (2+2) £10, Groups (15+) £4.50. Groups out of opening hours £6.50.

©NPL/Jerry Harpur

©NPL/Jerry Harpur

EMMETTS GARDEN
IDE HILL, SEVENOAKS, KENT TN14 6AY
www.nationaltrust.org.uk/emmetts

Tel: 01732 868381 (Chartwell office) **Fax:** 01732 868193 **Info:** 01732 751509
E-mail: emmetts@nationaltrust.org.uk
Owner: The National Trust
Contact: The Visitor Services Manager (Chartwell & Emmetts Garden, Mapleton Road, Westerham, Kent TN16 1PS)
Influenced by William Robinson, this charming and informal garden was laid out in the late 19th century, with many exotic and rare trees and shrubs from across the world. Wonderful views across the Weald of Kent – with the highest treetop in Kent. There are glorious shows of daffodils, bluebells, azaleas and rhododendrons, then acers and cornus in autumn, also a rose garden and rock garden.

Location: MAP 19:G11, OS Ref. TQ477 524. 1½m N of Ide Hill off B2042. M25/J5, then 4m.
Open: 13 Mar–31 Oct, Sat–Wed, 11am–5pm. Open BH Mons.
Admission: Adult £6.50, Child £1.70, Family (2+3) £14.70. Joint ticket with Quebec House: Adult £9.50. Group Adult £4.90. Gift Aid.
Special Events: Including family picnic day, school holiday activies and guided tours with the head gardener. Please see www.nationaltrust.org.uk for further details.
Partial, WCs. By arrangement. On leads.

THE GRANGE

St Augustine's Road, Ramsgate, Kent CT11 9NY
Tel: 01628 825925   **E-mail:** bookings@landmarktrust.org.uk
www.landmarktrust.org.uk
Owner/Contact: The Landmark Trust
Augustus Pugin built this house in 1843–4 to live in with his family. It was at The Grange that Pugin produced the designs for the interiors of the House of Lords and the Medieval Court at the Great Exhibition but he reserved some of his finest and most characteristic flourishes for his own home. The Landmark Trust, a building preservation charity, has undertaken a major restoration of the building which is now available for holidays all year round. Full details of The Grange and 189 other historic and architecturally important buildings are featured in the Landmark Trust Handbook (£10 plus p&p refundable against a booking) and on the website.
Location: MAP 4:O2, OS Ref: TR3764
Open: Available for holidays for up to 8 people throughout the year. Parts of the ground floor are open to the general public by appointment on Wednesday afternoons and there are 8 Open Days a year. Contact the Landmark Trust for full details.
Admission: Free on Wednesday afternoons & Open Days.

GROOMBRIDGE PLACE GARDENS   *See page 100 for full page entry.*

HALL PLACE & GARDENS   *See page 101 for full page entry.*

HEVER CASTLE & GARDENS 🏛   *See page 102 for full page entry.*

Hole Park

THE HISTORIC DOCKYARD CHATHAM

Chatham, Kent ME4 4TZ
Infoline: 01634 823807   **E-mail:** info@chdt.org.uk
www.thedockyard.co.uk
Owner/Contact: Chatham Historic Dockyard Trust
Costumed guides help you discover over 400 years of maritime history. Explore the most complete dockyard of the Age of Sail and 'meet' characters from the past. Set in a stunning 80 acre estate, all our maritime galleries and attractions will excite and entertain you – whatever your age!
Location: MAP 4:K2, OS Ref. TQ759 690. Signposted from M2/J1,3&4. From M2/J1&4 follow A289 to the Medway Tunnel. From M2/J3 follow the signs to Chatham, A229 then A230 and A231 and the brown tourist signs.
Open: 13 Feb - 31 Oct; daily, 10am – 4pm until 27 March, 10am - 6pm thereafter. Nov: Sat & Sun only, 10am – 4pm.
Admission: Adult £14.00; Child (5-15 yrs) £9.50; Conc. £11.50; Family (2+2 or 1+3) £39.50; Additional Family Child £6.50. Tickets valid for 12 months, terms & conditions apply.

HOLE PARK GARDENS 🏛
ROLVENDEN, CRANBROOK, KENT TN17 4JA

www.holepark.com

Tel: 01580 241344 / 241386   **Fax:** 01580 241882   **E-mail:** info@holepark.com
Owner/Contact: Edward Barham
A 15 acre garden with all year round interest, set in beautiful parkland with fine views. Trees, lawns and extensive yew hedges precisely cut are a feature. Walled garden with mixed borders, pools and water garden. Natural garden with bulbs, azaleas, rhododendrons and flowering shrubs. Bluebell walk and autumn colours a speciality.
Location: MAP 4:L4, OS Ref. TQ830 325. 1m W of Rolvenden on B2086 Cranbrook road.
Open: 4 Apr – 31 May Open daily incl. renowned bluebell season late April : 11am-6pm. Jun – end Oct. Wed & Thur: 2-6pm. Autumn Suns: 10, 17, 24 Oct. 2-6pm and by arrangement. Guided group visits available.
Admission: Adult £5, Child 50p. Group visits with conducted tour of the gardens by the owner or head gardener a speciality. Please contact us for details.
🚻♿🍴🎁🐾 Obligatory. By arrangement. 🅿🚻 Car park only. 🐾 12 Apr–10 May: Bluebell Spectacular.

IGHTHAM MOTE 🌿   *See page 103 for full page entry.*

KNOLE 🌿   *See page 104 for full page entry.*

LEEDS CASTLE   *See page 105 for full page entry.*

LESNES ABBEY

Abbey Road, Abbey Wood, London DA17 5DL
Tel: 01322 526574
Owner: Bexley Council   **Contact:** Lynda Weaver
The Abbey was founded in 1178 by Richard de Lucy as penance for his involvement in events leading to the murder of Thomas à Becket. Today only the ruins remain.
Location: MAP 19:G7, OS Ref. TQ479 788. In public park on S side of Abbey Road (B213), 500yds E of Abbey Wood Station, ¾m N of A206 Woolwich–Erith Road.
Open: Any reasonable time.
Admission: Free.

LULLINGSTONE CASTLE & WORLD GARDEN 🏰

Lullingstone, Eynsford, Kent DA4 0JA
Tel: 01322 862114 **Fax:** 01322 862115 **E-mail:** info@lullingstonecastle.co.uk
www.lullingstonecastle.co.uk
Owner/Contact: Guy Hart Dyke Esq
Fine State rooms, family portraits and armour in beautiful grounds. The 15th century gatehouse was one of the first ever to be made of bricks. This is also the site for the World Garden of Plants and for Lullingstone's Parish Church of St Botolph.
Location: MAP 19:G9, OS Ref. TQ530 644. 1m S Eynsford W side of A225. 600yds S of Roman Villa.
Open: Apr–Sept: World Garden Fris & Sats 12 noon–5pm; Suns & BHs, 2–6pm. House open BH weekends and for special events at same times, and for Guided Groups of over 20 persons on Weds & Thurs by arrangement. Closed Good Fri.
Admission: Adult £6, Child £3, OAP £5.50, Family £15, Groups (20+): £8 pp plus £40 for a dedicated guide (Weds & Thurs only).
ⓘ No interior photography. 🅿️ Partial. 🍴 Teas at visitor centre, 1km. 🐕 By arrangement. 🅿️ Limited for coaches. 🐕 Guide dogs only.

© English Heritage

LULLINGSTONE ROMAN VILLA ♯
LULLINGSTONE LANE, EYNSFORD, KENT DA4 0JA
www.english-heritage.org.uk/lullingstone

Tel: 01322 863467   **E-mail:** customers@english-heritage.org.uk
Owner: English Heritage   **Contact:** Visitor Operations Team
Recognised as a unique archaeological find, the villa has splendid mosaic floors and one of the earliest private Christian chapels. Step into the world of Roman Britain as a film and light show takes you back nearly 2,000 years. Marvel at the ruined rooms, amazing mosaic floors and wall paintings. Enjoy hands-on activities and see fascinating artefacts on display in an engrossing new exhibition.
Location: MAP 19:G9, OS Ref. TQ529 651. ½m SW of Eynsford off A225, M25/J3. Follow A20 towards Brands Hatch. 600yds N of Castle.
Open: 1 Apr–30 Sept: daily, 10am–6pm. 1 Oct–30 Nov: daily, 10am–4pm. 1 Dec–31 Jan '10: Wed–Sun, 10am–4pm. 1 Feb–31 Mar: daily, 10am–4pm. Closed 24–26 Dec & 1 Jan.
Admission: Adult £5.70, Child £2.90, Conc £4.80, Fam £14.30. EH Members Free. Group discount available. Opening times and prices are valid until 31st March 2010, after this date details are subject to change please see www.english-heritage.org.uk for the most up-to-date information.
🅿️🅿️🍴🐕🔲

MAISON DIEU ♯

Ospringe, Faversham, Kent ME13 8NS
Tel: 01795 534542   **E-mail:** customers@english-heritage.org.uk
www.english-heritage.org.uk/maisondieu
Owner: English Heritage   **Contact:** The Faversham Society
This forerunner of today's hospitals remains largely as it was in the 16th century with exposed beams and an overhanging upper storey. It now displays Roman artefacts from nearby sites.
Location: MAP 4:M3, OS Ref. TR002 608. In Ospringe on A2, ½m W of Faversham.
Open: 10 Apr–31 Oct: Sat–Sun & BHs, 2–5pm. Group visits at other times by appointment.
Admission: Adult £2, Child Free, Conc. £1. EH Members Free. Group discount available. Opening times and prices are valid until 31st March 2010, after this date details are subject to change please see www.english-heritage.org.uk for the most up-to-date information.
ⓘ WCs. 🐕

MILTON CHANTRY ♯

New Tavern Fort Gardens, Gravesend, Kent DA12 2BH
Tel: 01474 321520   **E-mail:** customers@english-heritage.org.uk
www.english-heritage.org.uk/miltonchantry
Owner: English Heritage   **Contact:** Gravesham Borough Council
A small 14th-century building which housed the chapel of the leper hospital and the chantry of the de Valence and Montechais families and later became a tavern.
Location: MAP 4:K2, OS Ref.TQ653 743. In New Tavern Fort Gardens ¼m E of Gravesend off A226.
Open: 1 Apr–30 Sept: Sat–Sun & BHs, 12pm–5pm. Admission outside these times by appointment. Opening times subject to change, please call to avoid disappointment.
Admission: Free. Opening times and prices are valid until 31st March 2010, after this date details are subject to change please see www.english-heritage.org.uk for the most up-to-date information.
🐕

NURSTEAD COURT

Nurstead Church Lane, Meopham, Nr Gravesend, Kent DA13 9AD
Tel: 01474 812368 (guided tours); 01474 812121 (weddings & functions)
E-mail: info@nursteadcourt.co.uk **www.nursteadcourt.co.uk**
Owner/Contact: Mrs S Edmeades-Stearns
Nurstead Court is a Grade I listed manor house built in 1320 of timber-framed, crown-posted construction, set in extensive gardens and parkland. The additional front part of the house was built in 1825. Licensed weddings are now held in the house with receptions and other functions in the garden marquee.
Location: MAP 4:K2, OS Ref. TQ642 685. Nurstead Church Lane is just off the A227 N of Meopham, 3m from Gravesend.
Open: All Wed & Thur in Sept 2010, 2–5pm. All year round by arrangement.
Admission: Adult £5, Child £2.50, OAP/Student £4. Group (max 54): £4.
🍴 Weddings & functions catered for. 🍷 Licensed. 🚻 WCs. 🐕 By arrangement. 🅿️ Limited for coaches. 🐕 On leads, in grounds. 🔲🔲

OLD SOAR MANOR 🐚

Plaxtol, Borough Green, Kent TN15 0QX
Tel: 01732 810378 **Info Line:** 01732 811145 **E-mail:** oldsoarmanor@nationaltrust.org.uk
Owner: The National Trust   **Contact:** The Property Manager
A solar chamber over a barrel-vaulted undercroft is all that remains of a late 13th century knight's dwelling of c1290 which stood until the 18th century.
Location: MAP 4:K3, OS Ref.TQ619 541. 1m E of Plaxtol.
Open: 1 Apr–30 Sept: Sat–Thu, 10am–6pm. Daily except Fridays.
Admission: Free.

OWLETTS 🐚

The Street, Cobham, Gravesend, Kent DA12 3AP
Tel: 01372 453401 **Fax:** 01372 452023 **E-mail:** owletts@nationaltrust.org.uk
Owner: The National Trust   **Contact:** The Property Manager
Former home of the architect Sir Herbert Baker. Highlights include an impressive Carolean staircase, plasterwork ceiling and large kitchen garden.
Location: MAP 4:K2, OS Ref. TQ669 686. 1m south of A2 at west end of village. Limited car parking at property. Parking nearby in Cobham village.
Open: 25 Mar–23 Oct: Thur & Sat, 2–5.30pm
Admission: Adult £3, Child £1.50, Family £7.50. Not suitable for groups.

PENSHURST PLACE & GARDENS   *See page 106 for full page entry.*

© The National Trust / J Rawlinson

QUEBEC HOUSE ✤
WESTERHAM, KENT TN16 1TD
www.nationaltrust.org.uk/quebechouse

Tel: 01732 868381 (Chartwell office) **E-mail:** quebechouse@nationaltrust.org.uk
Owner: The National Trust **Contact:** The Visitor Services Manager

This Grade I listed gabled house is situated in the centre of the beautiful village of Westerham. Many features of significant architectural and historical interest reflect its 16th century origins as well as changes made in the 18th and 20th centuries.

Quebec House was the childhood home of General James Wolfe, and rooms contain family and military memorabilia, prints and portraits. The Tudor Coach House contains an exhibition about the Battle of Quebec (1759) and the part played there by Wolfe, who led the British forces to victory over the French.

Location: MAP 19:F10, OS Ref. TQ449 541. At E end of village, on N side of A25, facing junction with B2026, Edenbridge Road.
Open: 13 Mar–31 Oct: House; Wed–Sun, 1pm–5pm. Garden & Exhibition; Wed–Sun, 12pm–5pm.
Admission: Adult £4.70, Child £1.70, Family (2+3) £11.00. Group: Adult £3.70. Joint ticket with Emmetts Garden £9.50. Gift Aid.
Special events: Including school holiday activities. Please see www.nationaltrust.org.uk for further details.

🖼 🔥 Partial. WCs. 🅵 By arrangement 🅿 🔁 In grounds. 🔞

© Heritage House Group/Nick McCann

POWELL-COTTON MUSEUM, QUEX HOUSE & GARDENS
Quex Park, Birchington, Kent CT7 0BH
Tel: 01843 842168 **E-mail:** enquiries@quexmuseum.org **www.quexmuseum.org**
Owner: Trustees of the Powell-Cotton Museum, Quex House & Gardens
Contact: Malcolm Harman, Curator.
World-class collections in a Regency/Victorian country residence. Walled gardens.
Location: MAP 4:N2, OS Ref. TR308 683. ½m from Birchington Church via Park Lane.
Open: 1 Apr–end Oct, Tue–Sun & BH Mons, 11am–5pm. Winter: Suns only, 1–4pm.
Admission: Summer: Adult £7, Child, OAP, Disabled & Carer £5, Student £4, Family (2+3) £20. Winter: Adult £5, Child, OAP, Disabled & Carer £4, Family (2+3) £16.

RECULVER TOWERS & ROMAN FORT ⚑
Reculver, Herne Bay, Kent CT6 6SS
Tel: 01227 740676 **E-mail:** customers@english-heritage.org.uk
www.english-heritage.org.uk/reculver
Owner: English Heritage **Contact:** Reculver Country Park
This 12th-century landmark of twin towers has guided sailors into the Thames estuary for seven centuries. Includes walls of a Roman fort, which were erected nearly 2,000 years ago.
Location: MAP 4:N2, OS Ref. TR228 693. At Reculver 3m E of Herne Bay by the seashore.
Open: Any reasonable time. External viewing only.
Admission: Free. Opening times and prices are valid until 31st March 2010, after this date details are subject to change please see www.english-heritage.org.uk for the most up-to-date information.

ℹ WCs. 🔥 🅿 🔁 On leads. ❄

Squerryes Court

David Winston, Period Piano Company

RESTORATION HOUSE 🏚

17–19 CROW LANE, ROCHESTER, KENT ME1 1RF

www.restorationhouse.co.uk

Tel: 01634 848520 **Fax:** 01634 880058
E-mail: robert.tucker@restorationhouse.co.uk
Owner: R Tucker & J Wilmot **Contact:** Robert Tucker

Unique survival of an ancient city mansion deriving its name from the stay of Charles II on the eve of The Restoration. Beautiful interiors with exceptional early paintwork related to decorative scheme 'run up' for Charles' visit. The house also inspired Dickens to situate 'Miss Havisham' here.

'Interiors of rare historical resonance and poetry', *Country Life*. Fine English furniture and pictures (Mytens, Kneller, Dahl, Reynolds and several Gainsboroughs). Charming interlinked walled gardens of ingenious plan in a classic English style. A private gem. 'There is no finer pre-Civil war town house in England than this' – Simon Jenkins, *The Times*.

Location: MAP 4:K2, OS Ref, TQ744 683. Historic centre of Rochester, off High Street, opposite the Vines Park.
Open: Sats 29 May & 3 Jul, 10am–5pm. 3 Jun–24 Sept, Thur & Fri, 10am–5pm.
Admission: Adult £6.50 (includes 32 page illustrated guidebook), Child £3.25, Conc £5.50. Booked group (8+) tours: £7.50pp.
ℹ️ No stiletto heels. No photography in house. 🏡 Garden by appointment.
🍽️ 1st, 2nd & 4th Thurs in month & other days by arrangement.
🎭 By arrangement. 🅿️ None. 🐕 Guide dogs only.

RICHBOROUGH ROMAN FORT ♯

Richborough, Sandwich, Kent CT13 9JW
Tel: 01304 612013 **E-mail:** customers@english-heritage.org.uk
www.english-heritage.org.uk/richborough
Owner: English Heritage **Contact:** Visitor Operations Team

This fort and township date back to the Roman landing in AD43. The fortified walls and the massive foundations of a triumphal arch which stood over 80 feet high still survive. The inclusive audio tour and the museum give an insight into life in Richborough's heyday as a busy township.

Location: MAP 4:O3, OS Ref. TR324 602. 1½m NW of Sandwich off A257.
Open: Amphitheatre: any reasonable time, access across grazed land from footpath, please call 01304 612013 for details. Fort: 1 Apr–30 Sept: daily, 10am–6pm.
Admission: Gardens: Adult £4.30, Child £2.20, Conc. £3.70. Family £10.80. EH Members Free. Group discount available. Opening times and prices are valid until 31st March 2010, after this date details are subject to change please see www.english-heritage.org.uk for the most up-to-date information.
ℹ️ Museum. 📷 ♿ 🔄 🅿️ 🎞️ 🐕 On leads.

RIVERHILL HOUSE GARDENS 🏛️

Sevenoaks, Kent TN15 0RR
Tel/Fax: 01732 458802 **E-mail:** jane@riverhillgardens.co.uk
www.riverhillgardens.co.uk
Owner: The Rogers Family **Contact:** Mrs Rogers

Calling all plant hunters and explorers! Discover our historic hillside garden and its unexpected treasures and be sure of a warm welcome, fabulous views and a fantastic tearoom.

Location: MAP 4:J3, OS Ref. TQ541 522. 2m S of Sevenoaks on A225.
Open: 21 Mar–12 Sept, Wed–Sun and BH Mondays, 10.30am–5pm. House open to pre-booked groups.
Admission & Events: See website.
📷 ♿ 🍽️ ☕ 🅿️ 🎞️ 🐕 ♿

ROCHESTER CASTLE ♯

The Lodge, Rochester-upon-Medway, Medway ME1 1SW
Tel: 01634 402276 **E-mail:** customers@english-heritage.org.uk
www.english-heritage.org.uk/rochester
Owner: English Heritage (Managed by Medway Council)
Contact: Visitor Operations Team

Built in the 11th century. The keep is over 100 feet high and with walls 12 feet thick. Strategically placed astride the London Road, guarding an important crossing of the River Medway, this mighty fortress has a complex history of destruction and re-building.

Location: MAP 4:K2, OS Ref. TQ741 686. By Rochester Bridge. Follow A2 E from M2/J1 & M25/J2.
Open: 1 Apr–30 Sep: daily, 10am–6pm. 1 Oct–31 Mar '10: daily, 10am–4pm. Last admission 45 mins before closing. Closed 24–26 Dec & 1 Jan. Group discount available.
Admission: Adult £5, Child £4.00 Conc £3.50, Family £13.50. EH Members Free. Opening times and prices are valid until 31st March 2010, after this date details are subject to change please see www.english-heritage.org.uk for the most up-to-date information.
ℹ️ WCs. 📷 🔄 🐕 ✳️ ♿

ROMAN PAINTED HOUSE

New Street, Dover, Kent CT17 9AJ
Tel: 01304 203279
Owner: Dover Roman Painted House Trust **Contact:** Mr B Philp

Discovered in 1970. Built around 200AD as a hotel for official travellers. Impressive wall paintings, central heating systems and the Roman fort wall built through the house.

Location: MAP 4:N4, OS Ref. TR318 414. Dover town centre. E of York St.
Open: Apr–Sept: 10am–5pm, except Mons. Suns 2–5pm.
Admission: Adult £2, Students/Child/OAP £1.

© NTPL / John Miller

© NTPL / Derek Croucher

SCOTNEY CASTLE ❧

LAMBERHURST, TUNBRIDGE WELLS, KENT TN3 8JN

www.nationaltrust.org.uk/scotneycastle

Tel: 01892 893868   **Fax:** 01892 890110   **E-mail:** scotneycastle@nationaltrust.org.uk

Owner: The National Trust   **Contact:** Property Manager

Scotney is not one but two houses. At the top of the hill is the new house, designed by Anthony Salvin in an Elizabethan style and built in 1837 for Edward Hussey III, who took the 'Picturesque' style as his inspiration. At the bottom of the valley are the romantic ruins of a medieval castle and moat. This is the focal point of the celebrated gardens featuring spectacular displays of rhododendrons, azaleas and kalmia in May and June with trees and shrubs providing autumnal colour. The estate is open all year, offering a variety of walks through beautiful parkland, woodland and farmland.

Location: MAP 4:K4, OS Ref. TQ688 353. Signed off A21 1m S of Lamberhurst village.

Open: House: 13 Mar–31 Oct, Wed–Sun, 11am–5pm; 4 Dec–19 Dec, Sat & Sun, 11am–4pm. Garden: 27 Feb–31 Oct, Wed–Fri, 11am–5.30pm, Sat & Sun, 10am–5.30pm; 6 Nov–19 Dec, Sat & Sun, 11am–4pm. Old Castle: 31 Mar–26 Sep, Wed–Sun, 11am–3pm. Shop & Tearoom: 27 Feb–31 Oct, Wed–Fri, 11am–5.30pm, Sat & Sun, 10am–5.30pm; 6 Nov–19 Dec, Wed–Sun, 11am–4.30pm. Estate walks: All year, Mon–Sun. Open Bank Holiday Mondays and Good Friday. Last admission to House and Garden one hour before closing. Timed tickets for the house are limited and may sell out on busy days.

*Admission: House & Garden: Adult £10, Child £5, Family £25.50. Garden only: Adult £7.75, Child £4.25, Family £21.50. NT members free. *includes a voluntary donation of at least 10% but visitors can choose to pay the standard prices displayed at the property and on the website.

⬚ ⬚ ⬚ Grounds (but steep parts). ⬚ ⬚ ⬚ ⬚

© NTPL / David Sellman

SISSINGHURST CASTLE GARDEN ❧

SISSINGHURST, CRANBROOK, KENT TN17 2AB

www.nationaltrust.org.uk/sissinghurst

Tel: 01580 710700   **Infoline:** 01580 710701

E-mail: sissinghurst@nationaltrust.org.uk

Owner: The National Trust   **Contact:** The Administrator

Visit one of the world's most celebrated gardens. The creation of Vita Sackville-West and her husband Sir Harold Nicolson. Sissinghurst Castle Garden developed around the surviving parts of an Elizabethan mansion with a central red-brick prospect tower. A series of small, enclosed compartments, intimate in scale and romantic in atmosphere, provide outstanding design and colour throughout the season. Peace and tranquillity after 4pm.

Location: MAP 4:L4, OS Ref. TQ807 383. 2m NE of Cranbrook, 1m E of Sissinghurst village (A262). Bus link from local station.

Open: Garden: 13 Mar–23 Oct, Mon, Tues, Fri, 11am–5.30pm; Sat & Sun, 10am–5.30pm; 23 Oct–31 Oct, Mon, Tues, Fri, 11am–4pm; Sat & Sun, 10am–4pm. Shop & Restaurant: 13 Feb–7 Mar, Sat & Sun only, 11am–4pm; 8 Mar–31 Oct, Mon, Tues, Fri, 10.30am–5.30pm; Sat & Sun, 10am–5.30pm; 23 Oct–31 Oct, Mon, Tues, Fri, 11am–4pm; Sat & Sun, 10am–4pm; 1 Nov–21 Dec, Sun–Wed, 11am–4pm. Vegetable Garden: 1 May–30 Sept, Mon, Tues, Fri, Sat, Sun, 12noon–4pm.

*Admission: Adult £10.50, Child £5.20, Family (2+3) £26.00, Groups £8.50. NT members Free. *includes a voluntary donation but visitors can choose to pay the standard prices displayed at the property and on the website.

⬚ ⬚ ⬚ ⬚ WCs. ⬚ ⬚ Licensed. ⬚ Ample, £2 per car (NT Members free). Limited for coaches. ⬚ Grounds only, on leads. Guide dogs only in Garden.

© NTPL / Joe Cornish

SOUTH FORELAND LIGHTHOUSE ❧

THE FRONT, ST MARGARET'S BAY, Nr DOVER CT15 6HP

www.nationaltrust.org.uk/southforeland

Tel: 01304 852463   **Fax:** 01304 215484

E-mail: southforeland@nationaltrust.org.uk

Owner: The National Trust   **Contact:** Volunteer Co-ordinator

Distinctive and historical Victorian Lighthouse at St Margaret's Bay, part of the White Cliffs of Dover. Built to guide ships safely past the Goodwin Sands, the lighthouse has the second highest light (above sea level) in the UK. Marconi and Faraday both used this lighthouse for their pioneering experiments.

Location: MAP 4:O3, OS138 Ref. TR359 433. 2m walk from White Cliffs car park, 1m walk from St Margaret's Village, short walk from bus stop Diamond route 15.

Open: 12 Mar–28 Mar, 19 Apr–30 May, 7 Jun–25 Jul, 6 Sept–24 Oct, Mon, Sat, Sun & Mon, 11am–5.30pm. 29 Mar–18 Apr, 31 May–6 Jun, 26 Jul–5 Sept, 25 Oct–31 Oct, daily, 11am–5.30pm.

Admission: Adult £4, Child £2, Family £10. NT members free.

⬚ Limited range of souvenirs. ⬚ Obligatory ⬚ In grounds only ⬚

SQUERRYES COURT 🏛

See page 107 for full page entry.

ST AUGUSTINE'S ABBEY ♯

Longport, Canterbury, Kent CT1 1TF
Tel: 01227 767345 **E-mail:** customers@english-heritage.org.uk
www.english-heritage.org.uk/staugustine
Owner: English Heritage **Contact:** Visitor Operations Team
The abbey, founded by St Augustine shortly after AD597, is part of a World Heritage Site. Take the free interactive audio tour which gives a fascinating insight into the abbey's history and visit the museum displaying artefacts uncovered during archaeological excavations of the site.
Location: MAP 4:N3, OS Ref. TR155 578. In Canterbury ½m E of Cathedral Close.
Open: 1 Apr–30 Jun: Wed–Sun, 10am–5pm. 1 Jul–31 Aug: daily, 10am–6pm. 1 Sep–1 Nov: Sat–Sun, 10am–5pm. 2 Nov–31 Mar '10: Sat & Sun, 10am–4pm. Closed 24–26 Dec & 1 Jan.
Admission: Adult £4.30, Child £2.20, Conc. £3.70. Family £10.80. 15% discount for groups (11+). EH Members Free. Opening times and prices are valid until 31st March 2010, after this date details are subject to change please see www.english-heritage.org.uk for the most up-to-date information.
🔲 ♿ 📷 Free. 🅿 Nearby. 🐕 On leads. ❄

ST JOHN'S COMMANDERY ♯

Densole, Swingfield, Kent CT15 7HG
Tel: 01304 211067 **E-mail:** customers@english-heritage.org.uk
www.english-heritage.org.uk/southeast
Owner: English Heritage **Contact:** Dover Castle
A medieval chapel built by the Knights Hospitallers. It has a moulded plaster ceiling, a remarkable timber roof and was converted into a farmhouse in the 16th century.
Location: MAP 4:N4, OS Ref. TR232 440. 2m NE of Densole on minor road off A260.
Open: Any reasonable time for exterior viewing. Internal viewing by appointment only, please call 01304 211067.
Admission: Free. Opening times and prices are valid until 31st March 2010, after this date details are subject to change please see www.english-heritage.org.uk for the most up-to-date information.
🐕 ❄

ST JOHN'S JERUSALEM 🌿

Sutton-at-Hone, Dartford, Kent DA4 9HQ
Tel: 01732 810378 **Fax:** 01732 811029 **E-mail:** stjohnsjerusalem@nationaltrust.org.uk
Owner: The National Trust **Contact:** Property Manager
The site of a former Knights Hospitaller Commandery chapel. See the garden, moated by the River Darent, and look inside one of the rooms.
Location: MAP 4:J2, OS Ref. TQ557 701. 3m south of Dartford at Sutton-at-Hone, on east side of A225. Turn into entrance gate near Balmoral Road; parking at end of drive.
Open: 1 Apr–30 Sept: Weds, 2–6pm. 1–31 Oct: Weds, 2–4pm.
Admission: Adult £2, Child £1, Family £5.

STONEACRE 🌿

Otham, Maidstone, Kent ME15 8RS
Tel/Fax: 01892 893842
Owner: The National Trust **Contact:** The Tenant
A late 15th century yeoman's house, with great hall and crownpost, surrounded by harmonious garden, orchard and meadow.
Location: MAP 4:L3, OS Ref. TQ800 535. In narrow lane at N end of Otham village, 3m SE of Maidstone, 1m S of A20.
Open: 20 Mar–2 Oct: Sats & BH Mons, 11am–5.30pm (last admission 5pm).
Admission: Adult £3.50, Child £1.50, Family (2+3) £8.50. Groups £3.

TEMPLE MANOR ♯

Strood, Rochester, Kent ME2 2AH
Tel: 01634 338110 **E-mail:** customers@english-heritage.org.uk
www.english-heritage.org.uk/templemanor
Owner: English Heritage **Contact:** Medway Council
The 13th-century manor house of the Knights Templar which mainly provided accommodation for members of the order travelling between London and the continent.
Location: MAP 4:K2, OS Ref. TQ733 685. In Strood (Rochester) off A228.
Open: 1 Apr–31 Oct: Sat & Sun, 11am–4pm. Closed 1 Nov–31 Mar. For group visits, please call 01634 402276.
Admission: Free. Opening times and prices are valid until 31st March 2010, after this date details are subject to change please see www.english-heritage.org.uk for the most up-to-date information.
♿ 🅿 🐕

TONBRIDGE CASTLE

Castle Street, Tonbridge, Kent TN9 1BG
Tel: 01732 770929 www.tonbridgecastle.org
Owner: Tonbridge & Malling Borough Council **Contact:** The Administrator
Location: MAP 19:H11, OS Ref. TQ588 466. 300 yds NW of the Medway Bridge at town centre.
Open: All year: Mon–Sat, 9am–4pm. Suns & BHs, 10.30am–4pm.
Admission: Gatehouse – Adult £6.50, Child/Conc. £3.90. Family £19 (max 2 adults). Admission includes audio tour. Last tour 1 hour before closing.
🔲 🅿 🐕 ❄

UPNOR CASTLE ♯

Upnor, Kent ME2 4XG
Tel: 01634 718742 **E-mail:** customers@english-heritage.org.uk
www.english-heritage.org.uk/upnorcastle
Owner: English Heritage **Contact:** Medway Council
Well preserved 16th-century gun fort built to protect Queen Elizabeth I's warships. However in 1667 it failed to prevent the Dutch Navy which stormed up the Medway destroying half the English fleet.
Location: MAP 4:K2, OS Ref. TQ759 706. At Upnor, on unclassified road off A228. 2 miles NE of Strood.
Open: 1 Apr–30 Sept: daily 10am–6pm. 1–31 Oct: daily, 10am–4pm. Last admission 45 mins before closing. Closed 24–26 Dec & 1 Jan. May close early on Fri & Sat for weddings. Please call in advance to check.
Admission: Adult £5.00, Child/Conc £3.50, Family £13.50. EH Members Free. Group discount available. Opening times and prices are valid until 31st March 2010, after this date details are subject to change please see www.english-heritage.org.uk for the most up-to-date information.
ⓘ WCs. ♿ ♨ 🔲 🐕 On leads in restricted areas.

©HHG/Peter Smith

Hall Place

© English Heritage

© English Heritage

WALMER CASTLE AND GARDENS ⌗

DEAL, KENT CT14 7LJ

www.english-heritage.org.uk/walmer

Tel: 01304 364288   **Venue Hire and Hospitality:** 01304 209889
E-mail: customers@english-heritage.org.uk
Owner: English Heritage   **Contact:** Visitor Operations Team

A Tudor fort transformed into an elegant stately home. The residence of the Lords Warden of the Cinque Ports, who have included HM The Queen Mother, Sir Winston Churchill and the Duke of Wellington. Take the inclusive audio tour and see the Duke's rooms where he died over 150 years ago. Beautiful gardens including the Queen Mother's Garden, The Broadwalk with its famous yew tree hedge, Kitchen Garden and Moat Garden. Lunches and cream teas available in the delightful Lord Warden's tearooms.

Location: MAP 4:O3, OS Ref. TR378 501. S of Walmer on A258, M20/J13 or M2 to Deal.
Open: 1 Apr–30 Sept: daily, 10am–6pm (closes 4pm Sat). 1 Oct–1 Nov: Wed–Sun, 10am–4pm. 2 Nov–28 Feb: Closed. 1–31 Mar: Wed–Sun, 10am–4pm. Closed 10/11 July and to 1pm July 12 when Lord Warden is in residence.
Admission: Adult £6.70, Child £3.40, Conc. £5.70, Family £16.80. 15% discount for groups (11+). English Heritage members free. Opening times and prices are valid until 31st March 2010, after this date details are subject to change please see www.english-heritage.org.uk for the most up-to-date information.
ℹ WCs. ⎙ Ⓣ Private & corporate hire. ♿ ⬛ 🏠 🅿 🚃 ♿

© NTPL / Paul Wakefield

WILLESBOROUGH WINDMILL

Mill Lane, Willesborough, Ashford, Kent TN24 0QG
Tel: 01233 661866

130 year old smock mill. Civil Wedding Licence.
Location: MAP 4:M4, OS Ref. TR031 421. Off A292 close to M20/J10. At E end of Ashford.
Open: Apr–end Sept; Sats, Suns & BH Mons, also Weds in Jul & Aug, 2–5pm or dusk if earlier.
Admission: Adult £3, Conc. £1.50. Groups 10% reduction by arrangement only.

WHITE CLIFFS OF DOVER ❧

UPPER ROAD, LANGDON CLIFFS, Nr DOVER CT16 1HJ

www.nationaltrust.org.uk/whitecliffs

Tel: 01304 202756   **Fax:** 01304 215484
E-mail: whitecliffs@nationaltrust.org.uk
Owner: The National Trust   **Contact:** Visitor Services

The White Cliffs Visitor Centre, Gift Shop and Coffee Shop offers spectacular views across the English Channel. Interpretation panels give visitors the opportunity to find out more about the formation of the cliffs, the importance of chalk grassland and the fascinating history of the property.
Location: MAP 4:O3, OS138 Ref. TR336 422. Follow White Cliffs brown signs from roundabout 1 m NE of Dover at junction of A2/A258.
Open: Visitor Centre: daily, 1 Mar–31 Oct, 10am–5pm. 1 Nov–28 Feb, 11am–4pm. Car park: daily, 1 Mar–31 Oct, 8am–6pm, 1 Nov–28 Feb, 8am–5pm.
Admission: Cars £3.00, Motorcycles & Blue Badge holders £2.00, Motor homes £4, Coaches £7. NT Members free.
⬛ ♿ ⬛ 🅿 ❄ ♿

HHG/Peter Smith

Hever Castle

ARDINGTON HOUSE 🏛

www.ardingtonhouse.com

■ **Owner**
The Baring Family

■ **Contact**
Nigel Baring
Ardington House
Wantage
Oxfordshire OX12 8QA

Tel: 01235 821566
Fax: 01235 821151
E-mail: info@
ardingtonhouse.com

■ **Location**
MAP 3:D1
OS Ref. SU432 883

12m S of Oxford,
12m N of Newbury,
2½ m E of Wantage.

■ **Opening Times**
1 August–10 September,
2010 (please phone to
check if visiting on a
Friday).

■ **Admission**
House & Gardens
Adult   £5.00
Child   Free

Just a few miles south of Oxford stands the tranquil and entirely beautiful Ardington House. Surrounded by manicured lawns, terraced gardens, peaceful paddocks, parkland and its own romantic temple on an island, this Baroque house is the private home of the Barings. You will find it in the attractive village of Ardington, close to the Ridgeway on the edge of the Berkshire Downs.

Built by the Strong brothers in 1720 with typical Georgian symmetry, the House is also famous for its Imperial Staircase. Leading from the Hall, the staircase is considered by experts to be one of the finest examples in Britain.

Away from the crowds and the hustle of the workplace Ardington House provides a private and secluded setting. The calm, exclusive use environment allows for weddings, offsite board meetings, conference and workshops utilising the stylish, splendid complimentary marquee, gardens and grounds. There is a heated outdoor swimming pool, tennis court, croquet lawn and trout river. Close by is the ancient Ridgeway Path, a popular place for walking.

Ardington House is licensed to hold Civil Wedding ceremonies. Receptions can range from drinks and intimate dining in the house, to a full dinner and dance reception using the marquee in the grounds.

Poet Laureate Sir John Betjeman wrote of the homeliness and warmth of Ardington House, and the rooms have seen many special occasions and important visitors in the past with this tradition being continued. The astonishing mixture of history, warmth and style you'll find at Ardington truly does place it in a class of its own.

i	Conferences, product launches, films, weddings.
🍸	Lunches and teas by arrangement for groups.
👥	By members of the family.
P	Free.
🐕	Guide dogs only.

Conference/Function

ROOM	MAX CAPACITY
Imperial Hall	
Theatre Style	80
U shape	30
Cabaret	40
Oak Room	
Theatre Style	40
U shape	20
Cabaret	30
Music Room	
Theatre Style	40
U shape	20
Cabaret	30

■ **Owner**
The Duke of Marlborough

■ **Contact**
Operations
Blenheim Palace
Woodstock OX20 1PX

Tel: 0800 849 6500
Fax: 01993 810570
E-mail: operations@
blenheimpalace.com

■ **Location**
MAP 7:A11
OS Ref. SP441 161

From London, M40, A44
(1½ hrs), 8m NW of
Oxford. London 63m
Birmingham 54m.

Air: Heathrow 60m.
Birmingham 50m.

Coach: From London
(Victoria) to Oxford.

Rail: Oxford Station.

Bus: No.S3 from Oxford
Station, Gloucester
Green & Cornmarket.

■ **Opening Times**
Sat 13 Feb–Sun 31 Oct
2010, Daily.

Wed 3 Nov–Sun 12 Dec
2010, Wed–Sun.

Palace
10.30am–5.30pm
(last admission 4.45pm).

**Palace and Formal
Gardens**
10.00am–5.30pm
(last admission 4.45pm).

Park
9am–6pm or dusk
during autumn and
winter months.

Except Christmas Day, all
areas to be vacated by
6.00pm.

Open daily except
Mondays & Tuesdays
from 3 November.

BLENHEIM PALACE 🏛

www.blenheimpalace.com

The state rooms of Blenheim Palace hold many treasures, from world famous tapestries to furniture, paintings, porcelain, clocks and sculptures. An unusually large collection of family portraits by great masters grace the walls. These include Joshua Reynolds' painting of the 4th Duke and family, a John Singer Sargent of the 9th Duke and family including Consuelo Vanderbilt, and a huge Clostermann of John Churchill, the 1st Duke, with his family. The collection of Chippendale and Boulle furniture is 'second to none in a historic home'.

The Palace, home of the Duke and Duchess of Marlborough and birthplace of Sir Winston Churchill, was built for John Churchill, 1st Duke of Marlborough by Sir John Vanbrugh between 1705 and 1722.

The original gardens were designed by Queen Anne's gardener Henry Wise, with later alterations by Lancelot 'Capability' Brown which included the creation of Blenheim Palace most outstanding feature, the lake. The French architect, Archille Duchêne created the Italian Garden and the beautiful Water Terraces. The newly restored Secret Garden lies to the east of the Palace. A new audio tour of the gardens is available.

The combination of house, gardens and park was recognised as uniquely important when Blenheim Palace was listed as a World Heritage Site in 1987.

'Blenheim Palace: The Untold Story', 300 years of enticing tales. This permanent visitor experience is open inside the Palace. It brings stories of the illustrious family and household staff who have lived here over the last 300 years, vividly to life. Follow our virtual lady's maid Grace Ridley as the dramatic stories are told by animated figures, talking portraits and touch screens.

The Pleasure Gardens, which can be reached by miniature train, includes the Marlborough Maze, the Butterfly House and Adventure Playground, making it a great area for young children.

Conference/Function

ROOM	SIZE (m)	MAX CAPACITY
Orangery	36.25 x 7.1	320
Marlborough Room	14.3 x 7.1	120
Saloon	13.3 x 9.9	150
Great Hall	13.3 x 13.1	250
with Great Hall & Library		500
Long Library	45.7 x 5	500
Oudenarde Room	7.9 x 4.9	14
Ramillies Room	4.9 x 4.9	14
Malplaquet Room	4.9 x 4.9	12
Spencer Churchill Room	10 x 8	70
Courtyard	19.4 x 10.7	180

The Long Library

■ Admission
Friends of Blenheim Palace tickets available.

Palace, Garden & Park

Individual:
13 Feb–12 Dec

Adult	£18.00
Conc.	£14.50
Child*	£10.00
Family (2+2)	£48.00

Groups (15+)
Main Season:
13 Feb–21 Feb
2 Apr–31 Oct

Adult	£12.30
Conc.	£10.80
Child*	£6.75

Groups (15+)
Low Season:
22 Feb–1 Apr,
3 Nov–12 Dec

Adult	£10.50
Conc.	£9.40
Child*	£6.00

Park & Gardens

Individual:
13 Feb–12 Dec

Adult	£10.30
Conc.	£7.70
Child*	£5.00
Family	£26.00

Groups (15+)
Main Season:
13 Feb–21 Feb
2 Apr–31 Oct

Adult	£6.90
Conc.	£5.70
Child*	£3.30

Groups (15+)
Low Season:
22 Feb–1 Apr,
3 Nov–12 Dec

Adult	£5.50
Conc.	£4.40
Child*	£2.00

*(5–16yrs)

Private tours by appointment only, prices on request.

ℹ Filming, product launches, activity days. No photography in house.

🛍 Four shops.

🍸 Corporate Hospitality includes weddings, receptions, dinners, meetings and corporate events.

♿ Car Park for disabled, adapted toilets, disabled lift into Palace.

☕ 3 cafés.

🍴 Group enquiries welcome (up to 150). Menus on request.

🚶 Guided tours except Sundays, BHs and extremely busy days.

🅿 Unlimited for cars and coaches.

Sandford Award holder since 1982. Teacher pre-visits welcome.

🐕 Dogs on leads in Park. Registered assistance dogs only in house and garden.

Full programme.

BROUGHTON CASTLE 🏛

www.broughtoncastle.com

Broughton Castle is essentially a family home lived in by Lord and Lady Saye & Sele and their family.

The original medieval Manor House, of which much remains today, was built in about 1300 by Sir John de Broughton. It stands on an island site surrounded by a 3 acre moat. The Castle was greatly enlarged between 1550 and 1600, at which time it was embellished with magnificent plaster ceilings, splendid panelling and fine fireplaces.

In the 17th century William, 8th Lord Saye & Sele, played a leading role in national affairs. He opposed Charles I's efforts to rule without Parliament and Broughton became a secret meeting place for the King's opponents.

During the Civil War William raised a regiment and he and his four sons all fought at the nearby Battle of Edgehill. After the battle the Castle was besieged and captured.

Arms and armour from the Civil War and other periods are displayed in the Great Hall. Visitors may also see the gatehouse, gardens and park together with the nearby 14th century Church of St Mary, in which there are many family tombs, memorials and hatchments.

Gardens

The garden area consists of mixed herbaceous and shrub borders containing many old roses. In addition, there is a formal walled garden with beds of roses surrounded by box hedging and lined by more mixed borders.

ℹ️	Photography allowed in house.
🛍️	
❄️	
♿	Partial.
☕	Teas on Open Days. Groups may book morning coffee, light lunches and afternoon teas.
🚶	Available for booked groups.
🅿️	Limited.
🐕	Guide dogs only in house. On leads in grounds.
❄️	Open all year for groups.

■ **Owner**

Lord Saye & Sele

■ **Contact**

Mrs J Hummer
Broughton Castle
Broughton
Nr Banbury
Oxfordshire OX15 5EB
Tel: 01295 276070
E-mail: info@broughton
castle.com

■ **Location**

MAP 7:A10
OS Ref. SP418 382

Broughton Castle is 2½m SW of Banbury Cross on the B4035, Shipston-on-Stour – Banbury Road. Easily accessible from Stratford-on-Avon, Warwick, Oxford, Burford and the Cotswolds. M40/J11.

Rail: From London/ Birmingham to Banbury.

■ **Opening Times**

Summer

Easter Sun & Mon,
1 May–15 September
Weds, Suns & BH Mons,
2–5pm.

Also Thurs in July and August, 2–5pm.

Last admission – 4.30pm.

Open all year on any day, at any time, for group bookings – by appointment only.

■ **Admission**

Adult	£7.00
Child (5–15yrs)	£3.00
OAP/Student	£6.00
Garden only	£3.00
Groups	
Adult	£7.00
OAP	£7.00
Child (5–10yrs)	£3.00
Child (11–15yrs)	£4.00
Garden only	£4.00

(There is a minimum charge for groups – please contact admin for details.)

■ **Owner**

Lord & Lady Camoys

■ **Contact**

The Administrator
Sue Gill
Stonor Park
Henley-on-Thames
Oxfordshire RG9 6HF

Tel: 01491 638587
E-mail:
administrator@stonor.com

■ **Location**

MAP 3:E1
OS Ref. SU743 893

1 hr from London,
M4/J8/9. A4130 to
Henley-on-Thames.
On B480 NW of Henley.
A4130/B480 to Stonor.
Rail: Henley-on-Thames
Station 5m.

■ **Opening Times**

4 April–19 September
Sundays and BH Mondays
Also Wednesdays, July
and August only.

Gardens
1–5.30pm

**House, Tea Room
& Giftshop**
2–5.30pm

Last entry to the house
4.30pm.

Private Groups (20+):
by arrangement
Tuesday–Thursday,
April–September

■ **Admission**

**House, Gardens,
Chapel, Exhibition**
Adults	£8.00
First Child (5–16)	£4.00
2 or more
Children (5–16)	Free
Under 5s	Free

Gardens
Adults	£4.00
First Child (5–16)	£2.00
2 or more
Children (5–16)	Free
Under 5s	Free

Groups
Adults	£9.00
Child (5–16)	£4.50

Includes guided tours.

■ **Special Events**

June 6
VW Owners' Rally.

August 7
Concert in the Park.

August 8
Concert in the Park.

August 27–30
Chilterns Craft Fair.

STONOR

www.stonor.com

Stonor is one of the very few houses in England that has remained in the same family from the earliest records to the present day and has been home to The Lord and Lady Camoys and the Stonor family for 850 years. The history of the house inevitably contributes to the atmosphere, at once unpretentious yet grand. A façade of warm brick with Georgian windows conceals much older buildings dating back to the 12th Century and a 14th Century Catholic Chapel sits on the south east corner. Stonor nestles in a fold of the beautiful wooded Chiltern Hills and has breathtaking views of the surrounding park where Fallow deer have grazed since medieval times.

It contains many family portraits, old Master drawings and paintings, Renaissance bronzes and tapestries, along with rare furniture and a collection of modern ceramics.

St Edmund Campion sought refuge at Stonor during the Reformation and printed his famous pamphlet 'Ten Reasons' here, in secret, on a press installed in the roof space. A small exhibition celebrates his life and work.

Mass has been celebrated since medieval times in the Chapel and is sited close by a pagan stone prayer circle. The painted and stained glass windows were executed by Francis Eginton, and installed in 1797. The Chapel decoration is that of the earliest Gothic Revival, begun in 1759, with additions in 1797. The Stations of the Cross seen in the lobby, were carved by Jozef Janas, a Polish prisoner of war in World War II and given to Stonor by Graham Greene in 1956.

The gardens offer outstanding views of the Park and valley and are especially beautiful in May and June, containing fine displays of daffodils, irises, peonies, lavenders and roses along with other herbaceous plants and shrubs.

 No photography in house.

 Unsuitable for physically disabled.

 Licensed.

For 20–60.

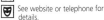 P 100yds away.

In Park on leads.

See website or telephone for details.

26A EAST ST HELEN STREET

Abingdon, Oxfordshire
Tel: 01865 242918 **E-mail:** info@oxfordpreservation.org.uk
www.oxfordpreservation.org.uk
Owner: Oxford Preservation Trust **Contact:** Mrs Debbie Dance
One of best preserved examples of a 15th century dwelling in the area. Originally a Merchant's Hall House with later alterations, features include a remarkable domestic wall painting, an early oak ceiling, traceried windows and fireplaces.
Location: MAP 7:A12, OS Ref. SU497 969. 300 yards SSW of the market place and Town Hall.
Open: By prior appointment.
Admission: Free.

ARDINGTON HOUSE 🏛

See page 117 for full page entry.

ASHDOWN HOUSE ❧

Lambourn, Newbury RG17 8RE
Tel: 01793 762209 **E-mail:** ashdownhouse@nationaltrust.org.uk
www.nationaltrust.org.uk
Owner: The National Trust **Contact:** Coleshill Estate Office
Location: MAP 3:C1, OS Ref. SU282 820. 3½m N of Lambourn, on W side of B4000.
Open: House & Garden: 3 Apr–30 Oct: Wed & Sat, 2–5pm. Admission by guided tour at 2.15, 3.15 & 4.15pm. Woodland: All year: daily except Fri, daylight hours.
Admission: House & garden: Adult £2.80, Child £1.40. Free to NT members. Woodland: Free.

BLENHEIM PALACE 🏛

See page 118 for full page entry.

BROOK COTTAGE

Well Lane, Alkerton, Nr Banbury OX15 6NL
Tel: 01295 670303/670590 **Fax:** 01295 730362
Owner/Contact: Mrs David Hodges
4 acre hillside garden. Roses, clematis, water gardens, colour co-ordinated borders, trees, shrubs.
Location: MAP 7:A10, OS Ref. SP378 428. 6m NW of Banbury, ½m off A422 Banbury to Stratford-upon-Avon road.
Open: Easter Mon–end Oct: Mon–Fri, 9am–6pm. Evenings, weekends and all group visits by appointment.
Admission: Adult £5, OAP £4, Child Free.

BROUGHTON CASTLE 🏛

See page 119 for full page entry.

BUSCOT OLD PARSONAGE ❧

Buscot, Faringdon, Oxfordshire SN7 8DQ
Tel: 01793 762209 **E-mail:** buscot@nationaltrust.org.uk
Owner: The National Trust **Contact:** Coleshill Estate Office
An early 18th century house of Cotswold stone on the bank of the Thames with a small garden.
Location: MAP 6:P12, OS Ref. SU231 973. 2m from Lechlade, 4m N of Faringdon on A417.
Open: 7 Apr–27 Oct, Weds, 2–6pm by written appointment with tenant.
Admission: Adult £2, Child £1, Family £5. Not suitable for groups. Free to NT members.
ℹ No WCs. ♿ Partial.

BUSCOT PARK ❧
BUSCOT, FARINGDON, OXFORDSHIRE SN7 8BU
www.buscotpark.com

Tel: Infoline 0845 345 3387 / Office 01367 240786 **Fax:** 01367 241794
E-mail: estbuscot@aol.com
Owner: The National Trust (Administered on their behalf by Lord Faringdon)
Contact: The Estate Office
This late 18th-century Palladian style house, set in an enchanting designed landscape, is home to the Faringdon Collection of art containing Old Master paintings by Rembrandt, Botticelli and Murillo, as well as works by Pre-Raphaelite artists such as Rossetti and Burne-Jones – including the latter's *The Legend of the Briar Rose* – and furniture designed by Robert Adam and Thomas Hope. The Pleasure Grounds include the renowned water garden designed by Harold Peto, the Four Seasons Walled Garden and extensive avenue walks. The colourful tearoom serves delicious home-made cream teas.

Location: MAP 6:P12, OS Ref. SU239 973. Between Faringdon and Lechlade on A417.
Open: 1 Apr–30 Sept: Wed–Fri, 2–6pm (last entry to house 5pm). Also open BH Mons and Good Fri, and the following weekends; 3/4, 17/18 Apr; 1/2, 15/16, 29/30 May; 12/13, 26/27 Jun; 10/11, 24/25 Jul; 14/15, 28/29 Aug; 11/12, 25/26 Sept. Grounds only: 6 Apr–28 Sept, Mon & Tue, 2–6pm. Tearoom open: as House, 2.30–5.30pm.
Admission: House & Grounds: Adult £8, Child £4. Grounds only: Adult £5, Child £2.50. NT members Free. Groups must book in writing, or by fax or e-mail. Disabled visitors may book single seater PMV in advance.
ℹ No photography in house. 🎭 Fully equipped theatre. ♿ Partial, tel for details.
🅿 Ample for cars, 2 coach spaces. 🐕 May be exercised in overflow car park only.

CHASTLETON HOUSE ❦

Chastleton, nr Moreton-in-Marsh, Oxfordshire GL56 0SU
Tel/Fax: 01608 674981 **Infoline:** 01494 755560
E-mail: chastleton@nationaltrust.org.uk
Owner: The National Trust **Contact:** The Custodian

An atmospheric gem of a Jacobean country house. Tucked away in its hidden Cotswold valley, Chastleton was built between 1607 and 1612 by a wealthy wool merchant as an impressive statement of wealth and power. Owned by the same, increasingly impoverished, family until 1991, it remained essentially unchanged for 400 years as the interiors and contents gradually succumbed to the ravages of time.

Location: MAP 6:P10, OS Ref. SP248 291. 6m ENE of Stow-on-the-Wold. 1½ miles NW of A436. Approach only from A436 between the A44 (W of Chipping Norton) and Stow.
Open: 24 Mar–30 Sept: Wed–Sat, 1–5pm, last admission 4pm. 1 Oct–30 Oct: Wed–Sat, 1–4pm, last admission 3pm.
Admission: Gift aid admission (Standard Admission prices in brackets): £8.65 (£7.85), Child £4.10 (£3.65), Family £21.25 (£19.30).
🔲 Partial. 🅿 Coaches limited to 25 seat minibuses. 🐕 Guide dogs only. 🎫 Special tour every Wednesday morning and special events throughout the season.

CHRIST CHURCH CATHEDRAL

The Sacristy, The Cathedral, Oxford OX1 1DP
Tel: 01865 276154
Contact: Tony Fox

12th century Norman Church, formerly an Augustinian monastery, given Cathedral status in 16th century by Henry VIII. Private tours available.

Location: MAP 7:A12, OS Ref. SP515 059. Just S of city centre, off St Aldates. Entry via Meadow Gate visitors' entrance on S side of college.
Open: Mon–Sat: 9am–5pm. Suns: 1–5pm (last entry 4.30pm) closed Christmas Day. Services: weekdays 7.20am, 6pm. Suns: 8am, 10am, 11.15am & 6pm. Areas of the college (especially the Great Hall & Cathedral) are closed at various times during the year. Please telephone to check before visit.
Admission: Adult £4.90, Child under 5 Free, Conc. £3.90, Family £9.80.

DEDDINGTON CASTLE ⌗

Deddington, Oxfordshire OX15
Tel: 01424 775705 **E-mail:** customers@english-heritage.org.uk
www.english-heritage.org.uk/deddington
Owner: English Heritage, managed by Deddington Parish Council
Contact: 1066 Battle Abbey

Extensive earthworks marking the site of an 11th century motte and bailey castle.

Location: MAP 7:A10, OS Ref. SP472 316. S of B4031 on E side of Deddington, 17 miles N of Oxford on A423. 5 miles S of Banbury.
Open: Any reasonable time.
Admission: Free. Opening times and prices are valid until 31st March 2010, after this date details are subject to change please see www.english-heritage.org.uk for the most up-to-date information.
🐕 On leads. ❋

DITCHLEY PARK

Enstone, Oxfordshire OX7 4ER
Tel: 01608 677346 **www.ditchley.co.uk**
Owner: Ditchley Foundation **Contact:** Brigadier Christopher Galloway

The most important house by James Gibbs, with magnificent interiors by William Kent and Henry Flitcroft. For three centuries the home of the Lee family, restored in the 1930s by Ronald and Nancy (Lancaster) Tree, it was frequently used at weekends by Sir Winston Churchill during World War II.

Location: MAP 7:A11, OS Ref. SP391 214. 2m NE from Charlbury. 13 miles NW of Oxford – 4 miles on from Woodstock (Blenheim Palace).
Open: Visits only by prior arrangement with the Bursar, weekdays preferred.
Admission: £7.50 per person (minimum charge £60).
🍴 🛏 🎫 🅿 ❋

Chastleton House

GREAT COXWELL BARN ❦

Great Coxwell, Faringdon, Oxfordshire
Tel: 01793 762209 **E-mail:** greatcoxwellbarn@nationaltrust.org.uk
Owner: The National Trust **Contact:** Coleshill Estate Office

A 13th century monastic barn, stone built with stone tiled roof, which has an interesting timber construction.

Location: MAP 3:C1, OS Ref. SU269 940. 2m SW of Faringdon between A420 and B4019.
Open: All year: daily at reasonable hours.
Admission: £1. Free to NT members.
❋

© NT/Paul Watson

GREYS COURT ❦
ROTHERFIELD GREYS, HENLEY-ON-THAMES, OXFORDSHIRE RG9 4PG

Infoline: 01494 755564 **Tel:** 01491 628529
E-mail: greyscourt@nationaltrust.org.uk
Owner: The National Trust **Contact:** The Custodian

Re-opening after a major conservation project, this enchanting and intimate family home in a sixteenth century mansion, is set amidst a patchwork of colourful walled gardens, courtyard buildings including a Tudor donkey wheel and medieval walls and towers. Beyond lies an estate and beech woodlands set in the rolling Chiltern Hills.

Location: MAP 3:E1, OS Ref. SU725 834. 3m W of Henley-on-Thames, E of B481.
Open: House: 1 Apr–26 Sept, Wed–Sun, 2–5pm. Garden & Tearoom: 1 Apr–26 Sept, Wed–Sun, 11am–5pm. Last entry 4.30pm. Open BH Mons but closed Good Fri.
*Admission: House & Garden: Adult £7.85, Child £5.15, Family £20.85. Group: Adult £6.75, Child £3.40. Garden Only: Adult £5.75, Child £3.05, Family £14.55. Group: Adult £4.95, Child £2.50. Groups must book in advance. Free to NT members. * Includes a voluntary donation but visitors can choose to pay the standard prices displayed at the property and on the website.
🔲 Grounds partial. WCs. 🍴 🐕 In car park only, on leads. 🎫 Contact Custodian.

RICHARD JEFFERIES FARMHOUSE AND MUSEUM

Marlborough Road, Coate SN3 6AA
Tel: 01793 783040 **E-mail:** R.Jefferies_Society@tiscali.co.uk
Owner: Swindon Borough Council

Dating from the early 18th century, the Museum was the home of Richard Jefferies, nature writer, who is cited by historians as an authority upon agriculture and rural life in Victorian England. The main house is a Grade II listed building.

Location: Adjacent to the Sun Inn on Marlborough Road A4259 close to Coate Water Country Park.
Open: 1st and 3rd Sundays from May to end Sept 2–5pm. 2nd Wed throughout the year. 10am–4pm. Open at other times by request.
Admission: Free

© NTPL / John Hammond

visit hudsons guide online

KINGSTON BAGPUIZE HOUSE 🏛
ABINGDON, OXFORDSHIRE OX13 5AX

www.kingstonbagpuizehouse.org.uk

Tel: 01865 820259 **Fax:** 01865 821659
E-mail: info@kingstonbagpuizehouse.org.uk
Owner: Mrs Francis Grant **Contact:** Virginia Grant

A family home, this beautiful house originally built in the 1660s was remodelled in the early 1700s in red brick with stone facings. It has a cantilevered staircase and panelled rooms with some good furniture and pictures. Set in mature parkland, the gardens, including shrub border and woodland garden, contain a notable collection of trees, shrubs, perennials and bulbs including snowdrops, planted for year round interest. A raised terrace walk leads to an 18th century panelled gazebo with views of the house and gardens, including a large herbaceous border and parkland. Licensed for Civil wedding ceremonies. Venue also available for wedding receptions, special events, corporate functions, product launches and filming. Facilities for small conferences.

Location: MAP 7:A12, OS Ref. SU408 981. In Kingston Bagpuize village, off A415 Abingdon to Witney road S of A415/A420 intersection. Abingdon 5m, Oxford 9m.
Open: House & Garden: 7, 14, 21 & 28 Feb; 7 & 28 Mar; 4, 5 & 25 Apr; 2, 3, 23, 30 & 31 May; 6, 7, 27 & 28 June; 4, 5, 25 & 26 July; 1, 2, 22, 23, 29 & 30 Aug; 5 & 19 Sept. Gates open 2pm and close at 5.30pm. Last admission to house 3.50pm.
Admission: House & Garden: Adult £6, Child (5–15) £2.50, (admission to house not recommended for children under 5yrs), Conc. £5. Gardens: £3.50 (child under 16yrs Free). Groups (20–60) by appointment throughout the year, prices on request.
Special events: see www.kingstonbagpuizehouse.org.uk.
ℹ No photography in house. Home made teas. 🖼🎁🍵♿ WCs. 🍴 Home-made cakes. Light lunches for groups by appointment. 🎦 Obligatory. 🅿 ♿ Guide dogs only. Dogs in car park area only. ▲✱🦌

MAPLEDURHAM HOUSE
MAPLEDURHAM, READING RG4 7TR

www.mapledurham.co.uk

Tel: 01189 723350 **Fax:** 01189 724016 **E-mail:** enquiries@mapledurham.co.uk
Owner: The Mapledurham Trust **Contact:** Mrs Lola Andrews

Late 16th century Elizabethan home of the Blount family. Original plaster ceilings, great oak staircase, fine collection of paintings and a private chapel in Strawberry Hill Gothick added in 1797. Interesting literary connections with Alexander Pope, Galsworthy's *Forsyte Saga* and Kenneth Grahame's *Wind in the Willows*. 15th century watermill fully restored producing flour and bran which is sold in the giftshop.
Location: MAP 3:E3, OS Ref. SU670 767. N of River Thames. 4m NW of Reading, 1½ m W of A4074.
Open: Easter –Sept: Sats, Suns & BHs, 2–5.30pm. Last admission 5pm. Midweek parties by arrangement only. Mapledurham Trust reserves the right to alter or amend opening times or prices without prior notification.
Admission: Please call 01189 723350 for details.
🖼🍵♿ Grounds. WCs. 🍴🅿♿ Guide dogs only. 🏠 8 holiday cottages (all year). 🦌

MAPLEDURHAM WATERMILL
MAPLEDURHAM, READING RG4 7TR

www.mapledurhamwatermill.co.uk

Tel: 01189 723350 **Fax:** 01189 724016 **E-mail:** enquiries@mapledurham.co.uk
Owner: The Mapledurham Trust **Contact:** Mrs Lola Andrews

The last working watermill on the Thames still produces excellent flour. It is a 600-year-old estate mill, powered by a wooden undershot waterwheel with parts of the original wooden structure still surviving inside the building. Sensitively repaired, visitors can see the milling process using French burr millstones with fine wooden and cast iron machinery.
Produce: 100% and 81% wholemeal flour, semolina, millers mix and bran with no additives. Outlets: local farmers markets, farm shops and many others.
Location: MAP 3:E3, OS Ref. SU670 767. N of River Thames. 4m NW of Reading, 1½ m W of A4074.
Open: Easter –Sept Saturdays and Sundays B BH's 2–5.30pm. Midweek parties by arrangement only. **Admission:** Please call 01189 723350 for details.
🖼🍴🅿✱🦌

For **accommodation** in the South East, see our special index at the back of the book.

MILTON MANOR HOUSE

MILTON, ABINGDON, OXFORDSHIRE OX14 4EN

www.miltonmanorhouse.com

Tel: 01235 831287 **Fax:** 01235 862321 **Email:** ask@miltonmanorhouse.com

Owner: Anthony Mockler-Barrett Esq   **Contact:** Alex Brakespear

Dreamily beautiful mellow brick house, traditionally designed by Inigo Jones. Celebrated Gothic library and Catholic chapel. Lived in by the family; pleasant relaxed and informal atmosphere. Park with fine old trees, stables, walled garden and woodland walk. Picnickers welcome. Free Parking, refreshments and pony rides usually available

Location: MAP 3:D1, OS Ref. SU485 924. Just off A34, village and house signposted, 9m S of Oxford, 15m N of Newbury. 3m from Abingdon and Didcot.

Open: Easter Sun & BH Mon; 2 May & BH Mon; then 16–31 May & 15–31 Aug. Guided tours of house: 2pm, 3pm & 4pm. For weddings/events etc. please contact the Administrator. Groups by arrangement throughout the year.

Admission: House & Gardens: Adult £7, Child £3.50. Garden & Grounds only: Adult £3, Child £1.50. Family tickets available for multiple visits throughout season. Garden & Grounds only (2+2): £30.

⬚ Grounds. 🅕 Obligatory. 🅟 Free. 🚶 Guide dogs only. ❋ 🖤

MINSTER LOVELL HALL & DOVECOTE ⌗

Witney, Oxfordshire OX29

Tel: 01424 775705   **E-mail:** customers@english-heritage.org.uk

www.english-heritage.org.uk/minsterlovell

Owner: English Heritage   **Contact:** 1066 Battle Abbey

The ruins of Lord Lovell's 15th century manor house stand in a lovely setting on the banks of the River Windrush.

Location: MAP 6:P11, OS Ref. SP325 113. Adjacent to Minster Lovell Church; 3 miles W of Witney off A40.

Open: Any reasonable time. Dovecote – exterior only.

Admission: Free. Opening times and prices are valid until 31st March 2010, after this date details are subject to change please see www.english-heritage.org.uk for the most up-to-date information.

🐕 On leads. ❋

PRIORY COTTAGES 🍂

1 Mill Street, Steventon, Abingdon, Oxfordshire OX13 6SP

Tel: 01793 762209

Owner: The National Trust   **Contact:** Coleshill Estate Office

Former monastic buildings, converted into two houses. South Cottage contains the Great Hall of the original priory.

Location: MAP 3:D1, OS Ref. SU466 914. 4m S of Abingdon, on B4017 off A34 at Abingdon West or Milton interchange on corner of The Causeway and Mill Street, entrance in Mill Street.

Open: The Great Hall in South Cottage only: 1 Apr–30 Sept: Thu, 2–6pm, by written appointment with the tenant.

Admission: Adult £2, Child £1, Family £5. Free to NT members.

© English Heritage

Minster Lovell Hall & Dovecote

ROUSHAM HOUSE
Nr STEEPLE ASTON, BICESTER, OXFORDSHIRE OX25 4QX
www.rousham.org

Tel: 01869 347110 / 07860 360407   **E-mail:** ccd@rousham.org
Owner/Contact: Charles Cottrell-Dormer Esq

Rousham represents the first stage of English landscape design and remains almost as William Kent (1685–1748) left it. One of the few gardens of this date to have escaped alteration. Includes Venus' Vale, Townesend's Building, seven-arched Praeneste, the Temple of the Mill and a sham ruin known as the 'Eyecatcher'. The house was built in 1635 by Sir Robert Dormer. Excellent location for fashion, advertising, photography etc.

Location: MAP 7:A10, OS Ref. SP477 242. E of A4260, 12m N of Oxford, S of B4030, 7m W of Bicester.
Open: Garden: All year: daily, 10am–4.30pm (last adm). House: Pre-booked groups, May–Sept. (Mon–Thur)
Admission: Garden: £5. No children under 15yrs.
Partial. P ⬚ ⬚

RYCOTE CHAPEL ⌗

Rycote, Oxfordshire OX9 2PE
Tel: 01844 210210   **E-mail:** customers@english-heritage.org.uk
www.english-heritage.org.uk/rycotechapel

Owner: English Heritage   **Contact:** Mr and Mrs Taylor - Rycote Building Charitable Foundation

A 15th century chapel with exquisitely carved and painted woodwork. It has many intriguing features, including two roofed pews and a musicians' gallery.
Location: MAP 7:B12, OS165 Ref. SP667 046. 3 miles SW of Thame, off A329. 1½ miles NE of M40/J7.
Open: 1 Apr–30 Sept: Fri–Sun, 2–6pm. Times may change at short notice, please telephone for details.
Admission: Adult £3.50, Child £1.50, Conc. £2.50. EH Members Free. Opening times and prices are valid until 31st March 2010, after this date details are subject to change please see www.english-heritage.org.uk for the most up-to-date information.
P ⬚

STONOR 🏠

See page 120 for full page entry.

SWALCLIFFE BARN

Swalcliffe Village, Banbury, Oxfordshire
Tel: 01295 788278   **Contact:** Jeffrey Demmar

15th century half cruck barn, houses agricultural and trade vehicles which are part of the Oxford County Museum Services Collection. Exhibition of 2500 years' of Swalcliffe history.
Location: MAP 7:A10, OS Ref. SP378 378. 6m W of Banbury Cross on B4035.
Open: Easter–end Oct: Suns & BHs, 2–5pm.
Admission: Free.

© Rousham House

Rousham House

THE COLLEGES OF OXFORD UNIVERSITY

For further details contact:
Oxford Information Centre,
15–16 Broad Street, Oxford OX1 3AS
Tel: +44 (0)1865 726871
Email: tic@oxford.gov.uk
Fax: +44 (0)1865 240261
www.visitoxford.org

All Souls' College
High Street
Tel: 01865 279379
Founder: Archbishop Henry Chichele 1438
Open: Mon–Fri, 2–4pm
          (4.30pm in summer)

Balliol College
Broad Street
Tel: 01865 277777
Founder: John de Balliol 1263
Open: Daily, 1–5pm (or dusk)

Brasenose College
Radcliffe Square
Tel: 01865 277830
Founder: William Smythe,
          Bishop of Lincoln 1509
Open: Daily, 10–11.30am (tour groups
          only) & 2–4.30pm
          (5pm in summer)

Christ Church
St. Aldates
Tel: 01865 286573
Founder: Cardinal Wolsey/Henry VIII 1546
Open: Mon–Sat, 9am–5.30pm;
          Sun, 1–5.30pm (last adm 4.30pm)

Corpus Christi College
Merton Street
Tel: 01865 276700
Founder: Bishop Richard Fox 1517
Open: Daily, 1.30–4.30pm

Exeter College
Turl Street
Tel: 01865 279600
Founder: Bishop Stapleden of Exeter 1314
Open: Daily, 2–5pm

Green College
Woodstock Road
Tel: 01865 274770
Founder: Dr Cecil Green 1979
Open: By appointment only

Harris Manchester College
Mansfield Road
Tel: 01865 271011
Founder: Lord Harris of Peckham 1996
Open: Chapel only: Mon–Fri,
          8.30am–5.30pm.
          Sat, 9am–12 noon

Hertford College
Catte Street
Tel: 01865 279400
Founder: TC Baring MP 1740
Open: Daily, l0am–noon & 2pm–dusk

Jesus College
Turl Street
Tel: 01865 279700
Founder: Dr Hugh Price
          (Queen Elizabeth I) 1571
Open: Daily, 2–4.30pm

Keble College
Parks Road
Tel: 01865 272727
Founder: Public money 1870
Open: Daily, 2–5pm

Kellogg College
Banbury Road
Tel: 01865 61200
Founder: Kellogg Foundation 1990
Open: Mon–Fri, 9am–5pm

Lady Margaret Hall
Norham Gardens
Tel: 01865 274300
Founder: Dame Elizabeth Wordsworth 1878
Open: Gardens: 10am–5pm

Linacre College
St Cross Road
Tel: 01865 271650
Founder: Oxford University 1962
Open: By appointment only

Lincoln College
Turl Street
Tel: 01865 279800
Founder: Bishop Richard Fleming
          of Lincoln 1427
Open: Mon–Sat, 2–5pm; Sun, 11am–5pm

Magdalen College
High Street
Tel: 01865 276000
Founder: William of Waynefleete 1458
Open: Oct–Jun: 1–6pm/dusk (whichever
          is the earlier) and Jul–Sept:
          12 noon–6pm

Mansfield College
Mansfield Road
Tel: 01865 270999
Founder: Free Churches 1995
Open: Mon–Fri, 9am–5pm

Merton College
Merton Street
Tel: 01865 276310
Founder: Walter de Merton l264
Open: Mon–Fri, 2–4pm; Sat & Sun,
          10am–4pm

New College
New College Lane
Tel: 01865 279555
Founder: William of Wykeham,
          Bishop of Winchester 1379
Open: Daily, 11am–5pm (summer);
          2–4pm (winter)

Nuffield College
New Road
Tel: 01865 278500
Founder: William Morris
          (Lord Nuffield) 1937
Open: Daily, 9am–5pm

Oriel College
Oriel Square
Tel: 01865 276555
Founder: Edward II/Adam de Brome 1326
Open: By arrangement with TIC

Pembroke College
St Aldates
Tel: 01865 276444
Founder: James I 1624
Open: By appointment only

The Queen's College
High Street
Tel: 01865 279120
Founder: Robert de Eglesfield 1341
Open: By arrangement with TIC

Somerville College
Graduate House, Woodstock Road
Tel: 01865 270600
Founder: Association for the Education of
          Women 1879
Open: 2–5.30pm

St. Anne's College
56 Woodstock Road
Tel: 01865 274800
Founder: Association for the Education
          of Women 1878
Open: 9am–5pm

St. Antony's College
62 Woodstock Road
Tel: 01865 284700
Founder: M. Antonin Bess 1948
Open: By appointment only

St. Catherine's College
Manor Road
Tel: 01865 271700
Founder: Oxford University 1964
Open: 9am–5pm

St. Edmund Hall
Queens Lane
Tel: 01865 279000
Founder: St. Edmund Riche of
          Abingdon c.l278
Open: Mon–Sun, Term time,
          12 noon–4pm

St. Hilda's College
Cowley Place
Tel: 01865 276884
Founder: Miss Dorothea Beale l893
Open: By appointment only

St. Hugh's College
St. Margarets Road
Tel: 01865 274900
Founder: Dame Elizabeth Wordsworth 1886
Open: 10am–4pm

St. John's College
St. Giles
Tel: 01865 277300
Founder: Sir Thomas White 1555
Open: 1–5pm (or dusk)

St. Peter's College
New Inn Hall Street
Tel: 01865 278900
Founder: Rev. Christopher Charvasse 1928
Open: 10am–5pm

Trinity College
Broad Street
Tel: 01865 279900
Founder: Sir Thomas Pope 1554–5
Open: Mon–Fri 10am–noon and 2–4pm.
          Sat & Sun in term, 2–4pm;
          Sat & Sun in vacation 10am–
          12 noon and 2–4pm

University College
High Street
Tel: 01865 276602
Founder: Archdeacon William of
          Durham 1249
Open: Contact College for details

Wadham College
Parks Road
Tel: 01865 277900
Founder: Nicholas & Dorothy
          Wadham 1610
Open: Term time: daily, 1–4.15pm.
          Vacation: daily, 10.30–11.45am
          & 1–4.15pm

Wolfson College
Linton Road
Tel: 01865 274100
Founder: Oxford University 1966
Open: Daylight hours

Worcester College
Worcester Street
Tel: 01865 278300
Founder: Sir Thomas Cookes 1714
Open: Daily, 2–5pm

Christchurch College, Oxford

This information is intended only as a guide. Times are subject to change due to functions, examinations, conferences, holidays, etc. You are advised to check in advance opening times and admission charges which may apply at some colleges, and at certain times of the year. Visitors wishing to gain admittance to the Colleges (meaning the Courts, not to the staircases and students' rooms) are advised to contact the Tourist Information Office. It should be noted that Halls normally close for lunch (12 noon–2pm) and many are not open during the afternoon. Chapels may be closed during services. Libraries are not normally open, and Gardens do not usually include the Fellows' garden. Visitors, and especially guided groups, should always call on the Porters Lodge first. Groups should always book in advance. Dogs, except guide dogs are not allowed in any colleges.

© NTPL / John Miller

© NT / David Sellman

CLANDON PARK & HATCHLANDS PARK

www.nationaltrust.org.uk/clandonpark

Clandon Park & Hatchlands Park were built during the 18th century and are set amidst beautiful grounds. They are two of England's most outstanding country houses and are only five minutes' drive apart.

Clandon Park is a grand Palladian Mansion, built c1730 for the 2nd Lord Onslow by the Venetian architect Giacomo Leoni. Clandon's interior is the most complete of his work to survive and is notable for its magnificent two-storied, white Marble Hall.

The Onslows have been active in the country's political history, being the only family ever to have produced three Speakers of the House of Commons. The last of these, Arthur Onslow, held the post from 1727 for over 30 years. Activity was not restricted to England; at the end of the 19th century the 4th Earl of Onslow served as Governor of New Zealand, whereupon the Maori meeting house came to be in the gardens at Clandon Park.

There is also an intimate sunken Dutch garden, at its best in May and June and a stunning bulb field flowering in spring.

Displayed inside the house is a superb collection of 18th century furniture, textiles and one of the finest collections of porcelain, including Meissen *Commedia Dell' Arte* figures.

Hatchlands Park was built in 1756 for Admiral Boscawen, hero of the Battle of Louisburg, and contains the earliest recorded decorations in an English country house by Robert Adam, whose ceilings appropriately feature nautical motifs.

The rooms are hung with the Cobbe Collection of Old Master paintings and portraits. The house is also home to the Cobbe Collection of keyboard instruments, the world's largest group of early keyboard instruments owned or played by famous composers such as Purcell, JC Bach, Mozart, Liszt, Chopin, Mahler and Elgar.

Hatchlands is set in a beautiful 430-acre Repton park, with a variety of way-marked walks offering vistas of open parkland and idyllic views of the house. The woodlands are a haven for wildlife and there is a stunning Bluebell wood in May.

There are frequent concerts on the instruments on the collection (for more details please contact: The Cobbe Collection Trust, 01483 211474, www.cobbecollection.co.uk).

© NTPL / Bill Batten

- No photography.
- For Clandon weddings and receptions tel: 01483 222502.
- WCs. Hatchlands suitable. Clandon please tel for details.
- Hatchlands: 01483 211120.
- Licensed. Clandon: 01483 222502.
- Clandon – by arrangement.
- Children's quizzes available.
- Hatchlands Parkland only.
- Clandon only.
- Tel: 01483 222482.

Owner

The National Trust

Contact

The Property Manager
Clandon Park &
Hatchlands Park
East Clandon
Guildford
Surrey GU4 7RT

Tel: 01483 222482
Fax: 01483 223176
E-mail: hatchlands@nationaltrust.org.uk

Location

MAP 19:A11

Clandon
OS Ref. TQ042 512
At West Clandon on the A247, 3m E of Guildford.

Rail: Clandon BR 1m.

Hatchlands
OS Ref. TQ063 516
E of East Clandon on the A246 Guildford–Leatherhead road.

Rail: Clandon BR 2½ m, Horsley 3m.

Opening Times

Clandon – House
14 March–31 October
Tue–Thur, Suns & BH Mons, Good Fri & Easter Sat
11am–5pm.

Garden
As house. 11am–5pm.

Museum
As house
12 noon–5pm.

Hatchlands – House
1 April–31 October
Tue–Thur, Suns & BH Mon, Plus Fris in August.
2–5.30pm.

Park Walks
1 April–31 October
Daily 11am–6pm.

*Admission

Clandon

House/Grounds	£8.60
Child	£4.20
Family	£23.10
Pre-booked Groups	
Adult	£7.00

Hatchlands

House/Grounds	£7.00
Child	£3.60
Family	£18.90
Park Walks only	£4.00
Child	£2.00
Pre-booked Groups	
Adult	£5.95

Combined ticket

Adult	£12.20
Child	£6.10
Family	£35.10

*includes a voluntary donation but visitors can choose to pay the standard prices displayed at the property and on the website.

Conference/Function

ROOM	SIZE	MAX CAPACITY
Marble Hall Clandon Pk	40' x 40'	160 seated 200 standing

■ **Owner**

Mr Michael
More-Molyneux

■ **Contact**

Sue Grant
Events Office
Loseley Park
Guildford
Surrey GU3 1HS

Tel: 01483 304440
Tel Events:
01483 405119/120
Fax: 01483 302036
E-mail: enquiries
@loseleypark.co.uk

■ **Location**

MAP 3:G3
OS Ref. SU975 471

30m SW of London, leave
A3 S of Guildford on to
B3000. Signposted.

Bus: 1¼m from House.

Rail: Farncombe 2m,
Guildford 3m,
Godalming 4m.

Air: Heathrow 30m,
Gatwick 30m.

■ **Opening Times**

Summer
Garden, Shop &
Tearoom
May–September
Tues–Sun & BH Mons
in May & August,
11am–5pm.

Loseley House
(guided tours)
May–August
Tues–Thurs,
Suns & BH Mons in
May & August,
1–5pm.

All Year (Private Hire)
Tithe Barn, Chestnut
Lodge, House, Garden
Marquee, Walled Garden
and Grounds. Civil
ceremonies and receptions.
Lunches and dinners. Off-
road 4x4 course and
showground. Activity Days.

■ **Admission**

House & Gardens
Adult	£8.00
Child (5–16yrs)	£4.00
Conc.	£7.50
Child (under 5yrs)	Free
Family (2 + 3)	£20.00

Booked Groups (10+)
Adult	£7.00
Child (5–16yrs)	£3.50
Garden tours	£3.00pp

Garden & Grounds only
Adult	£4.50
Child (5–16yrs)	£2.25
Conc.	£4.00
Family (2 + 3)	£12.00

Booked Groups (10+)
Adult	£3.50
Child (5–16yrs)	£1.75

Conference/Function

ROOM	SIZE	MAX CAPACITY
Tithe Barn	100' x 18'	180
Marquee sites available		up to 4,000
Great Hall	70' x 40'	80
Drawing Rm	40' x 30'	50
Chestnut Ldg	42' x 20'	50
White Garden Marquee		70

LOSELEY PARK 🏛

www.loseleypark.co.uk

Loseley Park, built in 1562 by Sir William More to entertain Queen Elizabeth I, is a fine example of Elizabethan architecture – its mellow stone brought from the ruins of Waverley Abbey now over 850 years old. The house is set amid magnificent parkland grazed by the Loseley Jersey herd. Many visitors comment on the very friendly atmosphere of the house. It is a country house, the family home of descendants of the builder.

Furniture, paintings and artefacts have been collected by the family since Loseley was built, including panelling from Nonsuch Palace, English and European furniture, a unique chalk fireplace and porcelain from the East. However, with all the history, it is still a family home.

Loseley Park is a stunning wedding venue with ceremonies in the Great Hall and receptions in the 17th century Tithe Barn. There are also flexible facilities for corporate and private functions. Highly rated film location. Christian Cancer/Parkinson's Disease Help Centre.

Garden

A magnificent Cedar of Lebanon presides over the front lawn. Parkland adjoins the lawn and a small lake adds to the beauty of Front Park. Walled Garden: Based on a Gertrude Jekyll design, the five gardens include the award-winning rose garden containing over 1,000 bushes, a magnificent vine walk, herb garden, colourful fruit and flower garden and the serene white garden. Other features include an organic vegetable garden and moat walk. HDRA Seed Library plants.

ℹ Lakeside walk. Picnic area. Chapel. Hire of gardens and grounds for corporate and private events. All group visits to be booked in advance. Group garden tours available. Lectures on history of house and contents by arrangement. South East Tourism Award Winner 2006, Runner-up 2008.

🛋

🎋

🍷 Corporate and private hire for special functions, conferences, meetings, civil ceremonies, wedding receptions, Elizabethan Banquets.

♿ May alight at entrance to property. Access to all areas except house first floor. WCs.

☕ Courtyard Tea Room & Garden Marquee serving light lunches, snacks and cream teas.

🚶 House tour obligatory: 40 mins. Group Garden tours available.

🅿 150 cars, 6 coaches. Summer overflow car park.

🐕 Guide dogs only.

🔔 100 max.

❄

🎭 Tel or see website for details.

PAINSHILL PARK 🏛

www.painshill.co.uk

Step into a 'living picture of paradise' and discover 158 acres of authentically restored Georgian landscape, created by the Hon. Charles Hamilton between 1738 and 1773 as a Living Work of Art … Stroll along the historic route from scene to scene through a series of unfolding vistas known as 'The Hamilton Landscapes'. The 18th century Grade I listed parkland has won the Europa Nostra Medal for exemplary restoration and is complete with a 14 acre lake, spectacular views across Surrey, an amazing crystal Grotto, plus many more interesting and unusual follies.

From Snowdrops to Autumn colour the pleasure grounds and plantings have something to offer the visitor throughout the year. Enjoy exploring the American Roots exhibition which tells an amazing story of the 18th century craze for new and exciting exotic plants from outside the British Isles or discover the NCCPG John Bartram Heritage Plant Collection of North American Trees and Shrubs. Guided walks for pre-booked groups give a fascinating insight into Hamilton's vision and it's a great way to discover the pleasure grounds. Throughout the year there are fun-filled family and adult events, as well as entertaining talks covering a wide range of subjects.

We have a choice of children's birthday parties and a full educational programme which explores the nature, art, history and geography unique to our landscape. Painshill is available for location filming, photographic shoots and in the walled garden 'The Conservatory' is available for weddings and corporate or private hire.

ℹ️ WCs. Filming, plays and photographic shoots.

🛍 Painshill Wine and Honey.

🍽 Private and Corporate Hospitality, Tel: 01932 584283, Email: events@painshillevents.co.uk, Website: www.painshillevents.co.uk.

♿ WCs. Accessible route. Free pre-booked wheelchair loan and guided Buggy Tours (Cap. Max. 3).

☕ Licensed. Picnic area.

🚶 By arrangement.

🎧 £2.50 pp. Free for Disabled person. English.

🅿️ Ample for Coaches (must book) and Cars.

🖼 By arrangement.

🐕 On leads.

❄️

🎪 All year – see website.

Owner
Painshill Park Trust

Contact
Visitor Manager
Painshill Park
Portsmouth Road
Cobham
Surrey KT11 1JE

Tel: 01932 868113
Fax: 01932 868001
E-mail:
info@painshill.co.uk
education@painshill.co.uk

Location
MAP 19:B10
OS Ref. TQ099 605

M25/J10/A3 to London. W of Cobham on A245. Entrance 200 mtrs E of A245/A307 roundabout.

Rail: Cobham/Stoke d'Abernon 2m.

Bus: Surrey Parks & Gardens Explorer Bus Route 515/515A.

Opening Times
All year
March–October:
10.30am–6pm or dusk (last entry 4.30pm),
November–February:
10.30am–4pm or dusk (last entry 3pm).
Closed Christmas Day and Boxing Day.

Admission
Adult   £6.60
Child (5–16)   £3.85
Conc.   £5.80
Family (2 adults,
4 children)   £22.00
Under 5s and carer of disabled person free.
Season Tickets available.

Pre-booked
groups (10+)
Adult   £5.80
Child   £2.00
(optional guided tour £1.00 per person). Free entry and refreshments for tour leader and coach driver.

Grotto has limited opening hours. Opened for Groups by prior arrangement.

Conference/Function

ROOM	MAX CAPACITY	
Abercorn and Small Courtyard	Standing 70 Seated 55 Theatre-style 55	
Discovery Centre Rooms	Standing 50 Seated 40	
The Conservatory in Walled Garden	Standing 400 Seated 320 Theatre-style 400	

BOX HILL 🌿

The Old Fort, Box Hill Road, Box Hill, Tadworth KT20 7LB
Tel: 01306 885502   **Fax:** 01306 875030   **E-mail:** boxhill@nationaltrust.org.uk
www.nationaltrust.org.uk
Owner: The National Trust   **Contact:** Head Warden
An outstanding area of woodland and chalk downland with wonderful walks and magnificent views across the weald. Long famous as a place for visitors and naturalists to enjoy as well as family picnics. Explore the newly opened Discovery Centre in the shop and 'Bee' amazed.
Location: MAP 19:C11, OS Ref. TQ171 519. 1m N of Dorking, 1.5m S of Leatherhead on A24.
Open: Shop, Information Centre and Servery: All year, daily (except 25 Dec). Shop and Information Centre: 1 Jan to 27 Mar 11-4pm; 28 Mar to 30 Oct 11–5pm or dusk if earlier; 31 Oct to 31 Dec 11-4pm. Tel. 01306 888793. Servery: 1 Jan to 27 Mar 10-4pm; 28 Mar to 30 Oct 9-5pm; 31 Oct to 31 Dec 10-4pm
Admission: Countryside: Free. Car/coach park £3, NT members Free.
Special Events: Friday 17 December - special Christmas shopping day.
🔲 🔲 Partial. WCs.🔲 🅿 🔲 🔲 🔲

CLANDON PARK & HATCHLANDS PARK 🌿

See page 127 for full page entry.

©NTPL/John Miller

CLAREMONT LANDSCAPE GARDEN 🌿

PORTSMOUTH ROAD, ESHER, SURREY KT10 9JG

www.nationaltrust.org.uk/claremont

Tel: 01372 467806   **Fax:** 01372 476420   **E-mail:** claremont@nationaltrust.org.uk
Owner: The National Trust   **Contact:** The Property Manager
One of the earliest surviving English landscape gardens, restored to its former glory. Begun by Sir John Vanbrugh and Charles Bridgeman before 1720, the garden was extended and naturalised by William Kent. 'Capability' Brown also made improvements. Features include a lake, island with pavilion, grotto, turf amphitheatre, viewpoints and avenues.
Location: MAP 19:B9, OS Ref. TQ128 632. On S edge of Esher, on E side of A307 (no access from Esher bypass).
Open: Garden open throughout the year. Jan–end Mar, Nov–end Dec: daily except Mons: 10am–5pm or sunset if earlier. Apr–end Oct: daily: 10am–6pm. Closed 25 Dec.
*Admission: Adult £6.40, Child £3.20. Family (2+2) £16 Groups (15+), £5.20. £1 tearoom voucher given if arriving by public transport. Coach groups must book; no coach groups on Sundays. *includes a voluntary donation but visitors can choose to pay the standard prices displayed at the property and on the website.
Special Events: Full events programme throughout the year. Please check website for details or send SAE for copy of Events Programme. Garden may close early in the event of bad weather (particularly high winds) and for certain events days in June & July. Please telephone property to check before travelling.
🔲 🔲 WCs. 🔲 Licensed 🔲 By arrangement. 🅿 Limited for coaches.
🔲 Guide dogs only. No dogs (Apr–Oct). 🔲

Properties that **open all year** appear in the special index at the end of the book.

FARNHAM CASTLE

Farnham, Surrey GU9 0AG
Tel: 01252 721194   **Fax:** 01252 711283   **E-mail:** conf@farnhamcastle.com
Owner: The Church Commissioners   **Contact:** Farnham Castle
Bishop's Palace built in Norman times by Henry of Blois. Tudor and Jacobean additions.
Location: MAP 3:F3, OS Ref. SU839 474. ½m N of Farnham town centre on A287.
Open: All year: Weds, Summer Sats & Suns (tel for details), 2–4pm except Christmas & New Year.
Admission: Adult £2.50, Child/Conc £1.50.

FARNHAM CASTLE KEEP ♯

Castle Hill, Farnham, Surrey GU9 0JA
Tel: 01252 713393   **E-mail:** customers@english-heritage.org.uk
www.english-heritage.org.uk/farnham
Owner: English Heritage   **Contact:** Visitor Operations Team
The impressive motte, shell-keep, bailey wall and other defences of a castle founded in 1138 and redeveloped by Henry II after 1155. Long a residence of the wealthy Bishops of Winchester, the fortress itself was abandoned after Civil War service; later attendant buildings remain in private occupation.
Location: MAP 3:F3, OS Ref. SU837 473. ½m N of Farnham town centre on A287.
Open: 1 Apr–30 Sep: Fri–Sun, 1–5pm.
Admission: Adult £3, Child £1.50, Conc. £2.60. EH Members Free. Group discount available. Opening times and prices are valid until 31st March 2010, after this date details are subject to change please see www.english-heritage.org.uk for the most up-to-date information.
🔲 🔲 Partial. 🅿 🔲 In grounds, on leads.

GODDARDS

Abinger Common, Dorking, Surrey RH5 6TH
Tel: 01628 825925   **E-mail:** bookings@landmarktrust.org.uk
www.landmarktrust.org.uk
Owner: The Lutyens Trust, leased to The Landmark Trust   **Contact:** The Landmark Trust
Built by Sir Edwin Lutyens in 1898–1900 and enlarged by him in 1910. Garden by Gertrude Jekyll. Given to the Lutyens Trust in 1991 and now managed and maintained by the Landmark Trust, a building preservation charity who let it for holidays. The whole house, apart from the library, is available for holidays. Full details of Goddards and 189 other historic and architecturally important buildings available for holidays are featured in The Landmark Handbook (price £10 plus p&p refundable against a booking) and on the website.
Location: MAP 19:B12, OS Ref. TQ120 450. 4½ m SW of Dorking on the village green in Abinger Common. Signposted Abinger Common, Friday Street and Leith Hill from A25.
Open: Available for holidays for up to 12 people. Other visits strictly by appointment. Must be booked in advance, including parking, which is very limited. Visits booked for Weds afternoons from the Wed after Easter until the last Wed of Oct, between 2.30–5pm. Only those with pre-booked tickets will be admitted. Visitors will have access to part of the garden and house only.
Admission: £4. Tickets available from Mrs Baker on 01306 730871, Mon–Fri, 9am & 6pm.
🔲

GREAT FOSTERS

Stroude Road, Egham, Surrey TW20 9UR
Tel: 01784 433822   **Fax:** 01784 472455   **E-mail:** enquiries@greatfosters.co.uk
www.greatfosters.co.uk
Owner: The Sutcliffe family   **Contact:** Amanda Dougans
Grade II listed garden. Laid out in 1918 by W H Romaine-Walker in partnership with G H Jenkins, incorporating earlier features. The site covers 50 acres and is associated with a 16th century country house, reputed to be a former royal hunting lodge and converted into an hotel by the owners in 1931. The main formal garden is surrounded on three sides by a moat, thought to be of medieval origin, and is modelled on the pattern of a Persian carpet. The garden also includes an amphitheatre, lake and a sunken rose garden.
Location: MAP 3:G2, OS Ref. TQ015 694. M25 J/13, follow signs to Egham. Under motorway bridge, first left at roundabout (The Avenue). Left at the mini roundabout into Vicarage Rd. Right at next roundabout. Over M25, left into Stroude Rd. 500 yds on left.
Open: All year.
Admission: Free.
🔲 🔲 Partial. WC. 🔲 🔲 Licensed. 🅿 🔲 Guide dogs only. 🔲 🔲 🔲 🔲

---

visit hudsons guide online

©HRP 2007

©HRP 2007

HAMPTON COURT PALACE
HAMPTON COURT PALACE, SURREY KT8 9AU
www.hrp.org.uk

Tel: 0844 482 7777
Venue Hire and Corporate Hospitailty: 02031 666505
Email: groupsandtraveltrade@hrp.org.uk **Web:** www.hrp.org.uk
Owner/Contact: Historic Royal Palaces

Henry VIII is most associated with this majestic palace, which he extended and developed in grand style after acquiring it from Cardinal Wolsey in the 1520s. The Tudor buildings that are among the most important in exisitence, but the elegance and romance of the palace owes much to the elegant Baroque buildings commissioned by William and Mary at the end of the 17th century. The palace is set in 60 acres of gardens, that include the famous Maze. The palace is decked out in splendour including a new Tudor Court garden. Visitors will revel in this moment of history that happened at Hampton Court in 1543.

Location: MAP 19:B9, OS Ref. TQ155 686. From M25/J15 and A312, or M25/J12 and A308, or M25/J10 and A307. Rail: From London Waterloo direct to Hampton Court (32 mins). 30 minutes from Waterloo, zone 6 travelcard.

Open: Mar–Oct: Daily, 10am–6pm (last admission 5.15pm). Nov–Feb: Daily, 10am–4.30pm (last admission 3.45pm). Closed 24–26 Dec.

Admission: Telephone Information Line for admission prices: 08444 827777. Advance Ticket Sales:08444 827799. Group Bookings 08444 827770, Quote Hudson's.

i Information Centre. No photography indoors. ◻ ⊤ 🅹 Partial. WCs.
🍽 ⅱ Licensed. 🎓 By arrangement ⌂ 🅿 Ample for cars, coach parking nearby. ■
Rates on request 0844 482 7777. 🐕 Guide dogs only ❄ 🍴

KEW GARDENS

Kew, Richmond, Surrey TW9 3AB

Tel: 020 8332 5655   **Fax:** 020 8332 5610   **E-mail:** info@kew.org   **www.kew.org**

Contact: Visitor Information

Kew Gardens is a World Heritage Site. It is a mixture of stunning vistas, magnificent glasshouses and beautiful landscapes beside the River Thames. This once Royal residence represents nearly 250 years of historical gardens and today its 300 acres are home to over 40,000 types of plants from rainforest to desert. There is always something to see … as the seasons change so does Kew.

Location: MAP 19:C7, OS Ref. TQ188 776. A307. Junc. A307 & A205 (1m Chiswick roundabout M4).

Open: All year: daily (except 24/25 Dec) from 9.30am. Closing time varies according to the season. Please telephone for further information.

Admission: 1 Nov '07–31 Mar '08: Adults £12.25, From 1 Apr: £13. Concessions available. Child (under 17) Free. Discounts for groups (10+). School groups: Free.

◻ ⊤ 🅹 ⅱ Licensed. 🅿 Limited. ■ 🐕 Guide dogs only. ▲ ❄

KEW PALACE, HISTORIC ROYAL PALACES

Kew Gardens, Kew, Richmond, Surrey TW9 3AB

Tel: Group Bookings 020 8332 5648   **E-mail:** groupsandtraveltrade@hrp.org.uk
www.hrp.org.uk **Contact:** Visitor Information 0844 482 7777

Kew Palace and Queen Charlotte's Cottage. The most intimate of the five royal palaces, Kew was built as a private house but became a royal residence between 1728 and 1818. Both the palace and the nearby Queen Charlotte's cottage, built in 1770, are most closely associated with King George III and his family. Discover their story.

Location: MAP 19:C7, OS Ref. TQ188 776.193. A307. Junc A307 & A205 (1m Chiswick roundabout M4). Rail: 30 minutes from Waterloo, zone 6 travelcard.

Underground: District Line station nearby. Boat: From Kingston or central London.

Open: 10 Apr–27 Sept: daily, 10am–5pm, Last admission 4.15pm.

Admission: By joint ticket purchased through Kew Gardens.

⊤ 🅹 WCs. 🍽 Licensed. ⅱ Licensed. 🎓 By arrangement. 🅿 Limited. 🐕

LEITH HILL ❧

Coldharbour, Surrey RH5 6LY
Tel: 01306 712711   **Email:** leithhill@nationaltrust.org.uk
www.nationaltrust.org.uk
Owner: The National Trust   **Contact:** Head Warden

The highest point in south-east England, crowned by an 18th century Gothic tower, from which there are magnificent views. Colourful display of rhododendrons in May–Jun. 2 circular nature trails with leaflet.

Location: MAP 19:B12, OS Ref. TQ139 432. 1m SW of Coldharbour A29/B2126.

Open: Tower: To 27 Mar, Sat & Sun, 10am–3.30pm, 28 Mar–30 Oct: Fri–Sun, and Weds 10am–5pm or dusk if earlier, 31 Oct–26 Mar 2011: Sats & Suns, 10am–3.30pm. Open all BHs (closed 25 Dec). Last adm. 30 mins before closing. Wood & Estate: All year: daily.

Admission: Tower: £1.20, Child 70p. Each child entry includes new Leith Hill Tower 360 degree panoramic leaflet/quiz, pencil and telescope token. Rhododendron Wood: £2 per car

i No vehicular access to summit. 🅹 Partial. 🍽 🅿 Parking at foot of hill, ½m walk from Tower. 🐕 Not in picnic area or Tower. ❄

LOSELEY PARK 🏛

See page 128 for full page entry.

Loseley Park

© NT / Geoff Hamilton

OAKHURST COTTAGE ✤

HAMBLEDON, GODALMING, SURREY GU8 4HF

www.nationaltrust.org.uk/main/w-oakhurstcottage

Tel: 01798 342207   **E-mail:** oakhurstcottage@nationaltrust.org.uk

Owner: The National Trust   **Contact:** Petworth House

A small 16th century timber-framed cottage, painted by both Helen Allingham and Myles Birket Foster, containing furniture and artefacts reflecting two or more centuries of continuing occupation. There is a delightful cottage garden and a small barn containing agricultural implements.

Location: MAP 3:G4, OS Ref. SU965 385. Hambledon, Surrey.

Open: 24 Mar–24 Oct: Weds, Thurs, Sats, Suns & BH Mons. Strictly by appointment, 2–5pm.

Admission: Adult £5, Child £3 (incl guided tour). No reduction for groups.

ⓘ No WC's. Please book appointment to visit at least 3 days in advance. ♿ Partial. 📷 Obligatory, by arrangement. 🅿 Limited. No coaches. 🐕 Guide dogs only.

PAINSHILL PARK 🏛   *See page 129 for full page entry.*

The Statue of Bacchus – Painshill Park

©NTPL/Nick Meers

POLESDEN LACEY ✤

GREAT BOOKHAM, Nr DORKING, SURREY RH5 6BD

www.nationaltrust.org.uk/polesdenlacey

Tel: 01372 452048 **Fax:** 01372 452023 **E-mail:** polesdenlacey@nationaltrust.org.uk

Owner: The National Trust   **Contact:** The Property Manager

Originally an elegant 1820s Regency villa in a magnificent landscape setting. The house was remodelled after 1906 by the Hon Mrs Ronald Greville, a well-known Edwardian hostess. Her collection of fine paintings, furniture, porcelain and silver are still displayed in the reception rooms and galleries. Extensive grounds (1,400 acre estate), walled rose garden, lawns and landscaped walks. New Restaurant, Farm shop & gift shop located outside the pay perimeter.

Location: MAP 19:B11, OS Ref. TQ136 522. 5m NW of Dorking, 2m S of Great Bookham, off A246.

Open: House: 3 Mar–31 Oct: Wed–Sun, & BH Mons, 11am–5pm. Garden, Restaurant, Gift Shop & Farm Shop: All year: daily, 10am–4pm, 1 Jan–12 Feb, 10am–5pm, 13 Feb–31 Oct, 10am–4pm, 1 Nov–31 Dec. Closed 24 & 25 Dec. Gift shop closed 24-26th Dec. Property closed 16th Mar 2010. Car Park: Daily 7.30am–dusk.

Admission: House & Gardens: Adults £11.60, Child £5.80, Family £29, Group £9.85. Gardens only: Adult £7.40, Child £3.70, Family £18.50, Group £6.30. Car park charge for non-members. Admissions to House by timed ticket at busy times. Tickets issued at reception on a first-come, first served basis cannot be booked in advance. Tickets may run out at peak times – please arrive early. Weekends in Feb, House open by guided tour, spaces limited. Last admission is 30 mins before closing.

📷 🔧 ♿ 🍴 Licensed. 🅿 🐕 In grounds on leads. ✳ Grounds only. ♿ Tel: 01372 452048 for info.

© NTPL / John Miller

RAMSTER GARDENS

Ramster, Chiddingfold, Surrey GU8 4SN

Tel: 01428 654167 **www.ramsterevents.com**

Owner/Contact: Mrs R Glaister

An idyllic, mature flowering shrub garden of 20 acres, with unusual and interesting plants. Spring colour changes from subtle daffodils and magnolias in April to the famous fiery display of rhododendrons, azaleas and bluebells in May, followed in June by the gentle pinks of climbing roses and cascades of primulas.

Location: MAP 3:G4, OS Ref. SU950 333. 1½ m S of Chiddingfold on A283.

Open: 2 Apr–20 Jun, daily, 10am–5pm.

Admission: Adult £5, Child (under 16) Free. Conc £4.50. Groups by arrangement.

⬛ 🔲 Partial. 🔲🔲 On leads. 🔲🔲 25 Apr: Ramster Food & Plant Fair.

RUNNYMEDE ❧

Egham, Surrey

Tel: 01784 432891 **Fax:** 01784 479007 **E-mail:** runnymede@nationaltrust.org.uk

www.nationaltrust.org.uk

Owner: The National Trust **Contact:** The Head Warden

An historic area alongside the River Thames where, in 1215, King John sealed Magna Carta, an event commemorated by the American Bar Association Memorial. The John F Kennedy Memorial was erected in 1965 to commemorate his life. The Commonwealth Air Forces Memorial is situated overlooking Runnymede and commemorates over 20,000 airmen and women with no known grave who died during World War II. Also here are the Fairhaven Lodges, designed by Lutyens, which host a summer art gallery and tearoom all year.

Location: MAP 3:G2, OS Ref. TQ007 720. 2m W of Runnymede Bridge, on S side of A308, M25/J13.

Open: All year. Riverside Car park (grass): Riverside open 15 Apr–15 Sept only, daily, 10am–7pm. Tearoom & car park (hard standing): daily, all year, 8.30am–5pm (later in Summer).

Admission: Fees payable for parking (NT members Free), fishing & mooring.

🔲 🔲 Partial. 🔲 🔲 🅿 🔲 On leads near livestock. ✱

THE SAVILL GARDEN
(WINDSOR GREAT PARK, BERKSHIRE)

See page 72 (Berkshire) for full page entry.

SHALFORD MILL ❧
SHALFORD, Nr GUILDFORD, SURREY GU4 8BS

www.nationaltrust.org.uk

Tel: 01483 561389 **E-mail:** shalfordmill@nationaltrust.org.uk

Owner: The National Trust **Contact:** The Navigations Office

This lovely 18th century watermill has remained virtually unaltered since ceasing operation in 1914. It was donated to the Trust by the mysterious Ferguson's Gang in 1932. Although the waterwheel no longer functions, it is possible to trace the remarkable journey of grain around the mill until it was bagged up and carted off to the bakers.

Location: MAP 3:G3, OS Ref. TQ001 476.

Open: 29 Mar–1 Nov, Wed & Sun, 11am–4.30pm.

Admission: Adult £2.50, Child £1.25, Family £5, Groups £3 (min 15, max 30).

ℹ No parking nor toilets at the mill. 🔲 Obligatory. 🔲 🔲 Guide dogs only.

Great Fosters

■ **Owner**
Arundel Castle
Trustees Ltd

■ **Contact**
Bryan McDonald
Castle Manager
Arundel Castle
Arundel
West Sussex BN18 9AB

Tel: 01903 882173
Fax: 01903 884581
E-mail: bryan.mcdonald@
arundelcastle.org

■ **Location**
MAP 3:G6
OS Ref. TQ018 072

Central Arundel, N of A27
Brighton 40 mins,
Worthing 15 mins,
Chichester 15 mins.
From London A3 or A24,
1½ hrs.
M25 motorway, 30m.

Bus: Bus stop 100 yds.

Rail: Station ½m.

Air: Gatwick 25m.

■ **Opening Times**
1 April–31 October 2010

Tuesday to Sunday

Closed on Mondays
Open Bank Holidays and
Mondays in August.

**Fitzalan Chapel,
Gardens & Grounds**
10am–5pm

Restaurant & Gift Shop
From 10.30am

Castle Keep
11.00am – 4.30pm

Main Castle Rooms
12 noon – 5pm

Last entry 4pm

■ **Admission**
Gold Plus
Castle Rooms &
Bedrooms, Castle Keep,
Fitzalan Chapel, The
Collector Earl's Garden,
Gardens & Grounds:
Adult £16, Child (5-16)
£7.50, Conc. £13.50,
Family (2+3 max) £39.00.

Gold
Castle Rooms, Castle
Keep, Fitzalan Chapel,
The Collector Earl's
Garden, Gardens &
Grounds: Adult £14,
Child £7.50, Conc.
£11.50, Family (2+3 max)
£36.00.

Silver
Castle Keep, Fitzalan
Chapel, The Collector
Earl's Garden, Gardens &
Grounds: Adult £9.00,
Child £7.50

Bronze
Fitzalan Chapel, The
Collector Earl's Garden,
Gardens & Grounds:
All £7.50.

Group rates available.

On special event days
admission prices may
vary.

For further information
visit our website, email
or telephone.

ARUNDEL CASTLE & GARDENS

www.arundelcastle.org

A thousand years of history is waiting to be discovered at Arundel Castle in West Sussex. Dating from the 11th century, the Castle is both ancient fortification and stately home of the Dukes of Norfolk and Earls of Arundel.

Set high on a hill, this magnificent castle commands stunning views across the River Arun and out to sea. Climb the Keep, explore the battlements, wander in the grounds and recently restored Victorian gardens and relax in the garden of the 14th century Fitzalan Chapel.

In the 17th century during the English Civil War the Castle suffered extensive damage. The process of structural restoration began in earnest in the 18th century and continued up until 1900. The Castle was one of the first private residences to have electricity and central heating and had its own fire engine.

Inside the Castle over 20 sumptuously furnished rooms may be visited including the breathtaking Barons' Hall with 16th century furniture; the Armoury with its fine collection of armour and weaponry, and the magnificent Gothic library entirely fitted out in carved Honduras mahogany. There are works of art by Van Dyck, Gainsborough, Canaletto and Mytens; tapestries; clocks; and personal possessions of Mary Queen of Scots including the gold rosary that she carried to her execution.

There are special event days throughout the season, including outdoor concerts and Shakespeare, jousting, and medieval re-enactments.

Do not miss the magnificent Collector Earl's garden based on early 17th century classical designs.

ℹ️ No photography or video recording inside the Castle.

🛍️ Wide choice of distinctive and exclusive gifts.

♿ Many areas accessible. Visitors may alight at the Castle gates. Free parking in the allocated areas in the town car park. Passenger buggy available. WCs.

☕
🍴 Licensed restaurant in Castle seats 140. Self-service. Serves morning coffee, lunch or afternoon tea.

🚶 By prior arrangement. Tour time 1½–2 hrs. Tours available in various languages - please enquire.

🅿️ Ample in town car park. Coaches visiting the castle can park for free in the town coach park. Free admission and refreshment voucher for coach driver.

▪️ Items of particular interest include a Norman Motte & Keep, Armoury & Victorian bedrooms. Special rates for schoolchildren (aged 5–16) and teachers.

🐕 Registered Assistance Dogs only

For further information please visit our website, e-mail or telephone.

BATEMAN'S ❧

www.nationaltrust.org.uk/batemans

Built in 1634 and home to Rudyard Kipling for over 30 years, Bateman's lies in the richly wooded landscape of the Sussex Weald. Visit this Sussex sandstone manor house, built by a local ironmaster, where the famous writer lived from 1902 to 1936. See the rooms as they were in Kipling's day, including the study where the view inspired him to write some of his well-loved works including *Puck of Pook's Hill* and *Rewards and Fairies*. Find the mementoes of Kipling's time in India and illustrations from his famous Jungle Book tales of Mowgli, Baloo and Shere Khan.

Wander through the delightful Rose Garden with its pond and statues, with Mulberry and Herb gardens and discover the wild garden, through which flows the River Dudwell. Through the wild garden, you will find the Mill where you can watch corn being ground on most Saturday and Wednesday afternoons and one of the world's first water-driven turbines installed by Kipling to generate electricity for the house. In the garage, see a 1928 Rolls Royce, one of several owned by Kipling who was a keen early motorist.

Savour the peace and tranquillity of this beautiful property which Kipling described as '*A good and peaceable place*' *and of which he said 'we have loved it, ever since our first sight of it …'.*

There is a picnic glade next to the car park, or you can enjoy morning coffee, a delicious lunch or afternoon tea in the licensed tearoom where there is special emphasis on using local produce. The well-stocked gift shop offers the largest collection of Kipling books in the area.

Partial. WCs.

Licensed.

Limited for coaches.

Guide dogs only.

■ Owner
The National Trust

■ Contact
The Administrator
Bateman's
Burwash
Etchingham
East Sussex TN19 7DS

Tel: 01435 882302
Fax: 01435 882811
E-mail: batemans@
nationaltrust.org.uk

■ Location
MAP 4:K5
OS Ref. TQ671 238

½ m S of Burwash
off A265.

Rail: Etchingham 3m,
then bus (twice daily).

Air: Gatwick 40m.

■ Opening Times
13 March–31 October:
Sat–Wed, Good Fri & BH
Mons, 11am–5pm. Last
admission 4.30pm.

■ *Admission
House & Garden
Adult   £8.20
Child   £4.10
Family (2+3)   £20.50
Groups   £6.45
*includes a voluntary donation but visitors can choose to pay the standard prices displayed at the property and on the website.

■ Special Events
Children's Fun Days. Jacobean and WWI re-enactment weekends. Lecture lunches. Edwardian Christmas weekends.

■ **Owner**

The Charleston Trust

■ **Contact**

Charleston
Firle
Nr Lewes
East Sussex BN8 6LL

Tel: 01323 811265
Fax: 01323 811628
E-mail: info@charleston.org.uk

■ **Location**

MAP 4:J6
OS Ref. TQ490 069

7m E of Lewes on A27 between Firle and Selmeston.

■ **Opening Times**

31 March – 31 October

Wed – Sat, 1–6pm (12–6pm in July and August) Last entry to the house 5pm

Sun & BH Mons, 1–5.30pm. Last entry to the house 4.30pm

Please check website for up to date information

■ **Admission**

House & Garden

Adult	£7.50
Children	£5.00
Disabled	£5.00
Family	£20.00
Conc. (Thur only)	£6.50
Themed tour	£9.00

Garden only

Adults	£3.00
Children	£1.50

Open by arrangement for groups
tel: 01323 811 626.

CHARLESTON

www.charleston.org.uk

Situated in the heart of the South Downs, Charleston was from 1916 the home of the artists Vanessa Bell and Duncan Grant. Influenced by Post Impressionists such as Picasso and Cezanne, they took painting beyond the canvas, decorating walls, doors, furniture, ceramics and textiles, transforming the house itself into a work of art over the decades they spent here. Within the walled garden they created a summer haven overflowing with flowers and punctuated by sculptures, mosaics and ponds.

Charleston was a country retreat for Bloomsbury, the group of artists, writers and intellectuals that included Virginia and Leonard Woolf, John Maynard Keynes, E M Forster, Lytton Strachey, Roger Fry and Clive Bell. Today, Charleston contains the only complete example of the domestic decorative art of Bell and Grant anywhere in the world;

alongside which hang their own easel paintings as well as works by the artists they knew and admired.

The Charleston shop stocks a range of original ceramics, painted furniture, textiles, clothes and books relating to Charleston and to Bloomsbury. The Outer Studio café provides light refreshment and the Charleston Gallery shows a changing programme of exhibitions.

The annual Charleston Festival is one of the UK's most successful independent literary events. Every May it presents a series of talks and lectures with an international cast of writers, performers and artists.

Charleston runs an exciting programme of events including walks, talks, discussions and workshops that use the collection as a catalyst for a wide range of creative activities to inform and inspire people about Bloomsbury and the arts.

ℹ️ Filming and photography by arrangement.

♿ Partial. Access leaflet. WC.

Obligatory, except Sun and BH Mons.

🅿️

Guide dogs only.

GOODWOOD HOUSE 🏛

www.goodwood.com

Goodwood is one of the finest sporting estates in the world. At its heart lies Goodwood House, the ancestral home of the Dukes of Richmond and Gordon, direct descendants of King Charles II. Today, it is still lived in by the present Duke's son and heir, the Earl of March and Kinrara, with his wife and family. Their home is open to the public on at least 60 days a year. This is the only house that belonged to a son of Charles II that can be visited.

Set in the exquisitely decorated and gilded interiors of Goodwood House, the art collection is at an international level, with a magnificent collection of British paintings from the 17th and 18th centuries. These include the celebrated and glorious views of London by Canaletto, and superb sporting scenes by George Stubbs, England's most famous animal painter. The rooms are filled with fine furniture, Gobelins tapestries and Sèvres porcelain, all from the 18th century, as well as English Regency furniture in the Egyptian Dining Room. One of the most important sets of French furniture in the world is on display. Special works of art are regularly rotated and displayed. Arrangements

to see the books can be made by written application to the Curator. (There is a special charge for these viewings).

This is a lively house to visit, in which the full calendar of both personal and public events mean that changes are always being made, whether it be fresh flowers for the rooms or an alteration in furniture layout. Something is always going on at Goodwood, giving the house the feel of a real living, working family home. It has a very special relaxed and friendly atmosphere.

Goodwood is not only a beautiful house to visit on an open day, but is also renowned for its entertaining. The house enjoys a reputation for excellence as a location for unforgettable weddings, parties and events. Goodwood's own organic farm, the largest in England, provides food for the table in the various restaurants on the estate. With internationally renowned horseracing and motor sport events, the finest Downland golf course in the UK, its own Aerodrome and hotel, Goodwood can offer an extraordinarily rich sporting experience.

i	Conference facilities. No photography. Highly trained guides. Shell House optional extra on Connoisseurs' Days or by Group Appointment, or written request.
🛍	Main shop at motor circuit.
⏣	
☕	
♿	
🚶	Obligatory.
P	Ample.
🎦	
🐕	In grounds, on leads. Guide dogs only in house.
🔔	Civil Wedding Licence.
🎭	

■ Owner
The Goodwood Estate Co.Ltd. (Earl of March and Kinrara).

■ Contact
Secretary to the Curator
Goodwood House
Goodwood
Chichester
West Sussex PO18 0PX

Tel: 01243 755048
01243 755042 (Weddings)
Recorded Info:
01243 755040
Fax: 01243 755005
E-mail: curator
@goodwood.com or
weddings@
goodwood.com

■ Location
MAP 3:F6
OS Ref. SU888 088

3½m NE of Chichester. A3 from London then A286 or A285. M27/A27 from Portsmouth or Brighton.

Rail: Chichester 3½m
Arundel 9m.

Air: Heathrow 1½ hrs
Gatwick ¾ hr.

■ Opening Times
Summer
21 March–11 October:
Most Sundays and
Mondays, 1–5pm
(last entry 4pm).
1–30 August: Sun–Thurs,
1–5pm.

Please check Recorded Info
01243 755040.

Connoisseurs' Days
17 March, 18 May
& 21 October.

Special tours for booked
groups only.

Closures
Closed for some special events and for two weekends between mid–June and mid–July for the Festival of Speed, and for one Sunday in September for the Revival Meeting.

Please ring Recorded
Information on 01243
755040 to check these
dates and occasional extra
closures.

■ Admission
House
Adult	£9.00
Young Person (12–18yrs)	£4.00
Child (under 12yrs)	Free
Senior Citizen	£7.50
Family	£20.00

Booked Groups (20–200)
Open Day (am)	£9.00
Open Day (pm)	£7.50
Connoisseur	£10.00

■ Special Events
Festival of Speed
Glorious Goodwood Race–
week
Vintage
Goodwood Revival

Please visit our website for up-to-date information. www.goodwood.com.

Conference/Function

ROOM	SIZE	MAX CAPACITY
Ballroom	79' x 23'	180
10 other rooms available.		

■ **Owner**

The Great Dixter
Charitable Trust

■ **Contact**

Perry Rodriguez
Northiam
Rye
East Sussex TN31 6PH

Tel: 01797 252878
Fax: 01797 252879
E-mail:
office@greatdixter.co.uk

■ **Location**

MAP 4:L5
OS Ref. TQ817 251.

Signposted off the A28
in Northiam.

■ **Opening Times**

1 April–31 October:
Tue–Sun, House 2–5pm.
Garden 11am–5pm.

■ **Admission**

House & Garden
Adult   £8.50
Child   £4.00

Gardens only
Adult   £7.00
Child   £3.50
Groups (25+) by
appointment.

■ **Specialist Nursery
Opening times**

April–October:
Mon–Fri, 9–5pm.
Sat 9–5pm
Sun 10–5pm.

Nov–end of March:
Mon–Fri 9–12.30pm,
1.30–4.30pm
Sat 9–12pm
Sun closed

GREAT DIXTER HOUSE & GARDENS 🏛

www.greatdixter.co.uk

Great Dixter, built c1450, is the birthplace of the late Christopher Lloyd, gardening author. Its Great Hall is the largest medieval timber-framed hall in the country, restored and enlarged for Christopher's father (1910–12). The house was largely designed by the architect, Sir Edwin Lutyens, who added a 16th century house (moved from elsewhere) and knitted the buildings together with service accommodation and bedrooms above. The house retains most of the collections of furniture and other items put together by the Lloyds early in the 20th century, with some notable modern additions by Christopher.

The gardens feature a variety of topiary, wild meadow areas and the famous Long Border and Exotic Garden. They featured regularly in "Country Life" from 1963, when Christopher was asked to contribute a series of weekly articles as a practical gardener – he never missed an issue in 42 years. There is a specialist nursery on site which offers an array of unusual plants of the highest quality, many of which can be seen in the fabric of the gardens. Light refreshments are available in the gift shop as well as tools, books and gifts.

The estate is 57 acres which includes ancient woodlands, meadows and ponds which have been consistently managed on a traditional basis. Coppicing the woodlands, for example, has provided pea sticks for plant supports and timber for fencing and repairs to the buildings.

There is a Friends programme available throughout the year. Friends enjoy invitations to events and educational courses as well as regular newsletters.

ℹ No photography in House.

📷

✻

🚶 Obligatory.

🅿 Limited for coaches.

🐕 Guide dogs only.

©NTPL/Edward Shorthouse

NYMANS

www.nationaltrust.org.uk/nymans

Set in the High Weald with splendid views, the Nymans estate was created by the Messel family and their gardeners. The garden is a series of experimental designs with spectacular planting and all-year-round beauty, created in the changing fashion of early 20th century gardening. Both a horticulturalist's dream and a peaceful country garden, it's easy to lose yourself in its intimate and surprising corners. Among the varied garden rooms and beautiful plants, you will discover intriguing ruins, summer houses and statues. The house, transformed into a gothic mansion in the twenties, burnt down shortly after, leaving romantic ruins. The remaining rooms are unexpectedly charming, filled with flowers reflecting the taste of Anne Messel, Countess of Rosse. The house contains a fine collection of 17th century furniture and Flemish tapestries, whilst Oliver Messel's television, draped in stage curtains is one of the more curious objects to discover. Ancient woods beyond the garden dip into the valley, providing wonderful walks among avenues, wild flowers, lake and cascades. There's much to explore – see if you can find the tallest tree in Sussex, a giant Redwood, near Conifer Avenue. Our wardens make charcoal for sale in the shop and you are welcome to walk your dogs in the woods. Nymans is open throughout the changing seasons with Rhododendron, Magnolia, Camellia and Azalea in spring, the renowned Summer Borders, the glorious colour of autumn and the scent of Daphne, the colour of Witch-hazel and the swathes of Snowdrops in winter.

©NTPL/John Miller

WCs
Licensed
Licensed
By arrangement

Limited for coaches

Guide dogs only

■ Owner
The National Trust

■ Contact
Nymans
Handcross
Haywards Heath
West Sussex
RH17 6EB

Tel/Fax: 01444 405250
E-mail: nymans@
nationaltrust.org.uk

■ Location
MAP 4:I4
OS Ref. SU187:TQ265 294

At Handcross on B2114, 12 miles south of Gatwick, just off London–Brighton M23.

Bus: 273 Brighton–Crawley, 271 Haywards Heath–Crawley.

Rail: Balcombe 4 miles; Crawley 5 miles.

Air: Gatwick airport 12 miles

Ferry: Dieppe or L'Havre to Newhaven then 20 miles by road

■ Opening Times
Garden, Shop & Restaurant
All year: Wednesday–Sunday, 10am–5pm, closes 4pm November–February.

House
10 March–31 October: Wednesday–Sunday, 11am–4pm.

■ *Admission
NT members Free

Adult	£9.00
Child	£4.50
Family	£22.00
Family (1 adult)	£13.50
Booked Groups (15+)	£7.50

Free cup of tea or coffee in restaurant when arriving by public transport. *Includes a voluntary donation but visitors can choose to pay the standard prices displayed at visitor reception and on the website.

■ Special Events
We have an all year round programme of events including family activities, summer openair theatre, horticultural workshops, compost demonstrations, bat walks and photography workshops.

■ Owner

Mr & Mrs
James A Sellick

■ Contact

Pashley Manor
Ticehurst
Wadhurst
East Sussex TN5 7HE

Tel: 01580 200888
Fax: 01580 200102
E-mail: info@
pashleymanorgardens
.com

■ Location

MAP 4:K4
OS Ref. TQ707 291

On B2099 between A21
and Ticehurst Village.

■ Opening Times

1 April–30 September:
Tues, Weds, Thurs, Sat,
Bank Holiday Mons and
Special Event days,
11am–5pm.

October: Garden only
Mon–Fri,10am–4pm.

■ Admission

Adult	£8.00
Children (6–16yrs)	£5.00
Groups (15+)	£7.50
Tulip Festival (no concessions)	£8.50
Season Ticket	£26.50

Coaches must book.
Please telephone for
details.

■ Special Events

23 April–3 May (inc.)
Tulip Festival

22–31 May (inc.)
Sculpture in Particular

11–13 June
Special Rose Weekend

18–20 June
Kitchen Garden Weekend

Mid July–Mid August
Lily Time

28–30 August
Sussex Guild Craft Show

PASHLEY MANOR GARDENS 🏛

www.pashleymanorgardens.com

A winner of HHA/Christie's Garden of the Year Award. The gardens offer a sumptuous blend of romantic landscaping, imaginative plantings and fine old trees, fountains, springs and large ponds. This is a quintessential English garden of a very individual character with exceptional views to the surrounding valleyed fields. Many eras of English history are reflected here, typifying the tradition of the English Country House and its garden.

The gardens first opened in 1992 and were brought to their present splendour with the assistance of the eminent landscape architect, Anthony du Gard Pasley. A number of different gardens have been created within the 11 acres allowing the visitor to travel from blazing colour to cool creams, greens and golds.

The gardens are always evolving and never static; it is hoped that they will be inspirational yet restful to the first-time visitor and will never disappoint those who return regularly. Pashley prides itself on its delicious food. During warm weather, visitors can enjoy their refreshments on the terrace overlooking the moat or in the Jubilee Courtyard. Home-made soups, ploughman's lunches with pickles and patés, fresh salad from the garden (whenever possible), home-made scones and delicious cakes, filter coffee, specialist teas and fine wines are served from the Garden Room café. The new gift shop caters for every taste … from postcards and local honey to traditional hand-painted ceramics and tapestry cushions. A selection of plants and shrubs, many of which grow at Pashley, are available for purchase.

Permanent exhibition and sale of sculpture and botanical art.

Excellent location for small corporate events, private parties and marquee wedding receptions.

Mariette Tulips and Lutyens Bench

'Mr Bennet's Daughter' by Philip Jackson

 Partial.
 Licensed.
 By arrangement.
 Guide dogs only.
 Telephone for details.

© NT / John Miller

PETWORTH HOUSE & PARK 🌿

www.nationaltrust.org.uk/petworth

Petworth House is one of the finest houses in the care of the National Trust and is home to an art collection that rivals many London galleries. Assembled by one family over 350 years, it includes works by Turner, Van Dyck, Titian, Claude, Gainsborough, Bosch, Reynolds and William Blake.

The state rooms contain sculpture, furniture and porcelain of the highest quality and are complemented by the Victorian kitchens in the Servants' Quarters. The Carved Room contains some of Grinling Gibbons' finest limewood carvings.

Petworth House is also the home of Lord and Lady Egremont and extra family rooms are open on weekdays by kind permission of the family (not Bank Holidays).

Petworth Park is a 700 acre park landscaped by 'Capability' Brown and is open to the public all year free of charge. Spring and autumn are particularly breathtaking and the summer sunsets over the lake are spectacular.

© NTPL / Bill Batten

ℹ️ Events & Exhibitions throughout the year. Baby feeding and changing facilities, highchairs, pushchairs admitted in house but no prams please. No photography or mobile phones in house.

📷

🎁

🍷 Contact Retail & Catering Manager on 01798 345521.

♿ Partial. WCs.

☕ Licensed

🍴 Licensed.

🏃 By arrangement with the Administration Office on variety of subjects.

🎧 Audio House Tours.

🅿️ 800 yards from house. Coach parties alight at Church Lodge entrance, coaches then park in NT car park. Coaches must book in advance.

🏫 Welcome. Must book. Teachers' pack available.

🐕 Guide dogs only

🎭

■ Owner
The National Trust

■ Contact
The Administration Office
Petworth House & Park
Church Street
Petworth
West Sussex GU28 0AE

Tel: 01798 342207
Info: 01798 343929
Fax: 01798 342963
E-mail: petworth@
nationaltrust.org.uk

■ Location
MAP 3:G5
OS Ref. SU976 218

In the centre of Petworth town (approach roads A272/A283/A285) Car park signposted.

Rail: Pulborough 5¼m.

■ Opening Times
House
13 March–3 November.Daily except Thur & Fri, but open Good Fri, 11am–5pm. Last admission to House 4.30pm. Extra rooms shown on Mon–Wed (closed BH Mons).

Pleasure Ground, Shop & Restaurant
27 February–10 March for spring bulbs and events, Sat–Wed 10.30am–3.30pm. 13 March–3 November, Sat–Wed 11am–5pm. 10 Nov–19 Dec, Wed–Sun, 10.30am–3.30pm.

Park
All year: Daily, 8am–dusk/9pm

■ *Admission
House & Pleasure Ground
Adult   £10.90
Child (5–17yrs)   £5.50
Child (under 5yrs) Free
Family (2+3)   £27.30

Groups (pre-booked 15+)
Adult   £9.00

Park Only   Free

Parking charge for non-NT members.

Pleasure Ground
Adult   £4.20
Child (5–17yrs) £2.10

NT Members Free.

*Includes a voluntary donation but visitors can choose to pay the standard prices displayed at the property and on the website.

Special Events
See website www.nationaltrust.org.uk /petworth for event details.

South East – England

■ **Owner**
The National Trust

■ **Contact**
Jo Hopkins
Visitor Services &
Marketing Manager
Sheffield Park
East Sussex
TN22 3QX

Tel: 01825 790231
Fax: 01825 791264
E-mail: sheffieldpark@
nationaltrust.org.uk

■ **Location**
MAP 4:I5

OS Ref. TQ415 240

Midway between East
Grinstead and Lewes, 5m
NW of Uckfield on E side
of A275.

Bus: Please call Traveline
on 0871 200 22 33 or
log onto their website
traveline.org.uk

Rail: Uckfield (6 miles),
Haywards Heath (7 miles)

■ **Opening Times**
Garden
Open all year, please call
01825 790231 or log
onto our website for
details of times.

Parkland
Open all year, dawn to
dusk.

■ ***Admission**
For 2010 prices &
opening times, please
call 01825 790231 or
log onto our website.

Groups discount
available (15+
prebooked)

NT, RHS Individual
Members and Great
British Heritage Pass
holders Free.

Joint Ticket available
with Bluebell Railway.

■ **Special Events**
Event programme
throughout the year.

SHEFFIELD PARK GARDEN ❧

www.nationaltrust.org.uk/sheffieldpark

A magnificent 120 acre landscaped garden. The centrepiece of this internationally renowned garden, is the four lakes that mirror the unique planting and colour that each season brings. Displays of spring bulbs as the garden awakens, and a stunning exhibition of colour in May, of rhododendrons and the National Collection of Ghent Azaleas. Water lilies dress the lakes during the summer. Visitors to the garden during the summer months can enjoy a leisurely walk perhaps pausing to sit on a seat to enjoy the tranquil ambience. In the autumn the garden is transformed by trees planted specifically for their autumn colour including Nyssa sylvatica, Amelanchier and Acer palmatum.

These and other fine specimen trees, particularly North American varieties, produce displays of gold, orange and crimson. The garden is open throughout the year and has something for all, whether a quiet stroll or a family gathering, allowing the children to participate in the many activities offered.

Whilst visiting the garden, take time to have a walk across our new parkland, South Park. 265 acres of beautiful parkland offer the chance for tranquil walks amongst stunning views. Special Events run throughout the year – please telephone for details.

WCs.

By arrangement.

Guide dogs only

©NTPL/Andrew Butler

ALFRISTON CLERGY HOUSE ✤
THE TYE, ALFRISTON, POLEGATE, EAST SUSSEX BN26 5TL

Tel: 01323 870001 **Fax:** 01323 871318 **E-mail:** alfriston@nationaltrust.org.uk

Owner: The National Trust **Contact:** The Property Manager

Step back into the Middle Ages with a visit to this 14th century thatched Wealden 'Hall House'. Trace the history of this building which in 1896 was the first to be acquired by the National Trust. Discover what is used to make the floor in the Great Hall and visit the excellent shop. Explore the delightful cottage garden and savour the idyllic setting beside Alfriston's parish church, with stunning views across the meandering River Cuckmere. An intriguing variety of shops, pubs and restaurants in Alfriston village make this a wonderful day out.

Location: MAP 4:J6, OS Ref. TQ521 029. 4m NE of Seaford, just E of B2108.

Open: 27 Feb–1 Aug daily except Tue & Fri, 10.30am–5pm; 2 Aug–29 Aug daily except Tue, 10.30am–5pm; 30 Aug–31 Oct daily except Tue & Fri, 1 Nov–19 Dec daily except Tue & Fri 11am–4pm.

Admission: Adult £4.50, Child £2.30, Family (2+3) £11.30. Pre-booked groups £3.85. ⓘ No WCs. 🖻 🅿 Parking in village car parks.

ANNE OF CLEVES HOUSE
52 SOUTHOVER HIGH STREET, LEWES, SUSSEX BN7 1JA

www.sussexpast.co.uk/anneofcleves

Tel: 01273 474610 **Fax:** 01273 486990 **E-mail:** anne@sussexpast.co.uk

Owner: Sussex Past **Contact:** Gina Meyer

This lovely timber-framed house was once owned by Anne of Cleves. It now displays period furnishings, everyday domestic objects and tells the story of Lewes from 15th century to modern times, political revolutionary Tom Paine, the Lewes Bonfire traditions and the Wealden iron industry. The enclosed rear garden gives a feeling of stepping back into an earlier age.

Location: MAP 4:I5, OS198 Ref. TQ410 096. S of Lewes town centre, off A27/A275/A26.

Open: 2 Jan-28 Feb Sat 10am- 5pm, Sun 11am-5pm. 1 Mar-31 Oct: Tues-Thurs 10am-5pm, Sun, Mon & Bank Hols 11am-5pm, (Closed Fri & Sat). Open Sat 2 Oct, Tudor Day. 1 Nov-28 Feb 2011: as 2 Jan-28 Feb 2010 . Special opening for halfterms and holidays Mon 15 Feb-Fri 19 Feb, and Mon 25 Oct-Fri 29 Oct and Sun 19 Dec-Wed 22 Dec. Last admission 30 mins before closing time.

Admission: Adult £4.20, OAP/Student £3.70, Child £2.10, Family (2+2 or 1+4) £11.30, Disabled/carer £2.10. Groups (15+), Adult £3.80, OAP/Student £3.30, Child £1.90, Disabled/carer £1.90. Combined ticket with Lewes Castle, Adult £8.80, OAP/Student £7.60, Child £4.40, Family (2+2 or 1+4) £23.80, Disabled/carer £4.40. Groups (15+), Adult £7.60, OAP/Student £6.80, Child £3.80, Disabled/carer £3.80.

🖻 🖌 By arrangement. 🅿 Limited (on road). 🔳 🐾 Guide dogs only. 🔺 ❋ ▣

ARUNDEL CASTLE
See page 134 for full page entry.

ARUNDEL CATHEDRAL
Parsons Hill, Arundel, West Sussex BN18 9AY

Tel: 01903 882297 **Fax:** 01903 885335 **E-mail:** aruncath1@aol.com

Contact: Rev. Canon T. Madeley

French Gothic Cathedral, church of the RC Diocese of Arundel and Brighton built by Henry, 15th Duke of Norfolk and opened 1873.

Location: MAP 3:G6, OS Ref. TQ015 072. Above junction of A27 and A284.

Open: Summer: 9am–6pm. Winter: 9am–dusk. Mon, Tues, Wed, Fri, Sat: Mass 10am; Thurs: Mass 8.30am (at Convent of Poor Clares, Crossbush); Sat: Vigil Mass 6.15pm (at Convent of Poor Clares, Crossbush); Sun: Masses 9.30am and 11.15am. Shop open in the summer, Mon–Fri, 10am–4pm and after services and on special occasions and otherwise on request.

Admission: Free.

BATEMAN'S ✤
See page 135 for full page entry.

Arundel Castle

English Heritage Photo Library

1066 BATTLE OF HASTINGS, ABBEY AND BATTLEFIELD ⌗
BATTLE, SUSSEX TN33 0AD
www.english-heritage.org.uk/1066

Tel: 01424 775705 **E-mail:** customers@english-heritage.org.uk
Owner: English Heritage **Contact:** Visitor Operations Team
Visit the site of the 1066 Battle of Hastings. An inclusive interactive audio tour will lead you around the battlefield and to the exact spot where Harold fell. Explore the magnificent abbey ruins and gatehouse and enjoy our new visitor centre with interactive displays and auditorium.
Location: MAP 4:K5, OS Ref. TQ749 157. Top of Battle High Street. Turn off A2100 to Battle.

Open: 1 Apr–30 Sept: daily, 10am–6pm. 1 Oct–31 Mar: daily 10am–4pm. Closed 24–26 Dec & 1 Jan.
Admission: Adult £6.70, Child £3.40, Conc. £5.70, Family £16.80. English Heritage members Free. 15% discount for groups (11+). Opening times and prices are valid until 31st March 2010, after this date details are subject to change please see www.english-heritage.org.uk for the most up-to-date information.
ℹ WCs. ⬚ ♿ WCs. ⬛ Inclusive. **P** Charge payable. 🐕 On leads. ❋ ⬛

© English Heritage

Bayham Old Abbey

BAYHAM OLD ABBEY ⌗
Lamberhurst, Sussex TN3 8DE
Tel/Fax: 01892 890381 **E-mail:** customers@english-heritage.org.uk
www.english-heritage.org.uk/bayhamoldabbey
Owner: English Heritage **Contact:** Visitor Operations Team
These riverside ruins are of a house of 'white' canons, founded c.1208 and preserved in the 18th century, when its surroundings were landscaped to create its delightful setting. Rooms in the Georgian Gothick dower house are also open to visitors.
Location: MAP 4:K4, OS Ref. TQ650 365. 1¾m W of Lamberhurst off B2169.
Open: 1 Apr–30 Sept: daily, 11am–5pm. 1 Oct–31 Mar: Closed.
Admission: Adult £3.80, Child £1.90, Conc. £3.20. English Heritage Members Free. Group discount available. Opening times and prices are valid until 31st March 2010, after this date details are subject to change please see www.english-heritage.org.uk for the most up-to-date information.
⬚ ♿ **P** 🐕 On leads.

BIGNOR ROMAN VILLA
Bignor Lane, Bignor, Nr Pulborough, West Sussex RH20 1PH
Tel/Fax: 01798 869259 **E-mail:** t.r.tupper@farming.me.uk
Owner: Mr J R Tupper **Contact:** John & Del Smith – Curators
One of the largest villas to be open to the public in Great Britain, with some of the finest mosaics all in situ and all under cover, including Medusa, Venus & Cupid Gladiators and Ganymede. Discovered in 1811 and open to the public since 1814. See the longest mosaic on display in Great Britain at 24 metres. Walk on original floors dating back to circa 350 AD. We have a small café and picnic area available.
Location: MAP 3:G5, OS Ref. SU987 146. 6m N of Arundel, 6m S of Pulborough A29. 7m S of Petworth A285.
Open: Mar & Apr: Tue–Sun & BHs, 10am–5pm; May & Oct: daily, 10am–5pm. Jun–Sept: daily, 10am–6pm.
Admission: Adult £4.60, Child £2, OAP £3.30. Groups (10+): Adult £3.70, Child £1.60, OAP £2.60. Guided tours (max 30 per tour) £30.
⬚ ♿ Partial. ⬛ 𝓘 By arrangement. **P** 🐕 ✗

Camber Castle

BOXGROVE PRIORY ⬢

Boxgrove, Chichester, West Sussex PO18
Tel: 01424 775705   **E-mail:** customers@english-heritage.org.uk
www.english-heritage.org.uk/boxgrove
Owner: English Heritage   **Contact:** 1066 Battle Abbey
Remains of the Guest House, Chapter House and Church of this 12th-century priory, which was the cell of a French abbey until Richard II confirmed its independence in 1383.
Location: MAP 3:G6, OS Ref. SU908 076. N of Boxgrove, 4 miles E of Chichester on minor road N of A27.
Open: Any reasonable time.
Admission: Free. Opening times and prices are valid until 31st March 2010, after this date details are subject to change please see www.english-heritage.org.uk for the most up-to-date information.

🅿 ✖ ✤

BRAMBER CASTLE ⬢

Bramber, Sussex BN44
Tel: 01424 775705   **E-mail:** customers@english-heritage.org.uk
www.english-heritage.org.uk/bramber
Owner: English Heritage   **Contact:** 1066 Battle Abbey
The remains of a Norman castle gatehouse, walls and earthworks in a splendid setting overlooking the Adur Valley.
Location: MAP 3:H5, OS Ref. TQ185 107. On W side of Bramber village NE of A283.
Open: Any reasonable time.
Admission: Free. Opening times and prices are valid until 31st March 2010, after this date details are subject to change please see www.english-heritage.org.uk for the most up-to-date information.

🅿 🐕 On leads. ✤

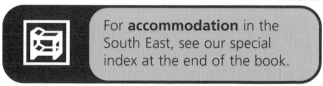

For **accommodation** in the South East, see our special index at the end of the book.

CAMBER CASTLE ⬢

Camber, Nr Rye, East Sussex TN31 7RS
Tel: 01797 223862   **E-mail:** customers@english-heritage.org.uk
www.english-heritage.org.uk/camber
Owner: English Heritage   **Contact:** Rye Harbour Nature Reserve
A fine example of one of many coastal fortresses built by Henry VIII to counter the threat of invasion during the 16th century. Monthly guided walks of Rye Nature Reserve including Camber Castle: telephone for details.
Location: MAP 4:L5, OS189, Ref. TQ922 185. Across fields off A259, 1 mile S of Rye off harbour road.
Open: 1 Jul–30 Sep: Sat & Sun, 2–5pm (plus BH weekends Apr–Sep). Last entry 4.30pm. Opening times subject to change.
Admission: Adult £2, Accompanied children Free, Conc. £1. Friends of Rye Harbour Nature Reserve & EH Members Free. Group discount available. Opening times and prices are valid until 31st March 2010, after this date details are subject to change please see www.english-heritage.org.uk for the most up-to-date information.
♿ ⓘ By arrangement. 🐕 Guide dogs only.

CHARLESTON

See page 136 for full page entry.

Arundel Castle

CHICHESTER CATHEDRAL
CHICHESTER, W SUSSEX PO19 1RP

www.chichestercathedral.org.uk

Tel: 01243 782595 **Fax:** 01243 812499 **E-mail:** visitors@chichestercathedral.org.uk
Contact: Visitor Services Officer
In the heart of Chichester, this magnificent 900 year old Cathedral has treasures ranging from medieval stone carvings to world famous 20th century artworks. Open every day and all year with free entry. Free guided tours and special trails for children. Regular exhibitions, free weekly lunchtime concerts and a superb Cloisters Restaurant and Shop. A fascinating place to visit.
Location: MAP 3:F6, OS Ref. SU860 047. West Street, Chichester.
Open: Summer: 7.15am–7.00pm, Winter: 7.15am–6.00pm. All are welcome. Choral Evensong daily (except Wed) during term time.
Admission: Free entry. Donations greatly appreciated.
🔲 🇹 Private functions and conferences. 🔲 🍽 🎦 ✳

COWDRAY
RIVER GROUND STABLES, MIDHURST, W SUSSEX GU29 9AL

www.cowdray.org.uk

Tel: 01730 810781 **E-mail:** info@cowdray.org.uk
Owner: Cowdray Heritage Trust **Contact:** The Manager
As a major new attraction, Cowdray is one of the most important survivals of a Tudor nobleman's house. Set within the stunning landscape of Cowdray Park, the house was partially destroyed by fire in 1793. Explore the Tudor Kitchens, Buck Hall, Chapel, Gatehouse, Vaulted Storeroom and Cellars, Visitor Centre and Shop.
Location: MAP 3:F5, OS Ref. TQ891 216. E outskirts of Midhurst on A272.
Open: 17 Mar–31 Oct: Wed–Sun & BH Mons, 10.30am–4pm (last admission). Groups all year round by arrangement.
Admission: Adult £6, Child (over 5yrs) £3.50, Conc. £5.50, Family £14. 10% discount for groups (10+).
🔲 🦽 Partial. WCs. 🎦 By arrangement. 🔲 🅿 Nearby. 🔲 🐕 🐕

©David Dixon

CLINTON LODGE GARDEN
FLETCHING, E SUSSEX TN22 3ST

Tel/Fax: 01825 722952 **e-mail:** garden@clintonlodge.com
Owner/Contact: Lady Collum
Caroline house enlarged by the Earl of Sheffield for his daughter when she married Sir Henry Clinton, one of three generals at Waterloo. The 18th century façade is set in a tree lined lawn, flanked by a newly created canal and overlooking parkland. The 6 acre garden reflects periods of English gardening history and includes a knot garden, mediaeval style herb garden with camomile paths and turf seats, potager, wild flower garden, pre-Raphaelite inspired allée, pleached lime walks; garden of old roses, double blue, white and yellow herbaceous borders; orchard planted with crinums and many yew and beech hedges.
Location: MAP 4:I5, OS Ref. TQ428 238. In centre of village behind tall yew and holly hedge.
Open: 9 May; 6, 7, 14, 21, 27 Jun; 5, 26 Jul; 2, 9 Aug, 2–5.30pm.
Admission: NGS Days: £5. Private groups by arrangement £7.
ℹ WCs. 🦽🦽 Unsuitable. 🔲 🎦 By arrangement. 🅿 Limited. 🐕 Guide dogs only.

DENMANS GARDEN

Denmans Lane, Fontwell, West Sussex BN18 0SU
Tel: 01243 542808 **Fax:** 01243 544064 **E-mail:** denmans@denmans-garden.co.uk
www.denmans-garden.co.uk
Owner: John Brookes MBE & Michael Neve **Contact:** Mrs Claudia Murphy
A unique 20th century 4 acre garden designed for year round interest – through use of form, colour and texture – owned by John Brookes MBE, renowned garden designer and writer and Michael Neve. Beautiful plant centre, gift shop, garden shop and fully licensed multi award winning Garden Café.
Location: MAP 3:G6, OS197 Ref. SZ947 070. Off the A27 (westbound) between Chichester (6m) and Arundel (5m).
Open: Daily all year round. Garden: 9am–5pm. Plant centre: 9am–5pm. Café: 10am–5pm. Please check website for winter opening times.
Admission: Adult £4.95, Child (4–16) £3.95, OAP £4.75, Pre-booked groups (15+) £4.50. 2009 prices – please telephone or check website for current prices.
🦽 WC. 🍴 Licensed. 🍴 Licensed. Group menus on request. 🐕 Guide dogs only.

Cowdray

©Jeremy Whitaker

FIRLE PLACE 🏛

FIRLE, LEWES, EAST SUSSEX BN8 6LP

www.firleplace.co.uk

Tel: 01273 858307 (Enquiries) **Events:** 01273 858567

Fax: 01273 858188 **Restaurant:** 01273 858307 **E-mail:** gage@firleplace.co.uk

Owner: The Rt Hon Viscount Gage

Firle Place is the home of the Gage family and has been for over 500 years. Set at the foot of the Sussex Downs within its own parkland, this unique house originally Tudor, was built of Caen stone, possibly from a monastery dissolved by Sir John Gage, friend of Henry VIII. Remodelled in the 18th century it is similar in appearance to that of a French château. The house contains a magnificent collection of Old Master paintings, fine English and European furniture and an impressive collection of Sèvres porcelain collected mainly by the 3rd Earl Cowper from Panshanger House, Hertfordshire.

Events: The Great Tudor Hall can, on occasion, be used for private dinners, with drinks on the Terrace or in the Billiard Room. A private tour of the house can be arranged. Events are held in the Park and House during the year and wedding receptions can be held in the Park or Old Riding School. For all event enquiries, contact the Estate Office on 01273 858567.

Restaurant: Enjoy the licensed restaurant and tea terrace with views over the garden for luncheon and cream teas.

Location: MAP 4:J6, OS Ref. TQ473 071. 4m S of Lewes on A27 Brighton / Eastbourne Road.

Open: Easter & BH Sun/Mon. Jun–Sept: Wed, Thur, Sun & BHs, 2–4.30pm. Dates and times subject to change without prior notice. Last admission 4.15pm. Garden Open Days 24th and 25th April 2010

Admission: Adult £6.50, Child £3.50, Conc. £6.

ℹ No photography in house. 🖸 🕎 ♿ Ground floor & restaurant. 🍴 Licensed. 🍵 Tea Terrace. 🎦 Wed & Thur. 🅿 ♿ In grounds on leads. 🛡

FISHBOURNE ROMAN PALACE

SALTHILL ROAD, FISHBOURNE, CHICHESTER, SUSSEX PO19 3QR

www.sussexpast.co.uk/fishbourne

Tel: 01243 785859 **Fax:** 01243 539266 **E-mail:** adminfish@sussexpast.co.uk

Owner: Sussex Past **Contact:** Christine Medlock

The remains of a palatial Roman building constructed in the 1st century AD. View the stunning Roman mosaics and the replanted Roman garden. Visitors may join a tour of the Palace site as well as the popular Behind the Scenes Tour during which they are able to handle original artefacts and learn about their storage and conservation.

Location: MAP 3:F6, OS Ref. SU837 057. 1½m W of Chichester in Fishbourne village off A27/A259. 5 minutes walk from Fishbourne railway station.

Open: Open Weekends 3/4, 10/11, 17/18 & 24/25 Jan 2009, 19/20 Dec and open daily 31 Jan–15 Dec. 31 Jan–Feb: 10am–4pm, Mar–July & Sept–Oct:10am–5pm, August: 10am–6pm, Nov–14 Dec: Daily, 10am–4pm and weekends 3/4, 10/11, 17/18, 24/25 Jan 2010.

Admission: Adult £7.30, Student £6.50, Child £3.80, Conc £7.30, Family (2+2) £20.30. Groups (20+): Adult/Student/Conc £6.00, Child £3.00. (2009 prices).

🖸 ℹ ♿ 🛝 🎦 By arrangement. 🅿 ♿ Guide dogs only. 🌐 🛡

Herstmonceux Castle 'Folly'

GLYNDE PLACE 🏛
GLYNDE, Nr LEWES, EAST SUSSEX BN8 6SX

www.glynde.co.uk

Tel/Fax: 01273 858224 **E-mail:** info@glynde.co.uk
Owners: Viscount & Viscountess Hampden   **Contact:** The Estate Office
Glynde Place is a magnificent example of Elizabethan architecture commanding exceptionally fine views of the South Downs. Amongst the collections of 400 years of family living can be seen 17th and 18th century portraits of the Trevors, furniture, embroidery and silver.
Location: MAP 4:J5, OS Ref. TQ456 092. Sign posted off of A27, 4m SE of Lewes at top of village. Rail: Glynde is on the London/Eastbourne and Brighton/Eastbourne mainline railway.
Open: May–Aug: Weds, Suns & BHs, 2–5pm (last tour 4pm). Group bookings by appointment.
Admission: House & Garden: Adult £6, Child (under 12yrs) Free, Conc. £5. CPRE 2 for 1. Groups (25+) by appointment. **Special Events:** Glynde Food & Drink Festival. 🚌 ♿ Unsuitable.WCs. 📷 📹 Obligatory 🅿 Free. 🐕 Guide dogs only.🏨

HAMMERWOOD PARK
EAST GRINSTEAD, SUSSEX RH19 3QE

www.hammerwoodpark.com

Tel: 01342 850594   **Fax:** 01342 850864   **E-mail:** latrobe@mistral.co.uk
Owner/Contact: David Pinnegar
Built in 1792 as an Apollo's hunting lodge by Benjamin Latrobe, architect of the Capitol and the White House, Washington DC. Owned by Led Zepplin in the 1970s, rescued from dereliction in 1982. Teas in the Organ Room; copy of the Parthenon frieze; and a derelict dining room still shocks the unwary. Guided tours (said by many to be the most interesting in Sussex) by the family. Also summer concerts.
Location: MAP 4:J4, OS Ref. TQ442 390. 3½ m E of East Grinstead on A264 to Tunbridge Wells, 1m W of Holtye.
Open: 1 June–end Sept: Wed, Sat & BH Mon, 2–5pm. Guided tour starts 2.05pm. Private groups: Easter–Jun. Coaches strictly by appointment. Small groups any time throughout the year by appointment.
Admission: House & Park: Adult £6, Child £2. Private viewing by arrangement. ℹ️ Conferences. 🚌 📹 📷 Obligatory. 🍴 🛏 In grounds. 🏠 B&B. ❊ 🏨 €

GOODWOOD HOUSE 🏛   *See page 137 for full page entry.*

GREAT DIXTER HOUSE & GARDENS 🏛   *See page 138 for full page entry.*

For unique **Civil wedding** venues see our index at the end of the book.

GARDENS AND GROUNDS OF HERSTMONCEUX CASTLE
HAILSHAM, E SUSSEX BN27 1RN
www.herstmonceux-castle.com

Tel: 01323 833816   **Fax:** 01323 834499   **E-mail:** c_cullip@isc.queensu.ac.uk
Owner: Queen's University, Canada   **Contact:** C Cullip
This breathtaking 15th century moated Castle is set within 500 acres of parkland and gardens (including Elizabethan Garden) and is ideal for picnics and woodland walks. At Herstmonceux there is something for all the family.
Location: MAP 4:K5, OS Ref. TQ646 104. 2m S of Herstmonceux village (A271) by minor road. 10m WNW of Bexhill.
Open: 3 Apr–31 Oct: daily, 10am–6pm (last adm. 5pm). Closes 5pm from Oct.
Admission: Grounds & Gardens: Adults £6.00, Child under 15yrs & Students £3 (child under 5 Free), Conc. £4.95, Family £14. Group rates/bookings available.
ⓘ Visitor Centre. ▣ ▣ Limited for Castle Tour. ▣ ▣ ▣ ▣ On leads. ▣ ▣

David Sellman

HIGH BEECHES WOODLAND 🏠 & WATER GARDENS
HIGH BEECHES, HANDCROSS, SUSSEX RH17 6HQ
www.highbeeches.com

Tel: 01444 400589   **Fax:** 01444 401543   **E-mail:** gardens@highbeeches.com
Owner: High Beeches Gardens Conservation Trust (Reg. Charity)
Contact: Sarah Bray
Explore 27 acres of magically beautiful, peaceful woodland and water gardens. Daffodils, bluebells, azaleas, naturalised gentians and glorious autumn colours. Rippling streams, enchanting vistas. Four acres of natural wildflower meadows. Marked trails. Recommended by Christopher Lloyd. Enjoy lunches and teas in the tearoom and tea lawn in restored Victorian farm building.
Location: MAP 4:I4, OS Ref. TQ275 308. S side of B2110. 1m NE of Handcross.
Open: 20 Mar–31 Oct: daily except Weds, 1–5pm (last adm. 4.30pm). Coaches/guided tours anytime, by appointment only.
Admission: Adult £6.00, Child (under 14yrs) Free. Concession for groups (20+). Guided tours for groups £10pp.
▣ Partial. WCs Tearoom fully accessible. ▣ Licensed ⑪ Licensed. ▣ By arrangement ▣ Limited for coaches ▣ Guide dogs only ▣

HIGHDOWN GARDENS
Littlehampton Road, Goring-by-Sea, Worthing, Sussex BN12 6PE
Tel: 01903 501054
Owner: Worthing Borough Council   **Contact:** Parks and Foreshore Manager
Unique gardens in disused chalk pit, begun in 1909.
Location: MAP 3:H6, OS Ref. TQ098 040. 3m WNW of Worthing on N side of A259, just W of the Goring roundabout.
Open: 1 Apr–30 Sept: daily, 10am–6pm. 1 Oct–30 Nov: Mon–Fri, 10am–4.30pm. 1 Dec–31 Jan: Mon–Fri, 10am–4pm.
Admission: Free.

LEWES CASTLE & BARBICAN HOUSE MUSEUM
169 HIGH STREET, LEWES, SUSSEX BN7 1YE
www.sussexpast.co.uk/lewescastle

Tel: 01273 486290   **Fax:** 01273 486990   **E-mail:** lamo@sussexpast.co.uk
Owner: Sussex Past   **Contact:** Michelle Browning
Lewes's imposing Norman castle offers magnificent views across the town and surrounding downland. Barbican House, towered over by the Barbican Gate, is home to an interesting museum of local history and archaeology. A superb scale model of Victorian Lewes provides the centrepiece of a 25 minute audio-visual presentation telling the story of the county town of Sussex. Lewes Castle reopened to the public on 2nd June 2009, after completion of a million-pound restoration project.
Location: MAP 4:I5, OS198 Ref. TQ412 101. Lewes town centre off A27/A26/A275.
Open: Castle & Barbican Museum open daily: Tues-Sat, 10am-5.30pm, Sun, Mon & Bank Hols 11am-5.30pm, except for Friday 24-Sunday 26 December. Last admission to both 30 mins before closing time and Castle closes at dusk in winter.
Admission: Adult £6, Child £3, Conc. £5.40, Disabled/Carer £3 Family (2+2) (1+4) £16.20. Groups (15+): Adult £5.40, Child £2.70, Conc. £4.85, Disabled/Carer £2.70 Combined tickets with Anne of Cleves House: Adult £8.50, Child £4.25, Conc. £7.50, Disabled/Carer £4.25, Family (2+2) (1+4) £23.
▣ ▣ Unsuitable. ▣ By arrangement. ▣ ▣ Guide dogs only. ▣ ▣

© NTPL / Eric Crichton

Monk's House, Virginia Woolf

MARLIPINS MUSEUM

HIGH STREET, SHOREHAM-BY-SEA, SUSSEX BN43 5DA

www.sussexpast.co.uk/marlipins

Tel: 01273 462994 or 01323 441279 **E-mail:** marlipins@sussexpast.co.uk
Owner: Sussex Past **Contact:** James Thatcher

Once a Customs House, it now holds artefacts from the long history of the Shoreham area and the maritime past plus a collection of local archaeological material from prehistoric to medieval times. In the upstairs gallery are displays on the local silent film industry and transport. A new extension hosts temporary visiting shows, activities and talks.

Location: MAP 3:H6, OS198 Ref. TQ214 051. Shoreham town centre on A259, W of Brighton.

Open: 1 May–30 Oct: Tue–Sat, 10.30am–4.30pm. (Closed Sundays & Mondays).

Admission: Adult £3.50, Child FREE, Conc. £3. Groups (15+): Adult £3, Child £1.50, Conc. £2.50, Disabled/Carer £1.55.

⬜ ♿ WC. 🎦 By arrangement. 🅿 None. ▣ 🐕 Guide dogs only. ♨

MONK'S HOUSE 🌿

Rodmell, Lewes BN7 3HF
Tel: 01323 870001 (Property Office)
Owner: The National Trust **Contact:** Property Office

A small weather-boarded house, the home of Leonard and Virginia Woolf until Leonard's death in 1969.

Location: MAP 4:I6, OS Ref. TQ421 064. 4 m E of Lewes, off former A275 in Rodmell village, near church.

Open: 3 Apr–31 Oct: Weds & Sats, 2–5.30pm. Last admission 5pm. Groups by arrangement with tenant.

Admission: Adult £4.00, Child £2.00, Family £10.00, Groups £3.50.

NYMAN'S 🌿

See page 139 for full page entry.

PALLANT HOUSE GALLERY

9 North Pallant, Chichester, West Sussex. PO19 1TJ
Tel: 01243 774557
Owner: Pallant House Gallery Trust **Contact:** Reception

Museum of the Year 2007, Pallant House Gallery houses one of the best collections of modern British art in the world alongside an exciting programme of temporary exhibitions.

Location: MAP 3:F6, OS Ref. SU861 047. City centre, SE of the Cross.

Open: Tue–Sat: 10am–5pm (Thur: 10am–8pm. Sun & BH Mons: 12.30–5pm).

Admission: Adult £6.50, Child (6–15yrs): £2, Students £3.50. Unemployed/Friends/Under 5s Free, Family (2 + 4): £15. Tue & Thur: 5–8pm, half price.

MICHELHAM PRIORY 🏛

UPPER DICKER, HAILSHAM, SUSSEX BN27 3QS

www.sussexpast.co.uk/michelham

Tel: 01323 844224 **Fax:** 01323 844030 **E-mail:** adminmich@sussexpast.co.uk
Owner: Sussex Past **Contact:** Chris Tuckett

Enter through the 14th-century gatehouse and wander through beautiful gardens or tour the historic house. Furniture and artefacts trace the property's religious origins and its development over 800 years to a grand country house. Explore the medieval watermill, working forge, rope museum and dramatic Elizabethan Great Barn. Plenty of free parking, restaurant and gift shop plus special events.

Location: MAP 4:J5, OS Ref. TQ557 093. 8m NW of Eastbourne off A22/A27. 2m W of Hailsham.

Open: 1 Mar-1 Nov: Tues-Sun from 10.30am. Closed Mondays except Bank Holidays

and in August. Closing Times: Mar & Oct - 4.30pm, April-July & Sept, 5pm, August, 5.30pm. Christmas Fair 5pm.

Admission: Adult £6.80, Student/OAP £5.80, Child £3.60, Disabled/Carer £3.60, Family (2+2) £17.50. Groups (15+): Adult/Student/OAP £5.40, Child £3.15, Disabled/Carer £3.40.

Game Fair: Adult £8.00, Student/OAP £6.00, Child £5.00, Disabled/Carer £5.00, Family (2+2) £23.50. Groups (15+): Adult £6.00, Student/OAP £ 5.20, Child £3.50, Disabled/Carer £5.00.

⬜🎦🍴♿🛍▣ Licensed. 🎦 By arrangement. 🅿 Ample for cars & coaches. ▣ 🐕 Guide dogs only. ⬆♨

PARHAM HOUSE & GARDENS 🏛
PARHAM PARK, STORRINGTON, Nr PULBOROUGH, WEST SUSSEX RH20 4HS
www.parhaminsussex.co.uk

Tel: 01903 742021 **Info Line:** 01903 744888 **Fax:** 01903 746557
Email: enquiries@parhaminsussex.co.uk
Owner: Parham Park Trust **Contact:** Richard Pailthorpe

One of the top twenty in Simon Jenkins's book *"England's Thousand Best Houses"*, Parham is one of the country's finest Elizabethan examples. Idyllically set in the heart of a 17th century deer park, below the South Downs, the house contains a particularly important collection of needlework, paintings and furniture. The spectacular Long Gallery is the third longest in England. The award winning gardens include a four acre walled garden with stunning herbaceous borders, greenhouse, orchard, potager and herbiary. All the flowers used in the house are home grown. Parham has always been a much-loved family home. Now owned by a charitable trust, the house is lived in by Lady Emma Barnard, her husband James and their family.

Location: MAP 3: G5, OS Ref. TQ060 143. Midway between Pulborough & Storrington on A283. Equidistant from A24 &A29.

Open: 4 Apr–30 Sept. House: Wed, Thur, Sun & BH Mons from 2–5pm, also Aug, Tue & Fri. Gardens: Tue, Wed, Thu, Fri, Sun and BH Mons from 12noon–5pm. Open Sundays in October

Admission: Please contact property for details.

ℹ No photography in house. ⬜⬜⬜ Partial. 🍴 Licensed. 🎫 By arrangement ⬜ 🅿 ⬜ ⬛ In grounds, on leads. ⬜ Special charges may apply. Please contact property for details.

PASHLEY MANOR GARDENS 🏛   *See page 140 for full page entry.*

PETWORTH COTTAGE MUSEUM

346 High Street, Petworth, West Sussex GU28 0AU
Tel: 01798 342100 **E-mail:** petworthcottagemuseum@yahoo.co.uk
www.petworthcottagemuseum.co.uk
Owner: Petworth Cottage Trust **Contact:** Curator

A Leconfield Estate Cottage as if it were 1910, when Mary Cummings lived here. A nostalgic and educational reconstruction that takes account of living memories, Mary's Irish Catholic background and her work as a seamstress. The range is lit, the tea table is laid, the kettle is boiling.

Location: MAP 3:G5
Open: Apr–Oct: Tue–Sat & BH Mons, 2–4.30pm.
Admission: Adult £2.50, Child (under 14yrs) 50p. Group visits by arrangement.
🎫

PETWORTH HOUSE & PARK 🌳   *See page 141 for full page entry.*

PEVENSEY CASTLE ⚑

Pevensey, Sussex BN24 5LE
Tel/Fax: 01323 762604 **E-mail:** customers@english-heritage.org.uk
www.english-heritage.org.uk/pevensey
Owner: English Heritage **Contact:** Visitor Operations Team

Originally a 4th-century Roman fort, Pevensey was where William the Conqueror landed in 1066 and established his first stronghold. The Norman castle includes remains of an unusual keep. An exhibition with artefacts found on site and an audio tour tells the story of the castle's 2,000 year history.

Location: MAP 4:K6, OS Ref. TQ645 048. In Pevensey off A259.
Open: 1 Apr–30 Sep: daily, 10am–6pm. 1 Oct–1 Nov, daily: 10am–4pm. 2 Nov–31 Mar '10: Sat & Sun, 10am–4pm. Closed 24–26 Dec & 1 Jan
Admission: Adult £4.30, Child £2.20, Conc. £3.70. Family £10.80. 15% discount for groups of 11+. EH Members free. Opening times and prices are valid until 31st March 2010, after this date details are subject to change please see www.english-heritage.org.uk for the most up-to-date information.
ℹ WC. ⬜⬜⬜⬜ Inclusive. 🅿 ⬛ On leads. ⬜

THE PRIEST HOUSE
NORTH LANE, WEST HOATHLY, SUSSEX RH19 4PP
www.sussexpast.co.uk/priest house

Tel: 01342 810479 **E-mail:** priest@sussexpast.co.uk
Owner: Sussex Past **Contact:** Antony Smith

Once a yeoman farmer's cottage, the 15th century timber-framed house, sits in the picturesque Wealden village of West Hoathly. Standing in a traditional cottage garden, it now contains country furniture, ironwork, textiles and domestic objects displayed in period rooms. The garden includes borders of perennials, shrubs, wild flowers and herbs. Guided tours available.

Location: MAP 4:J4, OS187 Ref. TQ362 325. In triangle formed by Crawley, East Grinstead and Haywards Heath, 4m off A22, 6m off M23.
Open: 1 Mar–31 Oct: Tue–Sat, 10.30am–5.30pm, Sun 12pm–5.30pm. Open on Bank Holiday Mondays and Mondays in August 10.30am–5.30pm.
Admission: Adult £3.50, Child £1.75, Conc. £3. Disabled/Carer £1.75. Garden only £1. Groups (15+) Adult £3.10, Child £1.55, Conc. £2.60. Disabled/Carer £1.55.
⬜⬜⬜ Partial. 🎫 By arrangement. 🅿 Limited (on street). ⬛⬛ In grounds, on leads.

Parham, Long Gallery

Michelham Priory

SACKVILLE COLLEGE

HIGH STREET, EAST GRINSTEAD, WEST SUSSEX RH19 3BX

www.sackvillecollege.co.uk

Tel: 01342 323414 **E-mail:** sackvillecollege@talktalkbusiness.net
Owner: Board of Trustees **Contact:** College Co-ordinator
Built in 1609 for Richard Sackville, Earl of Dorset, as an almshouse and overnight accommodation for the Sackville family. Feel the Jacobean period come alive in the enchanting quadrangle, the chapel, banqueting hall with fine hammerbeam roof and minstrel's gallery, the old common room and warden's study where "Good King Wenceslas" was composed. Chapel weddings by arrangement.
Location: MAP 4:I4, A22 to East Grinstead, College in High Street (town centre).
Open: 9 Jun–12 Sept: Wed–Sun, 2–5pm. Groups all year by arrangement.
Admission: Adult £3.50, Child £1. Groups: (10–60) no discount.
[i] Large public car park adjacent to entrance. 🖻 🔊 📶 🔽 Partial. 🖷
🅇 Obligatory. 🅿 Limited. 🔲 🔊 Guide dogs only. ⊛ By arrangement. ♿

SAINT HILL MANOR
SAINT HILL ROAD, EAST GRINSTEAD, WEST SUSSEX RH19 4JY

www.sainthillmanor.org.uk

Tel: 01342 326711 **Fax:** 01342 317057 **E-mail:** info@ hubbardfoundation.co.uk

Owner: Church of Scientology **Contact:** Liz Ostermann Saint Hill Manor

Built in 1792 by Gibbs Crawfurd, Saint Hill Manor is one of Sussex's finest sandstone buildings, with breathtaking views of unspoiled countryside. Impressive features include the magnificent black Spanish marble pillars added by the Maharajah of Jaipur, and the delightful 100-foot Monkey Mural, painted by Winston Churchill's nephew.

The final owner, author L Ron Hubbard, bought the Manor in 1959 and made it his family home, restoring much of the oak panelling and marble fireplaces. An impressive

collection of Mr. Hubbard's 590 published works is displayed in the library. There are 59 acres of grounds, lake and rose garden. Ideal for weddings and conferences.

Location: MAP 4:14, OS Ref. TQ383 359. 2 miles S of East Grinstead.

Open: All year. Guided tours of the house every afternoon 2–5 pm on the hour. Open in morning by arrangement. Gardens open all day.

Admission: Free of charge. Coach parties welcome, teas served.

Teas available. Obligatory. Group Visits Fair: Date TBC. Annual Open Air Theatre: Sunday 13 June, "The Importance of Being Earnest". Please phone for details.

ST MARY'S HOUSE & GARDENS
BRAMBER, WEST SUSSEX BN44 3WE

www.stmarysbramber.co.uk

Tel/Fax: 01903 816205 **E-mail:** info@stmarysbramber.co.uk

Owners: Mr Peter Thorogood MBE and Mr Roger Linton MBE

Features in Simon Jenkins' book *'England's Thousand Best Houses'*. St. Mary's is an enchanting, medieval timber-framed house, with fine panelled interiors, including the unique Elizabethan 'Painted Room', giving an air of tranquillity and timelessness. Interesting displays of family memorabilia and rare Napoleonic collection. The formal gardens with amusing topiary, include an exceptional example of the prehistoric *Ginkgo Biloba*, magnificent *Magnolia Grandiflora* and mysterious ivy-clad Monks' Walk.

The five acres of grounds include the Victorian 'Secret' Garden with original fruit wall and pineapple pits, Rural Museum, Jubilee Rose Garden, Terracotta Garden, Woodland Walk and newly-established Poetry Garden. In the heart

of the South Downs National Park, St. Mary's is a house of fascination and mystery, with picturesque charm and atmosphere of friendliness and welcome.

Location: MAP 3:H6, OS Ref. TQ189 105. Bramber village off A283. From London 56m via M23/A23 or A24. Bus from Shoreham to Steyning, alight St Mary's, Bramber.

Open: May–end Sept: Suns, Thurs & BH Mons, 2–6pm. Last entry 5pm. Groups at other times by arrangement.

Admission: House & Gardens: Adult £7.00, Conc. £6.50, Child £3. Groups (25+) £6.50.

No photography in house. Partial. Obligatory for groups (max 60). Visit time 2½hrs. 30 cars, 2 coaches.

SHEFFIELD PARK GARDEN ❧   *See page 142 for full page entry.*

©NTPL/John Miller

STANDEN ❧
EAST GRINSTEAD, WEST SUSSEX RH19 4NE

www.nationaltrust.org.uk/standen

Tel: 01342 323029   **Fax:** 01342 316424   **E-mail:** standen@nationaltrust.org.uk
Owner: The National Trust   **Contact:** The Property Manager

A late Victorian family home is brought vividly to life in this gem of the Arts & Crafts Movement. The House contains original furnishings by Morris & Co. and a nationally important Arts & Crafts collection, including works by De Morgan, Benson and Rossetti. The beautiful hillside Gardens offer year round interest, stunning views and woodland walks.

Location: MAP 4:I4, OS Ref. TQ389 356. 2m S of East Grinstead, signposted from B2110.

Open: House, Garden, Shop & Restaurant: 27 Feb–7 Mar: Sats & Suns, 11am–4.30pm. 13 Mar–31 Oct: Wed–Sun & BHs, 11am–4.30pm (last entry to house 4pm). Also Mons 5 Apr–18 Apr, 26 Jul–30 Aug and 25 Oct–31 Oct. 6 Nov–19 Dec: Sat & Sun, 11am–3pm (last entry to house 2.30pm).

*Admission: House & Garden: Adult £8.60, Child £4.30, Family £21.50. Garden only: Adult £5.20, Child £2.60, Family £13.00. Groups £7.30 only if booked in advance. *Includes a voluntary donation but visitors can choose to pay the standard prices displayed at the property or on the website.

🖾 ⬆ ♿ WCs. 🍴 Licensed 🍴 Licensed. 🅿 ♨ 🐕 In designated areas. ♿

© NTPL / Nadia Mackenzie

Uppark

STANSTED PARK 🏛
STANSTED PARK, ROWLANDS CASTLE, HAMPSHIRE PO9 6DX

www.stanstedpark.co.uk

Tel: 023 9241 2265   **Fax:** 023 9241 3773   **E-mail:** enquiry@stanstedpark.co.uk
Owner: Stansted Park Foundation   **Contact:** House and Events Manager

'One of the South's most beautiful stately homes'. The State Rooms and fully restored Servants' Quarters of Stansted House give the visitor a fascinating insight into the social history of an English Country House in its heyday in Edwardian times.

Location: MAP 3:F5, OS Ref. SU761 103. Follow brown heritage signs from A3 Rowlands Castle or A27 Havant. Rail: Mainline station, Havant.

Open: House & Chapel: Sun & BH from Easter Sun–end Sept: 1–4pm, June, Jul & Aug: Sun–Wed 1–4pm. Tea Room & Garden Centre open all year. Restricted access to grounds on Sats and during events. Stansted Park Light Railway runs through Arboretum. Tel: 02392 413324 for timetable.

Admission: House & Chapel: Adult £7, Child (5–15yrs) £3.50, Conc. £6, Family (2+3) £18. Groups/educational visits by arrangement other days.

⬆ 🍴 Private & corporate hire. 🖾 ⬛ 🐕 By arrangement. 🅿 ♨ By arrangement. 🐕 Guide dogs only. ⬆♿ Grounds. ♿

UPPARK HOUSE AND GARDEN ❧
SOUTH HARTING, PETERSFIELD GU31 5QR

www.nationaltrust.org.uk/uppark

NT/Raymond Woodham

Tel: 01730 825415   **Fax:** 01730 825873   **E-mail:** uppark@nationaltrust.org.uk
Owner: The National Trust   **Contact:** Administrator

Marvel at the historic elegance of Uppark – with fine, late-Georgian interiors and collections of paintings, ceramics and textiles, extensive basement rooms, famous dolls house, Regency garden (stunning views to the sea), children's activities, shop and restaurant – there is everything for a perfect day out.

Location: MAP 3:F5, OS Ref 197 SU781 181. Between Petersfield & Chichester on B2146.

Open: 21 Mar–31 Oct: Sun–Thur; Grounds, Shop & Restaurant: 11.30am–5pm; House: 12.30–4.30pm. BH Suns, Mons & Good Friday, 11.30am–4.30pm. Print Room open 1st Mon of each Month.

*Admission: Adult £8.40, Child £4.20, Family £21, Groups (15+) must book: £7.40.

*includes a voluntary donation but visitors can choose to pay the standard prices displayed at the property and on the website.

🖾 ⬆ ♿ WCs 🍴 Licensed 🐕 By arrangement. 🅿 🐕 Guide dogs only ♿

WEST DEAN GARDENS 🏛

WEST DEAN, CHICHESTER, WEST SUSSEX PO18 0QZ

www.westdean.org.uk

Tel: 01243 818210 **Fax:** 01243 811342 **E-mail:** gardens@westdean.org.uk

Owner: The Edward James Foundation **Contact:** Jim Buckland, Gardens Manager

West Dean Gardens, nestling in the South Downs National Park, is a place of tranquillity and beauty. Its features include a restored walled kitchen garden with some of the finest Victorian glasshouses in the country, rustic summerhouses, a 300ft Edwardian pergola, ornamental borders and a pond contrast with over 200 varieties of carefully trained fruit trees, rows of vegetables and exotic produce behind glass. For the more active a 21/2 mile circular walk offers breathtaking views of the estate and its fine flint house and parkland setting.

Location: MAP 3:F5, OS Ref. SU863 128. SE of A286 Midhurst Road, 6m N of Chichester, 7m S of Midhurst.

Open: Mar–Oct: daily, 10.30am–5pm (last adm 4.30pm). Feb & Nov–Mar 2011: daily, 10.30am–4pm. Closed Jan 2011.

Admission: Summer: Adult £7.50, Over 60s £7, Child £3.50, Family £18, Groups: Adult £7, Over 60s £6.50. Winter: Adult £4.75, Over 60s £4.25; Child £2.25, Family (2 Adults & 2 Children 5–15) £11.50, Groups: Adult £3.75, Over 60s £3.50. Yearly Friends Memberships: Single £27.50; Single and Guest £55; Family £60. The Chilli Fiesta garden event will incur a supplementary charge.

🖼 🚻 🍴 ♿ ☕ 🍽 Licensed. **P** Limited for coaches. 🎓 By arrangement. 🚗 🦮 Guide dogs only. 🌸 💶

Wilmington Priory.

WILMINGTON PRIORY

Wilmington, Nr Eastbourne, East Sussex BN26 5SW

Tel: 01628 825925 **E-mail:** bookings@landmarktrust.org.uk

www.landmarktrust.org.uk

Owner: Leased to the Landmark Trust by Sussex Archaeological Society

Contact: The Landmark Trust

Founded by the Benedictines in the 11th century, the surviving, much altered buildings date largely from the 14th century. Managed and maintained by the Landmark Trust, which lets buildings for self-catering holidays. Full details of Wilmington Priory and 189 other historic and architecturally important buildings available for holidays are featured in The Landmark Trust Handbook (price £10 plus p&p refundable against a booking) and on the website.

Location: MAP 3:F5, OS Ref. TQ543 042. 600yds S of A27. 6m NW of Eastbourne.

Open: Available for self-catering holidays for up to 6 people throughout the year. Grounds, Ruins, Porch & Crypt: on 30 days between Apr–Oct. Whole property including interiors on 8 of these days. Other visits by appointment. Contact the Landmark Trust for details.

Admission: Free entry on Open Days.

🏛

Stansted Park 'Library'

■ Owner
English Heritage

■ Contact
The House Administrator
Osborne House
Royal Apartments
East Cowes
Isle of Wight
PO32 6JX

Tel: 01983 200022
Fax: 01983 281380
E-mail: customers@
english-heritage.org.uk

Venue Hire and
Hospitality:
Tel: 01983 203055

■ Location
MAP 3:D6
OS Ref. SZ516 948

1 mile SE of East Cowes.

Ferry: Isle of Wight
ferry terminals.

Red Funnel, East Cowes
1½ miles
Tel: 02380 334010.

Wightlink, Fishbourne
4 miles
Tel: 0870 582 7744

■ Opening Times
1 April–30 September
Daily: 10am–6pm (House
closes 5pm, may close
early for special events on
occasional days in July &
August).
Last admission 4pm.

1 October–1 November
Daily: 10am–4pm.

4 Nov–31 March 2010,
Wed–Sun: 10am–4pm
(pre-booked guided tours
only. Last tour 2.30pm.
Christmas tour season 18
Nov–3 Jan). Pre-booking
essential on 01983
200022.

Closed 24–26 December
& 1 January.

■ Admission
House & Grounds
Adult	£10.20
Child (5–15yrs)	£5.10
Child under 5yrs	Free
Conc.	£8.70
Family (2+3)	£25.50

Grounds only
Adult	£8.40
Child (5–15yrs)	£4.20
Child under 5yrs	Free
Conc.	£7.20
Family (2+3)	£21.00

EH members free.

Groups (11+) 15%
discount. Tour leader and
driver have free entry.
1 extra free place for
every additional 20
paying.

Conference/Function
ROOM	MAX CAPACITY
Durbar Hall	standing 80 seated 50
Upper Terrace	standing 250
Walled Gardens	standing 100
Marquee	Large scale events possible

© English Heritage

OSBORNE HOUSE ⌗

www.english-heritage.org.uk/osborne

Osborne House was the peaceful, rural retreat of Queen Victoria, Prince Albert and their family; they spent some of their happiest times here.

Step inside and marvel at the richness of the State Apartments including the Durbar Room with its lavish Indian décor. The Queen died at the house in 1901 and many of the rooms have been preserved almost unaltered ever since. The nursery bedroom remains just as it was in the 1870s when Queen Victoria's first grandchildren came to stay. Children were a constant feature of life at Osborne (Victoria and Albert had nine). Don't miss the Swiss Cottage, a charming chalet in the grounds built for teaching the royal children domestic skills.

Enjoy the beautiful gardens with their stunning views over the Solent and the fruit and flower Victorian Walled Garden.

© English Heritage

ℹ️ WCs. Suitable for filming, concerts, drama. No photography in the House. Children's play area.

🛍️

🍽️ Private and corporate hire.

♿ Wheelchairs available, access to house via ramp and first floor via lift. WC.

☕

🍴 Hot drinks, light snacks & waiter service lunches in the stunning terrace restaurant.

🚶 Open from Nov–Mar for pre-booked guided tours only. These popular tours allow visitors to see the Royal Apartments and private rooms at a quieter time of the year, and in the company of one of our expert guides.

🅿️ Ample.

📖 Visits free, please book. Education room available.

❄️

🎭

Opening times and prices are valid until 31st March 2010, after this date details are subject to change please see www.english-heritage.org.uk for the most up-to-date information.

©English Heritage

APPULDURCOMBE HOUSE ⌗

Wroxall, Shanklin, Isle of Wight PO38 3EW
Tel: 01983 852484 **E-mail:** customers@english-heritage.org.uk
www.english-heritage.org.uk/appuldurcombehouse
Owner: English Heritage **Contact:** Mr & Mrs Owen

The bleached shell of a fine 18th-century Baroque style house standing in grounds landscaped by 'Capability' Brown. Once the grandest house on the Isle of Wight. An exhibition of photographs and prints depict the house and its history.

Location: MAP 3:D7, OS Ref. SZ543 800. ½mile W of Wroxall off B3327.

Open: 22 Mar–30 Sept: Sun–Fri, 10am–4pm; Sat, 10am–12pm. Last entry 1hr before closing. 1 Oct–31 Mar, Closed.

Admission: House: Adult £3.50, Child £2.50, Conc. £3.25, Family £12. EH members Free. Additional charge for the Falconry Centre. Group discount available. Opening times and prices are valid until 31st March 2010, after this date details are subject to change please see www.english-heritage.org.uk for the most up-to-date information.

▣ ⬛ ▣ ⬛ In grounds, on leads. ⬛

Appuldurcombe House

BEMBRIDGE WINDMILL ⬛

High Street, Bembridge, Isle of Wight PO35 5SQ
Correspondence to: NT Office, Strawberry Lane, Mottistone,
Isle of Wight PO30 4EA
Tel: 01983 873945 **www.nationaltrust.org.uk/isleofwight**
Owner: The National Trust **Contact:** The Custodian

Dating from around 1700, this is the only surviving windmill on the island and contains most of its original machinery. Four floors to explore plus small replica working model.

Location: MAP 3:E7, OS Ref. SZ639 874. ½m S of Bembridge off B3395.

Open: 13 Mar–31 Oct, daily, 11am–5pm.

*Admission: Adult £3, Child £1.50, Family £7.45. * includes a voluntary 10% donation but visitors can choose to pay the standard prices displayed at the property and on the website. Free to NT members. All school groups are conducted by a NT guide; special charges apply.

▣ ⬛ ⬛ By arrangement. ▣ 100 yds. ⬛ ⬛ Guide dogs only.

BRIGHSTONE SHOP & MUSEUM ⬛

North St, Brighstone, Isle of Wight PO30 4AX
Tel: 01983 740689 **www.nationaltrust.org.uk/isleofwight**
Owner: The National Trust **Contact:** The Manager

The traditional cottages contain a National Trust shop and Village Museum (run by Brighstone Museum Trust) depicting village life in the late 19th century.

Location: MAP 3:D7, OS Ref. SZ428 828. North Street, Brighstone, just off B3399.

Open: 2 Jan–1 Apr, Mon–Sat, 10am–1pm; 2 Apr–28 May, Mon–Sat, 10am–4pm; 29 May–25 Sept, Mon–Sat, 10am–5pm; 30 May–26 Sept, Sun, 12noon–5pm; 27 Sept–23 Dec, Mon–Sat, 10am–4pm.

Admission: Free.

⬛ Partial. ⬛

© English Heritage

CARISBROOKE CASTLE ⌗

NEWPORT, ISLE OF WIGHT PO30 1XY

www.english-heritage.org.uk/carisbrooke

Tel: 01983 522107 **E-mail:** customers@english-heritage.org.uk
Owner: English Heritage **Contact:** Visitor Operations Team

The island's royal fortress and prison of King Charles I before his execution in London in 1648. See the famous Carisbrooke donkeys treading the wheel in the Well House as donkeys would have done in the 18th century. Visit the on-site Carisbrooke Museum and take an invigorating battlements walk. Enjoy a fascinating presentation reflecting 800 years of colourful history at the castle, brought to life using dramatic film and interactive exhibits. Don't miss the new Edwardian-style Princess Beatrice Garden, designed by TV and radio gardening presenter Chris Beardshaw.

Location: MAP 3:E7, OS196 Ref. SZ486 877. Off the B3401, 1¼ miles SW of Newport.

Open: 1 Apr–30 Sept: daily, 10am–5pm. 1 Oct–31 Mar 2010: daily, 10am–4pm. Closed 24–26 Dec & 1 Jan.

Admission: Adult £6.70, Child £3.40, Conc. £5.70, Family (2+3) £16.80. 15% discount for groups (11+). EH Members Free. Opening times and prices are valid until 31st March 2010, after this date details are subject to change please see www.english-heritage.org.uk for the most up-to-date information.

ℹ WCs. ▣ ⬛ ⬛ Partial. WCs. ⬛ ⬛ ▣ ⬛ ⬛ Guide dogs only. ⬛ ⬛ Tel. for details.

ISLE OF WIGHT

MORTON MANOR

Brading, Isle of Wight PO36 0EP

Tel/Fax: 01983 406168   **E-mail:** mortonmanor-iow@amserve.com

Owner/Contact: Mr J A J Trzebski

Refurbished in the Georgian period. Magnificent gardens, vineyard and maize maze.

Location: MAP 3:E7, OS Ref. SZ603 863 (approx.). ¼m W of A3055 in Brading.

Open: Easter–end Oct: daily except Sats, 10am–5.30pm. Last admission 4.30pm.

Admission: Adult £5, Child £2.50, Conc. £4.50, Group (10+) £4.25.

MOTTISTONE MANOR GARDEN ✤

Mottistone, Isle of Wight PO30 4ED

Tel: 01983 741302   **Fax:** 01983 741154   **Email:** isleofwight@nationaltrust.org.uk

Web: www.nationaltrust.org.uk/isleofwight

Owner: The National Trust   **Contact:** The Gardener

Set in a sheltered valley this magical garden is full of surprises with shrub filled banks, hidden pathways and colourful herbaceous borders. Surrounding an Elizabethan manor house (not open) this 20th century garden is experimenting with a Mediterranean-style planting scheme to take advantage of its southerly location.

Location: MAP 3:D7, OS Ref. SZ406 838. Car: Between Brighstone & Brook on B3399.

Open: 14 March–28 October 2010: Sun–Thur, 11am–5pm. House: 31 May (BH) only: 2–5pm. Guided tours for NT members on that day 9.30am–12 noon by timed ticket available from visitor reception (advance booking not possible). Late night opening: garden open until 9pm on Wed 23 June.

***Admission:** Garden: Adult £4, Child £2, Family £9.90. Free to NT members. Extra charge for house. *Includes a voluntary 10% donation but visitors can choose to pay the standard prices displayed at the property and on the website.

▣ ▣ ♿ Partial. WCs ♨ ♒ By arrangement. Ⓟ 🚍 In grounds, on leads.

NEEDLES OLD BATTERY & NEW BATTERY ✤

Alum Bay, Totland, Isle of Wight PO39 0JH

Tel: 01983 754772   **Fax:** 01983 741154   **Email:** isleofwight@nationaltrust.org.uk

Web: www.nationaltrust.org.uk/isleofwight

Owner: The National Trust   **Contact:** The Fort Manager

Built in 1862 this spectacularly sited cliff top fort overlooking the Needles contains exhibitions about its involvement in both World Wars. Two original gun barrels are displayed on the parade ground and a tunnel leads to a searchlight emplacement perched above the Needles Rocks. Rocket exhibition at Needles New Battery.

Location: MAP 3:C7, OS Ref. SZ300 848. Needles Headland W of Alum Bay (B3322) Bus: Needles Tour Bus from Yarmouth or Alum Bay.

Open: Needles Old Battery: 13 Mar–31 Oct every day, 10.30am–5pm. Needles New Battery: 13 Mar–31 Oct, Sat, Sun & Tues, 11am–4pm. Closes in high winds; please telephone on day of visit to check.

***Admission:** Adult £4.85, Child £2.45, Family £12.10. Free to NT members. Needles New Battery: Free. *Includes a voluntary 10% donation but visitors can choose to pay the standard prices displayed at the property and on the website.

ⓘ No vehicular access. For disabled access please phone 01983 754772. ▣ ♿ WCs ♨ ♒ By appointment. 🔳 🚍

NEWTOWN OLD TOWN HALL ✤

Newtown, Isle of Wight PO30 4PA

Tel: 01983 531785   **Fax:** 01983 741154   **Email:** isleofwight@nationaltrust.org.uk

Web: www.nationaltrust.org.uk/isleofwight

Owner: The National Trust   **Contact:** The Custodian

The small, now tranquil village of Newtown once sent two members to Parliament and the Town Hall was the setting for often turbulent elections. This historic building contains an exhibition depicting the exploits of "Ferguson's Gang", a mysterious group of anonymous benefactors. Regular art exhibtions.

Location: MAP 3:D7, OS Ref. SZ424 905. Between Newport and Yarmouth, 1m N of A3054.

Open: 14 Mar–30 Jun, 1 Sept–20 Oct: Sun, Mon & Wed; 1 Jul–31 Aug: Sun–Thur, 2–5pm. Open Good Fri & Easter Sat.

Admission: Adult £2.20, Child £1.10, Family £5.50. Free to NT members.

♿ Partial. WCs ♨ By arrangement. Ⓟ No coaches. 🔳 🚍 Guide dogs only.

NUNWELL HOUSE & GARDENS

Coach Lane, Brading, Isle of Wight PO36 0JQ

Tel: 01983 407240

Owner: Col & Mrs J A Aylmer   **Contact:** Mrs J A Aylmer

Nunwell has been a family home for five centuries and reflects much architectural and Island history. King Charles I spent his last night of freedom here. Jacobean and Georgian wings. Finely furnished rooms. Lovely setting with Channel views and five acres of tranquil gardens including walled garden. Family military collections.

Location: MAP 3:E7, OS Ref. SZ595 874. 1m NW of Brading. 3m S of Ryde signed off A3055.

Open: 30/31 May & 5 Jul–8 Sept: Mon–Wed, 1–5pm. House tours: 2 & 3.30pm (extra tours when needed). Groups welcome by arrangement throughout the year.

Admission: Adult £5, Pair of Adults £9.50 (inc guide book), Child (under 10yrs) £1, OAP/Student £4.50. Garden only: Adult £3.

▣ ♨ Obligatory. Ⓟ 🚍 Guide dogs only. ✺

OSBORNE HOUSE ♯   *See page 156 for full page entry.*

YARMOUTH CASTLE ♯

Quay Street, Yarmouth, Isle of Wight PO41 0PB

Tel: 01983 760678   **E-mail:** customers@english-heritage.org.uk

www.english-heritage.org.uk/yarmouth

Owner: English Heritage   **Contact:** Visitor Operations Team

This last addition to Henry VIII's coastal defences was completed in 1547, unusually for its kind, square with a fine example of an angle bastion. Exhibition displays artefacts and an atmospheric recreation of how the rooms were used in the 16th century. Magnificent picnic spot, with views over the Solent.

Location: MAP 3:C7, OS Ref. SZ354 898. In Yarmouth adjacent to car ferry terminal.

Open: 1 Apr–30 Sep: Sun–Thu, 11am–4pm.

Admission: Adult £3.60, Child £1.80, Conc. £3.10. EH Members Free. Group discount available. Opening times and prices are valid until 31st March 2010, after this date details are subject to change please see www.english-heritage.org.uk for the most up-to-date information.

▣ ♿ Ⓟ 🚍 In grounds, on leads.

© NTPL / Martin Trelawny

Mottistone Manor Garden

Osborne House
©English Heritage
159

The Drawing Room, Hartland Abbey, Devon

South West

The moorlands of Devon and Cornwall are among the most dramatic in Britain, contrasting with the unspoilt beaches. The temperate climate means gardens (eg Abbotsbury Subtropical Gardens) can grow exotic plants that wouldn't survive in other parts of the country. Compare this with the bustling terraces of Georgian Bath, or the fascinating wildlife at Longleat in Wiltshire.

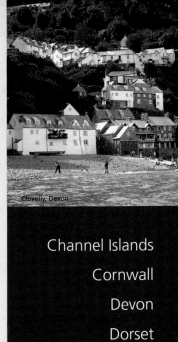
Clovelly, Devon

Channel Islands
Cornwall
Devon
Dorset
Gloucestershire
Somerset
Wiltshire

GLOCESTERSHIRE

WILTSHIRE

SOMERSET

DEVON

DORSET

CORNWALL

CHANNEL ISLANDS

Abbotsbury Subtropical Garden, Dorset

Blowinghouse Cottage Godolphin, Cornwall

Maze at Longleat, Wiltshire

■ Owner

The Seigneur de Sausmarez

■ Contact

Peter de Sausmarez
Sausmarez Manor
Guernsey
Channel Islands
GY4 6SG
Tel: 01481 235571/235655
Fax: 01481 235572
E-mail: sausmarezmanor @cwgsy.net

■ Location

Map 3:D10

2m S of St Peter Port, clearly signposted.

■ Opening Times

The Grounds:
Easter–End Oct
Daily: 10am–5pm

Guided tours of House
Easter–End Oct.
Mon–Thurs:
10.30 & 11.30am.
Additional 2pm tour during high season.

■ Admission

There is no overall charge for admission.

Sub Tropical Garden	£5.50
Sculpture Trail	£5.50
Pitch & Putt	£5.50
Putting	£2.00
House Tour	£7.00
Ghost Tour	£10.50
Train Rides	£2.00

Discounts for Children, Students, OAPs & Organised Groups.

SAUSMAREZ MANOR

www.sausmarezmanor.co.uk   www.artparks.co.uk

The home of the Seigneurs de Sausmarez since c1220 with a façade built at the bequest of the first Governor of New York.

An entrancing and entertaining half day encompassing something to interest everyone. The family have been explorers, inventors, diplomats, prelates, generals, admirals, privateers, politicians and governors etc, most of whom left their mark on the house, garden or the furniture.

The sub-tropical woodland garden is crammed with such exotics as banana trees, tree ferns, ginger, 300 plus camellias, lilies, myriads of bamboos, as well as the more commonplace hydrangeas, hostas etc. The RHS recommends the gardens to its own members.

The sculpture in the art park with its 200 or so pieces by artists from a dozen countries is the most comprehensive in Britain. The Little Green Island Gallery shows work by local and overseas artists and holds regular exhibitions. The pitch and put is a cruelly testing 500m 9 hole par 3. The Copper, Tin and Silversmith demonstrates his ancient skills in the large barn. The two lakes are a haven for ornamental wildfowl and some of the sculpture.

Sausmarez Manor is available for corporate hospitality functions and Civil weddings. It also offers guided tours, welcomes schools (has education programmes), and has a tearoom, café and gift shop.

There are concerts or plays on most Sunday afternoons in the summer and a Farmers' and Plantsmen's Market every Saturday morning.

Partial.

Guided tours of House Easter–Oct.

Two holiday flats are available see www.cottageguide.co.uk

NTPL/Andrew Butler

COTEHELE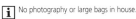

www.nationaltrust.org.uk

Cotehele, owned by the Edgcumbe family for nearly 600 years, is a fascinating and enchanting estate set on the steep wooded slopes of the River Tamar. Exploring Cotehele's many and various charms provides a full day out for the family and leaves everyone longing to return. The steep valley garden contains exotic and tender plants which thrive in the mild climate. Remnants of an earlier age include a medieval stewpond and domed dovecote, a 15th-century chapel and 18th-century tower with fine views over the surrounding countryside. A series of more formal gardens, terraces, an orchard and a daffodil meadow surround Cotehele House. One of the least altered medieval houses in the country, Cotehele is built in local granite, slate and sandstone. Inside the ancient rooms, unlit by electricity, is a fine collection of textiles,

tapestries, armour and early dark oak furniture. The chapel contains the oldest working domestic clock in England, still in its original position. A walk through the garden and along the river leads to the quay, a busy river port in Victorian times. A refurbished museum explains the vital role that the Tamar played in the local economy. As a living reminder, the restored Tamar sailing barge Shamrock is moored here. A further walk through woodland along the Morden stream leads to Cotehele Mill, a working water mill and workshops. This large estate with many footpaths offers a variety of woodland and countryside walks, opening up new views and hidden places. The Danescombe Valley, with its history of mining and milling, is of particular interest.

NTPL/Andrew Butler

ℹ️	No photography or large bags in house.
🛍️	National Trust shop, plant sales and gallery daily 13 Feb–24 Dec.
✽	
🍸	Available for up to 90 people.
♿	Partial. WCs.
🅿️	Licensed.
🍴	Licensed.
🚶	By arrangement.
🅿️	
🖼️	
🐕	Guide dogs only.
❄️	Tel for details of pre-Christmas opening of decorated hall.
🎭	

■ Owner
The National Trust

■ Contact
Charmian Saunders
General Manager
Cotehele
Saint Dominick
Saltash, Cornwall
PL12 6TA

Tel: 01579 351346
Fax: 01579 351222
E-mail:
cotehele@nationaltrust.
org.uk

■ Location
MAP 1:H8
OS Ref. SX422 685

1m SW of Calstock by foot. 8m S of Tavistock, 4m E of Callington, 15m from Plymouth via the Tamar bridge at Saltash.

Boats: Limited (tidal) service from Plymouth to Calstock Quay (Plymouth Boat Cruises).
Tel: 01752 822797

River ferry: Privately run from Calstock to Cotehele Quay.
Tel: 01822 833331

Buses: Western National (seasonal variations).
Tel: 01752 222666

Rail: Service from Plymouth to Calstock (1 1/4m uphill).

■ Opening Times
House
13 March–31 October:
Daily except Fridays (but open Good Friday),
11am– 4.30pm Last admission 30 mins before closing time.
Mill 13 March– 31 October: Daily 11am–5pm (4.30pm from 1 October).
Garden All year: Daily, 10am – dusk. Shop, Plant Sales, Restaurant, Tea Room & Gallery open from 13 March - 24 December.

■ *Admission
House, Garden & Mill
Adult	£9.60
Family	£24.00
1-Adult Family	£14.40
Pre-booked Groups	£8.20

Garden & Mill only
Adult	£5.20
Family	£13.00
1-Adult Family	£7.80

Groups must book in advance with the Property Office. No groups on BHS. NT members free. You may join here.
*includes a voluntary donation but visitors can choose to pay the standard prices displayed at the property and on the website.

Special Events: Hall of the House open until 24 December with unique garland

CORNWALL

■ Owner
The National Trust

■ Contact
General Manager
Lanhydrock
Bodmin
Cornwall PL30 5AD

Tel: 01208 265950
Fax: 01208 265959
E-mail: lanhydrock@
nationaltrust.org.uk

■ Location
MAP 1:F8
OS Ref. SX085 636

2½ m SE of Bodmin,
follow signposts from
either A30, A38 or
B3268.

■ Opening Times
House:
13 March – 31 October:
Daily except Mons (but
open BH Mons & Mons
during school holidays)
11am – 5.30pm. October:
11am – 5pm.
Last admission 1/2 hr
before closing.

Garden:
All year: Daily, 10am –
6pm. Charge levied from
13 February– 31 October.

Plant Sales:
Open as House

Shop & Refreshments:
2 January– 7 February: Sat
& Sun, 11am – 4pm.
13 February - 12 March:
Daily 11am – 4pm.
13 March - 30
September: Daily 11am –
5.30pm.
1 October – 31 October:
Daily, 11am – 5pm
1 November - 31
December: Daily 11am -
4pm (Closed 25,26
December)
Refreshments open
10.30am, 13 March - 31
October.

■ *Admission
**House, Garden &
Grounds**
Adult	£10.90
Child	£5.40
Family	£27.30
1-Adult Family	£16.40
Groups	£9.20

**Garden &
Grounds only** £6.40

*includes a voluntary
donation but visitors can
choose to pay the standard
prices displayed at the
property and on the website.

LANHYDROCK 🌿

www.nationaltrust.org.uk

Lanhydrock is the grandest and most welcoming house in Cornwall, set in a glorious landscape of gardens, parkland and woods overlooking the valley of the River Fowey.

The house dates back to the 17th century but much of it had to be rebuilt after a disastrous fire in 1881 destroyed all but the entrance porch and the north wing, which includes the magnificent Long Gallery with its extraordinary plaster ceiling depicting scenes from the Old Testament. Over 50 rooms are on show today and together they reflect the entire spectrum of life in a rich and splendid Victorian household, from the many servants' bedrooms and the fascinating complex of kitchens, sculleries and larders to the nursery suite where the Agar-Robartes children lived, learned and played, and the grandeur of the dining room with its table laid and ready.

Surrounding the house on all sides are gardens ranging from formal Victorian parterres to the wooded higher garden where magnificent displays of magnolias, rhododendrons and camellias climb the hillside to merge with the oak and beech woods all around. A famous avenue of ancient beech and sycamore trees, the original entrance drive to the house, runs from the pinnacled 17th-century gatehouse down towards the medieval bridge across the Fowey at Respryn.

ℹ No photography in house.

✳ By arrangement.

♿ Suitable. Braille guide. WC.

🍴 Licensed restaurant

🐕 In park, on leads. Guide dogs only in house.

🅿 Limited for coaches.

©Noel Chanan

PORT ELIOT

www.porteliot.co.uk

■ **Owner**
The Earl of St Germans

■ **Contact**
Port Eliot Estate Office
St Germans
Saltash
Cornwall
PL12 5ND

Tel: 01503 230211
Fax: 01503 230112
E-mail: jo@porteliot.co.uk

■ **Location**
MAP 1:H8
OS Ref. SX359 578

Situated in the village of St Germans on the Rame Peninsula in South East Cornwall. Parking signposted off B3249 (Tideford Cricket Ground/Port Eliot).

■ **Opening Times**
Beginning March to end of June 2010. Everyday except Friday. Open 2pm–6pm. Last admission at 5pm.

■ **Admission**
House, Garden
*Adult   £7.00
Children (under 16) £Free
Group (20+) Adult £6.00
*also vistors by public transport £6.00.
Grounds only
Adult   £4.00
Children (under 16) Free

Port Eliot is an ancient, hidden gem which only recently opened to the public. Set in stunning fairytale grounds, Port Eliot sits on the banks of a secret estuary. It has rare distinction of being a Grade I listed house, park and garden. This is due in part to the work of Sir John Soane, who worked his magic on the house and Humphrey Repton, who created the park and garden.

Port Eliot, once a monastery, has been continuously occupied for more than 1000 years, and home to the Eliot family for 445. It is still the family home of the Earl and Countess of St Germans. It is not an average Stately home, but has a fabulous atmosphere engendered by rooms like the Morning Room with it's nineteenth century red damask covered walls, an accumulation of wonderful treasures including a museum quality Boulle armoire, (which houses Lord St Germans record collection) alongside masterpieces by Van Dyck and Reynolds. The famous Round Room is considered to be Soane's masterpiece and is adorned with the greatest work of artist Robert Lenkiewicz, the 'Riddle Mural'.

Every year new light is shed on the hidden gems in the house when a tableau is created by Lady St Germans and Michael Howells (the acclaimed set designer to John Galliano and Ballet Rambert).

Walk by the estuary and meander through the woodland garden. Picnic by the maze with it's stunning views of the estuary and Brunel's viaduct or in the Orangery garden. Dogs very welcome.

i No photography.

WCs.

Limited for coaches.

On leads.

In July, Port Eliot Festival is an annual celebration of words, music, imagination, laughter, exploration and above all - fun in one of the most beautiful and secret gardens in England.

© NT / Peter Cade

ANTONY HOUSE & GARDEN ❧
& ANTONY WOODLAND GARDEN

TORPOINT, CORNWALL PL11 2QA

www.nationaltrust.org.uk

Antony House & Garden Tel: 01752 812191
Antony Woodland Garden Tel: 01752 814210
E-mail: antony@nationaltrust.org.uk
Antony House & Garden Owner: The National Trust
Antony Woodland Garden Owner: Carew Pole Garden Trust

Superb 18th-century house on the Lynher estuary, grounds landscaped by Repton. Formal garden with sculptures & National Collection of daylilies; woodland garden with magnolias, rhododendrons & National Collection of Camellia japonica.

Location: MAP 1:H9, OS Ref. SX418 564. 5m W of Plymouth via Torpoint car ferry, 2m NW of Torpoint.

Open: House: 16 Mar–31 Oct: Tue–Thur, Sun & BH's: 12noon–5pm (last entry to the house 4.30pm). Garden, Shop & Tea-Room, 6 Mar–31 Oct: Daily except Fri: 11am–5pm. Woodland Garden (not NT) 1 Mar–31 Oct: daily except Mon & Fri (open BH Mons), 11am–5.30pm. NB. Discover the *Alice in Wonderland* Experience in 2010!

Admission: House & Garden: £7.50, Child £4.80, Family £19.80, 1-Adult Family £12.30. Groups £6.30pp. NT Garden only: £4.95, Child £2.50. Woodland Garden: Adult £4.50, Child Free. (Free to NT members on days when the house is open.) Woodland Garden season ticket: £25. Joint Gardens-only tickets: Adult £6.95.

🔲 ♿ 🍴 🅿 ♿

BURNCOOSE NURSERIES & GARDEN

Gwennap, Redruth, Cornwall TR16 6BJ
Tel: 01209 860316   **Fax:** 01209 860011   **E-mail:** burncoose@eclipse.co.uk
www.burncoose.co.uk
Owner/Contact: C H Williams

The Nurseries are set in the 30 acre woodland gardens of Burncoose.

Location: MAP 1:D10, OS Ref. SW742 395. 2m SE of Redruth on main A393 Redruth to Falmouth road between the villages of Lanner and Ponsanooth.

Open: Mon–Sat: 9am–5pm, Suns, 11am–5pm. Gardens and Tearooms open all year (except Christmas Day).

Admission: Nurseries: Free. Gardens: Adult/Conc. £2. Child Free. Group conducted tours: £3.50 by arrangement.

🔲 ♿ ♿ Grounds. WCs. ▣ 🎦 By arrangement. 🅿 ♿ In grounds, on leads. ❋

Pencarrow

BOCONNOC

THE ESTATE OFFICE, BOCONNOC, LOSTWITHIEL, CORNWALL PL22 0RG

www.boconnocenterprises.co.uk

Tel: 01208 872507 **Fax:** 01208 873836 **E-mail:** adgfortescue@btinternet.com
Owner/Contact: Anthony Fortescue Esq

The fortunes of the greatest political dynasty in British History began with the sale of a diamond. Boconnoc was bought with the proceeds in 1717 by Governor Pitt of Madras. History from Domesday, Architecture by Sir John Soane, Thomas Pitt's picturesque landscape and one of the great Cornish gardens create ideal locations for Du Maurier and Rosamund Pilcher films. Groups visit Boconnoc House, the extensive woodland gardens with newly planted magnolias, the Church, Golden Jubilee lake walk, the Georgian Bath House and Pinetum. Ideal for romantic weddings, private and corporate events, conferences and filming with office space available, residential and holiday houses to let.

Location: MAP 1:G8, OS Ref. 148 605. A38 from Plymouth, Liskeard or from Bodmin to Dobwalls, then A390 to Middle Taphouse.

Open: House & Garden: 18 & 25 Apr; 2, 9, 16, 23 & 30 May: Suns: 2–5pm. Groups (15–255) by appointment all year.

Admission: House: £4, Garden £4.50. Child under 12yrs Free.

🔲 🎦 Conferences. ♿ Partial. ▣ 🎦 By arrangement. 🅿 ♿
♿ In grounds, on leads. 🛏 10 doubles (8 ensuite). ▲ ❋
🎗 7 Mar: Wedding Fair. 10–11 Apr: Cornwall Garden Society Spring Flower Show.
9 May: Dog Show. 11–12 May: Spring Fair. 25 June: Music in the Park.
4 July: Endurance Ride. 23–25 July: Boconnoc Steam Fair.

CAERHAYS CASTLE & GARDEN

CAERHAYS, GORRAN, ST AUSTELL, CORNWALL PL26 6LY

www.caerhays.co.uk

Tel: 01872 501310 **Fax:** 01872 501870 **E-mail:** estateoffice@caerhays.co.uk
Owner: F J Williams Esq **Contact:** Cheryl Kufel

One of the very few Nash built castles still left standing – situated within approximately 60 acres of informal woodland gardens created by J C Williams, who sponsored plant hunting expeditions to China at the turn of the century. As well as guided tours of the house from March to May visitors will see some of the magnificent selection of plants brought back by the intrepid plant hunters of the early 1900s these include not only the collection of magnolias but a wide range of rhododendrons and the camellias which Caerhays and the Williams familly are associated with worldwide.

Location: MAP 1:F9, OS Ref. SW972 415. S coast of Cornwall – between Mevagissey and Portloe. 9m SW of St Austell.

Open: House: 15 Mar–31 May: Mon–Fri only (including BHs), 12 noon–4pm, booking recommended. Gardens: 15 Feb–31 May: daily (including BHs), 10am–5pm (last admission 4pm).

Admission: House: £5.50. Gardens: £5.50. House & Gardens: £9.50. Guided group tours (15+) by Head Gardener, £6.50–by arrangement. Groups please contact Estate Office.

No photography in house. Partial. WC. Licensed. By arrangement. In grounds, on leads.

CAERHAYS CASTLE – THE VEAN

THE ESTATE OFFICE, CAERHAYS CASTLE, GORRAN, ST AUSTELL, CORNWALL PL26 6LY

www.thevean.co.uk

Tel: 01872 501310 **Fax:** 01872 501870 **E-mail:** manager@thevean.eclipse.co.uk
Owner: Mrs Lizzy Williams **Contact:** Sally Gammell

Staying at The Vean is like enjoying a house party where the owners have gone away for the weekend. The Vean is a luxury country house retreat, within the Caerhays Estate, that sleeps up to 16 people in its eight en-suite bedrooms. During the shooting season it is the shooting lodge for the guns at the Castle. The Vean is a restored former Georgian Rectory and is run with passion and a commitment to achieve the highest standards.

Location: MAP 1:F9, OS Ref. SW972 415. S coast of Cornwall – between Mevagissey and Portloe. 9m SW of St Austell.

Open: For bookings only. Licensed for Civil weddings.

Admission: Contact property for details.

Conferences & corporate breaks. Partial. Licensed. By arrangement. Ample for cars. In grounds, on leads. 8 x en-suite.

CHYSAUSTER ANCIENT VILLAGE ⌗

Nr Newmill, Penzance, Cornwall TR20 8XA
Tel: 07831 757934   **E-mail:** customers@english-heritage.org.uk
www.english-heritage.org.uk/chysauster
Owner: English Heritage   **Contact:** Visitor Operations Team
Set on a windy hillside, overlooking the wild and spectacular coast, explore this deserted Romano-Cornish village with a 'street' of nine well preserved houses, each comprising a number of rooms around an open court.
Location: MAP 1:C10, OS203 Ref. SW473 350. 2½m NW of Gulval off B3311.
Open: 1 Apr–31 Oct: daily, 10am–5pm (6pm Jul & Aug, 4pm Oct). Closed 1 Nov–31 Mar.
Admission: Adult £3, Child £1.50, Conc. £2.60, 15% discount for groups (11+). EH Members free. Opening times and prices are valid until 31st March 2010, after this date details are subject to change please see www.english-heritage.org.uk for the most up-to-date information.
ℹ️ WC. 🅿️ 🅿️ No coaches. ▣ ⊞ On leads.

COTEHELE ✤

See page 163 for full page entry.

GLENDURGAN GARDEN ✤

MAWNAN SMITH, FALMOUTH, CORNWALL TR11 5JZ

www.nationaltrust.org.uk

Tel: 01326 252020 (opening hours) or 01872 862090   **Fax:** 01872 865808
E-mail: glendurgan@nationaltrust.org.uk
Owner: The National Trust
A valley of great beauty with fine trees, shrubs and water gardens. The laurel maze is an unusual and popular feature. The garden runs down to the tiny village of Durgan and its beach on the Helford River. Replica Victorian school room, rebuilt in 2002 in traditional thatch and cob to replace the 1876 original.
Location: MAP 1:D10, OS Ref. SW772 277. 4m SW of Falmouth, ½m SW of Mawnan Smith, on road to Helford Passage. 1m E of Trebah Garden. Accessible by ferry from Helford.
Open: 13 Feb–30 Oct: Tue–Sat, BH Mons & Mons in Aug, 10.30am–5.30pm. Last admission 5pm. Closed Good Friday.
*Admission: Adult £6.60, Child £3.30, Family £16.70, 1-Adult Family £9.90. Booked groups: £5.70. *includes a voluntary donation but visitors can choose to pay the standard prices displayed at the property and on the website.
🅿️ ⊞ ♿ Unsuitable. ▣ 🖽 By arrangement. 🅿️ Limited for coaches. ⊞

Mount Edgcumbe

NTPL/Andrew Butler

GODOLPHIN ✤

GODOLPHIN CROSS, HELSTON, CORNWALL TR13 9RE

www.nationaltrust.org.uk/godolphinhouse

Tel: 01736 763194   **E-mail:** godolphin@nationaltrust.org.uk
Owner: The National Trust
One of Cornwall's most beautiful old houses at the heart of an historic estate, once the home of the illustrious Godolphin family. Centuries of benign neglect have given the place a haunting air of antiquity and peace. Extensive restoration is now needed, and visitors may find the opening arrangements changed at short notice to accommodate this. The garden is a rare survival from the 14th and 16th centuries and the estate has many fascinating walks.
Location: MAP 1:D10, OS Ref: SW602 318. On minor road from Godolphin Cross to Townshend. Some brown signs.
Open: House: Pre-booked, 'hard hat' tours limited to small groups. Please telephone the property for details. NB subject to change at short notice – please tel or visit website. Garden: 13 Mar–31 Oct: 10am–4pm, Sat–Weds. Estate: All year, daily.
Admission: Garden only: Adult £3, Child £1.50.
♿ 🅿️ ▣ Estate only. 🖽 Dogs on estate only. ☗

GODOLPHIN BLOWINGHOUSE

Blowinghouse Cottage, Godolphin Cross, Breage, Helston, Cornwall TR13 9RE
Tel: 01736 763218   **E-mail:** brian.portch@ndirect.co.uk
Owner/Contact: Mr & Mrs B J Portch
The Blowinghouse dates from the 16th century and was built as part of the Godolphin family tin mining works. The tin ingots weighed in excess of three hundredweight and were stamped with a cat's head that was the Godophin Mine logo.
Location: MAP 1:D10, OS Ref. SW508 521, Situated in the Godolphin Woods-National Trust opposite entrance to the Godolphin Manor House.
Open: 1 Aug 2010, 9.30am–4.30pm. Other times by appointment.
Admission: Free.
♿ 🅿️ Limited. ▣ 🖽 In grounds, on leads.

THE JAPANESE GARDEN & BONSAI NURSERY

St Mawgan, Nr Newquay, Cornwall TR8 4ET
Tel: 01637 860116   **Fax:** 01637 860887   **E-mail:** rob@thebonsainursery.com
Owner/Contact: Mr & Mrs Hore
Authentic Japanese Garden set in 1½ acres.
Location: MAP 2:E8, OS Ref. SW873 660. Follow road signs from A3059 & B3276.
Open: Summer: Daily, 10am–6pm. Winter: 10am–5.30pm. Closed Christmas Day–New Year's Day.
Admission: Adult £3.50, Child £1.50. Groups (10+): £3.

KEN CARO GARDENS

Bicton, Nr Liskeard PL14 5RF
Tel: 01579 362446
Owner/Contact: Mr and Mrs K R Willcock
5 acre plantsman's garden with woods and picnic area. Total 12 acres.
Location: MAP 1:G8, OS Ref. SX313 692. 5m NE of of Liskeard. Follow brown sign off main A390 midway between Liskeard and Callington.
Open: 22 Feb–30 Sept: daily, 10am–6pm.
Admission: Adult £4.50, Child £1.

LANHYDROCK ❧

See page 164 for full page entry.

LAUNCESTON CASTLE ⌘

Castle Lodge, Launceston, Cornwall PL15 7DR
Tel: 01566 772365 **Fax:** 01566 772396 **E-mail:** customers@english-heritage.org.uk
www.english-heritage.org.uk/launceston
Owner: English Heritage **Contact:** Visitor Operations Team
Set on the motte of the original Norman castle and commanding the town and surrounding countryside. The shell keep and tower survive of this medieval castle which controlled the main route into Cornwall. An exhibition shows the early history.
Location: MAP 1:H7, OS201 Ref. SX330 846. In Launceston.
Open: 1 Apr–30 Jun: daily, 10am–5pm. 1 Jul–31 Aug: daily, 10am–6pm. 1–30 Sep: daily, 10am–5pm. 1–31 Oct: daily, 10am–4pm. Closed 1 Nov–31 Mar.
Admission: Adult £3, Child £1.50, Conc. £2.60. 15% discount for groups (11+). EH members Free. Opening times and prices are valid until 31st March 2010, after this date details are subject to change please see www.english-heritage.org.uk for the most up-to-date information.
⌂⌖ Partial. Grounds. 🅿 NCP and coaches adjacent. Limited. ▣🖼 In grounds, on leads.

LAWRENCE HOUSE ❧

9 Castle Street, Launceston, Cornwall PL15 8BA
Tel: 01566 773277
Owner: The National Trust **Contact:** The Curator
A Georgian house given to the Trust to help preserve the character of the street, and now leased to Launceston Town Council as a museum and Mayor's Parlour.
Location: MAP 1:H7, OS Ref. SX330 848. Launceston.
Open: 29 Mar–29 Oct: Mon–Fri, 10.30am–4.30pm and occasional Saturdays. Other times by appointment.
Admission: Free, but contributions welcome.

Pentillie Castle

Planning a weekend away in Cornwall?

See Historic Places to Stay

MOUNT EDGCUMBE HOUSE & COUNTRY PARK

CREMYLL, TORPOINT, CORNWALL PL10 IHZ

www.mountedgcumbe.gov.uk

Tel: 01752 822236 **Fax:** 01752 822199 **E-mail:** mt.edgcumbe@plymouth.gov.uk
Owner: Cornwall County & Plymouth City Councils **Contact:** Secretary
Former home of the Earls of Mount Edgcumbe. Miraculously the walls of the red stone Tudor House survived the bombs in 1941. Restored by the 6th Earl. Now beautifully furnished with family possessions. Set in historic 18th century gardens on the dramatic sea-girt Rame peninsula. Follies, forts; National camellia collection. Grade I listed gardens. Exhibitions and events. Winner of the RHS Britain in Bloom UK Public Park of the Year.
Location: MAP 1:H9, OS Ref. SX452 527. 10m W of Plymouth via Torpoint.
Open: House & Earl's Garden: Apr–Sept: Sun–Thur, 11am–4.30pm. Group bookings by arrangement. Country Park: All year, daily, 8am–dusk.
Admission: House & Earl's Garden: Adult £6, Child (5–15) £3.50, Conc. £5, Family (2+2 or 1+3) £12.50. Groups (10+): Adult £5, Child £3.20. Park: Free.
⌂ ⌖ ⛝ ⌗ ▣ ⍓ Licensed. 🅇 By arrangement. 🅿 🖼 In grounds, on leads. ▦ ✽ ♥

Boconnoc

PENCARROW 🏛

BODMIN, CORNWALL PL30 3AG

www.pencarrow.co.uk

Tel: 01208 841369 **Fax:** 01208 841722 **E-mail:** info@pencarrow.co.uk

Owner: Molesworth-St Aubyn family **Contact:** Administrator

Still owned and lived in by the family. Georgian house and Grade II* listed gardens. Superb collection of pictures, furniture and porcelain. Marked walks through 50 acres of beautiful formal and woodland gardens, Victorian rockery, Italian garden, over 700 different varieties of rhododendrons, lake Iron Age hillfort and ice house.

Location: MAP 1:F8, OS Ref. SX040 711. Between Bodmin and Wadebridge. 4m NW of Bodmin off A389 & B3266 at Washaway.

Open: House, Peacock Café & Shop: 28 Mar–30 Sept, Sun–Thur. House tours from 11am–3pm, Cafe & shop 11am–5pm. Gardens: 1 Mar–31 Oct: daily.

Admission: House & Garden: Adult £8.50, Child £4, Family £22. Garden only: Adult £4, Child £1. Groups (by arrangement): House & Garden: groups (20–50) £7, 51+ £6; Gardens only: groups (20–50) £3.50, 51+ £3. Discounts not normally available on Fri & Sat or between 31 Oct and Easter.

ℹ Shop, small children's play area, self-pick soft fruit. 🗓 🎭 By arrangement. ♿ 📷 Licensed. 🍴 🎫 Obligatory. 🅿 📷 🚌 Grounds only. 🔔 🐕

Launceston Castle

PORT ELIOT 🏛 *See page 165 for full page entry.*

PENDENNIS CASTLE ⚏

FALMOUTH, CORNWALL TR11 4LP

www.english-heritage.org.uk/pendennis

Tel: 01326 316594 **E-mail:** pendennis.castle@english-heritage.org.uk

Venue and Hire Hospitality: 01326 310106

Owner: English Heritage **Contact:** Visitor Operations Team

Pendennis and its neighbour, St Mawes Castle, face each other across the mouth of the estuary of the River Fal. Built by Henry VIII in 16th century as protection against threat of attack and invasion from France. Extended and adapted over the years to meet the changing threats to national security from the French and Spanish and continued right through to World War II. It withstood five months of siege during the Civil War before becoming the penultimate Royalist Garrison to surrender on the mainland. Pendennis today stands as a landmark, with fine sea views and excellent site facilities including a hands-on discovery centre, exhibitions, a museum, guardhouse, shop and tearoom. An excellent venue for special events throughout the year.

Location: MAP 1:E10, OS Ref. SW824 318. On Pendennis Head.

Open: 1 Apr–30 Jun: daily, 10am–5pm (closes 4pm Sat). 1 Jul–31 Aug: daily, 10am–6pm (closes 4pm Sat). 1–30 Sep: daily 10am–5pm (closes 4pm Sat). 1 Oct–31 Mar: daily, 10am–4pm. The Keep will close for 1 hour at lunch on Saturdays if an event is booked. Closed 24 –26 Dec & 1 Jan.

Admission: Adult £5.70, Child £2.90, Conc. £4.80, Family £13.80. 15% discount for groups (11+). EH members Free. Opening times and prices are valid until 31st March 2010, after this date details are subject to change please see www.english-heritage.org.uk for the most up-to-date information.

ℹ WC. 🗓 🎭 ♿ Partial. 📷 🅿 No coaches. 📷 🚌 In grounds only. ☎ 0870 333 1187 🔔 ✳ 🐕 €

PRIDEAUX PLACE 🏛

PADSTOW, CORNWALL PL28 8RP

www.prideauxplace.co.uk

Tel: 01841 532411 **Fax:** 01841 532945 **E-mail:** office@prideauxplace.co.uk
Owner/Contact: Peter Prideaux-Brune Esq

Tucked away above the busy port of Padstow, the home of the Prideaux family for over 400 years, is surrounded by gardens and wooded grounds overlooking a deer park and the Camel estuary to the moors beyond. The house still retains its 'E' shape Elizabethan front and contains fine paintings and furniture. Now a major international film location, this family home is one of the brightest jewels in Cornwall's crown. The historic garden is undergoing major restoration work and offers some of the best views in the county. A cornucopia of Cornish history under one roof.

Location: MAP 1:E7, OS Ref. SW913 756. 5m from A39 Newquay/Wadebridge link road. Signposted by Historic House signs.

Open: Easter Sun 12–16 Apr, 10 May–8 Oct. Daily except Fris & Sats. Grounds & Tearoom: 12.30–5pm. House Tours: 1.30–4pm (last tour).

Admission: House & Grounds: Adult £7.50, Child £2. Grounds only: Adult £2.50, Child £1. Groups (15+) discounts apply.

🖻 🗵 By arrangement. 🗒 Ground floor & grounds. 🗖 🗵 Obligatory. 🅿
🖩 By arrangement. 🗕 In grounds, on leads. ✻

RESTORMEL CASTLE ♯

LOSTWITHIEL, CORNWALL PL22 0EE

www.english-heritage.org.uk/restormel

Tel: 01208 872687 **E-mail:** customers@english-heritage.org.uk
Owner: English Heritage **Contact:** Visitor Operations Team

Perched on a high mound, surrounded by a deep moat, the huge circular keep of this splendid Norman castle survives in remarkably good condition. It is still possible to make out Restormel's Keep Gate, Great Hall and even the kitchens and private rooms.

Location: MAP 1:F8, OS200 Ref. SX104 614. 1½m N of Lostwithiel off A390.

Open: 1 Apr–30 Jun: daily, 10am–5pm. 1 Jul–31 Aug: daily, 10am–6pm. 1–30 Sep: daily, 10am–5pm. 1–31 Oct: daily, 10am–4pm. Closed 1 Nov–31 Mar.

Admission: Adult £3, Child £1.50, Conc. £2.60. 15% discount for groups (11+). EH Members free. Opening times and prices are valid until 31st March 2010, after this date details are subject to change please see www.english-heritage.org.uk for the most up-to-date information.

ⓘ WC. 🖻 🅿 Limited for coaches. 🖩 🗕 In grounds, on leads.

ST CATHERINE'S CASTLE ♯

Fowey, Cornwall

Tel: 01326 310109 **E-mail:** customers@english-heritage.org.uk
Owner: English Heritage **Contact:** Visitor Operations Administrator

A small fort built by Henry VIII to defend Fowey harbour, with fine views of the coastline and river estuary.

Location: MAP 1:F9, OS200 Ref. SX118 508. 1½m SW of Fowey along footpath off A3082.

Open: Any reasonable time, daylight only.

Admission: Free. Opening times and prices are valid until 31st March 2010, after this date details are subject to change please see www.english-heritage.org.uk for the most up-to-date information.

🅿 🗕 ✻

Sausmarez Manor, Channel Islands

ST MAWES CASTLE ⌗
ST MAWES, CORNWALL TR2 5DE
www.english-heritage.org.uk/stmawes

Tel/Fax: 01326 270526   **Venue Hire and Hospitality:** 01326 310106
E-mail: stmawes.castle@english-heritage.org.uk
Owner: English Heritage   **Contact:** Visitor Operations Team

Situated on the edge of St. Mawes village, opposite Pendennis Castle, St. Mawes Castle shares the task of watching over the Fal estuary as it has done since Henry VIII built it as a defence against invasion. A fine example of Tudor military architecture, offering views of St. Mawes' little boat-filled harbour, the passenger ferry tracking across the Fal, and the splendid coastline which featured in the *Poldark* TV series.

Location: MAP 1:E10, OS204 Ref. SW842 328. W of St Mawes on A3078.

Open: 1 Apr–30 Jun: Sun–Fri, 10am–5pm. 1 Jul–31 Aug: Sun–Fri, 10am–6pm. 1–30 Sep: Sun–Fri, 10am–5pm. 1–31 Oct: daily, 10am–4pm. 1 Nov–31 Mar: Fri–Mon, 10am–4pm. Closed Sat. May close 4pm on Sun & Fri for private events. Closed 24–26 Dec & 1 Jan.

Admission: Adult £4, Child £2, Conc. £3.40. 15% discount for groups (11+). EH members Free. Opening times and prices are valid until 31st March 2010, after this date details are subject to change please see www.english-heritage.org.uk for the most up-to-date information.

◻ ⊤ 01326 310106 ⬓ Partial. Grounds. ⌂ ℙ Limited. ▣
⤬ Grounds only. ☏ 0870 333 1187 ▲ ✳

Tintagel Old Post Office

ST MICHAEL'S MOUNT ✶
MARAZION, Nr PENZANCE, CORNWALL TR17 0HT
www.stmichaelsmount.co.uk   www.nationaltrust.org.uk

Tel: 01736 710507 (710265 tide information)   **Fax:** 01736 719930
E-mail: mail@stmichaelsmount.co.uk
Owner: The National Trust   **Contact:** Clare Sandry, Manor Office, Marazion, Cornwall TR17 0EF

This beautiful island has become an icon for Cornwall and has magnificent views of Mount's Bay from its summit. There the church and castle, whose origins date from the 12th century, have at various times acted as a Benedictine priory, a place of pilgrimage, a fortress, a mansion house and now a magnet for visitors from all over the world. Following the Civil War, the island was acquired by the St Aubyn family who still live in the castle today.

Location: MAP 1:C10, OS Ref. SW515 300. 4m E of Penzance. At Marazion there is access on foot over causeway at low tide. In the main season, the property is reached at high tide by a short evocative boat trip.

Please note many paths are steep and cobbled.

Open: Castle: 28 March to 31st October Sun – Fri, 10.30am – 5pm (1 Jul–31 Aug, 10.30am–5.30pm). Last admission 45 mins before castle closing time, but allow plenty of time before this to reach the island. In winter, guided tours only, telephone in advance. Garden: May & Jun: Mon–Fri; Jul – Oct: Thur & Fri, 10.30am – 5.00pm. Church Service: Whitsun – end Sept (also Christmas Day, Good Fri & Easter Sun): Sun, 11.15am. All visits subject to weather and tides.

Admission: Adult £7.00 Child (under 17) £3.50, Family £17.50, 1-Adult Family £10.50 Booked groups £6.00 Garden £3.50 Child £1.50. Combined Adult £8.75 Child £4.25 Family £21.75 1-Adult Family £13.00 Groups £7.50

ℹ Parking on mainland (not NT). Dogs not permitted in the castle or gardens.◻ ⧉ ⬓ Partial. ▣ Licensed. ⊤ Licensed. ⟲ by arrangement. Tel for details. ℙ On mainland (not NT.) ▣ ⤬ Guide dogs only. ✳.

TINTAGEL CASTLE ⌗

TINTAGEL, CORNWALL PL34 0HE

www.english-heritage.org.uk/tintagel

Tel/Fax: 01840 770328 **E-mail:** tintagel.castle@english-heritage.org.uk
Owner: English Heritage **Contact:** Visitor Operations Team

Set spectacularly on the wild Cornish coast, Tintagel Castle is a place of magic where the legend of King Arthur was born. Clinging to the cliffs are the extensive ruins of a medieval castle – a stronghold of the Earls of Cornwall – representing only one phase in its long history. A place of mystery and romance, Tintagel will always jealously guard its marvellous secrets. Relax in our Beach Café which serves a delicious selection of refreshments.

Location: MAP 1:F7, Landranger Sheet 200 Ref. SX048 891. On Tintagel Head, ½m along uneven track from Tintagel.

Open: 1 Apr–30 Sep: daily, 10am–6pm. 1–31 Oct: daily, 10am–5pm. 1 Nov–31 Mar: daily, 10am–4pm. Closed 24–26 Dec & 1 Jan.

Admission: Adult £4.90, Child £2.50, Conc. £4.20. Family £11.80. 15% discount for groups (11+). EH members Free. Opening times and prices are valid until 31st March 2010, after this date details are subject to change please see www.english-heritage.org.uk for the most up-to-date information.

ℹ️ WC. 🅿️ No vehicles. Parking (not EH) in village only. ▣ ▣ ▣ ▣

TREBAH GARDEN

MAWNAN SMITH, Nr FALMOUTH, CORNWALL TR11 5JZ

www.trebah-garden.co.uk

Tel: 01326 252200 **Fax:** 01326 250781 **E-mail:** mail@trebah-garden.co.uk
Owner: Trebah Garden Trust **Contact:** Claire Vickers

Steeply wooded 26 acre sub-tropical valley garden falls 200 feet from 18th century house to private beach on Helford River. Stream cascading over waterfalls through ponds full of Koi Carp and exotic water plants winds through 2 acres of blue and white hydrangeas and spills out over beach. Huge Australian tree ferns and palms mingle with shrubs of ever-changing colours and scent beneath over-arching canopy of 100 year old rhododendrons and magnolias. The striking Visitor Centre houses a garden shop, plant sales and stylish catering.

Location: MAP 1:D10, OS Ref. SW768 275. 4m SW of Falmouth, 1m SW of Mawnan Smith. Follow brown and white tourism signs from Treliever Cross roundabout at A39/A394 junction through Mawnan Smith to Trebah.

Open: All year: daily, 10am–5pm (last admission). Winter opening times may vary.

Admission: 1 Mar–31 Oct: Adult £7.50, Child (5–15yrs) £2.50. Disabled £3. Child under 5yrs Free, OAP £6.50. 1 Nov–28 Feb: Adult £3, Child (5–15yrs)/Disabled £1, Child under 5yrs Free, OAP £2.50. NT members: free entry 1 Nov–end Feb. RHS members: free entry 1 Nov–end Mar.

🄿 ▣ 🅐 Partial. ▣ 🏠 🅧 By arrangement. 🅿️ ▣ ▣ On leads. ▣

TINTAGEL OLD POST OFFICE ⚜

Tintagel, Cornwall PL34 0DB

Tel: 01840 770024 or 01208 265200

Owner: The National Trust **Contact:** The Custodian

One of the most characterful buildings in Cornwall, and a house of great antiquity, this small 14th-century yeoman farmhouse is full of charm and interest.

Location: MAP 1:F7, OS Ref. SX056 884. In the centre of Tintagel.

Open: 13 Feb–21 Feb, daily 11am–4pm, 13 Mar–2 Apr, daily 11am–4pm, 3 Apr–28 May, daily 10.30am–5pm, 29 May–1 Oct, daily 10.30am–5.30pm, 2 Oct–31 Oct, daily 11am–4pm. Last admission 30 mins before closing.

Admission: Adult £3.20, Child £1.60, Family £8, 1-Adult Family £4.80. Booked Adult groups £2.60. Booked Child groups £1.30.

St Michael's Mount

©National Trust/Tony Kent

©Enterprise Boats

TRELISSICK GARDEN ❧
FEOCK, TRURO, CORNWALL TR3 6QL
www.nationaltrust.org.uk

Tel: 01872 862090 **Fax:** 01872 865808 **E-mail:** trelissick@nationaltrust.org.uk
Owner: The National Trust **Contact:** Administrator

A garden and estate of rare tranquil beauty with glorious maritime views over the Carrick Roads to Falmouth. The tender and exotic shrubs make this an attractive garden in all seasons. Extensive park and woodland walks beside the river. Art and Craft Gallery. Make your visit a really special day: travel to Trelissick by foot ferry from Truro, Falmouth and St Mawes by Fal River Links Partnerships Ferries, from May to September. Copeland Spode China on display in Trelissick House at 2pm on Thursdays, May and September, booking advisable 01872 864452.

Location: MAP 1:E10, OS Ref. SW837 396. 4m S of Truro on B3289 above King Harry Ferry.
Open: Garden, Shop, Restaurant, Gallery and Plant Sales: all year: daily, 10.30am – 5.30pm. (11am–4pm, Nov–Mid Feb). Closed 24–26 Dec & 1 Jan. Woodland Walks: All year: daily.
Admission: Adult £7.40, Child £3.70, Family £18.40, 1-Adult Family £11. Pre-arranged groups £6.30pp. Car Park £3.50 (refunded on admission). Garden & Copeland Spode China: £11.40 (NT members £4).

▢ ⊞ ⊤ By arrangement. ⬥ ⊞ ⊮ By arrangement. Ⓟ Limited for coaches. ⧈ In park on leads; only guide dogs in garden. ⊞ ⊎

©National Trust/Giles Clotworthy

©National Trust/Marcus Way

TRERICE ❧
KESTLE MILL, Nr NEWQUAY, CORNWALL TR8 4PG
www.nationaltrust.org.uk

Tel: 01637 875404 **Fax:** 01637 879300 **E-mail:** trerice@nationaltrust.org.uk
Owner: The National Trust **Contact:** Administrator

Trerice is an architectural gem – a small Elizabethan manor house hidden away in a web of narrow lanes and still somehow caught in the spirit of its age. An old Arundell house, it contains much fine furniture, ceramics, glasses and a wonderful clock collection. Several family activities. The garden has some unusual plants, an orchard with old varieties of south-west fruit trees and an experimental Tudor garden.

Location: MAP 1:E8, OS Ref. SW841 585. 3m SE of Newquay via the A392 & A3058 (right at Kestle Mill). Or from A30–signs at Summercourt and Mitchell. Bus: Western Greyhound 527 Newquay - St Austell
Open: 1 Mar–31 Oct: Daily except Fris, 11am–5pm. (Garden, shop & tearoom 10.30am.) Tel for details of pre-Christmas opening.
*Admission: Adult £7.40, Child £3.70, Family £18.20, 1-Adult Family £10.90. Pre-arranged groups £6.20. Garden only: Adult £2.50, Child £1.30, Family £6.30, 1-Adult Family £3.80, Groups £2.10. Discounted pre-Christmas rates. *includes a voluntary donation but visitors can choose to pay the standard prices displayed at the property and on the website.

▢ ⊞ ⊤ ⬥ WCs. ⬛ Licensed. ⊞ Licensed. Ⓟ Limited for coaches. ⬛ ⧈ Guide dogs only. ⊞ Holiday flat. ⊎

TRENGWAINTON GARDEN ❧
PENZANCE, CORNWALL TR20 8RZ
www.nationaltrust.org.uk

Tel: 01736 363148 **Fax:** 01736 367762
Owner: The National Trust **Contact:** Administrator

Plants from around the globe inspire around every corner. Champion Magnolias and vibrant Rhododendrons; lush banana plants and soaring Echiums. The restored walled kitchen garden showcases contemporary varieties of fruit and vegetables while a colourfully bordered stream leads up to a sunny terrace, with stunning views across Mount's Bay.

Location: MAP 1:B10, OS Ref. SW445 315. 2m NW of Penzance, ½m W of Heamoor on Penzance–Morvah road (B3312), ½ m off St. Just road (A3071).
Open: 14 Feb–31 Oct: Sun–Thur & Good Fri, 10.30am–5pm. Tearoom opens 10am. Last admission 15 mins before closing.
Admission: Adult £6.20, Child £3.10, Family £15.50, 1-Adult Family £9.30. Booked groups: £5.20. *includes a voluntary donation but visitors can choose to pay the standard prices displayed at the property and on the website.

▢ ⊞ ⬥ Partial. ⬛ Tea-house. ⊮ ⧈ On leads (except in Tea-house garden).

TREWITHEN 🏛

GRAMPOUND ROAD, NEAR TRURO, CORNWALL TR2 4DD

www.trewithengardens.co.uk

Tel: 01726 883647   **Fax:** 01726 882301   **E-mail:** info@trewithengardens.co.uk
Owner: A M J Galsworthy   **Contact:** The Estate Office

Trewithen is an historic estate near Truro, Cornwall. Owned and lived in by the same family for 300 years, it is both private home and national treasure. The woodland gardens are outstanding – with 24 champion trees and famously rare and highly prized plants. Tours of the house prove equally memorable.

Location: Grampound Road, near Truro, Cornwall

Open: The House is open Mon & Tues & August BH from 1 Apr–31 Jul, 2pm–4pm.

Admission: Adult £5.75 (groups 20+ £4.50), Child (5–15yrs) £2.50, Child under 5yrs Free, Free entry for under 16's Jul & Aug Inclusive. July–Sept: Adult £4.50 (groups 20+ £4), Child (5–15yrs) £1, Child under 5yrs Free. (2007 prices.) Combined Garden & House entry: Adult £8, Groups £7, Child £2.50. Garden tours available with garden guides and head gardener.

ⓘ No photography in house. 🚻 ♿ Partial. WC. ▣ 🎦 By arrangement.
🅿 Limited for coaches. 🐕 In grounds, on leads.

Trerice Musicians Gallery

Trebah Garden

■ Owner
Valerie Lister

■ Contact
Valerie Lister
Bicton Park
Botanical Gardens
East Budleigh
Budleigh Salterton
Devon
EX9 7BJ

Tel: 01395 568465
Fax: 01395 568374
E-mail: info@
bictongardens.co.uk

■ Location
MAP 2:L7
OS Ref. SY074 856

2m N of Budleigh
Salterton on B3178.

Follow the brown signs to
Bicton Park from M5/J30
at Exeter.

Rail: Exmouth 5mins,
Exeter St Davids 12m.

Air: Exeter Airport 5m.

■ Opening Times
Summer
10am–6pm.

Winter
10am–5pm.
Open all year except
Christmas Day &
Boxing Day.

■ Admission
Adult	£6.95
Child	£5.95
Conc	£5.95
Family (2+2)	£22.95

Groups (16-200)
Adult	£4.95
Child	£3.95
Conc.	£3.95

Children under 3yrs Free

BICTON PARK BOTANICAL GARDENS
www.bictongardens.co.uk

Spanning three centuries of horticultural history, Bicton Park Botanical Gardens are set in the picturesque Otter Valley, near the coastal town of Budleigh Salterton and 10 miles south of Exeter.

The 63 acre park's oldest ornamental area is the Italian Garden, created in the axial style of Versailles landscaper Andre le Notre, c1735. By that time formal designs were becoming unfashionable in England, which may explain why the garden was located out of view of the manor house. Today, the full grandeur of the Italian Garden can be seen from the spacious restaurant in the classically styled Orangery, built at the beginning of the 19th century.

Bicton's high-domed Palm House, one of the world's most beautiful garden buildings, was the first of many developments between 1820 and 1850. Others included an important collection of conifers in the Pinetum, now the subject of a rare species conservation project, and St Mary's Church, where Queen Victoria worshipped.

A large museum reflects changes in agriculture and rural life generally over the past 200 years. The Grade I listed gardens, which are open all year, also feature a narrow-gauge railway which meanders through the garden on its 1½ mile track. Gift shop, garden centre, children's inside and outdoor play areas, including an eco friendly Ice Rink.

i	Children's inside & outdoor play areas.	✶	By arrangement.
⬛		P	Free.
✿	Garden Centre.	⬛	
ⴹ		🐕	In grounds, on leads.
♿	WCs.	🔔	
☕	Licensed.	❄	
🍴	Licensed.	⬛	

CLOVELLY

www.clovelly.co.uk

From Elizabethan days until today, Clovelly Village has preserved its original atmosphere. The main traffic-free street, known as 'up-a-along' and 'down-a-long', tumbles its cobbled way down to the tiny harbour, which is protected by an ancient stone breakwater. It is a descent through flower-strewn cottages broken only by little passageways and winding lanes that lead off to offer the prospect of more picturesque treasures.

The New Inn, which is 400 years old, is halfway down the street, and another, the Red Lion, is right on the quayside. Both Inns have long histories and an atmosphere rarely found in the modern world. In addition you'll find the Visitor Centre, a range of gift shops, a café and an audio-visual theatre in which visitors are treated to a history of the village. Just below is the Stable Yard with a pottery and silk workshop. There are beautiful coastal and woodland walks.

Access is restricted to pedestrians only via the Visitor Centre with a Land Rover taxi service for those unable to walk.

- **i** Rubber soled, low heel shoes are recommended.
- Partial. Around the Visitor Centre.
- Licensed.
- Licensed.
- **P**
- On leads.
- 18 double, 1 single, all en suite.
- Civil Wedding Licence

Owner
The Hon John Rous

Contact
Visitor Centre
Clovelly
Nr Bideford
N Devon EX39 5TA

Tel: 01237 431781
Fax: 01237 431644

Location
MAP 1:H5
OS Ref. SS248 319

On A39 10 miles W of Bideford, 15 miles E of Bude. Turn off at 'Clovelly Cross' roundabout and follow signs to car park.

Air: Exeter & Plymouth Airport both 50 miles.

Rail: Barnstaple 19 miles.

Bus: from Bideford.

Opening Times
High season:
9am–6pm.

Low season:
10am–4.30pm.

Admission
The entrance fee covers parking and other facilities provided by Clovelly Estate. As well as admission to the audio-visual film, Fisherman's Cottage, and Kingsley Museum, your fee contributes to the ongoing maintenance of the village, itself part of a private estate.

Adult	£5.75
Child (7–16yrs)	£3.65
Child (under 7yrs)	Free
Family (2+2)	£15.50
Group Rates (20+)	
Adult	£4.70
Child	£3.40

Prices correct at time of going to press.

Special Events
April
Fantastic Fudge Hunt.

July
Clovelly Maritime Festival.
Woolsery Agricultural Show.

August
Lifeboat Weekend.

September
Lobster & Crab Feast.

November
Clovelly Herring Festival.

December
Christmas Lights.

©National Trust/David Garner

A LA RONDE 🌿
SUMMER LANE, EXMOUTH, DEVON EX8 5BD

www.nationaltrust.org.uk

Tel: 01395 265514 **E-mail:** alaronde@nationaltrust.org.uk

Owner: The National Trust **Contact:** Assistant Property Manager

A unique 16-sided house built on the instructions of two spinster cousins, Jane and Mary Parminter, on their return from a grand tour of Europe. Completed c1796, the house contains many 18th-century contents and collections brought back by the Parminters. The fascinating interior decoration includes a feather frieze and shell-encrusted gallery which, due to its fragility, can only be fully viewed by remote control on closed circuit television.

Location: MAP 2:L7, OS Ref. SY004 834. 2m N of Exmouth on A376.

Open: House: 27 Feb–7 Mar, Sat & Sun only; Sat–Wed from 13 Mar-30 Jun, Open Good Friday. Fri-Wed from 02 Jul-03 Sept. Sat-Wed 04 Sept-31 Oct. 11am–5pm. Last admission 1/2 hour before closing. Shop & Grounds: 10.30am–5.30pm.

Admission: Adult £6.70, Child £3.40, Family £16.80, 1-Adult Family £10.10, Pre-booked Groups (15+) £5.70. Reduced rate when arriving by public transport.

ANDERTON HOUSE

Goodleigh, Devon EX32 7NR

Tel: 01628 825925 **E-mail:** bookings@landmarktrust.org.uk

www.landmarktrust.org.uk

Owner/Contact: The Landmark Trust

Anderton House is a Grade II* listed building of an exceptional modern design by Peter Aldington of Aldington and Craig. It was commissioned in 1969 as a family home and is highly evocative of its time, retaining the contemporary features and materials. Anderton House is cared for by The Landmark Trust, a building preservation charity who let it for holidays. Full details of Anderton House and 189 other historic and architecturally important buildings are featured in the Landmark Trust Handbook (price £10 plus p&p refundable against a booking) and on the website.

Location: MAP 2:I14, OS Ref. SS603 343. In village.

Open: Available for holidays for up to 5 people throughout the year. 2 Open Days a year. Other visits by appointment. Contact Landmark Trust for details.

Admission: Free on Open Days.

© The Landmark Trust

Anderton House

NTPL/Nadia Mackenzie

ARLINGTON COURT 🌿
Nr BARNSTAPLE, NORTH DEVON EX31 4LP

www.nationaltrust.org.uk

Tel: 01271 850296 **Fax:** 01271 851108

E-mail: arlingtoncourt@nationaltrust.org.uk

Owner: The National Trust **Contact:** Ana Chylak – Property Manager

The 3,000-acre estate lies in the wooded Yeo valley on the edge of Exmoor. The intimate Victorian house is full of treasures including model ships, pewter and shells; there are formal and informal gardens, a restored walled kitchen garden and extensive parkland, woodland and lakeside walks. The Victorian stable block and purpose-built museum wing houses the National Trust's Carriage Museum. Working stables provide carriage rides around the grounds.

Location: MAP 2:I4, OS180 Ref. SS611 405. 7m NE of Barnstaple on A39.

Open: House & Carriage Museum: 13 Feb–21 Feb daily & 27 Feb–7 Mar Sat & Suns, 11am-3pm, guided tours only. 13 Mar–31 Oct daily, 11am–5pm. Last admission 4.30pm. Garden, shop, tearoom and Bat-cam, as house, plus 6 Nov–19 Dec: Sat & Sun, 11am–3pm. Grounds open all year.

*Admission: House, Garden & Carriage Museum: Adult £8.60, Child £4.30, Family £21.50, 1-Adult family £12.90. Group £7.30. Garden & Carriage Museum only: Adult £6.20, Child £3.10. Gardens only, Nov/Dec reduced winter admission, telephone for information. *includes a voluntary donation but visitors can choose to pay the standard prices displayed at the property and on the website.

▢ 🚻 ♿ WCs. ☕ Licensed. 🍴 Licensed. 🎭 By arrangement. 🅿 Limited for Coaches ▣ Teachers' pack. 🐕 On leads ▲ ✸ ♿

© English Heritage

BERRY POMEROY CASTLE ⌗
TOTNES, DEVON TQ9 6LJ

www.english-heritage.org.uk/berrypomeroy

Tel: 01803 866618 **E-mail:** customers@english-heritage.org.uk

Owner: The Duke of Somerset **Contact:** Visitor Operations Team

A romantic late medieval castle, dramatically sited half-way up a wooded hillside, looking out over a deep ravine and stream. It is unusual in combining the remains of a large castle with a flamboyant courtier's mansion. Reputed to be one of the most haunted castles in the country.

Location: MAP 2:J8, OS202 Ref. SX839 623. 2½m E of Totnes off A385. Entrance gate ½m NE of Berry Pomeroy village, then ½m drive. Narrow approach, unsuitable for coaches.

Open: 1 Apr–30 Jun: daily, 10am–5pm 1 Jul–31 Aug: daily, 10am–6pm. 1–30 Sep: daily, 10am–5pm. 1–31 Oct: daily, 10am–4pm. 1 Nov–31 Mar: Closed.

Admission: Adult £4.20, Child £2.10, Conc £3.60. 15% discount for groups (11+). EH members Free. Opening times and prices are valid until 31st March 2010, after this date details are subject to change please see www.english-heritage.org.uk for the most up-to-date information.

▢ ♿ Ground floor & grounds. ☕ Not EH. ▢🅿 No access for coaches. ▣ 🐕 Guide dogs only.

BICTON PARK BOTANICAL GARDENS

See page 176 for full page entry.

BRADLEY ❧

Newton Abbot, Devon TQ12 6BN
Tel: 01803 843235 **E-mail:** bradley@nationaltrust.org.uk
www.nationaltrust.org.uk
Owner: The National Trust
A delightful small medieval manor house set in woodland and meadows. Still a relaxed family home.
Location: MAP 2:K8, OS Ref. SX848 709. On Totnes road A381. ¾ m SW of Newton Abbot.
Open: 1 Apr–30 Sep: Tue–Thur, 2–5 pm. Last admission 4.30pm. 5 Oct–29 Oct: Mon–Fri by appointment only (1 day in advance).
Admission: Adult £4.40, Child £2.20, no reduction for groups.
ℹ No WC or refreshments. 🅿 From 1.30pm. Not suitable for coaches or large vehicles.

BRANSCOMBE MANOR MILL, THE OLD BAKERY & FORGE ❧

Branscombe, Seaton, Devon EX12 3DB
Tel: Manor Mill – 01752 346585 Old Bakery – 01297 680333 Forge – 01297 680481
www.nationaltrust.org.uk
Owner: The National Trust
Manor Mill, still in working order and recently restored, is a water-powered mill which probably supplied the flour for the bakery. There are regular working demonstrations. The Old Bakery was, until 1987, the last traditional working bakery in Devon. The old baking equipment has been preserved in the baking room and the rest of the building is now a tearoom. Information display in the outbuildings. The Forge opens regularly and ironwork is on sale - please telephone to check opening times.
Location: MAP 2:M7, OS Ref. SY198 887. In Branscombe ½ m S off A3052 by steep, narrow lane.
Open: Manor Mill: 28 Mar–31 Oct: Suns, 2–5pm; also Weds in Jul & Aug. The Old Bakery: 1 Apr–31 Oct, Wed–Sun, 10.30am–5pm. The Forge Open all year round.
Admission: Adult £3, Child £1.50. Manor Mill only.
◻ ▣

BUCKFAST ABBEY

Buckfastleigh, Devon TQ11 0EE
Tel: 01364 645500 **Fax:** 01364 643891 **E-mail:** education@buckfast.org.uk
Owner: Buckfast Abbey Trust **Contact:** The Warden
The original monastery at Buckfast was formed during the reign of King Cnut in 1018.
Location: MAP 2:J8, OS Ref. SX741 674. ½m from A38 Plymouth – Exeter route.
Open: Church & Grounds: All year: 9am–7pm.
Admission: Free.

Hartland Abbey, Bideford

BUCKLAND ABBEY ❧
YELVERTON, DEVON PL20 6EY
www.nationaltrust.org.uk/buckland

Tel: 01822 853607 **Fax:** 01822 855448
E-mail: bucklandabbey@nationaltrust.org.uk
Owner: The National Trust **Contact:** Jon Cummins – Visitor Services Manager
The spirit of Sir Francis Drake is rekindled at his home with exhibitions of his courageous adventures and achievements throughout the world. One of the Trust's most interesting historical buildings and originally a 13th century monastery, the abbey was transformed into a family residence before Sir Francis bought it in 1581. Fascinating decorated plaster ceiling in Tudor Drake Chamber. Outside there are monastic farm buildings, craft workshops estate walks. Introductory film presentation. Beautiful Elizabethan garden. Letterbox Trail through Great North Wood.

Location: MAP 2:I8, OS201 Ref. SX487 667. 6m S of Tavistock; 11m N of Plymouth off A386. Bus: 55/56 from Yelverton (except Sun).
Open: 12–21 Feb, Daily, 11am–4.30pm; 22 Feb–7 Mar, Fri–Sun, 11–4.30; 13 Mar–31 Oct, Daily, 10.30–5.30; 1 Nov–12 Dec, Fri–Sun, 11–4.30; 17–23 Dec, Daily 11–4.30 for Christmas event.
Admission: Abbey & Grounds: Adult £8.60, Child £4.30, Family £21.30, 1-Adult Family £12.80. Group (15+): Adult £7.30. Grounds only: Adult £4.40, Child £2.20.
ℹ No photography in house. Last admission 45 mins before closing. ◻ ⚹ ⊤ ⬤
WCs. ▣ Licensed. 🍴 Licensed. ✉ By arrangement. ■ 🅿 ⬛ Guide dogs only. ✾▣

CADHAY 🏛

OTTERY ST MARY, DEVON EX11 1QT

www.cadhay.org.uk

Tel: 01404 813511

Owner: Mr R Thistlethwayte   **Contact:** Jayne Covell

Cadhay is approached by an avenue of lime-trees, and stands in an extensive garden, with herbaceous borders and yew hedges, with excellent views over the original medieval fish ponds. The main part of the house was built in about 1550 by John Haydon who had married the de Cadhay heiress. He retained the Great Hall of an earlier house, of which the fine timber roof (about 1420–1460) can be seen. An Elizabethan Long Gallery was added by John's successor at the end of the 16th century, thereby forming a unique courtyard with statues of Sovereigns on each side, described by Sir Simon Jenkins as one of the 'Treasures of Devon'.

Location: MAP 2:L6, OS Ref. SY090 962. 1m NW of Ottery St Mary. From W take A30 and exit at Pattesons Cross, follow signs for Fairmile and then Cadhay. From E, exit at the Iron Bridge and follow signs as above.

Open: May–Sept, Fridays 2pm–5pm. Also: late May + Summer BH Sat–Sun–Mon. Last tour 4.15pm.

Admission: Guided tours: Adult £6.50, Child £2. Gardens: Adults £2.50, Child £1. Parties of 15+ by prior arrangement.

🚻 🚌 ♿ Ground floor & grounds. 🔲 🎫 Obligatory. 🅿 🚻 Guide dogs only. 🔲 🔼

Bicton Park Botanical Gardens

CASTLE DROGO ⚜

DREWSTEIGNTON, EXETER EX6 6PB

www.nationaltrust.org.uk

Tel: 01647 433306   **Fax:** 01647 433186   **E-mail:** castledrogo@nationaltrust.org.uk

Owner: The National Trust   **Contact:** David Bailey, Property Manager

Extraordinary granite and oak castle, designed by Sir Edwin Lutyens, which combines the comforts of the 20th century with the grandeur of a Baronial castle. Elegant dining and drawing rooms and fascinating kitchen and scullery. Terraced formal garden with colourful herbaceous borders and rose beds. Panoramic views over Dartmoor and delightful walks in the dramatic Teign Gorge.

Location: MAP 2:J7, OS191 Ref. SX721 900. 5m S of A30 Exeter–Okehampton road.

Open: Castle Drogo: 13 - 21 Feb, 27, 28 Feb, 6, 7 Mar; 13 Mar - 31 Mar (closed Tuesdays);1 April –5 Sept daily; 6 Sept - 31 Oct (closed Tuesdays)11am - 5pm. Garden, Shop & Tearoom open 13 - 21 Feb; 27,28 Feb, 6,7 Mar; 13 Mar - 31 Oct, daily, 8.30am - 5.30pm. Last admission 1/2 hr before closing. For pre- Christmas opening tel for details.

*Admission: House & Garden: Adult £8.60, Child £4.30, Family £21.60, 1-Adult Family £12.90. Group: £7.30. Garden only: Adult £5.50, Child £3.00, Group £4.70. *includes a voluntary donation but visitors can choose to pay the standard prices displayed at the property and on the website.

🔲 🚻 ♿ Partial. WCs. 🔲 🎫 By arrangement. 🅿 🔲 🚻 In grounds ✳

CHAMBERCOMBE MANOR

Ilfracombe, Devon EX34 9RJ
Tel: 01271 862624 **www.chambercombemanor.co.uk**
Owner: Chambercombe Trust   **Contact:** Angela Powell
Guided tours of Norman Manor House which is mentioned in Domesday Book. Hear the legend of Chambercombe and visit Haunted Room. Set in 16 acres of woodland and landscaped gardens. Lady Jane Tea Rooms offering light lunches and cream teas.
Location: MAP 2:I3, OS Ref. SS539 461. East of Ilfracombe between A399 and B3230, follow brown historic house signs. Private car park at end of Chambercombe Lane.
Open: Easter–end Oct: Mon–Fri, 10.30am–5pm; Sun, 1–5pm. Last tour 4.30pm.
Admission: Adult £7, Child/Conc. £5, Family £22, under 5s free. Group (max 50) discount – apply to Manor.
ℹ No photography in house. ♿ Partial. 📷 Obligatory. 🅿 Limited for coaches.
🐕 On leads, in grounds. ⬆

CLOVELLY

See page 177 for full page entry.

Clovelly, Nr Bideford

COLETON FISHACRE 🦋

BROWNSTONE ROAD, KINGSWEAR, DARTMOUTH TQ6 0EQ

www.nationaltrust.org.uk

Tel: 01803 752466   **Tea-room:** 01803 752984   **Fax:** 01803 753017
E-mail: coletonfishacre@nationaltrust.org.uk
Owner: The National Trust   **Contact:** Administrator
A 30 acre garden set in a stream-fed valley within the spectacular scenery of the South Devon coast. The Lutyens-style house with art deco-influenced interior was built in the 1920s for Rupert and Lady Dorothy D'Oyly Carte who created the delightful garden, planted with a wide range of rare and exotic plants giving year round interest. New for 2010: Open Mondays & Tuesdays.

Location: MAP 2:K9, OS202 Ref. SX910 508. 3m E of Kingswear, follow brown tourist signs.
Open: House, Garden & Tearoom: Sat–Wed 1 Mar–31 Oct. Closed Thurs and Fri, 10.30am–5pm. Last admission ½ hr before closing.
Admission: House & Garden: Adult £7.40, Child £3.70. Family £18.40, 1-Adult Family £11.00. Booked groups (15+): Adult £6.30, Child £3.15.
ℹ No photography in house. 📷 ♿ Limited access. WC. ☕
🅿 Limited. Coaches must book. 🐕 Assistance dogs only in garden.

Devon Coastline near Hartland Abbey

©NTPL/Andrew Butler

COMPTON CASTLE ❧
MARLDON, PAIGNTON TQ3 1TA

www.nationaltrust.org.uk

Tel: 01803 843235 **E-mail:** compton@nationaltrust.org.uk
Owner: The National Trust **Contact:** Administrator
Dramatic fortified manor house built by the Gilbert family between the 14th and 16th centuries. It has been the Gilberts' home for most of the last 600 years. Sir Humphrey Gilbert (1539-1583) was coloniser of Newfoundland and half-brother to Sir Walter Raleigh. There is a lovely rose garden and knot garden to complement the interior which includes great hall, solar, spiral staircases, old kitchen and chapel.
Location: MAP 2:K8, OS180 Ref. SX865 648. At Compton, 3m W of Torquay signed at Marldon. Coaches must approach from A381 Totnes Road at Ipplepen.
Open: 1 Apr–28 Oct: Mons, Weds & Thurs, 10.30am–4.30pm.
Admission: Adult £4.40, Child £2.20. Pre-arranged Groups Adult £3.70, Child £1.90.
🖻 🖵 (not NT) Castle Barton 01803 873314. 🖼 By arrangement.
🅿 Outside Castle or in Castle Barton Car Park. Coaches by appointment only.

CUSTOM HOUSE
THE QUAY, EXETER EX2 4AN

Tel: 01392 665521 **E-mail:** exeter.arch@exeter.gov.uk
Owner: Exeter City Council
The Custom House, located on Exeter's historic Quayside, was constructed from 1680–1682. It is the earliest substantial brick building in Exeter and was used by HM Customs and Excise until 1989. The building has an impressive sweeping staircase and spectacular ornamental plaster ceilings.
Location: MAP 2:K6, OS Ref. SX919 921. Exeter's historic Quayside.
Open: 1 Apr–31 Oct: Guided tour programme, telephone 01392 265203.
Admission: Free.
🦽 Partial. 🖼 Obligatory. 🎦 🖵 Guide dogs only.

CULVER HOUSE
LONGDOWN, EXETER, DEVON EX6 7BD

www.culver.biz

Tel: 01392 811885 **Fax:** 01392 811817 **E-mail:** info@culver.biz
Owner/Contact: Charles Eden Esq
Culver was built in 1836, but redesigned by the great Victorian architect, Alfred Waterhouse in a mock Tudor style. The distinctive interior of the house makes it a favoured location for functions and Culver was featured in BBC1's 'Down to Earth'. It has also been used by German and American film crews.
Location: MAP 2:J7, OS Ref. SX848 901. 5m W of Exeter on B3212.
Open: Not open to the public. Available for corporate hospitality.
Admission: Please telephone for booking details.
🍽

© English Heritage

DARTMOUTH CASTLE ⌗
CASTLE ROAD, DARTMOUTH, DEVON TQ6 0JN

www.english-heritage.org.uk/dartmouth

Tel: 01803 833588 **Fax:** 01803 834445
E-mail: dartmouth.castle@english-heritage.org.uk
Owner: English Heritage **Contact:** Visitor Operations Team
This brilliantly positioned castle juts out into the entrance to the Dart estuary. When begun in 1480s it was one of the most advanced fortifications in England, and was the first castle designed specifically with artillery in mind. For 500 years it kept its defences up-to-date in preparation for war. Today the castle is remarkably intact, along with excellent hands-on exhibitions, the history of the castle comes to life. A picnic spot of exceptional beauty.
Location: MAP 2:K9, OS202 Ref. SX887 503. 1m SE of Dartmouth off B3205, narrow approach road.
Open: 1 Apr–30 Jun: daily, 10am–5pm. 1 Jul–31 Aug: daily,10am–6pm. 1–30 Sep: daily, 10am–5pm. 1–31 Oct: daily, 10am–4pm. 1 Nov–31 Mar: Sat–Sun, 10am–4pm. Closed 24–26 Dec & 1 Jan.
Admission: Adult £4.20, Child £2.10, Conc. £3.60. 15% discount for groups (11+). EH members Free. Opening times and prices are valid until 31st March 2010, after this date details are subject to change please see www.english-heritage.org.uk for the most up-to-date information.
🅸 WC (not EH). 🖻🖵 Not EH. 🅿 Limited (charged, not EH). 🎦🖵 Guide dogs only. ✱🐾

DOCTON MILL & GARDEN

Spekes Valley, Hartland, Devon EX39 6EA
Tel/Fax: 01237 441369
Owner/Contact: John Borrett
Garden for all seasons in 8 acres of sheltered wooded valley, plus working mill.
Location: MAP 1:G5, OS Ref. SS235 226. 3m Hartland Quay. 15m N of Bude. 3m W of A39, 3m S of Hartland.
Open: 1 Mar–31 Oct: 10am–6pm.
Admission: Adult £4, Child (under 16 yrs) Free, OAP £3.75.

DOWNES

Crediton, Devon EX17 3PL
Tel: 01363 775142
Owner: Trustees of the Downes Estate Settlement   **Contact:** Amanda Boulton
Downes is a Palladian Mansion dating originally from 1692. As the former home of General Sir Redvers Buller, the house contains a large number of items relating to his military campaigns. The property is now predominantly a family home with elegant rooms hung with family portraits, and a striking main staircase.
Location: MAP 2:K6, OS Ref. SX852 997. Approx a mile from Crediton town centre.
Open: 5 Apr–6 Jul (and Aug BH Mon & Tues): Mons & Tues between Easter and 6 Jul, guided tours 2.15 & 3.30pm. Open to groups (15+) at other times between 5 Apr–6 Jul, by prior appointment.
Admission: Adult £6, Child (5–16yrs) £3, Child (under 5yrs) Free. Groups (15+) £5.
🅵 Obligatory.

THE ELIZABETHAN GARDENS

Plymouth Barbican Assoc. Ltd, New St, The Barbican, Plymouth PL1 2NA
Tel/Fax: 01822 611027/612983   **E-mail:** avdalo@dsi.pipex.com
Owner: Plymouth Barbican Association Limited   **Contact:** Mr Anthony P Golding
Very small series of four enclosed gardens laid out in Elizabethan style in 1970.
Location: MAP 1:H8, OS Ref. SX477 544. 3 mins walk from Dartington Glass (a landmark building) on the Barbican.
Open: Mon–Sat, 9am–5pm. Closed Christmas.
Admission: Free.

EXETER CATHEDRAL

Exeter, Devon EX1 1HS
Tel: 01392 285983 (Visitors' Officer)   **Fax:** 01392 285986
E-mail: visitors@exeter-cathedral.org.uk
Owner: Dean & Chapter of Exeter   **Contact:** Visitors' Officer
Fine example of decorated gothic architecture. Longest unbroken stretch of gothic vaulting in the world.
Location: MAP 2:K6, OS Ref. SX921 925. Central to the City – between High Street and Southernhay. Groups may be set down in South Street.
Open: All year: Mon–Fri, 9.30am–6.30pm, Sats, 9am–5pm, Suns, 7.30am–6.30pm.
Admission: Donation requested of £3.50 per person. Charges apply to groups.

FINCH FOUNDRY 🦋

Sticklepath, Okehampton, Devon EX20 2NW
Tel: 01837 840046
Owner: The National Trust
19th-century water-powered forge, which produced agricultural and mining hand tools, holding regular demonstrations throughout the day.
Location: MAP 2:I6, OS Ref. SX641 940. 4m E of Okehampton off the A30.
Open: 20 Mar–31 Oct: Daily except Tue, 11am–5pm.
Admission: Adult £4.40, Child £2.20.
🔲 🖻 🅿 Coach parking in road outside. 🔳 🐕 Except tearoom.

Fursdon House

FURSDON HOUSE 🏛

CADBURY, Nr THORVERTON, EXETER, DEVON EX5 5JS
www.fursdon.co.uk

Tel: 01392 860860   **Fax:** 01392 860126   **E-mail:** admin@fursdon.co.uk
Owner: Mr E D Fursdon   **Contact:** Mrs C Fursdon
The Fursdons have lived here for 750 years and the house, greatly modified in the 18th Century, is at the heart of a small estate within a wooded and hilly landscape. Family memorabilia is displayed including a letter to Grace Fursdon from King Charles during the Civil War as well as exceptional examples of costume and textiles. An almost secret terraced and walled garden with shrubs, roses and herbs has extensive views to Dartmoor. Newly opened woodland and Meadow Garden now included. Two private wings offer quality self catering accommodation.
Location: MAP 2:K6, OS Ref. SS922 046. 1½m S of A3072 between Thorverton & Crediton, 9m N of Exeter turning off A396 to Thorverton. Narrow lanes!
Open: House: BH Mons except Christmas. Jun, Jul & Aug, Suns & Weds. Guided tours at 2.30 & 3.30pm. Garden: as house 2–5pm. Tea Room. Groups welcome by prior arrangement.
Admission: House and Garden: Adult £7, Child (10–16yrs) £3, Child (under 10yrs) Free. Garden only: £3.
ℹ️ Conferences. No photography or video. 🆃 🔠 Partial. 🖻 🅵 Obligatory. 🅿
🐕 Guide dogs only. 🛏 Self-catering.

GREAT FULFORD

DUNSFORD, NR EXETER, DEVON EX6 7AJ

Tel: 01647 24205   **Fax:** 01647 24401   **E-mail:** francis@greatfulford.co.uk
Owner/Contact: Francis Fulford
The ancient home of the Fulford family since circa 1190. The house is built round a courtyard and is mainly early Tudor. There is a superb panelled Great Hall and a marvellous 17th century Great Staircase. Other rooms in the 'gothic' taste by James Wyatt when the house was remodelled in 1805.
Location: MAP 2:J7, OS Ref. SX790 917. In the centre of Devon. 10 miles west of Exeter. South of the A30 between the villages of Cheriton Bishop and Dunsford.
Open: All year by appointment only for parties or groups containing a minimum of 10 persons.
Admission: £7.50 per person.
🆃 🖻 🅵 Obligatory. 🅿 🐕 In grounds, on leads.

©NTPL/Andrew Butler

GREENWAY

GREENWAY ROAD, GALMPTON, CHURSTON FERRERS, DEVON TQ5 0ES

www.nationaltrust.org.uk/greenway

Tel: 01803 842382

E-mail: greenway@nationaltrust.org.uk

Owner: The National Trust   **Contact:** Administrator

The many collections, including archaeology, Tunbridgeware, silver, botanical china and books, the atmospheric house set in the 1950s, and the glorious woodland garden with wild edges and rare plantings, all allow a glimpse into the private holiday home of the famous and well-loved author Agatha Christie, and her family. Enjoy the adventure of arriving by ferry from Dartmouth, Brixham or Torquay and alighting at Greenway Quay, with dramatic views of the house from the river.

NB: Timed entry system for house. Tickets cannot be booked, and sell out fast. Cars must be pre-booked: tel or website above. Ferry: 0845 4890418 or www.greenwayferry.co.uk

Location: MAP 2:K8, OS Ref. SX876 548.

Open: 3 Mar–31 Oct, Wed–Sun plus Tues, 20 Jul–31 Aug. 10.30am–5pm (last admission 4.30pm).

Admission: Booked groups and visitors arriving on foot or by ferry: Adult £7.40, Child £3.70, 1-Adult Family £11, 2-Adult Family £18.40. Others (by booked car): Adult £8.60, Child £4.40, 1-Adult Family £13, 2-Adult Family £21.50.

⬚ ⬚ ⬚ ⬚ ⬚ Partial. WC. ⬚ Licensed. ⬚ Licensed. ⬚ ⬚ ⬚
P 1 midi size coach only. Groups must book. Please use river travel. ⬚

© Terry Squires

HALDON BELVEDERE (LAWRENCE CASTLE)

HIGHER ASHTON, NR DUNCHIDEOCK, EXETER, DEVON EX6 7QY

www.haldonbelvedere.co.uk

Tel/Fax: 01392 833668   **E-mail:** enquiries@haldonbelvedere.co.uk

Owner: Devon Historic Buildings Trust   **Contact:** Ian Turner

18th century Grade II* listed triangular tower with circular turrets on each corner. Built in memory of Major General Stringer Lawrence, founder of the Indian Army. Restored in 1995 to illustrate the magnificence of its fine plasterwork, gothic windows, mahogany flooring and marble fireplaces. Breathtaking views of the surrounding Devon countryside. Top floor holiday apartment available.

Location: MAP 2:K7, OS Ref. SX875 861. 7m SW of Exeter. Exit A38 at Exeter racecourse for 2½m.

Open: Feb–Oct: Suns & BHs, 1.30–5.30pm.

Admission: Adult £2, Child Free.

⬚ ⬚ Unsuitable. ⬚ Obligatory. By arrangement. P ⬚ ⬚ In grounds, on leads. ⬚ ⬚

HARTLAND ABBEY

HARTLAND, Nr BIDEFORD, N DEVON EX39 6DT

www.hartlandabbey.com

Tel: 01237 441264/234 or 01884 860225   **Fax:** 01237 441264/01884 861134

E-mail: ha_admin@btconnect.com

Owner: Sir Hugh Stucley Bt   **Contact:** The Administrator

In an enchanting valley leading to the Atlantic coast a mile away, this former Augustinian Abbey was given by Henry VIII to the Sergeant of his Wine Cellar, whose descendants live here today. Amongst the impressive interiors you can see the fabulous Alhambra Corridor by Sir George Gilbert Scott; the Gothic Library by Meadows and fireplace by Batty Langley. Important paintings by artists including Reynolds and Gainsborough, furniture, porcelain, early photographs, documents from 1160 and family memorabilia fascinate visitors. Woodland gardens of bulbs, rhododendrons, azaleas, camellias and hydrangeas lead to the restored Bog Garden and Victorian fernery by Jekyll and 18thC Walled Gardens, where herbaceous, tender and rare plants inc. *echium pininana* and vegetables thrive once again. Historic daffodils, carpets of bluebells and wildflowers in spring. Peacocks, donkeys and black sheep. Film Location of Jane Austen's Sense and Sensibility (BBC 2008) and Rosamund Pilcher's 'The Shell Seekers'. Stunning wedding venue. Holiday cottages, Light lunches and Cream Teas. **NEW FOR 2010; Daffodils and Spring Flowers Sunday 21st March; Bluebell Sundays 18th and 25th April.**

Location: MAP 1:G5, OS Ref. SS240 249. 15m W of Bideford, 15m N of Bude off A39 between Hartland and Hartland Quay.

Open: House: 21 March, 1 Apr–21 May: Wed, Thur, Sun & BHs; 23 May–3 Oct: Sun–Thurs, 2–5pm. Last adm. 4.30pm. Gardens & Grounds: Daily except Sats, 12 noon–5pm.

Admission: House, Gardens & Grounds: Adult £9.50, Child (5–15ys) £2.50, Family £21. Groups (15+) £8, (30+) £7.50. Gardens & Grounds only: Adult £5.00, Child (5–15ys) £1.50, Family £11.

⬚ ⬚ ⬚ Wedding receptions. ⬚ Partial. WC. ⬚ ⬚ By arrangement. P
⬚ In grounds, on leads. ⬚ ⬚ ⬚

Powderham Castle

Totnes Castle

HEMYOCK CASTLE

Hemyock, Cullompton, Devon EX15 3RJ
Tel: 01823 680745   **www.hemyockcastle.co.uk**
Owner/Contact: Mrs Sheppard
Former medieval moated castle, displays show site's history as fortified manor house, castle and farm.
Location: MAP 2:L6, OS Ref. ST135 134. M5/J26, Wellington then 5m S over the Blackdown Hills.
Open: BH Mons 2–5pm. Other times by appointment. Groups & private parties welcome.
Admission: Adult £1, Child 50p. Group rates available.

KILLERTON 🦌
BROADCLYST, EXETER EX5 3LE
www.nationaltrust.org.uk

Tel: 01392 881345   **E-mail:** killerton@nationaltrust.org.uk
Owner: The National Trust   **Contact:** Denise Melhuish – Assistant Property Manager
The spectacular hillside garden is beautiful throughout the year with spring flowering bulbs and shrubs, colourful herbaceous borders and fine trees. The garden is surrounded by parkland and woods offering lovely walks. The house is furnished as a family home and includes a costume collection dating from the 18th century in a series of period rooms and a Victorian laundry. New costume exhibition for 2010 'Elegance' dressing to impress from the 1770s to the 1970s. A selection of some of the most elegant fashions for men and women from the collection. Luxurious accessories and children's clothes are also displayed. With replica costumes to try on!

Location: MAP 2:K6,OS Ref. SS977 001. Off Exeter – Cullompton Rd (B3181). M5 N'bound J30, M5 S'bound J28.
Open: House: 13–21 Feb, 2pm–4pm, Wed–Sun; 10 Mar–31 Oct, 11am–5pm, daily; 4–23 Dec, 2–4pm, daily. Last entry half an hour before closing. Park & Garden: All year: daily, 10.30am–7pm (or dusk).
Admission: House & Garden: Adult £8.40, Child £4.20, Family £20.70, 1-Adult Family £12.90. Garden & Park: Adult £6.20, Child £3.10. Reduced rate when arriving by cycle or public transport. Garden & Park: reduced rate Nov–Feb.
▫️▫️▫️▫️▫️▫️▫️▫️▫️ Bookings required. 🐕 Guide dogs only in house. ▫️▫️

KNIGHTSHAYES COURT ✿

BOLHAM, TIVERTON, DEVON EX16 7RQ

www.nationaltrust.org.uk

Tel: 01884 254665 **E-mail:** knightshayes@nationaltrust.org.uk
Owner: The National Trust   **Contact:** Penny Woollams – Property Manager
The striking Victorian gothic house is a rare survival of the work of William Burges with
ornate patterns in many rooms. One of the finest gardens in Devon, mainly woodland
and shrubs with something of interest throughout the seasons. Drifts of spring bulbs,
summer flowering shrubs, pool garden and amusing topiary.
Location: MAP 2:K5, OS Ref. SS960 151. 2m N of Tiverton (A396) at Bolham.
Open: House: 13–21 Feb, daily except Fri, 27 Feb–7 Mar, Sat/Sun, 11am–4pm, 13

Mar–31 Oct, daily except Fri (open Good Fri), 11am–5pm. Last adm. ½hr before closing.
Garden: dates as house, daily 11am–5pm. Shop/plant centre & restaurant as garden.
Limited opening for garden/house and facilities in Nov & Dec, tel for details.
*Admission: House & Garden: Adult £8.60, Child £4.30, Family £21.50, 1 Adult Family
£12.90. Group: Adult £7.25, Child £3.60. Garden only: Adult £6.85, Child £3.45. Group:
Adult £5.75, Child £2.70. *includes a voluntary donation but visitors can choose to pay
the standard prices displayed at the property and on the website.
⊡ ⚑ ⊤ ⑤ Ground floor & grounds. WC. ⑪ ⊠ On leads in park.

LOUGHWOOD MEETING HOUSE ✿

Dalwood, Axminster, Devon EX13 7DU
Tel/Fax: 01752 346585
Owner: The National Trust
Around 1653 the Baptist congregation of the nearby village of Kilmington constructed
this simple thatched building dug into the hillside. It still contains the original box
pews.
Location: MAP 2:M6, OS Ref. SY253993. 4m W of Axminster.
Open: All year, daily.
Admission: Free.
ⓘ Pushchairs and baby carriers admitted. ⑤ Steep slope from the car park. Ground
floor only. ℙ Very narrow country lanes. No parking for coaches. ⊛

MARKER'S COTTAGE ✿

Broadclyst, Exeter, Devon EX5 3HR
Tel: 01392 881345 (Killerton House for information)
Owner: The National Trust   **Contact:** The Custodian
Thatched, medieval cob house containing a cross-passage screen decorated with a
painting of St Andrew and his attributes.
Location: MAP 2:K6, OS Ref. SX985 973. ¼m E of B3181 in village of Broadclyst.
Open: 4 Apr–31 Oct: Sun–Tue, 2–5pm. Last entry ½ hour before closing.
Admission: Adult £2.80, Child £1.40. Joint ticket with Clyston Mill: Adult £5.30,
Child £2.65.

MARWOOD HILL

Barnstaple, Devon EX31 4EB
Tel: 01271 342528   **Contact:** Patricia Stout
20 acre garden with 3 small lakes. Extensive collection of camellias, bog garden. National
collection of astilbes.
Location: MAP 2:I4, OS Ref. SS545 375. 4m N of Barnstaple. ½m W of B3230. Signs off
A361 Barnstaple – Braunton road.
Open: All year: 10am–5pm.
Admission: Adult £4.50, Child (under 12yrs) Free.

MORWELLHAM QUAY

Morwellham, Tavistock, Devon PL19 8JL
Tel: 01822 832766 Fax: 01822 833808
Owner: The Morwellham & Tamar Valley Trust   **Contact:** Anthony Power
Award-winning visitor centre at historic river port.
Location: MAP 1:H8, OS Ref. SX446 697. Off A390 about 15 mins drive from Tavistock,
Devon. 5m SW of Tavistock. 3m S of A390 at Gulworthy.
Open: Summer: daily, 10am–5.30pm, last adm. 3.30pm. Winter: daily, 10am–4.30pm,
last adm. 2.30pm.
Admission: Adult £8.90, Child £6, OAP £7.80, Disabled £3.70, Family (2+2) £19.50.
Group rate please apply for details. Usual concessions. Prices may be subject to change.

OKEHAMPTON CASTLE ⌗

Okehampton, Devon EX20 1JA
Tel: 01837 52844 **E-mail:** customers@english-heritage.org.uk
www.english-heritage.org.uk/okehampton
Owner: English Heritage   **Contact:** Visitor Operations Team
The ruins of the largest castle in Devon stand above a river surrounded by splendid
woodland. There is still plenty to see, including the Norman motte and the jagged
remains of the Keep. There is a picnic area and lovely woodland walks.
Location: MAP 2:I6, OS Ref. SX584 942. 1m SW of Okehampton town centre off
A30 bypass.
Open: 1 Apr–30 Jun: daily, 10am–5pm. 1 Jul–31 Aug: daily, 10am–6pm. 1–30 Sep: daily,
10am–5pm. Closed 1 Oct–31 Mar.
Admission: Adult £3.30, Child £1.70, Conc. £2.80. 15% discount for groups (11+).
EH members Free. Opening times and prices are valid until 31st March 2010, after this
date details are subject to change please see www.english-heritage.org.uk for the
most up-to-date information.
⊡ ⑤ WCs. Access difficult for ambulant disabilities. ⌂ ℙ ⊠ ⊠ In grounds, on leads.

OLDWAY MANSION
TORQUAY ROAD, PAIGNTON, DEVON TQ3 2CR

www.englishriviera.co.uk

Tel: 01803 207933 **E-mail:** fmhelpdesk@torbay.gov.uk
Owner: Torbay Council **Contact:** Stuart Left
Oldway Mansion, one of the grandest houses in the Torbay, was built in 1874 for Isaac Singer, the American millionaire sewing machine manufacturer. It was one of Isaac's sons, Paris Singer, who took over residency in the mansion and who gave it its present form. A regular visitor to Oldway was Paris's mistress, Isadora Duncan. Modelled on the Palace of Versailles, Oldway Mansion is where visitors can see The Gallery, a miniature reproduction of the 'Hall of Mirrors' and the Ballroom. The formal gardens were originally laid out by Achille Duchêne, of Blenheim Palace fame.
Location: MAP 2:K8, OS Ref. SX888 615. Off W side of A3022.
Open: All year: Apr–Oct, daily, 9am–5pm. Nov–Mar, Mon–Sat, 9am–5pm.
Admission: Free.
🔲🔲🔲🔲 By arrangement. 🅿 Limited. 🔲🔲 Guide dogs only. 🔲🔲

OVERBECK'S 🦋
SHARPITOR, SALCOMBE, SOUTH DEVON TQ8 8LW

www.nationaltrust.org.uk

Tel: 01548 842893 **E-mail:** overbecks@nationaltrust.org.uk
Owner: The National Trust **Contact:** Property Manager
Open the door to the most fascinating and exotic garden in the Southwest; explore the banana garden, meander through the towering purple echiums or just relax beneath palms and soak up the spectacular panorama of beautiful coastline. Continue your journey of discovery into the Edwardian house of Otto Overbeck.
Location: MAP 2:J10, OS Ref. SX728 374. 1½m SW of Salcombe. Signposted from Salcombe (single track lanes).
Open: Garden, Museum, Shop and Tea Room (4.15) Sat–Thurs, 13 March to 31 October 11am–5pm; Garden only - Monday to Thursday 1st November 10 to 31 January 11 from 11am–4pm. Open Fridays in holidays Feb–Oct.
Admission: Adult £6.70, Child £3.40, Family £16.80, 1-Adult Family £10.10. Groups £5.70.
ℹ No photography in house. 🔲🔲🔲🔲 Obligatory. By arrangement.
🅿 Limited. Charge refunded on admission. 🔲🔲🔲

POWDERHAM CASTLE 🏰
KENTON, Nr EXETER, DEVON EX6 8JQ

www.powderham.co.uk

Tel: 01626 890243 **Fax:** 01626 890729 **E-mail:** castle@powderham.co.uk
Owner: The Earl of Devon **Contact:** Mr Simon Fishwick – Estate Director
A splendid castle built in 1391 by Sir Philip Courtenay, remaining in the same family and currently home to the 18th Earl of Devon. Set in a tranquil deer park alongside the Exe estuary, its stunning location offers glorious views for miles around. A splendid Rose Garden terrace and walk through the Woodland Garden are very rewarding. Guided tours showcase the Castle's majestic rooms, stunning interiors and fine collection of treasures, while fascinating stories bring its intriguing history to life. The recently-restored Victorian kitchen offers an insight into domestic service at the Castle. The Victorian kitchen garden is now a children's play area with friendly animals.

Location: MAP 2:K7, OS Ref. SX965 832. 6m SW of Exeter, 4m S M5/J30. Access from A379 in Kenton village. Bus: No 2 Bus stops outside. Rail: Starcross Station – 2m. Ferry: Starcross Ferry – 2m
Open: 1 Apr–31 Oct: Sun–Fri, 11am–4.30pm (Last guided tour 1hr before closing). Available for private hire all year.
Admission: Adult £8.95, Child (5–14yrs) £6.95, Senior £7.95, Family: £25. Groups (15+) special rates available. (2009 prices).
ℹ Available for private hire all year round. 🔲🔲🔲🔲 Partial. WCs. 🔲 Licensed.
🔲 Licensed. 🔲 Included. 1hr. 🅿🔲🔲 Guide dogs only. 🔲

RHS GARDEN ROSEMOOR
GREAT TORRINGTON, DEVON EX38 8PH

www.rhs.org.uk/rosemoor

Tel: 01805 624067 **Fax:** 01805 624717 **E-mail:** rosemooradmin@rhs.org.uk
Owner/Contact: The Royal Horticultural Society

An enchanting 65-acre garden offering year-round interest and something for all interests and tastes. Visit us for inspiration, tranquility or simply a marvellous day out. Shop, plant centre, restaurant and tearoom on site offering exciting gifts and a relaxing place to enjoy a delicious meal.

Location: MAP 2:I5, OS Ref. SS500 183. 1m S of Great Torrington on A3124.
Open: All year except Christmas Day; Apr–Sept: 10am–6pm. Oct–Mar: 10am–5pm.
Admission: Adult £6.50, Child (6–16yrs) £2, Child (under 6yrs) Free. Groups (10+) £5.50pp. Companion for disabled visitor Free. RHS member & 1 guest Free.

Licensed. By arrangement. Guide dogs only.

SAND

SIDBURY, SIDMOUTH EX10 0QN
Tel: 01395 597230 **E-mail:** info@sandsidbury.co.uk **www.sandsidbury.co.uk**
Contact: Mrs Stella Huyshe-Shires

Sand is one of East Devon's hidden gems. The beautiful valley garden extends to 6 acres and is the setting for the lived-in house, the 15th century Hall House, and the 17th century Summer House. The family, under whose unbroken ownership the property has remained since 1560, provide guided house tours.

Location: MAP 2:L7, OS Ref. SY146 925. Well signed, 400 yards off A375 between Honiton and Sidmouth.
Open: House: Suns & Mons in July and on Bank Holidays, 4/5 Apr, 2/3 May, 30/31 May, 4/5, 11/12, 18/19, 25/26 July & 29/30 Aug: 2–6pm. Garden: 4 Apr–28 Sep: Sun–Tues, 2–6pm. Last admission to house & garden 5pm. Groups by appointment throughout the year.
Admission: House & Garden: Adult £6, Child/Student £1. Garden only: Adult £3, accompanied Child (under 16) Free.

No photography in house. Partial. Obligatory.
In grounds, on leads. Tel. for details.

Okehampton Castle

© NTPL/Joe Cornish
©NTPL/Rupert Truman

SALTRAM
PLYMPTON, PLYMOUTH, DEVON PL7 1UH

www.nationaltrust.org.uk

Tel: 01752 333500 **Fax:** 01752 336474 **E-mail:** saltram@nationaltrust.org.uk
Owner: The National Trust **Contact:** Administrator

Saltram stands high above the River Plym in a rolling and wooded landscaped park that now provides precious green space on the outskirts of Plymouth. The house, with its magnificent decoration and original contents, was largely created between the 1740s and 1820s by three generations of the Parker family. It features some of Robert Adam's finest rooms, exquisite plasterwork ceilings, original Chinese wallpapers and an exceptional collection of paintings including many by Sir Joshua Reynolds and Angelica Kauffman. The garden is predominantly 19th-century and contains an orangery and several follies, as well as beautiful shrubberies and imposing specimen trees.

The shop and art gallery offer work for sale from contemporary local artists, and National Trust gifts. The Park Restaurant offers refreshments for its visitors. Corporate business and special functions are very welcome.

Location: MAP 2:I9, OS Ref. SX520 557. From A38, exit 3 miles north of Plymouth City Centre at Marsh Mill's roundabout. Take Plympton exit; continue in right hand lane to third set of traffic lights then turn right onto Cott Hill. At the top of the hill turn right into Merafield Road then right again after 200 yards.
Open: House: 9 Feb–28 Feb weekends only; 13 Mar–31 Oct daily except Fris (open Good Fri), 12 noon–4.30pm. Last admission to house 3.45pm. Garden: all year, daily (except Fri, open Good Fri), 11am–5pm (4pm Nov–Mar). Restaurant: all year, daily, 11am–5pm (11am–4pm & closed Fri Nov–Mar). Tel for details of Christmas closure.
*Admission: House & Garden: Adult £9.60, Child £4.80, Family £23.90, 1–Adult Family £14.30. Groups (15+): £7.90. Garden only: Tickets available. *includes a voluntary donation but visitors can choose to pay the standard prices displayed at the property and on the website.

WC. Braille guide. Licensed.
On signed perimeter paths only, on leads. Guide dogs only in house & garden.

SHUTE BARTON 🦌

Shute, Axminster, Devon EX13 7PT
Tel: 01752 346585 www.nationaltrust.org.uk
Owner: The National Trust
One of the most important surviving non-fortified manor houses of the Middle Ages.
Location: MAP 2:M6, OS Ref. SY253 974. 3m SW of Axminster, 2m N of Colyton, 1m S of A35.
Open: 4 weekends 15 May–17 Oct 11am–5pm only. Tel. for dates.
Admission: Adult £3.20, Child £1.60. No group reductions.

TAPELEY PARK & GARDENS

Instow, Bideford, Devon EX39 4NT
Tel: 01271 860897 **Fax:** 01271 342371
Owner: Tapeley Park Trust
Extensive gardens and park.
Location: MAP 1:H4, OS Ref. SS478 291. Between Bideford and Barnstaple near Instow. Follow brown tourist signs from the A39 onto B3233.
Open: Good Fri–end Oct: daily except Sats, 10am–5pm.
Admission: Adult £4, Child £2.50, OAP £3.50. Groups (5+): Adult £3.20, Child £2 (under 5s Free), OAP £2.80 (2007 prices).

TIVERTON CASTLE 🏰

TIVERTON, DEVON EX16 6RP

www.tivertoncastle.com

Tel: 01884 253200/255200 **Fax:** 01884 254200 **E-mail:** tiverton.castle@ukf.net
Owner: Mr and Mrs A K Gordon **Contact:** Mrs A Gordon
Part Grade I Listed, part Scheduled Ancient Monument, few buildings evoke such an immediate feeling of history. All ages of architecture from medieval to modern. Fun for children - try on Civil War armour; ghost stories, secret passages, beautiful walled gardens, including working kitchen garden. Interesting furniture, pictures. Comfortable holiday apartments.
Location: MAP 2:K5, OS Ref. SS954 130. Just N of Tiverton town centre.
Open: Easter–end Oct: Sun, Thur, BH Mon, 2.30–5.30pm. Last admission 5pm. Open to groups (12+) by prior arrangement at any time.
Admission: Adult £6, Child (7–16yrs) £2.50, Child under 7 Free. Garden only: £1.50.
🔲 🔲 Partial. 🔲 By arrangement. 🅿 🔳 🔳 🔳 4 Apartments.

TORRE ABBEY

THE KING'S DRIVE, TORQUAY, DEVON TQ2 5JE

www.torre-abbey.org.uk

Tel: 01803 293593 **E-mail:** torre-abbey@torbay.gov.uk
Owner: Torbay Council **Contact:** Dr Michael Rhodes
A recent £6m restoration has brought this Devon gem to life. The medieval abbey, historic family home and garden, impressive art collection and lively contemporary exhibitions combine to make a thoroughly enjoyable visit. Torre Abbey, the historic and cultural heart of Torquay, is just minutes from the English Riviera's promenades.
Location: Map 2:K8 OS Ref. SX906 638. On Torquay seafront between rail station and harbour.
Open: Open daily from 10am to 6pm Apr-Oct, 10am to 5pm Nov-Mar. Last admission one hour before closing. Closed 25-26 Dec, all of Jan and Mondays in Feb.
Admission: Adult £5.75 Concessions £4.80 Child £2.45 (subject to change).
🔲 🔲 🔲 🔲 WC. 🔲 🔲 🔲 🔲 🔲 🔲 🅿 Nearby.

TOTNES CASTLE ⚔

Castle Street, Totnes, Devon TQ9 5NU
Tel/Fax: 01803 864406 **E-mail:** customers@english-heritage.org.uk
www.english-heritage.org.uk/totnes
Owner: English Heritage **Contact:** Visitor Operations Team
By the North Gate of the hill town of Totnes you will find a superb motte and bailey castle, with splendid views across the roof tops and down to the River Dart. It is a symbol of lordly feudal life and a fine example of Norman fortification.
Location: MAP 2:J8, OS202 Ref. SX800 605. In Totnes, on hill overlooking the town. Access in Castle St off W end of High St.
Open: 1 Apr–30 Jun: daily 10am–5pm. 1 Jul–31 Aug: daily, 10am–6pm. 1–30 Sep: daily, 10am–5pm. 1–31 Oct: daily, 10am–4pm. Closed 1 Nov–31 Mar.
Admission: Adult £3, Child £1.50, Conc. £2.60. 15% discount for groups (11+). EH members Free. Opening times and prices are valid until 31st March 2010, after this date details are subject to change please see www.english-heritage.org.uk for the most up-to-date information.
🔲 🔲 Very restricted. 🅿 Charged, 64 metres (70 yds), not EH. 🔳 🔳 In grounds, on leads.

See which properties offer **educational facilities** or **school visits** in our index at the end of the book.

Saltram

© Julien Lightfoot

■ Owner
The Hon
Mrs Townshend DL

■ Contact
Shop Manager
Abbotsbury
Weymouth
Dorset DT3 4LA

Tel: 01305 871387
E-mail: info@abbotsbury-tourism.co.uk

■ Location
MAP 2:N7
OS Ref. SY564 851

Off A35 nr Dorchester, on B3157 between Weymouth & Bridport.

■ Opening Times
Mar–Nov: daily,
10am–6pm.

Winter: daily,
10am–4pm.
(Closed Christmas and New Year.)

Last admission
1 hr before closing.

■ Admission
Adult	£9.50
Child	£6.50
OAP	£9.00

ABBOTSBURY SUBTROPICAL GARDENS 🏛

www.abbotsburygardens.co.uk   www.abbotsburyplantsales.co.uk

© Carole Drake

Established in 1765 by the first Countess of Ilchester. Developed since then into a 20-acre Grade I listed, magnificent woodland valley garden.

World famous for its camellia groves, magnolias, rhododendron and hydrangea collections. In summer it is awash with colour.

Since the restoration after the great storm of 1990 many new and exotic plants have been introduced. The garden is now a mixture of formal and informal, with charming walled garden and spectacular woodland valley views.

Facilities include a Colonial Tea House for lunches, snacks and drinks, a plant centre and quality gift shop. Events such as Shakespeare and concerts are presented during the year. The floodlighting of the garden at the end of October should not be missed.

The garden is now licenced for civil marriage cermonies.

Voted "Our Favourite Garden" by readers of *The Daily Telegraph*.

"One of the finest gardens I have ever visited and which is open to the public" *Alan Titchmarsh BBC Gardeners World magazine Sept 2008.*

Plants also for sale online.

Partial.

Licensed.

By arrangement.

Free.

In grounds, on leads.

Civil Wedding Licence

■ **Owner**
Mr & Mrs Julian Kennard

■ **Contact**
Carolyn Clay
Forde Abbey
Chard
Somerset TA20 4LU
Tel: 01460 220231
E-mail:
info@fordeabbey.co.uk

■ **Location**
MAP 2:N6
OS Ref. ST358 041
Just off the B3167
4m SE of Chard.

■ **Opening Times**
House
1st April–31 October
Tue–Fri, Sun & BH Mons
12 noon–4pm (last
admission).

Gardens
Daily all year:
10am–4.30pm (last
admission).

■ **Admission**
For current admission
prices phone
01460 221290.

FORDE ABBEY & GARDENS 🏛

www.fordeabbey.co.uk

Forde Abbey is a treasure in an area already known for its outstanding beauty. More than 900 years of history are encapsulated in this elegant former Cistercian monastery and its 30 acres of award-winning gardens. In the peaceful solitude of its secluded position it is possible to imagine just how it looked to its previous owners: monks going about their daily round of work and prayer, prosperous parliamentary gentlemen discussing the Cavalier threat, gifted philosophers debating the imponderable, elegant Victorian ladies fanning themselves by the fireside and country gentlemen going about their work on the estate.

Set on the banks of the River Axe, this beautiful home contains many treasures including the Mortlake Tapestries, woven from cartoons painted for the Sistine Chapel by Raphael. The intricacy of their original design is matched by the story behind these particular tapestries involving Civil war, rebellion and loyalty rewarded.

The garden has been described by Alan Titchmarsh as *"one of the greatest gardens of the West Country"* and includes a mature arboretum, rockery, bog garden, working kitchen garden, sloping lawns and a cascade of lakes surrounding the Centenary Fountain, the highest powered fountain in England. The fruits of the garden and estate can be sampled in the Undercroft restaurant with a wide selection of homemade lunches and cakes. A gift shop, plant centre and pottery exhibition add to the day.

Enjoy England Awards for Excellence Silver Winner 2008
South West Tourism's Small Visitor Attraction of the Year 2006 & 2007

i	Available for wedding receptions. No photography in house.
🛍	
✿	
♿	Partial.
🍷	Licensed.
🍴	Licensed.
🚶	By arrangement.
P	
🐕	On leads, in grounds.
🔔	
❄	

South West – England

■ Owner
The National Trust

■ Contact
The Property Manager
Kingston Lacy
Wimborne Minster
Dorset BH21 4EA

Tel: 01202 883402
Fax: 01202 882402

E-mail: kingstonlacy@
nationaltrust.org.uk

■ Location
MAP 3:A6
OS Ref. ST980 019

On B3082 – Blandford /
Wimborne road, 1½m NW
of Wimborne Minster.

Rail: Poole 8½m.

Bus: Wilts & Dorset
132/3, 182/3 from
Bournemouth, Poole,
alight Wimborne
Square. 2½m walk
or Fri & Sat Nordcat
Limited Service.

■ Opening Times
House
13 March–31 October
Wed–Sun, 11am–5pm.

Garden & Park
5 February–7 March, Fri,
Sat & Sun,
10.30am–4pm,
13 March–31 October,
10.30am–6pm, Mon–Sun
1 November–23
December, 10.30am–4pm,
Mon–Sun.

Shop & Restaurant
5 February–7 March,
Fri, Sat & Sun,
10.30am–3.30pm
13 March–31 October,
daily, 10.30am–5.30pm,
Mon–Sun.
1 November–23 December,
Mon–Sun,
10.30am–3.30pm.

Open Bank Holidays.
Admission by timed ticket
may operate on Bank
Holiday Sundays and
Mondays. Last admission
to house one hour before
closing. Garden, park,
shop and restaurant
closed 24–31 December
2010.

■ Admission
Gift Aid Admission
(Standard Admission
prices in brackets)

House & Garden
Adult   £12.00 (£10.50)
Child   £6.00 (£5.25)
Family   £26.50 (£30.00)

Park & Garden only
Adult   £6.00 (£5.25)
Child   £3.00 (£2.70)
Family   £15.00 (£13.00)

© NT / Kingston Lacy

KINGSTON LACY ❧

www.nationaltrust.org.uk/wessex

Kingston Lacy House lies at the heart of the 8,500 acre Bankes Estate. Opened to the public twenty five years ago, the 'secret estate' is still only slowly revealing itself. Lying 1½ miles from Wimborne Minster and 9 miles from the market town of Blandford Forum on the B3082, Kingston Lacy is the gateway to true, rural Dorset.

As the home of the Bankes family for 300 years, Kingston Lacy replaced the original family seat of Corfe Castle and is now presented by the National Trust as it was in its Edwardian heyday. This elegant country mansion contains an outstanding collection of fine works of art, including a Titian, two Rubens and the astounding Guido Reni detached fresco "Separation of Night from Day" returned to the Library ceiling following extensive restoration. Works by Spanish painters, including Velazquez, are hung in the extraordinary Spanish room created by William John Bankes. His collection of Egyptian artefacts is displayed within the House and outside in the Garden. Sculptures in wood, marble and bronze, much of it especially commissioned for the House, completes the magnificent interiors, while the Laundry adjacent to the House gives a glimpse of life "below stairs".

The 43 acres of formal gardens, many of them true to their Edwardian plantings, include the Fernery, Parterre and Sunk Gardens and the recently restored Japanese Gardens. The surrounding three hundred acre park and woodland are crossed by way-marked walks and include three child-friendly play areas.

Events occur throughout the year, including outdoor theatre, walks, talks and family activities.

© NT / Kingston Lacy

 Garden only. Braille guide & Induction Loop system. Interactive virtual tour. WC. Less-abled access info: 01202 883402.

Licensed.

By arrangement.

 On leads, in park & woodland walks only.

 Tel: 01202 883402.

ATHELHAMPTON HOUSE & GARDENS 🏛
DORCHESTER, DT2 7LG
www.athelhampton.co.uk

Tel: 01305 848363   **Email:** enquiry@athelhampton.co.uk
Owner: Patrick Cooke Esq   **Contact:** Owen Davies or Laura Dean
Topiary restaurant open as House & Gardens. Bookings taken for Sunday Carvery. Athelhampton's facilities are available for private visits & entertaining outside our opening hours throughout the year. We hold wedding Ceremonies & Receptions on Fridays and Saturdays. Please contact Owen Davies, Catering Manager.
Location: MAP 2:P6, OS Ref. SY771 942. Off A35 (T) at Puddletown Northbrook junction, 5m E of Dorchester. Nearest rail station Dorchester.

Open: 1 Mar–28 Oct, Sun–Thur (Open Sundays Nov–Feb), 10.30am–5pm/dusk. Last admission 4.30pm.
Admission: House & Gardens: Adult £9.25, Child (under 16) Free, Student/Disabled £6.50, Senior £8.75. Groups (12+) Adult £7.75 (£6.75 with pre-booked catering order). See our website for special offers and up-to-date admission charges.
By arrangement. Partial. WC. Licensed. Licensed. By arrangement. Guide dogs only. 2 May NCCPG Plant Sale, 13–17 Jun Flower Festival, 8 Aug MG Owners' Day, 30 Aug Village Fete.

ABBOTSBURY SUBTROPICAL GARDENS 🏛
See page 190 for full page entry.

BROWNSEA ISLAND 🌳
Poole Harbour, Dorset BH13 7EE
Tel: 01202 707744 **Fax:** 01202 701635 **E-mail:** brownseaisland@nationaltrust.org.uk
www.nationaltrust.org.uk/brownsea
Owner: The National Trust **Contact:** NT Office
Atmospheric island of heath and woodland with wide variety of wildlife. The island is dramatically located at the entrance to Poole harbour, offering spectacular views across to Studland and the Purbeck Hills. Its varied and colourful history includes use as a coastguard station, Victorian pottery, Edwardian country estate, daffodil farm, and as a decoy in the Second World War. In 1907 it was the site of Baden-Powell's experimental camp from which Scouting and Guiding evolved. Home to important populations of red squirrels and seabirds, the island provides a safe and relaxing place for walks and picnics, ideal for families to explore.
Location: MAP 3:A7, OS Ref. SZ032 878. In Poole Harbour. Boats run from Poole Quay and Sandbanks every 30 mins.
Open: 13 Mar–26 Mar: daily 10am–5pm*; 27 Mar–31 Oct, daily 10–5. *Boat service from Sandbanks only, full boat service from Poole Quay and Sandbanks from 27 Mar.
*Admission: Adult £5.50, Child: £2.70, Family (2+3) £13.70, Family (1+3) £8.20. *Price includes voluntary gift aid donation: visitors can however, choose to pay the standard admission charges which are displayed on the island and at www.nationaltrust.org.uk
Partial.

© Carole Drake
Abbotsbury Subtropical Gardens

CHURCH OF OUR LADY & ST IGNATIUS
North Chideock, Bridport, Dorset DT6 6LF
Tel: 01308 488348 **E-mail:** amyasmartelli40@hotmail.com
Owner: The Weld Family Trust **Contact:** Mrs G Martelli
The Church, dedicated to Our Lady Queen of Martyrs and St Ignatius, was built on the site of an existing chapel-barn in 1872 by Charles Weld of Chideock Manor. It is one of the gems of English Catholicism and is designed in the Italian Romanesque style. It is a pilgrimage centre of the Chideock martyrs who are depicted in portraits over the nave. 19th century wall paintings by the Weld family can be seen in the original barn-chapel (now priest's sacristry) by arrangement. The church is also a shrine to Our Lady and has been a centre of Catholicism since penal times. A Museum of village life is on view in the adjoining cloister.
Location: MAP 2:N6, OS Ref. SY419 937. A35 from Bridport into Chideock. Right at St Giles' Church. Continue towards North Chideock for ½m. The Church is on the right.
Open: All year: 10am–4pm.
Admission: Donations welcome.
Moveable ramp in Church Porch. Limited.

CLAVELL TOWER
Kimmeridge, near Wareham, Dorset
Tel: 01628 825925 **E-mail:** bookings@landmarktrust.org.uk
www.landmarktrust.org.uk
Owner/Contact: The Landmark Trust
Clavell Tower was built in 1830 by Reverend John Richards Clavell of Smedmore as an observatory and folly. It was designed by Robert Vining with four storeys and a distinctive Tuscan colonnade. Also known as the Tower of the Winds, it has a special place in literary history. Thomas Hardy often took his first love, Eliza Nicholl, there and used it as a frontispiece for his Wessex Poems. The Tower was also the inspiration for PD James' novel, The Black Tower. It was derelict from the 1930s and remained so up until 2007 when it was painstakingly rebuilt 25 metres inland by the Landmark Trust, safeguarding it from the cliff erosion and further neglect. Full details of Clavell Tower and 189 other historical and architecturally important buildings are featured in the Landmark Trust Handbook (price £10 plus p&p refundable against a booking) and on the website.
Location: Map 2:A7, OS Ref. SY909 786
Open: Available for holidays for up to 2 people throughout the year. Two Open Days a year. Other visits by appointment. Contact the Landmark Trust for details.
Admission: Free on Open Days.

©NTPL/Dennis Gilbert

CLOUDS HILL ❧
WAREHAM, DORSET BH20 7NQ

www.nationaltrust.org.uk

Tel: 01929 405616 **Email:** westdorset@nationaltrust.org.uk
Owner: The National Trust **Contact:** The Custodian
A tiny isolated brick and tile cottage, bought in 1929 by T E Lawrence (Lawrence of Arabia) as a retreat. The austere rooms inside are much as he left them and reflect his complex personality and close links with the Middle East. An exhibition details Lawrence's extraordinary life.
Location: (194:SY824909) Station: Wool 3½m; Moreton (U) 3½m. Road: 1m N of Bovington Tank Museum, 9m E of Dorchester, 1½m E of Waddock crossroads (B3390), 4m S of A35 Poole–Dorchester.
Open: 18 Mar - 31 Oct, Thurs–Sun & BH Mons, 12 noon–5pm or dusk if earlier; no electric light. Groups wishing to visit at other times must telephone in advance.
Admission: £4.50, Child £2
ℹ️ No WC. 🅿 No coaches. 🎦 Small groups.

©NTPL/Joe Cornish

CORFE CASTLE ❧
WAREHAM, DORSET BH20 5EZ

www.nationaltrust.org.uk

Tel: 01929 481294 **Fax:** 01929 477067 **E-mail:** corfecastle@nationaltrust.org.uk
Owner: The National Trust **Contact:** Visitor Services and Enterprises Manager
One of Britain's most majestic ruins, the Castle controlled the gateway through the Purbeck Hills and had been an important stronghold since the time of William the Conqueror. Defended during the Civil War by the redoubtable Lady Bankes, the Castle fell to treachery from within and was substantially destroyed afterwards by the Parliamentarians. Many fine Norman and early English features remain. Visitor Centre at Castle View.
Location: MAP 3:A7, OS Ref. SY959 824. On A351 Wareham–Swanage Rd. NW of the village.
Open: All year: daily. Mar & Oct: 10am–5pm; Apr–Sept: 10am–6pm; Nov–Feb (Closed 25/26 Dec), 10am–4pm.
***Admission:** Adult £6.20, Child £3.10, Family (2+3) £15.50, (1+3) £9.30. Groups: Adult £5, Child £2.45. *includes a voluntary donation but visitors can choose to pay the standard prices displayed at the property and on the website.
🎦 ♿ Limited. Braille guide. WC. 🎦🎦🎦🅿🎦 On leads. ❄️🎦

DEANS COURT 🏛
WIMBORNE, DORSET BH21 1EE

Tel: 07966 363791
Owner: Sir William Hanham **Email:** estateoffice.deanscourt@googlemail.com
This fine Georgian house and beautiful garden offers an oasis of tranquility just a few minutes walk from Wimborne Minster. The historic house, previously the Deanery to the Minster, is rich in family history and is surrounded by stunning gardens, which extend over 13 acres, include an 18th century organic kitchen garden bordered by a serpentine wall built by prisoners from the Napoleonic Wars, large monastic fishpond, a manicured herb garden, an apiary, a series of lawns giving way to semi-wild areas, mature specimen trees, a rose garden and Georgian stable block. The Gardens also include a delightful stretch of River Allen, well-known for its trout.
Dean's Court is a popular venue for weddings, civil ceremonies, photo shoots and filming.
Location: MAP 3:A6, OS Ref. SZ010 997. 2 mins walk S from centre of Wimborne Minster. Entrance signed from Deans Court Lane.
Open: Gardens only (for NGS): 2/3 May, 30/31 May, 2 & 9 June, 29/30 August: 11am–6pm. Guided tours of house & garden by prior appointment (not on garden open days).
Admission: Adult £4, Child under 16yrs Free, Senior Citizens £3.
ℹ️ Weddings and special events 🎦 Organic garden produce sales.
♿ Some gravel paths 🎦 Light lunches and home-made cream teas by fishpond or in tea room. 🅿 Free in Garden. 🐕 Well-behaved dogs on leads welcome.

EDMONDSHAM HOUSE & GARDENS 🏛

Cranborne, Wimborne, Dorset BH21 5RE
Tel: 01725 517207
Owner/Contact: Mrs Julia E Smith
Charming blend of Tudor and Georgian architecture with interesting contents. Organic walled garden, 6 acre garden with unusual trees and spring bulbs. 12th century church nearby.
Location: MAP 3:A5, OS Ref. SU062 116. Off B3081 between Cranborne and Verwood, NW from Ringwood 9m, Wimborne 9m.
Open: House & Gardens: All BH Mons & Weds in Apr & Oct 2–5pm. Gardens: Apr–Oct, Suns & Weds 2–5pm.
Admission: House & Garden: Adult £5, Child £1 (under 5yrs Free). Garden only: Adult £2.50, Child 50p. Garden Season Ticket (incl. children) £7. Groups by arrangement, teas for groups.
🎦 ♿ 🎦 Pre-booked (max 50). 🎦 Obligatory. 🚗 Car park only. 🎦 (max 50).

FORDE ABBEY & GARDENS 🏛   *See page 191 for full page entry.*

NTPL/Matthew Antrobus

Corfe Castle

HIGHCLIFFE CASTLE 🏛

ROTHESAY DRIVE, HIGHCLIFFE-ON-SEA, CHRISTCHURCH BH23 4LE

www.highcliffecastle.co.uk

Tel: 01425 278807   **Fax:** 01425 280423   **E-mail:** enquiries@highcliffecastle.co.uk

Owner: Christchurch Borough Council   **Contact:** David Hopkins

Built in the 1830s for Lord Stuart de Rothesay in the Romantic/Picturesque style and incorporating French medieval stonework and stained glass. The rooms in this Grade I listed building remain mostly unrepaired and now house a Heritage Centre and Gift Shop. They also provide a unique setting for changing exhibitions, featuring local and national artists. Programme of concerts and outdoor events. The refurbished Dining Room is available for wedding receptions, banquets and corporate use. Internal Guided Tours incorporating the upper floors. Cliff-top grounds. Access to Christchurch Coastal Path and beach.

Location: MAP 3:B6, OS Ref. SZ200 930. Off the A337 Lymington Road, between Christchurch and Highcliffe-on-Sea.

Open: 1 Feb–23 Dec: daily, 11am–5pm. Last admission 4.30 (4pm Fri/Sat). Grounds: All year: daily from 7am. Limited access for coaches. Tearooms closed Christmas Day.

Admission: Adult £2.75, accompanied U16 free. Group (10+) rates available. Guided tours of unrestored areas (may be unsuitable for people with mobility problems – please ring for details): Adult £3.75, accompanied U16 free. Grounds: Free.

📷 🍵 Wedding receptions. ♿ WC. 🎦 10am–5pm. 🍴 By arrangement.
🅿 Limited. Parking charge. ▣ By arrangement. 🐕 In grounds, on leads. 🔺 ❄ 📧

Forde Abbey, Nr Chard

HIGHER MELCOMBE

Melcombe Bingham, Dorchester, Dorset DT2 7PB
Tel: 01258 880251
Owner/Contact: Mr M C Woodhouse
Consists of the surviving wing of a 16th century house with its attached domestic chapel. A fine plaster ceiling and linenfold panelling. Conducted group tours by owner.
Location: MAP 2:P6, OS Ref. ST749 024. 1km W of Melcombe Bingham.
Open: May–Sept by appointment.
Admission: Adult £4.
Unsuitable. By written appointment only. Limited. Guide dogs only. Accommodation. Civil Wedding Licence.

KINGSTON LACY

See page 192 for full page entry.

KNOLL GARDENS & NURSERY

Stapehill Road, Hampreston, Wimborne BH21 7ND
Tel: 01202 873931 **Fax:** 01202 870842 **E-mail:** enquiries@knollgardens.co.uk
Owner: J & J Flude & N R Lucas **Contact:** Mr John Flude
Nationally acclaimed 6 acre gardens, with 6000+ named plants.
Location: MAP 3:B6, OS Ref. SU059 001. Between Wimborne & Ferndown. Exit A31 Canford Bottom roundabout, B3073 Hampreston. Signposted 1½m.
Open: May–Nov: Tue–Sun, 10am–5pm. Dec–Apr: Wed–Sat, 10am–4pm. Closed 21 Dec–31 Jan.
Admission: Adult £4.75, Child (5–15yrs) £3.25, Conc £4.25. RHS Free. Groups: Adult £3.75. Lower rates in low season.

Planning a weekend away in Dorset?

See Historic Places to Stay

Wooden Cabbage

Clavell Tower

LULWORTH CASTLE & PARK

EAST LULWORTH, WAREHAM, DORSET BH20 5QS
www.lulworth.com

Tel: 0845 4501054 **Fax:** 01929 400563 **E-mail:** office@lulworth.com
Owner: The Weld Estate
Surrounded by beautiful parkland with views of the Jurassic Coast this 17th century hunting lodge was destroyed by fire in 1929 and has been externally restored and internally consolidated by English Heritage. Steeped in history the Castle has remained in the same family since 1641. Features include a gallery on the Weld family, reconstructed kitchen, dairy and laundry rooms and a wine cellar. The Chapel is reputed to be one of the finest pieces of architecture in Dorset and houses an exhibition on vestments and recusant silver.
Location: MAP 3:A7, OS Ref. SY853 822. In E Lulworth off B3070, 3m NE of Lulworth Cove.
Open: Castle & Park: All year, Sun–Fri (but closed 3–16 Jan inc, 29 Jul–2 Aug inc, 24 & 25 Dec. Open Sat before Easter 3rd Apr and 18 Sept). See website for extensive list of Special Events: Entrance to Lulworth Castle House, the Weld family home, on Heritage Open Days 9th & 10th Sept or by appointment.
Admission: Off peak: Adults £8.50, Senior £7, Child (4–15) £4, Family (2+3) £25, Family (1+3) £16.50, Under 4's Free. Peak (25 Jul–30 Aug): Adults £10, Senior £9, Child (4–15) £5, Family (2+3) £30, Family (1+3) £20, Under 4's Free. Discount for Groups (10+). Season tickets available.
Concerts, corporate & private hire/events by arrangement. Partial. WC. Licensed. By arrangement. Free. Meal voucher & free access for coach drivers. In grounds, on leads. 5 holiday cottages, tel: 01929 400100. See website.

Max Gate sundial

MAPPERTON 🏛

BEAMINSTER, DORSET DT8 3NR

www.mapperton.com

Tel: 01308 862645   **Fax:** 01308 861082   **E-mail:** office@mapperton.com

Owner/Contact: The Earl & Countess of Sandwich

'The Nation's Finest Manor House' – *Country Life.* Jacobean mainly 1660s manor overlooking an Italianate upper garden with orangery, topiary and formal borders descending to fish ponds and shrub gardens. All Saints Church forms south wing opening to courtyard and stables. Area of Outstanding Natural Beauty with fine views of Dorset hills and woodlands.

Location: MAP 2:N6, OS Ref. SY503 997. 1m S of B3163, 2m NE of B3066, 2m SE Beaminster, 5m NE Bridport.

Open: House: 21 Jun–30 Jul, Mon–Fri, plus 31 May & 30 Aug, 2–4.30pm, last admission 4pm. Other times by appointment. Garden & All Saints Church: 1 Mar–31 Oct: daily (exc. Sat) 11am–5pm. Café: Mar–Sept: daily (exc. Sat) 11am–5.30pm, for lunch and tea. Tel: 01308 863348.

Admission: Gardens: Adult £5.00, Child (under 18yrs) £2.50, under 5yrs Free. House: £4.50. Group tours by appointment. House and Gardens combined £9.00 for groups over 20.

🖾 🗐 🖾 🖾 Partial. 🖳 Licensed. 🍴 🎦 By arrangement. 🅿 Limited for coaches. 🔲 🖾 Guide dogs only. 🖾

MAX GATE ✿

ALINGTON AVENUE, DORCHESTER, DORSET DT1 2AB

www.thomas-hardy.connectfree.co.uk

Tel: 01305 262538   **E-mail:** westdorset@nationaltrust.org.uk

Owner: The National Trust   **Contact:** The Tenant

Novelist and poet Thomas Hardy designed and lived in this house from 1885 until his death in 1928. Here he wrote Tess of the d'Urbervilles, Jude the Obscure and The Mayor of Casterbridge, as well as much of his poetry. The house contains several pieces of his furniture.

Location: MAP 2:P7, OS Ref. SY704 899. 1m E of Dorchester just N of the A352 to Wareham. From Dorchester follow A352 signs to the roundabout named Max Gate (at Jct. of A35 Dorchester bypass). Turn left and left again into cul-de-sac outside Max Gate.

Open: 28 Mar – 29 Sept: Mons, Weds & Suns, 2–5pm. Only hall, dining, drawing rooms and garden open. Private visits, tours and seminars for schools, colleges and literary societies at other times by appointment with the tenants, Mr & Mrs Andrew Leah.

Admission: Adult £3, Child £1.50.

ⓘ No WC. 🖾 🎦 Obligatory 🅿 Limited. No coaches 🔲 🖾

Portland Castle

DORSET

MILTON ABBEY CHURCH

Milton Abbas, Blandford, Dorset DT11 0BZ

Tel: 01258 880215

Owner: Diocese of Salisbury **Contact:** Chris Fookes

Abbey church dating from 14th century.

Location: MAP 2:P6, OS Ref. ST798 024. 3½m N of A354. Between Dorchester/Blandford Road.

Open: Abbey Church: daily 10.30am–5pm. Groups by arrangement please.

Admission: By donation except Easter & mid-Jul–end Aug. Adult £2, Child Free.

MINTERNE GARDENS 🏛

MINTERNE MAGNA, Nr DORCHESTER, DORSET DT2 7AU

www.minterne.co.uk

Tel: 01300 341370 **Fax:** 01300 341747 **E-mail:** enquiries@minterne.co.uk

Owner/Contact: The Hon Henry and Mrs Digby

Landscaped in the manner of 'Capability' Brown in the 18th century, Minterne's unique garden has been described by Simon Jenkins as *'a corner of paradise.'* Wander peacefully through 20 wild woodland acres where magnolias, rhododendrons and eucryphias provide a new vista at each turn, with small lakes, streams and cascades. Minterne also hosts private house tours, dinners, seminars, weddings and events, ensuring that guests leave with cherished memories of those special occasions.

Location: MAP 2:O6, OS Ref. ST660 042. On A352 Dorchester/Sherborne Rd, 2m N of Cerne Abbas.

Open: 1 Mar–9 Nov: daily, 10am–6pm.

Admission: Adult £5, accompanied children under 12 free.

🚻 ♿ Unsuitable. 📷 By arrangement. 🅿 Free. Picnic tables in car park. 🐕 In grounds on leads. 🏚

PORTLAND CASTLE ♯

CASTLETOWN, PORTLAND, WEYMOUTH, DORSET DT5 1AZ

www.english-heritage.org.uk/portland

Tel: 01305 820539 **Fax:** 01305 860853 **Email:** customers@english-heritage.org.uk

Owner: English Heritage **Contact:** Visitor Operations Staff

Discover one of Henry VIII's finest coastal fortresses. Perfectly preserved in a waterfront location overlooking Portland harbour, it is a marvellous place to visit for all the family whatever the weather. Explore the Tudor kitchen and gun platform, see the superb battlement views and enjoy a picnic in the Contemporary Heritage Garden or lunch in the Captain's Tearoom. An audio tour, included in the admission charge, brings the castle's long history to life.

Location: MAP 2:O7, OS Ref. SY684 743. Overlooking Portland harbour.

Open: 1 Apr–30 Jun: daily, 10am–5pm. 1 Jul–31 Aug: daily, 10am–6pm. 1–30 Sep: daily, 10am–5pm. 1 Oct–1 Nov: daily, 10am–4pm. Closed 2 Nov–31 Mar.

Admission: Adult £4, Child £2, Conc. £3.40. Family £10 .15% discount for groups (11+). EH members Free. Opening times and prices are valid until 31st March 2010, after this date details are subject to change please see www.english-heritage.org.uk for the most up-to-date information.

Special Events: Check the English Heritage website for details of special events.

🅿🚻♿ Partial. WCs. 🍴📷By arrangement. 🔊🅿Limited for coaches. 🏚 🐕Guide dogs only 🏚🛏

SANDFORD ORCAS MANOR HOUSE

Sandford Orcas, Sherborne, Dorset DT9 4SB

Tel: 01963 220206

Owner/Contact: Sir Mervyn Medlycott Bt

Tudor manor house with gatehouse, fine panelling, furniture, pictures. Terraced gardens with topiary and herb garden. Personal conducted tour by owner.

Location: MAP 2:O5, OS Ref. ST623 210. 2½m N of Sherborne, Dorset 4m S of A303 at Sparkford. Entrance next to church.

Open: Easter Mon, 10am–5pm. May & Jul–Sept: Suns & Mons, 2–5pm.

Admission: Adults £5, Child £2.50. Groups (10+): Adult £4, Child £2.

♿ Unsuitable. 📷 Obligatory. 🐕 In grounds, on leads. 🅿 Parking available

Minterne

SHERBORNE CASTLE

SHERBORNE, DORSET DT9 5NR

www.sherbornecastle.com

Tel: 01935 813182 (Line 2) **Fax:** 01935 816727 **E-mail:** enquiries@sherbornecastle.com

Owner: Mr & Mrs John Wingfield Digby **Contact:** Castle & Events Manager

Built by Sir Walter Raleigh in 1594, Sherborne Castle has been the home of the Digby family since 1617. Prince William of Orange was entertained here in 1688, and George III visited in 1789. Splendid interiors and collections of art, furniture and porcelain are on view in the Castle. Lancelot 'Capability' Brown created the lake in 1753 and gave Sherborne the very latest in landscape gardening, with magnificent vistas of the surrounding parklands. Today, some 30 acres of beautiful lakeside gardens and grounds are open for public viewing.

Location: MAP 2:O5, OS Ref. ST649 164. ³⁄₄m SE of Sherborne town centre. Follow brown signs from A30 or A352. ½m S of the Old Castle.

Open: Castle, Gardens, Shop & Tearoom: 1 Apr–31 Oct: daily except Mon & Fri (open BH Mons), 11am–4.30pm last admission. (On Sats, Castle interior from 2pm). Groups (15+) by arrangement during normal opening hours.

Admission: (2010 prices) Castle & Gardens: Adult £9.50, Child (0–15yrs) Free (max 4 per adult), Senior £9. Groups (15+): Adult/Senior £8.50, Child (0–15yrs) £3.50. Private views (15+): Adult/Senior £10.50, Child £5. Gardens only: Adult/Senior £5, Child (0–15yrs) Free (max 4 per adult), no concessions or group rates for gardens only.

🏠 🍴 ♿ Partial. 🍽 Licensed. 📷 By arrangement. 🐕 🐾 In grounds, on leads. 🔺 ♿

SHERBORNE OLD CASTLE

Castleton, Sherborne, Dorset DT9 3SA

Tel/Fax: 01935 812730 **Email:** customers@english-heritage.org.uk

www.english-heritage.org.uk/sherborne

Owner: English Heritage **Contact:** Visitor Operations Staff

The ruins of this early 12th century castle are a testament to the 16 days it took Cromwell to capture it during the Civil War, after which it was abandoned. A gatehouse, some graceful arcading and decorative windows survive.

Location: MAP 2:O5, OS Ref. ST647 167. ½m E of Sherborne off B3145. ½m N of the 'new' 1594 Castle.

Open: 1 Apr–30 Jun: daily, 10am–5pm. 1 Jul–31 Aug: daily, 10am–6pm. 1–30 Sept: daily, 10am–5pm. 1 Oct–1 Nov: daily, 10am–4pm. Closed 2 Nov–31 Mar.

Admission: Adult £3, Child £1.50, Conc. £2.60. 15% discount for groups of 11+. Joint ticket with Sherborne Castle grounds, £6.50. EH members Free. Opening times and prices are valid until 31st March 2010, after this date details are subject to change please see www.english-heritage.org.uk for the most up-to-date information.

🏠 ♿ Partial. WCs. 🍽 🅿 Limited for coaches. 🐕 🐾 Guide dogs only

---

STOCK GAYLARD HOUSE

Stock Gaylard, Sturminster Newton, Dorset DT10 2BG

Tel: 01963 23215 **E-mail:** langmeadj@stockgaylard.com

www.stockgaylard.com

Owner: Mrs J Langmead **Contact:** Mrs J Langmead

A Georgian house overlooking an ancient deer park with the parish church of St Barnabas in the garden. The grounds and principal rooms of the house are open to the public for 28 days a year.

Location: MAP 2:P5, OS Ref. ST722 130. 1 mile S of the junction of the A357 and the A3030 at the Lydlinch Common.

Open: 24th Apr–3rd May, 22–30 Jun & 22–30 Sept, 2–5pm. Large parties & coaches by appointment on Tue & Wed. Access to the Park by arrangement, please telephone for information.

Admission: Adult £5.00: Children £2.00.

Special Events: Stock Gaylard Oak Fair, 28th August, 2010

♿ Partial. 📷 Obligatory 🅿 🐾 Guide dogs only ♿

Sherborne Castle

WHITE MILL

Sturminster Marshall, Nr Wimborne, Dorset BH21 4BX

Tel: 01258 858051 **www.nationaltrust.org.uk**

Owner: The National Trust   **Contact:** The Custodian

Rebuilt in 1776 on a site marked as a mill in the Domesday Book, this substantial corn mill was extensively repaired in 1994 and still retains its original elm and applewood machinery (now too fragile to be operative).

Location: MAP 3:A6, OS Ref. ST958 006. On River Stour ½m NE of Sturminster Marshall. From the B3082 Blandford to Wimborne Rd, take road to Sturminster Marshall. Mill is 1m on right. Car park nearby.

Open: 27 Mar–31 Oct: Sats, Suns & BH Mons, 12 noon–5pm. Admission by guided tour only (last tour 4pm).

Admission: Adult £3, Child £2. Groups by arrangement.

ℹ️ No WC. 🅿️ Ground floor. 🔗 Obligatory. 🅿️ ⬛ 🐕 Under close control in grounds and car park.

Mapperton

WOLFETON HOUSE

Nr DORCHESTER, DORSET DT2 9QN

Tel: 01305 263500

E-mail: kthimbleby.wolfeton@gmail.com

Owner: Capt N T L L T Thimbleby   **Contact:** The Steward

A fine medieval and Elizabethan manor house lying in the water-meadows near the confluence of the rivers Cerne and Frome. It was much embellished around 1580 and has splendid plaster ceilings, fireplaces and panelling of that date. To be seen are the Great Hall, Stairs and Chamber, Parlour, Dining Room, Chapel and Cyder House. The medieval Gatehouse has two unmatched and older towers. There are good pictures and furniture.

Location: MAP 2:O6, OS Ref. SY678 921. 1½m from Dorchester on the A37 towards Yeovil. Indicated by Historic House signs.

Open: June–end Sept: Mons, Weds & Thurs, 2–5pm. Groups by appointment throughout the year.

Admission: £6.

🍴 By arrangement. 🅿️ Ground floor. 📷 By arrangement. 🔗 By arrangement. 🅿️ 🐕 ❄️

Sherborne Old Castle

BERKELEY CASTLE 🏛

www.berkeley-castle.com

Not many can boast of having their private house celebrated by Shakespeare nor of having held it in the possession of their family for nearly 850 years, nor having a King of England murdered within its walls, nor of having welcomed at their table the local vicar and Castle Chaplain, John Trevisa (1342–1402), reputed as one of the earliest translators of the Bible, nor of having a breach battered by Oliver Cromwell, which to this day it is forbidden by law to repair even if it was wished to do so. But such is the story of Berkeley.

This beautiful and historic Castle, begun in 1117, still remains the home of the famous family who gave their name to numerous locations all over the world, notably Berkeley Square in London, Berkeley Hundred in Virginia and Berkeley University in California. Scene of the brutal murder of Edward II in 1327 (visitors can see his cell and nearby the dungeon) and besieged by Cromwell's troops in 1645, the Castle is steeped in history but twenty-four generations of Berkeleys have gradually transformed a Norman fortress into the lovely home it is today.

The State Apartments contain magnificent collections of furniture, rare paintings by primarily English and Dutch masters, and tapestries. Part of the world-famous Berkeley silver is on display in the Dining Room. Many other rooms are equally interesting including the Great Hall upon which site the Barons of the West Country met in 1215 before going to Runnymede to force King John to put his seal to the Magna Carta.

The Castle is surrounded by lovely terraced Elizabethan Gardens with a lily pond, Elizabeth I's bowling green, and sweeping lawns.

ℹ Fashion shows and filming. No photography inside the Castle.

📷

❄

🍴 Wedding receptions and corporate entertainment.

♿ Visitors may alight in the Outer Bailey.

☕ Licensed. Serving lunches and home-made teas.

🚶 Free. Max. 120 people. Tour time: One hour. Evening groups by arrangement. Group visits must be booked.

🅿 Cars 150yds from Castle, 15 coaches 250yds away. Free.

📖 Welcome. General and social history and architecture.

🚫

Owner

Mr R J G Berkeley

Contact

The Custodian
Berkeley Castle
Gloucestershire
GL13 9BQ

Tel: 01453 810332
Fax: 01453 512995
E-mail: info@berkeley-castle.com

Location

MAP 6:M12
OS Ref. ST685 990

SE side of Berkeley village. Midway between Bristol & Gloucester, 2m W off the A38.

From motorway M5/J14 (5m) or J13 (9m).

Opening Times

28th March – 31st October 2010 11:00am – 5:30pm

Easter Holidays 28th March – 18th April Sunday – Thursday & Easter Weekend

April & May Sundays, Thursdays & Bank Holiday Mondays

May Half Term onwards 30th May – 5th September Sunday – Thursday

September & October Sundays & Thursdays

October Half Term 24th – 31st October Sunday –Thursday

Admission

Global Ticket including Castle & Gardens

Adult	£7.50
Child (5–16yrs)	£4.50
Child (under 5s)	Free
OAP	£6.00
Family (2+2)	£21.00

Groups (25+ pre-booked)

Adult	£7.00
Child (5-16yrs)	£3.50
OAP	£5.50

Gardens only

Adult	£4.00
Child	£2.00

Conference/Function

ROOM	MAX CAPACITY
Great Hall	150
Long Drawing Rm	100

■ Owner

Mr David Lowsley-Williams

■ Contact

D Lowsley-Williams
or Caroline
Lowsley-Williams
Chavenage
Tetbury
Gloucestershire
GL8 8XP

Tel: 01666 502329
Fax: 01666 504696
E-mail: info@
chavenage.com

■ Location

MAP 3:A1
OS Ref. ST872 952

Less than 20m
from M4/J16/17 or 18.
1⅞m NW of Tetbury
between the B4014 &
A4135. Signed from
Tetbury. Less than 15m
from M5/J13 or 14.
Signed from A46
(Stroud–Bath road).

Rail: Kemble Station 7m.

Taxi: Martin Cars
01666 503611.

Air: Bristol 35m.
Birmingham 70m.
Grass airstrip on farm.

■ Opening Times

Summer
May–September
Easter Sun, Mon
& BHs, 2–5pm.
Last admission 4pm.

Thurs & Suns 2–5pm.

NB. Will open on any day
and at other times by
prior arrangement for
groups.

Winter
October–March
By appointment only
for groups.

■ Admission

Tours are inclusive
in the following prices.

Summer
Adult   £7.00
Child (5–16 yrs) £3.50

Winter
Groups only
(any date or time)
Rates by arrangement.

Concessions:
By prior arrangement,
concessions may be given
to groups of 40+ and also
to disabled and to
exceptional cases.

© Skyscan

CHAVENAGE

www.chavenage.com

Chavenage is a wonderful Elizabethan house of mellow grey Cotswold stone and tiles which contains much of interest for the discerning visitor.

The approach aspect of Chavenage is virtually as it was left by Edward Stephens in 1576. Only two families have owned Chavenage; the present owners since 1891 and the Stephens family before them. A Colonel Nathaniel Stephens, MP for Gloucestershire during the Civil War was cursed for supporting Cromwell, giving rise to legends of weird happenings at Chavenage since that time.

Inside Chavenage there are many interesting rooms housing tapestries, fine furniture, pictures and many relics of the Cromwellian period. Of particular note are the Main Hall, where a contemporary screen forms a minstrels' gallery and two tapestry rooms where it is said Cromwell was lodged.

Recently Chavenage has been used as a location for TV and film productions including a Hercule Poirot story *The Mysterious Affair at Styles*, many episodes of the sequel to *Are you Being Served* now called *Grace & Favour*, episodes of *The House of Elliot* and *Casualty*, in 1997/98 *Berkeley Square* and *Cider with Rosie* and in 2002 the US series *Relic Hunter III*. In 2005 it was one of the homes Jeremy Musson visited in the BBC's *The Curious House Guest*. Chavenage has recently doubled as Candleford Manor in the BBC costume drama *Lark Rise to Candleford*. Scenes from the series *Bonekickers* and *Tess of the D'Urbervilles* were shot at Chavenage in 2008.

Chavenage is especially suitable for those wishing an intimate, personal tour, usually conducted by the owner, or for groups wanting a change from large establishments. Meals for pre-arranged groups have proved hugely popular. It also provides a charming venue for small conferences and functions.

ℹ️ Suitable for filming, photography, corporate entertainment, activity days, seminars, receptions and product launches.

🌳 Occasional.

🍸 Corporate entertaining. Private drinks parties, lunches, dinners, anniversary parties and wedding receptions.

♿ Partial. WC.

☕ Lunches, teas, dinners and picnics by arrangement.

🚶 By owner. Large groups given a talk prior to viewing. Couriers/group leaders should arrange tour format prior to visit.

🅿️ Up to 100 cars. 2–3 coaches (by appointment). Coaches access from A46 (signposted) or from Tetbury via the B4014, enter the back gates for coach parking area.

🪑 Chairs can be arranged for lecturing.

🐕 In grounds on leads. Guide dogs only in house.

❄️

Conference/Function

ROOM	SIZE	MAX CAPACITY
Ballroom	70' x 30'	120
Oak Room	25' x 20'	30

BERKELEY CASTLE 🏰

See page 201 for full page entry.

BLACKFRIARS PRIORY ⚑

Ladybellegate Street, Gloucester GL1 2HS
Tel: 0117 9750700 **Email:** customers@english-heritage.org.uk
www.english-heritage.org.uk/blackfriars
Owner: English Heritage **Contact:** The South West Regional Office
One of the most complete surviving friaries in England, later converted into a Tudor house and cloth factory. Most of the original 13th century church remains and a rare scissor- braced roof in the dormitory.
Location: MAP 6:N11, OS Ref. SO830 186. In Blackfriars Lane, off Ladybellegate St, Gloucester, off Southgate Street.
Open: Access usually only by guided tour, Jul–Aug, Sun 3pm. Please contact the South West Regional Office for 2010 opening times.
Admission: Non-members: Adult £3.50, EH members £3, Child Free. Opening times and prices are valid until 31st March 2010, after this date details are subject to change please see www.english-heritage.org.uk for the most up-to-date information.
🎫 Obligatory. 🅿 Nearby, not EH, charged. 🐕 Guide dogs only.

CHAVENAGE 🏰

See page 202 for full page entry.

CHEDWORTH ROMAN VILLA 🏛

Yanworth, Nr Cheltenham, Gloucestershire GL54 3LJ
Tel: 01242 890256 **Fax:** 01242 890909
E-mail: chedworth@nationaltrust.org.uk **www.nationaltrust.org.uk/chedworth**
Owner: The National Trust **Contact:** The Visitor Services Manager
Discover one of the largest Romano-British sites in the country. Located within the beautiful Cotswolds scenery, a mile of walls survives along with several marvellous mosaics, two bathhouses, hypocausts, latrines and a water shrine. First excavated in 1864 the site retains a Victorian museum and atmosphere. An audio-visual presentation available.
Location: MAP 6:O11, OS Ref. SP053 135. 3m NW of Fossebridge on Cirencester–Northleach road (A429) via Yanworth or from A436 via Withington. Coaches must approach from Fossebridge.
Open: 13 Mar–27 Mar: Tues–Sun, 10am–4pm. 28 Mar–31 Oct: Tues–Sun, 10am–5pm; 2 Nov–14 Nov: Tues–Sun, 10am–4pm. Open BH Mons. Shop open as Villa. Tea tent open weekends and school holidays. Shop and reception close at above time.
*Admission: Adult £7, Child £4, Family (2+3) £18. Booked group tours (max 30 per guide): Schools £25, others £50. *includes a voluntary donation but visitors can choose to pay the standard prices displayed at the property and on the website.
🅿 ♿ Partial. WCs. 🎫 By arrangement. 🐕 Adult £1.50 🅿 Limited for coaches. Child free. ⬛ By arrangement. 🎪 🎗 Full events programme available on www.nationaltrust.org.uk/chedworth.

© Sezincote

Sezincote, Temple to Surya, the Hindu God of the Sun, with Shivalinga Fountain and Pool

FRAMPTON COURT, THE ORANGERY AND FRAMPTON MANOR

FRAMPTON-ON-SEVERN, GLOUCESTERSHIRE GL2 7EP

www.framptoncourtestate.co.uk

Tel: 01452 740268 **Fax:** 01452 740698
E-mail: events@framptoncourtestate.co.uk
Owner: Mr & Mrs Rollo Clifford **Contact:** Janie Clifford, Frampton Manor

The Cliffords have lived in Frampton since the 11th century. Frampton Court, built in 1731, has a superb panelled interior housing period furniture, china and 19th century 'Frampton Flora' water-colours. Bed and breakfast and house parties available.

The 18th century 'Strawberry Hill gothic' Orangery sits – breath-takingly – at the end of the ornamental canal in the garden at Frampton Court, and is now a self-catering holiday house. Half-timbered Frampton Manor is said to be the birth-place of 'Fair Rosamund' Clifford, mistress of Henry II. The walled garden is a plantsman's delight. The 16th century Wool Barn is contemporary with the main part of the house. A whole day is recommended for tours of both houses and gardens.

Location: MAP 6:M12, OS Ref. SO750 078. In Frampton, ¼ m SW of B4071, 3m NW of M5/J13.
Open: Frampton Court and Frampton Manor by appointment for groups (10+). Frampton Manor Garden: Mon & Fri 2.30–5pm, 19 Apr–23 Jul.
Admission: Frampton Court House & Garden: £7. Manor, Garden & Wool Barn: £7. Garden only: £4. Wool Barn only £1.

ⓘ Filming, parkland for hire. 🌱 Pan Global Plants in walled garden (01452 741641). 🔲 Wedding receptions. 🔲 Partial. WC Frampton Manor. 🔲 For groups by arrangement in the Wool Barn at Frampton Manor. 🔲 Usually by family members. 🅿 For both houses at Frampton Manor. 🔲🔲 House parties and B&B at Frampton Court contact Gillian Keightley 01452 740267; self-catering holidays at The Orangery 01452 740698. 🔲 By arrangement. 🔲 Frampton Country Fair 12 Sep 2009.

GLOUCESTER CATHEDRAL

Cathedral Office, College Green, Gloucester GL1 2LR
Tel: 01452 508211 **Fax:** 01452 300469
E-mail: lin@gloucestercathedral.org.uk **www.gloucestercathedral.org.uk**
Contact: Mrs L Henderson

Daily worship and rich musical tradition continue in this abbey church founded 1300 years ago. It has a Norman nave with massive cylindrical pillars, a magnificent east window with medieval glass and glorious fan-vaulted cloisters. You can also find the tombs of King Edward II and Robert, Duke of Normandy.
Location: MAP 6:M11, OS Ref. SO832 188. Off Westgate Street in central Gloucester.
Open: Daily, 8am until after Evensong. Groups must book via the Cathedral Office.
Admission: £3 donation requested.

🔲🔲🔲 Partial. WC. 🔲🔲 By arrangement. 🔲🅿 None. 🔲 In grounds, on leads. 🔲

HAILES ABBEY ✠ 🐾

Nr Winchcombe, Cheltenham, Gloucestershire GL54 5PB
Tel/Fax: 01242 602398 **E-mail:** customers@english-heritage.org.uk
www.english-heritage.org.uk/hailes
Owner: English Heritage & The National Trust   **Contact:** Visitor Operations Staff

Seventeen cloister arches and extensive excavated remains in lovely surroundings of an abbey founded by Richard, Earl of Cornwall, in 1246. Let the audio tour bring this Cistercian Abbey to life and see sculptures, stonework and other site finds in the museum.
Location: MAP 6:O10, OS Ref. SP050 300. 2m NE of Winchcombe off B4632.
Open: 1 Apr–30 Jun: daily, 10am–5pm. 1 Jul–31 Aug: daily, 10am–6pm. 1–30 Sep: daily 10am–5pm. 1 Oct–1 Nov: daily, 10am–4pm. Closed 2 Nov–31 Mar 2010.
Admission: Adult £3.80, Child £1.90, Conc. £3.20. EH Members Free. NT members Free, but charge for audio tour (£1) and special events. Group discount available. Opening times and prices are valid until 31st March 2010, after this date details are subject to change please see www.english-heritage.org.uk for the most up-to-date information.

🔲🔲🔲 WCs. 🔲🔲 By arrangement. 🔲🅿 Limited for coaches. 🔲🔲 On leads.

Sezincote, Persian Garden of Paradise with Orangery behind

© Sezincote

Hailes Abbey

©NTPL/A Sparrow

© NTPL / Stephen Robson

HANHAM COURT

FERRY LANE, HANHAM ABBOTS, BRISTOL, BS15 3NT

www.hanhamcourt.co.uk

Owner: Isabel & Julian Bannerman   **E-mail:** info@hanhamcourt.co.uk
Contact: Isabel Bannerman

The Garden only of this unexpectedly rural Manor House (not open) is opening for a second year at the end of a tiny lane among fields. The Bannermans, award winning garden designers to the Prince of Wales, have created a deeply romantic, highly scented garden, with fountains, temples, treeferns, magnolias, old roses, delphiniums, lilies, hot summer plantings of dahlias, crocosmia, rudbeckia, heleniums as well as orchards and wild flowers.

Location: MAP 2:O1, OS Ref: AST649 702. 8km West of Bath, SE outskirts of Bristol.
Open: Easter Friday until October, Fri - Mon 11.30am until 5.30pm with Teas. Groups over 25, Coaches, Weddings, Functions by appointment. See website for details.
Admission: Adults £6.50, Child (under 14) £3.50, Groups by appointment.

⬛⬛ Partial ⬛⬛ By arrangement 🅿⬛

HIDCOTE MANOR GARDEN ✤

**HIDCOTE BARTRIM, Nr CHIPPING CAMPDEN,
GLOUCESTERSHIRE GL55 6LR**

www.nationaltrust.org.uk

Tel: 01386 438333   **Fax:** 01386 438817   **E-mail:** hidcote@nationaltrust.org.uk
Owner: The National Trust   **Contact:** Visitor Services Manager

One of the most delightful gardens in England, created in the early 20th century by the great horticulturist Major Lawrence Johnston; a series of small gardens within the whole, separated by walls and hedges of different species; famous for rare shrubs, trees, herbaceous borders, 'old' roses and interesting plant species.

Location: MAP 6:O9, OS Ref. SP176 429. 4m NE of Chipping Campden, 1m E of B4632 off B4081. At Mickleton ¼ m E of Kiftsgate Court. Coaches are not permitted through Chipping Campden High Street.
Open: 27 Feb–12 Mar: Sat & Sun, 11am–4pm; 13 Mar–1 Oct: Sat–Wed, 10am–6pm. Also open Thu & Fri July & Aug; 2 Oct–31 Oct: Sat–Wed, 10am–5pm. Last admission 1 hour before closing. Open Good Friday. 1 Nov–19 Dec: Sat & Sun, 12–4pm.
*Admission: Adult £9.50, Child £4.75, Family (2+3) £23.75. Groups (15+) Adult £8.20, Child £4.10. *includes a voluntary donation but visitors can choose to pay the standard prices displayed at the property and on the website.

⬛⬛⬛⬛ Limited. WC. ⬛⬛ Licensed. 🅿⬛⬛⬛ Send SAE for details.

©Chavenage

Chavenage

Nigel Fisher

KELMSCOTT MANOR 🏛

KELMSCOTT, Nr LECHLADE, GLOUCESTERSHIRE GL7 3HJ

www.kelmscottmanor.org.uk

Tel: 01367 252486 **Fax:** 01367 253754 **E-mail:** admin@kelmscottmanor.co.uk

Owner: Society of Antiquaries of London **Contact:** Jane Milne

Kelmscott Manor, a Grade I listed Tudor farmhouse adjacent to the River Thames, was William Morris' summer residence from 1871 until his death in 1896. Morris loved Kelmscott Manor, which seemed to him to have 'grown up out of the soil'. Its beautiful gardens with barns, dovecote, a meadow and stream provided a constant source of inspiration. The house, which is perhaps one of the most evocative of all the houses associated with Morris, contains an outstanding collection of the possessions and work of Morris, his family and associates, including furniture, original textiles, pictures, carpets and ceramics.

Location: MAP 6:P12, OS Ref. SU252 988. At SE end of the village, 2m due E of Lechlade, off the Lechlade – Faringdon Road.

Open: House and Garden Apr–Sept: every Wed and the 1st and 3rd Sat of each month, 11am–5pm (Ticket office opens 10.30am). Last admission to the house, 4.30pm. No advance bookings on public open days. House has limited capacity; timed ticket system operates. Group visits Apr–Sept: Thurs & Fri, must be booked in advance.

Admission: Adult £8.50, Child/Student £4.25. Garden only: £2. Carer accompanying disabled person Free.

Special Events: Please see the website

ⓘ No photography in house. 📷 ♿ Grounds. WCs.
🍷 Licensed. 🍴 Licensed. 🎦 By arrangement. 🅿 10 mins walk. Limited for coaches.
■ ♿ Guide dogs only. 🐾 See website www.24hourmuseum.org.uk.

KIFTSGATE COURT GARDENS 🏛

CHIPPING CAMPDEN, GLOUCESTERSHIRE GL55 6LN

www.kiftsgate.co.uk

Tel/Fax: 01386 438777 **E-mail:** info@kiftsgate.co.uk

Owner: Mr and Mrs J G Chambers **Contact:** Mr J G Chambers

Magnificently situated garden on the edge of the Cotswold escarpment with views towards the Malvern Hills. Many unusual shrubs and plants including tree peonies, abutilons, specie and old-fashioned roses. Winner HHA/Christie's Garden of the Year Award 2003.

Location: MAP 6:O9, OS Ref. SP173 430. 4m NE of Chipping Campden. ¼ m W of Hidcote Garden.

Open: May, Jun, Jul, Sat–Wed, 12 noon–6pm. August, Sat–Wed, 2pm–6pm. Apr & Sept, Sun, Mon & Wed, 2pm–6pm.

Admission: Adult: £6.50, Child £2. Groups (20+) £5.50.

📷 🚻 🍷 🅿 ✕

LODGE PARK & SHERBORNE ESTATE 🌿

Aldsworth, Nr Cheltenham, Gloucestershire GL54 3PP

Tel: 01451 844130 **Fax:** 01451 844131 **Email:** lodgepark@nationaltrust.org.uk

www.nationaltrust.org.uk/lodgepark

Owner: The National Trust **Contact:** The Visitor Services Manager

Lodge Park is a unique survival of a 17th-century Grandstand, Deer Course and Park. The interior has been reconstructed to its original form and is the first project of its kind undertaken by the Trust relying totally on archaeological evidence. The park was designed by Charles Bridgeman in 1725.

Location: MAP 6:O11, OS Ref. SP146 123. 3m E of Northleach, approach only from A40. Sherborne Park walks start from Ewe Pen car park. Approach from A40 towards Sherborne village.

Open: Grandstand & Deer Park: 12 Mar–14 Nov: Fri–Sun, 11 Dec - 12 Dec: Sat-Sun, BH Mons, 11am–4pm. Property occasionally closes for weddings. Please tel. to confirm opening times. Sherborne Park open all year round, walks start from the Ewe Pen car park near Sherborne village.

Admission: Adult £5.25, Child £3, Family £13.50.

ⓘ Video shows during the day. 🎗 Civil ceremonies & receptions. ♿ WCs. 🍷🎦 By arrangement. 🅿 Limited for coaches. ■ ♿ Guide dogs only. 🎭 Deerhound Racing Day in September. Outdoor theatre in August. Concerts, etc. Special childrens' trails and family events throughout the year. Full list of events on www.nationaltrust.org.uk/lodgepark.

©NTPL/Andreas von Einsiedel

Newark Park

NEWARK PARK ❦

OZLEWORTH, WOTTON-UNDER-EDGE, GLOUCESTERSHIRE GL12 7PZ

www.nationaltrust.org.uk

Tel: 01453 842644　**Fax:** 01453 845308　**Infoline:** 01793 817666
E-mail: newarkpark@nationaltrust.org.uk
Owner: The National Trust　**Contact:** Michael Claydon
A Tudor hunting lodge converted into a castellated country house by James Wyatt.
An atmospheric house, set in spectacular countryside with outstanding views.
Location: MAP 2:P1, OS Ref172. ST786 934. 1½ m E of Wotton-under-Edge, 1¾ m
S of Junction of A4135 & B4058, follow signs for Ozleworth, House signposted from
main road.
Open: House & Garden: 3rd Mar–27 May: Wed, Thurs & BH Mons; 2 Jun–31 Oct:
Wed, Thur, Sat, Sun & BH Mons, 11am–5pm (last entry 4.30pm). Also open Easter:
Good Fri–Mon, 11am–5pm.
Admission: Adult £6.25, Child £3.15, Family (2+3) £16.10. Groups by appointment.
ⓘ No photography in house.🖼 🏷 ♿ Partial.WCs 🍴 🎭 By arrangement. 🅿 🖼
🐕 In grounds 🛡

PAINSWICK ROCOCO GARDEN 🏛

PAINSWICK, GLOUCESTERSHIRE GL6 6TH

www.rococogarden.org.uk

Tel: 01452 813204　**Fax:** 01452 814888　**E-mail:** info@rococogarden.org.uk
Owner: Painswick Rococo Garden Trust　**Contact:** P R Moir
Unique 18th century garden restoration situated in a hidden 6 acre Cotswold combe.
Charming contemporary buildings are juxtaposed with winding woodland walks and
formal vistas. Famous for its early spring show of snowdrops. Anniversary maze.
Location: MAP 6:N11, OS Ref. SO864 106. ½ m NW of village of Painswick on B4073.
Open: 10 Jan–31 Oct: daily, 11am–5pm.
Admission: Adult £6.00, Child £3.00, OAP £5.00. Family (2+2) £15.
Free introductory talk for pre-booked groups (20+).
🖼 🏷 🚹 ♿ Partial. WC. 🍴 Licensed. 🍴 🅿 🖼 🐕 In grounds, on leads. 🔊 ❋ 🛡

Lodge Park

RODMARTON MANOR 🏠
CIRENCESTER, GLOUCESTERSHIRE GL7 6PF
www.rodmarton-manor.co.uk

Tel: 01285 841253

E-mail: sarahpoperodmarton@yahoo.co.uk

Owner: Mr & Mrs Simon Biddulph **Contact:** Sarah Pope

A Cotswold Arts and Crafts house, one of the last great country houses to be built in the traditional way and containing beautiful furniture, ironwork, china and needlework specially made for the house. The large garden complements the house and contains many areas of great beauty and character including the magnificent herbaceous borders, topiary, roses, rockery and kitchen garden. Available as a film location and for small functions.

Location: MAP 6:N12, OS Ref. ST943 977. Off A433 between Cirencester and Tetbury.

Open: House & Garden: Easter Monday & May–Sept (Weds, Sats & BHs), 2–5pm (Not guided tours). Garden only, for snowdrops,: 7, 14 & 18 and 21 Feb: from 1.30pm. Groups please book. Individuals need not book. Guided tours of the house (last about 1hr) may be booked for groups (15+) at any time of year (minimum group charge of £120 applies). Groups (5+) may book guided or unguided tours of the garden at other times.

Admission: House & Garden: £8, Child (5–15yrs) £4. Garden only: £5, Child (5–15yrs) £1. Guided tour of Garden: Entry fee plus £40 per group.

ℹ️ Colour guidebook & postcards on sale. Available for filming. No photography in house. WCs in garden. ♿ Garden & ground floor. 🐶 Most open days and groups by appointment. 🔧 By arrangement. 🅿 🔲 🖼 Guide dogs only. ❄️

ST MARY'S CHURCH ⌗

Kempley, Gloucestershire GL18 2AT

Tel: 0117 9750700 **E-mail:** customers@english-heritage.org.uk

www.english-heritage.org.uk/stmarys

Owner: English Heritage **Contact:** The South West Regional Office

A delightful Norman church with superb wall paintings from the 12th–14th centuries which were only discovered beneath whitewash in 1871.

Location: MAP 6:M10, OS Ref. SO670 313. On minor road. 1 mile N of Kempley off B4024; 6 miles NE of Ross-on-Wye.

Open: 1 Mar–1 Nov: daily, 10am–6pm. Telephone for appointment in winter.

Admission: Free. Opening times and prices are valid until 31st March 2010, after this date details are subject to change please see www.english-heritage.org.uk for the most up-to-date information.

🐶 Guide dogs only.

St Mary's Church

SEZINCOTE 🏠
MORETON-IN-MARSH, GLOUCESTERSHIRE GL56 9AW
www.sezincote.co.uk

Tel: 01386 700444

Owner/Contact: Dr E Peake

Exotic oriental water garden by Repton and Daniell. Large semi-circular orangery. House by S P Cockerell in Indian style was the inspiration for Brighton Pavilion.

Location: MAP 6:P10, OS Ref. SP183 324. 2½m SW of Moreton-in-Marsh. Turn W along A44 to Broadway and left into gateway just before Bourton-on-the-Hill (opposite the gate to Batsford Park, then 1m drive.

Open: Garden: Thurs, Fris & BH Mons, 2–6pm (dusk if earlier) throughout the year except Dec. House: Open as Garden but closed Oct–April. Groups at any time by written appointment. Tea and cake in Orangery when house open.

Admission: House: Adult £8 (guided tour). Garden: Adult £5, Child £1.50 (under 5yrs Free).

♿ Gravel paths. 🔧 Obligatory. 🐶 Guide dogs only. ❄️ 🔲 Café.

©NTPL/Dominic Hamilton

SNOWSHILL MANOR ❧

SNOWSHILL, Nr BROADWAY, GLOUCESTERSHIRE WR12 7JU

www.nationaltrust.org.uk

Tel: 01386 852410 **Fax:** 01386 842822 **E-mail:** snowshillmanor@nationaltrust.org.uk
Owner: The National Trust **Contact:** The Property Manager

Snowshill is no ordinary manor, as Charles Paget Wade was no ordinary Edwardian gentleman. He filled this Cotswold stone house to the rafters - quite literally - with a huge and diverse collection of extraordinary craftsmanship. From lowly fire buckets to exquisite ivory carvings, ancient musical instruments to Victorian toys, penny farthing bicycles to complete suits of Japanese armour, there's something to uncover in every room. The stunning garden, set on the edge of the Cotswolds, is laid out as a series of 'outdoor rooms' and run on organic principles.

Location: MAP 6:O10, OS Ref. SP096 339. 2½ m SW of Broadway, turning off the A44, at Broadway Green.

Open: Manor: 13 Mar to 31 Oct, Wed–Sun & BH Mons, 12–5pm. Last entry to Manor 4.10pm. Admission by timed ticket only. Gardens, restaurant and shop: dates as Manor, 11am–5.30pm, also 6 Nov to 12 Dec, 12–4pm.

*Admission: Manor, garden, shop and restaurant: Adult £9.00, Child £4.60, Family £22.80. Garden, restaurant and shop only: Adult £4.90, Child £2.50, Family £12.10. Visitors arriving by bicycle or on foot offered a voucher redeemable at Snowshill NT shop or tearoom. Coach & School groups by written appointment only. *includes a voluntary donation but visitors can choose to pay the standard prices displayed at the property and on the website. **Special events:** Apple Weekend 23 & 24 October 2010

🖼 🖩 T & Partial.WCs ⅋ Licensed. ⏀ By arrangement P Limited for coaches. ■ ⊞ Guide dogs only ⬚

STANWAY HOUSE & WATER GARDEN 🏠

STANWAY, CHELTENHAM, GLOS GL54 5PQ

www.stanwayfountain.co.uk

Tel: 01386 584528 **Fax:** 01386 584688 **E-mail:** stanwayhse@btconnect.com
Owner: The Earl of Wemyss and March **Contact:** Debbie Lewis

"As perfect and pretty a Cotswold manor house as anyone is likely to see" (Fodor's Great Britain 1998 guidebook). Stanway's beautiful architecture, furniture, parkland and village are now complemented by the restored 18th century water garden and the magnificent fountain – 300 feet – making it the tallest garden fountain and gravity fountain in the world. Teas available. Beer for sale. Wedding reception venue.

Location: MAP 6:O10, OS Ref. SP061 323. N of Winchcombe, just off B4077.

Open: House & Garden: June–Aug: Tue & Thur, 2–5pm. Private tours by arrangement at other times.

Admission: Adult £7, Child £2.00, OAP £5.00. Garden only: Adult £4.50, Child £1.50, OAP £3.50.

ⓘ Film & photographic location. 🖼 T Wedding receptions. ■ ⏀ By arrangement. P ⊞ In grounds on leads. ✱

SUDELEY CASTLE GARDENS & EXHIBITIONS

WINCHCOMBE , GLOUCESTERSHIRE GL54 5JD

www.sudeleycastle.co.uk

Tel: 01242 602308 **Fax:** 01242 602959 **E-mail:** enquiries@sudeley.org.uk

Owner: Lady Ashcombe, Henry and Mollie Dent-Brocklehurst **Contact:** The Secretary

Sudeley Castle sits nestled in the Cotswold Hills, surrounded by 1200 acres of grounds, award-winning gardens and historic medieval ruins.

Henry VIII's sixth wife, Queen Katherine Parr, lived here and is entombed in St Mary's Church within the grounds. Sudeley boasts royal connections dating back to Ethelred the Unready, many of which are explored in the fascinating exhibitions.

Location: MAP 6:O10, OS Ref. SP032 277. 8m NE of Cheltenham, at Winchcombe off B4632. From Bristol or Birmingham M5/J9. Take A46 then B4077 towards Stow-on-the-Wold. Bus: Castleways to Winchcombe. Rail: Cheltenham Station 8m. Air: Birmingham or Bristol 45m.

Open: Summer: 29 March–31 October, daily, 10.30am–5.00pm. Winter: Groups by appointment.

Admission: Gardens & Exhibitions: Adult £7.20, Child (5-15yrs) £4.20, Conc. £6.20, Family (2+2) £20.80. Group rates available.

Details may be subject to change – please ensure you telephone or visit our website for updated information.

ℹ️ Photographs & filming by prior arrangement. 📷🍴🎁 Corporate and private events, wedding receptions. ♿ Partial access to the grounds. WC. 🍴Licensed. 🎭 Tours and talks by prior arrangement for groups & Connoisseur Tours of the Castle Apartments Tue, Wed & Thur. 🅿️1,000 cars. Meal vouchers, free access for coach drivers. ✖️🏨 11 holiday cottages for 2–5 occupants. 🔼🔽 See website or call for details.

WESTBURY COURT GARDEN ❦

WESTBURY-ON-SEVERN, GLOUCESTERSHIRE GL14 1PD

www.nationaltrust.org.uk/wessex

Tel: 01452 760461 **E-mail:** westburycourt@nationaltrust.org.uk

Owner: The National Trust **Contact:** The Head Gardener

A Dutch water garden with canals and yew hedges, laid out between 1696 and 1705; the earliest of its kind remaining in England. Restored in 1971 and planted with species dating from pre-1700 including apple, pear and plum trees.

Location: MAP 6:M11, OS Ref. SO718 138. 9m SW of Gloucester on A48.

Open: 10 Mar–30 Jun & 1 Sept–31 Oct: Wed–Sun, 10am–5pm. 1 Jul–31 Aug: Daily, 10am–5pm. Open BH Mons. Other times of year by appointment.

Admission: Gift Aid: Adult £4.95, Child £2.45, Family £12.70; Standard: Adult £4.50, Child £2.20; Family £11.50.

Special events: Easter trail 2–5 Apr. Apple day 16–17 Oct.

♿ Partial. WCs. 🎭 By arrangement. 🅿️ Limited for coaches. 🐕 Guide dogs only 🔽

TYTHE BARN

Tanhouse Farm, Churchend, Frampton-on-Severn, Gloucestershire GL2 7EH

Tel: 01452 741072 **E-mail:** cottages@tanhouse-farm.co.uk

Owner/Contact: Michael Williams

Tythe Barn Grade II* c1650 recently restored in conjunction with English Heritage. Barn incorporating cow shed, the exceptional length and width of the timber framed structure upon a low stone plinth with box framing and undaubed wattle panels marks it out from other contemporary farm buildings.

Location: MAP 6:M12, OS Ref. SP014 206. Southern end of Frampton-on-Severn, close to church.

Open: By arrangement all year 10am–4pm.

Admission: Free.

♿ Partial. 🎭 Obligatory. By arrangement. 🅿️ Limited. None for coaches. ✖️

WHITTINGTON COURT 🏛️

Cheltenham, Gloucestershire GL54 4HF

Tel: 01242 820556 **Fax:** 01242 820218

Owner: Mr & Mrs Jack Stringer **Contact:** Mrs J Stringer

Elizabethan manor house. Family possessions including ceramics, antique and modern glass, fossils and fabrics.

Location: MAP 6:N11, OS Ref. SP014 206. 4m E of Cheltenham on N side of A40.

Open: 3–18 Apr & 14–30 Aug: 2–5pm.

Admission: Adult £5, Child £1, OAP £4.

📷🅿️

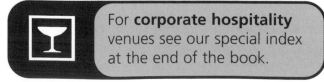

For **corporate hospitality** venues see our special index at the end of the book.

Blackfriars Priory

Frampton Court

WOODCHESTER MANSION

NYMPSFIELD, STONEHOUSE, GLOUCESTERSHIRE GL10 3TS

www.woodchestermansion.org.uk

Tel: 01453 861541 **Fax:** 01453 861337 **E-mail:** office@woodchestermansion.org.uk
Operated by: Woodchester Mansion Trust Ltd.
Location: MAP 6:M12, OS Ref. SO809 013. Near Nympsfield off the B4066 Stroud-Dursley road.

Hidden in a wooded valley near Stroud is one of the most intriguing houses in the country. Woodchester Mansion was started in the mid-1850s, but abandoned incomplete. It offers a unique insight into traditional building techniques. The Trust's repair programme includes courses in stone masonry and building conservation.

Open: Easter–Oct: Suns & 1st Sat of every month & BH weekends inc. Mon. Jul–Aug: Sat & Sun.
Admission: Adult £5.50, Child (under 14 yrs) Free, Conc £4.50. Group rates available.
⬚ ⊤ ⬚ 🅧 Obligatory. 🅿 Limited. 🅗 🅗 Guide dogs only.

©Sudeley Castle

Sudeley Castle

NO 1 ROYAL CRESCENT
BATH BA1 2LR

www.bath-preservation-trust.org.uk

Tel: 01225 428126 **Fax:** 01225 481850
E-mail: no1museum@bptrust.org.uk
Owner: Bath Preservation Trust **Contact:** Victoria Barwell – Curator
No. 1 Royal Crescent is a magnificently restored and authentically furnished Georgian Town House. From the elegant drawing room to the splendidly equipped Georgian kitchen, it creates a vivid picture of the fashionable life in the 18th century Bath.
Location: MAP 2:P2, OS Ref. ST746 653. M4/J18. A46 to Bath. ¼m NW of city centre.
Open: Mid Feb–end Nov: Tues–Sun, 10.30am–5pm. BH Mons. Closes 4pm in Nov. Open Good Fri. Last admission 30 mins before closing. Evening tours and other times by arrangement.
Admission: Adult £5, Child (5–16yrs) £2.50, Conc £4, Family £12. Groups: £3.
Unsuitable. The Royal Crescent & Bath centre.

THE AMERICAN MUSEUM & GARDENS
CLAVERTON MANOR, BATH BA2 7BD

www.americanmuseum.org

Tel: 01225 460503 **Fax:** 01225 469160 **E-mail:** info@americanmuseum.org
Owner: The Trustees of the American Museum in Britain **Contact:** Julian Blades
Claverton Manor (Jeffry Wyattville, 1820) now houses the finest collection of Americana outside the U.S. Interactive exhibitions; 18 furnished period rooms; inspiring quilt and textile collections. The stunning grounds contain a replica of George Washington's Mount Vernon garden and an Arboretum of North American specimens. Light lunches and teas available.
Location: MAP 2:P2, OS Ref. ST784 640. 2m SE of Bath city centre. Bus: No. 18 or 418 to University. Rail: Bath Spa.
Open: 13 Mar–31 Oct: Tues–Sun (open BH Mons and Mons in Aug) 12noon–5pm. 26 Nov –19 Dec: Tues–Sun, 12noon– 4.30pm. Last admission to museum 4pm.
Admission: Adult £8.00, Child £4.50, Conc. £7.00. Groups (15–70): Adult £6.50.
Special Events: Full programme of events including: live music, living history, craft workshops, kids events and lectures.
WCs. Licensed. By arrangement. On leads.

BARRINGTON COURT
BARRINGTON, ILMINSTER, SOMERSET TA19 0NQ

www.nationaltrust.org.uk

Tel: 01460 241938 **Info:** 01460 242614
E-mail: barringtoncourt@nationaltrust.org.uk
Owner: The National Trust **Contact:** Visitor Services Manager
The enchanting formal garden, influenced by Gertrude Jekyll, is laid out in a series of walled rooms, including the White Garden, the Rose and Iris Garden and the Lily Garden. The working Kitchen Garden has espaliered apple, pear and plum trees trained along high stone walls. The Tudor manor house was restored in the 1920s by the Lyle family. It is now presented empty, with the ghosts of the past echoing in evey room.
Location: MAP 2:N5, OS Ref. ST395 181. In Barrington village, 5m NE of Ilminster, on B3168.
Open: House, Garden & Shop: 27 Feb–31 Oct: daily except Weds, 11am–5pm. 6 Nov–28 Nov: Sats & Suns, 11am–4pm. Restaurant: 1 Apr–30 Sept (weekdays: lunches only, weekends: lunch & teas), 1–30 Mar & 2 Oct–2 Nov, daily except Weds, 11am–5pm. 31 Mar–30 Sept, Mon, Tues, Thurs & Fri, 12 noon–3pm, 29 Mar–28 Sep, Sats & Suns, 12 noon–5pm. 6–14 Dec: Sat & Suns, 11am–4pm. Café: 29 Mar–30 Sept: daily except Weds, 11am–5pm. 4–26 Oct: Sat & Suns, 11am–5pm. NB. Café may be closed in poor weather (Oct).
Admission: Gift Aid Admission (Standard Admission prices in brackets): Adult £9.05 (£8.20), Child £3.95 (£3.55), Family (2+3) £21.75 (£19.75).
Grounds. WC. Licensed.

For **accommodation** in the South West, see our special index at the end of the book.

BECKFORD'S TOWER & MUSEUM
Lansdown Road, Bath BA1 9BH
Tel: 01225 460705 **Fax:** 01225 481850 **E-mail:** beckford@bptrust.org.uk
Owner: Bath Preservation Trust **Contact:** The Administrator
Built in 1827 for eccentric William Beckford and recently restored by Bath Preservation Trust. The tower is a striking feature of the Bath skyline.
Location: MAP 2:P2, OS Ref. ST735 676. Lansdown Road, 2m NNW of city centre.
Open: Easter weekend–end of Oct: Sats, Suns & BH Mons, 10.30am–5pm.
Admission: Adult £3, Child £1.50, Conc. £2, Family £8. BPT & NACF members: Free. Groups by arrangement.

BREAN DOWN
Brean, North Somerset
Tel: 01934 844518 **www.nationaltrust.org.uk**
Owner: The National Trust **Contact:** Administrator
Brean Down, rich in wildlife and history, is one of the most striking landmarks of the Somerset coastline, extending 1½m into the Bristol Channel. A Palmerston Fort built in 1865 and then re-armed in World War II, provides a unique insight into Brean's past.
Location: MAP 2:M3, OS Ref. ST290 590. Between Weston-super-Mare and Burnham-on-Sea about 8m from M5/J22. Rail: Highbridge 5m.
Open: All year.
Admission: Free. Donations welcome.
The cliffs are extremely steep. Please stay on the main paths and wear suitable footwear. (Not NT.) Partial. WC in café. (Not NT.) Guided walks. On leads.

© Cothay Manor

The Book Room, Cothay Manor

THE BUILDING OF BATH MUSEUM

The Countess of Huntingdon's Chapel, The Vineyards, The Paragon, Bath BA1 5NA

Tel: 01225 333895 **Fax:** 01225 445473 **E-mail:** enquiries@bathmuseum.co.uk

Owner: Bath Preservation Trust **Contact:** The Administrator

Discover the essence of life in Georgian Bath.

Location: MAP 2:P2, OS Ref. ST751 655. 5 mins walk from city centre. Bath M4/J18.

Open: 15 Feb–30 Nov: Tue–Sun & BH Mons, 10.30am–5pm (last adm. 4.30pm).

Admission: Adult £4, Child £2, Conc. £3.50. Groups: £3.

CLEEVE ABBEY ⌘

Washford, Nr Watchet, Somerset TA23 0PS

Tel: 01984 640377 **Email:** customers@english-heritage.org.uk

www.english-heritage.org.uk/cleeve

Owner: English Heritage **Contact:** Visitor Operations Staff

There are few monastic sites where you will see such a complete set of cloister buildings, including the refectory with its magnificent timber roof. This Cistercian abbey was built in the 13th century and its fine collection of heraldic tiles is the subject of an ongoing high profile research project.

Location: MAP 2:L4, OS Ref. ST047 407. In Washford, ¼m S of A39.

Open: 1 Apr–30 Jun: daily, 10am–5pm. 1 Jul–31 Aug: daily, 10am–6pm. 1–30 Sep: daily, 10am–5pm. 1 Oct–1 Nov: daily, 10am–4pm. Closed 2 Nov–31 Mar '10.

Admission: Adult £3.80, Child £1.90, Conc. £3.20. 15% discount for groups (11+). EH Members free. Opening times and prices are valid until 31st March 2010, after this date details are subject to change please see www.english-heritage.org.uk for the most up-to-date information.

🅲 🅂 Partial. WCs. ⬛ 🎦 By arrangement. 🅿 Limited for coaches. ⬛ 🖾 In grounds.

CLEVEDON COURT ⚘

Tickenham Road, Clevedon, North Somerset BS21 6QU

Tel/Fax: 01275 872257 **E-mail:** clevedon.court@nationaltrust.org.uk

Owner: The National Trust **Contact:** The Administrator

Outstanding manor house, with much 14th-century work remaining, set in a beautifully landscaped 18th-century terraced garden. Home to the Elton family since 1709. Visitors will see striking examples of Eltonware pottery and a fascinating collection of Nailsea glass.

Location: MAP 2:N2, OS ref: 172:ST4237161 1.5m E of Clevedon, on Bristol road (B3130) signposted from M5, exit 20.

Open: 1 Apr–30 Sept, 2pm–5pm (entry to house by timed ticket, on a first come, first served basis, car park opens 1.15pm). Open Wed, Thur, Sun & BH Mons.

Admission: Gift Aid (Standard Admission prices in bracket): £6.60 (£6.00), Child £3.10 (£2.80). Garden only: Adult £3.10 (£2.80)

🅂 ⬛ (Not NT.) ⬛

COLERIDGE COTTAGE ⚘

35 Lime Street, Nether Stowey, Bridgwater, Somerset TA5 1NQ

Tel: 01278 732662 **E-mail:** coleridgecottage@nationaltrust.org.uk

Owner: The National Trust **Contact:** The Visitor Services Manager, Dunster Castle

The home of Samuel Taylor Coleridge for three years from 1797, with mementoes of the poet on display. It was here that he wrote *The Rime of the Ancient Mariner*, part of *Christabel, Frost at Midnight* and *Kubla Khan*.

Location: MAP 2:M4, OS Ref. ST191 399. At W end of Lime St, opposite the Ancient Mariner pub, 8m W of Bridgwater.

Open: 1 Apr–26 Sept: Thur–Sun & BHs, 2pm–5pm.

Admission: Adult £4, Child £2.

ℹ No WC. 🅂 Braille guide. 🅿 500yds (not NT). 🖾 ⬛ Details call 01643 821314.

COTHAY MANOR & GARDENS

GREENHAM, WELLINGTON, SOMERSET TA21 0JR

www.cothaymanor.co.uk

Tel: 01823 672283 **Fax:** 01823 672345 **E-mail:** cothaymanor@btinternet.com

Owner/Contact: Mr & Mrs Alastair Robb

The magical, romantic, gardens of Cothay surround what is said to be the most perfect example of a small classic medieval manor. Many garden rooms, each a garden in itself, are set off a 200yd yew walk. In addition there is a bog garden with azaleas, and drifts of primuli, fine trees, cottage garden, courtyards, and river walk. A plantsman's paradise. The manor is open to groups throughout the year.

Location: MAP 2:L5, OS Ref. ST085 212. From M5 W J/27, take A38 direction Wellington. 3½m left towards Greenham. From N J/26 take A38 direction Exeter. 3½m right towards Greenham (1½m). On LH corner at bottom of hill turn right. Cothay 1m, always keeping left.

Open: Garden: Easter–Sept: Tues, Weds, Thurs, Suns, & BHs, 11am–6pm, last entry 4.30pm. Groups: Daily all season by appointment. House: Groups (20+) by appointment throughout the year.

Admission: Please go to our website for details.

ℹ No photography in house. 🅸 🅃 🅂 ⬛ 🅿 🖾 🔼

DODINGTON HALL

Nr Nether Stowey, Bridgwater, Somerset TA5 1LF

Tel: 01278 741400

Owner: Lady Gass **Contact:** P Quinn (occupier)

Small Tudor manor house on the lower slopes of the Quantocks. Great Hall with oak roof. Semi-formal garden with roses and shrubs.

Location: MAP 2:L4, OS Ref. ST172 405. ½m from A39, 11m W of Bridgwater, 7m E of Williton.

Open: 5–15 Jun, 2–5pm.

Admission: Donations to Dodington Church.

ℹ No inside photography. 🅂 Unsuitable. 🅿 Limited. No coach parking. 🖾 Guide dogs only.

©NTPL/Rupert Truman

Clevedon Court

©NTPL/Nadia MacKenzie

DUNSTER CASTLE ✤
DUNSTER, Nr MINEHEAD, SOMERSET TA24 6SL

www.nationaltrust.org.uk

Tel: 01643 821314 **Fax:** 01643 823000 **E-mail:** dunstercastle@nationaltrust.org.uk
Owner: The National Trust **Contact:** Visitor Services Manager

Dramatically sited on a wooded hill, a castle has existed here since at least Norman times. The 15th century gatehouse survives, and the present building was remodelled in 1868–72 by Antony Salvin for the Luttrell family, who lived here for 600 years. The fine oak staircase and plasterwork of the 17th century house he adapted can still be seen. There is a sheltered terrace to the south which is home to palms, sub-tropical plant species, and a varied collection of citrus. The terraced gardens also house the National Collection of strawberry trees (arbutus) and there is a pleasant riverside walk beside the River Avill.

Location: MAP 2:K4, OS Ref. SS995 435. In Dunster, 3m SE of Minehead.
Open: Castle: 13 Mar–31 Oct, daily except Thur, 11am–5pm. Garden & Park: Open every day: 1 Jan–12 Mar, 11am–4pm; 13 Mar–31 Oct, 10am–5pm; 1 Nov–31 Dec, 11am–4pm.
Admission: Castle, Garden & Park: Adult £9, Child £4.40, Family (2+3) £21.50. Garden & Park only: Adult £5, Child £2.30, Family £12.20.
▢⬚ Braille guide. 🎦 Out of hours by arrangement. 🅿 £2. ◼
🐕 In park, on leads. 🛗⬚ Tel for details (01643 821314) or visit website.

DUNSTER WORKING WATERMILL ✤
Mill Lane, Dunster, Nr Minehead, Somerset TA24 6SW
Tel: 01643 821759 **www.nationaltrust.org.uk**
Owner: The National Trust **Contact:** The Tenant
Built on the site of a mill mentioned in the Domesday Survey of 1086. The mill is a private business and all visitors, including NT members, are asked to pay the admission charge.
Location: MAP 2:K4, OS Ref. SS995 435. On River Avill, beneath Castle Tor, approach via Mill Lane or Castle gardens on foot.
Open: 1 Apr–31 Oct, daily 11am–4.30pm. Tea Room open as Mill, 10.30am–4.45pm. Tearoom hours may vary (01643 821759).
Admission: Adult £3.25, Child £2.25, Senior Citizen £2.75, Family £8.50.
▢⬚ Ground floor. ◼ 🅿

ENGLISHCOMBE TITHE BARN
Rectory Farmhouse, Englishcombe, Bath BA2 9DU
Tel: 01225 425073 **E-mail:** jennie.walker@ukonline.co.uk
Owner/Contact: Mrs Jennie Walker
An early 14th century cruck-framed Tithe Barn built by Bath Abbey.
Location: MAP 2:P2, OS172 Ref. ST716 628. Adjacent to Englishcombe Village Church. 1m SW of Bath.
Open: BHs, 2–6pm. Other times by appointment or please knock at house. Closed 1 Dec–7 Jan.
Admission: Free.

FAIRFIELD
Stogursey, Bridgwater, Somerset TA5 1PU
Tel: 01278 732251
Owner: Lady Gass **Contact:** Fairfield Estate
Elizabethan and medieval house. Occupied by the same family (Acland-Hoods and their ancestors) for over 800 years. Woodland garden. Views of Quantocks and the sea.
Location: MAP 2:L4, OS Ref. ST187 430. 11m W of Bridgwater, 8m E of Williton. From A39 Bridgwater/Minehead turn North. House 1m W of Stogursey on road to Stringston.
Open: 14 Apr–31 May & 9–23 Jun: Wed–Fri and Bank Holiday Mondays. Guided house tours at 2.30 & 3.30pm. Groups at other times by arrangement. Garden also open for NGS and other charities on dates advertised in Spring. Advisable to contact to confirm dates.
Admission: £5 in aid of Stogursey Church.
ℹ No inside photography. ⬚🎦 Obligatory. 🅿 No coach parking.
🐕 Guide dogs only.

FARLEIGH HUNGERFORD CASTLE ⌗
Farleigh Hungerford, Bath, Somerset BA2 7RS
Tel/Fax: 01225 754026 **E-mail:** customers@english-heritage.org.uk
www.english-heritage.org.uk/farleighhungerford
Owner: English Heritage **Contact:** Visitor Operations Staff
Extensive ruins of a 14th century castle with a splendid chapel containing rare medieval wall paintings, stained glass and the fine tomb of Sir Thomas Hungerford, builder of the castle. Displays in the Priest's House and a complimentary audio tour tell of the castle's sinister past.
Location: MAP 2:P3, OS173, ST801 577. In Farleigh Hungerford 3½m W of Trowbridge on A366. 9 miles SE of Bath.
Open: 1 Apr–30 Jun: daily, 10am–5pm. 1 Jul–31 Aug: daily 10am–6pm. 1–30 Sep: daily, 10am–5pm. 1 Oct–1 Nov: daily, 10am–4pm. 2 Nov–31 Mar: Sat & Sun, 10am–4pm. Closed 24–26 Dec & 1 Jan.
Admission: Adult £3.60, Child £1.80, Conc. £3.10. 15% discount for groups of 11+. EH Members free. Opening times and prices are valid until 31st March 2010, after this date details are subject to change please see www.english-heritage.org.uk for the most up-to-date information.
▢ ⬚ Partial. WCs. ◼🎦 By arrangement. 🎧🅿 Limited for coaches. ◼
🐕 Guide dogs only. ❋

GATCOMBE COURT
Flax Bourton, Somerset BS48 3QT
Tel: 01275 393141 **Fax:** 01275 394274
Owner/Contact: Mrs Stella Clarke, CBE
www.gatcombecourt.co.uk
A Somerset manor house, dating from early 13th century, which has evolved over the centuries since. It is on the site of a large Roman village, traces of which are apparent. Rose and new Jekka McVicar roman herb garden. House described in Simon Jenkins' book, *England's Thousand Best Houses*.
Location: MAP 2:N2, OS Ref. ST525 698. 5m W of Bristol, N of the A370, between the villages of Long Ashton and Flax Bourton. Close to Tyntesfield.
Open: May–Aug: for groups of 15–40 people by appointment.
⬚ Unsuitable. 🎦 By arrangement. ◼ 🅿 🐕 ❋

THE GEORGIAN HOUSE
7 Great George Street, Bristol, Somerset BS1 5RR
Tel: 0117 921 1362
Owner: City of Bristol Museums & Art Gallery **Contact:** Karin Walton
Location: MAP 2:O2, OS172 ST582 730. Bristol.
Open: All year: Sat–Wed, 10am–5pm.
Admission: Free.

GLASTONBURY ABBEY

Abbey Gatehouse, Magdalene Street, Glastonbury BA6 9EL
Tel: 01458 832267   **Fax:** 01458 836117   **E-mail:** info@glastonburyabbey.com
www.glastonburyabbey.com
Owner: Glastonbury Abbey Estate   **Contact:** Francis Thyer
"Unique", "Peaceful", "Such atmosphere", "A hidden gem". Come and discover this wonderful place for yourself. From March to October hear, from our enactors, how the monks used to live and some of the history of this once great Abbey. See website for events. Outdoor Summer Café.
Location: MAP 2:N4, OS Ref. ST499 388. 50 yds from the Market Cross, in the centre of Glastonbury. M5/J23, then A39.
Open: Daily (except Christmas Day), 9.30am–6pm or dusk if earlier. Jun, Jul & Aug: opens 9am. Dec, Jan & Feb: opens 10am.
Admission: Adult £5, Child (5–15 yrs) £3, Conc. £4.50, Family (2+2) £14.50. Groups 10+ (booked): Adult £4.50, Group/Child £3.00 (2009).
🔲 ♿ 📧 Summer only. 🐾 🏠 🅿 🎫 📷 ✱ 🏛

GLASTONBURY TOR 🌿

Nr Glastonbury, Somerset
Tel: 01934 844518

Owner: The National Trust   **Contact:** The Regional Office
The dramatic and evocative Tor dominates the surrounding countryside and offers spectacular views over Somerset, Dorset and Wiltshire. At the summit of this very steep hill an excavation has revealed the plans of two superimposed churches of St Michael, of which only the 15th-century tower remains.
Location: MAP 2:N4, OS Ref. ST512 386. Signposted from Glastonbury town centre, from where seasonal park-and-ride (not NT) operates.
Open: All year.
Admission: Free.
🅿 Park & ride from town centre Apr–Sept. Also free at Rural Life Museum. Tel 01458 831197. 🐕 On leads only. ✱

GLASTONBURY TRIBUNAL ⬚

Glastonbury High Street, Glastonbury, Somerset BA6 9DP
Tel: 01458 832954   **Email:** customers@english-heritage.org.uk
www.english-heritage.org.uk/glastonbury
Owner: English Heritage   **Contact:** The TIC Manager
A well preserved medieval town house, reputedly once used as the courthouse of Glastonbury Abbey. Now houses Glastonbury Tourist Information Centre and the Glastonbury Lake Village Museum.
Location: MAP 2:N4, OS182 Ref. ST499 390. In Glastonbury High Street.
Open: 1 Apr–30 Sep: Mon–Thu, 10am–5pm; Fri–Sat, 10am–5.30pm. 1 Oct–31 Mar: Mon–Thu, 10am–4pm; Fri–Sat, 10am–4.30pm. Closed 25–26 Dec & 1 Jan.
Admission: TIC Free. Museum area: Adult £2, Child/Conc £1.50. Senior £1. EH Members free. Group discount available. Opening times and prices are valid until 31st March 2010, after this date details are subject to change please see www.english-heritage.org.uk for the most up-to-date information.
♿ Partial. 🅿 Charge. 🐕 Guide dogs only. ✱

Glastonbury Abbey

HESTERCOMBE GARDENS 🏛

CHEDDON FITZPAINE, TAUNTON, SOMERSET TA2 8LG

www.hestercombe.com

Tel: 01823 413923 **Fax:** 01823 413747
E-mail: info@hestercombe.com
Owner: Hestercombe Gardens Trust
Contact: The Administration Office
Lose yourself in 40 acres of walks, streams and temples, vivid colours, formal terraces, woodlands, lakes, cascades and views that take your breath away. This is Hestercombe: a unique combination of three period gardens. The Georgian landscape garden was created in the 1750s by Coplestone Warre Bampfylde, whose vision was complemented by the addition of a Victorian terrace and shrubbery and the stunning Edwardian gardens designed by Sir Edwin Lutyens and Gertrude Jekyll. All once abandoned, now being faithfully restored to their former glory. Each garden has its own quality of tranquillity, wonder and inspiration. Beautifully restored 17th century Mill & Barn open from Spring 2010. Fabulous Courtyard Café and Restaurant, excellent shop, conference and business facilities, weddings, parties, year round events.
Location: MAP 2:M5, OS Ref. ST241 287. 4m NE from Taunton, 1m NW of Cheddon Fitzpaine.
Open: All year: daily, 10am–6pm (last admission 5pm). Groups & coach parties by arrangement.
Admission: Adult £8.90, Conc. £8.30, Children (up to 2 per paying adult) £1 per child, Additional Children £3.30, Groups £6.50, Guided tours £12.
🔲 🎫 ♿ 🚻 Partial. WC. 📧 Licensed.
🍴 Licensed. 🐾 By arrangement. 🅿 Limited for coaches. 🐕 On short leads 🔼 ✱

HOLBURNE MUSEUM OF ART

Great Pulteney Street, Bath BA2 4DB

Tel: 01225 466669 **Fax:** 01225 333121

Owner: Trustees **Contact:** Katie Jenkins

This jewel in Bath's crown houses the treasures collected by Sir William Holburne: superb English and continental silver, porcelain, majolica, glass and Renaissance bronzes, and paintings by Turner, Guardi and Stubbs.

Location: MAP 2:P2, OS Ref. ST431 545. Via A4 or A431, follow brown signs.

Open: Mid Jan–Dec, please telephone for details.

Admission: Varies with exhibitions – telephone for details.

HOLNICOTE ESTATE

Selworthy, Minehead, Somerset TA24 8TJ

Tel: 01643 862452 **Fax:** 01643 863011 **E-mail:** holnicote@nationaltrust.org.uk

Owner: The National Trust **Contact:** The Estate Office

The Holnicote Estate covers 5042ha (12,500 acres) of Exmoor National Park. The Estate also covers 4 miles of coastline between Porlock Bay and Minehead. There are over 100 miles of footpaths to enjoy through the fields, woods, moors and villages.

Location: MAP 2:K3, OS Ref. SS920 469. Off A39 Minehead–Porlock, 3m W of Minehead. Station: Minehead 5m.

Open: Estate Office: All year: Mon–Fri, 8.30am–5pm, Closed Bank Hols. Estate: open all year.

Admission: Free.

(Not NT.)

KENTSFORD

Washford, Watchet, Somerset TA23 0JD

Tel: 01984 631307

Owner: Wyndham Estate **Contact:** Mr R Dibble

Location: MAP 2:L4, OS Ref. ST058 426.

Open: House open only by written appointment with Mr R Dibble. Gardens: 6 Mar–28 Aug: Tues & BHs.

Admission: House: £3, Gardens: Free.

Gardens only. Limited. In grounds, on leads.

KING JOHN'S HUNTING LODGE

The Square, Axbridge, Somerset BS26 2AP

Tel: 01934 732012 **www.nationaltrust.org.uk**

Owner/Contact: The National Trust

An early Tudor merchant's house, extensively restored in 1971. Note: the property is run as a local history museum by Axbridge & District Museum Trust in co-operation with Sedgemoor District Council, County Museum's Service and Axbridge Archaeological & Local History Society.

Location: MAP 2:N3, OS Ref. ST431 545. In the Square, on corner of High Street, off A371.

Open: 2 April–30 Sept 2010: 1–4pm daily. 1 Oct–31 Dec: open first Sat of month 10–4pm, to coincide with Farmers' Market.

Admission: Free. Donations welcome.

Ground floor. By arrangement.

LOWER SEVERALLS

Crewkerne, Somerset TA18 7NX

Tel: 01460 73234 **E-mail:** mary@lowerseveralls.co.uk

Owner/Contact: Mary Pring

2½ acre garden, developed over the last 25 years including herb garden, mixed borders and island beds with innovative features, ie a giant living dogwood basket and a wadi.

Location: MAP 2:N5, OS Ref. ST457 112. 1½m NE of Crewkerne, between A30 & A356.

Open: Mar–Sept: Tue & Wed & Fri & Sat, 10am–5pm. Closed Aug.

Admission: Adult £3.25, Child (under 16yrs) Free.

See which properties offer **educational facilities** or **school visits** in our index at the end of the book.

©NTPL/Nick Meers

LYTES CARY MANOR

Nr CHARLTON MACKRELL, SOMERSET TA11 7HU

www.nationaltrust.org.uk/lytescarymanor

Tel: 01458 224471 **E-mail:** lytescarymanor@nationaltrust.org.uk

Owner: The National Trust **Contact:** Visitor Services Manager

This charming manor house, with its 14th century chapel and 15th century Great Hall, was the former home of medieval herbalist Henry Lyte. In the 20th century it was rescued from dereliction by Sir Walter Jenner, who refurnished the interiors in period style. Its Arts & Crafts style garden is an intimate combination of outdoor rooms, topiary, statues and herbaceous borders.

Location: MAP 2:O5, OS Ref. ST529 269. 1m N of Ilchester bypass A303, signposted from Podimore roundabout at junction of A303. A37 take A372.

Open: 13 Mar – 31 Oct: Fri–Wed, 11am – 5pm. Closes dusk if earlier. Open Good Friday, BH Mons. Park and Walks open all year (dawn to dusk).

***Admission:** Adult £7.70, Child £3.90. Family £19.35. Garden only: Adult £5.50, Child £2.80.*includes a voluntary donation but visitors can choose to pay the standard prices displayed at the property and on the website.

WCs. Groups by arrangement. Free. Small coaches only by arrangement. On leads. Estate.

MAUNSEL HOUSE

NORTH NEWTON, Nr TAUNTON, SOMERSET TA7 0BU

www.maunselhouse.co.uk

Tel: 01278 661076 **Fax:** 01278 661074 **E-mail:** info@maunselhouse.co.uk

Owner: Sir Benjamin Slade Bt **Contact:** The Events Team

This imposing 13th century manor house offers the ideal location for wedding receptions, corporate events, private and garden parties, filming and family celebrations. The ancestral seat of the Slade family and home of the 7th baronet Sir Benjamin Slade, the house can boast such visitors as Geoffrey Chaucer, who wrote part of the *Canterbury Tales* whilst staying there. The beautiful grounds and spacious rooms provide both privacy and a unique atmosphere for any special event. Available for weekend/Christmas house parties, weddings, birthdays, dinner parties and conferences.

Location: MAP 2:M4, OS Ref. ST302 303. Bridgwater 4m, Bristol 20m, Taunton 7m, M5/J24, A38 to North Petherton. 2½m SE of A38 at North Petherton via North Newton.

Open: Coaches & groups welcome by appointment. Caravan rally field available.

Functions. Partial. In grounds, on leads.

MILTON LODGE GARDENS

Old Bristol Road, Wells, Somerset BA5 3AQ

Tel: 01749 672168 **www.miltonlodgegardens.co.uk**

Owner/Contact: S Tudway Quilter Esq

"The great glory of the gardens of Milton Lodge is their position high up on the slopes of the Mendip Hills to the north of Wells … with broad panoramas of Wells Cathedral and the Vale of Avalon", (Lanning Roper). Charming, mature, Grade II listed terraced garden dating from 1909. Replanned 1962 with mixed shrubs, herbaceous plants, old fashioned roses and ground cover; numerous climbers; old established yew hedges. Fine trees in garden and in 7-acre arboretum across old Bristol Road.

Location: MAP 2:O3, OS Ref. ST549 470. ½m N of Wells from A39. N up Old Bristol Road. Free car park first gate on left.

Open: Garden & Arboretum: Easter–end Oct: Tues, Weds, Suns & BHs, 2–5pm. Parties & coaches by prior arrangement.

Admission: Adult £5, Children under 14 Free.

Unsuitable.

©NTPL/Rupert Truman

MONTACUTE HOUSE

MONTACUTE, SOMERSET TA15 6XP

www.nationaltrust.org.uk

Tel: 01935 823289 **Fax:** 01935 826921 **E-mail:** montacute@nationaltrust.org.uk

Owner: The National Trust **Contact:** The Administrator

A glittering Elizabethan house, adorned with elegant chimneys, carved parapets and other Renaissance features, including contemporary plasterwork, chimney pieces and heraldic glass. The magnificent state rooms, including a long gallery which is the largest of its type in England, are full of fine 17th and 18th century furniture and Elizabethan and Jacobean portraits from the National Portrait Gallery.

Location: MAP 2:N5, OS Ref. ST499 172. In Montacute village, 4m W of Yeovil, on S side of A3088, 3m E of A303.

Open: House: 13 Mar–31 Oct: daily except Tue, 11am–5pm. Garden: 13 Mar–31 Oct: Wed–Mon, 11am–5.30pm. Closes dusk if earlier.

Admission: House, Park & Garden: Adult £10, Child £4.70, Family £24.70. Groups (15+): Adult £8.50. Group organisers please book in writing to House Manager with a SAE.

Partial. Braille guide. WC. Licensed. Christmas lunches in Dec (must book). In park, on leads.

MUCHELNEY ABBEY

Muchelney, Langport, Somerset TA10 0DQ

Tel: 01458 250664 **Fax:** 01458 253842 **Email:** customers@english-heritage.org.uk

www.english-heritage.org.uk/muchelney

Owner: English Heritage **Contact:** Visitor Operations Staff

Well-preserved ruins of the cloisters, with windows carved in golden stone, and abbot's lodging of the Benedictine abbey, which survived by being used as a farmhouse after the Dissolution. Tactile displays and interactive video illustrate monastic life.

Location: MAP 2:N5, OS193 Ref. ST428 248. In Muchelney 2m S of Langport.

Open: 1 Apr–30 Jun: daily, 10am–5pm. 1 Jul–31 Aug: daily, 10am–6pm. 1–30 Sep: daily, 10am–5pm. 1 Oct–1 Nov, daily, 10–4pm. Closed 2 Nov–31 Mar.

Admission: Adult £3.80, Child £1.90, Conc. £3.20. 15% discount for groups (11+). EH Members free. Opening times and prices are valid until 31st March 2010, after this date details are subject to change please see www.english-heritage.org.uk for the most up-to-date information.

Partial. WCs. By arrangement. Dogs on leads (in grounds only)

NUNNEY CASTLE

Nunney, Somerset BA11 4LQ

Tel: 0117 9750700 **Email:** customers@english-heritage.org.uk

www.english-heritage.org.uk/nunneycastle

Owner: English Heritage **Contact:** Visitor Operations Staff

A small 14th century moated castle with a distinctly French style. Its unusual design consists of a central block with large towers at the angles.

Location: MAP 2:P3, OS183 Ref. ST737 457. In Nunney 3½m SW of Frome, 1m N of the A361.

Open: Any reasonable time.

Admission: Free. Opening times and prices are valid until 31st March 2010, after this date details are subject to change please see www.english-heritage.org.uk for the most up-to-date information.

Partial. Limited for cars. No coaches. On leads.

ORCHARD WYNDHAM

Williton, Taunton, Somerset TA4 4HH

Tel: 01984 632309

Owner: Wyndham Estate **Contact:** Wyndham Estate Office

English manor house. Family home for 700 years encapsulating continuous building and alteration from the 14th to the 20th century.

Location: MAP 2:L4, OS Ref. ST072 400. 1m from A39 at Williton.

Open: Telephone for details.

Admission: Telephone for details.

Obligatory & pre-booked. Limited. No coach parking. In grounds, on leads.

PRIEST'S HOUSE

Muchelney, Langport, Somerset TA10 0DQ

Tel: 01458 253771 (Tenant) **www.nationaltrust.org.uk**

Owner: The National Trust **Contact:** The Administrator

A late medieval hall house with large gothic windows, originally the residence of priests serving the parish church across the road. Lived-in and recently repaired.

Location: MAP 2:N5, OS Ref. ST429 250. 1m S of Langport.

Open: 14 Mar–26 July 2010: Sun & Mon, 2–5pm. Admission by guided tour. Last tour commences at 4.30pm.

Admission: Adult £3.60, Child £1.80. Not suitable for groups.

No WC.

Hestercombe Gardens

The American Museum & Gardens

ROBIN HOOD'S HUT

Halswell, Goathurst, Somerset TA5 2EW
Tel: 01628 825925 **E-mail:** bookings@landmarktrust.org.uk
www.landmarktrust.org.uk
Owner/Contact: The Landmark Trust

Robin Hood's Hut is an 18th century garden building with two distinct faces. On one side it is a small rustic cottage, with thatched roof and bark clad door while on the other is an elegant pavilion complete with umbrello (or stone canopy). In the 1740s, Charles Kemeys Tynte began to transform the landscape around Halswell House into one of the finest Georgian gardens in the south west. He built several follies including Robin Hood's Hut in 1767. It is cared for by The Landmark Trust, a building preservation charity who let it for holidays. Full details of Robin Hood's Hut and 189 other historic and architecturally important buildings are featured in the Landmark Trust Handbook (price £10 plus p&p refundable against a booking) and on the website.
Location: MAP 2:M4, OS Ref. ST255 333.
Open: Available for holidays for up to 2 people throughout the year. Other visits by appointment. Please contact the Landmark Trust for details.
Admission: Free on Open Days.

STEMBRIDGE TOWER MILL 💐

High Ham, Somerset TA10 9DJ
Tel: 01935 823289 **www.nationaltrust.org.uk**
Owner: The National Trust **Contact:** The Administrator

The last thatched windmill in England, dating from 1822 and in use until 1910.
Location: MAP 2:N4, OS Ref. ST432 305. 2m N of Langport, ½m E of High Ham.
Open: 15 Mar–31 Oct 2010, daily 11am–5pm (outstide viewing only, please respect privacy of holiday tenants in cottage). To enter mill: interior open - 25 Apr, 27 Jun and 22 Aug, 12–5pm.
Admission: Adult £3.60, Child £1.80. Arrangements may be made for school groups on 01935 827767.
ⓘ No WC. 🅿 Limited. ▦ 💐

Robin Hood's Hut

STOKE-SUB-HAMDON PRIORY 💐

North Street, Stoke-sub-Hamdon, Somerset TA4 6QP
Tel: 01935 823289 **www.nationaltrust.org.uk**
Owner/Contact: The National Trust

A complex of buildings, begun in the 14th century for the priests of the chantry of St Nicholas, which is now destroyed. The Great Hall is open to visitors.
Location: MAP 2:N4, OS Ref. ST473 174. ½m S of A303. 2m W of Montacute between Yeovil and Ilminster.
Open: 14 Mar–26 Sept 2010: daily, 11am–5pm or dusk if earlier. Not suitable for coaches.
Admission: Free.
ⓘ No WC. 🅿 Limited. 💐

TINTINHULL GARDEN 💐

Farm Street, Tintinhull, Somerset BA22 9PZ
Tel: 01935 823289 **E-mail:** tintinhull@nationaltrust.org.uk
www.nationaltrust.org.uk
Owner: The National Trust **Contact:** The Administrator

A delightful formal garden, created in the 20th century around a 17th century manor house. Small pools, varied borders and secluded lawns are neatly enclosed within walls and clipped hedges and there is also an attractive kitchen garden.
Location: MAP 2:O5, OS Ref. ST503 198. 5m NW of Yeovil, ½m S of A303, on E outskirts of Tintinhull.
Open: 13 Mar–31 Oct: Wed–Sun (open BH Mon), 11am–5pm (Tearoom 11am–4.30pm) or dusk if earlier.
▦ ♿ Grounds. Braille guide. 🔊 🅿 Limited. ▦ 💐

TREASURER'S HOUSE 💐

Martock, Somerset TA12 6JL
Tel: 01935 825015 **www.nationaltrust.org.uk**
Owner/Contact: The National Trust

A small medieval house, recently refurbished by The Trust. The two-storey hall was completed in 1293 and the solar block is even earlier.
Location: MAP 2:N5, OS Ref. ST462 191. 1m NW of A303 between Ilminster and Ilchester.
Open: 14 Mar–26 Sept 2010: Sun–Tue, 2–5pm. Only medieval hall, wall paintings and kitchen are shown.
Admission: Adult £3.60, Child £1.80. Not suitable for groups.
ⓘ No WC. 🅿 Limited for cars. None for coaches & trailer caravans.

TYNTESFIELD 💐

Wraxall, North Somerset BS48 1NX
Tel: 01275 461900 **E-mail:** tyntesfield@nationaltrust.org.uk
www.nationaltrust.org.uk/tyntesfield
Owner/Contact: The National Trust

Situated on a ridge overlooking the beautiful Land Yeo Valley, Tyntesfield was inspired and remodelled by John Norton in c1864 for William Gibbs, a successful merchant. The mansion is an extraordinary Gothic Revival extravaganza and survives intact with an unrivalled collection of Victorian decorative arts, an insight into life below stairs and a sumptuously decorated private chapel. Its surrounding 200ha (500 acres) of land includes formal gardens and a wonderful walled kitchen garden. Tyntesfield was saved for the nation by the National Trust in June 2002 with funding from the National Heritage Memorial Fund, other heritage partners and a £3 million public appeal. The property is now one of the most exciting projects of the National Trust due to its innovative approach to giving access to the ongoing conservation. Visitors should expect to see building and conservation work in progress and access to parts of the estate will be restricted for health and safety reasons.
Location: MAP 2:N2, OS Ref. ST506 715. Off B3128.
Open: House & Chapel: 20 Mar–31 Oct, 11am–5pm, Sat–Wed. Gardens: 20 Mar–31 Oct, 10.30am-5.30pm, Sat-Wed, plus three weekends before Christmas 10am-4pm, Sat and Sun. Open Good Fri. Last admission to house 1 hr before closing. Entry cannot be guaranteed on busy days.
*Admission: House, Chapel & Gardens: Adult £11, Child £5.50, Family £27. Gardens only: Adult £5.50, Child £2.75, Family £13.75. Groups by appointment. *includes a voluntary donation but visitors can choose to pay the standard prices displayed at the property and on the website.
▦ ▦ ▦ ♿ WCs. 🔊 🅕 By arrangement. ▦ 🅿 ▦ 💐 🐕

WELLS CATHEDRAL

Cathedral Green, Wells, Somerset BA5 2UE
Tel: 01749 674483 **Fax:** 01749 832210
Owner: The Chapter of Wells   **Contact:** Mr John Roberts
Fine medieval Cathedral. The West Front with its splendid array of statuary, the Quire with colourful embroideries and stained glass, Chapter House and 1392 astronomical clock should not be missed.
Location: MAP 2:O3, OS Ref. ST552 458. In Wells, 20m S from both Bath & Bristol.
Open: Apr–Sept: 7am–7pm; Oct–Mar: 7am–6pm.
Admission: Suggested donation: Adult £5.50, Child/Student £2.50, OAP £4. Photo permit £3.

WOODLANDS CASTLE

Ruishton, Taunton, Somerset TA3 5LU
Tel: 01823 444955   **Fax:** 01823 444019   **E-mail:** info@woodlandscastle.co.uk
www.woodlandscastle.co.uk
Owner: Sir Benjamin Slade   **Contact:** Gemma Halliwell
Woodlands Castle is a beautiful period house in 12 acres of private grounds situated on Junction 25 of the M5. Woodlands is available for private functions from weddings and conferences to barbecues, birthdays and wakes. Ample free parking. Accommodation within walking distance.
Location: MAP 2:M5, OS Ref. ST258 248.
Open: All year to private bookings only.
Admission: No admission.
🅣 🅛 Partial. 🅟 Licensed. 🅧 Licensed. 🅧 By arrangement. 🅟 Ample for cars. Limited for coaches. 🅗 In grounds. 🅐 🅧

Muchelney Abbey

■ **Owner**
The Marquis of
Lansdowne

■ **Contact**
The Administrator
Bowood House and
Gardens
Calne
Wiltshire SN11 0LZ

Tel: 01249 812102
Fax: 01249 821757
E-mail:
houseandgardens@
bowood.org

■ **Location**
MAP 3:A2
OS Ref. ST974 700

From London M4/J17,
off the A4 in Derry Hill
village, midway between
Calne and Chippenham.
Swindon 17m, Bristol 26m,
Bath 16m.

Bus: to the gate,
1½ m through
park to House.

Rail: Chippenham
Station 5m.

Taxi: AA Taxis,
Chippenham 657777.

■ **Opening Times**
House & Garden
31 Mar–31 Oct. Daily,
11am–6pm.
Last admission 5pm (or
1hr earlier after the
autumn clock change).

Rhododendron Walks
Off the A342
Chippenham to Devizes
road, midway between
Derry Hill and Sandy Lane.

Open daily for 6 weeks
during the flowering
season, usually from late
April to early June,
11am–6pm.

We recommend visitors
telephone or visit the
website to check the
progress of the flowering
season.

■ **Admission**
House & Garden

Adult	£8.60
Child (5–15yrs)	£7.00
Child (2–4yrs)	£4.85
Senior Citizen	£7.60
Family (2+2)	£26.50
Groups (20+)	
Adult	£7.60
Child (5–15yrs)	£6.00
Child (2–4yrs)	£3.85
Senior Citizen	£6.60
Rhododendron Walks	
Adult	£5.70
Senior Citizen	£5.20

Season Tickets available,
ask for details.

£1 discount if combined
with a visit to the House
on the same day.

BOWOOD HOUSE & GARDENS 🏛

www.bowood.org

Bowood is the family home of the Marquis and Marchioness of Lansdowne. Begun c1720 for the Bridgeman family, the house was purchased by the 2nd Earl of Shelburne in 1754 and completed soon afterwards. Part of the house was demolished in 1955, leaving a perfectly proportioned Georgian home, over half of which is open to visitors. Robert Adam's magnificent Diocletian wing contains a splendid library, the laboratory where Joseph Priestley discovered oxygen gas in 1774, the orangery, now a picture gallery, the Chapel and a sculpture gallery in which some of the famous Lansdowne Marbles are displayed.

Among the family treasures shown in the numerous exhibition rooms are Georgian costumes, including Lord Byron's Albanian dress; Victoriana; Indiana (the 5th Marquess was Viceroy 1888–94); and superb collections of watercolours, miniatures and jewellery.

The House is set in one of the most beautiful parks in England. Over 2,000 acres of gardens and grounds were landscaped by 'Capability' Brown between 1762 and 1768, and are embellished with a Doric temple, a cascade, a pinetum and an arboretum. The Rhododendron Gardens are open for six weeks from late April to early June. All the walks have seats.

ℹ Receptions, film location, 2,000 acre park, 40 acre lake, 18-hole golf course and Country Club, open to all players holding a current handicap.

🛍

♿ Visitors may alight at the House before parking. WCs.

☕ Self-service snacks, teas etc.

🍴 The Restaurant (waitress service, capacity 85). Groups that require lunch or tea should book in advance.

🚶 On request, groups can be given introductory talk, or for an extra charge, a guided tour. Tour time 1¼ hrs. Guide sheets in French, German, Dutch, Spanish & Japanese.

🅿 1,000 cars, unlimited for coaches, 400 yds from house. Allow 2–3 hrs to visit house, gardens and grounds.

🎒 Special guide books. Picnic areas. Adventure playground.

🐕 Working assistance dogs only.

LONGLEAT

www.longleat.co.uk

Set within 900 acres of 'Capability' Brown landscaped parkland, Longleat House is widely regarded as one of the best examples of high Elizabethan architecture in Britain and one of the most beautiful stately homes open to the public.

Visited by Elizabeth I in 1574, Longleat House was built by Sir John Thynne from 1568 and is the current home of the 7th Marquess of Bath, Alexander Thynn.

Inspired by various Italian palace interiors, including the Ducal Palace in Venice, the ceilings are renowned for their ornate paintings and abundance of gilt made by the firm of John Dibblee Crace in the 1870s and 1880s. The furniture collection meanwhile includes English pieces from as early as the 16th century and fine French furniture of the 17th and 18th centuries.

The Murals are absolutely unique to Longleat as they have been painted by Lord Bath himself. Incorporating a mixture of oil paints and sawdust, these private works of art offer a unique insight into Lord Bath's personality and beliefs. Subject to availability, tours can be booked at the Front Desk of Longleat House on the day of your visit.

Following the success of the Longleat House VIP Tours for Groups in 2009, Longleat is now offering even more for November to March 2009/10. You may well have paid a visit to Longleat House in recent times but have you poked around in Longleat's cupboards, peeked behind closed doors and seen parts of the House previously closed to visitors… well, now's your chance! Tours are subject to availability and must be pre-booked. Please see www.longleat.co.uk for details.

■ Owner
Marquess of Bath

■ Contact
Longleat
Warminster
Wiltshire BA12 7NW
Tel: 01985 844400
Fax: 01985 844885
E-mail: enquiries@
longleat.co.uk
www.longleat.co.uk

■ Location
MAP 2:P4
OS Ref. ST809 430
Just off the A36 between Bath–Salisbury (A362 Warminster–Frome). 2hrs from London following M3, A303, A36, A362 or M4/J18, A46, A36.
Rail: Warminster (5m) on Cardiff/Portsmouth line. Westbury (12m) on Paddington/Penzance line. Taxis at Warminster & Westbury Stations.
Air: Bristol 30m.

■ Opening Times
House, Safari and all Attractions:
Open daily: Sat 13 Feb to Sun 21 Feb
Open weekends only: Sat 27 Feb to Sun 21 March
Open daily: Sat 27 March to Sun 31 Oct 2010
Longleat House also open for guided tours (12pm and 2pm). Mondays to Fridays only, Monday 22 February to Friday 26th March 2010.
Longleat House offers 'behind the scenes' VIP Tours for Groups in 'closed periods'. Subject to availability, pre booking essential. Please see www.longleat.co.uk for details

■ Admission
House & Grounds
Adult	£12.00
Child (3–14yrs)	£6.00
Senior (60yrs+)	£8.00

Groups (12+)
Adult	£8.40
Child (3–14yrs)	£4.20
Senior (60yrs+)	£5.60

Longleat Passport
(see below)
Adult	£24.00
Child (3–14yrs)	£17.00
Senior (60yrs+)	£19.00

Groups (12+)
Adult	£16.80
Child (3–14yrs)	£11.90
Senior (60yrs+)	£13.30

Longleat Passport includes:
Longleat House, Safari Park, Safari Boats, Longleat Hedge Maze, Pets Corner, Animal Adventure, Longleat Railway, Adventure Castle*, Motion Simulator**, Postman Pat Village*, Old Joe's Mine, Tea Cup Ride**, Grounds & Gardens.
*14yrs and under only
**Height restrictions in operation

 Rooms in Longleat House can be hired for conferences, gala dinners and product launches. Extensive parkland for company fun days, car launches and fishing. Film location.

 WCs.

 Licensed.

 Individuals & Groups (max 20; 15 for Murals). Booking essential.

 P Ample.

 Welcome with 1 teacher free entry per 8 children. Talks and packs available on request. Booking essential. Education sheets.

 Guide dogs only.
 Orangery.
House only.

Conference/Function

ROOM	SIZE	MAX CAPACITY
Great Hall	8 x 13m	120
Banqueting Suite	2 x (7 x 10m)	50
Green Library	7 x 13m	70

■ Owner
Dr Andrew Rickman

■ Contact
Diane Simmons
Rockley, Marlborough,
Wiltshire SN8 1RT
Tel: 01672 514120
Fax: 01672 511002
E-mail: diane.simmons
@rockleymanor.com

■ Location
MAP 3:B2
OS SU164 717
SAT NAV SN8 1RT

■ Opening Times
By arrangement.

■ Admission
By arrangement.

ROCKLEY MANOR

www.rockleymanor.com

The Rockley Estate has a history that spans more than a thousand years with previous owners including the daughter of a Duke, 9 Baronets, a Bishop and a High Sheriff of Wiltshire.

The current Manor, built in 1775 and reconstructed in 1820 by Sir Hugh Smyth, is a late Georgian masterpiece with many additional features being added by 'Paul' Geddes Hyslop, the renowned architect who specialised in salvaging Georgian features from fashionable Georgian houses in London and reinstating them elsewhere to great effect.

The Manor, set in its own magnificent parkland with its rolling hills and woodland, is situated within close proximity of the M4 with easy access to London and Bath, making it the perfect setting for entertaining in glorious style. With 10 bedrooms, indoor heated swimming pool, tennis court & pavilion and outstanding outdoor sporting facilities, the Manor makes the perfect location for corporate activities.

The Manor is licensed for Civil Marriage Ceremonies, both indoors and outdoors, and the Baronial Hall can accommodate up to 120 guests for Dinner Parties or Weddings. Rockley Manor has outstanding gardens and together with its private and entirely secure location the Estate makes the perfect rural retreat.

The Manor at Rockley is situated in the middle of Rockley Village 2 miles north of Marlborough.

 Partial.

 By arrangement.

P

 In grounds, On leads.

©NTPL / Nick Meers

STOURHEAD ❧

www.nationaltrust.org.uk

Often referred to as "Paradise", Stourhead is an exquisite example of an English landscape garden. It was once described by Horace Walpole as 'one of the most picturesque scenes in the world'.

Visitors can discover the inspiration behind Henry Hoare II's world famous garden, laid out between 1741 and 1780, and enjoy breathtaking views all year round.

The garden is dotted with Classical temples including the Pantheon and the Temple of Apollo, which provide dramatic backdrops to the majestic lake, secluded valley and mature woodland replete with exotic trees.

Stourhead House is an 18th century Palladian Mansion home to the beautifully restored Pope's Cabinet, furniture by the younger Chippendale and a magnificent collection of paintings. It is situated at the top of the gardens surrounded by lawns and parkland.

The Stourhead Estate extends east to King Alfred's Tower, a triangular folly 2¹/₂ miles from the House which affords stunning views across three counties, and is the perfect place for picnics.

Visitors can also enjoy breathtaking walks across Whitesheet Hill's chalk downs, and explore open countryside where native wildlife, including woodland birds, badgers, deer and wildflowers, can be seen.

The Restaurant offers fresh new flavours and local produce, there is an extensive Gift Shop and Plant Centre, and there are many opportunities to get involved with Stourhead's exciting Events Programme.

The Estate also comprises The Spread Eagle Inn, First View Art Gallery and Stourhead Farm Shop (all non NT).

New in 2010: Step back in time with our fascinating new Ricard Colt Hoare exhibition in the basement gallery of Stourhead House.

©NTPL/Stephen Robson

- WCs.
- Licensed.
- Licensed.
- Group tours, by arrangement.
- Limited for coaches.
- On leads.

■ Owner
The National Trust

■ Contact
The Estate Office
Stourton
Nr Warminster
BA12 6QD

Tel: 01747 841152
Fax: 01747 842005
E-mail: stourhead@
nationaltrust.org.uk

■ Location
MAP 2:P4
OS Ref. ST780 340

At Stourton off the B3092, 3m NW of A303 (Mere), 8m S of A361 (Frome).

Rail: Gillingham 6½m; Bruton 7m.

Bus: South West Coaches 80 Frome to Stourhead on Sat; First 58/0A.

■ Opening Times
House
13 Mar–31 Oct: Fri–Tue, 11am–5pm. Last admission 4.30pm.

Garden
All year: daily, 9am–7pm or dusk if earlier.

King Alfred's Tower
13 Mar–31 Oct: daily, 11am–5pm. or dusk if earlier. Last admission: 4.30pm.

Restaurant
All year, daily (closed 25 December), Mar & Oct: 10am–5.30pm; Nov–Feb: 10am–4.30pm.

Shop & Plant Centre
All year, daily, (closed 25 December) Mar & Oct: 10am–5pm; Apr–Sept: 10am–6pm; Nov–Feb: 10am–4pm.

Farm Shop
(closed 24 Dec–1 Jan) 2 Jan–28 Mar: 10am–4pm; 29 Mar–24 Oct: 10am–6pm; 25 Oct–23 Dec: 10am–5pm

■ *Admission
House & Garden
Adult	£12.80*
Child	£6.40*
Family	£30.40*
Groups (15+)	£11.20

House OR Garden
Adult	£7.70*
Child	£4.20*
Family	£18.30*
Groups (15+)	£6.70

NB. Groups must book.

*includes a 10% voluntary donation but visitors can however choose to pay the standard admission prices displayed at the property and on the website.

■ Special events
please contact us or visit the website for details of our full events programme.

■ **Owner**
The Earl of Pembroke

■ **Contact**
The Estate Office
Wilton, Salisbury SP2 0BJ

Tel: 01722 746720
Fax: 01722 744447
E-mail: tourism@
wiltonhouse.com

■ **Location**
MAP 3:B4
OS Ref. SU099 311

3m W of Salisbury
along the A36.

■ **Opening Times**
Summer
House, Old Riding School, Exhibitions
2–8 April & 1 May–31 August: Sun–Thurs & BH Sat 1st May & 28 Aug 11.30am–4.30pm, last admission 3.45pm.

House, Old Riding School and Exhibitions closed 24th–31st May inclusive.
Access to the House is generally by guided visit except during school holidays and other busy times. Please see website for full details.

South Ante Library and Dining Room
1–3 May, 1st July–1st Aug Suns–Thurs when house is open, 28th Aug–31st Aug.

Grounds & Restaurant
2nd–18th Apr, 1st May–31st Aug daily. Sept, weekends only.11am–5pm, last admission 4pm.

Grounds & Restaurant closed 24th – 31st May inclusive

Winter
At all other times, the House and Grounds are closed except for bespoke tours and groups by prior arrangement.

Closures
This information is correct at the time of publication, but may be subject to change. Please check recorded information on 01722 746720 or visit our website.

■ **Admission**
House, Grounds, ORS and Exhibitions
Adult	£12.00
Child (5–15)	£6.50
Concession	£9.75
Family	£29.50

Groups (15+)
Adult	£10.00
Child	£5.00
Concession	£8.00

Guided Tour
Adult	£6.00

Grounds
Adult	£5.00
Child (5–15)	£3.50
Concession	£4.50
Family	£15.00

Membership
From £20.00

WILTON HOUSE 🏛

www.wiltonhouse.com

Wilton House has been the ancestral home of the Earl of Pembroke and his family for over 460 years. In 1544 Henry VIII gave the Abbey and lands of Wilton to Sir William Herbert who had married Anne Parr, sister of Katherine, sixth wife of King Henry.

The Clock Tower, in the centre of the east front, is reminiscent of the part of the Tudor building which survived a fire in 1647. Inigo Jones and John Webb were responsible for the rebuilding of the house in the Palladian style, whilst further alterations were made by James Wyatt from 1801.

The chief architectural features are the magnificent 17th century state apartments (including the famous Single and Double Cube rooms) and the 19th century cloisters.

The house contains one of the finest art collections in Europe, with over 230 original paintings on display, including works by Van Dyck, Rubens, Joshua Reynolds and Brueghel. Also on show are Greek and Italian statuary, a lock of Queen Elizabeth I's hair, Napoleon's despatch case, and Florence Nightingale's sash.

The Old Riding School houses a dynamic introductory film (narrated by Anna Massey), the reconstructed Tudor kitchen and the Estate's Victorian laundry. The house is set in magnificent landscaped parkland, bordered by the River Nadder which is the setting for the majestic Palladian Bridge. The 17th Earl of Pembroke was a keen gardener who created four new gardens after succeeding to the title in 1969 including the North Forecourt Garden, Old English Rose Garden, Water and Cloister Gardens.

ℹ Film location, fashion shows, product launches, equestrian events, garden parties, antiques fairs, concerts, vehicle rallies. No photography in house. French, German, Spanish, Italian, Japanese and Dutch information.

🛍 Adjacent garden centre

🍽 Exclusive banquets.

♿ Visitors may alight at the entrance. WCs.

🍴 Licensed.

🚶 By arrangement. £6. Tours in French, German and Spanish.

🅿 200 cars and 12 coaches. Free coach parking. Group rates (min 15), drivers' meal voucher.

🏫 National Curriculum KS1/2. Free preparatory visit for teachers. Sandford Award Winner 2002 & 2008

🐕 Guide dogs only.

🎭 5–7 March Antiques Fair Please see our website for up to date information.

Conference/Function

ROOM	SIZE	MAX CAPACITY
Double cube	60' x 30'	150
Exhibition Centre	50' x 40'	140
Film Theatre	34" x 20"	67

©NTPL / David Norton

©NTPL / David Norton

AVEBURY MANOR & GARDEN, AVEBURY STONE CIRCLE ❦ ✠
& ALEXANDER KEILLER MUSEUM
AVEBURY, Nr MARLBOROUGH, WILTSHIRE SN8 1RF
www.nationaltrust.org.uk/avebury

Tel: 01672 539250 **E-mail:** avebury@nationaltrust.org.uk

Owner: The National Trust **Contact:** The Visitor Services Manager

Avebury Manor & Garden: A much-altered house of monastic origin, the present buildings date from the early 16th century, with notable 18th Century alterations and Edwardian renovation by Colonel Jenner. The garden comprises tranquil 'rooms', featuring topiary and a succession of seasonal colour and contrast. The Manor House has recently returned to the National Trust management after 15 years of tenanted occupancy. Many previously unseen rooms are now open to the public, including the former bedroom and dressing room of the charismatic Alexander Keiller. If there is prolonged wet weather it may be necessary to close the house and garden.

Avebury Stone Circle: One of Britain's finest, most impressive circles stands proud amidst the rolling Wiltshire landscape, steeped in 6,000 years of history.

Alexander Keiller Museum Barn & Stables Galleries: The investigation of Avebury Stone Circle was largely the work of archaeologist and 'marmalade millionaire' Alexander Keiller in the 1930s. He put together one of the most important prehistoric archaeological collections, which can be seen in the Stables Gallery. The 'Story of the Stones', the people who strove to reveal the true significance of Avebury's Stone Circle and the development of the Avebury landscape, are depicted through interactive displays in the spectacular Barn Gallery, a 17th century thatched threshing barn.

Location: MAP 3:B2, OS Ref. SU101 701 (Avebury Manor). OS Ref. SU102 699 (Stone Circle). OS Ref. SU100 699 (Alexander Keiller Museum). 7m W of Marlborough, 1m N of the A4 on A4361 & B4003.

Open: Avebury Manor: 2 Apr–31 Oct 2010, 12pm–5pm Fri–Tues inclusive*. (*Opening arrangements subject to change, visit website for details) Garden (subject to weather): 2 Apr–31 Oct, 11am–5pm Fri–Tues incl. **Stone Circle:** Open all year – Car Park open 9.15am–6.30pm, Apr–Oct. 9.15am–4.30pm, Nov–Mar. Pay and Display – NT and EH Members Free. **Alexander Keiller Museum Barn & Galleries:** 1 Jan–31 Mar, Daily, 10am–4.30pm. 1 Apr–31 Oct, Daily, 10am–6pm and 1 Nov–31 Dec, Daily, 10am–4.30pm. **Shop and Circle Restaurant:** 1 Jan–31 Mar Daily 10.30am–4pm, 1 Apr–31 Oct Daily 10am–5.30pm, 1 Nov–31 Dec Daily 10.30am–4pm. Musuem, Galleries, Shop and restaurant closed 24–26 Dec 2010.

Admission: Avebury Manor & Garden: Adult £4.20 and Child £2.10. Garden only: Adult £3.15 and Child £1.60. **Stone Circle:** Free. **Alexander Keiller Museum Barn & Stables Galleries:** *Gift Aid Admission: Adults £4.90, Children £2.45, Family (2+2) £13.45, Family (1+3) £8.70.

🖼 Alexander Keiller Museum & Shop. ♿ Avebury Manor: ground floor with assistance & grounds; Alexander Keiller Museum: fully accessible. WCs. Braille guide. 🍴 Avebury, licensed. 🅿 Pay & display. 🚫 🐕 No dogs in house, guide dogs only in garden (Avebury Manor). On leads in Stone Circle and museum galleries. ✠ Stone Circle.

©English Heritage

Bradford-on-Avon Tithe Barn

BOWOOD HOUSE & GARDENS 🏛 *See page 220 for full page entry.*

BRADFORD-ON-AVON TITHE BARN ✠
Bradford-on-Avon, Wiltshire BA15 2EF
Tel: 0117 975 0700 **Email:** customers@english-heritage.org.uk
www.english-heritage.org.uk/bradford
Owner: English Heritage **Contact:** South West Regional Office
A magnificent medieval stone-built barn with a slate roof and wooden beamed interior.
Location: MAP 2:P2, OS Ref. ST824 604. ½m S of town centre, off B3109.
Open: Daily, 10.30am–4pm. Closed 25 Dec.
Admission: Free. Opening times and prices are valid until 31st March 2010, after this date details are subject to change please see www.english-heritage.org.uk for the most up-to-date information.
♿ Partial. 🅿 Limited. Charged. 🐕 Guide dogs only ✠

BROADLEAS GARDENS
Devizes, Wiltshire SN10 5JQ
Tel: 01380 722035
Owner: Broadleas Gardens Charitable Trust **Contact:** The Administrator
10 acres full of interest, notably The Dell, where the sheltered site allows plantings of magnolias, camellias, rhododendrons and azaleas.
Location: MAP 3:A3, OS Ref. SU001 601. Signposted SW from town centre at S end of housing estate, (coaches must use this entrance) or 1m S of Devizes on W side of A360.
Open: Apr–Oct: Sun, Weds & Thurs, 2–6pm or by arrangement for groups.
Admission: Adult £5.50, Child (under 12yrs) £2.50, Groups (10+) £5. 🍴 🅿 🐕

CORSHAM COURT 🏛

CORSHAM, WILTSHIRE SN13 0BZ

www.corsham-court.co.uk

Tel/Fax: 01249 701610   **E-mail:** staterooms@corsham-court.co.uk

Owner: J Methuen-Campbell Esq   **Contact:** Mrs Leonora Martin

Corsham Court, a splendid Elizabethan house dating from 1582, was acquired in 1745 to display Sir Paul Methuen's celebrated collection of 16th and 17th century Old Master paintings. This internationally renowned collection includes important works by Van Dyck, Carlo Dolci, Filippo Lippi, Salvator Rosa, Reynolds and Romney.

Capability Brown was employed during the 1760's to enlarge the house, creating the magnificent Picture Gallery and suite of State Rooms. These rooms still retain their original silk wall-hangings and furniture designed by Chippendale, Johnson, Cobb and the Adam brothers.

Surrounding the Court are the delightful gardens and parkland which were initially designed by Brown and later completed by Humphry Repton. The gardens are particularly admired for the collection of magnolias, specimen trees and spring bulbs.

Location: MAP 3:A2, OS Ref. ST874 706. Car: Signposted from the A4, approx 4m W of Chippenham. Bus: Bath to Chippenham. Rail: Chippenham Station 6m.

Open: Spring / Summer: 20 March – 30 September. Daily, except Mons & Fris but including Bank Holidays 2–5.30pm. Last admission 5pm. Winter: 1 October – 19 March (closed December).Weekends only 2–4.30pm. Last admission 4pm. NB: Open throughout the year by appointment for groups. For further details and special viewings of the the collection, see our website.

Admission:.House & Garden: Adult £7.00, Child (5–15yrs) £3.00, OAP £6.00. Groups (includes guided tour) Adult £6.00. Garden only: Adult £2.50, Child (5–15yrs) £1.50, OAP £2.00.

ℹ No photography in house. 🔲🔽WCs 🔧 Max 50. If requested the owner may meet the group. Bookings for morning tours are preferred. Tour time 1hr. 🅿 120 yards from the house. Coaches may park in Church Square. Coach parties must book in advance. No camper vans, no caravans. ⬛ Available: rate negotiable. A guide will be provided. 🐕❄

GREAT CHALFIELD MANOR & GARDENS 🌿

Nr Melksham, Wiltshire SN12 8NH

Tel: 01225 782239   **www.nationaltrust.org.uk**

Owner: The National Trust   **Contact:** Mr & Mrs R. Floyd

Charming 15th century manor with Arts and Crafts gardens c1910. The manor sits between an upper moat, gatehouse and earlier parish church. Beautiful oriel windows and rooftop soldiers (c1480) adorn the house restored between 1905 and 1911 by Major R Fuller whose family live here and manage the property on behalf of the National Trust. Alfred Parsons designed the gardens, with walls, paths, terraces, gazebo and lily pond. There are large borders, lawn and roses surrounding a well. Grass paths offer romantic views across the spring fed fishpond which lies above the brook.

Location: MAP 3:A2, OS Ref. ST860 631. 3m SW of Melksham off B3107 via Broughton Gifford Common, sign for Atworth. Rail: Bradford-on-Avon 3m, Chippenham 10m.

Open: Manor (guided tours only): 1 Apr–31 Oct, Tue–Thur, 11am, 12am, 2pm, 3pm, 4pm; Sun 2pm, 3pm, 4pm. Garden: 1 Apr to 31 Oct, Tues–Thur, 11am–5pm; Sun, 2pm–5pm. The tours take 45 mins and numbers are limited to 25. Visitors arriving during a tour can visit the adjoining parish church and garden first. Note: Group visits are welcome on Fri & Sat (not BHs) by written arrangement with the tenant Mrs Robert Floyd, charge applies. Organisers of coach parties should allow 2 hrs because of limit on numbers in the house.

Admission: Manor & Garden: Adult £7.20, Child £3.60, Family £18.40, Group Adult £6.10, Group Child £3.10. Garden only: Adult £4.80, Child £2.40.

🔽 Ground floor with assistance. Limited access to Garden. WC. 🔧 Obligatory. 🅿 Limited. 🐕

Lions of Longleat

HAMPTWORTH LODGE 🏛

HAMPTWORTH, LANDFORD, SALISBURY, WILTSHIRE SP5 2EA

www.hamptworthestate.co.uk

Tel: 01794 390700   **Fax:** 01794 390644

E-mail: kate@hamptworthestate.co.uk

Contact: N D Anderson Esq/Miss K Anderson

Jacobean style manor house standing in mature deciduous woodland within the northern perimeter of the New Forest National Park. Grade II* with period furniture including clocks. The Great Hall has an unusual roof truss construction. There is a collection of prentice pieces and the Moffatt collection of contemporary copies. One room has late 17th century patterned wall hangings. Available for events.

Location: MAP 3:C5, OS Ref. SU227 195. 10m SE of Salisbury on road linking Downton on A338. (Salisbury to Ringwood road) to Landford on A36 (Salisbury to Southampton road).

Open: House and Garden: 15–18 Mar, 29 Mar–1 Apr, 12–15 Apr, 26–29 Apr, 12–17 Jul & 19–24 Jul. 2.15pm–last admission 4.15pm. Private Groups and coaches only by prior appointment 1 Apr–31 Oct.

Admission: Adult £6, Child (under 5yrs) Free.

🔲🔽 Ground floor & grounds. 🔧 Obligatory. 🅿🔊🦽

©NTPL/Andrew Butler

LACOCK ABBEY, FOX TALBOT MUSEUM & VILLAGE
LACOCK, CHIPPENHAM, WILTSHIRE SN15 2LG

www.nationaltrust.org.uk

Tel: 01249 730459 (Visitor Reception) **Fax:** 01249 730501 (Estate Office)

Owner: The National Trust **Contact:** The General Manager

Founded in 1232 and converted into a country house c1540, the fine medieval cloisters, sacristy, chapter house and monastic rooms of the abbey have survived largely intact. The handsome stable courtyard has half-timbered gables, a clockhouse, brewery and bakehouse. Victorian rose garden and a woodland garden boasting a fine display of spring flowers and magnificent trees. The Fox Talbot Museum commemorates William Fox Talbot, a previous resident of the Abbey and inventor of the modern photographic negative. The village has many limewashed half-timbered and stone houses, featured in the TV and film productions of *Pride & Prejudice*, *Cranford* and *Emma*. Lacock Abbey featured in some of the *Harry Potter* films and the recent *Other Boleyn Girl*.

Location: MAP 3:A2, OS Ref. ST919 684. In the village of Lacock, 3m N of Melksham, 3m S of Chippenham just E of A350.

Open: Abbey*: 2 Jan–12 Feb & 6 Nov–19 Dec, Sat & Sun, 11am–4pm. 13 Feb–31 Oct, daily, 11am–5pm. Abbey Grounds, Fox Talbot Museum, Exhibition & Bookshop: 2 Jan–12 Feb & 1 Nov–19 Dec, Sat & Sun, 11am–4pm. 13 Feb–31 Oct, daily, 11am–5.30pm. Shop: 2 Jan–12 Feb & 1 Nov–31 Dec, daily, 11am–4pm. 13 Feb–31 Oct, daily, 10am–5.30pm. Village: All Year. *Access to the Abbey on Tuesdays and Winter weekends is limited to Cloisters only. Last admission 30 mins before closing. Closed Good Friday (excluding Village and High Street Shop). High Street Shop closed 25/26 December and 1 January.

Gift Aid Admission: Abbey, Grounds, Museum & Exhibition: Adult £11, Child £5.50, Family (2+3) £28. Groups: Adult £9.40, Child £4.70. **Abbey (Cloisters only), Grounds, Museum & Exhibition:** Adult £8, Child £4, Family (2+3) £20.40. Groups: Adult £6.80, Child £3.40. Only ticket available Tues and winter weekend.

⬛ ♿ Braille guides. ▣ 𝕗 By arrangement. **P** ▣ ✖ ❀ ♿

LONGLEAT 🏛   *See page 221 for full page entry.*

© Jane Gifford

LYDIARD PARK
LYDIARD TREGOZE, SWINDON, WILTSHIRE SN5 3PA

www.lydiardpark.org.uk

Tel: 01793 770401 **Fax:** 01793 770968 **E-mail:** lydiardpark@swindon.gov.uk

Owner: Swindon Borough Council **Contact:** The Keeper

Lydiard Park is the ancestral home of the Viscounts Bolingbroke. This beautifully restored Palladian house contains the family's furnishings and portraits, exceptional plasterwork, rare 17th century window and room devoted to the 18th century society artist Lady Diana Spencer. The faithfully restored 18th century ornamental Walled Garden is a beautiful and tranquil place to stroll, with seasonal displays of flowers and unique garden features. Exceptional monuments, including the Golden Cavalier, in the adjacent church.

Location: MAP 3:B1, OS Ref. SU104 848. 4m W of Swindon, 1½ m N of M4/J16.

Open: House: Tues–Sun, 11am–5pm (4pm Nov–Feb). Grounds: all day, closing at dusk. Victorian Christmas decorations in December.

Admission: House & Walled Garden: Adult £4.50, Senior Citizen £4, Child £2.25. Pre-booked groups: Adult £4, Senior Citizen £3.50. Opening times and prices may change April 2010 – please telephone to confirm.

ℹ No photography in house. ⬛ ♿ ▣ Open all year, but groups must book. 𝕗 By arrangement. ⌂ **P** ▣ ⛟ In grounds on leads. ❀ ♿

THE MERCHANT'S HOUSE
132 HIGH STREET, MARLBOROUGH, WILTSHIRE SN8 1HN

www.merchantshouse.co.uk

Tel/Fax: 01672 511491 **E-mail:** manager@merchantshousetrust.co.uk

Owner: Marlborough Town Council, leased to The Merchant's House (Marlborough) Trust **Contact:** Michael Gray

Situated in Marlborough's world-famous High Street, The Merchant's House is one of the finest middle-class houses in England. Its well-preserved Panelled Chamber was completed in 1656. Both the Dining Room and Great Staircase display recently uncovered 17th century wall paintings which have aroused much expert interest. Latest attraction is our 17th century formal garden.

Location: MAP 3:B2, OS Ref. SU188 691. N side of High Street, near Town Hall.

Open: Easter–end Sept: Fris & Sats, guided tours 11am, 12noon, 2pm, 3pm. Booked groups at other times by appointment.

Admission: Adult £5, Child 50p. Booked groups (10–40): Adult £4, Child 50p.

ℹ Photography only by arrangement. ⬛ ♿ 𝕗 **P** Outside house, also in Hillier's Yard. ⛟ Guide dogs only. ♿

South West – England

©NTPL/Peter Cook

MOMPESSON HOUSE ✄

THE CLOSE, SALISBURY, WILTSHIRE SP1 2EL

www.nationaltrust.org.uk

Tel: 01722 335659 **Infoline:** 01722 420980 **Fax:** 01722 321559
E-mail: mompessonhouse@nationaltrust.org.uk
Owner: The National Trust **Contact:** The Property Manager

An elegant and spacious 18th century house in the Cathedral Close. Featured in the award-winning film Sense and Sensibility and with magnificent plasterwork and a fine oak staircase. As well as pieces of good quality period furniture the house also contains the Turnbull collection of 18th century drinking glasses. Outside, the delightful walled garden has a pergola and traditional herbaceous borders.

Location: MAP 3:B4, OS Ref. SU142 297. On N side of Choristers' Green in Cathedral Close, near High Street Gate.

Open: 13 Mar–31 Oct: Sat–Wed, 11am–5pm. Last admission 4.30pm. Open Good Fri.

*Admission: Adult £5.50, Child £2.75, Family (2+3) £13.75. Groups: £4.50. Garden only: £1. Reduced rate when arriving by public transport. *includes a voluntary donation but visitors can choose to pay the standard prices displayed at the property and on the website.

⬚⬚ Ground floor & grounds. Braille guide. WCs. ⬚⬚ By arrangement. ⬚⬚

NEWHOUSE 🏛

REDLYNCH, SALISBURY, WILTSHIRE SP5 2NX

Tel: 01725 510055
Owner: George & June Jeffreys **Contact:** Mrs Jeffreys

A brick, Jacobean 'Trinity' House, c1609, with two Georgian wings and a basically Georgian interior. Home of the Eyre family since 1633.

Location: MAP 3:B5, OS184, SU218 214. 9m S of Salisbury between A36 & A338.

Open: 1 Mar–8 Apr, Mon–Fri & 30 Aug: 2–5pm.

Admission: Adult £5.00, Child £3.00, Conc. £5.00. Groups (15+): Adult £4.00, Child £3.00, Conc. £4.00.

ⓘ No photography in house, except at weddings. ⬚⬚ By arrangement.
P Limited for coaches. 🐕 Guide dogs only. ⬚

© Longleat

Longleat: 'The Saloon'

NORRINGTON MANOR

Alvediston, Salisbury, Wiltshire SP5 5LL

Tel: 01722 780 259

Owner/Contact: Mr & Mrs J Sykes

Built in 1377 it has been altered and added to in every century since, with the exception of the 18th century. Only the hall and the 'undercroft' remain of the original. It is currently a family home and the Sykes are only the third family to own it.

Location: MAP 3:A5, OS Ref. ST966 237. Signposted to N of Berwick St John and Alvediston road (half way between the two villages).

Open: By appointment in writing.

Admission: A donation to the local churches is asked for.

⬧ Unsuitable. ⬧ By arrangement. P Limited for cars, none for coaches. ⬧ ⬧

Mompesson House

OLD WARDOUR CASTLE ⌗

Nr TISBURY, WILTSHIRE SP3 6RR

www.english-heritage.org.uk/oldwardour

Tel/Fax: 01747 870487 **E-mail:** customers@english-heritage.org.uk

Owner: English Heritage **Contact:** Visitor Operations Team

In a picture-book setting, the unusual hexagonal ruins of this 14th century castle stand on the edge of a beautiful lake, surrounded by landscaped grounds which include an elaborate rockwork grotto.

Location: MAP 3:A5, OS184, ST939 263. Off A30 2m SW of Tisbury.

Open: 1 Apr–30 Jun: daily, 10am–5pm. 1 Jul–31 Aug: daily, 10am–6pm. 1–30 Sep: daily, 10am–5pm. 1 Oct–1 Nov: daily, 10am–4pm. 2 Nov–31 Mar: Sat–Sun, 10am–4pm. Closed 24–26 Dec & 1 Jan.

Admission: Adult £3.60, Child £1.80, Conc. £3.10. 15% discount for groups (11+). EH Members Free. Opening times and prices are valid until 31st March 2010, after this date details are subject to change please see www.english-heritage.org.uk for the most up-to-date information.

Special Events: See the English Heritage website for details of special events.

ℹ WCs. ⬧ ⬧ ⬧ Partial. WCs. ⬧ ⬧ P Limited for coaches. ⬧ ⬧ On leads. ⬧ ⬧ ⬧

OLD SARUM ⌗

CASTLE ROAD, SALISBURY, WILTSHIRE SP1 3SD

www.english-heritage.org.uk/oldsarum

Tel: 01722 335398 **E-mail:** customers@english-heritage.org.uk

Owner: English Heritage **Contact:** Visitor Operations Team

Built by the Iron Age peoples, Old Sarum is the former site of the city of Salisbury. It was occupied by the Romans, Saxons, and eventually the Normans who made it into a major stronghold and thriving town. Today the remains of the medieval castle, cathedral and bishop's palace are a magnificent site covered with wild flowers with fine views of surrounding countryside. History comes alive at Old Sarum once again during regular special events.

Location: MAP 3:B4, OS184, SU138 327. 2m N of Salisbury off A345.

Open: 1 Apr–30 Jun: daily, 10am–5pm. 1 Jul–31 Aug: daily, 9am–6pm. 1–30 Sep: daily, 10am–5pm. 1 Oct–1 Nov: daily, 10am–4pm. 2 Nov–31 Jan: daily, 11am–3pm. 1–28 Feb: daily, 11am–4pm. 1–31 Mar: daily, 10am–4pm. Closed 24–26 Dec & 1 Jan.

Admission: Adult £3.30, Child £1.70, Conc. £2.80. 15% discount for groups (11+). EH Members Free. Opening times and prices are valid until 31st March 2010, after this date details are subject to change please see www.english-heritage.org.uk for the most up-to-date information.

Special Events: See English Heritage website for details of special events.

ℹ WCs. ⬧ ⬧ Partial. WCs. ⬧ By arrangement. P Limited for coaches. ⬧ ⬧ On leads. ⬧ ⬧

© F A H Bloemendal

THE PETO GARDEN AT IFORD MANOR ⌂

Bradford-on-Avon, Wiltshire BA15 2BA

www.ifordmanor.co.uk

Tel: 01225 863146 **Fax:** 01225 862364

Owner/Contact: Mrs E A J Cartwright-Hignett

This unique Grade I Italian-style garden is set on a romantic hillside beside the River Frome. Designed by the Edwardian architect Harold A Peto, who lived at Iford Manor from 1899–1933, the garden has terraces, a colonnade, cloister, casita, statuary, evergreen planting and magnificent rural views. Renowned for its tranquillity and peace, the Peto Garden won the 1998 HHA/Christie's *Garden of the Year* Award.

Location: MAP 2:P3, OS Ref. ST800 589. 7m SE of Bath via A36, signposted Iford. ½m SW of Bradford-on-Avon via Westwood on B3109.

Open: Apr & Oct: Suns only & Easter Mon, 2–5pm. May–Sept: Tue–Thur, Sats, Suns & BH Mons, 2–5pm. Children under 10yrs welcome weekdays only for safety reasons.

Admission: Adult £4.50, Conc, Students & Children £4. Groups (10+) welcome outside normal opening hours, by arrangement only, £5.

⬧ Partial. WCs. ⬧ Teas (May–Sep: Sats, Suns & BHs, 2.30–5pm). ⬧ By arrangement. P Limited for coaches. ⬧ On leads, in grounds.

© Ash Mills

ROCKLEY MANOR

See page 222 for full page entry.

SALISBURY CATHEDRAL

33 THE CLOSE, SALISBURY SP1 2EJ

www.salisburycathedral.org.uk

Tel: 01722 555120 **Fax:** 01722 555116 **E-mail:** visitors@salcath.co.uk

Owner: The Dean & Chapter **Contact:** Visitor Services

Be inspired by the peace and beauty of one of Britain's finest medieval cathedrals, Salisbury Cathedral offers a warm welcome to all who visit. Set within eight acres of lawn and surrounded by historic buildings and museums within the spectacular Cathedral Close, the Cathedral is unique in being built almost entirely in one architectural style - Early English Gothic. Britain's tallest spire (123m / 404ft) was added a generation later.

Inside the Cathedral discover nearly 800 years of history including the finest preserved original Magna Carta (1215), Europe's oldest working clock (1386) and most stunning font (2008). Boy and girl choristers sing daily services. Explore the roof spaces on a tower tour, climbing 332 steps to the base of the spire, and admire the magnificent views across Salisbury.

New this year – the Cathedral's beautiful new flowing water font, designed by sculptor William Pye, and a new West Front statue of Canon Ezra, a 20th Century Sudanese martyr.

Location: MAP 3:B4, OS Ref. SU143 295. S of City. M3, A303, A30 from London or A36.

Open: All year daily: 7.15am–6.15pm.

Admission: Suggested donation: Adult £5, Child (5–17) £3, Conc. £4.25, Family (2+2) £12. Some special events require ticket purchase. Group rates available.

🖻 🔁 🔁 🖾 Licensed. 🎬 🎞 Tower tour: 90 mins–Book in advance. 🅿 In city centre. 🔳 🔄 In grounds, on leads. ❀ ☙

STOURHEAD 🌿

See page 223 for full page entry.

STOURTON HOUSE FLOWER GARDEN

Stourton, Warminster, Wiltshire BA12 6QF

Tel: 01747 840417

Owner/Contact: Mrs E Bullivant

Four acres of peaceful, romantic, plantsman's garden. Rare daffodils, camellias, rhododendrons, roses, hydrangeas and wild flowers.

Location: MAP 2:P4, OS Ref. ST780 340. A303, 2m NW of Mere next to Stourhead car park. Follow blue signs.

Open: Apr–end Nov: Weds, Thurs, Suns, and BH Mons, 11am–6pm. Plants & dried flowers for sale during the winter on weekdays. Groups any day.

Admission: Adult £3.50, Child 50p.

WILTON HOUSE 🏛

See page 224 for full page entry.

© English Heritage

Old Wardour Castle

© English Heritage

STONEHENGE ⌗
AMESBURY, WILTSHIRE SP4 7DE

www.english-heritage.org.uk/stonehenge

Tel: 0870 3331181 (Customer Services) **Email:** customers@english-heritage.org.uk

Owner: English Heritage

The great and ancient stone circle of Stonehenge is unique; an exceptional survival from a prehistoric culture now lost to us. The monument evolved between 3,000BC and 1,600BC and is aligned with the rising and setting of the sun at the solstices, but its exact purpose remains a mystery. To this day Stonehenge endures as a source of inspiration and fascination and, for many, a place of worship and celebration. An awe-inspiring place to visit, visitors to Stonehenge can discover the history and legends which surround this unique stone circle with a complimentary audio tour available in 10 languages (subject to availability).

Location: MAP 3:B4, OS Ref. SU122 422. 2m W of Amesbury on junction of A303 and A344 / A360.

Open: 1 Apr–31 May: daily 9.30am–6pm. 1 Jun–31 Aug: daily, 9am–7pm. 1 Sept–15 Oct: daily, 9.30am–6pm. 16 Oct–15 Mar: daily, 9.30am–4pm. 16–31 Mar: 9.30am–6pm. Closed 24/25 Dec. 26 Dec & 1 Jan, 10am–4pm. Opening times from 20–22 June may be subject to change due to Summer Solstice. Please call 0870 333 1181 before you visit. Recommended last admission time no later than 30 minutes before the advertised closing time. Stonehenge will close promptly 20 minutes after the advertised closing time. When weather conditions are bad, access may be restricted and visitors may not be able to use the walkway around the stone circle.

Admission: Adult £6.60, Child £3.30, Conc £5.60, Family (2+3) £16.50. Groups (11+) 10% discount. NT/EH Members Free. Opening times and prices are valid until 31st March 2010, after this date details are subject to change please see www.english-heritage.org.uk for the most up-to-date information.

⬚ ♿ WCs. 🍴 🎧 🅿 📷 ✕ Guide dogs only. ✳

© English Heritage

Old Sarum

Layer Marney Tower, Essex

Eastern Region

East Anglia has magical coastal areas ranging from The Wash in Norfolk down to the Essex marshes. The half timbered houses in Suffolk villages such as Lavenham contrast with the Norfolk flint found further north. Among the major properties that welcome visitors are Sandringham, the country home of HM The Queen, Woburn Abbey and Hatfield House; but off the beaten track find time for Copped Hall or The Manor, Hemingford Grey.

St Edmundsbury Cathedral, Suffolk

Bedfordshire
Cambridgeshire
Essex
Hertfordshire
Norfolk
Suffolk

NORFOLK

CAMBRIDGESHIRE

SUFFOLK

BEDFORDSHIRE

HERTFORDSHIRE

ESSEX

Somerleyton Hall, Suffolk

Elton Hall, Cambridgeshire

Sandringham © Sandringham Estates

■ Owner:
The Duke and Duchess of Bedford &
The Trustees of the Bedford Estates

■ Contact
Woburn Abbey
Woburn
Bedfordshire MK17 9WA

Tel: 01525 290333
Fax: 01525 290271
E-mail: admissions@ woburnabbey.co.uk

■ Location
MAP 7:D10
OS Ref. SP965 325

On A4012, midway between M1/J13, 3m, J14, 6m and the A5 (turn off at Hockliffe). London approx. 1hr by road (43m).

Rail: London Euston to Leighton Buzzard, Bletchley/Milton Keynes. Kings Cross Thameslink to Flitwick.

Air: Luton 14m. Heathrow 39m.

■ Opening Times
Woburn Abbey
Please telephone or visit our website for details.

Deer Park
All year: Daily
10am–5pm.
(except 24–26 December).

Antiques Centre
All year: Daily
10am–5.30pm.
(except 24–26 December).

■ Admission
Woburn Abbey, Grounds, Deer Park & Car Park
Please telephone for details. Group rates available. Reduced rates apply when Private Apartments are in use by the family.

WOBURN ABBEY

www.woburn.co.uk

Set in a beautiful 3,000 acre deer park, Woburn Abbey has been the home of the Russell Family for nearly 400 years, and is now occupied by the 15th Duke of Bedford and his family.

The Abbey houses one of the most important private art collections in the world, including paintings by Cuyp, Gainsborough, Reynolds, Van Dyck and Canaletto, 21 of whose views of Venice hang in the Dining Room (photograph below).

The tour of the Abbey covers three floors, including the vaults, with 18th Century French and English furniture, silver and a wide range of porcelain on display. Amongst the highlights are a selection of pieces from the Sevres dinner service presented to the 4th Duke by Louis XV of France.

The Deer Park is home to ten species of deer, including the Père David, descended from the Imperial Herd of China, which was saved from extinction at Woburn and is now the largest breeding herd of this species outside china. In 1985 the 14th Duke gave 22 Père David deer to the People's Republic of China and herds are now well established in their natural environment and numbers several thousand.

Woburn Abbey is also noted for its excellent and unique Antiques Centre with over 40 dealers represented, housed behind original 18th century shop fronts and show cases. Woburn Abbey specialises in banqueting, conferences, receptions and company days; and the Sculpture Gallery overlooking the Private Gardens provides a splendid setting for weddings and wedding receptions for groups of 20 to over 1,000.

2010 will see a number of events in the Park including Craft Fairs and a variety of musical and theatrical performances.

Conference/Function

ROOM	SIZE	MAX CAPACITY
Sculpture Gallery	128' x 24'	300 250 (sit-down)
Lantern Rm	44' x 21'	60
Long Harness Room	35' x 21'	80

ℹ️ Suitable for fashion shows, product launches and company 'days out'. Use of parkland and garden. No photography in House.

🛍️

🍸 Conferences, exhibitions, banqueting, luncheons, dinners in the Sculpture Gallery, Lantern & Long Harness rooms.

☕ Group bookings in Sculpture Gallery and Duchess' Tea Room.

🍴 Licensed.

🧍 By arrangement, max groups of 8. Tours in French, German & Italian available. Guide book and audio guide available (additional charge). Special interest tours can be arranged.

🅿️ Please telephone for details.

🐕 In park on leads, and guide dogs in house.

🛏️ The Inn at Woburn

🔔

❄️

🛡️

BUSHMEAD PRIORY ⌗

Colmworth, Bedford, Bedfordshire MK44 2LD
Tel: 01525 860000 **E-mail:** customers@english-heritage.org.uk
www.english-heritage.org.uk/bushmead
Owner: English Heritage **Contact:** Visitor Operations Team
A rare survival of the medieval refectory of an Augustinian priory, with its original timber-framed roof almost intact and containing interesting wall paintings and stained glass.
Location: MAP 7:E9, OS Ref. TL115 607. On unclassified road near Colmworth; off B660, 2m S of Bolnhurst. 5m W of St. Neots (A1).
Open: 1 May–31 Aug. Entry by pre-booked guided tours on first Sat of the month only. Telephone: 01525 860000 to book.
Admission: Adult £5, Child £2.50, Conc. £4.30. Group discount. EH members Free. Opening times and prices are valid until 31st March 2010, after this date details are subject to change please see www.english-heritage.org.uk for the most up-to-date information.
ⓘ Picnickers welcome. 🅿 ⊠

DE GREY MAUSOLEUM ⌗

Flitton, Bedford, Bedfordshire
Tel: 01525 860094 (Key-keeper) **E-mail:** customers@english-heritage.org.uk
www.english-heritage.org.uk/degreymausoleum
Owner: English Heritage **Contact:** Mrs Stimson
A remarkable treasure-house of sculpted tombs and monuments from the 16th to 19th centuries dedicated to the de Grey family of nearby Wrest Park.
Location: MAP 7:D10, OS Ref. TL059 359. Attached to the church on unclassified road 1½m W of A6 at Silsoe.
Open: Weekends only. Contact the keykeeper in advance. Mrs Stimson, 3 Highfield Rd, Flitton. Tel: 01525 860094.
Admission: Free. Opening times and prices are valid until 31st March 2010, after this date details are subject to change please see www.english-heritage.org.uk for the most up-to-date information.

HOUGHTON HOUSE ⌗

Ampthill, Bedford, Bedfordshire
Tel: 01223 582700 (Regional Office) **E-mail:** customers@english-heritage.org.uk
www.english-heritage.org.uk/houghton
Owner: English Heritage **Contact:** East of England Regional Office
The shell of a 17th century mansion with magnificent views, reputedly the inspiration for the 'House Beautiful' in John Bunyan's *Pilgrim's Progress*. Built around 1615 for Mary, Dowager Countess of Pembroke, in a mixture of Jacobean and Classical styles: the ground floors of two Italianate loggias survive, possibly the work of Inigo Jones. New information panels describe the house, its owners and the surrounding hunting estate. There is also a downloadable audio tour – visit www.englishheritage.org.uk/audio.
Location: MAP 7:E9, OS Ref. TL039 394. 1m NE of Ampthill off A421, 8m S of Bedford.
Open: Any reasonable time.
Admission: Free. Opening times and prices are valid until 31st March 2010, after this date details are subject to change please see www.english-heritage.org.uk for the most up-to-date information.
ⓘ Picnickers welcome. 🅿 ⊠ ❋

MOGGERHANGER PARK

Park Road, Moggerhanger, Bedfordshire MK44 3RW
Tel: 01767 641007 **Fax:** 01767 641515
E-mail: enquiries@moggerhangerpark.com **www.moggerhangerpark.com**
Owner: Moggerhanger House Preservation Trust **Contact:** Mrs Carrie Irvin
Outstanding Georgian Grade I listed Country House, recently restored in keeping with the original design of architect, Sir John Soane and set in 33 acres of parkland originally landscaped by Humphry Repton. Moggerhanger House has 3 executive conference suites and 2 function rooms, making an ideal venue for conferences, promotions and corporate entertainment.
Location: MAP 7:E9, OS Ref. TL048 475. On A603, 3m from A1 at Sandy, 6m from Bedford.
Open: House Tours: Sun–Mon at 2.30pm, Grounds, Tearooms & Visitors' Centre: All year.
Admission: Please telephone 01767 641007.
ⓘ No photography. No smoking. 📷 🍽 ♿ 🛍 Licensed. 🍴 Licensed.
🎭 By arrangement. 🅿 Limited for coaches. 🐕 In grounds, on leads. ❋

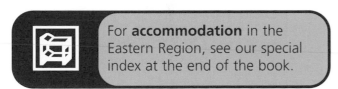

For **accommodation** in the Eastern Region, see our special index at the end of the book.

Woburn Abbey

BEDFORDSHIRE

QUEEN ANNE'S SUMMERHOUSE

Shuttleworth, Old Warden, Bedfordshire SG18 9DU
Tel: 01628 825925   **Email:** bookings@landmarktrust.org.uk
www.landmarktrust.org.uk
Owner/Contact: The Landmark Trust

The outstanding fine brickwork of this foursquare folly makes it likely to date from the early eighteenth century, as its name suggests. Surrounded by the floral and forna of a beautiful woodland, with the model village of Old Warden just down the drive, this is a magical spot. The Landmark Trust, a building preservation charity, has undertaken a major restoration of the building which is now available for holidays all year round. Full details of Queen Anne's Summerhouse and 189 other historic and architecturally important buildings are featured in the Landmark Trust Handbook (£10 plus p&p refundable against a booking) and on the website.

Location: MAP 7:E10, OS Ref. TL144436.
Open: Available for holidays for up to 2 people throughout the year. Six Open Days a year and visits by appointment. Contact the Landmark Trust for details.
Admission: Free on Open Days and visits by appointment.

SWISS GARDEN

Old Warden Park, Bedfordshire
Tel: 01767 627927   **www.shuttleworth.org**
Operated By: The Shuttleworth Trust

The Swiss Garden, Old Warden Park, Bedfordshire, created in the 1820s by Lord Ongley, is a late Regency garden and an outstanding example of the Swiss picturesque. The Swiss Cottage provides the main element for this unusual and atmospheric garden. It provides the principal aspect for a number of contrived vistas which lead the eye towards this attractive thatched structure. Interesting things to see in the garden are, a grotto and fernery, a thatched tree shelter, an Indian Pavilion, two ponds and many fine specimens of shrubs and conifers, plus some remarkable trees.

Location: MAP 7:E9, OS Ref. TL150 447. 1½m W of Biggleswade A1 roundabout, signposted from A1 and A600.
Open: Apr–Oct: 10am–5pm; Nov–Mar: 10am–4pm. Closed Christmas week.
Admission: Adult £5, Child Free, Conc. £4. Special rates for groups, tours & private hire.

🏠 ♿ 🕎 Catering. 🍴 Refreshments adjacent. 🅿 🚌 ▲ ❋

TURVEY HOUSE 🏠

Turvey, Bedfordshire MK43 8EL
Tel/Fax: 01234 881244   **E-mail:** danielhanbury@hotmail.com
Owner: The Hanbury Family   **Contact:** Daniel Hanbury

A neo-classical house set in picturesque parkland bordering the River Great Ouse. The principal rooms contain a fine collection of 18th and 19th century English and Continental furniture, pictures, porcelain, *objets d'art* and books. Walled Garden.

Location: MAP 7:D9, OS Ref. SP939528. Between Bedford and Northampton on A428.
Open: 1, 2, 3, 4, 6, 18, 20, 22, 31 May. 1, 3, 5, 15, 17, 19, 29 Jun. 1, 3, 13, 15, 17, 27, 29, 31 Jul. 14, 28, 29, 30 Aug, 2–5pm. Last Admission 4.30pm.
Admission: Adult £6, Child £3.

ℹ No photography in house. ♿ Partial. 🎫 Obligatory.
🅿 Ample for cars, none for coaches. 🚌

WOBURN ABBEY

See page 234 for full page entry.

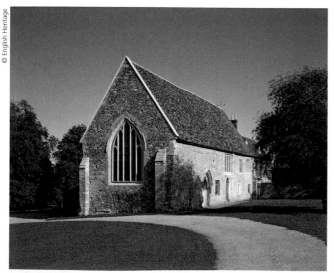
Bushmead Priory

Houghton House

WREST PARK ⚜

SILSOE, LUTON, BEDFORDSHIRE MK45 4HS

www.english-heritage.org.uk/wrest

Tel: 01525 860152   **E-mail:** customers@english-heritage.org.uk
Owner: English Heritage   **Contact:** Visitor Operations Team

Over 90 acres of enchanting gardens originally laid out in the early 18th century, and inspired by the great gardens of Versailles. Marvel at the magnificent collection of stone and lead statuary, the Bath House and the vast Orangery and dream of days gone by.

Location: MAP 7:E10, OS153, TL093 356. ¾m E of Silsoe off A6, 10m S of Bedford.
Open: 1 Apr–30 Jun: Sat–Sun & BHs, 10am–6pm. 1 Jul–31 Aug: Thu–Mon,10am–6pm. 1–30 Sep: Sat–Sun, 10am–6pm. 1 Oct–1 Nov: Sat–Sun, 10am–5pm. Last admission 1hr before closing. The house may be closed if an event is booked. The gardens may also close early. Please call to check.
Admission: Adult £5.20, Child £2.60, Conc. £4.40, Family £13.00. Group discounts. EH members Free. Opening times and prices are valid until 31st March 2010, after this date details are subject to change please see www.english-heritage.org.uk for the most up-to-date information.

ℹ WCs. Picnickers welcome. Buggies available. 📷 🕎 ♿ WCs. 🍴 🅿 🚌 On leads.
▲ ❤

©NT / Anglesey Abbey

ANGLESEY ABBEY, GARDENS & LODE MILL ❧
LODE, CAMBRIDGE, CAMBRIDGESHIRE CB25 9EJ

www.nationaltrust.org.uk/angleseyabbey

Tel: 01223 810080 **Fax:** 01223 810088 **E-mail:** angleseyabbey@nationaltrust.org.uk

Owner: The National Trust **Contact:** The Administrator

A passion for tradition and impressing guests inspired one man to transform a run-down country house and desolate landscape. At the age of 30, the future Lord Fairhaven began to create his first home. Wanting to inspire and surprise those who visited, he created a spectacular garden, with planting for all seasons, and a cosy house in which to entertain. Life revolved around horse racing and shooting, and guests enjoyed 1930s luxury. Inside, fine furnishings, books, paintings, silver and rare clocks give a feeling of opulence. Outside, 114 acres, offer vibrant colour, delicious scent, and the simple pleasures of nature.

Location: MAP 7:G8, OS Ref. TL533 622. 6m NE of Cambridge on B1102, signs from A14 jct35.

Open: House: 3 Mar–31 Oct: Wed–Sun: 11am–5pm; Garden, Shop, Plant Centre & Restaurant: 1 Mar–31 Oct: Mon–Sun; 10.30am–5.30pm. Winter: Garden, Shop, Plant Centre & Restaurant: 1 Jan–28 Feb & 1 Nov–31 Dec Mon–Sun, 10.30am–4.30pm; Picture Galleries & Dining Room: 1–17 Jan & 17 Nov–31 Dec: Wed–Sun: 11am–3.30pm; Lode Mill: 1 Jan-28 Feb & 1 Nov-31 Dec: Mon–Sun: 11am-3.30pm; 1 Mar–31 Oct: Mon–Sun: 11am–5pm. Groups must book, no groups on BHs. Open BH Mons & Good Fri. Snowdrop season: 18 Jan–21 Feb

*Admission: House, Garden & Mill: Adult £10.25, Child £5.15, Family £25.65, Family (1 adult) £15.40. Groups: Adult £8.70, Child £4.35. Garden, Mill & when appropriate winter house rooms: Adult £6.10, Child £3.05, Family £15.25, Family (1 adult) £9.15 Groups: Adult £5.20, Child £2.55. *includes a voluntary donation but visitors can choose to pay the standard prices displayed at the property and on the website.

Special Events: Exhibitions, activities, events and family events all year round. Further details available on the website.

ℹ️No photography in the house 🔲📧📺♿ WCs. 🍴 Licensed. 🎓 By arrangement 🅿️ ♿ Guide dogs only ✳️ ♿

©Nigel Luckhurst

CAMBRIDGE UNIVERSITY BOTANIC GARDEN
1 BROOKSIDE, CAMBRIDGE CB2 1JE

www.botanic.cam.ac.uk

Tel: 01223 336265 **Fax:** 01223 336278 **E-mail:** enquiries@botanic.cam.ac.uk

Owner: University of Cambridge **Contact:** Enquiries Desk

Opened in 1846 by John Henslow, teacher and mentor of Charles Darwin, this heritage-listed garden displays over 8000 plant species in a beautifully-designed landscape. Important collections include species tulips, geraniums and lavenders, and the finest arboretum in the East of England. The Garden also boasts the magnificent Glasshouses, recently restored to their original glory, which are planted with flamboyant tropical plants, extraordinary cacti and other plants requiring winter protection. Delicate alpines on the Rock Garden, Lake and Water Gardens teeming with aquatic life, and fabulous herbaceous plantings throughout make for a great day out whilst model gardens including the Dry Garden and Winter Garden provide year-round inspiration for the keen gardener.

Location: MAP 7:G9, OS Ref. TL453 573. 3/4 m S of Cambridge city centre; new Brookside Gate entrance on corner of Trumpington Road (A1309) and Bateman Street. Station Road Gate at the corner of Hills Road (A1307) and Station Road is 10mins walk from railway station with direct services to London, Birmingham and the north-west, and Norwich.

Open: Apr–Sept: daily, 10am–6pm; closes 5pm in Autumn & Spring and 4pm in winter. Closed over Christmas and New Year, please telephone for details.

Admission: Adult £4, Child (under 16yrs) Free, Conc. £3.50. Groups must book. Please use Trumpington Park & Ride, now open daily, and alight Bateman Street stop.

🔲♿📺🎓 By arrangement. 🅿️ Street/Pay & Display. ■ Schools and leisure groups must book. ♿ Guide dogs only. ✳️

DENNY ABBEY & THE FARMLAND MUSEUM ⌗

Ely Road, Chittering, Waterbeach, Cambridgeshire CB25 9PQ
Tel: 01223 860489   **E-mail:** customers@english-heritage.org.uk
www.english-heritage.org.uk/dennyabbey
Owner: English Heritage/Managed by the Farmland Museum Trust
Contact: Visitor Operations Team
What at first appears to be an attractive stone farmhouse is actually the remains of a 12th century Benedictine abbey which, at different times, also housed the Knights Templar and Franciscan nuns. Founded by the Countess of Pembroke. New family-friendly activities include hands-on interactives.
Location: MAP 7:G8, OS Ref. TL495 684. 6m N of Cambridge on the E side of the A10.
Open: 1 Apr–1 Nov: Mon–Fri, 12 noon–5pm, Sat & Sun 10.30am–5pm
Admission: Museum & Abbey: Adult £4, Child £2, Child under 5 Free, Conc. £3, Family £10. Museum charge: EH Members & OVP £2.60. Opening times and prices are valid until 31st March 2010, after this date details are subject to change please see www.english-heritage.org.uk for the most up-to-date information.
ℹ Farmland museum. Picnickers welcome. WC. ⬚⬚⬚⬚ Sat/Sun only. 🅿🔲 On leads. ⬚

DOCWRA'S MANOR GARDEN

Shepreth, Royston, Hertfordshire SG8 6PS
Tel: 01763 261473 **Information:** 01763 260677
Owner: Mrs Faith Raven   **Contact:** Peter Rocket
Extensive garden around building dating from the 18th century.
Location: MAP 7:F9, OS Ref. TL393 479. In Shepreth via A10 from Royston.
Open: All year: Weds & Fris, 10am–4pm & 1st Sun in month from Mar–Nov: 2–5pm.
Admission: £4.

ELTON HALL ⬚

Nr PETERBOROUGH PE8 6SH

www.eltonhall.com

Tel: 01832 280468   **Fax:** 01832 280584   **E-mail:** office@eltonhall.com
Owner: Sir William Proby Bt   **Contact:** The Administrator
Sir Peter Proby rose to prominence during the reign of Elizabeth I and by the early 17th century had acquired the mills at Elton. His grandson, Sir Thomas, was the first member of the family to establish himself at Elton Hall and he built a charming Restoration house attached to medieval buildings. Succesive generations, who later became the Earls of Carysfort, have added to the house greatly, both in architecture and contents. The house has many fine paintings and furniture. The library is one of the finest in private hands and includes Henry VIII's prayer book. Since 1983 the garden has been energetically restored and includes finely clipped topiary, a stunning new flower garden, Millennium Orangery and Box Walk.
Location: MAP 7:E7, OS Ref. TL091 930. Close to A1 in the village of Elton, off A605 Peterborough – Oundle Road.
Open: Late May bank holiday (Sun & Mon); June: Weds. Jul & Aug: Wed, Thur, Sun & Aug BH Mon, 2–5pm. Private groups by arrangement Apr–Sept.
Admission: House & Garden: £8.00, Conc. £7.00. Garden only: Adult £5.50, Conc. £5.00. Accompanied child under 16 Free.
ℹ No photography in house. ⬚⬚⬚⬚⬚ Garden suitable. ⬚⬚ Obligatory. 🅿🔲
🔲 Guide dogs in gardens only. ⬚

For **accommodation** in the Eastern Region, see our special index at the end of the book.

ELY CATHEDRAL

The Chapter House, The College, Ely, Cambridgeshire CB7 4DL
Tel: 01353 667735 ext.261 **Fax:** 01353 665658
Contact: Sally-Ann Ford (Visits & Tours Manager)
A wonderful example of Romanesque architecture. Octagon and Lady Chapel are of special interest. Superb medieval domestic buildings surround the Cathedral. Stained Glass Museum. Brass rubbing. Octagon and West Tower tours peak season.
Location: MAP 7:G7, OS Ref. TL541 803. Via A10, 15m N of Cambridge City centre.
Open: Summer: 7am–7pm. Winter: Mon–Sat, 7.30am–6pm, Suns and week after Christmas, 7.30am–5pm. Sun services: 8.15am, 10.30am and 4pm. Weekday services: 7.40am, 8am, and 5.30pm (Thurs only also 12.10pm).
Admission: Adult £5.20, Child Free, Conc. £4.50. Discounts for groups of 15+. Separate rates for school visits.
⊞

ISLAND HALL

GODMANCHESTER, CAMBRIDGESHIRE PE29 2BA

www.islandhall.com

Tel: (Groups) 01480 459676 (Individuals via Invitation to View) 01206 573948
E-mail: cvp@cvpdesigns.com
Owner: Mr Christopher & Lady Linda Vane Percy   **Contact:** Mr C Vane Percy
An important mid 18th century mansion of great charm, owned and restored by an award-winning interior designer. This family home has lovely Georgian rooms, with fine period detail, and interesting possessions relating to the owners' ancestors since their first occupation of the house in 1800. A tranquil riverside setting with formal gardens and ornamental island forming part of the grounds in an area of Best Landscape. Octavia Hill wrote *"This is the loveliest, dearest old house, I never was in such a one before."*
Location: MAP 7:F8, OS Ref. TL244 706. Centre of Godmanchester, Post Street next to free car park. 1m S of Huntingdon, 15m NW of Cambridge A14.
Open: Groups by arrangement: May–Jul & Sept. Individuals via Invitation to View.
Admission: Groups: (40+) Adult £5, (10–40) Adult £5.50. Under 20 persons, min charge £110 per group (sorry but no children under 13yrs).
⬚ Home made teas. ⬚

Elton Hall library

KIMBOLTON CASTLE

Kimbolton, Huntingdon, Cambridgeshire PE28 0EA
Tel: 01480 860505 **Fax:** 01480 861763
www.kimbolton.cambs.sch.uk/thecastle
Owner: Governors of Kimbolton School **Contact:** Mrs N Butler
A late Stuart house, an adaptation of a 13th century fortified manor house, with evidence of Tudor modifications. The seat of the Earls and Dukes of Manchester 1615–1950, now a school. Katharine of Aragon died in the Queen's Room – the setting for a scene in Shakespeare's Henry VIII. 18th century rebuilding by Vanbrugh and Hawksmoor; Gatehouse by Robert Adam; the Pellegrini mural paintings on the Staircase, in the Chapel and in the Boudoir are the best examples in England of this gifted Venetian decorator. New Heritage Room.
Location: MAP 7:E8, OS Ref. TL101 676. 7m NW of St Neots on B645.
Open: 7 Mar & 7 Nov, 1–4pm.
Admission: Adult £4, Child £2, OAP £3. Groups by arrangement throughout the year, including evenings, special rates apply.
⊤ ⑤ Unsuitable. ▣ ⒡ By arrangement. Ⓟ ▣ ⍒ On leads in grounds. ▲ ❋

OLIVER CROMWELL'S HOUSE

29 St Mary's Street, Ely, Cambridgeshire CB7 4HF
Tel: 01353 662062 **Fax:** 01353 668518 **E-mail:** tic@eastcambs.gov.uk
Owner: East Cambridgeshire District Council
The former home of the Lord Protector.
Location: MAP 7:G7, OS Ref. TL538 803. N of Cambridge, ¼m W of Ely Cathedral.
Open: 1 Nov–31 Mar: Sun–Fri, 11am–4pm; Sats, 10am–5pm. 1 Apr–31 Oct: daily, 10am–5.30pm.
Admission: Adult £4.40, Child £3, Conc. £3.95, Family (2+3) £12.75.

LONGTHORPE TOWER ⌗

Thorpe Rd, Longthorpe, Cambridgeshire PE1 1HA
Tel: 01536 203230 **E-mail:** customers@english-heritage.org.uk
www.english-heritage.org.uk/longthorpe
Owner: English Heritage **Contact:** Visitor Operations Team
The finest example of 14th century domestic wall paintings in northern Europe including the Wheel of Life, the Nativity and King David. The Tower that contains the paintings, is part of a fortified manor house.
Location: MAP 7:E6, OS Ref. TL163 983. 2m W of Peterborough just off A47.
Open: 1 Apr–30 Sep: Pre-booked guided tours on first Sun of the month only. Tel 01536 203230 during office hours to book.
Admission: Adult £5, Child £2.50, Conc. £4. Group discount. EH members Free. Opening times and prices are valid until 31st March 2010, after this date details are subject to change please see www.english-heritage.org.uk for the most up-to-date information.
ⓘ Picnickers welcome. ⌕ ⒡ By arrangement. ⍒

© English Heritage

Longthorpe Tower

Properties that **open all year** appear in the special index at the end of the book.

THE MANOR, HEMINGFORD GREY
HUNTINGDON, CAMBRIDGESHIRE PE28 9BN

www.greenknowe.co.uk

Tel: 01480 463134 **Fax:** 01480 465026 **E-mail:** diana_boston@hotmail.com
Owner: Mrs D S Boston **Contact:** Diana Boston
Built about 1130 and one of the oldest continuously inhabited houses in Britain. Made famous as 'Green Knowe' by the author Lucy Boston. Her patchwork collection is also shown. Four acre garden, laid out by Lucy Boston, surrounded by moat, with topiary, old roses, award winning irises and herbaceous borders.
Location: MAP 7:F8, OS Ref. TL290 706. Off A14, 3m SE of Huntingdon. 12m NW of Cambridge. Access is by a small gate on the riverside footpath.
Open: House: All year (except May), to individuals or groups by prior arrangement. In May guided tours will be daily at 2pm (booking advisable). Garden: All year, daily, 11am–5pm (4pm in winter).
Admission: Max: Adult £7, Child £2, OAP £5.50. Garden only: Adult £4, Child Free, OAP £3.50.
ⓘ No photography in house. ◩ ⑭ ⑤ Partial. ▣ ⒡ Obligatory. Ⓟ Disabled only. ▣ ⍒ In garden, on leads. ❋

PECKOVER HOUSE & GARDEN ❦
NORTH BRINK, WISBECH, CAMBRIDGESHIRE PE13 1JR

www.nationaltrust.org.uk

Tel/Fax: 01945 583463 **E-mail:** peckover@nationaltrust.org.uk
Web: nationaltrust.org.uk
Owner: The National Trust **Contact:** The Property Secretary
Peckover House is an oasis hidden away in an urban environment. A classic Georgian merchant's townhouse, it was lived in by the Peckover family for 150 years and reflects their Quaker lifestyle. The gardens are outstanding - two acres of sensory delight, complete with orangery, summer houses, croquet lawn.
Location: MAP 7:G6, OS Ref. TF458 097. On N bank of River Nene, in Wisbech B1441. Rail: 12m from March (Cambs) & Downham Market stations
Open: Garden, Shop & Tearoom: 13 Feb - 7 Mar, Sat & Sun, 11-4; 13 Mar–31 Oct, Sat–Wed, 12 noon–5pm House: 13 Mar - 31 Oct, Sat - Wed, 1 - 4:30pm. Open Good Friday and daily in Easter Week, and 1 & 2 July for Wisbech Rose Fair.
Admission: Adult £6, Child £3, Family £15. Groups discount (min 15 people)- book in advance with Property Secretary. **Special Events:** Call for leaflet.
ⓘ No picnics in grounds, no photography in House. PMV available for loan in grounds. Free garden tours most days. ◩ ⑭ ⊤ ⑤ Partial. WCs ▣ Licensed ⒡ By arrangement. Ⓟ Signposted ▣ ⍒ Guide dogs only ▲ ▣

CAMBRIDGESHIRE

PETERBOROUGH CATHEDRAL

Cathedral Office, Minster Precincts, Peterborough PE1 1XS
Tel: 01733 355300 **Fax:** 01733 355316
E-mail: andrew.watson@peterborough-cathedral.org.uk
www.peterborough-cathedral.org.uk
Contact: Andrew Watson

'An undiscovered gem.' With magnificent Norman architecture a unique 13th century nave ceiling, the awe-inspiring West Front and burial places of two Queens to make your visit an unforgettable experience. Exhibitions tell the Cathedral's story. Tours by appointment, of the cathedral, tower, Deanery Garden or Precincts. Group catering available – advance booking necessary. Cathedral gift shop and light refreshments at Coffee Shop. Business meeting facilities.

Location: MAP 7:E6, OS Ref. TL194 986. 4m E of A1, in City Centre.

Open: All year: Mon–Fri, 9am–6.30pm (restricted access after 5.30pm because of Evensong). Sat, 9am–5pm. Sun: services from 7.30am; visitors: 12 noon–5pm.

Admission: No fixed charge – donations are requested.

ℹ️ Visitors' Centre. 🏠 By arrangement. 🅿 None. Guide dogs only. See website for details.

Kimbolton Castle, Huntingdon

Wimpole Hall, Book Room

WIMPOLE HALL & HOME FARM

ARRINGTON, ROYSTON, CAMBRIDGESHIRE SG8 0BW

www.nationaltrust.org.uk   www.wimpole.org

Tel: 01223 206000 **Fax:** 01223 206000 **E-mail:** wimpolehall@nationaltrust.org.uk
Owner: The National Trust   **Contact:** General Manager

Wimpole is a magnificent country house built in The impressive mansion, at the heart of this country Estate, reflects how Elsie Bambridge made it into her home. Intimate rooms contrast with beautiful and unexpected Georgian interiors and a fascinating basement offers a glimpse into life below stairs. Stroll around the colourful Parterre and through the Pleasure Grounds to the Walled Garden, abundant with seasonal fruit, vegetables and herbaceous borders. At Home Farm discover rare breeds of cattle, sheep, pigs, poultry, goats and horses and see how we care for them. Stride out across the landscaped Park and imagine the previous owners planning their visions of grand avenues and vistas.

Location: MAP 7:F9, OS154. TL336 510. 8m SW of Cambridge (A603), 6m N of Royston (A1198). Rail: Shepreth 5ml. Royston with a taxi rank 8ml.

Open: Hall: 27 Feb–21 Jul & 28 Aug–31 Oct, Sat–Wed; 24 Jul–26 Aug, Sat–Thur, 11am–5pm. Timed guided tours may be in operation in the Hall between 11am–1pm. Hall open Sat–Thur during local school hols (Hall closed in Feb half-term). Hall open Good Friday 11am–5pm. Farm, Garden, Shop & Restaurant: 27 Feb-31 Oct Daily 10.30am-5pm. Garden, Shop & Restaurant: 2 Jan-24 Feb, 1 Nov–22 Dec, Sat–Wed, 11am–4pm; 27 Dec-30 Dec, Daily 11am-4pm. Farm: 2 Jan–21 Feb, 6 Nov-19 Dec, Sat-Sun 11am-4pm; 27 Dec-30 Dec, Daily 11am-4pm. Park: dawn–dusk, daily, all year.

*Admission: Hall: Adult £9.30, Child £5.20. Joint ticket with Home Farm: Adult £14, Child £7.60, Family £36.80. Garden: £3.90. Group rates (not Suns or BH Mons). Farm & Garden: Adult £7.70, Child (3yrs & over) £5.20, Family £24. Discount for NT members. *includes a voluntary donation but visitors can choose to pay the standard prices displayed at the property and on the website.

Partial. WCs Licensed. By arrangement. 🅿 Limited for coaches. Guide dogs only.

UNIVERSITY OF CAMBRIDGE

For further details contact:
(general enquiries): +44 (0)1223 337733

Christ's College
St Andrew's Street,
Cambridge CB2 3BU
Tel: 01223 334900
Website: www.christs.cam.ac.uk/admissn
Founder: Lady Margaret Beaufort
Founded: 1505

Churchill College
Madingley Road, Cambridge CB3 0DS
Tel: 01223 336000
Website: www.chu.cam.ac.uk
Founded: 1960

Clare College
Trinity Lane, Cambridge CB2 1TL
Tel: 01223 333200
Website: www.clare.cam.ac.uk
Founded: 1326

Clare Hall
Herschel Road, Cambridge CB3 9AL
Tel: 01223 332360
Website: www.clarehall.cam.ac.uk
Founded: 1965

Corpus Christi College
King's Parade, Cambridge CB2 1RH
Tel: 01223 338000
Website: www.corpus.cam.ac.uk
Founded: 1352

Darwin College
Silver Street, Cambridge CB3 9EU
Tel: 01223 335660
Website: www.dar.cam.ac.uk
Founded: 1964

Downing College
Regent Street, Cambridge CB2 1DQ
Tel: 01223 334800
Website: www.dow.cam.ac.uk
Founded: 1800

Emmanuel College
St Andrew's Street, Cambridge CB2 3AP
Tel: 01223 334200
Website: www.emma.cam.ac.uk
Founded: 1584

Fitzwilliam College
Huntingdon Road, Cambridge CB3 0DG
Tel: 01223 332000
Website: www.fitz.cam.ac.uk
Founded: 1966

Girton College
Huntingdon Road, Cambridge CB3 0JG
Tel: 01223 338999
Website: www.girton.cam.ac.uk
Founded: 1869

Gonville & Caius College
Trinity Street, Cambridge CB2 1TA
Tel: 01223 332400
Website: www.cai.cam.ac.uk
Founded: 1348

Homerton College
Hills Road, Cambridge CB2 2PH
Tel: 01223 507111
Website: www.homerton.cam.ac.uk
Founded: 1976

Hughes Hall
Wollaston Road, Cambridge CB1 2EW
Tel: 01223 334897
Website: www.hughes.cam.ac.uk
Founded: 1885

Jesus College
Jesus Lane, Cambridge CB5 8BL
Tel: 01223 339339
Website: www.jesus.cam.ac.uk
Founded: 1496

King's College
King's Parade, Cambridge CB2 1ST
Tel: 01223 331100
Website: www.kings.cam.ac.uk
Founded: 1441

Lucy Cavendish College
Lady Margaret Road, Cambs CB3 0BU
Tel: 01223 332190
Website: www.lucy-cav.cam.ac.uk
Founded: 1965

Magdalene College
Magdalene Street, Cambridge CB3 0AG
Tel: 01223 332100
Website: www.magd.cam.ac.uk
Founded: 1428

New Hall
Huntingdon Road, Cambridge CB3 0DF
Tel: 01223 762100
Website: www.newhall.cam.ac.uk
Founded: 1954

Newnham College
Grange Road, Cambridge CB3 9DF
Tel: 01223 335700
Website: www.newn.cam.ac.uk
Founded: 1871

Pembroke College
Trumpington Street, Cambs CB2 1RF
Tel: 01223 338100
Website: www.pem.cam.ac.uk
Founded: 1347

Peterhouse
Trumpington Street, Cambs CB2 1RD
Tel: 01223 338200
Website: www.pet.cam.ac.uk
Founder: The Bishop of Ely
Founded: 1284

Queens' College
Silver Street, Cambridge CB3 9ET
Tel: 01223 335511
Website: www.quns.cam.ac.uk
Founder: Margaret of Anjou,
Elizabeth Woodville
Founded: 1448

Ridley Hall
Ridley Hall Road, Cambridge CB3 9HG
Tel: 01223 741080
Website: www.ridley.cam.ac.uk
Founded: 1879

Robinson College
Grange Road, Cambridge CB3 9AN
Tel: 01223 339100
Website: www.robinson.cam.ac.uk
Founded: 1979

St Catharine's College
King's Parade, Cambs CB2 1RL
Tel: 01223 338300
Website: www.caths.cam.ac.uk
Founded: 1473

St Edmund's College
Mount Pleasant, Cambridge CB3 0BN
Tel: 01223 336086
Website: www.st-edmunds.cam.ac.uk
Founded: 1896

St John's College
St John's Street, Cambridge CB2 1TP
Tel: 01223 338600
Website: www.joh.cam.ac.uk
Founded: 1511

Selwyn College
Grange Road, Cambridge CB3 9DQ
Tel: 01223 335846
Website: www.sel.cam.ac.uk
Founded: 1882

Sidney Sussex College
Sidney Street, Cambridge CB2 3HU
Tel: 01223 338800
Website: www.sid.cam.ac.uk
Founded: 1596

Trinity College
Trinity Street, Cambridge CB2 1TQ
Tel: 01223 338400
Website: www.trin.cam.ac.uk
Founded: 1546

Trinity Hall
Trinity Lane, Cambridge CB2 1TJ
Tel: 01223 332500
Website: www.trinhall.cam.ac.uk
Founded: 1350

Wesley House
Jesus Lane, Cambridge CB5 8BJ
Tel: 01223 350127 / 367980
Website: www.wesley.cam.ac.uk

Wescott House
Jesus Lane, Cambridge CB5 8BP
Tel: 01223 741000
Website: www.ely.anglican.org/westcott

Westminster & Cheshunt
Madingley Road Cambridge CB3 0AA
Tel: 01223 741084
Website: www.westminstercollege.co.uk

Wolfson College
Grange Road, Cambridge CB3 9BB
Tel: 01223 335900
Website: www.wolfson.cam.ac.uk
Founded: 1965

Visitors wishing to gain admittance to the Colleges (meaning the Courts, not to the staircases & students' rooms) are advised to contact the Tourist Office for further information. It should be noted that Halls normally close for lunch (12–2pm) and many are not open during the afternoon. Chapels may be closed during services. Libraries are not normally open, and Gardens do not usually include the Fellows' garden. Visitors, and especially guided groups, should always call on the Porters Lodge first.

■ Owner
English Heritage

■ Contact
Visitor Operations Team
Audley End House
Audley End
Saffron Walden
Essex CB11 4JF

Tel: 01799 522842
Fax: 01799 521276
E-mail: customers@
english-heritage.org.uk

■ Location
MAP 7:G10
OS Ref. TL525 382

1m W of Saffron Walden
on B1383,
M11/J8 & J10.

Rail: Audley End 1¼ m.

■ Opening Times
House
1 Apr–30 Sept, Wed–Sun
& BHs, 11am–5pm
1–31 Oct, Wed–Sun,
11am–4pm.
1 Nov–31 Mar, House
closed. Last entry 1 hour
before closing.

**Gardens & Service
Wing***
1 Apr–30 Sept,
Wed–Sun, 10am–6pm.
1–31 Oct, Wed–Sun,
10am–5pm.
1 Nov–19 Dec, Sat–Sun,
10am–4pm.
20 Dec–31 Jan. closed.
1–13 Feb, Sat–Sun,
10am–4pm.
14–28 Feb, Wed–Sun,
10am–4pm. 1–31 Mar,
Wed–Sun, 10am–5pm.

■ Guided Tours House
1–30 Apr, Wed–Sun
(except Easter). 1
May–15 Jul, Wed–Fri
(except 3 and 29–31
May). 1 Sep–22 Oct,
Wed–Sun.

■ Admission
House & Gardens
Adult	£11.90
Child (5–15yrs)	£6.00
Child (under 5yrs)	Free
Conc.	£10.10
Family (2+3)	£29.80

**Service Wing &
Gardens**
Adult	£8.30
Child (5–15yrs)	£4.20
Child (under 5yrs)	Free
Conc.	£7.10
Family (2+3)	£20.80

Groups
(11+) 15% discount.
EH Members free.

AUDLEY END ▦

www.english-heritage.org.uk/audleyend

Audley End was a palace in all but name. Built by Thomas Howard, Earl of Suffolk, to entertain King James I. The King may have had his suspicions, for he never stayed there; in 1618 Howard was imprisoned and fined for embezzlement.

Charles II bought the property in 1668 for £50,000, but within a generation the house was gradually demolished, and by the 1750s it was about the size you see today. There are still over 30 magnificent rooms to see, each with period furnishings.

The house and its gardens, including a 19th century parterre and rose garden, are surrounded by an enchanting 18th century landscaped park laid out by 'Capability' Brown.

The Audley End Service Wing has become a firm favourite with visitors and gives a real flavour of what life was like for the servants of this grand country house in its Victorian hey day. The scullery, dairy, meat and game larders and laundries can all now be explored.

Visitors can also visit the working organic walled garden and seasonal produce is available to buy. Extending to nearly 10 acres the garden includes a 170ft long, five-bay vine house, built in 1802.

New attraction: From spring 2010 the Audley End Stable Block – claimed to be the "grandest surviving stables of the early 17th century" will come back to life. A new exhibition interprets the gardens, parkland and estate and links them to the working life of the house. There will also be a new café near to the acclaimed organic walled garden.

 Open air concerts and other events. WCs.

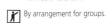 Service Yard and Coach House Shops.

 Partial. WCs.

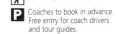 Audley End Tea Room and new Cart Yard Café

 By arrangement for groups.

 Coaches to book in advance. Free entry for coach drivers and tour guides.

School visits free if booked in advance. Contact the Administrator or tel 01223 582700 for bookings.

 On leads only.

■ **Owner/Contact**

Mr Nicholas Charrington
Tel: 01206 330784
E-mail: info@
layermarneytower.co.uk

■ **Location**
**MAP 8:J11,
OS Ref. TL929 175.**

7m SW of Colchester,
signed off B1022.

■ **Opening Times**
12noon–5pm:
April, May, June and
September,
Weds & Suns

July & August
Sun–Thurs

■ **Admission**
Adults £5.00
Children (3–15) £3.00
Family ticket £14.00

Group visits and guided
tours throughout the
year, by arrangement

Guided tours £8.50 per
person, minimum charge
for a group – £170.00

Group visits £4.50
person, minimum
group size 20

■ **Invitation to View**
Personal tours by the
owners – see
www.invitationtoview
.co.uk for info
and booking.

■ **Special Events**
See website
www.layermarneytower
.co.uk for details.

LAYER MARNEY TOWER

Nr COLCHESTER, ESSEX CO5 9US

www.layermarneytower.co.uk

Layer Marney Tower is a wonderful Tudor building of soft red brick and buff coloured terracotta, set within delightful gardens and parkland. In many respects the apotheosis of the Tudor gatehouse, Layer Marney Tower soars over the surrounding countryside offering spectacular views to those who climb the ninety nine steps to the top.

Built in the reign of Henry VIII by Henry, 1st Lord Marney, Layer Marney Tower is the tallest Tudor gatehouse in Great Britain and was intended to surpass the rival work being undertaken by Cardinal Wolsey at Hampton Court. Henry Marney died in 1523 before his ambition was realized and the death of his son John just two years later brought an end to the building work. By then the gatehouse and principal range were completed, as well as the stable block, some outbuildings and the parish church.

Layer Marney Tower has some of the finest terracotta work in the country, probably executed by Flemish craftsmen trained by Italian masters. The terracotta is used on the battlements, windows and, most lavishly of all, the tombs of Henry and John Marney. Much repair work has recently been undertaken to the upper parts of the gatehouse. Visitors may now wander through the recently restored tower rooms as they make their way up to the new viewing platform on the roof. The new lavatory block is a delight – worth a visit in its own right.

There are fine outbuildings, including the Long Gallery with its magnificent oak roof and the medieval barn, the principal timbers of which date to about 1450. The gardens follow a relatively formal Edwardian layout, with herbaceous borders, broad paths and plentiful roses that flourish in the heavy Essex clay.

One of the countries most desirable wedding venues, Layer Marney Tower is also used for conferences, banquets, trade shows, presentations and many corporate functions. During the year there are many special events ranging from plays to lantern tours to kite festivals.

ⓘ No photography inside the house. Suitable for conferences, business and social functions. Park and woodland for sports, corporate events, open air concerts, team building, balloon festivals and helicopter landing. Film location. Wedding ceremonies and receptions throughout the year.

🛍

🍷

♿ Partial. WC.

☕ Licensed

🍽 Banquets and pre-booked meals only

🚶 By arrangement – about 1½ hrs.

🅿 Cars & Coaches

🚷

🐕 On a lead.

🏠 Self catering cottage, 2 beds.

🔔

❄ By appointment for groups and special events.

AUDLEY END 🏠

See page 242 for full page entry.

BOURNE MILL ✂

Bourne Road, Colchester, Essex CO2 8RT
Tel: 01206 572422   **E-mail:** bournemill@nationaltrust.org.uk
www.nationaltrust.org.uk
Owner: The National Trust   **Contact:** The Custodian
Originally a fishing lodge built in 1591. It was later converted into a fulling mill with a 4 acre mill pond, then became a corn mill. Working waterwheel.
Location: MAP 8:J11, OS Ref. TM006 238. 1m S of Colchester centre, in Bourne Road, off the Mersea Road B1025.
Open: 6–27 June, Suns 2–5pm. 1 Jul–29 Aug: Thurs, Suns (& BH Mons), 2–5pm.
Admission: Adult £2.70, Child £1.20. No reduction for groups.
🏛 By arrangement 🅿 Limited. No coaches. 🐕 In grounds.

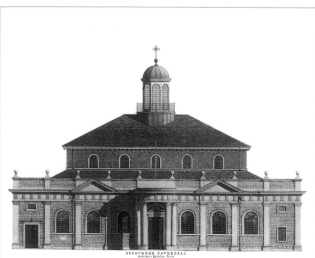

BRENTWOOD CATHEDRAL

INGRAVE ROAD, BRENTWOOD, ESSEX CM15 8AT

Tel: 01277 232266   **E-mail:** bishop@dioceseofbrentwood.org
Owner: Diocese of Brentwood   **Contact:** Rt Rev Thomas McMahon
The new (1991) Roman Catholic classical Cathedral Church of St Mary and St Helen incorporates part of the original Victorian church. Designed by distinguished classical architect Quinlan Terry with roundels by Raphael Maklouf. Architecturally, the inspiration is early Italian Renaissance crossed with the English Baroque of Christopher Wren. The north elevation consists of nine bays each divided by Doric pilasters. This is broken by a huge half-circular portico. The Kentish ragstone walls have a natural rustic look, which contrasts with the smooth Portland stone of the capitals and column bases. Inside is an arcade of Tuscan arches with central altar with the lantern above.
Location: MAP 4:J1, OS Ref. TQ596 938. A12 & M25/J28. Centre of Brentwood, opposite Brentwood School.
Open: All year, daily.
Admission: Free.
🛇 🅿 Limited. None for coaches. 🐕 ❄

CHELMSFORD CATHEDRAL

New Street, Chelmsford, Essex CM1 1TY
Tel: 01245 294489   **E-mail:** office@chelmsfordcathedral.org.uk
Contact: Mrs Bobby Harrington
15th century building became a Cathedral in 1914. Extended in 1920s, major refurbishment in 1980s and in 2000 with contemporary works of distinction and splendid new organs in 1994 and 1996.
Location: MAP 7:H12, OS Ref. TL708 070. In Chelmsford.
Open: Daily: 8am–5.30pm. Sun services: 8am, 9.30am, 11.15am and 6pm. Weekday services: 8.15am and 5.15pm daily. Holy Communion: Wed, 12.35pm & Thur, 10am. Tours by prior arrangement.
Admission: No charge but donation invited.

COGGESHALL GRANGE BARN ✂

Grange Hill, Coggeshall, Colchester, Essex CO6 1RE
Tel: 01376 562226   **email:** coggeshall@nationaltrust.org.uk
www.nationaltrust.org.uk
Owner: The National Trust   **Contact:** The Custodian
One of Europe's oldest timber-framed buildings with a cathedral-like interior. Exhibition of local woodcarving and tools.
Location: MAP 8:I11, OS Ref. TL848 223. Signposted off A120 Coggeshall bypass. West side of the road southwards to Kelvedon.
Open: 1 Apr–10 Oct: Thurs, Fri, Sat, Suns & BH Mons, 1–5pm.
Admission: Adult £2.70, Child £1.20. Joint ticket with Paycocke's: Adult £4.40, Child £2.20. 🛇 WCs 🅿 Coaches must book. 🐕 In Grounds.

COLCHESTER CASTLE MUSEUM

14 Ryegate Road, Colchester, Essex CO1 1YG
Tel: 01206 282939   **Fax:** 01206 282925
Owner: Colchester & Ipswich Museum Sevice   **Contact:** Museum Resource Centre
The largest Norman Castle Keep in Europe with fine archaeological collections on show. Hands-on & interactive display brings history to life.
Location: MAP 8:J11, OS Ref. TL999 253. In Colchester town centre, off A12.
Open: All year: Mon–Sat, 10am–5pm, also Suns, 11am–5pm.
Admission: Adult £5.10, Child (5–15yrs)/Conc. £3.30. Child under 5yrs Free. Saver ticket: £13.30. Prices may increase from April 2008.

©Alan Cox

COPPED HALL

CROWN HILL, EPPING, ESSEX CM16 5HS

www.coppedhalltrust.org.uk

Tel: 020 7267 1679   **E-mail:** Coxalan1@aol.com
Owner: The Copped Hall Trust   **Contact:** Alan Cox
Shell of 18th century Palladian mansion under restoration. Situated on ridge overlooking excellent landscaped park. Ancillary buildings including stables and small racquets court. Former elaborate gardens being rescued from abandonment. Large early 18th century walled garden – adjacent to site of 16th century mansion where 'A Midsummer Night's Dream' was first performed. Ideal film location.
Location: MAP 7:G12, OS Ref. TL433 016. 4m SW of Epping, N of M25.
Open: By appointment only for groups (20+) and events. Special open days.
Admission: Gardens £3.50. Part of Mansion and Stables £3.50, Child under 14yrs Free.
🛇 Partial. 🗊🚻🍴🏛 🅿 🐕 In grounds on leads. ❄🎭Concerts/plays.

FEERINGBURY MANOR

Coggeshall Road, Feering, Colchester, Essex CO5 9RB
Tel: 01376 561946
Owner/Contact: Mrs Giles Coode-Adams
Location: MAP 8:I11, OS Ref. TL864 215. 1¼m N of A12 between Feering & Coggeshall.
Open: From 1st Thur in Apr to last Fri in Jul: Thur & Fri only, 8am–4pm.
Admission: Adult £4, Child Free. In aid of National Gardens Scheme.

© NTPL/Nick Meers

Coggeshall Grange Barn

HARWICH REDOUBT FORT

Main Road, Harwich, Essex
Tel/Fax: 01255 503429 **E-mail:** info@harwich-society.co.uk
www.harwich-society.co.uk
Owner: The Harwich Society **Contact:** Mr A Rutter
180ft diameter circular fort built in 1808 to defend the port against Napoleonic invasion. Being restored by Harwich Society and part is a museum. Eleven guns on battlements.
Location: MAP 8:K10, OS Ref. TM262 322. Rear of 29 Main Road.
Open: 1 May–31 Aug: daily, 10am–4pm. Sept–Apr: Suns only, 10am–4pm. Groups by appointment at any time.
Admission: Adult £3, Child Free (no unaccompanied children).
✳ €

INGATESTONE HALL 🏛
HALL LANE, INGATESTONE, ESSEX CM4 9NR
www.ingatestonehall.com

Tel: 01277 353010 **Fax:** 01245 248979 **Email:** house@ingatestonehall.co.uk
Owner: The Lord Petre **Contact:** The Administrator
16th century mansion, set in 11 acres of grounds (formal garden and wild walk), built by Sir William Petre, Secretary of State to four Tudor monarchs, which has remained in the hands of his family ever since. The two Priests' hiding places can be seen, as well as furniture, portraits and family memorabilia accumulated over the centuries.
Location: MAP 7:H12, OS Ref. TQ654 986. Off A12 between Brentwood & Chelmsford. Take Station Lane at London end of Ingatestone High Street, cross level-crossing and continue for ½ m to SE.
Open: 4 Apr–26 Sept: Wed, Suns & BH Mons (not Weds in June), 12noon–5pm.
Admission: Adult £5, Child £2.50 (under 5yrs Free), Conc. £4. (Groups of 20+ booked in advance: Adult £4, Child £2, Conc. £3.50.)
ℹ️ No photography in house. 🔲 🔲 🔲 🔲 Partial. 🔲 🔲 By arrangement. 🅿️ 🔲 🔲 Guide dogs only. 🔲

HYLANDS HOUSE & ESTATE
HYLANDS PARK, LONDON ROAD, CHELMSFORD CM2 8WQ
www.chelmsford.gov.uk/hylands

Tel: 01245 605500 **Fax:** 01245 605510
E-mail: hylands@chelmsford.gov.uk
Owner: Chelmsford Borough Council **Contact:** Ceri Lowen
Hylands House is a beautiful Grade II* listed building, set in 574 acres of historic landscaped parkland, partly designed by Humphry Repton. Built c1730, the original house was a Queen Anne style mansion. Subsequent owners modernised and enlarged the property, added East and West wings and a colonnaded portico, and covered the house in white stucco, which produced today's neo-classical house. Restoration was completed in 2005 and visitors can explore the spectacular rooms, ranging from the exquisitely gilded neo-baroque Banqueting Room and Drawing Room, restored to their early Victorian splendour, to the Georgian Dining Room. There are stunning views from the Repton Room to the Serpentine Lake. The Stables Centre (Grade II listed)

incorporates a visitor centre, café, gift shop, artist studios, second hand bookshop and interpretation room. You can also visit the newly restored Pleasure Gardens and One World Garden. Group visits to house and gardens available by arrangement.
Location: MAP 7:H12, OS Ref. TL681 054. 2m SW of Chelmsford. Signposted on A414 from J15 of A12, near Chelmsford.
Open: House: Suns and Mons, 10am–5pm Apr-Sept, Sun only 10am-4pm Oct-Mar, Closed 25 Dec. Stables Centre and Park: Daily.
Admission: House: Adult £3.60, accompanied children under 16 Free, Conc. £2.60. Stables Centre and Park: Free.
ℹ️ Visitor Centre. No photography in house. 🔲 🔲 🔲 🔲 🔲 Daily. 🍽 🔲 By arrangement. 🔲 🅿️ 🔲 By arrangement. 🔲 In grounds. Guide dogs only in house. 🔲 ✳ 🔲

LAYER MARNEY TOWER

See page 243 for full page entry.

MISTLEY TOWERS

Colchester, Essex
Tel: 01206 393884 / 01223 582700 (Regional Office)
E-mail: customers@english-heritage.org.uk
www.english-heritage.org.uk/mistleytowers
Owner: English Heritage   **Contact:** The Keykeeper (Mistley Quay Workshops)
The remains of one of only two churches designed by the great architect Robert Adam. Built in 1776. It was unusual in having towers at both the east and west ends.
Location: MAP 8:K10, OS Ref. TM116 320. On B1352, 1½m E of A137 at Lawford, 9m E of Colchester.
Open: Key available from Mistley Quay Workshops, 01206 393884.
Admission: Free. Opening times and prices are valid until 31st March 2010, after this date details are subject to change please see www.english-heritage.org.uk for the most up-to-date information.
i Picnickers welcome. 🔾 Grounds only. 🔾 Restricted areas.

SIR ALFRED MUNNINGS ART MUSEUM

CASTLE HOUSE, CASTLE HILL, DEDHAM, ESSEX CO7 6AZ

www.siralfredmunnings.co.uk

Tel: 01206 322127   **E-mail:** info@siralfredmunnings.co.uk
Owner: Castle House Trust   **Contact:** The Administrator
In 1959 Castle House was set up as an art museum and memorial to Sir Alfred Munnings. The house is a mixture of Tudor and Georgian periods restored and with original Munnings' furniture. Over 200 of Munnings' works are exhibited, representing his life's work. The house stands in spacious grounds with well maintained gardens. Visitors may also view his original studio where his working materials are displayed.
Location: MAP 8:K10, OS Ref. TM060 328. Approximately ¾m from the village centre on the corner of East Lane.
Open: 1 Apr–30 Sep. Sun, Wed & BH Mon. Also Thurs & Sats in July and Sept.
Admission: Adult £5, Child £1, Conc. £4.
🔾 🔾 Partial. WC. 🔾 🅿 🔾 In grounds, on leads.

Layer Marney Tower

PAYCOCKE'S

West Street, Coggeshall, Colchester, Essex CO6 1NS
Tel: 01376 561305   **email:** paycockes@nationaltrust.org.uk
www.nationaltrust.org.uk
Owner: The National Trust   **Contact:** The Custodian
Marvel at the stunning woodcarving and elaborate panelling inside this merchant's house. Built around 1500 for Thomas Paycocke, the house is a grand example of the wealth generated by the cloth trade in the 16th century. Outside, there is a beautiful and tranquil cottage garden.
Location: MAP 8:I11, OS Ref. TL848 225. Signposted off A120.
Open: 6–28 Mar: Sat & Sun 1–5pm. 1 Apr–31 Oct: Wed–Sun 11–5pm. Open BH Mons.
Admission: Adult £3.40, Child £1.70. Groups (10+) by prior arrangement. Joint ticket with Coggeshall Grange Barn: Adult £4.40, Child £2.20.
i No WC, nearest one at Coggeshall Grange Barn. 🔾🔾 By arrangement 🅿 NT's at the Coggeshall Grange Barn. 🔾 Guide dogs only.

PRIOR'S HALL BARN

Widdington, Newport, Essex
Tel: 01223 582700 (Regional Office)   **E-mail:** customers@english-heritage.org.uk
www.english-heritage.org.uk/prior
Owner: English Heritage   **Contact:** East of England Regional Office
One of the finest surviving medieval barns in south-east England and representative of the group of aisled barns centred on north-west Essex.
Location: MAP 7:G10, OS Ref. TL538 319. In Widdington, on unclassified road 2m SE of Newport, off B1383.
Open: 1 Apr–30 Sep: Sat & Sun, 10am–6pm.
Admission: Free. Opening times and prices are valid until 31st March 2010, after this date details are subject to change please see www.english-heritage.org.uk for the most up-to-date information.
i Picnickers welcome. 🔾 🔾

TILBURY FORT

No. 2 Office Block, The Fort, Tilbury, Essex RM18 7NR
Tel: 01375 858489   **E-mail:** customers@english-heritage.org.uk
www.english-heritage.org.uk/tilbury
Owner: English Heritage   **Contact:** Visitor Operations Team
The best and largest example of 17th century military engineering in England, commanding the Thames. Learn more about the fascinating history of Tilbury Fort with a new interpretation scheme in the North East Bastion magazine passages.
Location: MAP 4:K2, OS Ref. TQ651 754. ½m E of Tilbury off A126. Near Port of Tilbury.
Open: 1 Apr–1 Nov: daily, 10am–5pm. 2 Nov–31 Mar: Thur–Mon, 10am–4pm. 24–26 Dec & 1 Jan: Closed.
Admission: Adult £3.90, Child £2, Under 5s Free. Conc. £3.30. Family £9.80. EH Members/OVP Free. Group discount available. Opening times and prices are valid until 31st March 2010, after this date details are subject to change please see www.english-heritage.org.uk for the most up-to-date information.
i Picnickers welcome. WCs. 🔾 🔾 Partial. 🔾 🅿 🔾 🔾 On leads. 🔾

WALTHAM ABBEY GATEHOUSE & BRIDGE

Waltham Abbey, Essex
Tel: 01992 702200 / 01223 582700 (Regional Office)
E-mail: customers@english-heritage.org.uk
www.english-heritage.org.uk/waltham
Owner: English Heritage   **Contact:** East of England Regional Office (01223 582700)
The late 14th century abbey gatehouse, part of the north range of the cloister and the medieval 'Harold's Bridge' of one of the great monastic foundations of the Middle Ages.
Location: MAP 7:G12, OS Ref. TL381 008. In Waltham Abbey off A112. Just NE of the Abbey church.
Open: Any reasonable time.
Admission: Free. Opening times and prices are valid until 31st March 2010, after this date details are subject to change please see www.english-heritage.org.uk for the most up-to-date information.
i Picnickers welcome. 🔾 Sensory trail guide. 🔾 On leads. 🔾

For **special events** held throughout the year, see the index at the end of the book.

HATFIELD HOUSE

www.hatfield-house.co.uk

Visit this stunning Jacobean house within an extensive Park. Home of the 7th Marquess of Salisbury and the Cecil family for 400 years, the house is steeped in Elizabethan and Victorian political history. Hatfield House has a fine collection of pictures, tapestries, furnishings and historic armour.

Delightful formal gardens, dating from 1611 when Robert Cecil employed John Tradescant the Elder to collect plants for the new scheme. The West garden includes scented garden, herb garden and knot garden. The adjoining wilderness areas are at their best in spring with masses of naturalised daffodils. The East garden's elegant parterres, topiary and rare plants are a delight for the gardening enthusiast and for those wishing to spend a quiet time in idyllic surroundings.

Within the gardens stands the surviving wing of The Royal Palace of Hatfield where Elizabeth I spent much of her childhood and held her first Council of State in November 1558. An oak tree marks the place where the young Princess Elizabeth first heard of her accession to the throne. Visitors can enjoy walking in the 1000 acres of park with woodland trails plus picnic areas and a children's play park.

The West Garden

The Marble Hall

Owner
The 7th Marquess of Salisbury

Contact
Director – Visitors & Events
Hatfield House
Hatfield
Hertfordshire AL9 5NQ
Tel: 01707 287010
Fax: 01707 287033
E-mail: visitors@
hatfield-house.co.uk

Location
MAP 7:F11
OS Ref. TL 237 084
21m N of London, M25/
J23 7m,A1(M)/J4, 2m.
Bus: Local services from
St Albans and Hertford.
Rail: From Kings Cross
every 30 mins. Station is
opposite entrance to Park.
Air: Luton (30 mins).
Stansted (45 mins).

Opening Times
Easter Sat–end September
House
Wed–Sun & BHs.
12 noon–4pm.
**Park, West Garden,
Restaurant & Shop**
Wed–Sun & BHs.
11am–5.30pm.
East Garden
Thurs only.
11am–5.30pm.

Admission
**House, Park
& West Garden**
Adult   £11.50
Child (5–15yrs)   £6.00
Senior   £10.50
Family (2+4)   £32.00
Groups (20+)
Adult   £10.00
Park & West Garden
Adult   £6.50
Child   £4.50
Park only
Adult   £3.00
Child (5–15yrs)   £2.00
East Garden
(Thursdays)   £4.00 extra
RHS members free entry
to Park & West Garden
daily during open season,
except during special
events.

Special Events
May 6–9
Living Crafts.
June 19–20
Rose Weekend. Summer
Garden Show.
Aug 6–8
Art in Clay.
Aug 20–22
Hatfield House Country
Show.

Please see website for details
of events programme.

No photography in house. National Collection of model soldiers, 5m of marked trails, children's play area. Film enquiries welcome.

Weddings, functions: tel 01707 287080. Banquets held in the Old Palace: tel 01707 262055.

WCs. Parking next to house. Lift.

Seats 150. Pre-booked lunch and tea for groups 20+. Tel: 01707 262030.

Wed–Fri only. Group tours available in French, German, Italian, Spanish or Japanese by prior arrangement.

Ample. Hardstanding for coaches.

Resource books, play area & nature trails. Living History days throughout the school year: tel 01707 287042. KS2 & 3 groups not permitted in house.

In grounds, on leads.

€

Conference/Function

ROOM	SIZE	MAX CAPACITY
The Old Palace	112' x 33'	280
Riding School Conference Centre	100' x 40'	170

■ Owner
The Hon Henry Lytton Cobbold

■ Contact
The Estate Office
Knebworth House
Knebworth
Hertfordshire SG3 6PY
Tel: 01438 812661
Fax: 01438 811908

E-mail: info@
knebworthhouse.com

■ Location
MAP 7:E11
OS Ref. TL230 224

Direct access off the
A1(M) J7 Stevenage, 28m
N of London, 15m N of
M25/J23.

Rail: Stevenage Station
2m (from Kings Cross).

Air: Luton Airport 15m

Taxi: 01438 811122.

■ Opening Times
2-18 April, 29 May-6
June, 3 July-31 August.
Weekends & BHs: 20-28
March, 24 April-23 May,
12-27 June, 4-26
September.

**Park, Playground &
Gardens**
11am-5pm, (last ticket
sold 4.15pm)

**House & Indian
Exhibition**
12 noon-5pm, (last tour
4.00pm).

■ Admission
Including House
Adult   £10.50
Child*/Conc   £10.00

Family Day Ticket
(4 persons)   £37.00

Groups (20+)
Adult   £9.50
Child*/Conc   £9.00

Excluding House
All Persons   £8.00

Family Day Ticket
(4 persons)   £28.00

Groups (20+)
All persons   £7.00

*4–16 yrs, under 4s Free.

Special Events
Check website for details.

KNEBWORTH HOUSE 🏛

www.knebworthhouse.com

Home of the Lytton family since 1490, and still a lived-in family house. Transformed in early Victorian times by Edward Bulwer-Lytton, the author, poet, dramatist and statesman, into the unique high gothic fantasy house of today, complete with turrets, griffins and gargoyles.

Historically home to Constance Lytton, the Suffragette, and her father, Robert Lytton, the Viceroy of India who proclaimed Queen Victoria Empress of India at the Great Delhi Durbar of 1877. Visited by Queen Elizabeth I, Charles Dickens and Sir Winston Churchill.

The interior contains various styles including the magnificent Jacobean Banqueting Hall, a unique example of the 17th century change in fashion from traditional English to Italian Palladian. The high gothic State Drawing Room by John Crace contrasts with the Regency elegance of Mrs Bulwer-Lytton's bedroom and the 20th century designs of Sir Edwin Lutyens in the Entrance Hall, Dining Parlour and Library.

25 acres of beautiful gardens, simplified by Lutyens, including pollarded lime avenues, formal rose garden, maze, Gertrude Jekyll herb garden and a walled kitchen garden. 250 acres of gracious parkland, with herds of red and sika deer, includes children's giant adventure playground and miniature railway. The Dinosaur Trail with 72 life-size dinosaurs is set grazing through the Wilderness Walk within the Formal Gardens. World famous for its huge open-air rock concerts, and used as a film location for *Batman*, *The Shooting Party*, *Wilde*, *Jane Eyre* and *The Canterville Ghost*, amongst others.

Conference/Function

ROOM	SIZE	MAX CAPACITY
Banqueting Hall	25' x 39'	100
Dining Parlour	21' x 36'	50
Library	21' x 32'	40
Manor Barn	25' x 70'	180
Lodge Barn	30' x 75'	180
Garden Terrace Barn	35' x 40'	30

ℹ Suitable for conferences and banquets, product launches, weddings, commercial photography, filming, exhibitions, garden shows, concerts and festivals.

🛍

❄

🍽

♿ Partial. WCs. Parking. Ground floor accessible.

☕ Licensed tearoom. Special rates for advance bookings, menus on request.

🚶 Obligatory.

🎧

🅿 Ample.

🏫 National Curriculum based school activity days.

🐕 Guide dogs only in House. Park, on leads.

💒 Licensed Knebworth House, Garden Gazebo & Manor Barn.

🎭 Telephone for details.

© Hatfield House

ASHRIDGE ⚜

Ringshall, Berkhamsted, Hertfordshire HP4 1LT
Tel: 01442 851227 **Fax:** 01442 850000 **E-mail:** ashridge@nationaltrust.org.uk
Owner: The National Trust **Contact:** The Visitor Centre
The Ashridge Estate comprises over 5000 acres of woodlands, commons and downland. At the northerly end of the Estate the Ivinghoe Hills are an outstanding area of chalk downland supporting a rich variety of plants and insects.
Location: MAP 7:D11 OS Ref. SP970 131. Between Northchurch & Ringshall, just off B4506.
Open: Visitor Centre & Shop: 13 Feb–19 Dec daily, 10am–5pm. Monument: 3 Apr–31 Oct: Sats, Suns & BHs 12 noon–last admission 4.30pm. Tearoom: 1 Jan–31 Dec: daily, 10am–5pm. *Tearoom opening hours may vary. Tearoom closes at 4pm 1 Jan–1 Apr and 1 Nov–31 Dec.
Admission: Monument: £1.70, Child 85p. Free to NT members.
ℹ Visitor Centre. 📷 ♿ Vehicles available. 🍴 🅿 Limited for coaches. 🏨
🐕 In grounds, on leads. 🐾

BENINGTON LORDSHIP GARDENS 🏠

Stevenage, Hertfordshire SG2 7BS
Tel: 01438 869668 **Fax:** 01438 869622 **E-mail:** garden@beningtonlordship.co.uk
www.beningtonlordship.co.uk
Owner: Mr R R A Bott **Contact:** Mr or Mrs R R A Bott
7 acre garden overlooking lakes in a timeless setting. Features include Norman keep and moat, Queen Anne manor house, James Pulham folly, formal rose garden, renowned herbaceous borders, walled vegetable garden, grass tennis court and verandah. Spectacular display of snowdrops in February. All location work welcome. Estate includes listed cottages, barns, buildings and airstrip.
Location: MAP 7:F11, OS Ref. TL296 236. In village of Benington next to the church. 4m E of Stevenage.
Open: Gardens only: Snowdrops: 6 Feb–28 Feb, daily, 12 noon–4pm. Easter & May BH weekends: Suns, 2–5pm. Mons, 12 noon–5pm. Floral Festival, 12 noon–6pm, 26/27 Jun. Chilli Festival, 10am–5pm, 29/30 Aug (adm £5). By request all year, please telephone. Coaches must book.
Admission: Adult £4 (Suns in Feb £4.50), Child under 12 Free.
🌱 February. ♿ Unsuitable. 🍴 🅿 🐕 🐾

BERKHAMSTED CASTLE ⚔

Berkhamsted, St Albans, Hertfordshire
Tel: 01223 582700 (Regional Office) **www.english-heritage.org.uk/berkhamsted**
Owner: English Heritage **Contact:** East of England Regional Office
The extensive remains of a large 11th century motte and bailey castle which held a strategic position on the road to London.
Location: MAP 7:D12, OS Ref. SP996 083. Adjacent to Berkhamsted rail station.
Open: Summer: daily, 10am–6pm. Winter: daily, 10am–4pm. Closed 25 Dec & 1 Jan.
Admission: Free. Opening times and prices are valid until 31st March 2010, after this date details are subject to change please see www.english-heritage.org.uk for the most up-to-date information.
ℹ Picnickers welcome. 🐕 🌱

CROMER WINDMILL

Ardeley, Stevenage, Hertfordshire SG2 7QA
Tel: 01438 861662/01763 271305
Owner: Hertfordshire Building Preservation Trust
Guardians: Simon Bennett/Robin Webb
Hertfordshire's last surviving post mill restored to working order. Ample parking, disabled access to video. Gifts and refreshments.
Location: MAP 7:F10, OS Ref. TL305 286. 4m E of Stevenage B1037. 2m NE of Walkern.
Open: Mid May–Mid-Sept: Sun & BH Mons, 2nd & 4th Sat, 2.30–5pm.
Admission: Adult £2, Child 25p.
📷 🍴 🅿 Ample.

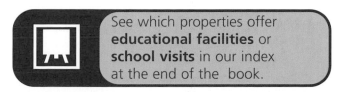
See which properties offer **educational facilities** or **school visits** in our index at the end of the book.

Hatfield House, Tomb

GORHAMBURY 🏠

St Albans, Hertfordshire AL3 6AH
Tel: 01727 854051 **Fax:** 01727 843675
Owner: The Earl of Verulam **Contact:** The Administrator
Late 18th century house by Sir Robert Taylor. Family portraits from 15th–21st centuries.
Location: MAP 7:E11, OS Ref. TL114 078. 2m W of St Albans. Access via private drive off A4147 at St Albans.
Open: May–Sept: Thurs, 2–5pm (last entry 4pm).
Admission: House & Gardens: Adult £7.50, Child £4, Conc £6.50. Visitors join guided tours. Special groups by arrangement (Thurs preferred).
♿ Partial. 🐕 🎧 Obligatory. 🅿

HATFIELD HOUSE
See page 247 for full page entry.

HERTFORD MUSEUM

18 Bull Plain, Hertford SG14 1DT
Tel: 01992 582686
Owner: Hertford Museums Trust **Contact:** Helen Gurney
Local museum in 17th century house, altered by 18th century façade, with recreated Jacobean knot garden.
Location: MAP 7:F11, OS Ref. TL326 126. Town centre.
Open: Tue–Sat, 10am–5pm.
Admission: Free.

KNEBWORTH HOUSE 🏠
See page 248 for full page entry.

THE NATURAL HISTORY MUSEUM AT TRING

Akeman Street, Tring, Hertfordshire HP23 6AP
Tel: 020 7942 6171   **Fax:** 020 7942 6150
Owner: The Natural History Museum   **Contact:** General Organiser
The museum was opened to the public by Lord Rothschild in 1892. It houses his private natural history collection. Over 4,000 species of animal in a Victorian setting.
Location: MAP 7:D11, OS Ref. SP924 111. S end of Akeman Street, ¼m S of High Street.
Open: All year, daily: Mon–Sat, 10am–5pm, Suns, 2–5pm. Closed 24–26 Dec.
Admission: Free.

OLD GORHAMBURY HOUSE ⌘

St Albans, Hertfordshire
Tel: 01223 582700 (Regional Office)   **E-mail:** customers@english-heritage.org.uk
www.english-heritage.org.uk/oldgorhambury
Owner: English Heritage   **Contact:** East of England Regional Office
The decorated remains of this Elizabethan mansion, particularly the porch of the Great Hall, illustrate the impact of the Renaissance on English architecture.
Location: MAP 7:E11, OS Ref. TL110 077. On foot by permissive 2m path. By car, drive to Gorhambury Mansion and walk across the gardens (1 May–30 Sep).
Open: All year (except 1 Jun), any reasonable time.
Admission: Free. Opening times and prices are valid until 31st March 2010, after this date details are subject to change please see www.english-heritage.org.uk for the most up-to-date information.
ℹ Picnickers welcome. 🐾 ❄

ST ALBANS CATHEDRAL

St Albans, Hertfordshire AL1 1BY
Tel: 01727 860780   **Fax:** 01727 850944   **E-mail:** mail@stalbanscathedral.org.uk
www.stalbanscathedral.org.uk
Owner: Dean and Chapter of St Albans   **Contact:** Susan Keeling, Visitors' Officer
Magnificent Norman abbey church built with recycled Roman bricks from the nearby city of Verulanium, the setting for the Shrine (1308) of Alban, Britain's first Christian martyr. Series of 12th–13th century wall paintings, painted Presbytery ceiling (1280), wooden watching loft (1400) and the tomb of Humphrey, Duke of Gloucester (1447).
Location: MAP 7:E12. OS Ref. TL145 071. Centre of St Albans.
Open: Daily, 9am–5.45pm.
Admission: Free, donations welcomed.
📷 ♿ WCs. 🍴 Licenced. 🎦 By prior arrangement. 🐾 In grounds, on leads.

©NTPL/Matthew Antrobus

SHAW'S CORNER 🌿

AYOT ST LAWRENCE, WELWYN, HERTFORDSHIRE AL6 9BX
www.nationaltrust.org.uk

Tel/Fax: 01438 820307   **E-mail:** shawscorner@nationaltrust.org.uk
Owner: The National Trust   **Contact:** The House Manager
The fascinating home of playwright George Bernard Shaw until his death in 1950. The modest Edwardian villa contains many literary and personal relics, and the interior is still set out as it was in Shaw's lifetime. The garden, with its richly planted borders and views over the Hertfordshire countryside, contains the revolving summerhouse where Shaw retreated to write.
Location: MAP 7:E11, OS Ref. TL194 167. At SW end of village, 2m NE of Wheathampstead, approximately 2m N from B653. A1(M)/J4, M1/J10.
Open: 13 Mar–31 Oct: Wed–Sun & BH Mons (open Good Fri), House: 1–5pm; Garden: 12 noon–5.30pm. Last admission to House & Garden 4.30pm. No large hand luggage inside house. Groups by prior appointment only.
Admission: Adult £5.50, Child £2.75, Family £13.75. Groups (15+ Adult £4.50, Child £2.25).
ℹ WC. 🎦 ♿ Partial, ground floor, no WC. 🅿 🎥 🐾 Car park only.
📷 Tel 01438 829221 for details.

ST PAULS WALDEN BURY

Hitchin, Hertfordshire SG4 8BP
Tel/Fax: 01438 871218/341   **E-mail:** spw@boweslyon.demon.co.uk
Owner/Contact: Simon & Caroline Bowes Lyon
Childhood home of the late Queen Mother. Formal woodland garden, covering about 60 acres, laid out 1730. Long rides lined with clipped beech hedges lead to temples, statues, lake and ponds, and to an outdoor theatre. Seasonal displays of snowdrops, daffodils, irises, cowslips, magnolias, rhododendrons, lilies and shrub roses. Wild flower areas. Grade I listed.
Location: MAP 7:E11, OS Ref. TL186 216. 30m N of London. 5m S of Hitchin on B651.
Open: Suns: 11 Apr, 25 Apr, 23 May & 20 Jun, 2–7pm. Other times by appointment.
Admission: Adult £4, Child 50p. Other times by appointment £7.
🎦 ♿ 🍴 🅿 🐾 On leads. €

SCOTT'S GROTTO

Ware, Hertfordshire S912 9SQ
Tel: 01920 464131
Owner: East Hertfordshire District Council   **Contact:** J Watson
One of the finest grottos in England built in the 1760s by Quaker Poet John Scott.
Location: MAP 7:F11, OS Ref. TL355 137. In Scotts Rd, S of the A119 Hertford Road.
Open: 1 Apr–30 Sept: Sat & BH Mon, 2–4.30pm. Also by appointment.
Admission: Suggested donation of £1 for adults. Children Free. Please bring a torch.

© Knebworth Estates

Knebworth House

HOLKHAM HALL 🏛

www.holkham.co.uk

This elegant Palladian style mansion, based on designs by William Kent, was built between 1734 and 1764 by Thomas Coke, the 1st Earl of Leicester, and is home to his descendants. It reflects Coke's natural appreciation of classical art, developed during his Grand Tour. Built from local yellow brick, with its pedimented portico, square corner towers and side wings, it has been little altered over the years, and has been described by Sir Nikolaus Pevsner as "The most classically correct house in Britain".

"The Marble Hall" is a spectacular introduction to this vast and imposing house, with its 50ft pressed plaster dome ceiling and walls of English alabaster, not marble as its name implies. Stairs from the hall lead to magnificent state rooms with superb collections of ancient statuary, original furniture, tapestries and paintings by Rubens, Van Dyck, Claude, Gaspar Poussin and Gainsborough.

On leaving the house visitors enter the lavender-fringed Pottery Courtyard. Here the original stable block houses the Bygones Museum; a display of more than 4,000 items of domestic and agricultural memorabilia, ranging from working steam engines, vintage cars and tractors to gramophones, craft tools and kitchenware. In the adjacent former brew house and malt house, the History of Farming Exhibition highlights how a great estate such as Holkham works and has evolved, explaining Coke of Norfolk's role in the great Agricultural Revolution of the 18th century.

In the same courtyard, the light and airy Gift Shop, once the former laundry for the Hall, offers a wide range of quality gifts, selected soft furnishings and souvenirs. Opposite, the Stables Café tempts visitors with delicious, local produce for a light snack, lunch or afternoon tea and an opportunity to sample Holkham's own, home-made, mouth-watering ice cream.

Set in a 3,000 acre deer park, visitors can enjoy designated walks, a nature trail and boat trips. The extensive 18th century walled gardens, designed by Samuel Wyatt, are being sensitively restored, along with the glasshouses, which are being renovated with the help of English Heritage - the gardens are open to be seen as work progresses. To the north of the park lies Holkham village with the estate's own hotel, "The Victoria". Directly opposite, the award-winning Holkham Beach with its panoramic vista and endless golden sands, is somewhere to catch your breath in a busy world.

- ℹ Grounds for shows, weddings, product launches, rallies and filming. Photography allowed in Hall. Central Ticket Office for admission & events tickets.
- Gift shop in the park.
- Hall & grounds.
- Access to first floor in the Hall is suitable for most manual wheelchairs. Elsewhere, full disabled access.
- Stables Café, licensed.
- The Victoria Hotel at Holkham and The Globe Inn, Wells-next-the-Sea.
- Private guided tours of Hall are available by arrangement when the Hall is not open to the public. Please tel for details.
- P Unlimited for cars, 12+ coaches. Parking charges.
- Bygones Museum, History of Farming Exhibition, Walled Gardens, Nature Trail and quiz.
- No dogs in Hall, on leads in grounds.
- Victoria Hotel and Globe Inn, Wells-next-the-Sea.
- Weddings and Civil Partnerships.
- Outdoor Theatre Productions, Marble Hall & Open-Air Concerts.

Owner
Trustees of the Holkham Estate. Home of the Coke family.

Contact
Marketing Manager
Laurane Herrieven
Holkham Estate Office
Wells-next-the-Sea
Norfolk NR23 1AB
Tel: 01328 710227
Fax: 01328 711707
E-mail: enquiries@holkham.co.uk

Location
MAP 8:I4
OS Ref. TF885 428

From London 120m
Norwich 35m
King's Lynn 30m.

Rail: Norwich Station 35m
King's Lynn Station 30m.

Air: Norwich Airport 32m.

Opening Times
Hall

1 April–31 October,
12noon–4pm, Sun, Mon & Thurs.

Bygones Museum, History of Farming Exhibition, Gift Shop, Stables Café

1 April–31 October,
10am–5pm every day.

Boat Trips

1 April–31 October,
11pm–5pm, Sun, Mon & Thurs (weather permitting).

Walled Gardens

1 April–31 October,
12noon–4pm every day.

The Libraries, Chapel & Strangers' Wing form part of the private accommodation and are open at the family's discretion.

Admission
Holkham Hall
Adult £9.00
Child (5–16yrs) £4.50
Bygones Museum
Adult £4.00
Child (5–16yrs) £2.00

Hall & Museum
Adult £11.00
Child (5–16yrs) £5.50
Family (2+2) £27.00

Groups (20+) 10% discount, organiser free entry, coach driver's refreshment voucher.

Private Guided Tours
£20.00
Price per person, min 12 people.

History of Farming Free

Walled Gardens Free

Boat trips on the lake
Adult £3.00
Child (5–16yrs) £2.50

BINHAM PRIORY ⌗

Binham-on-Wells, Norfolk
Tel: 01328 830362 / 01223 582700 (Regional Office)
E-mail: customers@english-heritage.org.uk
www.english-heritage.org.uk/binhampriory
Owner: English Heritage (Managed by Binham Parochial Church Council)
Contact: East of England Regional Office
Extensive remains of a Benedictine priory, of which the original nave of the church is still in use as the parish church, displaying a screen with medieval saints overpainted with Protestant texts.
Location: MAP 8:J4, OS Ref. TF982 399. ¼m NW of village of Binham-on-Wells, on road off B1388.
Open: Any reasonable time.
Admission: Free. Opening times and prices are valid until 31st March 2010, after this date details are subject to change please see www.english-heritage.org.uk for the most up-to-date information.
ℹ Picnickers welcome. ✳

BIRCHAM WINDMILL

Snettisham Road, Great Bircham, Norfolk PE31 6SJ
Tel: 01485 578393
Owner/Contact: Mr & Mrs S Chalmers
One of the last remaining complete windmills. Tearoom, bakery, windmill museum, gift shop, cycle hire, regular events and holiday cottage.
Location: MAP 8:I4, OS Ref. TF760 326. ½m W of Bircham. N of the road to Snettisham.
Open: Easter–end Sept: Daily 10am–5pm.
Admission: Adult £3.50, Child £2, OAP £3.

For **accommodation** in the Eastern Region, see our special index at the end of the book.

BRADENHAM HALL GARDENS

Bradenham, Thetford, Norfolk IP25 7QP
Tel: 01362 687279/243 **Fax:** 01362 687669 **E-mail:** info@bradenhamhall.co.uk
www.bradenhamhall.co.uk
Owner: Chris & Panda Allhusen **Contact:** Chris Allhusen
A plant-lover's garden for all seasons. The house and garden walls are covered with unusual climbers. Flower gardens, formal rose gardens, paved garden, herbaceous and shrub borders. Arboretum of over 800 different trees, all labelled. Traditional walled kitchen gardens, mixed borders, and two glasshouses. Massed daffodils in spring.
Location: MAP 8:J6, OS Ref. TF921 099. Off A47, 6m of Swaffham. 3m W of E Dereham. S on Dale Road, then S 2m to Bradenham.
Open: April: 3rd Sunday, June–Sept: 2nd & 4th Suns of each month, 2–5.30pm. Groups by appointment at other times.
Admission: Adult £4, Child Free. Group discounts available.
ℹ No commercial photography. House not open. ♿ Partial. 🍽
ℝ By arrangement. ℗ Ample. Limited for coaches. 🐕 Guide dogs only.

BURGH CASTLE ⌗

Breydon Water, Great Yarmouth, Norfolk
Tel: 01223 582700 (Regional Office) **E-mail:** customers@english-heritage.org.uk
www.english-heritage.org.uk/burghcastle
Owner: English Heritage **Contact:** East of England Regional Office
Impressive walls, with projecting bastions, of a Roman fort built in the late 3rd century as one of a chain to defend the coast against Saxon raiders.
Location: MAP 8:M6, OS Ref. TG475 046. At far W end of Breydon Water, on unclassified road 3m W of Great Yarmouth. SW of the church.
Open: Any reasonable time.
Admission: Free. Opening times and prices are valid until 31st March 2010, after this date details are subject to change please see www.english-heritage.org.uk for the most up-to-date information.
ℹ Picnickers welcome. 🐕✳

©NTPL/Nick Meers

BLICKLING HALL ✿
BLICKLING, NORWICH, NORFOLK NR11 6NF

www.nationaltrust.org.uk

Tel: 01263 738030 **Fax:** 01263 738035 **E-mail:** blickling@nationaltrust.org.uk
Owner: The National Trust **Contact:** The Property Manager
Built in the early 17th century and one of England's great Jacobean houses. Blickling is famed for its spectacular long gallery, superb library and fine collections of furniture, pictures and tapestries.
Location: MAP 8:K5, OS133 Ref. TG178 286. 1½m NW of Aylsham on B1354. Signposted off A140 Norwich (15m) to Cromer.
Open: House: 27 Feb–31 Oct: Wed–Sun & BH Mons, 11am–5pm. Also open Mons during local school holidays. Garden: 27 Feb–31 Oct: Daily, 10.15am–5.15pm. 4 Nov–end Jan 2011: Thurs–Sun, 11am–4pm. Park & Woods: daily, dawn–dusk.
***Admission:** Hall & Gardens: Adult £10.25, Child £5.10, Family £28.60. Garden only: Adult £7.00, Child £3.50, Family £20.50. Groups must book. *includes a voluntary donation but visitors can choose to pay the standard prices displayed at the property and on the website.
ℹ Cycle hire available in Orchard, ring for details. 📷 Open as garden. 🎁 ☕
♿ Mostly suitable. 🍽 🍴 Open as garden. Licensed. ℝ By arrangement. ℗ 🚌
🐕 In park, on leads. 🔺✳♿

CAISTER CASTLE CAR COLLECTION

Caister-on-sea, Great Yarmouth, Norfolk NR30 5SN

Tel: 01572 787649

Owner/Contact: Mr J Hill

Large collection of historic motor vehicles from 1893 to recent. Moated Castle built by Sir John Falstaff in 1432. Car park free.

Location: MAP 8:M6, OS Ref. TG502 122. Take A1064 out of Caister-on-sea towards Filby, turn left at the end of the dual carriageway.

Open: Mid May–End Sept: Sun–Fri (closed Sats), 10am–4.30pm.

Admission: Contact property for details.

No photography. Partial. WCs.

CASTLE ACRE PRIORY

Stocks Green, Castle Acre, King's Lynn, Norfolk PE32 2XD

Tel: 01760 755394 **E-mail:** customers@english-heritage.org.uk

www.english-heritage.org.uk/castleacre

Owner: English Heritage **Contact:** Visitor Operations Team

Explore the romantic ruins of this 12th century Cluniac priory, set in the picturesque village of Castle Acre. The impressive Norman façade, splendid prior's lodgings and chapel, and delightful recreated medieval herb garden should not be missed.

Location: MAP 8:I5, OS Ref. TF814 148. ¼m W of village of Castle Acre, 5m N of Swaffham.

Open: 1 Apr–30 Jun: daily, 10am–5pm. 1 Jul–31 Aug: daily, 10am–6pm. 1 Sep–30 Sep: daily, 10am–5pm. 1 Oct–31 Mar '10: Thu–Mon, 10am–4pm. Closed 24–26 Dec & 1 Jan. EH Members/OVP free.

Admission: Adult £5, Child £2.50, Conc. £4.30. Family £12.50. Group discount available. Opening times and prices are valid until 31st March 2010, after this date details are subject to change please see www.english-heritage.org.uk for the most up-to-date information.

Picnickers welcome. Partial. Limited for coaches. On leads.

CASTLE RISING CASTLE

CASTLE RISING, KING'S LYNN, NORFOLK PE31 6AH

Tel: 01553 631330 **Fax:** 01553 631724

Owner: Lord Howard **Contact:** The Custodian

Possibly the finest mid-12th century Keep left in England: it was built as a grand and elaborate palace. It was home to Queen Isabella, grandmother of the Black Prince. Still in surprisingly good condition, the Keep is surrounded by massive ramparts up to 120 feet high. Picnic area, adjacent tearoom. Free audio tour.

Location: MAP 7:H5, OS Ref. TF666 246. Located 4m NE of King's Lynn off A149.

Open: 1 Apr–1 Nov: daily, 10am–6pm (closes at dusk if earlier in Oct). 2 Nov–31 Mar: Wed–Sun, 10am–4pm. Closed 24–26 Dec.

Admission: Adult £4, Child £2.50, Conc. £3.30, Family £12 (2 adults & 2 children, each additional child £2). 15% discount for groups (11+). Prices include VAT. Opening times and prices are subject to change.

Picnic area. Grounds. WC.

GREAT YARMOUTH ROW HOUSES & GREYFRIARS' CLOISTERS

South Quay, Great Yarmouth, Norfolk NR30 2RQ

Tel: 01493 857900 **E-mail:** customers@english-heritage.org.uk

www.english-heritage.org.uk/greatyarmouth

Owner: English Heritage **Contact:** Visitor Operations Team

Two immaculately presented 17th century Row Houses, a type of building unique to Great Yarmouth. Row 111 House was almost destroyed by bombing in 1942/3 and contains items rescued from the rubble. Old Merchant's House boasts magnificent plaster-work ceilings and displays of local architectural fittings.

Location: MAP 8:M6, OS134, TG525 072. In Great Yarmouth, make for Historic South Quay, by riverside and dock, ½ m inland from beach. Follow signs to dock and south quay.

Open: 1 Apr–30 Sept: daily, 12 noon–5pm.

Admission: Adult £3.90. Child £2, Conc. £3.30, Family £9.80. EH Members Free. Group discount available. Opening times and prices are valid until 31st March 2010, after this date details are subject to change please see www.english-heritage.org.uk for the most up-to-date information.

Picnickers welcome. Museum.

GRIME'S GRAVES – PREHISTORIC FLINT MINE

Lynford, Thetford, Norfolk IP26 5DE

Tel: 01842 810656 **E-mail:** customers@english-heritage.org.uk

Owner: English Heritage **Contact:** Visitor Operations Team

www.english-heritage.org.uk/grimesgraves

These remarkable Neolithic flint mines, unique in England, comprise over 300 pits and shafts. The visitor can descend some 30 feet by ladder into one excavated shaft, and look along the radiating galleries, from where the flint used for making axes and knives was extracted.

Location: MAP 8:I7, OS 144, TL818 898. 7m NW of Thetford off A134.

Open: 1–31 Mar: Thu–Mon, 10am–5pm. 1 Apr–30 Jun: daily, 10am–5pm. 1 Jul–31 Aug: daily, 10am–6pm. 1 Sep–30 Sep: daily 10am–5pm, 1 Oct–1 Nov, Thu–Mon 10am–5pm, 2 Nov–28 Feb closed. Last visit to site 30 mins before close. No entry to the mines for children under 5 yrs.

Admission: Adult £3, Child £1.50 (Child under 5yrs free), Conc. £2.60, Family £7.50.EH Members/OVP free. Group discount available. Opening times and prices are valid until 31st March 2010, after this date details are subject to change please see www.english-heritage.org.uk for the most up-to-date information.

Picnickers welcome. Partial. Limited. On leads.

HOLKHAM HALL

See page 251 for full page entry.

Castle Acre Priory

©NTPL/Matthew Antrobus

OXBURGH HALL ❧
OXBOROUGH, KING'S LYNN, NORFOLK PE33 9PS

www.nationaltrust.org.uk

Tel: 01366 328258 **Fax:** 01366 328066 **E-mail:** oxburghhall@nationaltrust.org.uk
Owner: The National Trust **Contact:** The Property Secretary

No-one ever forgets their first sight of Oxburgh. A romantic moated manor house, it was built by the Bedingfeld family in the 15th century and they have lived here ever since. Inside, the family's Catholic history is revealed, complete with a secret priest's hole which you can crawl inside. See the astonishing needlework by Mary, Queen of Scots, and the private chapel, built with reclaimed materials. Outside, you can enjoy the panoramic views from the Gatehouse roof and follow the woodcarving trails in the gardens and woodlands. The late winter drifts of snowdrops and aconites are not to be missed.

Location: MAP 8:I6, OS143, TF742 012. At Oxborough, 7m SW of Swaffham on S side of Stoke Ferry road. Rail: 10miles from Downham Market station

Open: House: 27 Feb–31 Oct, Sat to Weds, 11am–5pm (closes at 4pm in October); daily in August 11am–5pm; open Good Fri & all Easter week daily 11am–5pm.

Garden, Shop & Tearoom: 2 Jan – 21 Feb & 6 Nov–19 Dec, Sat & Sun, 11am–4pm; 27 Mar– 31 Oct Sat–Wed, 11am–5pm; daily in August and Easter week.

Admission: House & Garden: Adult £7.80, Child £4, Family £20. Garden & Estate only: Adult £4.10, Child £2.30, Family £10.50. Groups discount (min 15)- must book in advance with the Property Secretary. Admission includes a voluntary 10% Gift Aid donation but visitors can choose to pay the standard prices displayed at the property and on the website. **Special Events:** Ask for leaflet

ℹ️ No picnics or dogs allowed in Garden; no photography in House. Free garden tours daily. Souvenir guides, gift shop, second-hand bookshop.⬜ 🎁 🔆 🔆 Partial. WCs. 🍴 Licensed. 🎫 By arrangement. 🅿️ Limited for Coaches. 🔆 🔆 Guide dogs only 🔆 🔆 Send SAE for details.

©NTPL/Nadia Mackenzie

©NTPL

RAVENINGHAM GARDENS 🏛️
RAVENINGHAM, NORWICH, NORFOLK NR14 6NS

www.raveningham.com

Tel: 01508 548152 **Fax:** 01508 548958
E-mail: info@raveningham.com
Owner: Sir Nicholas Bacon Bt **Contact:** Diane Hoffman

Superb herbaceous borders, 18th century walled kitchen garden, Victorian glasshouse, herb garden, Edwardian rose garden, contemporary sculptures, 14th century church and much more.

Location: MAP 8:L7, OS Ref. TM399 965. Between Norwich & Lowestoft off A146 then B1136.

Open: Easter–Aug: Mon–Fri, 11am–4pm (no teas). BH Suns & Mons, 2–5pm, (except Aug BH) Agapanthus weekend 24th–25th July.

Admission: Adult £4, Child (under 16yrs) Free, OAP £3. Groups by prior arrangement. 🍴 Teas only on Suns & BH Mons. 🅿️

ST GEORGE'S GUILDHALL ❧

29 King Street, King's Lynn, Norfolk PE30 1HA
Tel: 01553 765565 www.west-norfolk.gov.uk
Owner: The National Trust **Contact:** The Administrator

The largest surviving English medieval guildhall. The building is now converted into a theatre and arthouse cinema. Many interesting features survive.

Location: MAP 7:H5, OS132, TF616 202. On W side of King Street close to the Tuesday Market Place.

Open: Guildhall - all year, Mon–Fri, 10am–2pm. Crofters Coffee Shop - all year, Mon–Sat, 9.30am–5pm. Riverside Restaurant - all year, Mon–Sat, 12pm–2pm and 6.30pm–9.30pm. Closed first Mon in Jan, Good Fri, BH Mons and 24 Dec. Guildhall not open on days when there are performances in the theatre. Please telephone box office on 01553 764864 for details of opening dates and times.

Admission: Free.

⬜ 🔆 🍴 🍴 🅿️ Pay and Display 🔆 🔆

SHERINGHAM PARK ❧
Upper Sheringham, Norfolk NR26 8TL

Tel: 01263 820550 **E-mail:** sheringhampark@nationaltrust.org.uk
www.nationaltrust.org.uk
Owner: The National Trust **Contact:** Visitor Centre

One of Humphry Repton's most outstanding achievements, the landscape park contains fine mature woodlands, and the large woodland garden is particularly famous for its spectacular show of rhododendrons and azaleas (mid May–June). There are stunning views of the coast and countryside from the viewing towers and many delightful waymarked walks. Programme of special events.

Location: MAP 8:K4, OS133, TG135 420. 2m SW of Sheringham, access for cars off A148 Cromer–Holt road; 5m W of Cromer, 6m E of Holt.

Open: Park open all year, daily, dawn–dusk.

Admission: Pay & Display: Cars £4.50 (NT members Free–display members' sticker in car). Coaches Free must book in advance.

⬜ 🎁 🔆 Partial. WC. 🍴 Easter–end Sept, daily. Sats/Suns all year. 🅿️ Coaches free but must book in advance. 🔆 🔆 In grounds, on leads. 🔆 🔆

By gracious permission of HM Queen Elizabeth II

SANDRINGHAM

THE ESTATE OFFICE, SANDRINGHAM, NORFOLK PE35 6EN

www.sandringhamestate.co.uk

Tel: 01553 612908 **Fax:** 01485 541571 **E-mail:** visits@sandringhamestate.co.uk
Owner: H M The Queen **Contact:** The Public Enterprises Manager
Sandringham House, the charming Norfolk retreat of Her Majesty The Queen, is set in 60 acres of beautiful gardens. All the main ground floor rooms used by The Royal Family, full of their treasured ornaments, portraits and furniture and still maintained in the style of King Edward VII and Queen Alexandra, are open to the public. Don't miss the fascinating Museum and the charming parish church, to round off an absorbing day. There are also 600 acres of the Country Park open to all, with tractor tours running daily. Guided garden tours available; land train shuttle service inside the gardens.

Location: MAP 7:H5, OS Ref. TF695 287 8m NE of King's Lynn on B1440 off A148. **Rail:** King's Lynn. **Air:** Norwich.
Open: 3 April – late July & early Aug to 31 October.
Admission: House, Museum & Gardens, Adult £10.00, Child £5.00, Conc. £8.00, Family, £25.00. Museum & Gardens, Adult £7.00, Child £3.50, Conc. £6.00, Family £17.50 Groups (20+), Adult £9.00, Child £4.50 Conc. £7.00.
🛈 No photography in house. 🗖 ✤ Plant Centre. 🔳 Visitor Centre only. 🔳 🔳 Licensed. 🍴 Licensed. 🔳 By arrangement. Private evening tours. 🅿 Ample.🔳 🔳 Guide dogs only 🔳.

WALSINGHAM ABBEY GROUNDS & SHIREHALL MUSEUM 🔳

Little Walsingham, Norfolk NR22 6BP
Tel: 01328 820259 **Fax:** 01328 820098 **E-mail:** jackie@walsingham-estate.co.uk
Owner: Walsingham Estate Company **Contact:** Estate Office
Set in the picturesque medieval village of Little Walsingham, a place of pilgrimage since the 11th century, the grounds contain the remains of the famous Augustinian Priory with attractive gardens and river walks. The Shirehall Museum includes a Georgian magistrates' court and displays on the history of Walsingham.
Location: MAP 8:J4, OS Ref. TF934 367. B1105 N from Fakenham–5m.
Open: 13 Mar–24 Oct: daily, 10am–4.30pm. Also daily during snowdrop season (February) 10am–4pm. Abbey Grounds: many other times, please telephone for details.
Admission: Combined ticket: Adult £3.50, Conc. £2.50.
🗖 ✤ 🔳 🔳 By arrangement. 🔳 🔳 🔳 🔳

Kimberley Hall

WOLTERTON PARK 🔳

NORWICH, NORFOLK NR11 7LY

www.manningtongardens.co.uk

Tel: 01263 584175/768444 **Fax:** 01263 761214
email: laurelwalpole@manningtongardens.co.uk
Owner: The Lord and Lady Walpole **Contact:** The Lady Walpole
18th century Hall. Portrait collection annual exhibitions. Historic park with lake.
Location: MAP 8:K5, OS Ref. TG164 317. Situated near Erpingham village, signposted from Norwich–Cromer Rd A140.
Open: Park: daily from 9am. Hall: 23 Apr–29 Oct: Fridays, 2–5pm (last entry 4pm) and by appointment.
Admission: £5. £2 car park fee only for walkers. (Groups by application: from £4.)
🗖 Small. 🔳 🔳 Partial. WC. 🔳 🅿 🔳 🔳 In park, on leads. 🔳 🔳 Park. 🔳 €

FLATFORD BRIDGE COTTAGE

Flatford, East Bergholt, Colchester, Essex CO7 6UL
Tel: 01206 298260   **Fax:** 01206 297212
Email: flatfordbridgecottage@nationaltrust.org.uk   **www.nationaltrust.org.uk**
Owner: The National Trust   **Contact:** Visitor Services

In the heart of the beautiful Dedham Vale, the hamlet of Flatford is the location for some of John Constable's most famous paintings. Find out more about Constable at the exhibition in Bridge Cottage. Next door is the riverside tea-room and gift shop. Note: No public access to Flatford Mill.

Location: MAP 8:J10, OS Ref. TM077 332. On N bank of Stour, 1m S of East Bergholt B1070. Rail: Manningtree 2miles by footpath

Open: 2 Jan–28 Feb: Sats & Suns only, 11am–3.30pm. 3–31Mar: Wed–Sun, 11am–4pm. 1–30 Apr: daily, 11am–5pm. 1 May–30 Sept: daily, 10.30am–5.30pm. 1–31 Oct: daily, 11am–4.30pm. 3 Nov–23 Dec: Wed–Sun, 11am–3.30pm. Closed Christmas & New Year.

Admission: Guided walks (when guide available) £3, accompanied child Free.
ⓘ Car park is not NT. ⬛ ⬛ WCs. ⬛ Licensed ⬛ By arrangement. 🅿 Charge applies. Limited parking for coaches. ⬛ Guide dogs only. ⬛

FRAMLINGHAM CASTLE
FRAMLINGHAM, SUFFOLK IP13 9BP

www.english-heritage.org.uk/framlingham

Tel: 01728 724189   **E-mail:** customers@english-heritage.org.uk
Owner: English Heritage   **Contact:** Visitor Operations Team

A magnificent 12th century castle which, from the outside, looks almost the same as when it was built. From the continuous curtain wall linking 13 towers, there are excellent panoramic views of Framlingham and the charming reed-fringed Mere. Visitors can now experience life at Framlingham Castle through the ages with a new introductory exhibition, themed trails and a variety of indoor and outdoor interactive games. Throughout its colourful history the castle has been a fortress, an Elizabethan prison, a poor house and a school. The many alterations over the years have led to a pleasing mixture of historic styles. Entry also includes access to the Lanman Trust's Museum of local history.

Location: MAP 8:L8, OS Ref. TM287 637. In Framlingham on B1116. NE of town centre.

Open: 1 Apr–30 Jun: daily, 10am–5pm. 1 Jul–31 Aug: daily, 10am–6pm. 1 Sep–1 Nov: daily, 10am–5pm. 2 Nov–31 Mar: Thu–Mon, 10am–4pm. Closed 24–26 Dec & 1 Jan. The property may close early if an event is booked, please ring in advance for details.

Admission: Adult £5.70. Child £2.90, Children under 5 Free. Conc. £4.80, Family £14.30. EH Members/OVP Free. Group discount available. Opening times and prices are valid until 31st March 2010, after this date details are subject to change please see www.english-heritage.org.uk for the most up-to-date information.
ⓘ Picnickers welcome. ⬛ ⬛ Ground floor & grounds. WCs. ⬛ 🅿 ⬛ ⬛ ⬛

Freston Tower

Ickworth House

FRESTON TOWER

Nr Ipswich, Suffolk IP9 1AD
Tel: 01628 825925   **E-mail:** bookings@landmarktrust.org.uk
www.landmarktrust.org.uk
Owner/Contact: The Landmark Trust

An Elizabethan six-storey tower overlooking the estuary of the River Orwell. The tower was built in 1578 by a wealthy Ipswich merchant called Thomas Gooding, perhaps to celebrate the recent grant of his coat of arms. Freston Tower is cared for by The Landmark Trust, a building preservation charity who let it for holidays. Full details of Freston Tower and 189 other historic and architecturally important buildings are featured in the Landmark Trust Handbook (price £10 plus p&p refundable against a booking) and on the website.

Location: MAP 8:K9, OS Ref. TM177 397.

Open: Available for holidays for up to 4 people throughout the year. Please contact the Landmark Trust for details. Open Days on 8 days a year. Other visits by appointment.

Admission: Free on Open Days.
⬛

GAINSBOROUGH'S HOUSE
46 GAINSBOROUGH ST, SUDBURY, SUFFOLK CO10 2EU

www.gainsborough.org

Tel: 01787 372958   **Fax:** 01787 376991   **E-mail:** mail@gainsborough.org
Owner: Gainsborough's House Society   **Contact:** Rosemary Woodward

Gainsborough's House is the birthplace museum of Thomas Gainsborough (1727–1788), one of the greatest painters in the history of British art. More of his paintings, drawings and prints are on display here at any one time than anywhere else in the world. The collection encompasses Gainsborough's whole career, from early portraits or landscapes painted in Suffolk in the 1750s to later works from his London period of the 1770s and 80s. A varied programme of exhibitions of both historic British and contemporary art organised throughout the year. The historic house dates back to the 16th century with an attractive walled garden.

Location: MAP 8:I10, OS Ref. TL872 413. 46 Gainsborough St, Sudbury town centre.

Open: All year: Mon–Sat, 10am–5pm. Closed: Suns, Good Fri and Christmas to New Year.

Admission: Adult £4.50, Child/Student £2.00, Conc £3.60, Family Ticket £10. Tues, 1–5pm: Free.
ⓘ No photography. ⬛ ⬛ ⬛ WCs. ⬛ 🅿 None. ⬛ ⬛

GLEMHAM HALL 🏠
LITTLE GLEMHAM, WOODBRIDGE, SUFFOLK IP13 0BT

www.glemhamhall.co.uk

Tel: 01728 746704 **Fax:** 01728 747236 **E-mail:** events@glemhamhall.co.uk
Owner: Philip & Raewyn Hope-Cobbold
Contact: Mrs Kim Greenacre – Events Manager
Built around 1560, the Hall remained in the Glemham family until 1700 when it passed to the Norths (Earls of Guilford). Dudley North's wife Catherine was daughter of Elihu Yale, founder of the famous American University. The Cobbold's acquired the Hall in 1923. Old English: Gleam (happy) + ham (village) + Parva (small) hence Little Glemham.
Location: MAP 8:L9, OS Ref. TM212 GR347 592. Heritage signs off A12 between Woodbridge & Saxmundham.
Open: Various months/days/times throughout the year (see website).
Admission: Adult £15, Child under 13 Free, Groups min 10 max 30.
🅿 Partial.WC. 🖾 Obligatory, by arrangement. 🅿 Cars & coaches ample. ▣▣▲▣▣

HELMINGHAM HALL GARDENS 🏠
HELMINGHAM, SUFFOLK IP14 6EF

www.helmingham.com

Tel: 01473 890799 **Fax:** 01473 890776 **E-mail:** events@helmingham.com
Owner: The Lord & Lady Tollemache **Contact:** Events Office
Grade 1 listed gardens, redesigned by Lady Tollemache (a Chelsea Gold Medallist) set in a 400 acre deer park surrounding a moated Tudor Hall. Visitors are enchanted by the stunning herbaceous borders within the walled kitchen garden, the herb, knot, rose and wild gardens. Coach bookings are warmly welcomed and there are a variety of exciting events throughout the season.
Location: MAP 8:K9, OS Ref. TM190 578. B1077, 9m N of Ipswich, 5m S of Debenham.
Open: Gardens only 2nd May - 19th September 2010 (12-5pm Tuesdays, Wednesdays, Thursdays, Sundays).
Admission: Adults £6, Child (5-15yrs) £3. Groups (30+) £5.00.
▣▣▣▣ Grounds. WCs. ▣ 🖾 By arrangement. 🅿 ▣ Pre-booking required. 🖾 On leads. 🖾 Please contact us for details.

HADLEIGH GUILDHALL
Hadleigh, Suffolk IP7 5DT
Tel: 01473 827752
Owner: Hadleigh Market Feoffment Charity **Contact:** Jane Haylock
Fine timber framed guildhall, one of the least known medieval buildings in Suffolk.
Location: MAP 8:J9, OS Ref. TM025 425. S side of churchyard.
Open: mid Jun–end Sept: Building: Tues & Suns; Garden: Sun–Fri, 2–5pm.
Admission: Free. Donations welcome.

HAUGHLEY PARK 🏠
Stowmarket, Suffolk IP14 3JY
Tel: 01359 240701 www.haughleyparkbarn.co.uk
Owner/Contact: Mr & Mrs Robert Williams
Mellow red brick manor house of 1620 set in gardens, park and woodland. Original five-gabled east front, north wing re-built in Georgian style, 1820. 6 acres of well tended gardens including walled kitchen garden. 17th century brick and timber barn restored as meeting rooms. Woodland walks with bluebells (special Sun opening), lily-of-the-valley (May), rhododendrons and azaleas.
Location: MAP 8:J8, OS Ref. TM005 618. 4m W of Stowmarket signed off A14.
Open: Garden only: May–Sept: Tues & last Sun in Apr & 1st Sun in May, 2–5.30pm. Barn bookable for lectures, dinners, weddings etc (capacity 160).
Admission: Garden: £3. Child under 16 Free.
ℹ Picnics allowed. 🖾 Bluebell Sun. ▣▣▣ Bluebell Sun. 🅿🖾 On leads only. ▲▣

©NT/Fisheye Images

ICKWORTH HOUSE, PARK & GARDENS 🌼
HORRINGER, BURY ST EDMUNDS IP29 5QE

www.nationaltrust.org.uk/ickworth

Tel: 01284 735270 **Fax:** 01284 735175 **E-mail:** ickworth@nationaltrust.org.uk
Owner: The National Trust **Contact:** The Property Manager
One of the most unusual houses in East Anglia. The huge Rotunda of this 18th century Italianate house dominates the landscape. Inside are collections of Georgian silver, Regency furniture, Old Master paintings and family portraits.
Location: MAP 8:I9, OS155 Ref. TL816 611. In Horringer, 3m SW of Bury St Edmunds on W side of A143.
Open: House: 1 Mar–31 Oct: Fri–Tue, 11am–5pm. Garden: 1 Jan–28 Feb and 2 Nov–31 Dec, daily, 11am–4pm. 1 Mar–1 Nov, daily, 10am–5pm. Shop & Restaurant: 1 Jan–28 Feb and 2 Nov–31 Dec, Fri–Tue, 11am–4pm. 1 Mar–1 Nov, Fri–Tue, 10am–5pm. Park: Open all year.
Admission: Gift Aid Admission (Standard Admission prices in brackets) House, park & gardens: £9.15 (£8.30), child £3.65 (£3.30), family £21.90 (£19.90). Park & garden only: £4.65 (£4.20), child £1.15 (£1), family £10.40 (£9.45). House upgrade: £4.50 (£4.05), child £2.50 (£2.25), family £11.50 (£10.45).
▣▣▣▣▣▣ By arrangement. 🅿 Limited for coaches. ▣▣▲▣

Properties that **open all year** appear in the special index at the end of the book.

KENTWELL HALL & GARDENS 🏠
LONG MELFORD, SUFFOLK CO10 9BA

www.kentwell.co.uk

Tel: 01787 310207 **Fax:** 01787 379318 **E-mail:** info@kentwell.co.uk
Owner: Patrick Phillips Esq QC **Contact:** The Estate Office

A beautiful mellow redbrick Tudor Mansion, surrounded by a broad moat, with rare service building of c1500. Interior 'improved' by Thomas Hopper in 1820s. Still a lived-in family home. Famed for the long-time, long term, ongoing restoration works.

Gardens – Over 30 years' endeavour has resulted in gardens which are a joy in all seasons. Moats, massed spring bulbs, mature trees, delightful walled garden, with potager, herbs and ancient espaliered fruit trees. Much topiary including unique 'Pied Piper' story.

Re-Creations – Kentwell is renowned for its award-winning Re-Creations of Everyday Tudor Life. It also has occasional Re-Creations of WW2 Life. Re-Creations take place on selected weekends from April to October. Call or visit website for dates.

Corporate – House and upgraded 2500 sq ft Function Room for conferences, dinners, banquets of all sizes and Corporate Activity Days of originality.

Schools – Perhaps the biggest, most original and stimulating educational programme in the region enjoyed by about 20,000 schoolchildren each year.

Filming – Much used for medieval and Tudor periods for its wide range of perfectly equipped locations inside and out and access to Kentwell's 700 Tudors as extras.

Scaresville – Scariest Halloween Event 15–31 October. Also Christmas Wonderland.

Location: MAP 8:I9, OS Ref. TL864 479. Off the A134. 4m N of Sudbury.
Open: For full details see our website or call for Opening Leaflet.
Admission: Charges apply according to the Event (if any) on. Call for details.
ℹ️ No photography in house. 📷🎫 Conferences, dinners, Tudor feasts for groups of 40 or more. Car rallies. ♿🍴 Home-made food. 🅿️♿✖🔠 Including themed ceremonies. 🎭 Open-air theatre, opera and concert season Jul–Aug.

LANDGUARD FORT ⚜

Felixstowe, Suffolk
Tel: 07749 695523 **E-mail:** customers@english-heritage.org.uk
www.english-heritage.org.uk/landguard
Owner: English Heritage **Contact:** Visitor Operations Team
(Managed by Languard Fort Trust)

Impressive 18th century fort with later additions built on a site originally fortified by Henry VIII and in use until after World War II. Guided tours and audio tours of the fort are supplemented by a DVD presentation of the site's history and by guided tours of the substantial outside batteries.

Location: MAP 8:L10, OS Ref. TM284 318. 1m S of Felixstowe town centre – follow brown tourist signs to Landguard Point and Nature Reserve from A14.
Open: 1 Apr–31 May: daily, 10am–5pm. 1 Jun–30 Sep: daily, 10am–6pm. 1 Oct– 1 Nov: daily, 10am–5pm. Last admission 1 hour before closing. An average tour takes 1½ hours. Please call 07749 695523 to book Battery & group tours.
Admission: Adult £3.50, Child £1, Conc. £2.50. Free entry for children under 5yrs and wheelchair users. No unaccompanied children. EH Members Free. Group discount available. Opening times and prices are valid until 31st March 2010, after this date details are subject to change please see www.english-heritage.org.uk for the most up-to-date information.
ℹ️ Picnickers welcome. 📷🅿️🔄🎭 Contact David Morgan for details of tours of the outer batteries and charges for special events.

© Lavenham Photographic Studios

LAVENHAM: THE GUILDHALL OF CORPUS CHRISTI 🌿
THE MARKET PLACE, LAVENHAM, SUDBURY CO10 9QZ

www.nationaltrust.org.uk

Tel: 01787 247646 **E-mail:** lavenhamguildhall@nationaltrust.org.uk
Owner: The National Trust **Contact:** Jane Gosling

With its numerous timber-framed houses and magnificent church, a visit to picturesque Lavenham is a step back in time. The sixteenth-century Guildhall is the ideal place to begin with its exhibitions on the woollen cloth industry, agriculture and local history bringing to life the fascinating stories behind this remarkable village.

Location: MAP 8:J9, OS155, TL915 942. 6m NNE of Sudbury. Village centre. A1141 & B1071.
Open: Guildhall: 6–28 Mar, Wed–Sun, 11am–4pm; 29 Mar–31 Oct, daily, 11am–5pm; 6–28 Nov, 11am–4pm, Sat & Sun. Shop: 9 Jan–28 Feb, Sat & Sun, 11am–4pm; 6 Mar–31 Oct, As Guildhall; 6 Nov–19 Dec, Thur–Sun, 11am–4pm; Tea Room: 6 Mar– 31 Oct, As Guildhall; 6 Nov–19 Dec, Sat & Sun, 11am–4pm. Closed Good Friday and Parts of the building may be closed occasionally for community use.
Admission: Adult £4.30, Child £1.80, Family £10.50, Groups: Adult £3.55, Child £1.20. School parties by arrangement.
📷🍴♿💷✖🔠 Program of special talks, tours and events throughout year. Contact the property for an event calendar.

LEISTON ABBEY ⚜

Leiston, Suffolk
Tel: 01223 582700 (Regional Office) **E-mail:** customers@english-heritage.org.uk
www.english-heritage.org.uk/leiston
Owner: English Heritage **Contact:** The East of England Regional Office

The remains of this abbey for Premonstratensian canons, including a restored chapel, are amongst the most extensive in Suffolk.

Location: MAP 8:M8, OS Ref. TM445 642. 1m N of Leiston off B1069.
Open: Any reasonable time.
Admission: Free. Opening times and prices are valid until 31st March 2010, after this date details are subject to change please see www.english-heritage.org.uk for the most up-to-date information.
ℹ️ Picnickers welcome. ♿🅿️✖🔠

©NTPL/Fisheye Images

MELFORD HALL ✤
LONG MELFORD, SUDBURY, SUFFOLK CO10 9AA

www.nationaltrust.org.uk

Tel/Fax: 01787 379228 **Info:** 01787 376395
E-mail: melford@nationaltrust.org.uk
Owner: The National Trust **Contact:** Josephine Waters

For over two centuries Melford Hall has been the much loved family home of the Hyde Parkers. The interior charts their changing tastes and fashions and the stories about visits by Beatrix Potter and family life at Melford show that a home is far more than just bricks and mortar.

Location: OS Ref. TL867 462. In Long Melford off A134, 14m S of Bury St Edmunds, 3m N of Sudbury.
Open: 3–11 Apr, daily (except Tue), 17–25 Apr, Sat–Sun, 1 May–3 Oct, Wed–Sun, 9 Oct–31 Oct, Sat & Sun only. All 1.30pm–5pm.
Admission: House & Garden: Adult £6.30, Child (under 16yrs) £3.15, Family £15.50. Groups (15+): Adult £5.25, Child £2.60. Garden Only: Adult £3.15, Child (u16) £1.60, Family £8.
Special Events: Range of special events in the house and parkland throughout the year. Contact the property or National Trust website for details.

ℹ️ No photography in house. 🖼️🚻♿WCs. 🅿️Limited parking for coaches 🐕‍🦺

OTLEY HALL
OTLEY, IPSWICH, SUFFOLK IP6 9PA

www.otleyhall.co.uk

Tel: 01473 890264 **Fax:** 01473 890803 **E-mail:** enquiries@otleyhall.co.uk
Owner: Dr Ian & Mrs Catherine Beaumont **Contact:** Lucy Sheehan

A stunning medieval Moated Hall (Grade I) frequently described as "one of England's loveliest houses". Noted for its richly carved beams, superb linenfold panelling and 16th century wall paintings, Otley Hall was once the home of the Gosnold family and is still a family home. Bartholomew Gosnold voyaged to the New World in 1602 and named Cape Cod and Martha's Vineyard, (an account of the voyage is believed to have inspired Shakespeare's Tempest). Gosnold returned in 1607 and founded the Jamestown colony, the first English-speaking settlement in the US. The unique 10 acre gardens include historically accurate Tudor re-creations designed by Sylvia Landsberg (author of The Medieval Garden) and were voted among the top 10 gardens to visit in Great Britain.

Location: MAP 8:K9, OS Ref. TM207 563. 7m N of Ipswich, off the B1079.
Open: BH Suns (2 & 30 May, 29 Aug), 1–5pm. Afternoon teas available. Groups and individuals welcome all year by appointment for private guided tours.
Admission: BHs: Adult £5, Child £2.50.

🔲♿ Partial. 🖼️ℹ️ By arrangement. 🅿️🔆❄️🐕‍🦺

© English Heritage

ORFORD CASTLE ⌗
ORFORD, WOODBRIDGE, SUFFOLK IP12 2ND

www.english-heritage.org.uk/orford

Tel: 01394 450472 **E-mail:** customers@english-heritage.org.uk
Owner: English Heritage **Contact:** Visitor Operations Team

It has a warren of passageways and chambers to be explored, with a winding staircase right to the top where you can enjoy spectacular views of Orford Ness.

Location: MAP 8:M9, OS169, TM419 499. In Orford on B1084, 20m NE of Ipswich.
Open: 1 Apr–30 Jun: daily, 10am–5pm. 1 Jul–31 Aug: daily, 10am–6pm. 1 Sep–30 Sept: daily, 10am–5pm. 1 Oct–31 Mar '10: Thur–Mon, 10am–4pm. Closed 24–26 Dec & 1 Jan.
Admission: Adult £5, Child £2.50, Under 5s Free, Conc. £4.30, Family £12.50. EH Members/OVP Free. Group discount available. Opening times and prices are valid until 31st March 2010, after this date details are subject to change please see www.english-heritage.org.uk for the most up-to-date information.

🔲🔲🖼️🅿️❄️🔆

ST EDMUNDSBURY CATHEDRAL

Angel Hill, Bury St Edmunds, Suffolk IP33 1LS

Tel: 01284 748720 **Fax:** 01284 768655 **Email:** cathedral@stedscathedral.co.uk
www.stedscathedral.co.uk

Owner: The Church of England **Contact:** Sarah Friswell

The striking Millennium Tower, completed on 2005, is the crowning glory of St Edmundsbury Cathedral. Built from English limestone, brick and lime mortar, the 150ft Lantern Tower, along with new chapels, cloisters and North Transept, completes nearly fifty years of development in a style never likely to be repeated.

Location: MAP 8:I8, OS Ref. TL857 642. Bury St Edmunds town centre.
Open: All year: daily 8.30am–6pm.
Admission: Donation invited.

🔲♿ Partial. WC. 🖼️ℹ️🏛️🔆

SAXTEAD GREEN POST MILL ⌗

Post Mill Bungalow, Saxtead Green, Woodbridge, Suffolk IP13 9QQ

Tel: 01728 685789 **E-mail:** customers@english-heritage.org.uk
www.english-heritage.org.uk/saxtead

Owner: English Heritage **Contact:** Visitor Operations Team

The finest example of a Suffolk Post Mill. Still in working order, you can climb the wooden stairs to the various floors, full of fascinating mill machinery. Ceased production in 1947.

Location: MAP 8:L8, OS Ref. TM253 645. 2½m NW of Framlingham on A1120.
Open: 1 Apr–30 Sep: Fri–Sat & BHs, 12 noon–5pm.
Admission: Adult £3.30, Child £1.70, Conc. £2.80. EH Members Free. Group discount available. Opening times and prices are valid until 31st March 2010, after this date details are subject to change please see www.english-heritage.org.uk for the most up-to-date information.

ℹ️ Picnickers welcome. Museum. 🔲🔲🔆

SOMERLEYTON HALL & GARDENS 🏛

SOMERLEYTON, LOWESTOFT, SUFFOLK NR32 5QQ

www.somerleyton.co.uk

Tel: 08712 224244 (office) **Fax:** 01502 732143

E-mail: carolyn.ashton@somerleyton.co.uk

Owner: Hon Hugh Crossley **Contact:** Carolyn Ashton

Originally Jacobean the Hall was extensively re-modelled in 1844, guided tours of the state rooms are available on all open days. The 12 acres of fabulous landscaped gardens include the famous yew hedge maze, 300ft pergola, Vulliamy tower clock, Paxton glasshouses and walled, formal and arboreal gardens.

Location: MAP 8:M8, OS134 Ref. TM493 977. 5m NW of Lowestoft on B1074, 7m SW of Great Yarmouth off A143.

Open: Please visit our website for details – www.somerleyton.co.uk – or telephone our information line – 0871 222 4244

Admission: Hall Tour and Gardens: Adults £8.95, Over 60's £7.95, Children (5-16) £4.95, Under 5's are free, Family Ticket (2 adult & 2 child) £25.00. Garden's Only: Adults £5.50, Over 60's £4.50, Children £3.50. Season tickets, private tours and group discounts are available on request.

ℹ No photography in house. 📷 ♿ 🍽 Receptions/functions/conferences/weddings. 🔄 ♿ 🎧 Obligatory. 🅿 🏠 🚫 🏰 ❄

Saxtead Green

SOUTH ELMHAM HALL

ST CROSS, HARLESTON, NORFOLK IP20 0PZ

www.southelmham.co.uk   www.batemansbarn.co.uk

Tel: 01986 782526 **Fax:** 01986 782203 **E-mail:** enquiries@southelmham.co.uk

Owner/Contact: John Sanderson

A Grade I listed medieval manor house set inside moated enclosure. Originally built by the Bishop of Norwich around 1270. Much altered in the 16th century. Self guided trail through former deer park to South Elmham Minster, a ruined Norman chapel with Saxon origins.

Location: MAP 8:L7, OS30 Ref. TM778 324. Between Harleston and Bungay from the A143 take the B1062.

Open: Minster, Walks (Café: 1 May–30 Sept: Thurs, Fris & BH Mons). 1 Oct–30 Apr: Suns only, 10am–5pm. Hall: Guided tours only: 1 May–30 Sept: Thurs, 2pm, Sun & BH Mons, 3pm.

Admission: House: Adult £6.50, Child £3. Groups (15-50): Adult £4.50, Child £2.50. Walks (free).

🎧 ♿ WC. ♿ 🍽 🎧 Obligatory. ⬛ 🅿 🚫 In grounds, on leads. 🏰 🔺 ❄ ♿

SUTTON HOO 🦌

WOODBRIDGE, SUFFOLK IP12 3DJ

www.nationaltrust.org.uk/suttonhoo

Tel: 01394 389700 **Fax:** 01394 389702 **E-mail:** suttonhoo@nationaltrust.org.uk

Owner: The National Trust **Contact:** The Property Secretary

Anglo-Saxon royal burial site where priceless treasure was discovered in a ship grave in 1939. Site includes an exhibition hall, restaurant, shop, site walks and the famous burial mounds. Many special events. Exhibition 2010: The illustrations of Victor Ambrus.

Location: MAP 8:L9, OS Ref. TM288 487. Off B1083 Woodbridge to Bawdsey road. Follow signs from A12. Rail: Melton station 1/2 mile.

Open: Exhibition Hall, Shop & Restaurant: 1 Jan–14 Feb, Sat & Sun, 11am–4pm; 15 Feb–21 Feb, daily, 11am–4pm; 22 Feb–12 March, Sat & Sun, 11am–4pm; 13 Mar–4 Apr, Wed–Sun, 10.30am–5pm; 5 Apr–31 Oct, daily, 10.30am–5pm; 1 Nov–24 Dec, Sat & Sun, 11am–4pm; 27 Dec–31 Dec, daily, 11am–4pm. Open bank holidays, closed 25 & 26 Dec. Estate walks open daily all year 9am–6pm (except for some Thur, Nov–Jan 2011).

*Admission: Adult £6.85, Child £3.55. Family £17.30. Groups £5.80. Discount for visitors arriving by cycle or on foot. NT members free. Includes a voluntary donation but visitors can choose to pay the standard prices displayed at the property and on the website.

ℹ 📷 🎧 ♿ WCs. 🍽 Licensed. 🍽 Licensed. 🎧 By arrangement 🅿 Limited for Coaches ⬛ 🚫 In grounds, on leads. 🏰 ❄ ♿ Programme of events, tel for details.

St. Edmundsbury Cathedral

Somerleyton Hall & Gardens

WYKEN HALL GARDENS
STANTON, BURY ST EDMUNDS, SUFFOLK IP31 2DW

www.wykenvineyards.co.uk

Tel: 01359 250287 **Fax:** 01359 253821

Owner: Sir Kenneth & Lady Carlisle **Contact:** Mr Alan North

Wyken is an Elizabethan manor house surrounded by a romantic, plantlovers' garden with maze, knot and herb garden and rose garden featuring old roses. A walk through ancient woodlands leads to award-winning Wyken Vineyards. The 16th century barn houses the Vineyard Restaurant featured in Michelin and Good Food Guides, and the Leaping Hare Country Store, described in *Country Living* as 'a model of what a shop should be.'

Location: MAP 8:J8, OS Ref. TL963 717. 9m NE of Bury St. Edmunds 1m E of A143. Follow brown tourist signs to Wyken Vineyards from Ixworth.

Open: 5 Jan–24 Dec: daily, 10am–6pm. Garden: 1 Apr–1 Oct: daily except Sat, 2–6pm. Open for dinner from 7pm Fri & Sat (advisable to book).

Admission: Gardens: Adult £3.50, Child (under 12yrs) Free, Conc. £3. Groups by appointment.

Suitable. WC. Licensed. No dogs in garden.

See which properties offer **educational facilities** or **school visits** in our index at the end of the book.

■ Owner

Trustees of the Chatsworth Settlement. Home of the Devonshire family

■ Contact

The Booking Office
Chatsworth
Bakewell
Derbyshire DE45 1PP

Tel: 01246 565300
Fax: 01246 583536
E-mail: visit@
chatsworth.org

■ Location

MAP 6:P2
OS Ref. SK260 703

From London
3 hrs M1/J29,
signposted via
Chesterfield.

3m E of Bakewell,
off B6012,
10m W of Chesterfield.

Rail: Chesterfield
Station, 11m.

Bus: Chesterfield –
Baslow, 1½m.

■ Opening Times

House, garden and farmyard open daily, from Mid March to 23 December. The park is open every day.

■ Admission

The admission prices for the house, garden and farmyard are listed on our website at www.chatsworth.org, Discounted day tickets can be purchased online.

CHATSWORTH

www.chatsworth.org

The home of the Duke and Duchess of Devonshire is one of the country's greatest Treasure Houses, renowned for the quality of its art, landscape and hospitality, and the warm welcome all visitors receive. Home of the Cavendish family since the 1550s, it has evolved through the centuries to reflect the tastes, passions and interests of succeeding generations, and today contains works of art that span 4000 years, from ancient Roman and Egyptian sculpture, and masterpieces by Rembrandt, Reynold and Veronese, to work by outstanding modern artists, including Lucian Freud, Edmund de Waal, Sean Scully and David Nash. Chatsworth is also home to a growing collection of contemporary sculpture and temporary exhibitions.

2010 is a very special year. After 2 years of intensive work, we are delighted to open a new visitor route round the house, with full disabled access to all floors, some fascinating restored rooms on view for the first time, and exciting new displays of rare treasures. Our

programme of events includes a new spring festival of Tulips and a Russian Christmas. We are also celebrating the 90th birthday of Deborah Devonshire, the Dowager Duchess of Devonshire, with a special exhibition.

The garden is famous for its rich history, historic and modern waterworks and sculptures, the Victorian rock garden and the maze. Younger visitors enjoy the working farmyard and the woodland adventure playground and the 1,000 acre park is open for walks, picnics and play. Chatsworth's exciting events programme includes International Horse Trials and the Country Fair, and we offer interesting tours and talks about the house, garden and works of art throughout the year. You can stay with us, in the wide range of comfortable holiday accommodation across the estate. The elegant gift and farm shops and superb, seasonal home-made food will complete your visit.

5 gift shops, farm shop and pantry.

Rooms available for conferences and private functions. Contact Head of Catering.

WCs and full house access.

Cafes and food to go.

(Max 300; home-made food. Menus on request. Licensed

Daily tours (small charge). Private tours of house or greenhouses and Behind the Scenes Days, by arrangement only (extra charges apply). Groups please pre-book.

New adult and child audio tours, in English.

Cars 100 yds, Coaches drop off at house.

Guided tours, packs, and new self-guiding materials. Free preliminary visit recommended.

On leads.

Holiday cottages.

Conference/Function

ROOM	SIZE	MAX CAPACITY
Hartington Rm.		70
Racing Rm.		22

HADDON HALL

www.haddonhall.co.uk

Haddon Hall sits on a rocky outcrop above the River Wye close to the market town of Bakewell, looking much as is would have done in Tudor times. There has been a dwelling here since the 11th century but the house we see today dates mainly from the late 14th century with major additions in the following 200 years and some alterations in the early 17th century including the creation of the Long Gallery.

William the Conqueror's illegitimate son Peverel, and his descendants, held Haddon for 100 years before it passed to the Vernon family. In the late 16th century the estate passed through marriage to the Manners family, in whose possession it has remained ever since.

When the Dukedom of Rutland was conferred on the Manners family in 1703 they moved to Belvoir Castle, and Haddon was left deserted for 200 years. This was Haddon's saving grace as the Hall thus escaped the major architectural changes of the 18th and 19th centuries ready for the great restoration at the beginning of the 20th century by the 9th Duke of Rutland. Henry VIII's elder brother Arthur, who was a frequent guest of the Vernons, would be quite familiar with the house as it stands today.

Haddon Hall is a popular location for film and television productions. Recent films include *Pride & Prejudice* and the BBC dramatisation of *Jane Eyre*.

Gardens

Magnificent terraced gardens with over 150 varieties of rose and clematis, many over 70 years old, provide colour and scent throughout the summer.

■ Owner
Lord Edward Manners

■ Contact
Janet Blackburn
Estate Office
Haddon Hall
Bakewell
Derbyshire DE45 1LA
Tel: 01629 812855
Fax: 01629 814379
E-mail: info@
haddonhall.co.uk

■ Location
MAP 6:P2
OS Ref. SK234 663

From London 3 hrs
Sheffield ½ hr
Manchester 1 hr
Haddon is on the
E side of A6 1½m
S of Bakewell.
M1/J29.

Rail: Chesterfield
Station, 12m.

Bus: Chesterfield
Bakewell.

■ Opening Times
Summer
Easter: 1–6 April inc.
Apr & Oct: Sat–Mon;
May–Sept: Daily, 12
noon–5pm (closed 3 & 4
July).
Last admission 4pm.
Christmas: 4–12
December, 10.30am–4pm
(last admission 3.30pm).

■ Admission
Summer
Adult	£8.95
Child (5–15yrs)	£4.95
Conc	£7.95
Family (2+3)	£22.75
Regular Visitor Pass	£16.50

Groups (15+)
Adult	£7.95
Child (5–15yrs)	£4.00
Conc	£6.95
Parking	£1.50

 Haddon Hall is ideal as a film location due to its authentic and genuine architecture requiring little alteration. Suitable locations are also available on the Estate.

Unsuitable, steep approach, varying levels of house.

Self-service, licensed (max 75). Home-made food.

Special tours £11.00pp for groups of 15, 7 days' notice.

 Ample. 450 yds from house. £1.50 per car.

Tours of the house bring alive Haddon Hall of old. Costume room also available, very popular!

Guide dogs only.

■ **Owner**

The National Trust

■ **Contact**

Victoria Flanagan
Property Manager
Kedleston Hall
Derby DE22 5JH
Tel: 01332 842191
Fax: 01332 844059
Email: kedlestonhall@
nationaltrust.org.uk

■ **Location**
MAP 6:P4
OS ref. SK312 403

5 miles NW of Derby,
signposted from the
roundabout where the
A38 crosses A52 Derby
ring road

■ **Opening Times**
House
20 February–3 November:
Sat–Wed, 12noon–5pm,
last entry 4.15pm.
Open Good Friday

Pleasure Grounds
20 February–
3 November: daily,
10am–6pm

Park
20 February–3 November:
daily, 10am–6pm
4 November–18 February
2011: daily, 10am–4pm,
with occasional day
closures

Restaurant & Shop
13 February–3 November,
Sat–Wed, 11am–5pm;
plus 29 July–27 August,
Thu/Fri, 11am–3pm; 6
November–13 February
2011, Sat/Sun 11am–3pm

■ ***Admission**
House & Grounds
Adult   £9.45
Child   £4.70
Family   £23.60

Grounds only
Adult   £4.20
Child   £2.10
Family   £10.60

Winter admission £1 per
person (child 50p)

*includes a voluntary
donation but visitors can
choose to pay the standard
prices displayed at the
property and on the website.

Conference/Function

ROOM	SIZE	MAX CAPACITY
Caesars' Hall	40' x 60'	120 dining 150 reception 100 delegates theatre style
Saloon		Civil Weddings only – seats 110
Restaurant		90 dining split in 2 rooms

KEDLESTON HALL

www.nationaltrust.org.uk/kedleston

Kedleston was built between 1759 and 1765 for the Curzon family who have lived in the area since the 12th century. The hall boasts the most complete and least altered sequence of Robert Adam interiors in England, with the magnificent State rooms retaining much of their great collections of paintings and furniture. The Adam influence can be seen across the 18th century pleasure grounds and 800 acre park. Since 1987 the National Trust has undertaken a programme of work to return these interiors to their original appearance so that visitors can re-live the experience of coming to see a 'palace of the arts'. The Eastern Museum houses a remarkable collection, collected by Lord Curzon when he was Viceroy of India (1899–1905). Kedleston has a year wide programme of special events and can be used for corporate events and civil wedding ceremonies please ring the property or visit the website for more details.

New for 2010

Kedleston was used as a key location for the film, 'The Duchess' starring Keira Knightley, Ralph Fiennes and Charlotte Rampling which was released in the autumn of 2008. The film is based on the biography, Georgiana, Duchess of Devonshire, by Amanda Foreman which tells the life-story of Georgiana (1757–1806), wife of the 5th Duke of Devonshire. During the 2010 season visitors will able to walk in the 'footsteps' of the Duchess using a specially designed trail detailing more about how the property was used for filming.

No photography in the hall, welcomed in the park and pleasure grounds.

Also available as a filming location.

WCs

Licensed

Must be booked in advance.

Limited for coaches

Guide dogs only.

Please call us on 01332 842191 to be sent an events programme.

BOLSOVER CASTLE ⌗
CASTLE STREET, BOLSOVER, DERBYSHIRE S44 6PR
www.english-heritage.org.uk/bolsover

Tel: 01246 822844   **E-mail:** customers@english-heritage.org.uk
Owner: English Heritage   **Contact:** Visitor Operations Team

An enchanting and romantic spectacle, situated high on a wooded hilltop dominating the surrounding landscape. Built on the site of a Norman castle, this is largely an early 17th century mansion. Most delightful is the 'Little Castle', with intricate carvings, panelling and wall painting. See the restored interiors of the Little Castle including the only remaining copies of Titian's Caesar Paintings, and the Venus Fountain and statuary. There is also an impressive 17th century indoor Riding House built by the Duke of Newcastle. Enjoy the Visitor and Discovery Centre. Interesting interpretation scheme includes Audio/Visual and scale model of Little Castle. Also contemporary Visitor Centre with information about Bolsover town's development. Picnickers are welcome. (Bolsover is now available for Civil weddings, receptions and corporate hospitality.)

Location: MAP 7:A2, OS120, SK471 707. Signposted from M1/J29A, 6m from Mansfield. In Bolsover 6m E of Chesterfield on A632.

Open: 1 Apr–30 Jun: daily, 10am–5pm (closes 4pm Fri & Sat). 1 Jul–31 Aug: daily, 10am–6pm (closes 4pm Fri & Sat). 1 Sep–1 Nov: daily, 10am–5pm (closes 4pm Fri & Sat). 2 Nov–31 Mar: Thu–Mon, 10am–4pm. Closed 24–26 Dec & 1 Jan. Part of the castle may close for 1 hour if an event is booked. Please call to check.

Admission: Adult £7.30, Child £3.70, Conc. £6.20, Family £17.50. 15% discount for groups (11+). EH members Free. Opening times and prices are valid until 31st March 2010, after this date details are subject to change please see www.english-heritage.org.uk for the most up-to-date information.

ℹ️ Picnickers welcome. 🅾️🅃♿ WCs. ⬛🛈🅿️⬛✂️🔼✳️♨️

CALKE ABBEY ❧
TICKNALL, DERBYSHIRE DE73 7LE
www.nationaltrust.org.uk/calke

Tel: 01332 863822   **Fax:** 01332 865272   **E-mail:** calkeabbey@nationaltrust.org.uk
Owner: The National Trust   **Contact:** The Property Administrator

The house that time forgot, this baroque mansion, built 1701–3 for Sir John Harpur, is set in a landscaped park. Little restored, Calke is preserved by a programme of conservation as a graphic illustration of the English country house in decline; it contains the family's collection of natural history, a magnificent 18th century state bed and interiors that are virtually unchanged since the 1880s. Walled garden, pleasure grounds and orangery. Early 19th century Church. Historic parkland with Portland sheep and deer. Staunton Harold Church is nearby.

Location: MAP 7:A5, OS128, SK356 239. 10m S of Derby, on A514 at Ticknall between Swadlincote and Melbourne.

Open: House: 27 Feb–31 Oct, Mon–Wed & Sat & Sun, 12.30pm–5pm. last admission 4.30pm. Garden/Stables: 27 Feb–31 Oct, Mon–Wed & Sat & Sun, 1 Jul–3 Sept daily, 11am–5pm. Last admission 4.30pm. Restaurant/shop: 02 Jan–31 Dec, daily, 10.30am–5pm. closed 25 & 26 Dec and closes at 4pm Nov, Dec, Jan and Feb. Calke Park & National Nature Reserve: All year, 8am to 8.30pm or dusk if earlier. House & Garden open Good Friday 2 Apr 2010. Self guide West Wing Conservation Tours 11am to 12.30pm. Last Admission 12pm.

Admission: House & Garden, Adult £8.40, Child £4.30, Family £21.10. Garden only, Adult £4.60, Child £2.50, Family £11.70. Park & Stables, Adult £1.60, Child 50p, Family £4.20.

Special Events: Please telephone the property or visit www.nationaltrust.org.uk/calke for information on our extensive range of events that take place throughout the year.

🅾️🛈🅃♿⬛🍴 Licensed. 🅕 By arrangement. 🅿️ Limited for coaches. ⬛ 🔼✳️♨️

CATTON HALL 🏛

CATTON, WALTON-ON-TRENT, SOUTH DERBYSHIRE DE12 8LN

www.catton-hall.com

Tel: 01283 716311 **Fax:** 01283 712876 **E-mail:** r.neilson@catton-hall.com

Owner/Contact: Robin & Katie Neilson

Catton, built in 1745, has been in the hands of the same family since 1405 and is still lived in by the Neilsons as their private home. This gives the house, with its original collection of 17th and 18th century portraits, pictures and antique furniture, a unique, relaxed and friendly atmosphere. With its spacious reception rooms, luxurious bedrooms and delicious food and wine, Catton is centrally located for residential or non-residential business meetings/seminars, product launches and team-building activities, as well as for accommodation for those visiting Birmingham, the NEC, the Belfry, the Potteries and Dukeries – or just for a weekend celebration of family and friends. The acres of parkland alongside the River Trent are ideal for all types of corporate and public events.

Location: MAP 6:P5, OS Ref. SK206 154. 2m E of A38 at Alrewas between Lichfield & Burton-on-Trent (8m from each). Birmingham NEC 20m.

Open: By prior arrangement all year for corporate hospitality, shooting parties, wedding receptions, private groups. Guided tours: 5 Apr–11 Oct, Mons only, 2pm prompt. (Groups 15+ all year by prior arrangement).

ⓘ Conference facilities. 🍽 By arrangement. ♿🐕 By arrangement for groups. 🛏 4 x four posters, 5 twin, all en-suite. ▲ ♨

CHATSWORTH

See page 266 for full page entry.

Chatsworth

©Melbourne Hall

Melbourne Hall, Derbyshire

EYAM HALL 🏛

EYAM, HOPE VALLEY, DERBYSHIRE S32 5QW

www.eyamhall.co.uk

Tel: 01433 631976 **Fax:** 01433 631603 **E-mail:** info@eyamhall.co.uk

Owner: Mr R H V Wright **Contact:** Mr J Wright

Eyam Hall has been the home of the Wright family since 1671 and is a much loved family home. The tour includes tapestries, costumes, family portraits and anecdotes. The beautiful walled garden is nearing completion and forms part of the tour. There is also a working Craft Centre and a licensed restaurant.

Location: MAP 6:P2, OS119, SK216 765. Approx 10m from Sheffield, Chesterfield and Buxton, Eyam is off the A623 between Chesterfield and Chapel-en-le-Frith. Eyam Hall is in the centre of the village past the church.

Open: House and Garden: 30 Mar–30 April, Sun–Fri, 12noon–4pm. Craft Centre: Feb–Dec, Tues–Sun.

Admission: House & Garden: Adult £6.25, Child £4, Conc. £5.75, Family: (2+4). Group rates available during normal opening hours.

ⓘ Craft Centre, Free. 📷🍽♿ Partial. 🍴 Licensed. 📷 Obligatory. 🅿 Free. ▣ 🐕 In grounds, on leads. Guide dogs only in house. ▲ ✳ ♨

HADDON HALL 🏛

See page 267 for full page entry.

HARDSTOFT HERB GARDEN

Hall View Cottage, Hardstoft, Chesterfield, Derbyshire S45 8AH
Tel: 01246 854268
Owner: Mr Stephen Raynor/L M Raynor   **Contact:** Mr Stephen Raynor
Consists of two display gardens with information boards and well labelled plants.
Location: MAP 7:A3, OS Ref. SK436 633. On B6039 between Holmewood & Tibshelf, 3m from J29 on M1.
Open: Gardens, Nursery & Tearoom: 15 Mar–15 Sept: Wed–Sun, 10am–5pm. Closed Mon & Tue except Easter and BHs when open throughout.
Admission: Adult £1, Child Free.

KEDLESTON HALL 🌿

See page 268 for full page entry.

© English Heritage

© Haddon Hall & HHG / Nick McCann

Haddon Hall

HARDWICK OLD HALL ⊞
DOE LEA, NR CHESTERFIELD, DERBYSHIRE S44 5QJ

www.english-heritage.org.uk/hardwickoldhall

Tel: 01246 850431   **E-mail:** customers@english-heritage.org.uk
Owner: National Trust, managed by English Heritage
Contact: Visitor Operations Team
This large ruined house, finished in 1591, still displays Bess of Hardwick's innovative planning and interesting decorative plasterwork. Graphics panels focus on the rich interiors Bess created. The views from the top floor over the country park and 'New' Hall are spectacular.
Location: MAP 7:A3, OS120, SK463 638. 7½m NW of Mansfield, 9½m SE of Chesterfield, off A6175, from M1/J29.
Open: 14 Mar–1 Nov: Wed–Sun, 10am–5pm. Closed 2 Nov–31 Mar except 5 Dec–20 Dec, Sat ¶ Sun, 10am–4pm.
Admission: Adult £4, Child £2, Conc. £3.40, Family £10. 15% discount for groups (11+). NT members free, but small charge at events. EH members Free. Tickets for the New Hall (NT) and joint tickets for both properties available at extra cost. Opening times and prices are valid until 31st March 2010, after this date details are subject to change please see www.english-heritage.org.uk for the most up-to-date information.
ℹ Picnickers welcome. WC. ⬛ ⬛ Free with admission. 🅿 ⬛ On leads.

© NT / Giraffe Photography

© NT / Giraffe Photography

HARDWICK HALL, GARDENS, PARK & STAINSBY MILL 🌿
DOE LEA, CHESTERFIELD, DERBYSHIRE S44 5QJ

www.nationaltrust.org.uk/hardwickhall

Tel: 01246 850430   **Fax:** 01246 858424   **Shop/Restaurant:** 01246 858409
E-mail: hardwickhall@nationaltrust.org.uk
Owner: The National Trust   **Contact:** Property Administrator
Hardwick Hall: One of the most splendid houses in England. Built by the extraordinary Bess of Hardwick in the 1590's, and unaltered since: yet its huge windows and high ceilings make it feel strikingly modern. Rich tapestries, plaster friezes and alabaster fireplaces colour the rooms. Walled courtyards enclose fine gardens, orchards and a herb garden. The Parkland has circular walks, fishing ponds and rare breed animals. Hardwick Hall is now licensed for civil wedding ceremonies (Apr–Oct) and offers a marquee for receptions.
Location: MAP 7:A3, OS120, SK456 651. 7.5m NW of Mansfield, 9½m SE of Chesterfield: approach from M1/J29 via A6175 From M1/J29 take A6175, signposted to Clay Cross then first left and left again to Stainsby Mill.
Open: Hall: 17 Feb - 31 Oct (Tours only 17 Feb to 14 Mar). Wed to Sun, BH Mon and Good Friday; 12 noon - 4.30pm. Gardens, Shop and Restaurant: same days as the Hall; 11am - 5pm. Parkland: open daily. Stainsby Mill: same days as the Hall; 10am-4pm. Christmas opening: 4 - 19 Dec, Hall, Gardens, Shop, Restaurant and Stainsby Mill

weekends only; 11am-3pm
Admission: House & Garden: Adult £10.50, Child £5.25, Family £26.25. Garden only: Adult £5.30, Child £2.65, Family £13.25. Groups (15+) Adult £9.00
Stainsby Mill: Adult £3.50, Child £1.75, Family £8.75. Includes a voluntary donation but visitors can choose to pay the standard prices displayed at the property and on the website.
Special Events: Elizabethan Weekend - 25 & 26 September 2010
Hardwick Estate – Stainsby Mill is a 19th century water-powered corn mill in working order. Organic flour for sale.
Open: 18–22 Feb, Wed–Sun, 12noon–4pm. 28 Feb–8 Mar, Sat/Sun, 12noon–4pm. 14 Mar–1 Nov, Wed–Sun, 10am–4pm. 5–20 Dec, Sat/Sun, 11am–3pm. 26 Dec, 11am–3pm. 1 Jan 2010, 11am–3pm.
Location: MAP 7:A3, OS120, SK455 653. From M1/J29 take A6175, signposted to Clay Cross then first left and left again to Stainsby Mill.
ℹ Dogs welcome in the Parkland only, on leads. ⬛ ⬛ ⬛ Partial. WCs. ⬛ ⬛ Licensed. ⬛ By arrangement. 🅿 Limited for coaches. ⬛ ⬛ Guide dogs only. ⬛ ⬛

MELBOURNE HALL & GARDENS 🏛
MELBOURNE, DERBYSHIRE DE73 8EN

www.melbournehall.com

Tel: 01332 862502   **Fax:** 01332 862263

Owner: Lord & Lady Ralph Kerr   **Contact:** Mrs Gill Weston

This beautiful house of history, in its picturesque poolside setting, was once the home of Victorian Prime Minister William Lamb. The fine gardens, in the French formal style, contain Robert Bakewell's intricate wrought iron arbour and a fascinating yew tunnel. Upstairs rooms available to view by appointment.

Location: MAP 7:A5, OS Ref. SK389 249. 8m S of Derby. From London, exit M1/J24.

Open: Hall: Aug only (not first 3 Mons) 2–5pm. Last admission 4.15pm. Gardens: 1 Apr–30 Sept: Weds, Sats, Suns, BH Mons, 1.30–5.30pm. Additional open days possible in August, please telephone for details.

Admission: Hall: Adult £3.50, Child £2, OAP £3. Gardens: Adult £3.50, Child/OAP £2.50. Hall & Gardens: Adult £5.50, Child £3.50, OAP £4.50.

ℹ️ Crafts. No photography in house. 🅿️ Partial. 🍴 Obligatory in house Tue–Sat. 🅿️ Limited. No coach parking. 🐕 Guide dogs only.

PEVERIL CASTLE ⌘

Market Place, Castleton, Hope Valley S33 8WQ

Tel: 01433 620613   **E-mail:** customers@english-heritage.org.uk

www.english-heritage.org.uk/peveril

Owner: English Heritage   **Contact:** Visitor Operations Team

There are breathtaking views of the Peak District from this castle, perched high above the pretty village of Castleton. The great square tower of Henry II stands almost to its original height. A walkway opens up new areas and views from the first floor of the Keep. Peveril Castle is one of the earliest Norman castles to be built in England. The Peveril Castle Visitor Centre has displays which tell the story of Peveril as the focal point of the Royal Forest of the Peak as well as improved access and facilities.

Location: MAP 6:O2, OS110, SK150 827. S side of Castleton, 15m W of Sheffield on A6187.

Open: 1–30 Jun: daily, 10am–5pm. 1 Jul–31 Aug: daily, 10am–6pm. 1 Sep–1 Nov: daily, 10am–5pm. 2 Nov–31 Mar '10: Thu–Mon, 10am–4pm. Closed 24–26 Dec & 1 Jan.

Admission: Adult £3.90, Child £2, Conc. £3.30, Family £9.30. 15% discount for groups (11+). EH members Free. Opening times and prices are valid until 31st March 2010, after this date details are subject to change please see www.english-heritage.org.uk for the most up-to-date information.

ℹ️ Picnickers welcome. WCs. 🅿️ 🐕 ❄ ♿

Renishaw Hall Gardens

RENISHAW HALL GARDENS 🏛
RENISHAW, NR SHEFFIELD, DERBYSHIRE S21 3WB

www.renishaw-hall.co.uk

Tel: 01246 432310   **Fax:** 01246 430760   **E-mail:** info2@renishaw-hall.co.uk

Owner: Sitwell Estate   **Contact:** The Administrator

Home of the Sitwell family. Eight acres of Italianate gardens stand in 300 acres of mature parkland, encompassing statues, shaped yew hedges, herbaceous borders, a water garden and lakes. The Exhibition area is located in the Georgian stables alongside craft workshops and Gallery café. Separate childrens' garden featuring a maze and a willow tunnel. Renishaw Hall is available for exclusive hire as a film location. The Red Dining Room is available for Civil weddings.

Location: MAP 7:A2, OS Ref. SK435 786. On A6135 3m from M1/J30, equidistant from Sheffield and Chesterfield.

Open: 2010 Season Thur 1 Apr–26 Sept. Thursday through to Sunday and BH Mondays 10.30am to 4.30pm. Please note Renishaw Hall is not open to the general public. Guided Hall Tours are available for private groups of (25+) only, prior arrangement and booking essential.

Admission: £6.00 for Adults, £4.95 for Concessions. Children 12 years and under free of charge. Car Parking Fee £1.00. Season Tickets available @ £28.00. Optional information (HHA members welcome. RHS members entry to Gardens only, top-up tickets available for the exhibitions. Selected Buy-one-Get-one-Free scheme available Saturday only)

🅿️ 🍴 ☕ ♿ 🍴 By arrangement. 🅿️ 🐕 In grounds, on leads. 🅰️

♿ Bluebell Fortnight open daily for the limited period 22nd April to 9th May, 2010.

SUTTON SCARSDALE HALL

Chesterfield, Derbyshire
Tel: 01604 735400 (Regional Office) **E-mail:** customers@english-heritage.org.uk
www.english-heritage.org.uk/suttonscarsdale
Owner: English Heritage **Contact:** East Midlands Regional Office
The dramatic hilltop shell of a great early 18th century baroque mansion.
Location: MAP 7:A2, OS Ref. SK441 690. Between Chesterfield & Bolsover, 1½m S of Arkwright Town.
Open: Summer: daily, 10am–6pm; rest of year: daily, 10am–4pm. Closed 24–26 Dec & 1 Jan.
Admission: Free. Opening times and prices are valid until 31st March 2010, after this date details are subject to change please see www.english-heritage.org.uk for the most up-to-date information.
ℹ Picnickers welcome. 🚻 🅿 ❋

The Nursery at Eyam Hall

TISSINGTON HALL 🏛
ASHBOURNE, DERBYSHIRE DE6 1RA
www.tissingtonhall.co.uk

Tel: 01335 352200 **E-mail:** events@tissingtonhall.co.uk
Owner: Sir Richard FitzHerbert Bt **Contact:** Isobel James
Home of the FitzHerbert family for over 500 years. The Hall stands in a superbly maintained estate village, and contains wonderful panelling and fine old masters. A 10 acre garden and arboretum. Schools very welcome. Award-winning Old Coach House Tearoom, open Apr–Oct daily; Nov–Mar, Thurs–Sun, 11am–5pm for coffees, lunch and tea. Annual Well Dressings 2010: 13–19 May. Civil Weddings, Wedding Receptions, Private Hire.

Location: MAP 6:P3, OS Ref. SK175 524. 4m N of Ashbourne off A515 towards Buxton.
Open: Easter Week: Mon 5 Apr–Fri 9 Apr inc. Thur–Sun, 13–16 May 2010. Half-Term Week: Mon 31 May–Fri 4 Jun. 27 Jul–27 Aug, Tue–Fri inc. BH Mon 30 Aug.
Admission: Hall & Gardens: Adult £7.50, Child (10–16yrs) £4, Conc. £6.50. Gardens only: Adult £3.50, Child £1, Conc. £3.50.
Group visits very welcome throughout the year. Please apply.
ℹ No photography in house. 🖥 🎦 🍴 🚻 Partial. WCs at tearooms. 🍵 Tearoom adjacent to Hall. 🍽 ✗ Obligatory. 🅿 Limited. 🚌 🐕 Guide dogs only. 🏠 ❋ 🛏

Tissington Hall

■ Owner

Their Graces The Duke & Duchess of Rutland

■ Contact

Mary McKinlay
Castle Opening Office
Belvoir Castle
Grantham
Leicestershire NG32 1PE

Tel: 01476 871004
Fax: 01476 870443
E-mail: info@
belvoircastle.com

■ Location

MAP 7:C4
OS Ref. SK820 337

A1 from London 110m
Grantham Junction
York 100m. Leicester 30m
Grantham 7m.
Nottingham 20m.

Air: East Midlands &
Robin Hood Airports.
Helicopter Landing Pad.

Rail: Grantham Stn 7m

Bus: Melton Mowbray –
Vale of Belvoir via
Castle Car Park.

Taxi: Grantham Taxis
01476 563944 / 563988.

■ Opening Times

Castle:
Sun 14 Mar, 2–5 Apr, 2/3
30/31 May, Sun–Thur
Aug, 1–12 Dec
excluding 4 & 11

Gardens
14 Mar–3 Oct

■ Admission

Castle and Gardens
Adult	£10.00
Child (5–16yrs)	£6.00
Conc.	£9.00
Family (2+3)	£28.00

Gardens only
Adult	£5.00
Child (5–16yrs)	£3.00
Conc.	£4.00
Family (2+3)	£15.00

Groups
Adult	£9.00
Conc.	£8.00
Schools	£5.00

SEASON TICKETS
Castle and Gardens
Adult	£20.00
Child (5–16yrs)	£12.00
Conc.	£18.00
Family (2+3)	£56.00

Gardens only
Adult	£10.00
Child (5–16yrs)	£6.00
Conc.	£8.00
Family (2+3)	£30.00

Conference/Function

ROOM	SIZE	MAX CAPACITY
State Dining Room	52' x 31'	130
Old Kitchen	45' x 22'	100
Ballroom		90
Guards Room		175
Stewards Restaurant		100

BELVOIR CASTLE

www.belvoircastle.com

Belvoir Castle, home of the Duke and Duchess of Rutland, commands a magnificent view over the Vale of Belvoir. The name Belvoir, meaning beautiful view, dates back to Norman times, when Robert de Todeni, Standard Bearer to William the Conqueror, built the first castle on this superb site. Destruction caused by two Civil Wars and by a catastrophic fire in 1816 have breached the continuity of Belvoir's history. The present building owes much to the inspiration and taste of Elizabeth, 5th Duchess of Rutland and was built after the fire.

Inside the Castle are notable art treasures including works by Poussin, Holbein, Rubens, and Reynolds, Gobelin and Mortlake tapestries, Chinese silks, furniture, fine porcelain and sculpture.

Gardens

A remarkable survival of English garden history that are being sensitively restored to their former glory. The Duchess's Garden, opened to all day visitors in 2005, contain a collection of Victorian daffodils planted sympathetically with primroses and bluebells, against a background of rhododendrons and azaleas. There are also rare specimen trees, many the largest of their type in the British Isles.

Belvoir Castle is available for exclusive hire as a film location and for conferences, weddings and special events. It is also possible to put on events in conjunction with the open season.

- **i** Suitable for exhibitions, product launches, conferences, filming, photography welcomed (permit £2). Guide books £5.
- Banquets, private room available.
- Ground floor and restaurant accessible. Please telephone for advice. WC.
- Licensed. Groups catered for (100 max).
- Tue–Thur, twice daily. Tour time: 1¼ hrs. Specialist picture and costume tours.
- **P** Ample. Coaches can take passengers to entrance by arrangement but should report to the main car park and ticket office on arrival.
- Guided tours. Teacher's pack. Education room. Picnic area and adventure playground.
- Guide dogs only.
- Belvoir Castle is a day out for all the family and hosts different events every weekend from jousting to medieval re-enactments. Tel for details.

STANFORD HALL 🏛

www.stanfordhall.co.uk

Stanford has been the home of the Cave family, ancestors of the present owner, since 1430. In the 1690s, Sir Roger Cave commissioned the Smiths of Warwick to pull down the old Manor House and build the present Hall, which is an excellent example of their work and of the William and Mary period.

As well as over 5000 books, the handsome Library contains many interesting manuscripts, the oldest dating from 1150. The splendid pink and gold Ballroom has a fine coved ceiling with four *trompe l'oeil* shell corners. Throughout the house are portraits of the family and examples of furniture and objects which they collected over the

centuries. There is also a collection of Royal Stuart portraits, previously belonging to the Cardinal Duke of York, the last of the male Royal Stuarts. An unusual collection of family costumes is displayed in the Old Dining Room, which also houses some early Tudor portraits and a fine Empire chandelier.

The Hall and Stables are set in an attractive Park on the banks of Shakespeare's Avon. There is a walled Rose Garden behind the Stables. An early ha-ha separates the North Lawn from the mile-long North Avenue.

Owner
Mr & Mrs N Fothergill

Contact
Sarah Maughan
Stanford Hall
Lutterworth
Leicestershire
LE17 6DH

Tel: 01788 860250
Fax: 01788 860870
E-mail: s.maughan@
stanfordhall.co.uk

Location
MAP 7:B7
OS Ref. SP587 793

M1/J18 6m,M1/J19
(from/to the N only) 2m,
M6 exit/access at
A14/M1(N)J 2m, A14 2m.
Follow Historic
House signs.

Rail: Rugby Stn 7½ m.

Air: Birmingham
Airport 27m.

Taxi: Georges Taxi's
01455 559000.

Opening Times
Special two week easter
opening- Sunday
4 April to Sunday 18 April
2010. Also open
on selected days in
conjunction with park
events.
Please see our website or
telephone for details.

House open any day or
evening (except Saturdays)
for pre-booked groups.

Admission
House & Grounds
Adult	£6.00
Child (5–15yrs)	£2.50

Private Group Tours (20+)
Adult	£6.50
Child (5–15yrs)	£2.50

Grounds only
Adult	£3.50
Child (5–15yrs)	£1.50

ℹ️ Craft centre (most Suns). Corporate days, clay pigeon shoots, filming, photography, small conferences. Parkland, helicopter landing area, lecture room, Blüthner piano. Caravan site.

🛍

🍷 Lunches, dinners & wedding receptions.

♿ Visitors may alight at the entrance. WC.

🍽 Teas, lunch & supper. Groups must book (70 max.)

🚶 Tour time: ¾ hr in groups of approx 25.

🅿️ 1,000 cars and 6–8 coaches. Free meals for coach drivers, coach parking on gravel in front of house.

🐕 In Park, on leads.

🏨 Accomodation available.

🎭 Concerts/Theatre in the Ballroom or Park.

Conference/Function

ROOM	SIZE	MAX CAPACITY
Ballroom	39' x 26'	100
Old Dining Rm	30' x 20'	20
Crocodile Room	39' x 20'	60

ASHBY DE LA ZOUCH CASTLE ⌗

South Street, Ashby de la Zouch, Leicestershire LE65 1BR
Tel: 01530 413343   **E-mail:** customers@english-heritage.org.uk
www.english-heritage.org.uk/ashbydelazouch
Owner: English Heritage   **Contact:** Visitor Operations Team
The impressive ruins of this late medieval castle are dominated by a magnificent tower, over 80 feet high, which was split in two during the Civil War. Panoramic views. Explore the tunnel linking the kitchens to the Hastings Tower. New interpretation and audio tour.
Location: MAP 7:A7, OS128, SK363 167. In Ashby de la Zouch, 12m S of Derby on A511. SE of town centre.
Open: 1 Apr–30 Jun: Thu–Mon, 10am–5pm. 1 Jul–31 Aug: daily, 10am–5pm. 1 Sep–1 Nov: Thu–Mon, 10am–5pm. 2 Nov–31 Mar '10: Thur–Mon, 10am–4pm. Closed 24–26 Dec & 1 Jan.
Admission: Adult £3.90, Child £2, Conc. £3.30, Family £9.30. 15% discount for groups (11+). EH Members free. Opening times and prices are subject to change; please check the English Heritage website for up-to-date information.
ℹ Picnickers welcome. WC. ◻ ♿ Grounds. ⊙ Free with admission. 🅿 Restricted. 🐕 On leads. ❋ ♥

BELVOIR CASTLE 🏰

See page 274 for full page entry.

BRADGATE PARK & SWITHLAND WOOD COUNTRY PARK

Bradgate Park, Newtown Linford, Leics LE6 0HE
Tel: 0116 2362713
Owner: Bradgate Park Trust   **Contact:** M H Harrison
Includes the ruins of the brick medieval home of the Grey family and childhood home of Lady Jane Grey. Also has a medieval deer park.
Location: MAP 7:B6, OS Ref. SK534 102. 7m NW of Leicester, via Anstey & Newtown Linford. Country Park gates in Newtown Linford. 1¼ m walk to the ruins.
Open: All year during daylight hours.
Admission: No charge. Car parking charges.

DONINGTON-LE-HEATH MANOR HOUSE

Manor Road, Donington-le-Heath, Leicestershire LE67 2FW
Tel: 01530 831259 / 0116 2658326
Owner/Contact: Leicestershire County Council
Medieval manor c1280 with 16th–17th century alterations.
Location: MAP 7:A6, OS Ref. SK421 126. ½ m SSW of Coalville. 4½ m W of M1/J22, by A511.
Open: Mar–Nov: daily, 11am–4pm. Dec–Feb: Sat & Sun only, 11am–4pm. (Plus occasional weekdays. Tel for details.)
Admission: Free.

KIRBY MUXLOE CASTLE ⌗

Kirby Muxloe, Leicestershire LE9 2DH
Tel: 01162 386886   **E-mail:** customers@english-heritage.org.uk
www.english-heritage.org.uk/kirbymuxloe
Owner: English Heritage   **Contact:** Visitor Operations Team
Picturesque, moated, brick built castle begun in 1480 by William Lord Hastings. Recently reopened after extensive conservation work.
Location: MAP 7:B6, OS140, SK524 046. 4m W of Leicester off B5380.
Open: 1 May–31 Aug: Sat, Sun & BHs, 10am–5pm.
Admission: Adult £3, Child £1.50, Conc. £2.60. EH Members free. Group discount available. Opening times and prices are valid until 31st March 2010, after this date details are subject to change please see www.english-heritage.org.uk for the most up-to-date information.
ℹ Picnickers welcome. 🅿

LYDDINGTON BEDE HOUSE ⌗

Blue Coat Lane, Lyddington, Uppingham, Rutland LE15 9LZ
Tel: 01572 822438   **E-mail:** customers@english-heritage.org.uk
www.english-heritage.org.uk/lyddington
Owner: English Heritage   **Contact:** Visitor Operations Team
Located in this picturesque 'Cotswold' village of honey coloured stone cottages and public houses lies the splendid former 'palace' of the powerful medieval Bishops of Lincoln. In the 1600s the building was converted into an almshouse.
Location: MAP 7:D6, OS141, SP875 970. In Lyddington, 6m N of Corby, 1m E of A6003.
Open: 1 Apr–1 Nov: Thu–Mon, 10am–5pm.
Admission: Adult £3.90, Child £2, Conc. £3.30, Family £9.30. 15% group discount (11+). EH Members free. Opening times and prices are valid until 31st March 2010, after this date details are subject to change please see www.english-heritage.org.uk for the most up-to-date information.
ℹ Picnickers welcome. ◻ ♿ Ground floor only.

STANFORD HALL 🏰

See page 275 for full page entry.

STAUNTON HAROLD CHURCH 🍂

Staunton Harold Church, Ashby-de-la-Zouch, Leicestershire, LE65 1RW
Tel: 01332 863822   **Fax:** 01332 865272   **E-mail:** calkeabbey@nationaltrust.org.uk
www.nationaltrust.org.uk
Owner: The National Trust   **Contact:** Calke Abbey
One of the very few churches to be built during the Commonwealth, erected by Sir Robert Shirley, an ardent Royalist. The interior retains its original 17th century cushions and hangings and includes fine panelling and painted ceilings.
Location: MAP 7:A5, OS Ref. SK379 208. 5m NE of Ashby-de-la-Zouch, W of B587.
Open: 3 Apr–31 Oct, Sat & Sun, 2 Jun–27 Aug, Wed–Sun, 1–4.30pm.
Admission: £1 donation.
♿ ♥ ✍ By arrangement.

Belvoir Castle

©NTPL / Andrew Butler

BELTON HOUSE 🌿

www.nationaltrust.org.uk

The perfect English Country house, set in its own extensive deer park, Belton was designed to impress. Built in the late 17th century by 'Young' Sir John Brownlow, with family fortunes founded in law, it is one of the finest examples of Restoration architecture and was, for centuries, the scene of lavish hospitality. Opulent décor, stunning silverware, wonderful woodcarvings, imposing paintings – including many old masters – and personal mementos convey wealth, but also a family atmosphere. The Brownlow family had many Royal connections and Edward VIII was a frequent visitor before his abdication. Open Basements (11am – 12 noon during main season) provide a fascinating glimpse into life below stairs at a large country house.

Belton House featured in the BBC's adaptation of 'Pride and Prejudice' with Colin Firth and Jennifer Erhle, whilst the sundial, featuring the figure of Time, by Cibber, inspired 'The Moondial' Helen Cresswell's children's book and the subsequent BBC series of the same name.

Delightful gardens, luxuriantly planted Orangery and lakeside walks are a pleasure to explore all year round. Snowdrops, daffodils and bluebells provide a succession of springtime colour in the informal woodland gardens. Lavender, roses and sweetpeas give wonderful fragrance through the summer months. Deep red 'Bishop of Llandaff' dahlias add rich autumn colour. The newly restored boathouse on the lakeshore is a testament to traditional craftsmanship and a delightful feature in this tranquil location.

The Stables Restaurant (self service) features local produce including our award-winning Belton venison, reared on the estate, in season. A wide range of souvenirs can be found in the well-stocked Gift Shop whilst the Plant & Garden Shop provides year-round inspiration.

For families, we have the largest Children's Adventure Playground in Lincolnshire and the 'Moondial Express' miniature train. The Discovery Centre in the Estate Yard offers a variety of hands on activities at weekends. (Both open March – Oct).

Belton's varied events programme includes Theatre in the Garden, Easter and Halloween Trails, Garden Tours, costumed talks and special exhibitions. Please tel 01476 566116 for details.

Fine church (not NT) with many family monuments.

© NT / Rika Gordon

i Adventure playground opens 6 March 2010

& Partial. Please telephone for arrangements.

¶ Licensed.

P

♦ Civil Wedding Licence.

■ Owner
The National Trust

■ Contact
The Administrator/The Visitor Services Manager
Grantham
Lincolnshire NG32 2LS

Tel: 01476 566116
Fax: 01476 542980
E-mail: belton@ nationaltrust.org.uk

■ Location
MAP 7:D4
OS Ref. SK929 395

3m NE of Grantham on A607, Signed off the A1.

■ Opening Times
House
1–14 March:
Sat–Sun, 12.30–4pm;
15 Mar–31 Oct,
Wed–Sun, 11–5pm
(Last entry 30 mins before closing).
Basement only 11–12 noon (days as house).
Open BH Mons.

Garden, Park, Restaurant & Shop:
6–28 Feb: Sat–Sun, 12 noon–4pm; 1 Mar–31 Oct Wed–Sun, 11–5.30pm; 5 July–5 Sept: daily, 10.30am–5.30pm; 1 Nov–19 Dec, Fri–Sun, 12noon–4pm.

■ *Admission

Adult	£10.50
Child	£6.25
Family	£27.50

Garden, Park & Playground:
Adult	£8.50
Child	£4.75
Family	£21.50

Garden & Park (Winter):
Adult	£3.50
Child	£2.00

*Includes a voluntary Gift Aid donation but visitors can choose to pay the standard prices displayed at the property and on the website.

■ **Owner**

Burghley House
Preservation Trust Ltd

■ **Contact**

The House Manager
Burghley House
Stamford
Lincolnshire PE9 3JY

Tel: 01780 752451
Fax: 01780 480125
E-mail: burghley@
burghley.co.uk

■ **Location**

MAP 7:E7
OS Ref. TF048 062

Burghley House
is 1m SE of Stamford.
From London, A1 2hrs.

Visitors entrance
is on B1443.

Rail: London –
Peterborough 1hr (GNER).
Stamford Station
1½m, regular service to
Peterborough.

Taxi: Direct Line:
01780 481481.

■ **Opening Times**

Summer
House & Gardens
20 March–31 October
(closed 2–5 September):
Daily (Gardens only on
Fridays), 11am–5pm,
(last admission 4.30pm).

Winter
Orangery Restaurant &
Gift Shop only
3 February–20 March
Wed–Sun, 11am–4pm.

South Gardens
April: Daily (except
Fridays), 11am–4pm.

Park
All year. Admission is free
except on event days.

■ **Admission**

House & Gardens
Adult   £11.80
Child (5–15yrs)   £5.80
Conc.   £10.40
Family   £30.00

Groups (20+)
Adult   £10.00
School (up to 14yrs) £5.80

Gardens of Surprise only
Adult   £6.70
Child (5–15yrs)   £3.40
Conc.   £5.60
Family   £17.60

We are a charitable trust,
by paying an extra 10%
we can claim back the
tax paid on this and use
it for the benefit of the
house and collections.

■ **Conference/Function**

ROOM	SIZE	MAX CAPACITY
Great Hall	70' x 30'	150
Orangery	100' x 20'	120

BURGHLEY HOUSE 🏛

www.burghley.co.uk

Burghley House, home of the Cecil family for over 400 years, was built as a country seat during the latter part of the 16th century by Sir William Cecil, later Lord Burghley, principal adviser and Lord Treasurer to Queen Elizabeth.

The House was completed in 1587 and there have been few alterations to the architecture since that date thus making Burghley one of the finest examples of late Elizabethan design in England. The interior was remodelled in the late 17th century by John, 5th Earl of Exeter who was a collector of fine art on a huge scale, establishing the immense collection of art treasures at Burghley. Burghley is truly a 'Treasure House', containing one of the largest private collections of Italian art, unique examples of Chinese and Japanese porcelain and superb items of 18th century furniture. The remodelling work of the 17th century means that examples of the work of the principal artists

and craftsmen of the period are to be found at Burghley: Antonio Verrio, Grinling Gibbons and Louis Laguerre all made major contributions to the beautiful interiors.

Park and Gardens

The house is set in a 300-acre deer park landscaped by 'Capability' Brown. A lake was created by him and delightful avenues of mature trees feature largely in his design. The park is home to a large herd of Fallow deer, established in the 16th century. Opened in 2007, the Gardens of Surprise incorporates the existing Contemporary Sculpture Garden, containing many specimen trees and shrubs, and the new Elizabethan Garden, over an acre of yew mazes, revolving Caesars' heads and spurting fountains. The private gardens around the house are open in April for the display of spring bulbs.

ⓘ Suitable for a variety of events, large park, golf course, helicopter landing area, cricket pitch. No photography in house.

♿ Visitors may alight at entrance. WC. Chair lift to Orangery Restaurant, house tour has two staircases one with chairlift.

☕ Restaurant/tearoom. Groups can book in advance.

🍴

🚶 Available.

🅿 Ample. Free refreshments for coach drivers.

Welcome. Guide provided.

🐕 No dogs in house. In park on leads.

🔔 Civil Wedding Licence.

🎭

©Country Life Picture Library

■ Contact

Ray Biggs
Grimsthorpe Estate Office
Grimsthorpe
Bourne, Lincolnshire
PE10 0LY

Tel: 01778 591205
Fax: 01778 591259
E-mail: ray@
grimsthorpe.co.uk

■ Location

MAP 7:D5
OS Ref. TF040 230

4m NW of Bourne on A151, 8m E of Colsterworth Junction of A1.

■ Opening Times

Castle
April & May: Suns, Thurs & BH Mons.

June–September:
Sun–Thur.
1–4.30pm.

Park & Gardens
As Castle,
11am–6pm.

Groups: Apr–Sept: by arrangement.

■ Admission

Castle, Park & Garden
Adult	£10.00
Child	£4.00
Conc.	£9.00
Family (2+3)	£24.00

Park & Gardens
Adult	£5.00
Child	£2.00
Conc.	£4.00
Family (2+3)	£12.00

Special charges may be made for special events. Group rates on application.

GRIMSTHORPE CASTLE, 🏛 PARK & GARDENS

www.grimsthorpe.co.uk

Home of the Willoughby de Eresby family since 1516. Examples of 13th century architecture and building styles from the Tudor period. The dramatic 18th century North Front is Sir John Vanbrugh's last major work. State Rooms and picture galleries with magnificent contents including tapestries, furniture and paintings. Unusual collection of thrones, fabrics and objects from the old House of Lords, associated with the family's hereditary Office of Lord Great Chamberlain.

The Grounds and Gardens

3,000 acre landscaped park with lakes, ancient woods, woodland walk with all-weather footpath, adventure playground. Family cycle trail and cycle hire shop. Park tours in a vehicle with the Ranger.

Unusual ornamental vegetable garden and orchard, created in the 1960s by the Countess of Ancaster and John Fowler. Intricate parterres lined with box hedges. Herbaceous border with yew topiary framing views across to the lake. Woodland garden.

Groups can explore the park from the comfort of their own coach by booking a one-hour, escorted park tour, with opportunities to discover more about the site of the Cistercian Abbey, the ancient deer parks, historic woodland and extensive series of early tree-lined avenues. Special study days can be booked including 'How Grimsthorpe Works in the 21st Century', 'Hidden History' guided walking visits to the park and 'Garden Evolution' days. See website for full programme details.

©Country Life Picture Library

i	No photography in house.
🛍	
🍽	Conferences (up to 40), inc catering.
♿	Partial. WC.
🍷	Licensed.
👤	Obligatory except Suns.
P	Ample.
▥	
🐕	In grounds, on leads.
🎭	

AUBOURN HALL
LINCOLN LN5 9DZ

Tel: 01522 788224   **Fax:** 01522 788199   **E-mail:** estate.office@aubournhall.co.uk
Owner: Mr & Mrs Christopher Nevile   **Contact:** Ginny Lovell
Early 17th century house by John Smythson. Important staircase and panelled rooms. 10 acre garden.
Location: MAP 7:D3, OS Ref. SK928 628. 6m SW of Lincoln. 2m SE of A46.
Open: Garden: Open for Events, Groups and Garden visits. Please contact the property for details.
Admission: Please contact property for details.

BELTON HOUSE    *See page 277 for full page entry.*

BURGHLEY HOUSE   *See page 278 for full page entry.*

Burghley House, Queen Elizabeth's Bedroom

AYSCOUGHFEE HALL MUSEUM & GARDENS
CHURCHGATE, SPALDING, LINCOLNSHIRE PE11 2RA
www.ayscoughfee.org

Tel: 01775 764555   **E-mail:** museum@sholland.gov.uk
Owner: South Holland District Council   **Contact:** Museum Manager
Ayscoughfee Hall, a magnificent Grade II* listed building, was built in the 1450s. The Hall is set in extensive landscaped grounds which include, amongst other impressive features, a memorial designed by Edwin Lutyens. The building and gardens combined reflect the splendour of the Medieval, Georgian and Victorian ages.
The Hall has been fully restored and a number of important and rare features uncovered. The Museum explains the history of the Hall, and features the lives of the people who lived there and in the surrounding Fens.
Location: MAP 7:F5, OS Ref. TF249 223. E bank of the River Welland, 5 mins walk from Spalding town centre.
Open: 10.30am–4pm Wednesday to Sunday throughout the year (we are also open on Bank Holiday Mondays).
Admission: Free.
WCs. Guide dogs only.

© Heritage House Group

DODDINGTON HALL & GARDENS 🏛

LINCOLN LN6 4RU

www.doddingtonhall.com

Tel: 01522 694308 **Fax:** 01522 687213 **E-mail:** info@doddingtonhall.com
Owner: Mr & Mrs J J C Birch   **Contact:** The Estate Office

Romantic Smythson mansion which stands today as it was built in 1595 with its mellow walled gardens and gatehouse. Never sold since it was built, Doddington is still very much a family home and its contents reflect over 400 years of unbroken family occupation. There is an elegant Georgian interior with fine collections of porcelain, paintings and textiles. The five acres of beautiful gardens contain a superb layout of box-edged parterres filled with bearded Iris in midsummer, sumptuous borders that provide colour in all seasons, and a wild garden with a marvellous succession of spring bulbs and flowering shrubs set amongst mature trees. Exclusive private group visits with guided tours a speciality. Please call the Estate Office to discuss your requirements. Award winning facilities for disabled visitors, include sensory tours of house and gardens for the Visually Impaired; free use of electric buggy and panaoramic tour of upper floors – please call for details. Free audioguides and children's activity trail. Civil weddings and receptions at Doddington Hall and in The Littlehouse next door. Newly resurrected working walled Kitchen Garden.

Farm shop with kitchen garden and local produce plus café serving delicious, seasonal and freshly cooked teas and lunches. Open Tue–Sun, reservations advisable for lunch.

Location: MAP 7:D2, OS Ref. SK900 710. 5m W of Lincoln on the B1190, signposted off the A46.

Open: Gardens only: 14 Feb–28 Mar & throughout Oct: Suns only 11am–4pm. House & Gardens: 4 Apr (Easter Day)–29 Sep, every Wed, Sun & BH Mon 1pm–5pm (gardens open 11am). Last admission 4.30pm (Guided party tours of both House & Gardens welcome at other times by prior arrangement).

Admission: House & Gardens: Adult £8.50, Child £4.25, Family £22 (2+4, U4 free). House & Gardens Season Ticket £25 (single adult); £40 (2 adults), £45 (2+4). Group visits (20 or more): (Guided tours) private tour of House + free wander in Gardens, £8.50pp; private garden tour with Head Gardener, £7.25pp; private House + garden tour, £14.50pp. Groups (20 or more): (Self-guided tours) Gardens, £4.50pp, House + Gardens £7pp.

ℹ No photography in Hall. No stilettos. ◻ ☂ ♿ Gardens & ground floor. WC. ☞
🍴 In farm shop & café. Groups must book. 🅺 By arrangement. 📷 Free.
🅿 ♨ ♿ Guide dogs only. 🕮 1 Aug-1 Sept, Weds, Sun & BH Mon, 1-5pm, Exhibition of Wedding Dresses.

© Fred Cholmeley

EASTON WALLED GARDENS

THE GARDENS OFFICE, EASTON, GRANTHAM, LINCOLNSHIRE NG33 5AP

www.eastonwalledgardens.co.uk

Tel: 01476 530063 **Fax:** 01476 530063 **E-mail:** info@eastonwalledgardens.co.uk
Owner: Sir Fred & Lady Cholmeley   **Contact:** Landy Hosli

President Franklin Roosevelt described these award winning gardens as a *'Dream of Nirvana … almost too good to be true'*. 50 years later, the house was pulled down and the gardens abandoned. 100 years later see the ongoing revival of these magnificent gardens. Funded privately and with the support of visitors, this garden experience is like no other. Alongside the recovery of these 400 year old gardens are: fantastic snowdrops, David Austin Roses, Daffodil, Iris and Sweet Pea Collections, a cut flower garden, cottage vegetable garden and meadows. Teas and light lunches are served overlooking the garden. Groups can book out of hours if wished.

Location: MAP 7:D5, OS Ref. SK938 274. 1m from A1 (between Stamford and Grantham) North of Colsterworth, onto B6403 and follow signs.

Open: 13–21 Feb for snowdrops: 11am–4pm; Wed, Thurs, Fri, Suns & BH Mons. Mar–Oct Suns in Nov for Xmas shopping. Plant Fair 2–3 May. Sweet Pea Week 27 Jun–4 Jul: daily 11am–4pm. For other events and extended opening times please see our website.

Admission: Adult £5, Child £1.

◻ ⚑ ☂ ♿ Partial. WCs. ☞ 🅺 By arrangement. 🅿 ♿ Guide dogs only. 🕮

FULBECK MANOR

Fulbeck, Grantham, Lincolnshire NG32 3JN
Tel: 01400 272231 **Fax:** 01400 273545 **E-mail:** fane@fulbeck.co.uk
Owner/Contact: Mr Julian Francis Fane

Built c1580. 400 years of Fane family portraits. Open by written appointment. Guided tours by owner approximately 1¼ hours. Tearooms at Craft Centre, 100 yards, for light lunches and teas.

Location: MAP 7:D3, OS Ref. SK947 505. 11m N of Grantham. 15m S of Lincoln on A607. Brown signs to Craft Centre & Tearooms and Stables.

Open: By written appointment.

Admission: Adult £6. Groups (10+) £5.

ℹ No photography. ♿ Partial. WCs. ☞ 🍴 🅺 Obligatory. 🅿 Ample for cars. Limited for coaches. ♨ Guide dogs only. ❀

GAINSBOROUGH OLD HALL ⌗

Parnell Street, Gainsborough, Lincolnshire DN21 2NB
Tel: 01427 612669 **E-mail:** customers@english-heritage.org.uk
www.english-heritage.org.uk/gainsborough
Owner: English Heritage   **Contact:** Lincolnshire County Council

A large medieval manor house with a magnificent Great Hall and suites of rooms. A collection of historic furniture and a re-created medieval kitchen are on display.

Location: MAP 7:C1, OS121, SK815 895. In centre of Gainsborough, opposite library.

Open: 1 Apr–1 Nov: Mon–Sat, 10am–4pm; Sun, 1–4pm. 2 Nov–31 Mar '10: Mon–Sat, 10am–4pm. Closed 24–26 & 31 Dec & 1 Jan. Times and prices may vary, please call to check.

Admission: Adult £3.80, Child (5–15yrs) £2.60, Child under 5yrs Free, Conc. £2.60, Family (2+3) £10. Small charge to special events for EH Members. Discount for groups of 30 or more. Opening times and prices are valid until 31st March 2010, after this date details are subject to change please see www.english-heritage.org.uk for the most up-to-date information.

ℹ Picnickers welcome. WC. ♿ ☞ 📷 ❀

GRIMSTHORPE CASTLE, 🏛 PARK & GARDENS

See page 279 for full page entry.

LINCOLNSHIRE

LEADENHAM HOUSE

Leadenham House, Lincolnshire LN5 0PU
Tel: 01400 273256 **Fax:** 01400 272237
Owner: Mr P Reeve **Contact:** Mr and Mrs P Reeve
Late eighteenth century house in park setting.
Location: MAP 7:D3, OS Ref. SK949 518. Entrance on A17 Leadenham bypass (between Newark and Sleaford).
Open: 19–23 Apr, 4–7, 10–14, 17–21, 24–28 May, 20&21 Sept & Spring & Aug BHs. All 2–5pm.
Admission: £4.00. Please ring door bell. Groups by prior arrangement only.
ⓘ No photography. 🔲 🆃 Obligatory. 🅿 Limited for cars & coaches 🦮 Guide dogs only.

LINCOLN CATHEDRAL

Lincoln LN2 1PZ
Tel: 01522 561600 **Fax:** 01522 561634 **Contact:** Communications Office
One of the finest medieval buildings in Europe.
Location: MAP 7:D2, OS Ref. SK978 718. At the centre of Uphill, Lincoln.
Open: All year: Jun–Aug, 7.15am–8pm. Winter, 7.15am–6pm. Sun closing 6pm in Summer & 5pm in Winter. Tours of the floor, roof & tower available. Pre-booked groups welcome.
Admission: £4, Child (5–16yrs) £1, Child (under 5s) Free, Conc. £3, Family £10. Optional guided tours & photography Free. Audio guide £1. No charge on Sun or for services.

LINCOLN MEDIEVAL BISHOPS' PALACE ♯

Minster Yard, Lincoln LN2 1PU
Tel/Fax: 01522 527468 **E-mail:** customers@english-heritage.org.uk
www.english-heritage.org.uk/lincoln
Owner: English Heritage **Contact:** Visitor Operations Team
Constructed in the late 12th century, the medieval bishops' palace was once one of the most important buildings in England. Built on hillside terraces, it has views of the cathedral and the Roman, medieval and modern city. See a virtual tour of the Palace and explore the grounds.
Location: MAP 7:D2, OS121 Ref. SK981 717. S side of Lincoln Cathedral, in Lincoln.
Open: 1 Apr–1 Nov: daily, 10am–5pm. 2 Nov–31 Mar '10: Thu–Mon, 10am–4pm. Closed 24–26 Dec & 1 Jan. Open daily for Lincoln Christmas Market.
Admission: Adult £4, Child £2, Conc. £3.40, Family £10. 15% discount for groups (11+). EH Members free. Opening times and prices are valid until 31st March 2010, after this date details are subject to change please see www.english-heritage.org.uk for the most up-to-date information.
ⓘ Picnickers welcome. 📷 🎧 🦮 ✳ ♿

MARSTON HALL

Marston, Grantham NG32 2HQ
Tel/Fax: 07812 356237 **E-mail:** johnthorold@aol.com
Owner/Contact: J R Thorold
The ancient home of the Thorold family. The building contains Norman, Plantaganet, Tudor and Georgian elements through to the modern day. Marston Hall is undergoing continuous restoration some of it which may be disruptive. Please telephone in advance of intended visits.
Location: MAP 7:D4, OS Ref. SK893 437. 5m N of Grantham and about 1m E of A1.
Open: 27, 28 Feb, 1, 2, Mar, 24, 27 Apr, 3, 31 May, 10, 19 Jul, 27-30 Aug, 11, 14 Sept & 2–5 Oct: 1–6pm.
Admission: Adult £3.50, Child £1.50. Groups must book.
ⓘ No photography.

SIBSEY TRADER WINDMILL

Sibsey, Boston, Lincolnshire PE22 0SY
Tel: 07718 320449 **E-mail:** customers@english-heritage.org.uk
www.english-heritage.org.uk/sibseytrader
Owner: English Heritage **Contact:** Ian Ansell
An impressive old mill built in 1877, with its machinery and six sails still intact. Flour milled on the spot can be bought here. The award-winning tearoom sells produce made from the Mill's organic stoneground flour.
Location: MAP 7:F3, OS Ref. TF345 511. ½m W of village of Sibsey, off A16, 5m N of Boston.
Open: 1 Mar–30 Apr: Sat & BHs, 10am–6pm; Sun, 11am–6pm. 1 May–30 Sept: Sat & BHs, 10am–6pm; Sun & Tue 11am–6pm. 1 Oct–1 Nov: Sat & BHs, 10am–6pm; Sun, 11am–6pm. 2 Nov–28 Feb '10: Sat, 11am–5pm (Mill only). 1–31 Mar: Sat & BHs, 10am–6pm; Sun, 11am–6pm. Closed 25 Dec–1 Jan.
Admission: Adult £2, Child £1 (under 5yrs Free), Conc. £1.50. Members OUP Free. EH Members free. Opening times and prices are valid until 31st March 2010, after this date details are subject to change please see www.english-heritage.org.uk for the most up-to-date information.
ⓘ Picnickers welcome. WC. 🔲 Exterior only. 📷 🅿 🦮

© Ray Biggs

Grimsthorpe Castle, Park & Gardens

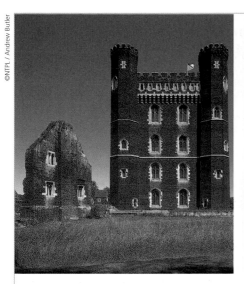

TATTERSHALL CASTLE 🌺
SLEAFORD ROAD, TATTERSHALL, LINCOLNSHIRE LN4 4LR
www.nationaltrust.org.uk/tattershall

Tel: 01526 342543   **E-mail:** tattershallcastle@nationaltrust.org.uk

Owner: The National Trust   **Contact:** The Property Manager

A vast fortified tower built c1440 for Ralph Cromwell, Lord Treasurer of England. The Castle is an important example of an early brick building, with a tower containing state apartments, rescued from dereliction and restored by Lord Curzon 1911–14. Four great chambers, with ancillary rooms, contain late gothic fireplaces and brick vaulting. There are tapestries and information displays in turret rooms.

Location: MAP 7:E3, OS122 Ref. TF209 575. On S side of A153, 12m NE of Sleaford, 10m SW of Horncastle.

Open: 13 Feb – 14 Mar - weekends only , 11am – 4pm; 15 Mar – 31 Mar, Open 5 days a week, 11am - 4pm, closed Thurs & Fri; 02 Apr – 29 Sept, Open 5 days a week, 11am - 5pm, closed Thurs & Fri; 02 Oct - 31 Oct, Open 5 days a week, 11am - 4pm, closed

Thurs & Fri; 06 Nov – 19 Dec - weekends only , 11am–4pm; last entry 3omin before closing; open 1pm some Sat's if hosting wedding, please ring to confirm 01526 342543

*Admission: Adult £5.30, Child £2.70, Family £13.30. Group discounts.

*includes a voluntary donation but visitors can choose to pay the standard prices displayed at the property and on the website. Property offers a host of events and activities throughout the year. Check out the website for the latest details. www.nationaltrust.org.uk/tattershall

ℹ️ Open Good Friday from 11am - 5pm. Free audio guide available up to one hr before closing. Shop serves light refreshments, hot & cold drinks and ice-creams. Family friendly. Picnic anywhere in the grounds.◻️ 🚹 Partial. WCs. 🅿️ Free. 🅿️ Limited for coaches. 🔲 🚌 Car park only. Guide dogs only in house. 🔲 ♿

WALCOT HALL
Nr Alkborough, North Lincolnshire DN15 9JT
Tel/Fax: 01724 720266   **E-mail:** WalcotHallEstate@gmail.com
www.WalcotHallEstate.com

Owner: Mr & Mrs Anthony Lane-Roberts   **Contact:** Cindy

Grade II listed Georgian hall built in 1726 with canted bays at either end and an imposing doric portico. Originally the family seat of Goulton-Constables. Set in glorious parkland in the North Lincolnshire countryside with five acres of beautifully landscaped gardens.

Location: MAP 11:D11, OS Ref. SE872 872. 15 mins SW of Humber Bridge & 15 mins N of M181. 45 mins from Robin Hood/Doncaster & Humberside international airports.

Open: Not open to the general public. Available for exclusive hire as a film location, corporate, weddings and for special events.

🍽️ 🅿️ 🔲 ♿

WOOLSTHORPE MANOR 🌺
WATER LANE, WOOLSTHORPE BY COLSTERWORTH, GRANTHAM NG33 5PD
www.nationaltrust.org.uk

Tel: 01476 860338   **Fax:** 01476 862826
E-mail: woolsthorpemanor@nationaltrust.org.uk
Owner: The National Trust   **Contact:** The Property Manager

Isaac Newton, scientist, Master of the Royal Mint and President of the Royal Society, was born in this modest 17th-century manor house in 1642 and developed his theories about light and gravity here. Visit the apple tree, explore his ideas in the brand-new Discovery Centre, see the short film.

Location: MAP 7:D5, OS130 Ref. SK924 244. 7m S of Grantham, ½ m NW of Colsterworth, 1m W of A1.

Open: House & Grounds: 19 Feb–14 Mar, 8 Oct–31 Oct, Fri–Sun, 11am–5pm; 17 Mar–3 Oct, Wed–Sun, 11am–5pm. Open BH Mons and Good Fri 11am-5pm.

*Admission: Adult £6.10, Child £3.05, Family £15.20, reduction for groups which must book in advance *includes a voluntary donation but visitors can choose to pay the standard prices displayed at the property and on the website.

Special Events: Programme of added-value events eg children's workshops, Apple Day, Summer Exhibition and short talks.

◻️ 🚹 Partial. WCs. 🔲 🎫 By arrangement. 🅿️ Limited for coaches. 🔲 🚌 Guide dogs only.

Woolsthorpe Manor

NORTHAMPTONSHIRE

■ Owner
E Brudenell Esq

■ Contact
The House Keeper
Deene Park
Corby
Northamptonshire
NN17 3EW

Tel: 01780 450278
or 01780 450223
Fax: 01780 450282
E-mail: admin@
deenepark.com

■ Location
MAP 7:D7
OS Ref. SP950 929

6m NE of Corby off A43.
From London via M1/J15
then A43, or via A1, A14,
A43 – 2 hrs.

From Birmingham via M6,
A14, A43, 90 mins.

Rail: Kettering Station
20 mins.

■ Opening Times
Summer
Open Easter Sun & Mon
Suns and BH Mons from
May to end August &
Weds 5,12,19, & 26 May
& 2 June 2–5pm

Refreshments available in
the Old Kitchen.

Open at other times by
arrangement for groups.

Winter
Open by arrangement for
groups.

Gardens only
Suns 14 & 21 Feb:
11am–4pm for
snowdrops.
Refreshments available in
the Old Kitchen.

■ Admission
Public Open Days
House & Gardens
Adult   £8.00
Child (10–14yrs)   £4.00
Conc.   £7.00

Gardens only
Adult   £5.50
Child (10–14yrs)   £2.50

Groups (20+)
by arrangement:
Weekdays   £7.00
                  (Min £140)
Weekends & BHs £8.00
                  (Min £160)

Child up to 10yrs free
with an accompanying
adult.

Conference/Function

ROOM	MAX CAPACITY
Great Hall	150
Tapestry Rm	75
East Room	18

DEENE PARK
www.deenepark.com

A most interesting house, occupied and developed by the Brudenell family since 1514, from a medieval manor around a courtyard into a Tudor and Georgian mansion. Visitors see many rooms of different periods, providing an impressive yet intimate ambience of the family home of many generations. The most flamboyant member of the family to date was the 7th Earl of Cardigan, who led the charge of the Light Brigade at Balaklava and of whom there are many historic relics and pictures on view.

Mr Edmund Brudenell, the current owner, has taken considerable care in restoring the house after the Second World War. The gardens have also been improved during the last thirty years or so, with long, mixed borders of shrubs, old-fashioned roses and flowers, together with a parterre designed by David Hicks and long walks under fine old trees by the water. The car park beside the main lake is a good place for visitors to picnic.

ⓘ Suitable for indoor and outdoor events, filming, specialist lectures on house, its contents, gardens and history. No photography in house.

🍽 Including buffets, lunches and dinners.

♿ Partial. Visitors may alight at the entrance, access to ground floor and garden. WC.

☕ Special rates for groups, bookings can be made in advance, menus on request.

🍴 By arrangement.

🚶 Tours inclusive of admittance, tour time 90 mins. Owner will meet groups if requested.

🅿 Unlimited for cars, space for 3 coaches 10 yds from house.

🐕 In car park only.

🏨 Residential conference facilities by arrangement.

❄

🎭

LAMPORT HALL & GARDENS 🏛

www.lamporthall.co.uk

Home of the Isham family from 1560 to 1976. The 17th and 18th century façade is by John Webb and the Smiths of Warwick. The Hall contains an outstanding collection of furniture, china and paintings including portraits by Van Dyck, Kneller and Lely and other important works of art, many brought back from a Grand Tour in the 17th century. The Library contains books dating back to the 16th century and the Cabinet Room houses rare Italian cabinets. The first floor includes a replicated 17th century bedchamber and a photographic record of Sir Gyles Isham, a Hollywood actor, who initiated the restoration. Refreshments are served in the Victorian dining room. The gardens owe much to the 10th Baronet who, in the mid 19th

century, created the famous rockery and populated it with the first garden gnomes. He also made a small Italian garden with a shell fountain, planted herbaceous borders and wisteria, which still thrives today. Other features include an 18th century box bower and a 17th century cockpit. The newly restored 2 acre walled garden, to be opened in 2010, now houses one of the largest cutting gardens in England and brings the total area of gardens to over 5 acres. Many of the plants used in the cutting garden were sourced from Piet Oudolf's Dutch nursery. The Lamport Hall Preservation Trust was formed in 1974 by Sir Gyles to complete the restoration work initiated by him and completed in 2007.

ℹ️ No photography in house, Available for filming.

🍽
♿ Partial. WCs.
☕ Licensed.
🍴 Licensed.
🚶 Obligatory other than Fair Days.
🅿️ Limited for coaches.
🐘
🐕 On leads.
🔔
❄️ Groups only.
🎭

■ Location
MAP 7:C8
OS Ref. SP759 745

Entrance on A508. 8m N of Northampton, 3m S of A14 J2.

Bus:
Limited Stagecoach from Northampton and Leicester.

■ Opening Times
House open for guided tours at 2.15 & 3pm Wed & Thu, from April 7th to October 7th and non guided tours on Bank Hol Suns & Mons from Easter Sunday and some event days to October 10. Private tours at other times by arrangement, minimum charge £200 for house & garden & £100 for garden only.

■ Admission
House & Garden,

Adult	£7.50
Child (11–16yrs)	£2.50
OAP	£7.00

Gardens only

Adult	£4.00
Child (11–16yrs)	£2.00
OAP	£3.50

■ Special Events

April 4/5 Easter Sunday and Monday – Antiques and Collectors Fair

May Bank Holiday Weekend 29/30/31 – Festival of Country Life

Shakespeare/jazz in the garden weekend June 26/27 & July 24/25

August 29/30 Bank Holiday Sunday and Monday Antiques and Collectors Fair

October 9/10 Autumn Gift and Craft Fair

Please see website for up-to-date list of educational courses, theatre, music and other events.

Conference/Function

ROOM	SIZE	MAX CAPACITY
Victorian Dining Room	7.5 x 9.5m	80
High Room	5.9 x 9.2m	60
Oak Room	6.1 x 8.2m	70
Complete stable yard and buildings available for fairs, exhibitions, corporate use, etc.		

East Midlands – England

■ **Owner**

James Saunders Watson

■ **Contact**

Andrew Norman
Operations Manager
Rockingham Castle
Market Harborough
Leicestershire
LE16 8TH

Tel: 01536 770240
E-mail: estateoffice@
rockinghamcastle.com

■ **Location**
MAP 7:D7
OS Ref. SP867 913.

1m N of Corby on A6003.
9m E of Market
Harborough. 14m SW of
Stamford on A427.

■ **Opening Times**
Easter (4 April)– to the
end of May: Suns & BH
Mons.

June–September:
Tues, Suns & BH Mon.
12 noon–5pm

Grounds: open at 12 noon

Castle opens at 1pm.

■ **Admission**
House & Grounds
Adult   £8.50
Senior Citizen   £7.50
Child (5–16yrs)   £5.00
Family ticket (2+2)£22.00

Grounds only
Including Gardens,
Salvin's Tower, Gift Shop
and Licensed Tea Room.

Adult & Child   £5.00
(Not available when
special events are held in
grounds.)

**Groups (min 20
visitors)**
Adult (on open days) £7.50
Adult (private guided
tour)   £9.50
Child (5–16yrs)   £4.25

**School groups (min 20
visitors)**
Adult   £7.50
Children   £4.25

(1 Adult Free with every
15 children). Groups and
school parties can be
accommodated on most
days by arrangement.

■ **Special Events**
April 4 & 5
Easter Sunday & Monday
May 2 & 3
American Civil War
Re-enactment
June 13
Jousting & Medieval
Living History Village
July 11
Falconry & Owl Day
August 29 & 30
Vikings! Of Middle
England
November 22–26
Christmas at Rockingham
Castle

ROCKINGHAM CASTLE

www.rockinghamcastle.com

Rockingham Castle stands on the edge of an escarpment giving dramatic views over five counties and the Welland Valley below. Built by William the Conqueror, the Castle was a royal residence for 450 years. In the 16th century Henry VIII granted it to Edward Watson and for 450 years it has remained a family home. The predominantly Tudor building, within Norman walls, has architecture, furniture and works of art from practically every century including, unusually, a remarkable collection of 20th century pictures. Charles Dickens was a regular visitor to the Castle and based *Chesney Wolds* in *Bleak House* on Rockingham.

Surrounding the Castle are some 18 acres of gardens largely following the foot print of the medieval castle. The vast 400 year old "Elephant Hedge" dissects the formal 17th century terraced gardens. The circular yew hedge stands on the site of the motte and bailey and provides shelter for the Rose Garden. Outside of which stands the newly planted 'Room Garden' created by Chelsea gold medal winner Robert Myers, using Yew hedging, shrubs and herbaceous planting. Below the Castle is the beautiful 19th century "Wild Garden" replanted with advice from Kew Gardens during the early 1960s. Included in the gardens are many specimen tress and shrubs including the remarkable Handkerchief Tree.

 No photography in Castle.

 Licensed.

 Partial. WC.

 By arrangement.

 In grounds, on leads.

78 DERNGATE: THE CHARLES RENNIE MACKINTOSH HOUSE & GALLERIES

82 Derngate, Northampton NN1 1UH   www.78derngate.org.uk
Tel: 01604 603407   **E-mail:** info@78derngate.org.uk
Owner: 78 Derngate Northampton Trust   **Contact:** House Manager
Winner Enjoy England Gold Award for Best Small Visitor Attraction 2009. 78 Derngate was remodelled by the world-famous architect and designer, Charles Rennie MacKintosh, in his iconic modernist style. Free entry to the impressive Gallery Upstairs, a boutique-style restaurant and shop offering unique gifts and contemporary craft. Truely is a must-see venue.
Location: MAP 7:C9, OS Ref. SP759 603. In the heart of Northampton close to the rear of the Royal & Derngate Theatres. Follow Derngate out of the centre of town.
Open: 2 Feb 2010 to 19 December 2010, Tues–Sun & BH Mons: 10am–5pm. Group and school bookings are also available.
Admission: Adult £6, Conc. £5.50. Family (2+2): £15. Groups (15+) £5pp.
ⓘ No indoor photography. ⬛ 🍴 ♿ Partial. ⬛ ✗ 🅿 None. ⬛ ✉ ♥

ALTHORP

See page 284 for full page entry.

BOUGHTON HOUSE 📖

See page 285 for full page entry.

Coton Manor Garden

CANONS ASHBY 🌿

CANONS ASHBY, DAVENTRY, NORTHAMPTONSHIRE NN11 3SD
www.nationaltrust.org.uk

Tel: 01327 861900   **Fax:** 01327 861909   **E-mail:** canonsashby@nationaltrust.org.uk
Owner: The National Trust   **Contact:** The Property Manager
Home of the Dryden family since the 16th century, this Elizabethan manor house was built c1550, added to in the 1590s, and altered in the 1630s and c1710; largely unaltered since. Within the house, Elizabethan wall paintings and outstanding Jacobean plasterwork are of particular interest. A formal garden includes terraces, walls and gate piers of 1710. There is also a medieval priory church and a 70 acre park.
Location: Map 7:B9, OS Ref. SP577 506. Access from M40/J11, or M1/J16. Signposted from A5, 3m S of Weedon crossroads. Then 7m to SW.
Open: Open 13 Feb - 1 Nov: Sats - Weds. 11:00 - 17:00 Guided house tours 11:00 - 13:00. 7 Nov - 19 Dec Open weekends only 12:00 - 16:00. Open Good Friday. Open all week in August.Closes dusk if earlier..
*Admission: Adult £8.30, Child £4.15, Family £20.75. Garden only: £3.10, Child £1.85. Winter grounds only, Adult £1.85, Child £1.05
*includes a voluntary donation but visitors can choose to pay the standard prices displayed at the property and on the website.
Special Events: Events throughout the year. Please see the website for details on www.nationaltrust.org.uk/canonsashby
ⓘ No photography. No high heeled shoes. ⬛ 🍴 ♿ Partial.WCs. ⬛ ✗ By arrangement. 🅿 Limited for coaches. ⬛ 🐕 Guide dogs only. ♥

COTON MANOR GARDEN

NR GUILSBOROUGH, NORTHAMPTONSHIRE NN6 8RQ
www.cotonmanor.co.uk

Tel: 01604 740219   **Fax:** 01604 740838
E-mail: pasleytyler@cotonmanor.co.uk
Owner: Ian & Susie Pasley-Tyler   **Contact:** Sarah Ball
Traditional English garden laid out on different levels surrounding a 17th century stone manor house. Many herbaceous borders, with extensive range of plants, old yew and holly hedges, rose garden, water garden and fine lawns set in 10 acres. Also wild flower meadow and bluebell wood.
Location: Map 7:B8, OS Ref. SP675 716. 9m NW of Northampton, between A5199 (formerly A50) and A428.
Open: 1 Apr–2 Oct: Tue–Sat & BH weekends; also Suns Apr–May: 12 noon–5.30pm.
Admission: Adult £5, Child £2, Conc. £4.50. Groups: £4.50.
⬛ 🍴 ♿ Partial. WCs. ⬛ Licensed. 🍴 Licensed. ✗ By arrangement. 🅿 ✉

Jerry Harpur, Harpur Garden Images

COTTESBROOKE HALL & GARDENS 🏛

COTTESBROOKE, NORTHAMPTONSHIRE NN6 8PF

www.cottesbrookehall.co.uk

Tel: 01604 505808 **Fax:** 01604 505619 **E-mail:** enquiries@cottesbrooke.co.uk
Owner: Mr & Mrs A R Macdonald-Buchanan   **Contact:** The Administrator

This magnificent Queen Anne house dating from 1702 is set in delightful rural Northamptonshire. Reputed to be the pattern for Jane Austen's *Mansfield Park*, the Hall's beauty is matched by the magnificence of the gardens and views and by the excellence of the picture, furniture and porcelain collections it houses. The Woolavington collection of sporting pictures at Cottesbrooke is possibly one of the finest of its type in Europe and includes paintings by Stubbs, Ben Marshall and many other artists renowned for works of this genre, from the mid 18th century to the present day. Portraits, bronzes, 18th century English and French furniture and fine porcelain are also among the treasures of Cottesbrooke Hall.

In the formal gardens huge 300-year-old cedars set off magnificent double herbaceous borders, pools and lily-ponds. In midsummer, visitors enjoy the splendid array of planters, a sight not to be missed. The Wild Garden is a short walk across the Park and is planted along the course of a stream with its small cascades and arched bridges. Previously winner of the HHA/Christie's *Garden of the Year* Award. Nominated as one of the best gardens in the world in "*1001 Gardens you must see before you die*".

Location: MAP 7:B8, OS Ref. SP711 739. 10m N of Northampton near Creaton on A5199 (formerly A50). Signed from Junction 1 on the A14.

Open: May–end of Sept. May & Jun: Wed & Thur, 2–5.30pm. Jul–Sept: Thur, 2–5.30pm. Open BH Mons (May–Sept), 2–5.30pm. The first open day is bank holiday Monday 3rd May 2010.

Admission: House & Gardens: Adult £8, Child £3.50, Conc £6.50. Gardens only: Adult £5.50, Child £2.50, Conc £4.50. RHS members receive free access to gardens. Group & private bookings by arrangement.

ℹ No photography in house. Filming & outside events. 🅃 🔱 Gardens. WC. Parking. 🖰 Home-made cakes. 🕊 Hall guided tours obligatory. 🅿 🚫 🍴

Cottesbrooke Hall & Gardens

DEENE PARK 🏛

See page 286 for full page entry.

© Deene Park/Nick McCann

Deene Park

ELEANOR CROSS ⌗

Geddington, Kettering, Northamptonshire

Tel: 01604 735400 (Regional Office)   **E-mail:** customers@english-heritage.org.uk

www.english-heritage.org.uk/eleanorcross

Owner: English Heritage   **Contact:** East Midlands Regional Office

One of a series of famous crosses, of elegant sculpted design, erected by Edward I to mark the resting places of the body of his wife, Eleanor, when brought for burial from Harby in Nottinghamshire to Westminster Abbey in 1290.

Location: MAP 7:D7, OS Ref. SP896 830. In Geddington, off A43 between Kettering and Corby.

Open: Any reasonable time.

Admission: Free. Opening times and prices are valid until 31st March 2010, after this date details are subject to change please see www.english-heritage.org.uk for the most up-to-date information.

ℹ Picnickers welcome. 🐕 ✳

HADDONSTONE SHOW GARDENS

The Forge House, Church Lane, East Haddon, Northampton NN6 8DB

Tel: 01604 770711   **Fax:** 01604 770027

E-mail: info@haddonstone.co.uk   **www.haddonstone.com**

Owner: Haddonstone Ltd   **Contact:** Marketing Director

See Haddonstone's classic garden ornaments in the beautiful setting of the walled manor gardens including: urns, troughs, fountains, statuary, bird baths, sundials and balustrading – even an orangery. The garden is on different levels with shrub roses, conifers, clematis and climbers. The Jubilee garden features a pavilion, temple and Gothic grotto. As featured on BBC *Gardeners' World*.

Location: MAP 7:B8, OS Ref. SP667 682. 7m NW of Northampton off A428. Signposted.

Open: Mon–Fri, 9am–5.30pm. Closed weekends, BHs & Christmas period.

Admission: Free. Groups by appointment only. Not suitable for coach groups.

📷 ✍ By arrangement. 🅿 Limited. 🐕 Guide dogs only.

Rockingham Castle

HOLDENBY 🏛

HOLDENBY, NORTHAMPTON NN6 8DJ

www.holdenby.com

Tel: 01604 770074   **Fax:** 01604 770962   **E-mail:** office@holdenby.com

Owner: James Lowther **Contact:** Caroline Houghton/Amanda Askew, Commercial Managers

Once the largest private house in England and subsequently the palace and prison of King Charles I, Holdenby has a special atmosphere all of its own. Its elegant rooms and acres of gardens and parkland make it a magnificent venue for corporate events, dinners and meetings, as well as an ideal location for films and TV. Visitors to the gardens can enjoy fascinating flying displays of birds from our famous Falconry Centre, while couples continue to choose Holdenby as an enchanting venue for weddings. Holdenby is five times winner of the Sandford Award for Heritage Education.

Location: MAP 7:B8, OS Ref. SP693 681. M1/J15a. 7m NW of Northampton off A428 & A5199.

Open: Gardens & Falconry: May–Aug, Suns & BH Mons, Easter Sun & Mon 1–5pm. Gardens only: Apr & Sep, 1–5pm. House: 15/16 May 2010, 29/30 Aug 2010.

Admission: (with Falconry Centre) Adult £5, Child £3.50, Conc. £4.50, Family (2+2) £15; (Gardens only) Adult £3, Child £2, Conc. £2.50, Family (2+2) £8. Different prices on event days. Groups must book.

ℹ Children's play area. 📷 ❄ 🍴 ♿ Partial. WC. ✍ By arrangement. 🅿 🔲 5 times Sandford Award Winner. 🐕 In grounds, on leads. 📷 ❄ 15/16 May 2010 Holdenby Garden Show. 29/30 Aug 2010 Holdenby Food Show.

291

NOTTINGHAMSHIRE

© NT / J Unell

CLUMBER PARK ❧

CLUMBER PARK, WORKSOP, NOTTINGHAMSHIRE S80 3AZ

www.nationaltrust.org.uk

Tel: 01909 544917 **Fax:** 01909 500721 **Email:** clumberpark@nationaltrust.org.uk
www.nationaltrust.org.uk

Owner: The National Trust **Contact:** Visitor Enquiry Point

Clumber Park was once the country estate of the Dukes of Newcastle and although the house was demolished in 1938 the Gothic Revival Chapel, the immense Lime Tree Avenue and the spectacular glasshouses all remain to give clues to its past.

Location: MAP 7:B2, OS120 Ref SK625 745. 4.5m SE of Worksop, 6½m SW of Retford, just off A1/A57 via A614. 11m from M1/J30.

Open: Parkland and Visitor Facilities (Restaurant, Shop, Plant Sales, The Clumber Story, Chapel): throughout year, daily. Walled Kitchen Garden: 13 Mar-31 Oct, daily. Cycle Hire Centre: Jan-27 Mar, Sat and Sun, 28 Mar-30 Oct, daily, 31 Oct-31 Dec, Sat and Sun. Chapel: as Visitor Facilities except 12 Jan-28 Mar when closed for conservation cleaning. Conservation Centre: 3 Apr-26 Sept, Sat, Sun and BH. See website or contact property for opening times.

Admission: Vehicle £5.20. Walled Kitchen Garden: Adults £3, children free. NT members free.

Special Events: Clumber holds a packed events programme throughout the year from open-air concerts to our ever-popular Christmas at Clumber. See website or contact property for details.

▢▢▢▢ WCs. ▢ Licensed. ▢ Licensed. ▢ By arrangement. ▢ ▣ Limited for coaches. ▢▢ Must be on leads in Walled Kitchen Garden, Pleasure Grounds and grazing areas. ▢▢

Wollaton Hall Natural History Museum

HODSOCK PRIORY GARDENS

Blyth, Nr Worksop, Nottinghamshire S81 0TY

Tel: 01909 591204 **www.snowdrops.co.uk**

Owner: Sir Andrew & Lady Buchanan **Contact:** George Buchanan

"A magical sight you will never forget". Myriads of flowers in the 5-acre garden plus a half mile walk through the woodland with sheets of snowdrops. Banks of *hellebores*, carpets of pink *cyclamen*, ribbons of golden *aconites*, blue *irises*, the red, orange, green, black and white stems of *Acers*, *Cornus* and *Willows* and the heady fragrance of *sarcococca*. There is a clearly marked trail, with plenty of seats. Shortcuts are signed for those who prefer a shorter walk.

Location: MAP 7:B1, OS Ref. SK612 853. W of B6045 Worksop/Blyth road, 1m SW of Blyth, less than 2m from A1.

Open: Every day in February 2010, 10am-4pm.

Admission: Adult £4.50, accompanied Child (6–16yrs) £1.

▢ Heritage shop. ▢ ▢ ▣

HOLME PIERREPONT HALL ▢

Holme Pierrepont, Nr Nottingham NG12 2LD

Tel: 0115 933 2371 **Fax:** 01636 821554 **www.holmepierreponthall.com**

Owner: Mr & Mrs Robin Brackenbury **Contact:** Robert Brackenbury

This charming 16th Century manor house set in thirty acres of Park and gardens with a carved Charles II Staircase, family portraits and furniture is still lived in by descendents of the Pierrepont family. The Ball Room, Drawing Room and Long Gallery are available for functions on an exclusive basis. Filming welcome.

Location: MAP 7:B4, OS Ref. SK628 392. 5m ESE of central Nottingham. Follow signs to the National Water Sports Centre and continue for 1½m.

Open: The house is open every Monday, Tuesday and Wednesday from 1st Feb–31stMar 2010. Also Hellebore Sunday, 7th Mar and Tulip Sun, 11 Apr 2010.

Admission: House & Garden: Adult £5, Child £1.50. Gardens only: Adult £3, Child £1.

▢ No photography or video recording in house when open to the public. ▢ Business and charity functions, wedding receptions, dinners, seminars and conferences. ▢ Please ring for details. ▢ In grounds on leads. ▢▢▢▢

NEWSTEAD ABBEY HISTORIC HOUSE & GARDENS

Newstead Abbey Park, Nottinghamshire NG15 8NA

Tel: 01623 455900 **Fax:** 01623 455904

www.mynottingham.gov.uk/newsteadabbey

Owner: Nottingham City Council **Contact:** Gillian Crawley

Historic home of the poet, Lord Byron, set in extensive formal gardens and parkland of 300 acres. See Byron's private apartments, period rooms and the medieval cloisters. The West Front of the Priory Church is a stunning local landmark.

Location: MAP 7:B3, OS Ref. SK540 639. 12m N of Nottingham 1m W of the A60 Mansfield Rd.

Open: House: 1 Apr–30 Sept: 12 noon–5pm, last adm. 4pm. Grounds: All year: 9am–6pm or dusk except for the last Friday in November and 25 Dec.

Admission: House & Grounds: Adult £7, Child £3, Conc. £4.50, Family (2+3) £17.50. Groups (10+) £4.50. Grounds only: Adult £3.50, Child £2, Conc. £3, Family £9.50. Groups (10+) £3.

▢▢▢▢▣▢▢▢▢

NOTTINGHAM CASTLE

Off Friar Lane, Nottingham NG1 6EL

Tel: 0115 9153700 **Fax:** 0115 9153653 **E-mail:** castle@ncmg.org.uk

www.mynottingham.gov.uk/nottinghamcastle

Owner: Nottingham City Council

17th century ducal mansion built on the site of the original medieval Castle, with spectacular views of the city. A vibrant museum and art gallery housing collections of paintings, silver, Wedgwood and 15 centuries of Nottingham history plus exhibitions of contemporary and historical art. Tour the underground caves system. Special events take place throughout the year, please visit www.nottinghamcity.gov.uk/whatson.

Location: MAP 7:B4, OS Ref. SK569 395. Just SW of the city centre on hilltop.

Open: Daily, 10am–5pm (4pm during winter). Closed 24–26 Dec & 1 Jan.

Admission: Joint admission with The Museum of Nottingham Life. Please call the castle on 0115 915 3700 for 2010 prices.

▢▢▢▢▢ Caves. ▢ ▢▢▢▢ Tel for details.

PAPPLEWICK HALL
PAPPLEWICK, NOTTINGHAMSHIRE NG15 8FE

www.papplewickhall.co.uk

Tel: 0115 9632623   **E-mail:** godwinaust@aol.com

Owner/Contact: Mr & Mrs J R Godwin-Austen

A beautiful classic Georgian house, built of Mansfield stone, set in parkland, with woodland garden laid out in the 18th century. The house is notable for its very fine plasterwork, and elegant staircase. Grade I listed.

Location: MAP 7:B3, OS Ref. SK548 518. Half way between Nottingham & Mansfield, 3m E of M1/J27. A608 & A611 towards Hucknall. Then A6011 to Papplewick and B683 N for ½m.

Open: 1st, 3rd & 5th Wed in each month 2–5pm, and by appointment.

Admission: Adult £5. Groups (10+): £4.

ℹ️ No photography. 📷 Obligatory. 🅿 Limited for coaches. 🐕 In grounds on leads. ❄

THRUMPTON HALL 🏛
THRUMPTON, NOTTINGHAM NG11 0AX

www.thrumptonhall.com

Tel: 07590818045   **E-mail:** enquiries@thrumptonhall.com

Owner: Miranda Seymour   **Contact:** Debbie Knox

Magnificent lakeside Jacobean house, built in 1607. Priest's hiding hole, carved Charles II staircase, panelled saloon, Byron memorabilia. Large lawns separated from landscaped park by ha-ha. Personal tours are led by family members. Dining room with capacity for 50 silver service or buffet for 100. Beautiful lakeside Pavilion for up to 250. Free access for coach drivers.

Location: MAP 7:A5, OS Ref. SK508 312. 7m S of Nottingham, 3m E M1/J24, 1m from A453, 4m from East Midlands Airport.

Open: By appointment throughout the year. Groups of (20+) 10.30am–6pm.

Admission: Adult £8, Child £3.50.

🖥 🍴 Wedding receptions, conferences, events. ♿ Ground floor & grounds. WC. 🍴 🅿 Unlimited. 🐕 In grounds on leads. ♿ ❄

RUFFORD ABBEY ⚏
Ruffford, Newark, Nottinghamshire NG22 9DF

Tel: 01623 821338   **E-mail:** customers@english-heritage.org.uk

www.english-heritage.org.uk/rufford

Owner: English Heritage   **Contact:** Nottinghamshire County Council

The remains of a 17th century country house; built on the foundations of a 12th century Cistercian Abbey, set in Rufford Country Park.

Location: MAP 7:B3, OS120, SK645 646. 2m S of Ollerton off A614.

Open: All year from 10am–5pm. Closed 25 Dec. Please call for full opening times and other site facilities.

Admission: Free – parking charge applies. Opening times and prices are valid until 31st March 2010, after this date details are subject to change please see www.english-heritage.org.uk for the most up-to-date information.

ℹ️ Picnickers welcome. WC. 🖥 ♿ 🍴 🅿 🐕 ❄

Properties that **open all year** appear in the special index at the end of the book.

WINKBURN HALL
Winkburn, Newark, Nottinghamshire NG22 8PQ

Tel: 01636 636465   **Fax:** 01636 636717

Owner/Contact: Richard Craven-Smith-Milnes Esq

A fine William and Mary house.

Location: MAP 7:C3, OS Ref. SK711 584. 8m W of Newark 1m N of A617.

Open: Throughout the year by appointment only.

Admission: £6.

WOLLATON HALL, GARDENS & DEER PARK
Wollaton, Nottingham NG8 2AE

Tel: 0115 915 3900   **E-mail:** wollaton@ncmg.org.uk

www.mynottingham.gov.uk/wollatonhall

Owner: Nottingham City Council   **Contact:** The Manager

A beautiful 16th century Grade I listed building designed by Robert Smythson featuring a Natural History Museum, set in a 500 acre historic deer park, home to red and fallow deer. Visitors have a choice of a variety of walks. Events held regularly – please visit www.mynottingham.gov.uk/whatson for details.

Location: MAP 7:B4, OS Ref. SK532 392. Wollaton Park, Nottingham. 3m W of city centre.

Open: All year.

Admission: Free. Car parking charge of £2 per car applies. Admission payable for some events and tours.

🖥 📺 ♿ 🍴 📷 🅿 🐕 ❄ 👶

Newstead Abbey & Gardens

Minworth Greaves at Selly Manor, West Midlands

Heart of England

Shakespeare's birthplace of Stratford-upon-Avon justly receives thousands of visitors each year, but travel further west too, into the gloriously unspoilt counties of Herefordshire and Worcestershire. Surrounded by the Malvern Hills, the fairytale Eastnor Castle has something to interest all visitors, whilst the fully restored Trentham Gardens offer something for everybody including "Barfuss Park" – Britain's first barefoot walk.

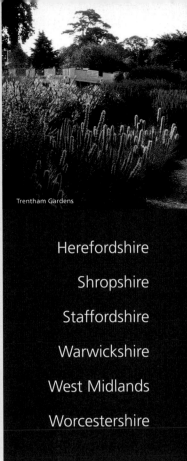

Trentham Gardens

Herefordshire

Shropshire

Staffordshire

Warwickshire

West Midlands

Worcestershire

STAFFORDSHIRE

SHROPSHIRE

WEST MIDLANDS

WORCESTERSHIRE

WARWICKSHIRE

HEREFORDSHIRE

Great Hall , Stokesay Court

Eastnor Castle

Heart of England

■ **Owner**
The National Trust

■ **Contact**
The Property Manager
Berrington Hall
Nr Leominster
Herefordshire
HR6 0DW

Tel: 01568 615721
Fax: 01568 613263

Restaurant:
01568 610134

Shop:
01568 610529

Costume Curator:
01568 613720

E-mail: berrington
@nationaltrust.org.uk

■ **Location**
MAP 6:L8

OS137 SP510 637

3m N of Leominster, 7m
S of Ludlow on
W side of A49.

Rail: Leominster 4m.

■ **Opening Times**
House
6 March–31 October:
Mon–Wed, Sats & Suns,
1pm–5pm (open Good
Friday). 7 Days Jul & Aug

House Tours
6 March–31 October:
Mon–Wed, Sats & Suns,
11am–1pm (open Good
Friday). 7 Days Jul & Aug

Garden
30 January–28 February,
6 November–
19 December: Sats &
Suns. 11am–4pm.
6 March–31 October:
Mon–Wed, Sats & Suns,
11am–5pm.
7 Days 1–18 April, 29
May–6 June, 1 July–31
August, 23 October–31
October, daily,
11am–5pm.

Park Walk
As Garden.

Shop & Tea-room
As Garden.

■ ***Admission**
Adult   £7.50
Child (5–12yrs) £3.75
Family (2+3)   £18.75
Groups (15–25)**
Adult   £6.05 (no GAOE)
Garden Ticket
Adult   £6.00
Child   £3.00
Joint Ticket
for Berrington &
Croft Castle   £10.50

**Groups must pre-
book. Two groups can
visit at a time.

Gift aid is not included in
group price.

*includes a voluntary
donation but visitors can
choose to pay the standard
prices displayed at the
property and on the website.

©NTPL / Rupert Truman

BERRINGTON HALL 🌿

www.nationaltrust.org.uk/berrington

Berrington Hall is the creation of Thomas Harley, the 3rd Earl of Oxford's remarkable son, who made a fortune from supplying pay and clothing to the British Army in America and became Lord Mayor of London in 1767 at the age of thirty-seven. The architect was the fashionable Henry Holland. The house is beautifully set above the wide valley of a tributary of the River Lugg, with views west and south to the Black Mountains and Brecon Beacons. This was the site chosen by 'Capability' Brown who created the lake with its artificial island. The rather plain neo-classical exterior with a central portico gives no

clue to the lavishness of the interior. Plaster ceilings decorated in muted pastel colours adorn the principal rooms. Holland's masterpiece is the staircase hall rising to a central dome. The rooms are set off with a collection of French furniture, including pieces which belonged to the Comte de Flahault, natural son of Talleyrand, and Napoleon's step-daughter Hortense.

In the dining room, vast panoramic paintings of battles at sea, three of them by Thomas Luny, are a tribute to the distinguished Admiral Rodney.

©NTPL / Andreas von Einsiedel

i No photography in the house. Groups by arrangement only.

1 single seater batricar for use outdoors; pre-booking essential. Audio tours for the visually impaired. Disabled lift access to tearoom.

Licensed tearoom: open as garden: 11am–5pm (4pm Oct–Dec).

By arrangement only. Tour time: 1 hr.

P Ample for cars. Parking for coaches limited; instructions given when booking is made.

Children's guide. Play area in walled garden.

Guide dogs only.

EASTNOR CASTLE 🏛

www.eastnorcastle.com

In the style of a medieval Welsh-border fortress, Eastnor Castle was built in the early 19th century by John First Earl Somers and is a good example of the great Norman and Gothic revival in architecture of that time. The Castle is dramatically situated in a 5000 acre estate in the Malvern Hills and remains the family home of the Hervey-Bathursts, his direct descendants.

This fairytale home is as dramatic inside as it is outside. A vast, 60' high Hall leads to a series of State Rooms including a Gothic Drawing Room designed by Pugin, with its original furniture, and a Library in the style of the Italian Renaissance, with views across the Lake.

The Hervey-Bathursts have lovingly restored the interiors and many of the Castle's treasures which have been buried away in the cellars and attics since the Second World War – early Italian Fine Art, medieval armour, 17th century Venetian furniture, Flemish tapestries and paintings by Van Dyck, Reynolds, Romney and Watts and early photographs by Julia Margaret Cameron.

Gardens

Castellated terraces descend to a 21 acre lake with a restored lakeside walk. The arboretum holds a famous collection of mature specimen trees. There are spectacular views of the Malvern hills across a 300 acre deer park, once part of a mediaeval chase and now designated a Site of Special Scientific Interest.

- ℹ Knight's maze, tree trail, children's adventure playground, junior assault course. Corporate events – off-road driving, country pursuits, outside adventure days, private dinners, exclusive hire, special events.

- 🎁 Gift shop open on public open days, also on-line shop.

- 🍷 Exclusive use for weddings, private and corporate events. Product launches, TV and feature films, concerts and charity events.

- ♿ Wheelchair stairclimber to main State rooms. DVD tour of first floor rooms. Visitors may alight at the Castle. Priority parking.

- 🍴 Snacks and lunches (open as Castle).

- 🚶 By arrangement, Mons & Tues all year, outside normal opening hours.

- 🅿 Ample 10–200 yds from Castle. Coaches phone in advance to arrange parking & catering. Tearoom voucher for drivers/courier.

- 🛡 Guides available.

- 🐕 On leads in house and grounds.

- 🏠 Exclusive use accommodation.

- 🔔 Exclusive use for weddings.

- 🛡 See website for details.

Owner
Mr J Hervey-Bathurst

Contact
Castle Office
Eastnor Castle
Nr Ledbury
Herefordshire HR8 1RL

Tel: 01531 633160
Fax: 01531 631776
E-mail: enquiries@
eastnorcastle.com

Location
MAP 6:M10
OS Ref. SO735 368

2m SE of Ledbury on the A438 Tewkesbury road. Alternatively M50/J2 & from Ledbury take the A449/A438.

Tewkesbury 20 mins, Malvern 20 mins, Gloucester 25 mins, Hereford 25 mins, Worcester 30 mins, Cheltenham 30 mins, B'ham 1 hr, London 2¼ hrs.

Taxi: Richard James 07836 777196.

Opening Times
Easter Weekend: Fri 2, Sat 3, Sun 4 & BH Mon 5 April.
May Bank Holiday Weekends: Sun 2/Mon 3 & Sun 30/Mon 31 May.
Every Sunday from 6 June–26 September.
Sun–Thurs from 18 July–31 August.

Admission
Summer

Castle & Grounds

Adult	£8.50
Child (5–15yrs)	£5.50
OAP	£7.50
Family (2+3)	£22.50

Grounds only

Adult	£5.50
Child (5–15yrs)	£3.50
OAP	£4.50
Family (2+3)	£14.50

Groups (20+)

Guided	£10.50
Freeflow	£7.00
Schools	£6.00

Privilege Pass
Valid for 1 year and includes all Castle special events (apart from theatre productions)

Adult	£24.00
Child (5–15yrs)	£15.00
OAP	£21.00
Family (2+3)	£63.00

Special Events
See website for further details.

Conference/Function

ROOM	SIZE	MAX CAPACITY
Great Hall	16 x 8m	150
Dining Rm	11 x 7m	80
Gothic Rm	11 x 7m	80
Octagon Rm	9 x 9m	50

© English Heritage

STOKESAY CASTLE ⌗
Nr CRAVEN ARMS, SHROPSHIRE SY7 9AH

www.english-heritage.org.uk/stokesaycastle

Tel: 01588 672544
Owner: English Heritage   **Email:** customers@english-heritage.org.uk
Contact: Visitor Operations Team

Nestling in a green valley, Stokesay Castle is England's most delightful fortified medieval manor. This beautiful house dates back to the 11th century with a magnificent great hall that has remained unaltered since it was built in 1291. The castle forms a picturesque grouping of castle, parish church and timber-framed Jacobean gatehouse set in the rolling Shropshire countryside. An audio tour will help you to imagine Stokesay as the centre of medieval life.

Location: MAP 6:K7, OS148, SO446 787. 7m NW of Ludlow off A49.

Open: 1 Apr–30 Sep: daily, 10am–5pm. 1 Oct–1 Nov: Wed–Sun, 10am–5pm. 2 Nov–28 Feb '10: Thur–Sun, 10am–4pm. 1–31 Mar: Wed–Sun, 10am–5pm. Closed 24–26 Dec & 1 Jan. Please note: castle may close early for functions. Please call to check.

Admission: Adult £5.20, Child £2.60, Conc. £4.40, Family £13.00. 15% discount for groups (11+). EH Members free. Opening times and prices are valid until 31st March 2010, after this date details are subject to change please see www.english-heritage.org.uk for the most up-to-date information.

ⓘ Guidebooks. Hazardous. Ovp. ⬚ ⬚ ⬚ ⬚ P ⬚ Family learning resources available. ⬚ ⬚ ⬚

STOKESAY COURT
ONIBURY, CRAVEN ARMS, SHROPSHIRE SY7 9BD

www.stokesaycourt.com

Tel: 01584 856238   **E-mail:** info@stokesaycourt.com
Owner/Contact: Ms Caroline Magnus

Unspoilt and secluded, Stokesay Court is an imposing late Victorian mansion with Jacobean style façade, magnificent interiors and extensive grounds containing a grotto, woodland and interconnected pools. Set deep in the beautiful rolling green landscape of South Shropshire near Ludlow, the house and grounds featured as the Tallis Estate in the award winning film 'Atonement'.

Location: MAP 6:K7, OS148, SO444 786. A49 Between Ludlow and Craven Arms.

Open: Guided tours all year for booked groups (20+). Groups (up to 60) can be accommodated. Tours for individuals take place on dates advertised on website. Booking essential. Tours are usually taken by the owner.

Admission: Adult £15pp to include light refreshments (full catering service available on request).

ⓘ No stilettos. No photography in house. ⬚ ⬚ Partial. WCs. ⬚ ⬚ Obligatory. P ⬚ Guide dogs only. ⬚ ⬚ €

Stokesay Court, Great Hall

Weston Park

WENLOCK GUILDHALL

Much Wenlock, Shropshire TF13 6AE
Tel: 01952 727509
Owner/Contact: Much Wenlock Town Council
16th century half-timbered building has an open-arcade market area.
Location: MAP 6:L6, OS Ref. SJ624 000. In centre of Much Wenlock, next to the church.
Open: 1 Apr–31 Oct: Mon–Sat, 10.30am–1pm & 2–4pm. Suns: 2–4pm.
Admission: Adult £1 (including guide), Child Free.

WENLOCK PRIORY ⌗

Much Wenlock, Shropshire TF13 6HS
Tel: 01952 727466   **Email:** customers@english-heritage.org.uk
www.english-heritage.org.uk/wenlock
Owner: English Heritage   **Contact:** Visitor Operations Team
The remains of this medieval monastery are set on the edge of beautiful Much Wenlock. The priory's grandeur can be traced in the ruins of its 13th century church, ornate Norman chapter house and rare monk's wash house. These majestic ruins are set in green lawns and topiary.
Location: MAP 6:L6, OS127, SJ625 001. In Much Wenlock.
Open: 1–30 Apr: Wed–Sun & BH Mons, 10am–5pm. 1 May–31 Aug: daily, 10am–5pm. 1 Sep–1 Nov: Wed–Sun, 10am–5pm. 2 Nov–28 Feb '10: Thur–Sun, 10am–4pm. 1–31 Mar: Wed–Sun & BH Mons, 10am–5pm. Closed 24–26 Dec & 1 Jan.
Admission: Adult £3.60, Child £1.80, Conc. £3.10. EH Members free. Group discount available. Opening times and prices are valid until 31st March 2010, after this date details are subject to change please see www.english-heritage.org.uk for the most up-to-date information.
ⓘ WC. Baby changing facilities. Gardens. Guidebooks. Ovp. 🔲 🔽 🔽 🅿 🔽 On leads. ✳

WESTON PARK    *See page 305 for full page entry.*

WROXETER ROMAN CITY ⌗

Wroxeter, Shrewsbury, Shropshire SY5 6PH
Tel: 01743 761330   **Email:** customers@english-heritage.org.uk
www.english-heritage.org.uk/wroxeter
Owner: English Heritage   **Contact:** Visitor Operations Team
The part-excavated centre of the fourth largest city in Roman Britain, originally home to some 6,000 men and several hundred houses. Impressive remains of the 2nd century municipal baths. There is a site museum in which many finds are displayed, including those from work by Birmingham Field Archaeological Unit.
Location: MAP 6:L6, OS126, SJ565 087. At Wroxeter, 5m E of Shrewsbury, on B4380.
Open: 1 Apr–1 Nov: daily, 10am–5pm. 2 Nov–28 Feb '10: Wed–Sun, 10am–4pm. 1–31 Mar: daily, 10am–5pm. Closed 24–26 Dec & 1 Jan.
Admission: Adult £4.20, Child £2.10, Conc. £3.60, Family £10.50. EH Members free. Group discount available. Opening times and prices are valid until 31st March 2010, after this date details are subject to change please see www.english-heritage.org.uk for the most up-to-date information.
ⓘ WC. Museum. Hazard. Ovp. 🔲 🔽 🔽 🅿 🔽 On leads. ✳

■ **Owner**
St Modwen Properties

■ **Contact**
Stone Road
Trentham
Staffordshire ST4 8AX

Tel: 01782 646646
Fax: 01782 644536
E-mail: mwalker@
trentham.co.uk
www.trentham.co.uk
Group Booking contact:
Jackie Grice.
Tel: 01782 645215 Email:
jgrice@trentham.co.uk

■ **Location**
MAP 6:N4
OS Ref. SJ864 408
SAT NAV: ST4 8JG

5 minute drive M6/J15.
45 minutes from
Birmingham, Manchester,
Liverpool & Nottingham.

■ **Opening Times**
Summer
1 April–31 October:
daily, 9am–6pm.
Exit by 8pm.

Winter
1 November–28 March:
daily, 10am–3pm.
Exit by 4pm.

The Italian Gardens are
open every day except
Christmas Day.

■ **Admission**
Summer
Adult	£7.25
Joint (2 Adults)	£13.50
Child	£5.70
Carers & Disabled.	£3.65
Concessions	£6.20
Family (2+3)	£24.85
Family (1+3)	£17.60

Special joint Garden and
Monkey Forest ticket
available.

Special group &
school rates:
Groups (12+) from £5.70
if pre booked and pre paid
Schools	£3.65

non supported entry
Schools	£7.75

for supported "Forest
School" activities
Educational groups can
now choose Bush craft
and Forest School
activities.

Winter
Reduced winter rates.

■ **Special Events**
Quilt Show,
Summer Music Festival,
Plant Festival and
seasonal events.

■ **New for 2010**
The garden has been
extended to enclose the
mile long lake and
circular walk. A special
joint ticket is now
available to combine the
garden with the Monkey
Forest.

TRENTHAM ESTATE
www.trentham.co.uk

Stunning Gardens described as the largest contemporary planting scheme in Europe. Utilising top designers Tom Stuart-Smith and Piet Oudolf, this is an iconic restoration, bringing such an important historic garden back to life with vast new plantings with in excess of 120,000 perennials, which will provide interest throughout the year.

The 10 acre Italian Gardens, planted by Tom Stuart-Smith, are now fully restored and the new plantings are well established. Also now established in the seven acre garden designed by Piet Oudolf consists of three distinct areas: the rivers of grass – swathes of ornamental grasses, the floral labyrinth with winding paths running through the brightly coloured, tall perennial planting and, finally, two sculptured viewing mounds flanked either side by choice shrub borders.

The western side of the garden is full of activity with show gardens offering a range of ideas for gardeners. The gardens include: 'The Winter Garden', 'Tropical Garden', a 'Pottager' with intimate beds of fruit and vegetables and the 'Sensory Garden' which is a garden to tantalise all the senses. "Barfuss Park" – Britain's first barefoot walk – has proved to be extremely popular as people exchange the comfort of their shoes and socks to experience the revitalising sensations of water, mud, sand, straw, and a range of other surfaces said to awaken the spirit. There are also extensive children's play areas and the stunning Italian Garden Tearoom.

A special joint ticket is now available to combine the garden with the unique Trentham Monkey Forest. Also set within the 725 acre estate are 60 individual shops and restaurants, an award winning Garden Centre and 120 room Premier Inn Hotel.

[i] Shopping, Hotel and several restaurants on site.

Wheelchair loan available.

Licensed.

By arrangement.

[P] Free Parking. Coach parking, drop-off, meet and greet available.

On leads.

Hotel.

THE ANCIENT HIGH HOUSE

Greengate Street, Stafford ST16 2JA
Tel: 01785 619131 **Fax:** 01785 619132 **E-mail:** ahh@staffordbc.gov.uk
www.staffordbc.gov.uk/heritage
Owner: Stafford Borough Council **Contact:** Mark Hartwell
Over four hundred years of history are waiting to be discovered within the walls of Stafford's Ancient High House – England's largest timber-framed town house and one of the finest Tudor buildings in the country. Now fully restored, the superb period room settings reflect its fascinating story.
Location: MAP 6:N5, OS Ref. SJ922 232. Town centre.
Open: All year: Tues–Sat, 10am–4pm.
Admission: Free. Check for events, charges may apply.
🔲 ♿ Unsuitable. 🎦 By arrangement. 🏫 School tours by arrangement.
🐕 Guide dogs only. ▲ ❄ ♿

BOSCOBEL HOUSE & THE ROYAL OAK ♯

BISHOP'S WOOD, BREWOOD, STAFFORDSHIRE ST19 9AR

www.english-heritage.org.uk/boscobel

Tel: 01902 850244   **E-mail:** customers@english-heritage.org.uk
Owner: English Heritage   **Contact:** Visitor Operations Team
This 17th century hunting lodge played a vital part in Charles II's escape from the Roundheads. A descendant of the Royal Oak, which sheltered the fugitive future King from Cromwell's troops after the Battle of Worcester in 1651, still stands in the fields near Boscobel House. The timber-framed house where the King slept in a tiny 'priest-hole' has been fully restored and furnished. Let our new interpretation guide you through Boscobel's more recent past as a farm, complete with dairy and smithy.
Location: MAP 6:N6, OS127, SJ838 082. On unclassified road between A41 & A5. 8m NW of Wolverhampton.
Open: 1 Apr–31 Oct: Wed–Sun & BH Mons, 10am–5pm. Last entry 1hr before closing.
Admission: Adult £5.20, Child £2.60, Conc. £4.40, Family £13. EH Members free. Group discount available. Opening times and prices are valid until 31st March 2010, after this date details are subject to change please see www.english-heritage.org.uk for the most up-to-date information.
ℹ️ Exhibition. Guidebooks. Picnic Area. Hazardous. Ovp. 🔲 ♿ 🎦 🅿️ 🏫 ✖ ♿

BIDDULPH GRANGE GARDEN ❧

GRANGE ROAD, BIDDULPH, STOKE-ON-TRENT ST8 7SD

Tel: 01782 517999 **Fax:** 01782 510624
Owner: The National Trust **Contact:** The Garden Office
E-mail: biddulphgrange@nationaltrust.org.uk
A rare and exciting survival of a High Victorian garden, restored by the National Trust. The garden is divided into a series of themed gardens within a garden, with a Chinese temple, Egyptian court, pinetum, dahlia walk, glen and many other settings. Difficult uneven levels, unsuitable for wheelchairs.
Location: MAP 6:N3, OS Ref. SJ891 592. E of A527, 3½m SE of Congleton, 8m N of Stoke-on-Trent.
Open: 15–19 Feb, Mon–Fri, 11am–3.30pm; 3–31 Mar, 11am–5pm, Wed–Sun; 1 Apr–31 Oct, 11am–5pm, daily; 6 Nov–19 Dec, 11am–3.30pm, Sat & Sun. Open BH Mons. Closes dusk if earlier. Tea-room last orders 4.30pm; winter menu in Nov & Dec.
*Admission: 3 Mar–31 Oct: Adult £7, Child £3.50, Family £17.50. Feb, Nov & Dec: Adult £3.50, Child £1.75, Family £8.75. Joint tickets available Wed–Sun only Biddulph Grange Gardens & Little Moreton Hall, 14 Mar–1 Nov. *includes a voluntary donation but visitors can choose to pay the standard prices displayed at the property and on the website. Gift Aid is not included in group prices.
🔲 ❄ ♿ Unsuitable for wheelchairs and people with mobility problems. ✖
🐕 In car park, on leads. ♿

CASTERNE HALL 🏛

Ilam, Nr Ashbourne, Derbyshire DE6 2BA
Tel: 01335 310489 **E-mail:** mail@casterne.co.uk **www.casterne.co.uk**
Owner/Contact: Charles Hurt
Manor house in beautiful location, a seat of the Hurt family for 500 years.
Location: MAP 6:O3, OS Ref. SK123 523. Take first turning on left N of Ilam and continue past 'Casterne Farms only' sign.
Open: 23 Jun–30 July: weekdays only. Tour at 2pm.
Admission: £5.
🎦 ♿ Partial. 🎦 Obligatory. 🅿️ 🏫 ▲€

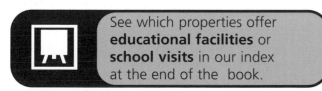

See which properties offer **educational facilities** or **school visits** in our index at the end of the book.

Biddulph Grange Garden

CHILLINGTON HALL 🏠
CODSALL WOOD, WOLVERHAMPTON, STAFFORDSHIRE WV8 1RE
www.chillingtonhall.co.uk

Tel: 01902 850236 **Fax:** 01902 850768 **E-mail:** info@chillingtonhall.co.uk

Owner/Contact: Mr & Mrs J W Giffard

Home of the Giffards since 1178. Built during 18th century by Francis Smith of Warwick and John Soane. Park designed by 'Capability' Brown. Smith's Staircase, Soane's Saloon and the Pool (a lake of 70 acres) are splendid examples of the days of the Georgian landowner.

Location: MAP 6:N6, OS Ref. SJ864 067. 2m S of Brewood off A449. 4m NW of M54/J2. SAT NAV. (off) Port Lane Brewood.

Open: House: Mon–Thur, 12 Apr–27 May, 2–5pm. Last entry 4pm. Grounds: As House. Parties by separate arrangement.

Admission: Adult £6, Child £3. Grounds only: half price.

⊤ ♿ Partial. 👣 Obligatory. 🅿 🚷 In grounds, on leads. €

Boscobel House

Dorothy Clive Garden

THE DOROTHY CLIVE GARDEN

Willoughbridge, Market Drayton, Shropshire TF9 4EU

Tel: 01630 647237 **Fax:** 01630 647902 **E-mail:** info@dorothyclivegarden.co.uk
www.dorothyclivegarden.co.uk

Owner: Willoughbridge Garden Trust **Contact:** Garden Office

The Dorothy Clive Garden accommodates a wide range of choice and unusual plants providing interest from Spring to Autumn. Features include a magnificent Rhododendron quarry garden with spectacular waterfall, beautiful seasonal flower borders, a scree and water garden. Tearoom serving home-baked hot and cold snacks throughout the day.

Location: MAP 6:M4, OS Ref. SJ753 400. A51, 2m S of Woore, 3m from Bridgemere.

Open: See website www.dorothyclivegarden.co.uk.

Admission: Adult £5.50, OAP £4.75, Child under 16 Free.
Pre-booked Groups (20+) £4.50.

🔳 🔳 🅿 🔳 In grounds on leads.

ERASMUS DARWIN HOUSE 🏛

Beacon Street, Lichfield, Staffordshire WA13 7AD
www.erasmusdarwin.org

Tel: 01543 306260 **E-mail:** enquiries@erasmusdarwin.org

Owner: The Erasmus Darwin Foundation **Contact:** Alison Wallis

Grandfather of Charles Darwin and a founder member of the Lunar Society, Erasmus Darwin (1731–1802) was a leading doctor, scientist, inventor and poet. This elegant Georgian house was his home and contains an exhibition of his life, theories, and inventions. There is also an 18th century herb garden. The house has been newly refurbished to make it more interactive, interesting and fun for all the family.

Location: MAP 6:P5, OS Ref. SK115 098. Situated at the West end of Lichfield Cathedral Close.

Open: All year. Please telephone for details and check our website.

Admission: Adult £3, Conc. £2, Child £1, Family £6. Groups (10–50) £2.

🔳 🔳 🔳 🔳 🔳 By arrangement. 🔳 🅿 Disabled only. 🔳 🔳 Guide dogs only. 🔆

THE HEATH HOUSE

Tean, Stoke-on-Trent, Staffordshire ST10 4HA
Tel: 01538 722212 / 01386 792110
E-mail: j-philips1@homecall.co.uk

Owner/Contact: Mr John Philips

The Heath House is an early Victorian mansion designed and built 1836–1840 in the Tudor style for John Burton Philips. The collection of paintings is a rare survival and has remained undisturbed since its acquisition. It is still a Philips family home. Large attractive formal garden.

Location: MAP 6:O4, OS Ref. SK030 392. A522 off A50 at Uttoxeter 5m W, at Lower Tean turn right.

Open: Easter Monday & August BH Mons & 26 May–8 Jun, Jul 23–5 Aug, 2.30–5pm. Please telephone in advance to confirm opening times.

Admission: £5. No Conc. No reductions for groups.

ℹ No photography or video recording. 🔳 🔳 Obligatory. 🅿
🔳 In grounds, on leads. 🔺

IZAAK WALTON'S COTTAGE

Worston Lane, Shallowford, Nr Stone, Stafford ST16 0PA
Tel/Fax: 01785 760278

E-mail: iwc@staffordbc.gov.uk **www.staffordbc.gov.uk/heritage**

Owner: Stafford Borough Council **Contact:** Mark Hartwell

Stafford's rural heritage is embodied in the charming 17th century cottage owned by the celebrated author of *The Compleat Angler*. Izaak Walton's Cottage gives a fascinating insight into the history of angling and the life of a writer whose work remains 'a unique celebration of the English countryside.'

Location: MAP 6:N5, OS Ref. SJ876 293. M6/J14, A5013 towards Eccleshall, signposted on A5013.

Open: May–Aug: Sun, 1–5pm.

Admission: Free. Check for events, charges may apply.

🔳 🔳 🔳 Partial. WCs. 🔳 🅿 Limited for cars. 🔳 Guide dogs only. 🔺 🔳

©NTPL/David Lee

MOSELEY OLD HALL ✤
FORDHOUSES, WOLVERHAMPTON WV10 7HY

Tel: 01902 782808   **E-mail:** moseleyoldhall@nationaltrust.org.uk
Owner: The National Trust   **Contact:** The Property Manager
An Elizabethan timber-framed house encased in brick in 1870; with original interiors. Charles II hid here after the Battle of Worcester. The bed in which he slept is on view as well as the hiding place he used. An exhibition retells the story of the King's dramatic escape from Cromwell's troops, and there are optional, free guided tours. The garden has been reconstructed in 17th century style with formal box parterre, only 17th century plants are grown. The property is a Sandford Education Award Winner.

© NTPL / Andreas von Einsiedel

Location: MAP 6:N6, OS Ref. SJ932 044. 4m N of Wolverhampton between A449 and A46.
Open: 6 Mar–31 Oct: Sats, Suns, Weds, BH Mons & following Tues, (excluding Tues 4 May), 12 noon–5pm also 5 Jul–14 Sept, Mon & Tues, 12 noon–5pm. 7 Nov–19 Dec: Suns, 12 noon–4pm (conducted tours only Nov & Dec), 28 Nov, 5 Dec & 12 Dec: Christmas activites. Last admission to the house 30 minutes before closing. Shop, Tearoom & Garden: Open 12 noon.
Admission: Adult £6.60, Child £3.30, Family £16.50. Groups (15+) £5.60pp (Weds £5.30). Private visits outside normal open times £7.70 (min £140). NT members free with valid membership card during normal opening times.
🖼 🚻 ♿ Ground floor & grounds. WC. 🖼 Tearoom in 18th century barn. 🖼 P 🖼 🖼 On leads. 🔺 🖼

Erasmus Darwin House

STAFFORD CASTLE & VISITOR CENTRE
Newport Road, Stafford ST16 1DJ
Tel/Fax: 01785 257698   **E-mail:** staffordcastle@staffordbc.gov.uk
www.staffordbc.gov.uk/heritage
Owner: Stafford Borough Council   **Contact:** Mark Hartwell
Stafford Castle has dominated the Stafford landscape for over 900 years. William the Conqueror first built Stafford Castle as a fortress to subdue the local populace. The visitor centre – built in the style of a Norman guardhouse – features an audio-visual area that brings its turbulent past to life.
Location: MAP 6:N5, OS Ref. SJ904 220. On N side of A518, 1½m WSW of town centre.
Open: Apr–Oct: Wed–Sun, 11am–4pm (open BHs). Nov–Mar: Sat & Sun, 11am–4pm.
Admission: Free (admission charges may apply for events).
🖼 🖼 By arrangement. P 🖼 Visitor centre – Guide dogs only. 🖼 🖼

TRENTHAM GARDENS   *See page 312 for full page entry*

© NTPL / Andreas von Einsiedel

Moseley Old Hall

©NTPL/Nik Meers

WALL ROMAN SITE (LETOCETUM) ♯ ❧

Watling Street, Nr Lichfield, Staffordshire WS14 0AW
Tel: 01926 852078 **E-mail:** customers@english-heritage.org.uk
www.english-heritage.org.uk/wallroman
Owner: English Heritage **Contact:** Visitor Operations Team
The remains of a staging post alongside Watling Street. The foundations of an inn and bathhouse can be seen, and many of the excavated finds are displayed in the on-site museum.

Location: MAP 6:O6, OS139, SK098 066. Off A5 at Wall, nr Lichfield.

Open: Site: 1 Mar–1 Nov: daily, 10am–5pm. Museum: 21 Mar–31 Oct: 11am–4pm on last Sat and Sun of each month and Bank Hols. 2 Nov–28 Feb '10: Closed.

Admission: Free. Opening times and prices are valid until 31st March 2010, after this date details are subject to change please see www.english-heritage.org.uk for the most up-to-date information.
ℹ Picnic area. 🅿 ♿

---

gift aid it Some properties will be operating the Gift Aid on Entry scheme at their admission points. Where the scheme is operating, visitors are offered a choice between paying the standard admission price or paying the 'Gift Aid Admission' which includes a voluntary donation of at least 10%. Gift Aid Admissions enable the charity to reclaim tax on the whole amount paid* – an extra 28% – potentially a very significant boost to property funds. Money raised from paying visitors in this way will go towards restoration projects at the property and will be very welcome.

Where shown, the admission prices are inclusive of the 10% voluntary donation where properties are operating the Gift Aid on Entry scheme, but both the standard admission price and the Gift Aid Admission will be displayed at the property and on their website.

*Gift Aid donations must be supported by a valid Gift Aid declaration and a Gift Aid declaration can only cover donations made by an individual for him/herself or for him/herself and members of his/her family.

WHITMORE HALL 🏛

WHITMORE, NEWCASTLE-UNDER-LYME ST5 5HW

Tel: 01782 680478 **Fax:** 01782 680906

Owner: Mr Guy Cavenagh-Mainwaring **Contact:** Mr Michael Cavenagh-Thornhill
Whitmore Hall is a Grade I listed building, designated as a house of outstanding architectural and historical interest, and is a fine example of a small Carolinian manor house (1676), although parts of the hall date back to a much earlier period. The hall has beautifully proportioned light rooms, curving staircase and landing. There are some good family portraits to be seen with a continuous line, from 1624 to the present day. It has been the family seat, for over 900 years, of the Cavenagh-Mainwarings who are direct descendants of the original Norman owners. The interior of the hall has recently been refurbished and is in fine condition. The grounds include a beautiful home park with a lime avenue leading to the house, as well as landscaped gardens encompassing an early Victorian summer house. One of the outstanding features of Whitmore is the extremely rare example of a late Elizabethan stable block, the ground floor is part cobbled and has nine oak-carved stalls.

Location: MAP 6:M4, OS Ref. SJ811 413. On A53 Newcastle–Market Drayton Road, 3m from M6/J15.

Open: 1 May–31 Aug: Tues, Weds, 2–5pm (last tour 4.30pm).

Admission: Adult £4, Child 50p.

♿ Ground floor & grounds.
🍽 Afternoon teas for booked groups (15+), May–Aug. ⚲ 🅿 ♿

Trentham Gardens

■ **Owner**

The Viscount Daventry

■ **Contact**

Miss Brenda Newell
Arbury Hall
Nuneaton
Warwickshire CV10 7PT

Tel: 024 7638 2804
Fax: 024 7664 1147
E-mail: brenda.newell@
arburyhall.net

■ **Location**
MAP 7:A7
OS Ref. SP335 893

London, M1, M6/J3
(A444 to Nuneaton),
2m SW of Nuneaton.
1m W of A444.

Chester A51, A34, M6
(from J14 to J3), 2½ hrs.
Nuneaton 10 mins.

London 2 hrs,
Birmingham ½ hr,
Coventry 20 mins.

Bus: Nuneaton 3m.

Rail: Nuneaton
Station 3m.

Air: Birmingham
International 17m.

■ **Opening Times**
All year
For corporate events.

Pre-booked visits to the
Hall and Gardens for
groups of 25+ on Tues,
Weds & Thurs from Easter
to the end of September.

Hall & Gardens open
2–5pm on BH weekends
only (Suns & Mons)
Easter–September.

■ **Admission**
Summer
Hall & Gardens

Adult	£7.00
Child (up to 14 yrs)	£4.50
Family (2+2)	£18.50

Gardens Only

Adult	£5.00
Child (up to 14 yrs.)	£3.50

Groups (25+)

Adult	£7.00

ARBURY HALL

www.arburyestate.co.uk

Arbury Hall has been the seat of the Newdegate family for over 450 years and is the ancestral home of Viscount Daventry. This Tudor/Elizabethan House was gothicised by Sir Roger Newdegate in the 18th century and is regarded as one of the finest examples of Gothic architecture in the country. The principal rooms, with their soaring fan vaulted ceilings and plunging pendants and filigree tracery, stand as a most breathtaking and complete example of early Gothic Revival architecture and provide a unique and fascinating venue for corporate entertaining, product launches, receptions, fashion shoots and activity days. Exclusive use of this historic Hall, its gardens and parkland is offered to clients. The Hall stands in the middle of beautiful parkland with landscaped gardens of rolling lawns, lakes and winding wooded walks. Spring flowers are profuse and in June rhododendrons, azaleas and giant wisteria provide a beautiful environment for the visitor.

George Eliot, the novelist, was born on the estate and Arbury Hall and Sir Roger Newdegate were immortalised in her book 'Scenes of Clerical Life'.

 Corporate hospitality, film location, small conferences, product launches and promotions, marquee functions, clay pigeon shooting, archery and other sporting activities, grand piano in Saloon, helicopter landing site. No cameras or video recorders indoors.

Exclusive lunches and dinners for corporate parties in dining room, max. 50, buffets 80.

Visitors may alight at the Hall's main entrance. Parking in allocated areas. Ramp access to main hall.

By arrangement for groups.

Obligatory. Tour time: 1hr.

200 cars and 3 coaches 250 yards from house. Follow tourist signs. Approach map available for coach drivers.

Welcome, must book. School room available.

In gardens on leads. Guide dogs only in house.

Conference/Function

ROOM	SIZE	MAX CAPACITY
Dining Room	35' x 28'	80
Saloon	35' x 30'	70
Stables Tearooms	31' x 18'	70

NTPL/Nadia Mackenzie

BADDESLEY CLINTON

www.nationaltrust.org.uk

Enjoy a day at Baddesley Clinton, the moated medieval manor house with hidden secrets! One of the most enchanting properties owned by the National Trust, Baddesley Clinton has seen little change since 1633 when Henry Ferrers 'the Antiquary' died. He was Squire at Baddesley for almost seventy years and remodelled the house over a long period of time, introducing much of the panelling and chimney pieces. Henry was proud of his ancestry and began the tradition at Baddesley of armorial glass, which has continued up to the present day. Henry let the house in the 1590s when it became a refuge for Jesuit priests, and hiding places, called 'priest's holes', created for their concealment, survive from this era. Pictures painted by Rebecca, wife of Marmion Edward Ferrers,

remain to show how the romantic character of Baddesley was enjoyed in the late 19th century when the family also created a sumptuously furnished Chapel.

The garden, which surrounds the house, incorporates many features including stewponds; a small lake (the 'Great Pool'); a walled garden with thatched summer house, and a lakeside walk with nature trail and wildflower meadow. Make a day of it! Complementary opening times and substantial discounts on joint ticket prices make a combined visit to Baddesley Clinton and Packwood House even more attractive, especially since both properties are only two miles apart.

NTPL/Andrew Butler

 WCs.
 Licensed.
 By arrangement.

 Guide dogs only.

■ Owner
The National Trust

■ Contact
The Estate Office
Baddesley Clinton
Rising Lane
Baddesley Clinton Village
Knowle
Solihull B93 0DQ

Tel: 01564 783294
Fax: 01564 782706
E-mail: baddesleyclinton@
nationaltrust.org.uk

■ Location
MAP 6:P8
OS Ref. SP199 715

¾ m W of A4141
Warwick/Birmingham
road at Chadwick End.

■ Opening Times
House
10 February–31 October:
Wed–Sun, Good Friday &
BH Mons, 11am–5pm.
29 March–18 April,
31 May–6 June, 26 July–
5 September &
25 October–31 October:
Mon–Sun, 11am–5pm.
1 December–19
December: Wed–Sun,
11am–4pm.

**Grounds, Shop &
Restaurant**
10 February–31 October:
Wed–Sun, Good Friday &
BH Mons, 11am–5pm.
29 March–18 April,
31 May–6 June, 26 July–
5 September &
25 October–31 October:
Mon–Sun, 11am–5pm.
3 November–
19 December: Wed–Sun,
11am–4pm.

■ *Admission
Adult	£9.25
Child	£4.65
Family	£23.10
Groups	£8.00
Guided tours (out of hours)	£16.00

Grounds only
Adult	£4.65
Child	£2.35

Combined Ticket with Packwood House
Adult	£13.00
Child	£6.55
Family	£32.50
Groups	£11.25

Gardens only
Adult	£6.95
Child	£3.50

*includes a voluntary donation but visitors can choose to pay the standard prices displayed at the property and on the website. This does not apply to group prices.

■ Owner
The National Trust

■ Contact
Visitor Services Manager
Charlecote Park,
Warwick CV35 9ER
Tel: 01789 470277
Fax: 01789 470544
E-mail: charlecotepark@
nationaltrust.org.uk

■ Location
MAP 6:P9
OS151, SP263 564

1m W of Wellesbourne,
5m E of Stratford-upon-
Avon.

Rail: Stratford-upon-
Avon 5 1/2ml.
Leamington Spa 8ml.

■ Opening Times
House*:
1 Mar–30 April, Fri–Tue,
12noon–4.30pm
1 May–28 Sept, Fri–Tue,
11am–5pm
1 Oct–31 Oct, Fri–Tue,
12noon–4.30pm
6 Nov–19 Dec, Sat &
Sun, 12noon–4pm
(Not all show rooms
are open)

House and Shop
also open:
Wed & Thu 31 Mar, 1,
7, 8 April and all of
Aug.

**Park, Gardens &
Outbuildings*:**
1 Jan-31 Dec, Mon-Sun,
10am-5.30pm.
Closes dusk if earlier

Restaurant:
1 Jan-31 Dec, Mon-Sun,
10.30am-5pm.
(11am–4pm, Jan, Feb,
Nov & Dec).

Shop:
6 Feb-28 Feb, 6 Nov-19
Dec, Sat & Sun, 11am-
4pm. 1 Mar-31 Oct, Fri-
Tue, 11am-5pm

*Last admission 30mins
before closing.

Property closed: 24-25
Dec

■ Gift Aid
Admission*

House, Garden & Park:
Adult £9, Child £4.50 &
Family £22.50
Garden & Park: Adult
£4.50, Child £2.25 &
Family £11.25
House, Garden & Park
Winter: Adult £5.50,
Child £2.75 & Family
£13.75

*Including a voluntary
donation; visitors can
however, choose to pay
the standard admission
prices which are
displayed at the property
and on the property web
site.
Gift aid is not included in
the group price.

CHARLECOTE PARK ❦

www.nationaltrust.org.uk

Enjoy a day at Charlecote Park, the home of the Lucy family for over 800 years. Built in the 1550's with warm red bricks and decorated in Warwickshire stone. The house has a fascinating history which includes a royal visit from Queen Elizabeth I and the arrest and trial of a young poacher. The young poacher was a local lad called William Shakespeare! Today, the visitors see the house as it was in Victorian times. The young bride of George Hammond Lucy, Mary Elizabeth, made extensive renovations to the house and gardens. These renovations included a new service wing and additional bedrooms as well as many of the plaster ceilings and stained glass windows that you will see. The gardens are interesting all year round and include the parterres on the west front, the sensory garden, herbaceous borders and beautifully manicured lawns. The outbuildings include the Victorian Kitchen, laundry, brew-house and carriage collections, while the Gatehouse hosts a family museum. There is also a children's quiz and you can play a game of croquet on the Croquet Lawn. The Orangery Restaurant, which is located next to the Cedar Lawn, serves hot and cold food. You could visit one of our two shops selling locally produced goods as well as a large range of gifts. There are various walks and talks throughout the season.

ℹ New project in the Victorian Kitchen which is bringing the room to life.

⬛

❋

🍴 Partial. WCs

🍷 Licensed.

🍴 Licensed.

⚒ For booked groups.

Ⓟ Limited for coaches.

⬛ By arrangement.

🦮 Guide dogs only.

⬛

❄

⬛ Special Events throughout the year. Please send SAE or tel. for details.

©English Heritage Photo Library

■ **Owner**
English Heritage

■ **Contact**
Visitor Operations Team
Kenilworth, Warwickshire
CV8 1NE

Tel: 01926 852 078
E-mail: customers
@english-heritage.org.uk

■ **Location**
MAP 6:P8
OS140, SP278 723

In Kenilworth off A46, W
end of town.

■ **Opening Times**

1 Apr–1 Nov: daily,
10am–5pm.

2 Nov–28 Feb '10, daily,
10am–4pm.

1–31 Mar: daily,
10am–5pm.

Closed 24–26 Dec & 1
Jan.

Gatehouse may close
early for private events.

■ **Gift Aid
Admission***

Adult	£7.00
Child	£3.50
Conc.	£6.00
Family	£17.50

15% discount for groups
(11+).

EH Members Free.

Opening times and prices
are valid until 31st March
2010, after this date
details are subject to
change please see
www.english-
heritage.org.uk for the
most up-to-date
information.

KENILWORTH CASTLE ▣
& ELIZABETHAN GARDEN
www.english-heritage.org.uk/kenilworth

A vast medieval fortress which became an Elizabethan palace, Kenilworth Castle is one of Britain's largest and most impressive historic sites. Extensive recent developments highlight its famous associations with Queen Elizabeth I and her favourite, Robert Dudley, including the recreation of the garden which was designed to astound visitors, including Elizabeth I at a time when Dudley still hoped to marry her.

The re-created garden features a bejewelled Renaissance aviary, an 18 foot high marble fountain, and a planting scheme abundant in colour, perfume and fruit.

As part of the multi-million pound English Heritage investment in Kenilworth Castle, Leicester's Gatehouse - long closed to the public - is now displayed fully restored. Chambers on its lower floors have been re-created as they might have appeared when the gatehouse was last inhabited in the 1930s, while the top floor houses 'The Queen and the Castle: Robert Dudley's Kenilworth'. Featuring items both from museums and private collections, this exhibition tells the story of Elizabeth I's relationship with Dudley, and her four visits to Kenilworth.

©English Heritage / John Watkins

©English Heritage Photo Library

ℹ WC. Guidebooks. Hazard. Ovp. Picnic area.

🛍

🍸

♿

☕

🎧

🅿

🖼 Exhibition. Family learning resources available.

🐕 On leads.

🔔

❄

🎭

■ **Owner**

The National Trust

■ **Contact**

The Estate Office
Packwood House
Lapworth
Solihull B94 6AT

Tel: 01564 783294
Fax: 01564 782706
E-mail: packwood@
nationaltrust.org.uk

■ **Location**
MAP 6:O8
OS Ref. SP174 722

2m E of Hockley Heath
(on A3400), 11m SE of
central Birmingham.

■ **Opening Times**
House
10 February–31 October:
Wed–Sun, Good Friday &
BH Mons, 11am–5pm.
29 March–18 April,
31 May–6 June, 26 July–
5 September &
25 October–31 October:
Mon–Sun, 11am–5pm.

Garden
10 February–31 October:
Wed–Sun, Good Friday &
BH Mons, 11am–5pm.
29 March–18 April, 31
May–6 June, 26 July–
5 September &
25 October–31 October:
Mon–Sun, 11am–5pm.

Park & Woodland Walks
All year: daily.

■ ***Admission***
Adult	£8.10
Child	£4.10
Family	£20.25
Groups	£7.00
Guided tours	
(out of hours)	£14.00

Garden only
Adult	£4.65
Child	£2.35

**Combined Ticket with
Baddesley Clinton**
Adult	£13.00
Child	£6.55
Family	£32.50
Groups	£11.25

Gardens only
Adult	£6.95
Child	£3.50

*includes a voluntary
donation but visitors can
choose to pay the standard
prices displayed at the
property and on the website.
This does not apply to group
prices.

PACKWOOD HOUSE ❧

www.nationaltrust.org.uk

Packwood lies in the pleasantly wooded Forest of Arden and was, for many years, the home of the Fetherstons who allowed Cromwell's General, Henry Ireton, to stay overnight before the Battle of Edgehill in 1642. There is also a tradition that Charles II was given refreshment at Packwood after his defeat at Worcester in 1651. Many of Packwood's interiors were designed in the 1920s and 30s in idealised Elizabethan or Jacobean styles for Graham Baron Ash. They offer a wonderful insight into the taste, rich decoration and way of life of a wealthy connoisseur in the period between the wars. Packwood still retains the intimate atmosphere of a real home, with lavishly furnished rooms containing French and Flemish tapestries and fine 17th & 18th century furniture. The oak panelled bedrooms with their sumptuous four-poster beds give you a glimpse of what it was like to stay the night as Baron Ash's guest. Queen Mary, another regal visitor, took refreshment here when she visited in August 1927. Look out for several reminders of that historic visit throughout the house.

The house is surrounded by its own delightful, tranquil grounds. The large flower garden complete with long herbaceous borders, enclosed by red brick walls with a gazebo in each corner, is a blend of the traditional country house garden and the Carolean Garden of the Fetherstons. The famous 17th century Yew Garden is traditionally said to represent 'The Sermon on the Mount' and is a highly unusual and attractive feature. Make a day of it! Complementary opening times and substantial discounts on joint ticket prices make a combined visit to Packwood House and Baddesley Clinton even more attractive, especially since both properties are only two miles apart.

 WCs.
 By arrangement.

🅿️

Guide dogs only.

Parkland only.

Shakespeare's Birthplace

Mary Arden's Farm

Anne Hathaway's Cottage

THE SHAKESPEARE HOUSES 🏛

www.shakespeare.org.uk

Five beautifully preserved Tudor Homes and gardens telling the complete Shakespeare story and all directly linked with William Shakespeare and his family. Each house has a unique story to tell and together they provide a unique experience of the dramatist's life and times.

Shakespeare's Birthplace

Start this fascinating journey with an introduction to William Shakespeare through a new Life, Love & Legacy exhibition before visiting this wonderful Tudor town house where the world's most famous playwright was born and grew up. See where prominent writers including Charles Dickens and Thomas Hardy have left their mark and watch demonstrations of the traditional craft practiced by Shakespeare's father, John, in the Glover's workshop. Meet your favourite Shakespeare characters in the garden with live impromptu performances from Shakespeare Aloud! Stroll round the traditional English garden, which features many plants and herbs mentioned in Shakespeare's plays, and remember your visit with a purchase from the gift shop.

Mary Arden's Farm - A Real Working Tudor Farm

Visit the childhood home of Shakespeare's mother and see the farm's history brought to life. Step back into the 1570s and see how Mary's neighbours, the Palmer family lived day-to-day Tudor style! Make friends with our Cotswold Sheep, Longhorn Cattle, Tamworth Pigs and many more rare breeds. Try hand-feeding the Bagot and Golden goats. Discover the nature trail and adventure playground and look out for special events over the school holidays.

Anne Hathaway's Cottage – The Most Romantic Shakespeare House.

Discover and fall in love with this beautiful English thatched cottage and family home of Shakespeare's wife, Anne Hathaway and see where he wooed her. Stroll through and admire the award winning cottage garden which overflows with old-fashioned plants, orchards and traditional vegetables. Sit in the romantic Willow Cabin and be inspired by Shakespeare's sonnets. Visit the Shakespeare Sculpture and Tree Garden and wander through the enchanting woodland walk.

Hall's Croft – The Jacobean Doctor's House

Explore the elegant house with its lavish rooms once owned by Shakespeare's daughter Susanna and wealthy physician husband John Hall.

Examine the fascinating collection of apothecary's equipment, books and medical instruments of the day. Relax in the tranquil gardens and savour the fragrant herb beds, like those used by John Hall in his remedies.

Nash's House & New Place – Where the Shakespeare Story Ended.

Take in the period splendour of Nash's House, once owned by Shakespeare's granddaughter and visit the site of New Place where Shakespeare's final beloved home once stood and where he died in 1616. Find out why New Place, Shakespeare's final home, came to be demolished and wander through the Elizabethan Knot Garden based on designs from Shakespeare's time.

The Shakespeare Houses and Gardens are owned and cared for by The Shakespeare Birthplace Trust which is an independent charity. Every admission to the Shakespeare Houses and purchase in the gift shops supports the work of the Shakespeare Birthplace Trust enabling the preservation of the houses and gardens for future generations.

■ Owner
The Shakespeare Birthplace Trust

■ Contact
The Shakespeare Birthplace Trust Henley Street Stratford-upon-Avon CV37 6QW
Tel: 01789 204016 (General enquiries)
Tel: 01789 201806/201836 (Group Visits)
Fax: 01789 263138
E-mail: info@ shakespeare.org.uk groups@ shakespeare.org.uk

■ Location
MAP 6:P9
OS Refs:
Birthplace – SP201 552
New Place – SP201 548
Hall's Croft – SP200 546
Hathaway's – SP185 547
Arden's – SP166 582
Rail: Direct service from London (Marylebone)
2 hrs from London
45 mins from Birmingham by car.
4m from M40/J15 and well signed from all approaches.

■ Opening Times
The Shakespeare Houses are open daily throughout the year.

1 November - 27 March: Last entry 4pm

Feb Half-Term, 28 March to end of October Half-Term: Last entry 5pm

July - August: last entry 5pm, except Shakespeare's Birthplace and Nash's House with last entry at 6pm

Please note that Mary Arden's Farm is open from 22 March–31 October.

■ Admission
Tickets to the Shakespeare Houses are valid for a full year, with unlimited entry. So for the price of one ticket, you can enjoy days out at the Shakespeare houses all year round –for free!

Visit the website for further details.

ℹ City Sightseeing guided bus tour service connecting the town houses with Anne Hathaway's Cottage and Mary Arden's Farm. No photography inside houses.

🎁 Gifts are available at all five Shakespeare properties.

❋ Plants are available for sale at Anne Hathaway's Cottage, Mary Arden's Farm and Hall's Croft.

🍴 Available, tel for details.

♿ Partial. WCs.

☕ Mary Arden's Farm

🍴 Hall's Croft

🧍 By special arrangement.

🅿 The Trust provides a free coach terminal for delivery and pick-up of groups, maximum stay 30 mins at Shakespeare's Birthplace. Parking at Anne Hathaway's Cottage and Mary Arden's.

📷 Available for all houses. For information 01789 201804.

🐕 Guide dogs only.

❄

🎭 Please check our website for further details.

Owner
Stoneleigh Abbey Ltd

Contact
Estate Office
Stoneleigh Abbey
Kenilworth
Warwickshire CV8 2LF

Tel: 01926 858535
Fax: 01926 850724
E-mail: enquire
@stoneleighabbey.org

Location
MAP 6:P8
OS Ref. SP318 712

Off A46/B4115,
2m W of Kenilworth.
From London 100m,
M40 to Warwick.

Rail: Coventry station 5m,
Leamington Spa
station 5m.

Air: Coventry Airport 3m
Birmingham International
17m.

Opening Times
Good Fri–end October

Tue–Thur, Suns & BHs:
House tours at
11am, 1pm & 3pm.

Grounds: 10am–5pm.

Admission
House Tour & Grounds
Adult   £7.00
1 Child Free with
each adult

Additional Child   £3.00
OAP   £6.50

Discounts for Groups
(20+).

Jane Austen Tours
Sundays and
Wednesdays, 1pm £7.00

Grounds only   £3.00

Parking

Car parking is free of
charge to purchasers of
tickets for a guided tour
or admission to the
grounds.

Groups are welcome
during the published
opening times or at other
times by arrangement.
Please telephone.

Conference/Function

ROOM	SIZE	MAX CAPACITY
Saloon	14 x 9m	100
Gilt Hall	7 x 7m	60
Servants' Hall	14 x 8m	100
Riding School	12 x 33m	490
Conservatory	19 x 6m	100

STONELEIGH ABBEY

www.stoneleighabbey.org

Stoneleigh Abbey was founded in the reign of Henry II and after the Dissolution was granted to the Duke of Suffolk. The estate then passed into the ownership of the Leigh family who remained for 400 years. The estate is now managed by a charitable trust.

Visitors will experience a wealth of architectural styles spanning more than 800 years: the magnificent State rooms and chapel of the 18th century Baroque West Wing contain original pieces of furniture including a set of library chairs made by William Gomm in 1763; a medieval Gatehouse; the Gothic Revival-style Regency Stables. Jane Austen was a distant relative of the Leigh family and in her description of 'Sotherton' in *Mansfield Park* she recalls her stay at Stoneleigh

Abbey. Parts of *Northanger Abbey* also use Stoneleigh for inspiration.

The River Avon flows through the estate's 690 acres of grounds and parkland which displays the influences of Humphry Repton and other major landscape architects. In June 1858 Queen Victoria and Prince Albert visited Stoneleigh Abbey – during their stay Queen Victoria planted an oak tree. In 2003 HRH Prince Charles visited Stoneleigh to mark the completion of the restoration of the Abbey and during his visit he also planted an English oak tree.

Stoneleigh Abbey has been the subject of a major restoration programme funded by the Heritage Lottery Fund, English Heritage and the European Regional Development Fund.

i Available for public and commercial hire.

House only. WCs.

Obligatory.

Schools welcome.

UPTON HOUSE & GARDENS

www.nationaltrust.org.uk

Join the guests of Lord & Lady Bearsted and experience the weekend house party of a 1930s millionaire. Walter Samuel, 2nd Viscount Bearsted was Chairman of Shell Transport & Trading Company and son of the company's founder. He was a passionate art collector, and adapted the building to display his paintings and porcelain. Today visitors can get close to internationally important works by artists such as Hogarth, Stubbs, Canaletto, Brueghel and El Greco. Visitors will also hear and discover more about family life and join the in the atmosphere of the party. Upton has all the elements of a millionaires country home – with swimming pool, squash court and a glamorous art deco interior in Lady Bearsted's bathroom.

Garden

The garden planting was principally designed by Kitty Lloyd-Jones with Lady Bearsted in the 1930's. The sweeping lawn gives way to a dramatic series of terraces and herbaceous borders, descending to over an acre of kitchen garden and tranquil water garden, with rills, ponds and ornamental fish. Upton is also home to the national collection of asters.

The licensed Pavilion Restaurant in the grounds serves full lunches and afternoon teas. It is also available for hire throughout the year for dinners, parties and functions, please call for details.

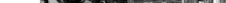

<table>
<tr><td></td><td>Children's Trail. No indoor photography.</td></tr>
<tr><td></td><td></td></tr>
<tr><td></td><td></td></tr>
<tr><td></td><td></td></tr>
<tr><td></td><td>Partial. WCs.</td></tr>
<tr><td></td><td>Licensed.</td></tr>
<tr><td>P</td><td>350 yds from House. Limited parking for coaches.</td></tr>
<tr><td></td><td>Guide dogs only</td></tr>
<tr><td></td><td></td></tr>
</table>

Owner
The National Trust

Contact
The Visitor Services Manager
Upton House & Gardens
Banbury
Oxfordshire OX15 6HT

Tel: 01295 670266
Fax: 01295 671144
E-mail: uptonhouse@nationaltrust.org.uk

Location
MAP 7:A9
OS Ref. SP371 461

On A422, 7m NW of Banbury. 12m SE of Stratford-upon-Avon

Rail: Banbury Station, 7m.

Opening Times
Spring & Summer
13 Feb–10 Mar, Sat - Wed, 11–5pm. House by guided tours only.
13 March–31 October.
House, Garden, Restaurant & Shop:
Fri–Wed, 11–5pm.
House by guided tours only 11am–1pm.
Last entry 4.30pm.

Winter
Exhibition, Garden, Restaurant & Shop:
1 November– 22 December, Sat–Wed, 26 Dec–3 Jan 2011 daily, 12noon–4pm.
House (ground floor):
Sat & Sun, 6 Nov–19 December, 12noon–4pm.

*Admission
House & Garden
Adult	£9.00
Child	£4.50
Family	£22.50
Groups (15+)	£7.35

Garden only
Adult	£5.50
Child	£2.70
Family	£13.70
Groups (15+)	£4.45

House & Garden
Winter
Adult	£5.50
Child	£2.70
Family	£13.70

*includes a voluntary donation but visitors can choose to pay the standard prices displayed at the property and on the website. This does not apply to group prices.

Special Events
All Year
Concerts, historical re-enactments, art tours, family fun days. Newly refurbished 1930's Squash Court with summer film and winter exhibition. Hands on activities in the house. 'Picture in Focus' and Conservation exhibitions.

© NTPL / Rupert Truman

© NTPL / Nadia Mackenzie

© NTPL / Robert Morris

COUGHTON COURT ❧
ALCESTER, WARWICKSHIRE B49 5JA

www.nationaltrust.org.uk

Tel: 01789 400777 **Fax:** 01789 765544 **Visitor Information:** 01789 762435
E-mail: coughtoncourt@nationaltrust.org.uk
Contact: The National Trust

Home to the Throckmorton family for 600 years, this finest of Tudor houses stands testament to a family's courage to maintain their beliefs. From high favour and fortunes to fear, oppression and danger following the Reformation, the Throckmortons were leaders in a dangerous age, and helped to bring about Catholic Emancipation in the nineteenth century. This is a story of fascinating personalities which you can explore through the 'family album' of portraits and Catholic treasures around the house. Coughton is still very much a family home with an intimate feel: the Throckmorton family live here and continue to manage the stunning gardens, which they have created.

Location: MAP 6:O9, OS Ref. SP080 604, Located on A435, 2m N of Alcester, 8m NW of Stratford-upon-Avon, 18m from Birmingham City Centre.

Open: House: 13–28 Mar; Sats & Suns, 1 Apr–30 Jun; Wed–Sun, 1 Jul–31 Aug; Tue–Sun, 1–30 Sept, Wed–Sun, 1 Oct–7 Nov; Thurs–Sun, 11am–5pm. 4–12 Dec; Mon–Sun, 12pm–6pm. Open BH Mons. Closed Good Friday & 12 Jun & 10 Jul. Admission by timed ticket at weekends and on busy days. Garden, Shop and Restaurant: As house, 11am–5.30pm. Walled Garden: As house, 11.30am–4.45pm but closed Mar, Thur & Fri in Oct, Dec.

*Admission: House & Garden: Adult £9.40, Child (5–16) £4.70, Family £23.50, Groups (15+) £7.45. Christmas Weekend; Adult £3, Child £1. Gardens only: Adult £6.50, Child (5–16) £3.25, Family £16.30, Groups (15+) £5.10. Walled Garden: NT members £2.50 (included in admission price for non-members). *includes a voluntary donation but visitors can choose to pay the standard prices displayed at the property and on the website. Not included in group prices.

ⓘSecrets Spies & Sacrifice trail and Mighty Mission Quiz for children; Outdoor Adventure Packs for families, 10 Highlights trail for adults; Children's play area. Ice Cream Parlour and Secondhand Bookshop. No indoor photography. ⬚⬚⬚ Private dinners can be provided by prior arrangement in restaurant. ⬚ Ground floor of house, gardens & restaurant. WC. ⬚ Licensed.⬚ Licensed. Capacity: 70 inside, Covered Courtyard 50. ⬚ Free introductory talks available most days. ⬚ ⬚ Guide dogs only. ⬚ There is an exciting events programme that includes walks, outdoor theatre, Christmas Wassail and a Christmas Festival. For further details call the property or see website.

COUGHTON COURT GARDENS ⬚
ALCESTER, WARWICKSHIRE B49 5JA

www.coughtoncourt.co.uk

Garden Tours: 01789 762542 **Fax:** 01789 764369
E-mail: office@throckmortons.co.uk
Contact: Throckmorton family

Heralded by the RHS as one of the finest gardens in Britain, the beautiful 25 acres of grounds include a walled garden, lake, riverside walk and bog garden, colour themed gardens, daffodils and orchards and fruit gardens. The Rose Labyrinth, designed by daughter Christina Williams, boasts spectacular displays of roses and received an **Award of Garden Excellence from the World Federation of Rose Societies** – a first for the UK. It is also the first private garden to be awarded a Gilt Medal from The Daffodil Society for an outstanding contribution to daffodils. A newly designed garden featuring the rare Throckmorton daffodils opened in 2009. Plants for sale are grown by the family.

Location / Open / Admission: see above.

⬚ ⬚⬚ ⬚ Partial. WCs. ⬚ Licensed. ⬚ Licensed. ⬚ ⬚ Guide dogs only.

©Coughton Court

©Coughton Court

ARBURY HALL 🏛	*See page 318 for full page entry.*
BADDESLEY CLINTON ❧	*See page 319 for full page entry.*
CHARLECOTE PARK ❧	*See page 320 for full page entry.*

For unique **Civil wedding** venues see our index at the end of the book.

COMPTON VERNEY
COMPTON VERNEY, WARWICKSHIRE CV35 9HZ

www.comptonverney.org.uk

Tel: 01926 645500 **Fax:** 01926 645501 **E-mail:** info@comptonverney.org.uk
Owner: Compton Verney House Trust   **Contact:** Ticketing Desk

Set in a Grade I listed mansion remodelled by Robert Adam in the 1760s, Compton Verney offers a unique art gallery experience. Relax, enjoy and explore the 120 acres of 'Capability' Brown landscaped parkland which it stands in.

Within the gallery discover a growing collection on nationally and internationally significant art from around the world including: paintings from the 'Golden Age' of Neapolitan art (1600-1800), Northern European art from (1450-1650) by Cranach and Schongauer; British portraits featuring work by Sir Joshua Reynolds and a collection of Tudor portraits; one of Europe's finest collections of Chinese bronzes; the UK's largest collection of British Folk Art and textiles by 1930s designer Enid Marx.

Contact us for details of our programme of changing exhibitions, talks, tours and workshops.

Location: MAP 7:A9, OS Ref. SP312 529. 9m E of Stratford-upon-Avon, 10 mins from M40/J12, on B4086 between Wellesbourne and Kineton. Rail: Nearest station is Banbury or Leamington Spa. Air: Nearest airport Birmingham International.

Open: 27 Mar–12 Dec: Tues–Sun & BH Mons, 11am–5pm. Last entry to Gallery 4.30pm. Groups welcome, please book in advance.

Admission: Adult £8, Child (5–16yrs) £2, Conc. £6, Family £18. Groups (15+): Adult £7.20, Conc. £5.40, group rate with tour, Adult £13, Conc. £11.

Special Events: 2010 Exhibitions: 27 Mar–20 Jun, Francis Bacon: In Camera. 24 July–31 October, Volcano. Autumn exhibition to be announced. Special events during the school holiday (Easter, May Bank Holiday, May Half Term, Summer Holidays, October Half Term and Christmas) please call or visit www.comptonverney.org.uk for details or sign up to our e-bulletin.

ⓘ No photography in the Gallery. ⬚ ⬚ ⬚ WCs. ⬚ Licensed. ⬚ Licensed. Ⓚ Obligatory. Ⓟ Ample. ⬚ ⬚ Guide dogs only. ⬚ ⬚

Coughton Court

NTPL / Matthew Antrobus

FARNBOROUGH HALL ❧
BANBURY, OXFORDSHIRE OX17 1DU

www.nationaltrust.org.uk

Tel: 01295 690002 (information line)

Owner: The National Trust

A classical stone house of the mid-18th century, the home of the Holbech family for 300 years. Collections include antiquities collected on the Grand Tour, whilst the interior plasterwork is some of the finest in the country. Superb Grade I listed grounds remain largely unchanged and include terraced walk with fine views, ornamented with temples.

Location: MAP 7:A9, OS151, SP430 490. 6m N of Banbury, ½ m W of A423.

Open: House & Terrace Walk: 3 Apr–29 Sept: Weds & Sats, 2–5.30pm. Also 2 & 3 May: Last admission 5pm.

Admission: House & Terrace Walk: Adult £5.25, Child £2.60, Family £13.20.

♿ House & grounds, but steep terrace walk. 🅿 Limited 🐾 In grounds, on leads.

©Coughton Court

Coughton Court Gardens, Alcester

THE HILLER GARDEN
Dunnington Heath Farm, Alcester, Warwickshire B49 5PD

Tel: 01789 491342 **Fax:** 01789 490439

Owner: A H Hiller & Son Ltd **Contact:** Mr Jeff Soulsby

2 acre garden of unusual herbaceous plants and over 200 rose varieties.

Location: MAP 6:O9, OS Ref. SP066 539. 1½ m S of Ragley Hall on B4088 (formerly A435).

Open: All year: daily 9am–5pm.

Admission: Free.

© NTPL

Farnborough Hall

HONINGTON HALL 🏛
SHIPSTON-ON-STOUR, WARWICKSHIRE CV36 5AA

Tel: 01608 661434 **Fax:** 01608 663717

Owner/Contact: Benjamin Wiggin Esq

This fine Caroline manor house was built in the early 1680s for Henry Parker in mellow brickwork, stone quoins and window dressings. Modified in 1751 when an octagonal saloon was inserted. The interior was also lavishly restored around this time and contains exceptional mid-Georgian plasterwork. Set in 15 acres of grounds.

Location: MAP 6:P9, OS Ref. SP261 427. 10m S of Stratford-upon-Avon. 1½ m N of Shipston-on-Stour. Take A3400 towards Stratford, then signed right to Honington.

Open: By appointment for groups (10+).

Admission: Telephone for details.

🎫 Obligatory. 🐾

KENILWORTH CASTLE ⌗   *See page 321 for full page entry.*

LORD LEYCESTER HOSPITAL
HIGH STREET, WARWICK CV34 4BH
www.lordleycester.com

Tel: 01926 491422

Owner: The Governors   **Contact:** The Master

This magnificent range of 14th and 15th Century half-timbered buildings was adapted into almshouses by Robert Dudley, Earl of Leycester, in 1571. The Hospital still provides homes for ex-Servicemen and their wives. The Guildhall, Great Hall, chantry Chapel, Brethren's Kitchen and galleried Courtyard are still in everyday use. The regimental museum of the Queen's Own Hussars is housed here. The historic Master's Garden was featured in BBC TV's Gardener's World, and the Hospital buildings in many productions including, most recently, "Dr Who" and David Dimbleby's "How We Built Britain".

Location: OS Ref. 280 648. 1m N of M40/J15 on the A429 in town centre. Rail: 10 minutes walk from Warwick station.

Open: All year: Tue–Sun & BHs (except Good Fri & 25 Dec), 10am–5pm (4pm in winter). Garden: Apr–Sept: 10am–4.30pm.

Admission: Adult £4.90, Child £3.90, Conc. £4.40. Garden only £2. 5% discount for adult groups (20+).

⬚⬚⬚⬚ Partial. WCs. ⬚⬚⬚ By arrangement. 🅿 Limited for cars. No coaches. ⬚⬚ Guide dogs only. ⬚⬚

PACKWOOD HOUSE 🌿   *See page 322 for full page entry.*

For **special events** held throughout the year, see the index at the end of the book.

Packwood House

NTPL / Stephen Robson

RAGLEY HALL & GARDENS
ALCESTER, WARWICKSHIRE B49 5NJ
www.ragleyhall.com

Tel: 01789 762090 **Fax:** 01789 764791 **E-mail:** ragley@ragleyhall.com

Owner: The Marquess of Hertford

Ragley Hall, the family home of the Marquess and Marchioness of Hertford, was designed by Robert Hooke in 1680 and is one of England's earliest Palladian Houses.

The Great Hall is adorned with exquisite baroque plasterwork by James Gibbs and Ragley houses a superb collection of paintings, china and furniture.

The house is set in 400 acres of parkland and gardens and the working stables houses a collection of carriages dating back to 1760.

For children there is the exciting Adventure Wood and 3D, and for walkers the delightful woodland walk.

Location: MAP 6:O9, OS Ref. SP073 555, Off A46/A435 1m SW of Alcester, From London 100m, M40 via Oxford and Stratford-on-Avon.

Open: House & State Rooms: Open Sundays and School Holidays Feb–Oct 12–4pm Gardens, Park, Adventure Wood & Jerwood Sculpture Park: Open Weekends and School Holidays Feb–Oct 10am–6pm.

Admission: House, Garden, Park, Adventure Playground & Jerwood Sculpture Park incl. Adult £8.50 Child (5–16yrs) £5 Conc. £7 Family (2+3) £27.

Season Tickets: Adult £32 Child £20 Family (2+3) £90

ℹ No video in the house. Visitors may alight at entrance. Parking. WCs. Lifts. Electric scooter for visiting the gardens may be available. Please enquire. Lakeside Café serving tea and light snacks. Drinks available from Harry's Bar open when House is open. Groups please book. By arrangement. P Coach drivers admitted free. Please advise of group visits. Education programme & outdoor classroom. Contact education officer. In grounds, on leads.

THE SHAKESPEARE HOUSES	*See page 323 for full page entry.*
STONELEIGH ABBEY	*See page 324 for full page entry.*
UPTON HOUSE & GARDENS	*See page 325 for full page entry.*

For unique **Civil wedding** venues see our index at the end of the book.

Stoneleigh Abbey Gardens

Ragley Hall, South Staircase Hall

©NTPL/Robert Morris

BACK TO BACKS ✿
55–63 HURST STREET, BIRMINGHAM B5 4TE

www.nationaltrust.org.uk/backtobacks

Tel: 0121 666 7671 (Booking line open Tues–Fri, 10am–4pm; Sat/Sun, 10am–12 noon)
E-mail: backtobacks@nationaltrust.org.uk

Owner: The National Trust   **Contact:** House & Visitor Services Manager

Take an exciting step back into Birmingham's industrial past by visiting the last remaining courtyard of Back to Back houses in Birmingham. Visitors are taken back in time to the start of the 1840s when Court 15 was both a home and workplace for its many inhabitants. Four houses have been restored to reflect the different time periods and lives of the people who lived there. Experience the sights, sounds and smells of the 1930s sweetshop and see what life was like for George Saunders, a tailor from St Kitts, who came to live and work in Birmingham in the 1950s.

Location: MAP 6:O7, OS Ref. SP071 861. In the centre of Birmingham next to the Hippodrome Theatre, within easy walking distance of bus and railway stations.

Open: 2 Feb–23 Dec, Tues–Sun, 10am–5pm. Admission is by timed ticket and guided tour only. Advance booking strongly advised. Open BH Mons, closed following Tues. Please note: during term time property will normally be closed for use by school groups on Tues, Weds, & Thurs mornings 10am–1pm. Last tour times vary due to light levels, please check with the property.

*Gift Aid Admission: Adult £6, Child £3, Family £15. *includes a voluntary donation but visitors can choose to pay the standard prices displayed at the property and on the website.

🏠 ♿ Partial, WCs. 🚻 Obligatory. ▓ 🐕 Guide dogs only. 🅿 ❋ ♿

BIRMINGHAM BOTANICAL GARDENS AND GLASSHOUSES
WESTBOURNE ROAD, EDGBASTON, BIRMINGHAM, B15 3TR

www.birminghambotanicalgardens.org.uk

Tel: 0121 454 1860 **Fax:** 0121 454 7835
E-mail: admin@birminghambotanicalgardens.org.uk
Owner: Birmingham Botanical & Horticultural Society

Tropical, Mediterranean and Arid Glasshouses contain a wide range of exotic and economic flora. 15 acres of beautiful gardens with the finest collection of plants in the Midlands. Home of the National Bonsai Collection. Children's adventure playground, aviaries, gallery and sculpture trail. An independent educational charity.

Location: MAP 7:N7, OS Ref. SP048 855. 2m W of city centre. Follow signs to Edgbaston then brown tourist signs.

Open: Daily: 9am–Dusk (7pm latest except pre-booked groups). Suns opening time 10am. Closed Christmas Day.

Admission: Adult £7.50, Family £22. Groups, Conc. £4.75, Children under 5 FREE.

🏠 🍴 🛍 ♿ 🅿 ▓ 🐕 Guide dogs only. 🅿 ❋ ♿

CASTLE BROMWICH HALL GARDENS
CHESTER ROAD, CASTLE BROMWICH, BIRMINGHAM B36 9BT

www.cbhgt.org.uk

Tel/Fax: 0121 749 4100   **E-mail:** admin@cbhgt.org.uk
Owner: Castle Bromwich Hall & Gardens Trust   **Contact:** Sue Brain

A unique example of 17th and 18th century formal garden design within a 10 acre walled area, comprising historic plants, vegetables, herbs and fruit, with a 19th century holly maze.

Location: MAP 7:O7, OS Ref. SP142 898. Off B4114, 4m E of Birmingham city centre, 1m from M6/J5 (exit northbound only). Southbound M6/J6 and follow A38 & A452.

Open: 1 Apr–31 Oct: Mon–Thurs, 10am–4.30pm, Fri 10am–3.30pm, Sats & Suns,BH Mon 1.30–5.30pm, 1 Nov–31 Mar: Mon–Fri, 10am–3.30pm. Café on request.

Admission: Summer: Adult £4, Child £1, Concs. £3.50. Winter: Adults £3, Child £1.

🏠 🍴 ♿ 🚻 🅿 ▓ ❋ ♿

COVENTRY CATHEDRAL

1 Hill Top, Coventry CV1 5AB
Tel: 024 7652 1200 **Fax:** 024 7652 1220
E-mail: information@coventrycathedral.org.uk
Owner: Dean & Canons of Coventry Cathedral **Contact:** The Visits Secretary
The remains of the medieval Cathedral, bombed in 1940, stand beside the new Cathedral by Basil Spence, consecrated in 1962. Modern works of art include a huge tapestry by Graham Sutherland, a stained glass window by John Piper and a bronze sculpture by Epstein. 'Reconciliation' statue by Josefina de Vasconcellos.
Location: MAP 7:P7, OS Ref. SP336 790. City centre.
Open: Cathedral: All year: 9am–5pm. Groups must book in advance.
Admission: Free – donations welcomed.

NT / Derek Wilbraham

KINVER EDGE
AND THE HOLY AUSTIN ROCK HOUSES ❦

COMPTON ROAD, KINVER, NR STOURBRIDGE, STAFFS DY7 6DL

Tel: 01384 872553
Owner: The National Trust **Contact:** The Custodian
These wonderful cave houses were inhabited until the 1950's and are now open to the public. Whilst you're here visit our new tea rooms and enjoy a 'rock cake at the rock houses'.
Location: MAP 7:A8, OS Ref. SO834 835 GB. 4m W of Stourbridge, 4m N of Kidderminster.
Open: Kinver Edge: all year. House grounds: daily 10am–4pm. Open BH Mons. Rockhouses: 4 Mar–28 Nov, Thur–Sun, 2–4pm. Tea Rooms: 4 Mar–28 Nov, Thurs–Sun, 11am–4pm.
Admission: Adult £2.10, Child £1.05, Family £5.25.

🖵 🖼 🅿 🖼 ✳

NTPL / Joe Cornish

Kinver Edge

SELLY MANOR
MAPLE ROAD, BOURNVILLE, WEST MIDLANDS B30 2AE

www.bvt.org.uk/sellymanor

Tel/Fax: 0121 472 0199 **E-mail:** sellymanor@bvt.org.uk
Owner: Bournville Village Trust **Contact:** Gillian Ellis
A beautiful half-timbered manor house in the heart of the famous Bournville village. The house has been lived in since the 14th century and was rescued from demolition by George Cadbury. It houses furniture dating back several centuries and is surrounded by a delightful typical Tudor garden.
Location: MAP 6:O7, OS Ref. SP045 814. N side of Sycamore Road, just E of Linden Road (A4040). 4m SSW of City Centre.
Open: All year: Tue–Fri, 10am–5pm. Apr–Sept: Sats, Suns & BHs, 2–5pm. Closed Mons.
Admission: Adult £3.50, Child £1.50, Conc. £2, Family £9.

🖵 🖼 🅢 Partial. WC. 🖼 By arrangement. 🖵 🅿 Limited. 🔳 🖼 In grounds, on leads. 🔺 ✳ 🖼

© NTPL / Andrew Butler

WIGHTWICK MANOR & GARDENS ❦
WIGHTWICK BANK, WOLVERHAMPTON, WEST MIDLANDS WV6 8EE

Tel: 01902 761400
Email: wightwickmanor@nationaltrust.org.uk
Owner: The National Trust **Contact:** The Property Manager
Begun in 1887, the house is a notable example of the influence of William Morris, with many original Morris wallpapers and fabrics. Also of interest are pre-Raphaelite pictures, Kempe glass and De Morgan ware. The 17 acre Victorian/Edwardian garden designed by Thomas Mawson has formal beds, pergola, yew hedges, topiary and terraces, woodland, two pools and kitchen garden.
Location: MAP 6:N6, OS Ref. SO869 985. 3m W of Wolverhampton, off the A454.
Open: 20 Feb–31 Oct: Wed–Sun, 6 Nov–19 Dec: Sat & Sun, 11am–5pm (last entry 4.30pm). Admission by timed ticket. (Taster Tour: 11am–12.30pm, access limited.) Guided groups through ground floor, freeflow upstairs (min. tour time approx. 1 hr). No guided tours on first Thur & Sat of the month – freeflow through the house from 12.30. Open BH Mons ground floor only. Garden, tea-room and shop also open seven days a week 1 Jul–31 Aug.
*Admission: Adult £8.70, Child £4.30. Garden only: £4.30, Child £2.10. *includes a voluntary donation but visitors can choose to pay the standard prices displayed at the property and on the website.
Special Events: Full calendar of events throughout the year.
🛈 No internal Photography. No Sharp Heeled Shoes. 🖵 🖼 🆃 🅢 Partial. WCs. 🖵 🖼 Obligatory. 🅿 400 yds. 🖼 Guide dogs only. 🔺 🖼

CROOME PARK ✄
NEAR HIGH GREEN, WORCESTERSHIRE WR8 9DW
www.nationaltrust.org.uk

Tel: 01905 371006 **Fax:** 01905 371090 **E-mail:** croomepark@nationaltrust.org.uk
Owner: The National Trust **Contact:** House & Visitor Services Manager
Enjoy the beautiful landscape of 'Capability' Brown's first complete landscape. Stroll through winding shrubberies to discover temples, statues and a lakeside garden and visit Croome Court which has at last been reunited with the parkland. The Court is presented empty of contents, giving visitors an opportunity to follow the restoration progress over the coming years.
Location: MAP 6:N9, OS150, SO878 448. 9m S of Worcester. Signposted from A38 and B4084.
Open: Park: 1 Jan–14 Feb, Sat & Sun, 10am–4pm. 20 Feb–31 Oct, Daily 10am–5.30pm. 6 Nov–19 Dec, Sat & Sun, 10am–4pm. 26 Dec–31 Dec, Daily, 10am–4pm. Last admission to park 45 mins before closing. Court: 9–31 Jan, Sat & Sun, 11am–3.30pm. 20 Feb–31 Oct, Wed–Mon 10am–4.30pm. 6 Nov–19 Dec, Sat & Sun, 11am–3.30pm. Last admission 30 mins before closing.
*Admission: Adult £6, Child (6–16) £3.00, Family £15.00, Group £5.25 *includes a voluntary donation but visitors can choose to pay the standard prices displayed at the property and on the website.

▢ ✦ ⧉ WCs ▣ 🅿 Limited parking for coaches. ⌂ On leads. ❄⊞

THE GREYFRIARS ✄
WORCESTER WR1 2LZ
www.nationaltrust.org.uk

Tel: 01905 23571 **E-mail:** greyfriars@nationaltrust.org.uk
Owner: The National Trust **Contact:** House and Visitor Services Manager
Built about 1480 next to a Franciscan friary in the centre of medieval Worcester, this timber-framed house has 17th and late 18th century additions. It was rescued from demolition at the time of the Second World War and was carefully restored. The panelled rooms have noteworthy textiles and interesting furniture. An archway leads through to a delightful walled garden.
Location: MAP 6:N9, OS150, SO852 546. Friar Street, in centre of Worcester.
Open: 3 Mar–12 Dec: Wed–Sun, 1–5pm. Open BH Mons.
*Admission: Adult £4.60, Child £2.30, Family £11.50. Booked Groups (8+) £4.00. *includes a voluntary donation but visitors can choose to pay the standard prices displayed at the property and on the website. This does not apply to group price.

✦ ▣ ⧉ Out of hours. ⌂▲ ⊞

Harvington Hall

©NTPL/David Levenson

©NTPL/Nadia Mackenzie

HANBURY HALL

DROITWICH, WORCESTERSHIRE WR9 7EA

www.nationaltrust.org.uk

Tel: 01527 821214 **Fax:** 01527 821251 **E-mail:** hanburyhall@nationaltrust.org.uk

Owner: The National Trust **Contact:** The Property Manager

Completed in 1701, this homely William & Mary-style house is famed for its fine painted ceilings and staircase, and has other fascinating features including an orangery, ice house, pavilions and working mushroom house. The stunning 8 hectare (20 acre) garden, recreated in keeping with the period of the house, is surrounded by 160 hectares (395 acres) of parkland, with beautiful views over the surrounding countryside.

Location: MAP 6:N8, OS150, SO943 637. 4½m E of Droitwich, 4m SE M5/J5.

Open: 27 Feb–31 Oct, daily 11am–5pm (House, Sat–Wed, 1–5pm); 6 Nov–26 Dec, Sat & Sun, 11am–4pm (House downstairs only, 11.30am–3.30pm by guided tour). Closed 25 Dec. Garden, Park, Stables Café & Shop, Jan & Feb 2011: wknds only, 11am–4pm. Open daily 26 Dec 2010–2 Jan 2011.

***Admission:** House & Garden: Adult £8, Child £4, Family £20. Garden & Park only, and house and grounds winter opening in Nov & Dec: Adult £5.40, Child £2.70, Family £13.50. Winter opening in Nov & Dec garden and grounds only: Adult £3.40, Child £1.70, Family £8.50. *includes a voluntary donation but visitors can choose to pay the standard prices displayed at the property and on the website.

Partial. WC. For pre-booked groups.

NTPL/Andrew Butler

Croome Park

HARTLEBURY CASTLE

HARTLEBURY, Nr KIDDERMINSTER DY11 7XZ

Tel: 01299 250416 **Fax:** 01299 251890 **E-mail:** museum@worcestershire.gov.uk

Owner: The Church Commissioners **Contact:** The County Museum

Hartlebury Castle has been home to the Bishops of Worcester for over a thousand years. In the Castle's North Wing the Worcestershire County Museum brings the county's past to life through a wide variety of exhibitions and a regular events programme. Collections include transport, costume, toys, archaeology and social history.

Location: MAP 6:N8, OS Ref. SO389 710. N side of B4193, 2m E of Stourport, 4m S of Kidderminster.

Open: 5 Jan–23 Dec: Tue–Fri, 10am–5pm. Sat, Sun & BHs, 11am–5pm. Closed Mons (except BHs) & Good Friday.

Admission: Adults £4, Conc. £2, Family (2+2) £10. Children under 5yrs Free. (2009 prices)

For pre-booked groups. Guide dogs only.

HARVINGTON HALL

HARVINGTON, KIDDERMINSTER, WORCESTERSHIRE DY10 4LR

www.harvingtonhall.com

Tel: 01562 777846   **Fax:** 01562 777190

E-mail: harvingtonhall@btconnect.com   **Contact:** The Hall Manager

Owner: Roman Catholic Archdiocese of Birmingham

Description: Harvington Hall is a moated, medieval and Elizabethan manor house. Many of the rooms still have their original Elizabethan wall paintings and the Hall contains the finest series of priest hides in the country. A full programme of events throughout the year including outdoor plays and music, living history weekends, candlelight tours and a pilgrimage is available.

Location: MAP 6:N8, OS Ref. SO877 745. On minor road, ½ m NE of A450/A448

crossroads at Mustow Green. 3m SE of Kidderminster.

Open: Mar & Oct: Sats & Suns; Apr–Sept: Wed–Sun & BH Mons (closed Good Fri), 11.30am–4pm. Open throughout the year for pre-booked groups and schools. Occasionally the Hall may be closed for a private function, please ring for up to date information.

Admission: Adult £7, Child (5-16) £4.50, OAP £6, Family (2 adults & 3 children) £20. Garden and Malt House Visitor Centre: £3.50. Garden only: £2.

⬛ 🏵 🎔 🔓 Partial. WCs ☕ 🎫 Obligatory 🔘 🅿 Limited for coaches. ⬛
🐕 Guide dogs only. ♿

LEIGH COURT BARN ⌘

Worcester

Tel: 01299 896636   **Email:** customers@english-heritage.org.uk

www.english-heritage.org.uk/leighcourt

Owner: English Heritage   **Contact:** Visitor Operations Administrative Assistant

Magnificent 14th century timber-framed barn built for the monks of Pershore Abbey. It is the largest of its kind in Britain.

Location: MAP 6:M9, OS150 Ref. SO783 535. 5m W of Worcester on unclassified road off A4103.

Open: 1 Apr–30 Sept: Thur–Sun & BH Mons, 10am–5pm.

Admission: Free. Opening times and prices are valid until 31st March 2010, after this date details are subject to change please see www.english-heritage.org.uk for the most up-to-date information.

⬛

LITTLE MALVERN COURT 🏠

Nr Malvern, Worcestershire WR14 4JN

Tel: 01684 892988   **Fax:** 01684 893057

Owner: Trustees of the late T M Berington   **Contact:** Mrs T M Berington

Prior's Hall, associated rooms and cells, c1480, of former Benedictine Monastery. Formerly attached to, and forming part of the Little Malvern Priory Church which may also be visited. It has an oak-framed roof, 5-bay double-collared roof, with two tiers of cusped windbraces. Library. Collections of religious vestments, embroideries and paintings. Gardens: 10 acres of former monastic grounds with spring bulbs, blossom, old fashioned roses and shrubs. Access to Hall only by flight of steps.

Location: MAP 6:M9, OS Ref. SO769 403. 3m S of Great Malvern on Upton-on-Severn Road (A4104).

Open: 21 Apr–22 Jul: Weds & Thurs, 2.15–5pm. 21 Mar & 3 May for NGS: 2–5pm. Last admission 4.30pm.

Admission: House & Garden: Adult £6.00, Child £2.00, Garden only: Adult £5.00, Child £1.00. Groups must book, max 30.

🔓 Garden (partial). 🎫 ⬛

MADRESFIELD COURT

Madresfield, Malvern WR13 5AU

Tel: 01684 579947   **E-mail:** helen.madresfield@yahoo.com

Owner: The Trustees of Madresfield Estate   **Contact:** Mrs Helen Sommerville

Elizabethan and Victorian house with medieval origins. Fine contents. Extensive gardens and arboretum.

Location: MAP 6:M9, OS Ref. SO809 474. 6m SW of Worcester. 1½ m SE of A449. 2m NE of Malvern.

Open: Guided tours: 14 Apr–29 Jul: mostly Wed & Thur, also Sats 17 Apr, 15 May, 10 Jul: 10.45am & 2.30pm. Numbers are restricted and prior booking, by telephone to Mrs Helen Somerville, is strongly recommended to avoid disappointment.

Admission: £10.

🎫 Obligatory. ⬛

ROSEDENE 🌿

Dodford, Worcestershire B61 9BU

Tel: 01527 821214   **www.nationaltrust.org.uk**

Owner: The National Trust   **Contact:** Property Manager

Mid 19th century Chartist cottage with organic vegetable garden and orchard.

Location: MAP 6:N8, OS Ref. SO393 273. 3½ m NW of Bromsgrove off A448.

Open: 4 Apr–26 Sept, Sun only by pre-booked guided tour (telephone to book).

Admission: Adult £4.60, Child £2.30, Family £11.50.

🎫 🅿 ⬛

SPETCHLEY PARK GARDENS 🏛

SPETCHLEY PARK, WORCESTER WR5 1RS

www.spetchleygardens.co.uk

Tel: 01453 810303 **Fax:** 01453 511915 **E-mail:** hb@spetchleygardens.co.uk

Owner: Spetchley Gardens Charitable Trust   **Contact:** Mr RJ Berkeley

A garden that inspired Elgar and helped WWII airmen recuperate must have something special. This lovely 30 acre private garden contains a large collection of trees, shrubs and plants, many rare or unusual. A garden full of secrets, every corner reveals some new vista, some treasure of the plant world. The exuberant planting and the peaceful walks make this an oasis of beauty, peace and quiet. Relax in the wonderful atmosphere of the old laundry tearoom and enjoy a traditional English tea or walk in the nearby deer park full of red and fallow deer.

Location: MAP 6:N9, OS Ref. SO895 540. 3m E of Worcester on A44. Leave M5/J6/J7.

Open: 21 Mar–30 Sept: Wed–Sun & BHs, 11am–6pm. Oct: Sats & Suns, 11am–4pm. (last admission 1hr before closing).

Admission: Adult £6, Child (under 16yrs) Free. Conc. £5.50. Groups (25+): Adult £5.50. Adult Season Ticket £25.

Special Events: Specialist Plant Fair 25th April 2010. Entry £5. M5 – History through the ages 14th & 15th August 2010.

ℹ️ Available for filming. 🚻 ♿WCs. 🎧📷By arrangement. 🅿️ Limited for coaches. 🔴🦮Guide dogs only. 💷

THE TUDOR HOUSE MUSEUM

16 Church Street, Upton-on-Severn, Worcestershire WR8 0HT

Tel: 01684 592447

Owner: Mrs Lavender Beard   **Contact:** Mrs Wilkinson

Upton past and present, exhibits of local history.

Location: MAP 6:N10, OS Ref. SO852 406. Centre of Upton-on-Severn, 7m SE of Malvern by B4211.

Open: Apr–Oct: Daily 2–5pm, including Bank Holidays. Winter: Suns only, 2–4pm.

Admission: Adult £1, Conc. 50p, Family £2.

© English Heritage

NTPL/Robert Morris

Rosedene

WITLEY COURT & GARDENS ✠

GREAT WITLEY, WORCESTER WR6 6JT

www.english-heritage.org.uk/witleycourt

Tel: 01299 896636 **E-mail:** customers@english-heritage.org.uk

Owner: English Heritage   **Contact:** Visitor Operations Team

Spectacular ruins of a palatial 19th century mansion with porticoes by John Nash. The adjoining church by James Gibbs has a remarkable 18th century baroque interior. The elaborate William Nesfield gardens contained immense fountains, which survive today; the largest is the Perseus and Andromeda Fountain. The Woodland Walks in the North Park include various species of tree and shrub acquired from around the world. From summer 2010, see the East Parterre Garden restored to its former glory.

Location: MAP 6:M8, OS150, SO769 649. 10m NW of Worcester off A443.

Open: 1 Apr–30 Jun: daily, 10am–5pm. 1 Jul–31 Aug: daily, 10am–6pm. 1 Sep–1 Nov: daily, 10am–5pm. 2 Nov–28 Feb '10: Wed–Sun, 10am–4pm. 1–31 Mar: Wed–Sun, 10am–5pm. Closed 24–26 Dec & 1 Jan.

Admission: Adult £5.80, Child £2.90, Conc. £4.90, Family £14.50. 15% discount for groups (11+). EH Members Free. Opening times and prices are valid until 31st March 2010, after this date details are subject to change please see www.english-heritage.org.uk for the most up-to-date information.

ℹ️ Visitor welcome point. Guidebooks. Hazard. Ovp. 📷🚻♿🎧🎁🅿️🔴 Family learning resources available. 🦮 On leads. 🏠 Holiday cottage available to let. ✳️ 💷

Sledmere House

Yorkshire and the Humber

York contains reminders of its medieval origins but is as well known for its elegant Jacobean and Georgian architecture. Within easy reach are grand palaces such as Castle Howard and Harewood House, but there are also more modest gems to be seen such as Sion Hill Hall, and the gardens at RHS Harlow Carr are amongst the finest in Britain.

York Gate Garden

Priory stepping stones, Bolton Abbey

YORKSHIRE

Longley Old Hall

Burton Constable Hall

Kiplin Hall

■ **Owner**
English Heritage

■ **Contact**
Visitor Operations Team
Brodsworth Hall
Brodsworth
Nr Doncaster
Yorkshire DN5 7XJ

Tel: 01302 722598
Fax: 01302 337165

E-mail: brodsworth.hall@
english-heritage.org.uk

■ **Location**
MAP 11:B12
OS Ref. SE506 070

In Brodsworth, 5m NW of
Doncaster off A635. Use
A1(M)/J37.

Rail: South Elmsall 4m;
Moorthorpe 4.5m;
Doncaster 5.5m.

■ **Opening Times**
Summer

House
1 April–30 September
Tue–Sun & BHs,
1–5pm.

1 October–1 November
Sat–Sun, 12 noon–4pm.

Gardens & Tearoom
1 April–1 November
Tue–Sun & BHs,
10am–5.30pm.

**Gardens, Tearoom,
Shop & Servants' Wing**

2 November–31 March
Sat–Sun, 10am–4pm.

Closed 24–26 December
& 1 January.

Last admission ½ hr
before closing.

■ **Admission**
House & Gardens
Adult   £8.50
Child (5–15yrs) £4.30
Child (under 5yrs) Free
Conc.   £7.20

Groups (11+) 15%
discount.

Gardens only
Adult   £5.00
Child (5–15yrs) £2.50
Child (under 5yrs) Free
Conc.   £4.30

EH members Free

Free admission for tour
leaders and coach drivers.

Opening times and prices
are valid until 31st March
2010, after this date
details are subject to
change please see
www.english-
heritage.org.uk for the
most up-to-date
information.

■ **Special Events**
Snow drop festival
during February half
term.

BRODSWORTH HALL & GARDENS ⊞

www.english-heritage.org.uk/brodsworth

Explore the changing fortunes of a wealthy Victorian family through the stories of a house and the memories of a home at Brodsworth Hall. This is no glossily restored showpiece, frozen in a single period of manicured grandeur, the hall was 'Conserved as found' and is a mansion which has grown comfortably old over 120 years, and reveals a country house as it really was: still reflecting its original opulence but well-used, patched up in places and full of unexpected family curios.

Built in the Italianate style of the 1860s by the fabulously wealthy Charles Sabine Augustus Thellusson, Brodsworth Hall served as the family home for over 120 years. The pillared, sculpture-lined and sumptuously furnished 'grand rooms' on the ground floor recall the house's Victorian heyday. The Thellusson family's sporting interests,

horse racing and yachtting, are reflected throughout the house, on display are the mumified hooves of 'Rataplan' who won the Doncaster Cup in 1855. Sporting successes also include the magnificent silver Goodwood Cup, won by a family racehorse in 1835.

In contrast to the house, the extensive gardens have been wonderfully restored to their original horticultural splendour as 'a collection of grand gardens in miniature'. Restoration work continues to reveal new features, along with visitas last enjoyed before World War 1. Explore the enghanted Grove with paths, banks and bridges winding over and under each other revealing an array of different views, which reflect the desires and apsorations of Victorian gentry. No matter what time of year visited the gardens at Brodsworth Hall are a delight in any season.

 Exhibitions about the family, the servants and the gardens. WCs. No Cameras (house only).

 WCs.

 Groups must book. Booked coach parties: 10am–1pm.

P 220 cars and 3 coaches. Free.

 Education Centre. Free if booked in advance.

※ Gardens, Tearoom and Servants' Wing only.

CASTLE HOWARD 🏛

www.castlehoward.co.uk

In a dramatic setting between two lakes with extensive gardens and impressive architecture, Castle Howard is undoubtedly one of Britain's finest private residences. Built by Sir John Vanbrugh in 1699 for Charles Howard, third Earl of Carlisle, Castle Howard remains the home of the Howard family.

With its impressive painted and gilded dome reaching 80ft, Castle Howard has collections of antique furniture; porcelain and sculpture, while the famous Holbein portraits of Henry VIII and the Duke of Norfolk dominate its fabulous collection of paintings.

The High South apartments, so disastrously destroyed by fire in 1940, are now open to the public for the first time. During the recent re-filming of *Brideshead Revisited* these bare rooms were converted into a film set and today visitors can witness this extraordinary transformation, with props and painted scenery, and see exhibitions that tell the story of the fire, and how Evelyn Waugh's famous novel came to be filmed not just once, but twice, at Castle Howard.

Designed on a heroic scale, the 1000 acres of gardens are dotted with statues and fountains, and include memorable sights such as The Temple of the Four Winds, the Mausoleum and New River Bridge. The walled garden has collections of old and modern roses, plus ornamental vegetable garden and Ray Wood, acknowledged by the Royal Botanical Collection, Kew, as a "rare botanical jewel" has a unique collection of rare trees, shrubs, rhododendrons, magnolias and azaleas.

Attractions include a changing programme of exhibition and events, plus a choice of shops and cafés. Families can also experience the new adventure playground and childrens activities.

i Filming, product launches, activity days. Suitable for helicopter landing. Photography allowed in the House for personal use only. Commercial photography with prior permission only.	Free outdoor guided tours for visitors Mar–Nov. Private tours & lectures available for special interest groups.
Choice of six shops including farm shop, plant centre, chocolate shop, bookshop and two gift shops. Free admission to Stable Courtyard shops and cafés.	**P** Plentiful free parking, including disabled.
Plant Centre & Tearoom open daily all year with free admission.	School parties welcome. Preferential rates available. Teacher pre-visits.
T Hospitality includes dinners, meetings, corporate events and wedding receptions.	Dogs on leads welcome. Registered assistance dogs in house only.
Car parking, toilets, ramped pathways and doors, wheelchair lift inside the House.	Holiday homes sales, plus camping and caravanning at the Lakeside Holiday Park.
Choice of four cafés to suit all the family.	Temple of the Four Winds.
Private group lunches and afternoon teas in the Grecian Hall. Menus upon request.	Gardens open all year except Christmas Day.
	Full programme for all the family.

■ Owner

The Hon Simon Howard

■ Contact

Visitor Services
Castle Howard
York, North Yorks
YO60 7DA

Tel: 01653 648333
Fax: 01653 648529
E-mail: house@
castlehoward.co.uk

■ Location

MAP 11:C8
OS Ref. SE716 701

Approaching from S, A64 to Malton, on entering Malton, take Castle Howard road via Coneysthorpe village.
Or from A64 following signs to Castle Howard via the Carrmire Gate
9' wide by 10' high.

York 15m (20 mins), A64. From London: M1/J32, M18 to A1(M) to A64, York/Scarborough Road, 3½ hrs.

Train: London Kings Cross to York 1hr. 50 mins. York to Malton Station 30 mins.

Bus: Service and tour buses from York Station.

■ Opening Times

House: 15 March–31 October & 27 November–19 December 2010. Daily, 11am–4pm (last admission).

Gardens: All year, daily from 10am (closed Christmas Day).

Stable Courtyard:
(Gift Shops, Farm Shop, Chocolate Shop, Plant Centre, Café):
All year, daily, 10am–5pm, free admission.

Access to Pretty Wood Pyramid 1 July–31 August. Special tours to newly restored rooms in the house are available by arrangement.
For more information please contact Castle Howard Estate Office on 01653 648444.

■ Admission

Annual Passes available

Summer
House & Garden
Adult	£12.00
Child (4–16yrs)	£7.00
Under 4yrs	Free
Conc.	£10.00

Garden only
Adult	£8.50
Child (4–16yrs)	£6.00
Under 4yrs	Free
Conc.	£8.00

Winter (when the house is closed) Gardens only
Adult	£5.00
Child (4–16yrs)	£2.50
Under 4yrs	Free

■ Conference/Function

ROOM	SIZE	MAX CAPACITY
Long Gallery	197' x 24'	200
Grecian Hall	40' x 40'	70

■ Owner
The National Trust

■ Contact
The National Trust
Fountains Abbey
and Studley Royal
Ripon
North Yorkshire
HG4 3DY

Tel: 01765 608888
E-mail: info@
fountainsabbey.org.uk

■ Location
MAP 10:P8
OS Ref. SE275 700

Abbey entrance:
4m W of Ripon off
B6265. 8m W of A1.

Rail: Harrogate 12m.

Bus: Regular
season service
tel: 0870 608 2608
for details.

■ Opening Times
March–October
Daily: 10am–5pm.

November–February
Daily: 10am–4pm or
dusk if earlier.

Closed 24/25 December,
& Fridays from Nov–Jan.

Deer Park: All year, daily
during daylight (closed
24/25 December).

■ *Admission
Adult	£8.50
Child† (5–16yrs)	£4.55
Family	£21.60
Groups (15+)	
Adult	£7.25
Groups (31+)	
Adult	£7

Group discount
applicable only with
prior booking.

Group visits and disabled
visitors, please telephone
in advance, 01765
643197.

Includes a voluntary
donation but visitors can
choose to pay the
standard prices displayed
at the property and on
the website. Does not
apply to group prices.

NT, EH Members &
Under 5s Free.

The Abbey is owned by
the National Trust and
maintained by English
Heritage. St Mary's
Church is owned by
English Heritage and
managed by the
National Trust.

FOUNTAINS ABBEY & STUDLEY ROYAL

www.fountainsabbey.org.uk

One of the most remarkable sites in Europe, sheltered in a secluded valley, Fountains Abbey and Studley Royal, a World Heritage Site, encompasses the spectacular remains of a 12th century Cistercian abbey with one of the finest surviving monastic watermills in Britain, an Elizabethan mansion, and one of the best surviving examples of a Georgian water garden. Elegant ornamental lakes, avenues, temples and cascades provide a succession of unforgettable eye-catching vistas in an atmosphere of peace and tranquillity. St Mary's Church, built by William Burges in the 19th century, provides a dramatic focal point to the medieval deer park with over 500 wild deer. Exhibitions, events, activities and guided tours throughout the year.

i	Events held throughout the year. Exhibitions. Seminar facilities. Outdoor concerts, meetings, activity days, walks..
	Two shops.
	Dinners.
	WCs.
	Licensed.
	Licensed.
	Free, but seasonal. Groups (please book on 01765 643197), please use Visitor Centre entrance.
	Audio tour £2.00.
P	Drivers must book groups.
	On leads.
	Fountains Hall, an Elizabethan Mansion is an ideal setting for weddings. For details or a Wedding pack tel: 01765 643198.

©NTPL/Matthew Antrobus

©NTPL/Andrew Butler

NEWBY HALL & GARDENS 🏛

www.newbyhall.com

The home of Richard and Lucinda Compton, Newby Hall is one of England's renowned Adam houses. In the 1760s William Weddell, an ancestor of the Comptons, acquired a magnificent collection of Ancient Roman sculpture and Gobelins tapestries. He commissioned Robert Adam to alter the original Wren designed house and Thomas Chippendale to make furniture. The result is a perfect example of the Georgian 'Age of Elegance' with the atmosphere and ambience of a family home.

Gardens

25 acres of stunning award-winning gardens contain rare and beautiful shrubs and plants, including a National collection of the Genus Cornus (Dogwoods). Newby's famous double herbaceous borders, framed by great bastions of yew hedges, make the perfect walkway to the River Ure. Formal gardens such as the Autumn and Rose Garden, the tranquillity of Sylvia's Garden and the Tropical Garden make Newby an inspiring and exciting place to explore. Walking through the curved pergolas leads to the Victorian Rock garden, which is an enchanting magical space for all ages. The gardens feature an exciting children's adventure garden and miniature railway. From 1st June there is an annual exhibition of contemporary sculptures in the mature woodland.

| i | Allow a full day for viewing house and gardens. Suitable for filming and for special events, craft and country fairs, vehicle rallies etc, promotions and lectures. No indoor photography. |

'The Shop @ Newby Hall' – Modern British Art and Craftsmanship.

Wedding receptions & special functions.

6 wheelchairs available. Access to ground floor of house and key areas in gardens. WC.

Obligatory.

Garden restaurant, teas, hot and cold meals. Booked groups in Grantham Room. Menus/rates on request.

P Ample. Hard standing for coaches.

Welcome. Rates on request. Grantham Room for use as wet weather base subject to availability. Woodland discovery walk, adventure gardens and train rides on 10¼" gauge railway.

Assistance Dogs only.

Globe Theatre.

Owner
Mr Richard Compton

Contact
The Administrator
Newby Hall
Ripon
North Yorkshire
HG4 5AE

Tel: 01423 322583
Information Hotline:
0845 450 4068
Fax: 01423 324452
E-mail:
via www.newbyhall.com

Location
MAP 11:A8
OS Ref. SE348 675

Midway between London and Edinburgh, 4m W of A1, towards Ripon. S of Skelton 2m NW of (A1) Boroughbridge.
4m SE of Ripon.

Taxi: Ripon Taxi Rank 01765 601283.

Bus: On Ripon–York route.

*SatNav users: please use postcode **HG4 5AJ**

Opening Times
Summer

House*
1 April–26 September.
April, May, June & September:
Tues–Sun & BH Mons;
July–August: Daily
12 noon–5pm.
Last admission 4pm.
*Areas of the House can be closed to the public from time to time, please check website for details.

Garden
Dates as House,
11am–5.30pm.
Last admission 5pm.

Winter
October–end March
Closed.

Admission
(2009 Prices)
House & Garden
Adult	£11.00
Child/Disabled	£8.50
OAP	£10.00

Group (15+)	
Adult/Conc	£9.50
Child/Disabled	£7.00

Family (2+2)	£36.00
Family (2+3)	£39.00

Garden only
Adult	£6.00
Child/Disabled	£6.50
OAP	£7.00

Group (15+)	
Adult	£7.00
Child (4–16yrs)	£5.20

Family (2+2)	£27.00
Family (2+3)	£32.00

Conference/Function

ROOM	SIZE	MAX CAPACITY
Grantham Room	90' x 20'	150

■ Owner

Sir Thomas Ingilby Bt

■ Contact

Tours: Jenny Carter
Meetings/Dinners:
Rebecca Riordan
Ripley Castle
Ripley, Harrogate
North Yorkshire
HG3 3AY

Tel: 01423 770152
Fax: 01423 771745
E-mail: enquiries@
ripleycastle.co.uk

■ Location

MAP 10:P9
OS Ref. SE283 605

W edge of village. Just off
A61, 3½ m N of
Harrogate, 8m S of Ripon.
M1 18m S, M62 20m S.
Rail: London–Leeds/York
2hrs. Leeds/York–
Harrogate 30mins.
Taxi: Blueline taxis
Harrogate
(01423) 503037.

■ Opening Times

Castle
Easter–end September:
Daily.
October, November &
March: Tues, Thurs,
Sat & Sun.
10.30am–3pm.
December–February:
Sats & Suns.
10.30am–3pm.
Gardens
All year, daily (except
Christmas Day),
10am–5pm (winter
4.30pm).

■ Admission

All Year
Castle & Gardens
Adult	£8.00
Child (5–16yrs)	£5.00
Child under 5yrs	Free
OAP	£7.50

Groups (25+)
Adult	£7.00
Child (5–16yrs)	£4.50

Gardens only
Adult	£5.50
Child (5–16yrs)	£3.50
OAP	£5.00

Groups (25+)
Adult	£5.50
Child (5–16yrs)	£3.00
Child under 5yrs	Free

■ Special Events

Check website or ring
for details.

Conference/Function

ROOM	SIZE	MAX CAPACITY
Morning Rm	27' x 22'	80
Large Drawing Rm	30' x 22'	80
Library	31 x 19'	70
Tower Rm	33' x 21'	70
Map Rm	19' x 14'	20
Dining Rm	23' x 19'	20
Long Gallery	19' x 6.5'	150
Amcotts Suite	10.2' x 6.6' 7.3' x 6'	120

RIPLEY CASTLE

www.ripleycastle.co.uk

Ripley Castle has been the home of the Ingilby family for twenty-six generations and Sir Thomas and Lady Ingilby, together with their five children, continue the tradition. The guided tours are amusing and informative, following the lives and loves of one family for 700 years and how they have been affected by events in English history. The Old Tower dates from 1555 and houses splendid armour, books, panelling and a Priest's Secret Hiding Place, together with fine paintings, china, furnishings and chandeliers collected by the family over the centuries.

The extensive Victorian Walled Gardens have been transformed and are a colourful delight through every season. In the Spring you can appreciate 150,000 flowering bulbs which create a blaze of colour through the woodland walks, and also the National Hyacinth Collection whose scent is breathtaking. The restored Hot Houses have an extensive tropical plant collection, and in the Kitchen Gardens you can see an extensive collection of rare vegetables from the Henry Doubleday Research Association.

Ripley village on the Castle's doorstep is a model estate village with individual charming shops, an art gallery, delicatessen and Farmyard Museum.

No photography inside Castle unless by prior written consent. Parkland for outdoor activities & concerts.

VIP lunches & dinners (max. 120): unlimited in marquees. Full catering service, wedding receptions, banquets, meetings and activity days.

5/7 rooms accessible. Gardens accessible (not Tropical Collection). WCs. Parking 50 yds.

The Castle Tearooms (seats 54) in Castle courtyard. Licensed. Pub lunches or dinner at hotel (100 yds). Groups must book.

Obligatory. Tour time 75 mins.

290 cars – 300 yds from Castle entrance. Coach park 50 yds. Free.

Welcome by arrangement, between 10.30am–7.30pm.

Guide dogs only.

Boar's Head Hotel (AA***) 100 yds. Owned and managed by the estate.

SKIPTON CASTLE
www.skiptoncastle.co.uk

■ Contact

Judith Parker
Skipton Castle
Skipton
North Yorkshire
BD23 1AW

Tel: 01756 792442
Fax: 01756 796100
E-mail: info@
skiptoncastle.co.uk

■ Location

MAP 10:O9
OS Ref. SD992 520

In the centre of
Skipton, at the N end
of High Street.

Skipton is 20m W of
Harrogate on the A59
and 26m NW of
Leeds on A65.

Rail: Regular services
from Leeds & Bradford.

■ Opening Times

All year
(closed 25 December)

Mon–Sat: 10am–6pm
Suns: 12 noon–6pm
(October–February 4pm).

■ Admission

Adult	£6.20
Child (0–4yrs)	Free
Child (5–17yrs)	£3.70
OAP	£5.60
Student (with ID)	£5.60
Family (2+3)	£19.50

Groups (15+)	
Adult	£5.20
Child (0–17yrs)	£3.70

Includes illustrated tour
sheet in a choice of nine
languages, plus free
badge for children.

Groups welcome:
Guides available for
booked groups at no
extra charge.

Guardian of the gateway to the Yorkshire Dales for over 900 years, this unique fortress is one of the most complete and well-preserved medieval castles in England. Standing on a 40-metre high crag, fully-roofed Skipton Castle was founded around 1090 by Robert de Romille, one of William the Conqueror's Barons, as a fortress in the dangerous northern reaches of the kingdom.

Owned by King Edward I and Edward II, from 1310 it became the stronghold of the Clifford Lords withstanding successive raids by marauding Scots. During the Civil War it was the last Royalist bastion in the North, yielding only after a three-year siege in 1645. 'Slighted' under the orders of Cromwell, the castle was skilfully restored by the redoubtable Lady Anne Clifford and today visitors can climb from the depths of the Dungeon to the top of the Watch Tower, and explore the Banqueting Hall, the Kitchens, the Bedchamber and even the Privy!

Every period has left its mark, from the Norman entrance and the Medieval towers, to the beautiful Tudor courtyard with the great yew tree planted by Lady Anne in 1659. Here visitors can see the coat of arms of John Clifford, the infamous 'Bloody' Clifford of Shakespeare's Henry VI, who fought and died in the Wars of the Roses whereupon the castle was possessed by Richard III. Throughout the turbulent centuries of English history, the Clifford Lords fought at Bannockburn, at Agincourt and in the Wars of the Roses. The most famous of them all was George Clifford, 3rd Earl of Cumberland, Champion to Elizabeth I, Admiral against the Spanish Armada and conqueror of Puerto Rico in 1598.

In the castle grounds visitors can see the Tudor wing built as a royal wedding present for Lady Eleanor Brandon, niece of Henry VIII, the beautiful Shell Room decorated in the 1620s with shells and Jamaican coral and the ancient medieval chapel of St John the Evangelist. The Chapel Terrace, with its delightful picnic area, has fine views over the woods and Skipton's lively market town.

Unsuitable.

Tearoom. Indoor and outdoor picnic areas.

By arrangement.

Large public coach and car park off nearby High Street. Coach drivers' rest room at Castle.

Welcome. Guides available. Teachers free.

In grounds on leads.

ALDBOROUGH ROMAN SITE

Main Street, Aldborough, Boroughbridge, North Yorkshire YO51 9ES

Tel: 01423 322768 **E-mail:** aldborough.roman_town@english-heritage.org.uk

www.english-heritage.org.uk/aldborough

Owner: English Heritage **Contact:** Visitor Operations Team

Aldborough was the 'capital' of the Romanised Brigantes, the largest tribe in Britain. One corner of the defences is laid out amid a Victorian arboretum, and two mosaic pavements can be viewed in their original positions. The site's fascinating museum has an outstanding collection of Roman finds.

Location: MAP 11:A8, OS Ref. SE405 662. Located in Aldborough 0.75m SE of Boroughbridge on a minor road off B6265; within 1 mile junction of A1 and A6055. Rail: Cattal 7.5m

Open: 1 Apr–30 Sept: Sat–Sun & BHs, 11am–5pm.

Admission: Adult £3, Child £1.50, Conc. £2.60. 15% discount for groups (11+). EH members Free. Opening times and prices are valid until 31st March 2010, after this date details are subject to change please see www.english-heritage.org.uk for the most up-to-date information.

WC. On leads (restricted areas only).

ASKE HALL

Richmond, North Yorkshire DL10 5HJ

Tel: 01748 822000 **Fax:** 01748 826611 **E-mail:** office@aske.co.uk

www.aske.co.uk

Owner: Earl of Ronaldshay **Contact:** Mandy Blenkiron

A good, predominantly Georgian collection of paintings, furniture and porcelain in house which has been the seat of the Dundas family since 1763.

Location: MAP 10:P6, OS Ref. NZ179 035. 4m SW of A1 at Scotch Corner, 2m from the A66, on the B6274.

Open: 9/10 Sept (Heritage Open Days). Tours 10.00, 11.00 & 12.00, limited to 15 max. Booking advisable and ID will be required (passport, driving licence etc). For further details contact Mandy Blenkiron.

Admission: Free.

Obligatory. Limited.

BAGSHAW MUSEUM

Wilton Park, Batley, West Yorkshire WF17 0AS

Tel: 01924 326155 **Fax:** 01924 326164

Owner: Kirklees Culture & Leisure Services **Contact:** Amanda Daley

A Victorian Gothic mansion set in Wilton Park.

Location: MAP10:P11, OS Ref. SE235 257. From M62/J27 follow A62 to Huddersfield. At Birstall, follow tourist signs.

Open: All year, 11am–5pm, Mon–Fri. 12noon–5pm, Sat–Sun.

Admission: Free.

BENINGBROUGH HALL & GARDENS

Beningbrough, North Yorkshire YO30 1DD

Tel: 01904 472027 **E-mail:** beningbrough@nationaltrust.org.uk

www.nationaltrust.org.uk/beningbrough

Owner: The National Trust **Contact:** Visitor Services Manager

Imposing 18th century house with new interpretation galleries with the National Portrait Gallery.

Location: MAP 11:B9, OS Ref. SE516 586. 8m NW of York, 3m W of Shipton, 2m SE of Linton-on-Ouse, follow signposted route.

Open: House: 1 Mar–31 Oct, 11am–5pm, Sat–Wed. Grounds, Shop & Walled Garden Restaurant: 2 Jan–28 Feb & 1 Nov–31 Dec, 11am–3.30pm Sat & Sun; 1 Mar–30 Jun & 1 Sept–31 Oct, 11am–5.30pm, Sat–Wed; 1 Jul–31 Aug, 11am–5.30pm, Daily. Galleries only: 2 Jan–28 Feb, 11am–3.30, Sat & Sun. 1 Nov–31 Dec, 11am–3pm, Sat & Sun. Note: Open 1 Jan, 13–17 Feb, Good Friday & 27 Dec. Closed 25 Dec.

***Admission:** Summer: Adult £8.40, Child £4.20, Family £20. Groups: £7.30. Winter: Adult £5.50, Child £2.60, Family £14. *includes a voluntary donation but visitors can choose to pay the standard prices displayed at the property and on the website.

Lift to all floors. WC. Reduced rates for groups (15+), not Suns or BHs.

BOLTON ABBEY

SKIPTON, NORTH YORKSHIRE BD23 6EX

www.boltonabbey.com

Tel: 01756 718009 **Fax:** 01756 710535 **E-mail:** tourism@boltonabbey.com

Owner: Chatsworth Settlement Trustees **Contact:** Visitor Manager

Set in the heart of the Yorkshire Dales on the banks of the River Wharfe, this historic estate is the Yorkshire home of the Duke and Duchess of Devonshire and a magnet for visitors drawn to its breathtaking landscape and excellent facilities.

Explore the ruins of the Priory and discover a landscape full of history and legend. Wander along the woodland and riverside paths or cross the exposed heights of heather moorland. Enjoy local produce in the excellent restaurants, tea rooms and cafés. Indulge in a little retail therapy in the gift and food shops. Or simply relax and enjoy a picnic whilst the children play.

Location: MAP 10:O9, OS Ref. SE074 542. On B6160, N from the junction with A59 Skipton–Harrogate road, 23m from Leeds.

Open: All year from 9am.

Admission: £6.00 per vehicle or 50p per person for groups of 12 or more travelling in one vehicle.

Licensed. Licensed. By arrangement. Devonshire Arms Country House Hotel & Devonshire Fell Hotel nearby.

BOLTON CASTLE
LEYBURN, NORTH YORKSHIRE DL8 4ET

www.boltoncastle.co.uk

Tel: 01969 623981 **E-mail:** info@boltoncastle.co.uk

Owner: Lord Bolton **Contact:** Tom Orde-Powlett

Location: MAP 10:O7, OS Ref. SE034 918. Approx 6m W of Leyburn. 1m NW of Redmire.

A stunning medieval castle preserved in outstanding condition. Completed in 1399, its scars bear testament to over 600 years of history, including being besieged during the Civil War and Mary, Queen of Scots' imprisonment. There is a medieval garden, including herbs, roses, a vineyard and maze. The tearoom provides tea and cakes, as well as sandwiches and light lunches. Wedding ceremonies and receptions can be held here, as well as parties, corporate events and themed activity days for children.

Open: 26 Mar–31 Oct daily, 10am–5pm. Closed Monday except school holidays/Bank holidays. Last admission 4.15pm. Pre-booked group visits and special events during winter months, see website for details.

Admission: Castle and Garden: Adults £6.50, Children/OAP/Students £5. Family ticket £20.

⬚ ⊤ Wedding receptions. ⬚ Partial. ⬚ P ⬚ ⬚ In grounds, on leads. ⬚ ⬚

BROCKFIELD HALL 🏛

Warthill, York YO19 5XJ

Tel: 01904 489362 **Fax:** 01904 488982 **E-mail:** simon@brockfieldhall.co.uk

www.brockfieldhall.co.uk

Owner: Mr & Mrs Simon Wood **Contact:** Simon Wood

A fine late Georgian house designed by Peter Atkinson, assistant to John Carr of York, for Benjamin Agar Esq. Begun in 1804, its outstanding feature is an oval entrance hall with a fine cantilevered stone staircase curving past an impressive Venetian window. It is the family home of Mr and Mrs Simon Wood. Mrs Wood is the daughter of the late Lord and of Lady Martin Fitzalan Howard. He was the brother of the 17th Duke of Norfolk and son of the late Baroness Beaumont of Carlton Towers, Selby. There are some interesting portraits of her old Roman Catholic family, the Stapletons, and some good English furniture. Permanent exhibition of paintings by Staithes Group Artists (by appointment outside August).

Location: MAP 11:C9, OS Ref. SE664 550. 5m E of York off A166 or A64.

Open: 31 July, Aug: daily except Mons (open BH Mon), 1–4pm. Other times by appt.

Admission: Adult £5, Child £2.

ⓘ No photography inside house. ⬚ Partial. ⬚ By arrangement. P
⬚ In grounds, on leads.

BRODSWORTH HALL ⌗
& GARDENS

See page 340 for full page entry.

For unique **Civil wedding** venues see our index at the end of the book.

BROUGHTON HALL
SKIPTON, YORKSHIRE BD23 3AE

www.broughtonhall.co.uk
www.aldouriecastle.co.uk

Tel: 01756 799608 **Fax:** 01756 700357 **E-mail:** tempest@broughtonhall.co.uk

Owner: Tempest Family **Contact:** The Estate Office

The Tempest family have been in the area since 1097. The new Grade I Hall was built in 1597 and has fine furniture and paintings. Set within 3,000 acres with parkland, Italianate gardens and stunning conservatory, it is an ideal venue for events and enterprise. Close by is the award-winning Broughton Hall Business Park which is home to over 51 companies and with first class meeting room and food facilities within the Utopia building.

Location: MAP 10:N9, OS Ref. SD943 507. On A59, 2m W of Skipton.

Open: Group tours by arrangement.

Admission: £8. ⊤ ⬚ P ⬚

BURTON AGNES HALL & GARDENS 🏛
DRIFFIELD, EAST YORKSHIRE YO25 4NB

www.burtonagnes.com

Tel: 01262 490324 **Fax:** 01262 490513 **E-mail:** office@burtonagnes.com

Owner: Burton Agnes Hall Preservation Trust Ltd **Contact:** Mr Simon Cunliffe-Lister

A lovely Elizabethan Hall containing treasures collected by the family over four centuries, from the original carving and plasterwork to modern and Impressionist paintings. The Hall is surrounded by lawns and topiary yew. The award-winning gardens contain a maze, potager, jungle garden, campanula collection and colour gardens incorporating giant game boards. Children's corner.

Location: MAP 11:E9, OS Ref. TA103 633. Off A614 between Driffield and Bridlington.

Open: Gardens, shops & café: Snowdrops 6 Feb–28 Feb, daily, 11am–4pm. Hall & Gardens: 1 Apr–31 Oct, daily 11am–5pm. Christmas opening: 14 Nov–22 Dec, daily, 11am–5pm.

Admission: Hall & Gardens: Adult £7, Child £3.50, OAP £6.50. Gardens only: Adult £4, Child £2.50, OAP £3.50. 10% reduction for groups of 30+.

⬚ Gift Shop and Home and Garden shop ⬚ ⊤ ⬚ Ground floor & grounds. ⬚
Café. Ice-cream parlour. ⬚ P ⬚ ⬚ In grounds, on leads. ⬚

BURTON CONSTABLE HALL 🏛

BURTON CONSTABLE, SKIRLAUGH, EAST YORKSHIRE   HU11 4LN

www.burtonconstable.com

Tel: 01964 562400   **Fax:** 01964 563229   **Email:** helendewson@btconnect.com
Owner: Burton Constable Foundation   **Contact:** Mrs Helen Dewson

One of the most fascinating country houses surviving with its historic collections, Burton Constable is a large Elizabethan mansion surrounded by extensive parkland. The interiors of faded splendour are filled with fine furniture, paintings and sculpture, a library of 5,000 books and a remarkable 18th century 'Cabinet of Curiosities'.

Location: MAP 11:E10 OS Ref TA 193 369. Beverley 14m, Hull 10m. Signed from Skirlaugh.

Open: Easter Sat–28 Oct, Sat–Thur, 1–5pm. Grounds & Tearoom, 12.30–5pm. Last admission 4pm. 20th Nov to 5 Dec, 12.30-4pm. Last admission 3pm. Tea room: 12.30-5pm.

Admission: Hall & Grounds, Adult £6, Child £3, OAP £5.50, Family £14.50, Groups (15–60) £5. Connoisseur Study Visits, prices on request. Grounds only Adult £2.50, Child £1.25, Family £6.25.

ℹ No photography in house. 📷 🖥 WCs. 🍴 🅿 🎦 🖼 Guide dogs only. 🏨

BYLAND ABBEY ⌗

Coxwold, Thirsk, North Yorkshire YO61 4BD
Tel: 01347 868614   **E-mail:** byland.abbey@english-heritage.org.uk
www.english-heritage.org.uk/byland
Owner: English Heritage   **Contact:** Visitor Operations Team

Once one of the greatest monasteries in England, Byland inspired the design of church buildings throughout the north. An outstanding example of early gothic architecture, it inspired the design of the famous York Minster rose window. The Abbey's collection of medieval floor tiles is a testament to its earlier magnificence.

Location: MAP 11:B8, OS Ref. SE549 789. 2m S of A170 between Thirsk and Helmsley, NE of Coxwold village. Rail: Thirsk 10m

Open: 1 Apr–30 Jun: Wed–Sun, 11am–6pm. 1 Jul–31 Aug: Daily, 11am–6pm. 1–30 Sep: 11am–5pm, Wed–Mon.

Admission: Adult £4, Child £2, Conc. £3.40. 15% discount for groups (11+). Opening times and prices are valid until 31st March 2010, after this date details are subject to change please see www.english-heritage.org.uk for the most up-to-date information.

ℹ WC. 🔥 🅿 Limited for coaches. 🖼 🖼 On leads.

CANNON HALL MUSEUM, PARK & GARDENS

Cawthorne, Barnsley, South Yorkshire S75 4AT
Tel: 01226 790270   **Fax:** 01226 792117   **E-mail:** cannonhall@barnsley.gov.uk
www.barnsley.gov.uk
Owner: Barnsley Metropolitan Borough Council   **Contact:** The Museum Manager

Set in 70 acres of historic parkland and gardens, Cannon Hall now contains collections of fine furniture, old master paintings, stunning glassware and colourful pottery, much of which is displayed in period settings. Plus 'Charge', the Regimental museum of the 13th/18th Royal Hussars (QMO) and the Light Dragoons. Events and education programme and an ideal setting for conferences and Civil wedding ceremonies.

Location: MAP 10:P12, OS Ref. SE272 084. 6m NW of Barnsley of A635. M1/J38.

Open: Please call for opening times.

Admission: Free except for some events. Charge for car parking.

📷 🍴 🔥 Partial. WC. 🍴 Weekends & school holidays. 🅿 🖼 🚆 Pre-booked. 🖼 In grounds, on leads. 🔺 ❋ 🏨

CASTLE HOWARD 🏛

See page 341 for full page entry.

CAWTHORNE VICTORIA JUBILEE MUSEUM

Taylor Hill, Cawthorne, Barnsley, South Yorkshire S75 4HQ
Tel: 01226 790545 / 790246
Owner: Cawthorne Village   **Contact:** Mrs Mary Herbert

A quaint and eccentric collection in a half-timbered building. Museum has a ramp and toilet for disabled visitors. School visits welcome.

Location: MAP 10:P12, OS Ref. SE285 080. 4m W of Barnsley, just off the A635.

Open: Palm Sun–end Oct: Sats, Suns & BH Mons, 2–5pm. Groups by appointment throughout the year.

Admission: Adult 50p, Child 20p.

CLIFFE CASTLE

Keighley, West Yorkshire BD20 6LH
Tel: 01535 618231
Owner: City of Bradford Metropolitan District Council   **Contact:** Daru Rooke

Victorian manufacturer's house of 1878 with tall tower and garden. Now a museum.

Location: MAP 10:O10, OS Ref. SE057 422. ¾ m NW of Keighley off the A629.

Open: All year: Tues–Sat & BH Mons, 10am–5pm. Suns, 12 noon–5pm. Closed 25/26 Dec.

Admission: Free.

CLIFFORD'S TOWER ⌗

TOWER STREET, YORK YO1 9SA

www.english-heritage.org.uk/clifford

Tel: 01904 646940   **E-mail:** customers@english-heritage.org.uk
Owner: English Heritage   **Contact:** Visitor Operations Team

Cliffords Tower is a must see attraction for any one that is planning a visit to York, with sweeping panaromic views of York and the surrounding countryside, it is clear to see how Clifford's Tower has played such a crucial role in York's history. Once the central stronghold of York Castle, the tower has survived turbulent centuries of fire, siege and attempted demolition.

Location: MAP 21, OS Ref. SE 605 515. York city centre.

Open: 1 Apr–30 Sep: daily, 10am–6pm; 1 Oct–1 Nov: daily, 10am–5pm. 2 Nov–31 Mar 2010: daily, 10am–4pm. Closed 24–26 Dec & 1 Jan.

Admission: Adult £3.50, Child £1.80, Conc. £3.00. Family ticket £8.80. 15% discount available for groups (11+). Opening times and prices are valid until 31st March 2010, after this date details are subject to change please see www.english-heritage.org.uk for the most up-to-date information.

Special Events: Throughout the holiday periods you can explore the part Clifford's Tower played in the history of England with special hidden history guided tours.

📷 🔥 Unsuitable. 🅿 Charged. 🖼 ❋ 🏨

For corporate hospitality venues see our special index at the end of the book.

CONISBROUGH CASTLE ⚑

Castle Hill, Conisbrough, South Yorkshire DN12 3BU
Tel: 01709 863329 **E-mail:** conisbrough.castle@english-heritage.org.uk
www.english-heritage.org.uk/conisbrough
Owner: English Heritage **Contact:** The Administrator

One of Yorkshire's best surviving examples of medieval military architecture, with a reinstated roof and floors; this 12th-century castle is a spectacular structure. Built of magnesium limestone, it is the only example of its kind in Europe, and was one of the inspirations for Sir Walter Scott's classic novel, Ivanhoe.

Location: MAP 7:A1, OS Ref. SK515 989. Located NE of Conisbrough town center off A630 4.5 miles SW of Doncaster. Rail: Conisbrough 0.5m.

Open: 1 Apr–30 Jun: Sat–Wed, 10am–5pm 1 Jul–31 Aug: daily, 10–5pm. 1–30 Sep: Sat–Wed 10am–5pm. 1 Oct–31 Mar 2011: Sat–Wed, 10am–4pm. (last admission 4.20pm). Closed 24–26 Dec & 1 Jan.

Admission: Adult £4, Child £2, Conc. £3, Family £10. Opening times and prices are valid until 31st March 2010, after this date details are subject to change please see www.english-heritage.org.uk for the most up-to-date information.

Partial. P Visitors with disabilities, please call the site to reserve a space. On leads (restricted areas only).

Burton Constable Hall

DUNCOMBE PARK 🏛
HELMSLEY, NORTH YORKSHIRE YO62 5EB

www.duncombepark.com

Tel: 01439 772625 **Fax:** 01439 771114 **E-mail:** liz@duncombepark.com
Owner/Contact: Hon Jake Duncombe

Built on a virgin plateau overlooking Norman Castle and river valley, Duncombe Park is surrounded by 35 acres of beautiful 18th century landscaped gardens and 400 acres of parkland with national nature reserve and veteran trees.

Location: MAP 11:B7, OS Ref. SE604 830. Entrance just off Helmsley Market Square, signed off A170 Thirsk–Scarborough road.

Open: 4 Apr–31 Oct: Sun–Thur. House by guided tour only: 12.30, 1.30, 2.30 & 3.30pm. Gardens & Parkland Centre: 11am–5.30pm. Last admission 4.30pm Closed 23/24 & 28 Jun.

Admission: House & Gardens: Adult £8.25, Conc. £6.25, Child (10–16yrs) £3.75, Child under 5yrs Free, Family (2+2 Chidren 5–16yrs) £17, Groups (15+) £5.75, EH Members £4.50. Gardens & Parkland: Adult £5, Conc £4.50, Child (5–16yrs) £3, Child under 5yrs Free, Groups (15+) £4, Group guided tour £5. Parkland: Adult £3, Child (10–16yrs) £2, Child under 10yrs Free. Season ticket: Family (2+2 Children 5–16yrs) £35, Adult £20.00.

Country walks, nature reserve, orienteering, conferences. Banqueting facilities. Partial. Licensed. Obligatory. P In park on leads.

Burton Agnes Hall

CONSTABLE BURTON HALL GARDENS 🏛
LEYBURN, NORTH YORKSHIRE DL8 5LJ

www.constableburtongardens.co.uk

Tel: 01677 450428 **Fax:** 01677 450622
Owner/Contact: M C A Wyvill Esq

A delightful terraced woodland garden of lilies, ferns, hardy shrubs, roses and wild flowers, attached to a beautiful Palladian house designed by John Carr (not open). Garden trails and herbaceous borders. Stream garden with large architectural plants and reflection ponds. Impressive spring display of daffodils and tulips.

Location: MAP 10:P7, OS Ref. SE164 913. 3m E of Leyburn off the A684.

Open: Garden only: 20 Mar–26 Sept: daily, 9am–6pm.

Admission: Adult £4, Children under 16 years 50p. OAP £3.50.

Partial, WC. Group tours of house & gardens by arrangement. P Limited for coaches. In grounds, on leads.

FAIRFAX HOUSE 🏛

FAIRFAX HOUSE, CASTLEGATE, YORK YO1 9RN

www.fairfaxhouse.co.uk

Tel: 01904 655543 **Fax:** 01904 652262 **E-mail:** info@fairfaxhouse.co.uk

Owner: York Civic Trust **Contact:** Hannah Phillip

Fairfax House was acquired and fully restored by the York Civic Trust in 1983/84. The house, described as a classic architectural masterpiece of its age and certainly one of the finest townhouses in England, was saved from near collapse after considerable abuse and misuse this century, having been converted into a cinema and dance hall.

The richly decorated interior with its plasterwork, wood and wrought-iron, is now the home for a unique collection of Georgian furniture, clocks, paintings and porcelain. The Noel Terry Collection, gift of a former treasurer of the York Civic Trust, has been described by Christie's as one of the finest private collections formed in the 20th century. It enhances and complements the house and helps to create that special 'lived-in' feeling, providing the basis for a series of set-piece period exhibitions which bring the house to life in a very tangible way.

Location: MAP 11:B9, OS Ref. SE605 515. In centre of York between Castle Museum and Jorvik Centre.

Open: 11 Feb–31 Dec, Mon–Thur: 11am –5pm. Fris: Guided tours only 11am and 2pm. Sats: 11am–5pm. Suns: 1.30–5pm. Last admission 4.30pm. Closed 1 Jan–10 Feb & 24–26 Dec.

Admission: Adult £6, Child Free with full paying adult, Conc. £5. Groups*: Prices start fro £4 for Concession and £5 for Adults *Min payment 10 persons.

ⓘ Suitable for filming. No photography in house. 📷 📺 Max. 28 seated. Groups up to 50. ♿ Partial. 🐕 🅿 🖥 ❊ ♿

For **accommodation** in Yorkshire, see our special index at the end of the book.

FOUNTAINS ABBEY & STUDLEY ROYAL 🌿

See page 342 for full page entry.

THE GEORGIAN THEATRE ROYAL

Victoria Road, Richmond, North Yorkshire DL10 4DW

Tel: 01748 823710 **Box Office:** 01748 825252

E-mail: admin@georgiantheatreroyal.co.uk

Owner: Georgian Theatre Royal Trust **Contact:** Trish Hoines

The most complete Georgian playhouse in Britain. Built in 1788 by actor/manager, Samuel Butler and restored to its Georgian grandeur in 2003.

Location: MAP 10:P6, OS Ref. NZ174 013. 4m from the A1 (Scotch Corner) on the A6108.

Open: All year: Mon–Sat, 10am–7.30pm (5pm on non-performance nights, 4pm until curtain up on performance Suns). Guided tours: On the hour, 10am–4pm.

Admission: Donation £3.50. Child Free.

Bolton Abbey

KIRKHAM PRIORY ⌗

Kirkham, Whitwell-on-the-Hill, North Yorkshire YO60 7JS
Tel: 01653 618768 **E-mail:** kirkham.priory@english-heritage.org.uk
www.english-heritage.org.uk/kirkhampriory
Owner: English Heritage **Contact:** Visitor Operations Team
The ruins of this Augustinian priory include a magnificent carved gatehouse, declaring to the world the Priory's association with the rich and powerful. Discover the stories of a monk's life and the Priory's involvement in WWII including a secret visit by the then Prime Minister Winston Churchill.
Location: MAP 11:C8, OS Ref. SE736 658. 5m SW of Malton on minor road off A64.
Open: 1 Apr–31 Jul: Thur–Mon, 10am–5pm. 1–31 Aug: daily, 10am–5pm. 1–30 Sep: Thu–Mon, 10am–5pm.
Admission: Adult £3, Child £1.50, Conc. £2.60. 15% discount for groups (11+). Opening times and prices are valid until 31st March 2010, after this date details are subject to change please see www.english-heritage.org.uk for the most up-to-date information.
ℹ️ WC. 🔲 ♿ 🅿️ Limited for coaches. ◼️ 🚻 On leads.

KNARESBOROUGH CASTLE & MUSEUM

Knaresborough, North Yorkshire HG5 8AS
Tel: 01423 556188 **Fax:** 01423 556130
Owner: Duchy of Lancaster **Contact:** Diane Taylor
Ruins of 14th century castle standing high above the town. Local history museum housed in Tudor Courthouse. Gallery devoted to the Civil War.
Location: MAP 11:A9, OS Ref. SE349 569. 5m E of Harrogate, off A59.
Open: Good Friday–5 Oct: daily, 10.30am–5pm.
Admission: Adult £2.60, Child £1.50, OAP £1.60, Family £7.50, Groups (10+) £2.40

LEDSTON HALL

Hall Lane, Ledston, Castleford, West Yorkshire WF10 2BB
Tel: 01423 523423 Fax: 01423 521373 **E-mail:** james.hare@carterjonas.co.uk
Contact: James Hare
17th century mansion with some earlier work.
Location: MAP 11:A11, OS Ref. SE437 289. 2m N of Castleford, off A656.
Open: Exterior only: May–Aug: Mon–Fri, 9am–4pm. Other days by appointment.
Admission: Free.

LONGLEY OLD HALL

Longley, Huddersfield, West Yorkshire HD5 8LB
Tel: 01484 430852 **E-mail:** gallagher@longleyoldhall.co.uk
www.longleyoldhall.co.uk
Owner: Christine & Robin Gallagher **Contact:** Christine Gallagher
This timber framed Grade II* hall dates from the 14th century. It was owned by the Ramsden family, the former Lords of the Manors of Almondbury and Huddersfield, for over 400 years. It is included in Simon Jenkins' England's Thousand Best Houses.
Location: MAP 10:P11, OS Ref. SE154 150. 1½ m SE of Huddersfield towards Castle Hill, via Dog Kennel Bank.
Open: Easter and Summer BH weekends and 27–30 Dec for pre-booked guided tours. Group viewings by appointment (min 15, max 25 in winter and 50 in the summer; smaller groups by arrangement). Gardens open for Heritage Open Days in September.
Admission: £6 for open days, £10 for groups.
🔲 ♿ Unsuitable. 🎦 Obligatory. 🅿️ Limited for coaches. 🚻 ❄️

Longley Old Hall

LOTHERTON HALL & GARDENS
ABERFORD, LEEDS, WEST YORKSHIRE LS25 3EB

www.leeds.gov.uk/lothertonhall

Tel: 0113 2813259 **E-mail:** lotherton@leeds.gov.uk
Owner: Leeds City Council **Contact:** Michael Thaw
A beautiful Edwardian country house with a bird garden, red deer park and formal gardens. Lotherton Hall is home to a treasure trove of arts and crafts and fine collections of paintings, silver, ceramics and beautiful costume galleries.
Location: MAP 11:B10, OS92, SE450 360. 2½ m E of M1/J47 on B1217 the Towton Road.
Open: 1 Mar–31 Oct: Tue–Sat, 10am–5pm, Suns, 1–5pm. 1 Nov–31 Dec: Tue–Sat, 10am–4pm, Sun, 12 noon–4pm. Last adm. ¾ hr before closing. Closed Jan & Feb. Open BH Mons.
Admission: Adult £3, Child £1, Conc. £1.50, Groups £2. Car parking: £3.50 per day or £15 per year (including one year free admission to house for driver). Coach parking £20 per day. Prices may be subject to change.
🔲 🛒 🎦 🅿️ ◼️ 🚻 ♿

MANSION HOUSE
ST HELEN'S SQUARE, YORK YO1 9QL

www.york.gov.uk/mansionhouse

Tel: 01904 552036 **Fax:** 01904 551052 **E-mail:** civicenquiries@york.gov.uk
Owner: City of York Council **Contact:** Richard Pollitt
The Mansion House is one of York's great historic treasures and the oldest surviving mayoral residence in the country. The beaiful simplicity of the hallway gives way to the magnificent grandeur of the stateroom. The extensive civic collection ranges from silver chamber pots to medieval ceremonial swords.
Location: MAP 21, SE601 518 situated in St Helen's Square, close to the post office and to York Minster.
Open: House tours: 11am & 2pm every Fri & Sat from Mar–Dec (no need to book in advance). Open all year for pre booked groups. For House, Silver & Connoisseur Tours, contact property for details.
Admission: House tours: Adult £5, Child (up to 16) Free, Conc £4. Pre-booked house tours 10% discount for groups 10+ (Fri & Sat). *Silver Tours £8.50, *Behind the scenes Tour £8.50 *Connoisseur Tours £12.95. *Includes refreshments.
ℹ️ No photography. 🔲 🛒 ♿ 🎦 Obligatory 🚻 Guide dogs only. ❄️ ♿

visit hudsons guide online

MARKENFIELD HALL 🏛

NR RIPON, NORTH YORKSHIRE HG4 3AD

www.markenfield.com

Tel: 01765 692303 **Fax:** 01765 607195
E-mail: info@markenfield.com
Owner: Lady Deirdre Curteis **Contact:** The Administrator

"This wonderfully little-altered building is the most complete surviving example of the meduim-sized 14th century country house in England" John Martin Robinson *The Architecture of Northern England*. Tucked privately away down a mile-long winding drive, Markenfield is one of the most astonishing and romantic of Yorkshire's medieval houses: fortified, completely moated, and still privately owned. Winner of the HHA and Sotheby's Finest Restoration Award 2008.

Location: MAP 10:P8, OS Ref. SE294 672. Access from W side of A61. 2½ miles S of the Ripon bypass.
Open: 2–15 May & 20 June–3 Jul: daily, 2–5pm. Groups all year round by appointment.
Admission: Adult £4, Conc £3. Booked groups £5 per person (min charge £80).
🄃 🄵 🄿 🄰 🕾

MIDDLEHAM CASTLE ⌗

Castle Hill, Middleham, Leyburn, North Yorkshire DL8 4QG
Tel: 01969 623899 **E-mail:** middleham.castle@english-heritage.org.uk
www.english-heritage.org.uk/middleham
Owner: English Heritage **Contact:** Visitor Operations Team

Once the childhood and favourite home of Richard III, where he learnt the military skills and the courtly manners appropriate for a future king. The massive keep, one of the largest in England, was both a defensive building and a self-contained residence for the Lords of this fortress palace.

Location: MAP 10:O7, OS Ref. SE128 876. At Middleham, 2m S of Leyburn on A6108. Rail: Leyburn (Wensleydale Railway) 2m
Open: 1 Apr–30 Sept: daily, 10am–6pm. 1 Oct–31 Mar 2011: Sat–Wed, 10am–4pm. Closed 24–26 Dec & 1 Jan.
Admission: Adult £4, Child £2, Conc. £3.40. 15% discount for groups (11+). Opening times and prices are valid until 31st March 2010, after this date details are subject to change please see www.english-heritage.org.uk for the most up-to-date information.
ℹ️ Exhibition. 🄾 🄳 Partial. 🐕 On leads. 🕾

MOUNT GRACE PRIORY ⌗

Staddlebridge, Nr Northallerton, North Yorkshire DL6 3JG
Tel: 01609 883494 **E-mail:** mountgrace.priory@english-heritage.org.uk
www.english-heritage.org.uk/mountgracepriory
Owner: English Heritage **Contact:** Visitor Operations Team

Set amid woodland, this enchanting monastery is the best preserved Carthusian priory in Britain. Discover how the monks lived 600 years ago in the reconstructed monk's cell and herb plot. The gardens, re-modelled in the Arts & Crafts style, are a haven for the famous 'Priory Stoats'.

Location: MAP11:A7, OS Ref. SE449 985. 12m N of Thirsk, 6m NE of Northallerton on A19. Rail: Northallerton 6m
Open: 1 Apr–30 Sept: Thur–Mon, 10am–6pm. 1 Oct–31 Mar 2010: Thur–Sun, 10am–4pm. Closed 24–26 Dec & 1 Jan. Please note on the days there are summer evening theatre events, the site will open at 12pm.
Admission: Adult £4.50, Child £2.30, Conc. £3.80, Family £11.30. 15% discount for groups (11+). NT Members Free, (except on event days). Opening times and prices are valid until 31st March 2010, after this date details are subject to change please see www.english-heritage.org.uk for the most up-to-date information.
ℹ️ WCs. 🄾 🄵 🄿 🄰 🕷 🕾 🕾

NATIONAL CENTRE FOR EARLY MUSIC

St Margaret's Church, Walmgate, York YO1 9TL
Tel: 01904 632220 **Fax:** 01904 612631 **E-mail:** info@ncem.co.uk **www.ncem.co.uk**
Owner: York Early Music Foundation **Contact:** Mrs G Baldwin

The National Centre for Early Music is based in the medieval church of St Margaret's York. The church boasts a 12th century Romanesque doorway and a 17th century brick tower of considerable note. The Centre hosts concerts, music education activities, conferences, recordings and events.

Location: MAP 21, OS Ref. SE609 515. Inside Walmgate Bar, within the city walls, on the E side of the city.
Open: Mon–Fri, 10am–4pm. Also by appointment. Access is necessarily restricted when events are taking place.
Admission: Free, donations welcome.
🄳 🄵 Obligatory. By arrangement. 🄿 Limited. No coaches. ▣ 🕷 🕾

York Gate Garden

NEWBURGH PRIORY
COXWOLD, NORTH YORKSHIRE YO61 4AS

Tel: 01347 868372

Owner/Contact: Sir George Wombwell Bt

Originally 1145 with major alterations in 1568 and 1720, it has been the home of the Earls of Fauconberg and of the Wombwell family since 1538. Tomb of Oliver Cromwell (3rd daughter Mary married Viscount Fauconberg) is in the house. Extensive grounds contain a water garden, walled garden, topiary yews and woodland walks.

Location: MAP 11:B8, OS Ref. SE541 764. 4m E of A19, 18m N of York, ½ m E of Coxwold.

Open: 4 Apr–30 Jun Wed & Sun + Easter Mon BH + End of May BH. House: 2.30–4.45pm. Garden: 2–6pm. Tours every ½ hour, take approximately 50–60mins. Booked groups by arrangement.

Admission: House & Gardens: Adult £6.00. Child £1.50. Gardens only: Adult £3, Child Free. Special tours of private apartment Sun only 4–25 Apr & Easter Mon £5pp.
ℹ No photography in house. 🚻♿ Partial. 🎫 Obligatory. 🅿 Limited for coaches. 🐕 In grounds, on leads. 🎩 And wedding receptions.

NORTON CONYERS 🏛
Nr RIPON, NORTH YORKSHIRE HG4 5EQ

Tel/Fax: 01765 640333　**E-mail:** norton.conyers@bronco.co.uk

Owner: Sir James and Lady Graham　**Contact:** Lady Graham

Visited by Charlotte Brontë, Norton Conyers is an original of 'Thornfield Hall'. House and garden have belonged to the Grahams since 1624. The charming and historically important mid-eighteenth century walled garden retains its original design. Herbaceous borders flanked by high yew hedges lead to central pleasure pavilion with attached peach-house (still in use). Small sales area specialising in unusual hardy plants. PYO fruit in season.

Location: MAP 11:A8, OS Ref. SF319 763. 4m N of Ripon. 3½ m from the A1.

Open: House will be closed for repairs during 2010. Garden: 2/3 & 30/31 May; Sun & Mon 6 Jun–9 Aug, also 29/30 Aug; daily 7–10 Jul. All 2–5pm; last admissions 4.40pm. Groups by appointment.

Admission: Admission to garden is free; donations are very welcome. A charge is made when the garden is open for charity.
ℹ No interior photography. No high-heeled shoes. 🚻♿ Partial. WC. 🎫 Garden charity openings only. 🎫 By arrangement. 🅿 🐕 Dogs must be on a lead in the grounds. 🛡

NEWBY HALL & GARDENS 🏛　　*See page 343 for full page entry.*

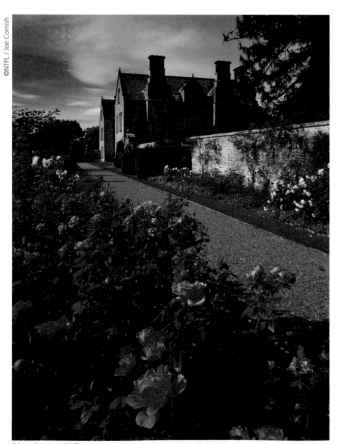

©NTPL / Joe Cornish

Nunnington Hall

NOSTELL PRIORY & PARKLAND 🌿

Doncaster Road, Wakefield, West Yorkshire WF4 1QE

Tel: 01924 863892　**E-mail:** nostellpriory@nationaltrust.org.uk

www.nationaltrust.org.uk

Owner: The National Trust　**Contact:** Visitor Services Manager

Set in over 350 acres of parkland, Nostell Priory is one of Yorkshire's jewels. It is an architectural treasure by James Pane with later additions by Robert Adam, and an internationally renowned Chippendale Collection.

Location: MAP 11:A11, OS Ref. SE403 175. 6m SE of Wakefield, off A638.

Open: Parklands open daily, 9am–7pm. House: 27 Feb–7 Nov, Wed–Sun, 11am–5pm, (last adm. 4.30pm). 4–12 Dec, daily, 12 noon–4pm. Open BH. Gardens Shop & Stables Tearoom: 27 Feb–7 Nov, Wed–Sun, 11am–5.30pm. 13 Nov–28 Nov, Wed–Sun, 11am–4.30pm, 4–12 Dec, Wed–Sun, 11am–4.30pm.

***Admission:** Parkland: Free. House & Garden: Adult £8.90, Child £4.20, Family (2+3) £20.00. Groups (15+) £6.50 (outside normal hours £12). Garden only: Adult £5.30, Child £2.70, Family £13.50. *Includes a voluntary donation but visitors can choose to pay the standard prices displayed at the property and on the website.
ℹ Baby facilities. 🍽🚻♿ WCs. 🎫 By arrangement. 🅿 Limited for coaches. 🐕 On leads. 🎩🛡

NUNNINGTON HALL 🌿

Nunnington, North Yorkshire YO62 5UY

Tel: 01439 748283　**E-mail:** nunningtonhall@nationaltrust.org.uk

Owner: The National Trust　**Contact:** The Property Manager

17th century manor house with magnificent oak-panelled hall, nursery, haunted room, and attics, with their fascinating Carlisle collection of miniature rooms fully furnished to reflect different periods.

Location: MAP 11:C8, OS Ref. SE670 795. In Ryedale, 4½ m SE of Helmsley, 1½ m N of B1257.

Open: 27 Feb–31 Oct, daily except Mons, 11am–5pm. 6 Nov–19 Dec, Sats & Suns, 11am–4pm. Last adm. 30 min before closing. Open BH Mons.

***Admission:** Adult £6.60, Child (under 17) £3.30, Family £16.50 Groups (15+) £5.60. National Trust Members Free. *includes a voluntary donation but visitors can choose to pay the standard prices displayed at the property and on the website.
🍽♿ Ground floor and grounds. WC. 🎫🐕 Guide dogs only. 🛡

RHS Garden Harlow Carr

ORMESBY HALL ✤

Ladgate Lane, Ormesby, Middlesbrough TS7 9AS
Tel: 01642 324188 **E-mail:** ormesbyhall@nationaltrust.org.uk
Owner: The National Trust **Contact:** Mr P Burton
A mid 18th century house with opulent decoration inside, including fine plasterwork by contemporary craftsmen.
Location: MAP 11:B6, OS Ref. NZ530 167. 3m SE of Middlesbrough.
Open: 13 Mar–31 Oct: 1.30–5pm, Sat & Sun & BH Mons & Good Fri. Tearoom: as House.
*Admission: Adult £5.10, Child £3.30, Family £13.35. Groups (15+) £4.20. Grounds Free. *includes a voluntary donation but visitors can choose to pay the standard prices displayed at the property and on the website.
🔽 Ground floor & grounds. WC. 🐕

PARCEVALL HALL GARDENS

Skyreholme, Skipton, North Yorkshire BD23 6DE
Tel:/Fax: 01756 720311 **E-mail:** parcevallhall@btconnect.com
Owner: Walsingham College (Yorkshire Properties) Ltd.
Contact: Phillip Nelson (Head Gardener)
Location: MAP 10:O8, OS Ref. SE068 613. E side of Upper Wharfedale, 1½ m NE of Appletreewick. 12m NNW of Ilkley by B6160 and via Burnsall.
Open: 1 Apr–31 Oct: 10am–6pm.
Admission: Adult £5.50, Child £2.50.
🖾 🍴 🐕 📷 P 🐾

PICKERING CASTLE ♯

Castlegate, Pickering, North Yorkshire YO18 7AX
Tel/Fax: 01751 474989 **E-mail:** pickering.castle@english-heritage.org.uk
www.english-heritage.org.uk/pickering
Owner: English Heritage **Contact:** Visitor Operations Team
Pickering Castle is set in an attractive market town. Built by William the Conqueror the splendid 13th Century Castle was used as a royal hunting lodge, holiday home and stud farm by a succession of medieval kings. Explore the walls, towers and mote and climb the steps to the motte.
Location: MAP 11:C7, OS Ref. SE998 845. In Pickering, 15m SW of Scarborough. Rail: Malton 9m, Pickering (N York Moors Railway) 0.5m
Open: 1 Apr–30 Jun: Thu–Mon, 10am–5pm. 1 Jul–31 Aug: Daily, 10am–5pm. 1–30 Sep: Thu–Mon, 10am–5pm.
Admission: Adult £3.50, Child £1.80, Conc. £3, Family £8.80. 15% discount for groups (11+). Opening times and prices are valid until 31st March 2010, after this date details are subject to change please see www.english-heritage.org.uk for the most up-to-date information.
ℹ️ WCs. 🖾 🔽 Partial Disabled Access (except motte). P Limited. 🔲 🐾 On leads.

PLUMPTON ROCKS 🏛

Plumpton, Knaresborough, North Yorkshire HG5 8NA
Tel: 01289 386360 **www.plumptonrocks.co.uk**
Owner: Edward de Plumpton Hunter **Contact:** Robert de Plumpton Hunter
Grade II* listed garden extending to over 30 acres including an idyllic lake, dramatic millstone grit rock formation, romantic woodland walks winding through bluebells and rhododendrons. Declared by English Heritage to be of outstanding interest. Painted by Turner. Described by Queen Mary as 'Heaven on earth'.
Location: MAP 11:A9, OS Ref. SE355 535. Midway between Harrogate and Wetherby on the A661, 1m SE of A661 junction with the Harrogate southern bypass.
Open: Mar–Oct: Sat, Sun & BHs, 11am–6pm.
Admission: Adult £2.50, Child/OAP £1.50. (2009 prices, subject to change)
🔽 Unsuitable. P Limited for coaches. 🔲 🐾 In grounds, on leads.

RHS GARDEN HARLOW CARR

Crag Lane, Harrogate, North Yorkshire HG3 1QB
www.rhs.org.uk/harlowcarr
Tel: 01423 565418 **Fax:** 01423 530663 **E-mail:** harlowcarr@rhs.org.uk
Owner/Contact: Royal Horticultural Society
One of Yorkshire's most relaxing yet inspiring gardens! Highlights of the beautiful garden include spectacular contemporary borders, Gardens Through Time, Streamside garden, alpines, scented and kitchen gardens, woodland and wildflower meadows, extensive RHS Shop and Plant Centre, Bettys Café Tea Rooms and free parking. Events all year including children's activities.
Location: MAP 10:P9. OS Ref. SE285 543. 1½m W from town centre on B6162 Otley Road.
Open: Daily: 9.30am–6pm (4pm Nov–Feb). Last entry 1 hour before closing. Closed Christmas Day.
Admission: Adult £7, Child (6–16yrs) £2.50, Child (under 6yrs) Free. Groups (10+): £6. Groups must book in advance. RHS Members (+1 family guest): Free.
ℹ️ Picnic area. 🖾 🍴 🔽 Partial. WC. 🐕 Licensed. 🍽 Licensed. 🎭 By arrangement. P 🔲 🐾 Guide dogs only. ❄ 🌂

© English Heritage

RICHMOND CASTLE ♯

TOWER ST, RICHMOND, NORTH YORKSHIRE DL10 4QW
www.english-heritage.org.uk/richmond
Tel/Fax: 01748 822493 **E-mail:** customers@english-heritage.org.uk
Owner: English Heritage **Contact:** Visitor Operations Team
Built shortly after 1066 on a rocky promontory high above the River Swale, this is the best preserved castle of such scale and age in Britain. The magnificent keep, with breathtaking views, is reputed to be the place where the legendary King Arthur sleeps. The castle's story is told in an interactive display exploring nine centuries of military history and is woven into the contemporary Cockpit Garden, created to reflect the stronghold's history and architecture.
Location: MAP 10:P6, OS Ref. NZ172 007. In Richmond.
Open: 1 Apr–30 Sep: daily, 10am–6pm. 1 Oct–31 Mar 2010: Thur–Mon, 10am–4pm. Closed 24–26 Dec & 1 Jan.
Admission: Adult £4.50, Child £2.30, Conc. £3.80 15% discount for groups (11+). Opening times and prices are valid until 31st March 2010, after this date details are subject to change please see www.english-heritage.org.uk for the most up-to-date information.
ℹ️ Interactive exhibition. WCs. 🖾 🔽 🔲 🐾 On leads. ❄ 🌂

© English Heritage

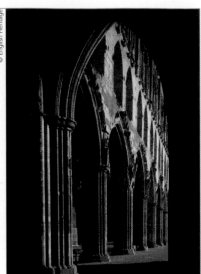

© English Heritage

RIEVAULX ABBEY ⌗

RIEVAULX, Nr HELMSLEY, NORTH YORKSHIRE YO62 5LB

www.english-heritage.org.uk/rievaulx

Tel: 01439 798228 **E-mail:** rievaulx.abbey@english-heritage.org.uk

Owner: English Heritage **Contact:** Visitor Operations Team

Rievaulx was the first Cistercian Abbey to be founded in the North of England in the 12th-century by St Bernard of Clairvaux. Set in a beautiful tranquil valley, it is among the most atmospheric and complete of all the ruined abbeys of the north.

"Everywhere peace, everywhere serenity, and a marvellous freedom from the tumult of the world", these words still describe Rievaulx today; written over eight centuries ago by the monastery's third abbot, St Aelred.

An exciting indoor exhibition "The Work of God and Man" explores the agricultural, industrial, spiritual and commercial aspects of Rievaulx's history, employing a variety of lively and interactive displays. The tearoom offers the chance to enjoy delicious Yorkshire fare; made with fresh locally sourced produce alongside the spectacular views.

Location: MAP 11:B7, OS Ref. SE577 850. In Rievaulx; 2¼m N of Helmsley on minor road off B1257.

Open: 1 Apr–30 Sep: daily, 10am–6pm. 1 Oct–1 Nov: Thu–Mon, 10am–5pm.2 Nov–31 Mar 2010: Thur–Mon, 10am–4pm. Closed 24–26 Dec & 1 Jan.

Admission: Adult £5, Child £2.50, Conc. £4.30. 15% discount for groups (11+). Opening times and prices are valid until 31st March 2010, after this date details are subject to change please see www.english-heritage.org.uk for the most up-to-date information.

ⓘ WCs. ▢ ▨ ⓓ ▣ ⓐ Audio tours (also available for the visually impaired, those with learning difficulties and in French and German). Ⓟ Pay and display parking, refundable to EH members and paying visitors upon admission. ▣ ⊞ On leads. ⊞ ⊡

RIEVAULX TERRACE & TEMPLES ⚘

Rievaulx, Helmsley, North Yorkshire YO62 5LJ

Tel: 01439 798340 (winter 01439 748283)

Owner: The National Trust **Contact:** The Property Manager

A ½m long grass-covered terrace and adjoining woodlands with vistas over Rievaulx Abbey and the Rye valley. There are two mid-18th century temples. Note: no access to the property Nov–end Mar.

Location: MAP 11:B7, OS Ref. SE579 848. 2½m NW of Helmsley on B1257. E of the Abbey.

Open: 27 Feb–31 Oct, daily, 11am–5pm.

*Admission: Adult £5.25, Child (under 17yrs) £2.90, Family (2+3) £12.60. Groups (15+): £4.40. NT Members Free. *includes a voluntary donation but visitors can choose to pay the standard prices displayed at the property and on the website.

▢ ⓓ Grounds. Batricar available. ⊞ In grounds, on leads. ⊡

RIPLEY CASTLE 🏰

See page 344 for full page entry.

RIPON CATHEDRAL

Ripon, North Yorkshire HG4 1QR

Tel: 01765 604108 (information on tours etc.) **Contact:** Canon Keith Punshon

One of the oldest crypts in Europe (672). Marvellous choir stalls and misericords (500 years old). Almost every type of architecture. Treasury.

Location: MAP 10:P8, OS Ref. SE314 711. 5m W signposted off A1, 12m N of Harrogate.

Open: All year: 8am–6pm.

Admission: Donations: £3. Pre-booked guided tours available.

©HortonDesign

RIPON MUSEUMS & HISTORIC WORKHOUSE GARDEN

RIPON HG4 1QS

www.riponmuseums.co.uk

Tel: 01765 690799 **Email:** info@riponmuseums.co.uk

Owner: Ripon Museum Trust **Contact:** Penny Hartley (Museums Manager)

Historic Workhouse Garden and three Museums, all within a 5 minute walk of the City Centre! The Workhouse and Prison & Police Museums have both had Heritage Lottery-funded refurbishments, retaining their original atmospheres, while the Georgian Courthouse is virtually unchanged since opening in 1830 – a unique trio of buildings.

Open: Daily, 13–20 Feb and 1 Apr–31 Oct, 1–4pm, extended in local school holidays 10am–4pm.

Location: MAP10:P8, OS Ref. SE314 711. All 3 museums are close to the main car/coach parks and bus station.

Admission: Family & '3 in 1' Passes for all 3 museums. Adult £7, Conc. £6, Child (U16 accom.) Free. Individual museum tickets are also available.

▢ ▨ ⓓ Garden, WH and P&P fully accessible. CH partial. ⓘ By arrangement. Ⓟ Ample for cars, limited for coaches. ▣ ⊞ Guide dogs only.

ROCHE ABBEY ♯

Maltby, Rotherham, South Yorkshire S66 8NW

Tel: 01709 812739 **E-mail:** roche.abbey@english-heritage.org.uk

www.english-heritage.org.uk/rocheabbey

Owner: English Heritage   **Contact:** Visitor Operations Team

Beautifully set in a valley landscaped by 'Capability' Brown in the 18th Century. It has one of the most complete ground plans of any English Cistercian monastery, laid out as excavated foundations. The most striking feature of this abbey is the Gothic transepts which still survive to their original height.

Location: MAP 7:B1, OS Ref. SK544 898. 1.5m S of Maltby off A634. Rail: Conisbrough 7m.

Open: 1 Apr–30 Sept: Thur–Sun & BHs, 11am–4pm.

Admission: Adult £3, Child £1.50, Conc. £2.60. 15% discount for groups (11+). Opening times and prices are valid until 31st March 2010, after this date details are subject to change please see www.english-heritage.org.uk for the most up-to-date information.

ℹ WCs. ▣ ⅏ 🅿 Limited. ▦ ✉

RYEDALE FOLK MUSEUM

Hutton le Hole, York, North Yorkshire YO62 6UA

Tel: 01751 417367 **E-mail:** info@ryedalefolkmuseum.co.uk

Owner: The Crosland Foundation

13 historic buildings showing the lives of ordinary folk from earliest times to the present day.

Location: MAP 11:C7, OS Ref. SE705 902. Follow signs from Hutton le Hole. 3m N of Kirkbymoorside.

Open: 20 Jan–18 Dec: 10am–5.30pm (last adm. 1 hour before dusk).

Admission: Adult £5, Child £3.50, Conc. £4.50. Family (2+2) £13.50. Season Ticket £30.

Scampston Hall

ST PETER'S CHURCH & BONES ALIVE! EXHIBITION ♯

Beck Hill, Barton upon Humber DN18 5EX

Tel: 01904 646940 (Clifford's Tower) **E-mail:** customers@english-heritage.org.uk

www.english-heritage.org.uk/stpeterschurch

Owner: English Heritage   **Contact:** Visitor Operations Team

With a history spanning a millennium, St Peter's is both an architectural and archaeological treasure. The thousand-year architecture includes a working Anglo-Saxon bell-tower and some surprising gargoyles. An exhibition includes the UK's largest resource for historic bone analysis from excavations of 2800 burials dating back over 900 years.

Location: MAP 11:E11, OS Ref TA03 3219. In Barton upon Humber town centre. Rail: Barton upon Humber 0.5m

Open: Open by appointment/guided tour only (call 01904 646940 Clifford's Tower)

Admission: Adult £5, Child £2.50, Conc. £4.30. Opening times and prices are valid until 31st March 2010, after this date details are subject to change please see www.english-heritage.org.uk for the most up-to-date information.

▣ ⅏ ℹ By arrangement. ✉

©Tim Imrie-Tait/Country Life Picture Library

SCAMPSTON HALL

SCAMPSTON, MALTON, NORTH YORKSHIRE YO17 8NG

www.scampston.co.uk

Tel: 01944 759111 **Fax:** 01944 758700 **E-mail:** info@scampston.co.uk

Owner: Sir Charles Legard Bt   **Contact:** The Administrator

Scampston is among the best examples of the English country house, combining fine architecture with a wealth of art treasures and set in 18th century 'Capability' Brown parkland. The double award winning house was featured in 'Hidden Treasure Houses' on FIVE in 2006. Guided tours around this family home are often led by the owner. Restaurant, disabled facilities and shop in The Walled Garden (see separate entry).

Location: MAP 11:D8, OS Ref. SE865 755. 4m E of Malton, off A64.

Open: 30 May–30 Aug, Tue–Fri & Sun and BH Mons, 1–3.45pm. All visits by guided tour. Last tour at 3pm. Also open in May for groups by appointment.

Admission: House, Front Garden & Woodland Walk: Adult £5, Child (12–16yrs) £2.50, Child (Under 12yrs) Free. Combined Ticket including Walled Garden: Adult £10, Child (12–16yrs) £5, Child (Under 12yrs) Free. Groups (15+) by appointment. HHA Members & Friends free admission to house only.

ℹ 🅿 ✉ ▲

THE WALLED GARDEN AT SCAMPSTON

SCAMPSTON HALL, MALTON, NORTH YORKSHIRE YO17 8NG

www.scampston.co.uk

Tel: 01944 759111 **Fax:** 01944 758700 **E-mail:** info@scampston.co.uk

Owner: Sir Charles Legard Bt   **Contact:** The Administrator

A contemporary garden with striking perennial meadow planting, as well as traditional spring/autumn borders, created by internationally acclaimed designer and plantsman Piet Oudolf. Described in *The Times* as "a gem". The garden is complemented by an excellent restaurant. "It's bold and beautiful – a must if you are heading to Yorkshire" *Toparius*.

Location: MAP 11:D8, OS Ref. SE865 755. 4m E of Malton, off A64.

Open: 2 Apr–31 Oct: daily (closed Mons except BHs), 10am–5pm, last adm. 4.30pm.

Admission: Walled Garden: Adult £5, Child (12–16yrs) £2.50, Child (11yrs & under) Free. Front Garden & Woodland Walk: Adult £3, Child (12–16yrs) £1.50, Child (11yrs & under) Free. Groups welcome by arrangement. See separate house listing for combined entry prices (30 May–30 Aug, Tues–Fri & Sun & BH Mons only). Please note: HHA membership does not give access to The Walled Garden.

▣ ⊺ ⅏ ☕ ℹ 🅿 ✉ ▲

SCARBOROUGH CASTLE ✠

CASTLE ROAD, SCARBOROUGH, NORTH YORKSHIRE YO11 1HY

www.english-heritage.org.uk/scarborough

Tel: 01723 372451 **E-mail:** scarborough.castle@english-heritage.org.uk
Owner: English Heritage **Contact:** Visitor Operations Team

Perched high in a dramatic setting overlooking the town of Scarborough, the castle has witnessed 3000 years of turbulent history from the Bronze Age to WWII. Gain fascinating insights into the past with an exhibition in the Master Gunner's house and see intriguing artefacts from the site. Specially constructed viewing platforms offer panoramic views. Less mobile visitors can enjoy a groundfloor touch-screen virtual tour of the displays, and virtual views reproducing those from the platforms.

Location: MAP 11:E7, OS Ref. TA050 892. Castle Road, E of the town centre. Rail: Scarborough 1m.

Open: 1 Apr–30 Sep: daily, 10am–6pm. 1 Oct–31 Mar 2010: Thur–Mon, 10am–4pm. Closed 24–26 Dec & 1 Jan.

Admission: Adult £4.50, Child £2.30, Conc. £3.80, Family £11.30. 15% discount for groups (11+). Opening times and prices are valid until 31st March 2010, after this date details are subject to change please see www.english-heritage.org.uk for the most up-to-date information.

ℹ️ WCs. ◻️♿🅿️ Tearoom open Summer only. 🎧 Inclusive. 🅿️ Limited. (pre-booked parking only for disabled visitors, otherwise located in town centre). ◼️🐕 On leads. ❋🎪

SION HILL 🏛

KIRBY WISKE, THIRSK, NORTH YORKSHIRE YO7 4EU

www.sionhillhall.co.uk

Tel: 01845 587206 **Fax:** 01845 587486 **E-mail:** sionhill@btconnect.com
Owner: H W Mawer Trust **Contact:** R M Mallaby

Sion Hill was designed in 1912 by the renowned York architect Walter H Brierley, 'the Lutyens of the North', receiving an award from the Royal Institute of British Architects as being of 'outstanding architectural merit'. The house is furnished with a fine collection of antique furniture, paintings, ceramics and clocks.

Location: MAP 11:A7, OS Ref. SE373 844. 6m S of Northallerton off A167, signposted. 4m W of Thirsk, 6m E of A1 via A61.

Open: April to October. Please contact the house for dates, times and booking arrangements. Admission strictly by pre-booked ticket.

Admission: £10 per person to include guided tour and admission to the grounds.

ℹ️ No photography in the house. ♿ Partial. WC. 🎭 By arrangement. 🅿️ Ample for cars and coaches. 🐕 Guide dogs only.

Sledmere House

SHIBDEN HALL

Lister's Road, Halifax, West Yorkshire HX3 6XG
Tel: 01422 352246 **Fax:** 01422 348440 **Email:** shibden.hall@calderdale.gov.uk
www.calderdale.gov.uk

Owner: Calderdale MBC **Contact:** Valerie Stansfield

A half-timbered 15th century manor house, the home of Anne Lister, set in a newly restored historic landscaped park. Oak furniture, 17th century aisled barn containing carriages and a folk museum, make Shibden an intriguing place to visit.

Location: MAP 10:O11, OS Ref. SE106 257. 1½ m E of Halifax off A58.

Open: 1 Mar–30 Nov: Mon–Sat, 10am–5pm (last admission 4.15pm), Sun, 12 noon–5pm (last admission 4.15pm). Dec–Feb: Mon–Sat, 10am–4pm, Sun, 12 noon–4pm (last admission 3.15pm).

Admission: Adult £3.50, Child/Conc. £2.50, Family £10. Prices subject to change April 2010.

◻️♿ Ground floor & grounds. 🎁🍴 Restaurant by the lake. 🎭 By arrangement. 🅿️◼️🐕 In grounds on leads. ❋🎪 Special events.

SKIPTON CASTLE

See page 345 for full page entry.

St Margaret's Church

SLEDMERE HOUSE 🏛

SLEDMERE, DRIFFIELD, EAST YORKSHIRE YO25 3XG

www.sledmerehouse.com

Tel: 01377 236637 **Fax:** 01377 236500 **Email:** info@sledmerehouse.com

Owner: Sir Tatton Sykes **Contact:** The House Secretary

At the heart of the Yorkshire Wolds, Sledmere House is the home of Sir Tatton Sykes, 8th Baronet. Built in 1751 and enlarged by Sir Christopher Sykes, 2nd Baronet, in the 1780s and sympathetically restored after a serious fire in 1911. The house exudes 18th Century elegance with each room containing decorative plasterwork by Joseph Rose Junior, and examples of the finest craftsmen of the period, including Chippendale, Hepplewhite & Sheraton. A tour of the house culminates in the magnificent Library which overlooks the 'Capability' Brown landscaped park. Award Winning Garden including Octagonal Walled Garden & Parterre, Wagoners' Special Reserve Military Museum, Children's Quiz, Adventure Playground, The Terrace Café & Gift Shop, The Triton Gallery, Park Walks, unspoilt Model Estate Village, Famous pipe organ played Weds & Suns 1.30pm–3.30pm.

Location: MAP 11:D9, OS Ref. SE931 648. Off the A166 between York & Bridlington. Scenic drive from York, Bridlington & Scarborough, 7 miles NW of Driffield.

Open: Friday 2 April to Sunday 26 September, Tues–Fri & Sun, BH Sat & Mon. Garden & Grounds, Shop, Terrace Café: Open 10am–5pm. House Open 11.00am closes 4.00pm, Sun & BH 4.30pm. The Triton Gallery Open 11.00am to 5.00pm.

Admission: House & Gardens: Adult £7.50, Conc. £7, Child £3, (Groups of 15+ £6.00 pp), Family Ticket £17 (2 Adults & 2 Children 5–16). Gardens & Park: Adult £5, Child £2, RHS members £4.50 (Gardens & Grounds only). Suggested visit time 4–5 hours.

ℹ️ No photography in house. 🅾️🍴🛗♿️📹 Licensed. 🅵 By arrangement: 🅿️🚹🚻 In grounds on leads. Guide dogs in house. 🔔

SUTTON PARK 🏛

SUTTON-ON-THE-FOREST, NORTH YORKSHIRE YO61 1DP

www.statelyhome.co.uk

Tel: 01347 810249 **Fax:** 01347 811239

E-mail: suttonpark@statelyhome.co.uk

Owner: Sir Reginald & Lady Sheffield **Contact:** Administrator

The Yorkshire home of Sir Reginald and Lady Sheffield. Early Georgian architecture. Magnificent plasterwork by Cortese. Rich collection of 18th century furniture, paintings and porcelain, put together with great style to make a most inviting house. Award winning gardens attract enthusiasts from home and abroad. Yorkshire in Bloom Award 2008.

Location: MAP 11:B9, OS Ref. SE583 646. 8m N of York on B1363 York–Helmsley Road.

Open: House: Apr–Sep: Wed, Sun & BHs, 1.30–5pm (last tour 4pm). Gardens: Apr–Sep: daily, 11am–5pm. Tearoom: Apr–Sep: Wed–Sun, 11am–5pm. Private groups any other day by appointment. House open Oct–Mar for private parties (15+) only.

Admission: House & Garden: Adult £6.50, Child £4, Conc. £5.50. Private Groups (15+): £7. Gardens only: Adult £3.50, Child £1.50, Conc. £3. Coaches £3. Caravans: £9.00 per unit per night. Electric hookup: £11.00 per unit per night.

Special Events: Specialist Plant Fair 18th April 2010

ℹ️ No photography. 🅾️🍴 Lunches & dinners in Dining Room. ♿️ Partial. WCs. 📹 Licensed. 🅵 Obligatory. 🅿️ Limited for coaches. 🔔🛏

STOCKELD PARK

WETHERBY, NORTH YORKSHIRE LS22 4AW

www.stockeldpark.co.uk

Tel: 01937 586101 **Fax:** 01937 580084 **Email:** enquiries@stockeldpark.co.uk

Owner: Mr and Mrs P G F Grant **Contact:** Mr P Grant

A gracious Palladian mansion by James Paine (1763), featuring a magnificent cantilevered staircase in the central oval hall. Surrounded by beautiful gardens and set in 18th Century landscaped parkland at the heart of a 2000 acre estate. Popular for filming and photography. Home of The Christmas Adventure www.thechristmasadventure.com

Location: MAP 11:A9, OS Ref. SE376 497. York 12m, Harrogate 5m, Leeds 12m.

Open: Privately booked events and tours only. Please contact the Estate Office: 01937 586101.

Admission: Prices on application.

Special Events: Outdoor Activities during Summer and Winter months October Half Term Activities, Halloween Events, Guy Fawkes Firework Display, Children in Need Ski-athon, Santa's Grotto, Fresh Christmas Tree Sale, The Christmas Adventure.

🅾️🍴♿️ WCs.📹 Licensed. 🍴 Licensed. 🅵 By arrangement 🅿️ Limited for coaches. 🛏❌📹

TEMPLE NEWSAM

LEEDS LS15 OAE

www.leeds.gov.uk/templenewsam

Tel: 0113 2647321 **E-mail:** temple.newsam.house@leeds.gov.uk

Owner: Leeds City Council **Contact:** Bobbie Robertson

One of the great country houses of England, this Tudor-Jacobean mansion was the birthplace of Lord Darnley, husband of Mary Queen of Scots and home to the Ingram family for 300 years. Rich in newly restored interiors, paintings, furniture (including Chippendale), textiles, silver and ceramics; an ever-changing exhibitions programme, audio-tours, family activities and children's trails are also on offer along with one of the largest working rare breed farms in Europe. Temple Newsam sits within 1500 acres of grand and beautiful 'Capability' Brown parkland with formal and wooded gardens as well as national plant collections.

Location: MAP 10:P10, OS Ref. SE358 321. 5m E of city centre, off A63 Selby Road. M1/J46.

Open: 30 Mar–2 Nov: Tue–Sun and BHs, House: 10.30am–5pm, Farm: 10am–5pm. 2 Nov–29 Mar 2011: Tue–Sun and BHs, House: 10.30am–4pm, Farm: 10am–4pm. Last admission ¾ hour before closing. Estate open free, dawn to dusk.

Admission: House only: Adult £3.43, Child £2.44, Family £8.81. House & Farm: Adult £5.63, Child £3.43, Family £14.19. Prices may be subject to change. Special group package and rates available. Free parking available or patrolled car park £3.50, coach parking for pre-booked groups is free.

🅾️🍴♿️🍴🎦📷🍴🅿️🛏🚻📹

THORNTON ABBEY AND GATEHOUSE ⧩

Ulceby DN39 6TU
Tel: 01469 541445   **E-mail:** thornton.abbey@english-heritage.org.uk
www.english-heritage.org.uk/thornton
Owner: English Heritage   **Contact:** Visitor Operations Team
The enormous fortified Gatehouse of Thornton Abbey is the finest surviving in Britain, trumpeting the prosperity of what was once one of the wealthiest Augustinian monasteries. Built in the nervous years following the Peasants' Revolt of 1381, it is thought to have protected the Abbey's treasures and his guests.
Location: MAP 11:E11, OS Map 284 Ref TA118 189. 18m NE of Scunthorpe on a road N of A160. 7m SE of Humber Bridge, on a road E of A1077. Rail: Thornton Abbey 0.25m.
Open: 1 Apr–30 Jun: Wed–Sun, 10am–5pm. 1 Jul–31 Aug: daily, 10am–5pm. 1 Sep–31 Mar, Fri–Sun, 10am–4pm. Closed 24–26 Dec & 1 Jan.
Admission: Adult £4, Child £2, Conc. £3.40. Opening times and prices are valid until 31st March 2010, after this date details are subject to change please see www.english-heritage.org.uk for the most up-to-date information.
⟨⟩ Partial. Except gatehouse interior & part of chapter ruins. **P** ⟨⟩
⟨⟩ On leads (restricted areas only).

THORP PERROW ARBORETUM, WOODLAND GARDEN BIRDS OF PREY & MAMMAL CENTRE

Bedale, North Yorkshire DL8 2PR
Tel/Fax: 01677 425323   **E-mail:** enquiries@thorpperrow.com
www.thorpperrow.com
Owner: Sir John Ropner Bt   **Contact:** Louise McNeill
85 acres of woodland walks. One of the largest collections of trees and shrubs in the north of England, including a 16th century spring wood and 19th century pinetum, and holds five National Collections – Ash, Lime, Walnut, Laburnum and Cotinus. The Bird of Prey and Mammal Centre is a captive breeding and conservation centre. Three flying demonstrations daily throughout the season.
Location: MAP 10:P7, OS Ref. SE258 851. Bedale–Ripon road, S of Bedale, 4m from Leeming Bar on A1.
Open: All year: dawn–dusk. Telephone for winter opening times.
Admission: Arboretum & Falcons: Adult £7, OAP £5.50, Child £4, Family (2+2) £20, (2+3) £23.50. Groups prices available.
⟨i⟩ Picnic area. Children's playground. ⟨⟩ ⟨⟩ ⟨⟩ Partial. WCs. ⟨⟩ Licensed.
⟨⟩ By arrangement. **P** Limited for coaches. ⟨⟩ ⟨⟩ In grounds, on leads. ⟨⟩ ⟨⟩

TREASURER'S HOUSE ⧩

Minster Yard, York, North Yorkshire YO1 7JL
Tel: 01904 624247   **E-mail:** treasurershouse@nationaltrust.org.uk
Owner: The National Trust   **Contact:** The Property Manager
Named after the Treasurer of York Minster and built over a Roman road, the house is not all that it seems! Nestled behind the Minster, the size and splendour and contents of the house are a constant surprise to visitors – as are the famous ghost stories. Free trails for children and free access to the National Trust tearoom.
Location: MAP 21, OS Ref. SE604 523. The N side of York Minster. Entrance on Chapter House St.
Open: 1 Apr–31 Oct: daily except Fri, 11am–4.30pm. 1–30 Nov: daily except Fri, 11am–3pm. (Tearoom, ghost cellar, partial access to show rooms via themed tours.)
Admission: House: Adult £6, Child £3, Family £15. Ghost Cellar: Adult £2.40, Child £1.90. November Opening: Adult £4, Child £2.80.
*includes a voluntary donation but visitors can choose to pay the standard prices displayed at the property and on the website.
⟨⟩ ⟨⟩ Partial. WC. ⟨⟩ Licensed. ⟨⟩ Licensed. **P** None. ⟨⟩ ⟨⟩ In grounds, on leads. ⟨⟩

WENTWORTH CASTLE GARDENS

Lowe Lane, Stainborough, Barnsley, South Yorkshire S75 3ET
Tel: 01226 776040   **Fax:** 01226 776042
Owner: Wentworth Castle Trust   **Contact:** Richard Evans – Heritage Director
This historic 18th century parkland estate features over 26 listed monuments and a magnificent 60-acre pleasure garden open on selected days from spring to autumn.
Location: MAP 10:P12, OS Ref. SE320 034. 5 mins from M1/J37.
Open: All year daily: Apr–Sept 10am–5pm, Oct–Mar 10am–4pm.
Admission: Garden: Adult £3.95, Conc. £3.25 Guided tours £2 extra.

WILBERFORCE HOUSE

25 High Street, Hull, East Yorkshire HU1 1NQ
Tel: 01482 613902   **Fax:** 01482 613710
Owner: Hull City Council   **Contact:** S R Green
Birthplace of slavery abolitionist William Wilberforce. Reopened 2007 following £1.6 million redevelopment. Displays chart the history of slavery, the abolition campaign and slavery today.
Location: MAP 11:E11, OS Ref. TA102 286. High Street, Hull.
Open: Mon–Sat, 10am–5pm, Sun 1.30–4.30pm.
Admission: Free.

WASSAND HALL
SEATON, HULL, EAST YORKSHIRE HU11 5RJ

www.wassand.co.uk

Tel: 01964 534488   **Fax:** 01964 533334   **E-mail:** reorussell.wassand@tiscali.co.uk
Owner/Contact: R E O Russell – Resident Trustee
Fine Regency house 1815 by Thomas Cundy the Elder. Beautifully restored walled gardens, woodland walks, Parks and vistas over Hornsea Mere, part of the Estate since 1580. The Estate was purchased circa 1520 by Dame Jane Constable and has remained in the family to the present day, Mr Rupert Russell being the great nephew of the late Lady Strickland-Constable. The house contains a fine collection of 18/19th century paintings, English and Continental silver, furniture and porcelain. Wassand is very much a family home and retains a very friendly atmosphere. Homemade afternoon teas are served in the conservatory on Open Days.

Location: MAP 11:F9, OS Ref. TA174 460. On the B1244 Seaton–Hornsea Road. Approximately 2m from Hornsea.
Open: 28–31 May; 10–14, 25–29 Jun; 9,10 & 12 Jul (Sunday the 11th– School concert "Music for a Summer's Afternoon" – Grounds open but hall closed) 30 & 31 (Evening review of Music & Mirth 7.30pm); 1–3, 6, 8, 9, 27–30 Aug.
Admission: Hall, all grounds & walks: Adult £5, Child (11–15yrs) £3. Hall: Adult £3, Child (11–15yrs) £1.50. Grounds & Garden: Adult £3, Child (11–15yrs) £1.50, Child under 10yrs Free. Guided tours and groups by arrangment – POA.
⟨⟩ Limited. ⟨⟩ ⟨⟩ By arrangement. **P** Ample for cars, limited for coaches.
⟨⟩ In grounds, on leads.

© English Heritage

WHITBY ABBEY ⌗
WHITBY, NORTH YORKSHIRE YO22 4JT
www.english-heritage.org.uk/whitbyabbey

Tel: 01947 603568 **E-mail:** whitby.abbey@english-heritage.org.uk
Owner: English Heritage **Contact:** Visitor Operations Team
The dramatic ruins of this once magnificent abbey stand high on the headland rich in over thirteen centuries of history.

Founded by St Hilda in AD657, Whitby Abbey soon acquired great influence, before being ransacked by the invading Viking army. It was to be 200 years before the monastic tradition was revived, but yet again the Abbey was plundered, this time following the dissolution.

Inspired by detailed archaeological investigation of the site, an interactive visitor centre provides visitors with a chance to discover the Abbeys history from St Hilda to Dracula with recreated images of the Abbey over time and "Talking Heads" of personalities from the past. A recent addition is the installation of a 'Borghese Gladiator' statue in front of the Mansion House.

Location: MAP 11:D6, OS Ref. NZ904 115. On cliff top E of Whitby. Rail: Whitby 0.5m
Open: 1 Apr–30 Sep: daily, 10am–6pm. 1 Oct–31 Mar 2010: Thur–Mon, 10am–4pm. Closed 24–26 Dec & 1 Jan.
Admission: Adult £5.50, Child £2.80, Conc. £4.70, Family £13.80. 15% discounts for groups (11+). EH members Free. Opening times and prices are valid until 31st March 2010, after this date details are subject to change please see www.english-heritage.org.uk for the most up-to-date information.

ℹ️ WCs. From the Whitby harbour area, the Abbey can only be directly reached on foot via the 199 'Abbey steps' (or Caedmon's Trod). Alternatively, a well-signposted road leads from the town outskirts to the cliff-top Abbey. ▣ ♿ Disabled access (south entrance, parking charged). ▣ ▣ P Parking not managed by English Heritage. Charge payable. ▣ ▣ On leads (restricted areas only). ▣ ▣

WORTLEY HALL

Wortley, Sheffield, South Yorkshire S35 7DB
Tel: 0114 2882100 **Fax:** 0114 2830695
Owner: Labour, Co-operative & Trade Union Movement **Contact:** Marc Mallender
15 acres of formal Italianate gardens surrounded by 11 acres of informal pleasure grounds.
Location: MAP 6:P1, OS Ref. SK313 995. 10kms S of Barnsley in Wortley on A629.
Open: Gardens: Daily 10am–4pm. Specialist Plant Fairs 1 Jun & 24 Aug. Walk & Dine evenings.
Admission: Donation. Garden tours with Head Gardener for groups (15+) £2pp.

YORK MINSTER

Deangate, York YO1 7HH
Tel: 01904 557216 **Fax:** 01904 557218 **E-mail:** visitors@yorkminster.org
Owner: Dean and Chapter of York **Contact:** Stephen Hemming
Large gothic church housing the largest collection of medieval stained glass in England.
Location: MAP 21, OS Ref. SE603 522. Centre of York.
Open: All year: Mon–Sat, 9.30am–5pm, Sun: 12 noon–3.45pm.
Admission: Adult £5.50, Child (under 16yrs) Free, Conc. £4.50. Groups: Adult £5, Child (under 16yrs) Free, Conc. £4.

Planning a weekend away in Yorkshire?

See Historic Places to Stay

Hazlewood Castle

YORK GATE GARDEN
BACK CHURCH LANE, ADEL, LEEDS, WEST YORKSHIRE LS16 8DW
www.perennial.org.uk/yorkgate

Tel: 0113 2678240
Owner: Perennial **Contact:** The Garden Co-ordinator
Inspirational one acre garden widely recognized as one of Britain's finest small gardens. A series of smaller gardens with different themes and in contrasting styles are linked by a succession of delightful vistas. Striking architectural features play a key role throughout the garden which is also noted for its exquisite detailing.
Location: MAP 10:P10, OS Ref. 275 403. 2¼m SE of Bramhope. ½m E of A660.
Open: 1 Apr–30 Sept: Thur, Sun & BH Mons, 2–5pm. Also selected evenings (see website for details).
Admission: Adult £3.80, Child (16yrs & under) Free.
Season Ticket £9.50.
ℹ️ Groups must book. ▣ ▣ Tea & Biscuits. ▣ By arrangement.
▣ Guide dogs only.

Leighton Hall, Lancashire

North West

Cheshire has two strikingly different faces; the East, more industrial and more rugged where it adjoins the Peak District National Park, and the West, the flatter 'Cheshire Plain', more densely farmed and with easily recognisable red brick buildings. On the edge of the Lake District is Levens Hall and to the west is Muncaster Castle and its fascinating Owl Centre. For children, a visit to the Beatrix Potter Gallery is a must.

Cholmondeley Castle Garden, Cheshire

Cheshire

Cumbria

Lancashire

Merseyside

CUMBRIA

LANCASHIRE

MERSEYSIDE

CHESHIRE

Capesthorne Hall, Cheshire

■ **Owner**
Mrs C J C Legh

■ **Contact**
Corporate Enquiries:
The Hunting Lodge
Adlington Hall
Macclesfield
Cheshire
SK10 4LF

Tel: 01625 827595
Fax: 01625 820797
E-mail: enquiries@
adlingtonhall.com

Hall Tours:
The Estate Office
Tel: 01625 829206

■ **Location**
MAP 6:N2
OS Ref. SJ905 804

5m N of
Macclesfield, A523,
13m S of Manchester.
London 178m.

Rail: Macclesfield
& Wilmslow
stations 5m.

Air: Manchester
Airport 8m.

■ **Opening Times**
July & August
Sunday, Tuesday &
Wednesday,
2.00pm–5.00pm.

■ **Admission**
House & Gardens
Adult	£8.00
Child	£4.00
Student	£4.00

Gardens only
Adult	£5.00
Child	FREE
Student	FREE
Groups of 20+	£7.50

ADLINGTON HALL

www.adlingtonhall.com

Adlington Hall, the home of the Leghs of Adlington from 1315 to the present day, was built on the site of a Hunting Lodge which stood in the Forest of Macclesfield in 1040. Two oaks, part of the original building, remain with their roots in the ground and support the east end of the Great Hall, which was built between 1480 and 1505.

The Hall is a manor house, quadrangular in shape, and was once surrounded by a moat. Two sides of the Courtyard and the east wing were built in the typical 'Black and White' Cheshire style in 1581. The south front and west wing (containing the Drawing Room and Dining Room) were added between 1749 and 1757 and are built of red brick with a handsome stone portico with four Ionic columns on octagonal pedestals. Between the trees in the Great Hall stands an organ built by 'Father' Bernard Smith (c1670-80). Handel subsequently played on this instrument and, now fully restored, it is the largest 17th century organ in the country.

Gardens
The Gardens have been laid out over many centuries. A lime walk planted in 1688 leads to a Regency rockery that surrounds the unique Shell Cottage. The Wilderness, a Rococo styled landscape garden of the Georgian period contains many follies such as the chinoserie T'Ing House, Pagoda bridge and a classical Temple to Diana. Newly created formal gardens around the house include an old fashioned rose garden yew maze and a flower parterre and water garden.

ℹ️ Suitable for corporate events, product launches, business meetings, conferences, concerts, fashion shows, garden parties, rallies, clay-pigeon shooting, filming and weddings.

🍽️ The Great Hall and Dining Room are available for corporate entertaining. Catering can be arranged.

♿ Visitors may alight at entrance to Hall. WCs.

☕

🍴 By arrangement.

🅿️ For 100 cars and 4 coaches, 100 yds from Hall.

❄️ By prior appointment.

■ **Conference/Function**

ROOM	SIZE	MAX CAPACITY
Great Hall	11 x 8m	80
Dining Rm	10.75 x 7m	80
Courtyard	27 x 17m	200
Hunting Lodge		130

ARLEY HALL & GARDENS

www.arleyhallandgardens.com

Owned by the same family for over 500 years, Arley is a delightful estate. The award-winning gardens, recently voted in the top 50 in Europe and in Britain's top 10, have been created gradually over 250 years with each generation of the family making its own contribution. The result is a garden of great atmosphere, interest and vitality, which blends strong elements of design from earlier centuries with modern ideas in both planting and design. Arley is, therefore, a wonderful example of the idea that the best gardens are living, changing works of art. Outstanding features are the renowned double herbaceous border (c1846), the Quercus Ilex and pleached Lime Avenues, Victorian Rootree, walled gardens, yew hedges and shrub rose collection. The family tradition continues today with the current Viscount Ashbrook, who over the last 30 years has created the less formal Grove and Woodland Walk, where 300 varieties of rhododendron grow amongst a collection of rare trees and shrubs in a delightful tranquil setting. One of Cheshire's most charming stately homes, the Hall (Grade II*) was built by the present Viscount Ashbrook's great, great grandfather, Rowland Egerton-Warburton between 1832 and 1885 and is a fine example of the Victorian Jacobean style. Each room is given its own individual character by the elaborate plasterwork, wood panelling, family portraits and porcelain. From the grandeur of the Gallery to the intimacy of the Library the Hall exudes charm. The Emperor's Room was even home to Prince Louis Napoleon, later Napoleon III of France, in the winter of 1847–48. Arley won the title of 2009 'Small Visitor Atraction of the Year' in the North West and with its new, purpose built conference facility 'Olympia' is also a wonderful, exclusive venue for weddings, corporate functions and private parties.

- **i** Suitable for weddings, corporate functions, product launches, conferences, filming, photography, concerts and fairs. Photography in Hall by permission only.
- Open while the Garden is open.
- Comprehensive set of menus available for entertaining in the Hall and Tudor Barn.
- Partial access to the Hall, full access to Gardens, WCs.
- Licensed Tudor Barn Restaurant.
- Welcomed by arrangement.
- **P** Free
- In the grounds on leads.

Sidebar

■ Owner
Viscount & Viscountess Ashbrook

■ Contact
Estate Manager –
Garry Fortune
The Estate Office
Arley
Nr Northwich
Cheshire CW9 6NA

Tel: 01565 777353
Fax: 01565 777465
E-mail: enquiries@ arleyhallandgardens.com
Arley Weddings: www.arleyweddings.com

■ Location
MAP 6:M2
OS Ref. SJ675 809

5m W Knutsford,
5m from M6/J19 & 20
and M56/J9 & 10.

■ Opening Times
2 April–24 October
(Plus November weekends)

Gardens: Tuesday–Sunday & BHs,
11am–5pm.

Hall: Tues, Suns & BHs,
12noon–4.30pm.

■ Admission
Gardens, Grounds & Chapel:

Adult	£6.00
Child (5–16yrs)	£2.00
Senior	£5.50
Family	£14.00
Groups:	
Adult	£5.00
Senior	£4.50

Hall & Gardens

Adult	£8.50
Child (5–16yrs)	£3.00
Senior	£7.50
Family	£21.00
Groups:	
Adult	£6.50
Senior	£5.75

Season tickets

Individual	£30.00
Joint	£50.00
Family (2+3)	£70.00

■ Special Events
February
Wedding Fair

March
Mothers Day Celebrations

April
Spring Plant Fair
Bluebell Walks

June
Arley Garden Festival

October
Halloween Murder Mystery Evening

December
Christmas Floral Extravaganza

■ **Owner**
Mr & Mrs W. A.
Bromley-Davenport

■ **Contact**
Christine Mountney
Hall Manager
Capesthorne Hall
Siddington
Macclesfield
Cheshire SK11 9JY

Weddings and Corporate enquiries

Tel: 01625 861221
Fax: 01625 861619
E-mail: info@
capesthorne.com

■ **Location**
MAP 6:N2
OS Ref. SJ840 727

5m W of Macclesfield.
30 mins S of Manchester
on A34.
Near M6, M63 and M62.
Air: Manchester
International 20 mins.
Rail: Macclesfield 5m
(2 hrs from London).
Taxi: 01625 533464.

■ **Opening Times**
Summer
April–Oct Suns, Mons &
BHs.
Hall 1.30–4pm. Last
admission 3.30pm.
Gardens & Chapel
12 noon–5pm. Groups
welcome by
appointment. Caravan
Park also open
Easter–end October.
Corporate enquiries:
March–December.

■ **Admission**
Sundays & BHs only
Hall, Gardens & Chapel
Adult   £7.00
Child (5–16yrs) £3.50
OAP   £6.00
Family*   £16.00

*Parents and children
aged up to 16yrs in the
same car.

Gardens & Chapel only
Adult   £4.50
Child (5–16yrs) £2.50
OAP   £3.50

**Transfers from Gardens
& Chapel to Hall**
Adult/OAP   £3.50
Child (5–16yrs) £2.00

**Mondays only: Hall,
Chapel & Gardens**
Car
(up to 4 pass.) £10.00
Additional person £2.50

Minibus
(up to 12 pass) £30.00

Coach
(up to 50 pass) £60.00

Caravan Park
Closed for 2010 season

CAPESTHORNE HALL

www.capesthorne.com

Capesthorne Hall, set in 100 acres of picturesque Cheshire parkland, has been touched by nearly 1,000 years of English history – Roman legions passed across it, titled Norman families hunted on it and, during the Civil War, a Royalist ancestress helped Charles II to escape after the Battle of Worcester. The Jacobean-style Hall has a fascinating collection of fine art, marble sculptures, furniture and tapestries. Originally designed by the Smiths of Warwick it was built between 1719 and 1732. It was altered by Blore in 1837 and partially rebuilt by Salvin in 1861 following a disastrous fire.

The present Squire is William Bromley-Davenport, Lord Lieutenant of Cheshire, whose ancestors have owned the estate since Domesday times when they were appointed custodians of the Royal Forest of Macclesfield.

In the grounds near the family Chapel the 18th century Italian Milanese Gates open onto the herbaceous borders and maples which line the beautiful lakeside gardens. But amid the natural spectacle and woodland walks, Capesthorne still offers glimpses of its man-made past … the remains of the Ice House, the Old Boat House and the curious Swallow Hole.

Facilities at the Hall can be hired for corporate occasions and family celebrations including Civil Wedding ceremonies.

ⓘ Available for corporate functions, meetings, product launches, promotions, exhibitions, presentations, seminars, activity days, Civil Weddings and receptions, family celebrations, still photography, clay shooting, car rallies, garden parties, barbecues, concerts, antique, craft, country and game fairs. No photography in Hall.

Ⳑ Catering can be provided for groups (full menus on request). Function rooms available for wedding receptions, corporate hospitality, meetings and other special events. 'The Butler's Pantry' serves light refreshments.

♿ Gravel paths, ramps. WCs.

Ⳑ Guided tours available for pre-booked parties (except Sunday and Monday).

🅿 100 cars/20 coaches on hard-standing and unlimited in park, 50 yds from house.

🐕 Guide dogs in Hall. Under control in Park.

LYME PARK 🌳

www.nationaltrust.org.uk

On the edge of the Peak District nestling within sweeping moor land Lyme Park is a magnificent estate. Its wild remoteness and powerful beauty contrast with one of the most famous country house images in England - the backdrop to where Darcy meets Elizabeth in Pride and Prejudice. Discover a colourful family history from rescuing the Black Prince, sailing into exile with the Duke of Windsor, to the writing of the hit series Upstairs Downstairs. Enjoy hearing visitors play the piano as you discover impressive tapestries, clocks and beautifully furnished rooms, or escape to the park and feel miles from anywhere.

There is plenty to see and do on a visit to Lyme Park. The Garden has a changing display of Spring and Summer bedding. The luxurious herbaceous borders and Rose Garden give scent and colour in the summer months. Children can let off steam, or you can enjoy a quiet moment as you admire the magnificent moor land.

Don't miss our interactive exhibition about living and working at Lyme in the Timber Yard. This exhibition contains archive pictures of some of the staff who worked at this magnificent estate.

Delicious food, including venison from the park, is prepared in the Lyme kitchens; and with retail therapy at hand, Lyme really is a glorious day out.

■ Owner
The National Trust

■ Contact
The Visitor Services Manager
Disley
Stockport
Cheshire
SK12 2NX

Tel: 01663 762023
Fax: 01663 765035

■ Location
MAP 6:N2
OS Ref. SJ965 825

Off the A6 at Disley. 6½m SE of Stockport. M60 J1.

■ Opening Times
House
27 Feb–31 Oct, 11am–5pm, Mon, Tue, Fri–Sun.

Park
open all year, 8am–6.00pm, Mon–Sun.

Garden
27 Feb–31 Oct, 11am–5pm, Mon–Sun; Please call for winter opening times.

■ Admission*
House & Gardens
Adult	£9.00
Child	£4.00
Family	£22.00

Garden only
Adult	£5.60
Child	£2.80

House only
Adult	£5.95
Child	£3.00

Park only
Car	£5.00
Motorbike	£3.00
Coach	£18.00

Booked coach groups park admission free. NT members free.

*includes a voluntary donation but visitors can choose to pay the standard prices displayed at the property and on the website.

 No photography in house.

 Licensed.
 Licensed.
By arrangement.

CHESHIRE

■ **Owner**
The National Trust

■ **Contact**
Visitor Services Manager
Styal, Wilmslow SK9 4LA
Tel: 01625 527468
Fax: 01625 539267
E-mail: quarrybankmill@
nationaltrust.org.uk

■ **Location**
MAP 6:N1
OS Ref. SJ835 835

1.5m N of Wilmslow off
B5166. 2.5m from
M56/J5. Styal Shuttle
Bus, Airport 2.5m

■ **Opening Times**
**Mill & Apprentice
House:** 1 Jan–28 Feb,
Wed–Sun, 11am–4pm,
last admission 3pm; 1
Mar–31 Oct, daily,
11am–5pm, last
admission 4pm; 1
Nov–12 Dec, Wed–Sun,
11am–4pm, last
admission 3pm; 13
Dec–23 Dec, Sat & Sun,
11am–4pm, last
admission 3pm; 26–31
Dec, daily, 11am–4pm,
last admission 3pm;
Closed 24 & 25 Dec.

Quarry Bank Garden:
1 Mar–31 Oct, daily,
11am–5pm, last
admission 4pm.

Shop and Restaurant:
1 Jan–28 Feb, Wed–Sun,
11am–4pm. 1 Mar–31
Oct, daily, 11am–5pm. 1
Nov–23 Dec, Wed–Sun,
11am–4pm.

**Shop, Restaurant and
Garden:** 26–31 Dec,
daily, 11am–4pm, last
admission to garden
3pm.

■ **Admission**
Estate: £4.00, Mill only:
Adult £7.35, Child
£3.90, Family (2+3)
£18.60, Group 15+
£6.30. Mill & Apprentice
House or Garden: Adult
£10.50, Child £5.25,
Family (2+3) £25.20,
Group (15+) £9.00. Mill
& Apprentice House &
Garden: Adult £14.20,
Child £7.05, Family
£35.40, Group (15+)
£12.00. Garden only:
Adult £5, Child £2.50,
Family £12.50, Group
(15+) £4.25. Includes a
voluntary 10% donation
but visitors can choose
to pay the standard
prices displayed at the
property and on the
website.

■ **Special Events**
Events throughout the
year. See website for
listing or telephone the
property for more details.
Family trails.

QUARRY BANK MILL & STYAL ESTATE

www.nationaltrust.org.uk

Quarry Bank overflows with the atmosphere of the Industrial Revolution. A visit to the cotton mill, powered by Europe's most powerful working waterwheel, will certainly stimulate the senses. The clatter of machinery and hiss of steam engines is astonishing. Take a guided tour of the Apprentice House, which housed the pauper children who worked in the mill. Visit the stunning garden - the Greg family's picturesque valley retreat adjoining the mill. Stroll to Styal village, built by the Greg family to house the mill workers and still a thriving community, or walk through woods along the River Bollin.

Experience the hands-on exhibits and demonstrations in to how cotton is processed into cloth; see how traditional spinning and weaving was transformed through the ingenuity of early textile engineers or follow a choice of family trails in the Mill, Village or on the Estate.

Delightful displays of daffodils, bluebells and rhododendrons in the Mill Garden. Explore the terrace paths, riverside walks or see the "hermit's cave" - you will be amazed by this magical place.

Tuck into a hearty meal in the Mill Restaurant or visit our shop.

Situated just near Manchester Airport - an ideal place to visit before you fly!

ℹ️ Picnic & play area. No pushchairs in the Mill or Apprentice House. Apprentice House guided tours: Limited availability & timed tickets only. Snacks availiable from the Pantry

🛏️

🍽️ Partial. WCs.

♿ Licensed.

🧍 By arrangement.

🅿️ Limited for coaches.

🐕 Guide dogs only.

ADLINGTON HALL

See page 366 for full page entry.

ARLEY HALL AND GARDENS

See page 367 for full page entry.

BEESTON CASTLE

Chapel Lane, Beeston, Tarporley, Cheshire CW6 9TX
Tel: 01829 260464   **Email:** beeston.castle@english-heritage.org.uk
www.english-heritage.org.uk/beestoncastle
Owner: English Heritage   **Contact:** Visitor Operations Team
Standing majestically on a sheer rocky crag, Beeston offers perhaps the most stunning views of any castle in England as well as fantastic woodland walks in the castle grounds. Its 4,000 year history spans Bronze Age settlement to Iron Age hill fort, to impregnable royal fortress.
Location: MAP 6:L3, OS Ref. SJ537 593. 11m SE of Chester on minor road off A49, or A41. 2m SW of Tarporley.
Open: 1 Apr–30 Sept: daily, 10am–6pm. 1 Oct–31 Mar: Thur–Mon, 10am–4pm. Closed 24–26 Dec & 1 Jan.
Admission: Adult £5, Child £2.50, Conc. £4.30. 15% discount for groups (11+). EH members Free. Opening times and prices are valid until 31st March 2010, after this date details are subject to change please see www.english-heritage.org.uk for the most up-to-date information.
ⓘ Exhibition. WCs. ▢ ⬓ Please note: Steep hill (no disabled access to the top of the hill). 🅿 The car park is not owned by English Heritage. There is a parking charge of £2. ■ ⬓ On leads. ✳ ⬓

CAPESTHORNE HALL

See page 368 for full page entry.

CHESTER CATHEDRAL

St. Werburgh Street, Chester, Cheshire
Tel: 01244 324756   **Fax:** 01244 341110   **E-mail:** visits@chestercathedral.com
www.chestercathedral.com
Owner: Church of England
Chester Cathedral opens a window onto a rich and varied story of monks, kings and craftsmen. 1000 years of history but a living thriving centre of community and Christian worship. A wonderful shop and unique 13th Century Refectory Café complement this magnificent National Treasure in the Heart of Chester.
Location: MAP 6:K2, OS Ref. SJ406 665. Chester city centre.
Open: Mon–Sat: 9am–5pm. Sun 1–4.30pm.
Admission: Adult £4, Child (5–16) £1.50, Senior Citizens/Groups £3, Family Ticket £10.

CHESTER ROMAN AMPHITHEATRE

Vicars Lane, Chester, Cheshire CH1 1QX
Tel: 01244 402009   **Email:** customers@english-heritage.org.uk
www.english-heritage.org.uk/chester
Owner: Managed by English Heritage and Chester City Council
Contact: Chester City Council
The largest Roman amphitheatre in Britain. Excavations carried out over 2004/05 indicate that there were two stone-built amphitheatres, one very similar to those in Pompeii, emphasising the great importance of Chester during the Roman era.
Location: MAP 6:K2, OS Ref. SJ408 662. On Vicars Lane beyond Newgate, Chester.
Open: Any reasonable time.
Admission: Free. Opening times and prices are valid until 31st March 2010, after this date details are subject to change please see www.english-heritage.org.uk for the most up-to-date information.
⬓ ✳

CHOLMONDELEY CASTLE GARDEN
MALPAS, CHESHIRE SY14 8AH
www.cholmondeleycastle.com

Tel: 01829 720383   **Fax:** 01829 720877   **E-mail:** dilys@cholmondeleycastle.co.uk
Owner: The Marchioness of Cholmondeley   **Contact:** The Secretary
Extensive ornamental gardens dominated by romantic Gothic Revival Castle built in 1801 of local sandstone. Visitors can enjoy the beautiful Temple Water Garden, Ruin Water Garden and memorial mosaic designed by Maggy Howarth. Rose garden and many mixed borders. Lakeside picnic area, children's play areas, farm animals, llamas, children's corner with rabbits, chickens and free flying aviary birds. Private chapel in the park.

Location: MAP 6:L3, OS Ref. SJ540 515. Off A41 Chester/Whitchurch Rd. & A49 Whitchurch/ Tarporley Road. 7m N of Whitchurch.

Open: Fri 2 Apr–Sun 26 Sept. Open for Autumn Tints, Sun 10 & 24 Oct, 11am–5pm. (The castle is only open to groups by prior arrangement on limited days).

Admission: Adult £5, Child £2, (reduction for groups to gardens of 25+).
▢ ✳ ⊤ ⬓ Limited. WCs. ■ ⬓ In grounds, on leads only.

Arley Hall & Gardens

Rode Hall

DUNHAM MASSEY ❧

ALTRINCHAM, CHESHIRE WA14 4SJ

www.nationaltrust.org.uk

Tel: 0161 941 1025 **Fax:** 0161 929 7508

E-mail: dunhammassey@nationaltrust.org.uk

Owner: The National Trust **Contact:** Visitor Services

An elegant Georgian mansion with a sumptuous Edwardian interior filled with fabulous collections of paintings, furniture and Huguenot silver. Enjoy the great plantsman's garden full of native favourites and exotic treasures and Georgian Orangery. Experience the creation of Britain's largest Winter Garden. Wander around the ancient deer park.

Location: MAP 6:M1, OS Ref. SJ735 874. 3m SW of Altrincham off A56. M6/J19. M56/J7. Station Altrincham (BR & Metro) 3m.

Open: House: 27 Feb–31 Oct, 11am–5pm, Mon–Wed, Sat & Sun. Taster Tours 11am–12 noon (restricted numbers, allocated upon arrival), last admission 4.30pm. Open Good Friday. Garden: 1 Jan–26 Feb & 1 Nov–31 Dec, 11am–4pm, Mon–Sun; 27 Feb–31 Oct, 11am–5.30pm, Mon–Sun. Winter closure at 4 or dusk if earlier. Park: Open all year, 9am–5pm, Mon–Sun. Mar–Oct Gates remain open till 7.30pm. Property closed, including park, 25 Dec. Also closed 25 Nov for staff training. Restaurant/Shop: 1 Jan–26 Feb & 1 Nov–31 Dec, 10.30am–4pm, Mon–Sun; 27 Feb–31 Oct, 10.30am–5pm, Mon–Sun. Mill: 27 Feb–31 Oct, 12noon–4pm, Mon–Wed, Sat & Sun. White Cottage: 28 Mar–31 Oct, 2–5pm, Last Sunday of the month only – all visits must be booked on 0161 928 0075 or by email to dunmasswhite@nationaltrust.org.uk.

*Admission: House & Garden: Adult £9.40, Child £4.70, Family (2+3 max) £23.50, Group £8. Garden only: Adult £6.60, Child £3.30, Family £16.50. Group £5.70 (only when House closed). Reduced rate when arriving by public transport. *includes a voluntary 10% donation but visitors can choose to pay the standard prices displayed at the property and on the website.

ℹ No photography in house. 📷 🖼 ♿ Partial. WC. Batricars. 🍴 Licensed.
🎟 Optional. No extra charge. 🅿 £5 per car. 🐕 🐾 In grounds, on leads. ❉

DORFOLD HALL 🏛

ACTON, Nr NANTWICH, CHESHIRE CW5 8LD

Tel: 01270 625245 **Fax:** 01270 628723

Owner/Contact: Richard Roundell

Jacobean country house built in 1616 for Ralph Wilbraham. Family home of Mr & Mrs Richard Roundell. Beautiful plaster ceilings and oak panelling. Attractive woodland gardens and summer herbaceous borders.

Location: MAP 6:L3, OS Ref. SJ634 525. 1m W of Nantwich on the A534 Nantwich–Wrexham road.

Open: Apr–Oct: Tue only and BH Mons, 2–5pm.

Admission: Adult £6, Child £3.

🎟 Obligatory. 🅿 Limited. Narrow gates with low arch prevent coaches.
🐾 In grounds on leads.

GAWSWORTH HALL
MACCLESFIELD, CHESHIRE SK11 9RN
www.gawsworthhall.com

Tel: 01260 223456 **Fax:** 01260 223469 **E-mail:** gawsworthhall@btinternet.com
Owner: Mr and Mrs T Richards **Contact:** Mr T Richards
Fully lived-in Tudor half-timbered manor house with Tilting Ground. Former home of Mary Fitton, Maid of Honour at the Court of Queen Elizabeth I, and the supposed 'Dark Lady' of Shakespeare's sonnets. Fine pictures, sculpture, furniture and beautiful grounds adjoining a medieval church.
Location: MAP 6:N2, OS Ref. SJ892 697. 3m S of Macclesfield on the A536 Congleton to Macclesfield road.
Open: Daily 2-5pm in July and August, other times see www.gawsworthhall.com
Special Events: Open-air theatre with covered grandstand, performances in July and August.
Admission: Adult £6, Child £3. Groups (20+): £5.
🖼 ♿ Partial. WCs. ☕ Licensed 🎨 By arrangement 🅿 🏠 ♨ 🍷

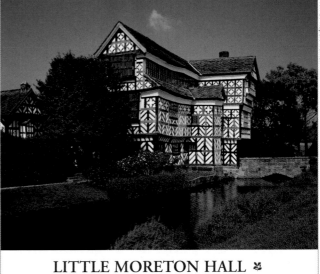

LITTLE MORETON HALL 🌿
CONGLETON, CHESHIRE CW12 4SD
www.nationaltrust.org.uk

Tel: 01260 272018
Owner: The National Trust **Contact:** The Property Administrator
Begun in 1504 and completed 100 years later, Little Moreton Hall is regarded as the finest example of a timber-framed moated manor house in the country.
Location: MAP 6:N3, OS Ref. SJ833 589. 4m SW of Congleton on E side of A34.
Open: 27 Feb–14 Mar, Sat & Sun, 11am–4pm; 17 Mar–31 Oct, Wed–Sun (& BH Mon), 11am–5pm; 6 Nov–19 Dec, Sat & Sun, 11am–4pm.
*Admission: Adult £7.00, Child £3.50, Family £17.50. Groups: £5.95 (must book).
*includes a voluntary donation but visitors can choose to pay the standard prices displayed at the property and on the website.
🖼 ♨ ♿ Partial. WCs. 🍴 Licensed. 🎨 🅿 Limited for coaches. 🔳 🍷 Guide dogs only. 🍷

HOLMSTON HALL BARN

Little Budworth, Tarporley, Cheshire CW6 9AY
Tel: 01829 760366/07778 510287
Owner/Contact: Mr Richard Hopkins
Newly restored 15th century oak framed barn. Sandstone base and floors, with twelve exterior oak doors.
Location: MAP 6:L3, OS Ref. SJ607 626. Off A49. 2m from Eaton village.
Open: All year by appointment only.
Admission: Free.
❄

LYME PARK 🌿

See page 369 for full page entry.

See page 369 for full page entry.

NESS BOTANIC GARDENS

Ness, Neston, Cheshire CH64 4AY
Tel: 0151 353 0123 **Fax:** 0151 353 1004
Owner: University of Liverpool **Contact:** Dr E J Sharples
New Visitor Centre opened in 2006. Leading garden in the North West for rhododendrons and azaleas.
Location: MAP 6:J2, OS Ref. SJ302 760 (village centre). Off A540. 10m NW of Chester. 1½m S of Neston.
Open: Mar–Oct: daily, 9.30am–5pm. Nov–Feb: 9.30am–4pm.
Admission: Adult £5.50, Conc £5, Child (5–16yrs) £2.50, Child (under 5yrs) Free., Family ticket (2+3) £13.50. 10% discount for groups. Please telephone for details.

NORTON PRIORY MUSEUM & GARDENS

Tudor Road, Manor Park, Runcorn WA7 1SX
Tel: 01928 569895 **E-mail:** info@nortonpriory.org www.nortonpriory.org
Owner/Contact: The Norton Priory Museum Trust
Discover the 800 year old priory range, excavated priory remains, museum gallery, the St Christopher statue – one of the great treasures of medieval Europe – exciting sculpture trail and award winning Walled Garden. Set in 38 acres of tranquil, woodland gardens, Norton Priory also has a coffee shop, retail area and temporary exhibitions gallery.
Location: MAP 6:K1, OS Ref. SJ545 835. 3m from M56/J11. 2m E of Runcorn.
Open: All year: daily, from 12 noon. Telephone for details.
Admission: Adult £5.20. Child/Conc. £3.70. Family £13.40. Groups £3.40, (as from Apr '08).
🖼 ♨ ♿ Wheelchairs, braille guide, audio tapes & WC. 🍷 🎨 By arrangement. 🅿 🔳 🍷 In grounds, on leads. ❄ 🍷

For unique **Civil wedding** venues see our index at the end of the book.

Norton Priory Museum & Gardens

PEOVER HALL 🏛

OVER PEOVER, KNUTSFORD WA16 9HW

Tel: 01565 632358

Owner: Randle Brooks   **Contact:** I Shepherd

An Elizabethan house dating from 1585. Fine Carolean stables. Mainwaring Chapel, 18th century landscaped park. Large garden with topiary work, and walled gardens.

Location: MAP 6:M2, OS Ref. SJ772 734. 4m S of Knutsford off A50 at Whipping Stocks Inn.

Open: May–Aug: Carolean Stables & Gardens, Mon & Thu except BHs, 2–5pm. Tours of the House at 2.30 & 3.30pm.

Admission: House, Carolean Stables & Gardens: Adult £5. Carolean Stables & Gardens only: Adult £4. Accompanied children free.

🖵 Mon & Thur. 🖊 Obligatory. ✠

RODE HALL 🏛

CHURCH LANE, SCHOLAR GREEN, CHESHIRE ST7 3QP

www.rodehall.co.uk

Tel: 01270 873237   **Fax:** 01270 882962

E-mail: richard.wilbra@btconnect.com

Owner/Contact: Sir Richard Baker Wilbraham Bt

The Wilbraham family have lived at Rode since 1669; the present house was constructed in two stages, the earlier two storey wing and stable block around 1705 and the main building was completed in 1752. Later alterations by Lewis Wyatt and Darcy Braddell were undertaken in 1812 and 1927 respectively. The house stands in a Repton landscape and the extensive gardens include a woodland garden, with a terraced rock garden and grotto, which has many species of rhododendrons, azaleas, hellebores and climbing roses following snowdrops and daffodils in the early spring. The formal rose garden was designed by W Nesfield in 1860; there is a large walled kitchen garden and a new Italian garden. The icehouse in the park has recently been restored.

Location: MAP 6:M3, OS Ref. SJ819 573. 5m SW of Congleton between the A34 and A50. Kidsgrove railway station 2m NW of Kidsgrove.

Open: 1 Apr–30 Sept: Weds & BHs and by appointment. Garden only: Tues & Thurs, 2–5pm. Snowdrop Walk: 30 Jan–7 March daily except Mons & Tues 12 noon–4pm.

Admission: House & Garden: Adult £6, Conc £5. Garden only and Snowdrop Walk: Adult £4, Conc £3.

🖼 🖵 Home-made teas. 🖊 P ✠ On leads.

QUARRY BANK MILL & STYAL ESTATE ✿   *See page 370 for full page entry.*

For rare and unusual plants visit the **plant sales** index at the end of the book.

Tatton Park

NTPL / Stephen Robson

TABLEY HOUSE
KNUTSFORD, CHESHIRE WA16 0HB
www.tableyhouse.co.uk

Tel: 01565 750151 **Fax:** 01565 653230 **E-mail:** tableyhouse@btconnect.com
Owner: The University of Manchester **Contact:** The Administrator
The finest Palladian House in the North West, Tabley a Grade I listing, was designed by John Carr of York for the Leicester family. Set in landscaped parkland it contains one of the first collections of English paintings, including works of art by Turner, Reynolds, Lawrence and Lely. Furniture by Chippendale, Bullock and Gillow and fascinating family memorabilia adorn the rooms. Interesting Tea Room and 17th century Chapel adjoin.

Location: MAP 6:M2, OS Ref. SJ725 777. M6/J19, A556 S on to A5033. 2m W of Knutsford.
Open: House: Apr–end Oct: Thurs–Suns & BHs, 2–5pm. Tea Room: 12 noon–5pm, Apr–Oct; 12 noon–3pm Thurs–Fri, 12 noon–4pm Sat–Sun, Nov–Mar. Closed 24 Dec 2009–9 Jan 2010.
Admission: Adult £4. Child/Student £1.50. Groups by arrangement.
🔲 ♿ Please telephone for easiest access. 💍 🅿️ 🖼️ Civil Wedding Licence plus Civil Naming Ceremonies & Re-affirmation of Vows. 🛡️

TATTON PARK 🌿
KNUTSFORD, CHESHIRE WA16 6QN
www.tattonpark.org.uk

Tel: 01625 374400 **Info:** 01625 374435 **Fax:** 01625 374403
Owner: The National Trust (Managed by Cheshire East County Council)
A stunning historic estate set in beautiful parkland. Over 1,000 acres of land are home to herds of red and fallow deer and provide the setting for the impressive Neo-Classical Mansion designed by Wyatt. The Egerton family's collection of Gillow furniture, Baccarat glass, porcelain and paintings by Dutch and Italian artists are on display. The gardens extend over 50 acres and include Japanese, walled and formal gardens. The 1930s working farm includes rare breed animals and events. An extensive year-round events programme includes the RHS Flower Show, picnic concerts and the Tatton Park Biennial 2010.
Location: MAP 6:M2, OS Ref. SJ745 815. From M56/J7 follow signs. From M6/J19, signed on A56 & A50.
Open: High (27 Mar–3 Oct 2010). Low (6 Oct 2009–26 Mar 2010), (4 Oct 2010–25 Mar 2011). Mansion: High, Tue–Sun 1–5pm, Low, Closed (except for Christmas events and October half term. See website). Parkland: High, Daily 10am–7pm. Low, Tue–Sun 11am–5pm. Gardens: Tue–Sun, High,10am–6pm. Low, 11am–4pm. Farm: High, Tue–Sun 12noon–5pm, Low, Sats & Suns 11am–4pm. Last entry for all attractions, one hour before closing. Old Hall open for pre-booked groups, educational tours and during certain events.
Admission: For prices see website www.tattonpark.org.uk or call 01625 374400. Park Entry charge applies (inc NT members). Coaches Free. (NT members, see website/handbook).
🔲 🎦 🍽️ Dinners, dances, weddings and conferences. ♿ Partial. WCs. 💍
🍴 Self-service. 🎦 By arrangement. 🅿️ Entry Charge applies. See website, 200–300 yds. Meal vouchers for coach drivers. ⬛ Please book. 🐕 In grounds, on leads. 🔺❄️🛡️

WOODHEY CHAPEL
Faddiley, Nr Nantwich, Cheshire CW5 8JH
Tel: 01270 524215
Owner: The Trustees of Woodhey Chapel **Contact:** Mr Robinson, The Curator
Small private chapel built in 1690, now restored.
Location: MAP 6:L3, OS Ref. SJ573 528. Proceeding W from Nantwich on A534, turn left 1m W of the Faddiley – Brindley villages onto narrow lane, keep ahead at next turn, at road end obtain key from farmhouse.
Open: Apr–Oct: Sats & BHs, 2–5pm, or apply for key at Woodhey Hall.
Admission: Donation box.

Gawsworth Hall, Suit of Armour

BLACKWELL,
THE ARTS & CRAFTS HOUSE

www.blackwell.org.uk

Blackwell is a superb house situated in the Lake District, set on the hillside overlooking Lake Windermere. Completed in 1900, it is the largest and most important surviving example of work by architect Hugh Mackay Baillie Scott, and the only one of his buildings open to the public.

This treasure trove of Arts and Crafts design contains fine examples of stained glass, decorative oak panelling and intricate plasterwork, their designs inspired by Lakeland birds and local wild flowers and trees. Blackwell's wealth of original detail also includes William de Morgan tiled fireplaces. The house was designed for relaxation, and visitors can sit and enjoy the stunning views and garden terraces from its many window seats and inglenooks.

Blackwell's period rooms are furnished with Arts and Crafts furniture and decorative arts. They are complemented by a series of first-floor galleries, where regular exhibitions of historical applied arts and contemporary craft are held.

 No photography.
No mobile phones.

 WCs.

 Licensed.

 By arrangement.

 Free for cars, coaches
by appointment.

 Guide dogs only.

HOLKER HALL & GARDENS 🏛

www.holker.co.uk

Holker is the family home of Lord and Lady Cavendish and you can discover the beauty and elegance of their home without the confines of ropes or barriers to restrict your viewing. Relax in 25 acres of National Award Winning Gardens and Parkland. Stroll through the formal gardens and thrill at the unique and rare treasures they offer. Treat yourself to a special lunch or afternoon tea in the Courtyard Restaurant or picnic in the grounds. Children will delight at the Adventure Playground. Unique gifts and speciality products, some hand selected by Lady Cavendish, are available in our Gift Shop.

The year round interest begins with breathtaking early spring bulbs, followed by magnificent ancient Rhododendrons and innumerable Azaleas and Magnolias. From late Spring the borders begin filling with skilful palettes of colour. A voluptuous crescendo of colour in the herbaceous borders is accompanied by impressive summer plantings. Throughout the year the unique collection of trees and shrubs provide scent and interest including late summer flowering Eucryphias. The national Collection of Styraceae and fragrant Rhododendrons are smothered in sweetly scented flowers in the summer. The formal gardens have splendidly sculptured Yew and box hedging and topiary trees and shrubs. In winter the woodland trees and shrubs have delightful architectural form. The colourful, twisted glades of Rhododendron trunks and the meadow and labyrinth are truly magical. The garden also is home to the huge Holker Lime, one of 50 of England's most magnificent trees, selected as part of Her Majesty's Jubilee celebrations.

■ **Owner**
Lord Cavendish of Furness

■ **Contact**
Sarah Ross
Holker Hall and Gardens
Cark-in-Cartmel
Grange-over-Sands
Cumbria LA11 7PL
Tel: 01539 558328
E-mail: info@holker.co.uk

■ **Location**
MAP 10:K8
OS Ref. SD359 773

Close to Morecambe Bay, 5m W of Grange-over-Sands by B5277. From Kendal, A6, A590, B5277, B5278: 16m. Motorway: M6/J36.

■ **Open**
Hall:
14 March–31 October 2010: daily (except Saturday), 11am–4pm.

Gardens:
14 March–31 October: daily (except Saturday), 10.30am–5.30pm.

■ **Admission**
House & Gardens
Adult	£10.00
Concession	£9.00
Child	£5.50

Gardens & Park
Adult	£6.50
Concession	£5.50
Child	£3.50

■ **Special Events**
4–6 June
The Holker Garden Festival
Tickets can be booked through the website: www.holker.co.uk

ℹ No photography in house.

🛍 Holker Food Hall – produce from the Estate.

❄

🍸

♿

🍴 Licensed.

☕ Menus using Estate produce according to season

🏃 By arrangement.

🅿 75 yds from Hall.

🎟

🐕 In grounds, on leads (not formal gardens).

🎭

■ Owner
Mrs Phyllida
Gordon-Duff-Pennington

■ Contact
Steve Bishop
Muncaster Castle
Ravenglass
Cumbria CA18 1RQ

Tel: 01229 717614
Fax: 01229 717010
E-mail: info@
muncaster.co.uk

■ Location
MAP 10:J7
OS Ref. SD103 965
SAT NAV – CA18 1RD

From S – M6/J36, A590, A595
From NE – M6/J40, A66, A595
From Carlisle (N) A59

On the A595 1m S of Ravenglass, 19m S of Whitehaven.

From Chester 2.5 hrs, Edinburgh 3.5 hrs, Manchester 2.5 hrs.

Rail: Ravenglass (on Barrow-in-Furness-Carlisle Line) 1½ m.

Air: Manchester 2½ hrs.

■ Opening Times
Full Season
Last Sun in March–first Sun in Nov. Castle open Sun–Fri inclusive 12–4pm. Gardens & World Owl Centre 10.30am–6pm (dusk if earlier).

Winter Season
11.30am–4pm (dusk if earlier). Castle open reduced hours, please see website or call for details.

Open for groups, conferences and weddings by appointment.

Darkest Muncaster
Explore the hauntingly beautiful gardens by night and light, see website or call for more details.

'Meet the Birds'
Daily at 2.30pm, Main season.
'Heron Happy Hour' daily 4.30pm (winter 3.30pm).

■ Admission
Castle, Gardens, Owl Centre & Meadow Vole Maze
Please see www.muncaster.co.uk for details.

Gardens, Owl Centre & Meadow Vole Maze
Please see www.muncaster.co.uk for details.

Special discounts groups (12+)

Conference/Function

ROOM	MAX CAPACITY
Drawing Room	100
Dining Room	50
Family Dining Rm	60
Great Hall	100
Old Laundry	120
Library	48
Guard Room	30
Marquee	200

©Brian Sherwen

MUNCASTER CASTLE
GARDENS & OWL CENTRE
www.muncaster.co.uk

Described by Ruskin as the 'Gateway to Paradise', Muncaster is set in 77 acres of historic woodland Grade 2 listed gardens of the Lake District National Park and is, uniquely, also the start of the famous 'Hadrian's Wall Country'.

With the Georgian Terrace (c.1780), 12th Century Church and home to the World Owl Centre (with more than 200 birds on display), the Gardens also house one of Europe's largest collection of Rhododendron's amongst the rich and diverse planting of this stunning landscape.

With influences dating back to Roman times, the Castle, (the jewel in the crown at Muncaster) is an iconic landmark in our rich history. Since 1208 Muncaster has been the family home of the Pennington family and is still a lived in family home to this day. The impressive library, beautiful barrel-vaulted drawing room and exquisite dining room are a real treasure trove and provide a unique view into our history. Muncaster's beautiful setting is perfect for unique weddings, team building events, conferences as well as parties and private dining experiences.

4* Guest B&B accommodation is available within the Castle Gardens or at the 3* luxuriously fitted Pennington Hotel in Ravenglass. The Pennington was once a coaching inn and has been bought back to life in stunning style. 3 holiday cottages are also available providing the idea base for your short break or family holiday.

Whether to relax, wonder, relish or enjoy, your experience will be as unique and personal as the service and setting of this beautiful estate.

©Brian Sherwen

- Church. Garden parties, film location, clay pigeon shooting. No photography inside the Castle.
- For wedding receptions, catering, & functions, tel: 01229 717614.
- By arrangement visitors can alight near Castle. Wheelchairs for loan. WCs. Audio tour tapes for partially sighted/those with learning difficulties. Allocated parking.
- Creeping Kate's Kitchen (licensed) (max 80) – full menu of light refreshments, afternoon tea and our famous home-made cakes. Groups can book: 01229 717614.
- Private tours with a personal guide (family member possible) can be arranged at additional fee.
- Individual audio tour (40mins) included in price.
- 500 cars 800 yds from Castle; coach park available at centre of estate, all parking free.
- Guides available. Historical subjects, horticulture, conservation, owl tours.
- In grounds, on leads.
- For details: www.muncaster.co.uk or telephone.

© NTPL / Val Corbett

SIZERGH CASTLE & GARDEN

www.nationaltrust.org.uk

■ **Owner**
The National Trust

■ **Contact**
Property Administrator
Sizergh, Nr Kendal,
Cumbria LA8 8AE

Tel: 01539 560951
E-mail: sizergh@
nationaltrust.org.uk

■ **Location**
MAP 10:L7,
OS Ref. SD498 878.

3½m S of Kendal, NW of
the A590 /A591
interchange.

■ **Opening Times**
14 Mar–1 Nov, Sun–Thu:
House *12 noon–5pm;
Garden, shop & café,
11am–5pm; Café & shop
only (11am–4pm), Sat &
Sun 2 Jan–13 Mar, 6
Nov–26 Dec (closed
Christmas Day), 15–19
Feb. *Access to the house
between 12 noon and
1pm will be by guided
tour only. Places are
limited and may be pre-
booked or booked on the
day if available. From
1pm, access will be
unguided only. During
very busy periods, a timed
ticket system may be in
operation.

■ ***Admission**
House & Garden: Adult
£7.90, Child £4.00,
Family £19.80, Family
One Adult £11.90.
Garden only: Adult
£5.15, Child £2.65.
*includes a voluntary
donation but visitors can
choose to pay the
standard prices displayed
at the property and on
the website.

This imposing house stands in a beautiful garden with herbaceous borders, kitchen garden, lake, national fern collection and magnificent limestone rock garden. The estate is crossed by footpaths, giving stunning views over Morecambe Bay and the Lakeland hills. Still lived in by the Strickland family, Sizergh has many tales to tell, showing centuries-old portraits and fine furniture alongside modern family photos – it certainly feels lived in! The exceptional wood panelling culminates in the inlaid chamber, previously at the Victoria & Albert Museum and returned in 1999. Take time to explore the house and garden, sample fine local produce in our contemporary café, then follow one of our trail leaflets around the estate.

The garden: Japanese Maples enhance the rock garden, notably Acer palmatum `Atropurpureum' with its coppery brown foliage. The mature green form of Acer palmatum here originated from seed collected in Japan in the early 1920's. You will also see herbaceous alpines, hellebores, hostas and many moisture loving plants in this spectacular rock garden.

During the spring the orchard is a blaze of colour with thousands of recently planted daffodils as well as fruit tree blossom. The orchard contains a curious mixture of eating, cooking and crab apples, several varieties of plum and damson trees, the unusual quince and medlar, and an assortment of ornamentals.

Sizergh is a great stop-off point when travelling into the Lake District, or visiting Kendal, 5ml from junction 36 of M6.

© NTPL / Andrew Butler

© NTPL / Val Corbett

© NTPL / Val Corbett

Partial.

ACORN BANK GARDEN & WATERMILL ✿

Temple Sowerby, Penrith, Cumbria CA10 1SP
Tel: 01768 361893   **E-mail:** acornbank@nationaltrust.org.uk
www.nationaltrust.org.uk
Owner: The National Trust   **Contact:** The Custodian
Seventeenth century walls enclose a herb garden with over 250 varieties of medicinal and culinary plants and orchards with traditional fruit trees surrounded by mixed borders. Beyond the walls, paths lead through woodland to a partially restored watermill. House not open. Tearoom serving delicious seasonal food.
Location: Gate: MAP 10:M5, OS Ref. NY612 281. Just N of Temple Sowerby, 6m E of Penrith 1m from A66.
Open: 27 Feb–12 Mar, weekends; 13 Mar–31 Oct, daily except Mon & Tue, 10am–5pm. Last admission 4.30pm. Tearoom 11am–4.30pm.
*Admission: Adult £4.20, Child £2.10, Family £10.50. *includes a voluntary 10% donation but visitors can choose to pay the standard prices displayed at the property and on the website. **Special events:** Apple Day 17 Oct, seperate charge including NT members.

🅾 🚻 ♿ 🍽 🅿 Limited. 🐾 On leads. ♿

BEATRIX POTTER GALLERY ✿

Main Street, Hawkshead, Cumbria LA22 0NS
Tel: 01539 436355   **Fax:** 01539 436187
E-mail: beatrixpottergallery@nationaltrust.org.uk   **www.nationaltrust.org.uk**
Owner: The National Trust   **Contact:** Ticket Office/House Steward
An annually changing exhibition of original watercolours and sketches by beloved children's author Beatrix Potter. See a new exhibition celebrating 100 years since the publication of 'The Tale of Mrs.Tittlemouse.' The gallery was once the office of Beatrix Potter's husband, William Heelis. Quiz for children.
Location: MAP 10:K7, OS Ref. SD352 982. 5m SSW of Ambleside. In the Square. Parking 300yards (pay and display, not NT). Tel. 01539 445161 for complete bus and ferry timetable.
Open: 13 Feb–25 Mar, 11am–3.30pm; 27 Mar–20 May, 11am–5pm; 22 May-2 Sept, 10.30am-5pm; 4 Sept-31 Oct, 11am-5pm: Sat–Thurs, Good Fri and 29 Oct. Closed other Fridays. Admission is by timed ticket (incl. NT members). Daily ticket quota, early sell outs possible. Last admission 30 mins before close. Shop: daily 13 Feb-31 Oct; Wed-Sun 1 Nov-31 Dec.
*Admission: Adult £4.40, Child £2.10, Family £10.50. No reduction for groups. Discount for Hill Top ticket holders. Group booking essential.
ℹ️ No photography inside. Accessible WC 300 yards (not NT) Assistance dogs only. Access- step to narrow entrance. Level access to 3 rooms downstairs. Illustrations upstairs via many stairs with handrail. 🅾 ♿ Partial. 🐾 Guide dogs only.

BLACKWELL – THE ARTS & CRAFTS HOUSE

See page 376 for full page entry.

BRANTWOOD

Coniston, Cumbria LA21 8AD
Tel: 01539 441396   **Fax:** 01539 441263   **E-mail:** enquiries@brantwood.org.uk
www.brantwood.org.uk
Owner: The Brantwood Trust
Brantwood, the former home of John Ruskin, is the most beautifully situated house in the Lake District. Explore Brantwood's estate and gardens or experience contemporary art in the Severn Studio. Brantwood's bookshop, the Jumping Jenny restaurant and Coach House Craft Gallery combine for a perfect day out.
Location: MAP 10:K7, OS Ref. SD313 959. 2½m from Coniston village on the E side of Coniston Water.
Open: Mid Mar–mid Nov: daily, 11am–5.30pm. Mid Nov–mid Mar: Wed–Sun, 11am–4.30pm.
Admission: Adult £6.95, Child £1.50, Student £5.50, Family (2+3) £14.50. Garden only: Adult £4.95, Family (2+3) £9.50. Groups: Adult £5.95, Child £1.50, Student £4.50 Garden only £3.00.
ℹ️ No photography in the house. 🅾 🚻 ♿ Licensed. 🍽 Licensed. 🍴 Licensed. 🎦 By arrangement. 🅿 Ample. Limited for coaches. 🏠 🐾 in grounds, on leads. 🅰 ❋

BROUGH CASTLE ⌗

Brough, Cumbria
Please call 0870 3331181 for details of opening times and charges
E-mail: customers@english-heritage.org.uk
www.english-heritage.org.uk/broughcastle
Owner: English Heritage   **Contact:** Visitor Operations Manager
This ancient site dates back to Roman times. The 12th century keep replaced an earlier stronghold destroyed by the Scots in 1174.
Location: MAP 10:M6, OS Ref. NY791 141. 8m SE of Appleby S of A66. South part of the village.
Open: 1 Apr–30 Sep: daily, 10am–5pm. 1 Oct–31 Mar: daily, 10am–4pm. Closed 24–26 Dec & 1 Jan.
Admission: Free. Opening times and prices are valid until 31st March 2010, after this date details are subject to change please see www.english-heritage.org.uk for the most up-to-date information.
🐾 On leads. 🅿 ❋

© English Heritage

Brougham Castle

Acorn Bank Garden

BROUGHAM CASTLE ⊞

Penrith, Cumbria CA10 2AA
Tel: 01768 862488 **E-mail:** customers@english-heritage.org.uk
www.english-heritage.org.uk/broughamcastle
Owner: English Heritage **Contact:** Visitor Operations Team
Come to the gentle banks of the River Eamont and discover the intriguing story of Lady Anne Clifford. Visit the exhibition highlighting her remarkable life at these impressive 13th-century ruins.
Location: MAP 10:L5, OS Ref. NY537 290. 1½ m SE of Penrith, between A66 & B6262.
Open: 1 Apr–30 Sep: daily, 10am–5pm.
Admission: Adult £3.50, Child £1.80, Conc. £3. Family £8.80. 15% discount for groups (11+). EH members Free. Opening times and prices are valid until 31st March 2010, after this date details are subject to change please see www.english-heritage.org.uk for the most up-to-date information.
ⓘ WCs. 🔲 ♿ 🅿 🖥 ♨ In grounds, on leads. ♿

Blackwell, The Arts & Crafts House

CARLISLE CASTLE ⊞

CARLISLE, CUMBRIA CA3 8UR

www.english-heritage.org.uk/carlisle

Tel: 01228 591922 **Email:** customers@english-heritage.org.uk
Owner: English Heritage **Contact:** Visitor Operations Team
One of Britain's best border castles, dating back over 900 years, this was a flashpoint of Anglo-Scottish border warfare, beating off sieges and serving as a grim prison for many generations of captives including Mary, Queen of Scots. Exhibition on Bonnie Prince Charlie and the Jacobite Rising.
Location: MAP 10:K3, OS Ref. NY396 562. In Carlisle town, at N end of city centre.
Open: 1 Apr–30 Sep: daily, 9.30am–5pm. 1 Oct–31 Mar '10: daily, 10am–4pm. Closed 24–26 Dec & 1 Jan.
Admission: Adult £4.50, Child £2.30, Conc £3.80. 15% discount for groups (11+). EH members Free. Opening times and prices are valid until 31st March 2010, after this date details are subject to change please see www.english-heritage.org.uk for the most up-to-date information.
🔲 ♿ 🎥 Obligatory. 🅿 Disabled parking only. 🖥 ✳ ♿

CARLISLE CATHEDRAL

Carlisle, Cumbria CA3 8TZ
Tel: 01228 548151 **Fax:** 01228 547049 **Contact:** Ms C Baines
Fine sandstone Cathedral, founded in 1122. Medieval stained glass.
Location: MAP 10:K3, OS Ref. NY399 559. Carlisle city centre, 2m from M6/J43.
Open: Mon–Sat: 7.40am–6.15pm, Suns, 7.40–5pm. Closes 4pm between Christmas Day & New Year. Sun services: 8am, 10.30am & 3pm. Weekday services: 8am, 5.30pm & a 12.30 service on Mons, Weds and Fris.
Admission: Donation.

CONISHEAD PRIORY & BUDDHIST TEMPLE

Ulverston, Cumbria LA12 9QQ
Tel: 01229 584029 **Fax:** 01229 580080 **E-mail:** visits@manjushri.org
www.manjushri.org
Owner: New Kadampa Tradition **Contact:** Geoffrey Roe
Romantic Gothic mansion with gardens and woodland walks to Morecambe Bay. Special features include reception rooms with decorative ceilings, a vaulted great hall, amazing stained glass windows, grand staircase, and 48m long cloister corridor. Home to international Buddhist Centre and unique Temple. Enjoy the Café, Gift shop, & Guided tours that bring alive the spiritual and healing work since 1160. Simon Jenkins says: *'There is no house in England like Conishead'.*
Location: MAP 10:K8, OS Ref. SD305 757. 2m S of Ulverston on A5087 Coast Road.
Open: Temple and grounds open everyday (except when closed for Buddhist Festivals). See website for opening times of Temple, Shop and Café.
Admission: Free. Guided Tours £2.50, Children Free.

Muncaster

© Heritage House Group/Nick McCann

DALEMAIN
PENRITH, CUMBRIA CA11 0HB
www.dalemain.com

Tel: 017684 86450 **Fax:** 017684 86223 **E-mail:** admin@dalemain.com
Owner: Robert Hasell-McCosh Esq **Contact:** Jennifer Little – House Administrator
Dalemain is a fine mixture of medieval, Tudor and early Georgian architecture. The imposing Georgian façade strikes the visitor immediately but in the cobbled courtyard the atmosphere of the north country Tudor manor is secure. The present owner's family have lived at Dalemain since 1679 and have collected china, furniture and family portraits. Delightful and fascinating 5 acre plantsman's gardens set against the picturesque splendour of the Lakeland Fells and Parkland. Richly planted herbaceous borders. Rose Walk with over 100 old-fashioned roses and ancient apple trees of named varieties. Magnificent Abies Cephalonica and Tulip Tree. Tudor Knot Garden. Wild Garden with a profusion of flowering shrubs and wild flowers and in early summer the breathtaking display of blue Himalayan Poppies. Giantess Earth Sculpture.

Location: MAP 10:L5, OS Ref. NY477 269. On A592 1m S of A66. 4m SW of Penrith. From London, M1, M6/J40: 5 hrs. From Edinburgh, A73, M74,M6/J40: 2½ hrs.
Open: Gardens & Tearoom: 31 Jan–25 Mar & 31 Oct–16 Dec:, Sun–Thur. 11am–4pm. Gardens, Tearoom & Gift Shop: 28 Mar–28 Oct:, Sun–Thur. 10.30am–5pm (4pm in Oct). House opens 11.15am–4pm (3pm in Oct). Groups (12+) please book.
Admission: House & Garden: Adult £9, Accompanied Children under 16 Free. Gardens only: Adult £6, Accompanied Children under 16 Free. Group prices on application.
ⓘ No photography in house. Moorings available on Ullswater. Phone for event enquiries 🔲 🔲 🔲 🔲 Partial WCs. 🔲 Licensed. 🔲 Licensed. 🔲 Obligatory, 1hr tours. German and French translations. Garden tour for groups extra. 🅿 Parking for coaches 50 yds. 🔲 🔲 Guide dogs only. 🔲

DOVE COTTAGE, THE WORDSWORTH MUSEUM & ART GALLERY

GRASMERE, CUMBRIA LA22 9SH

www.wordsworth.org.uk

Tel: 01539 435544 **Fax:** 01539 435748 **E-mail:** enquiries@wordsworth.org.uk

Owner: The Wordsworth Trust **Contact:** Bookings Officer

Situated in the heart of the Lake District, Dove Cottage is the beautifully preserved home of William Wordsworth. Visitors can take a guided tour of the cottage then discover more about the poet at the award-winning Wordsworth Museum next door. On site café/restaurant and bookshop.

Location: MAP 10:K6, OS Ref. NY342 070. Immediately S of Grasmere village on A591. Main car/coach park next to Restaurant.

Open: All year: daily, 9.30am–5.30pm (last admission 5pm). Closed 24–26 Dec & early Jan–early Feb. Winter opening hours apply Nov-Feb.

Admission: Adult £7.50, Child £4.50, Family and group rates available. Prices are subject to change without notice.

No photography. Partial. WC. Obligatory for Dove Cottage. Guide dogs only.

FURNESS ABBEY

Barrow-in-Furness, Cumbria LA13 0PJ

Tel: 01229 823420 **E-mail:** customers@english-heritage.org.uk

www.english-heritage.org.uk/furness

Owner: English Heritage **Contact:** Visitor Operations Staff

Set in the peaceful 'Valley of Nightshade'are the beautiful red sandstone remains of the wealthy abbey founded in 1123 by Stephen, later King of England. This abbey first belonged to the Order of Savigny and later to the Cistercians. There is a museum and exhibition.

Location: MAP 10:J8, OS Ref. SD218 717. 1½m N of Barrow-in-Furness off A590.

Open: 1 Apr–30 Jun: Thu–Mon, 10am–5pm. 1 July–31 Aug: Daily, 10am–5pm. 1–30 Sept: Thu–Mon, 10am–5pm. 1 Oct–31 Mar: Sat–Sun, 10am–4pm. Closed 24–26 Dec & 1 Jan.

Admission: Adult £3.50, Child £1.80, Conc. £3. 15% discount for groups (11+).EH members Free. Opening times and prices are valid until 31st March 2010, after this date details are subject to change please see www.english-heritage.org.uk for the most up-to-date information.

WC. Inclusive. In grounds, on leads.

HARDKNOTT ROMAN FORT

Ravenglass, Cumbria

Tel: 0161 242 1400 **E-mail:** customers@english-heritage.org.uk

www.english-heritage.org.uk/hardknottromanfort

Owner: English Heritage **Contact:** The North West Regional Office

This fort, built between AD120 and 138, controlled the road from Ravenglass to Ambleside.

Location: MAP 10:J6, OS Ref. NY218 015. At the head of Eskdale. 9m NE of Ravenglass, at W end of Hardknott Pass.

Open: Any reasonable time. Access may be hazardous in winter.

Admission: Free. Opening times and prices are valid until 31st March 2010, after this date details are subject to change please see www.english-heritage.org.uk for the most up-to-date information.

On leads.

HERON CORN MILL & MUSEUM OF PAPERMAKING

Beetham Trust, Waterhouse Mills, Beetham, Milnthorpe LA7 7AR

Tel: 015395 65027 **Fax:** 015395 65033 **E-mail:** info@heronmill.org

Owner: Heron Corn Mill Beetham Trust **Contact:** Audrey Steeley

A fascinating visitor attraction. An 18th century corn mill and museum of papermaking offers hand-made paper demonstrations and art workshops for visitors.

Location: MAP 10:L8, OS Ref. SD497 800. At Beetham. 1m S of Milnthorpe on the A6.

Open: Mar–Oct: daily except Mons (open BH Mons), 11am–5pm.

Admission: Please telephone for details. Redevelopment in progress causing some restrictions to visitors.

Furness Abbey

HOLEHIRD GARDENS

Patterdale Road, Windermere, Cumbria LA23 1NP
Tel: 01539 446008
Owner: Lakeland Horticultural Society   **Contact:** The Hon Secretary/Publicity Officer
Over 10 acres of hillside gardens overlooking Windermere, including a wide variety of plants, specimen trees and shrubs, extensive rock and heather gardens, a walled garden, alpine houses and herbaceous borders. The all year garden also is home to the national collections of Astilbe, Hydrangea and Polystichum ferns. Managed and maintained entirely by volunteers.
Location: MAP 10:K7, OS Ref. NY410 008. On A592, ¾m N of junction with A591. ½ m N of Windermere. 1m from Townend.
Open: All year: dawn till dusk. Groups strictly by arrangement. Reception: Apr–Oct, 10am–5pm.
Admission: Free. Donation appreciated (at least £3 suggested).

HILL TOP 🐾

NEAR SAWREY, AMBLESIDE, CUMBRIA LA22 0LF

www.nationaltrust.org.uk

Tel: 01539 436269 opt 5   **Fax:** 01539 436811   **E-mail:** hilltop@nationaltrust.org.uk
Owner: The National Trust   **Contact:** Administrator
Beatrix Potter wrote and illustrated many of her famous children's stories in this little 17th century house, which contains her furniture and china. There is a traditional cottage garden attached. A selection of the original illustrations may be seen at the Beatrix Potter Gallery in Hawkshead. Shop specialises in Beatrix Potter items.
Location: MAP 10:K7, OS Ref. SD370 955. 2m S of Hawkshead, in hamlet of Near Sawrey. Small car park. Bus: tel. 01539 445161 for complete ferry and bus timetable. Ferry: 3m from Bowness via ferry. 2m off-road path from ferry if walking.
Open: 13 Feb–25 Mar, 11am–3.30pm; 27 Mar–20 May 10.30am-4.30pm; 22 May-2 Sept 10am - 4.30pm; 4 Sept-31 Oct 10.30am-4.30pm:Sat–Thur,Good Fri & 29 Oct.Closed other Fridays.Garden & Shop: 13 Feb–24 Dec, daily: Call for winter details. Admission by timed ticket (incl. NT members). Daily quota, early sell-outs possible. Group booking essential.Last admission 30 mins before close.
Admission: Adult £6.50, Child £3.10, Family £16.00. No reduction for groups. Discount for Beatrix Potter Gallery ticket holders. Garden: Free on Fri.
Special Events: Children's Garden Trail during holiday periods.
ℹ️ No photography in house. Accessible WC 2m in Hawkshead. Assistance dogs only. 📷 ♿ Partial. 🅿️ None for coaches. 🐕 Guide dogs only ☸

HOLKER HALL & GARDENS 🏠   *See page 377 for full page entry.*

HUTTON-IN-THE-FOREST 🏠

PENRITH, CUMBRIA CA11 9TH

www.hutton-in-the-forest.co.uk

Tel: 017684 84449   **Fax:** 017684 84571   **E-mail:** info@hutton-in-the-forest.co.uk
Owner: Lord Inglewood   **Contact:** Leah Cameron
The home of Lord Inglewood's family since 1605. Built around a medieval pele tower with 17th, 18th and 19th century additions. Fine collections of furniture, paintings, ceramics and tapestries. Outstanding grounds with terraces, topiary, walled garden, dovecote and woodland walk through magnificent specimen trees.
Location: MAP 10:L5, OS Ref. NY460 358. 6m NW of Penrith & 2½ m from M6/J41 on B5305.
Open: 31 Mar-11 Apr, 28 Apr-3 Oct 2010. Wed, Thur, Sun, BH Mon, 12.30–4pm (last entry) Tearoom as House 11am–4.30pm. Gardens & Grounds 31 Mar–31 Oct 2010, daily except Sats, 11am–5pm.
Admission: Please see www.hutton-in-the-forest.co.uk or telephone 017684 84449 for details.
ℹ️ Picnic area. 🎁 Gift stall. 🍵 By arrangement. ♿ Partial. WCs 🍴 Licensed.
📷 Obligatory (except Jul/Aug & BHs). 🅿️ 🚻 🐕 On leads.☸

LANERCOST PRIORY ⚜

Brampton, Cumbria CA8 2HQ
Tel: 01697 73030   **E-mail:** angela.wareing@english-heritage.org.uk
www.english-heritage.org.uk/lanercost
Owner: English Heritage   **Contact:** Visitor Operations Team
This Augustinian priory was founded c1166. The nave of the church, which is intact and in use as the local parish church, contrasts with the ruined chancel, transepts and priory buildings.
Location: MAP 10:L3, OS Ref. NY556 637. 2m NE of Brampton. 1m N of Naworth Castle.
Open: 1 Apr–30 Sep: daily, 10am–5pm. 1 Oct–1 Nov: Thu–Mon, 10am–4pm.
Admission: Adult £3, Child £1.50, Conc. £2.60, Groups (11+): 15% discount. EH members Free. Opening times and prices are valid until 31st March 2010, after this date details are subject to change please see www.english-heritage.org.uk for the most up-to-date information.
📷 🅿️ Limited for coaches. 🚻 🐕 ☸

Hill Top, Sawrey

LEVENS HALL 🏚

LEVENS HALL, KENDAL, CUMBRIA LA8 0PD

www.levenshall.co.uk

Tel: 015395 60321 **Fax:** 015395 60669 **E-mail:** houseopening@levenshall.co.uk
Owner: C H Bagot **Contact:** The Administrator

Levens Hall is an Elizabethan mansion built around a 13th century pele tower. The much loved home of the Bagot family, with fine panelling, plasterwork, Cordova leather wall coverings, paintings by Rubens, Lely and Cuyp, the earliest English patchwork and Wellingtoniana combine with other beautiful objects to form a fascinating collection.

The world famous Topiary Gardens were laid out by Monsieur Beaumont from 1694 and his design has remained largely unchanged to this day. Over 90 individual pieces of topiary, some over nine metres high, massive beech hedges and colourful seasonal bedding provide a magnificent visual impact.

On Sundays and Bank Holiday Mondays 'Bertha', a full size Showman's Engine, is in steam.

Location: MAP 10:L7, OS Ref. SD495 851. 5m S of Kendal on the A6. Exit M6/J36.

Open: 4 April – 14 October Sun-Thurs (closed Fris & Sats). Garden, Tea Room, Gift Shop & Plant Centre 10am – 5pm. House 12 noon – 4.30pm (last entry 4pm) Groups (20+) please book.

Admission: House & Gardens or Gardens Only. Please see www.levenshall.co.uk for details. Group Rates on application.

ⓘ No indoor photography. 🏪 Gift shop 🚻 Partial. WC. Electric buggy hire. DVD of interior of house. 🍴 Licensed. 🎫 By arrangement. 🅿 Free on-site parking. ▣ 🐕 Assistance dogs only.

MIREHOUSE 🏚

KESWICK, CUMBRIA CA12 4QE

www.mirehouse.com

Tel: 017687 72287 **E-mail:** info@mirehouse.com
Owner: James Fryer-Spedding **Contact:** Janaki Spedding

Melvyn Bragg described Mirehouse as *'Manor from Heaven'*. Simon Jenkins in *The Times* said *'It is the Lake District with its hand on its heart'*. Literary house linked with Tennyson and Wordsworth. Live piano music and children's history trail in house. Natural playgrounds, serene bee garden and lakeside walk.

Location: MAP 10:J5, OS Ref. NY235 284. Beside A591, 3½ m N of Keswick. Good bus service.

Open: Apr–Oct: Gardens & Tearoom: daily, 10am–5.30pm. House: Suns & Weds (also Fris in Aug), 2–5pm (4.30pm last entry). Groups (15+) welcome by appointment.

Admission: House & Garden: Adult £6.50, Child £3.25, Family (2+4) £18.50. Gardens only: Adult £3, Child £1.50.

ⓘ No photography in house. 🚻 🍴 🎫 By arrangement. 🅿 Limited. ▣ 🐕 On leads only.

MUNCASTER CASTLE, GARDENS & OWL CENTRE 🏚

See page 378 for full page entry.

PENRITH CASTLE ⌗

Penrith, Cumbria
Tel: 0161 242 1400 **E-mail:** customers@english-heritage.org.uk
www.english-heritage.org.uk/penrith
Owner: English Heritage **Contact:** The North West Regional Office

This mainly 15th century castle, set in a park on the edge of the town, was built to defend Penrith against repeated attacks by Scottish raiders.

Location: MAP 10:L5, OS Ref. NY513 299. Opposite Penrith railway station. W of the town centre. Fully visible from the street.

Open: Park: Summer: 7.30am–9pm; Winter: 7.30am–4.30pm.

Admission: Free. Opening times and prices are valid until 31st March 2010, after this date details are subject to change please see www.english-heritage.org.uk for the most up-to-date information.

ⓘ WC 🐕 On leads.

SIZERGH CASTLE & GARDEN 🌿

See page 379 for full page entry.

STOTT PARK BOBBIN MILL ⌗

Low Stott Park, Nr Newby Bridge, Cumbria LA12 8AX
Tel: 01539 531087 **E-mail:** customers@english-heritage.org.uk
www.english-heritage.org.uk/stottpark
Owner: English Heritage **Contact:** Visitor Operations Team

Built in 1835, this mill was vital to the spinning and weaving industry in Lancashire. A remarkable opportunity to see demonstrations of the machinery and techniques of the Industrial Revolution. Free guided tours.

Location: MAP 10:K7, OS Ref. SD372 881. 1½m N of Newby Bridge off A590.

Open: 1 Apr–1 Nov: Mon–Fri, 11am–5pm. Last tour begins ½hr before closing.

Admission: Adult £4.50, Child £2.30, Conc £3.80, Family £11.30. Groups: discount for groups (11+). EH members Free. Opening times and prices are valid until 31st March 2010, after this date details are subject to change please see www.english-heritage.org.uk for the most up-to-date information.

🎫 Obligatory. Free. 🅿 🐕

Holker Hall & Gardens

TOWNEND 🌸

TROUTBECK, WINDERMERE, CUMBRIA LA23 1LB

www.nationaltrust.org.uk/townend

Tel: 015394 32628 **Fax:** 015394 32628 **E-mail:** townend@nationaltrust.org.uk
Owner: The National Trust **Contact:** The Custodian

The Brownes of Townend were just an ordinary farming family, but their home and belongings bring to life over 400 years of extraordinary stories. Townend contains carved woodwork, books, papers, furniture and fascinating implements of the past which were accumulated by the Browne family who lived here from before 1626 until 1943.

Location: MAP 10:K6, OS Ref. NY407 023. 3m SE of Ambleside at S end of Troutbeck village. 1m from Holehird, 3m N of Windermere.

Open: 13 Mar–31 Oct, Wed–Sun. Entry by guided tour at 11am & 12 noon, places limited and available on a first come first served basis. Self-guided opening 1pm –5pm with last admission 30 mins before closing.

***Admission:** Adult £4.70, Child £2.35, Family £11.75. No reduction for groups which must be pre-booked. Includes a voluntary donation but visitors can choose to pay the standard prices displayed at the property and on the website.

🖾 Partial. 🛈 By arrangement. 🅿 Limited. 🐾 🌸

Townend

THE WATERMILL

Little Salkeld, Penrith, Cumbria CA10 1NN
Tel: 01768 881523 **E-mail:** organicflour@aol.com
www.organicmill.co.uk
Owner: Nick and Ana Jones **Contact:** Nick Jones 01768 881047

Traditional 18th century Cumbrian watermill producing stoneground organic and biodynamic flours. Milltours. Tearoom. Millshop. Mail order service. Online shop. Breadmaking, baking courses. Childrens workshops. Near Long Meg Stone Circle, Lacy Caves, River Eden.

Location: MAP 10:L5, OS Ref. NY566 362. 7m from Penrith M6 (J40) in Eden Valley.
Open: Daily 10.30am–5pm. Closed Christmas to mid-Jan.
Admission: £1.00. Guided tour £3.50. (2009).

WORDSWORTH HOUSE AND GARDEN 🌸

Main Street, Cockermouth, Cumbria CA13 9RX
Tel: 01900 824805 **Fax:** 01900 820883 **Opening Info:** 01900 820884
E-mail: wordsworthhouse@nationaltrust.org.uk
www.wordsworthhouse.org.uk
Owner: The National Trust **Contact:** The Custodian

This Georgian townhouse was the birthplace of William Wordsworth. Imaginatively presented as his family home in the 1770s, it offers a lively and participative visit with costumed living history and hands-on rooms. The garden, with terraced walk, has been restored to its 18th-century appearance. Talks and tours available for groups.

Location: MAP 10:J5, OS Ref. NY118 307. Main Street, Cockermouth.

Open: During school terms 13 Mar–31 Oct: Sat–Wed; school holidays also open Thurs*. 11am–5pm. Last entry 4pm. Shop: 4–10 Jan: Mon–Sun, 10am–4.30pm; 13 Mar–31 Oct: Mon–Sun, 10am–5pm; 1 Nov–24 Dec, Mon–Sat, 10am–4.30pm. *Weeks starting: 29 Mar, 5 Apr, 31 May, 19 Jul–30 Aug and 25 Oct.

***Admission:** Adult £6.20, Child £3.10, Family £15.50. Pre-booked groups (15+): Adult £5.40, Child £2.50. Group out of hours £9. *Includes a voluntary donation but visitors can choose to pay the standard prices displayed at the property and on the website.

Special Events: Extensive events programme including talks, tours, concerts and school holiday activities. Also wedding photography packages. See website for details.

🛈 No photography. 🖾 🚻 WCs. 🛈 By arrangement only. 🐾 Guide dogs only. 🌸

Wordsworth House and Garden

ASTLEY HALL & PARK
www.chorley.gov.uk/astleyhall

Chorley's famous Astley Hall Museum and Gallery is often referred to as the 'Jewel in Chorley's crown' and features in Simon Jenkins book 'Britain's Best 1,000 Houses'.

The history of the Hall itself is full of intrigue, with stories of plotting and religious turmoil. It dates back to Elizabethan times with changes and additions over the centuries, all helping make a visit to the Hall a fascinating and enjoyable experience. This grade 1 listed building truly is the jewel in Chorley's crown, with stunning plaster work and architectural features. As the town's museum and art gallery it is also home to items of local historical interest.

Interiors include sumptuous plaster ceilings, fine 17th century oak furniture and tapestries. The Hall is spread over three floors; upstairs particularly of note are the Cromwell bedroom which has unusually enriched panelling and a plaster overmantel dating from the 16th century. A Priest's hole can be found and 'Cromwell's bed' in the Oak Room reveals an exquisite inlay on the canopy and floral carving on the headboard. The top floor houses the Long Gallery, and reveals the longest shovel-board in existence at 23 feet long, with twenty legs.

Situated within hundreds of acres of historic, recently restored parkland, which is home to outdoor theatre and music events, there is a walled garden and Grade II listed Coach House which houses two art galleries, offering exciting and changing exhibitions and Café Ambio.

Astley Hall can be hired for exclusive use, small conferences, evening events and weddings.

 No photography in period rooms. Hall not accessible to wheelchair users above ground floor level.

WCs.

Licensed.

Licensed.

By arrangement.

P Limited for coaches.

In grounds.

LANCASHIRE

ASTLEY HALL & GARDENS

See page 387 for full page entry.

BLACKBURN CATHEDRAL

Cathedral Close, Blackburn, Lancashire BB1 5AA
Tel: 01254 503090 **Fax:** 01254 689666 **Contact:** Pauline Rowe
www.blackburncathedral.com

On an historic Saxon site in town centre. The 1826 Parish Church dedicated as the Cathedral in 1926 with new extensions to give a spacious and light interior. Of special interest is '*The Journey*', a contemporary version of *The Stations of the Cross*, by Penny Warden commisioned by the Cathedral in 2005. The Cathedral is also noted for its outstanding music and significant contributions to the work of cultural understanding both locally and nationally.

Location: MAP 10:M11, OS Ref. SD684 280. 9m E of M6/J31, via A59 and A677. Town centre.

Open: Daily, 9am–5pm. Sun services: at 8am, 9am, 10.30am and 4pm. Catering: Tues–Sat, 10am–2.30pm.

Admission: Free. Donations invited.

BROWSHOLME HALL

Clitheroe, Lancashire BB7 3DE
Tel: 01254 827160 **E-mail:** rrp@browsholme.co.uk **www.browsholme.co.uk**
Owner/Contact: Robert Parker

Built in 1507 by Edmund Parker, 2007 was the 500th Anniversary of Browsholme Hall the ancestral Home of the Parker Family. This remarkable Tudor Hall has a major collection of oak furniture and portraits, arms and armour, stained glass and many unusual antiquities from the Civil war to a fragment of a Zeppelin. Browsholme, pronounced 'Brusom', lies in the Forest of Bowland, and is set in unspoilt parkland in the style of Capability Brown. The façade still retains the ' H' shape of the original house with later Queen Anne and Regency additions when the house was refurbished by Thomas Lister Parker a noted antiquarian and patron of artists such as Turner and Northcote.

Location: MAP 10:M10, OS Ref. SD683 452. 5m NW of Clitheroe off B6243.

Open: 31 May: 2–5pm. 26 Jun–2 Jul: Tue–Sun; 2–5pm. 8–31 Aug: 2–5pm Tue–Sun & BH Mon.

Admission: Adult £5.50, OAP & Groups £5, Child (under 16) £1.50, Grounds only £2.

GAWTHORPE HALL

Padiham, Nr Burnley, Lancashire BB12 8UA
Tel: 01282 771004 **Fax:** 01282 776663 **E-mail:** gawthorpehall@nationaltrust.org.uk
Owner: The National Trust, managed by Lancashire County Council
Contact: Property Office

Built in 1600–05 and restored by Sir Charles Barry in the 1850s, with Barry's designs recreated in the principal rooms. Gawthorpe was the home of the Shuttleworths and the Shuttleworth textile collection is on display, with private study by arrangement. Portrait collection on loan from the National Portrait Gallery.

Location: MAP 10:N10, OS Ref. SD806 340. M65/J8. On E outskirts of Padiham, ¾ m to house on N of A671. Signed to Clitheroe, then signed from 2nd set of traffic lights.

Open: Hall & Tearoom: 1 Apr– 31st Oct: daily except Mons & Fri, open Good Fri & BH Mons, 1–5pm. Last adm. 4.30pm. Garden: All year: daily, 10am–6pm.

Admission: Hall: Adult £4, Conc. £3, Child Free when accompanied by an adult. Prices subject to confirmation in 2010. Garden: Free. NT members Free, but charge to enter grounds may apply on special event days.

WCs. Limited for coaches. Guide dogs only.

HALL I'TH'WOOD

off Green Way, off Crompton Way, Bolton BL1 8UA
Tel: 01204 332370
Owner: Bolton Metropolitan Borough Council **Contact:** Liz Shaw
Late medieval manor house with 17/18th century furniture, paintings and decorative art.
Location: MAP 10:M12, OS Ref. SD724 116. 2m NNE of central Bolton. ¼m N of A58 ring road between A666 and A676 crossroads.
Open: Easter–31 Oct: Wed–Sun & BHs, 12 noon–5pm. Last adm. 4.15pm.
1 Nov–Easter '09: Sats & Suns, 12 noon–5pm. Last adm. 4.15pm.
Admission: Adult £2, Child/Conc. £1, Family £5.

For **corporate hospitality** venues see our special index at the end of the book.

Hoghton Tower

HEATON PARK
PRESTWICH, MANCHESTER M25 2SW

www.heatonpark.org.uk

Tel: 0161 773 1085 **Fax** 0161 798 0107 **E-mail:** heatonpark@manchester.gov.uk
Owner: Manchester City Council **Contact:** Graham Wightman

Heaton Park has been in public ownership since 1902 when the 5th Earl of Wilton sold it to the Manchester Corporation. The landscape surrounding the house was designed by William Emes and modified by John Webb and has recently been restored in partnership with the HLF, together with four of the park's historic buildings. The magnificent James Wyatt house was built for Sir Thomas Egerton in 1772, and is one of Manchester's most impressive and important buildings. The principal rooms have been beautifully restored and are used to display furniture, paintings and other decorative arts appropriate to the late 18th century.

Location: MAP 6:N1, OS Ref. SD833 044. NW Manchester, close to M60/J19. Main entrance off St Margaret's Road, off Bury Old Road – A665.

Open: House: 3 Apr–29 Aug, Thur–Sun & BH Mons, 11am–5.30pm. Park: all year, daily, 8am–dusk.

Admission: Free.

ⓘ No photography in house, no dogs in buildings. 🔲 🕐 ♿ Partial. WCs. ☕
🎓 By arrangement. 🅿 Ample for cars, but limited for coaches. ▮
🐕 In grounds, on leads. 🛏 Double x 2. ▲ ✳

Len Grant

HOGHTON TOWER 🏠
HOGHTON, PRESTON, LANCASHIRE PR5 0SH

www.hoghtontower.co.uk

Tel: 01254 852986 **Fax:** 01254 852109 **E-mail:** mail@hoghtontower.co.uk
Owner: Sir Bernard de Hoghton Bt **Contact:** Office

Hoghton Tower, home of 14th Baronet, is one of the most dramatic looking houses in northern England. Three houses have occupied the hill site since 1100 with the present house re-built by Thomas Hoghton between 1560–1565. Rich and varied historical events including the Knighting of the Loin 'Sirloin' by James I in 1617.

Location: MAP 10:L11, OS Ref. SD622 264. M65/J3. Midway between Preston & Blackburn on A675.

Open: Jul, Aug & Sept: Mon–Thur, 11am–4pm. Suns, 1–5pm. BH Suns & Mons excluding Christmas & New Year. Group visits by appointment all year.

Admission: Gardens & House tours: Adult £6, Child/Conc. £5, Family £18. Gardens, Shop & Tearoom only: £3. Children under 5yrs Free. Private tours by arrangement (25+) £6, OAP £5.

🔲 🕐 Conferences, wedding receptions. ♿ Unsuitable. ☕ 🎓 Obligatory. 🅿 ▮ ✳

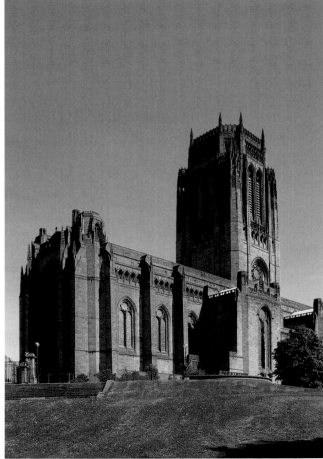

Liverpool Cathedral

LEIGHTON HALL 🏛

CARNFORTH, LANCASHIRE LA5 9ST

www.leightonhall.co.uk

Tel: 01524 734474 **Fax** 01524 720357 **E-mail:** info@leightonhall.co.uk

Owner: Richard Gillow Reynolds Esq **Contact:** Mrs C S Reynolds

Leighton Hall is one of the most beautifully sited houses in the British Isles, situated in a bowl of parkland, with the whole panorama of the Lakeland Fells rising behind. The Hall's neo-gothic façade was superimposed on an 18th century house, which, in turn, had been built on the ruins of the original medieval house. The present owner is descended from Adam d'Avranches who built the first house in 1246. The whole house is, today, lived in by the Reynolds family whose emphasis is put on making visitors feel welcome in a family home. Mr Reynolds is also descended from the founder of Gillow and Company of Lancaster. Connoisseurs of furniture will be particularly interested in the many 18th century Gillow pieces, some of which are unique. Fine pictures, clocks, silver and objéts d'art are also on display.

Gardens: The main garden has a continuous herbaceous border with rose covered walls, while the Walled Garden contains flowering shrubs, a herb garden and an ornamental vegetable garden with a caterpillar maze. Beyond is the Woodland Walk where wild flowers abound from early spring.

Location: MAP 10:L8, OS Ref. SD494 744. 9m N of Lancaster, 10m S of Kendal, 3m N of Carnforth. 1½ m W of A6. 3m from M6/A6/J35, signed from J35A.

Open: May–Sep, Tue–Fri (also BH Sun & Mon, Suns in Aug) 2–5pm. Booked groups (25+) at any time, all year by arrangement.

Admission: Adult £6.95, Child (5–12 Years) £4.75, Family £22, Conc. £6, Garden only £4. Booked groups (25+): Inside Leighton £5.50, Tea & Tour £9.95, Candelit Tour £9.95, Educational visits for Schools £4.75.

ℹ No photography in house. 📷 🌱 Unusual plants for sale. 🚻 ♿ Partial. WCs. 🍴 ⏰ Obligatory. 🅿 Ample for cars and coaches. 🐕 In Park, on leads.

Leighton Hall

MANCHESTER CATHEDRAL

Manchester M3 1SX

Tel: 0161 833 2220 **Fax:** 0161 839 6218 **www.manchestercathedral.org**

In addition to regular worship and daily offices, there are frequent professional concerts, day schools, organ recitals, guided tours and brass-rubbing. The cathedral contains a wealth of beautiful carvings and has the widest medieval nave in Britain.

Location: MAP 6:N1, OS Ref. SJ838 988. Manchester.

Open: Daily. Visitor Centre: Mon–Sat, 9am–3.30pm.

Admission: Donations welcome.

ℹ Visitor Centre.

MARTHOLME

Great Harwood, Blackburn, Lancashire BB6 7UJ

Tel: 01254 886463

Owner: Mr & Mrs T H Codling   **Contact:** Miss P M Codling

Part of medieval manor house with 17th century additions and Elizabethan gatehouse.

Location: MAP 10:M10, OS Ref. SD753 338. 2m NE of Great Harwood off A680 to Whalley.

Open: 2–11 & 23–26 May, 30 May–2 Jun, 22–31 Aug. Tours at 2pm & 4pm.

Admission: £5. Groups welcome by appointment.

RUFFORD OLD HALL 🌿
RUFFORD, Nr ORMSKIRK, LANCASHIRE L40 1SG

www.nationaltrust.org.uk

Tel: 01704 821254 **Fax:** 01704 823813 **Email:** ruffordoldhall@nationaltrust.org.uk
Owner: The National Trust **Contact:** The Property Manager
One of the finest 16th century buildings in Lancashire. The magnificent Great Hall contains an intricately carved movable screen and suits of armour, and is believed to have hosted Shakespeare. Collections of weapons, tapestries and oak furniture are found in the Carolean Wing and attractive gardens contain sculptures and topiary.
Location: MAP 10:L11, OS Ref. SD463 160. 7m N of Ormskirk, in Rufford village E of A59.
Open: Open: 13th Mar– 31st Oct: Mon–Wed, Sat & Sun, 11am–5.30pm. Last entry 4.30pm. Entry to house between 11am and 1pm is by guided tour only. 6 Nov–20 Dec: Shop, Tea Room and Garden open 12–4pm, Fri–Sun.
Admission: House & Garden: Adult £6.20, Child £3.10, Family £15.50. Garden only: Adult £4.30, Child £2.20. Booked groups (15+): Adult £5.30, Child £2.70.
ℹ No photography in house. ⬜ WCs. Licensed. Licensed. By arrangement. 🅿 Limited for coaches. Guide dogs only.

TOWNELEY HALL ART GALLERY & MUSEUMS
BURNLEY BB11 3RQ

www.towneleyhall.org.uk

Tel: 01282 424213 **Fax:** 01282 436138
Owner: Burnley Borough Council **Contact:** Mr. Ken Darwen
House dates from the 14th century with 17th and 19th century modifications. Collections include oak furniture, 18th and 19th century paintings. There is a Museum of Local History.
Location: MAP 10:N10, OS Ref. SD854 309. ½m SE of Burnley on E side of Todmorden Road (A671).
Open: All year: daily except Fri's, 12 noon–5pm. Closed Christmas–New Year.
Admission: Small charge. Guided tours: To be booked for groups.
⬜ WC.

SAMLESBURY HALL

Preston New Road, Samlesbury, Preston PR5 0UP
Tel: 01254 812010 **Fax:** 01254 812174
Owner: Samlesbury Hall Trust **Contact:** Mrs S Jones - Director
Built in 1325, the hall is an attractive black and white timbered manor house set in extensive grounds. Weddings and events welcome. Antiques and crafts all year.
Location: MAP 10:L11, OS Ref. SD623 305. N side of A677, 4m WNW of Blackburn.
Open: All year: daily except Sats: 11am–4.30pm.
Admission: Adult £3, Child £1. Free entry to Restaurant.

SMITHILLS HALL HISTORIC HOUSE

Smithills Dean Road, Bolton BL7 7NP
Tel: 01204 332377 **E-mail:** smithills@bolton.gov.uk
Owner: Bolton Metropolitan Borough Council **Contact:** Liz McNabb
14th century manor house with Tudor panelling. Stuart furniture. Stained glass.
Location: MAP 10:M12, OS Ref. SD699 119. 2m NW of central Bolton, ½m N of A58 ringroad.
Open: Apr–Oct: Tue–Fri & Sun, 12 noon–5pm. Last adm. 4pm. Nov–Mar: Fri & Sun, 12 noon–4pm. Last adm. 3pm. Open BH Mons: 12 noon–5pm.
Admission: Adult £3, Conc. £1.75, Family (2+3) £7.75.

TURTON TOWER

Tower Drive, Chapeltown Road, Turton BL7 0HG
Tel: 01204 852203 **Fax:** 01204 853759 **E-mail:** turtontower@mus.lancscc.gov.uk
Owner: The Trustees of Turton Tower (run by Lancashire County Museums Service)
Contact: Fiona Jenkins
Country house based on a medieval tower, extended in the 16th, 17th and 19th centuries.
Location: MAP 10:M11, OS Ref. SD733 153. On B6391, 4m N of Bolton.
Open: Mar, Apr & Nov, daily except Thurs & Fris, 12 noon–4pm. May–Sept, daily except Fris, 12 noon–5pm.
Admission: Adult £4, Child Free, Conc. £3.

WARTON OLD RECTORY ⌗

Warton, Carnforth, Lancashire
Tel: 0161 242 1400 **Email:** customers@english-heritage.org.uk
www.english-heritage.org.uk/warton
Owner: English Heritage **Contact:** The North West Regional Office
A rare medieval stone house with remains of the hall, chambers and domestic offices.
Location: MAP 10:L8, OS Ref. SD499 723. At Warton, 1m N of Carnforth on minor road off A6.
Open: 1 Apr–30 Sept: daily, 10am–6pm. 1 Oct–31 Mar '10: daily 10am–4pm. Closed 24–26 Dec & 1 Jan.
Admission: Free. Opening times and prices are valid until 31st March 2010, after this date details are subject to change please see www.english-heritage.org.uk for the most up-to-date information.
⬜ On leads.

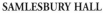

For unique **Civil wedding** venues see our index at the end of the book.

MERSEYSIDE

LIVERPOOL CATHEDRAL

Liverpool, Merseyside L1 7AZ

Tel: 0151 709 6271 **Fax:** 0151 702 7292

Owner: The Dean and Chapter   **Contact:** Eryl Parry

Sir Giles Gilbert Scott's greatest creation. Built last century from local sandstone with superb glass, stonework and major works of art, it is the largest cathedral in Britain.

Location: MAP 6:K1, OS Ref. SJ354 893. Central Liverpool, ½m S of Lime Street Station.

Open: All year: daily, 8am–6pm. Sun services: 8am, 10.30am, 3pm, 4pm. Weekdays: 8am & 5.30pm, also 12.05pm on Fri. Sats: 8am & 3pm.

Admission: Donation. Lift to Tower and Embroidery Exhibition: £4.25 (concessions available). Family Ticket (2+3) £10. Opened 2007: *'The Great Space'* panoramic film and audio tours £4.75 (concessions, family ticket and combination ticket to include tower available).

MEOLS HALL

Churchtown, Southport, Merseyside PR9 7LZ

Tel: 01704 228326 **Fax:** 01704 507185   **E-mail:** events@meolshall.com

www.meolshall.com

Owner: The Hesketh Family   **Contact:** Pamela Whelan

17th century house with subsequent additions. Interesting collection of pictures and furniture. Tithe Barn available for wedding ceremonies and receptions all year.

Location: MAP 10:K11, OS Ref. SD365 184. 3m NE of Southport town centre in Churchtown. SE of A565.

Open: 14 Aug–14 Sept: daily, 2–5pm.

Admission: Adult £4, Child £1. Groups welcome but Afternoon Tea is only available for bookings of 25+.

☂ Wedding ceremonies and receptions now available in the Tithe Barn.

© NTPL / Andrew Butler

SPEKE HALL GARDEN & ESTATE ❧
THE WALK, SPEKE, LIVERPOOL L24 1XD

www.nationaltrust.org.uk

Tel: 0151 427 7231   **Fax:** 0151 427 9860   **Info Line:** 0844 800 4799

Owner: The National Trust   **Contact:** The Property Manager

Superb half-timbered Tudor house, with rich Victorian interiors, fine gardens and estate. Close to Liverpool – but with room to breathe.

Location: MAP 6:K1, OS Ref. SJ419 825. North bank of the Mersey, 6m SE of city centre. Follow signs for Liverpool John Lennon airport.

Open: *House: 28 Feb–15 Mar: Sat & Suns only, 11am–4.30pm; 18 Mar–1 Nov: Wed–Sun, 11am–5pm; 7 Nov–13 Dec: Sats & Suns only, 11am–4.30pm. Grounds: 1 Feb–16 Mar: Tue–Sun, 11am–dusk; 18 Mar–1 Nov: Tue–Sun, 11am–5.30pm; 3 Nov–31 Jan 2010: Tue–Sun, 11am–dusk. Home Farm/restaurant/shop: 28 Feb–15 Mar: Sats & Suns only, 11am–4.30pm: 18 Mar–12 Jul: Wed–Sun, 11am–5pm: 14 Jul–13 Sep: Tue–Sun, 11am–5pm: 16 Sep–1 Nov: Wed–Sun, 11am–5pm: 7 Nov–13 Dec: Sats & Suns only, 11am–4.30pm. Open BH Mons. Grounds (garden and estate) closed 24–26 Dec, 31 Dec, 01 Jan. *28 Feb–13 Dec, 11am–1pm visit to house by guided tour only.

*Admission: Adult £8, Child £4, Family £20.50. Grounds only: Adult £4.75, Child £2.45, Family £12. *includes a voluntary donation but visitors can choose to pay the standard prices displayed at the property and on the website.

tage City
POOL

UNESCO seeks to encourage the identification, protection and preservation of the cultural and natural heritage around the world that is considered to be of outstanding universal value to humanity. Sites that meet the strict criteria of eligibility established by UNESCO are inscribed onto the World Heritage List.

Liverpool – Maritime Mercantile City was nominated by the UK government as "The supreme example of a commercial port at the time of Britain's greatest global influence" and was inscribed as a World Heritage Site by UNESCO's World Heritage Committee in July 2004. The status is a great honour as it acknowledges that Liverpool's architectural and technological heritage is of international significance and should rank alongside Stonehenge, the Taj Mahal and the Pyramids of Egypt.

Port of Liverpool Building
Completed 1907   Grade II*
The domed head office of the Mersey Docks and Harbour Board was designed by Briggs, Wolstenholme and Thorneley in 1901. Features include cast iron gates and gate piers decorated with maritime symbols and lamp holders in the form of naval monuments.

George's Dock Tunnel Ventilation Building and Offices
1931–1934   Grade II
This stylised obelisk, reminiscent of ancient Egypt, was designed by Sir Basil Mott and J A Brodie, with Herbert J Rowse, to serve the Mersey Road Tunnel. It has statues of Night and Day, symbols of the never-closing Mersey Tunnel and a black marble memorial to the workers who died in its construction.

Memorial to Heroes of the Engine Room (Titanic Memorial)
Circa 1916   Grade II
The memorial was originally intended to be for the engineers who stayed at their posts on 15th April 1912 when the Titanic sank. Its dedication was broadened to include all maritime engine room fatalities incurred during the performance of duty. The figures are naturalistic, the detail of their work-clothes being carefully studied.

Albert Dock's Warehouses
Albert Dock's warehouses form England's largest group of Grade I Listed Buildings. Jesse Hartley used well-established techniques adapted from textile mill methods. He introduced new solutions, such as the amazing stressed-skin iron roof. Raising of goods from the quaysides was performed with the first hydraulic cargo-handling installation. Today the dock is home to Tate Liverpool, Merseyside Maritime Museum and numerous bars and restaurants

Stanley Dock Warehouses
Stanley Dock opened in 1848, and between 1852–55 it was equipped with import warehouses. The complex includes: The North Stanley Warehouse 1852–5 Grade II*,The South Stanley Warehouse 1852–5 Grade II, The Stanley Dock Tobacco Warehouse The Hydraulic Tower 1852–55 Grade II, two entrances from Great Howard Street and two from Regent Road.

Liverpool Town Hall
Grade I
Liverpool's finest Georgian building, is the result of three building campaigns. The original design was by John Wood of Bath, and was built in 1749–54. Additions and alterations were designed by James Wyatt and carried out by the elder John Foster in 1789–92. Following a fire of 1795, it was reconstructed the work continuing until 1820.

India Building
1924–31   Grade II
This immense office block was built for the Blue Funnel Line and designed by Herbert J Rowse with Briggs, Wostenholme and Thorneley. It has stripped classical facades; Italian Renaissance detail is restricted to the top and bottom storeys. The building was badly damaged in the war, and restored under Rowse's supervision.

Martin's Building
1927–32   Grade II*
Originally Martin's Bank, designed by Rowse it is monumental and American influenced. The stylish top lit banking hall, with its Parisian jazz moderne fittings, survives well, as does the boardroom. Sculpture and carvings by Herbert Tyson Smith with Edmund Thompson and George Capstick celebrate maritime themes and commerce.

Oriel Chambers
1864   Grade I
Designed by Peter Ellis, the use of oriel windows was driven by a desire to provide good daylight. The oriels themselves are framed in the thinnest sections of iron. In its day, the building aroused much opposition. It is only recently that its futuristic qualities have become appreciated.

Bluecoat Chambers
Opened 1718   Grade I
Bluecoat Chambers was originally built as a charity school in 1717 in the Queen Anne style and in 1928 became one of the UK's first arts centres. The main is round headed with a broken pediment above containing a cartouche of the arms of Liverpool. To the rear is a landscaped garden. After a £12.5m refurbishment the building will reopen in early 2008, complete with a new wing. www.thebluecoat.org.uk

The Walker Art Gallery
Opened 1877   Grade II*
Known as the 'national gallery of the North', the Walker was designed by architects Sherlock and Vale and named after its principal benefactor, Alderman Sir Andrew Barclay Walker, at that time Lord Mayor of Liverpool. A classical portico is the centrepiece of the exterior, which includes friezes of scenes from the city's history, and is surmounted by a personification of Liverpool.
www.liverpoolmuseums.org.uk /walker/

Croxteth Hall
Originally built in 1575, the Croxteth Hall you see today is an Edwardian Country house with beautiful surroundings including a country park. The Hall and its outbuilding are a Grade II* Listed Building, as are 3 other buildings; another 15 on the estate are Grade II. The ancestral home of the Molyneux family (Earls of Sefton) until 1972, it is two miles from Aintree racecourse, which the family had owned and developed. For more information please visit www.croxteth.co.uk

Sudley House
This Grade II late Regency/Victorian red Liverpool sandstone mansion, believed to be the work of Thomas Harrison, was completed in 1824 for Nicholas Robinson, Lord Mayor of Liverpool in 1828–9. Today Sudley House contains the only surviving Victorian merchant art collection in Britain still hanging in its original location. For more information visit www.sudleyhouse.org.uk

Speke Hall
Built in 1530 Speke Hall was central to a 2,500 acre farm until it passed to the National Trust in 1944. This Grade I listed half-timbered Tudor house is set on the banks of the River Mersey with extensive views across to the mountains of North Wales. The Hall's atmospheric interior spans many periods – from its fine Tudor Great Hall and priest hole, to smaller more intimate rooms furnished by Speke's Victorian occupants. For information visit www.nationaltrust.org.uk

© NTPL / Andrew Butler

Lowlands
Built by renowned Liverpool architect Thomas Haigh as his residence in 1846, Grade II-listed Lowlands (13 Haymans Green, West Derby, Liverpool L12 7JG) is the home of the West Derby Community Association. Italianate stucco-faced mansion set in rare city woodland garden. Lowlands hosts many public events and has function rooms available for hire. Re-opens autumn 2008 following conservation work and improvements.

Bamburgh Castle, Northumberland
© Heritage House Group/Nick McCann

North East

Rugged and Roman – the North East region of Britain offers the visitor a wealth of history going back to the Roman occupation. As well as visiting the magnificent fortress castles at Alnwick, Bamburgh and Chillingham, time should be set aside to explore properties such as Wallington, with its exceptional murals depicting Northumbrian history, and The Lady Waterford Murals at Ford, with its 1860 biblical murals.

Alnwick Castle, Northumberland

Co. Durham

Northumberland

Tyne & Wear

NORTHUMBERLAND

TYNE & WEAR

CO. DURHAM

Raby Castle, Co. Durham

Alnwick Garden, Northumberland

Warkworth Castle, Northumberland

Raby Castle 'Octagon Drawing Room'
© Heritage House Group / Peter Smith

RABY CASTLE

www.rabycastle.com

The magnificent Raby Castle has been home to Lord Barnard's family since 1626, when it was purchased by his ancestor, Sir Henry Vane the Elder, the eminent Statesman and Politician. The Castle was built mainly in the 14th Century by the Nevill family on a site of an earlier Manor House. The Nevills continued to live at Raby until 1569, when after the failure of the Rising of the North, the Castle and its land were forfeited to the Crown.

A particular highlight of the Castle is the magnificent Barons Hall (below), where 700 knights met to plot The Rising of the North. Architect John Carr raised the floor level by 3 metres when constructing a carriageway below in the Entrance Hall and later William Burn extended the room by 17 metres over his elaborate Octagon Drawing Room. Today it houses an impressive Meissen bird collection. Other Raby treasures include fine furniture and artworks with paintings by Munnings, Reynolds, Van Dyck, Batoni, Teniers, Amigoni and Vernet.

There is a large Deer Park with two lakes and a beautiful walled garden with formal lawns, ancient yew hedges and ornamental pond. The 18th Century Stable block contains a horse-drawn carriage collection including the State Coach last used by the family for the Coronation of Edward VII in 1902. Parts of the Stables have been converted into a Gift Shop and Tearooms, where the former stalls have been incorporated to create an atmospheric setting.

© Heritage House Group Ltd

ℹ️ Film locations, product launches, corporate events, fairs and concerts. Raby Estates venison and game sold in tearooms. Soft fruit when in season. Lectures on Castle, its contents, gardens and history. No photography or video filming is permitted inside. Colour illustrated guidebook and DVD on sale. Christmas Shop in Stable Yard throughout December.

🛍️

🌷

☕

♿ Partial. WC. Castle DVD viewing area.

🍴 Licensed.

🚶 By arrangement for groups (20+) or min charge. VIP & Standard Castle Tours available. Tour time 1½ hrs.

🅿️

🚌 By arrangement (20+), weekday am. Primary & Junior £3.50; Secondary £4.

🐕 Guide dogs welcome. All dogs welcome in Park on leads.

🎭 Varied programme throughout the summer.

■ Owner
The Lord Barnard

■ Contact
Clare Owen /
Katie Blundell
Raby Castle
Staindrop
Darlington
Co. Durham DL2 3AH
Tel: 01833 660202
Fax: 01833 660169
E-mail: admin@
rabycastle.com

■ Location
MAP 10:O5
OS Ref. NZ129 218
On A688, 1m N of Staindrop. 8m NE of Barnard Castle, 12m WNW of Darlington.
Rail: Darlington Station, 12m.
Air: Durham Tees Valley Airport, 20m.

■ Opening Times
Castle
Easter weekend, May, June & September, Sun–Wed. July & August: Daily except Sats. (Open BH Sats), 1–5pm.

Park & Gardens
As Castle, 11am–5.30pm.

■ Admission
Castle, Park & Gardens
Adult	£9.50
Child (5–16yrs)	£4.00
OAP/Student	£8.50

Family discounts available.

Groups (12+)
Adult	£7.50
Child (5–16yrs)	£3.00

Park & Gardens
Adult	£5.00
Child (12–15yrs)	£3.00
Under 12s	Free
Conc.	£4.00

Groups (12+)
Adult	£3.50
Child (5–16yrs)	£2.50

Season Tickets available.

VIP Private Guided Tours (20+)*
(incl. reception, tea/coffee in entrance hall) Easter–Sept, Mon–Fri mornings.
£15.00

Standard Guided Tours (20+)*
(Easter–Sept, Mon–Fri.
Adult   £8.00

*Please book in advance.

Free RHS access to Park & Gardens.

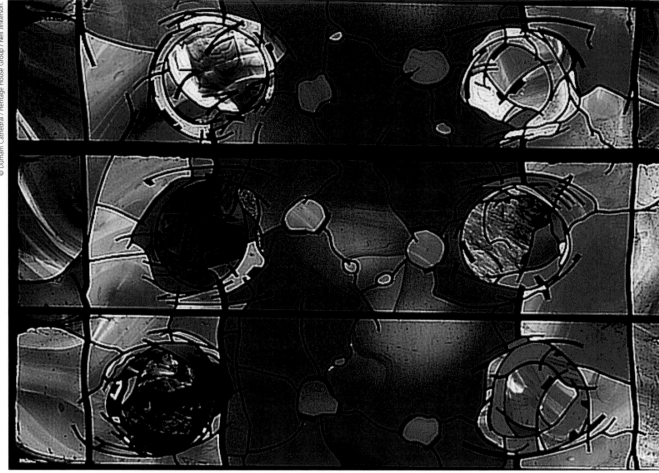

Durham Cathedral - detail 'The Daily Bread' Window

AUCKLAND CASTLE DEER HOUSE ⊞

Bishop Auckland, Durham DL14 7NR

Tel: 0191 2691200 **E-mail:** customers@english-heritage.org.uk

www.english-heritage.org.uk/aucklandcastle

Owner: English Heritage **Contact:** The North East Regional Office

A charming building erected in 1760 in the Park of the Bishops of Durham so that the deer could shelter and find food.

Location: MAP 10:P5, OS Ref. NZ216 304. In Bishop Auckland Park, just N of town centre on A68. About 500 yds N of the castle.

Open: Park: 1 Apr–30 Sept: daily, 10am–6pm 1 Oct–31 Mar: daily, 10am–4pm. Closed 24–26 Dec & 1 Jan.

Admission: Free. Opening times and prices are valid until 31st March 2010, after this date details are subject to change please see www.english-heritage.org.uk for the most up-to-date information.

🐕 On leads.

BARNARD CASTLE ⊞

Barnard Castle, Castle House, Durham DL12 8PR

Tel: 01833 638212 **E-mail:** barnard.castle@english-heritage.org.uk

www.english-heritage.org.uk/barnardcastle

Owner: English Heritage **Contact:** Visitor Operations Team

Barnard Castle is spectacularly set on a high rock above the river tees. Taking its name from its 12th-Century founder Bernard de Balliol, this huge and imposing fortress was later developed by the Beauchamp family and Richard III. Richard's boar emblem is carved above a window in the inner ward.

Location: MAP 10:O5, OS92, NZ049 165. In Barnard Castle Town.

Open: 1 Apr–30 Sept: daily, 10am–6pm. 1 Oct–1 Nov: daily, 10am–4pm. 2 Nov–31 Mar: Thur–Mon, 10am–4pm. Closed 24–26 Dec & 1 Jan.

Admission: Adult £4, Child £2, Conc. £3.40. 15% discount for groups (11+). EH members Free. Opening times and prices are valid until 31st March 2010, after this date details are subject to change please see www.english-heritage.org.uk for the most up-to-date information.

ℹ️ WCs in town. A 'sensory garden' of scented plants and tactile objects. 📷 ♿ 🐕 On leads. ▦

BINCHESTER ROMAN FORT

Bishop Auckland, Co. Durham

Tel: 01388 663089 / 0191 3834212 (outside opening hours)

Owner: Durham County Council **Contact:** Deborah Anderson

Once the largest Roman fort in Co Durham, the heart of the site has been excavated.

Location: MAP 10:P5, OS Ref. NZ210 312. 1½ m N of Bishop Auckland, signposted from A690 Durham–Crook and from A688 Spennymoor–Bishop Auckland roads.

Open: Easter–30 Sept: daily, 11am–5pm.

Admission: Adult £2, Child/Conc. £1.

CROOK HALL & GARDENS

Sidegate, Durham DH1 5SZ

Tel: 0191 3848028

Owner: Keith & Maggie Bell **Contact:** Mrs Maggie Bell

Medieval manor house set in rural landscape on the edge of Durham city.

Location: MAP 10:P4, OS Ref. NZ274 432. ½ m N of city centre.

Open: Easter weekend, 6 Mar–28 Sept: daily except Fri & Sat, 11am–5pm.

Admission: Adult £5.50, Conc. £5, Child. £4.50, Family £16.

DERWENTCOTE STEEL FURNACE ⊞

Newcastle, Durham NE39 1BA

Please call 0191 269 1200 (Mon–Fri) for opening details

E-mail: customers@english-heritage.org.uk

www.english-heritage.org.uk/derwentcote

Owner: English Heritage **Contact:** The North East Regional Office

Built in the 18th century, it is the earliest and most complete authentic steel-making furnace to have survived.

Location: MAP 10:O3, OS Ref. NZ130 566. 10m SW of Newcastle N of the A694 between Rowland's Gill and Hamsterley.

Open: Please call for details.

Admission: Free. Opening times and prices are valid until 31st March 2010, after this date details are subject to change please see www.english-heritage.org.uk for the most up-to-date information.

🅿️ 🐕 On leads in restricted areas.

DURHAM CASTLE

Palace Green, Durham DH1 3RW
Tel: 0191 3343800 **Fax:** 0191 3343801 **Contact:** Mrs Julie Marshall
Durham Castle, founded in the 1070s, with the Cathedral is a World Heritage Site.
Location: MAP 10:P4, OS Ref. NZ274 424. City centre, adjacent to Cathedral.
Open: Mar–Sept: 10am–12 noon & 2–4.30pm. Oct–Mar: Mon, Wed, Sat & Sun 2–4pm.
Admission: Adult £5, OAP £2.50, Family (2+2) £10. Guide book £2.50.

DURHAM CATHEDRAL

Durham DH13 3EH
Tel: 0191 3864266 **Fax:** 0191 3864267 **E-mail:** enquiries@durhamcathedral.co.uk
www.durhamcathedral.co.uk
Contact: Miss A Heywood
A World Heritage Site. Norman architecture. Burial place of St Cuthbert and the Venerable Bede.
Location: MAP 10:P4, OS Ref. NZ274 422. Durham city centre.
Open: Mon–Sat, 10am–4.30pm. Sun 12.45–5.30pm. School summer holidays – open to 8.00pm. Restricted access during services to which all are welcome. Please check if making a special visit of travelling far.
Admission: Free but donations very welcome. Tower: Adults £4, Child £2, Treasures of St Cuthbert: Adult £2.50, Child 70p, Family £6 Concessions £2.

EGGLESTONE ABBEY ♯

Durham
Tel: 0191 2691200 **E-mail:** customers@english-heritage.org.uk
www.english-heritage.org.uk/egglestone
Owner: English Heritage **Contact:** The North East Regional Office
The charming ruins of a small monastery set in a bend of the River Tees. Much of the 13th century church and a range of living quarters remain.
Location: MAP 10:O6, OS Ref. NZ062 151. 1m S of Barnard Castle on minor road off B6277.
Open: Daily, 10am–6pm.
Admission: Free. Opening times and prices are valid until 31st March 2010, after this date details are subject to change please see www.english-heritage.org.uk for the most up-to-date information.
🔾 🅿 🔾 On leads.

ESCOMB CHURCH

Escomb, Bishop Auckland DL14 7ST
Tel: 01388 602861
Owner: Church of England **Contact:** Mrs D Denham
Saxon church dating from the 7th century built of stone from Binchester Roman Fort.
Location: MAP 10:P5, OS Ref. NZ189 302. 3m W of Bishop Auckland.
Open: Summer: 9am–8pm. Winter: 9am–4pm. Key available from 26 Saxon Green, Escomb.
Admission: Free.

FINCHALE PRIORY ♯

Finchdale Priory, Brasside, Newton Hall DH1 5SH
Tel: 0191 269 1200 **E-mail:** customers@english-heritage.org.uk
www.english-heritage.org.uk/finchale
Owner: English Heritage **Contact:** The North East Regional Office
These beautiful 13th-century priory remains are located beside the curving River Wear.
Location: MAP 10:P4, OS Ref. NZ296 471. 3m NE of Durham.
Open: 1 Apr–30 Sept, Sat–Sun & Bank Hols, 10am–5pm.
Admission: Adult £3, Child £1.50, Conc. £2.60. Opening times and prices are valid until 31st March 2010, after this date details are subject to change please see www.english-heritage.org.uk for the most up-to-date information.
ⓘ WC. 🔾 🅿 (charge) on S side of river. 🔾

RABY CASTLE 🏛

See page 397 for full page entry.

ROKEBY PARK

Barnard Castle, Co. Durham DL12 9RZ
Tel: 01609 748612 **E-mail:** admin@rokebypark.com
www.rokebypark.com
A Palladian Country House c.1730 with unique print room, period furniture and paintings.
Location: MAP 10:O6, OS ref NZ 080 142. 3m SE of Barnard Castle, N of A66.
Open: 3 May, 31 May–7 Sept: Mons & Tues, 2–5 pm (last admission 4.30 pm). Groups by appointment.
Admission: Adult £6.50. Children under 16 Free. Over 60s £5.50. Students £4. Groups £5.50 on open days, by arrangement on other days.
ⓘ No photography in house. 🔾 Ground floor only, no WC. 🔾 By arrangement. 🔾 🅿

THE WEARDALE MUSEUM & HIGH HOUSE CHAPEL

Ireshopeburn, Co. Durham DL13 1EY
Tel: 01388 517433 **E-mail:** dtheatherington@ormail.co.uk
Contact: D T Heatherington
Small folk museum and historic chapel. Includes 1870 Weardale cottage room, John Wesley room and local history displays.
Location: MAP 10:N4, OS Ref. NZ872 385. Adjacent to 18th century Methodist Chapel.
Open: Easter & May–Sept: Wed–Sun & BH, 2–5pm. Aug: daily, 2–5pm.
Admission: Adult £1.50, Child 50p.

Rokeby Park

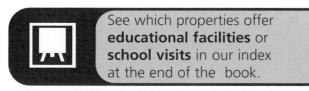

See which properties offer **educational facilities** or **school visits** in our index at the end of the book.

North East – England

■ Owner
His Grace the Duke of Northumberland

■ Contact
Alnwick Castle
Estate Office
Alnwick
Northumberland
NE66 1NQ

Tel: 01665 510777
Group bookings:
01665 511178
Fax: 01665 510876
E-mail: enquiries@
alnwickcastle.com

■ Location
MAP 14:M11
OS Ref. NU187 135

In Alnwick 1½ m
W of A1.
From London 6hrs,
Edinburgh 2hrs,
Chester 4hrs,
Newcastle 40mins
North Sea ferry
terminal 30mins.

Bus: From bus station
in Alnwick.

Rail: Alnmouth
Station 5m.
Kings Cross, London
3½hrs.

Air: Newcastle 40mins.

■ Opening Times
31 March–29 October
Daily, 10am–6pm.
State Rooms open
at 11am (last adm. to
State Rooms 4.30pm).

■ Admission
Adult	£11.95
Child (5–15yrs)	£4.95
Child (under 5yrs)	Free
Conc.	£9.95

Booked Groups
(14+, tel 01665 511178)
Adult	£7.95
Child	£4.50

(*2009 prices, may be
subject to change).

Seasonal and two day
joint tickets with The
Alnwick Garden are
available.

HHA members free
access to Castle only.

ALNWICK CASTLE 🏛
www.alnwickcastle.com

Set in a stunning landscape designed by 'Capability' Brown, Alnwick Castle is the family home of the Duke of Northumberland. Owned by his family since 1309, this beautiful castle, originally built to defend England from the Scots, now appeals to visitors of all ages from across the world.

Considered to be one of the finest castles in England, and known as the 'Windsor of the North', this has been the home of the Percy family for nearly 700 years. In the 1760s it was transformed from a fortification into a family home for the First Duke and Duchess. Today Alnwick Castle is an attraction of real significance, with lavish State Rooms, superb art treasures, fun activities and entertainment, all set in a beautiful landscape.

Visitors walking through the gates, set in massive stone walls, enter one of the most stunning castles in Europe. The Keep sits magnificently in the spacious grounds, with its medieval towers housing the castle's 14th century dungeon and the entrance to the remarkable State Rooms. The refurbished and restored dining room is worth a visit. Beautifully silked walls, a hand-woven carpet and intricate carved ceiling are among the delights. Important ceramics of the Meissen, Chelsea and Paris factories are impressively displayed in the china gallery.

Within the grounds are the museums and towers that tell the story of the Northumberland Fusiliers from 1674 to the present day, local archaeology of the area, the Percy Tenantry Volunteers and an exhibition on siege craft.

Adding to the magic of this castle is an interactive and fun activity area where children can enter the exciting and enchanting world of knights and dragons. They can learn how to become a Knight or Lady of Alnwick then take the ultimate challenge to win their spurs by facing the monster which rules the kingdom in Dragon's Quest.

ℹ	Conference facilities, events, fairs and exhibitions. Film location hire. No photography inside the castle. No unaccompanied children.	☕	Coffee, light lunches and teas.
		Ⓟ	Shared with Alnwick Gardens.
🖼		📖	Guidebook and worksheet, special rates for children and teachers.
🍽	Wedding receptions.		
♿	Partial. Parking.	🐕	Guide dogs only.
		🎭	

Conference/Function
ROOM	SIZE	MAX CAPACITY
The Guest Hall	100' x 30'	250

CHILLINGHAM CASTLE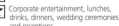

www.chillingham-castle.com

Only 20 minutes from the seaside. Rated 4-star (amongst the top 100!) in Simon Jenkins' *England's Thousand Best Houses*. *The Independent*: **First** of *The 50 Best Castles in Britain & Ireland*.

This remarkable castle, the home of Sir Humphry Wakefield Bt, with its alarming dungeons has, as now and since the 1200s, been continuously owned by the family of the Earls Grey and their relations. You will see active restoration of complex masonry, metalwork and ornamental plaster as the great halls and state rooms are gradually brought back to life with tapestries, arms and armour as of old and even a torture chamber.

At first a 12th century stronghold, Chillingham became a fully fortified castle in the 14th century (see the original 1344 Licence to Crenellate). Wrapped in the nation's history it occupied a strategic position as a fortress during Northumberland's bloody border feuds, often besieged and at many times enjoying the patronage of royal visitors. In Tudor days there were additions but the underlying medieval character has always been retained. The 18th and 19th centuries saw decorative extravagances including the lake, garden and grounds laid out by Sir Jeffrey Wyatville, fresh from his triumphs at Windsor Castle. These contrast with the prehistoric Wild Cattle in the park beyond (a separate tour).

Gardens

With romantic grounds, the castle commands breathtaking views of the surrounding countryside. As you walk to the lake you will see, according to season, drifts of snowdrops, daffodils or bluebells and an astonishing display of rhododendrons. This emphasises the restrained formality of the Elizabethan topiary garden, with its intricately clipped hedges of box and yew. Lawns, the formal gardens and woodland walks are all fully open to the public.

Corporate entertainment, lunches, drinks, dinners, wedding ceremonies and receptions.

 Partial.

 By arrangement.

 Avoid Lilburn route, coach parties welcome by prior arrangement.

 Self catering apartments.

Owner
Sir Humphry Wakefield Bt

Contact
Administrator
Chillingham Castle
Northumberland
NE66 5NJ

Tel: 01668 215359
Fax: 01668 215463
E-mail: enquiries@ chillingham-castle.com

Location
MAP 14:L11
OS Ref. NU062 258

45m N of Newcastle between A697 & A1. 2m S of B6348 at Chatton. 6m SE of Wooler.

Rail: Alnmouth or Berwick.

Opening Times
Summer
Easter–31 October
Closed Sats, Castle, Garden & Tearoom, 12 noon–5pm.

Winter
October–April: Groups & Coach Tours any time by appointment. All function activities available.

Admission
Summer
Adult	£7.00
Children	£3.50
Conc.	£5.50
Family Ticket	£18.00

(2 adults and 2 children under 16)

Conference/Function

ROOM	MAX CAPACITY
King James I Room	
Great Hall	100
Minstrels' Hall	60
2 x Drawing Room	
Museum	
Tea Room	35
Lower Gallery	
Upper Gallery	

North East – England

ALNWICK CASTLE 📖

See page 400 for full page entry.

Alnwick Castle, Dining Room

THE ALNWICK GARDEN

DENWICK LANE, ALNWICK, NORTHUMBERLAND NE66 1YU

www.alnwickgarden.com

Tel: 01665 511350   **Fax:** 01665 511351   **email:** info@alnwickgarden.com

Owner: The Alnwick Garden Trust

Experience the making of one of the most unusual and spectacular public gardens of the 21st century, The Alnwick Garden. This exciting new garden, with the Grand Cascade as its centrepiece, as well as the fascinating Poison Garden and enormous Treehouse, mixes the unique and the beautiful in an enchanting landscape.

Location: MAP 14:M11, OS Ref. NU192 132. Just off the A1 at Alnwick, Northumberland.

Open: Apr–Sept: 10am–6pm, Oct–Mar: 10am–4pm, Closed 25 Dec.

Admission: Includes Gift Aid donation: Adult £10, Conc. £7.50 Excludes Gift Aid donation: Adult £9, Conc. £6.50, Child 1p (for up to 4 per adult).

◻☷🅣🔊📶 Licensed. 🎦 By arrangement. 🅿 Cars & coaches. 🐕 Guide dogs only. 🔺❉♿ See website for details.

AYDON CASTLE ⌗

Corbridge, Northumberland NE45 5PJ

Tel: 01434 632450   **E-mail:** customers@english-heritage.org.uk

www.english-heritage.org.uk/aydoncastle

Owner: English Heritage   **Contact:** Visitor Operations Team

One of the finest fortified manor houses dating back from the late 13th century. Set in an area of outstanding natural beauty its survival, intact, can be attributed to its conversion to a farmhouse in the 18th century.

Location: MAP 10:O3, OS Ref. NZ001 663. 1m NE of Corbridge, on minor road off B6321 or A68.

Open: 1 Apr–30 Sept: Thur–Mon, 10am–5pm.

Admission: Adult £3.50, Child £1.80, Conc. £3.00. 15% discount for groups (11+). EH Members free. Opening times and prices are valid until 31st March 2010, after this date details are subject to change please see www.english-heritage.org.uk for the most up-to-date information.

ℹ WC. ◻♿🅿🔊🐕 In grounds, on leads. ♿

The Alnwick Garden

Planning a weekend away in Northumberland?

See Historic Places to Stay

The Otterburn Tower

CRAGSIDE

Rothbury, Morpeth, Northumberland NE65 7PX

Tel: 01669 620333 www.nationaltrust.org.uk

Owner: The National Trust   **Contact:** Property Manager

Revolutionary home of Lord Armstrong, Victorian inventor and landscape genius, Cragside sits on a rocky crag high above the Debdon Burn. Crammed with ingenious gadgets, it was the first house in the world to be lit with hydro-electricity.

Location: MAP 14:L12, OS Ref. NU073 022. ½m NE of Rothbury on B6341.

Open: House: 13-21 Feb & 6-7 Mar, Tues-Sun, 12-4pm; 13 Mar–1 April, 1pm–5pm Tues–Fri, 11am–5pm Sat & Sun; 2–18 April, 11am–5pm Tues–Sun; 20 Apr–28 May, 1pm–5pm Tues–Fri, 11am–5pm Sat & Sun; 29 May–6 Jun, 11am–5pm Tues–Sun; 8 Jun–23 Jul, 1pm–5pm Tues–Fri, 11am–5pm Sat & Sun; 24 Jul–5 Sept, 11am–5pm Tues–Sun; 7 Sept–22 Oct, 1pm–5pm Tues–Fri, 11am–5pm Sat & Sun; 23-31 Oct, 11am–5pm Tues–Sun.

Gardens, Estate, Shop & Restaurant: 28 13-21 Feb & 6-7 Mar, Tues-Sun, 11am-4pm; 13 Mar–31 Oct, 10.30am–5pm Tues–Sun; 2 Nov–19 Dec, 11am–4pm Wed–Sun.

*Admission: House, Gardens & Estate: Adult £13.90, Child (5–17 yrs) £7, Family (2+3) £34.70. Estate & Gardens: Adult £9, Child (5-17 yrs) £4.60, Family (2+3) £21.60, Groups (15+) £6.45. Gardens, Estate, Restaurant & Shop (House closed): Nov–Dec; Adult £4.40, Child (5-17 yrs) £2, Family (2+3) £10.40, Groups (15+) £3.40.

Please note: payment by CASH only at the admission point (to maintain speed of entry). Credit/debit cards can be used for purchases in the restaurant and shop. Includes a voluntary donation but visitors can choose to pay the standard prices displayed at the property and on the website.

In grounds, on leads.

DUNSTANBURGH CASTLE

Grieves Garage, Embleton, Northumberland NE66 3TT

Tel: 01665 576231   **E-mail:** customers@english-heritage.org.uk

www.english-heritage.org.uk/dunstanburgh

Owner: The National Trust   **Guardian:** English Heritage

Contact: Visitor Operations Team

Reached by a beautiful coastal walk, this wonderful 14th-century castle can be admired from afar in its dramatic setting. Built on the most magnificent scale and rivalling any castle of its day, it stands on a remote headland. The surviving ruins include the gatehouse and curtain walls.

Location: MAP 14:M11, OS75, NU257 219. 8m NE of Alnwick.

Open: 1 Apr–30 Sept: daily, 10am–5pm. 1 Oct–1 Nov: daily 10am–4pm. 2 Nov–31 Mar '10: Thur–Mon, 10am–4pm. Closed 24 - 26 December and 1 Jan

Admission: Adult £3.60, Child £1.80, Conc. £3.10. 15% discount for groups (11+). EH Members free. Opening times and prices are valid until 31st March 2010, after this date details are subject to change please see www.english-heritage.org.uk for the most up-to-date information.

P (in Craster village, 1½m walk. A charge is payable.) In grounds, on leads.

EDLINGHAM CASTLE

Edlingham, Alnwick, Northumberland

Tel: 0191 269 1200   **E-mail:** customers@english-heritage.org.uk

www.english-heritage.org.uk/edlingham

Owner: English Heritage   **Contact:** The North East Regional Office

The riverside ruins, principally the solar tower of a manor house, progressively fortified against the Scots during the 14th century.

Location: MAP 14:L11, OS Ref. NU116 092. At E end of Edlingham village, on minor road off B6341 6m SW of Alnwick.

Open: Any reasonable time.

Admission: Free. Opening times and prices are valid until 31st March 2010, after this date details are subject to change please see www.english-heritage.org.uk for the most up-to-date information.

In grounds, on leads.

ETAL CASTLE

Cornhill-on-Tweed, N

Tel: 01890 820332

www.english-herita

Owner: English Herita

A 14th century castle tells the story of the E

Location: MAP 14:K

Open: 1 Apr–30 Sep

Admission: Adult £3 (11+). EH Members fr this date details are most up-to-date info

WC in village.

HERTERTON H

Hartington, Camb

Tel: 01670 774278

Owner/Contact: C

One acre of formal small topiary garde

Location: MAP 10 (brown).

Open: 1 Apr–30 S

Admission: Adult

Unsuitable.

Guided tours f

HO

Tel: 01434

Owner: Th

Contact: V

The most

sites on H

wall, three

Location:

Open: 1 A

24–26 De

Admission

Group dis

after this

for the m

BAMBURGH CASTLE

BAMBURGH, NORTHUMBERLAND NE69 7DF

www.bamburghcastle.com

Tel: 01668 214515   **E-mail:** administrator@bamburghcastle.com

Owner: Trustees Lord Armstrong dec'd.   **Contact:** The Administrator

Welcome to the Royal Seat of the Kings of Northumbria and the Armstrong family home since 1894. These formidable stone walls have witnessed dark tales of royal rebellion, bloody battles, spellbinding legends and millionaire benefactors. With fourteen public rooms and over 3000 artefacts, including arms and armour, porcelain, furniture and artwork. The Armstrong and Aviation artefacts Museum houses a variety of artefacts spanning both World Wars as well as others relating to Lord Armstrongs ship building empire on the Tyne. Each summer sees live archaeology on the country's most important Anglo-Saxon excavation. You can even have a go yourself in the test pit! The summer sees a programme of re-enactments and concerts.

Location: MAP 14:M10, OS Ref. NU184 351. 42m N of Newcastle-upon-Tyne. 20m S of Berwick-upon-Tweed. 6m E of Belford by B1342 from A1 at Belford. Taxi: Parks Taxi 01665 306124. Bus: Bus service 200 yards. Rail: Berwick-upon-Tweed 20m. Air: Newcastle-upon-Tyne 1 hour.

Open: 1 March–31 October Daily, 10am–5pm. Last entry 4.00pm.

Admission: Adult £8, Child (5–15yrs) £4, OAP £7. Groups: Adult £6.40, Child (5–15yrs) £3.20, OAP £5.60. Winter: Group rates only quoted. For group bookings, phone 01668 214515.

No photography in the State Rooms. Partial. WCs. Licensed. By arrangement at any time, min charge out of hours £150. P 100 cars, coaches park on tarmac drive at entrance. Welcome. Guide provided if requested. Guide dogs only.

© English Heritage

BELSAY HALL, CASTLE & GARDENS

BELSAY, Nr PONTELAND, NORTHUMBERLAND NE20 0DX

www.english-heritage.org.uk/belsay

Tel: 01661 881636   **E-mail:** customers@english-heritage.org.uk

Owner: English Heritage   **Contact:** Visitor Operations Team

Belsay has something to captivate everyone. A 14th- century castle with adjoining Jacobean mansion ruins and an austerely classical Greek revival villa designed by Sir Charles Monck, a man inspired by buildings he had seen on his honeymoon in Athens. Thirty acres of spectacular Grade 1 gardens, including magnificent rhododendrons, provide the perfect backdrop. Enter another world in the romantic Quarry garden with ravines, pinnacles and sheer rock faces inspired by the quarries of Sicily.

Location: MAP 10:O2, OS87, NZ086 785. In Belsay 14m (22.4 km) NW of Newcastle on SW of A696. 7m NW of Ponteland. Nearest airport and station is Newcastle.

Open: 1 Apr–30 Sep: daily, 10am–5pm. Closed 19–30 Apr. 1 Oct–1 Nov: daily, 10am–4pm. 2 Nov–31 Mar: Thur–Mon, 10am–4pm. Closed 24–26 Dec and 1 Jan.

Admission: Adult £6.50, Child £3.30, Conc. £5.50, Family £16.30. 15% discount for groups (11+). Opening times and prices are valid until 31st March 2010, after this date details are subject to change please see www.english-heritage.org.uk for the most up-to-date information.

NORTHUMBERLAND

BERWICK-UPON-TWEED BARRACKS & MAIN GUARD ⌗

The Parade, Berwick-upon-Tweed, Northumberland TD15 1DF
Tel: 01289 304493   **E-mail:** customers@english-heritage.org.uk
www.english-heritage.org.uk/berwickbarracks
Owner: English Heritage   **Contact:** Visitor Operations Team
Among the earliest purpose built barracks, these have changed very little since 1717. They house an exhibition 'By Beat of Drum', which recreates scenes such as the barrack room from the life of the British infantryman, the King's Own Scottish Borderers Regimental Museum, the Gymnasium Gallery and the Berwick Museum.
Location: MAP 14:L9, OS Ref. NU001 531. On the Parade, off Church Street, Berwick town centre.
Open: Barracks: 1 Apr–30 Sept: Wed–Sun & Bank Hol Mon, 10am–5pm. Main Guard: Please call for details.
Admission: Adult £3.50, Child £1.80, Conc. £3. 15% discount for groups (11+). Opening times and prices are valid until 31st March 2010, after this date details are subject to change please see www.english-heritage.org.uk for the most up-to-date information.
🔲 🔲 🅿 In town. 🔲 On leads. 🔲 Main Guard.

BERWICK-UPON-TWEED CASTLE & RAMPARTS ⌗

Berwick-upon-Tweed, Northumberland TD15 1DF
Tel: 0191 269 1200   **E-mail:** customers@english-heritage.org.uk
www.english-heritage.org.uk/berwickcastle
Owner: English Heritage   **Contact:** The North East Regional Office
A remarkably complete system of town fortifications consisting of gateways, ramparts and projecting bastions built in the 16th century.
Location: MAP 14:L9, OS Ref. NT993 534. Surrounding Berwick town centre on N bank of River Tweed.
Open: Any reasonable time.
Admission: Free. Opening times and prices are valid until 31st March 2010, after this date details are subject to change please see www.english-heritage.org.uk for the most up-to-date information.
🔲 🅿 (Ramparts) 🔲 🔲

BRINKBURN PRIORY ⌗

Long Framlington, Morpeth, Northumberland NE65 8AR
Tel: 01665 570628   **E-mail:** customers@english-heritage.org.uk
www.english-heritage.org.uk/brinkburn
Owner: English Heritage   **Contact:** Visitor Operations Staff
Completely roofed and restored, this beautiful 12th-century church of the Augustinian priory of Brinkburn survives. Picturesquely set by a bend in the River Coquet, it is reached by a scenic 10-minute walk from the car park.
Location: MAP 14:L12, OS Ref. NZ116 983. 4½ m SE of Rothbury off B6344 5m W of A1.
Open: 1 Apr–30 Sept: Thur–Mon, 11am–4pm.
Admission: Adult £3, Child £1.50, Conc. £2.60. 15% discount for groups (11+). EH Members free. Opening times and prices are subject to change please see www.english-heritage.org.uk for the most up-to-date information.
🔲 🅿 🔲 On leads. 🔲

Aydon Castle

TYNE & WEAR

ARBEIA ROMAN FORT

Baring Street, South Shields, Tyne & Wear NE33 2BB
Tel: 0191 456 1369   **Fax:** 0191 427 6862
Owner: South Tyneside Metropolitan Borough Council   **Contact:** The Curator
Managed by: Tyne & Wear Museums
More than 1,500 years on, the remains at Arbeia represent the most extensively excavated example of a military supply base anywhere in the Roman Empire. Museum includes weapons, jewellery and tombstones.
Location: MAP 11:A3, OS Ref. NZ365 679. Near town centre and Metro Station.
Open: Easter–Sept: Mon–Sat: 10am–5.30pm, Suns, 1–5pm. Open BH Mons. Oct–Easter: daily except Suns, 10am–3.30pm. Closed 25/26 Dec, 1 Jan & Good Friday.
Admission: Free, except for Time Quest Gallery: Adult £1.50, Child/Conc. £1.

BEDE'S WORLD MUSEUM

Church Bank, Jarrow, Tyne & Wear NE32 3DY
Tel: 0191 489 2106   **Fax:** 0191 428 2361   **E-mail:** visitor.info@bedesworld.co.uk
Managed by: Bede's World   **Contact:** Visitor Services
Discover the world of the Venerable Bede, who lived and worked at the monastery of Wearmouth-Jarrow 1300 years ago.
Location: MAP 11:A3, OS Ref. NZ339 652. Just off A19, S end of Tyne Tunnel. 300yds N of St Paul's.
Open: Apr–Oct: Mon–Sat, 10am–5.30pm, Suns, 12 noon–5.30pm. Nov–Mar: Mon–Sat, 10am–4.30pm, Suns, 12 noon–4.30pm. Open BH Mons, closed Good Fri. Tel for Christmas opening times.
Admission: Adult £5.50, Child/Conc. £3.50, Family (2+2) £12.50. Groups by arrangement.

BESSIE SURTEES HOUSE ⌗

41–44 Sandhill, Newcastle, Tyne & Wear NE1 3JF
Tel: 0191 269 1200   **E-mail:** customers@english-heritage.org.uk
www.english-heritage.org.uk/bessiesurtees
Owner: English Heritage   **Contact:** Reception
These two five-storey 16th and 17th-century merchants' houses are fine examples of Jacobean domestic architecture, with splendid period interiors. Best known as the scene of the elopement of Bessie with John Scott, later Lord Chancellor of England. An exhibition illustrating the history of the houses is on the first floor.
Location: MAP 10:P3, OS Ref. NZ252 638. Riverside.
Open: All year: Mon–Fri: 10am–4pm. Closed BHs & 24 Dec–7 Jan.
Admission: Free. Opening times and prices are valid until 31st March 2010, after this date details are subject to change please see www.english-heritage.org.uk for the most up-to-date information.
ℹ WC. 🔲 🔲 🔲 🔲

GIBSIDE 🔲

Nr Rowlands Gill, Burnopfield, Newcastle-upon-Tyne NE16 6BG
Tel: 01207 541820   **E-mail:** gibside@nationaltrust.org.uk   **www.nationaltrust.org.uk**
Owner: The National Trust   **Contact:** The Property Manager
Gibside is one of the finest 18th century designed landscapes in the north of England. The Chapel was built to James Paine's design soon after 1760. Outstanding example of Georgian architecture approached along a terrace with an oak avenue. Walk along the River Derwent through woodland.
Location: MAP 10:P3, OS Ref. NZ172 583. 6m SW of Gateshead, 20m NW of Durham. Entrance on B6314 between Burnopfield and Rowlands Gill.
Open: Gardens, Walks & Stables: 1 Jan–7 Mar: daily, 10am–4pm. 8 Mar–31 Oct: daily, 10am–6pm. 1 Nov–31 Dec: daily, 10am–4pm. Chapel: 13 Mar–31 Oct, 11am–4.30pm. Stables: 1 Jan–7 Mar, 11am–3.30pm, 8 Mar–31 Oct, 11am–4.30pm. 1 Nov–31 Dec: daily, 11am–3.30pm. Larder, Shop & Tearoom: 1 Jan - 7 Mar, daily 11am-3.30pm; 8 Mar–31 Oct, daily, 11am-4.30pm; 1 Nov-31 Dec, daily, 11am-3.30pm. Closed 24 & 25 Dec.
***Admission:** Adult £6.50, Child £4, Family (2+4) £18.50, Family (1+3) £13. Booked groups £5.20. *includes a voluntary donation but visitors can choose to pay the standard prices displayed at the property and on the website.
🔲 🔲 🔲 🔲 🔲 🔲 By arrangement. 🅿 Limited for coaches. 🔲 🔲 On leads, in grounds. 🔲 🔲 🔲

Gibside

ST PAUL'S MONASTERY ⌗

Jarrow, Tyne & Wear
Tel: 0191 489 7052   **E-mail:** customers@english-heritage.org.uk
www.english-heritage.org.uk/stpauls
Owner: English Heritage   **Contact:** The Regional Office – 0191 269 1200
The home of the Venerable Bede in the 7th and 8th centuries, partly surviving as the chancel of the parish church. It has become one of the best understood Anglo-Saxon monastic sites.
Location: MAP 11:A3, OS Ref. NZ339 652. In Jarrow, on minor road N of A185. 300yds S of Bede's World.
Open: Monastery ruins: Any reasonable time.
Admission: Free. Opening times and prices are valid until 31st March 2010, after this date details are subject to change please see www.english-heritage.org.uk for the most up-to-date information.

SEGEDUNUM ROMAN FORT, BATHS & MUSEUM

Buddle Street, Wallsend, NE28 6HR

Tel: 0191 236 9347 **Fax:** 0191 295 5858

Explore life on the Roman frontier as it was 1,800 years ago, at the most completely excavated fort on Hadrian's Wall. See reconstructions of a section of the Wall together with an impressive Roman military bath house building.

Location: MAP 11:A3, OS Ref. N2 301 660.

Open: 1 Apr–31 Oct: daily, 10am–5pm. 1 Nov–31 Mar: daily, 10am–3pm.

Admission: Adults £3.95, Child (16 and under) Free. Conc. £2.25. Groups: Adult £3.20, Conc. £1.80.

SOUTER LIGHTHOUSE ✾

Coast Road, Whitburn, Sunderland, Tyne & Wear SR6 7NH

Tel: 0191 529 3161 **E-mail:** souter@nationaltrust.org.uk

www.nationaltrust.org.uk

Owner: The National Trust **Contact:** The House Manager

Dramatic red and white lighthouse tower on rugged coast. Built in 1871, the first to be powered by alternating electric current.

Location: MAP 11:A3, OS Ref. NZ408 641. 2½m S of South Shields on A183. 5m N of Sunderland.

Open: 13 Mar–31 Oct: daily except Fri (open Good Fri), 11am–5pm. Last adm 4.30pm.

*Admission: Adult £5.10, Child £3.30, Family £13.35. Booked Groups (10+): Adult £4.20, Child £2.90. NT members Free: membership available from shop. *includes a voluntary donation but visitors can choose to pay the standard prices displayed at the property and on the website.

▢ Ⓣ Ⓖ Partial. WCs. ▯ Ⓣ Ⓘ Ⓟ ▮ Ⓖ In grounds, on leads.

TYNEMOUTH PRIORY & CASTLE ⌗

North Pier, Tynemouth, Tyne & Wear NE30 4BZ

Tel: 0191 257 1090 **E-mail:** customers@english-heritage.org.uk

www.english-heritage.org.uk/tynemouth

Owner: English Heritage **Contact:** Visitor Operations Team

Set on a steep headland, Tynemouth has always been as much a fortress as a religious site, playing its role in the Civil War and both World Wars. The Life in the Stronghold exhibition tells the story of the site's 2000 year history from its original beginnings as an Anglo-Saxon settlement.

Location: MAP 11:A2, OS Ref. NZ373 694. In Tynemouth near North Pier.

Open: 1 Apr–30 Jun & 1-30 Sept: daily, 10am–5pm. 1 Jul–31 Aug: daily, 10am–6pm. 1 Oct–31 Mar '10: Thur–Mon, 10am–4pm. Closed 24–26 Dec & 1 Jan. Gun Battery: Access limited, please ask site staff for details.

Admission: Adult £4, Child £2, Conc. £3.40, Family £10. 15% discount for groups (11+). EH Members free. Opening times and prices are valid until 31st March 2010, after this date details are subject to change please see www.english-heritage.org.uk for the most up-to-date information.

▢ Ⓣ Ⓖ Ⓘ By arrangement. ▮ Ⓖ In grounds, on leads. ✳ ▯

Tynemouth Priory

WASHINGTON OLD HALL ✾

The Avenue, Washington Village, Washington, Tyne & Wear NE38 7LE

Tel: 0191 416 6879 **E-mail:** washington.oldhall@nationaltrust.org.uk

www.nationaltrust.org.uk

Owner: The National Trust **Contact:** The Manager

Delightful 17th century house incorporating parts of the medieval home of George Washington's ancestors, their surname of "Washington" was taken from here. Furnished with Delftware, paintings and oak furniture. The knot and parterre gardens lead you to the tranquil wildflower nut orchard. This little gem is well worth a visit.

Location: MAP 11:A3, OS Ref. NZ312 566. In Washington on E side of The Avenue. 5m W of Sunderland (2m from A1), S of Tyne Tunnel, follow signs for Washington then A1231 – follow brown signs to Washington Old Hall. The Old Hall is on The Avenue next to the church on the hill: Washington Village.

Open: House: 14 Mar–31 Oct: Sun–Wed, 11am–5pm. Garden: as house, 10am–5pm. Tearoom: as house, 11am–4pm. Open Good Fri & Easter Sat.

*Admission: Adult £5.10, Child £3.30, Family £13.35. Booked groups (10+): Adult £4.20, Child £2.90. NT Membership available from reception. *includes a voluntary donation but visitors can choose to pay the standard prices displayed at the property and on the website.

Ⓘ▢Ⓣ Conferences. Ⓖ ▯ Ⓘ By arrangement. Ⓟ Limited. ▮ Ⓖ In grounds, on leads. ▲

Washington Old Hall

Torosay Castle & Gardens, Isle Of Mull
© Phil McDermott

Scotland

First time visitors to Scotland can only scratch the surface of its cultural and social history. Edinburgh Castle is, of course, Scotland's most famous castle but there are so many others which merit a visit: fairytale Dunrobin on the east coast, Dunvegan on the Isle of Skye and Cawdor, home of the Thanes of Cawdor from the 14th century.

Cawdor Castle, Nairn

WESTERN ISLES

HIGHLANDS & SKYE

GRAMPIAN HIGHLANDS

SHETLAND ISLANDS

ORKNEY ISLANDS

PERTHSHIRE /FIFE

WEST HIGHLANDS & ISLANDS

GREATER GLASGOW

EDINBURGH

BORDERS

SOUTH WEST SCOTLAND

Drummond Castle Gardens, Perthshire

Inveraray Castle, Argyll

Mellerstain House, Berwickshire

■ Owner
His Grace the Duke of Roxburghe

■ Contact
Charlotte Newton
Castle Administrator
Roxburghe Estates Office
Kelso
Roxburghshire
Scotland TD5 7SF

Tel: 01573 223333
Fax: 01573 226056
E-mail: cnewton@
floorscastle.com

■ Location
MAP 14:J10
OS Ref. NT711 347

From South A68, A698.

From North A68, A697/9
In Kelso follow signs.

Bus: Kelso Bus Station 1m.

Rail: Berwick 20m.

■ Opening Times
Summer
Easter Weekend the 1
May – 31 October: Daily:
11am–5pm. Last
admission 4.30pm.

Winter
November–March Closed
to the general public,
available for events.

Please check our website
for details.

■ Admission
2009 (may be subject to
change in 2010)

Adult	£7.50
Child* (5–16yrs)	£3.50
OAP/Student	£6.50
Family	£19.00
Groups (20+)	
Adult	£6.00
Child* (5–16yrs)	£3.00
OAP/Student	£5.00

*Under 5yrs Free.

■ Special Events
Snowdrop Festival,
Easter Eggstravaganza,
Floors Castle Horse Trials,
Massed Pipe Bands Day.

Please check our website
for details.

Conference/Function

ROOM	SIZE	MAX CAPACITY
Dining Rm	18m x 7m	150
Ballroom	21m x 8m	150

FLOORS CASTLE

www.floorscastle.com

Floors Castle, home of the Duke and Duchess of Roxburghe, is situated in the heart of the Scottish Border Country. It is reputedly the largest inhabited castle in Scotland. Designed by William Adam, who was both masterbuilder and architect, for the first Duke of Roxburghe, building started in 1721. It was the present Duke's great-great-grand-father James, the 6th Duke, who embellished the plain Adam features of the building. In about 1849 Playfair, letting his imagination and talent run riot, transformed the castle, creating a multitude of spires and domes. The apartments now display the outstanding collection of French 17th and 18th century furniture, magnificent tapestries, Chinese and European porcelain and many other fine works of art. Many of the treasures in the castle today were collected by Duchess May, American wife of the 8th Duke. The castle has been seen on cinema screens worldwide in the film Greystoke, as the home of Tarzan, the Earl of Greystoke.

Gardens
The extensive parkland and gardens overlooking the River Tweed provide a variety of wooded walks. The garden centre and walled gardens contain splendid herbaceous borders and in the outer walled garden a parterre to commemorate the Millennium can be seen. An excellent children's playground and picnic area are very close to the castle.

Gala dinners, conferences, product launches, 4 x 4 driving, incentive groups, highland games and other promotional events. Extensive park, helicopter pad, fishing, clay pigeon and pheasant shooting. No photography inside the castle.

Exclusive lunches & dinners

Partial. WCs.

Licensed

Licensed

By arrangement

Unlimited for cars, 100 yds away, coach park 150 yds. Coaches can be driven to the entrance. Lunch or tea for coach drivers.

Welcome, guide provided. Playground facilities.

On leads, in grounds.

MANDERSTON 🏛

www.manderston.co.uk

Owner
The Lord Palmer

Contact
The Lord and Lady Palmer
Manderston
Duns
Berwickshire
Scotland TD11 3PP

Tel: 01361 883450
Secretary: 01361 882636
Fax: 01361 882010
E-mail: palmer@
manderston.co.uk

Location
MAP 14:K9
OS Ref. NT810 544

From Edinburgh
47m, 1hr.
1½ m E of Duns on
A6105.

Bus: 400 yds.

Rail: Berwick
Station 12m.

Taxi: 07970 221821.

Airport: Edinburgh or
Newcastle both
60m or 80 mins.

Opening Times
Summer
6 May–26 September
Thurs & Sun, 1.30–5pm
Last entry 4.15pm.
Gardens: 11.30am–dusk.

BH Mons, late May
& late August. Gardens
open until dusk.

Groups welcome all year
by appointment.

Winter
September–May
Group visits welcome
by appointment.

Admission
House & Grounds
Adult   £8.50
Child (under 12yrs)   Free
Conc.   £8.50

Groups (15+)   £8.00
(£8.50 outside opening
days).

**Grounds only including
Stables & Marble Dairy**
£4.50

On days when the house
is closed to the public,
groups viewing by
appointment will have
personally conducted
tours. The Gift Shop will
be open. On these
occasions reduced party
rates (except for school
children) will not apply.
Group visits (15+) other
than open days are
£8.50pp. Snaffles
Tearoom open on Open
Days or by arrangement.

Manderston, together with its magnificent stables, stunning marble dairy and 56 acres of immaculate gardens, forms an ensemble which must be unique in Britain today.

The house was completely rebuilt between 1903 and 1905, with no expense spared. Visitors are able to see not only the sumptuous State rooms and bedrooms, decorated in the Adam manner, but also all the original domestic offices, in a truly 'upstairs downstairs' atmosphere. Manderston boasts a unique and recently restored silver staircase.

There is a special museum with a nostalgic display of valuable tins made by Huntly and Palmer from 1868 to the present day. Winner of the AA/NPI Bronze Award UK 1994.

Gardens
Outside, the magnificence continues and the combination of formal gardens and picturesque landscapes is a major attraction unique amongst Scottish houses. The stables, still in use, have been described by *Horse and Hound* as 'probably the finest in all the wide world'.

Manderston has often been used as a film location, most recently it was the star of Channel 4's *'The Edwardian Country House'*.

ℹ Corporate & incentives venue. Ideal retreat: business groups, think-tank weekends. Fashion shows, air displays, archery, clay pigeon shooting, equestrian events, garden parties, shows, rallies, filming, product launches and marathons. Two airstrips for light aircraft, approx 5m, grand piano, billiard table, pheasant shoots, sea angling, salmon fishing, stabling, cricket pitch, tennis court, lake. Nearby: 18-hole golf course, indoor swimming pool, squash court. No photography in house.

📷

🍸 Available. Buffets, lunches and dinners. Wedding receptions.

♿ Special parking available outside the House.

☕ Snaffles Tearoom – home made lunches, teas, cakes and tray bakes. Can be booked in advance, menus on request.

👤 Included. Available in French. Guides in rooms. If requested, the owner may meet groups. Tour time 1¼ hrs.

P 400 cars 125yds from house, 30 coaches 5yds from house. Appreciated if group fees are paid by one person.

🎖 Welcome. Guide can be provided. Biscuit Tin Museum of particular interest.

🐕 Grounds only, on leads.

🛏 6 twin, 4 double.

❄

Conference/Function

ROOM	SIZE	MAX CAPACITY
Dining Rm	22' x 35'	100
Ballroom	34' x 21'	150
Hall	22' x 38'	130
Drawing Rm	35' x 21'	150

■ **Owner**

Historic Scotland

■ **Contact**

Castle Manager
Castle Hill, Edinburgh
EH1 2NG

Tel: 0131 225 9846

■ **Location**

MAP 21
OS NT252 736

At the top of the Royal Mile in Edinburgh. Rail: Edinburgh Waverley Station.

■ **Opening Times**

April–September: daily, 9.30am–6pm.

October–March, daily, 9.30am–5pm.

Last ticket 45 mins before closing.

■ **Admission**

Prices range from:

Adult £11.00-£13.00
Child £5.50–£6.50
Conc. £8.00–10.50

(2009 prices)

Visit www.edinburghcastle gov.uk for details.

Buy tickets on-line to beat the queues!

EDINBURGH CASTLE

www.edinburghcastle.gov.uk

Edinburgh Castle, built on the 340 million-year-old remains of an extinct volcano, dominates the skyline of Scotland's capital city just as it has dominated the country's history.

The 'stronghold of Eidyn' was first recorded before 600AD, and by the Middle Ages, it had become a mighty fortification and the favoured residence of Scotland's kings and queens. In 1140, it became the first recorded meeting place of the assembly now known as the Scottish Parliament. And in 1566, it was the birthplace of the only child of Mary Queen of Scots; a son who grew up to unite the crowns of Scotland and England.

The castle boasts a wealth of attractions including: The Honours of Scotland - the nation's crown jewels; The Stone of Destiny - the coronation stone of the ancient kings of Scots; The Great Hall, Laich Hall, King's Dining Room and St Margaret's Chapel - remarkable medieval rooms and buildings where royalty and great nobles wined, dined and worshipped; The Prisons of War Experience – showing what 18th century prison life was like for military prisoners held here; The National War Memorial - commemorating those who have died in conflict from World War I onwards; Mons Meg - a huge medieval siege gun; The One O'clock Gun - fired daily, except the Sabbath and certain holidays, as a time signal; The Dog Cemetery – the last resting place of regimental mascots and officers' pets.

[i] Parking only available for drivers with a blue disabled badge.

Private evening hire.

WCs.

Licensed.

In 8 languages.

€

HOPETOUN HOUSE

www.hopetounhouse.com

Hopetoun House is a unique gem of Europe's architectural heritage and undoubtedly 'Scotland's Finest Stately Home'. Situated on the shores of the Firth of Forth, it is one of the most splendid examples of the work of Scottish architects Sir William Bruce and William Adam. The interior of the house, with opulent gilding and classical motifs, reflects the aristocratic grandeur of the early 18th century, whilst its magnificent parkland has fine views across the Forth to the hills of Fife. The house is approached from the Royal Drive, used only by members of the Royal Family, notably King George IV in 1822 and Her Majesty Queen Elizabeth II in 1988.

Hopetoun is really two houses in one, the oldest part of the house was designed by Sir William Bruce and built between 1699 and 1707. It shows some of the finest examples in Scotland of carving, wainscotting and ceiling painting. In 1721 William Adam started enlarging the house by adding the magnificent façade, colonnades and grand State apartments which were the focus for social life and entertainment in the 18th century.

The house is set in 100 acres of rolling parkland including fine woodland walks, the red deer park, the spring garden with a profusion of wild flowers, and numerous picturesque picnic spots.

Hopetoun has been home of the Earls of Hopetoun, later created Marquesses of Linlithgow, since it was built in 1699 and in 1974 a charitable trust was created to preserve the house with its historic contents and surrounding landscape for the benefit of the public for all time.

i Private functions, special events, antiques fairs, concerts, Scottish gala evenings, conferences, wedding ceremonies and receptions, grand piano, helicopter landing. No smoking or flash photography in house.

Y Receptions, gala dinners.

& Partial.

☕ Licensed.

👤 By arrangement.

P Close to the house for cars and coaches. Book if possible, allow 1–2hrs for visit (min).

Special tours of house and/or grounds for different age/ interest groups.

No dogs in house, on leads in grounds.

■ Owner
Hopetoun House
Preservation Trust

■ Contact
Piers de Salis
Hopetoun House
South Queensferry
Edinburgh
West Lothian EH30 9SL

Tel: 0131 331 2451
Fax: 0131 319 1885
E-mail: marketing@
hopetounhouse.com

■ Location
MAP 13:F7
OS Ref. NT089 790

2½m W of Forth Road Bridge.

12m W of Edinburgh (25 mins. drive).

34m E of Glasgow (50 mins. drive).

■ Opening Times
Summer
Easter – End September:
Daily, 10.30am–5pm.
Last admission 4pm.

Winter
By appointment only for Groups (20+).

■ Admission
House & Grounds

Adult	£8.00
Child (5–16yrs)*	£4.25
Conc/Student	£7.00
Family (2+2)	£22.00
Additional Child	£3.00
Groups	£7.00

Grounds only

Adult	£3.70
Child (5–16yrs)*	£2.20
Conc/Student	£3.20
Family (2+2)	£10.00
Groups	£3.20

School Visits

Child	£5.50
Teachers	Free

*Under 5yrs Free.

Winter group rates on request.

Admission to Tearoom Free.

■ Special Events
July 25
Summer Fair

November 26–28
Christmas Shopping Fair

Conference/Function

ROOM	SIZE	MAX CAPACITY
Ballroom	92' x 35'	300
Tapestry Rm	37' x 24'	100
Red Drawing Rm	44' x 24'	100
State Dining Rm	39' x 23'	20
Stables	92' x 22'	200

ARNISTON HOUSE 🏛
GOREBRIDGE, MIDLOTHIAN EH23 4RY

www.arniston-house.co.uk

Tel/Fax: 01875 830515 **E-mail:** arnistonhouse@btconnect.com
Owner: Mrs A Dundas-Bekker **Contact:** Mrs H Dundas
Magnificent William Adam mansion started in 1726. Fine plasterwork, Scottish portraiture, period furniture and other fascinating contents. Beautiful country setting beloved by Sir Walter Scott.
Location: MAP 13:H9, OS Ref. NT326 595. Off B6372, 1m from A7, Temple direction.
Open: May & Jun: Tue & Wed; 1 Jul–12 Sept: Tue, Wed & Sun, guided tours at 2pm & 3.30pm. Pre-arranged groups (10–50) accepted all year.
Admission: Adult £6, Child £3, Conc. £5.
ℹ️ No inside photography. ♿ Partial. WCs. 🎫 Obligatory. 🅿️ Limited for coaches
🐕 In grounds, on leads ✳️

AMISFIELD MAINS

Nr Haddington, East Lothian EH41 3SA
Tel: 01875 870201 **Fax:** 01875 870620
Owner: Wemyss and March Estates Management Co Ltd **Contact:** M Andrews
Georgian farmhouse with gothic barn and cottage.
Location: MAP 14:I8, OS Ref. NT526 755. Between Haddington and East Linton on A199.
Open: Exterior only: By appointment, Wemyss and March Estates Office, Longniddry, East Lothian EH32 0PY.
Admission: Please contact for details.

BEANSTON

Nr Haddington, East Lothian EH41 3SB
Tel: 01875 870201 **Fax:** 01875 870620
Owner: Wemyss and March Estates Management Co Ltd **Contact:** M Andrews
Georgian farmhouse with Georgian orangery.
Location: MAP 14:I8, OS Ref. NT546 763. Between Haddington and East Linton on A199.
Open: Exterior only: By appointment, Wemyss and March Estates Office, Longniddry, East Lothian EH32 0PY.
Admission: Please contact for details.

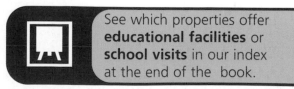

See which properties offer **educational facilities** or **school visits** in our index at the end of the book.

BLACKNESS CASTLE 🏰

Blackness EH49 7NH
Tel: 01506 834807 www.historic-scotland.gov.uk
Owner: In the care of Historic Scotland **Contact:** The Steward
One of Scotland's most important strongholds. Built in the 14th century and strengthened in the 16th century as an artillery fortress, it has been a royal castle, prison armaments depot and film location for Hamlet. It stands on a promontory in the Firth of Forth.
Location: MAP 13:F7, OS Ref. NT055 803. 4m NE of Linlithgow on the Firth of Forth, off the A904.
Open: 1 Apr–30 Sept: daily, 9.30am–5.30pm, 1 Oct–31 Mar 9.30am–4.30pm, closed Thurs & Fri. Last ticket 30 mins before closing.
Admission: Adult £4.20, Child £2.10, Conc. £3.20 (2009 prices).
ℹ️ Picnic area. bicycle racks 🖼 🅿️ 🍴 🐕 ✳️ €

CRAIGMILLAR CASTLE 🏰

Edinburgh EH16 4SY
Tel: 0131 661 4445 www.historic-scotland.gov.uk
Owner: In the care of Historic Scotland **Contact:** The Steward
Mary, Queen of Scots fled to Craigmillar after the murder of Rizzio. This well preserved medieval castle was built around an L-plan tower house. It also inlcudes a courtyard, gardens and a range of private rooms linked to the hall of the old tower.
Location: MAP 13:H8, OS Ref. NT286 708. 2½m SE of Edinburgh off the A7.
Open: 1 Apr–30 Sept: daily, 9.30am–5.30pm. 1 Oct–31 Mar 9.30am–4.30pm, closed Thurs & Fri. Last ticket 30 mins before closing.
Admission: Adult £4.20, Child £2.10, Conc. £3.20 (2009 prices).
ℹ️ Picnic area. bicycle racks 🖼 Partial. WCs. 🅿️ 🍴 🐕 ✳️ €

CRICHTON CASTLE 🏰

Pathhead EH37 5XA
Tel: 01875 320017 www.historic-scotland.gov.uk
Owner: In the care of Historic Scotland **Contact:** The Steward
Built as the lordly residence of the Crichtons, the castle later became home to the earls of Bothwell. This large and sophisticated castle has a spectacular Italian style façade added by the Earl of Bothwell in the 16th century. Mary Queen of Scots attended a wedding here.
Location: MAP 13:H8, OS Ref. NT380 612. 2½m SSW of Pathhead off the A68.
Open: 1 Apr–30 Sept: daily, 9.30am–5.30pm. Last ticket 5pm.
Admission: Adult £3.70, Child £1.85, Conc. £3.00 (2009 prices).
ℹ️ Closes for lunch 🖼 🐕 On leads 🅿️ €

DALMENY HOUSE 🏛 *See page 425 for full page entry.*

DUNGLASS COLLEGIATE CHURCH 🏰

Cockburnspath
Tel: 0131 668 8600 www.historic-scotland.gov.uk
Owner: In the care of Historic Scotland
Founded in 1450 for a college of canons by Sir Alexander Hume. A handsome cross-shaped building with vaulted nave, choir and transepts.
Location: MAP 14:J8, OS67 NT766 718. 1m NW of Cockburnspath off the A1.
Open: All year.
Admission: Free.
🐕 ✳️

EDINBURGH CASTLE 🏰 *See page 426 for full page entry.*

THE GEORGIAN HOUSE ♛

7 Charlotte Square, Edinburgh EH2 4DR
Tel: 0131 243 9300
Owner: The National Trust for Scotland
A good example of the neo-classical 'palace front'. Three floors are furnished as they would have been around 1796. There is an array of china and silver, pictures and furniture, gadgets and utensils.
Location: MAP 21, OS Ref. NT247 738. In Charlotte Square.

©Historic Scotland Photographic Library

DIRLETON CASTLE & GARDEN 🏛

DIRLETON, EAST LOTHIAN EH39 5ER

Tel: 01620 850330 **www.historic-scotland.gov.uk**

Owner: In the care of Historic Scotland **Contact:** The Steward

The oldest part of this romantic castle dates from the 13th century, when it was built by the De Vaux family. The renowned gardens, first laid out in the 16th century, now include a magnificent Arts and Crafts herbaceous border (the longest in the world) and a re-created Victorian Garden. In the picturesque village of Dirleton.

Location: MAP 14:I7, OS Ref. NT516 839. In Dirleton, 3m W of North Berwick on the A198.

Open: Apr–Sept: daily, 9.30am–5.30pm. Oct–Mar: daily, 9.30am–4.30pm. Last ticket 30 mins before closing.

Admission: Adult £4.70, Child £2.35, Conc. £3.70 (2009 prices).

ℹ️ Picnic area 🔲 🔲 P 🔲 Free if booked. 🔲 On leads 🔲 €

GOSFORD HOUSE 🏛

LONGNIDDRY, EAST LOTHIAN EH32 0PX

Tel: 01875 870201

Owner/Contact: The Earl of Wemyss

Though the core of the house is Robert Adam, the family home is in the South Wing built by William Young in 1890. This contains the celebrated Marble Hall and a fine collection of paintings and works of art. The house is set in extensive policies with an 18th century Pleasure Garden and Ponds. Greylag geese and swans abound.

Location: MAP 14:17, OS Ref. NT453 786. Off A198 2m NE of Longniddry.

Open: 5 Aug–16 Sep: Thurs–Sun, 1–4pm.

Admission: Adult £6, Child £1.

P 🔲 In grounds, on leads.

GLADSTONE'S LAND 🏛

477b Lawnmarket, Royal Mile, Edinburgh EH1 2NT

Tel: 0131 243 9300

Owner: The National Trust for Scotland

Gladstone's Land was the home of a prosperous Edinburgh merchant in the 17th century. Decorated and furnished to give visitors an impression of life in Edinburgh's Old Town some 300 years ago.

Location: MAP 21, OS Ref. NT255 736. In Edinburgh's Royal Mile, near the castle.

HAILES CASTLE 🏛

East Linton

Tel: 0131 668 8800 **www.historic-scotland.gov.uk**

Owner: In the care of Historic Scotland

Beautifully-sited ruin incorporating a fortified manor of the 13th century. It was extended in the 14th and 15th centuries. There are two vaulted pit prisons.

Location: MAP 14:I8, OS Ref. NT575 758. 1.5 m SW of East Linton off the A1.

Open: All year.

Admission: Free.

P 🔲

HARELAW FARMHOUSE

Nr Longniddry, East Lothian EH32 0PH

Tel: 01875 870201 **Fax:** 01875 870620

Owner: Wemyss and March Estates Management Co Ltd **Contact:** M Andrews

Early 19th century 2-storey farmhouse built as an integral part of the steading. Dovecote over entrance arch.

Location: MAP 14:I8, OS Ref. NT450 766. Between Longniddry and Drem on B1377.

Open: Exteriors only: By appointment, Wemyss and March Estates Office, Longniddry, East Lothian EH32 0PY.

Admission: Please contact for details.

HOPETOUN HOUSE 🏛 *See page 427 for full page entry.*

HOUSE OF THE BINNS 🏛

Linlithgow, West Lothian EH49 7NA

Tel: 0131 243 9300

Owner: The National Trust for Scotland

17th century house, home of the Dalyells, one of Scotland's great families, since 1612.

Location: MAP 13:F7, OS Ref. NT051 786. Off A904, 15m W of Edinburgh. 3m E of Linlithgow.

LIBERTON HOUSE

73 Liberton Drive, Edinburgh EH16 6NP

Tel: 0131 467 7777 **Fax:** 0131 467 7774 **E-mail:** practice@grovesraines.com

Owner/Contact: Nicholas Groves-Raines

Built around 1600 for the Littles of Liberton, this harled L-plan house has been carefully restored by the current architect owner using original detailing and extensive restoration of the principal structure. Public access restricted to the Great Hall and Old Kitchen. The restored garden layout suggests the original and there is a late 17th century lectern doocot by the entrance drive.

Location: MAP 13:H8, OS Ref. NT267 694. 73 Liberton Drive, Edinburgh.

Open: 1 Mar–31 Oct: 10am–4.30pm, by prior appointment only.

Admission: Free.

🔲 Unsuitable. P Limited. 🔲

LENNOXLOVE HOUSE 🏛

HADDINGTON, EAST LOTHIAN EH41 4NZ

www.lennoxlove.com

Tel: 01620 828614 **Fax:** 01620 825112 **Email:** ken-buchanan@lennoxlove.com
Owner: Lennoxlove House Ltd **Contact:** Kenneth Buchanan, General Manager
Service, Style and Seclusion. House to many of Scotland's finest artefacts, including
the Death Mask of Mary, Queen of Scots, furniture and porcelain collected by the
Douglas, Hamilton and Stewart families. Open to the public and available for events,
the House lends itself perfectly to intimate parties offering 11 luxury suites for an
overnight stay.
Location: MAP 14:I8, OS Ref. NT515 721. 18m E of Edinburgh, 1m S of Haddington.
Open: Easter–Oct: Weds, Thurs & Suns, 1.30-4pm. Guided Tours.

LINLITHGOW PALACE 🏛

LINLITHGOW, WEST LOTHIAN EH49 7AL

Tel: 01506 842896 **www.historic-scotland.gov.uk**
Owner: Historic Scotland **Contact:** The Steward
The magnificent remains of a great royal palace set in a picturesque park, beside
Linlithgow Loch. A favoured residence of the Stewart monarchs, James V and his
daughter Mary, Queen of Scots were born here. Bonnie Prince Charlie stayed here
during his bid to regain the British crown.
Location: MAP 13:F8, OS Ref. NT003 774. In the centre of Linlithgow off the M9.
Open: Apr–Sept: daily, 9.30am–5.30pm. Oct–Mar: daily, 9.30am–4.30pm. Last ticket
45 mins before closing.
Admission: Adult £5.20, Child £2.60, Conc. £4.20. (2009 prices)
ℹ️ Picnic area. Bicycle rack. 🔲 🔲 Partial. WCs. 🅿️ Cars only. 🔲
🐕 On leads ❄ 🔲 €

The Royal Yacht Britannia. The Drawing Room.

NEWLISTON 🏛

Kirkliston, West Lothian EH29 9EB
Tel: 0131 333 3231
Owner/Contact: Mrs Caroline Maclachlan
Late Robert Adam house. 18th century designed landscape, rhododendrons, azaleas and
water features. On Sundays there is a ride-on steam model railway from 2–5pm.
Location: MAP 13:G8, OS Ref. NT110 735. 8m W of Edinburgh, 3m S of Forth Road
Bridge, off B800.
Open: 1 May–4 Jun: Wed–Sun, 2–6pm. Also by appointment.
Admission: Adult £3, Conc. £2.
🐕 In grounds, on leads.

PALACE OF HOLYROODHOUSE

Edinburgh EH8 8DX
Tel: 0131 556 5100 **E-mail:** bookinginfo@royalcollection.org.uk
Owner: Official Residence of Her Majesty The Queen
Contact: Ticket Sales & Information Office
The Palace of Holyroodhouse, the official residence in Scotland of Her Majesty The
Queen, stands at the end of Edinburgh's Royal Mile against the spectacular backdrop of
Arthur's Seat. The Royal Apartments are used by The Queen for State ceremonies and
official entertaining. They are finely decorated with magnificent works of art from the
Royal Collection.
Location: MAP 21, OS Ref. NT269 739. Central Edinburgh, end of Royal Mile.
Open: Contact information office.
Admission: Contact information office.

PRESTON MILL 🦅

East Linton, East Lothian EH40 3DS
Tel: 0131 243 9300
Owner: The National Trust for Scotland **Contact:** Property Manager
For centuries there has been a mill on this site and the present one operated
commercially until 1957.
Location: MAP 14:I7, OS Ref. NT590 770. Off the A1, in East Linton, 23m E of Edinburgh.

RED ROW

Aberlady, East Lothian
Tel: 01875 870201 **Fax:** 01875 870620
Owner: Wemyss & March Estates Management Co Ltd **Contact:** M Andrews
Terraced Cottages.
Location: MAP 14:I7, OS Ref. NT464 798. Main Street, Aberlady, East Lothian.
Open: Exterior only. By appointment, Wemyss & March Estates Office, Longniddry, East
Lothian EH32 0PY.
Admission: Please contact for details.

ROYAL BOTANIC GARDEN EDINBURGH

20A Inverleith Row, Edinburgh EH3 5LR

Tel: 0131 552 7171 **Fax:** 0131 248 2901 **E-mail:** info@rbge.org.uk

Contact: Press Office

Scotland's premier garden. Discover the wonders of the plant kingdom in over 70 acres of beautifully landscaped grounds.

Location: MAP 21, OS Ref. NT249 751. Off A902, 1m N of city centre.

Open: Daily (except 25 Dec & 1 Jan): open 10am, closing: Nov–Feb: 4pm; Mar & Oct: 6pm; Apr–Sept: 7pm.

Admission: Free, with an admission charge on the Glasshouses.

THE ROYAL YACHT BRITANNIA

Ocean Terminal, Leith, Edinburgh EH6 6JJ

Tel: 0131 555 5566 **Fax:** 0131 555 8835

Email: enquiries@tryb.co.uk **www.royalyachtbritannia.co.uk**

Owners: The Royal Yacht Britannia Trust **Contact:** Julia Stephenson

Britain's last Royal Yacht; home to the Royal Family from 1953 to 1997. Learn about *Britannia's* history prior to boarding in the fascinating Visitor Centre. Enjoy a complimentary audio tour of 5 decks, available in 21 languages. Discover the heart and soul of this very special royal residence.

Location: MAP 13:H7, OS Ref. NT264 769. 2 miles from Edinburgh city centre, in historic port of Leith.

Open: Year round – 10.00am to last admission 3.30pm. Extended hours in summer.

Admission: Adult £10.50, Senior £9, Child £6.75, Group discount for 15 or more.

WCs. Licensed. Guide dogs only.

ST MARY'S EPISCOPAL CATHEDRAL

Palmerston Place, Edinburgh EH12 5AW

Tel: 0131 225 6293 **Fax:** 0131 225 3181

Contact: Cathedral Secretary

Neo-gothic grandeur in the classical new town. Designed by G Gilbert Scott.

Location: MAP 21, OS Ref. NT241 735. 1/2 m W of west end of Princes Street.

Open: Mon–Fri, 7.30am–6pm; Sat & Sun, 7.30am–5pm. Sun services: 8am, 10.30am & 3.30pm. Services: Weekdays, 7.30am, 1.05pm & 5.30pm; Thurs, 11.30am, Sat, 7.30am.

Admission: Free.

SCOTTISH NATIONAL PORTRAIT GALLERY

1 Queen Street, Edinburgh EH2 1JD

Tel: 0131 624 6200

Unique visual history of Scotland.

Location: MAP 21, OS Ref. NT256 742. At E end of Queen Street, 300yds N of Princes Street.

Open: All year to permanent collection: daily, 10am–5pm (Thurs closes 7pm). Closed 25 & 26 Dec. Open 1 Jan, 12 noon–5pm.

Admission: Free. (There may be a charge for special exhibitions.)

TRINITY HOUSE MARITIME MUSEUM

99 Kirkgate, Edinburgh EH6 6BJ

Tel: 0131 554 3289 **www.historic-scotland.gov.uk**

Owner: Historic Scotland

Contact: The Monument Manager

This fine Georgian mansion contains a treasure trove of maritime artefacts including paintings by Henry Raeburn. The site has been home to the Incorporation of Masters and Mariners since the Middle Ages. Many of the artefacts were donated by Leith sailors who travelled the world in centuries gone by.

Location: MAP 13:G8, OS Ref. NT269 760, Kirkgate, Leith, Edinburgh.

Admission: Adult £4.20, Child £2.10, Conc £3.20 (2009 prices).

Open: By prebooked visit only maximum of 10 - 15 people, telephone for details.

Max 10–15 people.

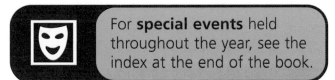

For **special events** held throughout the year, see the index at the end of the book.

TANTALLON CASTLE

BY NORTH BERWICK, EAST LOTHIAN EH39 5PN

Tel: 01620 892727 **www.historic-scotland.gov.uk**

Owner: In the care of Historic Scotland **Contact:** The Steward

Set atop cliffs, looking out to the Bass Rock, this formidable castle was a stronghold of the powerful Douglas family. The castle has earthwork defences and a massive 80-foot high 14th century curtain wall and has endured frequent sieges.

Location: MAP 14:I7, OS67 NT595 850. 3m E of North Berwick off the A198.

Open: 1 Apr–30 Sept: daily, 9.30am–5.30pm. 1 Oct–31 Mar 9.30am–4.30pm, closed Thurs & Fri. Last ticket 30 mins before closing.

Admission: Adult £4.70, Child £2.35, Conc. £3.70. (2009 prices)

Picnic area. Bicycle rack. Booked school visits free. On leads. €

The Royal Yacht Britannia

BURRELL COLLECTION

Pollok Country Park, 2060 Pollokshaws Road, Glasgow G43 1AT
Tel: 0141 287 2550   **Fax:** 0141 287 2597
Owner: Glasgow Museums
An internationally renowned, outstanding collection of art.
Location: MAP 13:C8, OS Ref. NS555 622. Glasgow 15 min drive.
Open: All year: Mon–Thur & Sats, 10am–5pm, Fri & Sun, 11am–5pm. Closed 25/26 Dec, 31 Dec (pm) & 1/2 Jan.
Admission: Free. Small charge may apply for temporary exhibitions.

COLZIUM HOUSE & WALLED GARDEN

Colzium-Lennox Estate, off Stirling Road, Kilsyth G65 0RZ
Tel/Fax: 01236 828156
Owner: North Lanarkshire Council   **Contact:** John Whittaker
A walled garden with an extensive collection of conifers, rare shrubs and trees, curling pond, picnic tables, woodland walks.
Location: MAP 13:D7, OS Ref. NS722 786. Off A803 Banknock to Kirkintilloch Road. ½m E of Kilsyth.
Open: Walled Garden: Apr–Sept: daily, 12noon–7pm; Oct–Mar: Sats & Suns, 12 noon–4pm.
Admission: Free.

COREHOUSE

Lanark, ML11 9TQ
Tel: 01555 663126
Owner: Colonel D A S Cranstoun of that Ilk TD   **Contact:** Estate Office
Designed by Sir Edward Blore and built in the 1820s, Corehouse is a pioneering example of the Tudor Architectural Revival in Scotland.
Location: MAP 13:E9, OS Ref. NS882 416. On S bank of the Clyde above the village of Kirkfieldbank.
Open: 1–19 May & 11–22 Sept: Sat–Wed. Guided tours: weekdays: 1 & 2pm, weekends: 2 & 3pm. Closed Thurs & Fri.
Admission: Adult £6, Child (under 14yrs)/OAP £3.
Partial. Obligatory. Limited. In grounds.

CRAIGNETHAN CASTLE

Lanark, Strathclyde, ML11 9PL
Tel: 01555 860364   www.historic-scotland.gov.uk
Owner: Historic Scotland   **Contact:** The Steward
In a picturesque setting overlooking the River Nethan and defended by a wide and deep ditch. The castle's defences include an unusual caponier, a stone vaulted artillery chamber, unique in Britain.
Location: MAP 13:E9, OS Ref. NS815 463. 5½m WNW of Lanark off the A72.
Open: 1 Apr–30 Sept: daily, 9.30am–5.30pm. 1 Oct –31 Mar 9.30am–4.30pm weekends only. Last ticket 30 mins before closing time.
Admission: Adult £3.70, Child £1.85, Conc. £3.00 (2009 prices).
Picnic area. WC. Bicycle Rack. No coaches.

© John Soury
New Lanark World Heritage Site

GLASGOW CATHEDRAL

Castle Street, Glasgow, G4 0QZ
Tel: 0141 552 6891   www.historic-scotland.gov.uk
Owner: Historic Scotland   **Contact:** The Steward
The only Scottish mainland medieval cathedral to have survived the Reformation complete. Built over the tomb of St Kentigern. Notable features in this splendid building are the elaborately vaulted crypt, the stone screen of the early 15th century and the unfinished Blackadder Aisle.
Location: MAP 13:D8, OS Ref. NS603 656. In Glasgow, off the M8, J15 next to the Royal Infirmary
Open: 1 Apr–30 Sept: Mon–Sat, 9.30am–5.30pm, Sun 1–5pm. 1 Oct–31 Mar: Mon–Sat, 9.30am–4.30pm, Sun 1–4.30pm. Last admission 30 mins before closing.
Admission: Free.
Obligatory.

MOTHERWELL HERITAGE CENTRE

High Road, Motherwell ML1 3HU
Tel: 01698 251000
Owner: North Lanarkshire Council   **Contact:** The Manager
VisitScotland 4-star attraction. Technopolois multi-media display tells the story of the area from the Romans, through the days of heavy industry, to the present time. Exhibition gallery, shop and tower viewing platform. A local studies and family history research room has census, newspaper and other databases on-line. Staff assistance available.
Location: MAP 13:E9, OS Ref. NS750 570. In High Road, 200yds N of A723 (Hamilton Road).
Open: All year, 10am–5pm. Sun, 12 noon–5pm (closed 25/26 Dec & 1/2 Jan and every Mon & Tues).
Admission: Free.

NEW LANARK WORLD HERITAGE SITE

New Lanark Mills, Lanark, S Lanarkshire ML11 9DB
Tel: 01555 661345   **Fax:** 01555 665738   **E-mail:** visit@newlanark.org
www.newlanark.org
Owner: New Lanark Trust   **Contact:** Trust Office
Surrounded by native woodlands and close to the famous Falls of Clyde, this cotton mill village was founded in 1785 and became famous as the site of Robert Owen's radical reforms. Now beautifully restored as both a living community and attraction, the fascinating history of the village is interpreted in an award-winning Visitor Centre. There is a Roof Garden and Viewing Platform giving panoramic views of the historic village and surrounding woodland. Accommodation is available in the New Lanark Mill Hotel and Waterhouses, a stunning conversion from an original 18th century mill. New Lanark is now a World Heritage Site.
Location: MAP 13:E9, OS Ref. NS880 426. 1m S of Lanark.
Open: All year: daily, 10.30am–5pm (11am–5pm Oct–March). Closed 25 Dec & 1 Jan.
Admission: Visitor Centre: Adult £6.95, Child/Conc. £5.95. Groups: 1 free/10 booked.
Conference facilities. Partial. WC. Visitor Centre wheelchair friendly. By arrangement. 5 min walk. In grounds, on leads.

NEWARK CASTLE

Port Glasgow, Strathclyde, PA14 5NH
Tel: 01475 741858   www.historic-scotland.gov.uk
Owner: In the care of Historic Scotland   **Contact:** The Steward
The oldest part of the castle is a tower built soon after 1478 with a detached gatehouse, by George Maxwell. The main part was added in 1597–99 in a most elegant style. Enlarged in the 16th century by his descendent, the wicked Patrick Maxwell who murdered two of his neighbours.
Location: MAP 13:B8, OS Ref. NS329 744. In Port Glasgow on the A8 at Newark roundabout.
Open: 1 Apr–30 Sept: daily, 9.30am–5.30pm. Last ticket 5pm.
Admission: Adult £3.70, Child £1.85, Conc. £3.00 (2009 prices).
WC. Closes for lunch. Limited for coaches.

For **corporate hospitality** venues see our special index at the end of the book.

POLLOK HOUSE 🦁

Pollok Country Park, Pollokshaws Road, Glasgow G43 1AT
Tel: 0131 243 9300
Owner: The National Trust for Scotland
The house contains an internationally famed collection of paintings as well as porcelain and furnishings appropriate to an Edwardian house.
Location: MAP 13:C8, OS Ref. NS550 616. In Pollok Country Park, off M77/J1, follow signs for Burrell Collection.

ST MARY'S EPISCOPAL CATHEDRAL

300 Great Western Road, Glasgow G4 9JB
Tel: 0141 339 6691   **Fax:** 0141 334 5669   **Email:** office@thecathedral.org.uk
Contact: The Office
Newly restored, fine Gothic Revival church by Sir George Gilbert Scott, with outstanding contemporary murals by Gwyneth Leech. Regular concerts and exhibitions.
Location: MAP 13:D8, OS Ref. NS578 669. ¼m after the Dumbarton A82 exit from M8 motorway.
Open: All year. Mon–Fri, 9.15–10am. Thur, 5.30–7.30pm. Sat, 9.30–10am.
Sun services: 8.30am, 10.30am & 6.30pm. Please telephone in advance to confirm up to date opening times.
Admission: Free

SUMMERLEE INDUSTRIAL MUSEUM

Heritage Way, Coatbridge, North Lanarkshire ML5 1QD
Tel: 01236 638460
Owner: North Lanarkshire Council   **Contact:** The Manager
Summerlee, the Scottish museum of industrial life, is a VisitScotland 4-star attraction. It is based around the site of the former Summerlee Ironworks and a branch of the Monklands Canal. The museum has recently reopened after a major Heritage Lottery Fund supported redevelopment. The main exhibition hall has been cleared and rebuilt with new displays, interactive features, children's activities and new shop and café.
Location: MAP 13:D8, OS Ref. NS729 655. 600yds NW of Coatbridge town centre.
Open: All year 10am–5pm (Oct–Mar to 4pm). Closed 25/26 Dec & 1/2 Jan.

THE TENEMENT HOUSE 🦁

145 Buccleuch Street, Glasgow G3 6QN
Tel: 0131 243 9300
Owner: The National Trust for Scotland
A typical Victorian tenement flat of 1892, and time capsule of the first half of the 20th century.
Location: MAP 13:D8, OS Ref. NS583 662. Garnethill (three streets N of Sauchiehall Street, near Charing Cross), Glasgow.

© Patrick Lane

Colzium Walled Garden

■ Owner
Blair Charitable Trust

■ Contact
Administration Office
Blair Castle
Blair Atholl
Pitlochry
Perthshire PH18 5TL

Tel: 01796 481207
Fax: 01796 481487
E-mail: bookings@blair-castle.co.uk

■ Location
MAP 13:E3
OS Ref. NN880 660

Car: Just off the main Perth/Inverness road (A9), 35 miles north of Perth. Approximately 90 minutes drive from Edinburgh and Glasgow.

Bus: Elizabeth Yule Service 87 (end March to early Nov), or Stagecoach 83 service from Perth.

Rail: Blair Atholl Station 1m. Serviced by main London Euston to Inverness line.

Taxi: Elizabeth Yule, 01796 472290.

■ Opening Times
Summer: 28 March– 29 October, Daily, 9.30am–5.30pm (Last admission to castle tour 4.30pm) **Winter:** Regular winter opening, please check website for details.

■ Admission
House & Grounds
Adult	£8.75
Child (5–16yrs)	£5.25
Senior	£7.50
Student (with ID)	£7.50
Family	£24.00
Disabled	£2.75
Groups* (12+) (Please book)	
Adult	£6.70
Child(5–16yrs)	£5.15
Primary School	£3.90
Senior/Student	£6.70
Disabled	£2.50

Grounds only
(inc. Restaurant, Gift Shop & WC)
Adult	£4.75
Child (5–16yrs)	£2.25
Senior/Student	£4.25
Family	£11.00
Disabled	Free
Scooter Hire	£3.75
Groups* (12+) (Please book)	
Adult	£3.50
Child (5–16yrs)	£2.00
Primary School	£2.00
Senior/Student	£3.50
Disabled	Free

*Group rates only apply when all tickets are bought by the Driver, Courier or Group leader at one time. Advance booking, particulary when guides are requested, is strongly recommended.

All prices are inclusive of VAT at the current rate.

Conference/Function
ROOM	SIZE	MAX CAPACITY
Ballroom	88' x 36'	400 or 220 dining
State Dining Room	36' x 26'	150 or 16–50 dining
Banvie Hall	55' x 32'	150

BLAIR CASTLE 🏛

www.blair-castle.co.uk

Nestling like a white jewel in the dramatic Highland Perthshire landscape, Blair Castle has a centuries old history as a strategic stronghold at the gateway to the Grampians and the route north to Inverness.

Famous as the last castle to be held under siege in 1746, Blair Castle is the ancient seat of the Dukes and Earls of Atholl and the home of the Atholl Highlanders, Europe's only remaining private army. More than 30 rooms are on display, crammed full of treasures and alive with the characters and personalities of their former occupants. Highlights of the visit include: the magnificent ballroom bedecked with 175 pairs of antlers; the superb China Room featuring more than 1700 individual pieces and an ornamental Victorian armoury housing targes and muskets used at the Battle of Culloden. There are also paintings by Sir Edwin Landseer, fine mortlake tapestries and plasterwork by Thomas Clayton.

Gardens & Grounds
Blair Castle is at the hub of a breath-taking historic landscape most of which was laid out in the 18th century and features a beautiful 9 acre walled garden with landscaped ponds, a peaceful wooded grove that is home to the UK's 2nd tallest tree, a ruined Celtic kirk; a red deer park and a whimsical gothic folly. Children will also enjoy the castle's woodland adventure playground.

ℹ	No photography inside the castle.
🛍	Licensed Gift Shop.
🍷	Civil and religious weddings may be held in the castle and receptions for up to 220 guests can be held in the ballroom. Banquets, dinners and private functions are welcome.
♿	Ground floor fully accessible. Disabled parking area adjacent to castle.
☕	Tea, coffee and lunches.
🍴	Tullibardine Self Service Restaurant seats 125. Private group lunches for up to 35 can be arranged in the Garry Room. Licensed
🧍	In English and German at no extra cost. Tour time 50mins (groups only). Illustrated guide books (English, German, French and Italian) available. Special interest tours also available.
🅿	200 cars, 20 coaches. Coach drivers/couriers free, plus meal and shop voucher, information pack.
🌳	Nature walks, deer park, ranger service, pony trekking and children's woodland adventure playground.
🐕	Guide dogs only in castle. Dogs on leads permitted in grounds.
🔔	Civil Wedding Licence.
❄	Regular winter opening.
🎫	Atholl Highlanders' Parade 29 May, Highland Games 30 May, Blair Castle International Horse Trials and Country Fair 26–29 August.

■ **Owner**
Grimsthorpe &
Drummond Castle Trust
A registered charity
(SCO39364) (507478)

■ **Contact**
The Caretaker
Drummond Castle
Gardens
Muthill
Crieff
Perthshire PH7 4HZ

Tel: 01764 681433
Fax: 01764 681642
E-mail: thegardens@
drummondcastle.sol.co.uk

■ **Location**
MAP 13:E5
OS Ref. NN844 181
2m S of Crieff off the
A822.

■ **Opening Times**
Easter weekend,
1 May–31 October:
Daily, 1–6pm.
Last admission 5pm.

■ **Admission**
Adult   £5.00
Child   £2.00
Conc.   £4.00

Groups (20+)
       10% discount.

DRUMMOND CASTLE GARDENS 🏛

www.drummondcastlegardens.co.uk

Scotland's most important formal gardens, among the finest in Europe. A mile of beech-lined avenue leads to a formidable ridge top tower house. The magnificent Italianate parterre is revealed from a viewpoint at the top of the terrace, celebrating the saltaire and family heraldry that surrounds the famous multiplex sundial by John Milne, master mason to Charles I. First laid out in the early 17th century by John Drummond, 2nd Earl of Perth and renewed in the early 1950s by Phyllis Astor, Countess of Ancaster.

The gardens contain ancient yew hedges and two copper beech trees planted by Queen Victoria during her visit in 1842. Shrubberies are planted with many varieties of maple and other individual ornamental trees including purple-leaf oaks, whitebeam, weeping birch and a tulip tree, *Liriodendron tulipifera*. The tranquility of the gardens makes them the perfect setting to stroll amongst the well-manicured plantings or sit and absorb the atmosphere of this special place.

Partial. WCS.
By arrangement.
Limited parking available for coaches.
 On leads.

■ **Owner**
The Earl of Mansfield

■ **Contact**
The Administrator
Scone Palace
Perth PH2 6BD

Tel: 01738 552300
Fax: 01738 552588
E-mail: visits@
scone-palace.co.uk

■ **Location**
MAP 13:G5
OS Ref. NO114 266

From Edinburgh
Forth Bridge M90,
A93 1hr.

Bus: Regular buses
from Perth.

Rail: Perth Station 3m.

Motorway: M90 from
Edinburgh.

Taxi: 01738 636777.

■ **Opening Times**
Summer
1 April–31 October.
Gates open at
9.30am–last admission
5.00pm, Mon–Fri & Sun.

9.30am–last admission
4.00pm, Sat.

Grounds Only open each
Friday during Winter,
10am–4pm.

Evening and Winter
tours by appointment.

Please check our website
for details of Winter
Events.

■ **Admission**
Admission prices correct
at time of going to print:

Palace & Grounds
Adult	£9.00
Conc.	£7.90
Child (5–16yrs)	£6.00
Family	£26.00

Groups (20+)
Adult	£7.90
Conc.	£6.75
Child (5–16yrs)	£5.50

Grounds only
Adult	£5.10
Conc.	£4.50
Child (5–16yrs)	£3.50

Under 5s Free
Private Tour £45
supplement.

■ **Special Events**
2010 Events Include:
2, 3 & 4 July: The
Scottish Game Fair.
7 & 8 August: Orchid
Festival.

For details of our 2010
event programme
please visit
www.scone-palace.co.uk

Conference/Function

ROOM	SIZE	MAX CAPACITY
Long Gallery	140' x 20'	200
Queen Victoria's Rm	20' x 20'	20
Drawing Rm	48' x 25'	80
Balvaird Rm	29' x 22'	50/60
Tullibardine Rm	19' x 23'	40/50

SCONE PALACE & GROUNDS 🏛

www.scone-palace.co.uk

Scone Palace is the home of the Earl and Countess of Mansfield and is built on the site of an ancient abbey. 1500 years ago it was the capital of the Pictish kingdom and the centre of the ancient Celtic church. In the intervening years, it has been the seat of parliaments and crowning place of Scottish kings, including Macbeth, Robert the Bruce and Charles II. The State Rooms house a superb collection of *objets d'art*, including seventeenth and eighteenth century ivories, mostly collected by the fourth Earl of Mansfield. Notable works of art are also on display, including paintings by Sir David Wilkie, Sir Joshua Reynolds, and Johann Zoffany. The Library boasts one of Scotland's finest collections of porcelain, including Sèvres, Ludwigsburg and Meissen, whilst the unique 'Vernis Martin' *papier mâché* may be viewed in the Long Gallery. An audio visual presentation explores centuries of Scone's history.

Gardens

The grounds of the Palace house magnificent collections of shrubs, with woodland walks through the Wild Garden containing David Douglas' original fir and the unique Murray Star Maze. A pavilion dedicated to Douglas and other Scottish plant hunters has recently been constructed. There are Highland cattle and peacocks to admire and an adventure play area for children. The 100 acres of mature Policy Parks, flanked by the River Tay, are available for a variety of events, including corporate and private entertaining.

ℹ️ Receptions, fashion shows, war games, archery, clay pigeon shooting, equestrian events, garden parties, shows, rallies, filming, shooting, fishing, floodlit tattoos, product launches, highland games, parkland, cricket pitch, helicopter landing, croquet, racecourse, polo field, firework displays, adventure playground. No photography in state rooms.

🛍 Gift shop & food shop.

🍸 Grand dinners in state rooms (inc. buffets & cocktail parties).

♿ All state rooms on one level, accessible by wheelchair, as are restaurants.

☕ Licensed. Teas, Lunches & Dinners, can be booked (menus upon request). Special rates for groups

🍴 Available for private hire.

🚶 By Arrangement. Guides in each room. Private tours in French, German, Italian and English by appointment only.

🧒 Welcome.

🅿️ 300 cars and 15 coaches (coaches – booking preferable). Couriers and coach drivers free meal and admittance.

🐕 In grounds on leads.

🔔 By Appointment.

❄️ Please telephone or see website for details.

ABERDOUR CASTLE

Aberdour, Fife, KY3 0SL

Tel: 01383 860519   www.historic-scotland.gov.uk

Owner: In the care of Historic Scotland   **Contact:** The Steward

This 12th century fortified residence was extended by the Douglas family. The gallery on the first floor gives an idea of how it was furnished at the time. The castle has a 14th century tower extended in the 16th and 17th centuries, a delightful walled garden and a circular dovecote.

Location: MAP 13:G7, OS Ref. NT193 854. In Aberdour 5m E of the Forth Bridge on the A921.

Open: 1 Apr–30 Sept: daily, 9.30am–5.30pm, last ticket 5pm. 1 Oct–31 Mar: 9.30am–4.30pm, last ticket 4pm. Closed Thurs & Fri during Oct–Mar.

Admission: Adult £4.20, Child £2.10, Conc. £3.20 (2009 prices).

ⓘ Picnic area. WCs. ♿ WCs. 🎦 🅿 Parking on site for disabled visitors only. Other parking available at the nearby railway station. 🔲🔳 On leads. 🔺❄€

ARBROATH ABBEY

Arbroath, Tayside, DD11 1EG

Tel: 01241 878756   www.historic-scotland.gov.uk

Owner: In the care of Historic Scotland   **Contact:** The Steward

The substantial ruins of a Tironensian monastery. Arbroath Abbey holds a very special place in Scottish history due to its association with the 'Declaration of Arbroath'. In this document Scotland's nobles swore their independence from England in 1320. The visitor centre includes an exhibition on the declaration.

Location: MAP 14:J4, OS Ref. NO644 414. In Arbroath town centre on the A92.

Open: 1 Apr–30 Sept: daily 9.30am–5.30pm, last ticket 5pm. 1 Oct–31 Mar: daily, 9.30am–4.30 pm, last ticket 4pm.

Admission: Adult £4.70, Child £2.35, Conc. £3.70 (2009 prices).

ⓘ WCs. Bicycle Rack. 📷 ♿ WCs. 🅿 🔲 🔳 On leads. ❄€

BALCARRES

Colinsburgh, Fife KY9 1HN

Tel: 01333 340520

Owner: Balcarres Heritage Trust   **Contact:** Lord Balniel

16th century tower house with 19th century additions by Burn and Bryce. Woodland and terraced gardens.

Location: MAP 14:I6, OS Ref. NO475 044. ½m N of Colinsburgh.

Open: Woodland & Gardens: 20 Mar–15 Aug, 2–5pm. House not open except by written appointment and 1–29 Apr, excluding Sun.

Admission: Adult £6. Garden only: £3.50.

🅕 By arrangement.

BALGONIE CASTLE

Markinch, Fife KY7 6HQ

Tel: 01592 750119   **Fax:** 01592 753103   **E-mail:** sbalgonie@yahoo.co.uk

Owner/Contact: The Laird of Balgonie

14th century tower, additions to the building up to 1702. Still lived in by the family. 14th century chapel for weddings.

Location: MAP 13:H6, OS Ref. NO313 006. ½ m S of A911 Glenrothes–Leven road at Milton of Balgonie on to B921.

Open: All year: daily, 10am–5pm.

Admission: Adult £3, Child £1.50, OAP £2.

BALHOUSIE CASTLE (BLACK WATCH MUSEUM)

Hay Street, North Inch Park, Perth PH1 5HR

Tel: 0131 310 8530

Owner: MOD   **Contact:** Major Proctor

Regimental museum housed in the castle.

Location: MAP 13:G5, OS Ref. NO115 244. ½ m N of town centre, E of A9 road to Dunkeld.

Open: May–Sept: Mon–Sat, 10am–4.30pm. Oct–Apr: Mon–Fri, 10am–3.30pm. Closed 23 Dec–5 Jan & last Sat in Jun.

Admission: Free.

BRANKLYN GARDEN

Dundee Road, Perth PH2 7BB

Tel: 01738 625535

Owner: The National Trust for Scotland

Small garden with an impressive collection of rare and unusual plants.

Location: MAP 13:F5, OS Ref. NO125 225. On A85 at 116 Dundee Road, Perth.

BLAIR CASTLE 🏰

See page 434 for full page entry.

BRECHIN CASTLE

Brechin, Angus DD9 6SG

Tel: 01356 624566   **E-mail:** mandyferries@dalhousieestates.co.uk

www.dalhousieestates.co.uk

Owner: Dalhousie Estates   **Contact:** Mandy Ferries

Dating from 1711 the Castle contains many family pictures and artefacts. Beautiful gardens.

Location: MAP 14:J3, OS Ref. NO593 602. Off A90 on A935.

Open: 29 May–27 Jun: guided tours only, 2 & 3.15pm.

Admission: Adult £5. Child under 12yrs Free.

ⓘ No photography. ♿ Unsuitable. 🅕 Obligatory. 🔳

© HHG / Peter Smith

Blair Castle

Drummond Castle Gardens

BROUGHTY CASTLE

Broughty Ferry, Dundee DD5 2TF
Tel: 01382 436916
Owner: Historic Scotland   **Contact:** The Monument Manager
A delightful castle originating from the 15th century and spectacularly positioned overlooking the Tay estuary. It was adapted over the centuries to reflect advances in warfare and defence. The castle houses a museum with fascinating displays on changing life, times and people of Broughty Ferry and about its wildlife.
Location: MAP 14:F4, OS Ref. NO464 304. On the shores of the River Tay at Broughty Ferry, Dundee off the A930.
Open: Apr–Sept, Mon–Sat, 10am–4pm, Sun 12.30pm–4pm. Oct–Mar, Tue–Sat, 10am–4pm, Sun 12.30pm–4pm.
Admission: Please telephone the site for details.
ℹ️ The museum is run by Dundee City Council. Visit www.dundeecity.gov.uk/broughtycastle

CASTLE CAMPBELL

Dollar Glen, Central District
Tel: 0131 243 9300
Owner: The National Trust for Scotland   **Contact:** Historic Scotland
Known as 'Castle Gloom' this spectacularly sited 15th century fortress was the lowland stronghold of the Campbells. Stunning views from the parapet walk.
Location: MAP 13:F6, OS Ref. NS961 993. At head of Dollar Glen, 10m E of Stirling on the A91.

CHARLETON HOUSE

Colinsburgh, Leven, Fife KY9 1HG
Tel: 01333 340249 **Fax:** 01333 340583
Location: MAP 14:I6, OS Ref. NO464 036. Off A917. 1m NW of Colinsburgh. 3m NW of Elie.
Open: Sept: daily, 12 noon–3pm. Admission every ½hr with guided tours only.
Admission: £12.
Ⓧ Obligatory.

CORTACHY ESTATE

Cortachy, Kirriemuir, Angus DD8 4LX
Tel: 01575 570108 **Fax:** 01575 540400
E-mail: office@airlieestates.com   **www.airlieestates.com**
Owner: Trustees of Airlie Estates   **Contact:** Estate Office
Countryside walks including access through woodlands to Airlie Monument on Tulloch Hill with spectacular views of the Angus Glens and Vale of Strathmore. Footpaths are waymarked and colour coded.
Location: MAP 13:H3, OS Ref. NO394 596. Off the B955 Glens Road from Kirriemuir.
Open: Woodland Walks: all year. Gardens: 2–5 Apr (Easter); 3 May & 17 May–6 Jun; 2 & 30 Aug. Castle not open. 10am–4pm. Last admission 3.30pm.
Admission: Please contact estate office for details.
Not suitable. **P** Limited.

CULROSS PALACE

Tel: 0131 243 9300
Owner: The National Trust for Scotland   **Contact:** Property Manager
Relive the domestic life of the 16th and 17th centuries at this Royal Burgh fringed by the River Forth. Enjoy too the Palace, dating from 1597 and the medieval garden.
Location: MAP 13:F7, OS Ref. NS985 860. Off A985. 12m W of Forth Road Bridge and 4m E of Kincardine Bridge, Fife.

DRUMMOND CASTLE GARDENS   *See page 435 for full page entry.*

DUNFERMLINE ABBEY & PALACE

Dunfermline, Fife, KY12 7PE
Tel: 01383 739026   **www.historic-scotland.gov.uk**
Owner: In the care of Historic Scotland   **Contact:** The Steward
The remains of the Benedictine abbey founded by Queen Margaret in the 11th century. The foundations of her church are under the 12th century Romanesque-style nave. Robert the Bruce was buried in the choir. Substantial parts of the abbey buildings remain, including the vast refectory.
Location: MAP 13:G7, OS Ref. NT090 873. In Dunfermline off the M90.
Open: All year 1 Apr–30 Sept: daily, 9.30am–5.30pm. 1 Oct–31 Mar: Mon–Sat, 9.30am–4.30pm. Closed Thurs pm, Fri and Sun. Closed for lunch 12.30pm–1.30pm.
Admission: Adult £3.70, Child £1.85, Conc. £3.00 (2009 prices).

DUNNINALD

Montrose, Angus DD10 9TD
Tel: 01674 672031   **Fax:** 01674 674860   **www.dunninald.com**
Owner: J Stansfeld   **Contact:** Mrs M Stansfeld
This house, the third Dunninald built on the estate, was designed by James Gillespie Graham in the gothic Revival style, and was completed for Peter Arkley in 1824. It has a fine walled garden and is set in a planned landscape dating from 1740. It is a family home.
Location: MAP 14:J3, OS Ref. NO705 543 2m S of Montrose, between A92 and the sea.
Open: 1 Jul–1 Aug, daily, closed Mondays 1–5pm, Garden from 12 noon.
Admission: Adult £5, Child (under 12) Free, Conc. £4. Garden only: £3.00.
ℹ️ No photography in house. Unsuitable. Ⓧ Obligatory. **P**
In grounds, on leads. €

EDZELL CASTLE AND GARDEN

Edzell, Angus, DD9 7UE
Tel: 01356 648631   www.historic-scotland.gov.uk
Owner: In the care of Historic Scotland   **Contact:** The Steward
The beautiful walled garden was created by Sir David Lindsay in 1604. The 'Pleasance', a delightful formal garden, has walls decorated with sculptured stone panels. The towerhouse dates from the late 15th century. Mary Queen of Scots held a council meeting here in 1562 as her army marched north against the Gordons.
Location: MAP 14:I2, OS Ref. NO585 691. At Edzell, 6m N of Brechin on B966.
Open: 1 Apr–30 Sept: daily, 9.30am–5.30pm, last ticket 5pm. 1 Oct–31 Mar: 9.30am–4.30pm, last ticket 4pm. Closed Thur and Fri.
Admission: Adult £4.70, Child £2.35, Conc. £3.70 (2009 prices).
ⅰ Picnic Area. Closes for lunch. 🖸 🖾 WCs. 🅿 Limited for coaches. 🔲 🖾 On leads. ✱ 🖲 €

ELCHO CASTLE

Perth, PH2 8QQ
Tel: 01738 639998   www.historic-scotland.gov.uk
Owner: In the care of Historic Scotland   **Contact:** The Steward
This handsome and complete fortified mansion of 16th century date has three projecting towers. The original wrought-iron grilles to protect the windows are still in place. Located on the River Tay, the castle is rich in bird life.
Location: MAP 13:G5, OS Ref. NO164 211. 5m NE of Bridge of Earn off the A912 and close to Rhynd.
Open: 1 Apr–30 Sept: daily, 9.30am–5.30pm. Last ticket 5pm.
Admission: Adult £3.20, Child £1.60, Conc. £2.70 (2009 prices).
ⅰ WC. Picnic area. 🖸 🅿 No coaches. 🔲🖾€

FALKLAND PALACE

Falkland KY15 7BU
Tel: 0131 243 9300
Owner: The National Trust for Scotland
Built between 1502 and 1541, the Palace is a good example of Renaissance architecture. Surrounded by gardens, laid out in the 1950s.
Location: MAP 13:G6, OS Ref. NO253 075. A912, 11m N of Kirkcaldy.

GLENEAGLES

Auchterarder, Perthshire PH3 1PJ
Tel: 01764 682388
Owner: Gleneagles 1996 Trust   **Contact:** Martin Haldane of Gleneagles
Gleneagles has been the home of the Haldane family since the 12th century. The 18th century pavilion is open to the public by written appointment.
Location: MAP 13:F6, OS Ref. NS931 088. ¾m S of A9 on A823. 2½m S of Auchterarder.
Open: By written appointment only.
✱

HILL OF TARVIT MANSIONHOUSE

Cupar, Fife KY15 5PB
Tel: 0131 243 9300
Owner: The National Trust for Scotland
House rebuilt in 1906 by Sir Robert Lorimer, the renowned Scottish architect, for a Dundee industrialist, Mr F B Sharp.
Location: MAP 13:F6, OS Ref. NO379 118. Off A916, 2½m S of Cupar, Fife.

HOUSE OF DUN

Montrose, Angus DD10 9LQ
Tel: 0131 243 9300
Owner: The National Trust for Scotland
Georgian house, overlooking the Montrose Basin, designed by William Adam and built in 1730 for David Erskine, Lord Dun.
Location: OS Ref. NO670 599. 3m W Montrose on A935.

HUNTINGTOWER CASTLE

Perth, PH1 3JL
Tel: 01738 627231   www.historic-scotland.gov.uk
Owner: In the care of Historic Scotland   **Contact:** The Steward
The splendid painted ceilings are especially noteworthy in this castle, once owned by the Ruthven family. Scene of a famous leap between two towers by a daughter of the house who was nearly caught in her lover's room. The castle is now home to two colonies of bats.
Location: MAP 13:F5, OS Ref. NO084 252. 3m NW of Perth off the A85 to Crieff.
Open: 1 Apr–30 Sept: daily, 9.30am–5.30pm, last ticket 5pm. 1 Oct–31 Mar: 9.30am–4.30pm, last ticket 4pm. Closed Thur & Fri.
Admission: Adult £4.20, Child £2.10, Conc. £3.20 (2009 prices).
ⅰ Closes for lunch. Picnic area. 🖸 🖾 WCs. 🎢 By arrangement. 🅿 No coaches. 🖾 On leads. ✱ €

INCHCOLM ABBEY

Inchcolm, Fife, KY3 0SL
Tel: 01383 823332   www.historic-scotland.gov.uk
Owner: In the care of Historic Scotland   **Contact:** The Steward
Known as the 'Iona of the East'. This is the best preserved group of monastic buildings in Scotland, founded in 1123. Includes a 13th century octagonal chapter house.
Location: MAP 13:H7, OS Ref. NT190 826. On Inchcolm in the Firth of Forth. Reached by ferry from South Queensferry (30 mins), or Newhaven (45 mins). Tel. 0131 331 5000 for times/charges.
Open: Depending on the availability of the ferry service: 1 Apr–30 Sept, daily, 9.30am–5.30pm. Last ticket 5pm.
Admission: Adult £4.70, Child £2.35, Conc. £3.70 (2009 prices). Additional charge for ferries.
ⅰ Visitor Centre. Picnic area. 🖸 🖾 On leads. €

© Scone Palace

Scone Palace

Brechin Castle

KELLIE CASTLE & GARDEN

Pittenweem, Fife KY10 2RF

Tel: 0131 243 9300

Owner: The National Trust for Scotland

Good example of domestic architecture in Lowland Scotland dates from the 14th century and was sympathetically restored by the Lorimer family in the late 19th century.

Location: MAP 14:I6, OS Ref. NO519 051. On B9171, 3m NW of Pittenweem, Fife.

LOCHLEVEN CASTLE

Loch Leven, Kinross, KY13 8UF

Tel: 01577 862670   **www.historic-scotland.gov.uk**

Owner: In the care of Historic Scotland   **Contact:** The Steward

Mary Queen of Scots endured nearly a year of imprisonment in this 14th century tower before her dramatic escape in May 1568. During the First War of Independence it was held by the English, stormed by Wallace and visited by Bruce.

Location: MAP 13:G6, OS Ref. NO138 018. On island in Loch Leven reached by ferry from Kinross off the M90.

Open: Apr–Sept 9.30am to last outward sailing at 4.30pm.

Admission: Adult £4.70, Child £2.35, Conc. £3.70 (2009 prices). Prices include boat trip.

ℹ Picnic area. 🅿 Limited for coaches. 🐕 On leads. €

MEGGINCH CASTLE

Errol, Perthshire PH2 7SW

Tel: 01821 642222   **Email:** catherine.herdman@gmail.com

Owner: Mr Giles Herdman & The Hon Mrs Drummond-Herdman

15th century castle, 1,000 year old yews, flowered parterre, topiary, double walled kitchen garden, astrological garden, heritage orchard. Early 19th century courtyard with Pagoda dovecote, part used as a location for the film *Rob Roy*.

Location: MAP 13:G5, OS Ref. NO240 245. 8m E of Perth on A90.

Open: Scottish Gardens Scheme. By Appointment. Gardens Only.

Admission: Contact property for details.

♿ Partial. 🕯 By arrangement. 🅿 Limited for coaches. 🐕 In grounds, on leads.

MONZIE CASTLE

Crieff, Perthshire PH7 4HD

Tel: 01764 653110

Owner/Contact: Mrs C M M Crichton

Built in 1791. Destroyed by fire in 1908 and rebuilt and furnished by Sir Robert Lorimer.

Location: MAP 13:E5, OS Ref. NN873 244. 2m NE of Crieff.

Open: 15 May–13 Jun: daily, 2–4.30pm. By appointment at other times.

Admission: Adult £5, Child £1. Group rates available, contact property for details.

❄

ST ANDREWS CASTLE
THE SCORES, ST ANDREWS KY16 9AR

www.historic-scotland.gov.uk

Tel: 01334 477196

Owner: Historic Scotland   **Contact:** Monument Manager

The main residence of the bishops of St Andrews. Explore the fascinating 16th century seige mine and counter-mine, rare examples of medieval siege techniques. There is also a bottle dungeon hollowed out of solid rock.

Location: MAP 14:I5, OS Ref. NO512 169. In St Andrews on the A91.

Open: Apr–Sept: daily, 9.30am–5.30pm. Oct–Mar: daily, 9.30am–4.30pm. Last ticket 30 mins before closing.

Admission: Adult £5.20, Child £2.60, Conc. £4.20 (2009 prices). 10% discount for groups (11+). Joint ticket with St Andrews Cathedral available.

ℹ Visitor centre. ♿ WCs. 🕯 By arrangement. 🎦 Free if booked. 🐕 ❄ €

For **corporate hospitality** venues see our special index at the end of the book.

ST ANDREWS CATHEDRAL

St Andrews, Fife, KY16 9QL
Tel: 01334 472563   www.historic-scotland.gov.uk
Owner: Historic Scotland   **Contact:** Monument Manager
Once the largest cathedral in Scotland, the remains still give a vivid impression of its impressive scale. See the associated domestic ranges of the priory and climb St Rule's Tower for spectacular views.
Location: MAP 14:I5, OS Ref: NO5143 167. In St Andrews on the A91.
Open: 1 Apr–30 Sept: daily, 9.30am–5.30pm, last ticket 4.45pm. 1 Oct–31 Mar: daily, 9.30am–4.30pm, last ticket 3.45pm.
Admission: Adult £4.20, Child £2.10, Conc. £3.20 (2009 prices). Joint entry ticket with St Andrews Castle available.
🖭 🖑 🖷 🖳 On leads. 🖷 €

SCONE PALACE & GROUNDS 🏛   *See page 436 for full page entry.*

STOBHALL 🏛

Stobhall, Cargill, Perthshire PH2 6DR
Tel: 01821 640332   www.stobhall.com
Owner: Viscount Strathallan
Original home of the Drummond chiefs from the 14th century. Romantic cluster of small-scale buildings around a courtyard in a magnificent situation overlooking the River Tay, surrounded by formal and woodland gardens. 17th century painted ceiling in Chapel depicts monarchs of Europe and North Africa on horse (or elephant) back.
Location: MAP 13:G4, OS Ref: NO132 343. 7m N of Perth on A93.
Open: 5 Jun–4 Jul: Tues–Sun, (closed Mons). Open by tour only. Tours at 2, 3 & 4pm of the Chapel, Drawing Room and Folly. Explore the garden at leisure after the tour. Library by prior appointment.
Admission: Adult £4, Child £2. Large group visits must be booked.
🖑 Partial. 🖻 Obligatory. 🅿 Limited. Coaches please book. 🖷 Guide dogs only.

STRATHTYRUM HOUSE & GARDENS

St Andrews, Fife
Tel: 01334 473600   **E-mail:** info@strathtyrumhouse.com
www.strathtyrumhouse.com
Owner: The Strathtyrum Trust   **Contact:** Henry Cheape
Location: MAP 14:I5, OS Ref: NO490 172. Entrance from the St Andrews/Guardbridge Road which is signposted when open.
Open: 3–7 May, 7–11 Jun, 5–9 Jul, 2–6 Aug and 6 –10 Sept: 2–4pm. Guided tours at 2 & 3pm.
Admission: Adult £5, Child + Conc. £2.50.
🖻 2pm and 3pm. 🅿 Free. 🖷 Guide dogs only.

TULLIBOLE CASTLE

Crook of Devon, Kinross KY13 0QN
Tel: 01577 840236   **E-mail:** visit@tulbol.demon.co.uk
www.tulbol.demon.co.uk/visit.htm
Owner: Lord & Lady Moncreiff   **Contact:** Lord Moncreiff
Recognised as a classic example of the Scottish tower house. Completed in 1608, the Moncreiff family have lived here since 1747. The Castle is in a parkland setting with ornamental fishponds (moat), a roofless lectarn doocot, with a short walk to a 9th century graveyard and a ruined church.
Location: MAP 13:F6, OS Ref: NO540 888. Located on the B9097 1m E of Crook of Devon.
Open: Last week in Aug–30 Sept: Tue–Sun, 1–4pm. Admission every ½ hr with guided tours only.
Admission: Adult £3.50, Child/Conc. £2.50. Free as part of "Doors Open Day" (last weekend of Sept).
🖑 Unsuitable. 🖻 Obligatory. 🅿 Ample for cars but limited for coaches. 🖷
🖷 Guide dogs only. 🛏 1 x twin, 1 bed holiday cottage.

© Historic Scotland

Edzell Castle & Garden

■ Owner
Duke of Argyll

■ Contact
Argyll Estates
Inveraray Castle
Inveraray
Argyll PA32 8XE

Tel: 01499 302203
Fax: 01499 302421
E-mail: enquiries@
inveraray-castle.com

■ Location
MAP 13:A6
OS Ref. NN100 090

From Edinburgh
2½–3hrs via Glasgow.

Just NE of Inveraray
on A83. W shore
of Loch Fyne.

Bus: Bus route stopping
point within ½m.

■ Opening Times
Summer
1 April–31 October: 7
Days 10am–5.45pm. Last
admission 5pm.

Winter
Closed.

■ Admission
Castle & Gardens

Adult	£9.00
	(£7.20)
Senior Citizen	£7.50
	(£6.00)
Student	£7.50
(on production of	(£6.00)
student card)	
Child (under 16yrs)	£6.10
	(£4.90)
Family	£25.00

(2 adults & 2 or
more children)

A 20% discount is
allowed on groups of
20 or more persons (as
shown in brackets).

Pre-booking available.

■ Special Events
Check website
www.inveraray-
castle.com for details of
forthcoming events.

INVERARAY CASTLE

www.inveraray-castle.com

The ancient Royal Burgh of Inveraray lies about 60 miles north west of Glasgow by Loch Fyne in an area of spectacular natural beauty. The ruggedness of the highland scenery combines with the sheltered tidal loch, beside which nestles the present Castle built between 1745 and 1790.

The Castle is home to the Duke and Duchess of Argyll. The Duke is head of the Clan Campbell and his family have lived in Inveraray since the early 15th century. Designed by Roger Morris and decorated by Robert Mylne, the fairytale exterior belies the grandeur of its gracious interior. The Clerk of Works, William Adam, father of Robert and John, did much of the laying out of the present Royal

Burgh, which is an unrivalled example of an early planned town.

Visitors enter the famous Armoury Hall containing some 1,300 pieces including Brown Bess muskets, Lochaber axes, 18th century Scottish broadswords, and can see preserved swords from the Battle of Culloden. The fine State Dining Room and Tapestry Drawing Room contain magnificent French tapestries made especially for the Castle, fabulous examples of Scottish, English and French furniture and a wealth of other works of art. The unique collection of china, silver and family artifacts spans the generations which are identified by a genealogical display in the Clan Room.

i No photography. Guide books in French, Italian, Japanese and German translations.

Partial. WCs.

Licensed.

Available for up to 100 people at no additional cost. Groups please book. Tour time: 1 hr.

P 100 cars. Car/ coach park close to Castle.

£2.50 per child. A guide can be provided. Areas of interest include a woodland walk.

Guide dogs only.

ANGUS'S GARDEN

Barguillean, Taynuilt, Argyll, West Highlands PA35 1HY
Tel: 01866 822335 **Fax:** 01866 822539
Contact: Sean Honeyman
Memorial garden of peace, tranquillity and reconciliation.
Location: MAP 12:P5, OS Ref. NM978 289. 4m SW on Glen Lonan road from A85.
Open: All year: daily, 9am–5pm (dusk during summer months).
Admission: Adult £2, Child Free.

ARDENCRAIG GARDENS

Ardencraig, Rothesay, Isle of Bute, West Highlands PA20 9BP
Tel: 01700 505339 **Fax:** 01700 502492
Owner: Argyll and Bute Council **Contact:** Allan Macdonald
Walled garden, greenhouses, aviaries. Woodland walk from Rothesay 1 mile (Skippers Wood.)
Location: MAP 13:A8, OS Ref. NS105 645. 2m from Rothesay.
Open: May–Sept: Mon–Fri, 10am–3.30pm, Sat & Sun, 1–4.30pm.
Admission: Free.

ARGYLL'S LODGING 🐾

Argyll's Lodging, Castle Wynd, Stirling, FK8 1EJ
Tel: 01786 450000 (Stirling Castle) **Fax:** 01786 448194
www.historic-scotland.gov.uk
Owners: Historic Scotland **Contact:** The Steward
An attractive townhouse decorated with rich materials and colours as it would have been during the 9th Earl of Argyll's occupation around 1680. During its restoration hidden secrets were revealed including a section of 17th century trompe l'oeil panelling in the dining room, created by painter David McBeath.
Location: MAP 13:E7, OS Ref. NS793 938. In Stirling's historic old town just below Stirling Castle off the M9. Rail: Stirling Train Station. Air:Edinburgh or Glasgow airport.
Open: Guided tours leave from Stirling Castle. Call 01786 450000 for times.
Admission: Included with entry to Stirling Castle.
ⓘ Access is by guided tour only. ☂ Evening receptions/dinners. ♿ WCs. 🎫 Obligatory. 🅿 Parking for cars and coaches available on Stirling Castle esplanade. ▮ Free pre-booked school visits scheme. ✖ ❋ ♥

BALLOCH CASTLE COUNTRY PARK

Balloch, Dunbartonshire G83 8LX
Tel: 01389 737000
Contact: West Dunbartonshire Council
A 200 acre country park on the banks of Loch Lomond.
Location: MAP 13:C7, OS Ref. NS390 830. SE shore of Loch Lomond, off A82 for Balloch or A811 for Stirling.
Open: All year: dawn–dusk.
Admission: Free.

BENMORE BOTANIC GARDEN

Dunoon, Argyll PA23 8QU
Tel: 01369 706261 **Fax:** 01369 706369
Contact: The Curator
A botanical paradise. Enter the magnificent avenue of giant redwoods and follow trails through the Formal Garden and hillside woodlands with its spectacular outlook over the Holy Loch and the Eachaig Valley.
Location: MAP 13:A7, OS Ref. NS150 850. 7m N of Dunoon on A815.
Open: 1 Mar–31 Oct: daily, 10am–6pm. Closes 5pm in Mar & Oct.
Admission: Adult £3.50, Child £1, Conc. £3, Family £8. Group discounts available.

BONAWE IRON FURNACE 🐾

Taynuilt, Argyll
Tel: 01866 822432
Owner: In the care of Historic Scotland **Contact:** The Steward
Founded in 1753 by Cumbrian iron masters this is the most complete remaining charcoal fuelled ironworks in Britain. Displays show how iron was once made here.
Location: MAP 12:P4, OS Ref. NN010 318. By the village of Taynuilt off the A85.
Open: 1 Apr–30 Sept: daily, 9.30am–5.30pm, last ticket 5pm. 1–31 Oct daily 9.30am–4.30pm. Last ticket 4pm.
Admission: Adult £4.20, Child £2.10, Conc. £3.20 (2008 prices).
🗐 🗺 🅿 €

Torosay

CASTLE STALKER

Portnacroish, Appin, Argyll PA38 4BA
Tel: 01631 730354 & 07789 597442 **www.castlestalker.com**
Owner: The Allward Family **Contact:** Messrs R & A Allward
Early 15th century tower house and seat of the Stewarts of Appin. Set on an islet 400 yds off the shore of Loch Linnhe. Reputed to have been used by James IV as a hunting lodge. Restored by the late Lt Col Stewart Allward and now retained by his family.
Location: MAP 12:P3, OS Ref. NM930 480. Approx. 20m N of Oban on the A828. On islet ¼m offshore.
Open: 10–14 & 17–21 May, 23–27 Aug, 30 Aug–3 Sept, 20–24 Sept. Telephone for appointments. Times variable depending on tides and weather.
Admission: Adult £8, Child £4.
ℹ Not suitable for coach parties. ♿ not suitable 📷 Obligatory 🅿 ⛔

DOUNE CASTLE

Doune, FK16 6EA
Tel: 01786 841742 **www.historic-scotland.gov.uk**
Owner: Earl of Moray (leased to Historic Scotland) **Contact:** The Steward
A formidable 14th century courtyard castle, built for the Regent Albany. The striking keep-gatehouse combines domestic quarters including the splendid Lord's Hall with its carved oak screen, musicians' gallery and double fireplace.
Location: MAP 13:D6, OS Ref. NN727 009. In Doune, 8m S of Callander on the A84.
Open: 1 Apr–30 Sept: daily, 9.30am–5.30pm. 1 Oct–31 Mar 9.30am–4.30pm, closed Thurs & Fri. Last ticket 30 mins before closing.
Admission: Adult £4.20, Child £2.10, Conc. £3.20 (2009 prices).
ℹ Picnic area. 🚻 ♿ WCs. 🅿 Limited for coaches. ⛔ On leads. 🏠⛔€

For **special events** held throughout the year, see the index at the end of the book.

Duart Castle

DUART CASTLE
ISLE OF MULL, ARGYLL PA64 6AP

www.duartcastle.com

Tel: 01680 812309 **E-mail:** duart.guide@btinternet.com
Owner/Contact: Sir Lachlan Maclean Bt
Duart is a fortress, one of a line of castles stretching from Dunollie in the east to Mingary in the north, all guarding the Sound of Mull. The earliest part of the Castle was built in the 12th century, the keep was added in 1360 by the 5th Chief Lachlan Lubanach and the most recent alterations were completed in 1673. The Macleans were staunchly loyal to the Stuarts. After the rising of 1745 they lost Duart and their lands were forfeited. Sir Fitzroy Maclean, 25th Chief, restored the Castle in 1910. Duart remains the family home of the Chief of the Clan Maclean.

Location: MAP 12:O4, OS Ref. NM750 350. Off A849 on the east point of the Isle of Mull.
Open: Castle & Tearoom open from 1st April Sun – Thur 11am – 4pm. Open daily from 1st May (including Shop) 10.30am – 5.30pm. Castle closes 18th Oct (Tearoom & Shop Close 11th Oct)
Admission: Adult: £5.30, Child (3–14) £2.65, Conc. £4.80, Family (2+2) £13.25.
🚻 🍴 ♿ Unsuitable. 📷 📷 By arrangement. 🅿 ⛔ In grounds, on leads. 🏠⛔

DUMBARTON CASTLE 🏛

Dumbarton, Strathclyde, G82 1JJ

Tel: 01389 732167 www.historic-scotland.gov.uk

Owner: Historic Scotland   **Contact:** The Steward

Dumbarton was the centre of the ancient kingdom of Strathclyde from the 5th century until 1018. Situated on a volcanic rock overlooking the Firth of Clyde, Dumbarton Castle was an important royal refuge sheltering both David II and Mary Queen of Scots.

Location: MAP 13:C8, OS Ref. NS 404 743. In Dumbarton off the A82.

Open: 1 Apr–30 Sept: daily, 9.30am–5.30pm. 1 Oct–31 Mar 9.30am–4.30pm, closed Thurs & Fri. Last ticket 30 mins before closing.

Admission: Adult £4.20, Child £2.10, Conc £3.20 (2009 prices).

ℹ Picnic Area. Bicycle Rack. 📷 🅿 No coaches. ⌨ ✳ €

DUNBLANE CATHEDRAL 🏛

Dunblane, FK15 0AQ

Tel: 01786 823388   www.historic-scotland.gov.uk

Owner: Historic Scotland   **Contact:** The Steward

One of Scotland's noblest medieval churches. The lower part of the tower is Romanesque but the larger part of the building is of the 13th century. It was restored in 1889–93 by Sir Rowand Anderson.

Location: MAP 13:E6, OS Ref. NN782 014. In Dunblane just off the B8033 close to Dunblane Station. Rail: Dunblane Station.

Open: 1 Apr–30 Sept: daily, 9.30am–5.30pm. 1 Oct–31 Mar 9.30am–4.30pm, closed Thurs & Fri. Last ticket 30 mins before closing. Closed for lunch daily 12.30–1.30pm.

Admission: Free.

📷 ♿ Partial. ⌨ ✳

THE HILL HOUSE ♦

Upper Colquhoun Street, Helensburgh G84 9AJ

Tel: 0131 243 9300

Owner: The National Trust for Scotland

Charles Rennie Mackintosh set this 20th century masterpiece high on a hillside overlooking the Firth of Clyde. Mackintosh also designed furniture, fittings and decorative schemes to complement the house.

Location: MAP 13:B7, OS Ref. NS300 820. Off B832, between A82 & A814, 23m NW of Glasgow.

INCHMAHOME PRIORY 🏛

Port of Menteith, FK8 3RA

Tel: 01877 385294   www.historic-scotland.gov.uk

Owner: In the care of Historic Scotland   **Contact:** The Steward

A beautifully situated Augustinian priory on an island in the Lake of Menteith founded in 1238 with much of the building surviving. The five year old Mary, Queen of Scots was sent here for safety in 1547.

Location: MAP 13:C6, OS Ref. NN574 005. On an island in Lake of Menteith. Reached by ferry from Port of Menteith, 4m E of Aberfoyle off A81.

Open: Open summer daily, 9.30am–5.30pm, last outward sailing at 4.30pm.

Admission: Adult £4.70, Child £2.35, Conc. £3.70 (2009 prices). Charge includes ferry trip.

ℹ Picnic area. 📷 🅿 Limited for coaches. ⌨ On leads. €

INVERARAY CASTLE 🏛   *See page 442 for full page entry.*

Inveraray Castle

DUNSTAFFNAGE CASTLE 🏛
BY OBAN, ARGYLL PA37 1PZ
www.historic-scotland.gov.uk

Tel: 01631 562465

Owner: In the care of Historic Scotland   **Contact:** The Steward

A fine 13th century castle built on a rock overlooking the Firth of Lorn. Captured by Robert the Bruce in 1309, it remained in royal possession for some years. The castle was briefly the prison of Flora Macdonald in 1746. Spectacular views from the huge curtain wall. Close by are the remains of a chapel.

Location: MAP 12:P4, OS49 NM882 344. Near Dunbeg 3m N of Oban off A85.

Open: 1 Apr–30 Sept: daily, 9.30am–5.30pm. 1 Oct–31 Mar 9.30am–4.30pm, closed Thurs & Fri. Last ticket 30 mins before closing.

Admission: Adult £3.70, Child £1.85, Conc. £3.00 (2009 prices). 10% discount for groups (11+).

📷 🎦 By arrangement. 🅿 Limited for coaches. ▣ Free pre-booked school visits. ⌨ On leads. ✳ €

West Highlands & Islands, Loch Lomond, Stirling and Trossachs

Torosay

IONA ABBEY & NUNNERY

Iona, Argyll, PA76 6SQ

Tel/Fax: 01681 700512   **www.historic-scotland.gov.uk**

Owner: In the care of Historic Scotland   **Contact:** The Steward

One of Scotland's most historic and venerated sites, Iona Abbey is a celebrated Christian centre and the burial place for many Scottish kings. The abbey and nunnery grounds house a superb collection of Christian carved stones and crosses, dating back to 600AD. Includes the Columba Centre and Fionnphort exhibition.

Location: MAP 12:L5, OS Ref. NM287 244. Ferry service from Fionnphort, Mull.

Open: All year, depending on the ferries.

Admission: Adult £4.70, Child (under 16yrs) £2.35, Conc. £3.70 (2009 prices). Columba Centre, exhibition & giftshop: Free.

On leads. €

KILCHURN CASTLE

Loch Awe, Dalmally, Argyll

Tel: 0131 668 8800   **www.historic-scotland.gov.uk**

Owner: In the care of Historic Scotland   **Contact:** The Steward

A square tower, built by Sir Colin Campbell of Glenorchy c1550. Much enlarged in 1693 it incorporates the first purpose-built barracks in Scotland. The picturesque castle ruins have spectacular views along Loch Awe.

Location: MAP 13:A5, OS Ref. NN133 276. At the NE end of Loch Awe, 2.5 m W of Dalmally off the A85.

Open: Summer only.

Admission: Free.

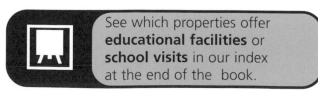

See which properties offer **educational facilities** or **school visits** in our index at the end of the book.

MOUNT STUART
ISLE OF BUTE PA20 9LR

www.mountstuart.com

Tel: 01700 503877   **Fax:** 01700 505313   **E-mail:** contactus@mountstuart.com

Owner: Mount Stuart Trust   **Contact:** Mount Stuart Office

Spectacular High Victorian gothic house, ancestral home of the Marquess of Bute. Splendid interiors, art collection and architectural detail. Set in 300 acres of stunning woodlands, mature Victorian pinetum, arboretum and exotic gardens.

Location: MAP 13:A9, OS Ref. NS100 600. SW coast of Scotland, 5m S of Rothesay. Local bus service to the Visitor Centre, frequent ferry service from Wemyss Bay, Renfrewshire and Colintraive, Argyll.

Open: Seasonal opening hours – please call for further information.

No photography. Licensed. Licensed. Obligatory. Ample. Guide dogs only. Exclusive.

©Phil McDermott Photography

ROTHESAY CASTLE

Rothesay, Isle of Bute, PA20 0DA
Tel: 01700 502691   **www.historic-scotland.gov.uk**
Owner: In the care of Historic Scotland   **Contact:** The Steward
A favourite residence of the Stuart kings, this is a wonderful example of a 13th century circular castle of enclosure with 16th century forework containing the Great Hall. Attacked by Vikings in its earlier days.
Location: MAP 13:A8, OS Ref. NS088 646. In Rothesay, Isle of Bute. Ferry from Wemyss Bay on the A78.
Open: 1 Apr–30 Sept: daily, 9.30am–5.30pm. 1 Oct–31 Mar 9.30am–4.30pm, closed Thurs & Fri. Last ticket 30 mins before closing.
Admission: Adult £4.20, Child £2.10, Conc. £3.20 (2009 prices).
ⓘ Closes for lunch. 🚻 On leads. €

ST BLANE'S CHURCH

Kingarth, Isle of Bute
Tel: 0131 668 8800   **www.historic-scotland.gov.uk**
Owner: In the care of Historic Scotland
This 12th century Romanesque chapel stands on the site of a 12th century Celtic monastery. A charming, tranquil spot.
Location: MAP 13:A9, OS Ref. NS090 535. At the S end of the Isle of Bute.
Open: All year: daily.
Admission: Free.
🅿 No coaches. 🚻 On leads.

STIRLING CASTLE

CASTLE WYND, STIRLING FK8 1EJ

www.stirlingcastle.gov.uk

Tel: 01786 450000
Owner: Historic Scotland   **Contact:** Castle Manager
Dominating the skyline, Stirling Castle is a shining example of Renaissance architecture. See the beautiful "Hunt of the Unicorn" tapestries in the Chapel Royal, watch the weavers at work in the tapestry studio, explore the vast Great Hall and visit the medieval kitchens. Enjoy views of the battlefields of Stirling Bridge where great medieval armies clashed. Home to generations of Scottish monarchs, Stirling Castle is an enduring and powerful reminder of Scotland's fascinating history.
Location: MAP 13:E7, OS Ref. NS790 941. At the top of Castle Wynd in Stirling's historic old town. Off the M9 junction 9 or 10.
Open: Apr–Sept: 9.30am–6pm. Oct–Mar: 9.30am–5pm. Last ticket 45 mins before closing.
Admission: Adult £9.00 Child £4.50, Conc. £7.00 (2009 Prices) Admission includes a tour of Argyll's Lodgings.
ⓘ Picnic area. 🚽 Private hire. ♿ WCs. 🎥 Obligatory. 🅿 Limited for coaches. €

TOROSAY CASTLE & GARDENS

CRAIGNURE, ISLE OF MULL PA65 6AY

www.torosay.com

Tel: 01680 812421   **E-mail:** torosay@aol.com
Owner/Contact: Mr Chris James
Torosay Castle was completed in 1858 by eminent architect David Bryce in the Scottish Baronial style, and remains a much loved family home. There are 12 acres of superb gardens, including three Italianate Terraces and the Statue Walk, and less formal woodland water gardens, rockery, Oriental and Alpine gardens, with a large collection of rare and tender plants, all offset by dramatic mountain and seascapes. The Castle offers family history, portraits, scrapbooks and antiques in an informal and relaxed atmosphere.
Location: MAP 12:O4, OS Ref. NM730 350. 1½m SE of Craignure by A849.
Open: House: 1 April–31 Oct: daily, 10.30am–5pm. Gardens: All year: daily, 9am–7pm (or till dusk if earlier).
Admission: Adult £7, Child £4, Conc. £6, Family £18. (2010 rates.)
ⓘ Children's adventure playground. ♿ WC. 🅿 Holiday cottages. €

Stirling Castle

GRAMPIAN HIGHLANDS

ALTYRE ESTATE

Altyre Estate, Forres, Moray IV36 2SH
Tel: 01309 672265 **Fax:** 01309 672270 **E-mail:** office@altyre.com
Contact: Sir Alastair Gordon Cumming
Altyre Estate comprises architecturally interesting buildings including Italianate farm buildings, standing stones and access to areas of natural and ornithological interest. Altyre Estate may interest scientific groups, students, and the general public.
Location: MAP 16:P8, OS Ref. NJ028 552. Details given on appointment.
Open: Visitors are welcome by appointment on the first working day of Apr, May Jun, Jul & Aug.
Admission: Free.

ARBUTHNOTT HOUSE & GARDEN

Arbuthnott, Laurencekirk AB30 1PA
Tel: 01561 361226 **E-mail:** keith@arbuthnott.co.uk **www.arbuthnott.co.uk**
Owner: The Viscount of Arbuthnott **Contact:** The Master of Arbuthnott
Arbuthnott family home for 800 years with formal 17th century walled garden on unusually steep south facing slope. Well maintained grass terraces, herbaceous borders, shrubs and greenhouses.
Location: MAP 14:K2, OS Ref. NO796 751. Off B967 between A90 and A92, 25m S of Aberdeen.
Open: House: 18–19 Apr, 2–3 May, 23–24 May, 11–12 Jul, 1–2 Aug and by arrangement. Guided tours: 2–5pm. Garden: All year: 9am–5pm.
Admission: House: £5. Garden: Adult £2.50, Child £1.
⬦ Ground floor. 🛈 Obligatory. 🅿 ⬛ ✳

BALFLUIG CASTLE

Alford, Aberdeenshire AB33 8EJ
Tel: 020 7624 3200
Owner/Contact: Mark Tennant of Balfluig
Small 16th century tower house in farmland, restored in 1967.
Location: OS Ref. NJ586 151. Alford, Aberdeenshire.
Open: Please write to M I Tennant Esq, 30 Abbey Gardens, London NW8 9AT. Occasionally let by the week for holidays. Graded *** by VisitScotland, see www.visitscotland.com/balfluigcastle
⬦ Unsuitable. ⬛ ⬛ 1 single, 4 double. ✳

BALMORAL CASTLE (GROUNDS & EXHIBITIONS)

Balmoral, Ballater, Aberdeenshire AB35 5TB
Tel: 013397 42534 **Fax:** 013397 42034 **E-mail:** info@balmoralcastle.com
www.balmoralcastle.com
Owner: Her Majesty The Queen **Contact:** Garry Marsden
Scottish home to The Royal Family. Ballroom, grounds and exhibitions, large café seating 120, quality gift shop. Excellent for coaches and groups. Holiday cottages, salmon fishing, Land Rover safaris and activity holidays.
Location: MAP 13:G1, OS Ref. NO256 951. Off A93 between Ballater and Braemar. 50m W of Aberdeen.
Open: 1 Apr–31 Jul: daily, 10am–5pm, last admission 4.30pm. Nov & Dec: Guided tours available – ring for details.
Admission: Adult £7, Child £3, OAP £6, Family £15 (Audio tour included). Discounts for groups (20+).
⬛ ⬛ 🛈⬛ ⬛

Cairness House

BALVENIE CASTLE 🏛

Dufftown, AB55 4DH
Tel: 01340 820121 **www.historic-scotland.gov.uk**
Owner: In the care of Historic Scotland **Contact:** The Steward
Picturesque ruins of 13th century moated stronghold originally owned by the Comyns. Visited by Edward I in 1304 and by Mary Queen of Scots in 1562. Occupied by Cumberland in 1746.
Location: MAP 17:B9, OS Ref. NJ326 408. At Dufftown on A941.
Open: 1 Apr–30 Sept: daily, 9.30am–5.30pm. Last ticket 5pm.
Admission: Adult £3.70, Child £1.85, Conc. £3.00 (2009 prices).
▣ ⬦ Partial. WCs. 🅿 ⬛ In grounds. €

BRODIE CASTLE ♜

Forres, Moray IV36 0TE
Tel: 0131 243 9300
Owner: The National Trust for Scotland
The lime harled building is a typical 'Z' plan tower house with ornate corbelled battlements and bartizans, with 17th & 19th century additions.
Location: MAP 16:P8, OS Ref. NH980 577. Off A96 4½m W of Forres and 24m E of Inverness.

CAIRNESS HOUSE

Lonmay, Fraserburgh, Aberdeenshire AB43 8XP
Tel: 01346 582078 **Email:** info@cairnesshouse.com **www.cairnesshouse.com**
Owners: Mr J Soriano-Ruiz / Mr K H Khairallah **Contact:** Property Manager
Cairness is Scotland's most extraordinary neoclassical house, recently brought back to life in a major restoration. Its exquisite interiors include the earliest Egyptian room in Britain, full of mysterious symbols. The house now contains one of the finest collections of furniture and paintings in the North East.
Location: MAP 17:F8, OS Ref. NK038 609. Off A90, 4m SE of Fraserburgh, ¼m W of B9033 about 2m S of St Comb's.
Open: Groups and special visits all year by prior arrangement.
Admission: Adult £7.50, tours with tea: £9.50. For special tours, lunches etc, please apply for details and rates. Minimum number for groups: 15.
🛈 No photography. No smoking. ⬛⬛🛈 Obligatory. 🅿 Limited. ⬛ ⬛⬛

Elgin Cathedral

visit hudsons guide online

Drum Castle, by Banchory

CASTLE FRASER & GARDEN ♛

Sauchen, Inverurie AB51 7LD
Tel: 0131 243 9300
Owner: The National Trust for Scotland
Begun in 1575, the two low wings contribute to the scale and magnificence of the towers rising above them, combining to make this the largest and most elaborate of the Scottish castles built on the 'Z' plan.
Location: MAP 17:D11, OS Ref. NJ723 125. Off A944, 4m N of Dunecht & 16m W of Aberdeen.

CORGARFF CASTLE ⛉

Strathdon, AB36 8YP
Tel: 01975 651460   **www.historic-scotland.gov.uk**
Owner: In the care of Historic Scotland   **Contact:** The Steward
A 16th century tower house converted into a barracks for Hanoverian troops in 1748. Corgarff Castle is surrounded by a distinctive star-shaped perimeter wall dating back to the 18th century.
Location: MAP 17:A11, OS Ref. NJ255 086. 8m W of Strathdon on A939. 14m NW of Ballater.
Open: 1 Apr–30 Sept: daily, 9.30am–5.30pm. Last ticket 5pm. 1 Oct–31 Mar 9.30am–4.30pm Sat & Sun only.
Admission: Adult £4.70, Child £2.35, Conc. £3.70 (2009 prices).
⌾ 🅿 Limited. ✳ €

CRAIG CASTLE

Rhynie, Huntly, Aberdeenshire AB54 4LP
Tel: 01464 861705   **Fax:** 01464 861702
Owner: Mr A J Barlas   **Contact:** The Property Manager
The Castle is built round a courtyard and consists of a 16th century L-shaped Keep, a Georgian house (architect John Adam) and a 19th century addition (architect Archibald Simpson of Aberdeen). The Castle was a Gordon stronghold for 300 years. It has a very fine collection of coats-of-arms.
Location: MAP 17:C10, OS Ref. NJ472 259. 3m W of Rhynie and Lumsden on B9002.
Open: May–Sept: Wed & every 2nd weekend in each month, 2–5pm.
Admission: Adult £5, Child £1.
🅣 🅖 Unsuitable. 🅧 By arrangement. 🅿 Limited for coaches. 🐕 Guide dogs only.

CRAIGSTON CASTLE

Turriff, Aberdeenshire AB53 5PX
Tel: 01888 551228   **E-mail:** wu-gen01@craigston.co.uk
Owner: William Pratesi Urquhart   **Contact:** The Housekeeper
Built in 1607 by John Urquhart Tutor of Cromarty, Craigston bears the marks of a client's brief rather than an architect's whim, which seems to belong to that strange slightly Gothic world. Few changes have been made to its exterior in its 400 years. A sculpted balcony unique in Scottish architecture depicts a piper, two grinning knights and David and Goliath. The interior dates from the early 19th century. Remarkable carved oak panels of Scottish kings' biblical heroes, mounted in doors and shutters of the early 17th century.
Location: MAP 17:D8, OS Ref. NJ762 550. On B9105, 4½m NE of Turriff.
Open: 29 May–13 Jun, 10 Jul–18 Jul: daily 1pm–4pm. Guided house tours: 1pm, 2pm & 3pm. Groups by appointment throughout the year.
Admission: Adult £6, Child £2, Conc. £4. Groups: Adult £5, Child/School £1.
🅖 Unsuitable. 🅧 Obligatory. 🅿 🐕 In grounds on leads. ✳

CRATHES CASTLE & GARDEN ♛

Banchory AB31 3QJ
Tel: 0131 243 9300
Owner: The National Trust for Scotland
The building of the castle began in 1553 and took 40 years to complete. Just over 300 years later, Sir James and Lady Burnett began developing the walled garden.
Location: MAP 17:D12, OS Ref. NO733 969: On A93, 3m E of Banchory and 15m W of Aberdeen.

CRUICKSHANK BOTANIC GARDEN

St Machar Drive, Aberdeen AB24 3UU
Tel: 01224 272704   **Fax:** 01224 272703
Owner: University of Aberdeen   **Contact:** R B Rutherford
Extensive collection of shrubs, herbaceous and alpine plants and trees. Rock and water gardens.
Location: MAP 17:E11, OS Ref. NJ938 084. In old Aberdeen. Entrance in the Chanonry.
Open: All year: Mon–Fri, 9am–4.30pm. Also May–Sept: Sat & Sun, 2–5pm.
Admission: Free.

DALLAS DHU DISTILLERY ⛉

Forres, IV36 2RR
Tel: 01309 676548   **www.historic-scotland.gov.uk**
Owner: In the care of Historic Scotland   **Contact:** The Steward
A completely preserved time capsule of the distiller's craft. Wander at will through this fine old Victorian distillery then enjoy a dram. Visitor centre, shop and audio-visual theatre.
Location: MAP 16:P8, OS Ref. NJ035 566. 1m S of Forres off the A940.
Open: 1 Apr–30 Sept: daily, 9.30am–5.30pm, 1 Oct–31 Mar 9.30am–4.30pm closed Thurs & Fri. Last ticket 30 mins before closing.
Admission: Adult £5.20, Child £2.60, Conc. £4.20 (2009 prices).
⌾ 🅖 WCs. 🅧 By arrangement. ⌾🅿 Limited for coaches. ✳ €

Provost Skene's House

DELGATIE CASTLE
TURRIFF, ABERDEENSHIRE AB53 5TD

www.delgatiecastle.com

Tel/Fax: 01888 563479   **E-mail:** joan@delgatiecastle.com

Owner: Delgatie Castle Trust   **Contact:** Mrs Joan Johnson

"Best Visitor Experience" Award Winner. Dating from 1030 the Castle is steeped in Scottish history yet still has the atmosphere of a lived in home. It has some of the finest painted ceilings in Scotland, Mary Queen of Scots' bed-chamber, armour, Victorian clothes, fine furniture and paintings are displayed. Widest turnpike stair of its kind in Scotland. Clan Hay Centre. 17th best place in Britain for afternoon tea.

Location: MAP 17:D9, OS Ref. NJ754 506. Off A947 Aberdeen to Banff Road.

Open: Daily, 10am–5pm. Closed Christmas & New Year weeks.

Admission: Adult £6, Child/Conc. £4, Family £16. Groups (10+): £4.

ⓘ No photography. 🄾🅃🅪 Ground floor. WC. 🄴 Home-baking and lunches. 🄵 By arrangement. 🄿 🄸 🄼 🄴 6 x houses for self catering. ❄

DRUM CASTLE & GARDEN ♨

Drumoak, by Banchory AB31 3EY

Tel: 0131 243 9300

Owner: The National Trust for Scotland

Owned for 653 years by one family, the Irvines. The combination over the years of a 13th century square tower, a very fine Jacobean mansion house and the additions of the Victorian lairds make Drum Castle unique among Scottish castles.

Location: MAP 17:D12, OS Ref. NJ796 004. Off A93, 3m W of Peterculter and 10m W of Aberdeen.

DRUMMUIR CASTLE

Drummuir, by Keith, Banffshire AB55 5JE

Tel: 01542 810332   **Fax:** 01542 810302

Owner: The Gordon-Duff Family   **Contact:** Alison Noakes

Castellated Victorian Gothic-style castle built in 1847 by Admiral Duff. 60ft high lantern tower with fine plasterwork. Family portraits, interesting artefacts and other paintings.

Location: MAP 17:B9, OS Ref. NJ372 442. Midway between Keith (5m) and Dufftown, off the B9014.

Open: Sat 28 Aug–Sun 26 Sept 2010: daily, 2–5pm (last tour 4.15pm).

Admission: Adult £2, Child £1.50. Pre-arranged groups: Adult £2, Child £1.50.

🅪 🄵 Obligatory. 🄿 🄼 In grounds on leads.

DUFF HOUSE

Banff AB45 3SX

Tel: 01261 818181   **Fax:** 01261 818900

Contact: The Manager

One of the most imposing and palatial houses in Scotland, with a strong classical façade and a grand staircase leading to the main entrance.

Location: MAP 17:D8, OS Ref. NJ691 634. Banff. 47m NW of Aberdeen on A947.

Open: Apr–Oct: daily, 11am–5pm. Nov–Mar: Thur–Sun, 11am–4pm.

Admission: Adult £6, Conc. £5, Family £16. Groups (10+): £5. Free admission to shop, tearoom, grounds & woodland walks. (Prices may change April 2008.)

ELGIN CATHEDRAL 🅪

Elgin, IV30 1HU

Tel: 01343 547171   www.historic-scotland.gov.uk

Owner: Historic Scotland   **Contact:** The Steward

Once one of the most beautiful Scottish cathedrals, known as the Lantern of the North. This magnificent ruin has many outstanding features including one of the country's finest octagonal chapter houses. See the bishop's home at Spynie Palace, 2m N. of the town.

Location: MAP 17:A8, OS Ref. NJ223 630. In Elgin on the A96.

Open: 1 Apr–30 Sept: daily, 9.30am–5.30pm, 1 Oct–31 Mar 9.30am–4.30pm, closed Thurs & Fri. Last ticket 30 mins before closing.

Admission: Adult £4.70, Child £2.35, Conc. £3.70 (2009 prices). Joint entry ticket available with Spynie Palace.

🄾 🅪 WCs. 🄸❄ €

FYVIE CASTLE ♨

Turriff, Aberdeenshire AB53 8JS

Tel: 0131 243 9300

Owner: The National Trust for Scotland

The five towers of the castle bear witness to the five families who have owned it. Fyvie Castle has a fine wheel stair and a collection of arms and armour and paintings.

Location: MAP 17:D9, S Ref. NJ763 393. Off A947, 8m SE of Turriff, and 25m N of Aberdeen.

HADDO HOUSE ♨

Tarves, Ellon, Aberdeenshire AB41 0ER

Tel: 0131 243 9300

Owner: The National Trust for Scotland

Designed by William Adam in 1731 for William, 2nd Earl of Aberdeen. Much of the interior is 'Adam Revival' carried out about 1880 for John, 7th Earl and 1st Marquess of Aberdeen and his Countess, Ishbel.

Location: MAP 17:E10, OS Ref. NJ868 348. Off B999, 4m N of Pitmedden, 10m NW of Ellon.

HUNTLY CASTLE 🅪

Huntly, AB54 4SH

Tel: 01466 793191   www.historic-scotland.gov.uk

Owner: In the care of Historic Scotland   **Contact:** The Steward

Known also as Strathbogie Castle, this glorious ruin stands in a beautiful setting on the banks of the River Deveron. Famed for its fine heraldic sculpture and inscribed stone friezes.

Location: MAP 17:C9, OS Ref. NJ532 407. In Huntly on the A96. N side of the town.

Open: 1 Apr–30 Sept: daily, 9.30am–5.30pm, 1–31 Oct 9.30am–4.30pm, Nov–Mar 9.30am–4.30pm closed Thurs & Fri. Last ticket sold 30 mins before closing.

Admission: Adult £4.70, Child £2.35, Conc £3.70 (2009 prices).

🄾 🅪 Partial. WCs. 🄿🄸🄼 On leads. ❄ €

KILDRUMMY CASTLE 🅪

Alford, Aberdeenshire, AB33 8RA

Tel: 01975 571331   www.historic-scotland.gov.uk

Owner: In the care of Historic Scotland   **Contact:** The Steward

Though ruined, the best example in Scotland of a 13th century castle with a curtain wall, four round towers, hall and chapel of that date. The seat of the Earls of Mar, it was dismantled after the first Jacobite rising in 1715.

Location: MAP 17:C11, OS Ref. NJ455 164. 10m W of Alford on the A97. 16m SSW of Huntly.

Open: 1 Apr–30 Sept: daily, 9.30am–5.30pm, last ticket 5pm.

Admission: Adult £3.70, Child £1.85, Conc. £3.00 (2009 prices).

🄾 🄿 Limited for coaches. 🄼 On leads. €

Pluscarden Abbey, The Altar reredos angels

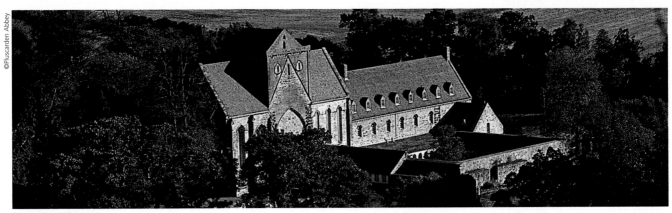

©Pluscarden Abbey

Pluscarden Abbey

KILDRUMMY CASTLE GARDEN

Kildrummy, Aberdeenshire
Tel: 01975 571203 / 563451   **Contact:** Alastair J Laing
Ancient quarry, shrub and alpine gardens renowned for their interest and variety. Water gardens below ruined castle.
Location: MAP 17:C11, OS Ref. NJ455 164. On A97 off A944 10m SW of Alford. 16m SSW of Huntly.
Open: Apr–Oct: daily, 10am–5pm.
Admission: Adult £3.50, Child Free.

LEITH HALL 🏰

Huntly, Aberdeenshire AB54 4NQ
Tel: 0131 243 9300
Owner: The National Trust for Scotland   **Contact:** The Property Manager
This mansion house, built around a courtyard was the home of the Leith family for almost 300 years.
Location: MAP 17:C10, OS Ref. NJ541 298. B9002, 1m W of Kennethmont, 7m S of Huntley.

LICKLEYHEAD CASTLE

Auchleven, Insch, Aberdeenshire AB52 6PN
Tel: 01651 821276
Owner: The Leslie family   **Contact:** Mrs C Leslie
A beautifully restored Laird's Castle, Lickleyhead was built by the Leslies c1450 and extensively renovated in 1629 by John Forbes of Leslie, whose initials are carved above the entrance. It is an almost unspoilt example of the transformation from 'Chateau-fort' to 'Chateau-maison' and boasts many interesting architectural features.
Location: MAP 17:C10, OS Ref. NJ628 237. Auchleven is 2m S of Insch on B992. Twin pillars of castle entrance on left at foot of village.
Open: 4–7, 10–14, 17–21 May: 12 noon–2pm. Also Sats only between 3 July–4 Sept: during the high season 12 noon–2pm.
Admission: Free.
🔗 Unsuitable. 🅿 Limited. No coaches. 🐾 In grounds, on leads.

PITMEDDEN GARDEN 🏰

Ellon, Aberdeenshire AB41 0PD
Tel: 0131 243 9300
Owner: The National Trust for Scotland
The centrepiece of this property is the Great Garden which was originally laid out in 1675 by Sir Alexander Seton, 1st Baronet of Pitmedden.
Location: MAP 17:E10, OS Ref. NJ885 280. On A920 1m W of Pitmedden village & 14m N of Aberdeen.

PLUSCARDEN ABBEY

Nr Elgin, Moray IV30 8UA
Tel: 01343 890257 **Fax:** 01343 890258 **E-mail:** monks@pluscardenabbey.org
Contact: Brother Michael
Valliscaulian, founded 1230.
Location: MAP 17:A8, OS Ref. NJ142 576. On minor road 6m SW of Elgin. Follow B9010 for first mile.
Open: All year: 4.45am–8.30pm. Shop: 8.30am–5pm.
Admission: Free.

PROVOST SKENE'S HOUSE

Guestrow, off Broad Street, Aberdeen AB10 1AS
Tel: 01224 641086 **Fax:** 01224 632133
Owner: Aberdeen City Council   **Contact:** Shonagh Bain
Built in the 16th century, Provost Skene's House is one of Aberdeen's few remaining examples of early burgh architecture. Splendid room settings include a suite of Georgian rooms, an Edwardian nursery, magnificent 17th century plaster ceilings and wood panelling. The house also features an intriguing series of religious paintings in the Painted Gallery and changing fashions in the Costume Gallery.
Location: MAP 17:E11, OS Ref. NJ943 064. Aberdeen city centre, off Broad Street.
Open: Mon–Sat, 10am–5pm, Closed Suns.
Admission: Free.

ST MACHAR'S CATHEDRAL TRANSEPTS 🏰

Old Aberdeen, AB24 1RQ
Tel: 01667 460232   www.historic-scotland.gov.uk
Owner: In the care of Historic Scotland
The nave and towers of the Cathedral remain in use as a church, and the ruined transepts are in care. In the south transept is the fine altar tomb of Bishop Dunbar (1514–32).
Location: MAP 17:E11, OS Ref. NJ939 088. In old Aberdeen. ½m N of King's College.
Admission: Free.
✳

SPYNIE PALACE 🏰

Elgin, IV30 5QG
Tel: 01343 546358   www.historic-scotland.gov.uk
Owner: In the care of Historic Scotland   **Contact:** The Steward
Spynie Palace was the residence of the Bishops of Moray from the 14th century to 1686. The site is dominated by the massive tower built by Bishop David Stewart (1461–77) and affords spectacular views across Spynie Loch.
Location: MAP 17:A8, OS Ref. NJ231 659. 2m N of Elgin off the A941.
Open: 1 Apr–30 Sept: daily, 9.30am–5.30pm, 1 Oct–31 Mar 9.30am–4.30pm weekends only. Last ticket 30 mins before closing.
Admission: Adult £3.70, Child £1.85, Conc. £3.00 (2009 prices) Joint entry ticket with Elgin Cathedral available.
ℹ Picnic area. Closes for lunch. 📷 🔗 Partial. WCs. 🅿 ✳ €

TOLQUHON CASTLE 🏰

Aberdeenshire, AB41 7LP
Tel: 01651 851286   www.historic-scotland.gov.uk
Owner: In the care of Historic Scotland   **Contact:** The Steward
Tolquhon was built for the Forbes family. The early 15th century tower was enlarged between 1584 and 1589 with a large mansion around the courtyard. Noted for its highly ornamented gatehouse and pleasance.
Location: MAP 17:E10, OS Ref. NJ874 286. 15m N of Aberdeen on the A920. 6m N of Ellon.
Open: 1 Apr–30 Sept: daily, 9.30am–5.30pm, 1 Oct –31 Mar 9.30am–4.30pm, weekends only. Last ticket 30 mins before closing.
Admission: Adult £3.70, Child £1.85, Conc. £3.00 (2009 prices).
ℹ Picnic area. Closes for lunch. 📷 🔗 WCs. 🅿 🚌 ✳ €

■ **Owner**
The Dowager Countess Cawdor

■ **Contact**
The Administrator
David Broadfoot MBE
Cawdor Castle
Nairn
Scotland IV12 5RD

Tel: 01667 404401
Fax: 01667 404674
E-mail: info@
cawdorcastle.com

■ **Location**
MAP 16:O9
OS Ref. NH850 500

From Edinburgh
A9, 3½ hrs,
Inverness 20 mins,
Nairn 10 mins.
Main road: A9, 14m.

Rail: Nairn
Station 5m.

Bus: Inverness to Nairn
bus route 200 yds.

Taxi: Cawdor Taxis
01667 404315.

Air: Inverness
Airport 5m.

■ **Opening Times**
Summer
1 May–10 October
Daily: 10am–5.30pm.
Last admission 5pm.

Winter
October–April
Groups by appointment,
admission prices on
application.

Auchindoune Garden
May–July: Tue & Thurs,
10am–4.30pm.

Otherwise by
appointment.

■ **Admission**
Summer
House & Garden
Adult	£8.30
Child (5–15yrs)	£5.20
OAP	£7.50
Student	£7.30
Family (2+5)	£26.00

Groups (20+)
Adult	£6.95
OAP/Student	£6.95
School Group (5–15yrs)	£4.50

Garden only
Per person	£4.50

RHS Access
Free admission to gardens
May, June, September &
October.

■ **Special Events**
June 5/6
Special Gardens
Weekend: Guided tours
of Gardens.

August 28/29
Special Gardens
Weekend: Guided tours
of Gardens.

September 25
'Living Food at Cawdor
Castle' – A celebration of
organic and local
produce.

CAWDOR CASTLE

www.cawdorcastle.com

This splendid romantic castle, dating from the late 14th century, was built as a private fortress by the Thanes of Cawdor, and remains the home of the Cawdor family to this day. The ancient medieval tower was built around the legendary holly tree.

Although the house has evolved over 600 years, later additions, mainly of the 17th century, were all built in the Scottish vernacular style with slated roofs over walls and crow-stepped gables of mellow local stone. This style gives Cawdor a strong sense of unity, and the massive, severe exterior belies an intimate interior that gives the place a surprisingly personal, friendly atmosphere.

Good furniture, fine portraits and pictures, interesting objects and outstanding tapestries are arranged to please the family rather than to echo fashion or impress. Memories of Shakespeare's *Macbeth* give Cawdor an elusive, evocative quality that delights visitors.

Gardens
The flower garden also has a family feel to it, where plants are chosen out of affection rather than affectation. This is a lovely spot between spring and late summer. The walled garden has been restored with a holly maze, paradise garden, knot garden and thistle garden. The wild garden beside its stream leads into beautiful trails through spectacular mature mixed woodland, in which paths are helpfully marked and colour-coded. The Tibetan garden and traditional Scottish vegetable garden are at the Dower House at Auchindoune.

ⓘ	9 hole golf course, putting green, golf clubs for hire, Conferences, whisky tasting, musical entertainments, specialised garden visits. No photography, video taping or tripods inside. No large day sacks inside castle.
🛍	Gift, book and wool shops.
🍷	Lunches, sherry or champagne receptions.
♿	Visitors may alight at the entrance. WC. Only ground floor accessible.
☕	Licensed Courtyard Restaurant, May–Oct, groups should book.
🚶	By arrangement.
Ⓟ	250 cars and 25 coaches. Two weeks' notice for group catering, coach drivers/couriers free.
🎗	£4.50 per child. Room notes, quiz and answer sheet can be provided.
🐕	Guide dogs only.

€

DUNVEGAN CASTLE & GARDENS 🏛

www.dunvegancastle.com

Any visit to the Isle of Skye would be incomplete without savouring the wealth of history offered by Dunvegan Castle & Gardens. Built on a rock in an idyllic loch side setting, Dunvegan is the oldest continuously inhabited castle in Scotland and has been the ancestral home of the Chiefs of MacLeod for 800 years.

Currently visitors can enjoy tours of an extraordinary castle and Highland estate steeped in history and clan legend, delight in the beauty of its formal gardens, take a boat trip onto Loch Dunvegan to see the seal colony (voted '1 of the Best UK Days Out' by *The Sunday Times Travel Magazine*), stay in one of its charming estate cottages, enjoy an appetising meal at the MacLeods Table Cafe or browse in one of its four shops offering a wide choice to suit everyone. There is a wealth of activities in the area ranging from walking, fishing and sightseeing to fine local cuisine, arts and craft and camping at the estate's Glenbrittle Campsite at the foot of the majestic Cuillin mountain range.

Over time, we have given a warm Highland welcome to visitors including Sir Walter Scott, Dr Johnson and Queen Elizabeth II and we now look forward to welcoming you. For more information, please visit www.dunvegancastle.com

Gardens

Dunvegan Castle's five acres of formal gardens began life in the 18th century. In stark contrast to the barren moorland and mountains that dominate Skye's landscape, the gardens are a hidden oasis featuring an eclectic mix of plants as you make your way through woodland glades, past shimmering pools fed by waterfalls and streams flowing down to the sea. Having experienced the Water Garden with its ornate bridges and islands replete with a rich and colourful plant variety, you can take a stroll through the elegant surroundings of the formal Round Garden featuring a Box-wood Parterre as its centrepiece. In what was formerly the castle's vegetable garden, the Walled Garden now features a diverse range of plants and flowers that compliment the attractive features including the stone worked MacLeod Clan Parliament Seating, a water lily pond and a Larch Pergola. A considerable amount of replanting and landscaping has taken place over the last thirty years to restore the gardens to their former glory and provide a legacy which future generations can enjoy.

■ Owner
Hugh Macleod of Macleod

■ Contact
The Administrator
Dunvegan Castle
Isle of Skye
Scotland IV55 8WF

Tel: 01470 521206
Fax: 01470 521205
E-mail: info@
dunvegancastle.com

■ Location
MAP 15:F9
OS Ref. NG250 480

1m N of village. NW corner of Skye.

From Inverness A82 to Invermoriston, A887 to Kyle of Lochalsh 82m. From Fort William A82 to Invergarry, A87 to Kyle of Lochalsh 76m.

Kyle of Lochalsh to Dunvegan 45m via Skye Bridge.

Ferry: Maillaig–Aradale (summer).

Rail: Inverness to Kyle of Lochalsh 3–4 trains per day – 45m.

Bus: Portree 25m, Kyle of Lochalsh 45m.

■ Opening Times
Summer
1 April–15 October
Daily: 10am–5.30pm.
Last admission 5pm.

Winter
16 October–31 March
Open by appointment weekdays only.

Castle & Gardens closed 20 December–3 January.

■ Admission
Summer
Castle & Gardens
Adult	£8.00
Child (3–15yrs)	£4.00
OAP/Student	£6.50
Family Ticket (2 Adults, 3 Children)	£23.00
Groups (10+)	£6.50
Cruise Ships using pontoon facilities.	£8.50

Gardens only
Adult	£6.00
Child (5–15yrs)	£3.00
Student/Group/OAP	£5.00

Seal Boats
Adult	£5.00
Child (5–12yrs)	£3.00
Student/Group/OAP	£4.00
Infant (under 2yrs)	Free

Loch Cruises & Fishing Trips
Adult	£35.00
Child (5–12yrs)	£25.00

Events & Weddings
Catering for up to 60 guests.

Film & TV
Unique location for film, TV or advertising.

The Gardens

The Dining Room

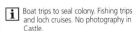

i	Boat trips to seal colony. Fishing trips and loch cruises. No photography in Castle.
	Gift and craft shops.
♿	Visitors may alight at entrance. WC.
	Licensed restaurant, (cap. 70) special rates for groups, menus upon request. Tel: 01470 521310.
🚶	By appointment in English or Gaelic at no extra charge. Self guided.
P	120 cars and 10 coaches. If possible please book. Seal boat trip dependent upon weather.
	Welcome by arrangement. Guide available on request.
	In grounds only, on lead. Guide Dogs allowed in Castle.
	3 self-catering units each sleeping 6.
❄	

BALLINDALLOCH CASTLE

Ballindalloch, Banffshire AB37 9AX

Tel: 01807 500205   **Fax:** 01807 500210   **E-mail:** enquiries@ballindallochcastle.co.uk
www.ballindallochcastle.co.uk

Owner: Mr & Mrs Oliver Russell   **Contact:** Mrs Clare Russell

Ballindalloch Castle is, first and foremost, a much-loved home, lived in by its original family, the Macpherson-Grants, since 1546. Filled with family memorabilia, including an important collection of 17th century Spanish paintings. Beautiful rock and rose gardens and river walks. The estate is home to the famous Aberdeen-Angus breed of cattle.

Location: MAP 17:A9, OS Ref. NJ178 366. 14 m NE of Grantown-on-Spey on A95. 22 m S of Elgin on A95.

Open: Good Fri–30 Sept: 10.30am–5pm. Closed Saturdays. Coaches outwith season by arrangement.

Admission: House & Grounds: Adult £8, Child (6–16) £4, Conc £6, Family (2+3) £20, Groups (20+) Adult £5, Child £2.50, Season Ticket £20. Grounds only: Adult £4, Child (6–16) £2, Conc £3, Family (2+3) £10, Season Ticket £12.

⊡🔽 Ground floor and grounds only. WCs. 🖬 🔽 🅿 🔽 In dog walking area.

CASTLE LEOD

Strathpeffer IV14 9AA

Tel/Fax: 01997 421264   **E-mail:** office@castleleod.org.uk

Owner/Contact: The Earl of Cromartie

Turreted 15th century tower house of rose-pink stone. Lived in by the Mackenzie family, chiefs of the clan, for 500 years and still very much a home where the family ensure a personal welcome. Magnificent setting below Ben Wyvis and amongst some of the finest trees in Scotland. Private tours, personally conducted by Lord Cromartie, can be arranged by emailing cromartie@castleleod.org.uk.

Location: MAP 16:M8, OS Ref. NH485 593. 1km E of Strathpeffer on the A834 Strathpeffer to Dingwall road.

Open: Public Open Days 27-30 May, 24-27 Jun, 29-31 Jul and 1 Aug, 12–15 Aug, 25-29 Aug, 23-26 Sept: 2–5.30pm (last admission 4.45pm).

Admission: Adult £7, Child £2, Conc £6.

ℹ️ No coaches. 🔽🔽 Grounds only. WC. 🔽 By arrangement, all year. 🅿 No coach parking. 🔽 Guide dogs only. 🔽

CASTLE OF OLD WICK 🔽

Wick, IV

Tel: 01667 460232   **www.historic-scotland.gov.uk**

Owner/Contact: Historic Scotland

This dramatically located castle is one of the best preserved Norse castles in Scotland. The castle is a simple square keep of at least three storeys. In addition to the tower the site contains the low-lying ruins of other buildings.

Location: MAP 17:B3, OS Ref. ND368 487. 1m S of Wick on Shore Road, signposted from Wick town centre.

Open: All year.

Admission: Free.

🔽

CAWDOR CASTLE 🔽

See page 452 for full page entry.

THE DOUNE OF ROTHIEMURCHUS 🔽

By Aviemore PH22 1QH

Tel: 01479 812345   **E-mail:** info@rothie.net   **www.rothiemurchus.net**

Owner: John Grant of Rothiemurchus, Lord Huntingtower

Contact: Rothiemurchus Centre

The family home of the Grants of Rothiemurchus since 1560, was nearly lost as a ruin and has been under an ambitious repair programme since 1975. The exterior and work on this exciting project in its unexpected setting may be visited on Mondays throughout the summer and the first Monday of every month. Book at the Rothiemurchus Centre or online for visits to restored rooms which can be enjoyed on the 1.5 hours 'Highland Lady Tour' which explores the haunts of Elizabeth Grant of Rothiemurchus, born 1797, author of 'Memoirs of a Highland Lady'. Her charming bestseller vividly describes the Doune of Rothiemurchus and its surroundings from the memories of her childhood.

Location: MAP 16:P11, OS Ref. NH900 100. 2m S of Aviemore on E bank of Spey river.

Open: Restoration and grounds open Apr-Aug: Mon 10am-12.30pm & 2-4.30pm (or dusk) also 1st Mon in the month during winter excl. Xmas & New Year. House open every Monday 11am as part of a Highland Lady Tour or by special arrangement excl. Xmas and New Year. Groups by special arrangement.

Admission: Restoration and grounds donation to charity; Tours: £16.50pp (min 2 people) 1¹/₂ hours; Groups: On application.

ℹ️ Rothiemurchus Centre. ⊡ 🔽 Obligatory. 🅿 Limited. 🔽 In grounds, on leads.

CASTLE OF MEY
THURSO, CAITHNESS KW14 8XH

www.castleofmey.org.uk

Tel: 01847 851473   **Fax:** 01847 851475   **E-mail:** enquiries@castleofmey.org.uk
Owner: The Queen Elizabeth Castle of Mey Trust   **Contact:** James Murray

The home of The Queen Mother in Caithness and the only property in Britain that she owned. She bought the Castle in 1952, saved it from becoming a ruin and developed the gardens. It became her ideal holiday home because of the beautiful surroundings and the privacy she was always given. Purpose-built Visitors' Centre with shop and tearoom and animal centre now open.

Location: MAP 17:B2, OS Ref. ND290 739. On A836 between Thurso and John O'Groats, just outside the village of Mey. 12m Thurso station, 18m Wick airport.

Open: 1 May–30 Sept: daily, 10.30am–4pm. Closed 29 Jul–9 Aug inclusive.

Admission: Adult £9.50, Child (16yrs and under) £4.00, Conc £8.50. Family £23.00. Booked groups (15+): £8.50. Gardens & grounds only: Adult £4.00.

ℹ️ No photography in the Castle. ⊡ 🔽 🔽 Partial. WCs. 🖬 🔽 By arrangement. 🅿 🔽 🔽 In grounds, on leads.

©Historic Scotland Photographic Library

DUNROBIN CASTLE 🏰
GOLSPIE, SUTHERLAND KW10 6SF
www.dunrobincastle.co.uk

Tel: 01408 633177   **Fax:** 01408 634081   **E-mail:** info@dunrobincastle.co.uk
Owner: The Sutherland Dunrobin Trust   **Contact:** Scott Morrison
Dates from the 13th century with additions in the 17th, 18th and 19th centuries. Wonderful furniture, paintings, library, ceremonial robes and memorabilia. Victorian museum in grounds with a fascinating collection including Pictish stones. Set in fine woodlands overlooking the sea. Magnificent formal gardens, one of few remaining French/Scottish formal parterres. Falconry display, telephone to confirm times.
Location: MAP 16:O6, OS Ref. NC850 010. 50m N of Inverness on A9. 1m NE of Golspie.
Open: 1 Apr–15 Oct: Mon–Sat, 10.30am–4.30pm, Sun, 12 noon–4.30pm. No Falconry display on Sundays. Last entry half an hour before closing.
Jun, Jul & Aug daily, 10.30am–5.30pm. Falconry displays every day. Last entry half an hour before closing. Falconry displays at 11.30am & 2pm.
Admission: Adult £8, Child £5, OAP/Student. £7, Family (2+2) £22. Booked groups (minimum 10): Adult £6.50, Child £4.70, OAP. £6. Please note these rates also include entry to the falconry display, museum and gardens.
🎦 🇹 ♿ Unsuitable for wheelchairs. 🖤 🍴 ⓧ By arrangement. 🅿 ✈

FORT GEORGE ⚜
ARDERSIER BY INVERNESS IV2 7TD
www.historic-scotland.gov.uk

Tel/Fax: 01667 460232
Owner: In the care of Historic Scotland   **Contact:** Brian Ford
Built following the Battle of Culloden to subdue the Highlands, Fort George never saw a shot fired in anger. One of the most outstanding artillery fortifications in Europe with reconstructed barrack room displays. The Queen's Own Highlanders' Museum.
Location: MAP 16:O6, OS Ref. NH762 567. 11m NE of Inverness off the A96 by Ardersier.
Open: Apr–Sep 9.30am–5.30pm daily, Oct–Mar 9.30am–4.30pm daily. Last ticket sold 45 mins before closing.
Admission: Adult £6.70, Child £3.35, Conc. £5.20. (2009 prices). 10% discount for groups (11+).
ℹ Picnic tables. 🎦 ♿ WCs. 🖤 🍴 🅿 🖼 Free if pre-booked. 🐕 On leads. ❄ ✡ €

DUNVEGAN CASTLE & GARDENS 🏰

See page 453 for full page entry.

©Historic Scotland Photographic Library

EILEAN DONAN CASTLE

Dornie, Kyle of Lochalsh, Wester Ross IV40 8DX
Tel: 01599 555202   **Fax:** 01599 555262   **E-mail:** eileandonan@btconnect.com
www.eileandonancastle.com   **Contact:** David Win – Castle Keeper
A fortified site for eight hundred years, Eilean Donan now represents one of Scotland's most iconic images. Located at the point where three great sea lochs meet amidst stunning highland scenery on the main road to Skye. Spiritual home of Clan Macrae with century old links to Clan Mackenzie.
Location: MAP 16:J10, OS Ref. NG880 260. On A87 8m E of Skye Bridge.
Open: Mar–Nov: 10am–5pm.
Admission: Adult £5.50, Conc £4.50.

URQUHART CASTLE ⚜
DRUMNADROCHIT, LOCH NESS, IV63 6XJ
www.historic-scotland.gov.uk

Tel: 01456 450551
Owner: In the care of Historic Scotland   **Contact:** Euan Fraser
One of the largest castles in Scotland, it dominates a rocky promontory on Loch Ness. Most of the existing buildings date from the 16th century. Explore the visitor centre with original artefacts, audio-visual presentation, shop and café.
Location: MAP 16:M10, OS Ref. NH531 286. On Loch Ness, 1½m S of Drumnadrochit on A82.
Open: 1 Apr–30 Sept: daily, 9.30am–6pm. Last ticket 5.15pm. 1–31 Oct 9.30–5pm, Nov–Apr 9.30am–4.30pm. Last entry 45 mins before closing.
Admission: Adult £7.00, Child £3.50, Conc £5.50 (2009 prices).
🎦 🇹 ♿ WCs. 🖤 🍴 🅿 Limited for coaches. 🖼 Free if pre-booked. 🐕 Guide dogs only. 🏠 ❄ €

Cawdor Castle

BALFOUR CASTLE

Shapinsay, Orkney Islands KW17 2DY

Tel: 01856 711282   **Fax:** 01856 711283

Owner/Contact: Mrs Lidderdale

Built in 1848. Now a small private hotel specialising in house parties, weddings etc. A beautiful island escape.

Location: MAP 14, OS Ref. HY475 164 on Shapinsay Island, 3½m NNE of Kirkwall.

Open: May–Sept: Suns only, 2.15–5.30pm.

Admission: Admission includes boat fare, guided tour, gardens & afternoon tea. Bookings essential. Contact property for details.

BISHOP'S & EARL'S PALACES 🏛

Kirkwall, Orkney, KW15 1PD

Tel: 01856 871918   **www.historic-scotland.gov.uk**

Owner: In the care of Historic Scotland   **Contact:** The Steward

The Bishop's Palace is a 12th century hall-house with a round tower built by Bishop Reid in 1541–48. The adjacent Earl's Palace built in 1607 has been described as the most mature and accomplished piece of Renaissance architecture left in Scotland.

Location: MAP 14, Bishop's Palace: OS Ref. HY447 108. Earl's Palace: OS Ref. HY448 108. In Kirkwall on A960.

Open: 1 Apr–30 Sept: daily, 9.30am–5.30pm. Last ticket 5pm.

Admission: Adult £3.70, Child £1.85, Conc. £3.00 (2009 prices). Explorer Pass available for entry to all Historic Scotland's Orkney attractions.

ℹ Closes for lunch. ⓘ 🐕 On leads. €

BLACKHOUSE 🏛

Arnol, Isle of Lewis, HS2 9DB

Tel: 01851 710395   **www.historic-scotland.gov.uk**

Owner: In the care of Historic Scotland   **Contact:** The Steward

A traditional Lewis thatched house, fully furnished, complete with attached barn, byre and stockyard. A peat fire burns in the open hearth. Includes an fascinating visitor centre.

Location: MAP 15, OS Ref. NB311 492. In Arnol village, 11m NW of Stornoway on A858.

Open: 1 Apr–30 Sept 9.30am–5.30pm, last ticket 5pm. 1 Oct–31 Mar: 9.30am–4.30pm, last ticket 4pm. Closed Sunday's all year round.

Admission: Adult £2.50, Child £1.25, Conc. £2.00 (2009 prices).

ⓘ ♿ WCs. 🅿 Limited for coaches. 🐕 On leads. ✳ €.

BROCH OF GURNESS 🏛

Aikerness, Orkney, KW17 2NH

Tel: 01856 751414   **www.historic-scotland.gov.uk**

Owner: In the care of Historic Scotland   **Contact:** The Steward

A noted icon of Orkney's rich archaeological heritage, the broch is one of the most outstanding surviving examples of a later prehistoric (Iron Age) settlement that is unique to northern Scotland.

Location: MAP 14, OS Ref. HY383 268. At Aikerness, about 14m NW of Kirkwall on A966.

Open: 1 Apr–30 Sept: daily, 9.30am–5.30pm, last ticket 5pm.

Admission: Adult £4.70, Child £2.35, Conc. £3.70 (2009 prices). Explorer Pass available for entry to all Historic Scotland's Orkney attractions.

ℹ Closes for lunch. ⓘ 🅿 Limited for coaches. 🐕 On leads. €

JARLSHOF PREHISTORIC & NORSE SETTLEMENT 🏛

Shetland, Sumburgh Head, ZE3 9JN

Tel: 01950 460112   **www.historic-scotland.gov.uk**

Owner: In the care of Historic Scotland   **Contact:** The Steward

Over 3 acres of remains spanning 3,000 years from the Stone Age. Oval-shaped Bronze Age houses, Iron Age broch and wheel houses. Viking long houses, medieval farmstead and 16th century laird's house.

Location: MAP 17, OS Ref. HU399 095. At Sumburgh Head, 22m S of Lerwick on the A970.

Open: 1 Apr–30 Sept: daily, 9.30am–5.30pm. Last ticket 30mins before closing.

Admission: Adult £4.70, Child £2.35, Conc. £3.70 (2009 prices).

ℹ Visitor Centre. Closes for lunch. ⓘ ⓘ 🅿 Limited for coaches. 🐕 On leads. €

KISIMUL CASTLE 🏛

Castlebay, Isle of Barra HS9 5UZ

Tel: 01871 810313   **www.historic-scotland.gov.uk**

Owner: In the care of Historic Scotland   **Contact:** The Monument Manager

The traditional seat of the chiefs of Clan Macneil, the castle stands on a rocky islet just off the island of Barra. It is the only significant surviving medieval castle in the Western Isles. It now makes a delightful place to visit, offering excellent views of the sea & the island.

Location: MAP 15 C:12. OS Ref. NL665 979. In Castlebay, Isle of Barra, five minute boat trip (weather permitting).

Open: 1 Apr–30 Sept: daily, 9.30am–5.30pm.

Admission: Adult £4.70, Child £2.35, Conc. £3.70 (2009 prices). Includes boat trip.

ℹ Closes for lunch. Sturdy footwear recommended. ⓘ €

© The Queen Elizabeth Castle of Mey Trust

Castle of Mey, Views of Orkney

© Dunrobin Castle

Dunrobin Castle, The Library

MAESHOWE CHAMBERED CAIRN

Orkney, KW16 3HA
Tel: 01856 761606   **www.historic-scotland.gov.uk**
Owner: In the care of Historic Scotland   **Contact:** The Steward
This world-famous tomb was built in Neolithic times, before 2700 BC. The large mound covers a stone-built passage and a burial chamber with cells in the walls. Runic inscriptions tell of how it was plundered of its treasures by Vikings.
Location: MAP 14, OS Ref. HY318 128. 9m W of Kirkwall on the A965.
Open: 1 Apr–30 Sept: daily, 9.30am–5.30pm. 1 Oct–31 Mar: daily, 9.30am–4.30pm.
Admission: Adult £5.20, Child £2.60, Conc. £4.20 (2009 prices) Timed ticketing in place – please telephone for details, and to book. Admission and shop at nearby Tormiston Mill. Ask about Explorer Passes, available for entry to all Historic Scotland's Orkney attractions.
ⓘ Timed Tours, booking in advance advisable. 📷 🎥 Obligatory.
Ⓟ Limited for cars. No coaches. 🐕 ♿ €

RING OF BRODGAR STONE CIRCLE & HENGE

Stromness, Orkney
Tel: 01856 841815   **www.historic-scotland.gov.uk**
Owner/Contact: In the care of Historic Scotland
A magnificent circle of upright stones with an enclosing ditch spanned by causeways, dating to the late Neolithic period. Part of the Heart of Neolithic Orkney World Heritage Site.
Location: MAP 14, OS Ref. HY294 134. 5m NE of Stromness on the B9055.
Open: All year.
Admission: Free.
ⓘ Ranger Service on site to give guided walks. Contact 01856 841 732 for details.
Ⓟ Limited for coaches. 🐕 On leads. ♿

© Heritage House Group Limited

Ballindalloch Castle

©Historic Scotland Photographic Library

SKARA BRAE & SKAILL HOUSE

SANDWICK, ORKNEY, KW16 3LR

www.historic-scotland.gov.uk

Tel: 01856 841815
Owner: Historic Scotland / Major M R S Macrae   **Contact:** Monument Manager
Skara Brae is one of the best preserved groups of Stone Age houses in Western Europe. Built before the Pyramids, the houses contain stone furniture, hearths and drains. Visitor centre and replica house with joint admission with Skaill House – 17th century home of the laird who excavated Skara Brae.
Location: MAP 14, OS6 HY231 188. 19m NW of Kirkwall on the B9056.
Open: Apr–Sept: daily, 9.30am–5.30pm. Oct–Mar: daily, 9.30am–4.30pm. Last ticket 45 mins before closing.
Admission: Apr–Sept: Adult £6.70, Child £3.35, Conc. £5.20. Oct–Mar: Adult £5.70, Child £2.85, Conc. £4.70 (2009 prices). 10% discount for groups (11+) Explorer Pass available for entry to all Historic Scotland's Orkney attractions.
ⓘ Visitor centre and picnic area. 📷♿ WCs. 🛍Ⓟ🅿 Free school visits when booked.
🐕 On leads. ♿ €

TANKERNESS HOUSE

Broad Street, Kirkwall, Orkney
Tel: 01856 873535   **Fax:** 01856 871560
Owner: Orkney Islands Council   **Contact:** Steve Callaghan
A fine vernacular 16th century town house contains The Orkney Museum.
Location: MAP 14, OS Ref. HY446 109. In Kirkwall opposite W end of cathedral.
Open: Oct–Apr: Mon–Sat, 10.30am–12.30pm & 1.30–5pm. May–Sept: Mon–Sat, 10.30am–5pm. Gardens always open. Please telephone in advance to confirm up to date opening times.
Admission: Free.

CALDICOT CASTLE & COUNTRY PARK

Church Road, Caldicot, Monmouthshire NP26 4HU
Tel: 01291 420241 **Fax:** 01291 435094
E-mail: caldicotcastle@monmouthshire.gov.uk **www.caldicotcastle.co.uk**
Owner: Monmouthshire County Council **Contact:** Castle Development Officer
Caldicot's magnificent castle is set in fifty acres of beautiful parkland. Founded by the Normans, developed in royal hands in the Middle Ages and restored as a Victorian home. Discover the Castle's past with an audio tour. Visitors can relax in tranquil gardens, explore medieval towers, discover children's activities and play giant chess. Medieval Banquet evenings and unique wedding location.
Location: MAP 2:N1, OS Ref. ST487 887. From M4 take J23a and B4245 to Caldicot. From M48 take J2 and follow A48 & B4245. Castle signposted from B4245.
Open: Castle: 1 Apr–31 Oct: daily, 11am–5pm. Active winter events programme, please telephone for winter opening times. Country Park: All year daily.
Admission: Adult £3.75, Child/Conc £2.50. Groups (10–100): Adult £3, Child/Conc £2. ▣ ⊤ 🅛 Partial. WCs. 🖤 🗾 By arrangement. 🖾 🅿 🎞 Free for formal educational visits. 🐾 In Castle, on leads. ▲ 🐾

CARDIFF CASTLE

Castle Street, Cardiff CF10 3RB
Tel: 029 2087 8100 **Fax:** 029 2023 1417
Owner: City and County of Cardiff **Contact:** Booking Office
2000 years of history, including Roman Walls, Norman Keep and Victorian interiors.
Location: MAP 2:M1, OS Ref. ST181 765. Cardiff city centre, signposted from M4.
Open: 1 Mar–31 Oct: daily, 9am–6pm. Tours 10am–5pm, last tour 4.50pm; 1 Nov–28 Feb: daily, 9.30am–5pm. Tours 10am–4pm, last tour 3.45pm. Closed 25/26 Dec & 1 Jan.
Admission: Full Tour: Adult £8.95, Child £6.35, OAP £7.50. Curator Tours: Adult/OAP £20.

CARMARTHEN CASTLE

Carmarthen, South Wales
Tel: 0126 7224923 **E-mail:** clgriffiths@carmarthenshire.gov.uk
Owner/Contact: The Conservation Department, Carmarthenshire County Council
The fortress, originally founded by Henry I in 1109, witnessed several fierce battles, notably in the 15th century when the Welsh hero Owain Glyndwr burnt the town and took the castle from the English.
Location: MAP 5:E11, OS Ref. SN413 200. In the town centre.
Open: Throughout the year.
Admission: Free.

CARREG CENNEN CASTLE ✠

Tir-y-Castell Farm, Llandeilo SA19 6TS
Tel: 01558 822291 **www.cadw.wales.gov.uk**
Owner: In the care of Cadw **Contact:** The Manager
Spectacularly crowning a remote crag 300 feet above the River Cennen, the castle is unmatched as a wildly romantic fortress sought out by artists and visitors alike. The climb from Rare Breeds Farm is rewarded by breathtaking views and the chance to explore intriguing caves beneath.
Location: MAP 5:G11, OS Ref. SN668 190. Minor roads from A483(T) to Trapp village. 5m SE of A40 at Llandeilo.
Open: 1 Apr–31 Oct: daily, 9.30am–6.30pm. 1 Nov–31 Mar, daily, 9.30am–4pm. Closed 25 Dec.
Admission: Adult £3.60, Child (under 16 yrs)/Conc. £3.25, Child under 5yrs Free, Family (2 adults and all children under 16yrs) £10.50. Under 16s must be accompanied by an adult. All opening times and prices are correct at time of going to press (Autumn 2009) but may be subject to change from March 2010 – Please see site for details.
ℹ️ Induction loop. Toilets. 🖾 🖤 🖾 🅿 🐾 ❄

CADW: Crown Copyright

CASTELL COCH ✠

TONGWYNLAIS, CARDIFF CF15 7JS

www.cadw.wales.gov.uk

Tel: 029 2081 0101
Owner: In the care of Cadw **Contact:** The Custodian
A fairytale castle in the woods, Castell Coch embodies a glorious Victorian dream of the Middle Ages. Designed by William Burges as a country retreat for the 3rd Lord Bute, every room and furnishing is brilliantly eccentric, including paintings of Aesop's fables on the drawing room walls.
Location: MAP 2:L1, OS Ref. ST131 826. M4/J32, A470 then signposted. 5m NW of Cardiff city centre.
Open: Apr–Oct: 9am–5pm, daily. Nov–Mar: Mon–Sat, 9.30am–4pm, Sun 11am–4pm. Closed 24, 25, 26 Dec, 1 Jan & 4 Jan–7 Feb 2010.
Admission: Adult £3.60, Child (under 16 yrs)/Conc. £3.20, Child under 5yrs Free, Family (2 adults and all children under 16yrs) £10.40. Under 16s must be accompanied by an adult. All opening times and prices are correct at time of going to press (Autumn 2009) but may be subject to change from March 2010 – Please see site for details.
ℹ️ Toilets. Cycle stands. Baby changing. Induction loop. 🖾 🖤 🅿 🐾 ▲ ❄

CHEPSTOW CASTLE ✠

Chepstow, Monmouthshire NP16 5EY
Tel: 01291 624065 **www.cadw.wales.gov.uk**
Owner: In the care of Cadw **Contact:** The Custodian
The oldest stone fortification in Britain. So powerful was this castle that it continued in use until 1690, being finally adapted for cannon and musket after an epic Civil War siege. This huge, complex, grand castle deserves to be explored.
Location: MAP 2:O1, OS Ref. ST533 941. Chepstow via A466, B4235 or A48. 1½m N of M48/J22.
Open: Apr–Oct: 9am–5pm ,daily. Nov–Mar: Mon–Sat, 9.30am–4pm, Sun 11am–4pm. Closed 24, 25, 26 Dec, 1 Jan. Last admission 30 minutes before closing.
Admission: Adult £3.60, Child (under 16 yrs)/Conc. £3.20, Child under 5yrs Free, Family (2 adults and all children under 16yrs) £10.40. Under 16s must be accompanied by an adult. All opening times and prices are correct at time of going to press (Autumn 2009) but may be subject to change from March 2010 – Please see site for details.
ℹ️ Induction loop. 🖾 🅛 Partial. 🅿 Pay and display. 🐾 ❄

National Botanic Garden of Wales

Cresselly

CILGERRAN CASTLE ♣ ❧

Cardigan, Pembrokeshire SA43 2SF

Tel: 01239 621339 **www.cadw.wales.gov.uk**

Owner: In the care of Cadw   **Contact:** The Custodian

Perched high up on a rugged spur above the River Teifi, Cilgerran Castle is one of the most spectacularly sited fortresses in Wales. It dates from the 11th–13th centuries.

Location: MAP 5:D10, OS Ref. SN195 431. Main roads to Cilgerran from A478 and A484. 3½m SSE of Cardigan.

Open: Apr–Oct: daily, 10am–5pm. Nov–Mar 10am–4pm. Last admission 30 minutes before closing.

Admission: Adult £3, Child (under 16 yrs)/Conc. £2.60, Child under 5yrs free, Family (2 adults and all children under 16yrs) £8.60. Under 16s must be accompanied by an adult. All opening times and prices are correct at time of going to press (Autumn 2009) but may be subject to change from March 2010 – Please see site for details.

ⅈ Toilets. Induction loop. 🖸 🖼 On leads. ❋

CLYNE GARDENS

Mill Lane, Blackpill, Swansea SA3 5BD

Tel: 01792 401737   **E-mail:** botanics@swansea.gov.uk

Owner: City and County of Swansea   **Contact:** Steve Hopkins

50 acre spring garden, large rhododendron collection, 4 national collections, extensive bog garden, native woodland.

Location: MAP 2:I1, OS Ref. SS614 906. S side of Mill Lane, 500yds W of A4067 Mumbles Road, 3m SW of Swansea.

Open: All year.

Admission: Free.

COLBY WOODLAND GARDEN ❧

Amroth, Narbeth, Pembrokeshire SA67 8PP

Tel: 01834 811885   **Fax:** 01834 831766

Owner: The National Trust

This 3½ ha (8 acre) garden has a fine display of colour in spring, with rhododendrons, magnolias, azaleas and camellias, underplanted with bluebells. Later highlights are the summer hydrangeas and autumn foliage. Open and wooded pathways through the valley offer lovely walks.

Location: MAP 5:D12, OS Ref. SN155 080. ½m inland from Amroth beside Carmarthen Bay. Signs from A477.

Open: 15 Mar–2 Nov: daily. Woodland Garden: 10am–5pm; Walled Garden: 11am–5pm.

*Admission: Adult £4.20, Child £2.10, Family £10.50. Groups (15+): Adult £3.60, Child £1.80. *includes a voluntary donation but visitors can choose to pay the standard prices displayed at the property and on the website.

ⅈ Gallery events. 🖸 🖼

CORNWALL HOUSE ☎

58 Monnow Street, Monmouth NP25 3EN

Tel/Fax: 01600 712031

Owner/Contact: Ms Jane Harvey

Town house, dating back to at least the 17th century. Red brick garden façade in Queen Anne style, dating from 1752. Street façade remodelled in Georgian style (date unknown). Many original features, including fine staircase. Delightful town garden with original walled kitchen garden.

Location: MAP 6:L11, OS Ref. SO506 127. Half way down main shopping street in Monmouth.

Open: 2–18 Apr, 1–3 May, 28–30 Aug, 11–12 Sept, 2–5pm.

Admission: Adult £4, Conc. £2.

🖬 Obligatory. 🅿 Public car park nearby. 🖼 €

CRESSELLY

Kilgetty, Pembrokeshire SA68 0SP

E-mail: hha@cresselly.com   **www.cresselly.com**

Owner/Contact: H D R Harrison-Allen Esq MFH

Home of the Allen family for 250 years. The house is of 1770 with matching wings of 1869 and contains good plasterwork and fittings of both periods. The Allens are of particular interest for their close association with the Wedgwood family of Etruria and a long tradition of foxhunting.

Location: MAP 5:C11, OS Ref. SN065 065. W of the A4075.

Open: 5–31 Jul; 1 Aug Inclusive, 10am–1pm. Guided tours only, on the hour. Coaches and at other times by arrangement.

Admission: Adult £4, no children under 12.

🖫 Ground floor only. 🖬 Obligatory. 🅿 Coaches by arrangement.

DINEFWR PARK AND CASTLE ❧

Llandeilo SA19 6RT

Tel: 01558 823902   **Fax:** 01558 825925   **E-mail:** dinefwr@nationaltrust.org.uk

Owner: The National Trust   **Contact:** Janet Philpin, Property Administrator

Historic site including 12th century Welsh castle, magnificent parkland with historic deer park and Newton House.

Location: MAP 5:G11, OS Ref. SN625 225. On outskirts of Llandeilo.

Open: House & Park: 15 Mar–2 Nov, Daily, 11am–5pm. 7 Nov–21 Dec, Fri–Sun, 11am–5pm. Tearoom open daily all year.

*Admission: House & Park: Adult £6.30, Child £3.15, Family £15.75. Groups (15+) £5.35. *includes a voluntary donation but visitors can choose to pay the standard prices displayed at the property and on the website.

🖫🖬🖬 By arrangement. 🅿 Limited for coaches. 🖫🖼 In grounds on leads.

© Skyscan

DYFFRYN GARDENS AND ARBORETUM

ST NICHOLAS, Nr CARDIFF CF5 6SU

www.dyffryngardens.com

Tel: 029 2059 3328   **Fax:** 029 2059 1966

Owner: Vale of Glamorgan Council   **Contact:** Ms G Donovan

Dyffryn Gardens is a beautiful Grade I registered Edwardian garden, set in the heart of the Vale of Glamorgan countryside. The 55-acre gardens are the result of a unique collaboration between the eminent landscape architect, Thomas Mawson, and the passionate plant collector, Reginald Cory. The garden includes great lawns, herbaceous borders, many individual themed garden 'rooms' and a well established Arboretum including 17 champion trees. The magnificent gardens have been undergoing extensive restoration work with assistance from the Heritage Lottery Fund, including a striking Visitor Centre and tearooms. Ongoing work includes the Walled Garden and new glasshouses, which are due for completion later this year.

Location: MAP 2:L2, OS Ref. ST095 723. 3m NW of Barry, J33/M4. 1½m S of St Nicholas on A48.

Open: All year. For details please telephone 029 2059 3328.

Admission: Summer: Adult £6.50, Child £2.50. Conc. £4.50. Winter: Adult £3.50, Child £1.50. Conc. £2.50. Discount for groups (15+).

FONMON CASTLE

FONMON, BARRY, VALE OF GLAMORGAN CF62 3ZN

Tel: 01446 710206   **Fax:** 01446 711687   **E-mail:** Fonmon_Castle@msn.com

Owner: Sir Brooke Boothby Bt   **Contact:** Anne Broadway

Occupied as a home since the 13th century, this medieval castle has the most stunning Georgian interiors and is surrounded by extensive gardens. Available for weddings, dinners, corporate entertainment and multi-activity days.

Location: MAP 2:L2, OS Ref. ST047 681. 15m W of Cardiff, 1m W of Cardiff airport.

Open: 1 Apr–30 Sept: Tue & Wed, 2–5pm (last tour 4pm). Other times by appointment. Groups: by appointment.

Admission: Adult £5, Child Free.

ⓘ Conferences. 🍽 By arrangement (up to 120). ♿ WC. 🅿 🖼 Guide dogs only. 🏠 ❋

KIDWELLY CASTLE ✿

Kidwelly, Carmarthenshire SA17 5BQ

Tel: 01554 890104   www.cadw.wales.gov.uk

Owner: In the care of Cadw   **Contact:** The Custodian

A chronicle in stone of medieval fortress technology this strong and splendid castle developed during more than three centuries of Anglo-Welsh warfare. The half-moon shape stems from the original 12th century stockaded fortress, defended by the River Gwendraeth on one side and a deep crescent-shaped ditch on the other.

Location: MAP 5:E12, OS Ref. SN409 070. Kidwelly via A484. Kidwelly Rail Station 1m.

Open: Apr–Oct: 9am–5pm. 1 Nov–31 Mar: Mon–Sat, 9.30am–4pm, Sun 11am–4pm. Closed 24, 25, 26 Dec, 1 Jan. Last admission 30 mintes before closing.

Admission: Adult £3, Child (under 16 yrs)/Conc. £2.60, Child under 5yrs Free, Family (2 adults and all children under 16yrs) £8.60. Under 16s must be accompanied by an adult. All opening times and prices are correct at time of going to press (Autumn 2009) but may be subject to change from March 2010 – Please see site for details.

ⓘ Baby changing. Induction loop. Toilets. 🖼 🅿 🖼 ❋

LAMPHEY BISHOP'S PALACE ✿

Lamphey, Pembroke SA71 5NT

Tel: 01646 672224   www.cadw.wales.gov.uk

Owner: In the care of Cadw   **Contact:** The Custodian

Lamphey marks the place of the spectacular Bishop's Palace but it reached its height of greatness under Bishop Henry de Gower who raised the new Great Hall. Today the ruins of this comfortable retreat reflect the power enjoyed by the medieval bishops.

Location: MAP 5:C12, OS Ref. SN018 009. A4139 from Pembroke or Tenby. N of village (A4139).

Open: 1 Apr–31 Oct: daily, 10am–5pm (last admission 30 mins before closing). The visitor centre will be closed during winter. Access will be via the side gate between 10am and 4pm.

Admission: Adult £3, Child (under 16 yrs)/Conc. £2.60, Child under 5yrs Free, Family (2 adults and all children under 16yrs) £8.60. Under 16s must be accompanied by an adult. All opening times and prices are correct at time of going to press (Autumn 2009) but may be subject to change from March 2010 – Please see site for details.

🖼 🅿 🖼 On leads. ❋

LAUGHARNE CASTLE ✤

King Street, Laugharne, Carmarthenshire SA33 4SA
Tel: 01994 427906 **www.cadw.wales.gov.uk**
Owner: In the care of Cadw   **Contact:** The Custodian
Picturesque Laugharne Castle stands on a low ridge overlooking the wide Taf estuary, one of a string of fortresses controlling the ancient route along the South Wales coast. Inspired Richard Huges and near to Dylan Thomas's Boathouse.
Location: MAP 5:E11, OS Ref. SN303 107. 4m S of A48 at St Clears via A4066.
Open: 1 Apr–31 Oct: daily, 10am–5pm. The Monument is closed at all other times.
Admission: Adult £3, Child (under 16 yrs)/Conc. £2.60, Child under 5yrs Free, Family (2 adults and all children under 16yrs) £8.60. Under 16s must be accompanied by an adult. All opening times and prices are correct at time of going to press (Autumn 2009) but may be subject to change from March 2010 – Please see site for details.
ℹ Induction loop. 📷 ♿

LLANCAIACH FAWR MANOR

Nelson, Treharris CF46 6ER
Tel: 01443 412248 **Fax:** 01443 412688
Owner: Caerphilly County Borough Council   **Contact:** The Administrator
Tudor fortified manor dating from 1530 with Stuart additions. Costumed guides.
Location: MAP 2:M1, OS Ref. ST114 967. S side of B4254, 1m N of A472 at Nelson.
Open: All year: daily, 10am–5pm. Last admission 1hour before closing. Nov–Feb: closed Mons. Closed Christmas week.
Admission: Adult £5.50, Child £4, Conc. £4.50, Family £16.50.

LLANVIHANGEL COURT

Nr Abergavenny, Monmouthshire NP7 8DH
Tel: 01873 890217 **E-mail:** jclarejohnson@googlemail.com
www.llanvihangel-court.co.uk
Owner/Contact: Julia Johnson
Grade I Tudor Manor. The home in the 17th century of the Arnolds who built the imposing terraces and stone steps leading to the house. The interior has a fine hall, unusual yew staircase and many 17th century moulded plaster ceilings. Delightful grounds. 17th century features, notably Grade I stables.
Location: MAP 6:K11, OS Ref. SO433 139. 4m N of Abergavenny on A465.
Open: 30 April-16 May & 11-18 August, incl, daily 2.30–5.30pm. Last tour 5pm.
Admission: Entry and guide, Adult £4.00, Child/Conc. £2.50.
ℹ No inside photography. ♿ Partial. ♿ 🅿 Limited. ♿ On leads. ▣

NATIONAL BOTANIC GARDEN OF WALES

See page 460 for full page entry.

The Judge's Lodging

Chepstow Castle

OXWICH CASTLE ✤

Oxwich SA3 1NG
Tel: 01792 390359 **www.cadw.wales.gov.uk**
Owner: In the care of Cadw   **Contact:** The Custodian
Beautifully sited in the lovely Gower peninsula, Oxwich Castle is a striking testament to the pride and ambitions of the Mansel dynasty of Welsh gentry.
Location: MAP 2:I1, OS159 Ref. SS497 864. A4118, 11m SW of Swansea, in Oxwich village.
Open: 1 Apr–30 Sept: daily, 10am–5pm. The Monument is closed at all other times.
Admission: Adult £2.60, Child (under 16 yrs)/Conc. £2.25, Child under 5yrs Free, Family (2 adults and all children under 16yrs) £7.45. Under 16s must be accompanied by an adult. All opening times and prices are correct at time of going to press (Autumn 2009) but may be subject to change from March 2010 – Please see site for details.
ℹ Baby changing. Toilets. Induction loop. Cycle stands. 📷 🅿 ♿ On leads.

PEMBROKE CASTLE
PEMBROKE SA71 4LA

www.pembrokecastle.co.uk

Tel: 01646 681510 **Fax:** 01646 622260 **E-mail:** info@pembrokecastle.co.uk
Owner: Trustees of Pembroke Castle   **Contact:** Mr D Ramsden
Pembroke Castle is situated within minutes of beaches and the breathtaking scenery of the Pembrokeshire Coastal National Park. This early Norman fortress, birthplace of the first Tudor King, houses many fascinating displays and exhibitions. Enjoy a picnic in the beautifully kept grounds, or on the roof of St. Anne's Bastion and take in the views along the estuary. Events every weekend in July and August.
Location: MAP 5:C12, OS Ref. SM983 016. W end of the main street in Pembroke.
Open: All year. 1 Apr–Sept: daily, 9.30am–6pm. Mar & Oct: daily, 10am–5pm. Nov–Feb: daily, 10am–4pm. Closed 24-26 Dec & 1 Jan. Cafe closed Dec–Jan. Brass rubbing centre open Summer months and all year by arrangement.
Admission: Adult £4.50, Child/Conc. £3.50, Family (2+2) £12. Groups (20+): Adult £4, OAP/Student £3.
📷 ♿ ♨ Closed Dec & Jan. ♿ End of May–Sept by arrangement. ▣
♿ In grounds, on leads. ❋ ♨

South Wales

PICTON CASTLE, GALLERY & GARDENS
THE RHOS, NEAR HAVERFORDWEST, PEMBROKESHIRE SA62 4AS

www.pictoncastle.co.uk

Tel/Fax: 01437 751326   **E-mail:** info@pictoncastle.co.uk

Owner: The Picton Castle Trust   **Contact:** Mr D W Evans

A stunning hybrid of 13th Century medieval castle and Georgian manor house, Picton Castle is set in 40 acres of magnificent woodland and walled garden. The medieval castle was modernised and extended during the 18th Century to create fine Georgian interiors. Well informed guides bring the history to life during castle tours, which are being extended through 2010 to include new features. Part of the RHS access scheme, the gardens contain unique rhododendrons and roses, rare conifers, tree ferns and bamboos. The Picton Gallery features a programme of exhibitions ranging from fine art to fine quality arts & crafts.

Events include plant sales, outdoor theatre, music evenings and family days.

Location: MAP 5:C11, OS Ref. SN011 135. 4m E of Haverfordwest, just off A40.

Open: 29 Mar–31 Sept, daily, 10.30am–5pm. Check website for dates and times of February and October half term opening and occasional winter weekend openings. Entrance to castle by guided tours only, between 11.30am and 3.30pm.

Admission: Gardens and Gallery ticket: Adult £4.95, Seniors £4.75, Child £2.50. With Castle Tour: Adult £7.45, Child £4.

Groups (20+): reduced prices by prior arrangement.

🛈 Ⓟ ♿ T ♿ ♿ ♿ Licensed. Obligatory. Ⓟ In grounds, on leads.

RAGLAN CASTLE ✤
RAGLAN NP15 2BT

www.cadw.wales.gov.uk

Tel: 01291 690228

Owner: In the care of Cadw   **Contact:** The Custodian

Undoubtedly the finest late medieval fortress-palace in Britain, it was begun in the 1430s by Sir William ap Thomas who built the mighty 'Yellow Tower'. His son William Lord Herbert added a palatial mansion defended by a gatehouse and many towered walls. Witness the Civil War effects and marvel at the lavish guest accommodation.

Location: MAP 6:K12, OS Ref. SO415 084. Raglan, NE of Raglan village off A40 (eastbound) and signposted.

Open: Apr–Oct: 9am–5pm, daily Nov–Mar: Mon–Sat, 9.30am–4pm, Sun 11am–4pm. Closed 24, 25, 26 Dec, 1 Jan. Last admission 30 minutes before closing.

Admission: Adult £3, Child (under 16 yrs)/Conc. £2.60, Child under 5yrs Free, Family (2 adults and all children under 16yrs) £8.60. Under 16s must be accompanied by an adult. All opening times and prices are correct at time of going to press (Autumn 2009) but may be subject to change from March 2010 – Please see site for details.

🛈 Toilets. Baby changing. Induction loop. Ⓟ On leads.

St. David's Cathedral

Picton Castle

ST DAVIDS BISHOP'S PALACE ✠

St Davids, Pembrokeshire SA62 6PE

Tel: 01437 720517 **www.cadw.wales.gov.uk**

Owner: In the care of Cadw   **Contact:** The Custodian

The city of St Davids boasts the most impressive medieval Bishops palace in Wales. Built in the elaborate 'decorated' style of gothic architecture, the palace is lavishly encrusted with fine carving. Be sure to explore the undercrofts and see the extensive conservation works already complete.

Location: MAP 5:B11, OS Ref. SM750 254. A487 to St Davids, minor road past the Cathedral.

Open: Apr–Oct: daily, 9am–5pm; Nov–Mar: Mon–Sat, 9.30am–4pm, Sun 11am–4pm. Closed 24, 25, 26 Dec, 1 Jan. Last admission 30 minutes before closing.

Admission: Adult £3, Child (under 16 yrs)/Conc. £2.60, Child under 5yrs Free, Family (2 adults and all children under 16yrs) £8.60. Under 16s must be accompanied by an adult. All opening times and prices are correct at time of going to press (Autumn 2009) but may be subject to change from March 2010 – Please see site for details.

ⓘ Induction loop. Cycle stands. 🔲 🅰 Partial. 🅿 🚌 On leads. ❋

ST DAVIDS CATHEDRAL

St Davids, Pembrokeshire SA62 6QW

Tel: 01437 720691 **Fax:** 01437 721885

Contact: Mr R G Tarr

Over eight centuries old. Many unique and 'odd' features.

Location: MAP 5:B11, OS Ref. SM751 254. 5–10 mins walk from car/coach parks: signs for pedestrians.

Open: Daily: 8.30am–5.30pm. Sun: 12.30–5.30pm, may be closed for services in progress. Sun services: 8am, 9.30am, 11.15am & 6pm. Weekday services: 8am & 6pm. Weds extra service: 10am. (2007 details).

Admission: Donations. Guided tours (Adult £4, Child £1.20) must be booked.

ST FAGANS: NATIONAL HISTORY MUSEUM

St Fagans, Cardiff CF5 6XB

Tel: 029 2057 3500 **Fax:** 029 2057 3490

One of the world's best-loved open-air museums. Original buildings have been moved from all over Wales and re-erected at the Museum – these include a Victorian school, industrial ironworkers' cottages and a rural chapel. St Fagans Castle, an Elizabethan Manor House, also stands within the grounds.

Location: MAP 2:L2, OS Ref. ST118 772. 4m W of city centre, 1½ m N of A48, 2m S of M4/J33. Follow the brown signs (Museum of Welsh Life). Entrance drive is off A4232 (southbound only).

Open: All year: daily, 10am–5pm. Closed 24–26 Dec & 1 Jan.

Admission: Free.

TINTERN ABBEY ✠

TINTERN NP16 6SE

www.cadw.wales.gov.uk

Tel: 01291 689251

Owner: In the care of Cadw   **Contact:** The Custodian

Tintern is the best preserved abbey in Wales and ranks among Britain's most beautiful historic sites. Elaborately decorated in 'gothic' architecture style this church stands almost complete to roof level. Turner sketched and painted here, while Wordsworth drew inspiration from the surroundings.

Location: MAP 6:L12, OS Ref. SO533 000. Tintern via A466, from M4/J23. Chepstow 6m.

Open: Apr–Oct: 9am–5pm, daily. Nov–Mar: Mon–Sat, 9.30am–4pm, Sun 11am–4pm. Closed 24, 25, 26 Dec, 1 Jan. Last admission 30 minutes before closing.

Admission: Adult £3.60, Child (under 16 yrs)/Conc. £3.20, Child under 5yrs Free, Family (2 adults and all children under 16yrs) £10.40. Under 16s must be accompanied by an adult. All opening times and prices are correct at time of going to press (Autumn 2009) but may be subject to change from March 2010 – Please see site for details.

ⓘ Induction loop. Toilets. Baby changing. 🔲 🅰 🅿 🚌 ❋

St David's Cathedral

TREBERFYDD

Bwlch, Powys LD3 7PX

Tel: 01874 730205 **E-mail:** david.raikes@btinternet.com **www.treberfydd.com**

Owner: David Raikes

Treberfydd is a Grade I listed Victorian country house, built in the Gothic style in 1847–50. The house was designed by J L Pearson, and the garden and grounds by W A Nesfield.

Location: MAP 6:I10, From A40 in Bwlch take road to Llangors, after ¼m turn left, follow lane for 2m until white gates and Treberfydd sign.

Open: 1–30 Aug. Guided tours of the House: 2 & 4pm, telephone or e-mail to secure a place on a tour. Grounds: 2–6pm.

Admission: House & grounds: Adult £4, Child (under 12yrs) Free. Grounds only: £2.50.
 ⟨⟩ Obligatory. 🅿 Limited. None for coaches. ⟨⟩ On leads, in grounds.

TREBINSHWN

Nr Brecon, Powys LD3 7PX

Tel: 01874 730653 **Fax:** 01874 730843

Owner/Contact: R Watson

16th century mid-sized manor house. Extensively rebuilt 1780. Fine courtyard and walled garden.

Location: MAP 6:I10, OS Ref. SO136 242. 1½m NW of Bwlch.

Open: Easter–31 Aug: Mon–Tue, 10am–4.30pm.

Admission: Free.
🅿

TREDEGAR HOUSE & PARK 🏛

NEWPORT, SOUTH WALES NP10 8YW

Tel: 01633 815880 **Fax:** 01633 815895 **E-mail:** tredegar.house@newport.gov.uk

Owner: Newport City Council **Contact:** The Manager

South Wales' finest country house, ancestral home of the Morgan family. Parts of a medieval house remain, but Tredegar owes its reputation to lavish rebuilding in the 17th century. Visitors have a lively and entertaining tour through 30 rooms, including glittering State Rooms and 'below stairs'. Set in 90 acres of parkland with formal gardens.

Location: MAP 2:M1, OS Ref. ST290 852. M4/J28 signposted. From London 2½hrs, from Cardiff 20 mins. 2m SW of Newport town centre.

Open: Easter–Sept: Wed–Sun & BHs, 11am–4pm. Evening tours & groups by appointment all year round.

Admission: Adult £6.25, Conc. £4.65. Children 15 & under free when accompanied by a paying adult (2008 prices).

ⓘ Conferences. No photography in house. ⟨⟩ ⟨⟩ ⟨⟩ Partial. WC. ⟨⟩ ⟨⟩ Obligatory.
🅿 ⟨⟩ ⟨⟩ In grounds, on leads. ⟨⟩ ⟨⟩

TREOWEN 🏚

Wonastow, Nr Monmouth NP25 4DL
Tel/Fax: 01600 712031 **E-mail:** john.wheelock@treowen.co.uk **www.treowen.co.uk**
Owner: R A & J P Wheelock **Contact:** John Wheelock
Early 17th century mansion built to double pile plan with magnificent well-stair to four storeys.
Location: MAP 6:L11, OS Ref. SO461 111. 3m WSW of Monmouth.
Open: May, Jun, Aug & Sept: Fri, 10am–4pm. Also 17/18 & 24/25 April; 8/9 & 15/16 May; 18/19 Sept: 2–5pm. HHA Friends Free on Fri only.
Admission: £5 (£3 if appointment made). Groups by appointment only.
🅃 📷 Entire house let, self-catering. Sleeps 25+. 🅰

TRETOWER COURT & CASTLE ✚

Tretower, Crickhowell NP8 1RD
Tel: 01874 730279 **www.cadw.wales.gov.uk**
Owner: In the care of Cadw **Contact:** The Custodian
A fine fortress and an outstanding medieval manor house, Tretower Court and Castle range around a galleried courtyard, now further enhanced by a beautiful recreated medieval garden.
Location: MAP 6:J11, OS Ref. SO187 212. Signposted in Tretower Village, off A479, 3m NW of Crickhowell.
Open: Closed until Spring 2010.
ℹ️ Toilets. Induction loop. Cycle stands. 📷 🅿 🐾

TUDOR MERCHANT'S HOUSE 🐾

Quay Hill, Tenby SA70 7BX
Tel/Fax: 01834 842279
Owner: The National Trust **Contact:** The Custodian
A late 15th century town house, characteristic of the area at the time when Tenby was a thriving trading port. The house is furnished to recreate family life from the Tudor period onwards. There is access to the small herb garden, weather permitting.
Location: MAP 5:D12, OS Ref. SN135 004. Tenby. W of alley from NE corner of town centre square.
Open: 17 Mar–2 Nov: daily (closed Sats, except BH weekends), 11am–5pm.
Admission: Adult £2.70, Child £1.30, Family £6.70. Groups: Adult £2.30, Child £1.15.
ℹ️ No indoor photography. 🅿 No parking. 🅸 🐾 Guide dogs only.

TYTHEGSTON COURT

Tythegston, Bridgend CF32 0NE
E-mail: cknight@tythegston.com **www.tythegston.com**
Owner/Contact: C Knight
Location: MAP 2:K1, OS Ref. SS857 789. 2m E of Porthcawl on Glamorgan coast.
Open: By written appointment (no telephone calls please).
Admission: Adult £10, Child £2.50, Conc. £5.
🅃 ♿ Partial. 🄵 Obligatory. 🅿 Limited. No coaches. 🐾 Guide dogs only.

USK CASTLE

Usk, Monmouthshire NP5 1SD
Tel: 01291 672563 **E-mail:** info@uskcastle.com **www.uskcastle.com**
Owner/Contact: J H L Humphreys
Romantic, ruined castle overlooking the picturesque town of Usk. Inner and outer baileys, towers and earthwork defences. Surrounded by enchanting gardens (open under NGS) incorporating The Castle House, the former medieval gatehouse.
Location: MAP 6:K12, OS Ref. SO376 011. Up narrow lane off Monmouth road in Usk, opposite fire station.
Open: Castle ruins: daily, 11am–5pm. Groups by appointment. Gardens: private visits welcome & groups by arrangement. House: May & BHs: 2–5pm, small groups & guided tours only.
Admission: Castle ruins: Adult £2, Child Free. Gardens: Adult £4. House: Adult £6, Child £3.
🅃 ♿ Partial. 🄵 By arrangement. 🅿 No coaches. 🅸 🐾 In grounds, on leads. 🌐

WEOBLEY CASTLE ✚

Weobley Castle Farm, Llanrhidian SA3 1HB
Tel: 01792 390012 **www.cadw.wales.gov.uk**
Owner: In the care of Cadw **Contact:** The Custodian
Perched above the wild northern coast of the beautiful Gower peninsula, Weobley Castle was the home of the Knightly de Bere family. Its rooms include a fine hall and private chamber as well as numerous 'garderobes' or toilets and an early Tudor porch block.
Location: MAP 2:I1, OS Ref. SN477 928. B4271 or B4295 to Llanrhidian Village, then minor road for 1½m.
Open: 1 Apr–31 Oct: daily, 9.30am–6pm (5pm, Nov–Mar). Closed 24, 25, 26 Dec, 1 Jan. Last admission 30 minutes before closing.
Admission: Adult £2.60, Child (under 16 yrs)/Conc. £2.25, Child under 5yrs Free, Family (2 adults and all children under 16yrs) £7.50. Under 16s must be accompanied by an adult. All opening times and prices are correct at time of going to press (Autumn 2009) but may be subject to change from March 2010 – Please see site for details.
ℹ️ Toilets. 📷 🅿 🐾 🌐

WHITE CASTLE ✚

Llantillio Crossenny, Monmouthshire NP7 8UD
Tel: 01600 780380 **www.cadw.wales.gov.uk**
Owner: In the care of Cadw **Contact:** The Custodian
With its high walls and round towers reflected in the still waters of its moat, White Castle is the ideal medieval fortress. Rebuilt in the mid-13th century to counter a threat from Prince Llywelyn the Last. Plenty of wildlife to discover.
Location: MAP 6:K11, OS Ref. SO380 167. By minor road 2m NW from B4233 at A7 Llantilio Crossenny. 8m ENE of Abergavenny.
Open: Open 1 Apr–31 Oct daily, 10am–5pm. Open at all other times generally between 10am–4pm, but unstaffed.
Admission: Adult £2.60, Child (under 16 yrs)/Conc. £2.25, Child under 5yrs Free, Family (2 adults and all children under 16yrs) £7.45. Under 16s must be accompanied by an adult. All opening times and prices are correct at time of going to press (Autumn 2009) but may be subject to change from March 2010 – Please see site for details.
ℹ️ Induction loop. Cycle stands. 📷 🅿 🐾 🌐

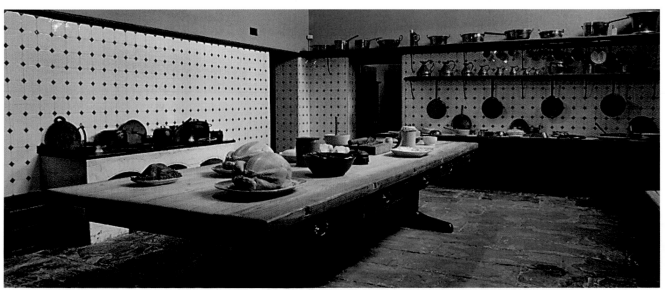

Tredegar House & Park

■ **Owner**

Paul and Victoria Humpherston

■ **Contact**

Paul Humpherston
The Hall at
Abbey-Cwm-Hir
Nr Llandrindod Wells
Powys LD1 6PH

Tel: 01597 851727
E-mail: info@
abbeycwmhir.com

■ **Location**

MAP 6:I8
OS Ref. SO054 711

7m NW of Llandrindod
Wells, 6m E of Rhayader,
turn for Abbey-Cwm-Hir
1 mile north of
Crossgates on the A483.

■ **Opening Times**

All year daily for pre-
booked tours only, at
10.30am, 2pm
and 7pm for couples,
small parties or groups.

■ **Admission**

House Tour & Gardens
Adult   £14.00
Child (under 12)   £5.00

Groups (10+) or
repeat visitors   £12.00

Gardens only
Adult   £5.00

■ **Gift Vouchers**

Gift vouchers for tours
may be purchased as a
heartfelt gift. They are
redeemable at any time
within 12 months of
purchase.

■ **Special Events**

6 November–6 January
Each of the 52 rooms is
decorated for Christmas,
for an entirely unique
experience. Morning,
afternoon and evening
tours for individuals, small
parties or groups.

**St. Valentines Day &
Easter**
Contact us for more
details.

THE HALL AT ABBEY-CWM-HIR

www.abbeycwmhir.com

In a mid Wales setting of breathtaking beauty, history and romance, The Hall and its 12 landscaped acres overlook the ruins of the 12th century Cisterian 'Abbey of the Long Valley' in which Llewellyn the Last is buried and the church. It is Grade II* listed as one of Wales' finest examples of Victorian Gothic Revival architecture.

Having spent nine years restoring the house and the gardens, the owners now personally conduct unique tours of all 52 rooms in a true family atmosphere. The tours are not just about the architecture of an historic house. Visitors also experience stunning interior designs in all rooms, and items from a lifetime of collecting used as furnishings.

Each of the 52 rooms contain their original features. In the formal reception rooms and bedrooms these include 14 marble fireplaces; rococco and stained glass ceilings; gothic windows and shutters; and a Minton Hollins tiled floor.

In the former domestic rooms, features include 10 further iron fireplaces; original slate slab surfaces; and vaulted cellar ceilings.

The house bursts with interior design ideas. These include images hand-painted on to existing wallpapers; bathrooms themed to trains, castles and the 1930s; bedrooms themed to schooldays, the seaside and transport; the Arthurian room; and the eclectic Garden Room.

Overall collections include clocks and phonographs; signs and packaging; kitchen memorabilia and children's books in original bindings; china and vehicles; and The Abbey-Cwm-Hir Art and Photographic Collections.

The beautiful gardens (also listed) include a romantic walled garden; a lake and a waterfall; sweeping lawns and terraces; 4 courtyards; and some particularly fine mixed woodland.

ⓘ Visitors are asked to remove outside shoes for the tour of the house, slippers can be provided.

⧖ Partial.

☕ Licensed.

🍴 Licensed.

🚶 Obligatory.

🅿 Ample for cars, limited for coaches.

🐕 In grounds on leads.

❄

☗

HAFOD

Hafod Estate Office, Pontrhydygroes, Ystrad-Meurig, Ceredigion SY25 6DX
Tel: 01974 282568 **Fax:** 01974 282579 **E-mail:** hafod.estate@forestry.gsi.gov.uk
www.hafod.org
Owner: Forestry Commission Wales **Contact:** The Hafod Trust
Picturesque landscape, one of the most significant in Britain located in a remote valley and improved by Col Thomas Johnes 1780–1816. Ten miles of restored walks featuring cascades, bridges and wonderful views in 500 acres of wood and parkland. The epitome of the Picturesque and Sublime. Georgian Group Award winner.
Location: MAP 5:G8, OS Ref. SN768 736. 15 miles E of Aberystwyth near Devils Bridge, car park, off B4574.
Open: All year, daylight hours.
Admission: Free – guide book available at local shops or website.
🔲 WC. 🔲 By arrangement. 🅿 🔲 🔲 In grounds on leads. 🔲

THE HALL AT ABBEY-CWM-HIR *See page 470 for full page entry.*

THE JUDGE'S LODGING

Broad Street, Presteigne, Powys LD8 2AD
Tel: 01544 260650 **E-mail:** info@judgeslodging.org.uk
www.judgeslodging.org.uk
Owner: Powys County Council **Contact:** Gabrielle Rivers
Explore the fascinating world of the Victorian judges, their servants and felonious guests at this award-winning, totally hands-on historic house. From sumptuous judge's apartments to the gas-lit servants' quarters below, follow an 'eavesdropping' audio tour featuring actor Robert Hardy. Damp cells, vast courtroom and local history rooms included.
Location: MAP 6:K8, OS Ref. SO314 644. In town centre, off A44 and A4113. Easy reach from Herefordshire and mid-Wales.
Open: 1 Mar–31 Oct: Tues–Sun, 10am–5pm. 1 Nov–31 Nov: Wed–Sun, 10am–4pm, 1 Dec–22 Dec: Sat–Sun 10am–4pm. Open BH Mon's. Bookings by arrangement accepted all year.
Admission: Adult £5.50, Child £3.95, Conc. £4.75. Groups (10-80): Adult £4.75, Child/Conc. £4.25, Family £15.
🔲 🔲 🔲 Partial (access via lift). 🔲 By arrangement. 🔲 🅿 In town. 🔲
🔲 Guide dogs only. 🔲 🔲

LLANERCHAERON 🔲

Ciliau Aeron, Nr Aberaeron, Ceredigion SA48 8DG
Tel: 01545 570200
Owner: The National Trust
This rare example of a self-sufficient 18th-century Welsh minor gentry estate has survived virtually unaltered. The Villa, designed in the 1790s, is the most complete example of the early work of John Nash. It has its own service courtyard with dairy, laundry, brewery and salting house, and walled kitchen gardens produce fruit, vegetables, herbs and plants, all on sale in season. The Home Farm complex has an impressive range of traditional and atmospheric outbuildings and is now a working organic farm with Welsh Black Cattle, Llanwenog Sheep and rare Welsh Pigs. Visitors can see farming activities in progress, such as lambing, shearing and hay-making.
Location: MAP 5:F8, OS Ref. SN480 602. 2½ miles East of Aberaeron off A482 / 2½ mile foot/cycle track from Aberaeron to property along old railway track.
Open: House: 15 Mar–20 Jul & 3 Sep–2 Nov, Wed–Sun; 22 Jul–31 Aug, Tues–Sun; 11.30am–4pm. Farm/Garden as House but 11am–5pm.
***Admission:** Adult £6.70, Child £3.40, Family £16.80, Groups: Adult £5.80, Child £2.90.*includes a voluntary donation but visitors can choose to pay the standard prices displayed at the property and on the website.

The Hall at Abbey-Cwm-Hir

For **educational facilities** or **school visits** in Mid Wales see our special index at the end of the book.

POWIS CASTLE & GARDEN 🔲

Nr Welshpool SY21 8RF
Tel: 01938 551929 **Infoline:** 01938 551944 **Fax:** 01938 554336
E-mail: powiscastle@nationaltrust.org.uk
Owner: The National Trust **Contact:** Visitor Services Manager
The world-famous garden, overhung with enormous clipped yew trees, shelters rare and tender plants in colourful herbaceous borders. Laid out under the influence of Italian and French styles, the garden retains its original lead statues and, an orangery on the terraces. Perched on a rock above the garden terraces, the medieval castle contains one of the finest collections of paintings and furniture in Wales.
Location: MAP 6:J6, OS Ref. SJ216 064. 1m W of Welshpool, car access on A483.
Open: Castle & Museum: 13 Mar–30 Jun; Thur–Mon, 1–5pm (Jul & Aug, Wed–Mon, 1–5pm); 1–21 Sept, 1–5pm; 25 Sept–2 Nov, 1–4pm). Shop & Restaurant: 1–9 Mar, Sat & Sun, 11am–4.30pm; 13 Mar–30 Jun, Thur–Mon, 11am–5.30pm; 2 Jul–31 Aug, Wed–Mon, 11am–5.30pm; 1–21 Sept, Thur–Mon, 11am–5.30pm; 25 Sept–2 Nov, Thur–Mon, 11am–5pm; 8 Nov–21 Dec, Sat & Sun, 10am–3pm. Garden: 1–9 Mar; Sats & Suns, 11am–4.30pm. 13 Mar–21 Sept; Thur–Mon (+ Wed Jul–Aug), 11am–5.30pm (25 Sept–2 Nov, 5pm). 8–29 Nov; 10am–3pm. Last entry 45 mins before closing.
***Admission:** Castle & Garden: Adult £10.50, Child £5.25, Family (2+3) £26.25. Groups (15+ booked): £9. Garden only: Adult £7.50, Child £3.75, Family (2+3) £18.75. Groups (15+ booked): £6.40. No group rates on Suns or BHs. NT members & under 5s Free.*includes a voluntary donation but visitors can choose to pay the standard prices displayed at the property and on the website.
🔲 No indoor photography. 🔲 🔲 🔲 Partial. 🔲 Licensed. 🔲 By arrangement. 🅿 Limited for coaches. 🔲 Guide dogs only.

STRATA FLORIDA ABBEY 🔲

Ystrad Meurig, Pontrhydfendigaid SY25 6ES
Tel: 01974 831261 **www.cadw.wales.gov.uk**
Owner: In the care of Cadw **Contact:** The Custodian
Remotely set in the green, kite-haunted Teifi Valley with the lonely Cambrian mountains as a backdrop, the ruined Cistercian abbey has a wonderful doorway with Celtic spiral motifs and preserves a wealth of beautiful medieval tiles. Explore the poetic connections with Dafydd ap Gwilym.
Location: MAP 5:H8, OS Ref. SN746 658. Minor road from Pontrhydfendigaid 14m SE of Aberystwyth by the B4340.
Open: 1 Apr–30 Sept: daily, 10am–5pm. Open at all other times generally between 10am–4pm, but unstaffed. Closed 24, 25, 26 Dec, 1 Jan. Last admission 30 minutes before closing.
Admission: Adult £3, Child (under 16 yrs)/Conc. £2.60, Child under 5yrs Free, Family (2 adults and all children under 16yrs) £8.60. Under 16s must be accompanied by an adult. All opening times and prices are correct at time of going to press (Autumn 2009) but may be subject to change from March 2010 – Please see site for details.
🔲 Induction loop. 🔲 🔲 🅿 🔲 On leads. 🔲

TREWERN HALL

Trewern, Welshpool, Powys SY21 8DT
Tel: 01938 570243
Owner: Chapman Family **Contact:** M Chapman
Trewern Hall is a Grade II* listed building standing in the Severn Valley. It has been described as *'one of the most handsome timber-framed houses surviving in the area'*. The porch contains a beam inscribed RF1610, though it seems likely that parts of the house are earlier. The property has been in the ownership of the Chapman family since 1918.
Location: MAP 6:J6 , OS Ref. SJ269 113. Off A458 Welshpool–Shrewsbury Road, 4m from Welshpool.
Opening: Last week in Apr, 1–31 May: Mon–Fri, 2–5pm.
Admission: Adult £2, Child/Conc. £1.
🔲 Unsuitable. 🅿 Limited. None for coaches. 🔲

ABERCONWY HOUSE ✣

Castle Street, Conwy LL32 8AY

Tel: 01492 592246 **Fax:** 01492 564818

Owner: The National Trust

Dating from the 14th century, this is the only medieval merchant's house in Conwy to have survived the turbulent history of this walled town for nearly six centuries. Furnished rooms and an audio-visual presentation show daily life from different periods in its history.

Location: MAP 5:H2, OS Ref. SH781 777. At junction of Castle Street and High Street.

Open: 21 Mar–2 Nov: Wed–Mon, 11am–5pm. Last adm. 30 mins before close. Shop: 1 Mar–31 Dec: daily (closed 25/26 Dec), 10am–5pm (5.30pm 25 Mar–29 Oct). Jan–Feb 2007: Wed–Sun, 11am–5pm. Suns open at 11am.

Admission: Adult £3, Child £1.50, Family (2+2) £7.50. Pre-booked groups (15+) Adult £2.50, Child £1. National Trust members Free.

ⓘ No indoor photography. 📷 All year. 🎭 By arrangement. 🅰
🅿 In town car parks only. ▣ 🐕 Guide dogs only.

BEAUMARIS CASTLE ✤

BEAUMARIS, ANGLESEY LL58 8AP

www.cadw.wales.gov.uk

Tel: 01248 810361

Owner: In the care of Cadw **Contact:** The Custodian

The most technically perfect medieval castle in Britain, standing midway between Caernarfon and Conwy, commanding the old ferry crossing to Anglesey. A World Heritage Inscribed Site.

Location: MAP 5:G2, OS Ref. SH608 762. 5m NE of Menai Bridge (A5) by A545. 7m from Bangor.

Open: Apr–Oct: daily, 9am–5pm. Nov–Mar: Mon–Sat, 9.30am–4pm, Sun 11am–4pm. Closed 24, 25, 26 Dec, 1 Jan. Last admission 30 minutes before closing.

Admission: Adult £3.60, Child (under 16 yrs)/Conc. £3.20, Child under 5yrs Free, Family (2 adults and all children under 16yrs) £10.40. Under 16s must be accompanied by an adult. All opening times and prices are correct at time of going to press (Autumn 2009) but may be subject to change from March 2010 – Please see site for details.

📷 ♿ 🐕 ❄

BODELWYDDAN CASTLE

Bodelwyddan, Denbighshire LL18 5YA

Tel: 01745 584060 **Fax:** 01745 584563 **E-mail:** enquiries@bodelwyddan-castle.co.uk

www.bodelwyddan-castle.co.uk

Owner: Bodelwyddan Castle Trust **Contact:** Bookings and Information Team

Journey back in time as you tour this magnificently restored Victorian country house and view exquisite pieces from the National Portrait Gallery, Royal Academy and Victoria & Albert Museum. Explore 260 acres of parkland including formal gardens, woodland walks and WW1 practice trenches. Hands on Victorian Toys and Games Room. Exciting events and exhibition schedule. Café specialising in traditional, freshly prepared products.

Location: MAP 6:I2, OS Ref. SH999 749. Follow signs Junction 25 off A55 expressway. 2m W of St Asaph, opposite Marble Church.

Open: Various dates throughout the year. Please telephone or visit our website to check opening dates and times.

Admission: Adult £6, Child (5–16yrs) £2.50 (under 4yrs free), Conc. £5, Disabled £3.50. Family (1+3) £12, (2+2) £15. Discounts for schools & groups. Season ticket available.

📷 🍴 ♿ Partial. WCs. ▣ 🎭 By arrangement. 🅰 Free. 🅿 ▣ 🐕 Assistance dogs only.
▣ ❄ 🥤

Conwy Castle

BODNANT GARDEN ✣

Tal-y-Cafn, Colwyn Bay LL28 5RE

Tel: 01492 650460 **Fax:** 01492 650448 **E-mail:** office@bodnantgarden.co.uk

www.bodnantgarden.co.uk

Owner: The National Trust

Bodnant Garden is one of the finest gardens in the country not only for its magnificent collections of rhododendrons, camellias and magnolias but also for its idyllic setting above the River Conwy with extensive views of the Snowdonia range.

Location: MAP 5:H2, OS Ref. SH801 723. 8 miles S of Llandudno and Colwyn Bay, off A470. Signposted from A55, exit at Junction 19.

Open: 8 Mar–2 Nov: daily, 10am–5pm. Tearoom: as garden. Plant Centre: Daily, 10am–5pm.

Admission: Adult £7.20, Child £3.60. Groups (20+): Adult £5.50, Child £3.25. RHS members free.

📷 🍴 ♿ Partial. WCs. ▣ 🅿 🐕 Guide dogs only.

BRYN BRAS CASTLE

Llanrug, Caernarfon, Gwynedd LL55 4RE

www.brynbrascastle.co.uk

Tel/Fax: 01286 870210 **E-mail:** holidays@brynbrascastle.co.uk

Owner: Mr & Mrs N E Gray-Parry **Contact:** Marita Gray-Parry

Built in the Neo-Romanesque style in c1830, on an earlier structure, and probably designed by Thomas Hopper, it stands in the Snowdonian Range. The tranquil garden includes a hill-walk with fine views of Mt Snowdon, Anglesey and the sea. Bryn Bras, a much loved home, offers a delightful selection of apartments for holidays for twos within the Grade II* listed castle. Many local restaurants, inns.

Location: MAP 5:F3, OS Ref. SH543 625. ½m off A4086 at Llanrug, 4½m E of Caernarfon.

Open: Only by appointment.

Admission: By arrangement. No children please.

🅿 🐕 ▣ Self-catering apartments for two within castle. ❄

Bryn Bras Castle

CAERNARFON CASTLE ✥

CASTLE DITCH, CAERNARFON LL55 2AY

www.cadw.wales.gov.uk

Tel: 01286 677617

Owner: In the care of Cadw **Contact:** The Custodian

The most famous, and perhaps the most impressive castle in Wales. Taking nearly 50 years to build, it proved the costliest of Edward I's castles. A World Heritage Inscribed Site.

Location: MAP 5:F3, OS Ref. SH477 626. In Caernarfon, just W of town centre.

Open: Apr–Oct: daily, 9am–5pm. Nov–Mar: Mon–Sat, 9.30am–4pm, Sun 11am–4pm. Closed 24, 25, 26 Dec, 1 Jan. Last admission 30 minutes before closing.

Admission: Adult £4.95, Child (under 16 yrs)/Conc. £4.60, Child under 5yrs Free, Family (2 adults and all children under 16yrs) £14.50. Under 16s must be accompanied by an adult. All opening times and prices are correct at time of going to press (Autumn 2009) but may be subject to change from March 2010 – Please see site for details.

ℹ Induction loop. Toilets. 🅾 🗶 ❋

For **educational facilities** or **school visits** in North Wales see our special index at the end of the book.

CHIRK CASTLE ✤

Chirk LL14 5AF

Tel: 01691 777701 **Fax:** 01691 774706 **E-mail:** chirkcastle@nationaltrust.org.uk

Owner: The National Trust

700 year old Chirk Castle, a magnificent marcher fortress, commands fine views over the surrounding countryside. Rectangular with a massive drum tower at each corner, the castle has beautiful formal gardens with clipped yews, roses and a variety of flowering shrubs. The dramatic dungeon is a reminder of the castle's turbulent history, whilst later occupants have left elegant state rooms, furniture, tapestries and portraits. The castle was sold for five thousand pounds to Sir Thomas Myddelton in 1595, and his descendants continue to live in part of the castle today.

Location: MAP 6:J4, OS Ref. SJ275 388. 8m S of Wrexham off A483, 2m from Chirk village.

Open: Castle & Shop: 2–10 Feb, Sat & Sun, 11am–4pm, 13–17 Feb, Wed–Sun; 11am–4pm, 15 Mar–30 Sept, Wed–Sun & BH Mons (+Tues Jul–Aug), 12 noon–5pm. 1 Oct–2 Nov, Weds–Sun, 11am–4pm, 6–14 Dec, Sat & Sun, 11am–5pm. Last admission ½hr before closing. Garden: as Castle, 10am–6pm (5pm in Oct), last admission 1hr before closing. Tearoom: as Castle, 10am–5pm (4pm in Oct). Shop: As Castle, 10am–6pm (5pm in Oct). NT shop as Castle, 11am–5pm (closes 4pm in Feb & Oct.) Home Farm & Estate: as Garden (not open Dec, closes 5pm in Oct).

*Admission: House & Garden: Adult £8.80, Child £4.40, Family £22. Pre-booked groups (15+): Adult £7.50, Child £3.75. Garden only: Adults £6.20, Child £3.10, Family £15.50. Pre-booked groups: Adult £5.20, Child £2.60. *includes a voluntary donation but visitors can choose to pay the standard prices displayed at the property and on the website.

ℹ No indoor photography. 🅾 🏠 🚻 🖷 Licensed. ✕ By arrangement. 🅿 🏢 🐕 Guide dogs only. 🅰 🎫

COCHWILLAN OLD HALL

Talybont, Bangor, Gwynedd LL57 3AZ

Tel: 01248 355853

Owner: R C H Douglas Pennant **Contact:** Miss M D Monteith

A fine example of medieval architecture with the present house dating from about 1450. It was probably built by William Gryffydd who fought for Henry VII at Bosworth. Once owned in the 17th century by John Williams who became Archbishop of York. The house was restored from a barn in 1971.

Location: MAP 5:G2, OS Ref. SH606 695. 3½m SE of Bangor. 1m SE of Talybont off A55.

Open: By appointment.

Admission: Please telephone for details.

❋

CONWY CASTLE ✥

CONWY LL32 8AY

www.cadw.wales.gov.uk

Tel: 01492 592358

Owner: In the care of Cadw **Contact:** The Custodian

The castle and town walls are the most impressive of the fortresses built by Edward I. Explore the almost complete medieval town walls and enjoy the spectacular views. A World Heritage Inscribed Site.

Location: MAP 5:H2, OS Ref. SH783 774. Conwy by A55 or B5106.

Open: Apr–Oct: 9am–5pm. Nov–Mar: Mon–Sat, 9.30am–4pm, Sun 11am–4pm. Closed 24, 25, 26 Dec, 1 Jan. Last admission 30 minutes before closing.

Admission: Adult £4.60, Child (under 16yrs)/Conc. £4.10, Child under 5yrs Free, Family (2 adults & and all children under 16yrs) £13.30. Joint ticket for Conwy Castle and Plas Mawr Town House: Adult £6.85, Conc. £5.85, Family (2 adults and all children under 16yrs) £19.55. Under 16s must be accompanied by an adult. All opening times and prices are correct at time of going to press (Autumn 2009) but may be subject to change from March 2010 – Please see site for details.

ℹ Induction loop. Toilets. 🅾 🅿 🗶 ❋

Dolbelydr

CRICCIETH CASTLE ✤

Castle Street, Criccieth, Gwynedd LL52 0DP
Tel: 01766 522227   www.cadw.wales.gov.uk
Owner: In the care of Cadw   **Contact:** The Custodian
Overlooking Cardigan Bay, Criccieth Castle is the most striking of the fortresses built by the Welsh Princes. Its inner defences are dominated by a powerful twin-towered gatehouse.
Location: MAP 5:F4, OS Ref. SH500 378. A497 to Criccieth from Porthmadog or Pwllheli.
Open: Apr–Oct : daily, 10am–5pm. 1 Nov–31 Mar: Fri & Sat, 9.30am–4pm, Sun, 11am–4pm. Last admission 30 minutes before closing. Closed 24, 25, 26 Dec, 1 Jan.
Admission: Adult £3, Child (under 16yrs)/Conc. £2.60, Child under 5yrs Free, Family (2 adults and all children under 16yrs) £8.60. Under 16s must be accompanied by an adult. All opening times and prices are correct at time of going to press (Autumn 2009) but may be subject to change from March 2010 – Please see site for details.
ⓘ Induction loop. Toilets. ⬜ ℗ Cycle stands. ✖ ✳

DENBIGH CASTLE ✤

Denbigh, Denbighshire LL16 3NB
Tel: 01745 813385   www.cadw.wales.gov.uk
Owner: In the care of Cadw   **Contact:** The Custodian
Crowning the summit of a prominent outcrop overlooking the Vale of Clwyd, the principal feature of this spectacular site is the great gatehouse dating back to the 11th century. Sections of the Town Walls are open to visitors. Don't miss Leicester's Church, Denbigh Friary and the Burgess Gate.
Location: MAP 6:I2, OS Ref. SJ052 658. Denbigh via A525, A543 or B5382.
Open: 1 Apr–31 Oct: daily, 10am–5pm. At all other times this monument will be open but unstaffed between 10am and 4pm.
Admission: Castle: Adult £3, Child (under 16yrs)/Conc. £2.60, Child under 5 yrs Free, Family (2 adults and all children under 16yrs) £8.60. Under 16s must be accompanied by an adult. All opening times and prices are correct at time of going to press (Autumn 2009) but may be subject to change from March 2010 – Please see site for details.
ⓘ Cycle stands. Induction loop. Toilets. ⬜ ℗ ✖ On leads. ✳

DOLBELYDR

Trefnant, Denbighshire LL16 5AG
Tel: 01628 825925   **E-mail:** bookings@landmarktrust.org.uk
www.landmarktrust.org.uk
Owner/Contact: The Landmark Trust
A 16th century, Grade II* listed building, a fine example of a 16th century gentry house and has good claim to be the birthplace of the modern Welsh language. It was at Dolbelydr that Henry Salesbury wrote his Grammatica Britannica. Dolbelydr is cared for by The Landmark Trust, a building preservation charity who let it for holidays. Full details of Dolbelydr and 189 other historic and architecturally important buildings are featured in the Landmark Trust Handbook (£10 plus p&p refundable against a booking) and on the website.
Location: MAP 6:I2, OS Ref. SJ031 709.
Open: Available for holidays for up to 6 people throughout the year. Open Days on 8 days throughout the year. Other visits by appointment. Contact the Landmark Trust for details.
Admission: Free on Open Days.
🖼

Erddig

For **Civil wedding** venues in North Wales see our special index at the end of the book.

DOLWYDDELAN CASTLE ✤

Dolwyddelan, Gwynedd LL25 0JD
Tel: 01690 750366   www.cadw.wales.gov.uk
Owner: In the care of Cadw   **Contact:** The Custodian
Standing proudly on a ridge, this stone keep tower remains remarkably intact and visitors cannot fail to be impressed with the great solitary square tower, built by Llewelyn the Great in the early 13th century.
Location: MAP 5:G3, OS Ref. SH722 522. A470(T) Blaenau Ffestiniog to Betws-y-Coed, 1m W of Dolwyddelan.
Open: Apr–Sept: Mon–Sat, 10am–5pm. Sun 11.30am–4pm. Oct–Mar: Mon–Sat, 10am–4pm. Sun, 11.30am–4pm. Closed 24, 25, 26 Dec, 1 Jan.Last admission 30 minutes before closing.
Admission: Adult £2.60, Child (5–16yrs)/Conc. £2.25, Child under 5 yrs Free, Family (2 adults and all children under 16yrs) £7.50. Under 16s must be accompanied by an adult. All opening times and prices are correct at time of going to press (Autumn 2009) but may be subject to change from March 2010 – Please see site for details.
℗ ✖ ✳

ERDDIG ❧

Nr Wrexham LL13 0YT
Tel: 01978 355314   **Fax:** 01978 313333   **Info Line:** 01978 315151
Owner: The National Trust
One of the most fascinating houses in Britain, not least because of the unusually close relationship that existed between the family of the house and their servants. The beautiful and evocative range of outbuildings includes kitchen, laundry, bakehouse, stables, sawmill, smithy and joiner's shop, while the stunning state rooms display most of their original 18th & 19th century furniture and furnishings, including some exquisite Chinese wallpaper.
Location: MAP 6:K3, OS Ref. SJ326 482. 2m S of Wrexham.
Open: House: 15 mar–2 Nov, Sat–Wed (+Thur Jul–Aug), 12 noon–5pm (Mar & Oct closes 4pm). 8 Nov–21 Dec, Sat & Sun, 12 noon–4pm (Limited Access). Garden & Outbuildings: 9 Feb–9 Mar, Sat & Sun, 11am–4pm ; 15–31 Mar, Sat–Wed, 11am–5pm; 1 Apr–30 Jun, Sun–Wed, 11am–6pm; 1 Jul–31 Aug, Sat–Thur, 10am–6pm; 1–30 Sept, Sat–Wed, 11am–6pm; 1 Oct–2 Nov, Sat–Wed, 11am–5pm; 8 Nov–21 Dec, Sat & Sun, 11am–4pm.
***Admission:** Adult £9.40, Child £4.70, Family (2+3) £23.50. Groups, Adult £7.20, Child £3.60. Garden & Outbuildings only: Adult £6, Child £3, Family £15. Groups, Adult £4.50, Child £2.25. NT members Free. *includes a voluntary donation but visitors can choose to pay the standard prices displayed at the property and on the website.
⬜ ✳ ♿ Partial. WCs. 🍴 Licensed. 🎧 AV presentation. ℗ ■ ✖ Guide dogs only.

FFERM

Pontblyddyn, Mold, Flintshire
Tel: 01352 770204
Owner: The Executors of the late Dr M Jones Mortimer
Contact: Miss Miranda Kaufmann
17th century farmhouse. Viewing is limited to 7 persons at any one time. Prior booking is recommended. No toilets or refreshments.
Location: MAP 6:J3, OS Ref. SJ279 603. Access from A541 in Pontblyddyn, 3½m SE of Mold.
Open: 2nd Wed in every month, 2–5pm. Pre-booking is recommended.
Admission: £4.
✖ ✳

GWYDIR CASTLE
LLANRWST, GWYNEDD LL26 0PN
www.gwydircastle.co.uk

Tel: 01492 641687 **E-mail:** info@gwydircastle.co.uk

Owner/Contact: Mr & Mrs Welford

Gwydir Castle is situated in the beautiful Conwy Valley and is set within a Grade I listed, 10 acre garden. Built by the illustrious Wynn family c1500, Gwydir is a fine example of a Tudor courtyard house, incorporating re-used medieval material from the dissolved Abbey of Maenan. Further additions date from c1600 and c1828. The important 1640s panelled Dining Room has now been reinstated, following its repatriation from the New York Metropolitan Museum.

Location: MAP 5:H3, OS Ref. SH795 610. ½m W of Llanrwst on B5106.

Open: 1 Mar–31 Oct: daily, 10am–4pm. Closed Mons & Sats (except BH weekends). Limited openings at other times. Please telephone for details.

Admission: Adult £4, Child £2, OAP £3.50. Group discount 10%.

⊤ ⟨&⟩ Partial. ⟨⟩ By arrangement. ⟨K⟩ By arrangement. P ⟨⟩ ⟨⟩ 2 doubles. ⟨⟩

ISCOYD PARK
Nr WHITCHURCH, SHROPSHIRE SY13 3AT

Tel: 01948 780785 **E-mail:** info@iscoydpark.com **www.iscoydpark.com**

Owner/Contact: Mr & Mrs P L Godsal

A Grade II* red brick Georgian house in an idyllic 18th century parkland setting, very much a family home. The house and garden will be available for weddings and events from May 2010.

Location: MAP 6:L4, OS Ref. SJ504 421. 2m W of Whitchurch off A525.

Open: By appointment.

⊤ Private dinners a speciality. ⟨&⟩ ⟨⟩ By prior arrangement. ⟨K⟩ Obligatory. P ⟨⟩ ⟨⟩ ⟨⟩ ⟨⟩

HARLECH CASTLE ♣

Harlech LL46 2YH

Tel: 01766 780552 **www.cadw.wales.gov.uk**

Owner: In the care of Cadw **Contact:** The Custodian

Set on a towering rock above Tremadog Bay, this seemingly impregnable fortress is the most dramatic of all the castles of Edward I. Discover the Castle's connections with Owain Glyn Dŵr and its importance in Welsh history. A World Heritage Inscribed Site.

Location: MAP 5:F4, OS Ref. SH581 312. Harlech, Gwynedd on A496 coast road.

Open: Apr–Oct: daily, 9am–5pm. 1 Nov–31 Mar: Mon–Sat, 9.30am–4pm. 11am–4pm Sun. Closed 24, 25, 26 Dec, 1 Jan. Last admission 30 minutes before closing.

Admission: Adult £3.60, Child (under 16yrs)/Conc. £3.20, Child under 5 yrs Free, Family (2 adults and all children under 16yrs) £10.40. Under 16s must be accompanied by an adult. All opening times and prices are correct at time of going to press (Autumn 2009) but may be subject to change from March 2010 – Please see site for details.

ⓘ Induction loop. Toilets. ⟨⟩ P Pay and Display. Cycle stands. ⟨⟩ ⟨⟩

HARTSHEATH 🏛

Pontblyddyn, Mold, Flintshire

Tel/Fax: 01352 770204

Owner: The Executors of the late Dr M Jones Mortimer

Contact: Miss Miranda Kaufmann

18th and 19th century house set in parkland. Viewing is limited to 7 persons at any one time. Prior booking is recommended. No toilets or refreshments.

Location: MAP 6:J3, OS Ref. SJ287 602. Access from A5104, 3½m SE of Mold between Pontblyddyn and Penyffordd.

Open: 1st, 3rd & 5th Wed in every month, 2–5pm.

Admission: £4.

⟨⟩ ⟨⟩

PENRHYN CASTLE ✻

Bangor LL57 4HN

Tel: 01248 353084 **Infoline:** 01248 371337 **Fax:** 01248 371281

Owner: The National Trust

This dramatic neo-Norman fantasy castle sits between Snowdonia and the Menai Strait. Built by Thomas Hopper between 1820 and 1845 for the wealthy Pennant family, who made their fortune from Jamaican sugar and Welsh slate. The castle is crammed with fascinating things such as a 1-ton slate bed made for Queen Victoria.

Location: MAP 5:G2, OS Ref. SH602 720. 1m E of Bangor, at Llandygai (J11, A55).

Open: Castle: 19 Mar–2 Nov, daily (except Tues), 12 noon–5pm. Grounds & Tearoom: as Castle. Shop & Museums: 19 Mar–2 Nov, daily (except Tues), 11am–5pm. Victorian kitchen, as Castle but last admission 4.45pm. Last audio tour 4pm.

Admission: Adult £9, Child £4.50, Family (2+2) £22.50. Pre-booked groups (15+) £7.50. Garden & Stableblock Exhibitions only: Adult £5.60, Child £2.80. Audio tour: £1 (including NT members). NT members Free.

⟨⟩ ⟨⟩ Licensed. ⟨⟩ ⟨⟩ ⟨⟩ Guide dogs only. ⟨⟩

PLAS BRONDANW GARDENS 🏛

Plas Brondanw, Llanfrothen, Gwynedd LL48 6SW

Tel: 01743 241181/07788 425713 **Email:** davinagriffiths@balfours.co.uk

Owner: Trustees of the Clough Williams-Ellis Foundation.

Italianate gardens with topiary.

Location: MAP 5:G4, OS Ref. SH618 423. 3m N of Penrhyndeudraeth off A4085, on Croesor Road.

Open: All year: daily, 9.30am–5.30pm. Coaches accepted, please book.

Admission: Adult £3.50, Child 12-18 £1, under 12 free.

Cadw: Crown Copyright

PLAS MAWR ✤

HIGH STREET, CONWY LL32 8DE

www.cadw.wales.gov.uk

Tel: 01492 580167

Owner: In the care of Cadw **Contact:** The Custodian

The best preserved Elizabethan town house in Britain, the house reflects the status of its builder Robert Wynn. A fascinating and unique place allowing visitors to sample the lives of the Tudor gentry and their servants, Plas Mawr is famous for the quality and quantity of its furnishings and plaster decoration "a worthy and plentiful house".

Location: MAP 5:H2, OS Ref. SH781 776. Conwy by A55 or B5106 or A547.

Open: 1 Apr–30 Sept: Tues–Sun, 9am–5pm. 1–31 Oct: Tues–Sun, 9.30am–4pm. Closed on Mons (except BH weekends) between 1 Apr–31 Oct. Closed at all other times.

Admission: Adult £4.95, Child (under 16yrs)/Conc. £4.60, Child under 5yrs Free, Family (2 adults) all children under 16yrs) £14.50. Children under 16 must be accompanied by an adult. Joint ticket for Plas Mawr and Conwy Castle: Adult £6.85, Conc. £5.85, Family (2 adults and all children under 16yrs) £19.55. Under 16s must be accompanied by an adult. All opening times and prices are correct at time of going to press (Autumn 2009) but may be subject to change from March 2010 – Please see site for details.

ℹ️ Toilets. Induction loop. 🖼️ ✖️

©NTPL/Nick Meers

PLAS NEWYDD 🌿

Llanfairpwll, Anglesey LL61 6DQ

Tel: 01248 714795 **Infoline:** 01248 715272 **Fax:** 01248 713673

Owner: The National Trust

Set amidst breathtaking beautiful scenery and with spectacular views of Snowdonia. Fine spring garden and Australasian arboretum with an understorey of shrubs and wildflowers. Summer terrace, and, later, massed hydrangeas and Autumn colour. A rhododendron garden open April–early June only. Elegant 18th century house by James Wyatt, famous for its association with Rex Whistler whose largest painting is here. Military museum contains relics of 1st Marquess of Anglesey and Battle of Waterloo. New coffee shop and second-hand bookshop. Children's adventure playground and quiz trails.

Location: MAP 5:F2, OS Ref. SH521 696. 2m S of Llanfairpwll and A5.

Open: from Sat 28 Mar until Wed 4 Nov (closed every Thurs & Fri). House 12–5pm (last admission 4.30pm) (Sat–Wed). Garden 11am–5.30pm (Sat–Wed). Coffee shop 11am–5pm (Sat–Wed). Free special interest tour at 11.15am every open day (subject to availability & for a maximum of 12 people). Tea room & Shop 28 Mar–20 May (Sat–Wed) 11am–5.30pm. 23 May–6 Sept (7 days a week) 11am–5.30pm. 7 Sept–4 Nov (Sat–Wed) 11am–5.30pm. 7 Nov–13 Dec (Sat & Sun only) 11am–4pm.

Admission: (Standard) House & Garden: Adult £7.50, Child £3.75 (under 5yrs free), Family (2+3) £18.75. Groups (15+) £6.50. Garden only: Adult £5.50, Child £2.75. NT members Free. (with Gift Aid) House & Garden: Adult £8.25, Child £4.25 (under 5yrs free), Family (2+3) £20.75. Groups (15+) £7.25. Garden only: Adult £6.25, Child £3.25.

ℹ️ No indoor photography. 🖼️ ♿ Partial. WCs. Minibus service operates from reception to the house.

▶️ Licensed. 🍴 ✖️ By arrangement. 🅿️ 🚐 ♿ Guide dogs only. 🛏️

©NTPL/Andreas von Einsiedel

Plas Newydd

PLAS YN RHIW 🌿

Rhiw, Pwllheli LL53 8AB

Tel/Fax: 01758 780219

Owner: The National Trust

A small manor house, with garden and woodlands, overlooking the west shore of Porth Neigwl (Hell's Mouth Bay) on the Llyn Peninsula. The house is part medieval, with Tudor and Georgian additions, and the ornamental gardens have flowering trees and shrubs, divided by box hedges and grass paths, rising behind to the snowdrop wood.

Location: MAP 5:D5, OS Ref. SH237 282. 16m SW of Pwllheli, 3m S of the B4413 to Aberdaron. No access for coaches.

Open: 20 Mar–30 Apr: Thur–Sun, 12noon–5pm. May & Jun; Thurs–Mon, 12noon–5pm. Jul & Aug; Wed–Mon, 12 noon–5pm. Sept; Thurs–Mon, 12noon–5pm. 1 Oct–2 Nov; Thurs–Sun, 12noon–4pm. Garden & snowdrop wood open occasionally at weekends in Jan & Feb, tel for details.

Admission: Adult £3.60, Child £1.80, Family (2+3) £9. Groups: £3, Child £1.50.

🖼️ ♿ Partial. WCs. ✖️ By arrangement. 🅿️ Limited. 🚶Guide dogs only.

PORTMEIRION

Portmeirion, Gwynedd LL48 6ET

Tel: 01766 770000 **Fax:** 01766 771331 **E-mail:** enquiries@portmeirion-village.com

Owner: The Portmeirion Foundation **Contact:** Mr R Llywelyn

Built by Clough Williams-Ellis as an 'unashamedly romantic' village resort.

Location: MAP 5:F4, OS Ref. SH590 371. Off A487 at Minffordd between Penrhyndeudraeth and Porthmadog.

Open: All year: daily, 9.30am–5.30pm. Closed 25 Dec.

Admission: Adult £7, Child £3.50, Senior £5.50, Family (2+2) £17, (2008 prices).

RHUDDLAN CASTLE ♣

Castle Street, Rhuddlan LL18 5AD
Tel: 01745 590777 **www.cadw.wales.gov.uk**
Owner: In the care of Cadw **Contact:** The Custodian
Guarding the ancient ford of the River Clwyd, Rhuddlan was the strongest of Edward I's castles in North-East Wales. Linked to the sea by an astonishing deep water channel nearly 3 miles long, it still proclaims the innovative genius of its architect.
Location: MAP 6:I2, OS Ref. SJ025 779. SW end of Rhuddlan via A525 or A547.
Open: 1 Apr–31 Oct: daily, 10am–5pm.
Admission: Adult £3, Child (under 16yrs)/Conc. £2.60, Child under 5 yrs Free, Family (2 adults and all children under 16yrs) £8.60. Under 16s must be accompanied by an adult. All opening times and prices are correct at time of going to press (Autumn 2009) but may be subject to change from March 2010 – Please see site for details.
ⓘ Cycle stands. Toilets. Induction loop. Baby changing. ⬚ 🅿 🚻 On leads.

RUG CHAPEL & LLANGAR CHURCH ♣

c/o Coronation Cottage, Rug, Corwen LL21 9BT
Tel: 01490 412025 **www.cadw.wales.gov.uk**
Owner: In the care of Cadw **Contact:** The Custodian
Prettily set in a wooded landscape, Rug Chapel's exterior gives little hint of the highly decorative and colourful wonders within. Nearby the attractive medieval Llangar Church still retains its charming early Georgian furnishings.
Location: Rug Chapel: MAP 6:I4, OS Ref. SJ065 439. Off A494, 1m N of Corwen. Llangar Church: MAP 6:I4, OS Ref. SJ064 423. Off B4401, 1m S of Corwen.
Open: **Rug** 1 Apr–31 Oct: Wed–Sun (open BH Mons), 10am–5pm. **Llangar** 1 Apr–31 Oct: Wed–Sun (open BH Mons), 1–2.30pm. Prior arrangement to access Llangar must be made through Custodian at Rug Chapel; please telephone 01490 412025 for details.
Admission: Adult £3.60, Child (under 16yrs)/Conc. £3.20, Child under 5 yrs Free, Family (2 adults and all children under 16yrs) £10.40. Under 16s must be accompanied by an adult. All opening times and prices are correct at time of going to press (Autumn 2009) but may be subject to change from March 2010 – Please see site for details.
ⓘ Toilets. Cycle stands. Induction loops. 🅿 🚻

TOWER

Nercwys Road, Mold, Flintshire CH7 4EW
Tel: 01352 700220 **E-mail:** enquiries@towerwales.co.uk **www.towerwales.co.uk**
Owner/Contact: Charles Wynne-Eyton
This Grade I listed building is steeped in Welsh history and bears witness to the continuous warfare of the time. A fascinating place to visit or for overnight stays.
Location: MAP 6:J3, OS Ref. SJ240 620. 1m S of Mold. SAT NAV – use CH7 4EF.
Open: 3–31 May incl. 30 Aug: 2–4.30pm. Groups also welcome at other times by appointment. It is strongly recommended that visitors travelling significant distances should phone in advance to check opening days.
Admission: Adult £3, Child £2.
🚻

TŶ MAWR WYBRNANT ✿

Penmachno, Betws-y-Coed, Conwy LL25 0HJ
Tel: 01690 760213
Owner: The National Trust
Situated in the beautiful and secluded Wybrnant Valley, Tŷ Mawr was the birthplace of Bishop William Morgan, first translator of the entire Bible into Welsh. The house has been restored to its probable 16th-17th century appearance and houses a display of Welsh Bibles. A footpath leads from the house through woodland and the surrounding fields, which are traditionally managed.
Location: MAP 5:H3, OS Ref. SH770 524. From A5 3m S of Betws-y-Coed, take B4406 to Penmachno. House is 2½m NW of Penmachno by forest road.
Open: 20 Mar–2 Nov, Thur–Sun, 12 noon–5pm, last adm 4.30pm.
Admission: Adult £3, Child £1.50, Child under 5 yrs Free, Family £7.50. Children under 16 must be accompanied by an adult. Groups: Adult £2.50, Child £1.
♿ Ground floor. 🅿 🚻 Guide dogs only.

VALLE CRUCIS ABBEY ♣

Llangollen, Denbighshire LL20 8DD
Tel: 01978 860326 **www.cadw.wales.gov.uk**
Owner: In the care of Cadw **Contact:** The Custodian
Set in a beautiful valley location, Valle Crucis Abbey is the best preserved medieval monastery in North Wales, enhanced by the only surviving monastic fish pond in Wales.
Location: MAP 6:J4, OS Ref. SJ205 442. B5103 from A5, 2m NW of Llangollen, or A542 from Ruthin.
Open: 1 Apr–31 Oct: daily, 10am–5pm. Unstaffed with no admission charge during winter, generally between 10am–4pm. Last admission 30 minutes before closing.
Admission: Adult £2.60, Child (under 16yrs)/Conc. £2.25, Child under 5 yrs Free, Family (2 adults and all children under 16yrs) £7.45. Under 16s must be accompanied by an adult. All opening times and prices are correct at time of going to press (Autumn 2009) but may be subject to change from March 2010 – Please see site for details.
ⓘ Induction loop. ⬚ 🅿 🚻 On leads. ❋

WERN ISAF

Penmaen Park, Llanfairfechan LL33 0RN
Tel: 01248 680437
Owner/Contact: Mrs P J Phillips
This Arts and Crafts house was built in 1900 by the architect H L North as his family home and it contains much of the original furniture and William Morris fabrics. It is situated in a woodland garden and is at its best in the Spring. It has extensive views over the Menai Straits and Conwy Bay. One of the most exceptional houses of its date and style in Wales.
Location: MAP 5:G2, OS Ref. SH685 75. Off A55 midway between Bangor and Conwy.
Open: 1–29 Mar: daily 1–4pm, except Tues.
Admission: Free.

©NTPL/Martin Trelawney

Plas Yn Rhiw

Carrick rope bridge, Ballintoy, County Antrim,
Northern Ireland © 2009 photolibrary.com

Ireland

Visitors come largely to enjoy the countryside and what it has to offer. Fishing (both river and sea) and golf are two of the most popular attractions. There are many heritage properties both in private ownership and owned by the National Trust for Ireland that have fascinating histories, among them Mount Stewart, once the home of Lord Castlereagh.

Ballywater Park, Co Down

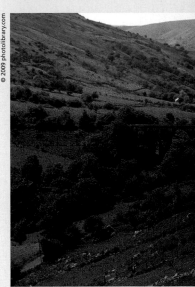
County Antrim, Northern Ireland

NORTHERN
IRELAND

ARDRESS HOUSE

64 Ardress Road, Portadown, Co Armagh BT62 1SQ

Tel 028 8778 4753 **Fax:** 028 3885 1236 **E-mail:** ardress@nationaltrust.org.uk

www.ntni.org.uk

Owner: The National Trust **Contact:** The Custodian

Nestled in the apple orchards of Armagh, Ardress is a 17th century house with elegant 18th century decoration. On display is the 1799 table made for the Speaker of the Irish Parliament upon which King George V signed the Constitution of Northern Ireland on 22 June 1921.

Location: MAP 18:N4, OS Ref. H912 561. On B28, 5m from Moy, 5m from Portadown, 3m from M1/J13.

Open: 21–22 Feb: 12pm–4pm. 14–28 Jun: weekends/BHs only, 2–6pm. 10–19 Apr: daily, 2–6pm. 2 Jul–30 Aug: Thu/Fri/Sat/Sun/BHs, 2–6pm. 5–27 Sep: weekends/BHs only, 2–6pm. Last admission 1 hour before closing. (2009).

***Admission:** House tour: Adult £4.60, Child £2.30, Family £11.50. Group prices available on request. *includes a voluntary donation but visitors can choose to pay the standard prices displayed at the property and on the website.

Ground floor. WC. Obligatory. On leads.

THE ARGORY

Moy, Dungannon, Co Tyrone BT71 6NA

Tel: 028 8778 4753 **Fax:** 028 8778 9598

E-mail: argory@nationaltrust.org.uk **www.ntni.org.uk**

Owner: The National Trust **Contact:** The Property Manager

The Argory was built in the 1820s on a hill and has wonderful views over the gardens and 320 acre wooded riverside estate. This former home of the McGeough-Bond family has a splendid stable yard with horse carriages, harness room, acetylene gas plant and laundry.

Location: MAP 18:N4, OS Ref. H871 577. On Derrycaw road, 4m from Moy, 3m from M1/J13 or J14 (coaches J13).

Open: House: 14–28 Jun: weekends/BHs only, 1–5.30pm. 10–19 Apr: daily, 1–5pm. 1 Jul–31 Aug: daily, 1–5pm. 5–27 Sep: weekends only, 1–5.30pm. Last admission 1 hour before closing. (2009).

***Admission:** House: Adult £5.80, Child £2.90, Family £14.50. Estate: Adult £2.50, Child £1, Family £6. *includes a voluntary donation but visitors can choose to pay the standard prices displayed at the property and on the website.

Ground floor. WC. Obligatory. On leads.

BALLYWALTER PARK

BALLYWALTER, NEWTOWNARDS, CO DOWN BT22 2PP

www.ballywalterpark.com

Tel: 028 4275 8264 **Fax:** 028 4275 8818 **E-mail:** enq@dunleath-estates.co.uk

Owner: The Lord and Lady Dunleath

Contact: Mrs Sharon Graham, The Estate Office

Ballywalter Park was built, in the Italianate Palazzo style, between 1846 and 1852 by Sir Charles Lanyon for the present owner's great, great, great, grandfather Andrew Mulholland. A single-storey Gentlemen's wing, comprising Billiard Room, Smoking Room and Conservatory, was added in 1870 for Andrew's son, John Mulholland, later 1st Baron Dunleath. Further Edwardian additions were made by W J Fennell. The house has a fine collection of original furniture and paintings, complemented by contemporary pieces added by the present owner. The house has undergone major conservation works over the past 20 years, with the magnificent domed conservatory being restored in 2008/9.

Location: MAP 18:P3, OS Ref. J610 723. Off A2 on unclassified road, 1 km S of Ballywalter village.

Open: By prior appointment only; please contact The Estate Office.

Admission: House or Gardens: £7. House & Gardens: £10. Groups (max 50): £7.

No photography indoors. By prior arrangement. Obligatory.

Tel for details. €

©NTPL/Andreas von Einsiedel

Ardress House

BARONS COURT

Newtownstewart, Omagh, Co Tyrone BT78 4EZ

Tel: 028 8166 1683   **Fax:** 028 8166 2059   **E-mail:** info@barons-court.com

www.barons-court.com

Contact: The Agent

The home of the Duke and Duchess of Abercorn, Barons Court was built between 1779 and 1782, and subsequently extensively remodelled by John Soane (1791), William and Richard Morrison (1819–1841), Sir Albert Richardson (1947–49) and David Hicks (1975–76).

Location: MAP 18:M3, OS Ref. H236 382. 5km SW of Newtownstewart.

Open: By appointment only.

Admission: Adult £8. Groups max. 50.

⬥ Partial. WCs. 🄵 By arrangement. 🅿 ⬛ ⬛ ❋ €

CASTLE COOLE ❧

Enniskillen, Co Fermanagh BT74 6JY

Tel: 028 6632 2690   **Fax:** 028 6632 5665   **E-mail:** castlecoole@nationaltrust.org.uk

www.ntni.org.uk

Owner: The National Trust   **Contact:** The Property Manager

Surrounded by its stunning landscape park on the edge of Enniskillen, this majestic 18th century home of the Earls of Belmore, designed by James Wyatt, was created to impress. The surrounding wooded landscape park sloping down to Lough Coole is ideal for long walks.

Location: MAP 18:L4, OS Ref. H245 436. On A4, 1.5m from Enniskillen on A4, Belfast–Enniskillen road.

Open: House: 17–31 May: 1–6pm. 10–19 Apr: Daily, 1–6pm. Jun: daily (except Thurs), 1–6pm. Jul & Aug: daily 12 noon–6pm. 5–27 Sept: Sats & Suns, 1–6pm. Grounds: 1 Apr–30 Sept, daily, 10am–8pm, 1 Oct–31 Mar: daily, 10am–4pm. (2009).

*Admission: House Tour & Grounds: Adult £5, Child £2.20, Family £12.20. Groups: £3.90 (outside normal hours £5).*includes a voluntary donation but visitors can choose to pay the standard prices displayed at the property and on the website.

⬛ 🅃 ⬥ Partial. WC. ⬛ 🄵 🅿 ⬛ In grounds, on leads. ⬛ ❋

CASTLE WARD & STRANGFORD LOUGH WILDLIFE CENTRE ❧

Strangford, Downpatrick, Co Down BT30 7LS

Tel: 028 4488 1204   **Fax:** 028 4488 1729   **E-mail:** castleward@nationaltrust.org.uk

www.ntni.org.uk

Owner: The National Trust   **Contact:** The Property Manager

Situated in a stunning location within an 820 acre walled demesne overlooking Strangford Lough, the lawns rise up to the unique 18th century house and its Gothic façade. This fascinating house features both Gothic and Classical styles of architectural treatment, internally and externally.

Location: MAP 18:P4, OS Ref. J573 498. On A25, 7m from Downpatrick and 1½m from Strangford.

Open: House: 21 Feb–28 Jun: Sats, Suns & BH/PHs (10–19 Apr: daily), 4 Jul–31 Aug: daily, Sept: Sats & Suns, 1–6pm. Grounds: All year: daily, 10am–4pm (8pm Apr–Sept). (2009).

*Admission: Grounds, Wildlife Centre & House Tour: Adult £6.50, Child £3, Family £16. Groups: £6.50. Grounds & Wildlife Centre: Adult £5, Child £2.50, Family £12.50, Groups £3.70. *includes a voluntary donation but visitors can choose to pay the standard prices displayed at the property and on the website.

⬛ 🅃 ⬥ Ground floor & grounds. ⬛ 🄵 Obligatory. 🅿 ⬛ In grounds, on leads. ⬛ Caravan park, holiday cottages, basecamp. ⬛ ❋

CROM ❧

Newtownbutler, Co Fermanagh BT92 8AP

Tel/Fax: 028 6773 8118 (Visitor Centre) 028 6773 8174 (Estate)

E-mail: crom@nationaltrust.org.uk   **www.ntni.org.uk**

Owner: The National Trust   **Contact:** The Visitor Facilities Manager

Crom is one of Ireland's most important nature conservation areas. It is set in 770 hectares of romantic and tranquil islands, woodland and ruins on the shores of Upper Lough Erne.

Location: MAP 18:M4, OS Ref. H359 246. 3m from A34, well signposted from Newtownbutler. Jetty at Visitor Centre.

Open: Grounds: 14 Mar–1 Nov: daily, 10am–6pm (1 Jan–31 Aug: 10am–7pm. Visitor Centre: 14–29 Mar: Sats, Suns & BH/PHs, 10am–6pm. 4 Apr–13 Sept: daily, 10am–6pm. 19 Sept–11 Oct: Sats & Suns, 10am–5pm. 18 Oct–1 Nov: Suns only, 10am–5pm. (2009).

*Admission: Demesne & Visitor Centre: Car/Boat £5.50. Minibus £15, Coach £19, Motorcycle £2.20. *includes a voluntary donation but visitors can choose to pay the standard prices displayed at the property and on the website.

🅃 ⬛ 🅿 ⬛ 7 x 4-star holiday cottages & play-area. ⬛

Crom Estate

THE CROWN BAR ❧

46 Great Victoria Street, Belfast BT2 7BA

Tel: 028 9027 9901

Belfast has many watering holes but none quite like The Crown! Rich in colour and design, it is famous for its special atmosphere, gas lamps, cosy snugs, fine ales and wines, and delicious lunch-time cuisine. The most famous pub in Belfast and one of the finest high-Victorian gin palaces in the UK, with an ornate interior of brightly-coloured tiles, carvings and glass. Wonderfully atmospheric setting in which to down a pint.

Location: MAP 18:O3, OS Ref. J336 736. Central Belfast.

Open: Mon–Sat: 11.30am–11pm, Sun: 12.30–10pm.

Admission: Free.

🍴 ❋

DERRYMORE ❧

Bessbrook, Newry, Co Armagh BT35 7EF

Tel: 028 8778 4753   **Fax:** 028 8778 9598   **E-mail:** derrymore@nationaltrust.org.uk

www.ntni.org.uk

Owner: The National Trust

An elegant late 18th century thatched cottage, built by Isaac Corry, who represented Newry in the Irish House of Commons. Park laid out in the style of 'Capability' Brown.

Location: MAP 18:O5, OS Ref. J059 276. On A25, 2m from Newry on road to Camlough.

Open: Grounds: May–Sep: daily, 10am–6pm. Oct–Apr: daily, 10am–4pm. Treaty Room: 4 & 25 May, 12 & 13 Jul, 13 Aug: 2–5.30pm. (2009).

*Admission: Treaty Room Tour: Adult £3.70, Child £1.80, Family £9.20. *includes a voluntary donation but visitors can choose to pay the standard prices displayed at the property and on the website.

🅿 ⬛ On leads.

DIVIS & THE BLACK MOUNTAIN ❧

12 Divis Road, Hannahstown, Belfast BT17 0NG

Tel: 028 9082 5434   **Fax:** 028 9082 5065   **E-mail:** divis@nationaltrust.org.uk

With spectacular panoramic views over Belfast, Divis and the Black Mountain is a haven for those seeking the wild countryside experience. On a clear day there are views of Strangford Lough, the Mournes and the Sperrins, as well as Scotland and Donegal.

Location: MAP 18:O3, OS Ref. J265 740. Access from Divis Road, off Upper Springfield Road. Signed from M1 Kennedy Way roundabout.

Open: All year.

Admission: Free

❋

©NTPL/Joe Cornish

IRELAND

Hezlett House

FLORENCE COURT ❦

Enniskillen, Co Fermanagh BT92 1DB

Tel: 028 6634 8249   **Fax:** 028 6634 8873   **E-mail:** florencecourt@nationaltrust.org.uk

www.ntni.org.uk

Owner: The National Trust   **Contact:** The Property Manager

Florence Court is a fine mid-18th century house and estate set against the stunning backdrop of the Cuilcagh Mountains. House tour includes service quarters popular with all ages. Beautiful walled garden and lots of walks in grounds.

Location: MAP 18:L4, OS Ref. H178 347. 8m SW of Enniskillen via A4 and then A32 to Swanlinbar.

Open: House: 21 Feb–10 May: Sats, Suns & BH/PHs (10–19 Apr: daily). 16 May–29 Jun: daily except Tues, 1–6pm; Jul & Aug: daily, 12 noon–6pm. 1–13 Sept: Daily, 19 Sept–Nov: Sats & Suns, 1–6pm. Grounds: All year, daily, 10am–4pm (8pm Apr–Sept). (2009).

*Admission: House tour: Adult £5, Child £2.20, Family £12.20. Groups: £3.90 (outside normal hours £5). Grounds only: Car £3.50, Minibus £16.50, Coach £22. *includes a voluntary donation but visitors can choose to pay the standard prices displayed at the property and on the website.

🅰 🇹 🔊 Ground floor. WC. 🖦 ⓕ Obligatory. 🅿 🔊 In grounds, on leads. 🏠 Holiday cottage. ▲

GIANT'S CAUSEWAY ❦

North Coast Office, 60 Causeway Road, Bushmills BT57 8SU

Tel: 028 2073 1582 / 2972   **Fax:** 028 2073 2963

E-mail: giantscauseway@nationaltrust.org.uk

The Giant's Causeway, renowned for its polygonal columns of layered basalt, is the only World Heritage Site in Northern Ireland. Resulting from a volcanic eruption 60 million years ago, this is the focal point of a designated Area of Outstanding Natural Beauty and has attracted visitors for centuries. It harbours a wealth of local and natural history. Geology, flora and fauna of international importance. Beautiful coastal path extends 11 miles to the Carrick-a-Rede rope bridge with wonderful views and coastal scenery.

Location: MAP 18:O1, OS Ref. C952 452. Off A2 Bushmills to Ballintoy road.

Open: Stones & North Antrim Coastal Path: all year. NT Shop & Tea Room: all year but closed 25 & 26 December. For opening times please contact property directly. (2009).

Admission: Guided Tours: Adult: £4, Child: £2.50, Family £12.50, Group £3.70. Group outside normal hours: £5. *includes a voluntary donation but visitors can choose to pay the standard prices displayed at the property and on the website.

ⓘ Suitable for picnics. 🅰 🇹 🔊 🖦 ⓕ For groups (15+), must be booked. 🅿 Charge (including NT). 🔊 On leads 🖦

GRAY'S PRINTING PRESS ❦

49 Main Street, Strabane, Co Tyrone BT82 8AU

Tel: 028 7188 0055   **E-mail:** grays@nationaltrust.org.uk   **www.ntni.org.uk**

Owner: The National Trust   **Contact:** The Administrator

An icon of Strabane's 18th century reputation as Ireland's capital of publishing, a local museum with a fine collection of print presses. Fascinating guided tours, demonstrations and audio-visual displays.

Location: MAP 18:M2, OS Ref. H345 976. in the centre of Strabane.

Open: 7 Apr–26 May & 1–29 Sept: Sats, 2–5pm; 2–30 Jun: Tue–Sat, 2–5pm; 3 Jul–31 Aug: Tue–Sat, 11am–5pm. (2009).

Admission: Press Tour: Adult £3.50, Child £2.10, Family £9.10. Group £2.60 (outside normal hours £4). *includes a voluntary donation but visitors can choose to pay the standard prices displayed at the property and on the website.

ⓕ 🅰

HEZLETT HOUSE ❦

107 Sea Road, Castlerock, Coleraine, Co Londonderry BT51 4TW

Tel/Fax: 028 8778 4753   **E-mail:** downhillcastle@nationaltrust.org.uk

www.ntni.org.uk

Owner: The National Trust   **Contact:** The Custodian

Charming 17th century thatched house with 19th century furnishings. One of only a few pre-18th century Irish buildings still surviving.

Location: MAP 18:N1, OS Ref. C773 356. 5m W of Coleraine on Coleraine–Downhill coast road, A2.

Open: Contact the property for visiting times.

*Admission: House Tour: Adult £3.50, Child £2.40, Family £9.40. Groups £2.50. (£4 outside normal hours.) *includes a voluntary donation but visitors can choose to pay the standard prices displayed at the property and on the website. (2009).

🔊 Ground floor. ⓕ Obligatory. 🅿 🔊 In grounds, on leads.

KILLYLEAGH CASTLE

Killyleagh, Downpatrick, Co Down BT30 9QA

Tel/Fax: 028 4482 8261   **E-mail:** gatehouses@killyleagh.plus.com

www.killyleaghcastle.com

Owner/Contact: Mrs G Rowan-Hamilton

Oldest occupied castle in Ireland. Self-catering towers available to sleep 4–15. Swimming pool and tennis court available by arrangement. Access to garden.

Location: MAP 18:P4, OS Ref. J523 529. At the end of the High Street.

Open: By arrangement. Groups (30–50): by appointment.

Admission: Adult £3.50, Child £2. Groups: Adult £2.50, Child £1.50.

ⓘ No photography in house. 🇹 Wedding receptions. 🔊 Unsuitable. ⓕ Obligatory. 🅿 🖦 ▲ ❄

LARCHFIELD ESTATE BARN & GARDENS

375 Upper Ballynahinch Road, Lisburn, Co Antrim BT27 6XL

Tel: 02892 638 025   **E-mail:** enquiries@larchfieldestate.co.uk

www.larchfieldestate.co.uk

Owner: Mr & Mrs G Mackie   **Contact:** Gavin Mackie

Just 20 minutes from Belfast City are the converted barns and spectacular walled gardens at Larchfield Estate. A stunning location year round, this venue offers exclusive use for private parties, weddings and corporate events. A private estate, viewings are strictly by appointment only.

Location: MAP 18:O4, OSNI J301 592. 4 Miles S of Lisburn, on the upper Ballynahinch Road, 10m SW of Belfast.

Open: Not open to general public. Weddings, events and conferences only.

🇹 🔊 Partial. WCs. ▲

MOUNT STEWART ❦

Newtonards, Co Down BT22 2AD

Tel: 028 4278 8387   **Fax:** 028 4278 8569   **E-mail:** mountstewart@nationaltrust.org.uk

Owner: The National Trust   **Contact:** The Property Manager

Home of the Londonderry family since the early 18th century, Mount Stewart was Lord Castlereagh's house and played host to many prominent political figures. The magnificent gardens planted in the 1920s have made Mount Stewart famous and earned it a World Heritage Site nomination.

Location: MAP 18:P3, OS Ref. J556 703. On A20, 5m from Newtownards on the Portaferry road.

Open: House: 10 Mar–29 Apr: Sats, Suns & BH/PHs (6–15 Apr: daily), 12 noon–6pm; 2 May–30 Jun: daily (except Tues in May), 1–6pm (12 noon–6pm Sats & Suns); 1 Jul–30 Sept: daily 12 noon–6pm (except Tues in Sept); 6–28 Oct: Sats & Suns, 12 noon–6pm. Lakeside Gardens: All year, daily, 10am–sunset. Formal Gardens: 10–31 Mar: Sats, Suns & BH/PHs, 10am–4pm; 1 Apr–31 Oct: daily, 10am–8pm (6pm in Apr & Oct). Temple of the Winds: 1 Apr–28 Oct: Suns & BH/PHs, 2–5pm. (2009).

*Admission: House Tour, Gardens & Temple of Winds: Adult £7.40, Child £3.70, Family £18.40. Group: £5.80 (outside normal hours £6.50). Gardens only: Adult £5.60, Child £2.80, Family £14. Group: £4.40. *includes a voluntary donation but visitors can choose to pay the standard prices displayed at the property and on the website.

🅰 ⓕ 🇹 🔊 🏠 ⓕ Obligatory. 🅿 🖦 🔊 In grounds, on leads. ▲ ❄ Lakeside area. 🖦 €

Properties that open all year appear in the special index at the end of the book.

MUSSENDEN TEMPLE & DOWNHILL DEMESNE ❧

North Coast Office, 60 Causeway Road, Bushmills BT57 8SU
Tel/Fax: 028 2073 1582 **E-mail:** downhilldemesne@nationaltrust.org.uk
www.ntni.org.uk
Owner: The National Trust
Set on a stunning and wild headland with fabulous views over Ireland's north coast is the landscaped demesne of Downhill.
Location: MAP 18:N1, OS Ref. C757 357. 1m W of Castlerock.
Open: Grounds: Dawn to dusk all year.
Admission: Contact property for admission rates.
🅿 🖼 On leads. ▲

PATTERSON'S SPADE MILL ❧

751 Antrim Road, Templepatrick BT39 0AP
Tel: 028 9443 3619   **Fax:** 028 9443 9713   **E-mail:** pattersons@nationaltrust.org.uk
Owner: The National Trust
Listen to the hammers, smell the grit, feel the heat and witness the thrill of the only surviving water-driven spade mill in Ireland. Visitors can watch as red-hot billets of steel are removed from the forge and fashioned into spades using the mill's massive trip hammer.
Location: MAP 18:O3, OS Ref. J263 852. 2m NE of Templepatrick on A6. M2/J4.
Open: 14 Mar–31 May: Sats, Suns & BH/PHs (10–19 Apr: daily); 1 Jun–30 Aug: daily (except Tues), 2–6pm; 5–27 Sept: Sats & Suns, 2–6pm. Last admission 1 hour prior to closing. (2009).
*Admission: Adult £4.30, Child £2.50, Family £11.10, Group £3.30, Group outside normal hours £5. *includes a voluntary donation but visitors can choose to pay the standard prices displayed at the property and on the website.
ℹ Suitable for picnics. 🔲 🔲 🔲 🖼 In grounds, on leads. 🔲

ROWALLANE GARDEN ❧

Saintfield, Ballynahinch, Co Down BT24 7LH
Tel: 028 9751 0721 **Fax:** 028 9751 1242 **E-mail:** rowallane@nationaltrust.org.uk
www.ntni.org.uk
Owner: The National Trust   **Contact:** Head Gardener
Rowallane is an enchanting garden enclosed within a demesne landscape of some 21 hectares, planted with an outstanding collection of trees, shrubs and other plants from many parts of the world, creating a beautiful display of form and colour throughout the year.
Location: MAP 18:P4, OS Ref. J405 585. On A7, 1m from Saintfield on road to Downpatrick.
Open: 1 Jan–30 Apr: daily, 10am–4pm; 1 May–31 Aug: daily, 10am–8pm. 1 Sep–30 Oct: daily, 10am–6pm. 1 Nov–31 Dec: daily, 10am–4pm. (2009).
*Admission: Adult £5, Child £2.50, Family £12.50, Group £3.70. Group outside normal hours £5.30. *includes a voluntary donation but visitors can choose to pay the standard prices displayed at the property and on the website.
🔲 Grounds. WC. 🔲 Apr–Aug. 🖼 In grounds, on leads. 🔲

SPRINGHILL HOUSE & COSTUME COLLECTION ❧

20 Springhill Road, Moneymore, Co Londonderry BT45 7NQ
Tel/Fax: 028 8674 8210 **E-mail:** springhill@nationaltrust.org.uk **www.ntni.org.uk**
Owner: The National Trust   **Contact:** The Property Manager
Described as 'one of the prettiest houses in Ulster'. A charming plantation house with portraits, furniture and decorative arts that bring to life the many generations of Lenox-Conynghams who lived here from 1680. The old laundry houses one of Springhill's most popular attractions, the Costume Collection with some exceptionally fine 18th to 20th century pieces.
Location: MAP 18:N3, OS Ref. H845 819. 1m from Moneymore on B18 to Coagh, 5m from Cookstown.
Open: 17 Mar–30 Jun: Sats, Suns & BH/PHs (6–15 Apr, daily); 1 Jul–31 Aug: daily; Sept: Sats & Suns, 1–6pm.
*Admission: House & Costume Collection Tour: Adult £4.80, Child £2.50, Family £12.10. Group £3.70 (outside normal hours £5.50). *includes a voluntary donation but visitors can choose to pay the standard prices displayed at the property and on the website. (2009).
🔲 🔲 🔲 Partial. WC. 🔲 🔲 🅿 🖼 In grounds, on leads. ▲

TEMPLETOWN MAUSOLEUM ❧

Templepatrick, Antrim BT39
Tel: 028 9082 5870
The mausoleum or monumental tomb was erected in 1789 by the Hon Sarah Upton to the Rt Hon Arthur Upton and displays some of Robert Adam's best classical work which is chaste, crisp and elegant. Given to the National Trust in 1965 by William Henderson Smith and Sir Robin Kinahan, it stands in the graveyard of Castle Upton. Castle Upton is privately owned and not open to the public.
Location: MAP 18:P4, OS Ref. J225 855. At Templepatrick on the Belfast-Antrim Road.
Open: All year.
Admission: Free access. Please contact Belfast Properties Office for further information.

WELLBROOK BEETLING MILL ❧

20 Wellbrook Road, Corkhill, Co. Tyrone BT80 9RY
Tel: 028 8674 8210/8675 1735 **E-mail:** wellbrook@nationaltrust.org.uk
www.ntni.org.uk
Owner: The National Trust   **Contact:** The Custodian
If you come to the mill when there is a flax pulling you will find a hive of industry and when the beetling engines are running their thunder fills the valley. There are hands-on demonstrations of the linen process, led by costumed guides, original hammer machinery, used to beat a sheen into the cloth, lovely walks and picnic opportunities by the Ballinderry River. A truly unique experience.
Location: MAP 18:N3, OS Ref. H750 792. 4m from Cookstown, following signs from A505 Cookstown–Omagh road.
Open: 14 Mar–28 Jun: Sats, Suns & BH/PHs (10–14 Apr, Fri–Tues); 1 Jul–31 Aug: daily except Fri; Sept: Sats & Suns; 2–6pm.
*Admission: Mill Tour: Adult £4, Child £2.30, Family £10.30. Group: £3.20 (outside normal hours £4.10).*includes a voluntary donation but visitors can choose to pay the standard prices displayed at the property and on the website. (2009).
🔲 🅿

Giant's Causeway

Opening Arrangements

at properties grant-aided by English Heritage

ENGLISH HERITAGE

I am very pleased to introduce this year's list of opening arrangements at properties grant-aided by English Heritage. The extent of public access varies from one property to another; the size and interest of the building or garden, their nature and function are all taken into account. Some buildings, such as town halls, museums or railway stations are, of course, open regularly. For other properties, especially those which are family homes or work places, access may need to be arranged in a way that also recognises the vulnerability of the building or the needs of those who live or work in it. Usually this will mean opening by arrangement or on an agreed number of days each year. This is made clear in each entry.

Some properties are open by written arrangement only. In most cases you should still be able to make initial contact by telephone, but you will be asked to confirm your visit in writing. This is to confirm the seriousness of your interest just as you would for example when making a hotel booking. It also provides a form of identification, enabling owners to feel more confident about inviting strangers into their house.

Over half the properties are open free, but we give details of admission charges where appropriate. There is also a brief description of each property, information on parking and access for people with disabilities.

It has always been a condition of grant-aid from English Heritage that the public should have a right to see the buildings to whose repair they have contributed. We therefore welcome feedback from visitors on the quality of their visit to grant-aided properties. In particular, please let us know if you are unable to gain access to any of the buildings on the list on the days or at the times specified, or if you have difficulty in making an appointment to visit and do not receive a satisfactory explanation from the owner. Please contact English Heritage Customer Services at PO Box 569, Swindon SN2 2YP (telephone: 0870 3331181; e-mail: customers@english-heritage.org.uk).

Information about public access is also included on our website (www.english-heritage.org.uk). The website is updated regularly to include new properties, any subsequent changes that have been notified to us or any corrections. We suggest that you consult our website for up-to-date information before visiting. If long journeys or special requirements are involved, we strongly recommend that you telephone the properties in advance, even if no appointment is required.

Finally, I would like to use this introduction to thank most warmly all those owners with whom we work; their support for these access arrangements is vital. The vast majority of this country's heritage is in the hands and care of private individuals. The public purse is pleased to be able to help through grant aid where it can, but it will only ever provide a fraction of the sums needed to pass on our historic environment to future generations. The private owners of listed buildings are today's principal custodians of tomorrow's heritage. Their contribution to the beauty and history of this country is vital.

I very much hope you enjoy the sites and properties you find in this list – from the famous to the many lesser-known treasures. They are all worth a visit – I hope we have helped you to find, and enjoy, them.

Baroness Andrews
Chair, English Heritage

BEDFORDSHIRE

ALL SAINTS CHURCH

Segenhoe, Bedfordshire MK43 0XW
Former parish church dating from 12th century, with many alterations between 12th–19th century. Now redundant and a consolidated ruin. Listed Grade II* and a Scheduled Monument.
Grant Recipient: Central Bedfordshire Council
Access Contact: Mr Robbie Ward-Booth
T: 07850 997026
E-mail: robert.wardbooth@centralbedfordshire.gov.uk
Open: At all reasonable times.
Heritage Open Days: No
P Spaces: 1
& No wheelchair access. No WC for the disabled. Guide dogs allowed.
£ No

MOGGERHANGER HOUSE

Moggerhanger, Bedford, Bedfordshire MK44 3RW
Grade I listed Country House. 18th century core, refurbished by Sir John Soane 1790-99 for Godfrey Thornton and further altered by Soane for Thornton's son, Stephen between 1806 and 1811. Set in 33 acre parkland originally landscaped by Humphry Repton.
www.moggerhangerpark.com
Grant Recipient: Harvest Vision Ltd
Access Contact: Mrs Carrie Irvin
T: 01767 641007   **F:** 01767 641515
E-mail: enquiries@moggerhangerpark.com
Open: Mid June–mid September: daily, guided tours Sunday and Monday at 2.30pm (some exceptions apply). Tea room and grounds throughout the year.
Heritage Open Days: Yes
P Spaces: 50
& Full. WC for the disabled. Guide dogs allowed.
£ Adult: £6.00. **Child:** Free. **Other:** £5.00 (concessions).

OLD WARDEN PARK

Old Warden, nr. Biggleswade, Bedfordshire SG18 9EA
Built in 1872 by Joseph Shuttleworth in a Jacobean design by Henry Clutton. Still housing original Gillows furniture, oak panelling and carvings, and a collection of 18th century paintings. The park was laid out by landscape architect Edward Milner.
www.shuttleworth.org
Grant Recipient: The Shuttleworth Trust
Access Contact: Ms Amanda Done
T: 01767 627972   **F:** 01767 627976
E-mail: amanda.Done@shuttleworth.org
Open: To the exterior of the building daily between May and September 9–5pm. Access to the interior by arrangement. Occasionally the site will be closed for private events, please call in advance: 01767 627972.
Heritage Open Days: No
P Spaces: 15
& Partial. Ramps and lifts available. WC for the disabled. Guide dogs allowed.
£ Free, except on event days.

SOMERIES CASTLE

Hyde, Bedfordshire LU2 9PL
Someries castle's name was derived from William de Someries who had a residence on the site. The site was acquired by Magnate Lord Wenlock in 1430 and work commenced on building the mansion. The house is unique in that it is regarded as one of the first brick buildings in England. Demolished in the 1700s, the fine brickwork can still be seen in the remains of the gatehouse.
Grant Recipient: Bedfordshire County Council
Access Contact: Mr Robert Ward Booth
T: 07850 997026
E-mail: robertwardbooth@centralbedfordshire.gov.uk
Open: At any reasonable time.
Heritage Open Days: No
P Roadside parking 400 yards from site.
& No wheelchair access. No WC for the disabled. Guide dogs allowed.
£ No

BERKSHIRE

BASILDON PARK

Lower Basildon, Reading, Berkshire RG8 9NR
Designed in the 18th century by Carr of York and set in parkland in the Thames Valley. Rich interiors with fine plasterwork. Small flower garden, pleasure ground and woodland walks.
www.nationaltrust.org.uk
Grant Recipient: The National Trust
Access Contact: Property Manager
T: 01189 843040   **F:** 01189 767370
E-mail: basildonpark@nationaltrust.org.uk
Open: House: 10 March to 31 October: Wednesday–Sunday (but open pm Bank Holiday Mondays and Good Friday), 12–5pm. Ground floor exhibitions, park, garden and woodland walks: as house, 11–5pm. 1–12 December: Wednesday, Thursday, Saturday and Sunday, 12–4pm.
Heritage Open Days: No
P Car park 400 metres from property.
& Partial. Wheelchair access to ground floor and garden, ramp available. Stairs with handrail to other floors. WC for the disabled. Guide dogs allowed.
£ Adult: £8.00 (house), £5.00 (park & garden only). Child: £4.40 (house), £2.50 (park & garden only). Other: Family: £20.35 (house), £11.00 (park & garden only) Free to National Trust members. Admission price includes voluntary gift aid donation.

SHAW HOUSE

Love Lane, Shaw-cum-Donnington, Berkshire RG14 2DR
Completed in 1581 by Thomas Dolman, a local clothier, Shaw House retains much of its original Tudor architecture. The house was used as headquarters by King Charles I during the battle of Newbury in 1644 and during World War II, it was requisitioned by the War Office as accommodation for troops. In 1943 it took on its final role as a school. Now open as a visitor attraction and for events, conferences and exhibitions.
www.shawhouse.org.uk
Grant Recipient: West Berkshire District Council
Access Contact: The House Team
T: 01635 279279
E-mail: shawhouse@westberks.gov.uk
Open: 13 February–31 March: Saturday and Sunday 11am–4pm; 1 April–31 July: Saturday and Sunday 11pm–5pm; 1–31 August: Wednesday to Sunday 11am–5pm; 1 September–19 December: Saturday and Sunday 11am–4pm. Special openings arranged during school holidays. Opening times subject to change, please check website for details.
Heritage Open Days: No
P Spaces: 35. Parking adjacent to the property for the disabled only.
& Partial. WC for the disabled. Guide dogs allowed.
£ Adult: £4.60 (subject to change, check website). Child: £2.30 (subject to change, check website). Other: £11.60 (family), £2.30 (students) subject to change (check website).

BRISTOL

29 QUEEN SQUARE RAILINGS

Bristol BS1 4ND
Fronted by repaired, grant-aided railings, 29 Queen Square is an early Georgian town house, 1709–11, listed Grade II*. One of the few surviving original houses in Queen Square which was laid out in 1699 and has claim to be the largest square in England.
Grant Recipient: The Queen Square Partnership
Access Contact: Ms Kate Difford
T: 0117 975 0700
E-mail: southwest@english-heritage.org.uk
Open: Access to the exterior at all reasonable times to view the railings from the pavement.
Heritage Open Days: No
P Paid parking in Queen Square and car park in The Grove (behind 29 Queen Square).
& No wheelchair access. WC for the disabled. Guide dogs allowed.
£ No

ARNOS VALE CEMETERY

Bath Road, Bristol BS4 3EW
Forty five acre burial grounds together with exterior of four Grade II* listed buildings and other listed structures. East Lodge and West Lodge gates and walls also Grade II*, now fully restored. Non-conformist and Anglican chapels fully restored in November 2009.
www.arnosvale.org.uk
Grant Recipient: Arnos Vale Cemetery Trust & Bristol City Council
Access Contact: Ms Sarah Cox
T: 0117 971 9117   **F:** 0117 971 5505
E-mail: sarah.cox@arnosvale.org.uk
Open: Cemetery: March–September: Monday–Friday 8.30am–5pm, Saturday 9am–5pm, Sunday and Public Holidays 9am–5pm; October to February: Monday–Friday 8.30am–4.30pm, Saturday 9am–4.30pm, Sunday and Public Holidays 10am–4.30pm, or dusk whichever is earlier. East Lodge Visitor Centre: Monday–Friday (except Bank Holidays) same as Cemetery opening times; Saturday 10am–1.00pm, Sundays and Bank Holidays: closed.
Heritage Open Days: Yes
P Spaces: 30
& Partial. Lower level Arcadian Garden area accessed from Bath Road. WC in non-conformist chapel. Guide dogs allowed.
£ No

LORD MAYOR'S CHAPEL

College Green, Bristol BS1 5TB
13th century church with 16th century floor of Spanish tiles in the Poyntz Chapel and a collection of stained glass. The only church in England that is owned, maintained and run by a City Council.
Grant Recipient: Bristol City Council
Access Contact: The Lord Mayors Chaplain
T: 0117 929 4350   **F:** 0117 929 4350
Open: Wednesday–Saturday 10am–12 noon and 1–4pm. Sunday service 11am.
Heritage Open Days: Yes
P On-street parking and multi-storey car park in Trenchard Street.
& No wheelchair access. No WC for the disabled. Guide dogs allowed.
£ No

ROYAL WEST OF ENGLAND ACADEMY

Queen's Road, Clifton, Bristol BS8 1PX
Bristol's first Art Gallery, founded in 1844, Grade II* listed and a registered museum. A fine interior housing five naturally lit art galleries, a new commercial gallery and a permanent fine art collection.
www.rwa.org.uk
Grant Recipient: Royal West of England Academy
Access Contact: Mrs Dee Smart
T: 0117 9735129   **F:** 0117 9237874
E-mail: info@rwa.org.uk
Open: Monday–Saturday 10am–5.30pm, Sunday 2–5pm. Bank Holidays 11am–4pm. Closed 25 December–3 January and Easter Day.
Heritage Open Days: Yes
P Parking for disabled badge holders only (5 spaces).
& Partial. Wheelchair access to New Gallery on ground floor and Main Galleries accessible by lift. Fedden Gallery not accessible. WCs fitted with handrails. Guide dogs allowed.
£ Adult: £4.00. **Child:** Free (under 16s) **Other:** £2.50 (students/senior citizens/groups)

BUCKINGHAMSHIRE

CLIVEDEN MANSION & CLOCK TOWER

Cliveden, Taplow, Maidenhead, Buckinghamshire SL6 0JA
Built by Charles Barry in 1851, once lived in by Lady Astor now let as an hotel. Series of gardens, each with its own character, featuring roses, topiary, water gardens, a formal parterre, informal vistas, woodland and riverside walks.
www.nationaltrust.org.uk
Grant Recipient: The National Trust
Access Contact: General Manager
T: 01628 605069   **F:** 01628 669461
E-mail: cliveden@nationaltrust.org.uk

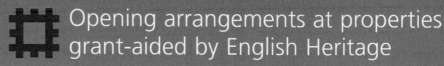
Open: House (main ground floor rooms) and Octagon Temple: 1 April–28 October, Thursday and Sunday 3–5.30pm. Estate and garden: 13 February–31 March, daily 11am–5pm, 1 April–23 December, daily 11am–5.30pm (closes at 4pm from 26 October).
Heritage Open Days: Yes
P Spaces: 300. Woodlands car park: open all year, daily 11am–5.30pm (closes at 4pm November–March). Overflow car park with 1000 spaces available.
Partial. Wheelchair access to ground floor of house and wheelchair route in grounds. WC for the disabled. Guide dogs allowed.
£ Adult: £1.00 extra (house), £8.00 (grounds), £3.00 (woodlands). **Child:** 50p extra (house), £4.00 (grounds), £1.50 (woodlands). **Other:** £20.00 (family: grounds), £7.50 (family: woodlands). Free to NT Members.

EDMUND WALLER TOMB

St Mary's Church, Beaconsfield, Buckinghamshire HP9 2JW
Grade II* listed, late 17th century ornate memorial tomb to poet and politician Edmund Waller (1608-87). Situated in St Mary's churchyard.
Grant Recipient: E L S Weiss & Richard Waller
Access Contact: E L S Weiss & Richard Waller
T: 01494 673479   **F:** 01494 671593
E-mail: eweiss@btopenworld.com
Open: Free access to exterior at all reasonable times.
Heritage Open Days: No
P Spaces: 25
Full. No WC for the disabled. Guide dogs allowed.
£ No

HALL BARN GOTHIC TEMPLE, OBELISK AND CLASSICAL TEMPLE

Hall Barn Estate, Beaconsfield, Buckinghamshire HP9 2SG
Garden buildings situated in landscaped garden, laid out in 1680s. Gothic temple in existence by 1740, but possibly c1725, by Colen Campbell. Gothic Revival style hexagonal-shaped building. Classical temple, mid 19th century, open fronted Doric style built of brick, rendered with a slate roof. Early 18th century stone obelisk, 9.5m high and rendered in coloured limestone slabs, topped with a stone ball finial with an iron spike protruding from its crown.
Grant Recipient: 5th Baron Burnham's Will Trust/Hall Barn Trustees Ltd
Access Contact: Colonel G S Brown
T: 01494 673 020
E-mail: geoff.brown@hallbarnestate.co.uk
Open: By prior telephone arrangement with the Estate Office (Colonel G S Brown, tel: 01494 673 020) or written arrangement with Mrs Farncombe, Hall Barn, Windsor End, Beaconsfield, Buckinghamshire HP9 2SG.
Heritage Open Days: No
P Spaces: 10. Parking 100 yards from garden buildings.
Full wheelchair access to the Gothic temple and obelisk. Grass track to the classical temple. No WC for the disabled. Guide dogs allowed.
£ No

STOWE HOUSE

Buckingham, Buckinghamshire MK18 5EH
Mansion built in 1680 and greatly altered and enlarged in the 18th century, surrounded by important 18th century gardens which are owned by the National Trust (see entry for Stowe Landscape Gardens). House and gardens variously worked on by Vanbrugh, Gibbs, Kent and Leoni and is one of the most complete neo-classical estates in Europe. The House is now occupied by the Preservation Trust's tenant, Stowe School.
www.shpt.org
Grant Recipient: The Stowe House Preservation Trust
Access Contact: Ms Anna McEvoy
T: 01280 818229 (Mon-Fri)   **F:** 01280 818186
E-mail: amcevoy@stowe.co.uk
Open: School holidays: Wednesday–Sunday 12 noon–5pm (last admission 4pm), tours at 2pm; July and August times vary, please check. Term time: Wednesday–Sunday tours at 2pm. Group visits (15 plus) by arrangement throughout the year. Please check opening arrangements before visiting (tel: 01280 818229 or 01280 818166 for 24 hour info line, or website: www.shpt.org).

Heritage Open Days: No
P Spaces: 520. Free parking. 20 spaces adjacent to site, 500 spaces 500 yards away.
Full. WC for the disabled. Guide dogs allowed.
£ Adult: £4.40 (NT members £3.80) **Child:** £2.70 (NT members £2.20)

STOWE LANDSCAPE GARDENS

Buckingham, Buckinghamshire MK18 5DQ
Extensive and complex pleasure grounds and park around a country mansion. Begun late 17th century but substantially developed in the 18th and 19th centuries by, among others, Charles Bridgeman, Sir John Vanbrugh, James Gibbs, William Kent and Lancelot 'Capability' Brown (Brown was originally head gardener here before leaving to set up his landscape practice). The park and gardens contain over 30 buildings, many of great architectural importance. Stowe was supremely influential on the English landscape garden during the 18th century.
www.nationaltrust.org.uk
Grant Recipient: The National Trust
Access Contact: Property Manager
T: 01280 822850
E-mail: stowegarden@nationaltrust.org.uk
Open: 2 January–28 February and 6 November–19 December: Saturday and Sunday 10.30am–4pm (last admission 3pm); 3 March–31 October: Wednesday–Sunday 10.30am–5.30pm (last admission 4pm). Open Bank Holiday Mondays. Closed 29 May. Contact property for Christmas opening arrangements.
Heritage Open Days: Yes
P Spaces: 100
Partial. Self-drive battery cars available. Uneven surfaces, map of accessible areas available. WC for the disabled. Guide dogs allowed.
£ Adult: £7.50. **Child:** £3.80. **Other:** £18.80 (family). Prices include voluntary gift aid donation. Free for National Trust members.

WIDMERE FARM CHAPEL

Widmere, nr. Marlow, Buckinghamshire SL7 3DF
Chapel attached to farmhouse, early 13th century with traces of 14th century windows and later alterations, listed Grade II*. 11th or 12th century crypt and medieval roof.
Grant Recipient: Mr G J White
Access Contact: Mr G J White
T: 01628 484204
Open: January–April: by prior arrangement.
Heritage Open Days: No
P Spaces: 6
No wheelchair access. No WC for the disabled. No Guide dogs allowed.
£ No

CAMBRIDGESHIRE

MINSTER PRECINCTS

Peterborough Cathedral, Peterborough, Cambridgeshire PE1 1XS
The Minster Precincts incorporate many remains from the medieval monastery of which the Cathedral church was a part. These include the richly decorated 13th century arcades of the former infirmary, the originally 13th century Little Prior's Gate and the 15th century Table Hall.
www.peterborough-cathedral.org.uk
Grant Recipient: The Dean & Chapter of Peterborough Cathedral
Access Contact: The Chapter of Peterborough Cathedral
T: 01733 355300   **F:** 01733 355316
E-mail: a.watson@peterborough-cathedral.org.uk
Open: All year (except Boxing Day): Monday–Friday 7.30am–6.30pm, Saturday 7.30am–5pm, Sunday 12 noon–5pm.
Heritage Open Days: Yes
P Spaces: 2. Disabled parking only. City centre car parks (nearest 5 minute walk).
Full. WC for the disabled in Cathedral restaurant, Tourist Information Centre and Cathedral Education Centre. Guide dogs allowed.
£ Adult: £4.00 (guided tour). **Child:** £3.00. **Other:** £3.00 (concession guided tour), £1.50 (school visit guided tour). Otherwise, donations welcome from Cathedral visitors.

THE MANOR

Hemingford Grey, Huntingdon, Cambridgeshire PE28 9BN
Built c1130 and one of the oldest continuously inhabited houses in Britain. Made famous by Green Knowe by the author Lucy Boston. Her patchwork collection is also shown. Four acre garden, laid out by Lucy Boston and surrounded by moat, with topiary, irises, old roses and herbaceous borders.
www.greenknowe.co.uk
Grant Recipient: Mrs Diana Boston
Access Contact: Mrs Diana Boston
T: 01480 463134   **F:** 01480 465026
E-mail: diana_boston@hotmail.com
Open: House: all year (except May) to individuals or groups by prior arrangement; May: guided tours daily at 2pm (booking advisable). Garden: all year, daily 11am–5pm (4pm in winter).
Heritage Open Days: No
P Spaces: 2. Parking for the disabled only adjacent to property.
Partial. Wheelchair access to garden and dining room only. WC for the disabled. Guide dogs allowed.
£ Adult: £7.00, £4.00 (garden only, maximum charges). **Child:** £2.00, free (garden only). **Other:** £5.50, £3.50 (garden only, maximum charges).

CHESHIRE

ADLINGTON HALL

Mill Lane, Adlington, Macclesfield, Cheshire SK10 4LF
Tudor/Elizabethan/Georgian manor house built around a Medieval hunting lodge. The Great Hall houses a 17th century organ, the most important of its type in the country, once played by Handel.
www.adlingtonhall.com
Grant Recipient: Mrs C J C Legh
Access Contact: Mrs Camilla J C Legh
T: 01625 829 206   **F:** 01625 828 756
E-mail: camilla@adlingtonhall.com
Open: July and August: Sunday, Tuesday and Wednesday 2–5pm, Special events: 30 May 10.30am–4pm for Plant Hunters Fair (admission £3.00) and 6 June 2–5pm for NGS opening (admission £5.00). Open to groups on weekdays throughout the year by prior arrangement.
Heritage Open Days: No
P Spaces: 100. Ample areas for parking at North front and East front.
Partial. Wheelchair access to ground floor and some areas of gardens. WC for the disabled. Guide dogs allowed.
£ Adult: £8.00 (house & gardens), £5.00 (gardens only). **Child:** £4.00 (house & gardens), free (gardens only). **Other:** £7.50 (groups).

CAPESTHORNE HALL

Macclesfield, Cheshire SK11 9JY
Jacobean style hall with a collection of fine art, sculpture, furniture, tapestry and antiques from Europe, America and the Far East. The Hall dates from 1719 when it was originally designed by the Smith's of Warwick. Altered in 1837 by Blore and rebuilt by Salvin in 1861 following a disastrous fire.
www.capesthorne.com
Grant Recipient: Mr William Arthur Bromley-Davenport
Access Contact: Hall Secretary
T: 01625 861221   **F:** 01625 861619
E-mail: info@capesthorne.com
Open: April–October: Sunday, Monday and Bank Holidays. Gardens and Chapel 12 noon–5pm, Hall from 1.30–4pm (last admission 3.30pm). Parties on other days by arrangement.
Heritage Open Days: No
P Spaces: 2000. 80 parking spaces in the car park and remainder in park.
Partial. Wheelchair access to ground floor and butler's pantry. WC for the disabled. Guide dogs allowed.
£ Adult: £7.00 (Sundays & Bank Holidays), £4.00 (garden & chapel only). **Child:** £3.50 (5-18 yrs), £2.00 (garden & chapel only). **Other:** £6.00 (senior citizen), £3.00 (senior citizen: garden & chapel), £16 (family). Mon only: £10 (car: 4 people) £30 (minibus) £60 (coach).

DODDINGTON HALL

Doddington Park, Nantwich, Cheshire CW5 7
Country house built between 1777-1790 designed by Samuel Wyatt. Listed Grade I. Park landscaped by Lancelot Brown in 1770s. Family seat of the Delves Broughton family. Occupied by the family until requisitioned by the MOD in WWII. A girls school (Goudhurst College) between 1946-1984. Vacant since 1985, a major programme of repairs is being undertaken.
Grant Recipient: Lady Delves Broughton
Access Contact: Mr Bruce Johnston
T: 01270 820263   **F:** 01270 820263
Open: Public access arrangements under review at time of publication, please check the English Heritage website or with the access contact for current information.
Heritage Open Days: No
P No.
& No wheelchair access. No WC for the disabled. No Guide dogs allowed.
£ No

HIGHFIELDS

Audlem, nr. Crewe, Cheshire CW3 0DT
Small half-timbered manor house dating back to c1600.
Grant Recipient: Mr J B Baker
Access Contact: Mrs Susan Baker
T: 01630 655479
Open: Guided tour of hall, drawing room, dining room, parlour, bedrooms and gardens by prior written arrangement.
Heritage Open Days: No
P Spaces: 20
& Partial. Wheelchair access to ground floor only. WC for the disabled with assistance (down 2 steps). Guide dogs allowed.
£ Adult: £5.00. Child: £2.50. Other: £5.00.

LYME HALL AND THE CAGE

Lyme Park, Disley, Stockport, Cheshire SK12 2NX
Early 18th century hunting tower within the 1400 acre medieval deer park of Lyme Park.
www.nationaltrust.org.uk
Grant Recipient: The National Trust
Access Contact: The Property Manager
T: 01663 762023   **F:** 01663 765035
E-mail: lymepark@nationaltrust.org.uk
Open: The Cage: 4 April–31 October, alternate weekends, 1–4pm. House: 27 February–31 October daily except Wednesdays and Thursdays 11am–5pm. Park: daily 8am–6pm. Garden: 27 February–31 October daily 11am–5pm; 6 November–19 December Saturdays and Sundays 12 noon–3pm.
Heritage Open Days: No
P Spaces: 1000. Park entry £4.60 per car.
& Partial. Wheelchair access to garden, first floor of house, parts of park, shop and restaurant. WC for the disabled. Guide dogs allowed.
£ Adult: Free (The Cage only), £9.00 (house & garden).Child: Free (The Cage only), £4.00 (house & garden). Other: National Trust members free.

CORNWALL

CAERHAYS CASTLE & GARDENS

Gorran, St Austell, Cornwall PL26 6LY
Built by John Nash in 1808. Set in 60 acres of informal woodland gardens created by J C Williams, who sponsored plant hunting expeditions to China at the turn of the 19th century.
www.caerhays.co.uk
Grant Recipient: The Trustees of Charles Williams (Caerhays Estate)
Access Contact: Mrs Cheryl Kufel
T: 01872 501144/501310   **F:** 01872 501870
E-mail: estateoffice@caerhays.co.uk
Open: House: 15 March–31 May (including Bank Holidays), Monday–Friday 12–4pm. Conducted tours every 45 minutes. Gardens: 15 February–31 May, daily 10am to 5pm (last entry 4pm).
Heritage Open Days: No
P Spaces: 500. Coaches can drive up to the castle by prior arrangement.
& Partial. Limited wheelchair access to gardens (area

around castle). Access to ground floor of castle with assistance, please telephone 01872 501144 or 01872 501310 in advance to check. WC for the disabled. Guide dogs allowed.
£ Adult: £9.50 (garden & house), £5.50 (house tour only), £5.50 (gardens). Child: £3.50 (garden & house), £2.50 (house tour only), £2.50 (gardens). Under 5s free. Other: £5.00 (groups 15+, house tour), £6.50 (groups, garden tour), £4.00 (groups, garden without tour).

COTEHELE

St Dominick, Saltash, Cornwall PL12 6TA
Cotehele, situated on the west bank of the River Tamar, was built mainly between 1485-1627. Home of the Edgcumbe family for centuries. Its granite and slate-stone walls contain intimate chambers adorned with tapestries, original furniture and armour.
www.nationaltrust.org.uk
Grant Recipient: The National Trust
Access Contact: Ms Charmian Saunders
T: 01579 351346   **F:** 01579 351222
E-mail: cotehele@nationaltrust.org.uk
Open: House and restaurant: 13 March– 31 October: daily except Friday (but open Good Friday), 11am–4pm. Mill: 13 March–30 September, daily 11–5pm; 1–31 October daily, 11am–4.30pm. Garden: daily all year 10.00am–dusk.
Heritage Open Days: Yes
P Spaces: 100. Parking space available for pre-booked coaches.
& Partial. Wheelchair access to house (hall, kitchen and Edgcumbe Room only), garden, area around house, restaurant and shop. Ramps available. Woodland walks: some paths accessible. WC for the disabled. No Guide dogs allowed.
£ Adult: £9.60 (house, garden & mill). £5.80 (garden & mill). Child: £4.80 (house, garden & mill), £2.90 (garden & mill). Other: Family: house, garden & mill: 1 adult £4.40, 2 adults £24.00. Family: garden & mill: 1 adult £8.70, 2 adults £13.00. £8.20 (pre-booked groups).

CULLACOTT FARMHOUSE

Werrington, Launceston, Cornwall PL15 8NH
Grade I listed medieval hall house, built in the 1480s as a long house, and extended 1579. Contains wall paintings of fictive tapestry, Tudor arms, St James of Compostella and remains of representation of St George and the Dragon. Extensively restored 1995-7 but still retains many original features. Now used as holiday accommodation.
www.cullacottholidays.co.uk
Grant Recipient: Mr & Mrs J Cole
Access Contact: Mr & Mrs J Cole
T: 01566 772631
E-mail: cullacott@btinternet.com
Open: By prior arrangement.
Heritage Open Days: No
P Spaces: 20
& Partial. Wheelchair access to Great Hall, through passage. WC for the disabled. WC for the disabled. Guide dogs allowed.
£ Adult: £3.00. Child: Free.

PENCARROW

Washaway Bodmin, North Cornwall, Cornwall PL30 3AG
A Grade II* Georgian house, completed in c1771, set in 50 acres of formal woodland gardens. Owned and lived in by the Molesworth-St Aubyn Family. Gardens include a sunken Italian Garden, Ice House, many specimen trees and 700 varieties of rhododendron.
www.pencarrow.co.uk
Grant Recipient: Trustees of Pencarrow House
Access Contact: Mrs Sally Harvey
T: 01208 841 369   **F:** 01208 841 722
E-mail: info@pencarrow.co.uk
Open: Gardens: 1 March–31 October, daily 9.30am–5.30pm. House: 28 March–30 September, Sunday to Thursday 11am–5pm (last entry 3pm).
Heritage Open Days: No
P Spaces: 270. Adjacent parking for disabled only. Main car park is 50 yards from house, also overflow car park with 220 spaces.
& Partial. Wheelchair access to ground floor only. If visitor cannot walk upstairs, admission is free. Video recording of the upstairs tour is provided. WC for the disabled. Guide dogs allowed.

£ Adult: £8.50 (house & garden) £4.00 (garden only). Child: £4.00 (house & garden) £1.00 (garden only). Under 5's free. Other: £22.00 (family ticket, 2 adults & 2 children).

PORTH-EN-ALLS LODGE

Prussia Cove, St Hilary, Cornwall TR20 9BA
Originally a chauffeur's lodge, built c1910-1914 and designed by Philip Tilden. It is built into the cliff and sits in close proximity to the main house. The Chauffeur's lodge is one of a number of historic houses on the Porth-en-Alls Estate.
www.prussiacove.com
Grant Recipient: Trustees of Porth-en-Alls Estate
Access Contact: Mr P Tunstall-Behrens
T: 01736 762 014   **F:** 01736 762 014
E-mail: penapc@dial.pipex.com
Open: Available as self-catering holiday lets throughout the year. Members of the public may view the property by arrangement, but only if it is unoccupied at the time. Most Fridays throughout the year 11am–3pm and other days out of season.
Heritage Open Days: No
P Spaces: 50. Public car park approximately 1/2 mile from the Lodge, off the A394 (near Rosudgeon village).
& Wheelchair access to the lodge is very difficult. No WC for the disabled. Guide dogs allowed.
£ Charges apply.

TREGREHAN

Par, Cornwall PL24 2SJ
Mid 19th century gardens and pleasure grounds designed by W A Nesfield together with significant 19th and 20th century plant collections. Concentrating on genera from warm temperate regions. An important green gene bank of known source plants. 1846 glasshouse range in walled garden. Set in 18th and 19th century parkland.
www.tregrehan.org
Grant Recipient: Mr T C Hudson
Access Contact: Mr T C Hudson
T: 01726 814 389   **F:** 01726 814389
E-mail: greengene@tregrehan.org
Open: Mid March–end of May: Wednesday–Sunday 10.30am–5pm. June–end August: Wednesdays only, 1pm–4.30pm.
Heritage Open Days: No
P Spaces: 50
& Partial. Wheelchair access to 10 acres of garden. WC for the disabled. Guide dogs allowed.
£ Adult: £5.00.
Child: Free.

WHEAL PEEVOR ENGINE HOUSE AND MINE COMPLEX

Wheal Peevor, Sinns Common, Redruth, Cornwall TR16 4BH
Engine houses and mine complex of former deep tin mine. The engine houses, listed Grade II, date from the 1870s. The buildings have been consolidated and viewing platforms installed allowing visitors to enter the structures. A network of trails have been created within the site to link up to the Coast to Coast multi-use trail.
www.cornwall.gov.uk/whealpeevor
Grant Recipient: Kerrier District Council
Access Contact: Cornwall Council
T: 0300 1234 202   **F:** 01209 614493
E-mail: adam.warden@corwall.gov.uk
Open: All reasonable times.
Heritage Open Days: No
P Spaces: 6. Access to Coast to Coast multi-use trail.
& Partial. Wheelchair access to the three key engine houses and main route throughout the site. No WC for the disabled. Guide dogs allowed.
£ No

CUMBRIA

BRIDGE OVER HELTONDALE BECK

Helton, Penrith, Cumbria CA10 2QB
17th century packhorse bridge with 5m limestone arch designed to carry pedestrians, riders and livestock over Heltondale Beck. Designed wide enough for just one horse

489

with a low parapet in order not to interfere with the panniers.
Grant Recipient: Mr George Robinson
Access Contact: Mr George Robinson
T: 01931 713 672
Open: At all reasonable times. (Advisable to call first at Widewath Farm, Helton, Penrith, Cumbria CA1 2QB).
Heritage Open Days: No
P No
No wheelchair access. No WC for the disabled. No Guide dogs allowed.
£ No

CHARGING HOUSE AT NEWLAND FURNACE, (NEWLAND CHARCOAL IRON FURNACE)
Ulverston, Cumbria LA12 7QG
Built 1747 and closed 1891, water powered and charcoal fuelled blast furnace producing pig iron from local haematite ore. The furnace and associated buildings are being preserved by the Newland Furnace Trust.
Grant Recipient: Newland Furnace Trust
Access Contact: Mr John Helme
T: 01539 731 020
E-mail: johnandjoanhelme@fsmail.net
Open: Access to exterior at all times. Guided tours: Heritage Open Days and by prior arrangement at other times for organised groups or societies.
Heritage Open Days: Yes
P Spaces: 3
Partial. Charging House is accessible for wheelchair users, but not all areas of the furnace. No WC for the disabled. Guide dogs allowed.
£ No

CROWN AND NISI PRIUS COURT
The Courts, English Street, Carlisle, Cumbria CA3 8NA
Former Crown Court in Carlisle situated at southern entrance to the city. One of a pair of sandstone towers built in the early 19th century as replicas of the medieval bastion. The towers were built to house the civil and criminal courts, used until the 1980s.
Grant Recipient: Cumbria Crown Court
Access Contact: Mr Mike Telfer
T: 01228 606116
Open: Guided Tours July and August: Monday–Friday 1.30pm and 3pm (excluding August Bank Holiday Monday).
Heritage Open Days: No
P Town centre car parks. Town Dyke Orchard upper viaduct.
Partial. Wheelchair access to Grand Jury Room, Court No.2 and Public Area Crown Court Room. WC for the disabled. Guide dogs allowed.
£ Adult: £4.00. Child: £2.00 (age 5-15). Other: £3.00.

DACRE HALL
Lanercost, Brampton, Cumbria CA8 2HQ
Part of the cloister of Lanercost Priory founded in 1168 and named Dacre Hall after its first owners since the dissolution in 1537. Contains unique remnants of 16th century murals in the 'grotesque' style. Given to the local community in 1952 as their Village Hall.
Grant Recipient: Lanercost Hall Committee
Access Contact: Mrs B Hall
T: 01697 746256
E-mail: david@lanerton.co.uk
Open: Dacre Hall is open when Lanercost Priory (managed by English Heritage) is open: 1 April–30 September, daily 10am–5pm; 1 October–1 November, Thursday – Monday 10am–4pm. For further information when the Hall is open contact Lanercost Priory (tel: 01697 73030). Otherwise, access outside the season can be arranged with Mrs B Hall, Secretary, Lanercost Hall Committee (tel: 01697 746256, email: david@lanerton.fsnet.co.uk).
Heritage Open Days: No
P Spaces: 1. Car parking uncertain at time of publication.
Full. Wheelchair access by prior appointment. WC for the disabled. Guide dogs allowed.
£ No

DIXON'S CHIMNEY
Shaddongate, Carlisle, Cumbria CA2 5TZ
270ft chimney, formerly part of Shaddongate Mill. Built in 1836 by Peter Dixon. At its original height of 306ft the chimney was the tallest cotton mill chimney to have been constructed. Structural problems meant that the decorative stone capping had to be removed in the 1950s.
Grant Recipient: Carlisle City Council
Access Contact: Mr Peter Messenger
T: 01228 871195 **F:** 01228 817199
E-mail: PeterMe@carlisle-city.gov.uk
Open: Chimney can be viewed from Shaddongate and Junction Street.
Heritage Open Days: No
P No
No wheelchair access. No WC for the disabled. Guide dogs allowed.
£ No

DRAWDYKES CASTLE
Brampton Old Road, Carlisle, Cumbria CA6 4QE
Pele tower, probably 14th century, converted to house 1676 by William Thackery and John Aglionby. Original tower with Classical Revival facade. Grade II* listed.
Grant Recipient: Mr J M Milbourn
Access Contact: Mr J M Milbourn
T: 01228 525 804
Open: By prior arrangement.
Heritage Open Days: No
P No
No wheelchair access. No WC for the disabled. No Guide dogs allowed.
£ No

ISEL HALL
Cockermouth, Cumbria CA13 0Q
An Elizabethan Range with a fortified Pele Tower dominates the landscape in its setting above the River Derwent. Interior of hall has Tudor panelling with traces of contemporary painting and contains furniture, paintings and textiles of historic interest.
www.visitcumbria.com/cm/iselhall.htm
Grant Recipient: Miss Mary Burkett
Access Contact: Miss Mary Burkett
T: 01900 826127 **F:** 01900 812436
Open: Mondays from the last Monday in March to the first Monday in October including Bank Holidays 1:30–4:30pm. Groups at other times by prior arrangement.
Heritage Open Days: No
P Spaces: 40
Roadside parking for coaches but small coaches can use the drive. Parking for the disabled at rear entrance.
Partial. Access to ground floor for wheelchair users. No WC for the disabled. Guide dogs allowed.
£ Adult: £5.00. Child: £2.50

LEAD MINES
Ore Works and Smeltmill, Nenthead, Alston Cumbria CA9 3PD
Standing and buried remains of lead mining operations. The smelt mill was in production from 1737 and by the time it closed in 1896 it had grown to six ore hearths, one slag hearth, two reverberatory furnaces, two refining furnaces and one de-silvering house.
www.npht.com
Grant Recipient: North Pennines Heritage Trust
Access Contact: North Pennines Heritage Trust
T: 01434 382294 **F:** 01434 382043
E-mail: management@npht.com
Open: During opening hours for the Nenthead Mines Visitor Centre. Dates and times not confirmed at time of publication. Please see website for current information.
Heritage Open Days: No
P Spaces: 50
Partial. Wheelchair access to all areas except mines. WC for the disabled. Guide dogs allowed.
£ Adult: £4.00 (£7.00 with mine tour). Child: Free (£3.00 with mine tour). Other: £3.25 (concessions). Admission charges subject to change.

LEVENS HALL
Kendal, Cumbria LA8 0PD
Elizabethan house built around a 13th century pele tower, containing fine furniture, panelling, plasterwork and an art collection. The gardens, which include much topiary, were laid out in the late 17th century by Monsieur Beaumont for Colonel James Grahme and are of national importance.
www.levenshall.co.uk
Grant Recipient: Mr C H Bagot
Access Contact: Mr P E Milner
T: 01539 560321 **F:** 01539 560669
E-mail: houseopening@levenshall.co.uk
Open: House: 4 April–14 October, Sunday–Thursday 12 noon–4.30pm (last admission 4pm). Garden: as house 10am–5pm. Opening times and admission prices under review at time of publication, please check with Mr Milner at the Estate Office for current information.
Heritage Open Days: No
P Spaces: 80
Partial. House unsuitable for wheelchair users due to stairs and narrow doorways but all other facilities (topiary garden, plant centre, gift shop, and tea room) are accessible. A DVD tour of the House is available in the Buttery during opening hours. A mobility buggy is available for hire. No WC for the disabled. No Guide dogs allowed.
£ Adult: £10.50. Child: £4.40. Other: Prices under review.

PERCY HOUSE
38-42 Market Place, Cockermouth, Cumbria CA13 9NG
Built in 1598 by Henry Percy the 9th Earl of Northumberland. Many of the original features of the building still remain, including carved plaster ceiling, Percy coat of arms, Tudor fireplace, oak plank and muslin screen and flag stone and oak floors.
www.percyhouse.co.uk
Grant Recipient: Mr R E Banks
Access Contact: Mr R E Banks
T: 01900 829667/ 07710 800973 **F:** 01900 85543
E-mail: banksrothersyke@mac.com
Open: Monday–Saturday 10am–5pm.
Heritage Open Days: Yes
P Spaces: 150. On-street parking in Market Place and public car park off Market Place.
Partial. Wheelchair access to ground floor only. WC for the disabled available in public toilets in nearby car park. No WC for the disabled. Guide dogs allowed.
£ No

RYDAL HALL MAWSON GARDENS
Rydal, Ambleside, Cumbria LA22 9LX
Formal Italianate gardens designed by Thomas Mawson in 1911 set in 34 acres. The gardens have been restored over a two year period returning them to their former glory. The gardens include an informal woodland garden, leading to a 17th century viewing station/summerhouse, fine herbaceous planting, community vegetable garden, orchard and apiary.
www.rydalhall.org
Grant Recipient: Church of England/Carlisle Diocesan Board of Finance
Access Contact: Mr Jonathon Green
T: 01539 432050 **F:** 01539 434887
E-mail: mail@rydalhall.org
Open: Daily, dawn to dusk.
Heritage Open Days: No
P Spaces: 40
Partial. Most garden paths are accessible for wheelchairs. WC for the disabled. Guide dogs allowed.
£ No

SCALEBY CASTLE
Scaleby, Carlisle, Cumbria CA6 4LN
Medieval ruins of Scaleby Castle which is a Scheduled Monument.
Grant Recipient: Lord Henley
Access Contact: Smiths Gore
T: 01228 527586 **F:** 01228 520802
E-mail: charles.baker@smithsgore.co.uk
Open: By prior written arrangement with the owner's agents Smiths Gore, 64 Warwick Road, Carlisle CA1 1DR.
Heritage Open Days: No

P Spaces: 10
Partial. All areas viewable but no wheelchair access to internal parts of the monument. No WC for the disabled. Guide dogs allowed.
£ No

SMARDALE GILL VIADUCT

Kirkby Stephen, Cumbria
Disused rail viaduct, built 1860-1 by Sir Thomas Bouch for the South Durham and Lancashire Union Railway. 550ft long with 14 arches, 90 ft high, spanning Scandal Beck at Smardale Gill, a National Nature Reserve. A well-preserved example of a large viaduct on this line.
www.nvt.org.uk
Grant Recipient: The Trustees of the Northern Viaduct Trust
Access Contact: Mr G J Biddle
T: 01539 560993
Open: All year, access by footpaths only from Newbiggin-on-Lune or Smardale. Path along former railway.
Heritage Open Days: No
P Spaces: 8. Parking at Smardale. Cumbria Wildlife Trust car park 1¼ miles.
Partial. Wheelchair access from Smardale only. No WC for the disabled. Guide dogs allowed.
£ No

WRAY CASTLE

Low Wray, Ambleside, Cumbria LA22 0JA
A large Gothic mock castle and arboretum. Built in the 1840s over looking the western shore of Lake Windermere.
www.nationaltrust.org.uk
Grant Recipient: The National Trust
Access Contact: Property Manager
T: 015394 47997   **F:** 015394 36811
E-mail: hawkshead@nationaltrust.org.uk
Open: Due to building work, access to the castle will be limited to possible tours and guided walks of the grounds. Details not finalised at time of publication. Please check the National Trust website or with the Property Manager (tel: 015394 47997) for current information.
Heritage Open Days: No
P Spaces: 30
Partial. No WC for the disabled. Guide dogs allowed.
£ **Adult:** £3.00. **Child:** Free. **Other:** National Trust members free.

DERBYSHIRE

ASSEMBLY ROOMS

The Crescent, Buxton, Derbyshire SK17 6BH
The Crescent was designed by John Carr of York and built by the Fifth Duke of Devonshire between 1780-89. It provided hotels, lodgings and a suite of elaborately decorated Assembly Rooms. The front elevation of three storeys is dominated by Doric pilasters over a continuous rusticated ground floor arcade.
Grant Recipient: Derbyshire County Council
Access Contact: Mr Allan Morrison
T: 01629 580 000 X3351   **F:** 01629 585 507
E-mail: allan.morrison@derbyshire.gov.uk
Open: Exterior accessible from public highway. No interior access until refurbishment works completed, other than by special agreement. Renovation works are likely to be in progress during 2010.
Heritage Open Days: No
P Spaces: 20. On-street pay and display parking available.
No wheelchair access. No WC for the disabled. No Guide dogs allowed.
£ No

BARLBOROUGH HALL

Barlborough, Chesterfield, Derbyshire S43 4TL
Built by Sir Francis Rhodes in the 1580s, the Hall is square in plan and stands on a high basement with a small internal courtyard to provide light. Contains Great Chamber, now a chapel, bearing a date of 1584 on the overmantel whilst the porch is dated 1583. Now a private school.
Grant Recipient: The Governors of Barlborough Hall School

Access Contact: Mr M J Lucas
T: 01246 435138   **F:** 01246 435090
E-mail: mlucas@msmcollege.com
Open: By prior arrangement only 26 March–16 April, 31 May–6 June, 8 July–3 September and most weekends throughout the year. External visits (without guide) any evening after 6pm or weekend.
Heritage Open Days: No
P Spaces: 50
No wheelchair access. No WC for the disabled. Guide dogs allowed.
£ No

BENNERLEY VIADUCT

Erewash Valley, Ilkeston, Derbyshire
Disused railway viaduct over the Erewash valley, c1878-9, and approximately 500 yards long with 15 piers. It is one of two remaining wrought iron lattice-girder bridges in the British Isles.
Grant Recipient: Railway Paths Ltd
Access Contact: Mr Huw Davies
T: 0121 633 1214   **F:** 0121 633 1214
E-mail: huw.davies@sustrans.org.uk
Open: There is access to the viaduct by a public footpath running underneath it, but the deck itself is inaccessible.
Heritage Open Days: No
P No
No wheelchair access. No WC for the disabled. No Guide dogs allowed.
£ No

CALKE ABBEY

Ticknall, Derbyshire DE73 1LE
Baroque mansion, built 1701-3 for Sir John Harpur and set in a landscaped park. Little restored, Calke is preserved by a programme of conservation as a graphic illustration of the English house in decline. It contains the natural history collection of the Harpur Crewe family, an 18th century state bed and interiors that are essentially unchanged since the 1880s.
www.nationaltrust.org.uk
Grant Recipient: The National Trust
Access Contact: Property Manager
T: 01332 863822   **F:** 01332 865272
E-mail: calkeabbey@nationaltrust.org.uk
Open: House (admission by timed ticket, delays may occur at peak times): 27 February–31 October: daily except Thursday and Friday, 12.30pm–5pm. Garden and Church: 27 February–31 October: daily except Thursday and Friday, 11am–5pm; 1 July–3 September: daily, 11am–5pm. Self guided West Wing Conservation Tours of House: 11am–12.30pm (by timed ticket only). Last admission 12noon. Park: All year 8am–8.30pm (or dusk if earlier).
Heritage Open Days: Yes
P Spaces: 75
Partial. Wheelchair access to ground floor of house, stables, shop and restaurant. Garden and park partly accessible. WC for the disabled. Guide dogs allowed.
£ **Adult:** £8.40, £4.60 (garden only). **Child:** £4.30, £2.50 (garden only). **Other:** £21.10 (family) £11.70 (family: garden only). Admission price includes voluntary gift aid donation.

CASTERNE HALL

Ilam, Ashbourne, Derbyshire DE6 2BA
Casterne Hall is a Grade II* manor house. The house was rebuilt in 1730, with a classic Georgian front and incorporating a 17th century and medieval back. Home of the Hurt family since the 16th century.
www.casterne.co.uk
Grant Recipient: Mr Charles Hurt
Access Contact: Mr Charles Hurt
T: 01335 310 489
E-mail: mail@casterne.co.uk
Open: 23 June–30 July: weekday afternoons. Tours at 2pm.
Heritage Open Days: No
P Spaces: 20
Partial. Wheelchair access to ground floor only. No WC for the disabled. Guide dogs allowed.
£ **Adult:** £5.00.

CATTON HALL

Catton, Walton-on-Trent, Derbyshire DE12 8LN
Country house built c1741 by Smith of Warwick for Christopher Horton. Property owned by the same family since 1405. Contains an interesting collection of 17th and 18th century pictures, including Royal and Family portraits; also Byron and Napoleon memorabilia. Gardens, which run down to the River Trent, include a family chapel.
www.catton-hall.com
Grant Recipient: Mr R Neilson
Access Contact: Mrs C Neilson
T: 01283 716311   **F:** 01283 712876
E-mail: kneilson@catton-hall.com
Open: 6 April–12 October: including tour of the house, chapel and gardens every Monday at 2pm. Group tours (15 or more) at any time of year by prior arrangement.
Heritage Open Days: Yes
P Unlimited parking available.
Partial. Wheelchair access by separate entrance to all ground floor rooms. No WC for the disabled. Guide dogs allowed.
£ **Adult:** £4.50. **Other:** £3.50 (concessions).

CROMFORD MIL

Mill Lane, Cromford, nr. Matlock, Derbyshire DE4 3RQ
Grade I listed mill complex established by Sir Richard Arkwright in 1771. The world's first successful water powered cotton spinning mill situated in the Derwent Valley Mills World Heritage Site. Currently being conserved by the Arkwright Society, an educational charity. The Mill is permanently home to four shops and two restaurants.
www.arkwrightsociety.org.uk
Grant Recipient: The Arkwright Society
Access Contact: Mrs Sarah McLeod
T: 01629 823256   **F:** 01629 825995
E-mail: smcleod@arkwrightsociety.org.uk
Open: Daily, 9am–5pm, closed on Christmas Day.
Heritage Open Days: No
P Spaces: 100
Partial. Wheelchair access to shops, lavatories and restaurant. WC for the disabled. Guide dogs allowed.
£ **Adult:** Free entry to main site, £3.00 for guided tour.
Child: Free entry to main site, £2.50 for guided tour.
Other: Free entry to main site, £2.50 for guided tour.

DEVONSHIRE ROYAL HOSPITAL

1 Devonshire Road, Buxton, Derbyshire SK17 6LX
Originally built as stables to service the adjacent Crescent, converted to a hospital in 1859. Central feature is a large circular colonnade capped with a spectacular dome added, along with the clock tower, in 1880. Listed Grade II*. Converted to and opened as the University of Derby Buxton campus in 2006.
www.derby.ac.uk/buxton
Grant Recipient: University of Derby
Access Contact: Professor Michael Gunn
T: 01332 594682
Open: University working site open throughout the year during normal working hours.
Heritage Open Days: No
P Spaces: 30. Access needs to be pre-arranged. 9 spaces for the disabled.
Full. WC for the disabled. Guide dogs allowed.
£ No

HARDWICK HALL AND STABLEYARD COTTAGES

Doe Lea, Chesterfield, Derbyshire S44 5QJ
A late 16th century 'prodigy house' designed by Robert Smythson for Bess of Hardwick. Contains an outstanding collection of 16th century furniture, tapestries and needlework. Walled courtyards enclosed gardens, orchards and herb garden. The Hall's environs include the late 16th century stableyard cottages, some of which have been converted to holiday cottages.
www.nationaltrust.org.uk
Grant Recipient: The National Trust
Access Contact: Property Manager
T: 01246 850430   **F:** 01246 858424
E-mail: hardwickhall@nationaltrust.org.uk
Open: 17 February–14 March: daily except Monday and Tuesday tours 11am–4.30pm, 15 March–31 October: daily except Monday and Tuesday 11am–4.30pm, tours 11am–12noon, 4 December–19 December Saturday and

Sunday 11am–3pm tours 11am–12noon. Garden: 17 February–31 October: daily except Monday and Tuesday 11am–5pm, 4–19 December: Saturday and Sunday 11am–3pm. Open Bank Holiday Mondays and Good Friday 12noon–4.30pm. The stableyard cottages are available to rent throughout the year and the public can view the cottages by prior arrangement with the access contact.
Heritage Open Days: Yes
P Spaces: 200
Partial. Wheelchair access to ground floor with audio guide. WC for the disabled in main car park. Guide dogs allowed.
£ Adult: £10.50, £5.30 (garden only). **Child:** £5.25, £2.65 (garden only). **Other:** £26.25 (family), £13.25 (Garden only). Admission price includes voluntary gift aid donation.

MASSON MILLS (SIR RICHARD ARKWRIGHT'S)
Derby Road, Matlock Bath, Derbyshire DE4 3PY
Sir Richard Arkwright's 1783 showpiece Masson Mills are the finest surviving example of one of Arkwright's cotton mills. The "Masson Mill pattern" of design was an important influence in nascent British and American mill development. Museum with historic working textile machinery. Part of the Derwent Valley Mills World Heritage Site.
www.massonmills.co.uk
Grant Recipient: Mara Securities Ltd
Access Contact: Museum Reception
T: 01629 581001 **F:** 01629 581001
Open: All year except Christmas Day and Easter Day: Monday–Friday 10am–4pm, Saturday 11am–5pm and Sunday 11am–4pm.
Heritage Open Days: No
P Spaces: 200
Partial. WC for the disabled. Guide dogs allowed.
£ Adult: £2.50. **Child:** £1.50. **Other:** £2.00 (school groups £1.00 per child).

NORTH LEES HALL
Birley Lane, Outseats, Hathersage, Derbyshire S30 1BR
Tower House built c1590 in the Peak District National Park and designed by the architect Robert Smythson. The Hall's tenants were the Eyre family. They were visited by Charlotte Bronte who is thought to have based Thornfield Hall on North Lees Hall.
www.vivat.org.uk
Grant Recipient: The Vivat Trust
Access Contact: Miss Lisa Simm
T: 0845 090 2212 **F:** 0845 090 0174
E-mail: enquiries@vivat.org.uk
Open: Heritage Open Days in September, 10am–4.30pm. At other times by prior arrangement with Laura Norris, The Vivat Trust, 70 Cowcross Street, London, EC1M 6EJ.
Heritage Open Days: Yes
P Spaces: 7
Partial. Wheelchair access to ground floor rooms by arrangement. No WC for the disabled. Guide dogs allowed.
£ No

SACHEVERELL-BATEMAN MAUSOLEUM
Churchyard of St Matthew's Church, Church Lane, Morley, Derbyshire
A Grade II* listed small rectangular mausoleum built in red sandstone designed in the Perpendicular Revival style by GF Bodley, in 1897. It contains a marble sarcophagus with a cut-glass cross incorporated in its lid, stained glass, a painted panelled roof and a framed memorial inscription written on vellum.
www.mausolea-monuments.org.uk
Grant Recipient: Mausolea & Monuments Trust
Access Contact: Miss Sheila Randall
T: 0115 875 8393
E-mail: se.randall@ntlworld.com
Open: Open when events are taking place in the Church (advertised locally). At other times by prior arrangement with Miss Sheila Randall (116 Kenilworth Drive, Kirk Hallam, Ilkeston, Derbyshire DE7 4EW. Tel: 0115 875 8393).
Heritage Open Days: Yes
P Spaces: 20

Full. Access for wheelchairs across churchyard but no designated path. No WC for the disabled. Guide dogs allowed.
£ No

ST ANN'S HOTEL
The Crescent, Buxton, Derbyshire SK17 6BH
The Crescent was designed by John Carr of York and built by the Fifth Duke of Devonshire between 1780–89. It provided hotels, lodgings and a suite of elaborately decorated Assembly Rooms. The front elevation of three storeys is dominated by Doric pilasters over a continuous rusticated ground floor arcade.
Grant Recipient: High Peak Borough Council
Access Contact: Mr Richard Tuffrey
T: 01457 851653 **F:** 01457 860290
E-mail: richard.tuffrey@highpeak.gov.uk
Open: Exterior accessible from public highway. No interior access until refurbishment works completed.
Heritage Open Days: No
P On-street parking available.
No wheelchair access. No WC for the disabled. No Guide dogs allowed.
£ No

SUDBURY HALL
Sudbury, Ashbourne, Derbyshire DE6 5HT
17th century house with rich interior decoration including wood carvings by Laguerre. The Great Staircase (c1676) with white-painted balustrade with luxuriantly carved foliage by Edward Pierce, is one of the finest staircases of its date in an English house. 19th century service wing houses the National Trust Museum of Childhood.
www.nationaltrust.org.uk
Grant Recipient: The National Trust
Access Contact: Property Manager
T: 01283 585305 **F:** 01283 585139
E-mail: sudburyhall@nationaltrust.org.uk
Open: Hall: 13 February–31 October: Wednesday–Sunday (but open Bank Holiday Mondays), 1–5pm. Schools and tours 11am–1pm. Museum: 13 February–28 March: Wednesday–Sunday 11am–5pm; 29 March–31 October: daily 11am–5pm, 4–19 December 11am–5pm weekends only. Grounds: 13 February–19 December: daily 10am–5pm.
Heritage Open Days: Yes
P Spaces: 100. Car park is a short distance from the Hall; six-seater volunteer driven buggy available.
Partial. Wheelchair access to tea room and shop. Ground floor access to museum. Access to Hall is difficult, please contact the Property Manager in advance. WC for the disabled. Guide dogs allowed.
£ Adult: £7.45. **Child:** £3.80 **Other:** £20.30 (family). Admission price includes voluntary gift aid donation.

TISSINGTON HALL
Tissington, Ashbourne, Derbyshire DE6 1RA
Grade II* listed Jacobean manor house altered in the 18th century and extended in the 20th. Contains fine furniture, pictures and interesting early 17th century panelling. Home of the FitzHerbert family for over 500 years.
www.tissingtonhall.co.uk
Grant Recipient: Sir Richard FitzHerbert Bt
Access Contact: Sir Richard FitzHerbert Bt
T: 01335 352200 **F:** 01335 352201
E-mail: tissington.hall@btinternet.com
Open: 5 and 9 April, 13–16 and 31 May, 1–4 June; 27 July–27 August: Tuesday–Friday and Monday 30 August 1.30–4pm. Tea rooms open daily in Old Coach House (tel: 01335 350501).
Heritage Open Days: Yes
P Spaces: 100
Partial. Wheelchair access to gardens and various rooms. Guide dogs: by arrangement. WC for the disabled.
£ Adult: £7.50 (house & garden), £3.50 (garden).
Child: £4.00 age 10-16 (house & garden), £1.00 (garden).
Other: £6.50 (house & garden), £3.50 (garden).

DEVON

21 THE MINT
off Fore Street Exeter, Devon EX4 3BL
The refectory range of St Nicholas Priory, converted into a substantial town house in the Elizabethan period and later into tenements. Features include medieval arch-braced roof, traces of the Norman priory and later Elizabethan panelling. Restored, now dwellings and meeting room with courtyard garden planted to represent the Tudor period.
www.ehbt.org.uk
Grant Recipient: Exeter Historic Buildings Trust
Access Contact: Ms Katharine Chant
T: 01392 436000 / 496653 **F:** 01392 496653
E-mail: enquiries@ehbt.org.uk
Open: House and meeting room: 29, 30, and 31 May; 24 and 25 July, Heritage Open Days (9–12 September), 11am–4pm. Meeting room: every Monday throughout the year, 2pm–4pm (except Bank Holidays). Also open for City's Redcoat guided tour 'Forgotten Exeter and 21 The Mint' starting from Cathedral Close on Saturdays at 2pm throughout the year and on Tuesdays (April–October) at 10:30am.
Heritage Open Days: Yes
P Car parks in Exeter.
Partial. Wheelchair access to ground floor and courtyard garden only. No WC for the disabled. Guide dogs allowed.
£ No

ANDERTON HOUSE/RIGG SIDE
Goodleigh, North Devon, Devon
Anderton House also known as Rigg Side. 1970-1 to the designs of Peter Aldington and John Craig for Mr and Mrs Anderton. The inspiration for its profile is taken from the longhouses of Devon. Timber frame, forming a two-row grid of double posts and beams with a tent roof, set half proud of concrete block walls and glazed clerestory and stained tiled gabled roof. Timber linings and ceilings internally, with tiled floors. Its sliding doors give views of the Devon countryside.
www.landmarktrust.org.uk
Grant Recipient: The Landmark Trust
Access Contact: Mrs Victoria O'Keeffe
T: 01628 825920 **F:** 01628 825417
E-mail: vokeeffe@landmarktrust.org.uk
Open: The Landmark Trust is an independent charity, which rescues small buildings of historic or architectural importance from decay or unsympathetic improvement. Landmark's aim is to promote the enjoyment of these historic buildings by making them available to stay in for holidays. Anderton House can be rented by anyone, at all times of the year, for periods ranging from a weekend to three weeks. Bookings can be made by telephoning the Booking Office on 01628 825925. As the building is in full-time use for holiday accommodation, it is not normally open to the public. However, the public can view the building by prior arrangement by telephoning the access contact (Victoria O'Keeffe on 01628 825920) to make an appointment. Potential visitors will be asked to write to confirm the details of their visit.
Heritage Open Days: Yes
P Parking at local playing fields.
Partial. Wheelchair access to kitchen, bedrooms and dining room. No WC for the disabled. Guide dogs allowed.
£ No

AYSHFORD CHAPEL
Ayshford, Burlescombe, Devon
Grade I listed private medieval chapel with a simple medieval screen. Distinctive stained glass of 1848 and 17th century monuments to the Ayshford family.
www.friendsoffriendlesschurches.org.uk
Grant Recipient: Friends of Friendless Churches
Access Contact: Mr & Mrs Kelland
T: 01884 820271
Open: At any reasonable time. Keyholder lives nearby.
Heritage Open Days: Yes
P Spaces: 2. On-street parking.
Partial. Wheelchair access possible with assistance. Access to church through field and up one step. No WC for the disabled. No Guide dogs allowed.
£ No

COLDHARBOUR MILL

Uffculme, Devon EX15 3EE

Woollen mill built by Thomas Fox between 1797-1799. Grade II* listed building. Now a working textile mill museum with demonstrations of textile machinery. Exhibition gallery, picnic area, café, waterside walks and shop.

www.coldharbourmill.org.uk

Grant Recipient: The Coldharbour Mill Trust

Access Contact: The Coldharbour Mill Trust

T: 01884 840960

E-mail: info@coldharbourmill.org.uk

Open: Daily 11am–4pm (walk through self guided tour of production factory, boiler room, steam engine, mill outbuildings). Power trail guided tours by prior arrangement, tour includes working water wheel, steam engines and gas and mill exhibitions). Tours of spinning mill for groups of 20 plus at other times by prior arrangement. 'Mill Tour' Steam Up event, see website for dates.

Heritage Open Days: No

🅿 Spaces: 100

♿ Partial. Wheelchair access to the mill via lift. Café not accessible but planning to relocate. WC for the disabled. Guide dogs allowed.

£ **Adult:** £7.50 (Mill tour), £5.00 (self guided tour and site) £4.00 (concessions). **Child:** £4.00 (Mill tour), £2.50 (self guided tour and site). **Other:** Mill tour: £20.00 (family), £6.50 (groups, per person, minimum of 20).

EXETER CUSTOM HOUSE,

The Quay, Exeter, Devon EX1 1NN

Located on the historic quayside, the Custom House was constructed in 1680-1 and is the earliest purpose-built customs house in Britain. Contains many original fittings and three exceptionally ornamental plaster ceilings by John Abbot of Frithelstock (amongst the finest such work of this date in the south west).

www.exeter.gov.uk/guidedtours

Grant Recipient: Exeter City Council

Access Contact: Mr Tim Gent

T: 01392 265914 or 01392 265203   **F:** 01392 665522

E-mail: guidedtours@exeter.gov.uk

Open: Red Coat guided tours from May–September: weekends. Times to be confirmed (please see website).

Heritage Open Days: Yes

🅿 Spaces: 400. Cathedral and Quay car park (75 metres). 5 public spaces for the disabled in front of Custom House.

♿ Partial. Wheelchair access to ground floor stair area only. WC for the disabled in car park. Guide dogs allowed.

£ No

KILWORTHY FARM COW HOUSES & GRANARY

Tavistock Hamlets, Devon PL19 0JN

Kilworthy Farm was part of the Duke of Bedford's Devon estates and demonstrates a pioneering approach to agriculture in the Victorian era. Built by the Seventh Duke of Bedford in 1851, the scale, technological innovation and extravagance of the farmstead make it of national significance. The farm buildings consist of three parallel ranges of cow houses and include a threshing barn with the largest water wheel in Devon, a granary, stables, cart shed and blacksmith's shop. The cow houses with underground dung pit are of exceptional interest. An unusually complete example of a planned Victorian 'factory farm' and still in use as a working farm. Restoration completed in 2003.

www.kilworthyfarm.co.uk

Grant Recipient: Mesdames Coren, Dennis & Edworthy

Access Contact: Mrs Sandra Vallance

T: 01822 614477   **F:** 01822 614477

E-mail: info@kilworthyfarm.co.uk

Open: Easter Friday, Saturday and Easter Monday; Saturdays and Mondays of both May and the August Bank Holiday weekends. 25 July–29 August: daily except Sunday and excluding Thursdays in August. At other times by prior arrangement with Mr & Mrs A Vallance 10am–5pm. Guided tour to start at 11am and 2pm or by special arrangement.

Heritage Open Days: No

🅿 Spaces: 8. Please ensure access for farm traffic is not obstructed.

♿ No wheelchair access. No WC for the disabled. No Guide dogs allowed.

£ **Adult:** £3.50 (to include information leaflet & guided tour). **Child:** £1.00 (under 10).

LAWRENCE CASTLE HALDON BELVEDERE

Higher Ashton, nr. Dunchideock, Exeter, Devon EX6 7QY

Grade II* listed building built in 1788 as the centrepiece to an 11,600 acre estate. Stands 244 metres above sea level overlooking the cathedral city of Exeter, the Exe estuary and the surrounding countryside. Contains a spiral staircase and miniature ballroom.

www.haldonbelvedere.co.uk

Grant Recipient: Devon Historic Buildings Trust

Access Contact: Mr Ian Turner

T: 01392 833668   **F:** 01392 833668

E-mail: enquiries@haldonbelvedere.co.uk

Open: 7 February–31 October: Sundays and Bank Holidays 1.30–5.30pm. At other times by prior arrangement. Grounds open all year.

Heritage Open Days: No

🅿 Spaces: 15. Parking for the disabled adjacent to building.

♿ Partial. Wheelchair access to ground floor only. WC for the disabled. Guide dogs allowed.

£ **Adult:** £2.00. **Child:** Free. **Other:** Free for wheelchair bound visitors.

LYNTON TOWN HALL

Lee Road, Lynton, Devon EX35 6HT

Grade II* listed Town Hall. Cornerstone laid 1898, opened by the donor Sir George Newnes, 15 August 1900. Neo-Tudor design with Art Nouveau details. In use as Town Hall and community facility.

www.lyntonandlynmouth.org.uk/towncouncil

Grant Recipient: Lynton & Lynmouth Town Council

Access Contact: Mr Dwyer

T: 01598 752384   **F:** 01598 752677

E-mail: ltc@northdevon.gov.uk

Open: Monday–Friday, 9.30–11.00am. Other times by arrangement.

Heritage Open Days: No

🅿 No

♿ Partial. Wheelchair access to part of ground floor. No WC for the disabled. Guide dogs allowed.

£ No

OLD QUAY HEAD

The Quay, Ilfracombe, Devon EX34 9EQ

Grade II* listed quay originally constructed early in the 16th century by William Bourchier, Lord Fitzwarren. The Quay was paved with stone in the 18th century and extended further in the 19th. This extension is marked by a commemorative stone plaque at its southern end. The Quay separates the inner harbour basin from the outer harbour.

Grant Recipient: North Devon District Council

Access Contact: Lieutenant Commander R Lawson

T: 01271 879130   **F:** 01271 862 108

E-mail: harbour_master@northdevon.gov.uk

Open: At all times.

Heritage Open Days: No

🅿 Spaces: 144. Charges apply. Places for disabled available.

♿ Full. WC for the disabled immediately adjacent to the Old Quay Head. Guide dogs allowed.

£ No

SALEM CHAPEL

East Budleigh, Budleigh Salterton, Devon EX9 7EF

Dating from 1719, built as a Presbyterian Chapel which later became congregational. Three galleries and school room added later in 1836 when the façade was re-designed.

www.hct.org.uk

Grant Recipient: Historic Chapels Trust

Access Contact: Mrs Kathy Moyle

T: 01395 445 236

Open: At any reasonable time by prior arrangement with the key holder, Kathy Moyle, 4 Collins Park, East Budleigh, Budleigh Salterton, Devon EX9 7EG. Occasional events during the summer; please check the Historic Chapels Trust website or contact the key holder for further information.

Heritage Open Days: Yes

🅿 2 parking spaces for the disabled, otherwise public parking close by.

♿ Partial. Wheelchair access to ground floor only. No WC for the disabled. Guide dogs allowed.

£ No

Adult: Donations invited.

SALTRAM HOUSE

Plympton, Plymouth, Devon PL7 1UH

A remarkable survival of a George II mansion, complete with its original contents and set in a landscaped park. Robert Adam worked here on two occasions to create the state rooms and produced what are claimed to be the finest such rooms in Devon. These show his development as a designer, from using the conventional Rococo, to the low-relief kind of Neo-Classical detail that became his hallmark and with which he broke new ground in interior design.

www.nationaltrust.org.uk

Grant Recipient: The National Trust

Access Contact: Carol Murrin

T: 01752 333500   **F:** 01752 336474

E-mail: saltram@nationaltrust.org.uk

Open: House: 14 March–1 November daily except Friday (but open Good Friday), 12 noon–4.30pm. Garden: 1 February–13 March daily except Friday, 11am–4pm; 14 March–1 November daily except Friday (but open Good Friday), 11am–5pm; 2 November–31 January daily except Friday, 11am–4pm.

Heritage Open Days: Yes

🅿 Spaces: 200. Parking 500 metres from house, 6 marked spaces for the disabled and 5 others on tarmac, remainder on grass. 200 spaces daily, 700 for events.

♿ Partial. Wheelchair access to ground floor. WC for the disabled. Guide dogs allowed.

£ **Adult:** £9.20 (house & garden), £4.60 (garden only). **Child:** £4.60 (house & garden), £2.40 (garden only). Under 5s free. **Other:** £13.80 (family: 1 adult), £23.00 (family: 2 adults). £7.50 (groups 15+).

SMEATON'S TOWER

The Hoe, Plymouth, Devon PL1 2NZ

Re-sited upper part of the former Eddystone Lighthouse. Built 1759 by John Smeaton, erected here on new base in 1882. Circular tapered tower of painted granite with octagonal lantern. When this lighthouse was first constructed it was considered to be an important technical achievement.

www.plymouthmuseum.gov.uk

Grant Recipient: Plymouth City Museum & Art Gallery

Access Contact: Mr Mark Tosdevin

T: 01752 304774   **F:** 01752 304775

E-mail: museum@plymouth.gov.uk

Open: 1 April–30 September: Tuesday–Friday 10am–12 noon, 1pm–4:30pm, Saturday and Bank Holiday Mondays 10am–12 noon, 1pm–4pm. October 1–March 31: Tuesday–Saturday and Bank Holiday Mondays 10am–12 noon, 1pm–3pm.

Heritage Open Days: Yes

🅿 Spaces: 40. On-street parking.

♿ No wheelchair access. No WC for the disabled. No Guide dogs allowed.

£ **Adult:** £2.00. **Child:** £1.00 (Under 5s free). **Other:** £4.80 (Family up to 2 adults & 3 children). Group rates available. Blue Badge guides & school groups (under 16s) free.

SOUTH MOLTON TOWN HALL AND PANNIER MARKET

South Molton, Devon EX36 3AB

Guild Hall, dating from 1743 and Grade I listed. Incorporates Court Room, Old Assembly Room and Mayors Parlour with Museum on ground floor. Adjacent to Pannier Market and New Assembly Room.

Grant Recipient: South Molton Town Council

Access Contact: Mr Malcolm Gingell

T: 01769 572501   **F:** 01769 574008

E-mail: smtc@northdevon.gov.uk

Open: Museum: March–October: Monday, Tuesday 10.30am–4.30pm, Thursday and Saturday 10.30am–1pm (times provisional). All other rooms used for meetings and functions as and when required.

Heritage Open Days: No

🅿 Parking available in Pannier Market except Thursdays and Saturdays.

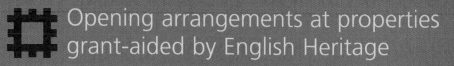
🖐 Partial. Wheelchair access to all areas except Court Room, Mayors Parlour and Old Assembly Room. WC for the disabled. Guide dogs allowed.
💷 No

DORSET

HIGHCLIFFE CASTLE

Rothesay Drive, Highcliffe-on-Sea, Christchurch, Dorset BH23 4LE

Cliff-top mansion built in the 1830s by Charles Stuart. Constructed in the romantic, picturesque style, much of its stonework is medieval coming from France. Exterior has been restored, interior houses changing exhibitions and the 16th century stained glass Jesse window. Gift shop and tea rooms on site with 14 acre cliff-top park.

www.highcliffecastle.co.uk
Grant Recipient: Christchurch Borough Council
Access Contact: Mr David Hopkins
T: 01425 278807   **F:** 01425 280423
E-mail: d.hopkins@christchurch.gov.uk
Open: 1 February–23 December: daily 11 am–5pm. Also some evenings for special events. Tea rooms open all year 10am–late afternoon. Grounds all year from 7am.
Heritage Open Days: Yes
🅿 Spaces: 120. Charged parking in Council car park with additional parking in Highcliffe Village (1 mile from Castle).
🖐 Full. Wheelchair access to all ground floor rooms and toilet facilities for the disabled at the site. WC for the disabled. Guide dogs allowed.
💷 **Adult:** £2.75 (from 1 February 2010). **Child:** Free. **Other:** HHA/Season ticket holders free.

MAPPERTON HOUSE

Beaminster, Dorset DT8 3NR

Grade I listed manor house, Elizabethan in origin, enlarged in late 1660s. Mapperton has remained almost unchanged since the plague of 1665-6. The buildings consist of the manor, church, stables, dovecote and outbuildings, forming a harmonious group. Set in a unique valley garden, in an area of outstanding natural beauty.

www.mapperton.com
Grant Recipient: Earl & Countess of Sandwich
Access Contact: Lord Sandwich
T: 01308 862645   **F:** 01308 861082
E-mail: office@mapperton.com
Open: 21 June–30 July: Monday–Friday; 31 May and 30 August, 2–4.30pm. At other times by prior arrangement.
Heritage Open Days: No
🅿 Spaces: 50. Space for one coach (pre-booked only).
🖐 Partial. WC for the disabled. Guide dogs allowed.
💷 **Adult:** £5.00. **Child:** £2.50 (under 18). Free (under 5).

NOTHE FORT

Barrack Road, Weymouth, Dorset DT4 8UF

Victorian fort constructed between 1860 and 1872 as part of the fortifications to protect Portland harbour. The fort is constructed on three levels, the lowest level provided the magazines for the storage of blackpowder (gunpowder) and shells. The parade ground level housed 12 heavy guns with the ramparts providing a high level observation platform.

www.nothefort.org.uk
Grant Recipient: Weymouth Civic Society
Access Contact: Mr David Joy
T: 01305 766 626   **F:** 01305 759 684
E-mail: hlnothefort@hotmail.com
Open: During Museum opening hours: 1 May–30 September 10.30am–5.30pm (last admission 4.30pm), Sundays out of season and 2 weeks at Easter and autumn half term school holidays 11am–4.30pm (4pm when summer time ceases).
Heritage Open Days: No
🅿 Public pay and display.
🖐 Full. WC for the disabled. Guide dogs allowed.
💷 **Adult:** £6.00. **Child:** £1.00 **Other:** £5.00 (senior citizens), £4.50 (groups).

DURHAM

BOWES MUSEUM

Newgate, Barnard Castle, Durham DL 12 8NP

French style chateau, built between 1869–c1885 as a museum by John and Joséphine Bowes, designed by Jules Pellechet and John Watson. The museum was the first building in the country to be designed in metric rather than imperial measurements. Opened in 1892, it houses a collection of European fine and decorative arts, and has a programme of exhibitions and special events.

www.thebowesmuseum.org.uk
Grant Recipient: Bowes Museum
Access Contact: Mr Matt Leng
T: 01833 690606
E-mail: matt.leng@thebowesmuseum.org.uk
Open: Daily, 10am–5pm. Closed Christmas Day, Boxing Day and New Years Day 2010.
Heritage Open Days: No
🅿 Spaces: 180
🖐 Full. WC for the disabled. Guide dogs allowed.
💷 **Adult:** £7.00 (includes donation). **Child:** Free to under 16s (as part of a family visit). **Other:** £6.00 (concessions, includes donation).

CROXDALE HALL

Durham DH6 5JP

18th century re-casing of an earlier Tudor building, containing comfortably furnished mid-Georgian rooms with Rococo ceilings. There is also a private chapel in the north elevation, walled gardens, a quarter-of-a-mile long terrace, an orangery and lakes which date from the mid-18th century.

Grant Recipient: Exors of Captain GM Salvin
Access Contact: Mr W H T Salvin
T: 01833 690100   **F:** 01833 637004
E-mail: williamsalvin@whtsalvin.co.uk
Open: By prior arrangement on Tuesdays and Wednesdays from first Tuesday in May to second Wednesday in July, 10am–1pm.
Heritage Open Days: Yes
🅿 Spaces: 20
🖐 Partial. WC for the disabled. No Guide dogs allowed.
💷 **Adult:** £7.50. **Child:** Free (under 16s).

DARLINGTON RAILWAY CENTRE AND MUSEUM (HEAD OF STEAM)

Station Road, Darlington DL3 6ST

Located on the 1825 route of the Stockton & Darlington Railway, the world's first steam-worked public railway. The site encompasses three significant railway buildings of the 1830s to 1850s. Interactive displays and audio visual equipment show the history of Darlington and the impact of the railways.

Grant Recipient: Darlington Borough Council
Access Contact: Mr David Tetlow
T: 01325 460532   **F:** 01325 287746
E-mail: david.tetlow@darlington.gov.uk
Open: 1 April–30 September: Tuesday–Sunday, 10am–4pm; 1 October–31 March 2011: Monday–Thursday, 11am–3.30pm.
Heritage Open Days: Yes
🅿 Spaces: 50. On-street parking.
🖐 Full. WC for the disabled. Guide dogs allowed.
💷 **Adult:** £4.95. **Child:** £3.00 (6 -16 years, under 5s free). **Other:** £3.75 (concession).

DURHAM CASTLE

Palace Green, Durham DH1 3RW

Dating from 1072, the Castle was the seat of the Prince Bishops until 1832. Together with the Cathedral, the Castle is a World Heritage site. It now houses University College, the Foundation College of Durham University, and is a conference, banqueting and holiday centre in vacations.

www.durhamcastle.com
Grant Recipient: University of Durham
Access Contact: University of Durham
T: 0191 374 4682
Open: University vacations: tours normally at 10 and 11am, 12 noon, 2, 3 and 4pm; term times: tours normally at 2, 3 and 4pm. Times may vary subject to events and functions, please phone the Castle Porter (tel: 0191 334 3800) in advance to confirm and for term dates, or check the website for term dates (www.dur.ac.uk). Heritage Open Days:10 and 11 September 10am–12pm.
Heritage Open Days: Yes
🅿 Parking for disabled only by arrangement. Public parking in city car parks.
🖐 Partial. Wheelchair access to courtyard only. WC for the disabled inaccessible to wheelchairs. Guide dogs allowed.
💷 **Adult:** £5.00, £4.50 (group rate 10+). **Child:** £3.50 (3-14), £3.00 (group rate 10+). **Other:** £3.50 (concessions), £12.00 (family).

HAMSTEELS HALL

Hamsteels Lane, Quebec, Durham DH7 9RS

Early 18th century farmhouse with 19th century alterations. Panelled window shutters, ground-floor room with full early 18th century panelling; similar panelling and cupboards in first-floor room. Good quality dogleg stair with turned balusters.

www.hamsteelshall.co.uk
Grant Recipient: Mr G F Whitfield
Access Contact: Mrs June Whitfield
T: 01207 520 388   **F:** 01207 520 388
E-mail: june@hamsteelshall.co.uk
Open: By prior arrangement.
Heritage Open Days: No
🅿 Spaces: 8
🖐 Partial. Wheelchair access to dining room and front parlour only. No WC for the disabled. No Guide dogs allowed.
💷 No

HARDWICK PARK BONO RETIRO

Sedgefield, Durham TS21 2DN

The gothic style Bono Retiro (a place of pleasant retirement) is one of a number of garden buildings set around a 17 acre lake in Hardwick Park. The 18th century landscape park and structures are being restored by Durham Country Council. The Bono Retiro has been consolidated as a ruin.

www.durham.gov.uk/hardwickpark
Grant Recipient: Durham County Council
Access Contact: Mr Darryl Cox
T: 0191 3833387   **F:** 0191 3834096
E-mail: darryl.cox@durham.gov.uk
Open: Daily, dawn to dusk, when the park is open.
Heritage Open Days: No
🅿 Spaces: 200
🖐 Partial. WC for the disabled. Guide dogs allowed.
💷 No

KEPIER FARM

Kepier Lane, West Range, Durham, DH1 1LB

Range of farm buildings which once formed a 'grange' to the abbey at Durham supplying it with food. Foundations date from the 12th century but current standing remains date from 14th-15th centuries.

Grant Recipient: Ruth Watson
Access Contact: Mrs Ruth Watson
T: 01913 842761
Open: By prior arrangement.
Heritage Open Days: Yes
🅿 Spaces: 12
🖐 Partial. No WC for the disabled. Guide dogs allowed.
💷 No

LOW BUTTERBY FARMHOUSE,

Croxdale & Hett, Durham DH6 5JN

Stone built farmhouse constructed on medieval site incorporating elements of 17th, 18th and 19th century phases of development.

Grant Recipient: The Trustees of Captain GM Salvin's 1983 Settlement
Access Contact: Mr W H T Salvin
T: 01833 690100   **F:** 01833 637004
E-mail: williamsalvin@whtsalvin.co.uk
Open: 1 January–5 July: By prior written or telephone arrangement with Mr W H T Salvin, The Estate Office, Egglestone Abbey, Barnard Castle, Co. Durham DL12 9TN.
Heritage Open Days: No
🅿 Spaces: 2
🖐 Partial. Limited wheelchair access with assistance (some changes in floor level). No WC for the disabled. No Guide dogs allowed.
💷 No

RABY CASTLE

PO Box 50, Staindrop, Darlington, Durham DL2 3AY

Medieval castle, built in the 14th century. Once the seat of the Nevills, it has been home to Lord Barnard's family since

1626. Contains collections of art, fine furniture and highly decorated interiors. Also has a deer park, gardens, carriage collection and woodland adventure playground.
www.rabycastle.com
Grant Recipient: Lord Barnard TD
Access Contact: Ms Katie Blundell
T: 01833 660888/660202   **F:** 01833 660169
E-mail: admin@rabycastle.com
Open: Easter and Bank Holiday weekends, Saturday–Monday; May, June and September: Sunday–Wednesday; July and August: daily except Saturday. Castle open 12.30–5pm. Garden and park 11am–5.30pm. Educational visits and private guided tours including tea/coffee reception (groups 20+) available weekday mornings from Easter to the end of September by prior arrangement.
Heritage Open Days: Yes
P Spaces: 500
♿ Partial. Limited wheelchair access to lower floor with assistance (3 steps to entrance and some internal steps to be negotiated). 3 wheelchairs available. WC for the disabled. Guide dogs allowed.
£ Adult: £9.50 (castle, park & gardens), £5.00 (park & gardens). **Child:** £4.00, age 5-15 (castle, park & gardens), £3.00, age 12-15 (park & gardens), under 12s free. **Other:** £8.50 (castle, park & gardens), £4.00 (park & gardens), £25 (family). Group rates available.

RECTORY FARM BARN,

Hall Walks, Easington, Peterlee, Durham SR8 3BS
Barn, possibly 13th century with extensive alterations. May originally have been an oratory connected with Seaton Holme. Limestone rubble construction; first floor contains medieval windows. Purchased by Groundwork in 1997 and recently renovated. Listed Grade II*.
Grant Recipient: Groundwork East Durham
Access Contact: Mr Peter Richards
T: 0191 5273333   **F:** 0191 5273665
E-mail: peter.richards@groundwork.org.uk
Open: Access to the exterior all year, Monday to Friday 9am–5pm.
Heritage Open Days: No
P Spaces: 10
♿ Full. WC for the disabled. Guide dogs allowed.
£ No

SHOTLEY HALL

Shotley Bridge, Consett, Durham DH8 9TE
Grade II* listed building designed in 1862 by Edward Robson in a Gothic style. Exceptionally complete and unaltered interior with stained glass, tiles and interior elements designed by Edward Burne-Jones and made by William Morris.
Grant Recipient: Mr Martell
Access Contact: Mr A Martell
T: 01207 582285
E-mail: lalla@martellhq.com
Open: 1 May–1 June: daily except Sundays 10am to 4pm. It is advisable to telephone the Hall before visiting. By prior arrangement only at other times between 1 April and 30 September to scholars, researchers and enthusiasts of William Morris and Edward Burne-Jones.
Heritage Open Days: No
P Spaces: 5
♿ Partial. Wheelchair access to ground floor only. No WC for the disabled. Guide dogs allowed.
£ No

UNTHANK HALL

Stanhope, Durham DL13 2PQ
Jacobean farmhouse dating from 1520s. Many original features still remain.
Grant Recipient: Alan Morton
Access Contact: Mr Alan Morton
T: 01388 526025
E-mail: alanunthank@sky.com
Open: 4, 11, 18 and 25 January; 1 and 8 February; 1, 8 and 15 March; 3, 10 and 17 May; 7, 14 and 21 June; 6, 13 and 20 September; 4, 11, 18 and 25 October; 8, 15, 22 and 29 November; 6 and 13 December: 10am–3pm. Please telephone beforehand to arrange visit.
Heritage Open Days: No
P Parking by river.

♿ No wheelchair access. No WC for the disabled. No Guide dogs allowed.
£ No

EAST RIDING OF YORKSHIRE

CONSTABLE MAUSOLEUM

Halsham, nr. Kingston-upon-Hull, East Riding of Yorkshire HU12 0DE
The Constable Mausoleum was commissioned by Edward Constable in 1792, built by Atkinson and York and completed in 1802 at a cost of £3,300. It comprises a central domed rotunda of stone, internally lined with black marble and surrounded by heraldic shields. The external raised and railed podium is part of a vaulted ceiling to the crypt below, in which various generation of the Constable family are interned.
Grant Recipient: Mr John Chichester-Constable
Access Contact: Mr John Chichester-Constable
T: 01964 562316   **F:** 01964 563283
E-mail: info@burtonconstable.co.uk
Open: By prior written arrangement with Mr John Chichester-Constable, South Wing–Estate Office, Burton Constable Hall, nr Kingston-upon-Hull, East Riding of Yorkshire HU11 4LN.
Heritage Open Days: No
P Spaces: 1. On-street parking.
♿ No wheelchair access. WC for the disabled at Halsham Arms approximately 300 metres. No Guide dogs allowed.
£ No

EAST SUSSEX

GREAT DIXTER HOUSE & GARDENS

Northiam, nr. Rye, East Sussex TN31 6PH
Original medieval hall house built c1450 comprising three rooms, the Great Hall, Parlour and Solar. Bought by Nathanial Lloyd in 1910 who employed Lutyens to restore and extend the property. A Yeoman's hall, originally located in Benenden, was dismantled and re-erected at Great Dixter.
www.greatdixter.co.uk
Grant Recipient: Ms O Eller
Access Contact: Mr Perry Rodriguez
T: 01797 252878 ext 3   **F:** 01797 252879
E-mail: office@greatdixter.co.uk
Open: 1 April–31 October: Tuesday–Sunday and Bank Holiday Mondays 2pm–5pm. Gardens open from 11am.
Heritage Open Days: No
P Spaces: 100
♿ Partial. Wheelchair access to most areas. Map of routes available. WC for the disabled. Guide dogs allowed.
£ Adult: £8.50 (house and garden), £7.00 (garden only). **Child:** £4.00 (house and garden), £3.50 (garden only). **Other:** Annual Tickets: 1 person £19.00, 2 person £27.50, Family £31.00.

LAMB HOUSE (COROMANDEL LACQUER PANELS)

3 Chapel Hill, Lewes, East Sussex, BN7 2BB
The incised lacquer panels in the study of Lamb House are a unique surviving example of imported late 17th century Chinese lacquer work that remains as decorative wall panelling. Recently restored.
Grant Recipient: Professor Paul Benjamin
Access Contact: Professor Paul Benjamin
T: 01273 475657
E-mail: p.r.benjamin@sussex.ac.uk
Open: Weekends only by prior telephone or e-mail arrangement.
Heritage Open Days: Yes
P On-street parking.
♿ Partial. Steps to front door. Wheelchair access to ground floor only. No WC for the disabled. No Guide dogs allowed.
£ No

ROTUNDA TEMPLE

Brightling Park, nr. Robertsbridge, East Sussex TN32 5HH
Built c1812 as an eye-catcher by Sir Robert Smirke for John Fuller, wealthy philanthropist and eccentric. Small circular building with colonnade and dome: the centre-piece of Brightling Park.

Grant Recipient: Mr H C Grissell
Access Contact: Mr H C Grissell
T: 01424 838207   **F:** 01424 838467
E-mail: henrygrissell@hotmail.co.uk
Open: At any time by prior arrangement. Otherwise Temple can be viewed from public footpaths and other permitted access routes through the Park.
Heritage Open Days: No
P Parking in surrounding roads.
♿ No wheelchair access. No WC for the disabled. Guide dogs allowed.
£ No

ST MARY-IN-THE-CASTLE

Pelham Crescent, Hastings, East Sussex TN34 3AF
Built in 1828, architect Joseph Kay, forming an integral part of the design of Pelham Crescent. The Church has a horseshoe-shaped auditorium with gallery and is now used as an arts centre and events venue.
www.stmaryinthecastle.com
Grant Recipient: Friends of St Mary in the Castle
Access Contact: Ms Barbara Rogers
T: 01424 717592
E-mail: contact@stmaryinthecastle.com
Open: Arts activities run throughout the year. Details of guided tours by local historians on website. Entry via the Café, 6-8 Pelham Arcade.
Heritage Open Days: No
P Spaces: 400. Pay and Display parking opposite.
♿ Full. WC for the disabled. Guide dogs allowed.
£ Adult: £3.50. **Child:** £2.50. **Other:** £2.50 (concessions).

STRAND GATE

Winchelsea, Rother, East Sussex TN36 4EA
Early 14th century medieval gateway built to defend the entrance to Winchelsea from its inner harbour. Stands astride a public highway.
Grant Recipient: Winchelsea Corporation
Access Contact: Mr Malcolm Pratt
T: 01424 215308
Open: Free access available at all times. Can also be viewed by pedestrians from footways to the north, south and east.
Heritage Open Days: No
P On-street parking nearby.
♿ Full. No WC for the disabled. Guide dogs allowed.
£ No

THE DOVECOTE

Alciston, East Sussex BN26 6UR
14th century dovecote of flint facings with green sand stone dressings on a chalk rubble core with chalk blocks and nesting boxes internally.
www.firleplace.co.uk
Grant Recipient: Trustees of the Firle Estate Settlement
Access Contact: Mr Josh Feakins
T: 01273 858567   **F:** 01273 858570
E-mail: josh@firleplace.co.uk
Open: Access to the dovecote is by prior arrangement with the Estate Office.
Heritage Open Days: No
P No
♿ No. Track to edge of property. No WC for the disabled. No Guide dogs allowed.
£ No

WINDMILL HILL WINDMILL

Herstmonceux, Hailsham, East Sussex BN27 4RT
Grade II* listed, dating from 1815, the second tallest and largest post mill in body size. The mill last worked by wind in 1894 and has recently been authentically restored.
www.windmillhillwindmill.co.uk
Grant Recipient: Windmill Hill Windmill Trust
Access Contact: Mrs B Frost
T: 01323 833033   **F:** 01323 833744
E-mail: admin@windmillhillwindmill.co.uk
Open: All year: first and third Sunday of the month and Bank Holidays 2.30–5pm. School parties and groups by prior arrangement.
Heritage Open Days: Yes
P Spaces: 4

♿ Partial. Wheelchair access to visitor centre. Film enables full visitor experience without climbing long ladder to mill body. WC for the disabled. Guide dogs allowed.
£ **No**

GLYNDE PLACE

Glynde, nr. Lewes, East Sussex BN8 6SX

Elizabethan manor house built in 1589 from local flint and stone from Normandy, then extensively added on to in the 18th century.

www.glynde.co.uk
Grant Recipient: Viscount Hampden
Access Contact: Viscount Hampden
T: 01273 858 224
Open: 1 May–31 August: Wednesdays, Sundays and Bank Holiday Mondays. House 2–5pm. Groups by prior arrangement (see website for details).
Heritage Open Days: No
P Spaces: 150
♿ Partial. WC for the disabled. Guide dogs allowed.
£ **Adult:** £6.00 (House). **Child:** Free (under 12).

ESSEX

57 CHURCH STREET

57 Church Street, Harwich, Essex CO12 3DS

16th century or earlier timber-framed two storey building. Pebble dashed upper storey, jettied to street.
Grant Recipient: Jamie Shrive
Access Contact: Mr Jamie Shrive
T: 01255 503507
E-mail: enquiries@thestingray.co.uk
Open: Free access to the exterior only.
Heritage Open Days: No
P On-street parking.
♿ Partial. No WC for the disabled. No Guide dogs allowed.
£ **No**

BICKNACRE PRIORY

Bicknacre, Essex CM3 4ES

Sole remaining arch of a priory founded in 1157 for Austin canons by Maurice Fitzgerald. The priory never flourished and the last canon died in 1507 and all that remains is the west arch of the crossing of the church of c1250. Information board showing a history of later developments is provided on site.
www.prioryfields.org.uk/arch.php
Grant Recipient: Wodham Ferrers and Bicknacre PC
Access Contact: Ms Karen Kuderovitch
T: 01245 328988
E-mail: clerk@wfandbpc.org.uk
Open: Can be viewed at all times from outside the protective fence. Entry to inside the fence by prior arrangement with the parish clerk (tel: 01245 328988) or via website www.prioryfields.org.uk.
Heritage Open Days: Yes
P Spaces: 30. Approximately 400 metres walk.
♿ Partial. Assistance needed for wheelchair users. No WC for the disabled. Guide dogs allowed.
£ **No**

HARWICH REDOUBT FORT

behind 29 Main Road, Harwich, Essex CO12 3LT

180ft diameter circular fort commanding the harbour entrance built in 1808 to defend the port against a Napoleonic invasion. Surrounded by a dry moat, there are 11 guns on the battlements. 18 casemates which originally sheltered 300 troops in siege conditions now house a series of small museums.
www.harwich-society.co.uk
Grant Recipient: The Harwich Society
Access Contact: Mr A Rutter
T: 01255 503429   **F:** 01255 503429
E-mail: info@harwich-society.co.uk
Open: 1 May–31 August: daily 10am–4pm. Rest of year: Sundays, 10am–4pm.
Heritage Open Days: Yes
P Parking for the disabled only (4 spaces).
♿ No wheelchair access. No WC for the disabled. Guide dogs allowed.
£ **Adult:** £3.00. **Child:** Accompanied children free.
Other: £3.00.

JOHN WEBB'S WINDMILL

Fishmarket Street, Thaxted, Essex CM6 2PG

Brick tower mill built in 1804 consisting of five floors. Has been fully restored as a working mill. On two floors there is a museum of rural and domestic bygones. There is also a small picture gallery of early photographs of the mill and the surrounding countryside.
http://www.thaxted.co.uk/?History_of_Thaxted
Grant Recipient: Thaxted Parish Council
Access Contact: Mr L A Farren
T: 01371 830285   **F:** 01371 830285
Open: 11 April–27 September: Saturday–Sunday and Bank Holidays 2–6pm. Groups during weekdays by special arrangement. For further information please contact Mr L A Farren, Borough Hill, Bolford Street, Thaxted, Essex CM6 2PY.
Heritage Open Days: No
P Spaces: 80. Public parking in Thaxted.
♿ Partial. Wheelchair access to ground floor only. WC for the disabled in public car park in Margaret Street. WC for the disabled. No Guide dogs allowed.
£ Donations welcome.

ST MARY

Mundon, Essex

Listed Grade I church, now redundant and owned by the Friends of Friendless Churches since 1975. Two-tier timber-framed weatherboarded tower of the 16th century and roughly contemporary north porch. The nave is partly 14th century and retains a complete set of 18th century box pews. The chancel is also Georgian but with simple 19th century fittings. Naïve Baroque trompe l'oeil painting of murals on the east wall.
www.friendsoffriendlesschurches.org.uk
Grant Recipient: Friends of Friendless Churches
Access Contact: Mr Matthew Saunders
T: 020 7236 3934   **F:** 020 7329 3677
E-mail: office@ancientmonumentssociety.org.uk
Open: At all reasonable times.
Heritage Open Days: Yes
P No
♿ Partial. Wheelchair access possible with assistance: access to church along rough track and up one step. Also interior poorly lit. No WC for the disabled. Guide dogs allowed.
£ **No**

THE GREAT DUNMOW MALTINGS

Mill Lane, Great Dunmow, Essex CM6 1BD

Grade II* maltings complex (listed as Boyes Croft Maltings, White Street), early 16th century and later, timber-framed and plastered, part weatherboarding and brick. The building exhibits the entire floor malting process whilst the Great Dunmow Museum Society occupies the ground floor with displays of local history. The first floor is available for community use.
www.greatdunmowmaltings.co.uk
Grant Recipient: Great Dunmow Maltings Preservation Trust
Access Contact: Mrs B A Ball
T: 01371 872097   **F:** 01371 872097
E-mail: bball_barnston@talktalk.net
Open: All year: Saturday, Sunday and Bank Holidays 11am–4pm. Groups at any reasonable time by prior arrangement. Closed over Christmas/New Year holiday week.
Heritage Open Days: No
P Spaces: 100. Public car park nearby (pay and display, free on Sundays and Bank Holidays).
♿ Full. WC for the disabled. Guide dogs allowed.
£ **Adult:** £1.50. **Child:** £1.00. **Other:** £1.00 (senior citizens).

THE SHELL HOUSE,

Hatfield Forest, Takeley, Nr Bishops Stortford, Essex CM22 6NE

Grade II* rare garden house/folly, c.1759, built by the Houblon family. Constructed of knapped and boulder flints, shells, glass fragments and brickwork with a low pitched pantile pediment gabled roof.
www.nationaltrust.org.uk/hatfieldforest
Grant Recipient: The National Trust
Access Contact: Nicky Daniel
T: 01279 870678   **F:** 01279 874044

E-mail: hatfieldforest@nationaltrust.org.uk
Open: Saturdays and Sundays, 10am–4.30pm.
Heritage Open Days: No
P Car park charge £4.60.
♿ Full. WC for the disabled. Guide dogs allowed.
£ **No**

VALENTINES MANSION,

Emerson Road, Ilford, Essex IG1 4XA

Valentines Mansion is a late 17th century house, largely Georgian in appearance with Regency additions. Of particular interest is the unusual curved early 19th century porte cochere. The exterior was extensively repaired and restored in 2007/8 and the house opened for public enjoyment in February 2009.
www.valentinesmansion.com
Grant Recipient: London Borough of Redbridge
Access Contact: Ms Nadia Brice
T: 020 8708 8101   **F:** 020 8708 3178
E-mail: Nadia.brice@redbridge.gov.uk
Open: All year: Tuesday and Wednesday 10am–5pm, Sunday 11am–4pm.
Open House London: Yes
P Spaces: 40. Charges may be introduced in 2010. On-street parking in Emerson Road.
♿ Full. WC for the disabled. Guide dogs allowed.
£ **No**

GLOUCESTERSHIRE

ACTON COURT

Latteridge Road, Iron Acton, Gloucestershire BS37 9TJ

Seat of the Poyntzes, an influential courtier family who occupied the house until 1680 when it was converted into a farm house. A Tudor range, constructed in 1535 to accommodate King Henry VIII and Queen Anne Boleyn survives along with part of the North range. The rooms are unfurnished but contain important traces of original decoration.
www.actoncourt.com
Grant Recipient: Rosehill Corporation
Access Contact: Ms Lisa Kopper
T: 01454 228224   **F:** 01454 227256
E-mail: actonct@dircon.co.uk or info@actoncourt.com
Open: Guided tours and events 15 June–22 August. Closed Mondays. Pre-booking essential. Ring information line for details 01454 228 224.
Heritage Open Days: No
P Spaces: 40
♿ Partial. Wheelchair access to grounds (grass) and ground floor. WC for the disabled. Guide dogs allowed.
£ **Adult:** £5.00. **Child:** £4.00. **Other:** £4.00 (senior citizens & the disabled), £100, daytime, £120, evening (exclusive group tours maximum 25). Special events priced separately.

CHAVENAGE

Tetbury, Gloucestershire GL8 8XP

Elizabethan Manor House (c1576), contains tapestry rooms, furniture and relics from the Cromwellian Period. Has been the home of only two families since the time of Elizabeth I. Used as a location for television and film productions. Recently seen as Candleford Manor in the BBC's 'Lark Rise to Candleford'.
www.chavenage.com
Grant Recipient: Trustees of the Chavenage Settlement
Access Contact: Miss Caroline Lowsley-Williams
T: 01666 502329   **F:** 01666 504696
E-mail: info@chavenage.com
Open: May–September: Thursday, Sunday and Bank Holidays plus Easter Sunday and Monday 2–5pm. Groups at other times by prior arrangement.
Heritage Open Days: Yes
P Spaces: 40. Access for coaches through Coach Entrance.
♿ Partial. Wheelchair access to ground floor only. Parking for the disabled near front door. WC for the disabled. Guide dogs allowed.
£ **Adult:** £7.00. **Child:** £3.50.

DEER PARK

Cirencester Park, Cirencester, Gloucestershire

The Deer Park is part of a much larger landscaped area. It

has recently been landscaped to remove concrete bases and roadways of World War II military hospitals, reinstating the original landscape designed in the 1700s by the First Earl and Alexander Pope.
Grant Recipient: Bathurst Estate
Access Contact: Mr Allsop
T: 01285 653135   **F:** 01285 656291
Open: All year: daily, 8am–5pm. Admission charge to park on weekend of Cotswold Show 3 and 4 July.
Heritage Open Days: No
P Car parking in the town and limited parking in Cecily Hill (short stay).
& Partial. Wheelchair access available but may be uneven due to unsurfaced tracks which may be rough or wet. Guide dogs should be accompanied due to farm hazards. WC for the disabled in the town. No WC for the disabled. Guide dogs allowed.
£ No

ELMORE COURT ENTRANCE GATES
Elmore, Gloucestershire GL2 3NT
Early 18th century carriage and pedestrian gateway, with 19th century flanking walls. By William Edney, blacksmith of Bristol for Sir John Guise at Rendcomb. Gateway was removed from Rendcomb and re-erected here in early 19th century.
www.elmorecourt.com
Grant Recipient: Trustees of the Elmore Court Estate
Access Contact: Trustees of the Elmore Court Estate
T: 01452 720293   **F:** 01452 724166
E-mail: anselm@elmorecourt.com
Open: Visible at all times from public highway.
Heritage Open Days: No
P Spaces: 5. Off-road parking on forecourt in front of gates.
& Full. No WC for the disabled. Guide dogs allowed.
£ No

FRAMPTON MANOR BARN (THE WOOL BARN, MANOR FARM)
The Green, Frampton-on-Severn, Gloucestershire GL2 7EP
Grade I listed timber-framed barn built c1560. Re-used worked stones in ashlar plinth wall were found during repair works.
www.framptoncourtestate.co.uk
Grant Recipient: Mr P R H Clifford
Access Contact: Mr P R H Clifford
T: 01452 740698   **F:** 01452 740698
E-mail: clifford@framptoncourt.wanadoo.co.uk
Open: During normal office hours (8.30am–4.30pm Monday–Friday). Other times by arrangement.
Heritage Open Days: No
P Spaces: 30
& Full. WC for the disabled. Guide dogs allowed.
£ **Adult:** £1.00. **Child:** Free (special rates for school parties). **Other:** Free.

HAT SHOP (OUT OF THE HAT)
100 Church Street, Tewksbury, Gloucestershire GL20 5AB
Known as the Hat Shop, 100 Church Street is an important Grade II* listed building with an exceptionally fine 17th century timber framed façade. Its proportions, with deep eaves and hipped roof, are influenced by the Dutch inspired classicism of the mid-17th century. It has had various uses and had been vacant for a number of years before being purchased and repaired by Tewkesbury Borough Council. Now restored and renovated, it houses a Tourist Information Centre on the ground floor. The two upper storeys incorporate interactive displays and information to allow visitors to contemplate the life of a 17th century glove maker.
outofthehat.org.uk
Grant Recipient: Tewkesbury Borough Council
Access Contact: Mr G Hill
Open: Monday–Saturday 9.30am–5pm; Bank Holidays 10am–4pm.
Heritage Open Days: Yes
P 5 minute walk to the nearest public car park.
& Full. WC for the disabled. Guide dogs allowed.
£ **Adult:** £3.50. **Child:** £2.50. **Other:** Concessions £3.00, Groups £2.50

STANCOMBE PARK TEMPLE
Dursley, Gloucestershire GL11 6AU
One in a series of buildings in the folly gardens at Stancombe Park, in the form of a Greek temple. Built in approximately 1815.
www.thetemple.info
Grant Recipient: Mr N D Barlow
Access Contact: Mrs G T Barlow
T: 01453 542815
E-mail: nicb@nicbarlow.com
Open: All year by prior telephone arrangement.
Heritage Open Days: No
P Spaces: 20. Limited parking at the site (4 cars)
& No wheelchair access. No WC for the disabled. Guide dogs allowed.
£ **Adult:** £3.00 (charity donation for visits to garden).
Other: No charge is made for anyone specifically wishing to see the temple only.

STANLEY MILL
King's Stanley, Stonehouse, Gloucestershire GL10 3HQ
Built 1813, with large addition c1825, of Flemish bond red brick with ashlar dressings and Welsh slate roof. Early example of fireproof construction (which survived a major fire in 1884).
Grant Recipient: Stanley Mills Ltd
Access Contact: Mark Griffiths/ Jill May
T: 01453 821800   **F:** 01453 791 167
E-mail: jill@marlings.co.uk
Open: By prior written arrangement as the Mill is used by various manufacturing companies.
Heritage Open Days: No
P Spaces: 30. By prior written arrangement as the Mill is used by various manufacturing companies.
& No wheelchair access. No WC for the disabled. No Guide dogs allowed.
£ No

TANHOUSE FARM TITHE BARN
Frampton-on-Severn, Gloucestershire GL2 7EH
17th century Tithe Barn with cattle Byre.
Grant Recipient: M R & C R Williams
Access Contact: Messrs M R & C A Williams
T: 01452 741 072
E-mail: tanhouse.farm@lineone.net
Open: All year by prior arrangement with M R or C R Williams (tel: 01452 741072).
Heritage Open Days: No
P Spaces: 20. Parking within 100 metres.
& Partial. Wheelchair access to main areas. WC for disabled 200 yards. Guide dogs allowed.
£ No

WEST BANQUETING HOUSE
Chipping Campden, Gloucestershire
The West Banqueting House stands opposite the East Banqueting House across a broad terrace. It is elaborately decorated with spiral chimney stacks, finials and strapwork parapets.
www.landmarktrust.org.uk
Grant Recipient: The Landmark Trust
Access Contact: Mrs Victoria O'Keeffe
T: 01628 825920   **F:** 01628 825417
E-mail: vokeeffe@landmarktrust.org.uk
Open: The Landmark Trust is an independent charity, which rescues small buildings of historic or architectural importance from decay or unsympathetic improvement. Landmark's aim is to promote the enjoyment of these historic buildings by making them available to stay in for holidays. West Banqueting House can be rented by anyone, at all times of the year, for periods ranging from a weekend to three weeks. Bookings can be made by telephoning the Booking Office on 01628 825925. The public can also view the building by prior arrangement; telephone the access contact Victoria O'Keeffe on 01628 825920 to make an appointment. Potential visitors will be asked to write to confirm the details of their visit.
Heritage Open Days: No
P Parking available in town only.
& No wheelchair access. No WC for the disabled. Guide dogs allowed.
£ No

WOODCHESTER PARK MANSION
Nympsfield, Stonehouse, Gloucestershire GL10 3TS
Grade I listed Victorian mansion, abandoned incomplete in 1870. One of the most important houses of its period and uniquely exhibiting its construction process. Set in a large landscaped park (possibly by 'Capability' Brown). The building is also a Site of Special Scientific Interest housing two nationally important populations of endangered bats.
www.woodchestermansion.org.uk
Grant Recipient: Woodchester Mansion Trust
Access Contact: Miss Hannah Jones
T: 01453 861541   **F:** 01453 861337
E-mail: office@woodchestermansion.org.uk
Open: Easter–End of October: every Sunday, first Saturday in month and Bank Holiday weekends; July–August: Saturday and Sunday, 21 March, and 12 September 11am–5.00pm (last admission to house at 4.00pm). Groups and private visits by prior arrangement.
Heritage Open Days: Yes
P Spaces: 60. Parking is 1 mile from Mansion, access via woodland walk. Minibus service available.
& Partial. Wheelchair access to ground floor only. No WC for the disabled. Guide dogs allowed.
£ **Adult:** £5.50. **Child:** Free with parents. **Other:** £4.50 (English Heritage & National Trust members, senior citizens & NUS card holders).

GREATER MANCHESTER

1830 WAREHOUSE
The Museum of Science & Industry, Liverpool Road, Castlefield, Manchester, Greater Manchester M3 4FP
Former railway warehouse, c1830, originally part of the Liverpool Road Railway Station (the oldest surviving passenger railway station in the world) which was the terminus of the Liverpool and Manchester Railway built by George Stephenson and his son Robert. Now part of The Museum of Science and Industry.
www.mosi.org.uk
Grant Recipient: The Museum of Science & Industry
Access Contact: Mr Robin Holgate
T: 0161 832 2244   **F:** 0161 606 0186
E-mail: collections@mosi.org.uk
Open: Daily (except 24, 25 and 26 December and 1 January) 10am–5pm.
Heritage Open Days: No
P Spaces: 50. Charge for use of Museum Car Park.
& Full. WC for the disabled. Guide dogs allowed.
£ Free entry to all to main museum building. Charge for special exhibitions.

FORMER CHURCH OF ST BENEDICT
Bennett Street, West Gorton, Manchester M12 5ND
Former church, built 1880 and the most original designed by JS Crowther. Includes notable stained glass and vestry furnishings. Now an indoor climbing centre with café and shop.
www.manchesterclimbingcentre.com
Grant Recipient: Manchester Climbing Centre Ltd
Access Contact: Mr John Dunne
T: 07798 857138   **F:** 0161 2307049
E-mail: info@manchesterclimbingcentre.com
Open: All year: Monday to Friday, 10am–10pm. Saturday, Sunday and Bank Holidays: 10am–6pm.
Heritage Open Days: Yes
P Spaces: 50. 200 spaces adjacent.
& Partial. Wheelchair access to main hall but not to café. WC for the disabled. Guide dogs allowed.
£ Café, shop and viewing free.

HALL I' TH' WOOD MUSEUM
Green Way, Bolton, Greater Manchester BL1 8UA
Grade I listed manor house, early 16th century, where Samuel Crompton invented and built his spinning mule in 1779. Part of the Hall is timber-framed and shows the development of a house in the 16th and 17th centuries. Now a museum.
www.boltonmuseums.org.uk
Grant Recipient: Bolton Council
Access Contact: Miss Danielle Hughes
T: 01204 332370   **F:** 01204 332241
E-mail: smithills@bolton.gov.uk

Open: For special events only at selected times throughout the year, for further information, please check website or telephone 01204 332370.
Heritage Open Days: No
P Spaces: 10
Partial. Wheelchair access to the Great Hall and Dining Room only. No WC for the disabled. Guide dogs allowed.
£ Adult: £2.00 (subject to change). **Child:** £1.00 (subject to change). **Other:** Family £5.00 (2 adults & 2 children, subject to change).

STAIRCASE HOUSE

30a/31 Market Place, Stockport, Greater Manchester SK1 1ES
Timber framed town house. Dating from 1460, enlarged in 16th and 17th centuries and altered in 18th, 19th and 20th centuries. Early panelled rooms and an important 17th century caged newel staircase from which the house takes its name. Damaged by fire, but restored by Stockport Council. Interpretation charts the history of the house and its evaluation to WWII. The house is fully interactive with visitors invited to touch all objects and furniture.
www.staircasehouse.org.uk
Grant Recipient: Stockport Metropolitan Borough Council
Access Contact: Ms Caroline Egan
T: 0161 480 1460 **F:** 0161 474 0312
E-mail: caroline.egan@stockport.gov.uk
Open: Daily: Tuesday–Friday, 1pm–5pm; Saturday 10am–5pm, Sunday, 11am–5pm. Closed Christmas Day, Boxing Day and New Years Day.
Heritage Open Days: Yes
P Spaces: 66. Town centre car parks and street parking.
Full. WC for the disabled. Guide dogs allowed.
£ Adult: £3.95. **Child:** Free (under 5s) £2.95 (age 5 -15).
Other: £2.95 (senior citizens), Free with leisure key.

VICTORIA BATHS

Hathersage Road, Manchester, Greater Manchester M13 0FE
An ornate and complete municipal swimming pool complex built 1903–1906, with 2 pools, Turkish and Russian Bath suite, Aeratone and extensive stained glass and tile work. Restoration Phase 1, comprising external and structural restoration to front of building has taken place.
www.victoriabaths.org.uk
Grant Recipient: The Manchester Victoria Baths Trust
Access Contact: Ms Gill Wright
T: 0161 224 2020
E-mail: info@victoriabaths.org.uk
Open: 1 March–31 October: first Sunday in each month 12–4pm; 1 April–30 September: Wednesday afternoons for guided tours from 2pm. Additional opening days include Heritage Open Days in September. At other times by prior arrangement with the Manchester Victoria Baths Trust (tel: 0161 224 2020). Group visits welcome. info@victoriabaths.org.uk
Heritage Open Days: Yes
P Spaces: 30
Partial. Wheelchair access to ground floor with assistance. Most of the building can be seen from the ground floor. No WC for the disabled. Guide dogs allowed.
£ Adult: £2.00. **Child:** Free. **Other:** Wednesday tours and group visits £4.00. Free admission for Friends of Victoria Baths.

HAMPSHIRE

AVINGTON PARK

Winchester, Hampshire SO21 1DB
Palladian mansion dating back to the 11th century, enlarged in 1670 by the addition of two wings and a classical Portico surmounted by three statues. Visited by Charles II and George IV. Has highly decorated State rooms and a Georgian church in the grounds.
www.avingtonpark.co.uk
Grant Recipient: Mrs Sarah Bullen
Access Contact: Mrs Sarah Bullen
T: 01962 779260 **F:** 01962 779202
E-mail: enquiries@avingtonpark.co.uk
Open: May–September: Sundays and Bank Holidays and Mondays in August, 2.30–5.30pm. Group booking and other times by prior arrangement.

Heritage Open Days: Yes
P Spaces: 150
Partial. Wheelchair access to ground floor only. Church with assistance (one step to interior). WC for the disabled. Guide dogs allowed.
£ Adult: £4.50. **Child:** £2.00.

BOATHOUSE NO. 6

Portsmouth Naval Base, Portsmouth P01 3LJ
Large Victorian naval boathouse constructed 1845. Designed by Captain James Beatson of the Royal Engineers, it is one of the first examples of a brick building constructed around a metal frame. Its massive cast iron beams are inscribed with their load-bearing capacity.
www.actionstations.org
Grant Recipient: Portsmouth Naval Base Property Trust
Access Contact: Mr Frank Nowosielski MBE
T: 02392 893305 **F:** 02392 862437
E-mail: fn@actionstations.org
Open: All year except Christmas Eve, Christmas Day and Boxing Day 10am–5.30pm (April–October) and 10am–5pm (November–March). Groups by prior arrangement.
Heritage Open Days: No
P Spaces: 350. Additional parking 500 metres from the site.
Full. WC for the disabled. Guide dogs allowed.
£ Adult: £12.50. **Child:** £8.50. **Other:** £33.00(family), £10.50 (senior citizens)

CALSHOT (ACTIVITIES SUNDERLAND SOPWITH HANGAR AND SCHNEIDER HANGER)

Calshot, Fawley, Hampshire SO45 1BR
Part of the most outstanding group of early aircraft structures of this type in Britain and the largest hangar built for use by fixed-wing aircraft during World War I. Now an activities centre.
www.calshot.com
Grant Recipient: Hampshire County Council
Access Contact: Mr Phil Quill
T: 023 8089 2077 **F:** 023 8082 1267
E-mail: phil.quill@hants.gov.uk
Open: Daily except Christmas Day, Boxing Day and New Year's Day: 8.30am–5pm.
Heritage Open Days: No
P Ample parking on-site. Disabled parking at Sunderland entrance.
Full. WC for the disabled. Guide dogs allowed.
£ No

HIGHCLERE CASTLE & PARK

Highclere, Newbury, Hampshire RG20 9RN
Early Victorian mansion rebuilt by Sir Charles Barry in 1842, surrounded by 'Capability' Brown parkland with numerous listed follies including Heavens Gate, an 18th century eye-catching hill-top landscape feature and The Temple, c1760, altered by Barry in mid 19th century, a regular classical circular structure. Family home of the 8th Earl and Countess of Carnarvon.
www.highclerecastle.co.uk
Grant Recipient: Executors of the 7th Earl of Carnarvon & Lord Carnarvon
Access Contact: Mr Alec Tompson
T: 01223 236996 **F:** 01223 234859
E-mail: agent@hwdean.co.uk
Open: 28 March–11 April: Sunday–Thursday; 4, 5 and 31 May, 1 June; 1 July–31 August: Sunday–Thursday: 11am–4. 30pm. Last admission 3.30pm. Temple: permissive path on days when Castle is open. At all other times by prior arrangement with the Castle Office (tel: 01635 253210). All opening times are provisional and visitors are recommended to confirm opening times with the Castle Office before travelling.
Heritage Open Days: No
P Spaces: 200. Unlimited parking.
Partial. Wheelchair access to ground floor only. WC for the disabled. Guide dogs allowed.
£ Adult: £8.00 (provisional). **Child:** £5.00 (provisional). **Other:** £7.00 (concession, provisional), family £24.00 (provisional).

HOUGHTON LODGE GARDENS

Stockbridge, Hampshire SO20 6LQ
Landscaped pleasure grounds and a park laid out c1800 with views from higher ground over informal landscape

(Grade II*) surrounding the 18th century Cottage Ornee (Grade II*). Chalk cob walls enclose ancient espaliers, greenhouses and herb garden. Formal topiary 'Peacock' Garden, snorting topiary dragon and wild flowers. A popular TV Film location. 14 acres of Meadow Walks through river valley.
www.houghtonlodge.co.uk
Grant Recipient: Captain M W Busk
Access Contact: Capt. M W Busk
T: 01264 810502 **F:** 01264 810063
E-mail: info@houghtonlodge.co.uk
Open: 1 March–30 October: daily 10am–5pm. Wednesdays by prior arrangement.
Heritage Open Days: No
P Spaces: 100
Partial. Sloping grass lawns to river. WC for the disabled. Guide dogs allowed.
£ Adult: £5.00. **Child:** Free. **Other:** £4.50 (group rate).

ST MICHAEL'S ABBEY

Farnborough, Hampshire GU14 7NQ
Grade I listed church and Imperial Mausoleum crypt of Napoleon III and his family. Abbey Church also built for the Empress Eugenie so the monks could act as custodians of the tombs. Initially a Benedictine priory, raised to Abbey status in 1903.
www.farnboroughabbey.org
Grant Recipient: Empress Eugenie Memorial Trust
Access Contact: Fr Cuthbert Brogan
T: 01252 546105 **F:** 01252 372822
E-mail: abbot@farnboroughabbey.org
Open: Saturdays and Public Holidays: guided tours at 3pm. Contact Fr D C Brogan, Abbot, for further information.
Heritage Open Days: No
P Spaces: 10
No wheelchair access. No WC for the disabled. No Guide dogs allowed.
£ No

THE VYNE

Sherborne St John, Basingstoke, Hampshire RG24 9HL
Built in the early 16th century for Henry VIII's Lord Chamberlain. The house acquired a classical portico mid 17th century (the first of its kind in England). Tudor chapel with Renaissance glass, Palladian staircase, old panelling and fine furniture. Grounds, containing wild garden, lakes and woodland walks.
www.nationaltrust.org.uk
Grant Recipient: The National Trust
Access Contact: The Property Manager
T: 01256 883858 **F:** 01256 881720
E-mail: thevyne@nationaltrust.org.uk
Open: House: 13 March–31 October: Saturday–Wednesday (but open Good Friday and Bank Holidays), Saturday and Sunday 11am–5pm, Monday–Wednesday 1–5pm (11am–12pm pre-booked groups only for guided tours). 4–19 December : Saturday–Wednesday 11am–5pm. Grounds: 6 February–7 March: weekends only 11am–5pm; 13 March–31 October, as house 11am–5pm.
Heritage Open Days: No
P Spaces: 140. Car park (with capacity for 140 cars and 3 coaches) located 450 metres from house (buggy service subject to volunteer availability). Disabled drivers will be able to park by house by prior arrangement.
Partial. Wheelchair access to ground floor, stairs to other floors. WC for the disabled. Guide dogs allowed.
£ Adult: £9.50, £5.80 (grounds only). **Child:** £4.75, £2.90 (grounds only). **Other:** £23.65 (family). Prices include voluntary gift aid contribution. Free to National Trust members.

WHITCHURCH SILK MILL

28 Winchester Street, Whitchurch, Hampshire RG28 7AL
Grade II* watermill built c1800 and has been in continuous use as a silk weaving mill since the 1820s. Now a working museum, the winding, warping and weaving machinery installed between 1890 and 1927 produces silks to order for theatrical costume, historic houses, fashion and artworks.
www.whitchurchsilkmill.org.uk

Grant Recipient: Hampshire Buildings Preservation Trust
Access Contact: General Manager
T: 01256 892065   **F:** 01256 893882
E-mail: silkmill@btinternet.com
Open: Mill and shop: Tuesday–Sunday 10.30am–5pm (last admission 4.15pm). Mill and shop closed Mondays (except Bank Holidays) and between Christmas and New Year.
Heritage Open Days: Yes
P Spaces: 20. Adjacent to Mill and additional parking in the town.
Ġ Partial. Wheelchair access to ground floor, shop and gardens. Stair lift to first floor and two steps to tea room. WC for the disabled. Guide dogs allowed.
£ Adult: £4.00. Child: £2.25. Other: £3.50, £9.25 (family).

HEREFORDSHIRE

EASTNOR CASTLE

nr. Ledbury, Herefordshire HR8 1RL
Norman-style castellated mansion set in the western slopes of the Malvern Hills. Constructed 1812–1820 and designed by Sir Robert Smirke, the castle has 15 state and other rooms fully-furnished and open to visitors. The decoration includes tapestries, paintings, armour and a drawing room by Augustus Pugin.
www.eastnorcastle.com
Grant Recipient: Mr J Hervey-Bathurst
Access Contact: Mr David Littlewood
T: 01531 633160   **F:** 01531 631776
E-mail: enquiries@eastnorcastle.com
Open: Easter weekend 2–5 April, May Bank holiday weekends 2, 3, 30 and 31 May; Sundays from 6 June–26 September; 18 July–31 August: Sunday–Thursday 11am–4.30pm (last admission 4pm).
Heritage Open Days: Yes
P Spaces: 150
Ġ Partial. Wheelchair access to grounds and ground and first floor with assistance (always available). WC for the disabled. No Guide dogs allowed.
£ Adult: £8.50. Child: £5.50. Other: £7.50 (senior citizens).

HERGEST COURT

Kington, Herefordshire HR5 3EL
House dates back to 1267 and was the ancestral home of the Clanvowe and Vaughan families. It is an unusual example of a fortified manor in the Welsh Marches. It has literary associations with Sir John Clanvowe and Lewis Glyn Cothi.
Grant Recipient: Mr W L Banks
Access Contact: Messrs W L Banks & R Banks
T: 01544 230160   **F:** 01544 232031
E-mail: gardens@hergest.co.uk
Open: 13 June and 12 September: 12 noon–5pm and by prior arrangement with the Hergest Estate Office, Kington, Herefordshire HR5 3EG. Bookings by phone or fax with five days' notice.
Heritage Open Days: No
P Spaces: 5
Ġ Partial. Wheelchair access to ground floor only. No WC for the disabled. Guide dogs allowed.
£ Adult: £5.00. Child: Free. Other: £3.50 (groups).

SHOBDON PARK GARDEN TEMPLE

Herefordshire HR6 9LZ
Garden Temple c1750 for the 2nd Viscount Bateman, set on a mound circled by sweet chestnut trees. Yellow limestone, four Ionic columns, enriched architrave and decorated frieze. Of considerable interest in terms of its unusual interpretation of the Ionic order and listed Grade AI*.
Grant Recipient: Corbett Farms Ltd
Access Contact: Mrs Penny Corbet
Open: During May and June, November to March, access for 4 to 6 hours a day without prior arrangement. (Access through arable field–please keep to path).
Heritage Open Days: No
P Spaces: 30. Designated car park at the end of the drive by the Church.
Ġ No wheelchair access. No WC for the disabled. No Guide dogs allowed.
£ No

THE WATERWORKS MUSEUM–HEREFORD (FORMERLY BROOMY HILL PUMPING STATION),

Broomy Hill, Hereford, Herefordshire HR4 0LJ
Set in the Victorian water pumping station of Hereford with working pumping engines telling the story of drinking water. Oldest triple-expansion steam engine working in Britain plus beam, gas and diesel engines and overshot waterwheel.
www.waterworksmuseum.org.uk
Grant Recipient: Herefordshire Waterworks Museum Ltd
Access Contact: Dr Noel Meeke
T: 01600 890 118   **F:** 01600 890 009
E-mail: info@waterworksmuseum.org.uk
Open: All year: every Tuesday (except two Tuesdays at Christmas/ New Year) 11am–4pm. Easter–October: in-steam with engines working on second and last Sundays in month. Plus Easter, Spring and August Bank Holidays 1–4pm.
Heritage Open Days: Yes
P Spaces: 30. Additional 50 spaces nearby, disabled parking in courtyard. Space for one full size coach.
Ġ Full. WC for the disabled. Guide dogs allowed.
£ Adult: £3.00 (Tuesdays), £5.00 (In steam days) **Child:** £1.00 (Tuesdays and In-steam days). **Other:** £2.00 (Tuesdays), £3.00 (senior citizens In-steam days).

WILTON CASTLE

Bridstow, nr. Ross on Wye, Herefordshire HR9 6AD
12th century castle, partly demolished for 16th century house which in turn became ruinous. A dry moat surrounds restored curtain walls which include three fortified accommodation towers.
www.wiltoncastle.co.uk
Grant Recipient: Mr & Mrs A K Parslow
Access Contact: A K Parslow
T: 07836 386317   **F:** 01985 212217
E-mail: sue@Wiltoncastle.co.uk
Open: Every Wednesday and Sunday in June, July and August plus Bank Holiday Mondays 31 May and 30 August 11am–5pm.
Heritage Open Days: No
P Spaces: 25
Ġ Partial. Wheelchair access throughout (except towers). WC for the disabled. Guide dogs allowed.
£ Adult: £4.00. Child: £2.00. (over 11years). **Other:** Free to English Heritage members.

HERTFORDSHIRE

173 HIGH STREET

Berkhamsted, Hertfordshire HP4 3QT
Grade II* listed 13th century timber framed building, thought to be one of the oldest shops in England. Covered by 19th century shop front until modernisation work in 2000. Dendrochronological analysis dated two structural timbers to between 1277 and 1297. Now housing offices on ground floor and accommodation on first floor.
Grant Recipient: Mr B Norman
Access Contact: Mr Barrie Norman
T: 01296 720981
E-mail: barrie@landfind.co.uk
Open: By prior arrangement with Claire Lloyd Properties (tel: 01442 879996), plus Heritage Open Days in September.
Heritage Open Days: Yes
P 1 hour maximum parking bay outside the building.
Ġ Partial. No WC for the disabled. Guide dogs allowed.
£ No

ALL SAINTS PASTORAL CENTRE

Shenley Lane, London Colney, St Albans, Hertfordshire AL2 1AF
Grade II* listed building, designed by architect Leonard Stokes. Chapel begun in 1927 by Ninian Comper and finished in 1964 by his son Sebastian Comper.
www.allsaintspc.org.uk
Grant Recipient: Diocese of Westminster
Access Contact: Mr Alan Johnstone
T: 01727 829306   **F:** 01 727 822 880
E-mail: conf.office@allsaintspc.org.uk
Open: Daily, 9am–5pm, except last week of December.
Heritage Open Days: No
P Spaces: 130

Ġ Full. WC for the disabled. Guide dogs allowed.
£ No

FOLLY ARCH

Hawkshead Road, Little Heath, Potters Bar, Hertfordshire EN6 1NN
Grade II* listed gateway and folly, once the entrance to Gobions estate. Circa 1740 for Sir Jeremy Sambrooke, probably by James Gibbs. Red brick with large round-headed arch and thin square turrets.
Grant Recipient: Mr RJ Nicholas
Access Contact: Mr & Mrs Nicholas
T: 01707 663553
E-mail: robnic@mac.com
Open: The Arch is on the boundary between public open space and a private garden and can be viewed from public ground at any time.
Heritage Open Days: No
P On-street parking.
Ġ Full. No WC for the disabled. Guide dogs allowed.
£ No

KNEBWORTH HOUSE

Knebworth, nr. Stevenage, Hertfordshire SG3 6PY
Originally a Tudor manor house, rebuilt in gothic style in 1843. Contains rooms in various styles, which include a Jacobean banqueting hall. Set in 250 acres of parkland with 25 acres of formal gardens. Home of the Lytton family since 1490.
www.knebworthhouse.com
Grant Recipient: Knebworth House Education & Preservation Trust
Access Contact: Mrs Christine Smith
T: 01438 812661   **F:** 01438 811908
E-mail: info@knebworthhouse.com
Open: Daily: 2 April–18 April, 29 May–6 June, 3 July–31 August. Weekends and Bank Holidays: 20–28 March, 24 April–23 May, 12–27 June, 4–26 September. House: 12 noon–5.00pm (last tour 4pm). Gardens, park and playground: 11am–5pm.
Heritage Open Days: No
P Spaces: 75. 50–75 parking spaces on gravel, unlimited space on grass.
Ġ Partial. Wheelchair access to ground floor of house only. Gravel paths around gardens and house but level route from car park to house entrance. WC for the disabled. Guide dogs allowed.
£ Adult: £10.50 (£9.50 group). Child: £10.00 (£9.00 group). **Other:** £10.00 (senior citizens, £9.00 group).

THE OLD CHURCH TOWER OF ALL SAINTS

Chapel Lane, Long Marston, Hertfordshire HP23 4QT
Grade II* listed 15th century tower set in small churchyard with ancient yew trees. The only remnant of a Chapel of Ease dating back to the 12th century, the rest of the church was demolished in 1883.
Grant Recipient: Tring PCC Tower Conservation
Access Contact: Dr Noakes
T: 01296 660 072
E-mail: john.noakes@btinternet.com
Open: Exterior (churchyard) open at all times. Interior by prior arrangement and under supervision only.
Heritage Open Days: No
P Parking in nearby village, 200 metre walk.
Ġ Partial. Wheelchair access to churchyard only. No WC for the disabled. Guide dogs allowed.
£ No

WOODHALL PARK

Watton-at-Stone, Hertfordshire SG14 3NF
Country house, now a school. Designed and built by Thomas Leverton in 1785 in neo-Classical style. Normally associated with London houses, this is one of his few country houses. Highly decorated interiors which include the Print Room with walls covered in engraved paper, reproductions of paintings with frames, ribbons, chains, busts, candelabra and piers with vases.
www.woodhallestate.co.uk
Grant Recipient: The Trustees of R M Abel Smith 1991 Settlement
Access Contact: The Trustees of R M Abel Smith 1991 Settlement
T: 01920 830286   **F:** 01920 830162

E-mail: rmas@woodhallestate.co.uk
Open: At all reasonable times, preferably school holidays, by prior arrangement with the Trustees.
Heritage Open Days: No
P Spaces: 30. Parking limited to 10 spaces during school terms.
Partial. Wheelchair access to ground floor only. No WC for the disabled. Guide dogs allowed.
£ No

KENT

ABBEY FARM BARNS–MINOR AND MAJOR BARNS
Faversham, Swale, Kent ME13 7BL
Monastic timber-framed, weatherboarding-clad barns. The two barns are amongst the few surviving buildings of Faversham Abbey. The larger, Major Barn, dates from circa 1500 with some early 19th century alterations and is listed Grade II*. The smaller, Minor Barn, dates from circa 1350 and listed Grade I. In use as a working sawmill.
Grant Recipient: Mr Robin Dane
Access Contact: Mr Robin Dane
T: 01795 537062 /07747117465   **F:** 01795 597666
E-mail: robin.dane@faveshamjoinery.co.uk
Open: 5 –27 June, Saturdays and Sundays, 11 and 12 September 12 noon–4pm. Access available to limited numbers and queuing may be necessary on busy days.
Heritage Open Days: Yes
P Spaces: 10
Not suitable for children under 14 as building is in use as a working sawmill.
Partial. Guide dogs not admitted when workshop is operating. Telephone before visit to check. Telephone in advance to arrange wheelchair assistance. No WC for the disabled.
£ **Adult:** £4.00. **Child:** Free. **Other:** £2.80 (over 65).

ALL SAINTS REDUNDANT CHURCH
Waldershare, Dover, Kent
Redundant Norman church with later chapels containing examples of classical funerary monuments, Victorian murals and stained glass. Still a consecrated building although not used for regular worship.
www.visitchurches.org.uk
Grant Recipient: Diocese of Canterbury
Access Contact: Mr John Vigar
T: 07884 436649
E-mail: jvigar@tcct.org.uk
Open: All year: daily, 10.30am–3.30pm.
Heritage Open Days: No
P Spaces: 4
Partial. Assistance needed at lychgate, thereafter church is accessible. No WC for the disabled. Guide dogs allowed.
£ No

AYLESFORD PRIORY
The Friars, Aylesford, Kent ME20 7BX
Home of a community of Carmelite Friars and a popular centre of pilgrimage. Chapels contain modern religious art created by Adam Kossowski and other notable artists.
www.thefriars.org.uk
Grant Recipient: The Carmelite Friars
Access Contact: Father Prior or Wendy Emery General Manger
T: 01622 717272   **F:** 01622 715575
E-mail: prior@thefriars.org.uk or Gm@the friars.org.uk
Open: At all times to site. Access to Gate House on Open day in September (please check web site)
Heritage Open Days: Yes
P Spaces: 1500
Full. Restricted access to ground floor of Gate House. WC for the disabled. Guide dogs allowed.
£ No

BARN AT HOWBURY FARM
Moat Lane, Slade Green, Kent DA8 2NE
Jacobean tithe barn standing to the west of Howbury Moat House. Queen post timber roof. In agricultural use. Situated in an urban area of Bexley. Due to the condition of the barn, access to the interior will be limited to viewing the space from the door.
Grant Recipient: Trustees of The Russell Stoneham Estate
Access Contact: Mr C Stoneham

T: 01322 333111   **F:** 01322 330347
E-mail: russellstoneham@aol.com
Open: By prior arrangement throughout the year (tel: 01322 333111). Due to the condition of the barn, access to the interior will be limited to viewing the space from the door.
Heritage Open Days: No
P Spaces: 4
Partial. Wheelchair access may be difficult due to rough road to the barn. No WC for the disabled. No Guide dogs allowed.
£ No

CHURCH HOUSE
72 High Street, Edenbridge, Kent TN8 5AR
Late 14th century timber-framed farmhouse, Tudor additions include fireplace and 18th century brick frontage. Now houses the Eden Valley Museum which illustrates economic and social changes during the 14th to 20th centuries and includes temporary exhibitions and archaeological displays.
www.evmt.org.uk
Grant Recipient: Edenbridge Town Council
Access Contact: Mrs Jane Higgs
T: 01732 868102
E-mail: curator@evmt.org.uk
Open: February–December (until Christmas): Wednesday and Friday 2–4.30pm, Thursday and Saturday 10am–4.30pm; June–August: Sundays 2–4.30pm. Closed Good Friday.
Heritage Open Days: Yes
P Spaces: 150. Free parking in town centre car park, 200 yards from House.
Partial. Wheelchair access to ground floor only (visual computer link to upstairs). WC for the disabled. Guide dogs allowed.
£ Except for out of hours pre-arranged visits.

COBHAM HALL AND DAIRY
Cobham, Kent DA12 3BL
Gothic-style dairy in grounds of Cobham Hall, built by James Wyatt c1790.
www.cobhamhall.com
Grant Recipient: Cobham Hall Heritage Trust
Access Contact: Mr N G Powell
T: 01474 823371   **F:** 01474 825904
E-mail: enquiries@cobhamhall.com
Open: Easter–July / August: Hall open Wednesday and Sunday, 2–5pm (last tour 4.30pm). Please telephone to confirm opening times. At other times (and coach parties) by prior arrangement. Self-guided tour of gardens and parkland (historical/conservation tour by prior arrangement).
Heritage Open Days: No
P Spaces: 100
Partial. Wheelchair access to ground floor, manual assistance required for first floor access. WC for the disabled. Guide dogs allowed.
£ **Adult:** £5.50. **Child:** £4.50. **Other:** £4.50 (senior citizens & groups).

DOVER TOWN HALL
Biggin Street, Dover, Kent CT16 1DL
The Town Hall incorporates the remains of a medieval hospital, 14th century chapel tower, 19th century prison, town hall and assembly rooms. The Maison Dieu Hall of c1325 was originally part of a hospital founded by Hubert de Burgh in the early 13th century. The Town Hall designed by Victorian Gothic architect William Burges was built in 1881 on the site of the hospital.
www.leisureforce.co.uk
Grant Recipient: Dover District Council
Access Contact: Mr Steve Davis
T: 01843 296111 (Admin)
E-mail: dover@leisureforce.co.uk
Open: Normally open during the week for functions and other bookings. Open on Wednesdays throughout the year. Guided tours can be arranged.
Heritage Open Days: No
P Parking at the rear of the building.
Full. WC for the disabled. Guide dogs allowed.
£ No

HERNE WINDMILL
Mill Lane, Herne Bay, Kent CT6 7DR
Kentish smock mill built 1789, worked by wind until 1952 and then by electricity until 1980. Bought by Kent County Council in 1985, which carried out some restoration. Now managed by Friends of Herne Mill on behalf of the County Council. Much of the original machinery is in place, some is run for demonstration and the sails used when the wind conditions permit.
www.herne-mill.btik.com
Grant Recipient: Kent County Council
Access Contact: Mrs Megan Taylor
T: 01227 722332
E-mail: megantaylor@yahoo.co.uk
Open: Easter–end September: Sunday and Bank Holidays, plus Thursdays in August, 2–5pm. National Mills Weekend, Saturday and Sunday, 2–5pm. For further information contact Megan Taylor, Secretary, Friends of Herne Mill (tel: 01227 722332) or John Fishpool (Chairman, tel: 01227 366863).
Heritage Open Days: Yes
P Spaces: 6. Six parking spaces in Mill grounds. Free on-street parking (Windmill Road).
Partial. Wheelchair and guide dog access to ground floor of Mill and meeting room. WC for the disabled. Guide dogs allowed.
£ **Adult:** £1.00. **Child:** 25p (of school age, accompanied by an adult). **Other:** Under 5s free.

IGHTHAM MOTE
Ivy Hatch, Sevenoaks, Kent TN15 0NT
Moated manor house covering nearly 700 years of history from medieval times to 1960s. Visitor route includes Tudor Chapel, Billiards Room, Drawing Room, apartments of Charles Henry Robinson, the American donor of Ightham Mote to the National Trust. Grade I listed dog kennel in the courtyard and Mote Cottages. Interpretation displays and special exhibition featuring conservation in action.
www.nationaltrust.org.uk/ighthammote
Grant Recipient: The National Trust
Access Contact: Property Manager
T: 01732 810378 exn 100   **F:** 01732 811 029
E-mail: ighthammote@nationaltrust.org.uk
Open: 13 March–31 October, daily except Tuesday and Wednesday. House, garden, shop and restaurant, 11am–5pm (last entry 4.30pm). 1 November–19 December (partial access to house and garden Thursday–Sunday 11am–3pm. Estate open all year dawn–dusk.
Heritage Open Days: No
P Spaces: 420
Partial. Wheelchair access to ground floor with assistance and part of the exterior only. WC for the disabled. Guide dogs allowed.
£ **Adult:** £11.00. **Child:** £5.50. **Other:** £27.50 (family), £8.85 (groups). All admission prices include voluntary Gift Aid donation.

ITALIANATE GREENHOUSE
King George VI Memorial Park, Ramsgate, Kent CT11 8BD
Early 19th century grade II* listed glasshouse, curved in design to maximise heat and light. Similar to works by J C Loudon and Sir George Mackenzie. Small formal garden outside, attached to former East Cliff Lodge.
www.thanet.gov.uk/pdf/greenhouse_lowres.pdf
Grant Recipient: Thanet District Council
Access Contact: Thanet District Council
Open: 1 April–30 September: Monday–Friday, 9am–5pm. At other times by prior arrangement with Philip Dadds Architect & Associates (tel: 01843 585588)
Heritage Open Days: No
P No
Partial. Wheelchair access to central part of glasshouse. No WC for the disabled. Guide dogs allowed.
£ No

KNOLE CARTOON GALLERY
Sevenoaks, Kent TN15 0RP
The largest private house in England, Knole is a fine example of late medieval architecture. It has been the home of the Sackville family since 1603. The Cartoon Gallery contains six large copies of Raphael's cartoons. It includes carved grotesque decoration and a fine plasterwork ceiling.
www.nationaltrust.org.uk/knole

Grant Recipient: The National Trust
Access Contact: The Property Manager
T: 01732 462100   **F:** 01732 465528
E-mail: knole@nationaltrust.org.uk
Open: House: 13 March–31 October Wednesday–Sunday
12noon–4pm. Garden: 6 April–28 September Tuesday only
11am–4pm.
Heritage Open Days: Yes
P Spaces: 200. £2.50 per car. National Trust members
free. Parking for the disabled 50 yards from house.
& Partial. Wheelchair access to the Great Hall, shop and
tea room, but not the Cartoon Gallery. Virtual reality tour
available. WC for the disabled. No Guide dogs allowed.
£ **Adult:** £10.50. **Child:** £5.25. **Other:** £26.25 (family).
Free to NT members. All admission prices include voluntary
Gift Aid donation.

MONASTIC GRANGE AND PRE-CONQUEST NUNNERY AT MINSTER ABBEY

Church Street, Minster-in-Thanet, Ramsgate, Kent CT12 4HF
Monastic Grange dating from the 11th and 12th centuries.
A scheduled Monument. The Abbey is home to a
community of Benedictine nuns.
www.minsterabbeynuns.org
Grant Recipient: The Trustees of Minster Abbey
Access Contact: Sister Benedict Gaughan
T: 01843 821254
Open: Free access to the exterior: 1 May–30 September,
Monday–Friday 2.45–3.45pm, Saturday 11am–12 noon; 1
October–30 April 2011, Saturdays 11am–12noon. At other
times by prior arrangement.
Heritage Open Days: No
P Spaces: 16
& Partial. WC for the disabled. Guide dogs allowed.
£ No

THE ARCHBISHOPS' PALACE

Mill Street, Maidstone, Kent ME15 6YE
14th century Palace built by the Archbishops of
Canterbury. Much altered and extended over the centuries,
the interior contains 16th century panelling and fine wood
or stone fireplaces. Now used as Kent County Council's
Register Office.
www.tour-maidstone.com
Grant Recipient: Maidstone Borough Council
Access Contact: Ms Lucy Stroud/ Corporate Property
assistant.
T: 01622 602015   **F:** 01622 602974
E-mail: lucystroud@maidstone.gov.uk
Open: One Sunday in September by prior arrangement
with the Registrar and Heritage Open Days.
Heritage Open Days: Yes
P Spaces: 100. Public parking in town centre car parks
(pay and display).
& Partial. Wheelchair access to ground floor via lift. WC
for the disabled. Guide dogs allowed.
£ No

THE GRANGE

St Augustine's Road, Ramsgate, Kent CT11 9PA
The Grange is a Grade I listed building that was designed
and lived in by Augustus Pugin, an influential 19th century
architect. The building fell into a state of severe disrepair
in the 1990s and was acquired and restored by the
Landmark Trust.
www.landmarktrust.org.uk
Grant Recipient: The Landmark Trust
Access Contact: Mrs Victoria O'Keeffe
T: 01628 825920   **F:** 01628 825417
E-mail: vokeeffe@landmarktrust.org.uk
Open: The Landmark Trust is an independent charity, which
rescues small buildings of historic or architectural
importance from decay or unsympathetic improvement.
Landmark's aim is to promote the enjoyment of these
historic buildings by making them available to stay in for
holidays. The Grange can be rented by anyone, at all times
of the year, for periods ranging from a weekend to three
weeks. Bookings can be made by telephoning the Booking
Office on 01628 825925. As the building is in full-time use
for holiday accommodation, it is not normally open to the
public. However, the public can view the building by prior
arrangement by telephoning the access contact (Victoria
O'Keeffe on 01628 825920) to make an appointment.
Potential visitors will be asked to write to confirm the details

of their visit. In addition, the main rooms will be open every
Wednesday afternoon by appointment. There is a small
exhibition in the Cartoon Room (a separate building next to
The Grange) which provides information about the building,
its history and the Pugin family. Open on Wednesday
afternoons (2–4pm), on Open Days and by appointment.
Heritage Open Days: Yes
P Parking on Royal Esplanade nearby.
& Partial. Parking on Royal Esplanade nearby. WC for the
disabled. Guide dogs allowed.
£ No

WESTENHANGER CASTLE AND WESTENHANGER CASTLE BARNS

Westenhanger, Kent CT21 4HX
Complex of 14th century castle and 16th century barns. By
1544 the Castle was extensive and of royal importance,
having been visited by Queen Elizabeth I. In mid 17th
century, Westenhanger was one of the largest houses in
Kent, but in 1701 much of it was taken down. Now mostly
ruinous, many features remain within the curtain wall
including Tudor fireplaces and a 13th century dovecote
tower. The uninhabited parts are scheduled. The Medieval
barn has a hammerbeam roof and four wagon porches.
www.westenhangercastle.co.uk
Grant Recipient: G Forge Ltd
Access Contact: Mr Graham Forge
T: 01227 738451 or 738223   **F:** 01227 738278
E-mail: grahamforge@btinternet.com
Open: 4 April–8 September: Tuesdays 10am–5pm. At
other times by prior arrangement with 24 hours notice.
Group tours also by arrangement.
Heritage Open Days: No
P Spaces: 100. Coaches by appointment only. Parking for
the disabled by arrangement at House.
& Partial. Access for wheelchairs within the keep. WC for
the disabled. Guide dogs allowed.
£ **Adult:** £5.00, £4.00 (English Heritage members).
Child: £3.50 (under 12), £2.50 (English Heritage
members), free (under 4s). **Other:** £7.00 (per person, pre-
arranged group visits). Free for organised Educational
Visits.

LANCASHIRE

BROWSHOLME HALL

nr. Clitheroe, Lancashire BB7 3DE
Browsholme Hall, pronounced 'Brewsom', was built in
1507 and the ancestral home of the Parker Family who
have lived there since it was built. Listed Grade I. The
house contains a collection of oak furniture, portraits and
stained glass.
www.browsholme.co.uk
Grant Recipient: Mr R R Parker
Access Contact: Mr Robert Redmayne Parker
T: 01254 826719
E-mail: rrp@browsholme.co.uk
Open: Monday 31 May, 26 –27 June and 29 June–2 July,
8–31 August (except Mondays but including Bank Holiday
Monday: 2- 5pm.
Heritage Open Days: No
P Spaces: 30
& Partial. Wheelchair access to ground floor. WC for the
disabled. Guide dogs allowed.
£ **Adult:** £5.50. **Child:** £1.50 (under 16). **Other:** £5.00
(senior citizens & groups), £2.00 (grounds only).

GAWTHORPE HALL

Padiham, nr. Burnley, Lancashire BB12 8UA
An Elizabethan property in the heart of industrial
Lancashire. Restored and refurbished in the mid 19th
century by Sir Charles Barry. There are many notable
paintings on display loaned to the National Trust by the
National Portrait Gallery, and a collection of needlework,
assembled by the last family member to live there, Rachel
Kay-Shuttleworth.
www.nationaltrust.org.uk
Grant Recipient: The National Trust
Access Contact: Property Manager
T: 01282 771004   **F:** 01282 770178
E-mail: gawthorpehall@nationaltrust.org.uk
Open: Hall: 1 April–31 October, daily except Monday and
Friday (but open Good Friday and Bank Holiday Mondays),
1–5pm. Garden: all year, 10am–6pm.

Heritage Open Days: Yes
P Spaces: 50
& Partial. Wheelchair access to garden only. WC for the
disabled. Guide dogs allowed.
£ **Adult:** £4.00. **Child:** Free when accompanied by an
adult. **Other:** £3.00 (concessions), garden: free

INDIA MILL CHIMNEY

Bolton Road, Darwen, Blackburn, Lancashire BB3 1AE
Chimney, 1867, built as part of cotton spinning mill. Brick
with ashlar base. Square section, 300 feet high, in the
style of an Italian campanile. Rests on foundation stone
said to have been the largest single block quarried since
Cleopatra's Needle. Listed Grade II*.
www.indiamill.com
Grant Recipient: Brookhouse Managed Properties Ltd
Access Contact: Ms Pamela Blackwell
T: 01254 777 788   **F:** 01254 777 799
E-mail: pam.blackwell@indiamill.com
Open: Chimney visible from public highway (no interior
access).
Heritage Open Days: No
P On-street parking.
& Full. No WC for the disabled. Guide dogs allowed.
£ No

LATHOM HOUSE

Lathom, Lancashire L40 5UQ
Grade II* listed wing of former country house built c1730
with an addition of c1862. Various outbuildings arranged
around a double courtyard to the rear.
Grant Recipient: TRU Ltd
Access Contact: Mr Arthur Edwardson
T: 01942 707 000   **F:** 01942 707 030
E-mail: trurehab@aol.com
Open: By prior arrangement to the exterior (subject to
building work).
Heritage Open Days: No
P Spaces: 2
& No wheelchair access. No WC for the disabled. Guide
dogs allowed.
£ No

LEIGHTON HALL

Carnforth, Lancashire LA5 9ST
Country House, 1765, probably by Richard Gillow, with
earlier remains. Gothic south-east front early 19th century,
possibly by Thomas Harrison. Tower at west end of the
façade 1870 by Paley and Austin. Ancestral home of the
Gillow family with fine furniture, paintings and objects d'art.
www.leightonhall.co.uk
Grant Recipient: Mr Richard Reynolds
Access Contact: Mr & Mrs Reynolds and Mrs Lucy
Arthurs
T: 01524 734474   **F:** 01524 720357
E-mail: leightonhall@yahoo.co.uk
Open: May–September: Tuesday–Friday (also Bank Holiday
Sundays and Mondays), 2–5pm. August only:
Tuesday–Friday and Sunday (also Bank Holiday
Monday),2.–5pm. Groups of 25+ all year by prior
arrangement. The owner reserves the right to close or
restrict access to the Hall and grounds for special events
(please see website for up- to-date information).
Heritage Open Days: No
P Spaces: 100. Parking for coaches on hard-standing.
Parking for the disabled at the front of Hall.
& Partial. Wheelchair access to ground floor, shop and
tea rooms. WC for the disabled. Guide dogs allowed.
£ **Adult:** £6.95. **Child:** £4.75 (age 5-12). **Other:** £6.00
(senior citizen/student), £22.00 (family), £5.50 (adult group
of 25+), £4.75 (child group).

QUEEN STREET MILL,

Queen Street, Harle Syke, Burnley, Lancashire BB10 2HX
Built in 1894, containing much of its original 19th century
equipment including over 300 Lancashire looms and steam
engine, which are demonstrated at intervals throughout
each working day. Believed to be the last remaining steam
powered textile mill in the world with collections
designated as being of national importance.
www.lancashire.gov.uk/museums
Grant Recipient: Lancashire County Council

Access Contact: Ms Catherine Pearson
T: 01282 412555   **F:** 01282 430220
E-mail: queenstreet.mill@lancashire.gov.uk
Open: March and November: Tuesday–Thursday, 12–4pm;
April and October: Tuesday–Friday, 12–5pm;
May–September: Tuesday–Saturday,12–5pm. Open Sunday
and Mondays on bank holiday weekends only. Closed
December, January and February.
Heritage Open Days: Yes
P Spaces: 40. Free parking.
Full. WC for the disabled. Guide dogs allowed.
£ Adult: £3.00. **Child:** Free if accompanied. **Other:**
£2.00 (concessions).

SAMLESBURY HALL

**Preston New Road, Samlesbury, Preston, Lancashire
PR5 0UP**
Built in 1325, the hall is a black and white timbered manor
house set in extensive grounds. Independently owned and
administered since 1925 by The Samlesbury Hall Trust
whose primary aim is to maintain and preserve the
property for the enjoyment and pleasure of the public.
Currently open to the public as a historic, educational,
craft, design and antique centre.
www.samlesburyhall.co.uk
Grant Recipient: Samlesbury Hall Trust
Access Contact: Ms Sharon Jones
T: 01254 812010/01254 812229   **F:** 01254 812174
E-mail: enquiries@samlesburyhall.co.uk
Open: Daily except Saturdays, 11am–4.30pm. Open Bank
Holidays. For Christmas closing times please contact the
Hall.
Heritage Open Days: Yes
P Spaces: 70. Additional parking for 100 cars in overflow
car park.
Partial. Free admission for wheelchair access to ground
floor of historical part of hall. WC for the disabled. Guide
dogs allowed.
£ Adult: £3.00. **Child:** £1.00 (ages 4-16).

THANKSGIVING SHRINE OF OUR LADY OF
LOURDES

Whinneys Hey Road, Blackpool, Lancashire
Roman Catholic chapel built 1955-7 in Portland stone and
designed by Frances Xavier Velarde. Exterior ornamented
with four statues, one at each corner and a relief on the
façade by sculptor David John. First stage of repairs have
been completed by the Historic Chapels Trust.
www.hct.org.uk
Grant Recipient: Historic Chapels Trust
Access Contact: Mr Terry Woodings
T: 01253 302373
E-mail: terence.woodings@fsmail.co.uk
Open: At any reasonable time to the exterior. Viewing to
the interior by prior arrangement.
Heritage Open Days: Yes
P Nearest on-street parking 100 metres.
Full. No WC for the disabled. Guide dogs allowed.
£ No

THE CHAPTER HOUSE

Cockersand Abbey, Lancaster, Lancashire
Part of ruins of Cockersand Abbey, built early 13th century
and used as a mausoleum for the Dalton family. Interior
has vaulted arch with interesting carvings. Situated on the
coast overlooking Morecambe Bay.
Grant Recipient: John Haydon Kellet
Access Contact: Mr John Haydon Kellet
T: 01524 751330
Open: At any reasonable time to the ruins of the abbey.
The interior of the Chapter house by prior arrangement (2
weeks notice required).
Heritage Open Days: Yes
P Spaces: 20. Car park ½ mile away along coastal
footpath.
Full. Uneven ground. No WC for the disabled. No
Guide dogs allowed.
£ No

TODMORDEN UNITARIAN CHURCH

Honey Hole Road, Todmorden, Lancashire OL14 6LE
Grade I listed church with a large wooded burial ground
and ornamental gardens designed by John Gibson, 1865-
69. Victorian Gothic style with tall tower and spire.

Detached smaller burial ground nearby and listed lodge in
churchyard. Lavish interior with highly decorated fittings
and furnishings. One of the most elaborate Non
conformist churches of the High Gothic Revival.
www.hct.org.uk
Grant Recipient: Historic Chapels Trust
Access Contact: Ms Mary Clear
T: 01706 815407
E-mail: fred.hunt@btopenworld.com
Open: At all reasonable times by application to the key
holder, Mary Clear, 5-6 Cockpit, Longfield Road,
Todmorden, Lancashire OL14 6LY or by calling at the
caretaker's house, Todmorden Lodge, at the entrance to
the churchyard.
Heritage Open Days: Yes
P Parking in local supermarket car park.
Full. WC for the disabled. Guide dogs allowed.
£ Donations invited.

LEICESTERSHIRE

7 KING STREET

Melton Mowbray, Leicestershire LE13 1XA
Dating from 1330, this is the oldest secular building in
Melton Mowbray. The building has Medieval roof timbers,
a 16th century timber-framed extension and has been
modified and gentrified through the centuries. Listed
Grade II*, the building was at risk for many years.
Restoration by Melton Mowbray Borough Council was
completed in 2004. Currently used as offices.
Grant Recipient: Mellton Borough Council
Access Contact: Mr Richard Spooner MA IHBC or Richard
Pearson
T: 01664 502387 or 502417   **F:** 01664 410283
E-mail: rspooner@melton.gov.uk or
rpearson@melton.gov.uk
Open: Monday–Friday 9.30am–3.30pm. Access to the
upper floors by prior arrangement.
Heritage Open Days: No
P Public car park adjacent (Pay and Display).
Partial. Wheelchair access to ground floor rooms. WC
for the disabled. No Guide dogs allowed.
£ No

BELVOIR CASTLE RIDING RING

Grantham, Leicestershire NG32 1PD
Grade II* listed circular exercise ring for horses, circa 1819.
Constructed of colour washed brick. Timber superstructure
and slate roof over curved rafters. It is 3 metres (12 feet)
wide, enclosing central space of 6.5 metres (20 feet) in
diameter, with two doorways access from the stable yard.
The building forms part of the intact stable block. The ring
is probably the earliest free-standing structure of its kind in
England.
www.belvoircastle.com
Grant Recipient: The Duke of Rutland
Access Contact: Mr Tim Stansby
T: 01476 870262   **F:** 01476 870443
Open: Exterior can be viewed when the gardens are open:
Sunday–Thursday 14 March–3 October. Access to the
interior: 1 May–31 August: Wednesday, 11am–5pm by
request at the Estate Office. Access at other times by prior
arrangement.
Heritage Open Days: No
P Two parking spaces at the ring.
Partial. No WC for the disabled. Guide dogs allowed.
£ Adult: £10.00 (castle & gardens), £5.00 (gardens) -
charge to view ring included in fee on specified Weds,
£2.50 at other times. **Child:** £5.00 (castle & gardens),
£3.00 (gardens)-charge to view ring incl. on specified
Weds, £2.50 at other times for age 16+.

REARSBY PACKHORSE BRIDGE

Rearsby, Leicestershire LE7 4YE
Low narrow medieval bridge, perhaps 16th century,
comprising five arches of random granite masonry and
brick coping. On the upstream side there are four
cutwaters, three of granite and one of brick. The bridge
has recently been restored.
Grant Recipient: Leicestershire County Council
Access Contact: Mr C Waterfield
T: 0116 305 7167   **F:** 0116 305 7135
E-mail: cwaterfield@leics.gov.uk
Open: At all times: in use as a public highway.

Heritage Open Days: No
P On-street parking.
Full. No WC for the disabled. Guide dogs allowed.
£ No

SIR JOHN MOORE'S SCHOOL

**Top Street, Appleby Magna, Swadlincote,
Leicestershire DE12 7AH**
Grade I listed school, built 1697, based on designs by Sir
Christopher Wren.
www.sirjohnmoore.org.uk
Grant Recipient: Trustees of Sir John Moore's Foundation
Access Contact: Mrs D Morris
T: 01530 273629
E-mail: deana@sirjohnmoore.org.uk
Open: Throughout the year for events and activities.
Group and school visits by prior arrangement.
Heritage Open Days: No
P Spaces: 50
Partial. Wheelchair access to ground floor and
telecentre gardens. WC for the disabled. Guide dogs
allowed.
£ £3.00 per person (for group visits). Some activities and
events have a fee.

TOMB OF ANDREW LORD ROLLO

St Margaret's Church, Canning Place, Leicester
Grade II* listed tomb of 1765. Each face has a large
rectangular plaque with ornate carved pilaster panels. The
west front has a long inscription on the slate plaque recording
the life and exploits of Andrew Lord Rollo, who died in 1765.
The remaining three fronts each have a shallow carved relief
of Lord Rollo's arms and military trophies.
www.stmargaretsleicester.org
Grant Recipient: The Abbey Parish PCC
Access Contact: Canon Barry Naylor
T: 0116 2487471   **F:** 0116 2487470
E-mail: barry.naylor@leccofe.org
Open: The churchyard is open at all times.
Heritage Open Days: No
P Spaces: 3. Additional street parking adjacent.
Full. No WC for the disabled. Guide dogs allowed.
£ No

LINCOLNSHIRE

ARABELLA AUFRERE TEMPLE

Brocklesby Park, Grimsby, Lincolnshire DN41 8PN
Garden Temple of ashlar and red brick with coupled doric
columns on either side of a central arch leading to a rear
chamber. Built c1787 and attributed to James Wyatt.
Inscription above inner door: "Dedicated by veneration
and affection to the memory of Arabella Aufrere."
Grant Recipient: The Earl of Yarborough
Access Contact: Mr R Barr
T: 01469 560214   **F:** 01469 561346
E-mail: office@brocklesby.co.uk
Open: 1 April–31 August: viewable from permissive paths
through Mausoleum Woods at all reasonable times.
Heritage Open Days: No
P Spaces: 10. Free parking in village or walks car park, ¾
mile from site.
No wheelchair access. No WC for the disabled. Guide
dogs allowed.
£ No

BROCKLESBY MAUSOLEUM

Brocklesby Park, Grimsby, Lincolnshire DN41 8PN
Family Mausoleum designed by James Wyatt and built
between 1787 and 1794 by Charles Anderson Pelham,
who subsequently became Lord Yarborough, as a
memorial to his wife Sophia who died at the age of 33.
The classical design is based on the Temples of Vesta at
Rome and Tivoli.
Grant Recipient: The Earl of Yarborough
Access Contact: Mr H A Rayment
T: 01469 560214   **F:** 01469 561346
E-mail: office@brocklesby.co.uk
Open: Exterior: 1 April–31 August: viewable from
permissive paths through Mausoleum Woods at all
reasonable times. Interior (excluding private crypt) by prior
arrangement with the Estate Office. Admission charge for
interior.
Heritage Open Days: No

P Spaces: 10. Free parking in village or walks car park, ½ mile from site.
& No wheelchair access. No WC for the disabled. No Guide dogs allowed.
£ Adult: £2.00 (charge for interior). **Child:** £2.00 (charge for interior). **Other:** £2.00 (charge for interior).

BURGHLEY HOUSE
Stamford, Lincolnshire PE9 3JY
Large country house built by William Cecil, Lord High Treasurer of England, between 1555 and 1587, and still lived in by descendants of his family. Eighteen State Rooms, many decorated by Antonio Verrio in the 17th century, housing a collection of artworks including 17th century Italian paintings, Japanese ceramics, European porcelain and wood carvings by Grinling Gibbons and his followers. There are also four State Beds, English and continental furniture, and tapestries and textiles. 'Capability' Brown parkland.
www.burghley.co.uk
Grant Recipient: Burghley House Preservation Trust Ltd
Access Contact: Mr Philip Gompertz
T: 01780 761 974   **F:** 01780 480125
E-mail: philip.gompertz@burghley.co.uk
Open: 20 March–31 October: daily (except Fridays and 2–5 September) 11am–4.30pm. Guided tours available at certain times.
Heritage Open Days: No
P Spaces: 500. Parking for the disabled available close to visitors' entrance.
& Full. Please telephone the Property Manager for information on wheelchair access. WC for the disabled. Guide dogs allowed.
£ Adult: £11.80. **Child:** £5.60. **Other:** £10.40 (senior citizens & students), £10.00 (per person for groups 20+), £30.00 (family).

FYDELL HOUSE GATES, PIERS AND RAILINGS
(The Boston Preservation Trust), South Street, Boston, Lincolnshire PE21 6HU
Fronted by renewed, grant-aided gate, gate piers and railings, Fydell House was built in 1726 with minor 19th century alterations. Example of a small 18th century stately home. It contains links between Boston England and Boston Mass and houses the Fydell House Centre Ltd, a provider of educational and cultural facilities.
www.fydellhousecentre.org.uk
Grant Recipient: Boston Preservation Trust Ltd
Access Contact: The Chairman
T: 01205 351520 or 01205 365949
E-mail: fydellhouse@btconnect.com
Open: Access to the exterior at all reasonable times. Open throughout the year (except Bank Holidays) but in term-time access to rooms is limited.
Heritage Open Days: No
P Public car park nearby.
& Full. WC for the disabled. Guide dogs allowed.
£ No

HARLAXTON GATEHOUSE
400 metres North West of Harlaxton Manor and attached boundary wall, Harlaxton, Grantham, Lincolnshire NG32 1AG
Gatehouse built c1835 by Anthony Salvin. Exterior structure and associated wing walls restored in 2008-9. Includes family crest stone shields related to the builder of Harlaxton Manor, Gregory Gregory.
www.harlaxton.ac.uk
Grant Recipient: Harlaxton College
Access Contact: Ms Suzanne Kingsley
T: 01476 403000   **F:** 01476 403030
Open: 10 July–8 August for viewing of exterior only. Building occupied by private residents. No access to Harlaxton Manor, other than Open House Day 8 August (charges apply).
Heritage Open Days: No
P No
& Full. No WC for the disabled. Guide dogs allowed.
£ No.

HARLAXTON MANOR RAILWAY TUNNEL
Harlaxton, Grantham, Lincolnshire NG32 1AG
Curved brick viaduct with buttresses and slate roof containing a narrow gauge railway for supplying the

service courtyard of Harlaxton Manor. The entrance vestibule has at the north end two 3-bay arcades with heavily rusticated round arches adorned with enormous ashlar trophies. Constructed between 1838-1844. The Elizabethan, Revival style Manor is now a university.
www.harlaxton.ac.uk
Grant Recipient: University of Evansville-Harlaxton College
Access Contact: Mr Ian Welsh
T: 01476 403000   **F:** 01476 403030
E-mail: iwelsh@harlaxton.ac.uk
Open: Guided tours (for approx. 20 plus) by prior arrangement. Open house: 8 August, 11am–5pm.
Heritage Open Days: No
P Spaces: 150
& Full. WC for the disabled. Guide dogs allowed.
£ Adult: £7.00. **Child:** £5.00. **Other:** £5.00 (concessions), £8.00 (guided tours, including refreshments).

KYME TOWER
Manor Farm, South Kyme, Lincoln, Lincolnshire LN4 4JN
23.5m high tower with one storey and a stair turret. Remainder of a fortified medieval manor house, built on the site of an Augustinian priory, itself built on an Anglo-Saxon religious establishment. There are also visible earthworks of the former moat and fishponds.
Grant Recipient: The Crown Estate Commissioners
Access Contact: Mr S Lamyman
T: 01526 860350
Open: By prior telephone arrangement with Mr S Lamyman of Manor Farm (tel: 01526 860350). At least one week's notice required.
Heritage Open Days: No
P Spaces: 3. Parking by church.
& No wheelchair access. No WC for the disabled. No Guide dogs allowed.
£ No

LINCOLN CASTLE
Castle Hill, Lincoln, Lincolnshire LN1 3AA
Lincoln Castle was begun by William the Conqueror in 1068. For 900 years the castle has been used as a court and prison. Many original features still stand and the wall walks provide magnificent views of the cathedral, city and surrounding countryside.
www.lincolnshire.gov.uk/lincolncastle
Grant Recipient: Lincolnshire County Council
Access Contact: Mrs Angie Clay
T: 01522 511068   **F:** 01522 512150
E-mail: angie.clay@lincolnshire.gov.uk
Open: Daily: 1 October–31 March 10am–4pm, April and September 10am–5pm, 1 May–31 August 10am–6pm. Closed 24–26 December, 31 December and 1 January.
Heritage Open Days: Yes
P Paid parking available in the Castle/Cathedral area.
& Partial. Wheelchair access to grounds, Magna Carta exhibition, audio visual presentation, Victorian Prison Experience and café. WC for the disabled. Guide dogs allowed.
£ Adult: £4.10. **Child:** £2.70 (under 5s free). **Other:** £2.70 (concessions), £10.90 (family).

MONKSTHORPE CHAPEL
Spilsby, East Lindsey, Lincolnshire, PE23 5PP
Resembling a brick barn, this remote chapel with outdoor baptistery was used by local Baptists as a secluded place of worship and is one of the two best surviving examples in England. It was substantially altered to its present appearance in the early 19th century.
www.nationaltrust.org.uk
Grant Recipient: The National Trust
Access Contact: Property Manager
T: 01526 342543   **F:** 01526 348826
E-mail: monksthorpe@nationaltrust.org.uk
Open: 1 April–30 September: Wednesday, Thursday 2pm–5pm. Access by key obtained from Gunby Hall (£10.00 returnable deposit). Also 3 April, 1 May, 5 June, 3 and 31 July and 4 September, Services at 3pm: 3 and 17 April, 15 May, 19 June, 17 July, 14 August, 18 September and 2 October (Harvest), carol service 4 December. Please contact The National Trust East Midlands Regional Office (tel: 01909 486411) for further details.
Heritage Open Days: No

P No
& No wheelchair access. No WC for the disabled. No Guide dogs allowed.
£ No

MOULTON WINDMILL
High Street, Moulton, Spalding, Lincolnshire PE12 6QB
Grade I listed tower mill. Built circa 1822 in brown brick by Robert King. Eight storeys plus basement, this was the tallest windmill in the country when built. Almost all the internal machinery survives intact.
www.moultonwindmill.co.uk
Grant Recipient: Moulton Windmill Project Ltd.
Access Contact: Mrs J Prescott
T: 01775 724929
E-mail: grumpygrower@aol.com
Open: All year: Thursday–Sunday, 10am–4pm; Monday–Wednesday by prior arrangement.
Heritage Open Days: No
P Spaces: 12. Secure area for bicycles.
& Partial. Wheelchair access to first two floors, granary, tea rooms, mill shop, interpretation centre and working stones on first floor. WC for the disabled. Guide dogs allowed.
£ Adult: £4.00. **Child:** £2.00. **Other:** £2.95 (concessions).

ST PETER
Sotby, Lincolnshire
Grade II* listed church dating from early 12th and 13th centuries.
Grant Recipient: Mr B F Cotton
Access Contact: Mrs Marlene Harvey
T: 01507 343 762
Open: Key available by prior arrangement with Marlene Harvey, Foremans Cottage, Wass Lane, Sotby, Lincolnshire LN8 5LP (tel: 01507 343762) or Mr A Cotton, Glebe Farm, Main Road, Sotby, Lincolnshire (tel: 01507 343801).
Heritage Open Days: No
P Roadside parking.
& Partial. Grass entry to building and small step. No WC for the disabled. Guide dogs allowed.
£ No

TATTERSHALL CASTLE
Tattershall, Lincoln, Lincolnshire LN4 4LR
A vast fortified and moated red-brick tower, built c1440 for Ralph Cromwell, Treasurer of England. The building was rescued from becoming derelict by Lord Curzon 1911-14 and contains four great chambers with enormous Gothic fireplaces, tapestries and brick vaulting. Gatehouse with museum room.
www.nationaltrust.org.uk
Grant Recipient: The National Trust
Access Contact: Property Manager
T: 01526 342543   **F:** 01526 342543
E-mail: tattershallcastle@nationaltrust.org.uk
Open: 13 February–14 March and 6 November–19 December: Saturday and Sunday 11am–4pm; 15–31 March Saturday–Wednesday 11am–4pm, 2 April–29 September: Saturday–Wednesday and Good Friday 11am–5pm, 2–31 October Saturday–Wednesday 11am–4pm, 6 November–19 December: Saturday and Sunday 11am–4pm. Castle opens at 1pm on Saturdays due to weddings except during July and August. Please ring in advance to confirm.
Heritage Open Days: Yes
P Spaces: 40
& Partial. Wheelchair access to ground floor via ramp. Photograph album of inaccessible parts of Castle. WC for the disabled. Guide dogs allowed.
£ Adult: £5.30. **Child:** £2.80. **Other:** £13.40 (family). Admission price includes voluntary gift aid donation.

WESTGATE HOUSE
Westgate, Louth, Lincolnshire LN11 9YQ
Grade II* listed Georgian town house in brick and stone, with 1775 neo-classical additions and proto-Regency remodelling c1799 on the Westgate façade. Interior contains fine plasterwork, mahogany doors, Carrara fireplaces and other fine details. Used as a school 1937-1980s but now in course of restoration as a residence by the present owners, after dereliction.
Grant Recipient: Professor P Byrne

Access Contact: Professor Byrne & Mrs Byrne
T: 01507 354388
E-mail: peterbyrnewestgate@keme.co.uk
Open: Ground floor only. Guided visits between 11.30am–4pm, by prior arrangement. Evening group visits for societies, etc, at any reasonable time by prior arrangement throughout the year.
Heritage Open Days: Yes
P Spaces: 6. Public parking in town centre (5 minutes walk).
& Partial. Wheelchair access by prior arrangement only. No WC for the disabled. Guide dogs allowed.
£ **Adult:** £4.00. **Child:** Free (when accompanied by an adult). **Other:** Evening group visits: £6.00 per person (maximum 30) including wine and canapés.

LONDON

19 PRINCELET STREET
London E1 6QH
Grade II* listed terraced house, 1719 by Samuel Worrall, builder; adapted and extended by the addition of a synagogue in 1870 by a Mr Hudson for the Loyal United Friends Friendly Society. Now an International Historic Site of Conscience. The building retains a wealth of original features and exemplifies the special history of Spitalfields, whose character has been marked by successive waves of immigrants. The upper portions retain associations with the Huguenot silk industry, whilst the rear extension is the best surviving small-scale Jewish prayer hall or 'shul' once distinctive in the area.
www.19princeletstreet.org.uk
Grant Recipient: Spitalfields Centre Charity
Access Contact: Co ordinator
T: 020 7247 5352   **F:** 020 7375 1490
E-mail: office@19princeletstreet.org.uk
Open: By prior arrangement for groups, booked well in advance (normally a minimum of 4 weeks ahead, as visits are in great demand). For further details see: www.19princeletstreet.org.uk/groupVisits.html. Public open days in May, June and September (dates to be announced), please check the website or with the access contact (tel: 020 7247 5352) for current information.
Open House London: No
P On-street parking.
& Partial. Wheelchair access to ground floor and synagogue. No WC for the disabled. Guide dogs allowed.
£ **Adult:** £5.00 (minimum donation normally requested per person for group visits). Free on open days. **Child:** £1.00 (minimum donation requested per person for group visits). Free on open days. **Other:** Special arrangements for unwaged, those in need, marginalised and refugee groups.

BENJAMIN FRANKLIN'S HOUSE
36 Craven Street, London WC2N 5NF
A 1730s terraced house with c1792 alterations. Part of the Craven family's 18th century development of their Brewhouse estate, laid out by Flitcroft. Listed Grade I for historical associations, retaining a majority of original features (central staircase; lathing; 18th century panelling; stoves; windows; fittings; beams; brick, etc,) 'unimproved' over time. The world's only remaining home of the diplomat, scientist, inventor, writer, and philosopher Benjamin Franklin. The house is a museum and educational facility.
www.benjaminfranklinhouse.org
Grant Recipient: Friends of Benjamin Franklin House
Access Contact: Dr Marcia Balisciano
T: 020 7839 2006   **F:** 020 7930 9124
E-mail: info@benjaminfranklinhouse.org
Open: All year: Wednesday–Sunday 10.30am–5.30pm.
Open House London: Yes
P No
& No wheelchair access. No WC for the disabled. Guide dogs allowed.
£ **Adult:** £7.00. **Child:** Free.

BOONE'S CHAPEL
Lee High Road, Lewisham, London SE13 5PH
Former chapel, 1680-83, to Boone's almshouses which were demolished in 1877. The Grade I listed chapel was removed from the buildings at risk register following

completion of repairs and conversion in 2008. Open days coincide with small exhibitions. (The grounds of the adjoining Merchant Taylors almshouses are not open to the public).
www.booneschapel.co.uk/home.html
Grant Recipient: Sir Ian Mills Blackheath Historic Buildings Trust
Access Contact: Ms Madeleine Adams
E-mail: info@boonschapel.co.uk
Open: 16 , 17, 23 and 24 January, 27 and 28 February, 6, 7, 20 and 21 March, 8, 9, 22 and 23 May, 12, 13, 26 and 27 June, 17 and 18 July. Further open days not confirmed at time of publication please check the English Heritage website or with the access contact for current information.
Open House London: Yes
P Red route parking restrictions: (10am–4pm: 20 minutes Monday–Saturday, 1 hour parking in side roads).
& Full. No WC for the disabled. Guide dogs allowed.
£ No

BRIXTON ACADEMY
211 Stockwell Road, Lambeth, London SW9 9SL
Built in 1929 as the largest of the four "Astoria" theatres. Retains many original features including elaborate presenium arch over stage and art deco interior. Presently used as a music venue.
www.brixton-academy.co.uk
Grant Recipient: McKenzie Group Ltd (Ex Magstack Ltd)
Access Contact: Mr Nigel Downs
T: 020 7787 3150   **F:** 020 7738 4427
E-mail: nigel@brixton-academy.co.uk
Open: Academy Open Day will normally be during Open House London weekend in September. Performances throughout the year.
Open House London: Yes
P NCP car park located on Popes Road. Restricted parking around Brixton Academy. Not open Sundays.
& Partial. Wheelchair access to ground floor and auditorium. WC for the disabled. Guide dogs allowed.
£ No

BROMLEY HALL
Gillender Street, Tower Hamlets, London E14 6RN
A rare surviving 15th century house and one of the oldest brick built houses in London. Tree ring analysis has established that the Hall was constructed around 1485 and it retains features from all periods dating back to Tudor times. The house has been used as a private residence, calico printing works and offices. The building now provides the new home for the London Voluntary Sector Training Consortium.
Grant Recipient: Leaside Regeneration
Access Contact: Messrs Peter Mitchell/ David Black
T: 0845 262 0846   **F:** 0845 262 0847
E-mail: pmitchell@leasideregeneration.co.uk
Open: By prior arrangement during working hours.
Open House London: Yes
P Spaces: 4
& Partial. Wheelchair access to ground floor only. WC for the disabled. Guide dogs allowed.
£ No

BRUNEL ENGINE HOUSE
Railway Avenue, Rotherhithe, Southwark, London SE16 4LF
Scheduled monument and international landmark, Isambard Kingdom Brunel's first project with his father Sir Marc Brunel. The Thames tunnel opened as a banquet hall, shopping arcade and underwater fairground, now the oldest tunnel in the oldest underground system in the world.
www.brunel-museum.org.uk
Grant Recipient: Trustees of the Brunel Museum
Access Contact: Mr Robert Hulse (Director)
T: 0207 231 3314
E-mail: director@brunel-museum.org.uk
Open: Daily, 10am–5pm. Closed Christmas Day, Boxing Day and New Years Day.
Open House London: Yes
P On-street parking. One disabled space on cobbled drive.
& Full. WC for the disabled. Guide dogs allowed.
£ **Adult:** £2.00. **Child:** Free. **Other:** £1.00 (concessions, Art Fund free).

BRUNSWICK SQUARE GARDENS
Brunswick Square, London WC1
A public park originally part of the grounds of the Foundling Hospital, founded by Sir Thomas Coram.
www.camden.gov.uk
Grant Recipient: London Borough of Camden
Access Contact: Mr Peter Stewart
T: 020 7974 1693   **F:** 020 7974 1543
E-mail: shaun.kidden@camden.gov.uk
Open: From 7.30am until dusk throughout the year.
Open House London: No
P On-street parking.
& Full. No WC for the disabled. Guide dogs allowed.
£ No

BUILDING 40
Royal Military Academy, Woolwich, London SE18 6ST
Building 40 is a Grade II* listed building on the historic Royal Arsenal site. Constructed in 1718 and 1723 of red brown stock brick with a slate roof, attributed to Nicholas Hawksmoor. One of four buildings now housing the Royal Artillery Museum called Firepower.
www.firepower.org.uk
Grant Recipient: Royal Artillery Museums Ltd
Access Contact: Mrs Eileen Noon
T: 020 8855 7755   **F:** 020 88557100
E-mail: eileen@firepower.org.uk
Open: Building 40: used for corporate events and temporary exhibitions. Museum: Wednesday–Sunday 10:30am–5pm, closed Monday and Tuesday.
Open House London: Yes
P Spaces: 400
& Partial. Wheelchair access through the rear of the building to the ground floor only. WC for the disabled. Guide dogs allowed.
£ **Adult:** £5.00. **Child:** £2.50. **Other:** £12.00 (Family), £4.50 (Concessions).

CATHEDRAL FOOTBRIDGE
Borough High Street, Southwark, London SE1 9DA
Victorian footbridge providing access from Borough High Street to the Cathedral churchyard.
www.southwarkcathedral.org.uk
Grant Recipient: Dean and Chapter of Southwark Cathedral
Access Contact: Mr Matthew Knight
T: 020 7367 6726   **F:** 020 7367 6725
E-mail: matthew.knight@southwark.anglican.org
Open: Daily: 7.30am–6.30pm. Closes Christmas Day at 1pm.
Open House London: No
P No
& Partial. Wheelchair access to footbridge but steps down to churchyard. Step-free access available via Borough Market. WC for the disabled. Guide dogs allowed.
£ No

CHURCH OF THE HOSPITAL OF ST JOHN AND ST ELIZABETH
60 Grove End Road, London NW8 9NH
Built in 1864 by Sir George Bowyer and designed by George Goldie, a leading Catholic architect of the day in the Italian Baroque style.
Grant Recipient: Trustees for the Hospital Church
Access Contact: Ms Christine Malcolmson, Matron
T: 0207 806 4000 (ext.4294)   **F:** 0207 806 4001
E-mail: christine.malcolmson@hje.org.uk
Open: At all times.
Open House London: No
P Public Car park.
& Partial. Wheelchair access is via the balconies on the first floor. Portable ramp available. WC for the disabled. Guide dogs allowed.
£ No

CROSSNESS BEAM ENGINE HOUSE, (OLD WORKS–THAMES WATER STW)
Belvedere Road, London SE2 9AQ
Grade I listed beam engine house, opened 1865. Engineer Joseph Bazalgette. Constructed in the Romanesque style. The interior includes important ornamental cast ironwork

and four original beam engines by James Watt and Co.
www.crossness.org.uk
Grant Recipient: Crossness Engines Trust
Access Contact: Mr Mike Jones
T: 020 8311 3711 (Tues & Sun)
E-mail: mike@jones86.freeserve.co.uk
Open: Site closed until July 2010 for re-development of
museum and visitor facility. Subsequent opening days to
be confirmed but will be at least 2 days per week. See
website for details or email Mike Jones
(mike@jones86.freeserve.co.uk).
Open House London: No
P Spaces: 50
& Partial. Wheelchair access to ground floor. Video link to
areas not accessible by wheelchairs (beam floor and
basement). WC for disabled to be provided as part of
current re-development. Guide dogs allowed.
£ Adult: £5.00, £6.00 (steaming days). Child: Under 16
free

DISSENTERS' CHAPEL
**Kensal Green Cemetery, Harrow Road, London W10
4RA**
Grade II* listed building within Grade II* Registered
cemetery. Cemetery dates from 1832 and is London's
oldest. The Chapel was designed in Greek Revival style by
John Griffith in 1834. It is now used by the Friends of
Kensal Green Cemetery as a headquarters, exhibition
space and art gallery and as a centre for their guided
walks, lectures and special events.
www.hct.org.uk or www.kensalgreen.co.uk
Grant Recipient: Historic Chapels Trust
Access Contact: Mr Henry Vivian-Neal
T: 020 8960 1030
E-mail: henry.vivianneal@btinternet.com
Open: Cemetery: daily: Dissenters' Chapel: Sunday
afternoons and at other times by prior arrangement. Guided
tours of chapels and cemetery for modest charge, also tours
of the Catacombs 1st and 3rd Sunday in every month.
Open House London: Yes
P Parking in adjacent streets, parking for the disabled in
cemetery.
& Full. WC for the disabled. Guide dogs allowed.
£ £5.00 (adult), £4.00 (child) donation requested for
guided tours of cemetery.

DR JOHNSON'S HOUSE
17 Gough Square, London EC4A 3DE
Fine 18th century town house in the heart of the City of
London. Here Dr Johnson compiled his dictionary
(published 1755). Original staircase and woodwork
throughout and collection of prints, paintings and Johnson
memorabilia. 2009 was the tercentenary of Johnson's
birth.
www.drjohnsonshouse.org
Grant Recipient: Dr Johnson's House Trust
Access Contact: The Curator Dr Johnson's House Trust
T: 020 7353 3745   **F:** 020 7353 3745
E-mail: curator@drjohnsonshouse.org
Open: Monday–Saturday: May–September 11am–5.30pm,
October–April 11am–5pm. Closed Sundays and Bank
Holidays. Check website for Christmas opening times.
Open House London: No
P For disabled only–2 spaces. On-street meter parking.
& No wheelchair access. WC for the disabled. Guide dogs
allowed.
£ Adult: £4.50. Child: £1.50. Other: £3.50
(student/senior citizens).

DULWICH OLD CEMETERY, (THE OLD BURIAL GROUND)
Dulwich Village, Dulwich, London SE21 7HN
Burial ground, consecrated in 1616, is unusual in not
being adjacent to any church or chapel. Group of 12
Grade II monuments form a group within 18th century
gates, walls and railings.
www.thedulwichestate.org.uk
Grant Recipient: The Dulwich Estate
Access Contact: Mr Simon Hoare / The Dulwich Estate
T: 020 8299 1000
E-mail: info@thedulwichestate.org.uk
Open: The exterior can be viewed at all times through
railings around the perimeter. Access to the interior by
prior arrangement with the Dulwich Estate Office.
Open House London: No

P On-street parking.
& Partial. Wheelchair access to the exterior on pavements.
No WC for the disabled. No Guide dogs allowed.
£ No

FINGERPOSTS IN ENFIELD
London EN1
Six historic cast iron finger posts, the only remaining
examples of traditional direction signs located at principal
junctions on the London Borough of Enfield's road
network. The destinations indicate long standing
settlements still recognisable within the modern borough.
Grant Recipient: London Borough of Enfield
Access Contact: Ms Christine White
E-mail: Christine.White@enfield.gov.uk
Open: At all times.
Open House London: No
P Parking availability varies at each location. See web site
www.park-up.com/
& Partial. No WC for the disabled. Guide dogs allowed.
£ No

GLOUCESTER GATE BRIDGE
Regents Park, London, NW1 7PS
Constructed 1877 to span a branch of the Regent's Canal,
of unusual width and remarkable for the amount of
artistic embellishment, including four elaborate bronze
lamp standards supporting large lanterns, two bronze
plaques commemorating the martyrdom of St Pancras and
quatrefoil fretwork designs on the balustrading.
Grant Recipient: London Borough of Camden
Access Contact: Mr Martin Reading
T: 020 7974 2018   **F:** 020 7974 4494
E-mail: martin.reading@camden.gov.uk
Open: Free access at all times.
Open House London: No
P Use of public transport strongly recommended.
& Full. No WC for the disabled. Guide dogs allowed.
£ No

GORDON SQUARE AND WOBURN SQUARE
Camden, London WC1
Two garden squares within the Bloomsbury conservation
area, first laid out as formal spaces in the 1830s.
Grant Recipient: University of London
Access Contact: Ms Suzanne Spooner
T: 020 7862 8236
E-mail: suzanne.spooner@london.ac.uk
Open: All year: dawn to dusk daily, except Christmas Day.
Open House London: No
P On-street pay and display parking available.
& Full. No WC for the disabled. Guide dogs allowed.
£ No

HACKNEY EMPIRE
291 Mare Street, London E8 1EJ
Hackney Empire, designed and built by Frank Matcham in
1901, is one of the finest surviving variety theatres in
Britain. Restoration and renovation completed 2004,
providing modern facilities and access for all.
www.hackneyempire.co.uk
Grant Recipient: Hackney Empire Ltd
Access Contact: Ms Clare Middleton
T: 020 8510 4500   **F:** 020 8510 4530
E-mail: info@hackneyempire.co.uk
Open: Performances throughout the year.
Open House London: Yes
P On-street parking. Permits available from box office to
use nearby Tesco car park when shows are on.
& Full. WC for the disabled. Guide dogs allowed.
£ Charges are made for performances and some
organised tours.

HEADSTONE MANOR
**Headstone Manor Recreation Ground, Pinner View,
Harrow, London HA2 6PX**
Grade I listed timber framed Manor House, surrounded by
a water filled moat. Earliest parts date from 1310, with
numerous extensions and adaptations through to 18th
century. Original residence of Archbishops of Canterbury
until the Reformation.
www.harrow.gov.uk/museum
Grant Recipient: London Borough of Harrow
Access Contact: Ms Lottie Collins

T: 020 8861 2626/ 020 8863 6720
E-mail: harrow.museum@harrow.gov.uk
Open: April–30 September: Saturdays and Sundays for
guided tours starting at 3pm.
Open House London: Yes
P Spaces: 50, Parking for disabled badge holders only
adjacent to property.
& Partial. WC for the disabled in adjacent tithe barn.
Wheelchair access to some exterior parts and ground floor
with assistance. WC for the disabled. Guide dogs allowed.
£ Adult: £3.00. Child: Free.

HIMALAYA PALACE CINEMA (FORMERLY LIBERTY CINEMA)
14 South Road, Southall, London UB1 1RT
Former cinema, later market hall. 1928. An early work by
George Coles; the only known example of cinema built in
the Chinese style. Street elevation faced with coloured
glazed tiles with red pantiled pagoda roofs. Interior badly
fire damaged. Repaired and returned to use as a three
screen cinema showing Bollywood, Tamil, Telugu and
Afghanistan movies.
www.himalayapalacecinema.co.uk
Grant Recipient: Himalaya Carpets Ltd
Access Contact: Mr S Pandher
T: 020 8574 6193   **F:** 020 8574 2317
E-mail: himalayacarpets@tiscali.co.uk
Open: Daily, 10.30am–11.30pm. Non-public areas by prior
arrangement.
Open House London: Yes
P Council car park at rear of cinema.
& Full. WC for the disabled. No Guide dogs allowed.
£ Adult: £3.95 (before 2pm), £5.95 other times. Child:
£4.95 (all times). Other: £4.95 (senior citizens).

LANDMARK ARTS CENTRE
Ferry Road, Teddington, London TW11 9NN
Grade II* listed former church, c1889, in French-Gothic
style by architect William Niven. A number of intended
architectural features were never built, due to insufficient
funds (hence the incomplete flying buttresses for
example). Redundant as a church in 1977. Following
renovation now used as an Arts Centre with a variety of
arts events, classes and private events.
www.landmarkartscentre.org
Grant Recipient: London Diocesan Fund
Access Contact: Mrs Lesley Bossine
T: 020 8977 7558   **F:** 020 8977 4830
E-mail: lesley@landmarkartscentre.org
Open: Normally open Monday–Friday 10am–5pm (shorter
hours at weekends when public events are held), visitors
are advised to contact the Arts Centre Manager at the
Landmark Arts Centre (tel: 020 8977 7558, fax: 020 8977
4830, email.lesley@landmarkartscentre.org) to check. Visits
at other times by prior arrangement with the Arts Centre
Manager, subject to staff availability.
Open House London: No
P Spaces: 4. Additional on-street parking nearby.
& Full. WC for the disabled. Guide dogs allowed.
£ Variable admission charges for some public events.

LSO ST LUKE'S
161 Old Street, London EC1V 9NG
Former Church of St Luke, 1727-33. The west tower, spire
and flanking staircase wings by Nicholas Hawksmoor.
Listed Grade I. Restored to become the home of the
London Symphony Orchestra's music education and
community programme. Conversion began in 2000 and
the building combines careful external restoration with an
impressive contemporary interior.
www.lso.co.uk/lsostlukes
Grant Recipient: St Luke Centre Management Company Ltd
Access Contact: Ms Alison Thompson
T: 020 7566 2871   **F:** 020 7566 2881
E-mail: lsostlukes@lso.co.uk
Open: By prior arrangement only.
Open House London: No
P Spaces: 6. Strictly limited to people attending events at
the site and for visitors with access requirements, by prior
arrangement only.
& Full. WC for the disabled. Guide dogs allowed.
£ Admission charges for events

LYCHGATE

Church Road, Beddington, London SM6 7NH
Designed by Joseph Clarke in 1875, the Lych Gate is a prominent feature in a public park at the entrance of a churchyard. Built of brick and carved stone with oak supports and a tiled roof.
Grant Recipient: London Borough of Sutton
Access Contact: Mr Bill Wyatt
T: 0208 770 5070
E-mail: bill.wyatt@sutton.gov.uk
Open: At any reasonable time.
Open House London: No
P Spaces: 50. On-street parking and car park nearby.
Full. WC in park pavillion. WC for the disabled. Guide dogs allowed.
£ No

MAPPIN TERRACE CAFÉ

ZSL London Zoo, Regents Park, London NW1 4RY
The café was designed by John James Joass and built between 1914-20. It was funded by John Newton Mappin. It is a single story red-brick building with a pantiled roof. It is characterised by paired Tuscan columns, French windows, bracketed eaves and pavilion towers at three angles.
www.zsl.org
Grant Recipient: Zoological Society of London
Access Contact: Ms Emily Sheath
T: 020 7449 6586   **F:** 020 7586 6177
E-mail: emily.sheath@zsl.org
Open: On view to visitors to London Zoo which is open daily except 25 December.
Open House London: No
P Spaces: 300. Car park £11.00 and 250 yards away.
Full. Guide dogs are housed and a personal guide provided. WC for the disabled.
£ **Adult:** £16.80. **Child:** £13.30 (under 3s free). **Other:** £15.30 (concessions).

MONUMENTS AND MEMORIALS

in the London Borough of Camden, London
Grade II listed monuments and memorials in the London Borough of Camden: Matilda statue, Regents Park; water pumps in Queens Square, 1840 cast iron with lion mask capital and coats of arms; water pump, Bedford Row, 19th century cast iron; cattle troughs, all granite in various locations; and Milkmaid statue, Gloucester Gate circa 1878 by Joseph Durham.
Grant Recipient: London Borough of Camden
Access Contact: Mr Martin Reading
T: 020 7974 2018   **F:** 020 7974 4494
E-mail: martin.reading@camden.gov.uk
Open: At all times.
Open House London: No
P Use of public transport strongly recommended.
Full. No WC for the disabled. Guide dogs allowed.
£ No

MORNINGTON STREET RAILWAY BRIDGE LAMP STANDARDS

Mornington Street, Camden, London NW1
The bridge, built by the London and North Western Railway circa 1900, crosses the West Coast Main line near Regent's Park linking John Nash's Park Village East with Camden Town. At each corner are refurbished cast iron lamp standards, now supporting new globe lanterns replacing those destroyed in WWII bombing.
Grant Recipient: London Borough of Camden
Access Contact: Mr Martin Reading
T: 020 7974 2018   **F:** 020 7974 4494
E-mail: martin.reading@camden.gov.uk
Open: At all times.
Open House London: No
P Spaces: 2. Pay and display.
Full. No WC for the disabled. Guide dogs allowed.
£ No

PITZHANGER MANOR HOUSE AND GALLERY

Walpole Park, Mattock Lane, London W5 5EQ
Pitzhanger Manor House is set in Walpole Park, Ealing and was owned and rebuilt by architect and surveyor Sir John Soane (1753-1837). Much of the house has been restored to its early 19th century style. Pitzhanger Manor Gallery opened in 1996 in a 1940s extension and exhibitions of professional contemporary art in all media are shown in both the House and Gallery.
www.ealing.gov.uk/pmgalleryandhouse
Grant Recipient: London Borough of Ealing
Access Contact: Ms Helen Walker
T: 020 8567 1227   **F:** 020 8567 0596
E-mail: pmgallery&house@ealing.gov.uk
Open: Tuesday–Friday 1pm–5pm, Saturday 11am–5pm. Summer Sunday openings (ring for details). Closed Bank Holidays, Christmas and Easter.
Open House London: Yes
P Parking meters and some free parking in Mattock Lane.
Partial. Access for certain types of wheelchair only with assistance (domestic lift and some steps), please phone in advance for further information and to check lift availability. WC for the disabled. Guide dogs allowed.
£ No

PRIORY CHURCH OF THE ORDER OF ST JOHN

St John's Square, Clerkenwell, London EC1M
Remains of the Priory Church of the Knights Hospitallers' London headquarters, including choir and 12th century crypt. Museum in adjacent St John's Gate presents information on the Order of St John and conducts guided tours.
www.sja.org.uk/museum
Grant Recipient: The Order of St John of Jerusalem
Access Contact: Ms Pamela Willis
T: 020 7324 4071   **F:** 020 7336 0587
E-mail: museum@nhq.sja.org.uk.
Open: Guided tours: Tuesday, Friday and Saturday 11am and 2.30pm. Other days and times by arrangement with the Museum. (Museum closed for refurbishment until June. Reopens from 1 June Monday–Saturday 10am–5pm).
Open House London: Yes
P Metered parking available in St John's Square.
Partial. Wheelchair ramp for access to Church but not the crypt. WC for the disabled at St John's Gate. WC for the disabled. Guide dogs allowed.
£ Donations requested for guided tours.

PUTNEY OLD BURIAL GROUND

Upper Richmond Road, Putney, London SW15
Mid-18th century cemetery with a small mortuary building. Cemetery has four listed tombs, two of which are for people of local importance; Harriet Thomson, an 18th century novelist and Robert Henry Wood, an 18th century traveller and author. Also tombs to Joseph Lucas and Stratford Canning.
Grant Recipient: Wandsworth Council
Access Contact: Ms Joanne Taylor
T: 020 8871 7530   **F:** 020 8871 7533
E-mail: jotaylor@wandsworth.gov.uk
Open: Free access at any reasonable time.
Open House London: No
P Parking meters in nearby residential streets.
Full. No WC for the disabled. Guide dogs allowed.
£ No

RED HOUSE

Red House Lane, Bexley DA6 8JF
Commissioned by William Morris, designed and built in 1859 by his friend and colleague, architect Philip Webb. Strongly influenced by Gothic medieval architecture and constructed with an emphasis on natural materials. Interior almost unaltered with numerous original features, including some items of fixed cupboards, settle and other furnishings designed by Morris and Webb, as well as wall paintings and stained glass by Edward Burne-Jones.
www.nationaltrust.org.uk
Grant Recipient: The National Trust
Access Contact: The Custodian
T: 020 8304 6359
E-mail: redhouse@nationaltrust.org.uk
Open: 3 March–28 November: Wednesday–Sunday, 3–19 December: Friday–Sunday and all Bank Holiday Mondays 11am–4:15pm. Pre booked guided tours 11am–1pm (tel: 020 8304 9878) Tuesday–Saturday 9.30am–1.30pm). Self guided tours from 1.30pm (booking not required).
Open House London: Yes
P Spaces: 2. Two spaces for pre-booked parking for the disabled. Additional parking at Danson Park (1 mile). Parking charge at weekends and Bank Holidays.
Partial. Wheelchair access to shop only. No WC for the disabled. Guide dogs allowed.
£ **Adult:** £6.90. **Child:** £3.45. **Other:** £17.50 (family). Free to NT members.

RICHMOND WEIR AND LOCK

Riverside, Richmond-upon-Thames, London
The lock and weir are important examples in the history of hydraulic engineering. Constructed in 1894 to control river levels between Richmond and Teddington at half-tide level, the weir was engineered to ensure that the river remained navigable at all times. Operated and maintained by the Port of London Authority since its establishment in 1909, the machinery was designed and built by Ransomes and Rapier.
www.pla.co.uk
Grant Recipient: Port of London Authority
Access Contact: Mr James Trimmer
T: 01474 562200   **F:** 01474 562398
E-mail: james.trimmer@pla.co.uk
Open: The lock and weir are open at all times for passage by river except for 3 weeks in November/December for major maintenance undertaken by the Port of London Authority. The footbridge over the lock is open 6.30am–9.30pm British Summer Time and 6.30am–7.30pm GMT.
Open House London: No
P No
No wheelchair access. No WC for the disabled. Guide dogs allowed.
£ No

ROBERT NELSON MONUMENT

St George's Gardens, Handel Street, Camden, London WC1
Monument to Robert Nelson, philanthropist and leading lay churchman d.1715. Portland stone, gadrooned urn on tall plinth, set within wrought-iron railings and now fully restored. Nelson was the first person to be buried in the new cemetery, choosing this place 'to overcome the aversion that has been discovered to its use'.
www.friendsofstgeorgesgardens.org.uk
Grant Recipient: London Borough of Camden
Access Contact: Parks and Open Spaces Liaison Officer
T: 020 7974 8280   **F:** 020 7974 8874
E-mail: gabi.howard@camden.gov.uk
Open: Daily, 7.30am to dusk (closing time changes from 4pm in mid winter to 9pm in mid summer).
Open House London: Yes
P No
Full. No WC for the disabled. Guide dogs allowed.
£ No

RUXLEY OLD CHURCH

Ruxley Manor Garden Centre, Maidstone Road, Bromley, London DA14 5BQ
Medieval church dating from 13th century. Deconsecrated in 1557 by Cardinal Pole. Excavated in the 1970s and used as a barn until recent times. Remains of an earlier church beneath the current structure.
www.ruxley-manor.co.uk
Grant Recipient: H Evans & Sons Ltd
Access Contact: Mr James Evans
T: 020 8300 0084   **F:** 020 8300 3370
E-mail: james@hevans.co.uk
Open: Free access to the exterior only: Monday to Saturday 9am–5.30pm, Sunday 10am–4.30pm. Closed Easter Sunday, Christmas Day, Boxing Day and New Year's Day.
Open House London: No
P Spaces: 500
Partial. Gravel path to church. WC for the disabled. Guide dogs allowed.
£ No

ST ANDREWS OLD CHURCH

Old Church Lane, Kingsbury, Brent, London
Possibly of Saxon origin, now of 15th century appearance with 19th century restoration work. Considered to be the oldest building in Brent. Contains brasses and memorials to well-known local families dating from the 16th to the 19th centuries.
Grant Recipient: The Churches Conservation Trust
Access Contact: Ms Rebecca Rees

T: 0790 0685 796   **F:** 020 7213 0678
Open: 31 May and Open House London, at other times by prior arrangement.
Open House London: Yes
P On-street parking.
& No wheelchair access. No WC for the disabled. Guide dogs allowed.
£ No

ST ETHELBURGA'S CENTRE FOR RECONCILIATION AND PEACE

78 Bishopgate, London EC2N 4AG
Church of St Ethelburga the Virgin built in the late 14th and early 15th centuries. Devastated by a terrorist bomb in April 1993 and re-opened in November 2002, after restoration, for use as a Centre for Reconciliation and Peace.
www.stethelburgas.org
Grant Recipient: St Ethelburga's Centre for Reconciliation & Peace
Access Contact: Mr Simon Keyes
T: 020 7496 1610   **F:** 020 7638 1440
E-mail: enquiries@stethelburgas.org
Open: Every Friday 11am–3pm. Groups may visit at other times by arrangement. Details of services, public lectures and other events available from the website or by telephone.
Open House London: Yes
P No
& Full. WC for the disabled. Guide dogs allowed.
£ No

ST GEORGE'S GERMAN LUTHERAN CHURCH

55 Alie Street, London E1 8EB
Oldest surviving German church in England from 1763 with mostly original furnishings including box pews on ground floor and in balconies. Double-decker central pulpit with sounding board set behind altar rails. 19th century Walcker organ.
www.hct.org.uk
Grant Recipient: Historic Chapels Trust
Access Contact: Dr Jennifer Freeman
T: 020 7481 0533   **F:** 020 7488 3756
E-mail: chapels@hct.org.uk
Open: By prior arrangement. Free monthly organ recital at 1pm on first Thursday of the month. Regular public concerts and talks. See website for details.
Open House London: Yes
P Multi-storey car park to rear and on-street parking.
& Partial. Wheelchair access to ground floor. WC for the disabled. Guide dogs allowed.
£ Donations invited.

ST LUKES MEMORIAL GARDEN WALL & PIERS

Knights Hill, West Norwood, London SE27 0HS
Memorial Gardens in front of St Luke's church include lawns, flowerbeds, paths and seating. Dedicated to West Norwood residents who lost their lives in WWII.
Grant Recipient: Lambeth Borough Council
Access Contact: Mr T Uprichard
T: 020 7926 6221   **F:** 020 7926 6201
E-mail: tuprichard@lambeth.gov.uk
Open: All reasonable times.
Open House London: No
P No
& Full. No WC for the disabled. Guide dogs allowed.
£ No

ST MATTHIAS OLD CHURCH COMMUNITY CENTRE

113 Poplar High Street, Poplar, London E14 0AE
Built by in 1650-54 by the East India Company, St Matthias Old Church is the oldest building in Docklands. Declared redundant in 1977, the building became derelict. In 1990 the building was restored and is now used as a community arts/cultural centre.
www.stmatthiascommunitycentre.com
Grant Recipient: London Diocesan Fund
Access Contact: Mr Nizam Uddin
T: 020 7987 0459   **F:** 020 7531 9973
E-mail: st.matthias@hotmail.com
Open: Monday–Friday: 10am–3pm.
Open House London: Yes

P Car park for limited number of cars.
& Full. WC for the disabled. Guide dogs allowed.
£ No

ST PAUL'S STEINER PROJECT

1 St Paul's Road, London N1 2QH
Grade II* listed church, 1826-28 by Sir Charles Barry. Perpendicular in style. Converted to a 'cradle to grave' education and cultural centre, including a Steiner school, multi use community performance space, adult education and information centre.
www.stpaulssteinerproject.org
Grant Recipient: St Paul's Steiner Project
Access Contact: Ms Jane Gerhard
T: 020 7226 4454   **F:** 102 7226 2062
E-mail: st.pauls.school@btinternet.com
Open: Weekdays: 19 January, 9 March, 11 May, 15 June, 15 September and 10 November. At other times by prior arrangement with 2 days notice. Weekends and evenings: as per events at the Nave: see www.thenave.org.
Open House London: No
P Pay and display.
& Partial. Wheelchair access to ground floor. WC for the disabled. Guide dogs allowed.
£ No

THE HOUSE MILL

Three Mill Lane, Bromley-by-Bow, London E3 3DU
Industrial water mill, originally built 1776 as part of a distillery. Contains four floors with remains of un-restored machinery, four water wheels and gearing. Originally had 12 pairs of millstones and has unique survival of Fairbairn-style "silent millstone machinery".
www.HouseMill.org.uk
Grant Recipient: River Lea Tidal Mill Trust
Access Contact: Miss Beverley Charters
T: 0208 980 4626 / 07968 063017   **F:** 0208 980 0725
E-mail: RLTMT@bcos.demon.co.uk or info@housemill.org.uk
Open: Sunday of National Mills Week, Open House London (check website for details) and first Sunday of each month April–December: 11am–4pm. Other Sundays May–October: 1–4pm. Groups by prior arrangement with Miss Beverley Charters.
Open House London: Yes
P Car park nearby.
& Full. WC for the disabled. Guide dogs allowed.
£ **Adult:** £3.00. **Child:** Free. **Other:** £1.50.

THE QUEEN'S CHAPEL OF THE SAVOY

Savoy Hill, Strand, London WC2R 0DA
Originally part of a hospital founded in 1512 by Henry VII. Rebuilt by Robert Smirke after a fire in 1864, from which time the ceiling covered with heraldic emblems dates. Recently restored.
www.duchyoflancaster.co.uk
Grant Recipient: Duchy of Lancaster
Access Contact: Mr Phillip Chancellor
T: 020 7836 7221
E-mail: pdc46@mailcity.com
Open: All year except August and September: Tuesday–Friday 11.30am–3.30pm; Sunday for Morning Service only. Closed the week after Christmas Day and the week after Easter Day.
Open House London: No
P No
& Full. No WC for the disabled. Guide dogs allowed.
£ No

THE ROUND CHAPEL (CLAPTON PARK UNITED REFORMED CHURCH)

1d Glenarm Road, London E5 0LY
Grade II* listed United Reformed Church, c1871. Horseshoe-shaped plan with roof and gallery supported by iron pillars. Detailed columns form a continuous iron arcade at roof level with latticework effects. Contemporary pulpit with double flight of stairs, organ and organ case.
www.hhbt.org.uk
Grant Recipient: Hackney Historic Buildings Trust
Access Contact: Ms Jill Truman
T: 020 8525 0706/ 02089860029   **F:** 020 8986 0029
E-mail: info@hhbt.org.uk
Open: Many public/community events take place in the Round Chapel which the public can attend; it is also

available to hire for private events, otherwise access by prior arrangement.
Open House London: Yes
P Spaces: 3
& Partial. Wheelchair access to ground floor only. WC for the disabled. Guide dogs allowed.
£ No

TOMB OF ELIZABETH AND ALEXIS SOYER

Kensal Green Cemetery, Harrow Road, London W10 4RA
Grade II* pedestal tomb of 1844 to popular painter Elizabeth Soyer who died in 1842 aged 29. Designed by her husband Alexis Soyer a leading chef and dietician of the 19th century who is also buried here. Carved by Pierre Puyenbroeck of Brussels and restored by Friends of Kensal Green Cemetery in 2009.
www.kensalgreen.co.uk
Grant Recipient: Friends of Kensal Green Cemetery
Access Contact: Mr H Vivian-Neal
E-mail: henry.vivianneal@btinternet.com
Open: Free access at any reasonable time. The tomb is occasionally included in guided tours of the cemetery (charges apply).
Open House London: Yes
P Limited parking in front of the main gate in Harrow Road.
& Full. Most paths are packed earth or gravel and there is uneven ground throughout the cemetery. No WC for the disabled. Guide dogs allowed.
£ **Adult:** £5.00. **Child:** £4.00, donation requested for guided tours of cemetery.

WAPPING HYDRAULIC POWER PUMPING STATION

Wapping Wall, London E1W 3ST
The Wapping Hydraulic Power Station was built by the London Hydraulic Power Company in 1890. One of the five London Stations of its kind, it harnessed Thames water to provide power throughout the central London area. The showcase building of the LHPC, it was used as a model for power stations in Argentina, Australia, New York and Europe. Now houses an art gallery and restaurant.
www.thewappingproject.com
Grant Recipient: Women's Playhouse Trust
Access Contact: Women's Playhouse Trust
T: 020 7680 2080   **F:** 020 7680 2081
E-mail: jules@thewappingproject.com
Open: Throughout the year (except 23 December–4 January): Monday–Friday: 12 noon–Midnight, Saturday 10am–Midnight and Sunday 10am–6pm.
Open House London: No
P Spaces: 30
& Full. WC for the disabled. Guide dogs allowed.
£ No

WHITECHAPEL GALLERY

77–82 Whitechapel High Street, London E1 7QX
Grade II* listed Arts and Crafts building constructed in the late 1890s by C H Townsend. Occupied by the Whitechapel Art Gallery, which was founded in 1901 by the Revd Canon Barnett 'to bring great art to the people of the East End'. Extensive redevelopment during 2009 incorporated the former Whitechapel library.
www.whitechapelgallery.org
Grant Recipient: Trustees of the Whitechapel Art Gallery
Access Contact: Ms Cookie Rameder
T: 020 7522 7886   **F:** 020 7377 1685
E-mail: cookierameder@whitechapelgallery.org
Open: All year, Tuesday–Sunday 11am–6pm, Thursday 11am–9am.
Open House London: Yes
P Paid parking in Spreadeagle Yard to the left of the gallery off Whitechapel High Street.
& Full. WC for the disabled. Guide dogs allowed.
£ One exhibition per year will have entrance fee.

MERSEYSIDE

74 LIVERPOOL ROAD

Birkdale, Sefton, Merseyside PR8 4PZ
Grade II* listed farmhouse, now house. Probably early to mid 17th century. Cruck frame with rendered walls and straw thatched roof.
Grant Recipient: Mr & Mrs Morris

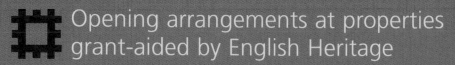

Access Contact: Mr & Mrs Morris
Open: Access to the exterior at all reasonable times.
Heritage Open Days: No
P No
No wheelchair access. No WC for the disabled. No Guide dogs allowed.
£ No

FORMER ST ANDREW'S CHURCH

Rodney Street, Liverpool
Former Scottish Presbyterian Church of 1824, now disused and partially ruinous. Listed Grade II*. Acquired by Liverpool City Council and temporarily repaired via holding works to make public access safe. A new use for the building is being sought. Pyramid monument in churchyard to civil engineer William Mckenzie (1794-1851).
Grant Recipient: Liverpool City Council
Access Contact: Mr Chris Griffiths
T: 0151 233 4488   **F:** 0151 233 4290
E-mail: chris.griffiths@liverpool.gov.uk
Open: Open week: 6–10 September, 10am–4pm (whilst in the ownership of Liverpool City Council).
Heritage Open Days: Yes
P Mount Pleasant car park 400 metres (pay and display).
No wheelchair access. No WC for the disabled. Guide dogs allowed.
£ No

GRAND ENTRANCE

Birkenhead Park, Park Road North, Birkenhead, Wirral, Merseyside CH41 4HD
Grand triple entrance archway to Birkenhead Park, with two-storey lodges on either side. Dated 1847, by L.Hornblower and J.Robertson for Sir Joseph Paxton. Full-height coupled Ionic columns which also continue across the flanking lodges. Balustraded parapet. Listed Grade II*.
www.wirral.gov.uk
Grant Recipient: Wirral Metropolitan Borough Council
Access Contact: Mr Adam King, Park Manager
T: 0151 652 5197   **F:** 0151 652 4521
E-mail: adamking@wirral.gov.uk
Open: March–September: Friday, tour 2–3pm; Heritage Open Days (9–12 September). At other times by prior arrangement.
Heritage Open Days: Yes
P Spaces: 20. Additional parking in park.
Partial. Entrance arches accessible but not internal buildings. WC for the disabled at Birkenhead Park Pavilion (visitor centre) and coffee shop. Guide dogs allowed.
£ No

LIVERPOOL COLLEGIATE APARTMENTS

Shaw Street, Liverpool, Merseyside L6 1NR
Grade II* listed former school built 1843 of red sandstone in Tudor Gothic style, gutted by fire and now converted into residential block.
Grant Recipient: Urban Splash Ltd
Access Contact: Ms Sue Kinsella
T: 0151 708 9449
E-mail: simonhumphreys@urbansplash.co.uk
Open: Exterior only, visible from Shaw Street.
Heritage Open Days: No
P No
Full. No WC for the disabled. No Guide dogs allowed.
£ No

SEFTON PARK

Liverpool, Merseyside L17 1AP
108 hectare public park, designed in 1867, the first to introduce French influence to the design of parks through the designer Edouard André who had worked on the design of major Parisian parks. Sefton Park is Grade II* registered and contains several listed statues and other features. The Grade II* listed Palm House, 1896 by Mackenzie and Moncur, is an octagonal iron frame structure glasshouse which appears as 3 domed roofs, one above the other.
www.palmhouse.org.uk
Grant Recipient: Liverpool City Council
Access Contact: Mrs Linda Barnes
T: 0151 726 9304
E-mail: info@palmhouse.org.uk
Open: Park open at all times. Palm House: 1 April–31 October: Monday–Saturday 10.30am–5pm, Sunday 10.30am-4pm, may be closed on Tuesdays and Thursdays

and from 4pm for events; 1 November–31 March: Monday–Sunday 10.30am–4pm, may be closed on Tuesdays and Thursdays for events. The Trust reserves the right to shut the Palm House on other occasions and will endeavour to give as much notice as possible on the website and information line (tel: 0151 726 2415).
Heritage Open Days: Yes
P On-street parking available on edge of park and at Iron Bridge on Mossley Hill Drive.
Full. No WC for the disabled. Guide dogs allowed.
£ No

THE ARCHES

136 High Street, Newton-le-Willows, Merseyside WA12
Early 19th century entrance archway with flanking buildings. Originally at Haydock Lodge a mile away and rebuilt on the present site in 1840 as a centre piece of Newton's revived market. Later, the entrance to Randall's Nurseries, now a restaurant. The archway has been glazed to form the entrance lobby to the restaurant. Grade II* listed.
Grant Recipient: Mr Bahman Rashidi
Access Contact: Mr Bahman Rashidi
T: 07855 824269   **F:** 0161 4488900
E-mail: bahmancasatapas@hotmail.com
Open: Daily, 9am–10pm.
Heritage Open Days: No
P Spaces: 4
Full. WC for the disabled. Guide dogs allowed.
£ No

WALLASEY UNITARIAN CHURCH

Manor Road, Liscard, Wallasey, Merseyside CH44 1BU
Arts and Crafts chapel interior dating from 1899 with fittings by Bernard Sleigh and craftsmen associated with Bromsgrove Guild.
www.hct.org.uk
Grant Recipient: Historic Chapels Trust
Access Contact: Mr Terry Edgar
T: 0151 639 9707
E-mail: terryedgar@hotmail.com
Open: At all reasonable times by prior arrangement with key holder, Terry Edgar, 5 Mere Lane, Wallasey Village, Wirral CH45 3HY.
Heritage Open Days: Yes
P Restricted on-street parking.
Full. WC for the disabled. Guide dogs allowed.
£ Donations invited.

WEST DERBY COURTHOUSE

Almonds Green, Liverpool L12 5HP
Mid 17th century sandstone Courthouse. Its interior, lit by four mullioned windows contains original court furniture such as stewards and jury benches as well as muniment cupboards for rolls of parchment documents produced by the Manor and Hundred Courts.
www.croxteth.co.uk
Grant Recipient: Liverpool City Council
Access Contact: Ms Irene Vickers
T: 0151 233 6910   **F:** 0151 228 2817
E-mail: croxtethcountrypark@liverpool.gov.uk
Open: 1 April–31 October: Sundays, 2–4pm. All other times by prior arrangement, seven days notice required.
Heritage Open Days: Yes
P On-street parking nearby.
No wheelchair access. No WC for the disabled. Guide dogs allowed.
£ No

NORFOLK

15 ST MARTIN AT PALACE PLAIN (MOVE ON EAST)

Norwich, Norfolk NR3 1RW
Medieval former church, now housing 'Move on East'. Has a fine 16th century tomb for Lady Elizabeth Calthorpe.
www.moveoneast.org
Grant Recipient: Norwich Historic Churches Trust
Access Contact: Ms Amanda Payne
T: 01603 763555   **F:** 01603 220524
E-mail: amanda@moveoneast.org
Open: By prior written arrangement.
Heritage Open Days: No

P In city centre car parks.
Partial. Wheelchair access to ground floor only, by prior arrangement. WC for the disabled. Guide dogs allowed.
£ No

BINHAM PRIORY

Warham Road, Binham, Fakenham, Norfolk NR21 0DQ
One of the most complete monastic ruins in Norfolk. The Benedictine priory was founded in the late 11th Century and has a well-documented history. The nave, with its 13th century west front and great (bricked-up) window, is now the parish church, displaying a screen with medieval saints over-painted with Protestant texts. Church is maintained by Binham PCC. (The ruins are in the guardianship of English Heritage).
www.binhampriory.org
Grant Recipient: Binham PCC
Access Contact: Mr David Frost
T: 01328 830362
E-mail: davidfrost226@btinternet.com
Open: Free access to the ruins at any reasonable time. Church open daily until 6pm in summer and 4pm in winter.
Heritage Open Days: No
P Spaces: 8
Full. WC available when church is open. No WC for the disabled. Guide dogs allowed.
£ Donations welcome.

CHURCH OF ALL SAINTS,

Hargham, Norfolk NR16 2JW
Redundant church of medieval origins with Victorian restorations. The tower stands alone to the west of the body of the church and the nave is a single narrow bay. Chancel is decorated with late 19th century stencilling.
Grant Recipient: Norfolk Churches Trust
Access Contact: Mr & Mrs Amos
T: 01953 455 553
Open: At all times. Key available from Mr and Mrs Amos, Soma House, Station Road, Attleborough, Norfolk NR17 2AS. (Tel: 01953 455 553).
Heritage Open Days: No
P Limited roadside parking.
No wheelchair access. Steps difficult for wheelchair users. No WC for the disabled. Guide dogs allowed.
£ No

CHURCH OF ST MARY THE VIRGIN

Houghton-on-the-Hill, Norfolk PE37 8DP
Ancient church at least 900 years old. Many original features remain including double splay windows, keyhole chancel, Roman brick arch, 12th century North door and early wall paintings. All areas open.
www.saintmaryschurch.org.uk and
www.hoh.org.uk
Grant Recipient: Norfolk County Council
Access Contact: Mr K Simpson
T: 01953 882790
E-mail: kevin-simpson@tiscali.co.uk
Open: All year 2pm–4pm or by prior arrangement.
Heritage Open Days: Yes
P Spaces: 40
Full. No WC for the disabled. Guide dogs allowed.
£ No

FELBRIGG HALL

Felbrigg, Norwich, Norfolk NR11 8PR
17th century house containing its original 18th century furniture and paintings. The walled garden has been restored and features a working dovecote, small orchard and the National Collection of Colchicums. The park is renowned for its fine and aged trees.
www.nationaltrust.org.uk/felbrigg
Grant Recipient: The National Trust
Access Contact: Property Manager
T: 01263 837444   **F:** 01263 837032
E-mail: felbrigg@nationaltrust.org.uk
Open: House: 1 March–31 October: Saturday–Wednesday 11am–5pm. Garden: 1 March–31 October: daily 11am–5pm; 27–31 December: daily 11am–3pm. Estate walks: All year, dawn to dusk.
Heritage Open Days: Yes

P Spaces: 200. Separate parking for disabled and drop-off point.
♿ Partial. Wheelchair access to ground floor, photograph album of first floor. Garden, shop and bookshop (ramp), tea room and restaurant accessible. WC for the disabled. Guide dogs allowed.
£ **Adult:** £8.70 (house & garden), £4.10 (garden). **Child:** £4.10 (house & garden), £1.80 (garden). **Other:** £21.50 (family, house & garden). Admission prices include voluntary Gift Aid. £1.00 off admission price when arriving by public transport.

GATEHOUSE AT BINHAM PRIORY
Binham, Norfolk NR21 0DQ
Ruined 15th century gatehouse to ruined 13th century monastic Binham Priory.
www.norfarchtrust.org.uk or
www.binhampriory.org
Grant Recipient: Norfolk Archaeological Trust
Access Contact: Mr Peter Wade-Martins
T: 01362 667043
Open: Free access to exterior at all times.
Heritage Open Days: No
P Spaces: 10
♿ Full. No WC for the disabled. Guide dogs allowed.
£ No

GREAT HOSPITAL
Bishopgate, Norwich NR1 4EL
Almshouse founded in 1249 to care for aged priests, scholars and paupers. Eagle ward, created in the former chancel of St Helen's church after the Reformation has furnished cubicles and painted ceiling. 15th century refectory and cloisters. Now provides sheltered housing and a care home.
www.greathospital.org.uk
Grant Recipient: Trustees of the Great Hospital
Access Contact: Air Commodore Kevin Pellat
T: 01603 622022   **F:** 01603 766093
E-mail: enquiries@thegreathospital.org
Open: Guided tours for groups by arrangement (tel: 01603 622022) or email enquiries@greathospital.org. Occasional public open days to view church and Eagle ward. See website or local press.
Heritage Open Days: Yes
P Public car park (pay and display) at St Helen's Wharf, Bishopgate.
♿ Partial. St Helen's Church, Refectory and Birkbeck Hall accessible for wheelchairs. WC for the disabled. Guide dogs allowed.
£ Admission charge under review at time of publication.

HOLKHAM HALL VINERY
Wells-next-the-Sea, Norfolk NR23 1AB
Range of late 19th century Glasshouses. Six houses in the range, four of which have been repaired.
www.holkham.co.uk
Grant Recipient: Coke Estates Ltd
Access Contact: Mr D Horton-Fawkes
T: 01328 710227   **F:** 01328 711707
E-mail: enquiries@holkham.co.uk
Open: The walled gardens are not currently open to the public. Access to view the glasshouses by prior arrangement only.
Heritage Open Days: No
P Spaces: 25
♿ Full. WC for disabled available at Holkham Hall. No WC for the disabled. Guide dogs allowed.
£ No

NELSON'S MONUMENT
Great Yarmouth, Norfolk
Grade I listed monument, also knows as Norfolk Pillar. 1817–19 by William Wilkins. The first monument in England to Admiral Lord Nelson (Nelson's Column in Trafalgar Square is 1840-43). Consists of a fluted Greek Doric column on a square pedestal standing on a raised plinth. The column is surmounted by a figure of Britannia in fibreglass standing on a disc supported by Caryatid figures. The figures were of Coade stone when built, replaced in concrete in 1896 and finally in fibreglass during the restoration of 1982–4. Fully restored for the bicentenary celebrations in 2005.
www.nelsonsmonument.org.uk
Grant Recipient: Norfolk Historic Buildings Trust
Access Contact: Dr Douglas Munro

T: 01603 629048   **F:** 01603 629048
E-mail: nhbt@btconnect.com
Open: Exterior can be viewed at all times. The interior and tower are open on 10 days throughout the year (dates to be set), please check the website or with the access contact for dates.
Heritage Open Days: No
P On-street parking.
♿ Partial. Wheelchair access to exterior only. No WC for the disabled. Guide dogs allowed.
£ £6.00 (open days only).

OLD HALL
Norwich Road, South Burlingham, Norfolk NR13 4EY
Small Elizabethan manor house with a painted stucco fireplace, painted stucco mermaids and scrollwork on the front porch, and a long gallery of hunting scenes in grisaille, c1600.
Grant Recipient: Mr P Scupham
Access Contact: Mr P Scupham
T: 01493 750804
E-mail: margaret@moonshinecat.fsnet.co.uk
Open: 1 January–31 March: by prior telephone arrangement with Mr P Scupham or Ms M Steward. No access for guide dogs to the Long Gallery.
Heritage Open Days: Yes
P Spaces: 8. 12 extra parking spaces available in small attached meadow.
♿ Partial. Wheelchair access to ground floor and garden, painted gallery inaccessible. No WC for the disabled. Guide dogs allowed.
£ No

ST ANDREW'S CHURCH
Illington, Norfolk
Medieval Church, restored 1887. Listed Grade II*.
Grant Recipient: St Andrew's Church
Access Contact: Mrs Shaw
T: 01953 498546
Open: Three services a year. At other times, key is available from Mrs Shaw (tel: 01953 498546).
Heritage Open Days: No
P Spaces: 12. Parking in the farmyard.
♿ Partial. Steps into the Church. No WC for the disabled. Guide dogs allowed.
£ No

ST BENET'S LEVEL MILL
Ludham, Norfolk
Typical example of a Broadland drainage mill with tapering red brick tower, white boat shaped cap, sails and fantail. Built in 18th century and altered over the years, it became redundant in the 1940s. Ground and first floors accessible. Information boards on site.
Grant Recipient: Crown Estates Commissioners
Access Contact: Mrs Alison Ritchie
T: 01692 678232
E-mail: alison@ludhamhall.co.uk
Open: Second Sunday in May and first Sunday in August. At other times by prior arrangement with Mrs Alison Ritchie at Hall Farm, Ludham, Great Yarmouth, Norfolk NR29 5NU (tel: 01692 678232) or Mrs Jenny Scaff, Carter Jonas, 6-8 Hills Road, Cambridge CB2 1NH (tel: 01223 346628).
Heritage Open Days: No
P No
♿ No wheelchair access. Guide dog access possible to ground floor only. No WC for the disabled. Guide dogs allowed.
£ No

ST CLEMENT,
Colegate, Norwich, Norfolk NR3 1BQ
15th century church, now a pastoral care and counselling centre. Has a slender tower decorated with lozenges of flushwork (patterns made from flint and stone).
www.norwichchurches.org
Grant Recipient: Norwich Historic Churches Trust
Access Contact: Ms Lucy Tetlow
T: 07921 252951
E-mail: lucy.tetlow@norwich-churches.org
Open: By prior arrangement (tel: 07921 252951 for details) or Saturday mornings.

Heritage Open Days: Yes
P In city centre car parks.
♿ Partial. Wheelchair access to Nave at street level. No WC for the disabled. Guide dogs allowed.
£ No

ST MARGARET-DE-WESTWICK
St Benedict's Street, Norwich, Norfolk
Medieval church, now redundant. Used for art exhibitions.
www.norwichchurches.org
Grant Recipient: Norwich Historic Churches Trust
Access Contact: Ms Lucy Tetlow
T: 07921 252 951
E-mail: lucytetlow@norwich-churches.org
Open: By prior arrangement with Lucy Tetlow (tel: 07921 252 951). Also open for art exhibitions during the summer months and limited exhibitions during winter months.
Heritage Open Days: Yes
P No
♿ Full. No WC for the disabled. Guide dogs allowed.
£ No

ST MARTIN AT OAK
Oak Street, Norwich, Norfolk
15th century former church, now redundant.
www.norwichchurches.org
Grant Recipient: Norwich Historic Churches Trust
Access Contact: Ms Lucy Tetlow
T: 07921 252 951
E-mail: lucy.tetlow@norwich-churches.org
Open: By arrangement with the tenant. Please telephone 07867 801995 for details.
Heritage Open Days: Yes
P Parking meters in St Martin Lane and city centre car parks.
♿ No wheelchair access. No WC for the disabled. No Guide dogs allowed.
£ No

ST MARY, FORDHAM
Downham Market, Norfolk
Medieval aisleless church in rural landscape, now redundant. Listed Grade II*.
Grant Recipient: Fordham St Mary Preservation Trust
Access Contact: Mr Robert Bateson
T: 01366 388399   **F:** 01366 385859
E-mail: bateson@rannerlow.co.uk
Open: By prior arrangement or key may be available from farm opposite church.
Heritage Open Days: No
P Spaces: 12
♿ No wheelchair access. No WC for the disabled. Guide dogs allowed.
£ No

ST PETER AND ST PAUL
Tunstall, Norfolk
Origins of church date to early years of 14th century as evidenced by double piscinas in chancel. Ruined tower and nave never rebuilt. Overlooks Halvergate Marshes, on the edge of the Broads National Park and Weavers Way.
Grant Recipient: Tunstall (Norfolk) Church Preservation Trust
Access Contact: The Secretary
T: 01493 700279   **F:** 01493 700279
E-mail: smore@fsmail.net
Open: Normally all year. If locked, it is due to severe weather. Key available at the Manor House in Tunstall.
Heritage Open Days: No
P Spaces: 6
♿ Full. Wheelchair access is across uneven path. No WC for the disabled. Guide dogs allowed.
£ No

THE DEANERY
56 The Close, Norwich, Norfolk NR1 4EG
13th century with later additions, originally the Prior's lodgings. It remains the residence of the Dean of Norwich. The interior is closed to the public.
www.cathedral.org.uk
Grant Recipient: The Chapter of Norwich Cathedral
Access Contact: The Chapter Steward
T: 01603 218303   **F:** 01603 766032
E-mail: akefford@cathedral.org.uk

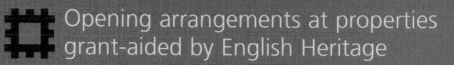

Opening arrangements at properties grant-aided by English Heritage

Open: Exterior visible from The Close which is open to visitors during daylight hours throughout the year.
Heritage Open Days: No
🅿 No
♿ No wheelchair access. No WC for the disabled. No Guide dogs allowed.
💷 No

THURNE DYKE DRAINAGE MILL
Thurne Staithe, Thurne, Norfolk NR29 3BU
Broadland drainage mill c1820 with classic 'hained' appearance and turbine pump. Originally 2 storey tapering circular whitewashed brick tower but raised to 3 storeys in mid 19th century, with timber weatherboarded boat shaped cap, sails and fan.
www.norfolkwindmills.co.uk
Grant Recipient: Norfolk Windmills Trust
Access Contact: Mrs Amanda Rix
T: 01603 222705   **F:** 01603 224413
E-mail: amanda.rix@norfolk.gov.uk
Open: April–September: second and fourth Sunday of each month; National Mills weekend (second weekend in May) 2–5pm and at other times by arrangement.
Heritage Open Days: No
🅿 Spaces: 4. Parking at parish staithe, approx. 100 yards. Pub also allows parking for visitors.
♿ No wheelchair access. No WC for the disabled. No Guide dogs allowed.
💷 Donations invited.

WAXHAM GREAT BARN
Sea Palling, Norfolk NR12 0DY
Grade I listed barn, 1570s-80s, with later additions. Flint with ashlar dressings and thatched roof. Much of its fabric is reused material from dissolved monasteries.
Grant Recipient: Norfolk County Council
Access Contact: Mrs Helen Wiggins
T: 01603 222705   **F:** 01603 224413
E-mail: helen.wiggins@norfolk.gov.uk
Open: Provisional: 4 May–31 October, daily 10.30am–4.30pm. Visitors should ring nearer the time to confirm opening times.
Heritage Open Days: No
🅿 Spaces: 100. Free parking.
♿ Partial. Wheelchair access with assistance (gravel path from car park to Barn). WC for the disabled. Guide dogs allowed.
💷 No

NORTH YORKSHIRE

BENINGBROUGH HALL
Beningbrough, North Yorkshire YO30 1DD
Country house, c1716, contains an impressive Baroque interior exhibiting over one hundred 18th century portraits in partnership with the National Portrait Gallery. A very high standard of craftsmanship is displayed throughout, most of the original work surviving with extremely fine woodcarving and other ornate decoration, and an unusual central corridor running the full length of the house. There is a fully equipped Victorian laundry and a working walled garden which supplies produce for the restaurant.
www.nationaltrust.org.uk/beningborough
Grant Recipient: The National Trust
Access Contact: Property Manager
T: 01904 472027   **F:** 01904 472020
E-mail: beningbrough@nationaltrust.org.uk
Open: House: 1 March–30 June (plus Good Friday), 1 July–31 August, 1 September–31 October: daily except Thursday and Friday 11am–5pm. Grounds and shop: 2 January–28 February Saturday and Sunday 11am–3.30pm; 13–17 February: daily except Thursday and Friday 11am–3.30pm, 1 March–30 June (plus Good Friday) daily except Thursday and Friday 11am–5.30pm, 1 July–31 August: daily 11am–5.30pm, 1 September–31 October: daily except Thursday and Friday 11am–5.30pm, 1 November–20 December Saturday and Sunday 11am–3.30pm.
Heritage Open Days: No
🅿 Spaces: 250
♿ Full. Wheelchairs available on all floors, as well as seating. Steps to entrance with handrail or lift available as well as alternative entrance. Access to ground floor and stairs with handrail or lift to other floors. WC for the disabled. Guide dogs allowed.

💷 **Adult:** £8.40 (house & grounds). **Child:** £4.20 (house & grounds). **Other:** £20.00 (Family: 2 Adults & 3 Children/1 Adult & 4 Children). Group: £6.50 (adult), £4.00 (child). Reduced rate when arriving by cycle.

CASTLE HOWARD,
York, North Yorkshire YO60 7DA
Large stately home dating from the beginning of the 18th century and designed by Sir John Vanbrugh. Situated in 10,000 acres of landscaped grounds, which includes numerous monuments.
www.castlehoward.co.uk
Grant Recipient: The Hon. Simon Howard, Castle Howard Estate Ltd
Access Contact: Hon Simon Howard
T: 01653 648444
E-mail: sh@cashow.net
Open: 15 March–31 October, 27 November–19 December: daily, 11am–4.00pm (grounds only from 10am); November–mid March: grounds open most days but please telephone for confirmation in November, December, January and February. Access to interior of Temple of the Four Winds by prior arrangement only.
Heritage Open Days: No
🅿 Spaces: 300
♿ Partial. Wheelchair access to all but chapel and first floor of exhibition wing. WC for the disabled. Guide dogs allowed.
💷 **Adult:** £12.00. **Child:** £7.00. **Other:** £10.00.

FOUNTAINS HALL
Ripon, North Yorkshire HG4 3DY
Elizabethan mansion, built between 1589 and 1604 for Stephen Proctor. Three rooms; the Stone Hall, the Arkell Room, and the Reading Room, all unfurnished, are open to the public. The conservation of a fourth room, the Great Chamber, has been completed. This upper room features an ornate chimney piece depicting the Biblical story of the Judgement of Solomon. The mansion is situated within a World Heritage Site which also includes the ruins of a 12th century Cistercian Abbey, monastic water mill and Georgian water garden.
www.fountainsabbey.org.uk
Grant Recipient: The National Trust
Access Contact: Property Manager
T: 01765 608888   **F:** 01765 601002
E-mail: fountainsenquiries@nationaltrust.org.uk
Open: As part of the Fountain's Abbey and Studley Royal Estate. 1 March–31 October: daily 10am–5pm; 1 November–31 January 2011 daily (except Friday), 10am–4pm. Estate closed 24, 25 December and Fridays in January, November and December. Deer Park: open all year, dawn to dusk.
Heritage Open Days: Yes
🅿 Spaces: 1200
♿ Partial. Wheelchair access to paved areas only. WC for the disabled. Guide dogs allowed.
💷 **Adult:** £8.25. **Child:** £4.40. **Other:** £22.00 (family). £6.50 (adult, groups 15–30), £3.50 (child, groups 15-30). £6.00 (adult, groups 31+), £3.00 (child, 31+). EH Members free.

GIGGLESWICK SCHOOL CHAPEL
Giggleswick, Settle, North Yorkshire BD24 0DE
Built 1897-1901 by T G Jackson for Walter Morrison as a gift to the school to commemorate the Diamond Jubilee of Queen Victoria. Constructed of Gothic banded rock-faced millstone grit sandstone and limestone, with lead hipped roof to nave and copper covered terracotta dome to chancel. Contains Italian grafitto work throughout.
www.giggleswick.org.uk
Grant Recipient: The Governors of Giggleswick School
Access Contact: The Bursar and Clerk to the Governors
T: 01729 893012   **F:** 01729 893151
E-mail: bursar@giggleswick.org.uk
Open: Monday–Friday 9am–5pm, closed Bank Holidays. Other times by arrangement. Visitors must report to reception to obtain the key to the Chapel.
Heritage Open Days: Yes
🅿 Spaces: 40
♿ Partial. Wheelchair access to ground floor only. WC for the disabled in main school premises. WC for the disabled. No Guide dogs allowed.
💷 No

HOVINGHAM HALL
Hovingham, York, North Yorkshire YO62 4LU
Palladian house built c1760 by Thomas Worsley to his own design. Unique entry through huge riding school. Extensive gardens in a parkland setting. The private cricket ground in front of the house is reported to be the oldest in England.
www.hovingham.co.uk
Grant Recipient: Mr William Worsley
Access Contact: Mrs Kathryn Lamprey
T: 01653 628771   **F:** 01653 628668
E-mail: office @hovingham.co.uk
Open: 1–28 June, 12.30–4.30pm. Last tour 3.30pm.
Heritage Open Days: No
🅿 Spaces: 80
♿ Partial. Wheelchair access to ground floor. WC for the disabled in adjacent village hall. WC for the disabled. Guide dogs allowed.
💷 **Adult:** £7.50. **Child:** £3.00. **Other:** £7.00 (concessions), £5.00 (gardens).

JERVAULX ABBEY
Ripon, North Yorkshire HG4 4PH
Ruins of Cistercian Abbey moved to this site in 1156, built of sandstone ashlar in Early English style. Remains of nave, transepts and choir, with a cloister on the south side of the nave, flanked by a chapter house to the east and a kitchen and dorter to the south.
Grant Recipient: Mr Ian Burdon
Access Contact: Mr Ian Burdon
T: 01677 460391/01677 460226
E-mail: ba123@btopenworld.com
Open: At any reasonable time throughout the year.
Heritage Open Days: No
🅿 Spaces: 55
♿ Partial. Wheelchair access to church, infirmary, frater and cloisters. Uneven terrain and steps on other parts of site. WC for the disabled. Guide dogs allowed.
💷 **Adult:** £2.00 (honesty box). **Child:** £1.50 (honesty box).

MARKENFIELD HALL
Ripon, North Yorkshire HG4 3AD
Fortified moated manor house, built 1310-1323 for John de Markenfield (Chancellor of the Exchequer to Edward II), with further additions and alterations in the 16th, 18th and 19th centuries. Restored 1981-4 and 2001-3.
www.markenfield.com
Grant Recipient: Lady Deirdre Curteis
Access Contact: Mrs Sarah Robson
T: 01765 692303   **F:** 01765 607195
E-mail: info@markenfield.com
Open: 2–15 May and 20 June–3 July: 2–5pm (last entry 4.30pm). Groups with guided tour by prior arrangement all year round.
Heritage Open Days: No
🅿 Spaces: 25
♿ Partial. Wheelchair access to ground floor only. No WC for the disabled. Guide dogs allowed.
💷 **Adult:** £4.00. **Child:** £3.00. **Other:** £3.00 (senior citizens), £80.00 (minimum charge groups out of opening times).

MOWBRAY POINT
The Ruin, Hackfall, Harrogate, North Yorkshire
Folly, built c1750, standing in the Grade I registered remains of the 18th century garden at Hackfall. It is a small pavilion above a steep wooded gorge.
www.landmarktrust.org.uk
Grant Recipient: The Landmark Trust
Access Contact: Mrs Victoria O'Keeffe
T: 01628 825920   **F:** 01628 825417
E-mail: vokeeffe@landmarktrust.org.uk
Open: The Landmark Trust is an independent charity, which rescues small buildings of historic or architectural importance from decay or unsympathetic improvement. Landmark's aim is to promote the enjoyment of these historic buildings by making them available to stay in for holidays. Mowbray Point can be rented by anyone, at all times of the year, for periods ranging from a weekend to three weeks. Bookings can be made by telephoning the Booking Office on 01628 825925. As the building is in full-time use for holiday accommodation, it is not normally open to the public. However, the public have access to and across the terrace all year 11am–4pm and to the

interior by prior arrangement by telephoning the access contact (Victoria O'Keeffe on 01628 825920) to make an appointment. Potential visitors will be asked to write to confirm the details of their visit.
Heritage Open Days: Yes
P Spaces: 2. Parking in Woodland Trust car park.
⟨⟩ No wheelchair access. No WC for the disabled. Guide dogs allowed.
£ No

NATIONAL CENTRE FOR EARLY MUSIC

St Margaret's Church, Walmgate, York, North Yorkshire YO1 9TL
14th century church with highly decorated 12th century Romanesque doorway (removed from chapel of the ruined hospital of St Nicholas, probably during 1684-5 rebuilding of church (orange-red brick tower of same date) occasioned by Civil War damage). Now houses the National Centre for Early Music and used for concerts, music educational activities, conferences, recordings and events.
www.ncem.co.uk
Grant Recipient: York Early Music Foundation
Access Contact: Mrs G Baldwin
T: 01904 632220   **F:** 01904 612631
E-mail: info@ncem.co.uk
Open: All year: Monday–Friday 10am–4pm. Also by prior arrangement. Access is necessarily restricted when events are taking place.
Heritage Open Days: No
P Spaces: 9. 2 parking places for the disabled.
⟨⟩ Full. WC for the disabled. Guide dogs allowed.
£ No

NORTON CONYERS

Wath, Ripon, North Yorkshire HG4 5EQ
Medieval house with Stuart and Georgian additions. Listed Grade II*. Family pictures, furniture and costumes. Visited by Charlotte Bronte in 1839; a family legend of a mad woman confined in an attic room contributed towards the mad Mrs Rochester in 'Jane Eyre' and the house was a model for 'Thornfield Hall'. Located within the walled garden to the west of the house, the 18th century Pleasure Pavillion (Orangery) is a five bay arcaded sandstone building, flanked by Victorian glasshouses. The Orangery is listed Grade II.
Grant Recipient: Sir James Graham Bt
Access Contact: Sir James Graham Bt
T: 01765 640333 or 641290   **F:** 01765 640333
E-mail: norton.conyers@bronco.co.uk
Open: Garden and Orangery: 2 and 3 May, 30 and 31 May: Sundays and Mondays; 6 June–9 August: daily, 7–10 July, 29 and 30 August: 2–5pm (last admission 4.40pm). House: Closed for major repairs.
Heritage Open Days: No
P Spaces: 45. Free car park approx. 50 metres from the garden; parking for the disabled available near garden entrance by arrangement.
⟨⟩ Partial. Main garden path is gravelled and runs up a slight slope. Rest of garden is accessible for wheelchairs. No WC for the disabled. Guide dogs allowed.
£ Entry to Gardens is free, charge is made on charity open days. At other times, donations are welcome.

RIBBLEHEAD VIADUCT

Ribblehead, North Yorkshire
Railway viaduct, 1870-74, rockfaced stone and brick. 104 feet high at highest point. Largest and most impressive of the viaducts of the Settle–Carlisle line of the Midland Railway.
www.settle-carlisle.org
Grant Recipient: British Rail
Access Contact: Mr Keith Lumley
T: 0161 880 3142   **F:** 0161 880 3994
E-mail: keith.lumley@networkrail.co.uk
Open: Viewing from ground level only. Strictly no access from Network Rail property.
Heritage Open Days: No
P On-street parking in Cave.
⟨⟩ No wheelchair access. No WC for the disabled. Guide dogs allowed.
£ No

ST MARY'S CHURCH STAIRS

Whitby, North Yorkshire
Flight of steps originally built of wood in 14th century, replaced in stone now largely 18th and 19th century. Flight of 199 stone steps leading up to the parish church. Listed Grade I.
www.whitbyparish.org.uk
Grant Recipient: PCC of St Mary's Whitby
Access Contact: Canon David Smith
T: 01947 606578   **F:** 01974 602798
E-mail: whitbyparishoffice@btconnect.com
Open: At all times.
Heritage Open Days: No
P Pay and display parking.
⟨⟩ Partial. Wheelchair access for viewing only. WC for the disabled in the church. Guide dogs allowed.
£ No

ST PAULINUS

Brough Park, Richmond, North Yorkshire DL10 7PJ
Catholic neo-Gothic chapel designed by Bonomi with priest's accommodation and school room in undercroft.
Grant Recipient: Mr Greville Worthington
Access Contact: Mr Greville Worthington
T: 01748 812127
E-mail: grev@saintpaulinus.co.uk
Open: By prior arrangement.
Heritage Open Days: No
P Spaces: 2
⟨⟩ Partial. Wheelchair access to downstairs. No WC for the disabled. Guide dogs allowed.
£ No

THORPE PREBEND HOUSE

High St. Agnesgate, Ripon, North Yorkshire HG4 1QR
Late medieval house with 17th century alterations. Restored 2002-4 to form a heritage interpretation centre for the region. The house also has facilities for small scale public events and meetings.
Grant Recipient: Chapter of Ripon Cathedral
Access Contact: The Administrator
T: 01765 603462/ 01765 609076   **F:** 01765 690398
E-mail: ianhorsford@riponcathedral .org.uk
Open: April–end of October: daily except Sunday, 10.30am- 4pm. Occasionally closed for special events, please telephone to check before visiting.
Heritage Open Days: No
P Spaces: 5. Parking available for the disabled.
⟨⟩ Full. WC for the disabled. Guide dogs allowed.
£ **Adult:** £2.00. **Child:** £1.00. **Other:** £1.00 (students).

TRINITY CHURCH TOWER

Market Place, Richmond, North Yorkshire DL10 4QN
Church clock tower to the former castle church, now in the centre of Richmond Market Place.
Grant Recipient: Richmond Town Council
Access Contact: Town Clerk
T: 01748 850 808
E-mail: towncouncil@richmond.org.uk
Open: Access to the exterior at all times from Richmond Market Place.
Heritage Open Days: No
P Spaces: 120. Market Place parking restricted to 2 hours.
⟨⟩ Full. WC for the disabled available in Town Hall opposite. Guide dogs allowed.
£ No

NORTHAMPTONSHIRE

BOUGHTON PARK

Boughton, Northamptonshire NN16 9UP
Extensive remains of formal gardens of late 17th and early 18th century around a country house rebuilt at the same time, set in a park developed from a late medieval deer park. Beyond the park are avenues and rides, also part of the landscape of the late 17th and early 18th centuries. The grant aided Lily pool is approximately 100 meters south of the House.
www.boughtonhouse.org.uk
Grant Recipient: Boughton Estates Ltd
Access Contact: Mr Christopher B Sparrow MRICS
T: 01536 482308   **F:** 01536 410 452

E-mail: csparrow@boughtonestate.co.uk
Open: House: daily 1 August–1 September 2pm–5pm; Grounds: 1 May–1 September, daily (except Saturdays in May–July) 1pm–5pm. The Lily Pond is open as part of the House opening and by appointment when the grounds are open.
Heritage Open Days: No
P Spaces: 100
⟨⟩ Partial. Wheelchair access to ground floor fully accessible, first floor viewable on virtual tour in gift shop. No WC for the disabled. Guide dogs allowed.
£ **Adult:** £3.00 (grounds), £9.00 (house and grounds). **Child:** £1.50 (grounds), £7.00 (house and grounds). **Other:** Family (2+2) £20.00 (house and grounds), family (2+2) £8.00 (grounds only).

HARROWDEN HALL GARDEN STATUES

Wellingborough, Northamptonshire NN9 5AD
Early 18th century Harrowden Hall retains its surprisingly unaltered contemporary garden containing a number of garden features, including statues by the Dutch sculptor Van Nost, of which one has recently been repaired.
Grant Recipient: Wellingborough Golf Club
Access Contact: Mr David Waite
T: 01933 677234   **F:** 01933 679379
E-mail: secretary@wellingboroughgolfclub.com
Open: 27 March to 2 October: Mondays 9am–dusk.
Heritage Open Days: No
P Spaces: 100
⟨⟩ Full. WC for the disabled. Guide dogs allowed.
£ No

LAXTON HALL

Corby, Northamptonshire NN17 3AU
Stone built 18th century manor house, enlarged and modified in 19th century and set in 60 acres of parkland. Stable block by Repton. Formerly a boys school, now a residential home for elderly Poles.
Grant Recipient: Polish Benevolent Housing Association Ltd
Access Contact: Sister Teresa Sabok
T: 01780 444 292   **F:** 01780 444 574
E-mail: Teresa@pbfgroup.co.uk
Open: By prior written arrangement with Sister Teresa at Laxton Hall.
Heritage Open Days: Yes
P Spaces: 10
⟨⟩ Partial. Wheelchair access to ground floor only. WC for the disabled. Guide dogs allowed.
£ No

NORTHUMBERLAND

ALNWICK TOWN HALL

Market Place, Alnwick, Northumberland NE66 1HS
Situated in Alnwick Market Place. Property includes the Hall, the Freemens' Council Room and the Clock Tower. The 18th century building houses the Freemen's Shields and various items of Freemen's History.
Grant Recipient: The Freemens' Common Council
Access Contact: Mr Bob Shepherd
T: 01665 604297
Open: To the exterior at all times and to the interior by prior arrangement.
Heritage Open Days: Yes
P No
⟨⟩ Partial. No WC for the disabled. Guide dogs allowed.
£ No

BRIZLEE TOWER

Hulne Park, Alnwick, Northumberland NE66 3JE
Elaborate Gothick style ornamental tower, dated 1781. An important landscape feature; built as a viewing platform for the 1st Duke of Northumberland. Listed Grade I.
Grant Recipient: Duke of Northumberland
Access Contact: The Estate Office
T: 01665 510777   **F:** 01665 510876
E-mail: enquiries@alnwickcastle.co.
Open: Access to the exterior of the tower when Hulne Park is open: all year, daily 11am–5pm. Please note that the Park is closed to the public on certain days due to shooting activities. Before making a visit, it is strongly recommended that you contact the Park Manager, Mr Gary Whitfield (tel: 07980 630923), to confirm that the

date of your proposed visit does not coincide with a day when the park will be closed.
Heritage Open Days: No
P Roadside parking, 3km from the Tower.
No wheelchair access. No WC for the disabled. No Guide dogs allowed.
£ No

COANWOOD FRIENDS MEETING HOUSE

Coanwood nr. Haltwhistle, Northumberland NE49
Built in 1760, remaining relatively unchanged. Located in a remote valley south of Hadrian's Wall.
www.hct.org.uk
Grant Recipient: Historic Chapels Trust
Access Contact: Michael Long
T: 01661 852104
Open: At all reasonable times.
Heritage Open Days: Yes
P Spaces: 20. On-street parking.
Full. No WC for the disabled. Guide dogs allowed.
£ Donations invited.

CRAGSIDE

Rothbury, Morpeth, Northumberland NE65 7PX
High Victorian mansion by Norman Shaw, with original furniture and fittings including William Morris's stained glass and earliest wallpapers. Built for the inventor-industrialist and armaments manufacturer, Lord Armstrong, who installed the world's first hydro-electric lighting. The mansion is set in a 1,000-acre wooded estate, with rock garden, formal garden, man-made lakes and hydro-electric machinery.
www.nationaltrust.org.uk
Grant Recipient: The National Trust
Access Contact: Ms Justine James
T: 01669 622034   **F:** 01669 620066
E-mail: justine.james@nationaltrust.org.uk
Open: 6-7 March: Saturday and Sunday 12noon–4pm; 13 March–1 April: Tuesday–Friday 1pm–5pm, Saturday and Sunday 11am–5pm; 2–18 April: Tuesday–Sunday 11am–5pm; 20 April–28 May: Tuesday–Friday 1pm–5pm, Saturday and Sunday 11am–5pm; 29 May–6 June: Tuesday–Sunday 11am–5pm; 8 June–23 July: Tuesday–Friday 1pm–5pm, Saturday and Sunday 11am–5pm; 24 July–5 September: Tuesday–Sunday 11am–5pm; 7 September–22 October: Tuesday–Friday 1pm–5pm, Saturday and Sunday 11am–5pm; 23–31 October 11am–5pm. Open Bank Holiday Mondays. Last admission 1 hour before closing. On occasions the house may have to open late or close early if light or temperature levels are too low. Occasional guided tours of house 11am–1pm.
Heritage Open Days: No
P Spaces: 450
Partial. Please telephone 01669 622001 for details of areas accessible for wheelchairs. WC for the disabled. Guide dogs allowed.
£ **Adult:** £13.90 (house, garden & estate), £9.00 (garden & estate). **Child:** £7.00 (house, garden & estate), £4.60 (garden & estate) for 5-17 years. **Other:** £34.70 family (house, garden & estate), £21.60 (garden & estate). Admission prices include Gift Aid donation.

GRACE DARLING MONUMENT

St Aidans Churchyard, Bamburgh, Berwick-upon-Tweed, Northumberland NE69 7AE
Grade II* listed churchyard memorial of 1842. Designed by Anthony Salvin in Gothic Revival style. The tomb was repaired in 1885 by Frederick Wilson, when a new life-size effigy was carved by C R Smith in Portland stone. (The original is in the church). Surrounded by railings with spear-head finials. Grace Darling became a national heroine following the wreck of the steamship Forfarshire on the Farne Islands in September 1838 when she and her father, the keeper of the Longstone Lighthouse, rowed out and rescued 9 survivors.
Grant Recipient: Grace Darling Memorial Trust
Access Contact: Ms Christine Bell
T: 01665 720364
Open: At all reasonable times.
Heritage Open Days: No
P Spaces: 200. Parking in village car park or roadside parking in Radcliffe Road..
Full. WC for the disabled 100 yds away. Guide dogs allowed.
£ No

HEXHAM MOOTHALL,

Market Place, Hexham, Northumberland NE46 1XD
Built c1400 and used as a home, office and court for the Archbishop of York's bailiff who administered Hexhamshire from the Hall. The former stores on the ground floor are now an art gallery, the first floor courtroom houses Northumberland County Council's Museum West Area offices and the second floor hall is used for community activities.
Grant Recipient: Tynedale District Council
Access Contact: Ms Lynn Turner
T: 01434 652346
E-mail: lynn.turner@tnorthumberland.gov.uk
Open: Ground floor is used throughout the year for art exhibitions, craft fairs and other activities. Courtroom and second floor are open for community activities.
Heritage Open Days: Yes
P No
No wheelchair access. WC for the disabled. Guide dogs allowed.
£ No

LAMBLEY VIADUCT

Lambley, Tynedale, Northumberland
17 arch stone viaduct, 100ft high and 1650ft long, spanning the South Tyne river. Originally carried single track, now used as a footpath.
www.npht.com
Grant Recipient: British Rail Property Board/North Pennines Heritage Trust
Access Contact: Ms Carol Robinson
T: 01434 382 294   **F:** 01434 382 043
E-mail: trust@npht.com
Open: At all times as part of the South Tyne Trail between Featherstone Park and Alston.
Heritage Open Days: No
P Spaces: 30
Full. No WC for the disabled. Guide dogs allowed.
£ No

NETHERWITTON HALL

Morpeth, Northumberland NE61 4NW
Grade I listed mansion house built c1685 by Robert Trollope for Sir Nicholas Thornton. Access to main ground floor rooms and external elevations. Built as a family home and remains the current family home.
Grant Recipient: Mr J H T Trevelyan
Access Contact: Mr J H T Trevelyan
T: 01670 772 249
Open: By prior arrangement at least 24 hours in advance. 3–27 May and 7–17 June: Monday–Friday 11am–2pm by compulsory tour. Groups at other times by prior arrangement.
Heritage Open Days: No
P Spaces: 20
Partial. Use of ramps up external steps. WC for the disabled available at village hall. No Guide dogs allowed.
£ **Adult:** £5.00. **Child:** £1.00.

ROCK HALL

Rock, Northumberland NE66 3SB
Grade II* listed manor house, parts dating back to 13th century or early 14th century. Remodelled in early 17th century, and partly ruined after serious fire in 1752. Restorations and extensions in 19th century include south front (c1820) and north-west wing. Set in five acres of grounds. Now a school with additional community use.
Grant Recipient: Rock Hall School Charitable Trust
Access Contact: Rock Hall School Charitable Trust
T: 01665 579224   **F:** 01665 579467
E-mail: rockhallschool@btinternet.com
Open: Access to the exterior all year. To the interior by prior arrangement. Visitors must be accompanied during school term times.
Heritage Open Days: No
P Spaces: 100
Partial. Wheelchair access to ground floor and grounds. WC for the disabled. Guide dogs allowed.
£ Donations for church welcome.

ST CUTHBERT'S CHAPEL

Farne Islands, Northumberland
St Cuthbert's Chapel was completed in 1370. By the early 19th century it was in a ruinous condition. Restored in 1840 by Archdeacon Thorp it includes some fine 17th century woodwork from Durham Cathedral and a memorial to Grace Darling. Remains of an original window.
www.nationaltrust.org.uk
Grant Recipient: The National Trust
Access Contact: Mr John Walton
T: 01665 720651   **F:** 01665 720651
E-mail: john.walton@nationaltrust.org.uk
Open: 1–30 April and 1 August–31 October: daily 10.30am–6pm; 1 May–31 July (breeding season) daily Staple Island 10.30am–1.30pm, Inner Farne 1.30–5pm.
Heritage Open Days: Yes
P Public parking in Seahouses (nearest mainland village).
Partial. Inner Farne is accessible for wheelchairs (telephone the Property Manager in advance). Staple Island is not accessible. WC for the disabled on Inner Farne. Guide dogs are allowed on boat but not on islands.
£ **Adult:** £6.00 (breeding season), £5.00 (outside breeding season). **Child:** £3.00 (breeding season), £2.50 (outside breeding season). **Other:** £3.00 (booked school parties, breeding season, per island), £2.50 (outside breeding season, per island). Admission fees do not include boatmen's charges.

ST MICHAEL'S PANT,

Alnwick, Northumberland
St Michael's Pant (drinking fountain) was built in 1765 by Matthew Mills, designed by Mr Bell. St Michael and Dragon (the symbol of the Town) on top of an octagonal drum, gargoyle for the water spout with large square trough which measures approximately ten square metres. Listed Grade II*.
Grant Recipient: The Freemen of Alnwick
Access Contact: Mr Bob Shepherd
T: 01665 604297
Open: To the exterior at all times.
Heritage Open Days: Yes
P No
Full. No WC for the disabled. Guide dogs allowed.
£ No

SWINBURNE CASTLE

Hexham, Northumberland NE48 4DQ
Kitchen range 1600-1650, incorporating earlier fabric and with later alterations, stands at right angles to the footprint of the now demolished (1966) mid 18th century house which stood on the site of the medieval castle. East (laundry) wing 1770, restored in 2000. Orangery early 19th century.
Grant Recipient: Trustees of R W Murphy
Access Contact: Major R P Murphy
T: 01434 681610
Open: 1, 5–9, 12–16, 19–23, 26–30 April; 3–7, 31 May and 30 August 12 noon–4.30pm.
Heritage Open Days: No
P Spaces: 6
Partial. Wheelchair access to East Wing ground floor only. No WC for the disabled. No Guide dogs allowed.
£ No

VINDOLANDA ROMAN FORT

Bardon Mill, Hexham, Northumberland, NE47 7NJ
Roman Fort and civilian settlement in central sector of Hadrian's Wall with active excavation and education programmes. The site is owned and administered by the Vindolanda Charitable Trust and has an on-site museum, with full visitor services, reconstructed Roman buildings and gardens.
www.vindolanda.com
Grant Recipient: Vindolanda Trust
Access Contact: Mrs Patricia Birley
T: 01434 344277   **F:** 01434 344060
E-mail: info@vindolanda.com
Open: During March and October: daily 10am–5pm, November and December: daily 10am–4pm, April –September: daily 10am–6pm. January and February opening times uncertain at time of publication – please telephone the museum for current information. (Tel: 01434 344277).

Heritage Open Days: No
P Spaces: 60. Coach parking available on-site.
& Partial. Wheelchair access to parts of the archaeological site and all of the museums, gardens and open air museum. WC for the disabled. Guide dogs allowed.
£ **Adult:** £5.90. **Child:** £3.50. **Other:** Senior citizens & students £4.90. Discount for English Heritage members.

WALLINGTON HALL & CLOCK TOWER

Cambo, Morpeth, Northumberland NE61 4AR
Dating from 1688, the house was home to many generations of the Blackett and Trevelyan family. Contains Rococo plasterwork, fine ceramics, paintings and a doll's house collection. Pre-Raphaelite central hall with scenes from Northumbrian history. House, Clock Tower and stable buildings set among lawns, lakes and woodland with walled garden.
www.nationaltrust.org.uk/wallington
Grant Recipient: The National Trust
Access Contact: General Manager
T: 01670 773600   **F:** 01670 774420
E-mail: wallington@nationaltrust.org.uk
Open: House: daily (except Tuesday), 1 March–31 October 1pm–5pm on week days outside school holidays and 11am–5pm at weekends and during school holidays. Walled garden: daily, 1 April–30 September 10am–7pm; October and March; 10am–6pm, 1 November–28 February 10am–4pm. Grounds: daily in daylight hours.
Heritage Open Days: Yes
P Spaces: 500
& No wheelchair access. Lift to first floor for visitors with mobility problems. No WC for the disabled. No Guide dogs allowed.
£ **Adult:** £10.20 (house & gardens), £7.10 (gardens only). **Child:** £5.10 (house & gardens), £3.55 (gardens only). **Other:** £25.50 (family, house & gardens), £17.75 (family, gardens only), £8.30 (groups 15+ house & gardens), £5.75 (groups 15+ gardens only).

NOTTINGHAMSHIRE

CHURCH OF ST MARY

New Road, Colston Bassett, Rushcliffe, Nottinghamshire NG12 3FP
Grade I listed and scheduled monument dating from 1130, now ruined in isolated hill-top position. Former parish church of Colston Bassett set in an open graveyard.
Grant Recipient: P.C.C. of St John the Divine.
Access Contact: Rev E B Gamble
T: 0115 989 3172
E-mail: brongamble@hotmail.com
Open: Access at all times.
Heritage Open Days: No
P Spaces: 7. Additional unlimited on-street parking on New Road.
& Full. No WC for the disabled. Guide dogs allowed.
£ No

KILN WAREHOUSE

Mather Road, Newark, Nottinghamshire NG24 1FB
Grade II* former warehouse. Early example of the use of massed concrete construction. Interior completely destroyed by fire in the early 1990s, the exterior walls have been restored and warehouse converted into offices.
Grant Recipient: British Waterways Midlands & South West
Access Contact: Mr Tom Woodcock
T: 01636 704481 x 4359   **F:** 01636 705584
E-mail: tom.woodcock@britishwaterways.co.uk
Open: The exterior walls for which the property is notable can be viewed without arrangement. Access to the internal courtyard is by prior arrangement with Nick Pogson (tel: 01636 704481 ext. 4314) or Tom Woodcock (tel: 01636 704481 ext. 4359)
Heritage Open Days: No
P Parking is available on adjacent land.
& Full. WC for the disabled. Guide dogs allowed.
£ No

PLEASLEY COLLIERY

Pit Lane, Pleasley, nr. Mansfield, Nottinghamshire
Victorian winding engine house and associated buildings. Engine house contains two steam winding engines under restoration, one turns on electronic motor and work to

dismantle the second engine has started.
www.pleasley-colliery.org.uk
Grant Recipient: Pleasley Pit Trust
Access Contact: Mr Peter Chambers
T: 01623 811231
E-mail: peter-chambers@tiscoli.co.uk
Open: All year: Thursdays 10am–1pm and Sundays 9am–3pm. Group visits by prior arrangement. Access may be restricted January–June due to restoration work.
Heritage Open Days: No
P Spaces: 50. Free parking.
& No wheelchair access. No WC for the disabled. No Guide dogs allowed.
£ No

OXFORDSHIRE

ASTON MARTIN HERITAGE TRUST

Drayton St Leonard, Wallingford, Oxfordshire OX10 7BG
15th century tithe barn, 6 bays. Constructed of elm with hipped roof. Listed Grade II*.
www.amheritrust.org
Grant Recipient: Aston Martin Owners Club
Access Contact: Mrs Anne Wright
T: 01865 400414   **F:** 01865 400200
E-mail: secretary@amheritrust.org
Open: Wednesday afternoons: 2–5pm. At other times by prior arrangement
Heritage Open Days: No
P Spaces: 30
& Partial. Wheelchair access to ground floor only. WC for the disabled. Guide dogs allowed.
£ No

BAPTIST CHAPEL

Shifford Road, Cote, Oxfordshire OX18 2EG
Built around 1739-40 on earlier site and enlarged in 1756.
www.hct.org.uk
Grant Recipient: Historic Chapels Trust
Access Contact: Dr Jennifer Freeman
T: 020 7481 0533   **F:** 020 7488 3756
E-mail: chapels@hct.org.uk
Open: By prior arrangement with the Historic Chapels Trust, St George's German Lutheran Church, 55 Alie Street, London E1 8EB (tel: 020 7481 0533, email: chapels@hct.org.uk).
Heritage Open Days: Yes
P Spaces: 20. On-street parking.
& Full. WC for the disabled. Guide dogs allowed.
£ Donations invited.

BLENHEIM PALACE & PARK

Woodstock, Oxfordshire OX20 1PX
Ancestral home of the Dukes of Marlborough and birthplace of Winston Churchill. Built between 1705-22 for John Churchill, the 1st Duke, in recognition of his victory at the Battle of Blenheim in 1704. Designed by Sir John Vanbrugh, the house contains in its many state rooms a collection of paintings, furniture, bronzes and the Marlborough Victories tapestries. A five-room Churchill Exhibition includes his birth room. 'Capability' Brown park and gardens.
www.blenheimpalace.com
Grant Recipient: Duke of Marlborough
Access Contact: Mrs Heather Carter
T: 01993 810570   **F:** 01993 810580
E-mail: hcarter@blenheimpalace.com
Open: Palace: 13 February–12 December, daily 10.30am–5.30pm (last admission 4.45pm). November and December closed Monday and Tuesday. Park: daily (except Christmas Day) 9am–6pm (last admission 4.45pm).
Heritage Open Days: No
P Spaces: 10000
& Partial. Some rough terrain in the park. WC for the disabled. Guide dogs allowed.
£ **Adult:** £17.50. **Child:** £10.00. **Other:** £14.00.

CHANTRY HOUSE

St Mary the Virgin, Hart Street, Henley on Thames, Oxfordshire RG9 2AR
Grade I listed 14th -15th century, three storey timber framed building with exposed interior timbering and early leaded glazing.

www.stmaryshenley.org.uk
Grant Recipient: PCC of St Mary the Virgin
Access Contact: Mr M Parish Secretary
T: 01491 577340   **F:** 01491 571827
E-mail: office.hwr@lineone.net
Open: May–September: Sundays 2–5pm. At other times by prior telephone arrangement (tel: 01491 577340).
Heritage Open Days: No
P No
& Partial. Wheelchair access to middle floor only. WC for the disabled. Guide dogs allowed.
£ No

CHASTLETON HOUSE

Chastleton, Moreton-in-Marsh, Oxfordshire GL56 0SU
Jacobean house filled with a mixture of rare and everyday objects, furniture and textiles collected since 1612. Continually occupied for 400 years by the same family. Emphasis lies on conservation rather than restoration.
www.nationaltrust.org.uk
Grant Recipient: The National Trust
Access Contact: The Custodian
T: 01608 674981
E-mail: chastleton@nationaltrust.org.uk
Open: 24 March–30 October: Wednesday–Saturday, 1–5pm (last admission 4pm); 29 September–30 October: Wednesday–Saturday, 1–4pm (last admission 3pm). Visitor numbers limited, pre-booking advised (tel: 01608 674981, Monday–Friday between 10am–2pm). Groups by written arrangement with the Custodian.
Heritage Open Days: Yes
P Spaces: 50
& Partial. Wheelchair access to ground floor with assistance and parts of garden only. WC for the disabled. Guide dogs allowed.
£ **Adult:** £8.65. **Child:** £4.10. **Other:** £21.25 (family). Admission prices include voluntary Gift Aid donation. Free to NT members.

CORNBURY PARK

Charlbury, Oxford, Oxfordshire OX7 3EH
400 acre deer park adjacent to Wychwood Forest containing newly restored/replanted beech avenues, ancient English oak trees and several ancient monuments.
www.cornburypark.co.uk
Grant Recipient: The Lord Rotherwick
Access Contact: The Lord Rotherwick
T: 01608 811276   **F:** 01608 811252
E-mail: estate@cpark.co.uk
Open: 1 March–31 October: Tuesdays and Thursdays 10am–4pm. Please note that a permit is required for access to the Park; permit must be applied for in advance. Organised educational access walks for groups by prior arrangement.
Heritage Open Days: No
P Spaces: 20
& No wheelchair access. No WC for the disabled. No Guide dogs allowed.
£ No

FARNBOROUGH HALL

Farnborough, Banbury, Oxfordshire OX17 1DU
Mid-18th century honey-coloured stone built home of the Holbech family for over 300 years, contains impressive plasterwork. Set in grounds with 18th century temples, a terrace walk and an obelisk.
www.nationaltrust.org.uk
Grant Recipient: The National Trust
Access Contact: Mrs Julie Smith
T: 01295 670266   **F:** 01295 671144
E-mail: julie.smith@nationaltrust.org.uk
Open: House and garden: 3 April–29 September, Wednesday and Saturday 2–5.30pm; 2–3 May: Sunday and Monday 2–5.30pm.
Heritage Open Days: No
P Spaces: 10. Additional free parking, 200 yards.
& Partial. Wheelchair access to ground floor of house and garden. Terrace walk may be difficult as it is very steep. No WC for the disabled. Guide dogs allowed.
£ **Adult:** £5.00. **Child:** £2.50. **Other:** £12.00.

MARTYRS' MEMORIAL

St. Giles, Oxford, Oxfordshire OX1
Erected in 1841-3 and designed by Sir George Gilbert Scott, in commemoration of Protestant martyrs, Archbishop Cranmer, Bishops Ridley and Latimer who were burnt to death in 1555 and 1556. The memorial is hexagonal in plan and takes the form of a steeple of three stages reaching a height of 21 metres.
Grant Recipient: Oxford City Council
Access Contact: Mr Nick Worlledge
T: 01865 252147   **F:** 01865 252144
E-mail: nworlledge@oxford.gov.uk
Open: Accessible at all times.
Heritage Open Days: No
🅿 No
♿ Full. No WC for the disabled. Guide dogs allowed.
£ No

SHOTOVER PARK GOTHIC TEMPLE

Wheatley, Oxfordshire OX33 1QS
Early 18th century garden folly. The Gothic Temple/eyecatcher (designer unknown) lies east of the house at the end of a long canal vista. Has a battlemented gable with a central pinnacle and a rose-window, below which is an open loggia of three pointed arches.
Grant Recipient: Shotover Estate Company
Access Contact: Sir Beville Stanier Bt
T: 07778 305419   **F:** 01865 875838
E-mail: BDStanier@aol.com
Open: Access to Temple at all reasonable times (lies close to public rights of way).
Heritage Open Days: No
🅿 Spaces: 50. Parking for a few cars on the drive near the Gothic Temple, otherwise other arrangements can be made in advance with Sir Beville Stanier on 07778 305419.
♿ Partial. Wheelchair access to the Gothic Temple with assistance. No WC for the disabled. Guide dogs allowed.
£ No

SWALCLIFFE TITHE BARN

Shipston Road, Swalcliffe, nr. Banbury, Oxfordshire OX15 5DR
15th century barn built for the Rectorial Manor of Swalcliffe by New College, who owned the Manor. Constructed between 1400 and 1409, much of the medieval timber half-cruck roof remains intact. It is now a museum operated by Oxfordshire Museums Service for the display storage of agricultural and trade vehicles.
www.oxfordshire.gov.uk
Grant Recipient: Oxfordshire Historic Building Trust Ltd
Access Contact: Ms C Anderson
T: 01993 814105   **F:** 01993 813239
E-mail: carol.anderson@oxfordshire.gov.uk
Open: Easter–end of September: Sunday and Bank Holidays, 2–5pm. At other times by prior arrangement (contact Carol Anderson tel: 01993 814105).
Heritage Open Days: No
🅿 Spaces: 10
♿ Full. WC for the disabled. Guide dogs allowed.
£ No

REDCAR AND CLEVELAND

MARSKE HALL

Marske by the Sea, Redcar and Cleveland TS11 6AA
Country house built by Sir William Pennyman in 1625. 2 storeys with 3-storey projecting towers in a 9-bay range forming a symmetrical front approx. 115ft long. Altered in the late 19th and 20th centuries. Varied uses during 20th century include as quarters for the Royal Flying Corps in WWI, Army quarters in WWII, school 1948-58 and since 1963 a Cheshire Foundation nursing home.
Grant Recipient: Teesside Cheshire Homes
Access Contact: Mrs Sue O'Brien or Karen Hutchinson
T: 01642 482672   **F:** 01642 759973
E-mail: marske@ney.leonard-cheshire.org.uk
Open: Hall by prior arrangement only. Grounds open to public at all fund raising events such as the Summer Fete (one Saturday in June).
Heritage Open Days: No
🅿 Spaces: 20
♿ Full. WC for the disabled. Guide dogs allowed.
£ No

SHROPSHIRE

2/3 MILK STREET

Shrewsbury, Shropshire SY1 1SZ
Timber-framed two and a half storey building dating from the 15th century with later alterations and additions. Medieval shop front to rear. Still a shop.
Grant Recipient: Mr M J Cockle
Access Contact: Mr H Carter
T: 01743 276600   **F:** 01743 242140
E-mail: htc@pooks.co.uk
Open: Ground floor shop open 6 days a week all year. Monday–Saturday 9.30am–5.30pm. 1 January–16 February only: upper floor flats can be visited only by prior arrangement with Mr H Carter, Pooks, 26 Claremont Hill, Shrewsbury, Shropshire SY1 1RE.
Heritage Open Days: No
🅿 No
♿ Partial. Wheelchair access to ground floor only. No WC for the disabled. Guide dogs allowed.
£ No

ATTINGHAM PARK

Atcham, Shrewsbury, Shropshire SY4 4TP
Built 1785 by George Steuart for the 1st Lord Berwick, with a picture gallery by John Nash. Contains Regency interiors, Italian neo-classical furniture and Grand Tour paintings. Park landscaped by Humphry Repton in 1797.
www.nationaltrust.org.uk
Grant Recipient: The National Trust
Access Contact: The Property Manager
T: 01743 708162/708123   **F:** 01743 708155
E-mail: attingham@nationaltrust.org.uk
Open: House: 13 March–7 November, daily except Wednesday 1–5.30pm. Guided tours from 11am. 9 January–7 March and 13–28 November for guided tours Saturday and Sundays 11am–3pm. Park: Open daily 9 am–6pm or dusk if earlier. Closed Christmas Day.
Heritage Open Days: Yes
🅿 Spaces: 150. free parking.
♿ Partial. Wheelchair access: to lower ground and ground floors only (house), drives and paths (grounds), shop and carriage house café. WC for the disabled. Guide dogs allowed.
£ **Adult:** £9.40 (house & grounds) £4.20 (park & grounds). **Child:** £5.70 (house & grounds) £2.20 (park & grounds). **Other:** £20.50 (family: house & grounds), £10.40 (family: grounds only), £7.30 (booked parties 15+).

CASTLE HOUSE

Castle Square, Ludlow, Shropshire SY8 1AY
Grade II* listed house within Ludlow Castle. Probably 14th–15th century with late 16th to early 17th century additions. Late 18th century railings and gate. Interior includes decorative plaster ceilings and pendants; fireplaces with fireback and imported 16th–19th century panelling.
www.ludlowcastle.com
Grant Recipient: Powis Castle Estate
Access Contact: Mr Tom Till
T: 01938 552554   **F:** 01938 556617
Open: As part of Ludlow Castle the house is open January and December: Saturday and Sunday 10am–4pm; February, March, October and November: daily 10am–4pm; April–July: daily 10am–5pm; August: daily 10am–7pm. September: daily 10am–5pm. Closed Christmas Day. Please check website for other closed days which may vary.
Heritage Open Days: No
🅿 Town square parking nearby and on-street meter parking.
♿ Full. WC for the disabled. Guide dogs allowed.
£ No

DORTER HOUSE

15 Barrow Street, Much Wenlock, Shropshire TF13 6EN
A detached portion of the former Wenlock Priory Guesten hall, comprising solar chamber and ground floor service accommodation, of early 14th century origin. Some medieval window openings exist. Converted to residential use.
Grant Recipient: Mr and Mrs L de Wet

Access Contact: Mr & Mrs L de Wet
T: 01952 727911
Open: Access to exterior only, 10–14 May and 13–17 September (inclusive) 12 noon–4pm.
Heritage Open Days: No
🅿 Spaces: 35. Public car park off Barrow Street, within 200 meters of Dorter House.
♿ No wheelchair access. No WC for the disabled. No Guide dogs allowed.
£ No

HALSTON CHAPEL

Ellesmere Road, Halston, nr. Whittington, Shropshire
Timber framed chapel dating from mid 16th century with altered additions including west tower of circa 1725. The Chapel stands across the fields from Halston Hall and remains a private chapel. Listed Grade I.
Grant Recipient: Major and Mrs J L Harvey
Access Contact: Mr T Perkins
T: 01691 662 335
Open: By prior arrangement with Mr T Perkins (tel: 01691 662 335). Further public access under review at time of publication, please check the English Heritage website or with the access contact for current information.
Heritage Open Days: No
🅿 Spaces: 20
♿ No wheelchair access. No WC for the disabled. No Guide dogs allowed.
£ No

HOFFMAN KILN CHIMNEY AND DRAW KILN

Llanymynech, Oswestry, Shropshire
Disused lime production buildings of 1899. The smelt flue chimney (Hoffman chimney) built in red brick in English garden-wall bond is a prominent landmark and part of the Llanymynech Limeworks. The brick kiln has 2 tunnel vaults which are entered through 14 round-headed arches and covered by a massive oval earth covered mound.
www.llanymynech.org.uk
Grant Recipient: Shropshire County County
Access Contact: Shropshire Council
T: 01743 255053   **F:** 01743 255001
E-mail: mark.blount@shropshire.gov.uk
Open: At all reasonable times.
Heritage Open Days: Yes
🅿 Spaces: 10. Parking behind Post Office.
♿ Partial. WC for the disabled. No Guide dogs allowed.
£ No

JACKFIELD TILE MUSEUM & FACTORY

Jackfield, Telford, Shropshire TF8 7LJ
Home to the Craven Dunnill factory, where decorative tiles were mass-produced from 1874 until just after the Second World War. Surviving example of a purpose-built Victorian tile factory and continues to manufacture products today.
www.ironbridge.org.uk
Grant Recipient: Ironbridge Gorge Museum Trust
Access Contact: Carol Bowsher or Adrian Vreede
T: 01952 435900   **F:** 01952 435999
E-mail: carol.bowsher@ironbridge.org.uk
Open: Daily, 10am–5pm. Closed 24 and 25 December and 1 January 2010
Heritage Open Days: No
🅿 Spaces: 30. £1.00 per day charge.
♿ Full. WC for the disabled. Guide dogs allowed.
£ **Adult:** £6.75. **Child:** £4.50. **Other:** £6.25 (senior citizens, provisional) Discounted educational rates.

JOHN ROSE BUILDING

High Street, Coalport, Telford, Shropshire TF8 7HT
A range of china painting workshops, centre part dating from late 18th century, outer wings rebuilt early 20th century. Restored and converted to a Youth Hostel, craft workshops and shop. Main entrance is paved with mosaic celebrating the amalgamation of Coalport, Swansea and Nantgarw brands. Coalbrookdale cast iron windows of large dimension line both major elevations.
www.ironbridge.org.uk
Grant Recipient: Ironbridge Gorge Museum Trust
Access Contact: Ms Cath Young/ Manager
T: 01952 588 755   **F:** 01952 588 722
E-mail: ironbridgemanager@yha.org.uk

Open: Access to exterior at all times. This is a working Youth Hostel and access to interior by prior telephone arrangement.
Heritage Open Days: No
P Spaces: 65. Museum car park.
& Partial. Youth Hostel: wheelchair access to ground and first floor (stair lift) with WC and shower facilities for the disabled. China Museum: majority accessible, visiting guide available on arrival. WC for the disabled. Guide dogs allowed.
£ No

LANGLEY GATEHOUSE

Acton Burnell, Shropshire SY5 7PE
This gatehouse has two quite different faces: one is of plain dressed stone; the other, which once looked inwards to long demolished Langley Hall, is timber-framed. Probably used for the Steward or important guests. It was rescued from a point of near collapse and shows repair work of an exemplary quality.
www.landmarktrust.org.uk
Grant Recipient: The Landmark Trust
Access Contact: Mrs Victoria O'Keeffe
T: 01628 825920   **F:** 01628 825417
E-mail: vokeeffe@landmarktrust.org.uk
Open: The Landmark Trust is an independent charity, which rescues small buildings of historic or architectural importance from decay or unsympathetic improvement. Landmark's aim is to promote the enjoyment of these historic buildings by making them available to stay in for holidays. Langley Gatehouse can be rented by anyone, at all times of the year, for periods ranging from a weekend to three weeks. Bookings can be made by telephoning the Booking Office on 01628 825925. As the building is in full-time use for holiday accommodation, it is not normally open to the public. However, the public can view the building by prior arrangement by telephoning the access contact (Vicky O'Keeffe on 01628 825920) to make an appointment. Potential visitors will be asked to write to confirm the details of their visit.
Heritage Open Days: No
P Spaces: 2
& No wheelchair access. No WC for the disabled. Guide dogs allowed.
£ No

LOTON HALL

Alberbury, Shropshire SY5 9AJ
Country house, c1670, but extensively altered and enlarged in the early 18th and 19th centuries. Set in parkland which includes the ruins of the early 13th century Alberbury Castle. Home of the Leighton family since the 14th century.
Grant Recipient: Sir Michael Leighton
Access Contact: Mr Paul Dalton
T: 01691 655334   **F:** 01691 657798
Open: House: 5 January–9 April, Mondays and Thursdays by guided tour only at 10am or 12 noon. Garden and castle can also be viewed at the same times.
Heritage Open Days: No
P Spaces: 30. Access for coaches via back drive.
& Partial. Wheelchair access to ground floor only. 5 steps at front door–ramp can be put in place for wheelchair access. No WC for the disabled. Guide dogs allowed.
£ Adult: £5.00. **Child:** Free. **Other:** £5.00 (senior citizens).

OLD MARKET HALL

The Square, Shrewsbury, Shropshire SY1 1HJ
Old market hall and court house, dated 1596 and listed Grade I. Recently repaired and refurbished to accommodate a Film and Digital Media Centre, including auditorium and cafe/bar.
www.oldmarkethall.co.uk
Grant Recipient: Shrewsbury & Atcham Borough Council
Access Contact: Mr David Jack
T: 01743 256502   **F:** 01743 281283
E-mail: davidjack@musichall.co.uk
Open: Daily, 10am–11pm. Auditorium closed to public when film being screened. Current screening times: Monday–Sunday evening films. Matinee films on most days.
Heritage Open Days: No
P No

& Full. WC for the disabled. Guide dogs allowed.
£ Charges for performances only (Adult £5.50, Child £4.50).

THE LYTH

Ellesmere, Shropshire SY12 0HR
Grade II* listed small country house, c1820, with minor later additions. Cast-iron verandah with trellised supports, one of the earliest and largest examples in the country. Birthplace of E and D Jebb, founders of Save the Children.
Grant Recipient: Mr L R Jebb
Access Contact: Mr L R Jebb
T: 01691 622339   **F:** 01691 624134
Open: To the exterior: 28 March, 16 May, 19 September, 10 October 2–6pm. At other times by arrangement with Mr Lionel Jebb.
Heritage Open Days: No
P Spaces: 40
& Full. No WC for the disabled. Guide dogs allowed.
£ No

THE OLD MANSION

St Mary's Street, Shrewsbury, Shropshire SY1 1UQ
Early 17th century house with original staircase. The building was renovated in 1997 and now provides 4 bedroom suites for the Prince Rupert Hotel.
www.prince-rupert-hotel.co.uk
Grant Recipient: Mr A Humphreys
Access Contact: Mr Michael Matthews
T: 01743 499 955   **F:** 01743 357 306
E-mail: ikematthews@prince-rupert-hotel.co.uk
Open: By prior arrangement with the Prince Rupert Hotel (tel: 01743 499 955).
Heritage Open Days: No
P No
& Partial. Access to ground floor via external entrance, to first floor via Prince Rupert Hotel. WC for the disabled on ground floor of hotel. Guide dogs allowed.
£ No

YEATON PEVEREY HALL

Yeaton Peverey, Shrewsbury, Shropshire SY4 3AT
Mock Jacobean country house, 1890-2 by Aston Webb. Previously a school, now reinstated as a family home. Principal rooms on the ground floor open to visitors.
Grant Recipient: Mr Martin Ebelis
Access Contact: Mr Martin Ebelis
T: 01743 851185   **F:** 01743 851186
E-mail: mae@earlstone.co.uk
Open: By prior arrangement with written confirmation or introduction through known contact.
Heritage Open Days: No
P Spaces: 6. Parking adjacent to the property for the disabled.
& Full. No WC for the disabled. Guide dogs allowed.
£ Adult: £5.00. **Child:** £2.00. **Other:** £5.00.

SOMERSET

BATH ASSEMBLY ROOMS

Bennett Street, Bath, Somerset BA1 2QH
Built in 1771 by John Wood the Younger, now owned by the National Trust and administered by Bath and North East Somerset District Council. Each of the rooms has a complete set of original chandeliers. The Fashion Museum is located on the lower ground floor.
www.fashionmuseum.co.uk
Grant Recipient: Bath City Council/National Trust
Access Contact: Mr Iain Johnston
T: 01225 477752 or 477753
E-mail: iain_johnston@bathnes.gov.uk
Open: Daily: January, February, November and December 10.30am–5pm; March–October 10.30am–6pm when not in use for pre-booked functions. Last admission is one hour before closing. Telephone in advance (01225 477789) to check availability. Closed Christmas Day and Boxing Day.
Heritage Open Days: No
P On-street car parking (pay and display).
& Full. WC for the disabled. Guide dogs allowed.
£ But charge for Museum of Costume.

CHARD GUILDHALL

Fore Street, Chard, Somerset TA20 2PP
Grade II* listed building dating to 1834. Former Corn Exchange and Guildhall, now Town Hall.
www.chard.gov.uk
Grant Recipient: Chard Town Council
Access Contact: Ms Sandra Pittwood
T: 01460 260 371   **F:** 01460 260 372
E-mail: sandra.pittwood@chard.gov.uk
Open: Monday–Friday 9am–5pm, Saturdays 9am–1pm. Public events throughout the year. Also available for hire and the Tourist Information Centre is based in the Guildhall. Access at any other time by prior arrangement.
Heritage Open Days: No
P Public car parks nearby. Disabled parking at the front of the building.
& Full. WC for the disabled. Guide dogs allowed.
£ No

CLEVEDON PIER

The Beach, Clevedon, Somerset BS21 7QU
Pier with attached toll house built c1860s to serve steamers bound for South Wales. Wrought and cast iron structure and shelters consisting of eight 100ft arched spans leading to a landing stage. The exceptionally slender spans are constructed from riveted broad-gauge railway track as designed by W H Barlow for the Great Western Railway. Scottish baronial style toll house contains shop and art gallery. Pier restored in 1999 after partial collapse 30 years earlier and is one of only two Grade I listed piers. This pier is of outstanding importance for its delicate engineering and the relationship of pier to landward buildings, which creates an exceptionally picturesque ensemble.
www.clevedonpier.com
Grant Recipient: The Clevedon Pier and Heritage Trust
Access Contact: Mrs Linda Strong
T: 01275 878846   **F:** 01275 790077
E-mail: enquiries@clevedonpier.com
Open: All year daily (except Christmas Day): 1 January–29 March 10am–4pm; 30 March–26 October 10am–5pm; 27 October–23 December 10am–4pm; 24 and 31 December 10am–1pm. Please check opening times on website prior to visit.
Heritage Open Days: No
P Car parking on seafront.
& Partial. No wheelchair access to art gallery. No WC for the disabled. No Guide dogs allowed.
£ Adult: £1.50. **Child:** 75p. **Other:** £1.00 (over 60s).

ENGLISHCOMBE TITHE BARN,

Rectory Farmhouse, Englishcombe, Bath, Somerset BA2 9DU
Early 14th century cruck framed tithe barn. Recently restored with new crucks, masonry and straw lining to the roof, and filigree windows unblocked. There are masons and other markings on the walls.
Grant Recipient: Mrs Jennie Walker
Access Contact: Mrs Jennie Walker
T: 01225 425073
E-mail: jennie.walker@ukonline.co.uk
Open: Bank Holidays 2–6pm; all other times by arrangement with Mrs Walker (tel: 01225 425073). Closed 18 December 2009–2 April 2010.
Heritage Open Days: Yes
P Spaces: 34. Drop off at door facility.
& Full. WC for the disabled. Guide dogs allowed.
£ Donations invited.

FAIRFIELD

Stogursey, nr. Bridgwater, Somerset TA5 1PU
Elizabethan and medieval house and Grade II* listed. Undergoing repairs. Occupied by the same family (Acland-Hoods and their ancestors) for over 800 years. Woodland garden with views of the Quantocks and the sea.
Grant Recipient: Lady Gass
Access Contact: Lady Gass
T: 01278 732251   **F:** 01278 732277
Open: House: 14 April–31 May and 9–23 June: Wednesday, Thursday, Friday and Bank Holiday Mondays by guided tour at 2.30pm and 3.30pm. Groups also at other times by prior arrangement. Garden: also open for NGS and other charities on dates advertised in Spring. No inside photography. No dogs except Guide Dogs.
Heritage Open Days: No

Opening arrangements at properties grant-aided by English Heritage

P Spaces: 30. No parking for coaches.

& Full. WC for the disabled. Guide dogs allowed.

£ Adult: £5.00. Child: £1.00. Other: Admission charges in aid of Stogursey Church.

FORDE ABBEY

Chard, Somerset TA20 4LU

Cistercian monastery founded in 1140 and dissolved in 1539 when the church was demolished. The monks quarters were converted in 1640 into an Italian style "palazzo" by Sir Edmund Prideaux. Interior has plaster ceilings and Mortlake tapestries.

www.fordeabbey.co.uk

Grant Recipient: Trustees of the Roper Settlement

Access Contact: Mrs Clay

T: 01460 220231

E-mail: info@fordeabbey.co.uk

Open: Gardens; daily, 10am–4.30pm. House: April–October; Tuesday–Friday, Sunday and Bank Holidays 12 noon–4pm.

Heritage Open Days: No

P Spaces: 500

& Partial. Wheelchair access to ground floor and garden. WC for the disabled. Guide dogs allowed.

£ Adult: £9.00. Child: Free. Other: £8.50 (senior citizen).

HIGHER FLAX MILLS (JOHN BOYD TEXTILES LTD)

Torbay Road, Castle Cary, Somerset BA7 7DY

Listed Grade II*, Higher Flax Mills is one of the largest and unusually complete examples of an integrated rope and twine works in the West Country, a significant regional industry in the 19th century. Part of the site is used by John Boyd Textiles, Horsehair fabric manufacturer, established in 1837 and still using the original looms of 1870. The company is unique in being the only horsehair weaving factory in the world that uses power looms.

www.johnboydtextiles.co.uk

Grant Recipient: South Somerset District Council

Access Contact: John Boyd Textiles Ltd

T: 01963 350 451   **F:** 01963 351 078

E-mail: enquiries@johnboydtextiles.co.uk

Open: By prior arrangement only: Tuesdays, Wednesdays or Thursdays. Individual visitors are invited to join groups of 10 or more (maximum 25) for tours. 1–2 tours per week during summer months. First tour 10am, last tour 2.30pm.

Heritage Open Days: No

P Spaces: 7. By the Gatehouse.

& No wheelchair access. WC for the disabled. No Guide dogs allowed.

£ Adult: £4.00. Child: £2.00. Other: By prior arrangement only.

MANOR FARM HOUSE

Meare, Glastonbury, Somerset BA6 9SP

14th century summer residence of The Abbots of Glastonbury, now a farmhouse with 16th century alterations. L shaped in plan, the interior has a former open hall with large stone hooded fireplace. Two storey south porch with a stone figure finial in robes postulated as Abbot Richard Whiting of Glastonbury. Range of 18th and 19th century outbuildings incorporating remains of medieval fabric.

Grant Recipient: Mr Look

Access Contact: Mr Robyn Look

T: 01458 860242

E-mail: robynlook@yahoo.co.uk

Open: 3, 4 and 5 April; 1, 2, 3, 29, 30 and 31 May; 3, 4, 10, 11, 17, 18, 24, 25, and 31 July; 1, 7, 8, 14, 15, 21, 22, 28, 29 and 30 August 9am–5pm. In addition, wall paintings can be viewed on these dates by prior arrangement (tel: 01458 860242).

Heritage Open Days: No

P Spaces: 4. Visitors need to take care as the buildings are on a working farm.

& No wheelchair access. No WC for the disabled. Guide dogs allowed.

£ No

PRIOR PARK COLLEGE OLD GYMNASIUM

Ralph Allen Drive, Bath, Somerset BA2 5AH

Built for Ralph Allen in the mid-18th century as an early and successful demonstration of the quality of Bath stone. The Old Gymnasium is part of the mid-19th century

additions to adapt the property as a Catholic seminary for Bishop Baines. Now a boarding and day school.

www.priorpark.co.uk

Grant Recipient: Governors of Prior Park College

Access Contact: Mrs J K Barr

T: 01225 837491   **F:** 01225 835753

E-mail: bursar@priorpark.co.uk

Open: 23–27 August: daily 10.30am–4pm. Group tours during school holidays, otherwise by prior arrangement. Please telephone in advance.

Heritage Open Days: No

P Spaces: 50

& Partial. Limited by slope of the ground. Uneven ground and steps make wheelchair access difficult. WC for the disabled in school theatre nearby. Guide dogs allowed.

£ No

ROWLANDS MILL

Rowlands, Ilminster, Somerset TA19 9LE

Grade II* stone and brick 3-storey millhouse and machinery, c1620, with a mill pond, mill race, overshooting wheel and waterfall. The millhouse is now a holiday let but the machinery has separate access and is in working condition.

Grant Recipient: Mr P G H Speke

Access Contact: Mr P G H Speke

T: 01460 52623   **F:** 01460 52623

Open: Millhouse Fridays and machinery Monday–Friday 10am–4pm by prior written arrangement (at least 1 week's notice required). Heritage Open Days machinery only unless a Friday, then whole building.

Heritage Open Days: Yes

P Spaces: 7

& Partial. Wheelchair access to ground floor only. WC for the disabled at Rowlands House nearby. Guide dogs allowed.

£ No

ST ANDREWS

Stogursey, Somerset

Benedictine priory church, now parish church. Listed Grade I.

Grant Recipient: St Andrews PCC, Church of England

Access Contact: Mr D Mott

T: 01278 632670

E-mail: derekmott401@msn.com

Open: Daily during daylight hours.

Heritage Open Days: No

P Spaces: 6

& Partial. Wheelchair access to most areas except the High Altar, ramp available on request. No WC for the disabled. Guide dogs allowed.

£ No

ST GEORGE'S BRISTOL

Great George Street, Bristol BS1 5RR

Grade II* listed Georgian former church, c1821-3, by Robert Smirke in Greek Revival style, now 550 seater concert hall. A Waterloo church, built as a chapel-of-ease to Cathedral of St Augustine, and converted to a concert hall in 1987. The crypt now houses a café and art gallery.

www.stgeorgesbristol.co.uk

Grant Recipient: St George's Bristol

Access Contact: Ms Jennifer Hutchinson

T: 0117 929 4929   **F:** 0117 927 6537

E-mail: j.hutchinson@stgeorgesbristol.co.uk

Open: For seasonal concert programmes; mainly evenings, some lunchtimes and Sunday afternoons, contact the Box Office on 0845 40 24 001 for brochure. Free access to crypt and art gallery from 1 hour before concerts. Tours can be arranged if dates comply with events schedule.

Heritage Open Days: No

P Spaces: 3

& Partial. Wheelchair access via Charlotte Street. The auditorium stalls, crypt, café, gallery and Box Office are accessible but preferable if you ring in advance as entry is not straightforward. WC for the disabled. Guide dogs allowed.

£ Tickets required for concerts.

ST MARGARET'S ALMSHOUSES

Taunton, Somerset TA1 2EQ

Converted 16th century almshouses built on site of 12th century leper hospital. Listed Grade II*. 16th century conversion/repair undertaken through services of Abbot Bere of Glastonbury Abbey. Remained as almshouses until

1938 when it became HQ of the Rural Community Council and Somerset Guild of Craftsmen. Building stood unused from the late 1980s and became derelict. Purchased, repaired and converted into social housing by the Somerset Building Preservation Trust in 1999. Occupied by tenants of Falcon Rural Housing.

Grant Recipient:

Access Contact: Ms Sam Southam

T: 01823 667 343   **F:** 01823 661726

E-mail: sam@falconhousing.co.uk

Open: By prior arrangement only on the following days: Wednesdays, 24 March, 26 May, 21 July and 22 September 10am–2pm.

Heritage Open Days: No

P No

& Full. Level access only for wheelchair users. No WC for the disabled. Guide dogs allowed.

£ No

SOUTH YORKSHIRE

HICKLETON HALL

Hickleton, South Yorkshire DN5 7BB

Georgian Mansion, Grade II* listed, built in the 1740s to a design by James Paine with later additions. The interior is noted for its plasterwork ceilings. Set in 15 acres of formal gardens laid out in the early 1900s, the Hall is now a residential care home.

Grant Recipient: Sue Ryder Care

Access Contact: The Administrator

T: 01709 892070   **F:** 01709 890140

E-mail:

Open: By prior arrangement with the administrator at Sue Ryder Care, Monday–Friday 2–4pm.

Heritage Open Days: No

P Parking available.

& Partial. WC for the disabled. Guide dogs allowed.

£ Donations welcome.

THE LYCEUM THEATRE

Tudor Square, Sheffield, South Yorkshire S1 1DA

Grade II* listed theatre built 1897. The only surviving example of the work of WGR Sprague outside London. Its special features include a domed corner tower, a lavish Rococo auditorium (1097 seats) and a proscenium arch with a rare open-work valance in gilded plasterwork. A notable example of a theatre of the period, with a largely unaltered interior.

www.sheffieldtheatres.co.uk

Grant Recipient: The Lyceum Theatre Trust

Access Contact: Mr Dan Bates

T: 0114 201 3832   **F:** 0114 249 6003

E-mail: info@sheffieldtheatres.co.uk

Open: Performances throughout the year. 21 scheduled backstage tours per year. All tours commence at 10.30am. Group guided tours by prior arrangement. Contact the Box Office (tel: 0114 249 6000) or check the website for further information.

Heritage Open Days: Yes

P Spaces: 600. National Car Park adjacent to the theatre.

& Partial. Wheelchair access to all areas except two private entertaining rooms. WC for the disabled. Guide dogs allowed.

£ Adult: £3.00 (backstage tour). Other: Admission charge for performances.

WENTWORTH CASTLE GARDENS AND STAINBOROUGH PARK

Lowe Lane, Stainborough, nr. Barnsley, South Yorkshire S75 3ET

Wentworth Castle and Stainborough Park is a Grade I registered landscape comprising a 500 acre parkland and a 60 acre pleasure gardens and containing 26 listed buildings and monuments. The gardens were laid out in the 18th century by Sir Thomas Wentworth, 1st Earl of Strafford and his son William, 2nd Earl. The gardens fell into neglect during the 20th century. In 2005, work began on a major programme to restore the estate. The gardens are home to the National Plant collections of rhododendrons, camellias and magnolias.

www.wentworthcastle.org

Grant Recipient: Wentworth Castle and Stainborough Park Heritage Trust

Access Contact: Ms Vicky Martin

T: 01226 776040 **F:** 01226 776042
E-mail: heritage@wentworthcastle.org
Open: Parkland: daily, all year; Gardens: daily, summer
(April–September) 10am–5pm, winter (October–March)
10am–4pm. Last admission one hour before closing.
Closed Christmas day.
Heritage Open Days: Yes
P Spaces: 200. Disabled parking adjacent to Visitor
Centre.
& Full. WC for the disabled. Guide dogs allowed.
£ **Adult:** £4.50. **Child:** £2.50. **Other:** £3.50
(concession). Admission prices subject to change in 2010.

STAFFORDSHIRE

10 THE CLOSE

Lichfield, Staffordshire WS13 7LD
Early 15th century timber-framed house, originally one-up one-
down and part of a five-dwelling range in the Vicar's Close.
Notable doors and solid tread staircase remains in attic.
Grant Recipient: Dean & Chapter of Lichfield Cathedral
Access Contact: Administrator
T: 01543 306100 **F:** 01543 306109
E-mail: enquiries@lichfield-cathedral.org
Open: By prior written arrangement with Cathedral
Chapter Office.
Heritage Open Days: No
P Public car parks nearby.
& No wheelchair access. WC for disabled available in The
Close. Guide dogs allowed.
£ No

BISHTON HALL DORIC SCREEN

Woseley Bridge, Staffordshire ST17 0XN
1840s screen with a summerhouse at the centre, in the
form of a Greek Doric temple, with flanking porticos and
terrace. Listed Grade II*. The screen might have been built
to screen the gardens from the nearby Trent Valley Railway
Line, which was built in 1845-7.
Grant Recipient: St Bede's School Limited
Access Contact: The Administrator
T: 01889 881277 **F:** 01889 882749
E-mail: admin@saintbedes.com
Open: 4–8 January, 29 March–1 April, 13–16 April, 19–23
July, 26–30 July, 2–6 August 10am–2pm. Please report to
the School Office on arrival.
Heritage Open Days: No
P Spaces: 5
& Partial. Steps up to the screen. No WC for the disabled.
No Guide dogs allowed.
£ No

CHEDDLETON FLINT MILL,

**Cheddleton, Leek, nr. Stoke-on-Trent, Staffordshire
ST13 7HL**
18th century complex for grinding flint comprising two
working watermills. South Mill modified in 19th century
and now contains displays relating to the pottery industry.
www.people.ex.ac.uk/akoutram/cheddleton-mill
Grant Recipient: Cheddleton Flint Mill Industrial Heritage
Trust
Access Contact: Mr E E Royle, MBE
T: 01782 502907
Open: April–September (including Bank Holidays),
Saturday–Sunday 1pm–5pm. Weekdays by arrangement
(tel: 01782 502907).
Heritage Open Days: No
P Spaces: 16
& Partial. Wheelchair access to ground floor only. WC for
the disabled. Guide dogs allowed.
£ No

CHILLINGTON HALL

**Codsall Wood, nr. Wolverhampton, Staffordshire
WV8 1RE**
House by Sir John Soane with earlier wing by Francis Smith
(1724). Home of the Giffard family for over 800 years.
Extensive grounds with gardens landscaped by Capability
Brown.
www.chillingtonhall.co.uk
Grant Recipient: Mr J W Giffard
Access Contact: Mr J W Giffard
T: 01902 850236 **F:** 01902 850 768
E-mail: info@chillingtonhall.co.uk

Open: Hall & Grounds: 12 April–27 May
Monday–Thursday 2pm–5pm (last admission 4pm). Parties
at other times by prior arrangement.
Heritage Open Days: No
P Spaces: 100. Unlimited parking.
& Full. WC for the disabled. Guide dogs allowed.
£ **Adult:** £6.00. **Child:** £3.00. **Other:** Free to HHA
members.

CLIFTON HALL

Clifton Campville, Staffordshire B79 0BE
Small country house built in 1705, perhaps by Francis
Smith of Warwick for Sir Charles Pye. Two monumental
wings flanking a courtyard, the intention being to link
them with a central main building which was never
constructed. This strange history explains why the Hall
unusually developed out of what would have been the
servants wing.
www.richardblunt.com
Grant Recipient: Mr Richard Blunt
Access Contact: Mr Richard Blunt
T: 01827 373111 **F:** 01827 373111
E-mail: richard@richardblunt.com
Open: By prior arrangement only, any weekday 9am–5pm
all year.
Heritage Open Days: No
P Spaces: 10
& Full. No WC for the disabled. Guide dogs allowed.
£ **Adult:** £5.00. **Child:** £2.00. **Other:** £2.00.

HAMSTALL HALL

Hamstall Ridware, Staffordshire WS15 3RS
Small scheduled monument known as 'The Porch', with
stone balcony, now restored and two stone fireplaces.
Restored oak doors and windows. Some carvings on the
stone balcony. Interior is made up of two rooms.
Grant Recipient: Mr and Mrs Shore
Access Contact: Mr & Mrs Shore
T: 0121 382 6540 office hrs only
Open: By prior arrangement with Mr and Mrs Shore.
Heritage Open Days: No
P No
& No wheelchair access. No WC for the disabled. No
Guide dogs allowed.
£ No

MALTHOUSE

Malthouse Road, Alton, Staffordshire ST10 4AG
Rare underground malthouse. Brick vaulted cellars and
network of tunnels. Listed Grade II*. Used to produce malt
for brewing from late 17th century.
enquiries@the-malthouse.com
Grant Recipient: Owen John Venables
Access Contact: Mr Owen John Venables
T: 01538 703 273
E-mail: enquiries@the-malthouse.com
Open: 5 April–11 October: Sundays 10am–2pm (last
admittance 1.30pm).
Heritage Open Days: Yes
P On-street parking.
& No wheelchair access. No WC for the disabled. Guide
dogs allowed.
£ No

MIDDLEPORT POTTERY

**Port Street, Middleport, Stoke on Trent,
Staffordshire ST6 3PE**
Grade II* listed pottery works built 1888-9 in brick and
terracotta. The site includes a Burgundy bottle oven, the
largest now standing in Stoke-on-Trent. In use by
Burleigh–a family pottery business established in 1851 and
still manufacturing using Victorian methods and
machinery.
www.burleigh.co.uk
Grant Recipient: Burgess Dorling & Leigh
Access Contact: Mrs Rosemary Dorling
T: 01782 577 866 **F:** 01782 575 529
E-mail: sales@burleigh.co.uk
Open: All year: Wednesdays 10am guided tour only,
except during Potters holidays (usually last week of June,
first week of July, last week of August and 2 weeks over
Easter). At all other times by prior arrangement. Due to
hazardous nature of the site, minimum age for children is
10 years.

Heritage Open Days: Yes
P Spaces: 12. Weekday parking, 12 spaces. Weekend
parking, 24 spaces. Additional on-street parking available.
& Partial. Wheelchair access to shop only. No WC for the
disabled. Guide dogs allowed.
£ **Adult:** £5.00 (tours only).

SHUGBOROUGH

Milford, Stafford, Staffordshire ST17 0XB
The present house was begun c1695. Between 1760 and
1770 it was enlarged and refashioned by James
"Athenian" Stuart and again partly remodelled by Samuel
Wyatt at end of 18th century. The interior is particularly
notable for its plaster work and other decorations.
Ancestral home of the Earls of Lichfield. Houses the
Staffordshire County Museum in the Servants Quarters,
Georgian working farm, restored Walled Garden and Rare
Livestock Breed project. The estate is set in 900 acres of
parkland with monuments of national importance and 22
acres of grade I listed formal gardens.
www.shugborough.org.uk
Grant Recipient: The National Trust
Access Contact: Ms Liz Carruthers / Group Manager
T: 01889 881388 **F:** 01889 881323
E-mail: shugborough.promotions@staffordshire.gov.uk
Open: Estate open 19 March–28 October: daily
11am–5pm (last admission 4.30pm). Open Bank Holiday
Mondays. Tours for groups throughout the year, daily
10.30am. Evening tours also available.
Heritage Open Days: No
P Spaces: 250. The estate is car free and parking is close
to the walled garden. Accessible transport runs throughout
the day from the car park to the Servants quarters and
House.
& Partial. Wheelchair access to ground floor of house and
museum only. Access to the Mansion House is via 8 steps,
stair climber available for these. WC for the disabled.
Guide dogs allowed.
£ **Adult:** £12.00. **Child:** £7.00. **Other:** £30.00 (family
2+3), £9.50 (concessions), £15.00 (family 1+1), free to
house for NT members.

SINAI HOUSE

**Shobnall Road, Burton on Trent, Staffordshire DE14
2BB**
Timber-framed E-shaped house, two-thirds derelict, on
moated hill-top site, dating from the 13th century. House
built variously during 15th, 16th and 17th centuries with
later additions, including wall paintings and carpenters
marks. 18th century bridge and plunge pool in the
grounds.
Grant Recipient: Ms C A Newton
Access Contact: Ms C A Newton
T: 01283 544161/01283 840732 **F:** 01283 841084
E-mail: kate@brookesandco.net
Open: By prior arrangement only. Minimum of one week's
notice required.
Heritage Open Days: No
P Spaces: 10
& Partial. Temporary ramps to internal steps can be
arranged. No WC for the disabled. Guide dogs allowed.
£ Donations requested.

TRENTHAM MAUSOLEUM

Stone Road, Trentham, Stoke on Trent
Built circa 1808 in a neo-Egyptian style, designed by
Charles Heathcote Tatham. Monumental exterior. Stone
vaulted ceiling inside. Erected for the Marquis of Stafford,
later Duke of Sutherland. All tombs of the Sutherland
family have been removed. Listed Grade I.
Grant Recipient: Stoke on Trent City Council
Access Contact: Mr Richard Marsland
T: 01782 232154
E-mail: heritage@stoke.gov.uk
Open: To the exterior at all reasonable times and to the
interior by prior arrangement.
Heritage Open Days: No
P On-street parking.
& Partial. Wheelchair access to exterior unrestricted on flat
land. Access to interior is restricted by two steps to entrance.
No WC for the disabled. No Guide dogs allowed.
£ No

SUFFOLK

ABBEY FARM BARN

Snape, Saxmundham, Suffolk IP17 1RQ
Grade II* listed Aisled barn. Circa 1300. Built by resident monks living in adjacent Priory (no remains standing above ground). Refurbished and still used by farmer for storage.
Grant Recipient: Mr & Mrs Raynor
Access Contact: Mr & Mrs Raynor
T: 01728 688088
Open: By prior arrangement.
Heritage Open Days: No
P Spaces: 10
Full. No WC for the disabled. Guide dogs allowed.
£ No

BARDWELL WINDMILL

School Lane, Bardwell, Suffolk IP31 1AD
Grade II* listed tower mill, under restoration. Circa 1830; a beam in the cap frame bears the date 1823. Ground floor and 3 upper floors, with tarred red brick tower. Machinery largely intact. Sails being built on the premises. Two pairs of over-driven millstones a flour sifter and underground driving shaft in adjacent out building.
www.bardwellvillage.info/
Grant Recipient: Messrs Jonathan & David Wheeler & Ms Susan Wooster
Access Contact: Messrs Jonathan & David Wheeler & Ms Susan Wooster
T: 01359 251331/07887 912624
E-mail: jwheeler@wheeler-steam.co.uk
Open: Daily (except Christmas and New Year), 10am–4pm. Advisable to telephone before visiting to check open.
Heritage Open Days: Yes
P On-street parking.
Partial. Wheelchair access to exterior. No WC for the disabled. Guide dogs allowed.
£ Donations welcome.

BUNGAY CASTLE

Waveney, Suffolk NR35 1DD
Two remaining towers of gatehouse to castle built in 1294 by Roger Bigod. Visitor centre houses tourist information, heritage area with interactive material and a model of medieval Bungay.
Grant Recipient: Bungay Castle Trust
Access Contact: Mr Peter Morrow
T: 01986 892361
Open: Winter: 1 January–1 April, 1 November–31 December Tuesday–Sunday 11am–3pm; Summer: 2 April–31 October Monday–Sunday 10am–5pm.
Heritage Open Days: No
P Public car park approximately 150 metres.
Partial. Access to keep area may be difficult for wheelchair users. WC for disabled in Visitor Centre. Guide dogs allowed.
£ No

FRESTON TOWER

Freston, Babergh, Suffolk IP9 1AD
Elizabethan six-storey tower built in 1578 by Thomas Gooding, an Ipswich Merchant, to demonstrate his wealth and status and probably used as a look-out tower. Overlooks the estuary of the River Orwell.
www.landmarktrust.org.uk
Grant Recipient: The Landmark Trust
Access Contact: Mrs Victoria O'Keeffe
T: 01628 825920   **F:** 01628 825417
E-mail: vokeeffe@landmarktrust.org.uk
Open: The Landmark Trust is an independent charity, which rescues small buildings of historic or architectural importance from decay or unsympathetic improvement. Landmark's aim is to promote the enjoyment of these historic buildings by making them available to stay in for holidays. Freston Tower can be rented by anyone, at all times of the year, for periods ranging from a weekend to three weeks. Bookings can be made by telephoning the Booking Office on 01628 825925. The public can also view the building on eight Open Days throughout the year (dates to be set) or by prior arrangement; telephone the

access contact Victoria O'Keeffe on 01628 825920 to make an appointment. Potential visitors will be asked to write to confirm the details of their visit.
Heritage Open Days: No
P Spaces: 2
No wheelchair access. No WC for the disabled. Guide dogs allowed.
£ No

ICKWORTH HOUSE, PARK AND GARDEN

Horringer, Bury St Edmunds, Suffolk IP29 5QE
The Earl of Bristol created this eccentric house, with its central rotunda and curved corridors, in 1795 to display his collections. These include paintings by Titian, Gainsborough and Velazquez and a Georgian silver collection. The house is surrounded by an Italianate garden set in a 'Capability' Brown park with woodland walks, deer enclosure, vineyard, Georgian summerhouse, church, canal and lake.
www.nationaltrust.org.uk/ickworth
Grant Recipient: The National Trust
Access Contact: Property Manager
T: 01284 735270   **F:** 01284 735175
E-mail: ickworth@nationaltrust.org.uk
Open: House: 1 March–31 October Friday–Tuesday, 11am–5pm (gardens open 10am); Gardens: 1 February–12 March daily 11am–4pm, 13 March–1 November daily 10am–5pm, 2 November–31 December daily 11am–4pm. Park open daily, 8am–8pm (closes dusk if earlier). Park and Gardens open daily during Suffolk County Council school holidays. Closed 24, 25 and 26 December.
Heritage Open Days: Yes
P Spaces: 200
Partial. Wheelchair access to House: ramped access (restricted access in House for large powered vehicles/chairs); lift to first floor; stair-lift to basement (shop and restaurant) suitable for wheelchair users able to transfer; wheelchair on each floor. Garden largely accessible, some changes of level, gravel drive and paths. West Wing: all floors accessible. Separate parking in visitor car park (200 yards). WC for the disabled. Guide dogs allowed.
£ **Adult:** £9.15 (House & garden), £4.65 (garden). **Child:** £3.65 (House & garden), £1.15 (garden). **Other:** £21.90 (family, house & garden), £10.40(family, garden). Admission prices include Gift Aid donation.

LEISTON ABBEY (FIRST SITE) WITH LATER CHAPEL AND PILL BOX

Westleton, Saxmundham, Suffolk IP17 3BY
Premonstratensian house, founded 1182. Abandoned in 1363 for Leiston Abbey (second site) further inland. Old abbey remains retained as remote cell of new house. A small chapel was built on the site, circa 16th century, and later, a WW2 pill box. The remains are situated near the coast within the RSPB's Minsmere Nature Reserve.
www.rspb.org
Grant Recipient: RSPB
Access Contact: Mr Andy Needle
T: 01728 648074 or 648780   **F:** 01728 648701
E-mail: andy.needle@rspb.org
Open: Access to ruin from public road at any time. Minsmere Reserve open daily (except 25 and 26 December) 9am–dusk.
Heritage Open Days: No
P Approximately one mile from limited roadside parking in Eastbridge and from RSPB car park (160 spaces).
Partial. Wheelchair access possible for All Terrain powered wheelchairs. WC for the disabled in Reserve centre. Guide dogs allowed.
£ No charge to ruin if accessed from road. Admission charge to non RSPB members to the reserve.

METTINGHAM CASTLE

Mettingham, Bungay, Suffolk NR35 1TH
Ruins of a moated fortified manor house founded in 1342 by Sir John de Norwich and a late 14th-15th century monastic college. The chief remains are the flint gatehouse, barbican and curtain wall of the original manor house. A Scheduled Monument.
Grant Recipient: Jenny Gormley
Access Contact: Ms Jenny Gormley
T: 01986 895669
Open: 24 April, 15 May, 26 June, 14 August, 18 September and 9 October, 10am–4pm or by telephone appointment (tel: 01986 895669).

Heritage Open Days: No
P Spaces: 10
No wheelchair access. No WC for the disabled. Guide dogs allowed.
£ No

MORETON HALL

Mount Road, Bury St Edmunds, Suffolk IP32 7BJ
White brick residence designed by Robert Adam in 1773 for Dr. John Symonds, noted Cambridge professor and author. The design was inspired by the ruins of Emperor Diocletian's palace and many of the original Adam features remain on the ground and first floors. It is now the home of Moreton Hall Preparatory School.
www.moretonhall.net
Grant Recipient: Moreton Hall School Trust Ltd
Access Contact: Mrs Doreen Young
T: 01284 753 532   **F:** 01284 769 197
E-mail: office@moretonhall.net
Open: By prior arrangement at any reasonable time, plus the Saturday of Heritage Open Days weekend.
Heritage Open Days: Yes
P Spaces: 20. Free parking.
Partial. Wheelchair access to ground floor only. WC for the disabled. Guide dogs allowed.
£ No

RUINED CHURCH TOWER

Fornham St Genevieve, St Edmundsbury, Suffolk
Only the tower remains of the 15th century church. Church destroyed by fire in 1782.
Grant Recipient: Rossfleet Investments Ltd
Access Contact: Mr Steve Stuteley
T: 01953 717176   **F:** 01953 717173
E-mail:
Open: By prior arrangement with Steve Stuteley (Rossfleet Investments, Manor Farm, Bridgham, Norfolk).
Heritage Open Days: No
P No
No wheelchair access. No WC for the disabled. Guide dogs allowed.
£ No

SOMERLEYTON HALL & GARDENS

Somerleyton, Lowestoft, Suffolk NR32 5QQ
Early Victorian stately home, built in Anglo-Italian style for Sir Morton Peto by John Thomas upon former Jacobean mansion. Contains fine furnishings, paintings, ornate carved stonework and wood carving, and state rooms. Set in twelve acres of historic gardens including a yew hedge maze.
www.somerleyton.co.uk
Grant Recipient: The Rt Hon Lord Somerleyton GCVO
Access Contact: Ms Carolyn Ashton
T: 01502 734901 or 734904   **F:** 01502 732143
E-mail: carolyn.ashton@somerleyton.co.uk
Open: House: 5 April–1 November, Thursday, Sunday and Bank Holidays plus Tuesday and Wednesday 19 July–20 September 11.30am–3.30pm. Half hourly guided tours. Closed Saturdays. Gardens: 10am–5pm. Please check website in advance www.somerleyton.co.uk or telephone 0871 222 4244.
Heritage Open Days: No
P Spaces: 200. Parking for disabled and coach park.
Full. WC for the disabled. Guide dogs allowed.
£ **Adult:** £5.50 (gardens only), £8.95 (Hall & gardens). **Child:** £3.50 (gardens only), £4.95 (Hall & gardens). **Other:** Over 60's : £4.50 (gardens only), £7.95 (Hall & gardens).

ST LAWRENCE

Dial Lane, Ipswich, Suffolk IP1 1DL
15th century aisleless church with a 97 foot west tower, enlarged in the 19th century and recently restored. Declared redundant in 1975. Owned by Ipswich Borough Council and re-opened in 2008 as 'The St Lawrence Centre', a community centre for the people of Ipswich.
www.stlawrencecentre.co.uk
Grant Recipient: Ipswich Historic Churches Trust
Access Contact: Mr Billy Brenan
T: 0844 736 9710
E-mail: admin@stlawrencecentre.co.uk
Open: Daily, Monday–Friday 10am–4pm; Saturdays 10.30am–3.30pm (café).

Heritage Open Days: Yes
P Public car park in town centre car parks (10 minute walk).
♿ Full. WC for the disabled. Guide dogs allowed.
£ No

ST MARGARET'S CHAPEL

Old Chapel Farm, Mells, Halesworth, Suffolk IP19 9DE

Constructed circa 1100 on a steep-sided promontory overlooking the river Blyth, abandoned c1467. A two-celled building constructed of flint and rubble in a ruinous state. Chancel arch subjected to stabilisation repairs in 2008. No recorded burials.
Grant Recipient: David George
Access Contact: Mr David George
T: 01986 874141
E-mail: dmeg@btinternet.com
Open: Appointments can be made at any reasonable time by telephone, email or calling at the farm. Please ensure gates remain closed when visiting the site.
Heritage Open Days: No
P Spaces: 20. Cars or cycles may be left in the main yard or on grass to the front of farm buildings. Farm and vehicle access should not be obstructed.
♿ Partial. Wheelchair access through pedestrian gate and into ruin but access around site difficult due to steep embankment. No WC for the disabled. Guide dogs allowed.
£ No

WARREN LODGE

Thetford Road, Mildenhall, Suffolk IP28 7JH

14th century lodge, one of only two remaining in Breckland. Constructed of mortared flint with stone quoins it was built to house the warrener and his family on the first floor, with the ground floor used for storage of nets, traps, pelts and rabbit meat. Strong barred door and thick walls pierced by small windows protected against poachers. Altered in the 19th century and inhabited by a gamekeeper until 1949.
www.fotfp.org.uk
Grant Recipient: Forest Enterprise
Access Contact: Ms Anne Mason
T: 01842 810271 or 01760 755685
E-mail: anne@providence28.fsnet.co.uk
Open: Free access to the exterior at any reasonable time. Heritage Open Day Sunday 12 September.
Heritage Open Days: Yes
P Spaces: 10. From car park there is a 10 minute walk up the hill.
♿ Partial. Barrier can be opened on request for cars to drive to the site for access for the disabled. No WC for the disabled. Guide dogs allowed.
£ No

SURREY

CLANDON PARK

West Clandon, Guildford, Surrey GU4 7RQ

Palladian mansion, built c1730 by Venetian architect Giacomo Leoni with a two-storeyed Marble Hall, collection of 18th century furniture, porcelain, textiles, carpets, the Ivo Forde Meissen collection of Italian comedy figures and a series of Mortlake tapestries. Grounds contain grotto, sunken Dutch garden, Maori Meeting House and Museum of the Queen's Royal Surrey Regiment.
www.nationaltrust.org.uk
Grant Recipient: The National Trust
Access Contact: Property Manager
T: 01483 222482   **F:** 01483 223479
E-mail: clandonpark@nationaltrust.org.uk
Open: House: 14 March–31 October, daily except Monday, Friday and Saturday (but open Good Friday, Easter Saturday and Bank Holiday Mondays) 11am–5pm (last admission 4.30pm). Museum: as house 12 noon–5pm. Garden: as house 11am–5pm.
Heritage Open Days: No
P Spaces: 200.
♿ Partial. Lift provides access to all areas of the house open to the public, some restrictions apply; please telephone for details. Grounds partially accessible, with some slopes and uneven terrain. WC for the disabled. Guide dogs allowed.
£ Adult: £8.60. Child: £4.20. Other: £23.10 (family), £7.00 (groups). All admission prices include voluntary Gift Aid donation.

GREAT HALL

Virginia Park, Christchurch Road, Virginia Water, Surrey GU25 4BH

By W H Crossland for Thomas Holloway and opened 1884. Built of red brick with Portland stone dressings and slate roofs in Franco-Flemish Gothic style. Formerly part of the Royal Holloway Sanatorium.
Grant Recipient: Virginia Park Management Co Ltd
Access Contact: Estate Manager
T: 01344 849232   **F:** 01344 842428
E-mail: virginia.park@btinternet.com
Open: Entrance Hall, Staircase and Great Hall of former Sanatorium: 10 and 21 February, 17, 21 and 28 March, 7, 18 and 21 April, 12, 26 and 30 May, 16, 23 and 27 June, 7, 21 and 25 July, 4, 18 and 22 August, 12, 15 and 29 September, 6, 20 and 24 October, 17 and 21 November, 10am–4pm.
Heritage Open Days: No
P Parking for the disabled only. Public car park nearby at Virginia Water Station.
♿ Partial. Wheelchair access with assistance (steps into building to be negotiated). Downstairs entrance Hall but not the Great Hall (no lift). Key required from security for access to WC for the disabled. Guide dogs allowed.
£ No

IVY CONDUIT

Holy Cross Preparatory School, George Road, Kingston, Surrey KT2 7NU

Conduit house built c1514, part of an elaborate water system built in 16th century to provide water to Hampton Court Palace situated over 5km away. A scheduled monument.
Grant Recipient: Holy Cross Preparatory School
Access Contact: Mr Michael Harrison
T: 020 8942 0729   **F:** 020 8336 0764
E-mail: michael@holycrossprep.co.uk
Open: By prior arrangement on weekdays, with 24 hours notice.
Heritage Open Days: Yes
P Spaces: 20
♿ Partial. Steep gradient through gardens, about 150m from car park. Refreshments and WC. No WC for the disabled. Guide dogs allowed.
£ No

PAINSHILL PARK

Portsmouth Road, Cobham, Surrey KT11 1JE

Restored Grade I Registered 18th century landscape garden of 158 acres, created by Charles Hamilton between 1738 and 1773. Contains a Gothic temple, Chinese bridge, ruined abbey, Turkish tent, crystal grotto, vineyard and 14 acre serpentine lake fed by a large waterwheel. Europa Nostra medal winner for 'Exemplary Restoration'. National plant collection of North American trees and shrubs.
Grant Recipient: Painshill Park Trust Ltd
Access Contact: Ms Jayne Newman
T: 01932 868113   **F:** 01932 868001
E-mail: info@painshill.co.uk
Open: March–October: 10.30am–6pm (last admission 4.30pm) or dusk if earlier; November–February: 10.30am–4pm (last admission 3pm) or dusk if earlier. Closed Christmas Day and Boxing Day. Guided tours by prior arrangement at additional cost of £1.00 per person.
Heritage Open Days: Yes
P Spaces: 400. Parking for 15 coaches.
♿ Partial. Wheelchair access to most of the site. Pre booked wheelchair loan and guided buggy tours (max 3 persons) available on request. Free admission for carer of disabled person. WC for the disabled. Guide dogs allowed.
£ Adult: £6.60. Child: £3.85 (under 5s free). Other: £5.80 (concessions); £22.00 (family–2 adults and 4 children); Group £5.80 (adult).

TYNE AND WEAR

FREEMASONS HALL

Queen Street East, Sunderland, Tyne and Wear SR1 2HT

Grade I listed oldest purpose-built Masonic meeting place in the world, c1785. Contains an ornate Lodge Room which remains virtually unaltered with elaborate thrones from 1735. Also has a cellar is in its original condition and one of the last remaining examples of a Donaldson organ which was specially constructed for the building in 1785.
Grant Recipient: Queen Street Masonic Temple Ltd
Access Contact: Mr Colin Meddes
T: 0191 522 0115   **F:** 0191 522 0115
E-mail: colinmeddes@tiscali.co.uk
Open: Guided tours throughout the year by prior arrangement. Heritage Open Days (times to be confirmed).
Heritage Open Days: Yes
P Spaces: 80
♿ Full. WC for the disabled. No Guide dogs allowed.
£ No

GIBSIDE CHAPEL

Orangery and stables, Gibside, nr. Rowlands Gill, Burnopfield, Tyne and Wear NE16 6BG

Palladian chapel, 1760-69 and completed 1812; designed by James Paine for George Bowes, MP and coal owner. Palladian style stables built 1746 by Daniel Garrett. The Orangery, built 1771-5, is one tall storey with seven bays. Situated south-west of Gibside Hall, overlooking the River Derwent.
www.nationaltrust.org.uk
Grant Recipient: The National Trust
Access Contact: Visitor Services Manager
T: 01207 541 820   **F:** 01207 541 830
E-mail: gibside@nationaltrust.org.uk
Open: Chapel: daily, 8 March–31 October 11am–4.30pm. Stables: daily, 1 January–7 March 10am–pm; 8 March–31 October 10am–6pm; 1 November–31 December 10am–4pm. Orangery: daily, 8 March–31 October 10am–6pm; 1 November–31 December 10am–4pm.
Heritage Open Days: Yes
P Spaces: 500. Limited coach parking.
♿ Full. Assisted access to chapel. WC for the disabled. Guide dogs allowed.
£ Adult: £6.50. Child: £4.00. Other: £18.50 (family).

HIGH LEVEL BRIDGE

linking Newcastle & Gateshead, Tyne and Wear

Grade I listed railway and road bridge of ashlar and cast iron, 1849, designed by Robert Stephenson. One of the finest pieces of architectural iron work in the world.
Grant Recipient: Network Rail
Access Contact: Mr Stephen Hyde
T: 01904389 876   **F:** 01904 389 802
E-mail: stephen.hyde@networkrail.co.uk
Open: Best viewed from adjacent riverbanks or via access road/footpath under bridge. Also may be viewed from the footways which cross the lower deck of the bridge. No access to the upper deck of the bridge.
Heritage Open Days: No
P On-street parking.
♿ Partial. Footways across the lower deck of the bridge are accessible for wheelchairs. No WC for the disabled. Guide dogs allowed.
£ No

OLD HOLLINSIDE FORTIFIED HALL HOUSE

Clockburn Lonnen, Whickham, Gateshead, Tyne and Wear NE9 1PT

Fortified manor, first recorded in 1317. Originally occupied by Thomas de Holinside. In 1730 it became part of the Gibside estate owned by the Bowes family. Listed Grade I and a Scheduled Monument.
Grant Recipient: Gateshead Metropolitan Borough Council
Access Contact: Mr Stuart Norman
T: 0191 433 3451
E-mail: stuartnorman@gateshead.gov.uk
Open: At all times.
Heritage Open Days: No
P No
♿ No wheelchair access. No WC for the disabled. Guide dogs allowed.
£ No

THEATRE ROYAL

100 Grey Street, Newcastle-upon-Tyne, Tyne and Wear NE1 6BR

Victorian theatre opened in 1837, rebuilt in 1899 by Frank Matcham in a richly-ornamented style. Classical façade with rare Hanoverian coat of arms. Traditional 4-tier 1,294 seat auditorium hosting annual programme of touring productions and international companies.

www.theatreroyal.co.uk
Grant Recipient: Newcastle Theatre Royal Trust Ltd
Access Contact: Mr Philip Bernays
T: 0191 232 0997   **F:** 0191 261 1906
E-mail: philip.bernays@theatreroyal.co.uk
Open: Regular tours available depending on production schedule, contact theatre on 08448 112121 for details. Regular public programme except Sundays. Café and Foyer: Monday–Saturday from 10am.
Heritage Open Days: No
P Public car parks in city centre.
Partial. Wheelchair access to foyer, café, stalls and box office. WC for the disabled. Guide dogs allowed.
£ **Adult:** £3.50 (tours, some free). **Child:** £3.50 (tours, some free).

WARWICKSHIRE

CHARLECOTE PARK

Wellesbourne, Warwick, Warwickshire CV35 9ER

Owned by the Lucy family since 1247, Sir Thomas built the house in 1558. Now much altered, it is shown as it would have been a century ago. The balustraded formal garden gives onto a deer park landscaped by 'Capability' Brown.

www.nationaltrust.org.uk
Grant Recipient: The National Trust
Access Contact: Stephen Bennett, Property Manager
T: 01789 470277   **F:** 01789 470544
E-mail: charlecote.park@nationaltrust.org.uk
Open: House: 1 March–31 October, Friday–Tuesday 12 noon–4.30pm (11am–5pm May–September); 1 November–31 December Saturday and Sunday 12 noon–4pm. Park, gardens and outbuildings: daily, all year 10am–5.30pm in summer, 10am–4pm in winter.
Heritage Open Days: Yes
P Spaces: 200. Overflow car park available. Parking for the disabled available on request.
Partial. Wheelchair access to ground floor of house, restaurant, shop, Green Court and Paddock. WC for the disabled. Guide dogs allowed.
£ **Adult:** £9.00. **Child:** £4.50. **Other:** £22.50 (family), £7.70 (group).

LORD LEYCESTER HOSPITAL

High Street, Warwick, Warwickshire CV34 4BH

14th century chantry chapel, Great Hall, galleried courtyard and Guildhall. Acquired by Robert Dudley, Earl of Leicester in 1571 as a home for his old soldiers. Still operating as a home for ex-servicemen.

www.lordleycester.com
Grant Recipient: Patron & Governors of Lord Leycester Hospital
Access Contact: Mr G F Lesinski
T: 01926 491422
E-mail: lordleycester@btinternet.com
Open: Tuesday–Sunday 10am–4pm (winter), 10am–5pm (summer), plus Bank Holiday Mondays. Closed Good Friday and Christmas Day.
Heritage Open Days: No
P Spaces: 10
Partial. Wheelchair access to ground floor only. WC for the disabled. Guide dogs allowed.
£ **Adult:** £4.90, £2.00 (garden only). **Child:** £3.90. **Other:** £4.40, £2.00 (garden only).

STONELEIGH ABBEY

Kenilworth, Warwickshire CV8 2LF

16th century house built on site and incorporating remains of Cistercian Abbey founded in 1155. West wing designed by Francis Smith of Warwick between 1714-26 and northern wing reconstructed in 19th century by Charles S Smith of Warwick. South wing c1820. West wing contains a range of State Apartments. Also has restored Regency riding stables, 19th century conservatory and Humphrey Repton landscaped riverside gardens.

www.stoneleighabbey.org
Grant Recipient: Stoneleigh Abbey Preservation Trust (1996) Ltd
Access Contact: Estate Office
T: 01926 858535   **F:** 01926 850274
E-mail: enquire@stoneleighabbey.org
Open: Good Friday–end of October: Tuesday, Wednesday, Thursday and Sunday, plus Bank Holidays 10am–5pm. Guided tours only at 11am, 1pm and 3pm. Opening arrangements may change, please check with the Preservation Trust for current information.
Heritage Open Days: No
P Spaces: 400
Partial. Gravel paths to grounds. WC for the disabled. Guide dogs allowed.
£ **Adult:** £7.00. **Child:** £3.00. **Other:** £6.50 (senior citizens), £3.00 grounds only. Jane Austen tour £7.00.

UMBERSLADE BAPTIST CHAPEL

Spring Lane, Tanworth in Arden, Warwickshire B94 6QH

Exceptionally fine nonconformist estate chapel by George Ingall, opened in 1877 and built for George Frederick Muntz who owned nearby Umberslade Hall. Timber furnishings and interior features remain largely intact.

www.hct.org.uk
Grant Recipient: Historic Chapels Trust
Access Contact: Simon Willcock
T: 0121 704 2694
E-mail: simon_willcock@eigmail.com
Open: At any reasonable time by prior arrangement with keyholder Simon Willcock (tel: 0121 7042694). Occasional events held throughout the year, please check website.
Heritage Open Days: Yes
P Spaces: 10
Partial. No WC for the disabled. Guide dogs allowed.
£ Donations invited.

WEST MIDLANDS

119-123 UPPER SPON STREET

Coventry, West Midlands CV1 3BQ

Late medieval (15th century) terrace of houses, known as Black Swan Terrance, with 16th to 20th century alterations. One of few timber framed structures in Coventry to survive in situ. Listed Grade II*. Restored by the Spon End Building Preservation Trust. No.122 has been restored as a Medieval weavers cottage, furnished with appropriate artefacts and loom on upper floor. Garden at rear restored with plants typical of Tudor period (1540). Activity centre in adjacent building (No. 121) with information and displays.

www.sebpt.org.uk
Grant Recipient: Spon End Building Preservation Trust
Access Contact: Ms Carol de Rose
T: 024 7625 7117
Open: Open Days: 10 April, 12 June, 10 July and Heritage Open weekend in September. School and group visits throughout the year by prior arrangement.
Heritage Open Days: Yes
P Limited on-street parking.
No. WC for the disabled. Guide dogs allowed.
£ No

BETHESDA METHODIST CHAPEL

Albion Street, Stoke-on-Trent, West Midlands ST1 1QF

Largest Methodist chapel outside London built 1819 with additions of 1859 and 1887. Closed and unused for 20 years. BBC2 Restoration series finalist in 2003. Phase I repairs to roof and front elevation were completed in 2007 and fundraising continues for phase II.

www.bethesda-stoke.org.uk
Grant Recipient: Historic Chapels Trust
Access Contact: John Booth
T: 01782 856810
E-mail: john.booth5@ntlworld.com
Open: March–December: 2nd Saturday of the month, afternoons and at any reasonable time by arrangement with keyholder Mr John Booth, 9 Hammerton Avenue, Eaton Park, Stoke-on-Trent ST2 9NL (tel: 01782 856810, email: john.booth5@ntlworld.com).
Heritage Open Days: Yes

P Public multi-storey car park (5 minutes walk, off Bethesda Street).
Partial. Wheelchair access to ground floor only. No WC for the disabled. Guide dogs allowed.
£ Donations invited.

FOUR ASHES HALL STABLE BLOCK

Four Ashes, Enville, Stourbridge, West Midlands DY7 5JG

Grade II* listed Georgian stable block, incorporating extensive outbuilding ranges. Courtyard plan, with stable front intended as the architectural focus within the same vista as Four Ashes Hall.

www.four-ashes-hall.com
Grant Recipient: Mr S Thompson
Access Contact: Mr S Thompson
T: 01384 221224   **F:** 01384 221042
E-mail: four.ashes@virgin.net
Open: By prior arrangement for interested groups and individuals.
Heritage Open Days: No
P No
No wheelchair access. No WC for the disabled. No Guide dogs allowed.
£ No

MEDIEVAL UNDERCROFT

38 & 39 Bayley Lane, (The Herbert Art Gallery & Museum), Jordan Well, Coventry, West Midlands CV1 5QP

Late medieval stone-vaulted undercroft, beneath numbers 38 and 39 Bayley Lane. Listed Grade I. Building of an extension to the Herbert Art Gallery & Museum on the site has included works to preserve the undercroft and provide access.

www.theherbert.org
Grant Recipient: Coventry City Council
Access Contact: Mr David Bancroft
T: 024 7683 4094   **F:** 024 7629 4790
E-mail: david.bancroft@theherbert.org
Open: Daily, Tuesday–Saturday 11.30am–4.15pm. Free access normally provided by Visitor Services Staff on request at main reception desk
Heritage Open Days: Yes
P No
No wheelchair access. WC for the disabled. Guide dogs allowed.
£ No

MOLINEUX HOTEL

Whitmore Hill, Wolverhampton, West Midlands WV1 1RY

Grade II* listed house of c1720 with mid 18th century additions. Used as an hotel from 1860 onwards. Vacant since 1979 and acquired by Wolverhampton City Council in 2004. The first stage of repairs was undertaken during 2004-2005. Restoration and conversion to house the City's Archives and Local Studies service was completed in 2009.

www.wolverhampton.gov.uk
Grant Recipient: Wolverhampton City Council
Access Contact: Mr Jon Beesley
T: 01902 555 622   **F:** 01902 555 637
E-mail: jon.beesley@wolverhampton.gov.uk
Open: All year: Tuesday, Thursday and Friday 10am–5pm, Wednesday 10am–7pm, Saturday 10am–1pm. Closed for 2 weeks in November for stock review (dates unknown at time of publication), advisable to check prior to any visit.
Heritage Open Days: Yes
P Spaces: 8. Limited parking available evenings and most weekends.
Full. Wheelchair access to ground floor and most of the site. Full access by lift to the Archives. WC for the disabled. Guide dogs allowed.
£ No

OLD GRAMMAR SCHOOL

81 Kings Norton Green, Birmingham, West Midlands B38 8RU

Early 15th century house, probably built as the priests house to St Nicholas Church, used as a place of learning. Half-timbered first floor, with faint remnants of Tudor decoration throughout. Schoolmaster and Puritan Thomas Hall taught here from 1629–1662. Subjected to decay and

vandalism from the 1950s, it was restored after winning the 2004 BBC TV series ' Restoration'.
www.saintnicholasplace.co.uk
Grant Recipient: Kings Norton PCC
Access Contact: Canon Rob Morris and Emma Banks
T: 0121 458 1223
E-mail: info@saintnicholasplace.co.uk
Open: All year (except Christmas and New Year) Fridays and Saturdays, 10am–4pm. Guided tours for groups (minimum 10 people) at any time by prior arrangement (tel: 0121 458 1223).
Heritage Open Days: No
P Spaces: 25. Limited public and parking for the disabled on The Green. Free public car park 5 minutes walk in Pershore Road.
 Partial. Wheelchair access to ground floor. WC for the disabled. Guide dogs allowed.
£ **Adult:** £4.00 guided tour, £2.00 self guided. **Child:** £3.00 guided tour, £1.50 self guided.

RED HOUSE GLASSCONE
Wordsley, Stourbridge, West Midlands DY8 4AZ
Built around 1790, the Cone was used for the manufacture of glass until 1936 and is now one of only four left in the Country. Reaching 100ft into the sky, the Cone enclosed a furnace where glass was made for 140 years. In its 200 year history, the site has remained virtually unaltered and therefore provides an interesting insight into the history and tradition of glassmaking. Glassmaking and exhibitions tell the story of glassmaking in the area and the history of the glassworks.
www.dudley.gov.uk/redhousecone
Grant Recipient: Dudley Metropolitan Borough Council
Access Contact: Ms Sarah Hall
T: 01384 812752   **F:** 01384 812751
E-mail: sarah.hall@dudley.gov.uk
Open: All year: daily 10am–4pm.
Heritage Open Days: Yes
P Spaces: 40. 4 parking spaces for the disabled.
 No wheelchair access. No WC for the disabled. No Guide dogs allowed.
£ Free audio guide.

ST JAMES
Great Packington, Meriden, nr. Coventry, West Midlands CV7 7HF
Red brick building with four domes topped by finials in neo-classical style. Built to celebrate the return to sanity of King George III. The organ was designed by Handel for his librettist, Charles Hennens, who was the cousin of the 4th Earl of Aylesford, who built the church.
www.packingtonestate.net
Grant Recipient: St James Great Packington Trust
Access Contact: Packington Estate Office
T: 01676 522020   **F:** 01676 523399
E-mail: jameschurch@packingtonestate.co.uk
Open: Monday–Friday 9am–5pm: key can be obtained from the Estate Office at Packington Hall, preferably by phoning in advance (01676 522020). At other times by prior arrangement with Lord Aylesford (tel: 01676 522274).
Heritage Open Days: No
P Spaces: 10
 Partial. Wheelchair access with assistance (entrance steps and heavy door to be negotiated). No WC for the disabled. Guide dogs allowed.
£ Donations towards restoration welcomed.

THE BIG HOUSE
44 Church Street, Oldbury, West Midlands B69 3DE
Grade II* 3-storey house dating from c1730. Originally with agricultural land and later the house and offices of a solicitor in 1857 when the land was sold. Restored and reopened in 2002 as Civic offices.
www.sandwell.gov.uk
Grant Recipient: Sandwell Metropolitan Borough Council
Access Contact: Sandwell Metropolitan Borough Council
T: 0121 569 3041   **F:** 0121 569 3050
E-mail: ann_oneill@sandwell.gov.uk
Open: By arrangement with the Mayor's office via the Civic Affairs officer (tel: 0121 569 3041). The Mayor will also hold 'Open House' at various times throughout the year.
Heritage Open Days: No
P No

 No wheelchair access. No WC for the disabled. No Guide dogs allowed.
£ No

WEST SUSSEX

OUSE VALLEY VIADUCT
Balcombe, West Sussex
The most important surviving architectural feature of the original layout of the London–Brighton railway, the grade II* Ouse Valley Viaduct has 37 circular arches, is 492 yards long and 92 feet high. Designed by John Rastrick with stonework accredited to David Mocatta, it is known for its pierced piers, ornate limestone parapets and pavilions. Built 1839-1841.
Grant Recipient: Railtrack plc (now Network Rail)
Access Contact: Network Rail
Open: Public access at all times on the footpath running underneath the viaduct. It is possible to view the viaduct from Borde Hill Lane without walking across the field.
Heritage Open Days: No
P Limited on-street parking.
 No wheelchair access. Wheelchair users can view viaduct from Borde Hill Lane. No WC for the disabled. No Guide dogs allowed.
£ No

PARHAM HOUSE
Parham Park, Storrington, nr. Pulborough, West Sussex RH20 4HS
Dating from 1577, Parham is listed Grade I and is one of the country's finest examples of an Elizabethan House. From the panelled Great Hall to the Long Gallery, the house contains an important collection of paintings, furniture and needlework.
www.parhaminsussex.co.uk
Grant Recipient: Parham Park Ltd
Access Contact: Mr Richard Pailthorpe, General Manager
T: 01903 742021   **F:** 01903 743260
E-mail: enquiries@parhaminsussex.co.uk
Open: Easter–End of September: Wednesday, Thursday, Sunday and Bank Holiday Mondays. Tuesdays and Fridays during August. Gardens open at 12 noon, house at 2pm with last entry at 4.15pm.
Heritage Open Days: No
P Spaces: 300. Parking for the disabled close to the house.
 Partial. Wheelchair access to ground floor only by prior arrangement, there is a reduced admission charge for wheelchair users and carers. Free loan of recorded tour tape. WC for the disabled. Guide dogs allowed.
£ **Adult:** £7.50 (provisional). **Child:** £3.50 (age 5 -15) (provisional). **Other:** £6.50 (senior citizens), £15.50 (family) (provisional).

PETWORTH HOUSE
Petworth, West Sussex GU28 0AE
Late 17th century mansion in 'Capability' Brown landscaped park. The house contains the Trust's largest collection of pictures including Turners and Van Dycks, as well as sculpture, furniture and Grinling Gibbons' carvings. Also there are the Servants' Quarters with interesting kitchens and other service rooms. Extra rooms open Monday, Tuesday and Wednesday afternoon by kind permission of Lord and Lady Egremont.
www.nationaltrust.org.uk/petworth
Grant Recipient: The National Trust
Access Contact: Property Manager
T: 01798 342207   **F:** 01798 342963
E-mail: petworth@nationaltrust.org.uk
Open: House and Servants' Quarters: 13 March–3 November, daily except Thursday and Friday (but open Good Friday), 11am–5pm (last admission to house 4.30pm). Extra rooms shown weekday afternoons (but not Bank Holiday Mondays) as follows: Monday: White and Gold Room and White Library; Tuesday and Wednesday: three bedrooms on first floor. Park: All year, daily.
Heritage Open Days: Yes
P Spaces: 150. Car park for house and park off the A283, 800m from house.
 Partial. Wheelchair access to ground floor of house, shop and tea room. WC for the disabled. Guide dogs allowed.
£ **Adult:** £10.90. **Child:** £5.50. **Other:** £27.30 (family),

£9.00 (booked groups of 15+). All admission prices include voluntary Gift Aid donation.

ST HUGH'S CHARTERHOUSE,
Henfield Road, Partridge Green, Horsham, West Sussex RH13 8EB
Large monastery covering 10 acres. The main cloister is 598 yards long and links 34 four-room hermitages where the monks live. The fore part is a smaller cloister 260 yards long linking the cells of the Brothers and their work places. There is also a large church, library, refectory, Brothers Chapel and other monastic buildings. The large quad encloses a cemetery. The spire is 203ft high and has a five-bell chime.
www.parkminster.org.uk
Grant Recipient: St Hugh's Charterhouse
Access Contact: Dr Simon Brennan
T: 01403 864231 **F:** 01403 864231
E-mail: simon.brennan@chartreuse.info
Open: By prior arrangement, with due respect for the rules of the Charterhouse monastery. For further details please contact the monastery.
Heritage Open Days: No
P Spaces: 20
 Partial. Wheelchair access to ground level only. No WC for the disabled. Guide dogs allowed.
£ No

WEST YORKSHIRE

BRAMHAM PARK LEAD LADS TEMPLE
Wetherby, West Yorkshire LS23 6ND
Park folly, in the form of an open temple in the classical style, built in the 1750s by local craftsmen on the instructions of Harriet Benson (about a mile from the house in woodland called Black Fen, close to a public footpath). The 'Lead Lads' were classical lead figures that stood on the three small blocks at the apex and base of the front pediment, and were lost to vandals many years ago.
www.bramhampark.co.uk
Grant Recipient: Trustees of the Bramham Settled Estate
Access Contact: The Estate Office
T: 01937 846000   **F:** 01937 846007
E-mail: enquiries@bramhampark.co.uk
Open: All year: Monday–Friday 10am–4.30pm. Closed weekends, Bank Holidays, 17 May–11 June for Horse Trials and 9 August–17 September for Leeds Festival. Ring estate office (tel: 01937 846000) when visiting to enable gates to be opened.
Heritage Open Days: No
P Spaces: 50. No charge made for visitors via the footpath but charge made for visitors to the house and gardens.
 Partial. WC for the disabled is not on site, but in visitors car park via footpath. Lift to House rooms. Guide dogs allowed.
£ **Adult:** £4.00 (gardens only), £10 for house (pre booked, 10 plus visitors). **Child:** £2.00 (gardens only, under 5's free). **Other:** £2.00 (senior citizens, gardens only). No charge made for visitors via the footpath but charge made for visitors to the house and gardens.

FARFIELD FRIENDS MEETING HOUSE
off Bolton Road, Addingham, nr. Ilkley, West Yorkshire LS29
Land for burial ground purchased in 1666, followed by construction of Meeting House in 1669. A simple single cell building with rubblestone walls, mullioned windows, stone-slated roof and stone-flagged floor. Contains loose benches and an oak minister's stand of an unusual panelled design with turned balusters.
www.hct.org.uk
Grant Recipient: Historic Chapels Trust
Access Contact: Mr and Mrs Barry Cody
T: 01756 710587
Open: At all reasonable times. Burial ground open for viewing and picnics.
Heritage Open Days: No
P Spaces: 2
 Partial. Step down from road and into building. No WC for the disabled. Guide dogs allowed.
£ Donations invited.

521

HAREWOOD HOUSE

Harewood, Leeds, West Yorkshire LS17 9LQ

Designed in neo-classical style by John Carr commenced 1750 and completed in 1771. Contains Adam interiors, Chippendale furniture, an fine art and archive collection and museum. Home of the Earl and Countess of Harewood.

www.harewood.org
Grant Recipient: The Trustees of Harewood House Trust Ltd
Access Contact: Ms Anna Robinson
T: 0113 218 1036   **F:** 0113 218 1002
E-mail: anna.robinson@harewood.org
Open: Daily 12 February–1 November: Grounds and Bird Garden 10am–6pm (last admission 4pm). House 2 April–31 October: 11am–4.30pm (last admission 4pm). Grounds close at 6pm. Grounds and Bird Garden also open weekends between 7 November and 13 December. Guide dogs are not allowed in the Bird Garden but a free sound guide is available for the partially sighted visitor and a minder for the dog.
Heritage Open Days: No
🅿 Spaces: 200. Unlimited overflow parking on grass.
♿ Full. WC for the disabled. Guide dogs allowed.
💷 **Adult:** £12.00. (to be confirmed, check website).
Child: £7.70. (to be confirmed, check website). **Other:** £11.00 (senior), £42.00 (family), season ticket & concessions for disabled groups, 50% reduction for arrivals by public transport, students free Wednesday.

HUDDERSFIELD STATION

St George's Square, Huddersfield, West Yorkshire HD1 1JF

Designed by J P Pritchett of York and built by local builder Joseph Kaye using local ashlar sandstone, the station is the oldest of the seven Grade I listed station buildings in use for railway passengers having opened on 3 August 1847. When the foundation stone was laid the year before a public holiday was declared and church bells were rung from dawn till dusk. The grandeur of the station is the result of it having been built at the joint expense of the Huddersfield and Manchester Rail and Canal Company and the Manchester and Leeds Railway Company.

Grant Recipient: Kirkless Council
Access Contact: Head of Design & Property Service
T: 01484 226154   **F:** 01484 226086
E-mail: cheryl.noble@kirklees.gov.uk
Open: Operational building open to the public every day except Christmas Day and Boxing Day. Please note that the building may also be closed on other days specified by Network Rail or other railway operators.
Heritage Open Days: No
🅿 Spaces: 20. One hour stay maximum in station car park. Pay and display car park.
♿ Full wheelchair access to main buildings. Access with assistance to inner platforms. No WC for the disabled. Guide dogs allowed.
💷 No

KIRKSTALL ABBEY

Leeds, West Yorkshire LS5 3EH

One of the best preserved examples of a ruined Medieval Cistercian Monastery in the country. Founded by monks from Fountains and the primary building work was completed in 1182. The Reredorter has been restored as a Visitor Centre.

www.leeds.gov.uk/kirkstallabbey
Grant Recipient: Leeds City Council
Access Contact: Ms Samantha Flavin
T: 0113 230 5492   **F:** 0113 230 5499
E-mail: sam.flavin@leeds.gov
Open: 1 October–31 March: Tuesday, Wednesday, Thursday, Saturday, Sunday (closed Mondays and Fridays) 10am–4pm. 1 April–30 September: Tuesday–Sunday (closed Mondays) 11am–4pm.
Heritage Open Days: No
🅿 Spaces: 70. Parking for 3 coaches and for the disabled.
♿ Full. WC for the disabled. Guide dogs allowed.
💷 No

NATIONAL COAL MINING MUSEUM FOR ENGLAND

Caphouse Colliery, New Road, Wakefield, West Yorkshire WF4 4RH

A colliery complex dating back to the 18th century with an underground tour into authentic coal workings and major galleries covering social history, science and technology within mining. Most of the historic buildings are open to the public. Facilities include a research library, restaurant, shop and education services.

www.ncm.org.uk
Grant Recipient: The National Coal Mining Museum for England Trust Ltd
Access Contact: Dr M Faull
T: 01924 848806   **F:** 01924 840694
E-mail: info@ncm.org.uk
Open: All year: daily 10am–5pm except 24–26 December and 1 January.
Heritage Open Days: Yes
🅿 Spaces: 200. Some accessible parking bays close to museum reception.
♿ Partial. Wheelchair access to all galleries and historic buildings and underground (limited tour) but not the screens. Guide dogs not permitted underground. WC for the disabled. Guide dogs allowed.
💷 No

NOSTELL PRIORY

Doncaster Road, Nostell, Wakefield, West Yorkshire WF4 1QE

Country house, c1736-1750, by James Paine for Sir Rowland Winn 4th baronet. Later Robert Adam was commissioned to complete the State Rooms. On display is a collection of Chippendale furniture, designed especially for the house, an art collection with works by Pieter Breughel the Younger and Angelica Kauffmann, an 18th century dolls house, complete with its original fittings and Chippendale style furniture and an 18th century Muniments Room. Other attractions include lakeside walks, historic park, family croquet, giant chess set and open days for cabinets.

www.nationaltrust.org.uk
Grant Recipient: The National Trust
Access Contact: Property Manager
T: 01924 863892   **F:** 01924 866846
E-mail: nostellpriory@nationaltrust.org.uk
Open: House: 27 February–7 November, daily (except Monday and Tuesday) 11am–4.30pm; 4–12 December, daily except Monday and Tuesday 11am–4.30pm; 8–9 December 5pm–8pm. Grounds, shop and tea room: 1–3 January 11am–4pm; 8 January–27 February Saturday and Sunday 11am–4pm. 27 February–7 November, daily (except Monday and Tuesday) 11am–5.30pm; 13–28 November Saturday and Sunday 11am–4.30pm; 4–12 December, daily except Monday and Tuesday 11am–4.30pm; 8–9 December, 5pm–8pm; 26–28 December 11am–4pm. February school half term 11am–5pm. Parkland open all year 9am–7pm.
Heritage Open Days: No
🅿 Spaces: 700. Parking £2.00, refundable on purchase of House and Garden ticket. Blue Badge parking adjacent to House.
♿ Partial. Wheelchair access to ground floor of house with lift to first floor, tea room, children's playground and shop. WC for the disabled. Guide dogs allowed.
💷 **Adult:** £8.80 (house & gardens), £5.30 (gardens only), parkland free. **Child:** £4.10 (house & gardens), £2.70 (gardens only), parkland free. **Other:** £20.00 (family, house & gardens), £13.50 (family, gardens only), parkland free.

PONTEFRACT OLD TOWN HALL AND ASSEMBLY ROOMS

Bridge Street, Pontefract, West Yorkshire WF8 1PG

Grade II and II* Listed buildings. Old Town Hall built in 1785 and designed by Bernard Hartley. Assembly Rooms later added in 1882 and designed by Perkin and Bulmer. Currently used for events and hospitality.

Grant Recipient: Wakefield Metropolitan District Council
Access Contact: Ms Lisa Casey
T: 01924 305 297   **F:** 01924 306 963
E-mail: lcasey@wakefield.gov.uk
Open: 3 days per week (days and times vary, please telephone Events & Function Office (on 01924 305830). All other times by prior arrangement.

Heritage Open Days: Yes
🅿 Car park in the town centre nearby, disabled parking adjacent to property.
♿ Full. WC for the disabled. Guide dogs allowed.
💷 No

THE ROUNDHOUSE

Wellington Road, Leeds, West Yorkshire LS12 1DR

Grade II* railway roundhouse built in 1847 for the Leeds and Thirsk Railway by Thomas Granger. In full use by the North-Eastern Railway until 1904, now home to Leeds Commercial Van and Truck Hire.

Grant Recipient: Wellbridge Properties Ltd
Access Contact: Mr J D Miller
T: 0113 2435964   **F:** 0113 246 1142
E-mail: sales@leedscommercial.co.uk
Open: By prior written arrangement with the occupiers, Leeds Commercial, who manage the property as a working garage, or call in during office hours.
Heritage Open Days: Yes
🅿 Spaces: 100. Free parking.
♿ Full. WC for the disabled. Guide dogs allowed.
💷 No

WILTSHIRE

AVONCLIFF AQUEDUCT

Kennet & Avon Canal, Westwood, Wiltshire

19th century limestone aqueduct carrying the Kennet and Avon Canal over the River Avon and the railway line. The canal towpath crosses alongside the canal providing a foot link to Bradford-on-Avon or Bath.

www.britishwaterways.co.uk/southwest
Grant Recipient: British Waterways
Access Contact: Mr David Viner
T: 01452 318000   **F:** 01452 318076
E-mail: david.viner@britishwaterways.co.uk
Open: At all times.
Heritage Open Days: No
🅿 Spaces: 12
♿ Partial. Wheelchair access to top of aqueduct from the small car park beside the canal. No WC for the disabled. Guide dogs allowed.
💷 No

BARTON GRANGE FARM WEST BARN

Bradford on Avon, Wiltshire

Part of Barton Farm, once a grange of Shaftesbury Abbey (the richest nunnery in England), which includes the adjacent 14th century Tithe Barn. The West Barn was destroyed by fire in 1982 but has subsequently been rebuilt by the Preservation Trust and is now used as an 'Interpretation Centre' and as a Community Hall.

www.bradfordheritage.co.uk/PAGES/project.htm
Grant Recipient: Bradford on Avon Preservation Trust Limited
Access Contact: The Secretary
T: 01225 865733
E-mail: boapt@boapres.totalserve.co.uk
Open: May–September: weekends and Bank Holidays 12 noon–4pm. Also open at other times throughout the year, please check with the secretary or the Tourist Information Centre for further details.
Heritage Open Days: Yes
🅿 Pay parking (15 spaces) near the site. Pay parking (200 spaces) at railway station.
♿ Partial. Wheelchair access to main building but not galleries. Entrance pathways are loose gravel. WC for the disabled. Guide dogs allowed.
💷 No

HEMYNGSBY

56 The Close, Salisbury, Wiltshire SP1 2EL

14th century canonical residence with spacious 18th century rooms and medieval Great Hall. Contains 15th century linenfold panelling. Large and interesting garden. Home of Canon William Fideon, a Greek scholar who escaped from Constantinople in 1453, and Canon Edward Powell, advocate of Catherine of Aragon and later hanged for denying the Act of Supremacy.

Grant Recipient: The Dean & Chapter of Salisbury Cathedral
Access Contact: Mr Peter Edds
T: 01722 555115   **F:** 01722 555140
E-mail: p.edds@salcath.co.uk

Open: By prior arrangement only. Exterior can be viewed at all times.
Heritage Open Days: No
P No
No wheelchair access. No WC for the disabled. Guide dogs allowed.
£ Donations invited.

LACOCK ABBEY

Lacock, nr. Chippenham, Wiltshire SN15 2LG
Founded in 1232 and converted into a country house c1540, the fine medieval cloisters, sacristy, chapter house and monastic rooms of the Abbey have survived largely intact. The handsome 16th century stable courtyard has half timbered gables, a clockhouse, brewery and bakehouse. Victorian woodland garden. Former residents include William Fox Talbot 'the father of modern photography' and the Abbey now houses the Fox Talbot Museum.
www.nationaltrust.org.uk
Grant Recipient: The National Trust
Access Contact: Property Manager
T: 01249 730459   **F:** 01249 730501
E-mail: lacockabbey@nationaltrust.org.uk
Open: Abbey: 13 February–31 October, daily 11am–5pm (closed Tuesdays and Good Friday). Museum, cloisters and garden: 2 January–12 February 11am–4pm, 13 February–31 October, daily 11am–5.30pm (closed Good Friday). Museum also open 1 November–19 December 11am–4pm.
Heritage Open Days: Yes
P Spaces: 300
Partial. Wheelchair access to Abbey is difficult as four sets of stairs. Garden, cloisters and museum are accessible (non-wheelchair stair lift in museum). Limited parking in Abbey courtyard by arrangement. WC for the disabled at Red Lion car park, High Street, and abbey courtyard, RADAR lock. Guide dogs allowed.
£ **Adult:** £11.00 (Abbey, museum, cloisters & garden), £8.00 (Abbey cloister, museum & garden), £6.50 (garden, cloisters & museum). **Child:** £5.50 (Abbey, museum, cloisters & garden), £4.00 (Abbey, cloisters & garden), £3.60 (garden, cloisters & museum). **Other:** £28.00 (family: Abbey, museum, cloisters & garden), £20.40 (family: Abbey, cloisters & garden), £16.60 (family: garden, cloisters & museum). Group rates.

LADY MARGARET HUNGERFORD ALMSHOUSES

Pound Pill, Corsham, Wiltshire SN13 9HT
Fine complex of Grade I listed 17th century almshouses, schoolroom, Warden's house and stables. Schoolroom with original 17th century furniture and exhibition room. Lady Margaret Hungerford founded the almshouses for the care of six poor people and the schoolroom for educating poor children. Arms of the foundress are well displayed.
Grant Recipient: Trustees Of The Lady Margaret Hungerford Charity
Access Contact: Mr R L Tonge
T: 01225 742471   **F:** 01225 742471
E-mail: rtonge@northwilts.gov.uk
Open: 4 April–30 September: Tuesday, Wednesday, Friday and Saturday 1.30–4.00pm; October, November, February and March: Saturdays 1.30pm–4.00pm. Closed December and January and Bank Holidays. Groups welcome by prior arrangement.
Heritage Open Days: No
P Spaces: 100. Parking in the town within 100 yards.
Partial. Wheelchair access to ground floor only. WC for the disabled. Guide dogs allowed.
£ **Adult:** £2.00. **Child:** 50p. **Other:** £1.75 (senior citizens and concession).

LARMER TREE GARDENS

nr Tollard Royal, Salisbury, Wiltshire SP5 5PY
Created by General Pitt Rivers in 1880 as a pleasure grounds for 'public enlightenment and entertainment', the Larmer Tree Gardens are set high on the Cranbourne Chase providing exceptional views of the surrounding countryside. One of the most unusual gardens in England containing an extraordinary collection of colonial and oriental buildings, a Roman Temple and an Open Air Theatre.
www.larmertree.co.uk

Grant Recipient: Trustees of MALF Pitt-Rivers No. 1 Discretionary Settlement
Access Contact: Estate Secretary
T: 01725 516225   **F:** 01725 516321
E-mail: larmertree@rushmoreuk.com
Open: Summer opening: Easter Sunday–End of August: Sunday–Thursday 11am–4.30pm. Closed July and September, Fridays and Saturdays for private hire. Winter opening: October, November, February and March: Monday–Friday 11am–4pm. Tea rooms: Sundays and August Bank Holiday. Please check website to confirm opening arrangements.
Heritage Open Days: No
P Spaces: 500
Partial. Wheelchair access to the sunken dell is difficult. WC for the disabled. Guide dogs allowed.
£ **Adult:** £3.75. **Child:** £2.50 (over 5 yrs). **Other:** £3.00 (Admission charges apply on Sundays only, other times donations invited).

LOCK-UP 20M SOUTH OF LITTLE LONDON COTTAGE

High Street, Heytesbury, Wiltshire BA12 0EA
18th century blind house, village lock-up. Octagonal limestone construction with stone slate covering roof, heavy studded plank door and small iron barred window. Roof with ball finial at apex, interior with simple fitted wooden bench. Scheduled Monument.
Grant Recipient: Heytesbury, Imber and Knook PC
Access Contact: Heytesbury Post Office
E-mail: jackiekirkby@btinternet.com
Open: Access at any reasonable time. Keyholder details displayed on nearby noticeboard. Key held at Heytesbury Post Office which is open daily except Sunday (closed 1-2pm Monday–Friday, from 12 noon on Saturdays and from 1pm on Wednesdays) £10.00 deposit required for key.
Heritage Open Days: No
P On-street parking.
Partial. Narrow door may not accommodate wheelchairs. No WC for the disabled. Guide dogs allowed.
£ £10.00 deposit required for key.

MERCHANT'S HOUSE

132 High Street, Marlborough, Wiltshire SN8 1HN
17th century town house built by the Bayly family, mercers between 1653 and c1700. Situated prominently in the High Street it contains a unique stripe-painted dining room c1665, painted balustrading to the oak staircase and a panelled chamber of the Commonwealth period.
www.merchantshouse.co.uk
Grant Recipient: Merchant's House (Marlborough) Trust
Access Contact: Mr Michael Gray
T: 01672 511491 **F:** 01672 511491
E-mail: manager@merchantshousetrust.co.uk
Open: Easter–end September: Fridays and Saturdays 11am–4pm. Tours at 11am, 12 noon, 2pm and 3pm. Other times by arrangement with the Secretary at Merchant's House.
Heritage Open Days: No
P Parking for the disabled outside the building. Public parking in High Street.
Partial. Wheelchair access to part of ground floor. No WC for the disabled. Guide dogs allowed.
£ **Adult:** £5.00.
Child: £1.00.

OLD BISHOP'S PALACE,

Salisbury Cathedral School, 1 The Close, Salisbury, Wiltshire SP1 2EQ
13th century building, much altered over the centuries, with 13th century undercroft, Georgian drawing room and a chapel.
Grant Recipient: Salisbury Diocesan Board of Finance
Access Contact: Mrs Esther Horwood
T: 01722 555302   **F:** 01722 410910
E-mail: bursar@salisburycathedralschool.com
Open: Guided tours on 10 days in July and August. Details can be obtained from the Visitors' Office at Salisbury Cathedral (tel: Fiona Nelder: 01722 555124).
Heritage Open Days: No
P No
No wheelchair access. There is a WC for the disabled in the cloister (100 yards). No Guide dogs allowed.
£ **Adult:** £5.00.

SALISBURY CATHEDRAL EDUCATION CENTRE (WREN HALL)

56c The Close, Salisbury, Wiltshire SP1 2EL
Originally north wing of adjacent Braybrook House, early 18th century. Former choristers' school (founded 13th century). Many of the original fixtures and fittings are still present. Items of particular interest are the teacher's and head teacher's desks, original wood panelling and various photographs and artefacts from the history of the schoolroom.
www.salisburycathedral.org.uk/education.php
Grant Recipient: The Dean & Chapter of Salisbury Cathedral
Access Contact: Mr Peter Edds
T: 01722 555115   **F:** 01722 555140
E-mail: p.edds@salcath.co.uk
Open: By prior arrangement.
Heritage Open Days: No
P As part of The Close parking arrangements for members of the public.
No wheelchair access. WC for the disabled available within the Close. Guide dogs allowed.
£ No

WILTON HOUSE

Wilton, Salisbury, Wiltshire SP2 0BJ
Ancestral home of the Earls of Pembroke for over 450 years, rebuilt by Inigo Jones and John Webb in the Palladian style with further alterations by James Wyatt c1801. Contains 17th century state rooms and an art collection including works by Van Dyck, Rubens, Joshua Reynolds and Brueghel. Surrounded by landscaped parkland.
www.wiltonhouse.com
Grant Recipient: Wilton House Charitable Trust
Access Contact: Mr Chris Rolfe
T: 01722 746720   **F:** 01722 744447
E-mail: tourism@wiltonhouse.com
Open: House: Easter weekend 2–8 April, 1 May–31 August Sunday–Thursday plus Bank Holiday Saturdays; 1 May and 28 August 11.30am–4.30pm (last admission 3.45pm). Grounds: 2–18 April, 1 May–31 August, Saturdays and Sundays in September: 11am–5pm (last admission 4pm). House and grounds closed 24–31 May.
Heritage Open Days: Yes
P Spaces: 200
Full. WC for the disabled. Guide dogs allowed.
£ **Adult:** £12.00. **Child:** £6.50. **Other:** £9.75 (senior citizens), £29.50 (family); Group rates on application.

WORCESTERSHIRE

ABBERLEY HALL CLOCK TOWER

Great Witley, Worcester, Worcestershire WR6 6DD
Victorian folly, built 1883-4, by J P St Aubyn in a fantastic mixture of 13th and 14th century Gothic styles. 161ft tall, it can be seen from six counties.
Grant Recipient: Abberley Hall Ltd
Access Contact: Mr John G W Walker
T: 01299 896275   **F:** 01299 896875
E-mail: johnwalker@abberleyhall.co.uk
Open: 15 and 16 July; other times by prior arrangement.
Heritage Open Days: No
P Spaces: 20
No wheelchair access. No WC for the disabled. No Guide dogs allowed.
£ **Adult:** £4.00. **Child:** £2.00.

HANBURY HALL

School Road, Hanbury, Droitwich, Worcestershire WR9 7EA
Built in 1701, this William and Mary-style house contains painted ceilings and staircase. It has an orangery, ice house and Moorish gazebos. The re-created 18th century garden is surrounded by parkland and has a parterre, wilderness, fruit garden, open grove and bowling green pavilions. The recently redecorated Long Gallery houses an exhibition of the Vernon family and the history of Hanbury Hall. Original 17th century panelling to the study.
www.nationaltrust.org.uk
Grant Recipient: The National Trust
Access Contact: Property Manager
T: 01527 821214   **F:** 01527 821251

E-mail: hanburyhall@nationaltrust.org.uk
Open: House: 27 February–30 June , 1 September–31 October Saturday–Wednesday 11am– 5pm; 1 July–31 August Saturday–Thursday 11am–5pm; 6 November–19 December (downstairs only in house) for guided tours 11.30am–3.30pm. Garden, grounds, tea room, Long Gallery and shop: 2 January–21 February Saturdays and Sundays 11am–4pm; 27 February–31 October daily 11am–5pm; 6 November–19 December Saturday and Sundays 11am–4pm. Open daily during spring half term 13–21 February and 26 December–2 January 2011.
Heritage Open Days: No
P Spaces: 300. Car parking 200 metres from house. Buggy transfer available.
Partial. Wheelchair access to ground floor, gardens, tea room, shop and café. WC for the disabled. Guide dogs allowed.
£ Adult: £8.00 (house & garden), £5.40 (garden & park only and house and grounds in November and December). **Child:** £4.00 (house & garden), £2.70 (garden & park only and house & grounds in November and December). **Other:** £19.00 (family, house & garden), £12.50 (family, garden & park only and house and grounds in November and December).

HAWFORD GRANGE DOVECOTE
Hawford, Worcestershire WR3 7SG
16th century half-timbered dovecote.
www.nationaltrust.org.uk
Grant Recipient: The National Trust
Access Contact: Property Manager
T: 01527 821 214
E-mail: hanburyhall@nationaltrust.org.uk
Open: 28 February–1 November, 9am–6pm.
Heritage Open Days: No
P Spaces: 3
Partial. View from exterior. No WC for the disabled. Guide dogs allowed.
£ Adult: £1.00.

HOPTON COURT CONSERVATORY
Cleobury Mortimer, Kidderminster, Worcestershire DY14 0EF
Grade II* listed conservatory, c1830, of cast iron with a rounded archway leading to a rear room roofed with curved glass. Two rooms either side, one housing the boiler beneath to supply heat by way of cast iron grilles running around the floor of the interior.
www.hoptoncourt.co.uk
Grant Recipient: Mr C R D Woodward
Access Contact: Mr Christopher Woodward
T: 01299 270734   **F:** 01299 271132
E-mail: info@hoptoncourt.co.uk

Open: Weekends of 8/9 May, and 28/29 August 10am–4.30pm. At other times by prior arrangement.
Heritage Open Days: No
P Spaces: 150
Full. WC for the disabled. Guide dogs allowed.
£ Adult: £5.00.

LOWER BROCKHAMPTON
Bringsty, Worcestershire WR6 5UH
A late 14th century moated manor house with a detached half-timbered 15th century gatehouse. Also, the ruins of a 12th century chapel. Woodland walks.
www.nationaltrust.org.uk
Grant Recipient: The National Trust
Access Contact: Property Manager
T: 01885 488099   **F:** 01885 482151
E-mail: brockhampton@nationaltrust.org.uk
Open: House: 6–21 March Wednesday–Sunday 12 noon–4pm; 22 March–11 April daily 11am–5pm; 14 April–30 June Wednesday–Sunday 11am–5pm; 1 July–31 August daily 11am–5pm; 1 September–31 October Wednesday–Sunday 11am–5pm; 6 November–19 December Saturday and Sunday 11am–4pm. Open Bank Holiday Mondays. Estate: All year daily, dawn to dusk.
Heritage Open Days: Yes
P Spaces: 60. Parking for the disabled near house. Car parking free when visiting house.
Partial. Ground floor of house, gardens, courtyard, shop & tea room accessible for wheelchairs. WC for the disabled. Guide dogs allowed.
£ Adult: £5.80 (admission price includes voluntary gift aid donation). **Child:** £2.85. **Other:** £14.30 (family) £4.90 (15+groups) £2.75 (park only).

ST MICHAEL'S RUINED NAVE AND WEST TOWER
Abberley, Worcestershire
Ruins of tower, nave (both 12th century) and south aisle (c1260). Walls standing approximately 4ft high with many surviving features from Medieval church. 12th century chancel and south chapel, c1260, repaired in 1908 and still used for services.
Grant Recipient: Abberley Parochial Church Council
Access Contact: Mrs M A Nott
T: 01299 896392
Open: At all times.
Heritage Open Days: No
P Spaces: 7. Also parking at Manor Arms Hotel.
Full wheelchair access to ruins but assistance required to visit interior of church. No WC for the disabled. Guide dogs allowed.
£ Donations welcome (place in Green Box).

WALKER HALL
Market Square, Evesham, Worcestershire WR11 4RW
16th century timber-framed building adjoining Norman gateway, much altered. In the late 19th century the floor was removed and it became an open hall. In 1999 it was repaired and refitted to form offices (first floor) and a retail unit (ground floor).
www.wds.gb.com
Grant Recipient: Messrs Saggers & Rhodes
Access Contact: Messrs Saggers & Rhodes
T: 01386 446623   **F:** 01386 48215
E-mail: peter.rhodes@wds.gb.com
Open: Access to interior by prior arrangement only.
Heritage Open Days: No
P Spaces: 500. Parking in town centre car parks.
Partial. Wheelchair and guide dog access to ground floor only. WC for the disabled. Guide dogs allowed.
£ Charitable donation only.

WHITBOURNE HALL AND PALM HOUSE
Whitbourne, Worcester, Worcestershire WR6 5SE
Victorian Greek Revival style country house with large palm house built later (circa 1865-77) in the space between main block and service wing. The south front has an imposing Ionic portico. The main hall, with Maw and Co. mosaic tiled floor, is lit entirely by glazed blue-glass ceiling and surrounded by a gallery accessed by a white marble staircase with limestone balustrade.
www.whitbournehall.com
Grant Recipient: Whitbourne Hall Community Ltd
Access Contact: Ms H D Colley
T: 01886 821165
E-mail: heatherdcolley@aol.com
Open: 25 April 10am- 6pm; 3, 10, 17, 24 and 31 May, 7, 14, 21and 28 June: 11am–4pm. At other times for groups by prior arrangement.
Heritage Open Days: No
P Spaces: 100. Parking around the House for 30 cars.
Partial. Wheelchair access to part of the garden. Mobile ramp available for access to the house (three steps). Open areas of the house accessible for wheelchairs (wide doors). WC for the disabled. Guide dogs allowed.
£ Adult: £5.00.
Child: £2.50.

Heritage Open Days: an annual event over four days in September (9–12) which aims to increase opportunities for access to properties outside London which are predominantly inaccessible to the general public or usually charge an admission fee. English Heritage funds the Civic Trust to co-ordinate Heritage Open Days.

Open House London: a similar annual event, co-ordinated by Open House, for buildings in the Capital over one weekend in September (18 and 19).

H

Historic Places to Stay

HAZLEWOOD CASTLE

Yorkshires best kept secret

Hazlewood Castle Paradise Lane, Tadcaster, Leeds, LS24 9NJ   Owner - Ashdale Hotels
Weddings & Conference enquiries Tel- 01937 535313 Fax- 01937 530630 Email- info@hazlewood-castle.co.uk

The recorded history of Hazlewood Castle starts with the Domesday Book carried out for King William.

The Domesday Book introduced for the first time taxation to the country. The entry is for Sir Mauger the Vavasour, and resides in the Hall of a Thane at Hazlewood. (Mauger was a Saxon and they only had the one name!

The Normans introduced the second name as a defining name i.e. your title or occupation). He was given his name by the De Percy's.

The Duke of Northumbria had been given Northumbria, which began at The Wash and stretched up the east coast to Scotland, by King William. He was a vassal to the King. The name Vavasour described Mauger as the vassal of a vassal or the tenant for a greater tenant.

In 1283 Sir William built on the site of the Hall of a Thane, a manor house i.e. Great Hall and Pele Tower but as a result of the Barons' Wars, he applied to the King to crenellate and fortify his manor. The licence was granted in 1290, transforming the Hall of a Thane into a castle and his title went to a Baron as only Barons were allowed to live in a castle.

The 29th March 1461 saw the War of the Roses take place on Towton Moor, which is directly in front of the castle to the south and south east (which is the valley of the River Cock which ran red with blood from this battle for many a day after the fight had finished. (70,000 people took part with 28,000 killed).

The Tudor reign then followed (all the families from Mauger through to the Carmelites of 1996 were Catholic). When Henry outlawed the Catholic Church, priest holes were added to the Tudor Tower and an underground passage went to Crossroads Farm on the A1/A64 crossroads. These were imperative as the priest if caught would be hung, drawn and quartered and the person aiding or abetting him hung!

In 1908, the Vavasours left Hazlewood after 900 years and went to the Attewe Valley near Marlborough in New Zealand, and began vineyards (Hazlewood Castle Hotel stock a Vavasour Sauvignon Blanc, introducing the ancestors back on site). Mr Simpson, a solicitor, bought the castle and he and descendent families were here until 1953.

During the Second World War, from 1939 to June 1953, the castle was requisitioned as a maternity hospital.

The Fawcett family then bought the castle and they still reside just down the lane from the castle (Mr Fawcett married the great grand-daughter of the Vavasours, so a member of the family moved back on site for a few years.)

In 1958 the castle was sold to the Hart family, who expressed a desire to the Bishop of Leeds that the castle would make a nice place to be used as a retreat. To avoid gift taxes, the castle was sold to the Carmelite Friars who opened the castle in 1971 as a retreat until 1996, when it was closed and put up for sale. Hazlewood Castle Hotel opened on the 1st October 1997 having been sympathetically restored to reflect it's former glory.

Recently the castle held a garden party for 'Hazlewood babies' born in the castle during its spell as a maternity hospital from 1939- 1953, all who attended received a lifetime privilege card entitling them to various benefits and giving them chance to share their stories.

visit hudsons guide online

THE NATIONAL TRUST

THE THREE HISTORIC HOUSE HOTELS

PAST, PRESENT AND FUTURE PERFECT

Since 1980, Historic House Hotels has acquired three rundown country houses, beautifully and accurately restoring them back to what they once were, and reinstating many lost features. More than just hotels, the beauty of the exterior of the buildings is matched by the meticulous attention to the detail of their contents.

The grounds surrounding each house are worthy of a visit in their own right, with walled gardens, follies, greenhouses, statues, woodland gardens and parterres of great beauty. The award-winning food, cooked to perfection in the hotel kitchens, also pursues the theme of tradition coupled with excellence. Each house has its own Spa, with a superb indoor pool, exercise facilities and a selection of therapeutic and invigorating treatments for the mind, body and soul. First class business facilities featuring the latest technologies satisfy the need of the discerning business traveller.

These beautifully restored houses provide the very best of British hospitality, retaining the atmosphere of a well-kept, well furnished private country house.

BODYSGALLEN HALL & SPA

Standing in over 200 acres of its own parkland to the south of Llandudno in North Wales, with spectacular views of Snowdonia and Conwy Castle and providing the best in country house hospitality. With a choice of 15 bedrooms in the main house and 16 adjacent cottage suites, it is ideally situated as a base for exploring and discovering some of the most attractive scenery in Europe.

HARTWELL HOUSE & SPA

One of Buckinghamshire's finest houses, in the tranquil Vale of Aylesbury, just one hour by car or rail from central London. Formally the home in exile of King Louis XVIII of France, the house now stands in 90 acres of parkland and provides 46 individual bedrooms, magnificent drawing rooms and superb dining rooms. It is easily reached from both LHR, Luton and Gatwick airports.

MIDDLETHORPE HALL & SPA

A distinguished 30 bedroom William III house standing in its own grounds, and very close to York Racecourse. An obvious choice for the racegoer, it is also only a mile and a half from York railway station and the historic city centre. The beauty of the Yorkshire Dales, the open splendour of the North York Moors, the Howardian Hills and the wonderful coastal scenery are all within easy reach.

BODYSGALLEN HALL & SPA
Llandudno North Wales LL30 1RS
T 01492 584466   F 01492 582519
info@bodysgallen.com
www.bodysgallen.com

HARTWELL HOUSE & SPA
Oxford Road nr Aylesbury
Buckinghamshire HP17 8NR
T 01296 747444   F 01296 747450
info@hartwell-house.com
www.hartwell-house.com

MIDDLETHORPE HALL & SPA
Bishopthorpe Road
York YO23 2GB
T 01904 641241   F 01904 620176
info@middlethorpe.com
www.middlethorpe.com

Discover the magic of Lumley Castle Hotel

Standing proud for more than 600 years, Lumley Castle Hotel dominates the County Durham landscape. The Castle's location makes it an ideal base to explore North East England, with the culturally diverse city of Newcastle and the historical city of Durham just minutes away.

The Hotel itself boasts 73 individually designed bedrooms each offering a magical special touch. The well renowned Black Knight Restaurant offers a feast for all taste buds, while year round events such as Elizabethan Banquets and Murder Mystery Evenings all add to making your stay at Lumley Castle an unforgettable experience.

Come and discover the magic of Lumley Castle for yourself.

LUMLEY CASTLE
no ordinary hotel

Lumley Castle Hotel Chester-le-Street
County Durham DH3 4NX England
T: + 44 (0) 191 389 1111   F: + 44 (0) 191 389 5871
E: reservations@lumleycastle.com
www.lumleycastle.com

Discover the charms of Coombe Abbey Hotel

Originally a 12th Century Cistercian Abbey, Coombe Abbey Hotel is set in England's historic heartland in Warwickshire. Surrounded by 500 acres of breathtaking parkland, majestically overlooking a moat, the hotel boasts a stunning garden that was designed by Lancelot 'Capability' Brown in 1771.

Coombe Abbey Hotel is home to 119 specially designed bedrooms each with a unique décor. A meal at the elegantly subtle Garden Room Restaurant is sure to tantalise a wide range of taste buds while the entertainment offered by events such as the Mediaeval Banquets and Murder Mystery Evenings will make your stay at the Abbey a truly memorable experience.

Come and discover the charms of Coombe Abbey for yourself.

COOMBE ABBEY
no ordinary hotel

Coombe Abbey Hotel Brinklow Road Binley
Coventry Warwickshire CV3 2AB England
T: + 44 (0) 2476 450 450   F: + 44 (0) 2476 635 101
E: reservations@coombeabbey.com
www.coombeabbey.com

Lumley Castle and Coombe Abbey Hotel - Your special place in history

Park House Hotel
Sandringham

Award winning holiday and short break destination

Operated by the charity Leonard Cheshire Disability, located on the Royal Sandringham estate near King's Lynn in West Norfolk, Park House Hotel offers a holiday experience for people with mobility difficulties or disabilities, with or without their carer or companion.

Park House is an impressive Victorian country house set in its own grounds amidst the soaring trees and rolling parklands of the Estate. The main house was the birthplace of Princess Diana.

Fully accessible, the hotels is equipped to the very highest standards:

- 16 ensuite bedrooms (8 single/8 twin)
- Digital T.V., radio, direct dial telephone
- Tea/Coffee making facilities
- Well stocked library. Broadband enabled computer
- Relaxing lounge with 42" television
- Movie/games room, piano and art equipment
- Optional Entertainment most evenings

The picturesque grounds are fully accessible; both garden and woodland areas. A heated outdoor swimming pool with Arjo hoist is available May-September.

Only the finest, locally sourced ingredients are used by our team of chefs in preparing international menus complemented by a comprehensive wine list.

Optional, escorted excursions ensure that all guests have a chance to visit their choice of local attractions. The Royal residence at Sandringham House is adjacent to the hotel and is a popular destination, along with the myriad other stately homes within the local area.

Park House Hotel is the ideal country house destination for people with mobility difficulties or disabilities providing peace of mind and a holiday for everyone.

Park House Hotel, Sandringham,
King's Lynn, Norfolk PE35 6EH
t 01485 543000 e parkinfo@LCDisability.org
w www.parkhousehotel.org.uk

enjoyEngland.com
★★
HOTEL

Leonard Cheshire Disability

OPEN BRITAIN

Pentillie
CASTLE AND ESTATE

www.pentillie.co.uk

Experience the magic of Pentillie Castle and Estate ...

Standing in its own magnificent riverside gardens, Pentillie Castle, had been closed to visitors for 40 years. Now, following its inheritance by the latest generation of the Coryton family, the 17th Century castle has been extensively refurbished, under the watchful eye of Channel 4's Country House Rescue, and is now open as an exclusive wedding venue, luxury B&B and events venue.

Its location is stunning but highly accessible: the Castle is just a few miles from the historic harbour town of Plymouth on the banks of the River Tamar, in an area of outstanding natural beauty. St Mellion International Golf resort is minutes away, and it is surprisingly close to the A38, and major rail and air links.

Luxury B&B ...

A stay at Pentillie is relaxing and memorable. The Castle boasts 5 star accommodation for 18, and all the beautifully decorated spacious bedrooms have elegant en-suites and views overlooking the river or gardens. Guests can enjoy dinner in the beautiful Georgian dining room and breakfast on the terrace. Then explore the gardens, which are studded with delightful secrets: the bathing house, the lime tree avenue, the American Gardens, and a walk across the estate will reveal Jimmy Tillie's intriguing mausoleum.

Weddings ...

Weddings at Pentillie are beautifully romantic and luxurious. The bride and groom can enjoy private and exclusive use of the house and its magical grounds. And the friendly and experienced staff will tailor the event to ensure it's the wedding of your dreams. Civil marriages can take place in 4 licensed areas around the house, including outside under the Southern Loggia. Weddings for 60 can be accommodated in the main house, or with marquees on the lawns, up to 250.

Guests can also be treated to a candlelit dinner in the bathing house by the river. The grounds can accommodate helicopters or hot air balloons, or, if the bride and groom wish to leave in style, a boat can pick them up from the jetty to take them on honeymoon. Pentillie is full of beautiful photo opportunities.

Events ...

Whether it's the launch of an exciting new project, a party that no-one will forget, or a business strategy day which delivers results, Pentillie has the flexibility, privacy and magic to ensure your event is special. With catering facilities, break out areas, conference rooms and beautiful open spaces.

Pentillie will be memorable and a pleasure to visit. The staff are friendly, efficient and will tailor things to suit your requirements.

Tel: 01579 350044

Shrewsbury's Historic Royal Hotel

Situated in the heart of medieval Shrewsbury, the Prince Rupert Hotel is firmly established as one of the town's finest hotels. The former home of Prince Rupert, the grandson of King James I, it combines old-world charm with modern comforts and hosts an array of historic period features.

Surrounded by cobblestone streets and Tudor buildings, the Prince Rupert is perfectly located to explore all of the town's main attractions.

Privately owned since 1996 by the Matthews family the hotel has benefited from a significant investment programme.

The Prince Rupert has 70 unique ensuite bedrooms including 12th century Mansion House Suites (some with a 4-poster beds), 15th century Tudor Suites, three fabulous restaurants, Camellias Tearooms, a garden courtyard and a fully equipped health suite. Valet parking in our own private car park.

Butcher Row Shrewsbury SY1 1UQ
Tel. 01743 499955 Fax 01743 357306
reservations@prince-rupert-hotel.co.uk

PRINCE RUPERT
HOTEL

www.prince-rupert-hotel.co.uk

CLASSIC
BRITISH HOTELS

★★★
AA GRADED 83%

The Angel & Royal Hotel

*I love everything that is old,
the old angel, old manners,
old times. old books,
old wines"*

Oliver Goldsmith, 1764

High Street, Grantham,
Lincolnshire, NG31 6PN
Reservations: 0808 178 7666
www.angelandroyal.co.uk

Widely regarded and fondly known as the oldest surviving English Inn, the main façade of the building that stands today was built approximately 600 years ago. The site then, however, had already been an Inn for 200 years, and was built as a hostel for the chivalrous Brotherhood of the Knights Templar. It was then that the beautifully carved building caught the eye of King John, who decided it would make a suitable location for a visit of his Royal Court in 1213.

In 1483 Richard III held court in the Chambre de Roi known today as the Kings Room restaurant, where he dispatched the letter to his great Chancellor bidding for the Great Seal to proclaim the treachery of his cousin, upon it's receipt his death warrant was duly signed.

Charles I made use of the Kings Room during his visit in 1633 and his arch enemy Oliver Cromwell also stayed at the Angel after his successful battle near Grantham in 1643. No less than 7 kings of England and various other royal figures including George IV have patronised the inn. However it wasn't until 1866 after the visit of Queen Victoria eldest son and heir to the throne Edward VII it was universally agreed that this should be celebrated by the incorporation of the 'Royal' into the inns name thus the Angel and Royal came into being as it is known throughout the world.

The Inn has been beautifully and sympathetically restored with many of its original features having been retained. Owner - Ashdale hotels

Situated in the south west corner of Lincolnshire in the historic market town of Grantham, The Angel and Royal Hotel offers 29 high quality and recently refurbished bedrooms, the historic Angel bar with large selection of speciality whiskeys, The Kings room restaurant offering fine cuisine in regal surroundings, Simply Berties our informal bustling Bistro perfect for meeting for drinks and al fresco dining courtyard.

Three venues within the hotel, the Kings room, Simply Berties and the Prince of Wales function room are licensed for civil marriages and partnerships, for weddings for up to 75 guests.

BOVEY CASTLE.
YOU'VE ARRIVED.

Luxurious yet relaxed, Bovey Castle is nestled in the heart of the Dartmoor National Park.

A round of golf, a spa treatment, afternoon tea in front of a roaring log fire, fine dining and even finer views.

For more information please call 01647 445 000 or visit www.boveycastle.com

BOVEY CASTLE
on
DARTMOOR NATIONAL PARK

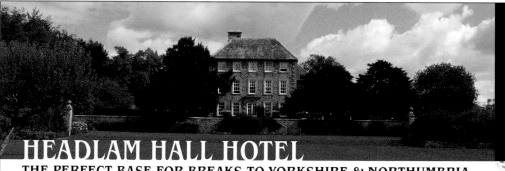

The perfect retreat.

Come home to luxury at Stapleford Park, the country house hotel in the heart of England's beautiful and scenic countryside. With an extensive array of sporting activities and a tranquil spa, Stapleford is the perfect retreat.

Stapleford Park
COUNTRY HOUSE HOTEL & SPORTING ESTATE

Stapleford, Nr. Melton Mowbray, Sunny Leicestershire LE14 2EF
Tel: 01572 787 000   Fax: 01572 787 001
www.staplefordpark.com   reservations@stapleford.co.uk

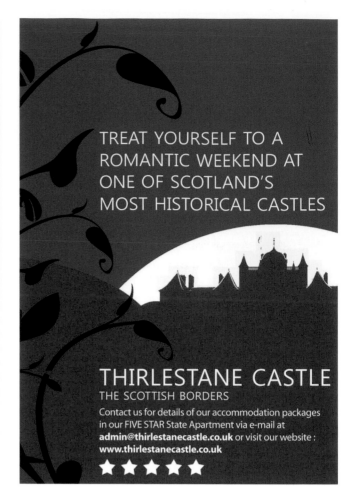

TREAT YOURSELF TO A ROMANTIC WEEKEND AT ONE OF SCOTLAND'S MOST HISTORICAL CASTLES

THIRLESTANE CASTLE
THE SCOTTISH BORDERS

Contact us for details of our accommodation packages in our FIVE STAR State Apartment via e-mail at **admin@thirlestanecastle.co.uk** or visit our website : **www.thirlestanecastle.co.uk**

★★★★★

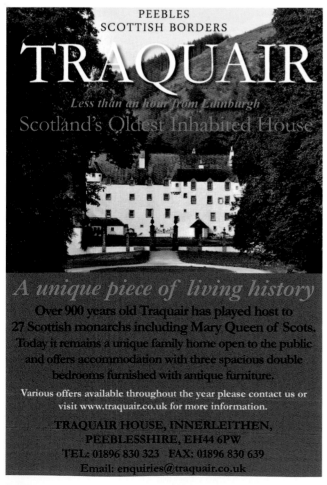

PEEBLES
SCOTTISH BORDERS

TRAQUAIR

Less than an hour from Edinburgh

Scotland's Oldest Inhabited House

A unique piece of living history

Over 900 years old Traquair has played host to 27 Scottish monarchs including Mary Queen of Scots. Today it remains a unique family home open to the public and offers accommodation with three spacious double bedrooms furnished with antique furniture.

Various offers available throughout the year please contact us or visit www.traquair.co.uk for more information.

TRAQUAIR HOUSE, INNERLEITHEN, PEEBLESSHIRE, EH44 6PW
TEL: 01896 830 323   FAX: 01896 830 639
Email: enquiries@traquair.co.uk

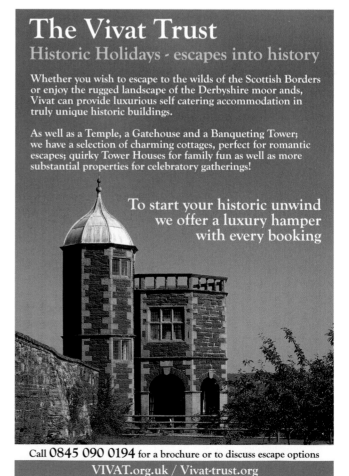

The Vivat Trust
Historic Holidays - escapes into history

Whether you wish to escape to the wilds of the Scottish Borders or enjoy the rugged landscape of the Derbyshire moor ands, Vivat can provide luxurious self catering accommodation in truly unique historic buildings.

As well as a Temple, a Gatehouse and a Banqueting Tower; we have a selection of charming cottages, perfect for romantic escapes; quirky Tower Houses for family fun as well as more substantial properties for celebratory gatherings!

To start your historic unwind we offer a luxury hamper with every booking

Call **0845 090 0194** for a brochure or to discuss escape options

VIVAT.org.uk / Vivat-trust.org

Ashridge
©HHG/Neil Jinkerson

Indexes

Plant Sales   **542**

Properties and gardens offering rare and
unusual plants not generally available.

Corporate Hospitality   **546**

Properties able to accommodate corporate
functions, wedding receptions and events.

Education   **550**

Properties providing facilities for
schools / educational groups.

Accommodation   **555**

Historic properties which offer accommodation -
from basic comfort to ultimate luxury.

Civil Wedding Venues   **558**

Places where the ceremony itself can take place
and may also provide facilities for reception.

Open All Year   **562**

Properties and/or their grounds that are
open for all or most of the year.

Special Events   **568**

Historical re-enactments, festivals, country &
craft fairs, concerts, fireworks, car & steam rallies.

RHS Partner Gardens   **574**

Properties in Hudsons that offer free garden
access at specified times to RHS Members

Plant Sales

Properties where plants are offered for sale.

ENGLAND

LONDON

NORTH WEST

NORTH EAST

SCOTLAND

WALES

SOUTH WALES

MID WALES

NORTH WALES

NORTHERN IRELAND

Coughton Court

© Simon Hadley / Throckmorton Estates

THE 2010 RHS SHOWS.
WE'RE GETTING READY. ARE YOU?
TICKETS NOW AVAILABLE.

Royal
Horticultural
Society

RHS SHOW CARDIFF 16-18 April
MALVERN SPRING GARDENING SHOW 6-9 May
RHS CHELSEA FLOWER SHOW 25-29 May
BBC GARDENERS' WORLD LIVE 16-20 June
HAMPTON COURT PALACE FLOWER SHOW 6-11 July
RHS SHOW TATTON PARK 21-25 July
MALVERN AUTUMN SHOW 26-27 September

rhs.org.uk/flowershows
020 7649 1885

Registered charity no: 222879/SC038262

The RHS, the UK's leading gardening charity

Corporate Hospitality

Properties which are able to accommodate corporate functions, wedding receptions and events. Some properties specialise in corporate hospitality and are open, only rarely, if ever, to day visitors. Others do both. See entry for details.

ENGLAND

LONDON

SOUTH EAST

HEART OF ENGLAND

YORKSHIRE & THE HUMBER

NORTH WEST

NORTH EAST

SCOTLAND

WALES

SOUTH WALES

MID WALES

NORTH WALES

NORTHERN IRELAND

Beaulieu, Hampshire

Education

The properties listed below provide special facilities for schools' groups. The range of these services varies, so it is vital that you contact the property directly when preparing to arrange a school trip. English Heritage offers free admission for pre-booked educational groups. For a free teacher's information pack: e-mail: education@english-heritage.org.uk or visit the website www.english-heritage.org.uk/education

ENGLAND

LONDON

SOUTH EAST

SOUTH WEST

SCOTLAND

WALES

SOUTH WALES

MID WALES

MID WALES

NORTHERN IRELAND

Historic Dockyard Chatham

©Britainonview / Daniel Bosworth

Accommodation

Accommodation for individuals in historic hotels is listed on page 525. The historic properties listed below are not hotels. Their inclusion indicates that accommodation can be arranged, often for groups only. The type and standard of rooms offered vary widely – from the luxurious to the utilitarian. Full details can be obtained from each individual property.

ENGLAND

SCOTLAND

WALES

SOUTH WALES

NORTH WALES

NORTHERN IRELAND

The Italian Bedroom at Eastnor Castle

©Britainonview / Joanna Henderson

Lulworth Castle, Dorset

Civil Wedding Venues

Places at which the marriage or Civil partnership ceremonies can take place – many will also be able to provide facilities for wedding receptions.

Full details about each property are available in the regional listings. There are numerous other properties included within *Hudson's* which do not have a Civil Wedding Licence but which can accommodate wedding receptions. In Scotland religious wedding ceremonies can take place anywhere, subject to the Minister being prepared to perform them.

ENGLAND

LONDON

SOUTH EAST

SOUTH WEST

DREAM WEDDINGS

FINEST VENUES AND SERVICES

THE FINEST VENUES FOR CIVIL CEREMONIES AND RECEPTIONS

Beautiful photographs, informative profiles, and invaluable quick-check Fact File for each venue. At-a-glance information covering all important details from capacity and price range to whether red wine and confetti is permitted.

Fabulous articles written by the 'finest in their field' of expertise giving tips on everything from dress trends for 2010, cakes, flowers, make-up and much, much more. Interesting reading to help with all aspects of wedding planning from 'who does what' to 'transport' and 'toasts'

Plus Services Section to make organising your wedding even easier

Everything you need to ensure your Dream Wedding comes true

www.hudsonsweddings.com
the UK's most stylish and sophisticated wedding website

Open All Year

Properties included in this list are open to some extent for all or most of the year. See individual entries for details.

ENGLAND

EAST MIDLANDS

HEART OF ENGLAND

YORKSHIRE & THE HUMBER

NORTH WEST

NORTH EAST

SCOTLAND

WALES

SOUTH WALES

MID WALES

NORTH WALES

NORTHERN IRELAND

©Britainonview / - Britain on View

Winter night, Lincoln

Special Events

This is merely a selection of special events being staged in 2010 – more information can be obtained from individual property websites – for quick access to these sites visit: www.hudsonsguide.co.uk

JANUARY

January–March

Hodsock Priory, Nottinghamshire
Snowdrops

FEBRUARY

Arley Hall & Gardens, Cheshire
Wedding Fair

Savill Gardens, Surrey
Camellias & Daffodils

6–7

Kelmarsh Hall and Gardens,
Northamptonshire
Snowdrop Weekend

MARCH

6–7

Wilton House, Wiltshire
Antiques Fair

7

Boconnoc, Cornwall
Weddings Fair

13–31

Exbury Gardens, Hampshire
Lachenalia Exhibition

14

Exbury Gardens, Hampshire
Mothering Sunday Weekend

27–June 20

Compton Verney, Warwickshire
Francis Bacon: In Camera

APRIL

Clovelly, Devon
Fantastic Fudge Hunt

Arley Hal & Gardens, Cheshire
Spring Plant Fair and Bluebell Walks

2–5

Groombridge Place Gardens, Kent
Easter Eggstravaganza

2–June 6

Exbury Gardens, Hampshire
Four Seasons Artists Exhibition

3–5

Exbury Gardens, Hampshire
Easter at Exbury – Parrot Trail and
Family train rides

© Exbury Gardens

Easter at Exbury Gardens, Hampshire

3–5

Arundel Castle, Sussex
Normans & Crusaders – Armourer,
archery, mounted display

4–5

Kelmarsh Hall & Gardens,
Northamptonshire
Kelmarsh Country Fair

5

Chenies, Buckinghamshire
Easter fun for children

10-11

Boconnoc, Cornwall
Cornwall Garden Society Spring Flower
Show

11

Arundel Castle, Sussex
MG Rally

12

Traquair, Scotland
Easter Egg Extravaganza

12–May 10

Hole Park Gardens, Kent
Bluebell Spectacular

23–May 3

Pashley Manor Gardens, Sussex
Tulip Festival

18

Chenies, Buckinghamshire
Tulip Festival

19–May 31

Exbury Gardens, Hampshire
The Glory of the Garden

25

Beaulieu, Hampshire
Boat Jumble

22 April– May 9

Renishaw Hall Gardens, Derbyshire
Bluebell Fortnight

MAY

Winchester Cathedral, Hampshire
Fine Food & Wine Show

Tissington Hall, Derbyshire
Well Dressing

1–Oct 31

National Maritime Museum, London
Toy Boats Exhibition

2–3

Groombridge Place Gardens, Kent
The Myth & Magic of Robin Hood

2–3

Kelmarsh Hall and Gardens,
Northamptonshire
Hardy Plant Fair

2–3

Rockingham Castle, Northamptonshire
American Civil War Re-enactment

6–9

Hatfield House
Living Crafts

9

Boconnoc, Cornwall
Dog Show

11–12

Boconnoc, Cornwall
Spring Fair

15–16

Beaulieu, Hampshire
Spring Motormart & Autojumble

16

Arundel Castle, Sussex
Murder Mystery

Jousting, Arundel Castle

22–May 31

Pashley Manor Gardens, Sussex
Sculpture in Particular

23

Kelmarsh Hall and Gardens,
Northamptonshire
Marie Curie Daffodil Run

23–24

Traquair, Scotland
Medieval Fayre

29

Blair Castle, Scotland
Atholl Highlanders' Parade

30

Blair Castle, Scotland
Highland Games

30–31

Arundel Castle, Sussex
Castle in Siege

31

Chenies, Buckinghamshire
The British Driving Society
Competitive Event with many classes

JUNE

Arley Hall & Gardens
Garden Festival

4

Arundel Castle, Sussex
Pirates – archery, fencing, story-teller

4–6

Hollker Hall & Gardens, Cumbria
The Holker Garden Festival

5–6

Cawdor Castle, Scotland
Special Gardens Weekend

5–6

Exbury Gardens, Hampshire
Petal Fall Weekend

6

Stonor, Oxfordshire
VW Owners' Rally

11–13

Pashley Manor Gardens, Sussex
Special Rose Weekend

13

Rockingham Castle, Northamptonshire
Jousting & Medieval Living History
Village

13

Saint Hill Manor, Sussex
Open Air Theatre – "The Importance of
Being Earnest"

18–20

Pashley Manor Gardens, Sussex
Kitchen Garden Weekend

19–20

Hatfield House, Hertfordshire
Rose Weekend Summer Garden Show

©Britainonview / David Sellman

Annual Tulip Festival at Pashley Manor Gardens

19–20

Exbury Gardens, Hampshire
Models and Miniatures Weekend

20

Kelmarsh Hall and Gardens,
Northamptonshire
Kelmarsh at Home

25

Boconnoc, Cornwall
Music in the Park

25–27

Cottesbrooke Hall & Gardens,
Northamptonshire
Plant Finders Fair

26–27

Groombridge Place Gardens, Kent
40's weekend with Spa Valley Railway

26–28

Arundel Castle, Sussex
Medieval Tournament

JULY

Clovelly, Devon
Maritime Festival.
Woolsery Agricultural Show

Port Eliot, Cornwall
Festival – Words, Music, Imagination

Winchester Cathedral, Hampshire
Art, Craft & Design Fair

2–4

Scone Palace, Scotland
The Scottish Game Fair

11

Groombridge Place Gardens
Wings, Wheels & Steam

11

Rockingham Castle, Northamptonshire
Falconry & Owl Day

Mid July–Mid August

Pashley Manor Gardens, Sussex
Lily Time

18

Arundel Castle, Sussex
Pirates – archery, fencing, story-teller

18

Chenies, Buckinghamshire
Plant & Garden Fair

23–25

Boconnoc, Cornwall
Steam Fair

24 July–October 31

Compton Verney, Warwickshire
Volcano Exhibition

25

Hopetoun House, Scotland
Summer Fair

The Harbour, Clovelly, Devon.

© Britainonview / - Britain on View

25–26

Kelmarsh Hall and Gardens,
Northamptonshire
Festival of History – Highlight of English
Heritage event calendar

26–27

Groombridge, Kent

26–Aug 31

Exbury Gardens, Hampshire
Summer Holiday Family Trail

27–Aug 1

Arundel Castle, Sussex
Medieval Encampment/tournament

July–August

Kentwell Hall & Gardens, Suffolk
Open-air theatre, opera and concert
season

AUGUST

Clovelly, Devon
Lifeboat Weekend

1–Sept 1

Doddinghton Hall & Gardens,
Lincolnshire
Exhibition of Wedding Dresses

1

Groombridge Place Gardens
Balloon, Bikes & Ferraris

1–2

Traquair, Scotland
Craft & Country Fair

6–8

Hatfield House, Hertfordshire
Art in Clay

7–8

Exbury Gardens, Hampshire
Woodland Adventures

7–8

Stonor, Oxfordshire
Concert in the Park

7–8

Scone Palace, Scotland
Orchid Festival

12

Arundel Castle, Sussex
Pirates – Archery, fencing, story-teller

14–15

Arundel Castle, Sussex
Medieval encampment/tournament

14–15

Exbury Gardens, Hampshire
New Forest Fuchsia Society Display

14–15

Rockingham Castle, Northamptonshire
Victorian Garrison

20–22

Arundel Castle, Sussex
Concerts

24

Arundel Castle, Sussex
Opera

26

Arundel Castle, Sussex
Shakespeare

Bagpipers marching at the Braemar Highland Games.

© Britainonview / Andy Sewell

20–22

Hatfield House, Hertfordshire
Country Show

27–30

Stonor, Oxfordshire
Chilterns Craft Fair

26–29

Blair Castle, Scotland
International Horse Trials & Country Fair

28–30

Pashley Manor Gardens, Sussex
Sussex Guild Craft Show

28–29

Cawdor Castle, Scotland
Special Gardens Weekend

29–30

Rockingham Castle, Northamptonshire
Vikings! Of Middle England

SEPTEMBER

Clovelly, Devon
Lobster & Crab Feast

11–12

Beaulieu, Hampshire
International Autojumble

19

Arundel Castle, Sussex
Murder Mystery

25

Cawdor Castle, Scotland
'Living Food' – Organic and local produce

25–26

Groombridge Place Gardens
Fairies & Crystals

26

Kelmarsh Hall, Northamptonshire
Wedding Fair

OCTOBER

1–Nov 7

Exbury Gardens, Hampshire
Nerine Exhibition and Wild Autumn Art Display

9–Nov 7

Exbury Gardens, Hampshire
Festival of Autumn Colours

9–10

Exbury Gardens, Hampshire
Big Draw

©Britainonview / Jenny Woodcock

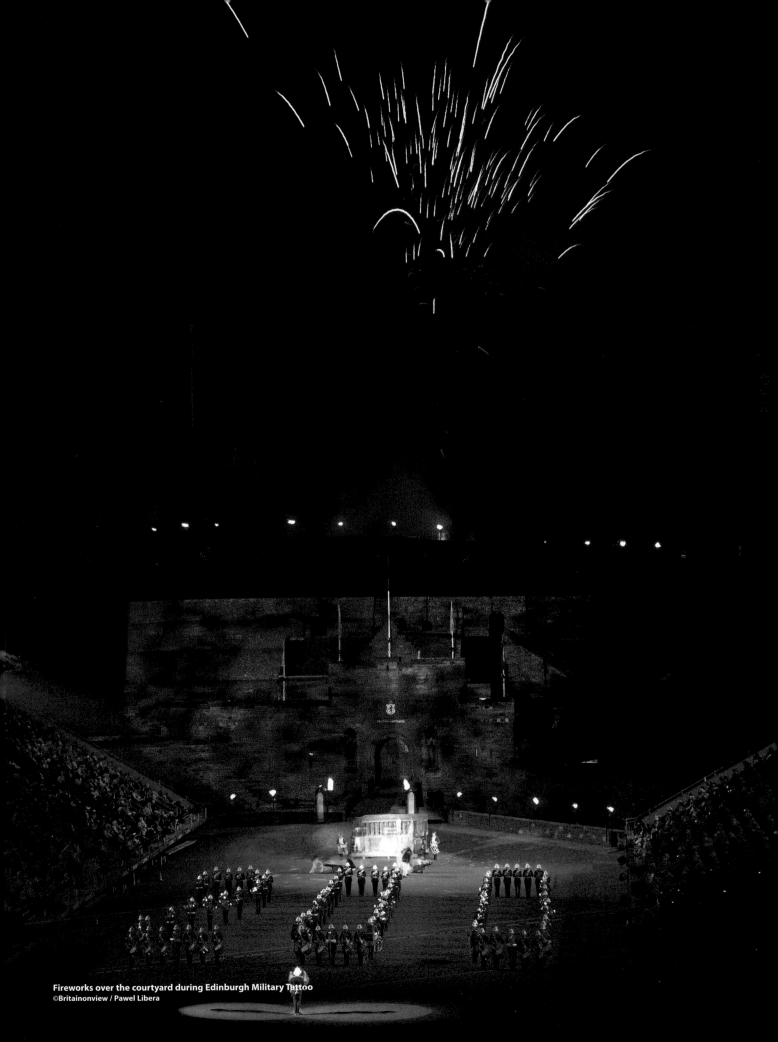

Fireworks over the courtyard during Edinburgh Military Tattoo
©Britainonview / Pawel Libera

RHS Partner

Properties in Hudson's that offer free garden access at specified times to RHS Members.

Abbotsbury Sub-Tropical Gardens
Jan – Feb & Oct-Dec

Aberglasney Gardens
Jan-Mar & Dec (except 5-6 Dec)

Alnwick Garden
Jan – Apr

Anglesey Abbey Gardens
When open (gardens only and not special event days)

Arley Hall & Gardens
Apr-May & Sept-Oct (Gardens only and not special event days)

Belvoir Castle
Apr & Jul

Benington Lordship Gardens
6-12 Feb, 12-4pm & May Bank Holiday, Sun 2-5pm, Mon 12-5pm

Bicton Park Botanical Gardens
Jan-Feb & Nov (excl train rides)

Blenheim Palace Park & Gardens
13 Feb – 28 May (excl. Easter) & 20 Sept – 12 Dec. Park & Gardens only

Bodnant Garden
When open

Branklyn Gardens
When open

Broadleas Gardens
When open (excluding NGS days)

Burton Agnes Hall
When open (except special event days)

Cae Hir Gardens
When open

Caerhays Castle Garden
15 Feb - 14 Mar

Cawdor Castle & Gardens
May - Jun & Sept - Oct (Gardens only)

Cholmondeley Castle Garden
May

Corsham Court Gardens
When open (Gardens only) Excl NGS days 21 Mar and 6 Jun)

Cottesbrooke Hall & Gardens
When open (Gardens only) Excl special event days.

Coughton Court
When open (Gardens only) Excl special event days.

Dalemain
1-30 Apr, 1-30 Sept and 1-28 Oct (gardens only and not special event days)

Docton Mill & Garden
Saturdays 1 Mar - 31 Oct inclusive

Doddington Hall
When open

The Dorothy Clive Garden
Jul - Sept

Drummond Castle
May, Sept and Oct

Duncombe Park
When open (not special event days)

Dunrobin Castle Gardens
When open

Dyffryn Gardens
When open (except special event days)

Elton Hall
May-Jul (gardens only)

Exbury Gardens
Mar and Sept

Floors Castle Gardens
When open (gardens only)

Forde Abbey & Gardens
Jan-Feb & Oct - Dec (Gardens only)

Furzey Gardens
When open

Glenwhan Garden
1 Aug -31 Oct by appointment

Grimsthorpe Castle
Apr, May & Sept

Harewood House
13 Feb – 20 Jun & 6 Sept – 12 Dec (excl. special event days and bank holidays)

Hatfield House & Gardens
Easter Saturday to end of Sept, Wed-Sun and bank holidays (not special event days)

Hergest Croft
Weekends in Mar & 1 Apr- 30 Apr and 1 Jul-30 Sept

Hestercombe Gardens
Jan – Mar & Oct – Dec (Gardens only)

Hill of Tarvit Mansionhouse & Garden
When open (Gardens only)

Holker Hall & Gardens
When open (Gardens only) Excl special event days.

Houghton Hall
June (Gardens only)

Royal Horticultural Society

Kellie Castle & Garden
When open

Kelmarsh Hall
When open (except special event days)

Leith Hall and Garden
When open (except special event days)

Loseley Park
May & Sept (Garden only) except NGS day 9th May

Mannington Gardens
When open (Gardens only, not special event days)

Mapperton Gardens
When open (except special event days)

Muncaster Castle Garden
1 Jul – 31 Dec

National Botanic Garden of Wales, The
Jan - Mar & Oct - Dec

Newby Hall & Gardens
Apr, May & Sept (Gardens only, not special event days)

Nymans
When open

Painswick Rococo Garden
When open (except Feb)

Parcevall Hall Gardens
Aug-Sept

Parham House and Gardens
When open (except group visits)

Penshurst Place & Gardens
When open (except group bookings)

Picton Castle
Apr – Sept, gardens and gallery only (except special event days and group visits).

Plas Brondanw Gardens
When open

Portmeirion
When open

Raby Castle
When open (except special event days)

Ragley Hall
When open (Gardens only, not special event days)

Renishaw Hall
When open (except special event days and bank holidays)

Ripley Castle
When open (not special event days)

Rode Hall
When open

Sandringham
When open (Gardens only)

Sausmarez Manor
First week of every month when open

Scone Palace & Grounds
When open

Sheffield Park Garden
When open (not special event days)

Syon Park
When open (Gardens only, not special event days)

Tapeley Park
8 Jun - 31 Jul

Tatton Park
When open (gardens only)

Thorp Perrow Arboretum
Jan, Jul, Sept and Dec (except special event days)

Threave Garden & Estate
Apr-May and Sept-Oct

Torosay Castle & Gardens
When open

Trentham Estate
Jan-Mar and Oct-Dec (except special event days)

Trebah Garden
1 Jan- 31 Mar and 1 Nov- 31 Mar '11

Trewithen Gardens
Jul - Sept

Waddesdon Manor
Mar & Sept - Oct

Wentworth Castle Gardens
When open

West Dean
Jan-Mar and Nov-Dec (except special event days)

Wilton House
When open (except regular access to adventure playground)

Wyken Hall Gardens
When open

York Gate Garden
Apr-May and Sept (except 4-5 Apr, 2-3 May and 30-31 May)

N.B. Information correct at time of going to print. Please check before travelling. Free access applies to one member per policy. For more information log on to www.rhs.org.uk/rhsgardenfinder/gardenfinder.asp

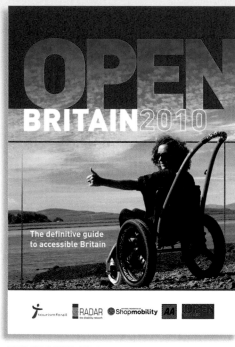 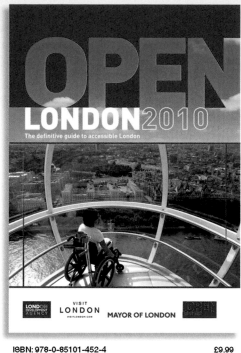

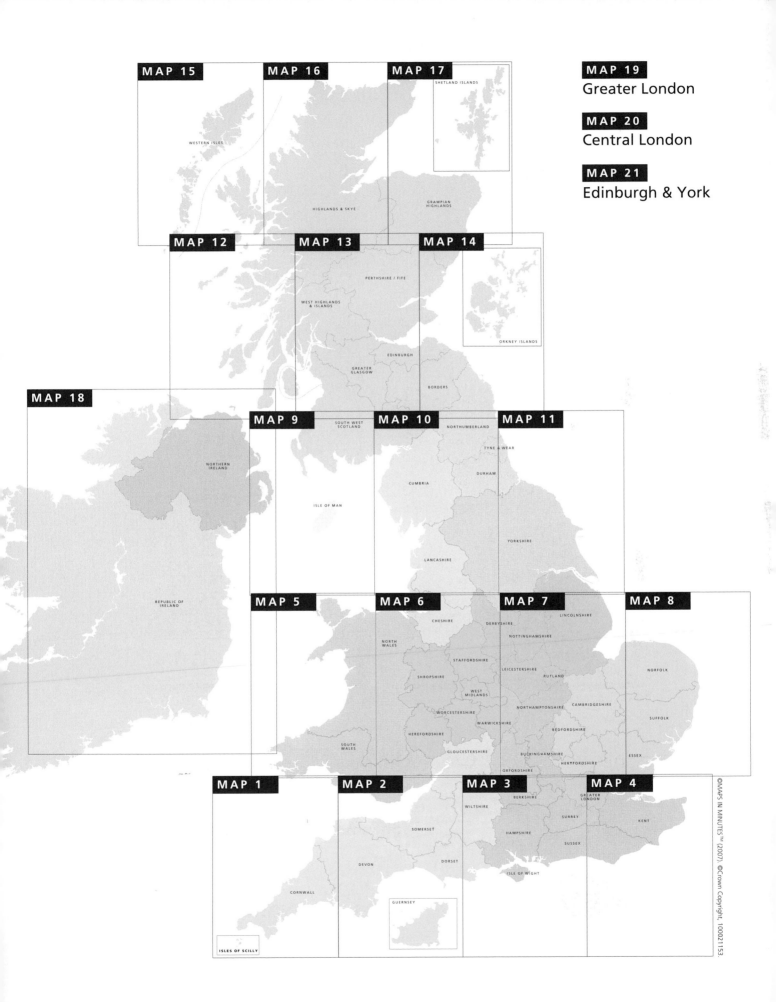

MAP 15

MAP 16

MAP 17

SHETLAND ISLANDS

MAP 19
Greater London

MAP 20
Central London

MAP 21
Edinburgh & York

WESTERN ISLES

HIGHLANDS & SKYE

GRAMPIAN
HIGHLANDS

MAP 12

MAP 13

MAP 14

PERTHSHIRE / FIFE

WEST HIGHLANDS
& ISLANDS

ORKNEY ISLANDS

EDINBURGH

GREATER
GLASGOW

BORDERS

MAP 18

MAP 9

MAP 10

MAP 11

SOUTH WEST
SCOTLAND

NORTHUMBERLAND

TYNE & WEAR

NORTHERN
IRELAND

DURHAM

CUMBRIA

ISLE OF MAN

YORKSHIRE

LANCASHIRE

REPUBLIC OF
IRELAND

MAP 5

MAP 6

MAP 7

MAP 8

CHESHIRE

DERBYSHIRE

LINCOLNSHIRE

NOTTINGHAMSHIRE

NORTH
WALES

STAFFORDSHIRE

LEICESTERSHIRE

RUTLAND

NORFOLK

SHROPSHIRE

WEST
MIDLANDS

NORTHAMPTONSHIRE

CAMBRIDGESHIRE

SUFFOLK

WORCESTERSHIRE

WARWICKSHIRE

BEDFORDSHIRE

HEREFORDSHIRE

BUCKINGHAMSHIRE

HERTFORDSHIRE

ESSEX

SOUTH
WALES

GLOUCESTERSHIRE

OXFORDSHIRE

MAP 1

MAP 2

MAP 3

MAP 4

WILTSHIRE

BERKSHIRE

GREATER
LONDON

SURREY

KENT

SOMERSET

HAMPSHIRE

SUSSEX

DEVON

DORSET

ISLE OF WIGHT

CORNWALL

GUERNSEY

ISLES OF SCILLY

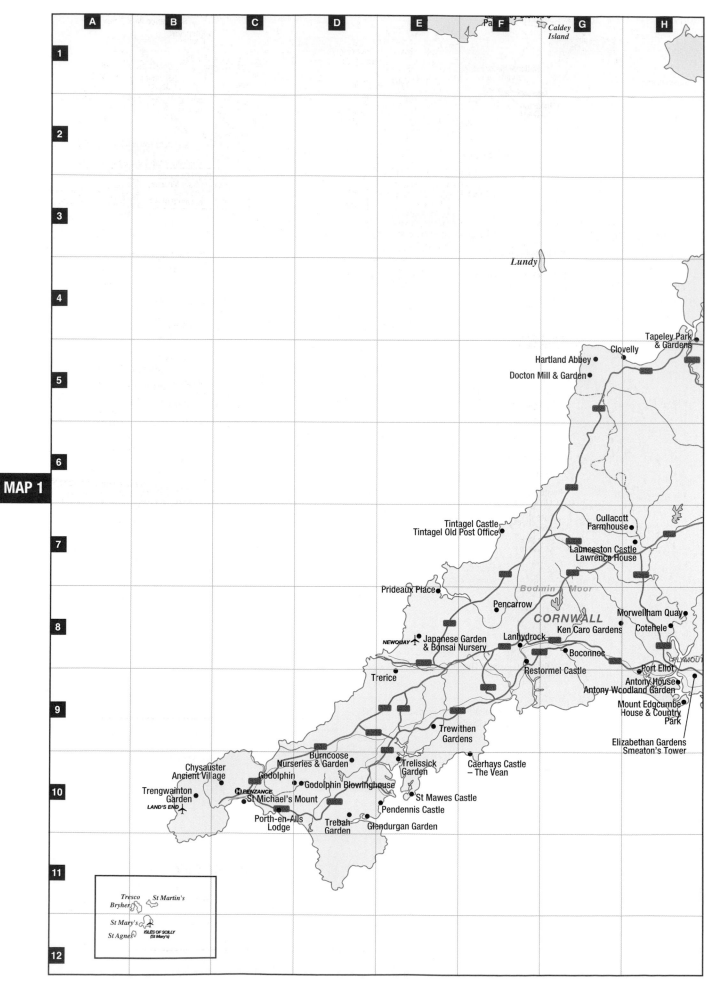

MAP 1

MAP 3

582

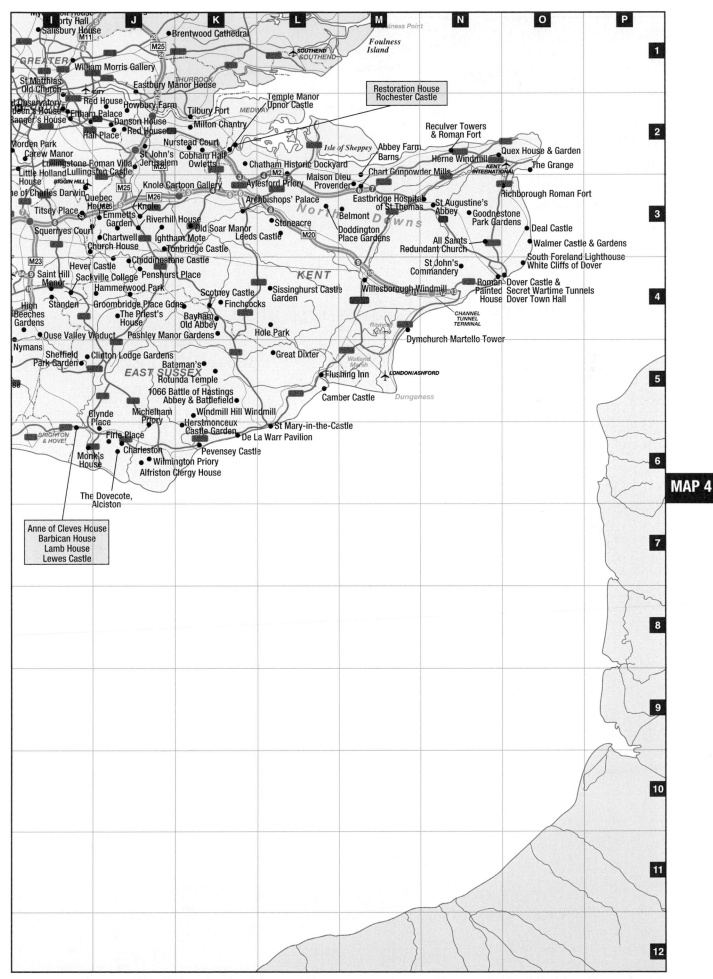

MAP 4

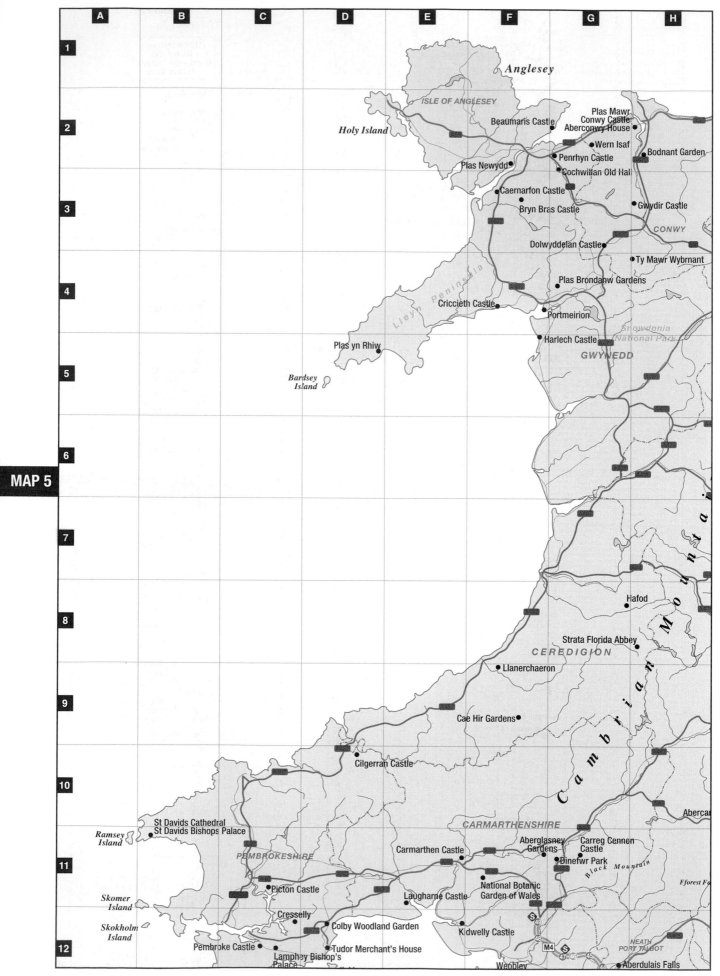

MAP 5

A   B   C   D   E   F   G   H

Anglesey

ISLE OF ANGLESEY

Holy Island

Plas Mawr
Conwy Castle
Beaumaris Castle   Aberconwy House

Wern Isaf
Bodnant Garden
Plas Newydd   Penrhyn Castle
Cochwillan Old Hall

Caernarfon Castle

Bryn Bras Castle   Gwydir Castle

CONWY

Dolwyddelan Castle

Ty Mawr Wybrnant

Plas Brondanw Gardens

Lleyn Peninsula

Criccieth Castle   Portmeirion

Snowdonia National Park

Plas yn Rhiw   Harlech Castle

GWYNEDD

Bardsey Island

Hafod

Strata Florida Abbey

CEREDIGION

Llanerchaeron

Cae Hir Gardens

Cambrian Mountains

Cilgerran Castle

Abercar

St Davids Cathedral
St Davids Bishops Palace

CARMARTHENSHIRE

Ramsey Island

Aberglasney   Carreg Cennen
Gardens   Castle

Carmarthen Castle   Dinefwr Park

PEMBROKESHIRE

Black Mountain

Fforest Fa

Picton Castle   National Botanic
Garden of Wales

Skomer Island

Laugharne Castle

Cresselly

Skokholm Island   Colby Woodland Garden

Kidwelly Castle

M4   *NEATH PORT TALBOT*

Pembroke Castle   Tudor Merchant's House

Aberdulais Falls

Lamphey Bishop's Palace   Weobley

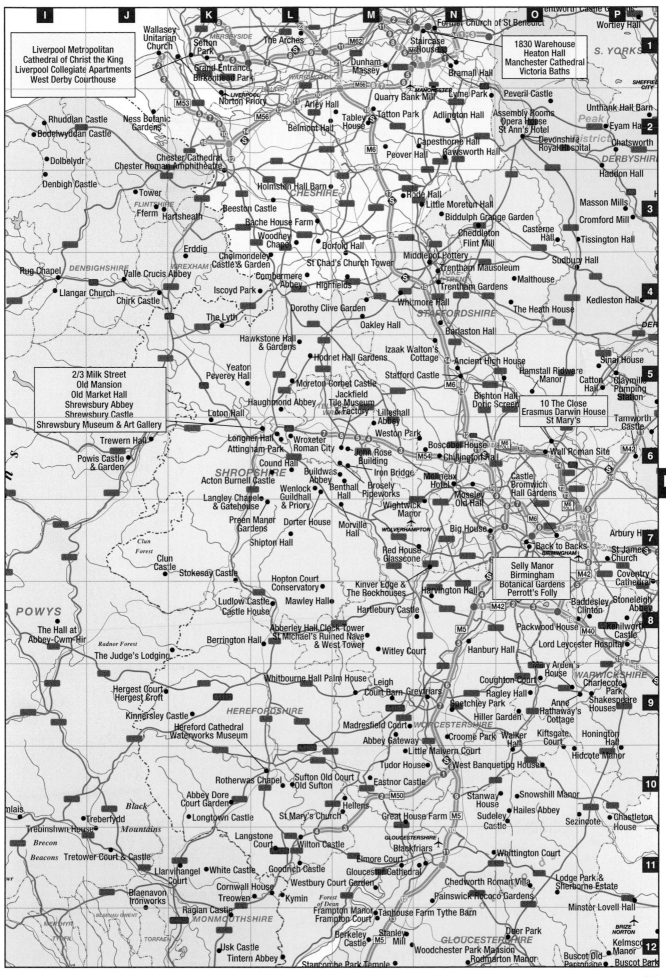

I   J   K   L   M   N   O   P

1

Wortley Hall
S. YORKS

Former Church of St Benedict
Staircase
Dunham Massey
Bramall Hall

Wallasey Unitarian Church
Sefton Park
The Arches
Grand Entrance Birkenhead Park

Liverpool Metropolitan Cathedral of Christ the King
Liverpool Collegiate Apartments
West Derby Courthouse

1830 Warehouse
Heaton Hall
Manchester Cathedral
Victoria Baths

2

Unthank Hall Barn
Eyam Hall
Chatsworth
DERBYSHIRE

Rhuddlan Castle
Bodelwyddan Castle
Ness Botanic Gardens
Liverpool
Norton Priory
Arley Hall
Tabley House
Belmont Hall
Tatton Park
Quarry Bank Mill
Lyme Park
Adlington Hall
Peveril Castle
Assembly Rooms
Opera House
St Ann's Hotel
Devonshire Royal Hospital
Peak District

Dolbelydr
Denbigh Castle
Chester Cathedral
Chester Roman Amphitheatre
Capesthorne Hall
Gawsworth Hall
Peover Hall

Haddon Hall

3

Masson Mills
Cromford Mill

Tower
Fferm
Hartsheath
Beeston Castle
Bache House Farm
Holmston Hall Barn
Rode Hall
Little Moreton Hall
Biddulph Grange Garden
Cheddleton Flint Mill
Casterne Hall
Tissington Hall

FLINTSHIRE
CHESHIRE

4

Rug Chapel
DENBIGHSHIRE
Valle Crucis Abbey
WREXHAM
Erddig
Llangar Church
Chirk Castle
Woodhey Chapel
Dorfold Hall
Cholmondeley Castle & Garden
Combermere Abbey
Highfields
St Chad's Church Tower
Middleport Pottery
Trentham Mausoleum
Trentham Gardens
Malthouse
Kedleston Hall
DER

Iscoyd Park
The Lyth
Dorothy Clive Garden
Oakley Hall
Whitmore Hall
STAFFORDSHIRE
The Heath House
Barlaston Hall

5

Sinai House
Catton Hall
Claymills Pumping Station
Tamworth Castle

Hawkstone Hall & Gardens
Yeaton Peverey Hall
Hodnet Hall Gardens
Moreton Corbet Castle
Izaak Walton's Cottage
Stafford Castle
Ancient High House
Hamstall Ridware Manor

2/3 Milk Street
Old Mansion
Old Market Hall
Shrewsbury Abbey
Shrewsbury Castle
Shrewsbury Museum & Art Gallery

Haughmond Abbey
Jackfield Tile Museum & Factory
Lilleshall Abbey
Weston Park
Bishton Hall Doric Screen

10 The Close
Erasmus Darwin House
St Mary's

6

Loton Hall
Longner Hall
Wroxeter Roman City
John Rose Building
Boscobel House
Chillington Hall
Wall Roman Site
MAP 6

Trewern Hall
Attingham Park
Cound Hall
Iron Bridge
Brosely Pipeworks
Molineux Hotel
Castle Bromwich Hall Gardens

Powis Castle & Garden
SHROPSHIRE
Acton Burnell Castle
Buildwas Abbey
Benthall Hall
Moseley Old Hall

7

Langley Chapel & Gatehouse
Wenlock Guildhall & Priory
Wightwick Manor
Arbury Hall

Preen Manor Gardens
Dorter House
Morville Hall
WOLVERHAMPTON
Big House
Back to Backs
BIRMINGHAM
St James's Church

Clun Forest
Shipton Hall
Red House Glasscone
Selly Manor
Birmingham Botanical Gardens
Perrott's Folly
Coventry Cathedral

Clun Castle
POWYS
Stokesay Castle
Hopton Court Conservatory
Kinver Edge & The Rockhouses
Harvington Hall
Baddesley Clinton
Stoneleigh Abbey

8

Ludlow Castle
Castle House
Mawley Hall
Hartlebury Castle
Packwood House
Kenilworth Castle

The Hall at Abbey-Cwm-Hir
Berrington Hall
Abberley Hall Clock Tower
St Michael's Ruined Nave & West Tower
Witley Court
Hanbury Hall
Lord Leycester Hospital

The Judge's Lodging
Radnor Forest

9

Hergest Court
Hergest Croft
Whitbourne Hall Palm House
Leigh
Court Barn Greyfriars
Coughton Court
Ragley Hall
Spetchley Park
Mary Arden's House
Charlecote Park
Shakespeare Houses
Anne Hathaway's Cottage
WARWICKSHIRE

Kinnersley Castle
HEREFORDSHIRE
Hereford Cathedral
Waterworks Museum
Madresfield Court
WORCESTERSHIRE
Hiller Garden
Croome Park
Walker Hall
Kiftsgate Court
Honington Hall

10

Rotherwas Chapel
Sufton Old Court
Old Sufton
Abbey Gateway
Little Malvern Court
Tudor House
West Banqueting House
Hidcote Manor

Abbey Dore Court Garden
Hellens
Stanway House
Snowshill Manor

Treberfydd
Longtown Castle
St Mary's Church
Great House Farm
Sudeley Castle
Hailes Abbey
Sezincote
Chastleton House

Trebinshwn House
Black Mountains
Langstone Court
Wilton Castle
Blackfriars
GLOUCESTERSHIRE
Whittington Court

11

Tretower Court & Castle
Brecon Beacons
Llanvihangel Court
White Castle
Goodrich Castle
Westbury Court Garden
Gloucester Cathedral
Chedworth Roman Villa
Painswick Rococo Gardens
Lodge Park & Sherborne Estate

Cornwall House
Treowen
Kymin
Frampton Manor
Frampton Court
Tanhouse Farm Tythe Barn
Minster Lovell Hall

12

Raglan Castle
MONMOUTHSHIRE
BLAENAU GWENT
Usk Castle
Tintern Abbey
Stancombe Park Temple
Berkeley Castle
Stanley Mill
Woodchester Park Mansion
Rodmarton Manor
Deer Park
GLOUCESTERSHIRE
BRIZE NORTON
Buscot Old Parsonage
Kelmscott Manor
Buscot Park

585

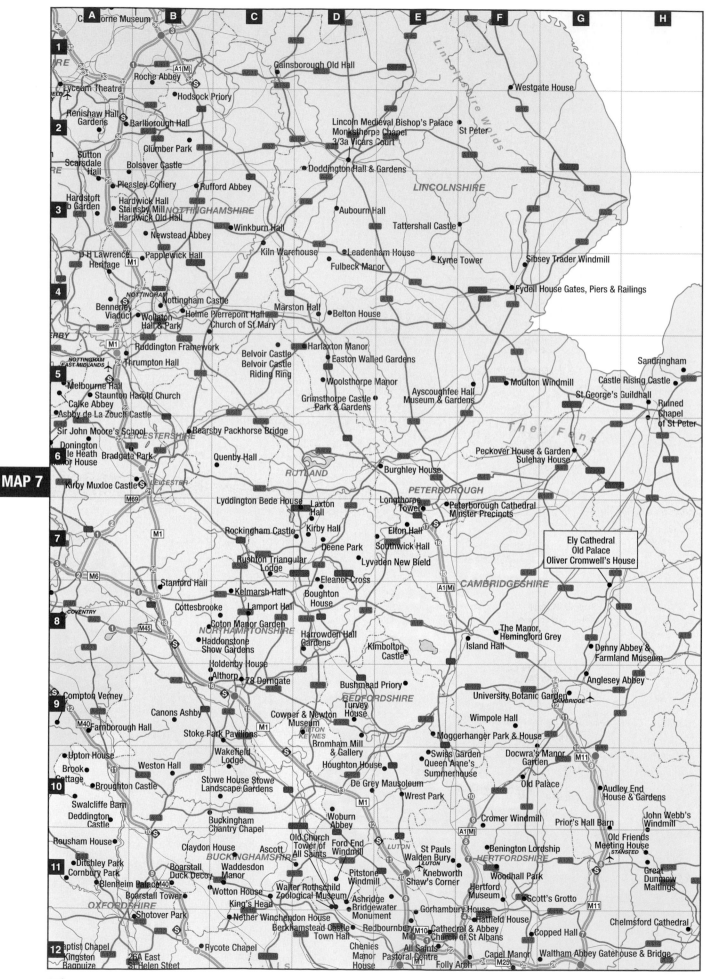

MAP 7

A B C D E F G H

1

- Clumber Museum
- Roche Abbey
- Lyceum Theatre
- Renishaw Hall Gardens
- Barlborough Hall
- Hodsock Priory
- Gainsborough Old Hall
- Westgate House

2

- Clumber Park
- Sutton Scarsdale Hall
- Bolsover Castle
- Lincoln Medieval Bishop's Palace
- Monksthorpe Chapel
- 3/3a Vicars Court
- St Peter

3

- Hardstoft Herb Garden
- Pleasley Colliery
- Hardwick Hall
- Stainsby Mill
- Hardwick Old Hall
- Rufford Abbey
- Doddington Hall & Gardens
- LINCOLNSHIRE
- Aubourn Hall
- Tattershall Castle
- Winkburn Hall
- Newstead Abbey

4

- D H Lawrence Heritage
- Papplewick Hall
- Kiln Warehouse
- Leadenham House
- Kyme Tower
- Sibsey Trader Windmill
- Fulbeck Manor
- Fydell House Gates, Piers & Railings
- Bennerley Viaduct
- Wollaton Hall & Park
- Nottingham Castle
- Holme Pierrepont Hall
- Church of St Mary
- Marston Hall
- Belton House

5

- Ruddington Framework
- Thrumpton Hall
- Belvoir Castle
- Belvoir Castle Riding Ring
- Harlaxton Manor
- Easton Walled Gardens
- Woolsthorpe Manor
- Grimsthorpe Castle Park & Gardens
- Ayscoughfee Hall Museum & Gardens
- Moulton Windmill
- Sandringham
- Castle Rising Castle
- St George's Guildhall
- Ruined Chapel of St Peter
- Melbourne Hall
- Staunton Harold Church
- Calke Abbey
- Ashby de La Zouch Castle

6

- Sir John Moore's School
- Bearsby Packhorse Bridge
- Donington le Heath Manor House
- Bradgate Park
- Quenby Hall
- RUTLAND
- Burghley House
- Peckover House & Garden
- Sulehay House
- The Fens
- Kirby Muxloe Castle
- LEICESTER
- PETERBOROUGH

7

- Lyddington Bede House
- Laxton Hall
- Longthorpe Tower
- Peterborough Cathedral Minster Precincts
- Rockingham Castle
- Kirby Hall
- Elton Hall
- Deene Park
- Southwick Hall
- Ely Cathedral
- Old Palace
- Oliver Cromwell's House
- Rushton Triangular Lodge
- Lyveden New Bield
- CAMBRIDGESHIRE
- Stanford Hall

8

- Eleanor Cross
- Kelmarsh Hall
- Boughton House
- Cottesbrooke
- Lamport Hall
- Coton Manor Garden
- NORTHAMPTONSHIRE
- Harrowden Hall Gardens
- The Manor, Hemingford Grey
- Haddonstone Show Gardens
- Kimbolton Castle
- Island Hall
- Denny Abbey & Farmland Museum
- Anglesey Abbey

9

- Holdenby House
- Althorp
- 78 Derngate
- Bushmead Priory
- University Botanic Garden
- CAMBRIDGE
- Compton Verney
- Canons Ashby
- Cowper & Newton Museum
- Turvey House
- Wimpole Hall
- Farnborough Hall
- Stoke Park Pavilions
- Bromham Mill & Gallery
- MILTON KEYNES
- Moggerhanger Park & House

10

- Upton House
- Brook Cottage
- Weston Hall
- Wakefield Lodge
- Houghton House
- Swiss Garden
- Queen Anne's Summerhouse
- Docwra's Manor Garden
- Broughton Castle
- Stowe House Stowe Landscape Gardens
- De Grey Mausoleum
- Old Palace
- Audley End House & Gardens
- Swalcliffe Barn
- Deddington Castle
- Wrest Park
- John Webb's Windmill

11

- Rousham House
- Buckingham Chantry Chapel
- Woburn Abbey
- Cromer Windmill
- Prior's Hall Barn
- Ditchley Park
- Cornbury Park
- Blenheim Palace
- Boarstall Duck Decoy
- Waddesdon Manor
- Claydon House
- Ascott
- Old Church Tower of All Saints
- Ford End Windmill
- St Pauls Walden Bury
- LUTON
- Benington Lordship
- Woodhall Park
- Old Friends Meeting House
- STANSTED
- Great Dunmow Maltings
- Boarstall Tower
- Wotton House
- King's Head
- Pitstone Windmill
- Knebworth
- Shaw's Corner
- Hertford Museum
- Shotover Park
- Walter Rothschild Zoological Museum
- Ashridge
- Bridgewater Monument
- Gorhambury House
- Hatfield House
- Scott's Grotto
- Chelmsford Cathedral
- Copped Hall
- Nether Winchendon House
- Berkhamstead Castle
- Town Hall
- Redbournbury Mill
- Cathedral & Abbey
- Church of St Albans
- Capel Manor
- Waltham Abbey Gatehouse & Bridge

12

- Baptist Chapel Kingston Bagpuize
- 26A East St Helen Street
- Rycote Chapel
- Chenies Manor House
- All Saints Pastoral Centre
- Folly Arch
- BUCKINGHAMSHIRE
- OXFORDSHIRE
- HERTFORDSHIRE
- BEDFORDSHIRE

586

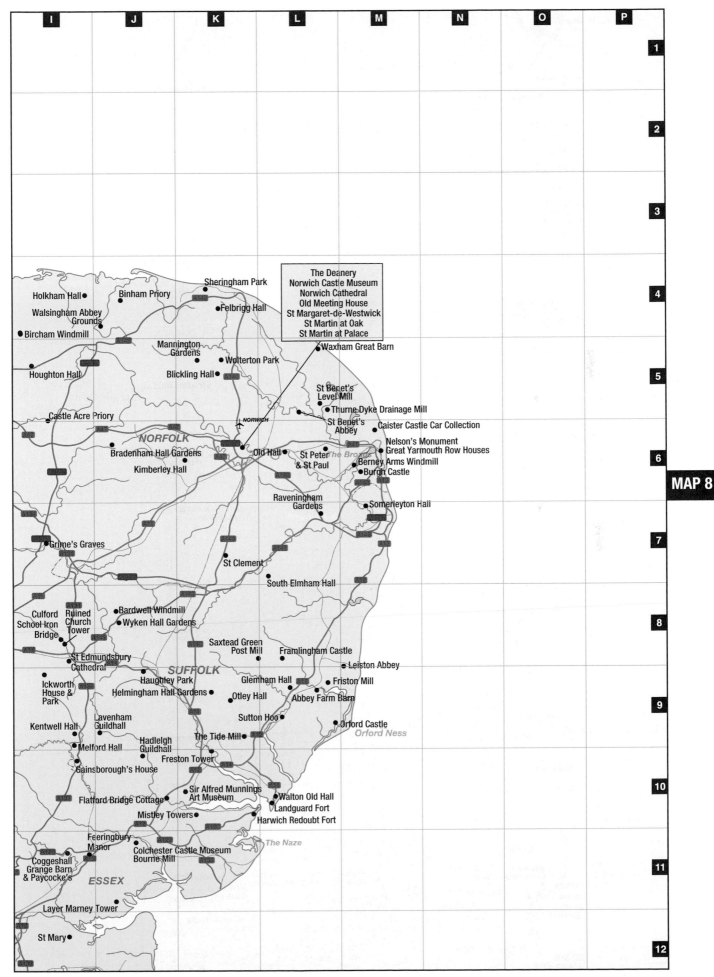

I J K L M N O P

1 2 3 4 5 6 7 8 9 10 11 12

The Deanery
Norwich Castle Museum
Norwich Cathedral
Old Meeting House
St Margaret-de-Westwick
St Martin at Oak
St Martin at Palace

Holkham Hall ●
Binham Priory
Sheringham Park
Walsingham Abbey Grounds
Felbrigg Hall
● Bircham Windmill
Mannington Gardens
● Wolterton Park
Houghton Hall
Blickling Hall ●
Waxham Great Barn

St Benet's Level Mill
● Thurne Dyke Drainage Mill
Castle Acre Priory
St Benet's Abbey
● Caister Castle Car Collection
NORWICH
NORFOLK
Nelson's Monument
● Great Yarmouth Row Houses
Bradenham Hall Gardens
Old Hall
St Peter & St Paul
The Broads
● Berney Arms Windmill
Kimberley Hall
● Burgh Castle

Raveningham Gardens
● Somerleyton Hall

● Grime's Graves
St Clement
South Elmham Hall

● Bardwell Windmill
Culford School Iron Bridge
Ruined Church Tower
● Wyken Hall Gardens
Saxtead Green Post Mill
Framlingham Castle
● Leiston Abbey
St Edmundsbury Cathedral
SUFFOLK
Haughley Park
Glemham Hall
● Friston Mill
Ickworth House & Park
Helmingham Hall Gardens
Otley Hall
Abbey Farm Barn
Kentwell Hall
Lavenham Guildhall
Sutton Hoo
● Orford Castle
● Melford Hall
Hadleigh Guildhall
The Tide Mill
Orford Ness
Gainsborough's House
Freston Tower

Sir Alfred Munnings Art Museum
● Walton Old Hall
Flatford Bridge Cottage
● Landguard Fort
Mistley Towers ●
Harwich Redoubt Fort
Feeringbury Manor
The Naze
Colchester Castle Museum
Bourne Mill
Coggeshall Grange Barn & Paycocke's
ESSEX

● Layer Marney Tower

St Mary ●

MAP 8

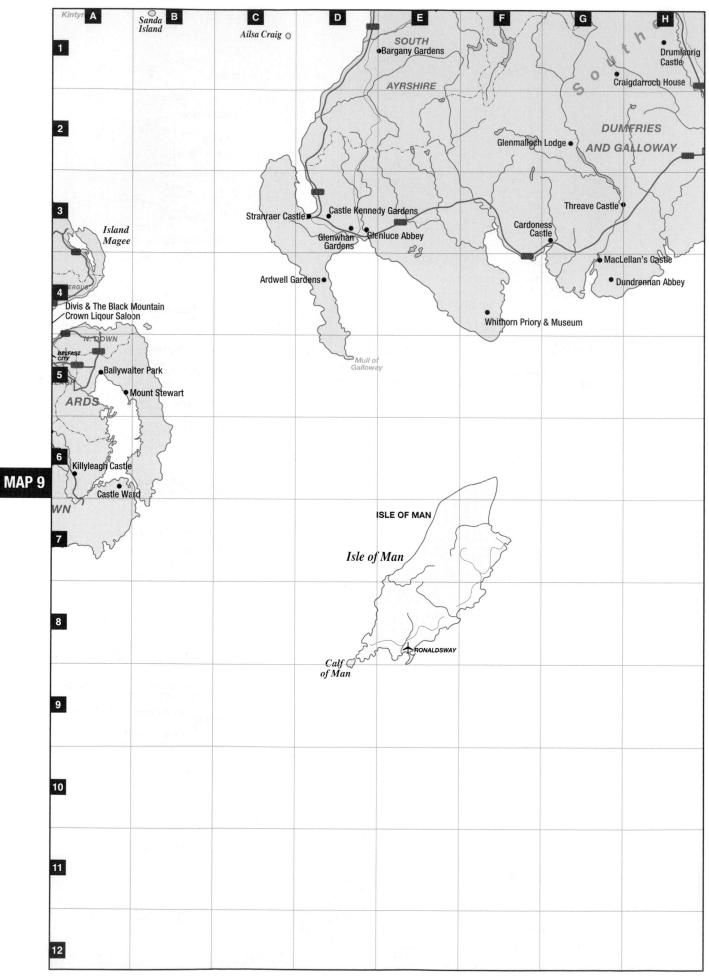

MAP 9

A B C D E F G H

1
Kintyre
Sanda Island
Ailsa Craig
SOUTH
Bargany Gardens
AYRSHIRE
Drumlanrig Castle
Craigdarroch House
South

2
DUMFRIES AND GALLOWAY
Glenmalloch Lodge

3
Island Magee
Stranraer Castle
Castle Kennedy Gardens
Glenwhan Gardens
Glenluce Abbey
Threave Castle
Cardoness Castle
MacLellan's Castle

4
FERGUS
Divis & The Black Mountain
Crown Liqour Saloon
N. DOWN
Ardwell Gardens
Dundrennan Abbey
Whithorn Priory & Museum
Mull of Galloway

5
BELFAST CITY
Ballywalter Park
Mount Stewart
ARDS
LEAGH

6
Killyleagh Castle
Castle Ward

7
WN
ISLE OF MAN
Isle of Man

8
RONALDSWAY

9
Calf of Man

10

11

12

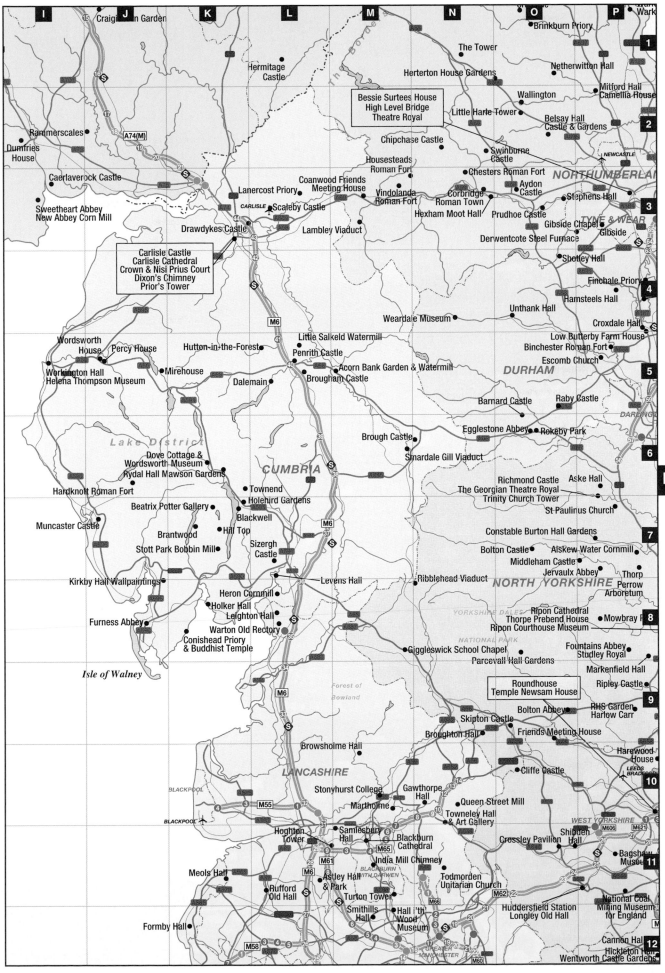

I   J   K   L   M   N   O   P

Craigieburn Garden

15

16 S

17

Hermitage Castle

Rammerscales

18 A74(M)

19

20

Dumfries House

Caerlaverock Castle

21 S

Sweetheart Abbey
New Abbey Corn Mill

Drawdykes Castle

CARLISLE

Scaleby Castle

13

42

Carlisle Castle
Carlisle Cathedral
Crown & Nisi Prius Court
Dixon's Chimney
Prior's Tower

Lanercost Priory

Coanwood Friends
Meeting House

Vindolanda
Roman Fort

Lambley Viaduct

S

M6

41

Wordsworth
House

Percy House

Hutton-in-the-Forest

Little Salkeld Watermill

Penrith Castle

Acorn Bank Garden & Watermill

Workington Hall
Helena Thompson Museum

Mirehouse

Dalemain

Brougham Castle

40

S

Lake District

Dove Cottage &
Wordsworth Museum
Rydal Hall Mawson Gardens

CUMBRIA

Townend

Holehird Gardens

Blackwell

Hardknott Roman Fort

Brantwood

Hill Top

Beatrix Potter Gallery

Muncaster Castle

Stott Park Bobbin Mill

Sizergh
Castle

Kirkby Hall Wallpaintings

Heron Cornmill

Holker Hall

Leighton Hall

Furness Abbey

Warton Old Rectory

Conishead Priory
& Buddhist Temple

Isle of Walney

Levens Hall

39

38

37

S

M6

S

36

35 S

34

Forest of
Bowland

M6

33

S

Browsholme Hall

LANCASHIRE

Stonyhurst College

Gawthorpe
Hall

14

13

Queen Street Mill

Martholme

Towneley Hall
& Art Gallery

BLACKPOOL

M55

32

S

Hoghton
Tower

Samlesbury
Hall

Blackburn
Cathedral

M65

India Mill Chimney

BLACKPOOL

31

M61

S

6

M6

Meols Hall

Astley Hall
& Park

BLACKBURN
WITH DARWEN

Todmorden
Unitarian Church

M66

M62

Rufford
Old Hall

Turton Tower

Smithills
Hall

Hall i' th'
Wood
Museum

Formby Hall

M58

GREATER
MANCHESTER

M60

The Tower

Herterton House Gardens

Bessie Surtees House
High Level Bridge
Theatre Royal

Chipchase Castle

Housesteads
Roman Fort

Little Harle Tower

Swinburne
Castle

Wallington

NEWCASTLE

NORTHUMBERLAND

Chesters Roman Fort

Corbridge
Roman Town

Aydon
Castle

Hexham Moot Hall

Prudhoe Castle

Stephens Hall

TYNE & WEAR

Gibside Chapel

Gibside

Derwentcote Steel Furnace

S

65

64

63

Shotley Hall

Finchale Priory

Hamsteels Hall

4

Weardale Museum

Unthank Hall

Croxdale Hall

S

Low Butterby Farm House

DURHAM

Binchester Roman Fort

Escomb Church

5

Barnard Castle

Raby Castle

Egglestone Abbey

Rokeby Park

DARLINGTON

57

56

Brough Castle

Smardale Gill Viaduct

6

Richmond Castle

Aske Hall

MAP 10

The Georgian Theatre Royal
Trinity Church Tower

St Paulinus Church

Constable Burton Hall Gardens

Bolton Castle

Alskew Water Cornmill

Middleham Castle

Jervaulx Abbey

Thorp
Perrow
Arboretum

7

Ribblehead Viaduct

NORTH YORKSHIRE

YORKSHIRE DALES

Ripon Cathedral

Thorpe Prebend House

Ripon Courthouse Museum

Mowbray P

8

NATIONAL PARK

Giggleswick School Chapel

Parcevall Hall Gardens

Fountains Abbey
Studley Royal

Markenfield Hall

Ripley Castle

Roundhouse
Temple Newsam House

Bolton Abbey

RHS Garden
Harlow Carr

9

Skipton Castle

Broughton Hall

Friends Meeting House

Harewood
House

LEEDS
BRADFORD

Cliffe Castle

10

M621

M606

Shibden
Hall

27

28

Crossley Pavilion

WEST YORKSHIRE

S

Bagshaw
Museum

11

Brinkburn Priory

1

Netherwitton Hall

Mitford Hall
Camellia House

Belsay Hall
Castle & Gardens

2

Longley Old Hall

Huddersfield Station

National Coal
Mining Museum
for England

Cannon Hall

Hickleton Hall

Wentworth Castle Gardens

12

589

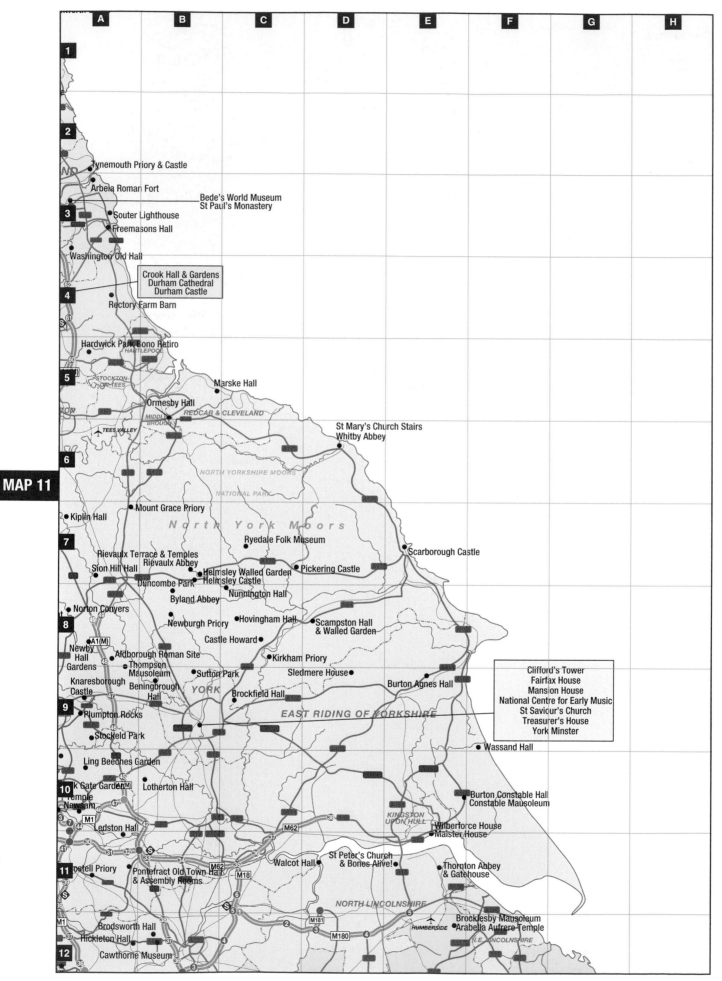

MAP 11

A **B** **C** **D** **E** **F** **G** **H**

Tynemouth Priory & Castle

Arbela Roman Fort

Bede's World Museum
St Paul's Monastery

Souter Lighthouse

Freemasons Hall

Washington Old Hall

Crook Hall & Gardens
Durham Cathedral
Durham Castle

Rectory Farm Barn

Hardwick Park Bono Retiro

HARTLEPOOL

STOCKTON-ON-TEES

Marske Hall

Ormesby Hall

MIDDLESBROUGH

REDCAR & CLEVELAND

TEES VALLEY

St Mary's Church Stairs
Whitby Abbey

NORTH YORKSHIRE MOORS

NATIONAL PARK

Mount Grace Priory

Kiplin Hall

North York Moors

Ryedale Folk Museum

Scarborough Castle

Rievaulx Terrace & Temples
Rievaulx Abbey

Sion Hill Hall

Helmsley Walled Garden
Helmsley Castle

Pickering Castle

Duncombe Park

Byland Abbey

Nunnington Hall

Norton Conyers

Hovingham Hall

Newburgh Priory

Scampston Hall
& Walled Garden

Castle Howard

Newby
Hall
Gardens

A1(M)

Aldborough Roman Site

Thompson
Mausoleum

Sutton Park

Kirkham Priory

Sledmere House

Burton Agnes Hall

Knaresborough
Castle

Beningbrough
Hall

YORK

Brockfield Hall

Clifford's Tower
Fairfax House
Mansion House
National Centre for Early Music
St Saviour's Church
Treasurer's House
York Minster

Plumpton Rocks

EAST RIDING OF YORKSHIRE

Stockeld Park

Wassand Hall

Ling Beeches Garden

k Gate Garden

Lotherton Hall

Burton Constable Hall
Constable Mausoleum

Temple
Newsam

M1

KINGSTON
UPON HULL

Wilberforce House
Maister House

Ledston Hall

M62

Walcot Hall

St Peter's Church
& Bones Alive!

Thornton Abbey
& Gatehouse

ostell Priory

Pontefract Old Town Hall
& Assembly Rooms

M62

M18

NORTH LINCOLNSHIRE

Brodsworth Hall

M1

M181

M180

HUMBERSIDE

Brocklesby Mausoleum
Arabella Aufrere Temple

Hickleton Hall

N.E. LINCOLNSHIRE

Cawthorne Museum

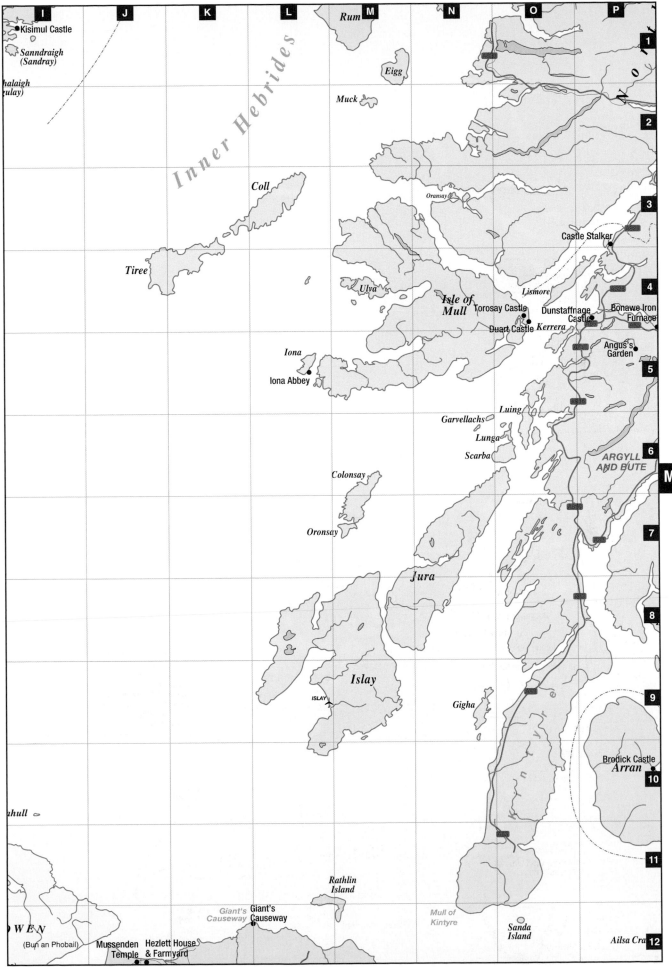

Kisimul Castle

Sanndraigh
(Sandray)

halaigh
gulay)

Rum

Eigg

Muck

I n n e r   H e b r i d e s

Coll

Oransay

Castle Stalker

Tiree

Ulva

Lismore

Isle of Mull
Torosay Castle   Dunstaffnage Castle   Bonawe Iron Furnace

Duart Castle   *Kerrera*

Angus's Garden

Iona

Iona Abbey

Luing
Garvellachs

Lunga

Scarba

Colonsay

ARGYLL AND BUTE

MAP 12

Oronsay

Jura

Islay

Islay ISLAY ✈

Gigha

Brodick Castle
Arran

ahull

Rathlin Island

Mull of Kintyre

Sanda Island

Ailsa Cra

O W E N
(Bun an Phobail)

Mussenden Temple

Hezlett House & Farmyard

Giant's Causeway   Giant's Causeway

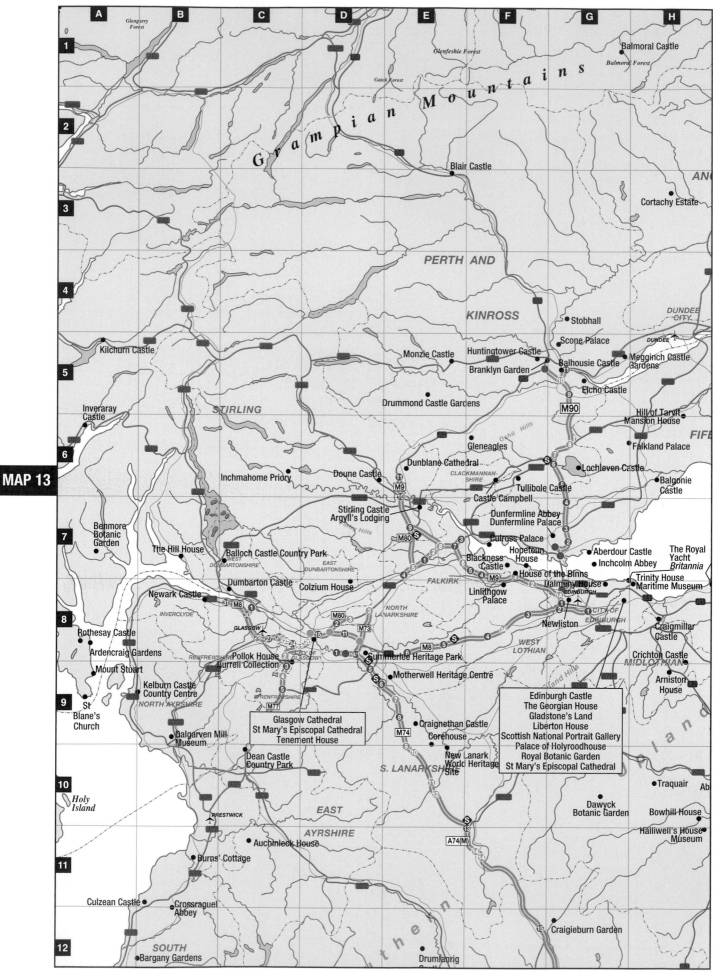

MAP 13

Grid references (columns A–H, rows 1–12):

- Glengarry Forest
- Balmoral Castle
- Balmoral Forest
- Glenfeshie Forest
- Gaick Forest
- Grampian Mountains
- Blair Castle
- ANG
- Cortachy Estate
- PERTH AND
- KINROSS
- DUNDEE CITY
- Stobhall
- Scone Palace
- DUNDEE
- Kilchurn Castle
- Monzie Castle
- Huntingtower Castle
- Balhousie Castle
- Megginch Castle Gardens
- Branklyn Garden
- M90
- Elcho Castle
- Inveraray Castle
- STIRLING
- Drummond Castle Gardens
- Hill of Tarvit Mansion House
- Gleneagles
- Falkland Palace
- FIFE
- Ochil Hills
- Dunblane Cathedral
- CLACKMANNAN-SHIRE
- Lochleven Castle
- Benmore Botanic Garden
- Inchmahome Priory
- Doune Castle
- Tullibole Castle
- Balgonie Castle
- M9
- Castle Campbell
- Stirling Castle
- Argyll's Lodging
- Dunfermline Abbey
- Dunfermline Palace
- The Hill House
- Balloch Castle Country Park
- WEST DUNBARTONSHIRE
- EAST DUNBARTONSHIRE
- Culross Palace
- Hopetoun House
- Aberdour Castle
- The Royal Yacht Britannia
- M80
- Blackness Castle
- Inchcolm Abbey
- Dumbarton Castle
- Colzium House
- FALKIRK
- House of the Binns
- Trinity House Maritime Museum
- Newark Castle
- INVERCLYDE
- M9
- Dalmeny House
- M8
- Linlithgow Palace
- EDINBURGH
- GLASGOW
- NORTH LANARKSHIRE
- Newliston
- CITY OF EDINBURGH
- Craigmillar Castle
- Rothesay Castle
- M80
- M73
- WEST LOTHIAN
- Crichton Castle
- Ardencraig Gardens
- RENFREWSHIRE
- Pollok House
- Burrell Collection
- CITY OF GLASGOW
- Summerlee Heritage Park
- M8
- MIDLOTHIAN
- Mount Stuart
- Arniston House
- Kelburn Castle Country Centre
- EAST RENFREWSHIRE
- Motherwell Heritage Centre
- NORTH AYRSHIRE
- St Blane's Church
- M77
- Glasgow Cathedral
- St Mary's Episcopal Cathedral
- Tenement House
- Craignethan Castle
- Edinburgh Castle
- The Georgian House
- Gladstone's Land
- Liberton House
- Scottish National Portrait Gallery
- Palace of Holyroodhouse
- Royal Botanic Garden
- St Mary's Episcopal Cathedral
- Dalgarven Mill Museum
- Corehouse
- Dean Castle Country Park
- New Lanark World Heritage Site
- Traquair
- Holy Island
- M74
- Dawyck Botanic Garden
- Bowhill House
- PRESTWICK
- EAST AYRSHIRE
- S. LANARKSHIRE
- Halliwell's House Museum
- Auchinleck House
- A74(M)
- Burns' Cottage
- Culzean Castle
- Crossraguel Abbey
- Craigieburn Garden
- SOUTH
- Bargany Gardens
- Drumlanrig

592

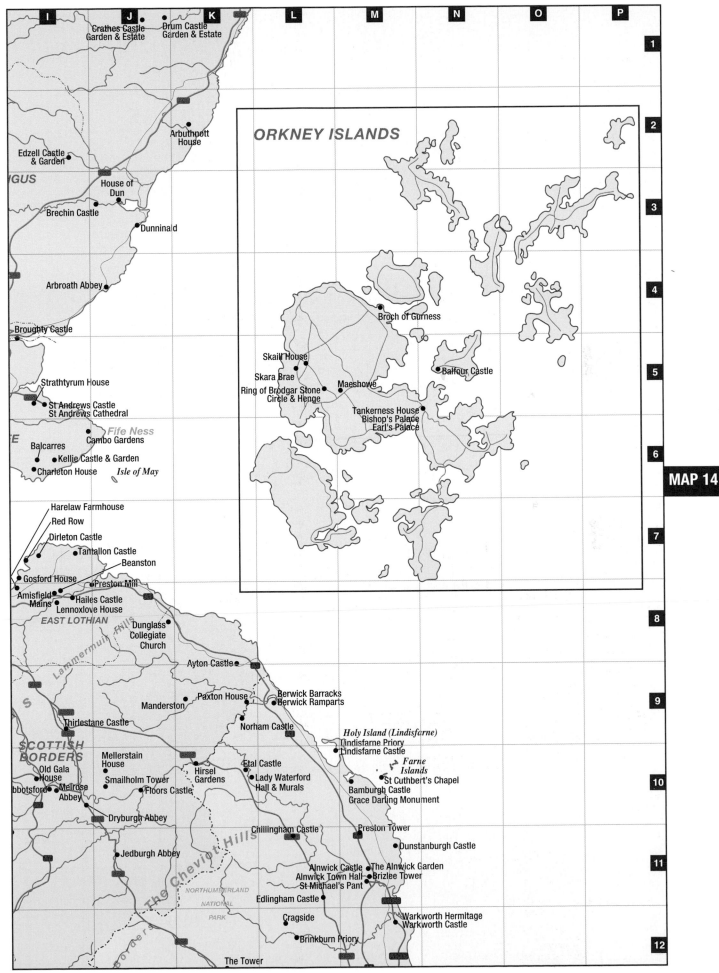

ORKNEY ISLANDS

Arbuthnott House

Edzell Castle & Garden

House of Dun

Brechin Castle

Dunninald

Arbroath Abbey

Broughty Castle

Strathtyrum House

St Andrews Castle
St Andrews Cathedral

Fife Ness

Cambo Gardens

Balcarres
Kellie Castle & Garden
Charleton House

Isle of May

Harelaw Farmhouse
Red Row
Dirleton Castle
Tantallon Castle
Beanston
Gosford House
Preston Mill
Amisfield
Mains
Hailes Castle
Lennoxlove House

EAST LOTHIAN

Dunglass Collegiate Church

Ayton Castle

Paxton House
Berwick Barracks
Berwick Ramparts

Manderston

Thirlestane Castle

Norham Castle

SCOTTISH BORDERS

Holy Island (Lindisfarne)
Lindisfarne Priory
Lindisfarne Castle

Mellerstain House

Hirsel Gardens

Etal Castle

Farne Islands

Old Gala House

Smailholm Tower

Floors Castle

Lady Waterford Hall & Murals

St Cuthbert's Chapel

bbotsford
Melrose Abbey

Bamburgh Castle
Grace Darling Monument

Dryburgh Abbey

Chillingham Castle

Preston Tower

Dunstanburgh Castle

Jedburgh Abbey

The Cheviot Hills

Alnwick Castle
Alnwick Town Hall
St Michael's Pant

The Alnwick Garden
Brizlee Tower

NORTHUMBERLAND NATIONAL PARK

Edlingham Castle

Cragside

Warkworth Hermitage
Warkworth Castle

Brinkburn Priory

The Tower

Broch of Gurness

Skaill House
Skara Brae
Ring of Brodgar Stone Circle & Henge
Maeshowe

Balfour Castle

Tankerness House
Bishop's Palace
Earl's Palace

Crathes Castle Garden & Estate

Drum Castle Garden & Estate

Lammermuir Hills

MAP 14

593

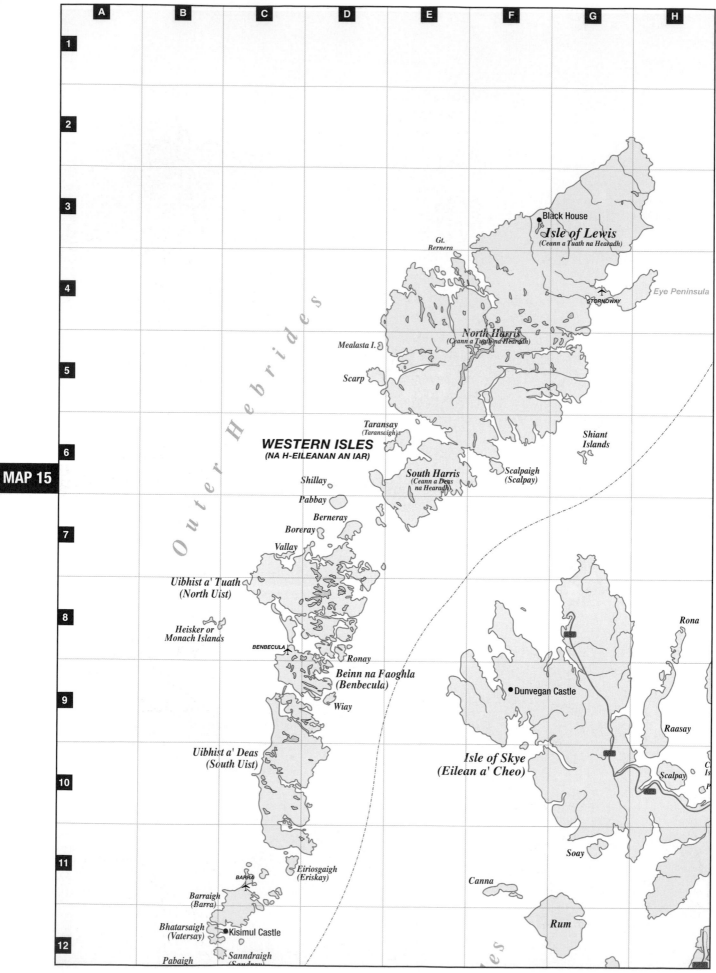

MAP 15

A B C D E F G H

1
2
3
4
5
6
7
8
9
10
11
12

Isle of Lewis
(Ceann a Tuath na Hearadh)

Black House

Gt.
Bernera

Eye Peninsula

STORNOWAY

North Harris
(Ceann a Tuath na Hearadh)

Mealasta I.

Scarp

Taransay
(Taransaigh)

Shiant
Islands

WESTERN ISLES
(NA H-EILEANAN AN IAR)

South Harris
(Ceann a Deas
na Hearadh)

Scalpaigh
(Scalpay)

Shillay

Pabbay

Berneray

Boreray

Vallay

Uibhist a' Tuath
(North Uist)

Rona

Heisker or
Monach Islands

BENBECULA

Ronay

Beinn na Faoghla
(Benbecula)

Dunvegan Castle

Wiay

Raasay

Uibhist a' Deas
(South Uist)

Isle of Skye
(Eilean a' Cheo)

Scalpay

C
Is

Eiriosgaigh
(Eriskay)

Soay

BARRA

Barraigh
(Barra)

Canna

Bhatarsaigh
(Vatersay)

Kisimul Castle

Rum

Pabaigh

Sanndraigh
(Sandray)

Outer Hebrides

594

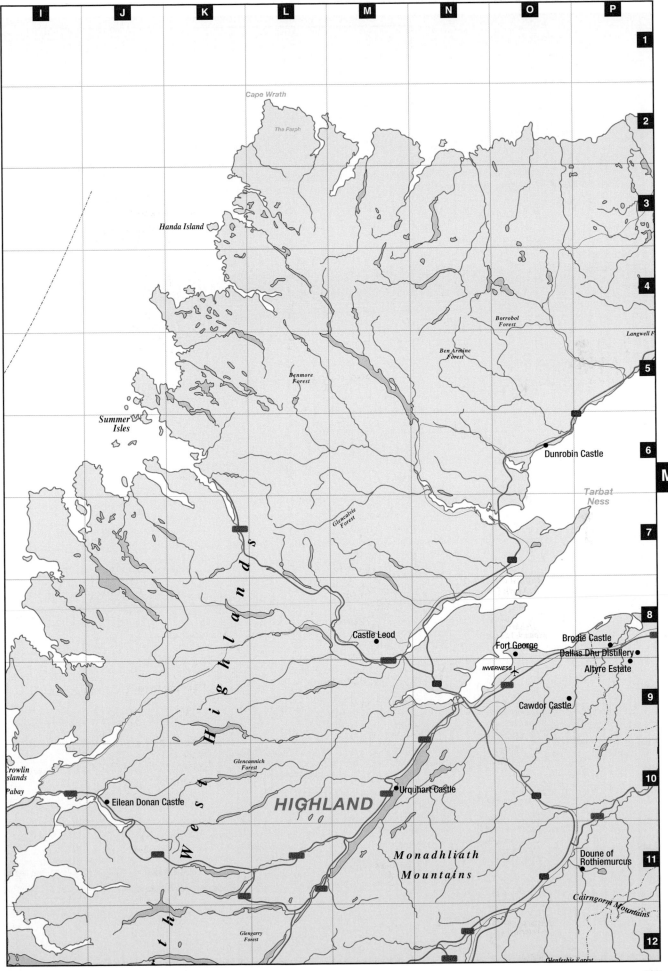

MAP 16

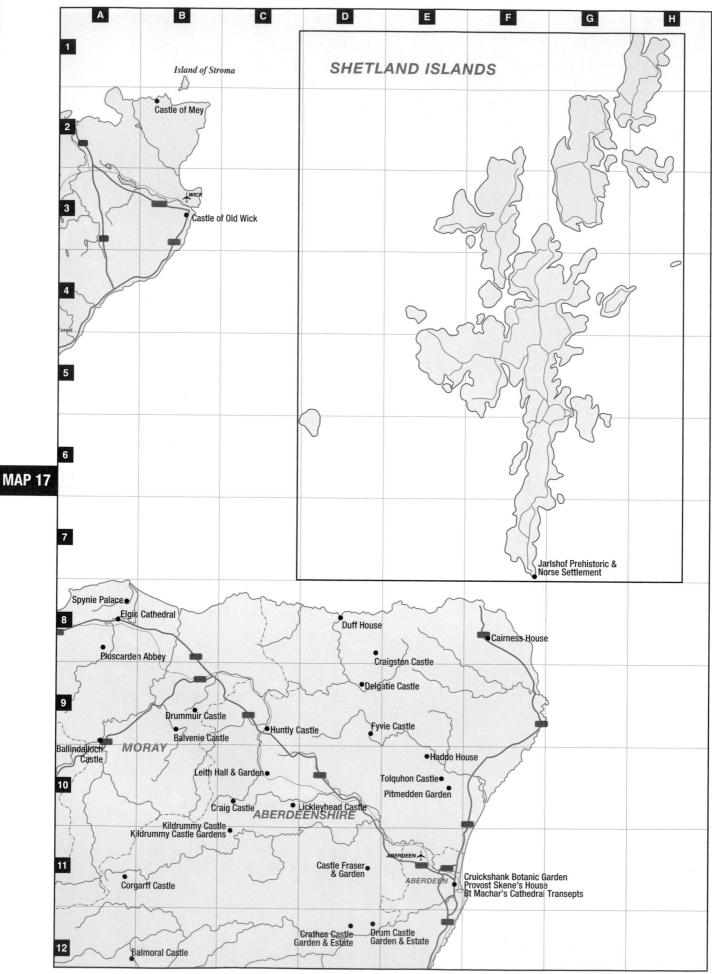

MAP 17

A **B** **C** **D** **E** **F** **G** **H**

1

Island of Stroma

Castle of Mey

SHETLAND ISLANDS

2

3

WICK

Castle of Old Wick

4

Forest

5

6

7

Jarlshof Prehistoric &
Norse Settlement

Spynie Palace

Elgin Cathedral

Duff House

Cairness House

8

Pluscarden Abbey

Craigston Castle

Delgatie Castle

9

Drummuir Castle

Fyvie Castle

Balvenie Castle

MORAY

Huntly Castle

Ballindalloch
Castle

Haddo House

Leith Hall & Garden

Tolquhon Castle

10

Pitmedden Garden

Craig Castle

Lickleyhead Castle

ABERDEENSHIRE

Kildrummy Castle
Kildrummy Castle Gardens

ABERDEEN

11

Castle Fraser
& Garden

Cruickshank Botanic Garden
Provost Skene's House
St Machar's Cathedral Transepts

Corgarff Castle

ABERDEEN

Crathes Castle
Garden & Estate

Drum Castle
Garden & Estate

12

Balmoral Castle

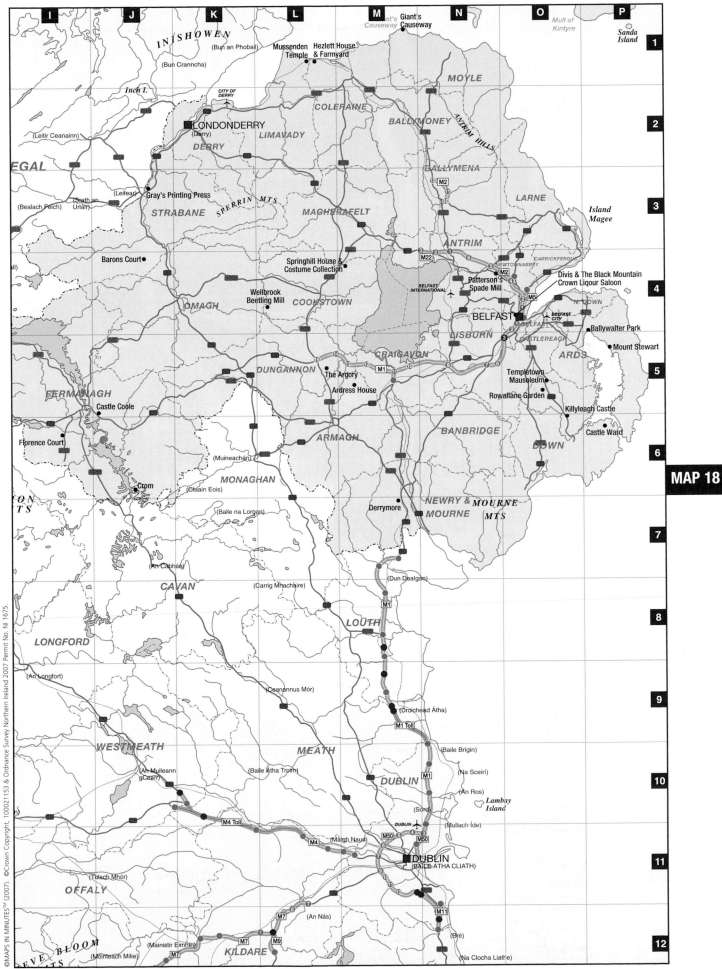

MAP 18

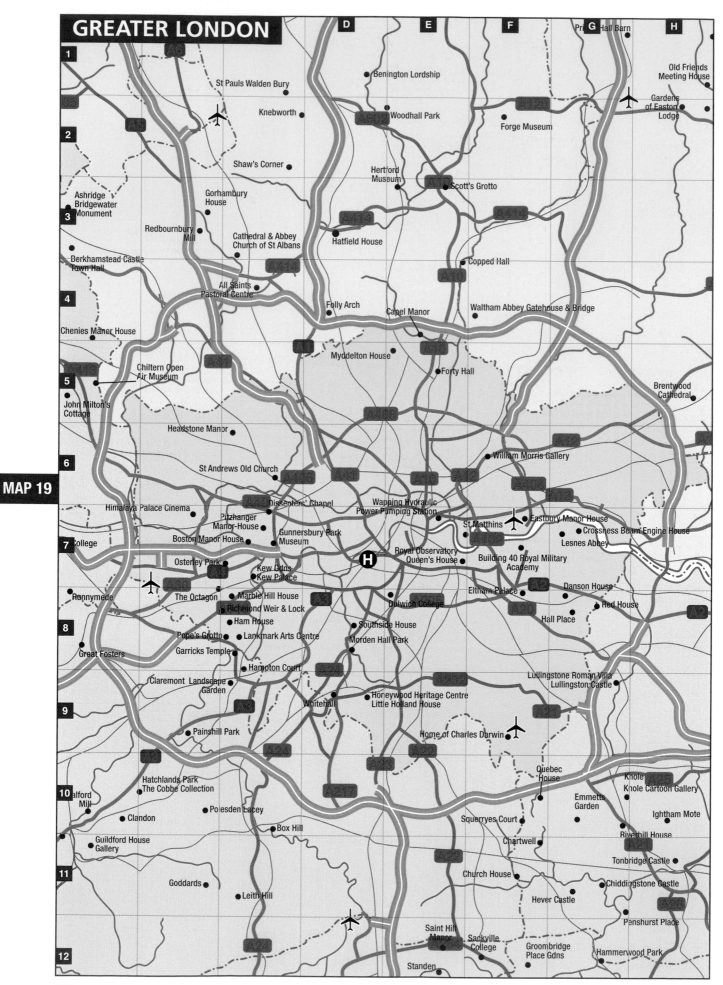

GREATER LONDON

MAP 19

D E F G H

1

St Pauls Walden Bury
Knebworth

Benington Lordship
Woodhall Park
Forge Museum

Old Friends
Meeting House
Gardens
of Easton
Lodge

2

Shaw's Corner

Hertford
Museum
Scott's Grotto

3

Ashridge
Bridgewater
Monument
Redbournbury
Mill
Gorhambury
House

Cathedral & Abbey
Church of St Albans

Hatfield House
Copped Hall

Berkhamstead Castle
Town Hall

4

All Saints
Pastoral Centre

Folly Arch
Capel Manor
Waltham Abbey Gatehouse & Bridge

Chenies Manor House

Myddelton House
Forty Hall

Brentwood
Cathedral

5

Chiltern Open
Air Museum

John Milton's
Cottage

6

Headstone Manor

St Andrews Old Church
William Morris Gallery

7

Himalaya Palace Cinema
Pitzhanger
Manor-House
Boston Manor House

Dissenters' Chapel
Gunnersbury Park
Museum

Wapping Hydraulic
Power Pumping Station

St Matthins
Royal Observatory
Queen's House

Eastbury Manor House
Crossness Beam Engine House
Lesnes Abbey

Building 40 Royal Military
Academy

College

Osterley Park

Kew Gdns
Kew Palace

Eltham Palace
Danson House

Runnymede

The Octagon
Marble Hill House
Richmond Weir & Lock
Ham House

Dulwich College

Hall Place
Red House

8

Pope's Grotto
Lankmark Arts Centre
Garricks Temple

Southside House
Morden Hall Park

Great Fosters

Hampton Court

Luilingstone Roman Villa
Lullingston Castle

9

Claremont Landscape
Garden

Whitehall

Honeywood Heritage Centre
Little Holland House

Home of Charles Darwin

Painshill Park

Quebec
House

Knole
Knole Cartoon Gallery

10

alford
Mill
Clandon

Hatchlands Park
The Cobbe Collection

Polesden Lacey

Box Hill

Squerryes Court
Chartwell

Emmetts
Garden

Ightham Mote

Riverhill House

Guildford House
Gallery

Church House
Tonbridge Castle

11

Goddards

Leith Hill

Hever Castle

Chiddingstone Castle

Penshurst Place

12

Saint Hill
Manor
Sackville
College

Groombridge
Place Gdns

Hammerwood Park

Standen

598

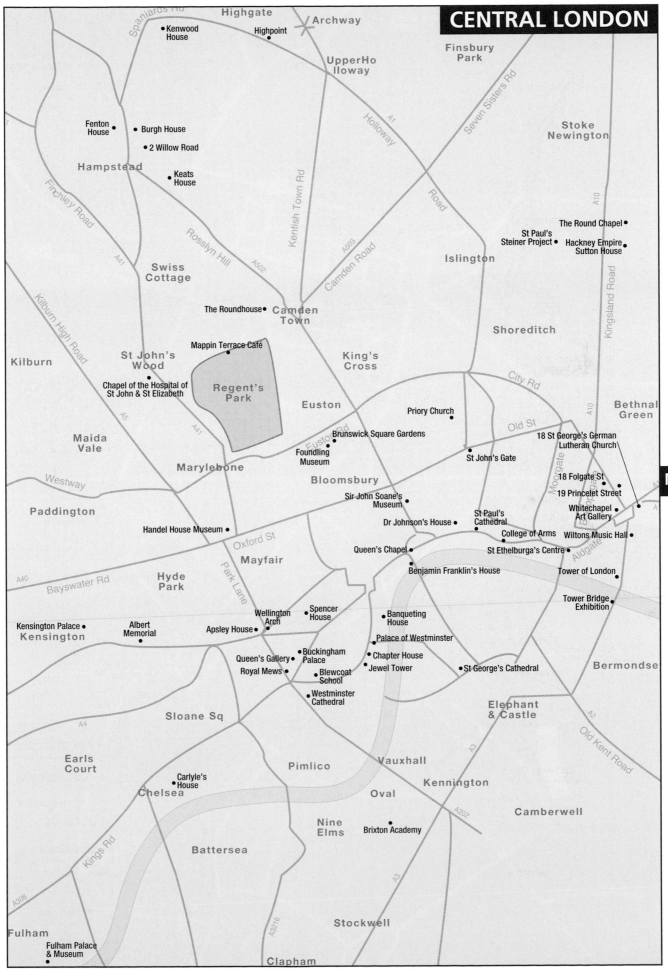

MAP 20

Highgate

Archway

Finsbury Park

UpperHo lloway

Kenwood House

Highpoint

Stoke Newington

Seven Sisters Rd

Spaniards Rd

Fenton House

Burgh House

2 Willow Road

Hampstead

Keats House

Finchley Road

Rosslyn Hill

Kentish Town Rd

Holloway

A1

Camden Road

A503

Islington

A502

Kingsland Road

A10

The Round Chapel

St Paul's Steiner Project

Hackney Empire

Sutton House

Swiss Cottage

A41

Kilburn High Road

Kilburn

St John's Wood

The Roundhouse

Camden Town

Shoreditch

City Rd

Bethnal Green

A5

Chapel of the Hospital of St John & St Elizabeth

Mappin Terrace Café

Regent's Park

King's Cross

Old St

A10

Moorgate

Maida Vale

A41

Euston

Priory Church

St John's Gate

18 St George's German Lutheran Church

Westway

Marylebone

Euston Rd

Brunswick Square Gardens

Foundling Museum

Bloomsbury

18 Folgate St

19 Princelet Street

Paddington

Sir John Soane's Museum

Dr Johnson's House

St Paul's Cathedral

Whitechapel Art Gallery

A1

Handel House Museum

Oxford St

College of Arms

Wiltons Music Hall

A40

Bayswater Rd

Mayfair

Park Lane

Queen's Chapel

St Ethelburga's Centre

Aldgate

Hyde Park

Benjamin Franklin's House

Tower of London

Kensington Palace

Albert Memorial

Wellington Arch

Spencer House

Banqueting House

Tower Bridge Exhibition

Kensington

Apsley House

Palace of Westminster

Queen's Gallery

Buckingham Palace

Chapter House

Jewel Tower

St George's Cathedral

Bermondse

Royal Mews

Blewcoat School

Westminster Cathedral

Elephant & Castle

A2

Sloane Sq

A4

Old Kent Road

Earls Court

Carlyle's House

Pimlico

Vauxhall

Kennington

A3

Chelsea

Kings Rd

Oval

Camberwell

A202

Nine Elms

Brixton Academy

A308

A3216

Battersea

A3

Stockwell

Fulham

Fulham Palace & Museum

Clapham

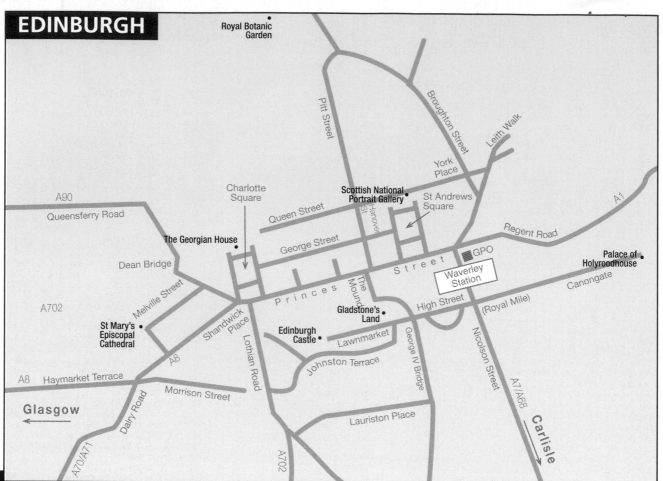

EDINBURGH

Royal Botanic Garden

Pitt Street

Broughton Street

Leith Walk

York Place

A90

Queensferry Road

A1

Charlotte Square

Queen Street

Scottish National Portrait Gallery

St Andrews Square

Hanover St

Regent Road

The Georgian House

George Street

GPO

Palace of Holyroodhouse

Dean Bridge

Street

Waverley Station

Melville Street

Princes

The Mound

High Street

(Royal Mile)

Canongate

A702

Gladstone's Land

Nicolson Street

St Mary's Episcopal Cathedral

Shandwick Place

Edinburgh Castle

Lawnmarket

George IV Bridge

A7/A68

A8

Lothian Road

Johnston Terrace

A8 Haymarket Terrace

Morrison Street

Carlisle

Glasgow

Dairy Road

Lauriston Place

A70/A71

A702

MAP 21

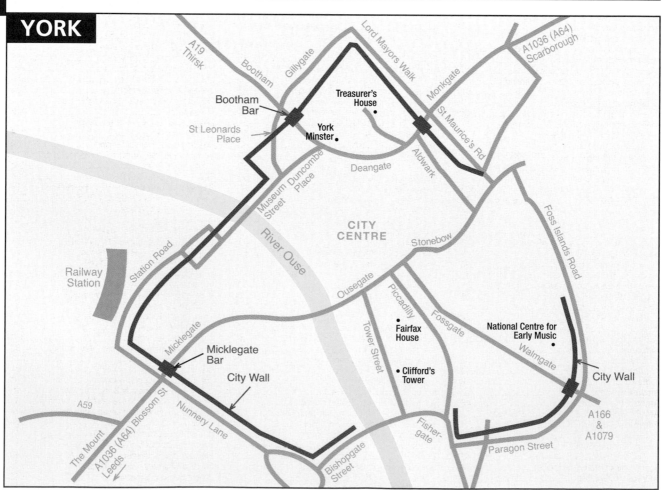

YORK

A19 Thirsk

Bootham

Gillygate

Lord Mayors Walk

A1036 (A64) Scarborough

Monkgate

Bootham Bar

Treasurer's House

St Leonards Place

York Minster

St Maurice's Rd

Museum Duncombe Street Place

Deangate

Aldwark

CITY CENTRE

Foss Islands Road

River Ouse

Stonebow

Railway Station

Station Road

Ousegate

Piccadilly

Fossgate

National Centre for Early Music

Micklegate

Fairfax House

Tower Street

Walmgate

Micklegate Bar

Clifford's Tower

City Wall

A59

Nunnery Lane

Fisher-gate

A166 & A1079

The Mount

A1036 (A64) Blossom St

Bishopgate Street

Paragon Street

Leeds

Y

visit hudsons guide online